International Directory of
COMPANY HISTORIES

International Directory of
COMPANY HISTORIES

VOLUME 13

Editor
Tina Grant

ST. JAMES PRESS
An ITP Information/Reference Group Company

Changing the Way the World Learns

NEW YORK • LONDON • BONN • BOSTON • DETROIT • MADRID
MELBOURNE • MEXICO CITY • PARIS • SINGAPORE • TOKYO
TORONTO • WASHINGTON • ALBANY NY • BELMONT CA • CINCINNATI OH

STAFF

Tina Grant, *Editor*

Laura Berger, Joann Cerrito, David Collins, Nicolet V. Elert, Miranda H. Ferrara, Paula Kepos, Janice Jorgensen, Margaret Mazurkiewicz, Mike Tyrkus, *Contributing Editors*

The paper used in this publication meets the minimum requirements of American National Standard for Information Sciences—Permanence Paper for Printed Library Materials, ANSI Z39.48-1984.

Library of Congress Catalog Number: 89-190943

British Library Cataloguing in Publication Data

International directory of company histories. Vol. 12
I. Tina Grant
338.7409

ISBN 1-55862-341-8

Printed in the United States of America
Published simultaneously in the United Kingdom

The trademark **ITP** is used under license.

Cover photograph of the Lloyd's of London headquarters building courtesy of Lloyd's of London.

10 9 8 7 6 5 4 3 2 1

CONTENTS

Company Histories

PREFACE

International Directory of Company Histories provides detailed information on the development of the world's largest and most influential companies. To date, *Company Histories* has covered more than 2000 companies in thirteen volumes.

Inclusion Criteria

Most companies chosen for inclusion in *Company Histories* have achieved a minimum of US$200 million in annual sales and are leading influences in their industries or geographical locations. State-owned companies that are important in their industries and that may operate much like public or private companies also are included. Wholly owned subsidiaries and divisions are presented if they meet the requirements for inclusion.

St. James Press does not endorse any of the companies or products mentioned in this book. Companies that appear in *Company Histories* were selected without reference to their wishes and have in no way endorsed their entries. The companies were given the opportunity to participate in the compilation of the articles by providing information or reading their entries for factual accuracy, and we are indebted to many of them for their comments and corrections.

Entry Format

Each entry in this volume begins with a company's legal name, the address of its headquarters, its telephone number and fax number, and a statement of public, private, state, or parent ownership. A company with a legal name in both English and the language of its headquarters country is listed by the English name, with the native-language name in parentheses.

Also provided are the company's founding or earliest incorporation date, the number of employees, and the most recent sales figures available. Sales figures are given in local currencies with equivalents in U.S. dollars. For some private companies, sales figures are estimates. The entry lists the exchanges on which a company's stock is traded, as well as the company's principal Standard Industrial Classification codes. American spelling is used, and the word ''billion'' is used in its American sense of one thousand million.

Sources

The histories were compiled from publicly accessible sources such as general and academic periodicals, books, annual reports, and material supplied by the companies themselves. *Company Histories* is intended for reference use by students, business people, librarians, historians, economists, investors, job candidates, and others who want to learn more about the historical development of the world's most important companies.

Cumulative Indexes

An Index to Companies and Persons provides access to companies and individuals discussed in the text. Beginning with Volume 7, an Index to Industries allows researchers to locate companies by their principal industry.

ABBREVIATIONS FOR FORMS OF COMPANY INCORPORATION

A.B.	Aktiebolaget (Sweden)
A.G.	Aktiengesellschaft (Germany, Switzerland)
A.S.	Atieselskab (Denmark)
A.S.	Aksjeselskap (Denmark, Norway)
A.Ş.	Anomin Şirket (Turkey)
B.V.	Besloten Vennootschap met beperkte, Aansprakelijkheid (The Netherlands)
Co.	Company (United Kingdom, United States)
Corp.	Corporation (United States)
G.I.E.	Groupement d'Intérêt Economique (France)
GmbH	Gesellschaft mit beschränkter Haftung (Germany)
H.B.	Handelsbolaget (Sweden)
Inc.	Incorporated (United States)
KGaA	Kommanditgesellschaft auf Aktien (Germany)
K.K.	Kabushiki Kaisha (Japan)
LLC	Limited Liability Company (Middle East)
Ltd.	Limited (Canada, Japan, United Kingdom, United States)
N.V.	Naamloze Vennootschap (The Netherlands)
OY	Osakeyhtiöt (Finland)
PLC	Public Limited Company (United Kingdom)
PTY.	Proprietary (Australia, Hong Kong, South Africa)
S.A.	Société Anonyme (Belgium, France, Switzerland)
SpA	Società per Azioni (Italy)

ABBREVIATIONS FOR CURRENCY

DA	Algerian dinar
A$	Australian dollar
Sch	Austrian schilling
BFr	Belgian franc
Cr	Brazilian cruzado
C$	Canadian dollar
DKr	Danish krone
E£	Egyptian pound
Fmk	Finnish markka
FFr	French franc
DM	German mark
HK$	Hong Kong dollar
Rs	Indian rupee
Rp	Indonesian rupiah
IR£	Irish pound
L	Italian lira
¥	Japanese yen
W	Korean won
KD	Kuwaiti dinar
LuxFr	Luxembourgian franc
M$	Malaysian ringgit
Dfl	Netherlands florin
NZ$	New Zealand dollar
N	Nigerian naira
NKr	Norwegian krone
RO	Omani rial
P	Philippine peso
Esc	Portuguese escudo
SRls	Saudi Arabian riyal
S$	Singapore dollar
R	South African rand
W	South Korean won
Pta	Spanish peseta
SKr	Swedish krona
SFr	Swiss franc
NT$	Taiwanese dollar
B	Thai baht
£	United Kingdom pound
$	United States dollar
B	Venezuelan bolivar
K	Zambian kwacha

International Directory of COMPANY HISTORIES

Nielsen

A. C. Nielsen Company

Nielsen Plaza
Northbrook, Illinois 60062
U.S.A.
(708) 498-6300
Fax: (708) 498-7286

Wholly Owned Subsidiary of The Dun & Bradstreet Corporation
Incorporated: 1929
Employees: 20,000
Operating Revenues: $1.87 billion
SICs: 8732 Commercial, Economic, Sociological, and Educational Research

A. C. Nielsen Company is the nation's leading consumer research concern, offering comprehensive information that tracks sales, volume, shares, trends, pricing, promotions, distribution, and inventory levels for corporate clients worldwide. The company is a subsidiary of The Dun & Bradstreet Corporation, the world's largest supplier of business information and services.

Nielsen's enormous scope has justified the formation of distinct divisions to optimize the management of the company's most valuable services. Nielsen Marketing Research, for example, measures consumer response at point-of-sale for suppliers of groceries, drugs, health and beauty aids, and other packaged goods. It also measures and evaluates promotions that influence consumer sales at the retail level. The patronage of 40 of the 50 largest consumer packaged goods companies in the United States have bolstered Nielsen Marketing Research's position as the world leader in providing these services. The other key division, Nielsen Media Research, provides similar marketing information and services to media-related businesses and advertisers.

The company's origins date back to 1923, when an engineer by the name of Arthur C. Nielsen borrowed $45,000 to start a business running quality tests and offering buying suggestions on conveyor belts, turbine generators, and other machine-related parts. After that business was nearly bowled over by the Depression, Nielsen shifted to measuring consumer sales. In 1933, Nielsen introduced measurements for drugstore and retail store sales. A year later, similar measurements were introduced for food and department store sales. By going beyond conventional consumer questionnaires and having auditors actually survey store shelves and accounting books to determine sales patterns, Nielsen helped pioneer key market research tools—including the concept of market share in 1935.

While he was pioneering the discipline of marketing research, Nielsen faced the difficult task of drumming up demand for his services. The labor required to gather and tabulate useful data was expensive, and many businesses were skeptical about paying top dollar for data that they thought they could gather almost as effectively themselves. "For years my father would go around and try and explain that his work was worth something. He'd quote the price. And he couldn't get any takers," Arthur C. Nielsen Jr. told Barry Stavro of *Forbes* in 1984. Nielsen recalled that his father's attempts to sell his services to Kellogg Co. were rebuffed on the grounds that the cereal giant already had its own, cheaper alternative: "a guy stationed outside the gates trying to see how many carloads General Foods shipped out."

Though sales did not always come easily to the budding leader in marketing research, A. C. Nielsen Company enjoyed continued growth into the 1950s. That decade saw the emergence of new industries in mass media through radio and television—areas that called for new forms of marketing measurement that Nielsen was equipped to provide. Indeed, as early as 1942, Nielsen began measurement of radio audiences on a national scale. In radio's heyday following World War II, determining radio ratings was a labor-intensive endeavor: listeners would send cards to advertisers, who would actually weigh the mailbags to determine which shows were most popular. Improving upon this technique, Nielsen attached meters to radios in sample households and, eventually, installed cameras that took pictures of the meter readings. The heads of the households then mailed the pictures in to the rating company on a regular basis. In the 1950s, the advent of television and the need for ever-quicker rating techniques spurred the development of meter readers that Nielsen attached to telephone lines for "overnight" TV ratings. This method saved time over past techniques, but costs were extremely high. Still, the relatively young company persisted, driven by the belief that the TV market would grow—and communications technology along with it—enough to compensate for the high costs of tracking market trends.

Nielsen's projections were right on the mark, and the rapid growth of television worked to the overwhelming advantage of the marketing research company. By the mid-1980s, more than $19 billion was spent on national TV advertising; Nielsen metered more than 5,500 homes and generated approximately $100 million in revenue from that business segment alone. Encouraged by the continued success of its media rating service, the company established a separate division to manage it. Nielsen Media Research provided television advertisers, advertising agencies, syndicates, cable operators, networks, and stations with TV-rating information to increase the effectiveness of television advertising and programming into the 21st century.

A. C. Nielsen Sr.'s efforts gained momentum in 1945 when his son, A. C. Nielsen Jr., joined the firm, bringing new energy and ideas. The time-consuming tasks of sorting through data cards and doing calculations on slide rules prompted the younger Nielsen to consider emerging computer technology as a way to reduce the time and costs involved in managing the data so crucial to their business. In 1952, the company acquired one of the first computers manufactured by IBM. Although it was unwieldy in size and function compared to later models, it nonetheless marked a milestone in efficiency. Nielsen Jr. also helped implement a training program that allowed the company to disseminate its expertise in cutting-edge marketing research tools to its growing employee base.

Such technological and administrative advances helped position A. C. Nielsen Company for decades of growth and diversification. From the 1960s through the 1980s, the company developed new information-management systems and attracted a broader client base. In 1963, Nielsen introduced measurement of sales at mass merchandisers, providing a bulk of consumer-related information that would have been virtually unmanageable just a decade earlier. Three years later, a system of warehouse withdrawal reporting was introduced. In addition, the company established a coupon clearinghouse segment that would top $91 million in volume by the mid-1980s, with no sign of slowing down.

A momentous advancement for Nielsen was the development of scanning technology, which allowed the company to collect accurate and instantaneous data on consumer purchases as they occurred. Scanning of universal product codes at retail stores was introduced in 1977. By 1979, Nielsen offered local SCANTRACK service, which gave clients proprietary means of tracking specific market trends and producing custom reports to develop better marketing and distribution plans. A year later, such services were available on the national level. Scanning technology and data processing software continued to improve, and by the mid-1990s Nielsen considered retail scanning information "the nerve center of the changes now underway," according to the company's promotional literature. "Not only do scanning databases bring a speed and precision never previously possible, they also provide the foundation for a range of diagnostic and analytical applications which can help clients find and implement solutions that grow their revenues and minimize the cost of delivering their products to their consumers." In 1993, Nielsen became the first in the industry to offer scanning-based information from warehouse clubs with the introduction of the Nielsen Warehouse Club Service.

Nielsen's unparalleled status as a marketing research leader drew the attention of The Dun & Bradstreet Corporation, and Arthur C. Nielsen Jr. sold A. C. Nielsen Company to the financial data giant for $1.3 billion in stock, a remarkable 26 times earnings, in May 1984. In fact, the two companies had been considering such a merger for over 15 years, as Nielsen Jr. and Harrington Drake, chairman and chief executive officer of Dun & Bradstreet, told the *New York Times.* "We both have the ability to collect a lot of data and deliver it efficiently to clients," Nielsen Jr. explained. "I'm sure Nielsen will take advantage of our technology as well as our data bases," Drake added.

With the backing of its powerful parent, Nielsen continued to grow rapidly, entering several alliances and introducing new products in the late 1980s. In June 1987, Nielsen Marketing Research and The NPD Group signed a contract to establish electronic household panel services through a joint venture, NPD/Nielsen Inc. The venture had three main objectives: to measure all marketing stimuli received by sample households, including TV commercials and product purchases; to measure consumer response to promotions at the local market level; and to provide profiles by product category and brand by integrating facts from store, retail-promotion, TV-commercial, coupon distribution, and household databases. The scope of the project was enormous, offering detail and complexity unprecedented in the marketing research industry. By 1991—just three years after its inception—the National Electronic Household Panel announced coverage of 40,000 homes.

Nielsen also formed other key alliances. In August 1987, Dun & Bradstreet acquired Information Resources Inc. (IRI), bringing the market research "wonderkid" together with its rival, Nielsen. IRI's flagship product, BehaviorScan, provided a highly effective method for analyzing the effectiveness of TV commercials. Under the auspices of the same parent, IRI and Nielsen were freed from the "upward battle" of head-on competition and were better positioned to focus on new product development, according to David Snyder in *Crain's Chicago Business.* A similar collaboration of formerly competitive forces occurred in 1988, when Nielsen acquired Logistics Data Systems, the market leader whose software product, SPACEMAN, helped retailers profitably manage shelf space and display areas.

Capitalizing on new developments in networking, information modeling, and forecasting, Nielsen was able to introduce a wave of new products in the early 1990s. The company's decision-support and software services enabled customers to retrieve data and analyze information via terminals and personal computers installed in their offices. Such information was accessible in a number of ways, including on-line connection to mainframes or permanent downloading of information into customers' in-house information systems. In 1990 alone, new product introductions included: a national Convenience Store Service representing all major U.S. chains; the SCANTRACK Food/Drug Combo Retail Outlet Service, representing all major U.S. chains; the Discount Drug Service for health and beauty aids (HBA) customers; WealthWise, a modeling tool for consumer-oriented financial services firms; and ScorePlus, which provided demographic and product-use data applicable to specific trading areas.

New product introductions kept pace with rapid growth in demand, as ever more powerful computer processing systems were made available to Nielsen's customer base. In 1991, the company introduced Spotlight, a system that enabled users to locate and account for volume and share changes for given brands. That system would win an award for outstanding artificial intelligence application from the American Association for Artificial Intelligence in 1992. Other products introduced that year included: Nielsen Sales Advisor, SCANTRACK Category Manager, and ScanQuick. In addition, PROCISION provided a single source for tracking all components of HBA marketing, and the Nielsen Workstation provided Windows-based support for marketers. In 1993, the company introduced Nielsen Opportunity Explorer to help marketing and sales professionals understand category dynamics and pinpoint sales opportunities. Along with Nielsen Promotion Simulator, that product placed first in the software applications category at the Information Industry Association's Product Achievement Awards in 1993.

Responding to overwhelming demand for its efficiency-related solutions in the consumer packaged goods industry, in 1993 Nielsen created a separate division for Efficient Consumer Response (ECR) and began forging ties within the industry to enhance its capabilities. The key objectives of ECR were to streamline distribution and sales processes, eliminate waste, and deliver product to consumers faster and at a lower cost. One example was the 1993 implementation of a Micro-Marketing system—Nielsen's Eagle Eye—to help the Anheuser-Busch Company work with its retailers to organize space plans, marketing, and distribution for maximum sales. One retail chain that implemented the system saw an annual potential increase in beer category sales of $3.2 million, according to Nielsen literature.

In a joint effort aimed at ECR implementation around the globe, the company worked together with suppliers and distributors to form the Nielsen Solution Partners program in 1994. The program was designed to align the "best practices" of industry leaders, such as NON-STOP Logistics, a state-of-the-art cross-docking network focused on reducing warehouse inventory and speeding up the delivery process from plants to stores. Into the 21st century, one of Nielsen's key objectives was to strengthen that partnership and thereby contribute innovative solutions to ECR in general.

Nielsen also continued to increase its global presence, with marketing-information clients in more than 34 countries by the mid-1990s. Indeed, the company's international reach grew steadily after its first overseas office was opened in England in 1939. By 1991, the company had opened an office in its 28th country, Hungary. In 1993, the company was looking into a subsidiary office in Israel. In April 1994, Nielsen expanded into South Africa through a partnership with Integrated Business Information Services (IBIS), the premier market research company in that country. Serge Olun, president and chief executive officer of A. C. Nielsen, told *Business Wire* in 1994 that "Nielsen is moving aggressively today to negotiate further partnerships in South America, Africa, Eastern Europe, the Middle East and elsewhere." He cited plans to increase the company's coverage to 70 countries worldwide by 1995. In April 1995, the company made significant progress toward achieving that goal when it extended its global coverage to six countries in Central America: Costa Rica, Guatemala, Honduras, Nicaragua, El Salvador, and Panama. Since its origin as a strictly American concern in the 1920s, Nielsen branched out until 70 percent of its business came from outside the United States in the 1990s.

By the mid-1990s, Nielsen asserted its dominance in the marketing information industry by successfully consolidating or winning back 26 consumer packaged goods clients, such as Dole Foods, Tambrands, Johnson & Johnson, Bristol Myers Squibb, and Clairol. It also remained king of the hill in media rating services—especially since its main TV-rating competitor, Arbitron Co., stopped providing local TV ratings at the end of 1993. Nielsen, a company that started as a rating service for conveyor belts, became a global success story by gathering information from an ever-increasing variety of sources and turning it into valuable products.

Principal Subsidiaries: Nielsen Marketing Research, Nielsen Media Research.

Further Reading:

"A. C. Nielsen Extends Global Reach to Six Countries in Central America," *Canada News Wire,* April 18, 1995.

"A. C. Nielsen Signs Pan-European Contract with Reckitt & Colman; Global Expansion Continues at Record Pace," *PR Newswire,* March 14, 1994.

"A. C. Nielsen to Israel; Plans Subsidiary," *Israel Business Today,* July 2, 1993, p. 5.

Clark, Kenneth R., "CBS Taps 2nd Ratings Firm in Jab at Nielsen," *Chicago Tribune,* November 5, 1991, p. C1.

——, "Maxwell Firm to Challenge Nielsen," *Chicago Tribune,* June 20, 1990, p. C3.

——, "Nielsen Acts to Upgrade TV Monitoring System," *Chicago Tribune,* June 6, 1990, p. C1.

"Dun & Bradstreet to Link Nielsen and IMS Data with Manugistics' Supply Chain Management Software to Provide Integrated ECR Solution," *PR Newswire,* August 8, 1994.

Farhi, Paul, "Maryland-Based 'Peoplemeter' Firm Is Suspending Its Operation; Demise Leaves Nielsen as Only TV Ratings Firm in U.S.," *Washington Post,* July 30, 1988, p. D10.

"GTE Interactive Services and Nielsen to Conduct Market Test," *PR Newswire,* May 6, 1992.

Haire, Kevlin C., "TV Stations Rate Need for Nielsen," *Baltimore Business Journal,* October 22, 1993, p. 5.

Millenson, Michael L., "Arbitron Leaves TV to Nielsen," *Chicago Tribune,* October 19, 1993, p. N1.

"Nielsen Expands into South Africa through Partnership with IBIS," *PR Newswire,* April 6, 1994.

"Nielsen Marketing Research Announces Joint Venture with the NPD Group," *Business Wire,* June 15, 1987.

"Nielsen's New Magazine Measurement Service a Boon to Marketers and Advertisers," *PR Newswire,* March 25, 1991.

"Revlon Signs Agreement with Nielsen; Significantly Expands Current Relationship," *PR Newswire,* July 26, 1994.

Salibian, Catherine E., "Marketing Firm Lodges Action against Nielsen," *Rochester Business Journal,* July 24, 1989, p. 1.

Salmans, Sandra, "Dun and Nielsen: Compatible Goals," *New York Times,* May 21, 1984, p. D1.

Snyder, David, "Why Archrivals IRI, A. C. Nielsen Merged," *Crain's Chicago Business,* August 31, 1987, p. 1.

Stavro, Barry, "Rating Nielsen," *Forbes,* December 17, 1984, p. 100.

—Kerstan Cohen

Acme-Cleveland Corp.

1242 East 49th Street
Cleveland, Ohio 44114
U.S.A.
(216) 432-5400
Fax: (216) 432-5401

Public Company
Incorporated: 1904
Employees: 1,105
Sales: $107.87 million
Stock Exchanges: New York
SICs: 3661 Telephone and Telegraph Apparatus; 3829 Measuring and Controlling Devices, Not Elsewhere Classified; 6719 Holding Companies, Not Elsewhere Classified

For over a century, Acme-Cleveland Corp. was a leading producer of machine tools, the heavy implements used by other manufacturers to shape metal into useful parts. But after a devastating drop in machine tool demand in the early 1980s, the company transformed itself into a significantly smaller high-tech firm with interests in telecommunications, industrial sensors, and quality assurance. From the early 1980s to the early 1990s, Acme-Cleveland's annual revenues shrunk drastically, from nearly $500 million to just over $100 million, as the company shed its historic focus.

Acme-Cleveland was created through the 1968 merger of the Cleveland Twist Drill Company and the National Acme Company. At that time, the manufacturers' combined interests included machine tools, foundry equipment and electrical controls. Acme-Cleveland's earliest predecessor, The Cleveland Twist Drill Company, was founded in 1876. Founder Jacob D. Cox, Sr., used $2,000 borrowed from his father to buy a 50 percent stake in C. C. Newton's small twist drill factory in western New York. Later that year, Cox convinced his partner to move the company to the bustling Great Lakes port city of Cleveland, Ohio. Armed with eight years of experience in that area's steel mills, Cox hoped to parlay his connections there into increased business.

The partnership split up after four difficult years. Cox bought Newton's stake and was left with $9,000 in debt and few prospects. Nonetheless, he soon invited a nephew, Frank F. Prentiss, to take a 40 percent equity position in the firm and become Cleveland Twist Drill's first true salesman. The presence of Prentiss freed Cox to design and build tools and machines and attend to the company's bookkeeping.

Cleveland Twist Drill remained highly leveraged throughout its first decade in business. For example, Cox once told his sons of a $2,000 loan that went totally unpaid for six years in the 1880s. The founder noted that it took him 14 years to pay the obligation during these lean early years. At one point, the business deteriorated so much that Cox tried to sell it for $75,000 in 1886. When he could find no investors, he decided to struggle on.

In spite of a major economic depression in 1893, Cox was able to eradicate Cleveland Twist Drill's debt in the early 1890s. By the turn of the twentieth century the company's steady growth had necessitated the ten-fold expansion of its manufacturing floor space. Cleveland Twist Drill incorporated in 1904, and Jacob Cox, Sr., retired the following year. He was succeeded as president by Frank Prentiss, described as an optimistic foil to the founder's conservatism in a 1976 corporate history. Prentiss has been credited with expanding the company's manufacturing capacity during his tenure.

In the meantime, the company that would later merge with Cleveland Twist Drill was undergoing birth pains of its own. After more than a decade of "great difficulties, Edward C. Henn and Reinhold Hakewessell built and patented their first multiple spindle automatic lathe in 1894. Acme-Cleveland's centenary history noted that "the basic principles used by Henn and Hakewessell in their first machine still stand today as the foundation for the economical, reliable, mass production of accurate interchangeable parts." A friend contributed the cash necessary to found Acme Machine Screw Company of Hartford, Connecticut, and begin production, but the company continued to struggle.

When the partners ran out of money again just three years later, Edward Henn sent his brother A.W. to Cleveland in search of an investor. His successful efforts gave the company a new lease on life and a stake in a joint venture; Henn traded 25 Acme machines for a combination of cash and a 50 percent stake in a new Cleveland-based firm called the National Manufacturing Company. The infusion of cash and confidence sustained Acme through the remainder of the nineteenth century, and in 1901 the two enterprises merged to become The National Acme Manufacturing Company. By 1914, it had grown to become one of Cleveland's top employers.

Bored with retirement, Jacob Cox, Sr., rejoined Cleveland Twist Drill as president in 1910 and served in that role until 1919, when he advanced to chairman. He continued to provide guidance to Cleveland Twist Drill until his death in 1930. After just eight years with his father's firm, Jacob Cox, Jr., was elected president in 1919. The new leader, who had studied and written about social economics, put these theories to work at Cleveland Twist Drill. In 1915 he established an employee profit sharing plan.

National Acme continued to grow during the early twentieth century. It was boosted in part by the 1915 acquisition of the Windsor Manufacturing Company, a Vermont firm that produced Gridley brand multiple spindle automatic machines. The machines were named for their designer, George Gridley; they became known as Acme-Gridleys after the acquisition. Demand for multiple spindle automatic machines and their output skyrocketed during World War I. National Acme expanded accordingly, adding on to existing plants and even building a new one to accommodate defense needs. As a leading-edge manufacturer, the company was "left in the lurch" at war's end; it was overstocked, had overcapacity, and was undercapitalized. A company history noted that National Acme was "almost wrecked" in the postwar period. After a massive contraction, the company was able to get back on its feet on the strength of product redesign and vertical diversification, but only barely survived the Great Depression that followed soon after.

Many years of research at Cleveland Twist Drill culminated in the patent of "Mo-Max" brand high speed steel, the first successful molybdenum-tungsten high speed steel. This development proved especially important in the Depression and World War II years, when the material helped Cleveland Twist Drill cut costs and avoid chronic shortages of tungsten steel.

Support of the Allied effort during World War II drove increased production at both Cleveland Twist Drill and National Acme. A company history asserted that "more than 90 percent of all the 30- and 50-caliber bullet cores produced . . . for the United States and Canadian military were made on Acme-Gridley machines." Ironically, future partners National Acme and Cleveland Twist Drill received Army-Navy "Star" Awards for wartime production excellence on the same day.

National Acme emerged from World War II in a much better strategic position than from the previous global conflict. The company made important design changes in anticipation of shifting postwar demand. When the conflict concluded, National Acme was not handicapped by the excess capacities and inventories that had weighed it down after World War I.

Arthur S. Armstrong was elected president of Cleveland Twist Drill in 1952 after Jacob, Jr., advanced to chairman and chief executive officer. Jacob died the following year. Armstrong led the establishment of a Scottish subsidiary as well as the acquisition of Bay State Tap and Die Company in Massachusetts. The company expanded manufacturing into Canada and the Netherlands in the 1960s, and acquired Eastern Machine Screw Products Co. in New Haven, Connecticut.

National Acme was on the acquisition trail as well during the postwar era. In 1959 it purchased Shalco Systems, a six-year-old California producer of foundry shell and core mold machines. These tools were vital to the production of heavy-duty metal parts like engine blocks and heads, and enjoyed high demand from the automotive and heavy equipment industries.

The 1968 merger of the Cleveland Twist Drill Company and the National Acme Company created Acme-Cleveland Corporation. The new corporation had interests in the machine tool, foundry equipment, and electrical controls businesses. The firm's primary markets were the automotive, capital equipment, and screw machine products industries. Cleveland Twist president Arthur Armstrong was selected to lead the unified corporation.

The 1970s brought more acquisitions. In 1972 Acme-Cleveland acquired LaSalle Machine Tool, Inc., a 36-year-old producer of total manufacturing systems. The company's products included systems for the automated production of many internal combustion engine parts. The target markets for this machinery were the automotive, farm, and construction equipment industries. At the time, the total manufacturing concept was the vanguard of the machine tool industry. These systems were intended to increase productivity through automation and thereby cut costs, especially in the area of labor. At the time of its acquisition by Acme-Cleveland, LaSalle had nine plants in the United States, Canada, and Italy.

Problems within and without Acme-Cleveland hounded the company throughout the 1980s. External forces in the early 1980s, including an economic recession, brought on the machine tool industry's worst years since before World War II. From 1982 to 1983 alone, total annual shipments of metal cutting machine tools plummeted from $5 billion to less than $3 billion. Acme-Cleveland was especially dependent on cyclical industries like auto and steel makers, which were hit hard during these years. To make matters worse, imports rose from ten percent of the U.S. machine tool market in 1974 to 41.5 percent by 1984.

At the same time, rising demand for precise, flexible automated systems required ever-increasing investment in research and development. After wasting desperately-needed funds on what CEO B. Charles Ames called "costly but unproductive research and development programs," Acme-Cleveland acquired and formed joint ventures with firms that could provide it with less cyclical, higher-margin niches within the machine tool market. The company bought into laser and water jet machining, high-tech coatings, and remanufacturing during the early 1980s.

Under the direction of Ames, Acme-Cleveland made drastic efforts to cut costs from 1981 to 1987. From 1981 to 1984, the company slashed its work force from 6,300 to 2,600. It closed, wrote off, or consolidated 15 manufacturing facilities, thereby eliminating over half (1.4 million square feet) of its 2.5 million square feet of manufacturing floor space. Acme-Cleveland's sales dropped proportionately, from well over $400 million in fiscal 1980 to $164 million in fiscal 1983—their lowest level in a decade. In February 1984 CEO Ames told *Tooling & Production* magazine that, "while these actions were painful, a less aggressive course would have risked allowing the whole business to sink deeper into a hole that might have made recovery impossible."

Ames and his management team initially believed that they had successfully executed a dramatic restructuring effort in 1984. But by the middle of the decade it became clear that Acme-Cleveland's leaders had begun to lose faith in their company's traditional business. A second, decade-long, reorganization utterly and irrevocably transformed the company. The LaSalle division was the first important divestment. Its 1984 loss of $15.7 million was a major factor in that year's overall net shortfall of $11.4 million, and its spin-off in 1985 helped free Acme-Cleveland from dependence on the auto market. Acquisitions provided the cornerstones upon which Acme-Cleveland hoped to build a stable new business. Purchased in 1984, Communications Technology Corp. (CTC), a Los Angeles-based manufacturer of industrial communications equipment, was expected to be an important brick in that foundation. Although the subsidiary floundered in its first few years with Acme-Cleveland, by 1993 the telecommunications market accounted for almost 75 percent of the company's operating earnings.

Other issues plagued Acme-Cleveland during this trying period. The company's top two executives vacated within a twelve-month period in 1986 and 1987. President James T. Bartlett was first to go, then B. Charles Ames resigned to take a new position. David L. Swift, who had previously served as a vice-president, was appointed as president, CEO, and director in 1987. Strikes in 1986 and 1989 also disrupted the company as workers registered their resistance to wage and benefit concessions. In the latter year, the company lost a $10 million lawsuit brought against it by Vickers Inc., a subsidiary of TRINOVA Corp. The plaintiff alleged that Acme-Cleveland—through then-subsidiary LaSalle Machine Tool Inc.—had reneged on a 1983 contract to deliver a fully-automated flexible manufacturing system. Acme-Cleveland appealed the federal court decision, then settled with Vickers for $4 million in cash and an additional $4.5 million in machine tools.

The sum of all these factors was decidedly negative. From 1982 to 1992, Acme-Cleveland lost $45.5 million more than it made. Sales dropped from nearly $500 million to $112.67 million over the same period. Nonetheless, the company recorded its third successive fiscal year of profitability in 1990, and was proclaimed "Turnaround of the Year" by the Turnaround Management Association in 1991.

The true climax of Acme-Cleveland's drawn out reorganization, however, actually came three years later, with the late 1994 divestment of the company's primary metalworking subsidiary and the acquisition of several telecommunications firms. Although Cleveland Twist Drill was Acme-Cleveland's founding business, accounting for two-thirds of overall sales, it was sold in the fall of 1994 to longtime rival Greenfield Industries Inc. for $45.2 million in cash. Acme-Cleveland's leaders reasoned that since the cutting-tool industry in general was gearing for an upturn and the divestment of Cleveland Twist Drill was inevitable, this was the best time for an asset sale. At the same time, the company boosted its telecommunications interests with the purchases of TxPort Inc. (pronounced "transport") and Phoenix Microsystems Inc., thereby adding about $25 million in annual sales to its Communications Technology Corp. subsidiary.

While Acme-Cleveland's annual sales declined steadily in the early 1990s from $125.5 million in 1990 to $107.9 million in 1994, Wall Street clearly registered its approval of the company's strategy. In January 1995 alone, the company's stock spurted from about $10.50 to $16, and a jubilant CEO Swift told the *Cleveland Plain Dealer*'s that shareholder equity had "more than doubled to $75 million." Having overseen the company's historic transformation, Swift planned to shore up Acme-Cleveland's competitive position with what he called "good" acquisitions and overseas expansion in the late 1990s.

Principal Subsidiaries: Communications Technology Corporation; TxPort, Inc.; Namco Controls Corporation; M&M Precision Systems Corporation; The National Acme Company.

Further Reading:

"Acme-Cleveland Continues its Return to Profit Lane," *Cleveland Plain Dealer,* January 26, 1990, p. B9.

"Acme-Cleveland Selling Twist Drill," *Cleveland Plain Dealer,* September 2, 1994, p. C1.

"Acme-Cleveland Settlement Erases $10 Million Judgment," *Cleveland Plain Dealer,* April 2, 1991, p. 5D.

"Acme-Cleveland: 'We Tried to do Too Much,' " *American Metal Market,* January 28, 1985, p. 8.

"Acme-Cleveland's Chairman Thrives on New Challenges," *Cleveland Plain Dealer,* January 12, 1992, p. E3.

Armstrong, Arthur S., *The Persistence of Struggle: The Story of Acme-Cleveland Corporation.* New York: The Newcomen Society, 1976.

Clifford, Mark, "Slow Recovery for a Vulnerable Giant," *Financial World,* October 17, 1984, p. 24.

Freeh, John, "Acme-Cleveland Turning Profitable Again," *Cleveland Plain Dealer,* January 27, 1989, p. B7.

Gerdel, Thomas W., "Acme-Cleveland Loses Suit," *Cleveland Plain Dealer,* October 5, 1988, p. G1.

"On Corporate Darwinism," *Tooling & Production,* February 1984, p. 14.

Sabath, Donald, "Acme-Cleveland Moves in a Brand New Direction," *Cleveland Plain Dealer,* January 27, 1995, p. C1.

Solov, Diane, "Holding Its Own: Acme-Cleveland Evolving to Meet the Times," *Cleveland Plain Dealer,* January 12, 1992, p. E1.

"Twist Drill Sold to Rival Tool Maker," *Cleveland Plain Dealer,* September 14, 1994, p. C1.

Weiss, Barbara, "Reshaped Acme Assessed by Departing Bartlett," *American Metal Market,* March 17, 1986, p. 16.

—April D. Gasbarre

Adolph Coors Company

12th and Ford Streets
Golden, Colorado 80401
U.S.A.
(303) 279-6565
Fax: (303) 277-6564

Public Company
Incorporated: 1913 as the Adolph Coors Brewing and Manufacturing Company
Employees: 6,300
Sales: $1.66 billion
Stock Exchanges: NASDAQ
SICs: 2082 Malt Beverages

The Adolph Coors Company is the only family-owned brewery in America that was able to survive the late 20th-century consolidation of the U.S. beer industry without relinquishing family control. The regional brewer gained national prominence in the 1960s and 1970s, but only officially achieved national distribution in 1986. In the mid-1990s, Coors ranked a distant third to market leaders Anheuser-Busch Company, Inc. and Miller Brewing Company. By that time, Coors operated the world's largest brewery at its headquarters in Golden, Colorado, and distributed its 16 branded malt beverages in 17 countries worldwide. Prodded from its conservative management tendencies by stagnant sales and meager profits in the late 1980s, a new generation of Coors family leaders sought to revitalize the business in the early 1990s.

Adolph Herman Joseph Coors emigrated to the United States from Germany in 1868 at the age of 21. After purchasing a Denver bottling company in 1872, Coors formed a partnership with Jacob Schueler in 1873. Although Schueler invested the lion's share of the $20,000 necessary to build a brewery in nearby Golden, Coors was able to buy out his partner by 1880. His acquisition inaugurated more than a century of Coors family control.

The fledgling brewery's sales increased steadily in the ensuing decades. In 1887 the brewery sold 7,049 barrels of beer (31 gallons per barrel). Three years later that figure more than doubled, reaching 17,600 barrels. Over the years Adolph Coors slowly expanded his market. By the time he officially incorporated his brewery as the Adolph Coors Brewing and Manufacturing Company, Coors's beer was being distributed throughout Colorado.

Even at this early point in the company's history, the distinctive Coors philosophy was emerging. The main tenets of this philosophy adhered to by three successive generations of Coors beermakers, each generation further refining the knowledge inherited from the preceding generation were the following: Adolph Coors believed in sparing no effort or expense in producing the best beer possible. To this end, he believed that only Colorado spring water was good enough for his beer. He also commissioned farmers to grow the barley and hops that he needed for his brewing process. The second tenet of the philosophy was that his family always came first, without exception; the Coors family brewery has remained a tight-knit, protective, and almost secretive enterprise. The last tenet was that "a good beer sells itself." Until 1980 Coors spent substantially less on advertising than any other brewer.

Prohibition came early to Colorado. In 1916 the state's legislature passed a law banning the production and consumption of alcoholic beverages within the state. Obviously, Prohibition was detrimental to Adolph Coors's brewery; however, some business historians would assert that the legislation strengthened the burgeoning company. The obvious changes in product offerings—Coors manufactured "near beer" and malted milk during this period—were reflected in a name change, to the "Adolph Coors Company." Adolph Coors and his son, Adolph Jr., also used the opportunity to diversify their company, creating what was eventually to become a small-scale vertical monopoly: Coors acquired all that it needed to produce its beer, from the oil wells that created the energy necessary to run the brewery to the farms that grew the ingredients, and from the bottling plant that made the containers to the trucks used for distribution. This expansion was financed entirely with family money.

The repeal of Prohibition did not result in as dramatic a sales increase for Coors as it did for many other producers of alcoholic beverages. Instead, the Adolph Coors Company, under the direction of Adolph Jr. and his two brothers, expanded its market slowly in the 1930s. Their insistence on the use of all natural ingredients and no preservatives—in accordance with the brewery's founding tenets—made wider distribution prohibitively expensive. The beer had to be brewed, transported, and stored under refrigeration, and its shelf life was limited to one month. But if Coors growth and development in the decades following the repeal of Prohibition was less dramatic than that of brewing powerhouses like Anheuser-Busch and Miller, it was no less amazing. For while other regional breweries were squeezed out of the market—the number of independents shrunk from 450 in 1947 to 120 in 1967—Coors grew steadily into one of America's leading beer brands. Coors's production increased 20-fold, from 123,000 barrels in 1930 to 3.5 million barrels in 1960, as the brewer expanded its reach into 11 western states. Coors's ranking among the nation's beer companies advanced accordingly, from 14th in 1959 to fourth by 1969.

So how did Coors grow 1500 percent between 1947 and 1967, with only one product, made in a single brewery, and sold in only ten states? A quality product was certainly one reason for Coors's success. The company's technological innovations, including the development of both the first cold-filtered beer and the first aluminum can in 1959, also placed it in the vanguard of the beer industry. Another reason was a unique marketing ploy that Coors perfected during the 1960s. When Coors entered a new market, it would lead with draught beer only. The company would sell kegs to taverns and bars at a price under that of its lowest competition. Then Coors would encourage the barkeepers to sell the beer at a premium price. Once Coors's premium image was established, the company would then introduce the beer in retail stores. Since Coors spent so little on advertising, the company was able to offer a better profit margin to its wholesalers. These profit incentives to both wholesalers and retailers worked well. Through the 1970s Coors was the leading beer in nine of the 11 western states in which it was sold. In California, the second largest beer market in the country (New York was first), Coors at one time held an astonishing 43 percent of the market.

However, marketing, innovation, and product quality could not account for what was later considered one of the strangest phenomena in American business history. Beginning in the late 1960s and culminating in the mid-1970s Coors developed, without any effort by the company, an unusual reputation as a "cult" beer. Limited availability created intense demand on the East Coast. Westerners, keen to flaunt their perceived superiority to easterners, got caught up in a "we have what you want" syndrome and unwittingly became the company's unpaid advertisers. As a result, Coors virtually eliminated its competition in nine western states. Those nine states provided Coors with all the market it needed to become the fourth largest brewery in America.

But all was not well with the company and its enigmatic founding family. The 1960 kidnapping and murder of Adolph III intensified the clan's already-strong tendency toward secrecy. Their cautious, elusive nature produced circumspect hiring practices, including polygraphs and sworn statements of loyalty. Outsiders saw these practices as both unfair and as a means of enforcing racial discrimination: the limited numbers of African Americans and Hispanics employed by the company seemed to support this view. Lawsuits were filed alleging discrimination and, more importantly, a coalition of minority and labor groups organized a boycott, which intensified the negative publicity surrounding the company. The boycott and lawsuits provoked more public scrutiny of the Coors dynasty. A series of articles appeared in the *Washington Post* in May of 1975 documenting Joe Coors's ultra-conservative political philosophy. Not only did these revelations exacerbate the boycott, they also influenced the average consumer and generally undermined Coors's market position.

At first, the Coors family response was retrenchment and litigation. However, when sales dropped ten percent in California in 1975 (at the time that state accounted for 49 percent of total sales), the family changed its tactics. They settled the lawsuits, agreed to a minority hiring plan, and launched advertising campaigns aimed at showing the company's "good side." Television advertisements showed that minorities were happily employed in the brewery. Bill Coors took the initiative on environmental issues and proclaimed that the company was well ahead of the industry and the government in keeping the environment clean. The replacement of pull-tabs with "pop-down" tabs and the first aluminum recycling program were cited as proof of Coors's commitment.

After a decrease in sales through the late 1970s, the company appeared to revive in 1980. Sales volume dropped by one million barrels between 1976 and 1978, bottoming out at 12.5 million barrels before rebounding in 1980 to 13.7 million. Bill and Joe Coors, the third generation of the family to take charge, concluded that their sales problem emanated from their image problem and that they had successfully solved both.

Two separate situations, one in 1975 and the other in 1976, should have signaled that the company's problems went beyond that of image. In 1975 the Coors family was forced for the first time to offer shares to the public to raise $50 million to pay inheritance tax for a family member. The original offering was successful, raising over $130 million. The stock sold was of a non-voting class, so the family did not relinquish any control over the company. However, analysts suggested that the reluctance with which the company undertook the offering disclosed a disdain for modern methods of capitalization. The second situation involved a Federal Trade Commission (FTC) ruling, later upheld by the Supreme Court, striking down Coors's strong-arm tactics over distribution. Coors refused to sell its product to distributors that the company regarded as unable to handle the beer properly. Once again, many industry analysts remarked that the company exhibited a disdain for mass marketing techniques.

Indeed, Coors remained committed to its founder's decidedly outdated idea that "a good beer sells itself." In 1975, William Coors claimed that "We don't need marketing. We know we make the best beer in the world." Throughout its entire history, Coors had spent far less than its competitors on advertising. In the 1970s, Coors's ad budget amounted to about $.65 per barrel, compared to the $3.50 per barrel promoting the leading beers. Anheuser-Busch and Miller spent billions of dollars on promotion in a market which they continually expanded with new products. Coors, on the other hand, only reluctantly joined the light beer movement and grudgingly increased its meager marketing outlay. As a result, Coors's 1982 sales volume declined to less than 12 million barrels for the first time in ten years, and the company relinquished its third-place ranking to Stroh Brewing Company.

Although Coors's sales increased from $1.1 billion in 1983 to $1.8 billion in 1989, profits declined from $89 million to $13 million, and the company's return on sales dropped from eight percent to less than one percent. Some observers blamed the brewery's entrenched family management, which they characterized as reactionary. But larger industry wide trends also contributed to the low earnings. The beer market's customer base began to stagnate in the mid-1980s, forcing brewers to use margin-lowering tactics to build volume and share. These included brand segmentation, increased (and increasingly malicious) advertising, international expansion, and heavy discounting.

Under the direction of Peter Coors beginning in 1986, the brewery eagerly sought to catch up with its larger rivals. The new leader had been a driving force behind Coors's ground swell of change and continued on that course in the late 1980s and early 1990s. Under his direction, the brewery completely reversed its advertising course: by the early 1990s, Coors began to spend more—in terms of advertising per barrel of beer sold—than its bigger rivals. Coors Light became the company's best-selling beer, America's third-ranking light beer, and the number-one light beer in Canada. The company embraced the concept of brand segmentation and discounting, introducing the "economy" or "popularly priced" Keystone and Keystone Light in 1989. Ostensibly offering "bottled-beer taste in a can," these beers boosted sales volume, raising overall Coors sales to ten percent of the beer market and winning back the number three spot. But at the same time, such new products took market share away from other Coors brands, including the family's original label, which lost one-third of its sales volume from the mid-1980s to the mid-1990s.

While Keystone appealed to the budget-minded beer drinker, other new beverages targeted the higher-margin "specialty" and "boutique" markets. The domestic company craftily entered the fast-growing import market with the introduction of "George Killian's Irish Red," a defunct Irish brand licensed by Coors and produced in the United States. Even without the support of television advertising, the faux import was able to compete with Boston Beer Co.'s domestically-microbrewed Samuel Adams brand for leadership of the specialty beer segment.

In 1992, Coors launched Zima, one of the beer industry's most creative new beverages. The clear, foam-free malted brew created a whole new beverage category. The drink's novelty won it instant popularity that fizzled even before Coors could introduce its first derivative, Zima Gold, in 1995. Analysts noted the telling fact that neither Anheuser-Busch nor Miller, both noted for savvy marketing, followed Coors's lead into the clearmalt category.

Peter Coors wasn't afraid to buck decades of family tradition, chalking up several firsts that had previously been renounced. With Coors running up against its lone brewery's 20 million barrel annual capacity, Peter floated the company's first long-term debt offering in 1990. Shortly thereafter, he tried to negotiate the $425 million acquisition of Stroh Brewing Co., but ended up buying its three million-barrel-capacity Memphis, Tennessee, brewery for about $50 million. If, as Peter Coors hinted to a reporter in a March 1991 *Forbes* article, the company wanted to mount a challenge to second-ranking Miller Brewing Co., it would still need to double its U.S. brewing capacity.

In 1992, Coors spun off the company's non-beer assets—including the high-tech ceramics division, as well as the aluminum and packaging businesses—as ACX Technologies. Coors's shareholders received one share of ACX for every three shares of the brewing company. The divestment was considered successful: ACX's sales increased from $544 million in 1991 to $732 million in 1994, and profits multiplied from $1.3 million to $20 million over the same period.

In 1993, Peter Coors broke with 121 years of history by hiring the first nonfamily member to the presidency of the brewing business. His choice, W. Leo Kiely, reflected Coors's new emphasis on marketing. Kiely had been a top marketing executive with PepsiCo's Frito-Lay division. The new president was given a straightforward, but arduous mandate: increase Coors's return on investment from less than five to ten percent by 1997.

Principal Subsidiaries: Coors Brewing Company.

Further Reading:

Burgess, Robert J., "Popular Keystone Hurt Other Coors Brands," *Denver Business Journal*, April 30, 1993, p. A1.

——, *Silver Bullets : A Soldier's Story of How Coors Bombed in the Beer Wars*, New York: St. Martin's Press, 1993.

Conny, Beth Mende, *Coors, A Catalyst for Change: The Pioneering of the Aluminum Can*, Golden, Colo.: Adolph Coors Co., 1990.

"Coors: The Adolph Coors Story," Golden, Colo,: Corporate Communication Department Adolph Coors Co., 1984.

Fulscher, Todd James, *A Study of Labor Relations at the Adolph Coors Brewery*, M.A. Thesis, Denver: University of Denver, 1994.

Hunter, Kris, "Battle of the Beers," *Memphis Business Journal*, March 13, 1995, p. 34.

Lane, Randall, "Splitsville in Coors Country," *Forbes*, April 10, 1995, p. 52.

Lang, Tam, *Coors: A Report on the Company's Environmental Policies and Practices*, New York: Council on Economic Priorities, Corporate Environmental Data Clearinghouse, 1992.

Poole, Claire, "Shirtsleeves to Shirtsleeves," *Forbes*, March 4, 1991, p. 52.

The Pre-Prohibition History of Adolph Coors Company, 1873–1933, Golden, Colo.: Adolph Coors Co., 1973.

Sellers, Patricia, "A Whole New Ball Game in Beer," *Fortune*, September 19, 1994, p. 79.

"Time in a Bottle: Adolph Coors Company," Golden, Colo.: Corporate Communications Dept., Adolph Coors Co., 1984.

—updated by April Dougal Gasbarre

AES Corporation

1001 North 19th Street
Arlington, Virginia 22209
U.S.A.
(703) 522-1315
Fax: (703) 528-4510

Public Company
Incorporated: 1981 as Applied Energy Sources
Employees: 1,664
Sales: $532.7 million
Stock Exchanges: NASDAQ
SICs: 4911 Electrical Services

AES Corporation is one of the largest independent producers of electrical power in the world, with an ownership stake in 14 power-generating facilities in six U.S. states (California, Connecticut, Pennsylvania, Texas, Hawaii, and Oklahoma) and four foreign countries (the United Kingdom, Pakistan, China, and Argentina). The company supplies more than 3,567 megawatts of electricity worldwide, with most of its production taking place in the United States and Great Britain. New projects slated for completion in the late 1990s, however, were expected to add at least 1,500 megawatts of electricity to the company's total production output; an estimated 85 percent of such new production was slated to occur in emerging overseas markets in Asia, the Near East, and Latin America. In 1995, AES generated, sold, or marketed electricity in more than 25 countries, ranging from Italy to Vietnam and India to Mexico, all with the aim of building on its role as one of the world's chief suppliers of electricity. AES assets totaled more than $2 billion in 1995, and over $5 billion worth of projects were either in construction or the late stages of development.

AES was the invention of Roger W. Sant and Dennis W. Bakke, who had served together in the Federal Energy Administration (FEA) during the Nixon and Ford administrations in the early to mid-1970s. Sant had been a lecturer at the Stanford School of Business; Bakke, a Harvard MBA and career government employee, was his assistant. As part of their work at the FEA, the two had been instrumental in drafting preliminary versions of the Public Utility Regulatory Policies Act (PURPA).

The law was part of the federal government's attempt to deal with America's energy crisis, which, according to prevailing opinion at the time, was caused largely by American dependence on foreign oil. Seeking to reduce this dependence, PURPA mandated that electrical utilities fulfill any need they might have for new power by seeking out qualified cogenerators and independent, small-scale, private-sector power producers. The law further stipulated that the cost of power provided by these facilities be less than a utility's "avoided cost"—that is, the cost incurred by the utility if it generated the power itself.

Prior to PURPA, by contrast, utilities typically secured additional power by building a new power-generating facility, which was usually oil dependent. Otherwise they purchased new power on the open market from yet another oil-dependent utility. PURPA, however, changed that, since it effectively required utilities to fulfill their energy needs by turning instead to cogenerators and other oil-independent power producers.

PURPA was enacted into law in 1978—four years after Sant and Bakke had left the government to found an energy research institute or "think tank" at Carnegie Mellon University. That was also the year in which President Carter declared America's energy crisis to be the "moral equivalent of war," as Americans experienced oil and gas shortages, long lines at the gas pumps, and fear of what the crisis portended for its future. Because of their formative work experience in government at the height of this crisis and their subsequent related work experience in academe, Sant and Bakke were well familiar with the contours of this problem—and familiar as well with the rapidly emerging business opportunities spawned by the new law.

What Sant and Bakke were quick to realize—and, at the time, were virtually alone in recognizing—was that PURPA had the paved the way for a burgeoning market in independent, private-sector power production. In part this was because of the new law's mandate that outside purchases of power be made from cogenerators and independent, small-scale, private-sector power producers. It also stemmed, however, from the fact that PURPA shielded new producers from costly state government regulation and subjected them instead to less onerous federal rules and strictures. In practice, this meant that new producers typically could undercut a utility's "avoided cost."

AES was founded in 1981 as Applied Energy Sources, and it took several years for Sant and Bakke to taste real success. The novelty of their idea and the untested nature of the market in which they sought to do business made it difficult to attract capital financing. Investors were understandably wary and skeptical of the firm's chances for success. One year's worth of effort netted the firm only $1.1 million in venture capital—a inadequate sum on which to build an electric power company. "From 1981 to 1985," reported *The Washington Post,* "one potential project participant after another—including ARCO, IBM, Bechtel Corp. and other large companies—marched in and then backed out of agreements with tiny AES."

The firm's luck took a turn for the better in 1985, when Sant and Bakke invested all of AES's assets in a single deal: a Beaver Valley, Pennsylvania, coal-burning plant. The deal was closed in September 1985 and the plant commenced production in 1987, marking a turning point for the company, which would never again have to depend upon the success of a single project for its very survival.

By then, in fact, AES had two plants up and running. Its Beaver Valley facility, supplied 125 megawatts of electricity to residents and commercial outfits in the Pittsburgh area, and its Deepwater, Texas, power plant, which, fueled by petroleum coke, went on line in June 1986 and supplied 143 megawatts of electricity to homeowners and businesses in the Houston area. Financial arrangements for Deepwater had been completed on December 30, 1983, and, in addition to AES, involved 12 other companies: ARCO, Bechtel, J.P. Morgan, eight supporting banks, and the General Electric Credit Corporation.

It was an auspicious start for the struggling company, which, over the course of the next 11 years (1984–1994), proceeded to build or acquire ten new power plants. According to an article in a 1993 issue of *Financial World (FW)* magazine, the average utility, by contrast, might "build one large facility every 10 or 15 years." AES sales, consequently, more than tripled in two years, rising from only $55.4 million in 1988 to $190.2 million in 1990. Sales grew an additional 75 percent the following year, while net company income witnessed similarly spectacular growth, soaring from $1.6 million in 1988 to $42.6 million in 1991.

Buoyed by its success, the company changed its name from Applied Energy Sources to AES and became a publicly traded company on the NASDAQ stock exchange in 1991. Company stock began and closed the year priced at $22.18 a share, with investors earning 66 cents per share. Sant assumed the position of company chairman, while Bakke became the firm's president and CEO. Together, they owned approximately 27 percent of all AES stock.

In these early growth years, AES's primary source of profits and revenue was the domestic U.S. power market. Bakke, for instance, estimated that up until about the mid-1992, 70 percent of the money that AES spent on new business activity was spent in the United States. The remaining 30 percent, he noted, was spent in the United Kingdom.

These investments yielded very good results. A November 1993 report by the investment banking firm of Kidder Peabody, for example, found that from 1988 to 1992 AES revenues grew at an annual compounded rate of 64 percent. Company earnings during that same time period, the report noted, likewise soared at an annual rate of 136 percent. In 1991, AES was recognized by the leading chronicler of American business, *Forbes* magazine, as one of "America's fastest growing companies," an honor it again earned in 1992 and 1993.

In conjunction with this success, AES staked out a reputation as one of the world's most socially conscious and organizationally innovative companies. Such distinctions were a legacy of Sant and Bakke and a direct consequence of their backgrounds. Bakke, was a devout Christian who readily acknowledged that Christian beliefs formed the basis of his world view. Sant, too, was raised a Christian, specifically a Mormon, and was an ardent environmentalist. Moreover, Bakke and Sant shared a common formative work experience in the federal bureaucracy, which inspired in them a deep and abiding distrust of centralized bureaucracies in either the public or private sector. Nevertheless, their youthful and idealistic desire to work for the government resulted in a strong and life-long commitment to public service.

Such principles and beliefs made AES a rather unique company. Indeed, Bakke and Sant maintained that the firm's primary goal was to build and nurture a firm that embodied their shared values, specifically integrity, fairness, fun, and social responsibility. A company that embodied these values, they felt, would in all likelihood make money. For AES, however, profits were neither an end in and of themselves nor the chief reason for the firm's existence. Rather, according to Bakke and Sant, money was the natural and inevitable byproduct of the firm's shared values. As Bakke told *CFO, The Magazine for Senior Financial Executives* in 1995: "The most socially responsible thing we can do is to do a really good job of fulfilling our business mission, which is to provide clean, reliable, safe, low-cost electricity around the world."

By conscious design, in fact, AES plants were among the safest and cleanest in the world, with pollution-emissions rates, accident rates, and plant 'availability' time all setting the standard for the electric power industry. Plant 'availability,' referred to the percentage of total potential capacity at which a plant was able to operate; taken as a group, AES power-generating facilities consistently averaged at least 90 percent availability. Moreover, in 1993 *FW* magazine reported that "the company's number of lost-time accidents is 44 percent below the national average." Regarding its pollution-emissions rates, AES plants were reportedly running an estimated 58 percent below permitted emission levels for sulphur dioxide and nitrogen oxide, averaging nearly one-sixth the rate reported by the majority of American plants.

To further protect the environment, AES committed itself to a tree planting and preservation program, whereby the company agreed to plant or preserve enough trees to offset the carbon dioxide emissions from its power-generating facilities. Study into such a program was initiated in 1987 after growing concern by company executives that such emissions were contributing to global warming and therefore having a deleterious effect on the environment. The program got underway in earnest two years later when AES committed itself to planting more than 52 million trees in Guatemala over roughly a ten-year period. The project cost the company an estimated $2 million, an amount that reportedly nearly equaled AES profits for that year.

Similar company efforts to plant and preserve trees, woodlands, and forests followed, including a $3 million effort undertaken in conjunction with Oxfam America, an international development group, to preserve 3.7 million acres of South American forest. The program was unique in that to save this land from development and exploitation, AES and Oxfam were helping pioneer a private property-rights approach to environmental protection by helping indigenous peoples in South America establish ownership rights to their territorial homelands. It also involved developing land-management programs that would help keep this land in good stead for decades to come.

Other company-sponsored social programs included the funding and construction of a $1.5 million public elementary school in Panama, Oklahoma, the site of one of its power-generating facilities. According to AES Chief Financial Officer Barry

Sharp, this was done to give something back to the town, which had given AES generous tax breaks to build the facility. In 1994, when construction of the school was completed, it was dedicated and turned over to the local school district. AES also established a consulting arm, AES Greenhouse Offset Group, to help other electric power companies be environmentally responsible and progressive. In recognition of these efforts, Harvard University honored AES in 1994 with its George S. Dively Award for Corporate Public Initiative.

Organizationally, AES established a decentralized corporate culture that gave company employees responsibility for most all aspects of business management. "Frequent and intensive cross-training, role rotation, and finance education for everyone are the rule," reported *CFO.* At AES, no more than three layers of management separated an AES entry-level employee from the firm's plant supervisor, each power-generating facility was responsible for its own affairs, and there were no company-wide departments for finance, human resources, operations, purchasing, or public relations. Consequently, the few company officers assigned to these areas acted typically as distant in-house advisors to the plant project management team responsible for a given project rather than as more conventional hands-on corporate facilitators. For plant financing, for example, CFO Barry Sharp raised less than ten percent of the estimated $3.5 billion needed for AES's first ten power plants; most of the necessary financing was raised by each plant's own multidisciplinary project team, composed of a broad cross-section of AES employees. By all accounts, this management system worked spectacularly well for AES. By giving workers a greater sense of involvement in, and responsibility for, their own professional destiny, employee morale was boosted. In 1995, annual employee turnover was averaging less than one percent, according company executives.

Like all management systems, however, the AES program faced challenges. One of the earliest and most significant breakdowns occurred in 1992 when the company disclosed that employees at its plant in Oklahoma had falsified the results of waste-water test samples in order to retain pollution permits from the Environmental Protection Agency (EPA). The workers responsible for the infraction said they feared losing their jobs if their violation of EPA pollution standards became known. In fact, the infraction actually had little substantive impact on AES since the pollution effect being covered up proved negligible and since the company itself disclosed to the government that it had broken the law. The workers responsible were fined, demoted, and placed on probation, but not fired. Sant and Bakke voluntarily cut their bonus pay for that year by 65 percent and 85 percent, respectively. The company publicly apologized for the incident and paid a $125,000 EPA fine. And employees at the Oklahoma plant imposed upon themselves an additional layer of management supervision and environmental monitoring before eventually readopting AES's standard management system.

Also in 1992 the state of Florida charged AES with misleading state officials about the environmental impact of a coal-fired power plant then under construction in Jacksonville. A subsequent state investigation cleared AES of any wrongdoing. By the time the state eventually concluded its investigation, however, the banks providing financing for the facility had cut off funding for the power plant, thus forcing AES to sell off its financial interest in the facility, cut its losses, and abandon the project, despite the fact that construction was nearly complete.

In spite of these difficulties, AES appeared to have a bright and promising future. In the early 1990s, independent, small-scale, private-sector power producers generated only nine percent of electricity in the United States. The U.S. Department of Energy estimated, however, that they would account for nearly 40 percent of all new electrical generating capacity added in the United States by the turn of the century. Certainly, AES's growth record bore this out, as company profits grew by some 650 percent from 1990 to 1994 and earnings per share during that same time period also grew dramatically, by approximately 500 percent.

Despite the opportunities for continued growth in the U.S. power market, however, AES began to look abroad for most of its new business ventures in the early 1990s. In fact, by 1995, the firm was spending an estimated 85 percent of its venture capital abroad. Six AES divisions worldwide emerged: AES Electric, which serviced Europe, the Middle East, and Africa; AES Enterprise, AES Chigen, which serviced China; AES Transpower (Asia, Hawaii, and the American West Coast); AES Shady Point; and AES Americas (Latin America).

The company's shift to the developing world was in part a natural reaction to its experience with its defunct Jacksonville power plant. The plant's failure underscored the relative difficulty independent power producers had doing business in the United States as opposed to overseas, where environmental restrictions were more flexible in part because the cost of pollution there was more easily offset by the benefits of electrical power. As AES company executive Sheryl Sturges told *The Washington Post* in 1995: "In the developing world, electricity produced from coal and other sources can make the difference between life and death. It can mean refrigeration for medicines and light for schoolchildren to study by."

AES's U.S. government tax levy rose sharply in the mid-1990s, from an effective rate of taxation of 23 percent in 1993 to 40 percent in 1996. In the developing world, by contrast, which was hungry for electrical energy, governments were eliminating tax and regulatory barriers that stymied the efforts of independent power producers.

In fact, the developing world's heightened need for electrical power was the chief reason AES shifted most of its new business ventures abroad. Electricity consumption in the United States, for instance, was expected to grow at an average annual rate of 1.9 percent until the year 2010, according to the Edison Electric Institute. The demand for electricity in the rest of the world, however, was projected to grow at nearly twice that rate, at an estimated annual rate of four percent during that same time period, according to the International Energy Agency.

According to Sant, the world needed $30 billion worth of new power plants a year through the year 2000. China and India alone, he suggested, would need three times more generating power over the next ten years than all of North America combined, and thus would require some $500 billion in power plant financing. It was expected therefore that, well into the next century, as the demand for electricity continues to grow, AES would remain one of the world's foremost producers of electrical power.

Further Reading:

''The AES Corporation (AESC),'' *The Wall Street Transcript,* February 27, 1995, pp. 117,669–117,748.

''AES Corp.: Sparking Competition,'' *Financial World,* June 8, 1993, p. 43.

Birchard, Bill, ''Power to the People,'' *CFO: The Magazine for Senior Financial Executives,* March 1995, pp. 38–43.

Buchanan, Leigh, ''The Way We Work,'' *CIO: The Magazine for Information Executives,* August 1994, pp. 33–77.

Cropper, Carol M., ''A Four-Letter Dirty Word,'' *Forbes,* January 17, 1994, p. 83.

Egan John, ''Power Plays,'' *Financial World,* February 4, 1992, pp. 28–29.

Markels, Alex, ''A Power Producer Is Intent on Giving Power to Its People,'' *The Wall Street Journal,* July 3, 1995.

Rubino, John, ''Powering the Planet—and Saving It,'' *Virginia Business,* September 1993, pp. 49–52.

Southerland, Daniel, ''The International Power Generators: Arlington's AES Corporation Leads a Battery of U.S. Energy Companies Expanding Overseas,'' *The Washington Post,* May 22, 1995, Bus. Sec., pp. 1, 12–13.

Waterman, Jr., ''Values from the Start: Culture Is Strategy at the AES Corporation,'' in *What America Does Right,* New York: Penguin Books, 1994, pp. 111–136.

—John R. Guardiano

AGCO Corp.

5295 Triangle Pkwy.
Norcross, Georgia 30092
U.S.A.
(404) 447-5546
Fax: (404) 246-6158

Public Company
Incorporated: 1985 as Deutz-Allis
Employees: 3,500
Sales: $1.20 billion
Stock Exchanges: New York
SICs: 3523 Farm Machinery & Equipment

AGCO Corp. is a major global manufacturer and distributor of tractors and other farm equipment. Through its extensive dealer network, AGCO builds and distributes products under brands that include AGCO Allis, GLEANER, Hesston, White, and Massey Ferguson, among others. AGCO achieved explosive growth during the early 1990s through savvy business management and by acquiring competitors.

Although AGCO itself was not created until 1990, the company boasts a rich history of success and innovation in the farm machinery industry. In fact, AGCO is the successor to Deutz-Allis, which was formed in 1985 when Klockner-Humboldt-Deutz AG purchased the agricultural unit of Allis-Chalmers Corp. In 1990, Klockner spun off Deutz-Allis to a group of executives who formed AGCO. Thus, AGCO is effectively the offspring of the renowned Allis-Chalmers Corp.

The Allis-Chalmers Corp. was the progeny of an American named Edward P. Allis. Allis was born in New York in 1824 and graduated from Geneva College in 1845. After college, Allis and a friend, William Allen, moved to Milwaukee, Wisconsin, where they opened the Empire Leather Store. This venture was a natural progression for Allis because his family was already involved in the leather business in that area. Through either sheer luck or great foresight, Allis sold his interest in Empire Leather shortly before the Financial Panic of 1857. A number of businesses, including Empire Leather, failed during the economic downturn. For the cash-rich Allis, the disaster was an opportunity. In 1861, he used his savings to purchase the financially troubled Reliance Works at a Sheriff's auction. Reliance Works was a leading manufacturer of sawmills, flour milling equipment, and castings. Before 1857, Reliance had been one of Milwaukee's largest employers with a payroll of about 75 men.

During the 1860s, Reliance Works of Edward P. Allis & Co., as the company was called, employed about 40 men working 55 hours per week. Allis constructed a new plant in 1868, and one year later he purchased his biggest rival, Bay State Iron Manufacturing Co. The company enjoyed strong profits until the Financial Panic of 1873, during which Allis went bankrupt. Chiefly due to the goodwill and faith of his creditors, Allis successfully renegotiated his debt and eventually recovered from the depression. The company remained intact, and even enjoyed a period of strong growth during much of the 1880s. By 1889, Allis employed 1,500 workers and shipped about $3 million worth of equipment annually. Allis died on April 1 of that year. He is still recognized as a pioneer in several machinery industry segments.

A number of gifted inventors and managers contributed to Allis's business efforts during the late 1800s. George M. Hinkley, for example, was a talented engineer and salesman who joined Allis in 1873. Among his most notable inventions was the bandsaw, which replaced the circular saw in many milling applications. The innovation was credited with revolutionizing the logging industry at the time, and the great demand for the saw helped the Edward P. Allis Company achieve a global presence in the machinery industry. Throughout his career, Hinkley accrued 35 patents on a wide range of sawmill machinery and accessories. Other notable Allis Company inventors included William Dixon Gray, who invented important new milling devices, and Edwin Reynolds, a pioneer in steam engine technology.

After Allis's death, his company continued to introduce breakthrough machines to the industry, particularly steam and pumping equipment. By the turn of the 20th century, the Edward P. Allis Company was the largest supplier of steam engines in the world. In 1901, Allis merged with another prominent machinery manufacturer, Fraser & Chalmers, to form Allis-Chalmers Company. Chalmers brought several new lines of machinery, particularly mining equipment, to the newly formed group, giving Allis-Chalmers a comprehensive product line. Further acquisitions during the next few years significantly broadened the company's product offerings, and Allis-Chalmers (the name was changed to Allis-Chalmers Manufacturing Company in 1913) continued to enter new machinery industries throughout the coming decades. Of greatest import to the history of AGCO was Allis-Chalmers's foray into the farm tractors market. Allis-Chalmers made many significant contributions to the farm machinery industry during the 1920s and 1930s, although its participation in that burgeoning market was dwarfed by competitors like International Harvester and John Deere.

Although it trailed a few industry leaders, Allis-Chalmers was recognized as a major U.S. manufacturer of farm equipment following its acquisition of Advance-Rumely Thresher Co. in 1931. The company parlayed its legacy of innovation into substantial gains with the division, introducing the first rubber-tired tractor in 1932 and, a few years later, a machine called the "All-Crop" harvester, which eventually eliminated the grain binder and threshing machine. One of the company's most profitable early innovations was the color it chose for its tractors—orange, in contrast to the industry-standard green. That move, devised by Allis-Chalmers's clever tractor division manager, Harry Merritt, proved to be a savvy publicity gimmick. The company's distinctive bright orange tractors eventually dotted the American landscape and became an excellent advertising tool.

During the 1940s and 1950s, Allis-Chalmers's farm machinery division assumed an increasingly prominent position within the company's many product groups. Ongoing innovation, such as the landmark multiple V-belt drive (Texrope drive) which the company introduced in the 1940s, spurred steady growth of the agricultural unit. To compete more effectively within its various markets, the company reorganized into separate tractor and general machinery divisions in the 1950s and several non-farm equipment lines were gradually phased out. Simultaneously, the company moved to expand its presence in foreign markets with the creation of Allis-Chalmers International. By the early 1960s, Allis-Chalmers operated factories in Mexico, Australia, England, France, and several other countries.

During the 1960s and early 1970s, Allis-Chalmers Corp., as it was named in 1971, experienced turbulence in several of its key markets. Fortunately, demand for agricultural equipment boomed during this period, and the company was able to offset losses in other areas with sales of tractors and other farm machinery. Despite the success of the agricultural division, general mismanagement and faulty strategy resulted in huge overall losses for the company. To make matters worse, the demand for farm equipment dropped significantly in the late 1970s. Battered by years of poor planning and a sagging economy, Allis-Chalmers's executives began searching in the early 1980s for a way to bring capital into the cash-starved organization.

During this period, Allis-Chalmers's farm equipment division became so depressed that the company was forced to close down its tractor and combine production plants for three months in 1984. This move stunned long-time Allis-Chalmers employees, many of whom were laid off. Desperate for cash and impatient with agricultural markets, Allis-Chalmers executives reached an agreement within six months of the shutdown to sell the farm machinery division. In 1985, the Allis-Chalmers Agricultural Equipment Co., along with a related credit subsidiary, was sold to Klockner-Humboldt-Deutz AG (KHD) for approximately $132 million and other consideration. At the time, the division was producing about $260 million in annual sales. KHD combined the new purchase with its established Deutz Farm Equipment subsidiary to create a new company called Deutz-Allis Corp.

Between 1985 and 1989, KHD labored to cut costs and restore profitability to the ailing Deutz-Allis Corp. It closed down U.S. tractor production facilities and began relying solely on its imported German-built tractors. However, KHD continued to operate the Allis-Chalmers combine manufacturing facility in Independence, Missouri, and even invested about $8 million in capital improvements at the plant. Importantly, KHD drastically reduced the number of equipment dealers from about 1,800 to just 800 and slashed its U.S. work force from more than 1,800 to just 900. The company also eliminated some unprofitable product lines and worked to reduce unnecessary operational costs. The effort succeeded in reducing Deutz-Allis's losses from about $82 million in 1987 to just $1.9 million in 1989.

Despite these noteworthy gains with its new Deutz-Allis unit, KHD was disappointed with the performance of its U.S. farm equipment operations. Importantly, the company had underestimated the loyalty of American farmers, many of whom were World War II veterans, to U.S.-built machinery. One of the Deutz-Allis gleaners, for example, was nicknamed the "Kraut Can" by import-wary farmers, despite the fact that the machine was built in Missouri. By 1989, KHD had tired of its Deutz-Allis experiment and was ready to sell the division. Robert Ratliff, the head of Deutz-Allis in the United States, recognized the company's potential; along with a group of fellow executives, Ratliff arranged to purchase the division by selling off Deutz-Allis receivables and using the money to finance a management buyout. Ratliff's management group completed the acquisition of Deutz-Allis in 1990 and renamed the company Allis-Gleaner Corp., or AGCO.

Ratliff was well acquainted with both AGCO's operations and the machinery industry when he took control of the company. He had worked at Uniroyal and at International Harvester, where he headed the truck group, before KHD hired him in 1988 to turn around the ailing Deutz-Allis. Upon purchasing the company, he and four other executives, with the help of investment firm Hamilton, Robinson & Co., moved quickly to assume control of the $200-million-per-year equipment manufacturer. "We never looked back," Ratliff recalled in the October 30, 1994, *Topeka Capital-Journal.* Ratliff and his partners moved AGCO's headquarters to Atlanta, Georgia, where the company could get a clean start by taking advantage of strong transportation and labor markets. Among other changes, they brought back the distinguished bright orange color to the farm equipment, which KHD had previously jettisoned in favor of dark green.

In the early 1990s, AGCO executives launched an aggressive plan to cut costs and increase efficiency. More importantly, they devised an ambitious strategy for growth. In 1991, Ratliff went to his home state of Kansas to negotiate the purchase of Hesston Corporation, a small hay handling equipment company with an excellent reputation for quality but a long history of financial problems. Founded by a group of Mennonite farmers, the company prospered for a short time before giant round-balers were introduced to the industry. Hesston was then purchased by Fiat, of Italy, which achieved uneven success in attempting to turn the company around. Ratliff believed that his team stood a better chance of reviving the company. A few months after the Hesston purchase, AGCO bought the White Tractor division of Allied Products. The acquisition of both Hesston and White Tractor not only rounded out AGCO's product line, but it also added 1,100 dealerships for the distribution of AGCO's existing machinery.

The Hesston and White Tractor acquisitions provided an insight into Ratliff's long-term profit strategy for AGCO. He realized that AGCO would be fighting an uphill battle if it was going to try to compete with manufacturing giants like John Deere and J.I. Case. "You've got 70 percent of the industry in North America controlled by two companies . . . neither of which has made money for a number of years," explained Allen Ritchie, head of AGCO's acquisition team, in the May 1994 issue of *Georgia Trend.* ''[Those] businesses were really being driven by the manufacturing side of the business—low cost production . . . and nobody won.'' Thus, instead of profiting by building more farm equipment, AGCO hoped to succeed by beating Deere and Case in the marketing and distribution arenas. To that end, AGCO executives planned to concentrate on building a comprehensive, efficient network of dealers that could supply an expansive, reputable product line.

AGCO paid $36 million for both Hesston and White Tractor, financing each deal by selling more receivables. To help stabilize the ballooning organization, Ratliff hired John Shumejda to serve as chief operating officer. Shumejda was an engineer and an expert at farm machinery technology. While Shumejda worked to streamline AGCO's manufacturing and distribution operations, Ratliff and Ritchie continued to make acquisitions. In January 1993, AGCO paid $94.8 million to Varity Corp. for the assets of farm-tractor giant Massey Ferguson's North American operations. This move represented a major coup for AGCO in that Massey added 1,100 new dealers to AGCO's network and $200 million in sales. In addition, AGCO bought a related credit company for about $45 million which became a primary profit center for the corporation. Later that year, AGCO acquired White-New Idea for $53 million. This baling equipment manufacturer added $83 million to AGCO's revenue and tagged 300 new dealers onto its burgeoning network.

By mid-1994, AGCO had established itself as the top North American distributor of tractors and a leading distributor of a wide range of farm machinery. Its giant distribution network had swelled to include 2,600 dealers, compared to John Deere's 1,400. AGCO was selling 20 different tractor models under the AGCO Allis name, four different GLEANER combines, 11 White tractors, and a range of equipment marketed under the names of Massey Ferguson and other brands. Although AGCO's debt burden had increased significantly, sales rocketed from about $220 million in 1990 to $314 million in 1992 and then $596 million in 1993. More importantly, AGCO's net income bounded to a healthy $34 million in 1993 (including a $14 million charge related to the Massey Ferguson buyout).

In 1994, AGCO transformed itself from a mid-sized North American farm equipment company to an international industry leader when it paid the equivalent of about $330 million for the international operations of Massey Ferguson. Prior to the buyout, only about two percent of AGCO's revenue came from outside North America. That figure shot up past 50 percent after the sale, giving AGCO immediate access to 140 different countries where Massey Ferguson was active. Furthermore, the giant division more than doubled AGCO's revenues, which surged in 1994 to an impressive $1.32 billion, about $76 million of which was net income. Going into the mid-1990s, AGCO continued to cut costs, particularly in its foreign operations, and to enhance its distribution network. It was the fourth largest farm machinery distributor in the world and was selling its machines and parts under seven different brand names. Improving agriculture industry dynamics, combined with AGCO's proven marketing and distribution strategies, gave the company a foundation for long-term growth.

Principal Subsidiaries: AGCO Allis; Agrecredit Acceptance Company; GLEANER; Hesston; Massey Ferguson; White; White-New Idea.

Further Reading:

Baldo, Anthony, ''Tricks With Tractors,'' *Financial World,* January 4, 1994, p. 68.

Connola, Jon, and John Fauber, ''Allis-Chalmers Files State Plant Closing Notice,'' *Business Journal-Milwaukee,* July 27, 1987, p. 1.

Fogarty, Bill, and Scott Nesbitt, ''Deutz and Allis Get Hitched,'' *Implement & Tractor,* July 1985, p. 8.

Hitchcock, Doug, ''Analysts Say Deutz-Allis Slowdown at Combine Factory to Be Temporary,'' *Kansas City Business Journal,* February 8, 1988, p. 11.

Mallory, Maria, ''AGCO Tractors Roar Down the Fast Track,'' *Business Week,* February 7, 1994.

McNaughton, David, ''Sharp Jump in Earnings Drives Up AGCO Stock, Analysts' Projections,'' *Atlanta Constitution,* October 28, 1994, p. D1.

Nesbitt, Scott, ''Deutz-Allis Execs Buy U.S. Operation,'' *Implement & Tractor,* May 1990, p. 2.

Ritchie, Allen W., ''AGCO to Acquire Assets of McConnell Tractor,'' *PR Newswire,* October 10, 1994.

Rubinger, David, ''Biggest Deal in Southeast This Year Brings Allis Home to U.S.,'' *Atlanta Business Chronicle,* July 23, 1990, p. A1.

Sparks, Debra, ''Betting the Farm; Can the New Massey Ferguson Reap Rewards in the Depressed European Market?'' *Financial World,* October 25, 1994, p. 74.

Suber, Jim, ''A Farm Equipment Company Led By a Native Kansan Has Quietly Pulled Off a Machinery Miracle,'' *Topeka Capital-Journal,* October 30, 1994, p. C1.

Wendel, Charles H., *The Allis Chalmers Story,* Sarasota, Fla.: Crestline Publishing, 1988.

Wilkinson, Bruce, ''Well-Run Companies Always Make Money,'' *Georgia Trend,* May 1994, p. 43.

—Dave Mote

Air Express International

Air Express International Corporation

120 Tokeneke Road
Darien, Connecticut 06820
U.S.A.
(203) 655-7900
Fax: (203) 655-5779

Public Company
Incorporated: 1946
Employees: 4,700
Sales: $1 billion
Stock Exchanges: NASDAQ
SICs: 4731 Freight Transportation Arrangement

A diverse transportation and logistics concern, Connecticut-based Air Express International Corporation (AEI) faced the brink of bankruptcy in the mid-1980s and emerged with unique strengths. In fact, AEI has become one of only two U.S. companies known worldwide for freight forwarding.

In 1935, Chester Mayer noticed that PanAmerican Airlines was having troubles expediting its air freight. At that time, most freight was still shipped by truck, so air shipments tended to be fairly small. Nonetheless, many airlines found it difficult to keep track of their freight, and Mayer saw an opportunity. He created AEI to help PanAm manage its air freight services. AEI quickly expanded its services to act as an agent for other airlines as well. Before long, the company had locations in New York, Los Angeles, and Chicago.

Despite the fact that the airline industry was growing, surface transportation remained the most popular way to ship freight until World War II. During that time, the military's need for swifter deliveries led to a boom in air transportation. AEI stepped in to become the contractor for the U.S. military throughout World War II. This role laid the foundation—in terms of experience and adaptability—for the company's later expansion to become the logistics provider of choice in a rapidly changing market.

With the war's end, AEI concentrated on extending its expertise to new markets, both at home and abroad. It opened offices in Paris and London by 1953, and it also became an exclusive agent in Argentina. This strategy proved to be an important factor in the company's later success. In fact, about 60 percent of AEI's revenues were generated outside of the United States by 1994.

In 1960, the company's operations expanded into the South Pacific and the Far East. By 1968, AEI also began doing business in Africa. Also in that year, AEI merged with Wings & Wheels, an international company with impressive financial strength. AEI continued to grow in the United States and Canada during the 1970s, and it opened offices in South America in 1979 and in the Middle East in the early 1980s.

Through the years, AEI faced keen competition in the air freight forwarding industry. In order to carve a niche for itself, the company introduced innovations such as scheduled charter services across the Atlantic and the first door-to-door package service. By the 1980s, however, the highly competitive environment began putting a strain on the company. For example, companies like Federal Express, United Parcel Service, and Airborne Express emerged to challenge AEI in small package and overnight door-to-door delivery.

Another significant problem for AEI involved a large-scale federal investigation of extortion charges against the Teamsters Union. Payoffs to Teamsters Union members at Kennedy International Airport in New York came to light, sullying the reputation of AEI and many other transportation companies. AEI also became the target of a takeover attempt by Consolidated Freightways Inc. The company's 1985 annual report admitted that it was "incurring substantial losses, suffering from cash flow problems, operating [its] airplanes unprofitably, had low employee morale and was in search of a strategic direction" at this time.

Salvation came from Hendrik Hartong, who—with his investment company, Brynwood Partners—gave AEI a $5 million cash infusion. Hartong became chairman and CEO, and he made Guenter Rohrmann president. An AEI veteran, Rohrmann had been vice-president of international operations. Together, the men took a hard look at the company and decided to scale back its involvement in the highly competitive overnight small-package service segment and concentrate on the less colorful heavy cargo forwarding business. They sold off AEI's two airplanes—that act alone cut yearly fixed costs by more than $1 million—and turned instead to leasing space on commercial carriers' planes to ship customer freight. This transformed Federal Express from a competitor into a supplier, as AEI began leasing space on FedEx planes.

An even bolder and more innovative step was the development and installation of a costly automated communications system. Rohrmann recognized that this gamble could make or break AEI. The freight forwarding business involved shepherding quantities of heavy cargo from one place to another via leased space on trucks, planes, or ships, often in combination, through various stops and nations. In the mid-1980s, the industry was often viewed as a black hole, or "dump the freight in, hope it comes out," as an AEI executive put it. With all the potential snafus inherent in shipping freight internationally, the creation of a computer system that could track shipments from point of origin to destination, using a single invoice number, could give the company responsible an obvious edge. Customers could instantly monitor the status of their freight from anywhere in the world. AEI committed itself to this task, with Rohrmann confidently staking his own salary against the investment.

In 1993, the company's $50 million LOGIS system was considered the best in the industry. Rohrmann received his salary intact, as AEI zoomed to the head of the freight-forwarding industry. After losing money in 1987 and 1988, AEI turned itself around by working with high-weight, high-volume business clients—shipping items such as heavy machinery and electronic components. This type of sale generated a larger margin than overnight letter-sized deliveries, and by 1989 business was growing at a compounded annual rate of 20 percent. That same year, Rohrmann replaced Hartong as CEO. AEI's nearest competitor was the San Francisco-based Harper Group, Inc., which set out to develop its own information system.

During its turnaround, AEI worked at keeping its fixed costs low and declined business that did not offer solid margins. It also invested wisely. In 1987, for example, AEI became one of the first U.S. forwarders to forge a pan-European freight network by acquiring Pandair, based in Holland. AEI also maintained its technological edge by achieving the first mainframe-to-mainframe electronic data interchange (EDI) with an airline in 1990.

By 1992, AEI was enjoying solid growth, with record revenues and earnings. Rather than resting on its laurels, however, the company began to shop around in the sea freight industry. Its reasoning was that customers prefer to rely on a single forwarder for all their shipping needs—whether by air or sea. Some of the tasks involved in shipping by sea include warehousing the freight after it arrives in a port and taking care of ground distribution. Since AEI was already well-poised in a consolidating market by virtue of its computerized tracking capabilities and worldwide presence, the next step was logical.

In 1993, the company purchased Votainer International, one of the world's oldest and largest worldwide Non-Vessel Operating Common Carrier concerns. Headquartered in Rotterdam, Votainer had offices in 12 countries with annual revenues of more than $100 million. AEI thus acquired an instant network of global offices and ocean freight experts. The $15 million purchase took a bite out of AEI's earnings for that year, but innovations were steady. For example, AEI linked its New York gateway with the U.S. Custom Service's Automated Manifest System in 1993. This link-up allowed AEI to speed up customs clearance—by starting the process before items even arrived at Kennedy International Airport—and reduce transit times by up to 24 hours. AEI also acquired two air freight companies in the United Kingdom, as well as Banner International in New Zealand and Pace Express Pty. Ltd. in Australia. These companies, which had combined annual revenues of $50 million, were blended into AEI's existing operations.

By the end of 1994, sea-freight forwarding accounted for about 12 percent of AEI's revenues. Business was booming in Asia, where manufacturers were active air-freight forwarders. Also in 1994, AEI became the first major U.S. transportation company to obtain ISO 9002 status. This designation, part of the ISO 9000 quality standards series set by the International Organization of Standardization, was highly valued by European clients. Since AEI was absorbing Votainer's losses for two years, the company projected a return to profitability by the second half of 1995. In May of 1995, AEI acquired Radix Group, Inc., a leader in customs brokerage services. Radix had a network of 23 domestic offices, gross revenues of $65 million, and air freight and ocean freight forwarding services of its own. AEI fared well during the worldwide recession of the early 1990s and expected to see continued growth as the transportation sector rebounded.

Principal Subsidiaries: AEI Occan Services Corp.; Air Charter Express International Limited; Air Express International Agency, Inc.; Air Express International USA, Inc.; Couriaire Express International, Inc.; Roadstar Corporation; Surface freight Corp.; Wings & Wheels Express, Inc.; Air Express International Finland Oy (Finland); Maruzen Air Express International Limited (Japan); AEI Ocean Services Sdn. Bhd. (Malaysia); Air Express International Holding B.V. (The Netherlands); Air Express International (U.K.) Ltd.; Air Express International GmbH (Germany); Air Express International (Canada) Limited.

Further Reading:

"AEI Seeking to Bolster Global Presence," *Journal of Commerce and Commercial,* August 2, 1994, p. 2B.
"Air Express Chief Talks of Wings and Wheels," *Journal of Commerce and Commercial,* July 25, 1994, p. S14.
"Air Express International Corp.," *Insiders' Chronicle,* June 15, 1992, p. 2.
"Air Express International Units Expand Singapore Cargo Facilities," *Journal of Commerce and Commercial,* May 18, 1992, p. 4B.
"Air Express Links with Customs in NY," *Journal of Commerce and Commercial,* January 11, 1993, p. 3B.
"Air Express to Buy Votainer," *American Shipper,* July 1993, p. 46.
"Air Express to Close Votainer Purchase," *American Shipper,* August 1993, p. 6.
Armbruster, William, "AEI Lands Contracts for GM Parts Shipments," *Journal of Commerce and Commercial,* July 6, 1994, p. 3B.
——, "AEI President Stands by Votainer Acquisition," *Journal of Commerce and Commercial,* September 27, 1994, p. 3B.
——, "Air Express International Offices Recognized for Quality Management," *Journal of Commerce and Commercial,* May 26, 1994, p. 3.
——, "Air Express Opens Texas Facility," *Journal of Commerce and Commercial,* April 13, 1994, p. 3B.
Byrne, Harlan, "Flying High," *Barron's,* November 14, 1994, p. 22.
Cone, Edward, "The Revolution Came Just in Time," *Information Week,* May 24, 1993.
Kimelman, John, "Fire Bird," *Financial World,* March 16, 1993, pp. 26–27.
Malkin, Richard, "AEI Enters a New Phase," *Distribution,* February 1993, p. 60.
Sanborn, Stephen, "Air Transport Industry," *Value Line Investment Survey,* September 25, 1992, p. 251.
Schuman, Michael, "Survive Now, Thrive Later," *Forbes,* January 3, 1994, p. 173.
Solomon, Mark, "Air Express' Profit Surged 60 Percent in Third Quarter," *Journal of Commerce and Commercial,* November 2, 1992, p. 2B.
——, "Technology is Freight's Weapon," *Knight-Ridder/Tribune Business News,* December 26, 1993, p. 122.
Tucker, Timothy, "Air Transport Industry," *Value Line Investment Survey,* June 24, 1994, p. 251; September 23, 1994, p. 251; December 23, 1994, p. 251.
Vail, Bruce, "U.S. Logistics for a European Operation," *American Shipper, September 1994, p. 70.*
Watson, Ric, "Air Express to Buy Votainer," *Journal of Commerce and Commercial,* May 13, 1993, p. 3B.

—Carol I. Keeley

Akzo Nobel N.V.

Velperweg 76
NL-6824 BM Arnhem
Netherlands
(85) 663761
Fax: (85) 664505

Public Company
Incorporated: 1969 as Akzo N.V.
Employees: 70,000
Sales: US $11.5 billion
Stock Exchanges: Many different European exchanges
SICs: 1479 Chemical and Fertilizer Mineral Mining, Not Elsewhere Classified; 2812 Alkalies and Chlorine; 2834 Pharmaceutical Preparations; 2841 Soap and Other Detergents; 2851 Paints, Varnishes, Lacquers, Enamels, and Allied Products; 2869 Industrial Organic Chemicals; 2890 Miscellaneous Chemical Products

The Dutch company Akzo Nobel N.V. stands as a highly diversified conglomerate which conducts business in more than 50 different countries. In the mid-1990s, the company ranked among the ten largest chemical producers in the world and was the leading global manufacturer of paints and coatings. Akzo Nobel was also active in an expansive array of other industries, including health care, fibers, electronics, and energy. Akzo Nobel was formed in 1994 by the merger of Akzo N.V. of the Netherlands, and Nobel Industries of Sweden. Its operations are centered in the Netherlands, Germany, and the United States.

The merger of Akzo and Nobel represented the culmination of more than a century of acquisitions and mergers between two companies boasting rich pasts. Akzo's history can be traced as far back as the 18th century. For example, one of the coating units that it acquired, Sikkens, was formed in 1792. Another subsidiary, a food company named Duyvis, was founded in 1806. Further, Akzo's chemical interests in the U.S. were tied to Armour & Company, a leading meat packing organization that commenced operations in the 1860s. However, the foundation for Akzo originally sprang from Vereinigte Glanzstoff-Fabriken, a German chemical company formed in 1899. In the early decades of the 20th century, Vereinigte established itself in the chemical industry as a leading producer of rayon and various paints and coatings. In 1929, Vereinigte merged with Nederlandsche Kunstzijdebariek (NK), a competing Dutch manufacturer of rayon. The resulting organization was named AKU.

From the 1930s to the 1960s, AKU became a solid market leader in the development and manufacture of synthetic fibers. In addition to Rayon, AKU began producing such breakthrough man-made materials as nylon and polyester. Chief among the company's significant innovations was the invention of a material called aramid, a derivative of nylon. AKU experimented with this synthetic fiber in the late 1960s, and by the 1980s the company was selling the product under the name of Twaron. Unfortunately for AKU, fiber industry leader Du Pont was simultaneously developing the fabric under the name of Kevlar, and Du Pont succeeded in beating AKU to market. As a result, AKU was not only shut out of the lucrative U.S. market for the product, but it also faced stiff competition in its home market of Europe. AKU's failure to carve out a market for Twaron proved to be the culmination of a series of setbacks which adversely affected its synthetic fibers operations throughout the 1970s.

Indeed, AKU had enjoyed generous profits from its core man-made fiber products during the 1960s, and its corporate strategy looked sound for the 1970s. AKU joined forces with KZO—a major Dutch producer of chemicals, drugs, detergents, and cosmetics—in 1969, and the resultant organization became Akzo. Further expansion plans on the part of Akzo were thwarted in the early 1970s, however, when actions by the OPEC oil cartel wreaked havoc with petrochemical markets. Akzo's businesses, particularly those related to man-made fibers, suffered. In addition to these oil-related problems, the fibers market was affected by turbulence from other quarters. During this period, many synthetic fibers became a commodity product, and low-cost Far-Eastern manufacturers took control of many industry segments. Burdened by weak demand and manufacturing overcapacity, Akzo's profits plunged. By the late 1970s, some analysts speculated that Akzo was headed for bankruptcy.

Throughout this turbulent period, Akzo executives scrambled to overcome adversity. They reduced the percentage of revenues attributable to man-made fibers from more than 50 percent in the early 1970s to less than 30 percent going into the 1980s. Further, they tried to supplant income from the struggling fiber division with higher margin products like paint coatings, non-commodity chemicals, and pharmaceuticals. Akzo executives made another significant move toward reorganizing their operations in 1982 when they appointed Arnout A. Loudon chief executive of the company. Loudon, a 46-year-old attorney turned executive, had demonstrated an impressive financial acumen in turning around Akzo subsidiaries in France and Brazil. Upon assuming leadership of the company, Loudon initiated an aggressive restructuring strategy designed to stabilize Akzo's unwieldy balance sheet and to ensure long-term profitability.

Among other maneuvers, Loudon further reduced Akzo's man-made fibers emphasis to just 20 percent of corporate revenues and boosted its position in coatings and health care related industries. He also decentralized decision-making and eliminated management layers. Furthermore, Loudon launched an ambitious acquisition drive in 1984 chiefly designed to increase Akzo's presence in the important U.S. market and to diversify into higher profit-margin chemical businesses. Between 1984 and 1990, Akzo purchased more than 30 companies, most of which were located in the United States, at a cost of about US $1.8 billion. The units were primarily involved in the production of salt, chemicals, and pharmaceuticals. To fund these purchases, Loudon simultaneously jettisoned poorly performing assets which were worth more than US $1.5 billion. By the end of the acquisition campaign, Akzo had emerged as the leading global producer of salt and peroxides and one of the top 20 chemical companies in the world. 1990 sales approached $10 billion as profits surged.

During the early 1990s, Akzo concentrated on improving efficiency. Indeed, compared to chemical companies in Japan and the United States, its operations were bloated, chiefly due to restrictive government and organized-labor regulations in Europe. Gradual improvements in efficiency led to marked success in key divisions such as pharmaceuticals, which captured a key position in the reproductive medicine market. Its most notable product was Desogen, the top-selling birth control formula in the world. Similarly, Akzo enjoyed steady market share gains in some of its paints and coatings divisions. The net result was that Akzo sustained steady sales and profits throughout the early 1990s, despite a global economic downturn.

Going into the mid-1990s, Akzo continued to reduce its emphasis on low-profit commodities like salt and fibers and to boost its dependence on coatings and specialty chemicals. To that end, Akzo consummated a pivotal merger early in 1994 with Nobel Industries of Sweden. Nobel was a major contender in global paint, coatings, and specialty chemical industries. It operated subsidiaries worldwide and enjoyed a relatively strong position in U.S. markets. The company that resulted—Akzo Nobel N.V.—elevated Akzo's revenue figure by more than 25 percent, gave the new company a leadership role in the global paints and coatings industry, and bolstered the former Akzo's stance in the European and U.S. markets. The former Nobel Industries benefitted from economies of scale offered by Akzo, such as inexpensive access to raw materials like salt and chlorates.

Akzo's merger partner Nobel Industries was founded in 1864 by Alfred Nobel, the progenitor of the Nobel Peace prize. Nobel was born in 1833 into a Swedish family that claimed heritage to the 17th-century Swedish prodigy Olaf Rudbeck. Alfred Nobel's father, Immanuel, was a self-educated inventor with an interest in explosives. An unsuccessful businessman, Immanuel was forced to file for bankruptcy in 1832 after the family's home burned down. In 1837, Immanuel moved to Russia, leaving his family behind, to start a new business. There, he invented an explosive device for which demand gradually increased. By 1842, Immanuel had achieved modest success with his invention, and he sent for his family. Alfred's exposure to that environment, combined with his natural interest in chemistry, prompted him to form his own company in 1864 called Nitroglycerin AB.

Alfred's key invention was a process of making nitroglycerine that did not explode during production and handling. However, the perfection of this technique came at a great personal cost for Nobel in that an explosion killed Alfred's brother and four other workers during the testing process. This breakthrough led to Nobel's development of dynamite in 1866, which combined nitroglycerine and an absorbent earthy substance. Nobel went on to create blasting gelatin and smokeless powder, and eventually claimed 350 patents. In an effort to overcome opposition from established gunpowder manufacturers and other competitors, Nobel and several associates formed the Nobel Dynamite Trust in 1886. This cartel eventually dominated five continents and Nobel dynamite factories dotted the globe.

A surprising turn of events occurred for Nobel in 1888 when his brother, Ludwig, died and a local French newspaper accidentally reported Alfred's death instead. To his dismay, Alfred read his own obituary, in which he was described as the inventor of dynamite and the "merchant of death," despite the fact that most of his explosives were used in nonmilitary applications. This experience motivated Nobel to demonstrate his true intent. Thus, when he died in 1896, Alfred directed that his entire fortune be entrusted to the Norwegian parliament and distributed annually as a reward to individuals who "shall have conferred the greatest benefit on mankind." Subsequently, the Nobel Foundation was established and the first prize was awarded in 1901.

After his death, Nobel's conglomeration of businesses was divided into various corporations. Nobel's Swedish companies evolved into two separate organizations. His original company, Nitroglycerin AB, continued to make explosives. Its name was changed to Nitro Nobel in 1965 before it was bought out by a chemical group controlled by the prominent Wallenberg family in 1978. The resultant organization was called KemaNobel. The other segment of the Swedish Nobel operations became Bofors, a manufacturer of munitions. In 1982, Erik Penser, a young Swedish stock broker, engineered the purchase of Bofors. Two years later, he purchased KemaNobel, reuniting the two divisions in a company he called Nobel Industries.

In 1986, Penser's company won a five-year, $1.2 billion contract to supply field artillery to the Indian government. Business analysts lauded the deal as one of the largest orders ever secured by a Swedish company until it was discovered that Penser may have made illegal, covert payments of $4.5 million into a secret Swiss bank account to get the contract. To make matters worse, it was discovered in 1987 that Nobel Industries had illegally shipped arms to Iran, Iraq, and other countries not sanctioned for arms trade by the Swedish government. Meanwhile, Nobel's U.S. chemical subsidiary, Bofors Nobel Inc., filed for bankruptcy in 1985, largely because the U.S. Department of Natural Resources had sued the division for $15 million in environmental clean-up costs. Initially, Bofors Nobel had agreed to pay the clean up expenses, but once the higher-than-expected costs accrued, the division elected to file for bankruptcy instead.

Despite Nobel Industries's setbacks, Akzo executives viewed the company as a potential asset to their organization. In 1994, Akzo completed the merger of Nobel's six business groups, making Akzo Nobel one of the ten largest chemical companies in the world. Shortly before the merger, Akzo had implemented a sweeping reorganization drive to dismantle the company's five major business divisions and recreate them in four new groups—chemical, fibers, coatings, and pharmaceuticals. Akzo continued to develop its U.S. markets aggressively, while it worked simultaneously to penetrate Asian and South American markets. Going into the mid-1990s, Akzo had invested about 33 percent of its resources in the Netherlands, 20 percent in Germany, and 22 percent in the United States, with much of its remaining investments scattered throughout Europe. Akzo Nobel's 1994 sales rose slightly to about US $11.5 billion, roughly five percent of which was netted as income. Company executives continued to view long-term growth as resulting from ongoing geographic and market diversification as well as improved operational efficiency.

Principal Subsidiaries: Akzo Nobel Chemicals B.V. (Netherlands); Akzo Nobel Coatings B.V. (Netherlands); Akzo Nobel Fibers B.V. (Netherlands); Organon Teknika N.V. (Belgium).

Further Reading:

''Akzo Nobel Combination Look Like a Perfect Fit,'' *Chemical Marketing Reporter,* April 18, 1994, p. 8.

Hunter, David, and Lyn Tattum, ''Akzo Shapes Up with a New Organization,'' *Chemical Week,* October 27, 1993, p. 26.

Mendes, Joshua, ''A New, Improved Chemical Stock at Half-Price,'' *Fortune,* July 2, 1990, p. 28.

Moskowitz, Milton, *The Global Marketplace,* New York: Macmillan, 1987.

Reier, Sharon, ''Master of the Hunt: While Most of Europe's Chemical Industry is Hurting, Akzo Surges Ahead,'' *Financial World,* January 5, 1993, p. 26.

Sommers, Nick, ''Akzo Nobel Launches New Generic Pharmaceutical Firm,'' *Business Wire,* September 6, 1994.

Srodes, James, ''Dutch Treat,'' *Financial World,* January 9, 1990, p. 32.

—Dave Mote

Aldi Group

Eckenbergstr. 16
D-45307 Essen
Germany
201 85930
Fax: 201 8593252

Private Company
Founded: 1913
Employees: 20,000
Sales: $US21 billion (1993)
SICs: 5400 Food Stores

Privately held by brothers Theo and Karl Albrecht, Aldi Group is Germany's leading grocery store chain and a top competitor in the global retail food industry. Cited by some as Europe's largest retailer, the chain has found success by going against virtually every standard of supermarketing, from its legendary reticence to the "Spartan atmosphere" of its stores. By the early 1990s the company operated an estimated 3,000 stores under the Aldi, Hofer, and Combi names in Germany, the Netherlands, Belgium, Denmark, Austria, the United States, France, and the United Kingdom.

Established in 1913 in Germany, Aldi operates what are known in the grocery business as "limited-assortment" stores or "hard discounters." Aldi has taken this retail concept, which features low overhead and scanty selection, to its leanest, meanest extreme. Unlike the vast majority of supermarket chains, which are continuously increasing their product offerings and selling space, Aldi holds selection at its stores to about 500 items. The bulk of these items are packaged grocery or dry goods. All other grocery formats carry at least ten times Aldi's typical 500-item lineup. Up to 95 percent of Aldi's offerings are sold under private or packer labels, and some of these products are made expressly for the chain. A 1993 examination of the limited-assortment niche noted that successful discounters (like Aldi) work closely with manufacturers to design products that are cheaper to transport, stock, and sell than name-brand goods. National brands are sometimes offered, but many industry observers speculate that Aldi only stocks them to highlight its own discounts.

By limiting consumer choice, Aldi saves money in several ways. Aldi stores are correspondingly small—usually 8,000 to 15,000 square feet—compared to the 50,000 to 125,000 square feet typically utilized by competitors with larger catalogs of items. Aldi's outlets also bypass expensive barcode scanners that are used by other stores to inventory and price products. Instead, a stockperson (who may double as the store's manager) simply sets out cases of goods, opens them, and posts a sign with the price nearby. Cashiers memorize price lists, and some sources claim that they're quizzed on their knowledge of the store's prices. Aldi's decision not to sell fresh meat also saves the company money because it is able to avoid steep refrigeration costs as well as the high wages demanded by meat-cutters' unions.

Aldi keeps labor costs low in other ways, too. Shoppers are charged four cents per bag and must bag their own groceries. Customers can "rent" a shopping cart for 25 cents; they get their quarter back when they bring the cart to the front of the store. Under this system Aldi doesn't have to pay someone to collect carts in the parking lot or replace stolen ones. The company even keeps the telephone numbers of their stores unlisted so that employees don't "waste" time answering the phone. Aldi-style austerity holds labor costs to an estimated four percent of store sales, compared to ten percent to 12 percent for most supermarkets.

Although precise figures on Aldi's financial performance are not available, limited-assortment stores in general are known to garner gross margins of about ten percent, compared to 26 percent for the average supermarket. Limited-assortment stores make up for this low gross margin by stocking only fast-moving products, thereby making more inventory turns than a typical supermarket. In 1989 Carol Fischman estimated in *Supermarket News* that limited-assortment stores made nearly twice as many annual inventory turns than the average supermarket. An examination of the industry by the *Economist* in 1993 noted that hard discounters also enjoy a favorable cash flow because they often sell their goods before suppliers' bills come due.

An anecdotal example of this extraordinary volume of goods sold was cited by Suzanne Bidlake in 1989 in *Marketing*. She quoted an unnamed competitor who claimed that, although Aldi "only sells one flavoured yoghurt, it sells more yoghurt than anyone else in Germany." Aldi also enjoys tremendous success with a variety of other goods. Aldi's Tandil laundry detergent led the German market in volume in the early 1990s, and industry observers have asserted that some of Aldi's canned goods have more than a 50 percent market share. As a result, a 1993 *Forbes* article estimated Aldi's net U.S. profit margin at 1.5 percent of sales, nearly double the industry average.

Jon Hauptman of Willard Bishop Consulting Ltd. in Barrington, Illinois, reported that Aldi's many efficiencies gave its customers 24 percent savings over membership in a warehouse club during the early 1990s. Hauptman noted in the *Business Journal-Milwaukee* that Aldi's "low prices attract people because it creates a lot of excitement and heavy word-of-mouth advertising," thereby allowing the chain to eschew traditional—and costly—media promotion. Hauptman also asserted that the Aldi phenomenon was not simply recession-driven, but that "no matter what happens to our [U.S.] economy, there is going to be 20 percent or more of the population that is going to find Aldi pretty attractive from a price standpoint." Although it does not use advertising regularly, Aldi has been known to position itself as "The Stock-Up Store" in infrequent print and television placements.

Maintaining an attractive facade isn't a priority at Aldi stores. Instead, the company often purchases second-rate locations as part of its cost-cutting strategy. Harsh strip lighting emphasizes the "pile it high, sell it cheap" atmosphere of which Aldi seems proud. Mark Kass of the *Business Journal-Milwaukee* quoted from a rare company brochure in July 1994 that summarized Aldi's philosophy: "When you buy a can of peas at Aldi, you're paying almost entirely for the can of peas. Aldi doesn't need to tack on one more penny to pay for any army of stackers or piped-in music or fancy display or check cashing or gimmicks and games. So your food dollar pays for what it's supposed to pay for . . . food."

To some consumers, the low-budget ambiance is a turn-off. Fiona Gilmore, managing director of Great Britain's largest design consultancy, Michael Peters and Partners, told Suzanne Bidlake of *Marketing* that Aldi's stores were so depressing that "people charge around the shelves to get out as soon as possible." Other analysts, however, count the chain's counter-culture aura as one of its most powerful selling points. Industry observer L. Craig Carver speculated in a 1989 interview with Richard Turcsik of *Supermarket News* that "certain customers are overwhelmed by the large formats and wide selections offered by modern superstores. They are intimidated in large stores and prefer the lack of assortment."

The Aldi Group's management executives have long been regarded as reticent and secretive, and the chain's policy of evading the press is widely known. The international chain's reserved reputation is attributed to its founders and owners, Theo and Karl Albrecht. A June 1992 *Supermarket News* story reported that the Albrecht brothers hadn't been seen in public "for many years."

In a characteristically brief 1989 phone interview, Aldi's United Kingdom Managing Director Trevor Coats told Suzanne Bidlake of *Marketing* that "we're not being mysterious at all. Its just that we're one of the largest retailers in Europe and we don't want to discuss our business with the media." In fact, the company's policy of secrecy—which is nevertheless often broken by "unnamed sources close to the company"—appears to be a key part of its competitive strategy. Jim Baska, the president and CEO of Associated Wholesale Grocers, operators of a U.S. limited-assortment chain, told *Supermarket News*' Richard Turcsik in 1989 that "it's when limited-assortment stores are ignored that they proliferate and become ubiquitous in the market. If they're taken seriously by the competition, limited-assortment stores won't grow or be a threat in any given market." Marcia Berss of *Forbes* concurred, noting in her 1993 coverage of the chain, "Why let competitors in on a good thing?"

Aldi's stealthy and successful international expansion to its present stature was undertaken gradually. Originally founded in 1913, the company refined its strategy and built up significant reserves in the post-World War II German grocery market. Aldi quietly expanded into other areas of Europe. The company made a big impact in Belgium, where analysts estimated the chain had 260 stores and US$1 billion sales by 1992. The private company also garnered approximately five percent of the grocery business in the Netherlands in the early 1990s. In addition, Aldi set up about 130 outlets in Austria and another 110 in Denmark. But while Aldi established its presence in a number of neighboring countries in the latter half of the twentieth century, its home country remained its primary market. By the late 1980s Aldi operated about fifty separate companies, which in turn ran over 2,000 stores in West Germany alone. Estimated sales of DM17 billion to DM20 billion (US$9.3 billion to US$10.99 billion) ranked the chain as that country's top food retailer with about 13 percent of the grocery market.

The 1970s and 1980s were marked by Aldi's initial attempts to establish itself in three key international markets: the United States, the United Kingdom, and France. Aldi established its U.S. arm in 1976, when limited-assortment stores first gained a foothold. At that time, other national retailers in the country, including the Great Atlantic and Pacific Tea Company (A&P), Kroger Company, Jewel Food Stores, and Dominick's Finer Foods, experimented with the format. All of those companies eventually abandoned the concept.

Aldi's first American outlets were launched in rural areas of the Midwest. A warehouse was established in Batavia, Illinois; the company's U.S. headquarters was still located at the site in the early 1990s. Less than a decade after opening its first store in the United States, Aldi had nearly 150 stores in Illinois, Indiana, Iowa, Kansas, Missouri, and Wisconsin. New distribution hubs were installed in Kansas, Iowa, and Missouri, and warehouses in Indiana and Ohio were completed by the end of the decade. By 1989 U.S. sales estimates ranged from US$515 million to US$780 million.

The company increased the pace of U.S. expansion in the late 1980s and early 1990s, expanding from its base in the Midwest to the East Coast. The company began construction of a huge warehouse outside Allentown, Pennsylvania. The distribution center was slated for completion by mid-1994, and Aldi officials informed local planners that they expected the building to be operating at full capacity—and therefore supplying 60 new stores—by the turn of the century. Analysts estimated that Aldi's American operations increased from about 200 stores in 1990 to nearly 400 in 1993, a year in which the grocery chain registered sales of approximately US$1.2 billion.

Aldi made its first foray into the British market in 1989. Some observers surmised that the chain was well-prepared to exploit that country's high-margin grocery industry, especially in light of the general economic downturn that hit the United Kingdom in the late 1980s. Others noted that Aldi was bigger than any of the country's indigenous chains, had more buying power, enjoyed lower overhead costs, had "deep pockets," and was not answerable to shareholders. Nonetheless, some analysts questioned the chain's prospects for success there. Fiona Gilmore correctly predicted in Suzanne Bidlake's 1987 *Marketing* piece that Aldi would have a tough time appealing to British shoppers accustomed to posh supermarkets and national brands. It was rumored that Aldi had hoped to open 200 outlets from 1989 to 1994, but the company fell short of that mark by almost 100 stores.

In order to survive in the United Kingdom, Aldi made a dramatic deviation from its own-label policy. *Marketing* reported in 1990 that a "source close to the secretive company revealed . . . that Aldi has 'come to the conclusion that the UK market, and the discount market in particular, is very brand sensitive.' Thus 'they will have to stock predominantly national brands.' " Aldi also found its adaptation to Britain's harsh market conditions hindered by Kwik Save, a fierce "soft discount" competitor. Kwik Save helped head off Aldi's expansion in the early 1990s by acquiring 100 stores. This maneuver made the efforts of the German firm to secure a healthy base for growth considerably more difficult.

Undaunted, Aldi continued to adapt to market conditions. In 1991 the chain forged an agreement with Britain's Gateway Foodmarkets Ltd. to establish outlets on the latter's sites. The partners hoped that their cooperation would be mutually beneficial—Aldi's exceptionally low prices would attract new customers to Gateway's stores, which could then fill in the gaps left by the discounter's scanty selection. Both rivals and analysts claimed that the cooperative venture was just another sign of the chains' inherent weaknesses in the face of market pressures.

Expansion in France was difficult as well, hampered by heavy price competition from entrenched rivals like Leclerc and Intermarche. David Shriver, an analyst with County NatWest (London) told Mark Tosh of *Supermarket News* that "to create a real differential in terms of price, Aldi has had to lower gross margins [in France] even more than it has had to in the U.K." As a result, Aldi only had an estimated 37 stores there by 1992.

Setbacks in Great Britain and France fueled skepticism about Aldi's invulnerability. Some attributed the chain's German success to historically restrictive market conditions that did not necessarily exist in other countries. Others surmised that economic recovery would spell the demise of limited assortment chains forced to "cannibalize" each other's market share. For its part, Aldi appeared to turn its attentions to Eastern Europe. In the former East Germany it built distribution centers and set up temporary "teaser" stores.

While Aldi has experienced uneven success in its efforts to expand its influence around the world, its activities have had a pronounced effect. Aldi's pioneering internationalization, as well as the competitive threat it posed, spurred the transformation of the global retail food industry. In 1993 the *Economist* confirmed that "cross-border mergers, acquisitions and alliances in [European Community] food-retailing, almost unknown a few years ago, are already growing. They could soon soar as companies seek pan-European economies of scale in areas like logistics as a response to cut-price competition. Those that stand still could find themselves right in the discounters' sights."

Further Reading:

"Aldi Reverses Policy to Compete in the UK," *Marketing,* March 1, 1990, p. 3.

Bennett, Stephen, "Right for the Times," *Progressive Grocer,* November 1993, p. 57.

Berss, Marcia, "Bag Your Own," *Forbes,* February 1, 1993, p. 70.

Bidlake, Suzanne, "Counter Revolution," *Marketing,* July 6, 1989, p. 22.

"Business: Europe's Discount Dogfight," *Economist,* May 8, 1993, pp. 69–70.

Fallon, James, "Aldi's European Stores Offer Price," *Supermarket News,* August 31, 1987, p. 33.

Giles, Martin, "Store Wars," *Economist,* December 4, 1993, pp. SS5–SS7.

Kass, Mark, "Aldi Quietly Spreads its No-Frills, Low-Price Grocery Message," *Business Journal-Milwaukee,* July 2, 1994, p. 2A.

Mitchell, Alan, "Aldi and Gateway Seal Site Deal in Move that Puzzles Supermarkets," *Marketing,* December 12, 1991, p. 5.

Schwarz, Michel, "Land of the Giants," *Marketing Week,* September 24, 1993, pp. SS14–SS17.

Tosh, Mark, "The Quiet Giant," *Supermarket News,* June 1, 1992, p. 1.

Turcsik, Richard, "They're Back: Limited-Assortment Stores," *Supermarket News,* September 25, 1989, p. 1.

Zimmerman, Susan, "New Aldi Depot Heralds One-Third More Stores?" *Supermarket News,* August 31, 1987, 1.

—April D. Gasbarre

Alfa Romeo

Fiat S.p.A.
Corso Marconi 10
Turin
Italy
011 39 11 65651
Fax: 011 39 11 6863525
Alfa Romeo Distributors of North America
P.O. Box 598026
Orlando, FL 32859
U.S.A.
(407) 856-5000

Wholly Owned Subsidiary of Fiat S.p.A.
Incorporated: 1910 as Societa Anonima Lombarda Fabbrica Automobili
Employees: 1,500
SICs: 5012 Automobiles & Other Motor Vehicles; 5013 Motor Vehicle Supplies & New Parts

Alfa Romeo is one of the most famous sports cars in the world, along with Porsche, Ferrari, Maserati, Corvette, Lamborghini, and Jaguar. Unfortunately, Alfa Romeo and its parent company, Fiat, have experienced severe economic difficulties during the early 1990s. Although Alfa Romeo accounted for over 50 percent of Fiat's domestic sales in Italy during 1990, Alfa Romeo's market share in the United States has continued to dwindle over the years. As a result, Fiat management has decided not to sell models of the new Spider convertible and new Spider 165 sedan in the United States. This decision will significantly alter the manner in which Alfa Romeo sells cars in North America.

Alfa Romeo was founded in Portello, just north of Milan, in 1910. Cav Ugo Stella, managing director of a Portello assembly plant for the Darracq, a French automobile, decided to organize a group to purchase the plant and build a car more suitable for the harsh and mountainous Italian roads. Along with a few Milanese businessmen, he took out a loan to purchase the Darracq plant. The group named itself the Lombardy Car Manufacturing Company (Societa Anonima Lombarda Fabbrica Automobili), and was soon known by its initials—ALFA.

Ugo Stella hired Giuseppi Merosi as chief automotive designer of the new company. Merosi had previously worked as a designer for Marchand, Fiat, and Bianchi car companies, and was well qualified to design both touring cars and cars for the racing circuit. His first design for ALFA included a monobloc engine, high tension magneto ignition, three-bearing crankshaft, side valves, and pressure lubrication. A radiator badge was also designed for the new firm's cars, including the soon-to-be famous red cross and snake, symbols that were part of the emblems of the city of Milan and the Visconti family. A blue border surrounded the edge of the circular badge, with the word "ALFA" at the top and "MILANO" at the bottom. First inscribed in brass lettering, the lettering was shortly afterward replaced with white enamel. During the first year of business, ALFA manufactured ten cars each of a 12hp and a 24hp model; one year later, production had increased to 40 cars of each model. By the time World War I began in 1914, ALFA was manufacturing 272 chassis a year with a staff of almost 300.

Although revenues from car sales seemed to provide adequate funds for ALFA to continue business, in 1915 the company was suddenly and surprisingly acquired by Nicola Romeo. From rather humble beginnings, Romeo had graduated from the University of Liege with a degree in electrical engineering. After working for a short time in Germany and then France, he returned to his native Italy and started a business in Milan in association with the American company Ingersoll-Rand. Romeo's business was so successful that he soon formed his own business to manufacture mining equipment. This business was so successful, and the expansion of his company was so rapid, that the number of employees he hired increased from 100 to over 1,200 in three months during the summer of 1915.

When Romeo purchased ALFA in 1915, there were fears among the remaining management and workers that the company was doomed for extinction. Romeo had not only purchased ALFA, but also numerous other firms in the area. His goal was to create an engineering combine that manufactured compressors, tractors, air brakes, ploughs, railway equipment, and other assorted products for use in heavy industry. Fortunately, Romeo was also a motoring enthusiast and had always dreamed of making a prestigious Italian sports car. As a result, he immediately expanded the production facilities at the ALFA factory in Portello. In February 1918, he changed the name of the firm to Societe Anonima Italiana Ing. Nicola Romeo & Company. In addition, he decided to place his own name next to the well-respected ALFA name on the company's radiator badge, and after 1918 all the firm's cars appeared with "Alfa Romeo" on the hood.

During the 1920s Alfa Romeos on the racing circuit established the company as one of the premier sports car manufacturers in the world. Alfa Romeo relied heavily on modified versions of its prewar racing cars, while designer Merosi labored frantically to design more up-to-date models. As Merosi's new designs were introduced on the raceways, the company began to win such prestigious competitions as the Parma-Berceto, the Consuma Hill Climb, the Coppa Florio, the Aosta-Great St. Bernard Hill Climb, the Autumn Grand Prix, the Circuit of Savio race, the Circuit of Mantua race, the European Grand Prix, and many, many more. Nicola Romeo was determined to wrest the European racing crown from Italian competitor and rival Fiat, and he employed the best drivers and mechanics in order to do so. Enzo Ferrari, who was to become famous in his own right as an Italian sports car manufacturer, won the 1927 Circuit of Modena in a six-cylinder 150 Alfa Romeo.

As Alfa Romeo continued to win races, the innovations that led to the successes of the racing cars directly affected the design and production of the company's touring cars and roadsters; for example, front wheel brakes, adapted from the Alfa Romeo racing cars, were installed on touring cars for the first time.

Vittorio Jano, who replaced Merosi as head of design at Alfa Romeo in 1926, continued the tradition of improving the company's cars through his creations for the racing circuit. Jano's first design for general production was the NR (Nicola Romeo) touring car, which included a single overhead camshaft, coil ignition, a four-speed gearbox, and rod-operated brakes. Despite the growing success and reputation of the company, Nicola Romeo suddenly and inexplicably retired in 1928, and management of the company was assumed by the board of directors. Unfortunately, the firm began to experience financial difficulties as soon as Romeo retired.

During the early 1930s, management changed the name of the firm from Ing Nicola Romeo and Company to Societe Anonomie Alfa Romeo. Alfa Romeo's revenues continued to diminish, and in 1933 the government-sponsored Istituto Riconstruzione Industriale (IRI) assumed control of the company. Although Alfa Romeo technically retained its status as a private corporation with its own board of directors, the company had essentially been nationalized. Under the auspices of IRI, and with the rise of Benito Mussolini as dictator of Italy, Alfa Romeo's production facilities at Portello were expanded to include airplane engines, armaments, diesel engines, and even light aircraft. Jano continued to design touring cars and racing cars for the company through the mid-1930s, but car production became less and less important as Mussolini prepared Italy for war.

Alfa Romeo's fortunes during the Second World War slipped even further. In 1936 a Spanish engineer by the name of Wilfredo Ricart was hired to replace Jano as head of the design office at Alfa Romeo. Ricart had extensive experience designing diesel engines and sports and racing cars, and had also organized public transportation in the city of Valencia before arriving in Italy. Expectations of his potential for designing Alfa Romeo cars was very high. But Ricart, it was soon discovered, exhibited some very strange habits, including a penchant for wearing enormously thick rubber-soled shoes. When asked by Enzo Ferrari why he affected these shoes, Ricart replied in all seriousness that a genius's brain must be cushioned against the harsh unevenness of the ground lest its delicate mechanics be disrupted. Upon hearing Ricart's response, Ferrari left Alfa Romeo. During the war years, Ricart's designs for the company never went beyond the prototype stage.

After the end of World War II, Alfa Romeo's factory at Portello needed rebuilding due to the damage inflicted by American and British bombing raids. At the same time, the company's board of directors decided to release Ricart from his contract and hire Orazio Satta to replace him. Satta was the last of the great Alfa Romeo designers. Educated as an aeronautical engineer, Satta guided the company into an era of racing success and economic prosperity. Satta was responsible for designing the 6C 2500 Super Sport, the 1900 Sprint, the Giulietta Sprint Special, and the famous Spider Veloce. All of these cars sold extremely well abroad, with the Spider Veloce selling especially well in both Britain and the United States. During Satta's tenure, Alfa Romeo also continued to be successful in racing, winning such prestigious races as the 1950 and 1951 Swiss Grand Prix and the 1953 Grand Prix of Supercortmaggiore at Merano.

By the early 1960s, the factory at Portello was unable to produce enough cars to suit the growing demand of Alfa Romeo customers, so the company built a new assembly plant at Arese, about ten miles away from Portello. In 1963 the first Giulia Sprint GT rolled out of the plant at Arese, and by 1970 manufacturing capacity had increased to 150,000 automobiles per year. Still striving for the best performance from its vehicles, the company built a test track at Balocco, west of Milan. Numerous prototypes were tested on this track, and Satta's reputation as a designer continued to grow with each successful production. As sales increased, Alfa Romeo laid the foundation for a new plant just outside Naples, the place of Nicola Romeo's birth.

In 1970 Alfa Romeo sold 109,598 cars worldwide, primarily in Europe and the United States. The company was at the height of its success, with a growing share of the sports car market in every country where it sold cars. When Satta retired, accolades were heaped upon him, both by his peers and by the Italian government. After Satta's retirement, however, Alfa Romeo began to experience managerial and financial problems. Rising production costs and increased competition from Ferrari, Maserati, Jaguar, Porsche, and American car manufacturers led to declining revenues. In addition, the tradition of testing new Alfa Romeo models through the racing circuit was growing less important to the design office, and technical problems began to occur in cars purchased by customers expecting high levels of performance. By the early 1980s, the manufacturer's financial position had deteriorated so rapidly that the state-owned holding company Finmeccanica had taken control of the Alfa Romeo factories.

Under the auspices of Finmeccanica, Alfa Romeo's fortunes fared no better. Management was unable to stop the company's financial hemorrhaging and, as a result, Alfa Romeo became an attractive takeover target. Ford Motor Company expressed interest, but in 1986 Fiat outbid Ford, acquiring Alfa Romeo and all its holdings for $1.75 billion. Fiat, a well-established Italian car manufacturer owned by the Agnelli family, regarded Alfa Romeo as the perfect complement to its own line of European sports cars.

Alfa Romeo benefitted from Fiat's largesse—Fiat decided to invest over $1 billion in rehabilitating and improving the company's manufacturing plants in Portello, Naples, and Arese, while more than $1.25 billion was earmarked for research and development. Yet Fiat's direct management and supervision of Alfa Romeo car production and distribution was unable to reverse the company's fortunes. In 1989 Fiat formed Alfa Romeo Distributors of North America, a 50–50 joint venture with Chrysler. This arrangement, it was hoped, would enable Alfa Romeo to increase its presence in the American automobile market. Since Alfa Romeo had sold 8,201 cars in 1986 in the United States, it was not an unwarranted prediction that annual sales would increase to 12,000 by 1991. With new designs ready to roll from the company's Italian factories, Chrysler and Fiat were even confident enough to project annual sales figures of $40,000 to $50,000 by 1995. Fiat depended on Chrysler's knowledge of the American car market, and gave Chrysler management a free hand in advertising and distributing Alfa Romeo cars.

From the beginning of the collaboration, however, almost nothing went according to plan. The first Alfa Romeo car produced under Fiat ownership, the 164 sedan, was delayed so that Fiat engineers could improve its quality and add a 2.0-liter turbo engine. The delay lasted months longer than expected, and distributors in the United States were left with nothing to sell except the Milano sedan and the old-version of the Spider convertible. Unfortunately, the Alfa Romeo Milano, another design significantly influenced by Fiat engineers, was plagued with mechanical problems and quickly developed a reputation for unreliability. Chrysler, dissatisfied with the results of the joint venture, decided to dissolve the partnership in 1991. Chrysler's withdrawal left Fiat to market Alfa Romeo cars alone in the United States, and, as a result, Alfa Romeo's presence in the United States began to decline dramatically. During 1991 only 649 Alfa Romeo cars were sold in the United States.

In an attempt to improve Alfa Romeo's dwindling market share, Fiat engineers conceived the 155, introducing the car in Europe in 1992. However, the car didn't sell well, which industry analysts attributed to the lackluster exterior and interior design. With earnings decreasing and debt rising for its U.S. operation, Fiat decided not to export the 155 to America. In 1993 Alfa Romeo's car production dropped 24 percent to only 109,598 units, most of which were sold in Europe.

With a decision by Fiat management not to sell the new Spider convertible, the Spider coupe, or the newly designed 145 three-door and five-door hatchback in the United States, Alfa Romeo's presence in America has virtually disappeared. Unless Fiat can effectively design and market new sports cars in the Alfa Romeo tradition, the company that bears Nicola Romeo's name might not survive.

Further Reading:

Ciferri, Luca, "Fiat Performs CPR to Revive Alfa Romeo," *Automotive News,* May 16, 1994, p. 26.

Henry, Jim, "Fiat Weighs Alfa's Fate in U.S.," *Automotive News,* July 5, 1993, p. 4.

Pitt, Barrie, *Alfa Romeo,* New York: Ballantine Books, Inc., 1971.

—Thomas Derdak

Alpine Electronics, Inc.

1-1-8 Nishi-Gotanda
Shinagawa-ku
Tokyo 141
Japan
03 3494 1101
Fax: 03 3494 1109

Wholly Owned Subsidiary of Alps Electric Company, Ltd.
Founded: 1967 as Alps Motorola Company, Ltd.
Sales: $1.1 billion
Employees: 1,459
Stock Exchanges: Tokyo
SICs: 3661 Telephone & Telegraph Apparatus; 5064 Electrical Appliances (Television & Radio); 3663 Radio and Television Communications Equipment

Alpine Electronics, Inc., is one of the world's leading manufacturers of sophisticated audio, navigational, and electronic automobile products. These include in-dash compact disc changers, CD head units, Ai-NET-compatible CD changers, multifunctional audio systems, amplifiers, in-dash color television monitors, security systems, and speakers. Alpine also makes one of the world's most precise and reliable high-speed car navigation systems. The company manufactures custom audio systems for such prestigious automakers as Honda, BMW, Chrysler, Mercedes Benz, Volvo, and Lamborghini.

Alpine Electronics was established in 1967 as a joint venture between Alps Electric Company, one of Japan's leading manufacturers of electronic components for consumer appliances, and Motorola, Inc.; the company was originally called Alps Motorola Company, Ltd. With headquarters in Tokyo, the company focused on developing and manufacturing new electronic products for the burgeoning Japanese automotive market. The company's first product, an eight-track cartridge tape player, was introduced in 1968. One year later, Alps Motorola Company began producing car radios.

During the early 1970s, Alps Motorola Company introduced the ''Handy-8,'' a lightweight, portable eight-track cartridge tape player that was initially successful; however, by the mid-1970s sales had slipped. In order to offset shrinking sales in Japan and expand its product line, Alps Motorola began to export tape decks to Europe and North America and entered the automotive audio market. This change in strategy brought with it a change of name, from Alps Motorola Company to Alpine Electronics, Inc.

At the first consumer electronics show Alpine attended, the company introduced the 7206 AM/FM Cassette Tape Player, which included the brand-new Strontium Colbat long-playing tape head. Soon afterward, Alpine introduced the 7308 AM/FM Cassette Tape Player, which was specifically designed for the automotive audio market. In order to distribute its products, Alpine established sales subsidiaries in Dusseldorf, Germany; Torrence, California; and Toronto, Canada. In addition, Alpine entered into an agreement with Lamborghini, the Italian sports car manufacturer, to place its electronic audio products in one of the most glamorous vehicles in the world, the Lamborghini Countach. Suddenly, other automobile manufacturers were competing for the opportunity to place Alpine audio equipment in their cars.

As revenues increased rapidly, the company began to investigate digitalized electronic products. In 1980 the company introduced the 7128 and 7308 electronically tuned radios, the first of their kind. In 1981, in a venture with Honda Motor Corporation, Alpine introduced the world's first gyrocator. One year later, Alpine introduced the revolutionary 3015 computerized graphic equalizer, the first such product in the world. In 1982 the company was awarded the Japanese ''Good Design'' Award for its computerized equalizer and garnered worldwide attention for redefining the electronic car audio market.

Alpine captured additional ''Good Design'' awards during the following years and began to capitalize on its publicity as a leader in the field. The company established new sales subsidiaries in Paris and Melbourne, as well as its first manufacturing subsidiary outside Japan, in Greenwood, Indiana, which was the first Japanese car audio plant in North America. Alpine also constructed a new company building in Iwaki, Japan. Automotive manufacturers from around the world contracted Alpine to place state-of-the-art audio equipment in their vehicles, including such prestigious companies as Volvo, BMW, and Mercedes Benz. By 1988, Alpine had grown large enough to have its shares listed on the Second Section of the Tokyo Stock Exchange.

The worldwide enthusiasm for high-quality automotive audio equipment led Alpine to establish competitions such as the Japan Car Audio Nationals; the competitive focus on high performance and reliability generated by this competition, in turn, led Alpine to develop the 7907 AM/FM compact disc player. With a widely recognized brand name, products that garnered high marks from customers, a marketing campaign that capitalized on its identification with sports car manufacturers such as Lamborghini, and the support of an effective specialty dealer network, Alpine had grown into the most successful car audio products manufacturer.

In 1989 Alpine made a commitment to the development of compact disc products and began investing heavily in research and development in this area. In 1990 the company introduced the CD Shuttle 5952, a six-disc compact disc automatic changer that was the first to fit into a car's dashboard, thanks to a miniature mechanism for ultrathin pickup. Almost overnight, the CD Shuttle became Japan's best-selling compact disc automatic changer. Continuing to build on micro-mechatronics technology, Alpine later introduced the smallest six-disc CD autochanger in the world. Small enough to fit into the glove compartment of a car, the CD Shuttle 5960 also become one of the company's best-selling products.

During 1990 and 1991, Alpine Electronics achieved significant financial goals. More capital was raised for the development of new products and expansion of existing facilities, and for a worldwide marketing campaign. Alpine stock was listed on the First Section of the Tokyo Stock Exchange, and Alpine issued Eurodollar-based warrants for the European Union market.

Alpine also introduced the revolutionary AV Shuttle 2913, an in-dash, full-color, high resolution television monitor. Mounted in a car's dashboard, the 5-inch display system was brought up with the touch of a finger and could be tucked away inside the console when no longer in use. The screen displayed television broadcasts as well as automotive navigation maps. The AV Shuttle was complemented by another Alpine development, a completely automated, high-speed navigation system that could be displayed on it, providing driver and passengers with the best route to a destination and rerouting if the car should stray off its course. The system included voice guidance, optimized timing for both expressways and local roads, and specific information on intersections. A gyro-sensing device within the system provided precise, reliable tracking.

As Alpine continued to grow, the company built a new facility to house its European headquarters in Dusseldorf, Germany, and established Singapore Alpine Electronics Asia Pte. Ltd. as a parts procurement and liaison subsidiary. A division of the Singapore subsidiary included a cassette production facility providing component parts to other plants in Southeast Asia. The cassette mechanisms, when completed, were then sent to China for final assembly.

During the 1990s, Alpine invested heavily in China. Recognizing the importance of applied computer technology, especially in car navigation systems, in 1991 Alpine created NEU Alpine Software, Inc., to recruit and train young software engineers in China. In 1994 the company built a manufacturing facility in China and entered into a Chinese joint venture called Dandong Alpine Electronics, Inc. Dandong Alpine planned to establish a huge production facility in China that would export products to the Japanese, European, and American markets.

In 1994 the company also moved into Mexico, establishing a Mexican manufacturing plant to produce car stereos, tuners, and other electronic component parts. Plans called for the plant to initially export all of its products to the United States and later expand distribution to Asia and Europe.

Principal Subsidiaries: Alpine Electronics of America, Inc.; Alpine Electronics Manufacturing of America, Inc.; Alpine Electronics of Canada, Inc.; Alpine Electronics (Europe) GmbH; Alpine Electronics GmbH; Alpine Electronics of U.K., Ltd.; Alpine Electronics France S.A.R.L.; Alpine Italia S.p.A.; Alpine Electronics de Espana, S.A.; Alpine Electronics of Australia Pty. Ltd.; Alpine Electronics of New Zealand, Ltd.; Alpine Do Brasil Ltda.; Alpine Electronics Asia Pte. Ltd.; Alpine Electronics Research of America, Inc.; Alcom Electronics de Mexico; Dandong Alpine Electronics, Inc.

Further Reading:

Alpine Car and Communications Systems: Corporate Profile 1994–1995, Tokyo: Alpine Electronics, Inc., 1995.
The Alpine Story, 1995, Company Document.

—Thomas Derdak

American Colloid Co.

1500 W. Shure Co.
Arlington Heights, Illinois 60004-1434
U.S.A.
(708) 392-4600
Fax: (708) 506-6199

Public Company
Founded: 1924 as Bentonite Mining and Manufacturing Company
Employees: 2,400
Sales: $265 million
Stock Exchanges: NASDAQ
SICs: 1459 Clay & Related Minerals, Not Elsewhere Classified; 2821 Plastics Materials & Resins; 4213 Trucking Except Local

American Colloid Co. is a leading U.S. manufacturer of materials, such as absorbent polymers and bonding agents, consumed in mineral, environmental, and consumer products industries. Its offerings range from cat litter and absorbent polymers used in diapers to bentonite clay used in metal casting and for other industrial applications. The company operated 37 production/research facilities throughout the world in 1995 and was posting record profits, largely as a result of innovative new products.

American Colloid Co. was built on a single product; bentonite clay. Although various types and grades of Bentonite clay were in existence, the material that American Colloid began selling in the early 1900s was located in deposits as deep as 100 feet in the northern plains of the United States. That clay was formed from volcanic ash that, over millions of years, was transformed into a highly-absorbent, paste-like substance. Native Americans used the clay in several applications, including as a soap for buffalo hide, an ingredient in soils for decorative plants, and possibly even as a dietary supplement during pregnancy. Later, settlers began using the clay to seal log homes, pack inflamed horses hooves, and grease wheel axles.

In the late 1800s a Wyoming rancher named William Taylor sent some of the clay that he found on his ranch to the University of Wyoming to be studied. He first dubbed the clay ''Taylorite,'' but soon thereafter changed the name to ''Bentonite'' because he had found it near Fort Benton. In the early 1900s that deposit became one of the first commercial Bentonite mines in the world. The substance was originally mined from the earth's surface by horse and wagon, shipped to Chicago, milled into a fine powder, and processed into a skin-wrinkle cream called ''Denver Mud''—the clay was still a chief ingredient in beauty mask products in the 1990s. Bentonite was later utilized in the manufacture of laundry detergent, asphalt, and insulation. Because few other commercial uses were known for the absorbent material, the Bentonite industry languished for several years.

It was eventually discovered that Bentonite could be used in foundries to improve the quality of molding sands used to manufacture metal castings. That important discovery was followed by the realization that Bentonite was a useful additive to the slurry applied as a lubricant to oil and gas well drills. Among the few Bentonite mining companies that emerged early was the Bentonite Mining and Manufacturing Company, which was located in the gold-mining town of Deadwood, South Dakota. The company was formed one night in 1924—by a group of frustrated gold miners in a local tavern—and was extracting Bentonite from nearby deposit shortly afterward.

Enter Paul Bechtner, an entrepreneur, inventor, and workaholic with a background in the foundry industry. Bechtner was born in Wisconsin in 1882, served in a stateside cavalry unit during World War I after typhoid nearly took his life, and then started a chicken farm in his home state. When he tired of that venture, he took a job with a sand company, quickly rising to the position of vice-president and then promptly quitting in 1922. Next, he was employed by a metal casting company, where he worked on developing better foundry molds to make engine blocks for the burgeoning automobile industry. After experimenting with numerous additive and bonding materials, Bechtner became convinced that Bentonite was superior to all other materials. Armed with that knowledge, Bechtner left his job and headed west.

Bechtner struck a partnership with the founders of Bentonite Mining in 1927. The two parties each agreed to contribute $15,000 to form two new companies; American Colloid Company, which would be headed by the original founders, and American Colloid Company Sales Division, which would buy Bentonite from its sister company and sell it in the East for a profit. The name ''Colloid'' was derived from the Greek 'kolloid,' meaning glue-like, and the English 'colloid,' which defined a degree of fitness. American Colloid built its first plant in Upton, Wyoming, in 1928 adjacent to the original mining facility. Bechtner named the Bentonite material that he sold ''Volcay,'' referring to its volcanic origin, and he even advertised that ''Bentonite is our sole product.''

Bechtner had finally discovered his niche. Indeed, during the 1930s and through the 1950s he became a sort of apostle of Bentonite (Volcay). He worked relentlessly, often from early morning until late at night, to build the business. During the start up, Bechtner effectively lived out of his Ford, traveling non-stop to promote his product before setting up shop in a Chicago apartment. Then, when he wasn't on the road he was writing literature and responding to customer inquiries in an effort to build American Colloid's client base. At a rate of about two tons per hour, the South Dakota mine generated about 740 tons of Bentonite during its first full year of production. As a result of Bechtner's sales push, that figure bolted to more than 3,000 tons in 1929. And demand was growing.

The Great Depression slowed American Colloid's growth. To make matters worse, a fire destroyed the Upton plant. But the enterprise managed to survive the downturn and even to record meager profits during most of the 1930s. In fact, Bechtner managed to turn the misfortune into a positive experience. When he and his crew were surveying the fire damage, one of the men angrily picked up a handful of Bentonite clay and hurled it against a burned wall. The clay stuck to the wall extremely well, sending Bechtner's mental gears into motion. Within several weeks he had filed a patent covering the use of vermiculite bonded with Bentonite as insulation. He then sold the patent to help pay for reconstruction costs. Although output rose during the early 1930s to more than 4,500 tons, American Colloid struggled. At one point, when the company was on the edge of bankruptcy, an investor named John Owen paid just $5,000 for 17 percent of the organization's stock to keep it afloat.

By 1935 American Colloid's shipments had grown to the point where a second processing plant had to be built. The second plant was capable of producing granular and powder Bentonite products, for which demand was growing. By 1936, American Colloid was shipping 9,000 tons from the new plant and about 8,000 from the old facility. Also in 1936, the sales and production divisions of American Colloid merged to form a single company; American Colloid Co. In the late 1930s, the company began mining and processing "southern" Bentonite clay in Mississippi. Southern Bentonite clay, found primarily in Mississippi and Alabama, was similar to material in the plains states, but the former had significant amounts of calcium rather than sodium and swelled much less when exposed to moisture. Southern Bentonite was found to be favorable to plains clay in many foundry applications, although combining the two materials often produced the best effect.

By 1940 American Colloid was selling more than 35,000 tons of clay annually. Because of the U.S. war effort, that figure leapt to 60,000 in 1941. Unfortunately, the company's profit growth failed to keep pace with output, largely because of increased competition from new Bentonite manufacturers. As competition increased, the company's profit per ton plunged to 20 cents. Worse yet, in 1941 fire again destroyed the Upton plant. American Colloid quickly rebuilt as its order backlog swelled. Three years later, however, a third blaze wreaked havoc and again leveled the Upton plant. Again, American Colloid rebuilt. Soon after the plant reopened, however, demand plunged with the end of the war. Bechtner and his discouraged associates struggled for a few years to reposition the company for growth in the postwar era.

Fortunately, a major new market opened up for American Colloid in the late 1940s. Because a competitor's patent expired, American Colloid was able to start selling Bentonite as an ingredient in oil-drilling lubricants. That new product line quickly took off and the company was forced to expand its manufacturing operations and headquarters to keep up with demand. Despite a fourth fire—this time at the Mississippi plant—and a 1954 tornado that wrecked the rebuilt facility, the company steamed into the mid-1950s with record revenues and profits. Boosting sales were new minerals being mined and processed by Bechtner's team including lignite/leonardite, a type of low-grade coal used in the petroleum industry and later as a fertilizer. To keep pace with gains, the company opened another plant in Mississippi in 1957.

Paul Bechtner died from a stroke in 1961 at the age of 79. Until his death, he had been intimately involved in the leadership of the company, overseeing its growth from a single plant to the world's largest Bentonite producer with sales throughout the world. Bechtner was succeeded by Everett Weaver. Weaver had joined the company straight out of high school in 1940. After a two-year stint in Europe during the war, he had returned to American Colloid to develop the company's marketing program for the oil well drilling industry and to manage some manufacturing plants. He was also joined at the company by his younger brother, Bill. Everett was hand-picked by Bechtner to lead the company and assumed the chief executive slot in 1960.

Under Weaver's direction, American Colloid continued to flourish. The company opened a new Alabama calcium Bentonite processing center in 1961. In 1965, moreover, the company inaugurated its first overseas production plants, which were located in Germany and England. Also during the early 1960s, Weaver purchased a trucking company as part of an effort to vertically integrate the company and reduce distribution costs. Everett Weaver handed off some of the day-to-day control of American Colloid to his brother, Bill, in 1968. Before doing so, he added a new production facility in Wyoming, initiated a distribution agreement with a Japanese company that eventually became American Colloid's biggest overseas customer, and broke ground for a new production facility in Illinois. That new facility reflected American Colloid's increasing emphasis on the growing well-drilling market.

The Weaver brothers continued to expand the company's reach overseas in the 1970s. In the early 1970s they oversaw the creation of divisions in Spain and Australia, for example. They also purchased a foundry blend-processing center in Detroit that allowed the company to create new products in demand by the foundry industry. Throughout the 1970s the brothers helped to boost the company's international exposure and to raise sales and profits. Importantly, American Colloid benefited from growing demand for its lubricating mud products from oil and gas drillers. That increase was largely a result of the OPEC oil embargo that began in 1973 and buoyed the U.S. oil industry through the early 1980s.

Indeed, American Colloid's revenues went from $20 million in the early 1970s to more than $100 million by the decade's end. During the same period, the company's work force increased from 450 to more than 1,000. By the early 1980s, at the height of the oil industry boom, American Colloid was shipping more than 80,000 tons of its clay-based gel each month. To keep up with growing demand, the organization invested millions of dollars in new facilities. At the same time, American Colloid began a concerted effort to diversify its product lines to include specialty, high-margin items. The Weaver brothers relinquished hands-on control of the company when it was at its height in terms of sales and profits. That left Roy Harris, who became chief executive in 1981, holding the bag when the bottom dropped out of the U.S. oil industry.

Because American Colloid had become so dependent on the oil industry, but also because of a downturn in its industrial and export divisions, the early 1980s dealt an ugly blow to the company. Almost instantly, orders from the company's oil accounts stopped. American Colloid's management was stunned by the almost unimaginable drop in business. Sales plunged from $134.3 million in 1981 to $77.3 million in 1986. As management scrambled to cut costs and pay its bills, the company's work force shrunk from 1,250 to just 475 during the same time period. American Colloid was eventually forced to shutter its gleaming, eight-year-old, state-of-the art Bentonite plant in Malta, Montana.

Roy Harris, one of the last top executives to have worked with Bechtner in the early days, stepped aside in 1985. He was replaced by John Hughes, who would face the task of revitalizing American Colloid and leading it onto a new path toward growth and prosperity. The hard-charging, outspoken Hughes had joined American Colloid straight out of college in 1965 as a research chemist. Almost from the start, he had pressed top management to reduce its dependence on the oil well market. In fact, it was he who had pushed for American Colloid to diversify into other specialty products derived from Bentonite, rather than commodity goods, during the late 1970s. As he rose through the ranks, Hughes became known as a workaholic, and some executives had even left the company upon discovering that they would be required to report to him.

After the oil market crashed, Hughes was tapped to help engineer the company's consolidation and work force reduction. His efforts during that period only added to his intimidating presence within the company. Still, Hughes aggressive, hard-driving style was exactly what American Colloid needed during the mid-1980s to turn it around. Just as important as his management style and personality, though, was his strategy. "When he first started . . . John had a dream: to develop a line of specialized products and decentralized management," explained Everett Weaver in the May 1989 *Business Marketing.* "He doesn't waste time when he knows what he wants to do," Weaver said.

Indeed, Hughes didn't waste time. In 1986 he moved the company's corporate offices to Arlington Heights, Illinois, demolished the Malta plant, sold the plant in Germany, and opened a new polymer processing operation in Wyoming. The company raised cash in 1987 by going public for the first time, and Hughes launched aggressive new cost-control and quality initiatives. As American Colloid slashed costs and reorganized during the mid-1980s, Hughes pursued his goal of developing a diverse mix of high-margin specialty applications for Bentonite. To that end, the company set up several relatively autonomous industry-specific divisions designed to attack key market niches. The units usually had about 12 people, depending on the market, and were headed by a profit manager. For example, American Colloid's desiccant division was set up to develop and market clays used to absorb moisture in packaging. Similarly, in 1988 American Colloid purchased Absorbent Clay Products, Inc., a cat litter company in Illinois. Other Bentonite niches included winemaking and new uses in the fertilizer industry.

An important new arena for American Colloid beginning in the late 1980s was an absorbent powder that it sold primarily to manufacturers of diapers and feminine products. The powder was first developed in Japan for the drilling industry, but American Colloid managed to get rights to the product in all countries but Japan and was marketing the powder for new specialty applications. The amazing powder was capable of expanding to hold more than 40 times its volume in water, making it potentially useful in a range of applications that Hughes believed American Colloid could develop and market. An added benefit of the polymer was that it could be shipped much more inexpensively than Bentonite. In 1987, Hughes set up a subsidiary—Chemdal Corp.—to produce and market the superabsorbent polymer. A separate European division of that subsidiary was established in England in 1989.

Also in 1989, American Colloid purchased a feed processing operation in Pennsylvania. Meanwhile, the company continued to cut operating costs and to update manufacturing facilities. The results of Hughes's strategy were quickly visible. After falling to a 1980s low of $77 million in 1986, revenues shot up to $85 million in 1987 and then to $111 million in 1988; the oil well industry accounted for less than ten percent of those sales. Profits rose similarly, jumping 21 percent in 1987 and then 20 percent in 1988 to a healthier $4.6 million. The profit gains reflected Hughes financial goal of raising sales at double the rate at which operating costs increased. As demand for American Colloid's new products surged, revenues continued to climb to $125 million in 1989 and then to nearly $150 million in 1991.

Early 1990s gains were largely the result of the success of American Colloid's superabsorbent polymer division, Chemdal. That division was churning out 20,000 tons of product annually by 1993 after more than doubling sales to $31 million between 1990 and 1992. The kitty litter division was also posting gains. At the same time, American Colloid's Bentonite operations were enjoying steady sales and profit jumps, and they continued to account for the bulk of the company's income. As American Colloid expanded production capacity and bolstered product lines, sales reached $265.4 million in 1994, far surpassing the company's revenues during the oil-industry peak of the early 1980s. Meanwhile, net income rose 17 percent to more than $15 million.

Going into the mid-1990s, American Colloid was operating three major product divisions: 1) minerals, which encompassed traditional metalcasting and oil drilling markets for Bentonite, as well as cat litter and other specialty Bentonite products; 2) absorbent polymers, which had grown to account for about 25 percent of company sales by 1994; and 3) environmental materials—the smallest product division—which produced groundwater chemicals, building materials, wastewater treatment products, and other environmental products. The company was operating manufacturing facilities throughout the world and was selling its products in more than 60 countries.

Principal Subsidiaries: Chemdal; Colloid Environmental Technologies Company; Ameri-Co Carriers, Inc.; Nationwide Freight Service, Inc.

Further Reading:

"American Colloid Company," *Foundry Management & Technology,* February 1994, p. 51.

Cleaver, Joanne, "Polymer Broadens Colloid's Markets," *Crain's Chicago Business,* June 27, 1988, p. 23.

Cochran, Thomas N., ''American Colloid Co.,'' *Investment News & Views,* May 23, 1988, pp. 65–66.

Kapp, Sue, ''Niche Nitter,'' *Business Marketing,* May 1989, pp. 10–11.

Murphy, H. Lee, ''Colloid Polymer Group Bolsters Bottom Line,'' *Crain's Chicago Business,* May 31, 1993, p. 68.

Rountree, David, ''Company Celebrates Anniversary,'' *Montgomery Advertiser,* October 30, 1994, p. F6.

Warner, Jodi, ''American Colloid Co. Announces Chemdal Superabsorbent Polymer Production Expansion,'' *PR Newswire,* August 29, 1994.

——, ''New American Colloid Co. Cat Litter Operation to Come on Line in First Quarter,'' *PR Newswire,* November 30, 1994.

Young, Linda, ''Aberdeen Polymer Plant to Double Production,'' *Mississippi Business Journal,* December 7, 1992, p. 11.

—Dave Mote

Amway Corporation

7575 Fulton Street East
Ada, Michigan 49355-0001
U.S.A.
(616) 6766000
Fax: (616) 6768140

Private Company
Incorporated: 1959 as Amway Sales Corporation and Amway Services Corporation
Employees: 12,500
Sales: $5.3 billion
SICs: 2844 Toilet Preparations; 2841 Soap & Other Detergents

"Don't let anyone steal your dream" is a popular rallying cry for many Amway distributors, independent businessmen and women whose goals of financial independence have led to the success of the Amway Corporation. The slogan indicates that this company is more than just a business; it has some traits of a social movement. Amway is well known as one of the largest network, or multilevel marketing (MLM), firms in the world. Its own products and services and brandname goods from other companies are marketed by over two million self-employed distributors in the United States and 70 other countries and territories. Unlike many other MLM firms, Amway offers a wide variety of items, ranging from cleaning products, cosmetics, and vitamins to travel services, discount car purchases, and catalog merchandise. Its rapid growth, zealous distributors, unusual corporate culture, and certain political and legal controversies have made Amway a well-recognized name since its founding in 1959.

Amway's independent distributors are different from sales forces for more traditional, retail companies. Credentials, such as education and work skills, are irrelevant to becoming a distributor. Sociologist Nicole W. Biggart, in her book *Charismatic Capitalism,* quoted an Amway distributor to illustrate this point: "It still gives me goose bumps just to think about how a person could come in with no experience in business or sales [and succeed]. I've listened to chicken farmers. I mean chicken farmers. . . . they get up on the stage and they're crown direct distributors. And they say, 'Aw, hell, me and Mabel, we just decided we needed some money one day.' And they're multimillionaires." Relationships among Amway distributors are based on cooperation; emotional rallies and close interpersonal relations in a familylike atmosphere contrast with the impersonal usual corporate world. Moreover, charismatic leadership and few bureaucratic rules characterize Amway.

Amway's history is a recent chapter in the long history of direct selling, which began in America's colonial period with unorganized Yankee peddlers selling tools and other items door to door. By the 1800s, direct selling decreased with the advent of mass merchandising, such as department stores and mail order sales. In the later 19th century and early 20th century, however, some manufacturers found direct sales had advantages over the sales of their products in large stores. They preferred the personal touch, with salesmen making home demonstrations of their products exclusively. By the 1920s door-to-door salesmen were marketing brushes, cooking utensils, and other products.

Retail stores fought back with local laws on peddlers. The federal government's regulations of company-employee relations led to the independent contractor solution. As independent contractors, salesmen were no longer employees: they were independent businessmen who bought products for resale. The first network marketing began in 1941 when two men created a mechanism to distribute Nutrilite vitamins. Within this mechanism, in addition to making money in retail sales, distributors earned a bonus on the sales of those individuals whom they personally recruited.

Amway's story began with the friendship between two youths who would become the founders. Jay Van Andel, born in Grand Rapids, Michigan, in 1924, and Richard M. DeVos, born in the small nearby community of Ada in 1926, became friends at Christian High School in Grand Rapids. Their common Dutch heritage of hard work, thrift, and entrepreneurship drew them together.

Both served in the Army Air Corps during World War II. Returning to Michigan after the war, they founded Wolverine Air Service to offer flying lessons. After selling Wolverine and a couple of other small businesses, the two young men bought a schooner and sailed off to see Latin America. The vessel sank in the Caribbean, and the two spent the next six months in South America; when they returned to Michigan, they started the JaRi Corporation to import and sell Caribbean handicraft.

In 1949 DeVos and Van Andel became distributors of vitamins for the Nutrilite Company of California. They enjoyed modest success from their own retail sales and from bonuses earned on the sales force they created in the Midwest. However, increasing government regulations and an internal conflict in Nutrilite led Van Andel, DeVos, and several other leading Nutrilite distributors to start their own venture. In April 1959 they created The American Way Association, later renamed the Amway Distributors Association, to protect the independent distributors. They chose as their first product a biodegradable liquid organic cleanser made by a small Michigan firm, the kind of high-demand merchandise that could be easily sold by MLM. By September 1959 the Amway Sales Corporation and the Amway Services Corporation were begun to assist the distributors. Van Andel and DeVos, with the help of their wives and a handful of employees, began operations from offices in their basements. Van Andel created sales literature and supervised new product development; DeVos motivated and trained new distributors.

The company rapidly expanded. The first full year of operations in 1960 resulted in gross sales of $500,000. That figure doubled in each of the next two years, and in 1964 it reached $10 million. Thousands of distributors signed up each month. The expansion was so rapid that as soon as the company moved into new facilities, they were already crowded. In the company history, *Commitment to Excellence; The Remarkable Amway Story,* DeVos noted, ''We were always scrambling, just trying to catch up on back orders, working to train people adequately.''

In 1964 the business underwent a major reorganization. The three divisions—sales, services, and manufacturing—were merged to create the Amway Corporation, with Van Andel as chairman of the board and DeVos as president. Major business decisions were always made jointly by the two founders.

A laundry detergent, SA8, was introduced in 1960. Amway's reputation for selling soap was based primarily on its experience with this product. Other products included a dishwashing liquid, aerosol shoe spray, cookware, hair products, and cosmetics. In 1962 Amway started international growth, with its expansion into Canada. In 1968 the Personal Shoppers Catalog allowed distributors to sell merchandise made by other companies. Catalog sales increased thereafter.

The 1960s also brought some false starts and problems for the new firm. It began marketing underground fallout shelters, for example, in an era when civil defense against atomic warfare was a priority, but gradually consumers lost interest in the shelters. Other short-lived products included 110volt automobile generators and waterconditioning units. It was not surprising that some items were not successful, however, for by 1968 the company was selling more than 150 products through its 80,000 distributors.

In July 1969 Amway's aerosol manufacturing plant burned completely to the ground. Losses were estimated at $700,000. The next day plans were made for a temporary substitute supplier and a new facility. Six months later the new facility was completed and the company moved in.

The 1970s began with a change in corporate structure. Van Andel and DeVos remained board chairman and president, respectively, but four vice-presidents were added to handle the daily burden of a rapidly expanding firm. In addition, 30 regional warehouses were replaced by seven new regional distribution centers in Georgia, Michigan, Texas, California, New Jersey, Washington, and Colorado.

Overseas expansion in the 1970s began with Australia in 1971, a choice that was partly influenced by the common culture, language, and economic system. Operations in the United Kingdom began in 1973. Other European operations began with West Germany in 1975, France in 1977, and the Netherlands and the Republic of Ireland in 1978. The Asian market was opened with ventures into Hong Kong in 1974, Malaysia in 1976, and Japan in 1979.

Diversification and acquisitions marked Amway's experience during this time. In 1972 the company purchased Nutrilite Products, Inc., the firm that had introduced Van Andel and DeVos to direct selling. Moreover, to reward and train its key distributors, the company acquired a yacht, Enterprise II, to serve as a floating conference center. A luxury resort and hotel complex on Peter Island in the British Virgin Islands was purchased in 1978, another amenity used to motivate Amway distributors. To house distributors coming to corporate headquarters, the firm bought the dilapidated Pantlind Hotel in Grand Rapids. The hotel, renovated and renamed Amway Grand Plaza Hotel, along with the newly constructed adjoining Grand Plaza Tower, marked a significant addition to downtown Grand Rapids.

Amway's growth was predicated on the success of its independent distributors. Lacking formal control over the distributors, Amway relied on bonuses and incentives to motivate them. As the company grew, distributors built larger and larger sales organizations. Their status and income increased and were marked by achievement levels identified as ''pin levels.'' The first major milestone of a successful distributor was reaching the level of Direct Distributor (DD), thus buying products and literature directly from the corporation instead of from a sponsor or other DD. Soon after Amway's origin, it began recognizing further sales milestones by using the names of jewels in achievement awards. The first Ruby DD was awarded in 1962, followed by Pearl, Emerald, and Diamond, in each instance the award including a decorative pin in which the specific stone was mounted. In 1966 the first Double Diamond level was reached, the Triple Diamond in 1969, Crown in 1970, and the highest level, Crown Ambassador DD, in 1977. By Amway's 25th anniversary in 1984, there were 24 Crown DDs and 15 Crown Ambassador DDs. Almost all of these 39 distributors were married couples; 28 were based in the United States.

The corporation kept in touch with its distributors through a monthly magazine, the *Amagram,* and provided a wide variety of sales literature, audio cassettes, and video cassettes. Although much of the product promotion was done by distributors, Amway also sponsored advertising in magazines, newspapers, radio, and TV. Its advertising costs were much less than other corporations, allowing Amway to introduce new products inexpensively.

Amway's most important legal battle was its successful defense against the allegation that it was engaged in an illegal ''pyramid scheme,'' characterized in part by making money on recruiting new distributors. The Federal Trade Commission (FTC) in 1969 began investigating several companies, including Amway and Nutrilite, filing formal charges against Amway in 1975. Three months of FTC hearings began in May 1977, and a ruling by the full FTC in 1979 declared Amway's MLM plan legitimate. The decision was based on findings that distributors were not being paid to recruit new distributors, that products had to be sold for distributors to receive bonuses, and that the firm was willing to buy back excess distributor inventory. Lawyer Rodney K. Smith in his book *Multilevel Marketing,* after reviewing several cases, concluded, ''Amway is not and never has been an illegal pyramid scheme.''

In another legal controversy, the Canadian government charged Amway with not paying millions of dollars in customs duties on goods imported from the United States. In 1983, after pleading guilty in the criminal case, Amway paid a C$25 million fine in an out-of-court settlement. *Maclean's,* Canada's weekly news magazine, reported in a November 1983 issue that the fine was "the largest sum that a Canadian court has ever levied and one of the heaviest criminal penalties ever imposed against any corporation in the world." A separate civil case was continued by the Canadian government to collect the duties it should have been paid in the 1970s. Amway again settled out of court, this time in 1989 for C$45 million, 40 percent of the amount the Canadian government tried to collect.

Other serious problems occurred in the first half of the 1980s, when, for the first time, Amway sales declined. Some of the major distributors sold their businesses, and a substantial number of top executives either quit or were demoted or fired. The pyramid allegations surfaced again, not against the corporation, but against certain distributors who advised their sales groups to downplay retail sales, buy Amway merchandise for their own use, and purchase many motivational items, such as tapes and books, from the distributor.

One corporate executive, COO William W. Nicholson, previously a secretary to President Gerald R. Ford and a key player at Amway headquarters since 1984, oversaw the introduction of many new products and services. According to Nicholson, a turning point was reached in 1985 when MCI decided to market its long distance telephone services through Amway. By 1990 Amway was gaining more than 40,000 new clients per month for MCI. Offering its customers discount purchases on new cars was another Amway innovation; by 1988 this service competed with five other discount autobuying services, including the American Automobile Association. Other new items in the Amway inventory included Visa credit cards, prepaid legal services, real estate, and Tandy computers. The increase in hightech merchandise and services was a dramatic shift for Amway, but the bulk of its sales remained in traditional products such as home care items. According to some analysts, Amway's transition to include more services reflected a general U.S. movement from a goods-and-manufacturing economy toward a service economy.

Not all new ventures worked well for Amway. The Mutual Broadcasting System (MBS), with its hundreds of affiliated radio stations, was purchased in 1977, but inexperience in the field, unfulfilled goals, and lack of profitability, according to DeVos, led to the sale of MBS in 1985. Having retained one satellite division from the original purchase, Amway manufactured and sold satellite dishes for some time, but the last division was eventually sold in 1989.

Probably the most publicized Amway activity in the late 1980s was its failed bid to take over Avon Products Inc. Amway and corporate raider Irwin L. Jacobs jointly acquired 5.5 million Avon shares, 10.3 percent of the company's stock, in 1989. One week later, without Jacobs' cooperation, Amway offered to buy Avon for $2.1 billion in cash. Although a billion dollars in debt, Avon rejected the bid, citing Amway's evasion of Canadian customs duties and an incompatible corporate culture. In May 1989 Amway withdrew its bid. *Business Week,* in a May 1989 issue, characterized the bid as Amway "flexing its muscles for the first time"; although the bid failed, it was a good indication of Amway's financial strength.

Amway and its founders also became significant sponsors of the arts in the 1980s. In 1982 Jay Van Andel chaired the NetherlandsAmerican Bicentennial Commission, while the company sponsored an art exhibit at Amsterdam's Stedelijk Museum. Amway also supported tours of the Hong Kong Children's Choir and the Malaysian Youth Symphony Orchestra. In Grand Rapids, Michigan, the company helped fund an Art Museum, Arts Council, and the Gerald R. Ford Presidential Museum.

Amway also made several commendable efforts to be environmentally responsible. Several of Amway's early products were biodegradable, and its SA8 detergent was available in a phosphatefree formula to limit pollution of waterways, and products were concentrated, reducing the amount of packaging that ended up in landfills. After chlorofluorocarbons were reported as hazardous to the ozone layer, Amway modified its aerosol products to delete those compounds. In 1989 Amway was a main sponsor of the two-month-long Icewalk, an expedition to the North Pole, designed to focus attention on environmental issues. In cooperation with the American Forestry Association, Amway also participated in the Global ReLeaf Program, to plant 100 million trees by 1992. In fact, on June 5, 1989, Amway received the United Nation's Environmental Programme's Achievement Award for Excellence, becoming one of two corporations to gain that honor. That same day the firm announced that it would end all animal testing in its research programs and that it would not cooperate with the Cosmetics, Toiletry and Fragrance Association's campaign against the ban on animal testing. In the area of recycling, Amway was named Michigan Recycling Coalition's 1992 Recycler of the Year, for its on-site recycling center and recycling practices in its operations and product development.

Despite the legal battles and occasionally unfavorable media characterizations of Amway, and direct selling in general, the concept was becoming increasingly popular. According to the Direct Selling Association (DSA), total retail sales were approximately $9.7 billion in 1988, up 10.3 percent from 1987, and Amway accounted for about 16 percent of that total. A 1976 Harris poll of U.S. households found that 16 percent of the respondents had tried direct selling. The boom was influenced by shifts in employment trends. First, more women had moved into the work place and were selling Amway products; in fact, the DSA reported that in 1988, 81.4 percent of all salespeople were women. Moreover, instability in corporate employment had prompted increasing numbers of workers to consider alternative vocations, particularly those in which much of the administrative activities might be handled in home offices.

Amway's European expansion also continued throughout the 1980s, with operations established in Switzerland and Belgium in 1980, and in Spain and Italy in 1986. In 1985, Panama became the first Latin American base of Amway operations, followed by Guatemala in 1986. Amway de Mexico was established in June 1990 with headquarters in Monterrey and distribution centers in Mexico City, Guadalajara, Tijuana, and Juarez. Amway's success depended in part on its ability to adapt its product line to suit local cultures. In Japan, for example, the company began marketing a small induction range made by

Japan's Sharp Company, which proved ideal for the small homes of Japan and sold well when demonstrated in the home by Amway distributors. Perseverance and high quality goods resulted in 1988 sales of $536 million for Amway (Japan) Ltd, Amway's largest overseas subsidiary.

Based on rapid international expansion, strong family leadership, and good financial condition, Amway remained a strong force in the 1990s. When Van Andel and DeVos, whose children had begun in the business in the mid-1970s, retired from the company in the early 1990s, all eight of the Van Andel and DeVos children were in leadership positions. Dick DeVos was named president in 1992, and Steve Van Andel was appointed company chairperson. Jay Van Andel planned to remain active with the company as senior chairman and member of the policy board.

With the failure of communist economies in Eastern Europe and other nations, Amway's promotion of free enterprise became increasingly noteworthy in the years ahead. During the first half of the 1990s, Amway's territories expanded into Korea, Hungary, Brazil, Portugal, Indonesia, Poland, Argentina, Czech Republic, Turkey, and Slovakia. In addition to tapping into new, emerging economies, foreign expansion was possibly part of Amway's strategy to offset slowing U.S. sales, prompted, according to one article in an October 1994 *U.S. News & World Report,* by regulatory investigations and media criticism of the company. In 1991, for example, Procter & Gamble won a $75,000 judgment from a group of Amway distributors, who were accused of spreading rumors that Procter & Gamble's products were instruments of Satan. Nevertheless, Amway's overall performance didn't suffer; in 1994, sales increased by 18 percent over 1993 to total $5.3 billion. Dick DeVos estimated that 70 percent of 1994 sales came from abroad and predicted that figure would increase to 75 percent by fiscal 1996. In 1994 Amway moved its entrepreneurial business into the Eastern European market and also targeted Vietnam and China as its newest markets.

Japan was probably one of Amway's most successful foreign markets in the 1990s. In a culture where many Japanese business people were accustomed to staying with one company for their entire career, Amway offered new economic freedom. In fact, word of mouth recommendations allowed Amway to operate in Japan without spending any money on advertising up until around 1989. In 1990, over 500,000 Japanese belonged to Amway, making the company one of the largest and most profitable foreign companies in Japan. In 1989, Amway (Japan) Ltd. had over $500 million in sales and $164 million in pretax profits, comprising about one-third of Amway's worldwide business. By the mid-1990s, revenues had more than doubled and the Japanese subsidiary had grown to include 816,000 salespeople. Public offerings of stock in Amway Japan and Hong Kong-based Amway Asia Pacific in 1994 proved a huge success.

In fact, the success of Amway had brought the founders Richard DeVos and Jay Van Andel into the exclusive ranks of America's ten richest people, according to *Forbes* magazine in the mid-1990s. Their collective net worth was estimated at about $9 billion. As the next generation led Amway into the 21st century, they too pursued continued success and expansion. According to *U.S. News & World Report,* if the heirs made the right decisions and the company continued its strong growth in foreign countries, the DeVos and Van Andel families would earn a place beside the Rockefellers and du Ponts as America's most prominent and wealthy families.

Principal Subsidiaries: Nutrilite Products, Inc.; Amway Gesellschaft m.b.H. (Austria); Amway of Australia Pty. Ltd.; Amway Belgium Company; Amway (U.K.) Limited; Amway France; Amway (HK) Limited (Hong Kong); Amway Italia s.r.l. (Italy); Amway (Japan) Limited; Amway (Malaysia) Sdn. Bhd.; Amway Nederland Ltd. (Netherlands); Amway of New Zealand Ltd.; Amway de Panama, S.A.; Amway (Schweiz) AG (Switzerland); Amway De España S.A. (Spain); Amway (Taiwan) Limited; Amway (Thailand) Ltd.; Amway GmbH (Germany); Amway de Mexico; Amway Communications Corporation; Amway Hotel Corporation; Amway Global, Inc.; Amway International, Inc.

Further Reading:

Biggart, Nicole Woolsey, *Charismatic Capitalism: Direct Selling Organizations in America,* Chicago: University of Chicago Press, 1989.

Butterfield, Stephen, *Amway: The Cult of Free Enterprise,* Boston: South End Press, 1985.

Conn, Charles Paul, *An Uncommon Freedom: The Amway Experience & Why It Grows,* New York: Berkley Publishing Group, 1983.

——, *Promises to Keep: The Amway Phenomenon and How It Works,* New York: G. P. Putnam's Sons, 1985.

Cross, Wilbur, and Gordon Olson, *Commitment to Excellence: The Remarkable Amway Story,* Elmsford, N.Y.: The Benjamin Company, 1986.

Eisenstodt, Gale and Hiroko Katayama, "Soap and Hope in Tokyo," *Forbes,* September 3, 1990, p. 62.

"The $4-Billion Man: Rich DeVos Bet on Capitalism and Won," *Success,* May 1993, p. 10.

Grant, Linda, "How Amway's Two Founders Cleaned Up: Strong Overseas Sales Helped Richard DeVos and Jay Van Andel Add Billions to Their Fortunes," *U.S. News & World Report,* October 31, 1994, p. 77.

Holzinger, Albert G., "Selling America to the Japanese," *Nation's Business,* October 1990, p. 54.

Klebnikov, Paul, "The Power of Positive Inspiration," *Forbes,* December 9, 1991, p. 244.

Morgello, Clem, "Richard Johnson of Amway Japan: Challenging Japan's Sales Culture," *Institutional Investor,* May 1994, p. 23.

Muller, Joann, "Amway Tailors Marketing Approach to Individual Foreign Cultures," *Journal of Commerce and Commercial,* July 8, 1991, p. 4A.

Ruzicka, Milan, "Amway Wins Converts in Former East Bloc," *Journal of Commerce and Commercial,* June 3, 1994, p. 1A.

Smith, Rodney K., *Multilevel Marketing: A Lawyer Looks at Amway, Shaklee, and Other Direct Sales Organizations,* Grand Rapids, Mich.: Baker Book House, 1984.

Tate, Nancy Ken, "Amway's Green Roots Go Deep," *American Demographics,* April 1991, p. 18.

Xardel, Dominique, *The Direct Selling Revolution,* Cambridge, Mass.: Blackwell, 1993.

—David M. Walden
—updated by Beth Watson Highman

Anchor Hocking Glassware

1115 West Fifth Avenue
P.O. Box 600
Lancaster, Ohio 43130-0600
U.S.A.
(614) 681-6144
Fax: (614) 681-6076

Wholly Owned Subsidiary of Newell Co.
Founded: 1905
Employees: 1,400
Sales: $150 million (est.)
SICs: 3229 Pressed & Blown Glass Nec

Anchor Hocking Glassware has been one of the world's leading producers and marketers of glass tableware and ovenware for most of its nine decades in business. Acquisitions and mergers expanded the company's interests into glass containers, plastics, and hardware, increasing annual sales to a peak of more than $900 million in the early 1980s, but intense competition forced Anchor Hocking to sell out to the Newell Co. in 1987. The various operations that made up Anchor Hocking before the merger contributed $440 million to Newell's 1994 sales of $2.08 billion. The sales of the Anchor Hocking Glassware unit were estimated to make up $150 million of that figure.

The company's roots can be traced to 1905, when founder Ike Collins convinced a group of seven investors led by E. B. Good to contribute to the Hocking Glass Company's original capitalization of $25,000. By the end of its first year of manufacturing and marketing lamp chimneys and other glass items, the company had generated sales of $20,000, offered its first dividend, and acquired the equipment of a defunct competitor. Technological innovation helped promote speedy growth in those early days. Within its first year, the company upgraded its facilities to incorporate new continuous furnace technology, as opposed to outdated day-tank operations. By 1919, Hocking boasted 300 employees (many of them highly skilled glass blowers) and $900,000 in annual sales, and had diversified from lamp chimneys (which were made obsolete by the invention of the incandescent light bulb) into glass tableware.

Even a disastrous fire, which destroyed the Lancaster, Ohio, plant and offices in 1924, could not hinder the company's progress. Engineer William V. Fisher, who had been hired in 1919 and would go on to become company president, decided that this was the perfect time to build a new, state-of-the-art plant. The rebuilt factory featured gravity-fed glass tanks and small-batch feeders that provided flexibility, especially in the area of color changes. Fisher also worked with a local machinist to develop a device that would automatically manufacture pressed, rather than hand-blown, pieces. As a 1965 corporate memoir declared, it was "a turning point in Hocking Glass history." Automation expanded Hocking Glass's rate of production from one piece per minute to 20, then to 35. By 1928, the company had introduced a full array of pressed, colored dinnerware. These inexpensive manufacturing methods would become a company hallmark, and propel it to the forefront of the glass tableware market.

In order to remain competitive during the Great Depression, Hocking's Fisher developed a machine that could manufacture 90 glasses per minute at half the previous cost. Technological advances such as this enabled the company to gain an advantage over competitors. In 1931 Hocking entered the glass container market with the acquisition of Turner Glass Company, which was renamed General Glass Corporation. Fisher turned his engineering expertise to this new aspect of the business, developing lightweight glass jars and tumblers in 1932.

In 1937 the Hocking Glass Company merged with the Anchor Cap Corporation of Long Island, New York, creating a powerful force in the glass container industry, with sales of $21.5 million in 1938. The unified firm went on to convert the baby food industry, among others, from tin packaging to the now-familiar glass jar. Vertical consolidation through acquisition over the ensuing years expanded or established capabilities in glass containers, closures, cartons, mold equipment, and closure machines. The company even built a 38-mile natural gas pipeline to supply its growing energy needs in the 1940s.

The company's lines of inexpensive glassware were expanded as well. In 1944 Anchor acquired Carr-Lowrey Glass Co., a 55-year-old Maryland manufacturer of small specialty bottles for the cosmetics and toiletries markets. Other glass products included automotive lenses and reflectors. By the 1960s, Anchor Hocking was producing more than 2,500 different items and adding hundreds of new products and designs each year. These were sold in supermarkets and mass merchandise chains and were used as premiums by fast food chains, gas stations, and banks. The Anchor Hocking brand enjoyed a strong reputation among price- and quality-conscious consumers.

Anchor Hocking benefitted from the rapid growth of the container industry in the 1960s. More than three decades after William Fisher had first developed the non-returnable bottle, rapidly rising consumption of soft drinks and beer led to increased profitability. Anchor Hocking ranked among the top three producers of glass containers nationwide, as well as retaining its leading position in glass tableware. Annual sales topped $150 million by 1963, and profits reached more than $6 million.

The company formalized its overseas operations around this time as well, establishing an International Division in 1963. With operations in 105 countries in 1965, the company became the world's leading manufacturer of glass tableware and ovenware.

In spite of its indisputable success in the 1960s—sales and profits increased to $199 million and $10.38 million, respectively, by 1967—Anchor Hocking began to be criticized for managerial conservatism. Bill Fisher, who had succeeded founder Ike Collins as president, was honored for his many contributions to the company, but was also viewed by some as an aging symbol of that conservatism. Some observers pointed out that the company's risk-averse leadership had never officially taken on debt, while others criticized the company's lack of a coherent succession plan. In 1961 Anchor Hocking's board of directors recruited an outsider, John L. Gushman, to breathe new life into Anchor Hocking's corporate strategy.

Gushman succeeded to the chief executive office in 1967 and quickly set a new course for the company. A subtle, but telling name change in 1969, when the company dropped the word "Glass" from its title, signaled the transformation that was to come. Over the course of Gushman's first decade in office, Anchor Hocking experienced a comprehensive turnover of managers and acquired nine companies. In 1968 Anchor acquired Plastics, Inc., a top manufacturer of disposable tableware for the airline industry, through an exchange of shares, giving Anchor a "hedge" in the container market, where injection-molded plastic packaging had begun to replace many glass packages. In 1975 the company acquired Amerock Corp., the leading U.S. producer of cabinet and window hardware, for $32 million from the Stanley Works. Gushman financed these purchases with more than $35 million in long-term debt. A modernization program that included automation helped reduce operating costs in an era of rising labor expenditures. Centralized distribution at a massive warehouse (the largest in the U.S. glass industry) also reduced expenses.

Although sales increased steadily from $293.2 million in 1970 to $411 million in 1974, earnings did not follow suit, peaking at $20.7 million in 1972, then declining to $18.7 million in 1973 and $16.3 million in 1974. Industry analysts blamed short supplies of raw materials, surging fuel costs, and a 10-week strike, which combined with price controls and "stagflation" to squeeze profit margins. Fuel expenses alone shot up 25 percent during this period. The middle of the decade brought good news, however, when both supplies of raw materials and demand for glass containers briefly rebounded.

Nonetheless, Anchor Hocking's return on equity had dropped from 17.2 percent in 1969 to nine percent in 1974, far short of the 16 percent average for all industries. In 1975 company leaders set their sights on recovering that level of return. As plastic bottles and lightweight aluminum cans quickly replaced glass throughout the packaging industry, especially in the beverage sector, Anchor Hocking struggled in the early 1980s to maintain any level of return, let alone a double-digit percentage.

J. Ray Topper, an Anchor Hocking executive since 1971, succeeded Gushman as president in the late 1970s and assumed the role of chief executive officer in 1982. Although Topper decreased Anchor Hocking's dependence on the rapidly declining glass container market from over 60 percent of annual sales to just over one-third, the company's annual return from 1975 to 1982 averaged a meager one percent. In 1982 the company elected to divest its $300 million container division—dubbed an "albatross" in a May 1983 *Forbes* article—to Wesray Corp. for a mere $68 million. Anchor walked away from the deal with $55 million in cash, only to attract the unwanted advances of corporate raider Carl Ichan. By mid-1982, Ichan had accumulated six percent of the undervalued, cash-rich firm. Anchor maintained its independence only by buying back his shares at 35 percent more than their book value. The company subsequently adopted a "poison pill plan" in an attempt to deter future takeover attempts.

The divestment left Anchor Hocking with a strong focus on consumer goods, including plastic dinnerware and food storage containers, decorative hardware, and its traditional glassware. More than one industry observer predicted that Topper's decision to shed the glass packaging division would bring a swift turnaround. However, intense competition from imported glassware and a strong dollar hammered Anchor's earnings both domestically and abroad. The company lost more than $4 million in 1983 and nearly $19 million in 1984 despite sales growth from $678 million to nearly $713 million during that same period. The company closed a major glassware plant in its hometown of Lancaster, Ohio, in 1985, eliminating 650 employees in the process.

Anchor's readily apparent weaknesses brought a new takeover threat, this time from Newell Co., a burgeoning housewares manufacturer. Daniel Ferguson, chief executive officer and son of one of Newell's four founders, had formulated a program of expansion through acquisition that had given the company a seemingly diverse collection of manufacturing subsidiaries ranging from Mirro brand cookware to BernzOmatic propane torches. Newell's acquisitions were united by their distribution through mass merchandisers and their leading positions in their respective product categories.

Neither Anchor's size—over twice Newell's—nor J. Ray Topper's clear aversion to selling out deterred Newell. When negotiations with Topper proved fruitless, Ferguson went over the CEO's head to Anchor's board of directors and shareholders. In 1986 Anchor accepted a so-called "friendly" $338.2 million offer ($32 per share). Topper, who reportedly wept at the deciding shareholders' meeting, and more than 100 other Anchor executives and headquarters personnel were sacked within a week of the merger's approval.

Ferguson himself took charge of Anchor Hocking, applying his customary post-purchase measures—known internally as "Newellization"—to the new acquisition. First, the CEO focused on selling off non-core divisions like packaging products, food services, and a retail chain, and applying the proceeds to acquisition-related debt. Next, he installed new managers who were already acclimated to Newell's high standards of customer service and fiscal performance. The parent split Anchor Hocking's remaining operations into separate subsidiaries: Anchor Hocking Glassware, Anchor Hocking Plastics, and Plastics Inc., all of which were added to the parent's housewares division, and Amerock Corp., which became part of Newell's hardware division. Newell centralized Anchor Hocking Glassware's administrative offices at the corporate headquarters in Illinois, and consolidated all manufacturing at Lancaster, Ohio, which reduced capacity and tightened supply in the process. Although Anchor's annual sales dropped by about one-third to

$100 million as a result, the subsidiary was left with more efficient operations.

In 1992 a reinvigorated Anchor Hocking Glassware was able to acquire the assets of Toscany Co., a bankrupt manufacturer of upscale glassware. Known as Anchor Hocking Specialty Glassware after the merger, Toscany gave Anchor access to high-end retailers like Macy's, May Co., Williams-Sonoma, and the Pottery Barn. Anchor maintained Toscany's exclusive image by resisting the temptation to offer the brand in its mass merchandising outlets. Anchor Hocking Glassware also launched new lines of its own featuring popular licensed cartoon characters and fashion colors. Ovenware, including pieces specially designed for use in microwave ovens, were also introduced. New sales programs, some of which were formulated in concert with mass merchandisers like Kmart and Wal-Mart, included point-of-purchase displays, gift with purchase promotions, and special packaging.

Despite a relatively high rate of turnover in top positions (Anchor Glassware had as many presidents from 1986 to 1995 as it had had in its entire pre-merger history), Anchor's businesses appear to be thriving under their new management, which has worked to trim expenses, boost product development, and improve retail distribution.

Further Reading:

''Anchor Hocking Branches Out,'' *Business Week,* May 10, 1976, pp. 69, 72.

''Beginning Anew: Anchor Hocking Molds Bright Future with New Products, Packaging Innovations,'' *Discount Store News,* January 8, 1990, p. H11.

Bernard, Sharyn, ''Glass Acts,'' *HFN: The Weekly Newspaper for the Home Furnishing Network,* March 27, 1995, p. 25.

Brown, Paul B., ''We Couldn't Afford Excellence,'' *Forbes,* May 23, 1983, p. 134.

''Glass Firm Accepts Bid for Buy-Out,'' *Plain Dealer,* February 25, 1987, p. D1.

Greene, Joan, ''Anchor Hocking to Cap Another Earnings Peak,'' *Barron's,* April 19, 1976, pp. 31–32.

Gushman, John L., *Living Glass: The Story of the Anchor Hocking Glass Corporation,* New York: Newcomen Society, 1965.

''It's a Question of Technical Skill,'' *Forbes,* March 1, 1969, p. 41.

Lappen, Alyssa A., ''Still Expanding,'' *Forbes,* October 19, 1987, p. 8.

Longo, Don, ''Ferguson Guides Newell to the Top,'' *Discount Store News,* September 25, 1989, p. 82.

Simon, Ruth, ''Of Pots and Paintbrushes,'' *Forbes,* November 3, 1986, p. 110.

Slovak, Julianne, ''Companies to Watch: Newell,'' *Forbes,* February 12, 1990, p. 118.

Wendlinger, Lisa D., ''Firmly Anchored,'' *Forbes,* January 27, 1992, p. 51.

—April D. Gasbarre

ANNTAYLOR.

Ann Taylor Stores Corporation

142 West 57th Street
New York, New York 10019
U.S.A.
(212) 541-3300
Fax: (212) 541-3379

Public Company
Incorporated: 1988
Employees: 3,099
Sales: $658 million
Stock Exchanges: New York
SICs: 5621 Women's Clothing Stores; 6719 Holding Companies Not Elsewhere Classified

Through its wholly owned subsidiary, Ann Taylor Inc., Ann Taylor Stores Corporation is a retailer of women's apparel, with stores in major downtown city locations and shopping malls across the United States. Over 90 percent of the retailer's merchandise consists of its proprietary Ann Taylor brand of clothing, shoes, accessories, and even a perfume. Noted for its classic, tailored designs for career women, Ann Taylor strives to provide what it referred to as "a head to toe concept of dressing with an edited assortment of tasteful, fashion-updated classic apparel and accessories in a one-stop shopping environment." Having faced several challenges in the early 1990s, in the form of falling sales and management shakeups, the company was regaining its poise in 1995.

The original Ann Taylor store was founded in New Haven, Connecticut, in 1954, by Robert Liebskind. Interestingly, there was never an actual Ann Taylor; the name was simply selected to characterize the target customer. The company's line of classic clothing became popular and eventually new shops were opened primarily in such eastern college towns as New Haven, Providence, Boston, Cambridge, and Georgetown. In 1977, Liebskind sold his stores to Garfinckel, Brooks Brothers, Miller & Rhodes Corporation (known as Garfinckels). Under new management, Ann Taylor stores began to spread rapidly during the late 1970s.

During this time, Ann Taylor began showcasing the work of Perry Ellis, who designed clothing for the Ann Taylor label, and also had exclusive contracts with Marimeko and other cutting-edge, upscale designers. The stores eventually began to offer European fashions, as management found that loyal Ann Taylor customers were generally willing to spend a little more for unique, less conservative styles but still less likely to pay the prices or risk the fashion statements available in designer boutiques. Moreover, by refraining from carrying a wide variety of designer labels and brands offered by department stores, Ann Taylor had less competition and thus more pricing flexibility; the company could also produce fast reactions to fashion trends and regional needs.

The value of Ann Taylor's name as a brand increased steadily, and the stores became increasingly popular. The flagship store for the company, on 57th Street in Manhattan, featured a chic restaurant on the third floor. The Ann Taylor customer during this time was characterized as a new breed of well-dressed career women who favored classic fabrics in fashionable designs. Describing a 1978 Ann Taylor catalog, one writer for *Working Woman* magazine noted that the catalog showed "a duo of well-dressed working women ganging up on a would-be mugger, hitting him with their Ann Taylor purses. The message: The Ann Taylor woman might wear silk and cashmere, but watch out—she's taken karate."

In 1981, Ann Taylor, as part of Garfinckels, was acquired by Allied Stores Corporation and quickly became the most profitable among the group of Allied retailers, outperforming even Brooks Brothers and Bonwit Teller. Allied subsequently unloaded unprofitable subsidiaries and further polished its core stores' image of upscale, high-profile specialty and department stores. In 1983, Sally Frame Kasaks, who had started in the fashion industry as a salesperson, was named president of the company, and she served in that capacity until 1985, when she left to join Talbots, and, eventually, Abercrombie & Fitch.

A new president and CEO, Mark Shulman, faced new challenges. A Canadian financier, Robert Campeau, was attracted by Allied's cache of healthy, upscale stores with recognizable names. In 1986, his Campeau Corporation made an overture to acquire Allied but was rebuffed. Campeau was tiny compared to Allied; it had 1985 revenues of $153 million, while Allied reported $4.1 billion for the same year. Nevertheless, in the leveraged buyout-crazed 1980s, it wasn't hard for Campeau to get financial backing. After securing $3 billion in credit, Campeau launched a hostile takeover of Allied. The final price for the deal was more than $5 billion by some estimates, and Campeau had to sell off many of Allied's units in order to pay for the purchase, retaining only the best performers, like Brooks Brothers and Ann Taylor. By the end of 1987, more than $1 billion of Allied's holdings had been sold off, and Campeau was able to pay down some of its debts.

Though it was ahead of schedule on debt payments, Campeau was still feeling the effects of the transaction, earning only $44 million in the first three quarters of 1987. Moreover, its interest payments for that same time period were $244 million. Thus, some analysts were surprised when Campeau quickly set its sights on Federated Department Stores, Inc., a giant holding company of department stores then three times the size of Allied. With more than $4 billion in fresh loans, Campeau initiated a similar takeover, again increasing the initial per share offer, until the final cost for Federated reached $6.6 billion.

Campeau sold off Brooks Brothers to a British Department store to get cash for its debts and for Federated stock. Although Campeau vowed he would not sell Ann Taylor, the retailer was put on the block by June 1988, when Campeau claimed that Ann Taylor's spot in specialty retailing no longer complemented Campeau's department store holdings. At the time, Ann Taylor had 100 stores nationwide and accounted for eight percent of Allied's $3.96 billion in sales in 1988. Taylor was the last of Allied's specialty stores. Proceeds from the sale would go towards Allied's bank debt, as well as for Federated stock.

It wasn't hard to find a buyer for Ann Taylor. Joseph E. Brooks, formerly the chief executive officer of Lord & Taylor, led a group of investors that included Merrill Lynch Capital Partners, Inc. and some of Ann Taylor's management. The price paid was $430 million, which, to some observers, seemed a tad high for a company that, like many companies in the women's apparel industry, had recently reported flat earnings. In fact, although Ann Taylor had more than 36 percent annual growth in both earnings and sales between 1983 and 1987, its earnings seemed to have peaked in 1986. But expectations soared now that Brooks was in charge.

Brooks was noted for making Lord & Taylor over into an upscale store offering classic merchandise. Under his leadership, Lord & Taylor had expanded from 19 to 46 units and sales had quadrupled. Brooks moved quickly at Ann Taylor, bringing in a new management team, some of whom had been with him at Lord & Taylor, including his son, Thomas H.K. Brooks, who was named Ann Taylor's president. Faced with staggering interest payments and a tricky debt-to-equity load, the company focused on rapid expansion and cost-cutting tactics.

By 1991, Ann Taylor had spread as far from its East Coast roots as Jackson, Mississippi, and now boasted 58 new outlets and a total of 176 stores. With new stores helping to boost sales, Brooks felt confident enough to make bids for Saks Fifth Avenue and Bloomingdale's. However, he was outbid for Saks, and the $1 billion he offered for Bloomingdale's failed to tempt its owners, Federated Stores. With the debt load still pressuring Ann Taylor to perform, the company's buyout bosses proposed a public offering of Ann Taylor stock. The industry was limping and a stock offering seemed a good way to raise equity enough to tide Ann Taylor over the rough spots. Despite the fact that Ann Taylor was not faring well in same-store sales, the indication of a retail store's ability to increase stock, the offering went well. Seven million shares were sold at $26 per share, providing the cash flow necessary to continue planned expansions.

However, the offering also increased Ann Taylor's burden to perform well in sales and earnings growth, and it was in the face of such pressures that some decisions were made that would eventually prove detrimental to the company. The new management decided that the typical Ann Taylor customer of 1990 was not as affluent as its earlier clientele had been, and, in an effort to broaden its appeal and cut expenses, the company began using fabrics of lesser quality for the first time.

Management also opted to end Ann Taylor's long and profitable relationship with Joan & David shoes, a product that had accounted for roughly 14 percent of Ann Taylor's sales for 30 years, and had a fine reputation of its own, pulling many customers into Ann Taylor stores. Ann Taylor began offering its own line of shoes instead, at about half the price. Early reviews of these shoes bordered on snide, and earnings and revenues became weak. Stock collapsed and some stockholders sued, alleging misrepresentation of the facts by the prospectus that accompanied the public offering.

Then, in December 1991, Joseph E. Brooks abruptly announced his retirement from his position as chairman. His son, Thomas Brooks had quit the presidency just as suddenly a few weeks earlier as had Gerald H. Blum, the company's vice-chairman. With their company suddenly being run by a committee, stockholders and investors became anxious. The company had lost about two-thirds of its market value since going public in 1991 and was daily losing its most loyal customers. That year, Ann Taylor lost $15.8 million on sales of $438 million.

In February of 1992, Ann Taylor wooed former president Sally Frame Kasaks back. Her first action, like Brooks's, was to install a solid management team. Kasaks chose a largely female management staff, comprised of seasoned veterans of the specialty retail trade. Kasaks then worked to reestablish Ann Taylor's reputation for high-quality clothing, getting rid of the cheap synthetic fabrics and overseeing a new autumn line of clothes that borrowed heavily from popular and costly designs of Donna Karan and Ralph Lauren. Four months after Kasaks rejoined Ann Taylor, the company's same-store sales were up ten percent.

After reassuring the customer of the quality of Ann Taylor merchandise, Kasaks sought a strategy for keeping prices reasonable. Toward that end, she explored several manufacturing options, finally reaching an agreement with Cygne Designs for the joint manufacture of apparel. A private-label company with factory contracts mainly overseas, Cygne worked with Ann Taylor to produce items made to specification more cheaply and quickly. As a result, what few designer labels the Ann Taylor stores stocked nearly disappeared, and lines of casual and weekend clothes were added, as were lines of petite sizes and whole new lines meant to attract younger women.

Sales at stores opened in 1993 grew an impressive 13.6 percent by March of 1994, and the Merrill Lynch Capital Partners and other affiliates still holding 52 percent of Ann Taylor's stock prepared to make another public offering. During the first six months of 1994, same-store sales grew 10.6 percent, while other popular specialty stores, such as The Gap and Nordstrom's, were reporting gains of less than half that amount.

By early 1995, Ann Taylor's prices had been cut ten to 15 percent across the board. A new fragrance line had been introduced, five free-standing shoe and accessory stores had been opened, and a mail-order catalog had been launched. Moreover, the company was progressing with its plan for aggressive expansion, calling for 15 new stores in 1995 and the further expansion of existing stores. With formerly loyal customers returning to Ann Taylor, the company's sales and earnings were increasing considerably in the mid-1990s. Quoted in a 1993 issue of *Working Woman,* Kasaks asserted that "the best way to satisfy Wall Street is to satisfy the customer."

Principal Subsidiaries: Ann Taylor Inc.

Further Reading:

''Brooks Group Gets Ann Taylor for $430 Million,'' *Women's Wear Daily,* November 30, 1988, pp. 1, 26.

Caminiti, Susan, ''How to Win Back Customers,'' *Fortune,* June 14, 1993, p.118.

Coleman, Lisa, ''Welcome Back,'' *Forbes,* August 17, 1992, p. 124.

Colodny, Mark, ''Mr. Ann Taylor,'' *Fortune,* March 11, 1991, p. 105.

Contavski, Vicki, ''Who'll Mind the Store?,'' *Forbes,* December 9, 1991, p. 16.

Donahue, Christine, ''Ann Taylor Turns Barbara Bush Into a Fashion Plate,'' *Adweek's Marketing Index,* September 4, 1989, p. 31.

Furman, Phyllis, ''Fashionable Ann Taylor to Sell Stock,'' *Crain's New York Business,* March 25, 1991, pp. 3, 34.

Jeresky, Laura, ''Rags to Riches,'' *Forbes,* April 15, 1991, p. 42.

Mahar, Maggie, ''Mission Impossible?,'' *Working Woman,* December 1993, pp. 60–68.

McNally, Pamela, ''The Ann Taylor Footwear Formula,'' *Footwear News,* August 1, 1994, p. S6.

McNish, Jacquie, ''Campeau Plans to Sell Allied's Ann Taylor Unit,'' *The Wall Street Journal,* June 16, 1988, p. 10.

Power, William, ''Soaring Ann Taylor May Need Some Caution as Accessory,'' *The Wall Street Journal,* April 15, 1994.

Trachtenberg, Jeffrey, ''Ann Taylor Plans Expansion to Pay $37 Million in Interest from Buy-Out,'' *The Wall Street Journal,* May 11, 1989, p. A4.

Wachs Book, Esther, ''The Treachery of Success,'' *Forbes,* September 12, 1994, pp. 88–90.

Wilson, Marianne, ''Reinventing Ann Taylor,'' *Chain Store Age Executive,* January 1995, pp. 26–45.

Zinn, Laura, ''Trouble Stalks the Aisles at Ann Taylor,'' *Business Week,* December 9, 1991, p. 38.

—Carol I. Keeley

Anthem Electronics, Inc.

1160 Ridder Park Drive
San Jose, California 95131
U.S.A.
(408) 453-1200

Wholly Owned Subsidiary of Arrow Electronics, Inc.
Founded: 1968
Employees: 678
Sales: $618 million
Stock Exchanges: New York
SIC: 3674 Semiconductors & Related Devices

Anthem Electronics, Inc. is one of the most successful and one of the largest semiconductor distributors in the United States. The company specializes in highly advanced, sophisticated technology products such as computer subsystems and other computer accessories, including RAMs (random access memory units), ROMs (read-only memory units), PROMs (programmable random access memory units), video display terminals, disk-drive controls, and various switching component supplies. Anthem's products are used by such diverse industries as telecommunications, electronic data processing, the aerospace industry, and the U.S. Department of Defense. In the mid-1990s, the company was concentrating on advanced electronic storage devices.

Founded in 1968 by a group of electronic experts and businessmen, Anthem initially focused on providing semiconductors for both the burgeoning computer systems industry and the consumer electronic component parts industry. The company contracted to distribute semiconductors to a number of companies on the west coast of the United States, and in doing so developed an extensive network throughout the region. Contracts with the U.S. Department of Defense and NASA (National Aeronautical and Space Administration) provided the company with a stable source of income and enough funds to expand its distributor network.

Throughout the 1970s, Anthem continued to provide semiconductors to an ever-wider range of industries. At the same time, management decided to increase its market share of military semiconductors and programmable logic devices. Yet, despite increasing revenues, Anthem remained a regional firm, expanding up and down the California coastline, but keeping the development of its distributor network primarily within the western region of the United States.

It wasn't until the mid-1980s that Anthem burst onto the national scene. Management at Anthem decided to acquire Lionex Corporation, a privately owned and operated semiconductor and computer subsystems distributor located in Wilmington, Massachusetts. For approximately $17 million, Anthem purchased the east coast distributor which reported sales of over $50 million in 1985. The acquisition was a watershed for Anthem.

With this single purchase, Anthem immediately expanded its distribution network throughout the northeastern region of the United States. Besides a formidable presence in the semiconductor industry, Lionex possessed a line of electromechanical products. Most importantly, however, Lionex operated six branches in New York, Connecticut, Maryland, Pennsylvania, New Jersey, and Massachusetts.

Within a few months of the acquisition, Anthem implemented a complete reorganization of Lionex. The owner and founder of Lionex, Leonard Schley, retired soon after the purchase was finalized, and Anthem brought in a new management team to smooth the process of incorporating the distribution network of the newly acquired company. Anthem management decided to retain the Lionex name, due to its high profile and reputation in the northeastern region, in order to focus on satisfying the customers and suppliers already within the Lionex network.

In early 1986, Anthem expanded its distribution network to include the Midwest. The company opened new distribution offices in Chicago, Milwaukee, and Minneapolis in order to fill the gap between its home base on the West Coast and its expansion into the northeastern part of the United States. In 1986, Anthem reported an impressive sales figure of $798 million in its western region, almost a 40 percent share of the total U.S. market for distribution. The acquisition of Lionex provided an additional $573 million, which added up to sales of $1.3 billion, or an astounding 65 percent share of the entire distribution market. By expanding into the Midwest, Anthem projected that it would grab another $135 million in market sales, increasing its share of the distribution market to approximately 75 percent.

Yet management did not expect this expansion strategy to encompass a national distribution network. Anthem was content to focus on regional markets, thereby avoiding the possibility of a downturn in the national distribution market. During this time, the company began to focus on providing products such as data storage systems for the commercial market, and also to develop new products for the new Winchester disk drives and 32-bit microprocessors that had just been introduced. In the military market, Anthem began to establish itself as the premier supplier of military-grade semiconductors. With a market in excess of $350 million, the company used Lionex's well-established military support organization and distribution network to sell advanced technological equipment.

By 1988, Anthem was the sixth largest distributor of semiconductors in the United States, and boasted a customer base of over 6,500 companies, including huge original equipment manufacturers and small engineering firms. With 16 distribution locations in the western, midwestern, and eastern parts of the United States, the company reported a 32 percent increase in sales from 1987 to 1988. The semiconductor industry was developing products for computer-related equipment, and Anthem received more and more orders destined for desktop work stations, desktop publishing systems, and microcomputers with large memories. With a yearly percentage of sales increasing more than any company in the industry, Anthem reported that its revenues had grown from $119.5 million in 1984 to over $196 million by the end of fiscal 1987.

In 1989, Anthem scored another major coup when it arranged to become the sole distributor for Seeq Technology. Seeq Technology, a manufacturer of EEpROMs and flash EEpROMs with sales of $55 million in 1988, reached an exclusive agreement with Anthem for the latter firm to function as its sole nationwide distributor. Anthem's distribution network was highly efficient in the West, Midwest, and Northeast, and provided Seeq with the opportunity to significantly increase its sales in those regions.

Although sales of electronic components slowed drastically during the year, Anthem remained almost untouched by the industry downturn. Sales rose over 20 percent, or about $319 million, and profits rose even more, increasing by 33 percent to over $15 million. In an industry with extremely thin profit margins, Anthem recorded the widest of any major distributor—an impressive 4.9 percent. One reason for this success was due to the formation of a Technology Systems Division which sold disk drives and tape drives by telephone. With almost no overhead, or burdensome service expenses, the division doubled its sales figures in 1989. Another highly innovative, and extremely lucrative unit, was the Turnkey Division. This division accepted a customer's product list, purchased the items, built all the component parts, tested its effectiveness and reliability, and then delivered a completed system to the company ready for use.

In 1993, one of the largest manufacturers of semiconductors in the world, Intel Corporation, reached an agreement with Anthem to distribute its entire line of semiconductor products. By franchising Anthem to distribute its semiconductor items in locations throughout the United States, Anthem was given the opportunity to develop into one of the largest semiconductor suppliers in the Northern Hemisphere. Working out the details of a franchise relationship took nearly eight years, but Intel was satisfied with Anthem's operations and distribution network, and estimated that sales for its products would increase significantly. International Business Machines Corporation (IBM), which had seriously considered making a similar franchising agreement with Anthem, was forced to drop the company from its list of potential candidates.

As Anthem continued to develop its distribution network, and provide semiconductor equipment to a growing list of customers, the company was approached by Arrow Electronics, Inc. Arrow Electronics, one of the largest distribution companies in the United States with sales near the $3 billion mark, was looking to expand its distribution network in certain niche areas within particular industries, and within certain geographical regions. An agreement was worked out and Arrow purchased Anthem in late 1994 for an approximate price of $370 million. The acquisition of Anthem by Arrow was mutually beneficial for both companies, but Arrow was the immediate and most noticeable beneficiary. Arrow grabbed the number one position in distributor sales away from Avnet Inc., another large American distributor of semiconductor equipment and data storage systems. The acquisition was projected to increase Arrow's worldwide sales to over $4.5 billion, with over $3 billion in sales coming from the United States alone. Arrow was also fortunate in gaining between $40 to $50 million in cash which Anthem had squirreled away to meet the contingencies of the marketplace.

With the acquisition of Anthem, Arrow had created the largest distributor network in the world, far ahead of all its competition, and the company also became the largest supplier of semiconductor equipment and computer-related subsystems. In early 1994, before the acquisition, Avnet was approximately $80 million ahead of Arrow, also nearing the $3 billion mark in distributor sales. Other large companies within the industry included Pioneer-Standard, with $950 million in sales, Marshall, with over $750 million in sales, Future at $650 million in sales, Anthem at $610 million in sales, Wyle, with sales of $525 million, Premier at $502 million, Bell Industries at $286 million, and TTI at $208 million. With sales estimated at over $15 billion in the industry, Arrow seized the largest share of the market with its new acquisition. Most of Arrow's sales had previously come from outside the United States. The purchase of Anthem was intended to strengthen the company's position within the domestic market.

Anthem was fortunate to be purchased by Arrow. During the early 1990s, the company's revenues had declined, and the acquisition provided Anthem with the financial stability and resources to continue to expand its distributor network within certain regions of the United States. Anthem had been in the midst of a limited expansion program when acquired by Arrow. But the industry was volatile, and Anthem's extremely thin profit margin was beginning to grow even thinner. After the merger, it was believed that if Arrow used Anthem's distributor network wisely, the two companies would have a very promising future together.

Principal Subsidiaries: Lionex Corporation.

Further Reading:

''Anthem Electronics Agrees to Buy Lionex,'' *Electronic News,* July 14, 1986, p. 50.

''Anthem Electronics Inc.,'' *Barrons,* April 11, 1988, pp. 59–60.

''Anthem Sets Expansion Into Midwest,'' *Electronic News,* January 19, p. 50.

Autry, Ret, ''Anthem Electronics,'' *Fortune,* September 10, 1990, p. 95.

''CEO: Anthem to Avoid National Focus,'' *Electronic News,* March 23, 1987, p. 35.

Ferguson, Bob, ''Seeq Terminates Schweber, Time In Favor of Exclusive Anthem Pact,'' *Electronic News,* November 13, 1989, p. 61.

Levine, Bernard, ''Industry Buzzing About Arrow/Anthem,'' *Electronic News,* October 3, 1994, p. 4.

McCausland, Richard, ''Intel Trumps IBM With Anthem Deal,'' *Electronic News,* January 18, 1993, pp. 1–19.

—Thomas Derdak

Aramark Corporation

Aramark Tower
1101 Market Street
Philadelphia, Pennsylvania 19107
U.S.A.
(215) 238-3326
Fax: (215) 238-3333

Private Company
Incorporated: 1959 as Automatic Retailers of America, Inc.
Employees: 124,000
Sales: $5.2 billion
SICs: 7299 Miscellaneous Personal Services, Nec; 7213 Linen Supply; 6719 Holding Companies, Nec

Aramark Corporation is a diversified service company with five major lines of business: food service, health care, child care, uniform services, and periodicals distribution. Its food service operations serve such diverse customers as Fortune 500 executives, prison inmates, college students, Olympic athletes, and tourists. Its Spectrum Health Care Services subsidiary offers emergency care, correctional medical services, primary care, and anesthesia services. Child care is provided through its Children's World Learning Centers subsidiary. Aramark's two uniform companies, WearGuard, a direct mail retailer, and Aramark Uniform Services, a producer of uniforms and work clothes, are the largest in the United States. Its Magazine and Book Services is also the largest wholesale distributor of periodicals in the United States, serving more than 18,000 retail locations. In 1994 the company's revenues topped $5 billion.

Aramark was founded by Davre Davidson and Bill Fishman, both owners of peanut-vending businesses. The two had never met when they started expanding the boundaries of the traditional vending industry in the early 1940s. In Los Angeles, Davidson began moving his machines from traditional outlets like drug stores, bowling alleys, and restaurants to factories and offices. In Chicago, Fishman was attempting to transform his vending operation from a "fringe benefit" into a bona fide food service operation. The two met when each won a contract to serve Douglas Aircraft plants in Santa Monica and Chicago. In the following years, they frequently discussed their desire to provide food service along with their vending operations. Finally, after a number of unsuccessful attempts to subcontract to catering companies, the two decided to merge their operations in 1959. Their company was incorporated under the name Automatic Retailers of America, Inc., and earned $24 million in its first year.

Almost immediately, the company began expanding through acquisitions. Between 1959 and 1964, ARA merged with or acquired more than 150 smaller vending companies. Its largest acquisition (and one that fulfilled a dream for both Fishman and Davidson) was the 1961 purchase of Slater Systems, Inc., the largest food service business in the United States, for $15 million. The purchase made ARA a diversified food service company, and gave it a strong foothold in institutional markets such as colleges and universities. During the early 1960s ARA led the trend among vending companies to expand into the food service industry. "We recognized that vending was moving into food service and that this more sophisticated business would require skills we couldn't attain individually," Davidson told *Business Week* in 1964. By 1964, ARA operated 95,000 vending machines, offering freshly brewed coffee, hot soup, sandwiches, and other items. It had 750 cafeterias or other "manual food service" outlets, and total revenues of $200.6 million.

The company's dominance of the vending industry grew so quickly that in 1964 the Federal Trade Commission required ARA to divest itself of a number of vending companies, worth about $7.6 million in annual sales. The company complied, selling a third of the required portion by 1965 and the remainder in the following year. Fishman and Davidson had other plans for their company's growth. "We're in the service business," ARA vice-president Harry Stephens told *Business Week*, "And food is only one of the services necessary to keep an institution operating. There's janitorial services, cleaning, lawn care, security, laundry, accounting, many things." This concept became the cornerstone of ARA's expansion. The company established a division to run resorts, sports parks, and amusement parks; acquired Air La Carte Inc., a private company that provided in-flight meals for more than 20 domestic and international airlines; and ventured into periodicals distribution, purchasing 39 local distributorships over a period of about four years.

In 1972 the FTC again charged ARA with anti-competitive practices. The first complaint stated that its recent purchase of 39 distributorships posed a potential monopolistic threat. The second charged the company (which by then had grown to be the nation's biggest vending machine company) with anti-competitive practices through the purchase of 97 separate vending companies. ARA vigorously defended itself against the charges, stating that "approximately 80 percent" of ARA's revenues were not earned by the segments under question. In 1973 the court ordered ARA to cease purchasing "certain types of wholesale operations in the paperback books and periodicals field" and to divest itself of a portion of its vending business. The company's image suffered again in 1973 when a federal grand jury indicted ARA, Western Vending, and AAV Cos. of Cleveland with colluding to fix prices and illegally control the customers and locations of cigarette vending machines. ARA filed a "no contest" plea, stating the that the charges dealt with a market segment that was too small to warrant the cost of defending them in court.

ARA's earnings grew at a compound annual rate of 10 percent from 1970 to 1975, fueled primarily by internal expansion. In addition to its food and distribution services, ARA had branched into student bus services, maintenance and housekeeping, and merchandising. The majority of the company's income, however, came from food service. According to analysts, its growth was remarkable given the rising foods costs that had adversely affected many companies in the food service industry. "We try to manage our services like an investment portfolio," Fishman told *Financial World* in 1975. "While one area may be down another is up. That's why we've been able to hold our margins." During this time, the company also ventured into the somewhat unpopular nursing home management field, purchasing National Living Centers in 1973 and Geriatrics Inc. in 1974. Although many in the investment community questioned the move (leading to a drop in stock prices), Fishman defended it, stating, "We've been in the medical market for over thirty years, so it was just a natural transition."

By 1977, the company had divested almost all of its vending operations. That year, the FTC asked the federal Justice Department to force ARA to further divest itself of four periodicals distribution companies in the South and Midwest, stating that the purchases were in violation of its 1973 order. ARA complied with the order, paid a $300,000 fine, and continued to grow through the purchase of several service-oriented companies, including Aratex Inc., a uniform laundry and delivery service, Daybridge Learning Centers, a chain of day care centers, Smith Transfer Corp., a trucking company, and Physicians Placement, a management support and physician service for hospital emergency rooms. As it had with its other operations, ARA expanded each new division by purchasing other small companies and consolidating them.

The company also continued to develop internally. By 1979 ARA operated more than 6,000 food service establishments in the United Kingdom, Belgium, France, and Germany. In Canada, ARA purchased VS Services, a food service operation which quickly grew to become the largest food service operation in that country. Its student transport division, which operated school bus fleets throughout the United States, also grew at a rapid rate during the last half of the 1970s, providing 9.5 percent of revenues by 1979. ARA president and chief operating officer Marvin Heaps attributed the company's success during difficult economic times to its effective management of three factors: food costs, energy costs, and labor costs. Sales for the first six months of 1979 topped $1 billion. Earnings per share rose to $2.80, ten cents below the hourly wage the company paid a large number of its employees.

ARA's reputation was tarnished once again in 1981, as a federal grand jury began investigating the company's student transport division to determine whether it engaged in a bid-rigging strategy designed to squeeze out local competition. ARA management maintained that the company was a victim of a "smear campaign" started by disgruntled former employees and local transport companies angry that ARA had won certain bids. ARA's earnings dropped from $63 million in 1980 to $39 million in 1982, and share prices steadily declined, although sales had risen to $3 billion by fiscal 1983. Many investors believed that "the company's many divisions had gotten out of control from too much growth too fast." Although profits in its geriatrics, health care, textile-service, and distribution divisions were strong, profits in its trucking and food service divisions were severely affected by recessions, and its European food service operations also posted heavy losses.

Led by the newly appointed president and chief executive Joseph Neubauer, ARA management responded to the company's uneven results by reorganizing its divisions by geography as well as type of operation. Its acquisition program slowed slightly, focusing on companies in profitable markets such as geriatrics and distribution. The company also embarked on a major public relations campaign, with two specific goals: to make ARA a respected household word, and to generate a sense of corporate identity among its 112,000 employees. "Originally the strategy was 'we are servants in other people's homes and ought to be invisible,' " Neubauer told the *Wall Street Journal* in 1984. "But now we are going to stand for something." Advertising expenditures jumped to around $2 million as the company took out ads in major weekly magazines such as *Time* and *Newsweek.* Employees began wearing company uniforms embroidered with the ARA logo, and managers began receiving incentives, worth up to 45 percent of their annual salaries, as rewards for work well done.

Perhaps the largest change that year was an unexpected, $850 million leveraged buy-out, which was orchestrated by ARA management in the surprisingly short time span of 99 days from start to finish. Deemed an "absolute necessity" by management to prevent undesired investors from bidding for control of the company (although the only known bid was for $720 million from former food service division president William Siegel), the buyout was financed by borrowing from Chemical Bank and Morgan Guaranty Trust Co. After the buyout, ARA neither cut its operating expenditures, nor (with the exception of its unprofitable Smith Transfer division) sold any major assets to pay down the debt. ARA actually acquired three companies within its first three years of going private, while paying $100 million on its debt.

In the early 1990s, the company began selling assets, including its Ground Services Inc., which cleaned aircraft and handled cargo and baggage at airports. And in 1992, ARA spun off a portion of its geriatrics division in an initial public offering that raised $112.7 million. ARA held a 10 percent interest in the new company, which took the name Living Centers of America, and used $76 million of the money raised in the IPO to pay "certain intercompany indebtedness." By 1992, ARA's annual revenues totaled $4.8 billion. Its image was greatly improved, especially in its food service and leisure service divisions, where "customized service" allowed the company to expand throughout Europe and into Japan, and even serve Olympic athletes their native foods at the 1992 Barcelona Olympics. Its day care division was growing more slowly than desired, as corporations and government cut back on expenditures, but the rest of its operations remained relatively healthy.

Having transformed itself from a collection of vending machines into a mature, $5 billion corporation, in 1994 ARA developed a new logo and changed its name to Aramark Corporation, reflecting the changes that it has undergone during its 36-year history.

Principal Subsidiaries: Aramark Business Dining Services; Aramark Correctional Services; Aramark Refreshment Services; Aramark Campus Services; Aramark School Nutrition Services; Aramark Health Care Support Services; GMARA; Aramark Leisure Services; Aramark International Services; Aramark Uniform Services; WearGuard; Spectrum Health Care Services; Children's World Learning Centers; Aramark Magazine and Book Services.

Further Reading:

Allen, Frank, "ARA, Betting on Pride, Approves Plan to Give Its Managers Voting Control," *Wall Street Journal*, March 16, 1988, p. 25.

Engelmayer, Paul A., "ARA Attempts Revival Using a High Profile," *Wall Street Journal*, June 8, 1984, p. 1.

"Has ARA Misstepped?" *Financial World*, February 5, 1975, p. 12.

"Vendors Outgrow Machines," *Business Week*, October 10, 1964, p. 136.

Weber, Joseph, "Catering to the Olympics: A Gold Medal—But Not Much Gold," *Business Week*, July 27, 1992, p. 38.

—Maura Troester

Associated British Foods plc

Weston Centre
Bowater House
68 Knightsbridge
London, SW1X 7LR
United Kingdom
(44) 171 589-6363
Fax: (44) 171 584-8560

Public Company
Incorporated: 1935 as Food Investments Ltd.
Employees: 50,241
Sales: £4.48 billion
Stock Exchanges: London
SICs: 2051 Bread, Cake and Related Products; 2041 Flour and Other Grain Mill Products; 2099 Food Preparations, Not Elsewhere Classified; 5411 Grocery Stores; 5331 Variety Stores; 2063 Beet Sugar; 6719 Holding Companies, Not Elsewhere Classified; 5141 Groceries, General Lines

With high-ranking positions in several categories of foodstuffs, Associated British Foods plc (ABF) stands as one of the United Kingdom's top producers of consumables. From its roots as a Canadian bakery, the company grew and evolved to become Britain's top manufacturer of bread, with over one-third of the U. K. market. By the early 1990s, the company had diversified within the food business into tea and coffee (sold under the Twinings and Jackson brands), biscuits and crispbread (marketed under the Burtons and Ryvita names, respectively), as well as frozen foods and edible oils. Its British Sugar subsidiary ranked as the country's dominant producer of sugar. The company's activities in Ireland, Australia, and the United States encompassed grocery retailing, milling and baking, and soft goods retailing. Notwithstanding its geographic diversity, the vast majority (over 89 percent) of its revenues continued to be generated in the United Kingdom and Ireland in the early 1990s.

ABF is a multibillion dollar international conglomerate that characterizes itself as a ''family of businesses.'' ABF subsidiaries, whether self-developed or acquired through merger or acquisition, retain their individuality in name, operations, and clientele, yet maintain strong connections with the parent's central management core. Advertising and marketing of ABF's wide range of products and services—bakeries, supermarkets, restaurants, catering companies, and clothing stores—are geared to the family as consumers. And for more than half a century one family has controlled ABF: the Westons. In the early 1990s, the Westons owned just over half of ABF's equity through Wittington Investments Ltd., which was controlled by then-Chairman G.H. Weston. About one-third of ABF's shares were traded publicly during this time.

The family saga began in Toronto, Canada, in 1882, when George Weston, then 18, bought a bread-delivery route. During the following 36 years, he built a number of successful bakeries in that area. George Weston Ltd., the Toronto-based chain of bakeries and supermarkets that resulted from that growth, consistently ranked among North America's top businesses throughout the 20th century.

When George Weston's son Garfield took over the bakery business at his father's death in 1924, he had much more in mind than simply maintaining or building up the chain of local bakeries his father had founded; he was determined that it grow into an international business. Eleven years later, in November 1935, he took a giant step toward that goal by purchasing seven bakeries in England, Scotland, and Wales and added them to his newly formed Food Investments Ltd., which was promptly renamed Allied Bakeries Limited. All seven bakeries remained in operation throughout the 20th century, three under their original names.

Within four years, Garfield had 18 bakeries and four biscuit factories throughout the British Isles, beginning decades of expansion into Europe, Africa, Australia, Asia, and North America. The expansion went beyond food products to encompass seed production, milling, canning, retail grocery and clothing outlets, restaurants, vehicle parts, fuel, and basic research.

The expansion was not always steady. At the onset of World War II, wartime restrictions and shortages of supplies began to slow production, while high taxes and voluntary defense contributions reduced profits. But expansion picked up again in the postwar period. A postwar excess-profits tax refund was wholly invested in expansion and equipment. In 1948 Garfield's son Garry joined the board of directors. The following year, the company purchased two Australian firms: Gold Crust Bakeries in Adelaide and Gartrell White in Sydney. By the end of the decade, profits had surpassed £2 million a year.

A growth spurt in the 1950s added dozens of new bakeries, tea shops, restaurants, and catering businesses, many of them in newly constructed shopping centers, which provided one-stop convenience for consumers. Food stores purchased by the company were refashioned into supermarkets to suit new shopping habits. This diversification led to a name change in 1960, to Associated British Foods. By 1964, the company claimed to be the largest baker in the world and one of the largest millers, in addition to being one of the largest grocers in the United Kingdom.

Rapid growth continued during the 1960s, with the acquisition of A.B. Hemmings, Ltd., a chain of 230 bakery shops in the London area, the entire chain of Fine Fare food shops, and a 51 percent interest in the South African Premier Milling Company.

In 1970 ABF also opened the largest bakery in western Europe, in Glasgow, Scotland. A year later, ABF's Fine Fare opened its first two "superstores." As the 1970s progressed, the Stewart Cash Stores in Ireland, which ABF had acquired some 20 years before, followed suit, opening their first hypermarket. In 1978, ABF expanded into a new market—frozen foods—by buying an ice cream factory and a pizza bakery.

Garfield died in October 1978 and Garry advanced to the chairmanship of ABF. The family no longer sought the public eye, keeping a low profile since 1983, when an attempt by six Irish Republican gunmen to kidnap Galen was foiled.

Despite difficulties such as fluctuation of the pound and climatic conditions affecting crops, ABF has continued to expand and prosper. In 1980, a subsidiary, Twinings Tea, opened its first North American factory, in Greensboro, North Carolina, and also opened the Grosvenor Marketing Company in Paramus, New Jersey. Additional bakeries and other businesses have been acquired, and ABF's continual program of monitoring and modernizing has kept products and services up to date and operations efficient.

Some of ABF's subsidiaries are much older than their parent. The Twining Crosfield Group, for example, dates back to a coffee shop purchased by Thomas Twining in 1706, when coffee was the fashionable drink for men. Tea, introduced early in the 17th century, had been popularized as a drink for ladies by Queen Catherine, the wife of Charles II, at mid-century. But men usually drank it for medicinal purposes only (it was widely regarded as a remedy for headaches). When Twining introduced tea as a sideline, he found it was so popular that in 1717 he converted Tom's Coffee House into the Golden Lyon, London's first tea shop.

Twinings Tea, exported to 90 countries, may be ABF's most widely-known brand name. It has won the Queen's Award for export achievement, and consistently dominated its market. The tea was blended in several factories in the British Isles and one in the United States; ABF marketing companies in both countries manage distribution.

The Ryvita Company, purchased by ABF in 1949, also won the Queen's Award for export with the crispbread that has long been its principal product and probably ABF's second-best-known brand name. Increasing interest in health foods made Ryvita and the company's other main product, Crackerbread, popular in many countries in the 1980s. By the early 1990s, Ryvita eclipsed its competition with an 80 percent share of the market. ABF hoped to parlay the brand's strength into increased sales with the late 1988 introduction of a crossover product. Ryvita High Fibre Corn Flakes coupled the original product's reputation as a health food with a marketing emphasis on environmentalism; the product came in recycled packaging. Demand for high-fiber foods and the availability of new extrusion technology resulted in the development of Allinson's branded products, Croustipain, as well as other extruded breakfast cereals and cereal products.

Allied Bakeries, the group of bakeries Weston purchased at the time of its incorporation, continued to function as part of ABF's largest subsidiary. Over the course of the company's history, this segment grew to include some 40 wholesale bakeries and close to 1,200 retail bakery shops and restaurants throughout the British Isles. When the addition of in-house bakeries in many supermarkets put a slight crimp in the wholesale baked-goods business, Allied Bakeries countered this trend with a line of partially baked goods and a line of frozen bakery products, both of which could be completed at an in-house bakery or by the retail consumer at home. But by mid-1994, a string of losses in the Baker's Oven retail chain led to that operation's divestment. The sale, which encompassed two bakeries and over 400 retail locations, generated £18.95 million.

Cereal Industries, a holding company for six subsidiaries, also worked closely with Allied Foods Group. Fishers Agricultural Holdings, one of the six cereal industries subsidiaries, included Fishers Nutrition, which supplied animal feeds and livestock marketing services and Fishers Seed and Grain, which produced agricultural seeds. The Allied Grain Group, another of the six, marketed seeds and fertilizers. Mardorf, Peach and Company imported and exported cereals. ABR Foods supplied wheat by-products to several types of industry: baking and brewing, food and pharmaceutical manufacturers, animal feed, and packaging products. The Aughton Group, which, with ABR, comprised the fifth Cereal Industries group, supplied computerized process-control systems to a variety of industries. Finally, Westmill Foods and Alric Packing supplied retail grocers and caterers with Allinson's flour, yeast, bran, and wheatgerm, among other products.

ABF's Burtons Gold Medal Biscuits long ranked as one of the largest biscuit manufacturers in the United Kingdom. As it grew, rumors surfaced that it was planning to take over a competitor, such as United Biscuits. Burtons pursued an aggressive program of investment in new and modernized equipment and cost-effective production techniques in order to maintain its leadership in the market.

The Irish retail group was the largest supermarket chain in Ireland (Quinnsworth stores in the Irish Republic and Stewarts and Crazy Prices in Northern Ireland). This group also included retail clothing stores—Penneys in Ireland and Primark in the United Kingdom—focusing on fashions for young people. Many of these stores opened in the 1960s; although they continued to do a thriving business through the 1980s, they were battered by cutthroat price wars in the early 1990s. Early in 1995, markets were rife with speculation that the Stewarts chain was on the auction block.

AB Ingredients, formed in 1982, and AB Technology, formed in 1987, constituted new directions for ABF. AB Ingredients developed and manufactured new ingredients and additives for Allied Bakeries and for other independent companies. It also developed improved bakery processes. AB Technology specialized in high-tech improvements for several types of industry, including food production.

It took a strong central management, an efficient reporting system, and vigilant personnel and investment programs to hold together so many relatively independent companies of disparate size and design, in widely separated geographical locations. ABF's continual expansion testified to its strength, but its structure, marked by an intricate system of holding companies and representation, was difficult to penetrate and analyze.

An early 1990s recession put ABF in what an anonymous analyst with Charles Stanley & Co., Ltd. called "an unenviable situation." Cautious consumers and ready-to-please retailers squeezed profit margins on virtually all the company's products. Sales declined from £4.81 billion in 1991 to £3.95 billion in 1992, and pre-tax profits dropped from £332.3 million to £267 million during the same period. The company responded with a major reorganization encompassing the core bakery division as well as the British Sugar plc operations acquired in 1991, closing factories and eliminating a net of nearly 1,500 jobs from 1992 to 1994. Net results rebounded in 1993, when the company recorded £4.39 billion in revenues and £338 million in pre-tax profits. Financial performance continued to improve in 1994, as sales increased to £4.48 billion and pre-tax profits increased to £360 million.

Principal Subsidiaries: AB Ingredients Limited (95%); ABR Foods Limited; AB Technology Limited; Allied Bakeries Limited; Allied Foods Co. Limited (New Zealand); Allied Foods Limited; Allied Grain Limited; Allied Mills Limited; J Bibby Agriculture Limited; British Sugar plc; Burtons Gold Medal Biscuits Limited; Crazy Prices; C.W.I.I. Limited (Channel Islands); Eastbow Securities Limited; Fishers Agricultural Holdings Limited; Foods International S.A. (France; George Weston Foods Limited (78%) (Australia); Germain's (UK) Limited; Germain's (Ireland) Limited Gregg & Company Limited; Grosvenor Marketing Limited (US); Jacksons of Piccadilly Limited; KW Agriculture Limited; Lax & Shaw Limited; Mauri Products Limited (50%); Namosa Limited; N.B. Love Industry Pty Ltd (Australia); Power Supermarkets Limited (Ireland); Primark (Ireland); Primark Stores Limited; Provincial Merchants Limited; The Ryvita Company Limited; Serpentine Securities Limited; Stewarts Supermarkets Limited; Sugarpol (Poland); Trident Feeds; R Twining & Company Limited; R Twining & Co. Ltd (US); Walmsley Limited; Westmill Foods Limited; Weston Research Laboratories Limited; Wesfeeds Pty Limited (50%) (Australia); Wesmilk Pty Limited (50%) (Australia).

Further Reading:

"Associated British Foods," *Pensions & Investments,* May 25, 1992, p. 32.

"Associated British Foods: Company Report," Charles Stanley & Co., Ltd., November 16, 1994.

"British Deal with Kraft," *The New York Times,* July 12, 1995, p. C4.

Davies, Charles, *Bread Men: How the Westons Built an International Empire,* Toronto: Key Porter Books, 1987.

Hoggan, Karen, "Ryvita Cereal Shows Its Fibre," *Marketing,* January 11, 1990, p. 2.

Tigert, D., *George Weston Limited: A Corporate Background Report,* Toronto: Royal Commission on Corporate Concentration, 1977.

—updated by April Dougal Gasbarre

The Associated Press

50 Rockefeller Plaza
New York, New York 10020-1666
U.S.A.
(212) 621-1500
Fax: (212) 621-1723

Private Company
Incorporated: 1848 as Associated Press of New York
Employees: 3,100
Sales: $350 million
SICs: 7383 News Syndicates

The Associated Press (AP) describes itself as the largest newsgathering organization in the world. Organized as a nonprofit cooperative, AP provides news and graphics by wire to over 1,700 member newspapers and 5,500 member television and radio stations. To collect the news and photographs it supplies to its members, AP maintains 143 bureaus in the United States, as well as dozens more in 67 countries across the world. In addition to its basic news wire service, AP also operates a commercial-free All News Radio network, and in 1994 launched APTV, its London-based video newsgathering service. Another video-oriented service offered by AP is NewsCenter, a Microsoft Windows based software system that provides a number of television newsroom functions.

The Associated Press was first established in 1848, when six of the most prominent daily newspapers in New York City decided to pool their resources in order to cut costs. Representatives of the six papers—the *Journal of Commerce,* the *New York Sun,* the *Herald,* the *Courier and Enquirer,* the *Express,* and the *New York Tribune*—were able to put aside their competitive differences, and the Associated Press of New York was created. David Hale, publisher of the *Journal of Commerce,* was its first president. The purpose of the organization at the beginning was strictly a financial one. By sharing all the news that arrived by telegraph wire and dividing the expenses evenly, each member was spared the dangers of losing wire-borne information to a higher bidder.

By 1850, the group had its first paying customers, the Philadelphia *Public Ledger* and the *Baltimore Sun,* which were given access to AP dispatches for a fee, without becoming actual members of the collective. A seventh full member (another New York paper) was admitted in 1851. Over the next several years, the number of client newspapers outside of New York grew, and the AP was able to recover about half of its expenses through its sales of news to those papers. The AP kept its transmission costs in check by sending out news to each geographical area only one time. The newspapers in each area were left to distribute the news among themselves. This led to the formation of several regional associations modeled on the original AP. The Western Associated Press (WAP) was created by a group of midwestern daily newspapers in 1862. Other groups that sprang up over the next few years were the Northwestern Associated Press, the New England Associated Press, the Philadelphia Associated Press, and the New York State Associated Press.

As the regional associations, especially the WAP, gained strength, friction developed between them and their New York parent. The western papers felt that they were being overcharged for European news, which by the 1860s was flowing steadily to the United States by underwater telegraph cable. Concessions were made, and peace reigned for several years. Several competitors to the AP arose during the 1870s, but none were able to break the virtual monopoly the AP held on the transmission of domestic and international news by wire. The first serious rival emerged in 1882, when the United Press (UP), led by William M. Laffan of the *New York Sun,* was formed.

In 1891, Victor Lawson of the *Chicago Daily News* produced evidence that top executives of the AP and the UP had engaged in a secret agreement that gave the UP free access to AP News. Outraged by this revelation, the AP's western members broke from the association, and in 1892 established the Associated Press of Illinois under the leadership of general manager Melville Stone. The New York AP quickly folded, and its original members defected to the UP. Stone then pulled off a major coup for the new AP by obtaining exclusive arrangements with three major European news agencies: Reuters in England, Havas in France, and Wolff in Germany. These contracts put the UP in an untenable position, and by 1897, the UP had thrown in the towel. All of the New York dailies except the *Sun* and William Randolph Hearst's's *Journal* were given memberships in the new AP.

Another controversy erupted in 1898, and again Laffan of the *Sun* was involved. Laffan had set up his own agency, the Laffan News Bureau, following the collapse of the UP. When the AP discovered that one of its client papers, the *Chicago Inter Ocean,* had used Laffan copy, it sought to punish the *Inter Ocean* by cutting off its AP service. The *Inter Ocean* sued to block the AP from severing its service. The Illinois Supreme Court ruled in 1900 that the AP's bylaws were broad enough to make the organization akin to a public utility. The Court's decision meant that the AP must provide service to anybody who wanted it. Rather than comply with the Illinois Court's conclusion, the Associated Press of Illinois was dissolved, and the organization set up shop once again in New York. The new AP was organized under New York State law as a nonprofit membership association, with Stone continuing in his role as general manager.

By reorganizing, rather than by complying with the Illinois Supreme Court's decision, the AP was able to maintain control over who was allowed to become a member. The new AP of

1900 was a cooperative, whose members were to share their news with each other and share the costs of maintaining staff to control the flow of news among members. By 1914, the AP had about 100 member newspapers. Until 1915, AP members were prohibited from buying news from other services. By that time, there were actually two viable competitors from whom AP members could be getting additional news: the United Press Association, formed in 1907, and the International News Service, founded by Hearst in 1909. Laffan's agency, after thriving for a few years, was out of the picture by 1916.

In 1910, a young Indiana journalist named Kent Cooper approached general manager Stone with the idea of using telephone rather than telegraph to feed news to out-of-the-way newspapers. Although this method was only put to use for a few years—due mainly to the emergence of the teletype machine in 1913—Stone was impressed, and he hired Cooper as AP's traffic chief. Cooper worked his way up to assistant general manager by 1920. A year later, Stone retired, and was succeeded by Frederick Roy Martin. Cooper replaced Martin as general manager in 1925, and he remained with the AP for a total of 41 years.

It was under Cooper that the AP grew into a gigantic international news machine. From the beginning, Cooper saw countless ways to improve the organization's methods of collecting and distributing information. One of his most important moves was his ongoing battle to free the AP from its obligations to import European news by way of news agencies there—ironically,these were the same arrangements that had given the AP its decisive edge over the UP years earlier. Cooper saw that news from European agencies was often slanted in favor of their home governments. He believed that the only way for the AP to receive accurate accounts of events abroad was to use its own reporters. The AP opened bureaus in Great Britain, France, and Germany in 1929, but it took until 1934 to break free of those confining arrangements completely.

One of Cooper's most important domestic improvements was the development of state bureaus as the organization's primary operating units. Cooper also widened the AP's coverage to better reflect the public's changing interests, adding an afternoon sports service, financial information, and features. The AP's new acceptance of human interest stories, which it had historically disdained, led to the organization's first Pulitzer Prize, awarded to Kirke L. Simpson in 1922 for a series on the Unknown Soldier buried in Washington D.C.'s Arlington Cemetery. In 1927, the AP started up a news photo service, and the improved AP Wirephoto system gained approval in 1935.

In 1931, the Associated Press Managing Editors Association, a group composed of editors of AP member newspapers for the purpose of reviewing the organization's work, was formed. By 1940, AP membership had grown to more than 1,400 papers. The AP began selling its news reports to radio stations in 1940, and by 1946, radio stations were allowed to become associate AP members, without voting rights. Meanwhile, another legal skirmish forced the AP to change its bylaws concerning membership. Since 1900, the AP had generally been regarded as a private association with the right to refuse membership to any outfit it did not want to admit. When the *Chicago Sun*—a paper launched by Marshall Field in 1941 to compete with the *Tribune*—sought entry into the AP collective, it was denied membership by the publishers of the AP's member newspapers. At the *Sun*'s urging, the matter was investigated by the Justice Department, which found the AP's exclusionary rules to be in violation of federal antitrust regulations. The AP changed its rules at its next meeting, and the *Sun* became a member. As a result, since 1945, any publisher that wanted access to AP news reports could become an AP member.

World War II brought further breakthroughs in international news coverage, including the additions of transatlantic cable and radio-teletype circuits, leased land circuits in Europe, and an overseas radiophoto network. In 1946, the AP launched its World Service. Cooper retired in 1948, and was succeeded as general manager by Frank J. Starzel, who had joined the AP in 1929. The organization continued to grow steadily through the 1950s under Starzel. Broadcast media began playing an increasing role in news coverage in the United States, and in 1954, the Associated Press Radio-Television Association was formed. By 1960, that subgroup was already representing over 2,000 domestic stations. Meanwhile, the AP's newspaper count had risen to nearly 1,800. In addition, about 3,500 news outlets outside of the United States were receiving AP reports.

Starzel retired in 1962, and the general manager position was taken up by Wes Gallagher, who had led the AP's World War II coverage as a reporter. By 1962, the organization had a total revenue of $44 million. Although the number of domestic newspapers subscribing to AP reports was beginning to decline, broadcast members were joining at a brisk pace. Meanwhile, advancing technology was making it easier to collect and spread news faster than ever before. Use of computers was expanded to include typesetting. Wire systems were overhauled and modernized, and a direct Teletype line connecting Moscow, London, and New York was set up. The AP also established a book division during 1963.

AP teamed with Dow Jones & Co., Inc. in 1967 to launch a new, ambitious business reporting service. The AP-Dow Jones Economic Report was an in-depth business news wire service transmitted to governments, corporations, trading firms, and other interested entities in nine European, Asian, and African countries. The following year, the same team launched the AP-Dow Jones Financial Wire, a teleprinter news service aimed primarily at stockbrokers in all of Europe's financial centers. By 1970, these services were being offered in 17 countries. Broadcast stations continued to join the AP in droves, with a total net increase of 1,224 member stations for the 1960s as a whole.

Technological progress continued to improve AP services during the 1970s. One of its breakthroughs during this period was the Laserphoto news picture system, developed jointly with researchers at the Massachusetts Institute of Technology (MIT). The Laserphoto system allowed the AP to transmit photographs of a much higher quality than was previously possible to both print and broadcast members. Another new general manager, Keith Fuller, was named upon Gallagher's retirement in 1976. The following year, three new seats, bringing the total to 21, were added to the AP board of directors, in order to give AP broadcast members board representation for the first time. In 1977, the same MIT team that had developed Laserphoto broke through again with the Electronic Darkroom, a system capable of transmitting, receiving, and storing pictures in digital form.

By the early 1980s, newspapers were generating about half of AP's revenues, as new media, particularly cable television, emerged to dilute print's role in delivering news to Americans. In 1982, the organization amended its bylaws to allow the use of its news reports by member newspapers on cable systems. The AP also began developing ways of transmitting news reports via satellite. By 1984, the AP's global network included over 300 news and photo bureaus throughout the world, and it was delivering reports to 1,300 daily newspapers and 5,700 broadcast stations in the United States alone. In addition, there were 8,500 subscribers in foreign countries. Fuller retired as both president and general manager that year, and was replaced by Louis D. Boccardi, a 17-year veteran of the AP.

Under Boccardi, the AP continued to enhance its services through the rest of the 1980s. A new graphics department was added in 1985, and a year later, a transition began that made all photographs offered to member newspapers available in color. By this time, the AP's network of satellite receiving dishes had grown to 3,000. Further improvements were made on transmission speed, business coverage, and graphics over the next few years. In 1989, the organization developed a fully designed sports page that could be delivered over its GraphicsNet system. Other new services included state weather maps and a biweekly package of stories and columns aimed at senior citizens.

The AP collected revenue of $329 million in 1991. As the 1990s progressed, the organization focused on ways to make more money from non-traditional sources, such as the sale of photo technology and through its AP-Dow Jones financial services outside the United States. By early in the decade, all of the AP's photo members had the Leaf Picture Desk—a digital photo compression and transmission system—and PhotoStream—its high-speed digital photo service—in place. American newspapers began to take on a more colorful look in the 1990s, and the combination of Leaf and PhotoStream was a big part of this trend.

As the 1990s continued, the AP focused on adding video news coverage to its arsenal. In 1994, the organization launched APTV, an international video newsgathering service based in London. Other developments included All News Radio, and the commercial sales of AP's television newsroom software, called NewsCenter. In order to remain a leader in the international newsgathering community, the AP expressed its intention to devote vast resources to research and development for the rest of the century, in recognition of the fact that technology had become perhaps the most important element in the battle for the attention of news consumers.

Principal Subsidiaries: La Prensa Asociada, Inc.; Press Association, Inc.; SaTellite Data Broadcast Networks, Inc.; Wide World Photos, Inc.; The Associated Press A/S (Norway); The Associated Press A/S (Denmark); The Associated Press AB (Sweden); The Associated Press (Belgium) S.A.; The Associated Press GmbH (Germany); The Associated Press, Ltd. (United Kingdom); The Associated Press, Ltd. (Canada); The Associated Press de Venezuela.

Further Reading:

"AP in 'Healthiest Condition,' 1963—$44 Million News Year," *Editor & Publisher,* April 25, 1964, p. 20.
"AP Offers New Member Services," *Editor & Publisher,* April 29, 1989, p. 20.
"AP's Digital Darkroom Breaks New Ground," *Editor & Publisher,* June 11, 1977, p. 15.
"AP Upgrades," *Editor & Publisher,* April 30, 1994, p. 14.
"Associated Press Taps Boccardi as President and General Manager," *Wall Street Journal,* September 14, 1984, p. 24.
Brown, Robert U., "Transition at AP," *Editor & Publisher,* April 21, 1979, p. 130.
Consoli, John, "Improvements at AP," *Editor & Publisher,* April 26, 1986, p. 20.
"Dow Jones, AP Plan International Service to Report Business News, Starting April 1," *Wall Street Journal,* January 23, 1967, p. 26.
Emery, Edwin, and Michael Emery, *The Press and America,* Englewood Cliffs, N.J.: Prentice-Hall, 1977.
"Gallagher: AP Geared for 'News Explosion'," *Editor & Publisher,* March 21, 1970, p. 11.
Gersh, Debra, "State of the AP," *Editor & Publisher,* May 1, 1993, p. 15.
"Keith Fuller Chosen as A.P.'s President at Annual Meeting," *New York Times,* May 4, 1976, p. 14.
Kobre, Sidney, *Development of American Journalism,* Dubuque, Iowa: Wm. C. Brown Co., 1969.
Lenett, Joe, "The Rivals . . . AP and UPI," *Editor & Publisher,* June 27, 1959, p. 222.
Mott, Frank Luther, *American Journalism,* New York: MacMillan, 1962.
Rathbun, Elizabeth, "Associated Press Tackles International Video," *Broadcasting & Cable,* July 18, 1994, p. 44.
Scully, Sean, "AP Determined to Stay on Cutting Edge," *Broadcasting & Cable,* September 27, 1993, p. 44.
Shmanske, Stephen, "News as a Public Good: Cooperative Ownership, Price Commitments, and the Success of the Associated Press," *Business History Review,* Spring 1986, p. 55.
Stein, M. L., "AP Reports to its Member Editors," *Editor & Publisher,* November 10, 1990, p. 18;
"A Strong Year for Associated Press," *Editor & Publisher,* May 9, 1992, p. 16.
"What's New? That's a $42 Million Question," *Editor & Publisher,* April 6, 1963, p. 12.

—Robert R. Jacobson

AT&T Bell Laboratories, Inc.

600 Mountain Avenue
Murray Hill, New Jersey 07974
U.S.A.
(908) 582-3000

Wholly Owned Subsidiary of AT&T Corporation
Incorporated: 1925
Employees: 29,000
Operating Revenues: $3 billion
SICs: 8731 Commercial Physical Research

AT&T Bell Laboratories is the research and development arm of AT&T. Bell Labs designs and develops all the systems and services required by its parent company, conducts experiments for application to AT&T's manufacturing facilities, and provides the technological foundation for the company's future. Much of modern society as we know it, with its emphasis and dependence on technological innovation, has been formed within the research facilities of Bell Labs. The organization's renowned scientists have created such innovations as solar cells, lasers, transistors, cellular mobile radios, long-distance television transmission, stereo recording, communications satellites, and sound motion pictures. The Nobel Prize in physics has been awarded to seven scientists at Bell Labs. Since its founding, the facility has received an average of one patent a day. Entering the mid-1990s, Bell Labs had claims to more then 25,000 total patents.

One of the most influential private research laboratories in the entire world, AT&T Bell Laboratories was established in 1925. The process of centralizing research and development operations with AT&T started in 1907 when AT&T merged its engineering department with the engineering department of Western Electric Company.

Bell Labs was formed in an effort to combine the resources and talent of various research laboratories into a single operation. At the beginning of its existence, Bell Labs employed 4,000 individuals, many of whom were reputable engineers, physicists, chemists, metallurgists, and mathematicians from the United States and Europe. This technical staff conducted some of the initial—and famous—experiments in the burgeoning fields of electronics, magnetics, and radio. Freedom to pursue research in various areas, including those outside the telecommunications field, was encouraged and rewarded. Frank B. Jewitt, the first president of Bell Labs, knew that applied and fundamental research would ultimately benefit AT&T's telephone business.

In 1927 Bell Labs scientist Clinton Davisson conducted an experiment during which he bombarded a small crystal of nickel with electrons. The dispersement of the electrons in waves as they bounced off the nickel corresponded to their momentum. Davisson's documentation of this research provided the initial experimental proof that electrons display wave characteristics. Ten years later, Davisson received the Nobel Prize in Physics for his work in the field of electron wave characteristics.

The year 1927 also marked Harold S. Black's first experiments in the field of negative feedback circuitry. Black eventually proved the principles that gave rise to the negative feedback amplifier, one of the most important discoveries in the communications field. The practical application of these principles resulted in the design and success of long-distance multichannel systems. Taking this research one step further, H.W. Bode investigated the problems of distortion and noise interference, which were the consequences of using amplifiers for long-distance telephone communication. Through intensive mathematical analysis, Bode discovered a way to eliminate the noise and distortions, thereby improving the quality of transcontinental telephone communication.

Bell Labs was contacted by the U.S. Navy in 1937 to develop research already initiated in the emerging field of radar technology. Between 1934 and 1937, the Naval Research Laboratory and the U.S. Army Signal Corps had conducted experiments in the field of radio detection and ranging device. Bell Labs' involvement in the project proved worthwhile. In 1939 the facility demonstrated to U.S. federal government and Navy officials a model radar instrument that accurately plotted the course of ships between New York and New Jersey. Impressed with the accuracy and reliability of the new technology, the government awarded numerous contracts to the research facility. According to the arrangement, Bell Laboratories designed the radar and Western Electric Laboratories manufactured the final equipment. By the time America entered World War II in December of 1941, the development of radar technology had become the single largest activity engaged in by Bell Labs. During the war, scientists at Bell Labs designed over 100 different kinds of radar equipment, including submarine radar, fire control radar for large guns on Navy vessels, and bombing radar for the United States Air Force.

In 1942 Bell Labs engaged in one of its most secret projects—the design and manufacture of a successful acoustic homing torpedo. The homing torpedo was dropped in the vicinity of a hostile submarine from an aircraft. When the torpedo entered the water, it was electrically propelled by an acoustical design system that focused on the propulsion mechanisms of the submarine. The torpedo was designed to pursue the propulsion mechanism and then explode upon impact with the vessel. According to U.S. Navy statistics, approximately 55 enemy submarines were rendered inoperable by the homing torpedo model.

In 1943 Bell Labs designed the famous echo-ranging sonar device. Developed to detect underwater objects, the device emitted a pulse of sound waves that registered an echo from underwater objects. This echo was then transformed back into a pulse that helped U.S. vessels locate the actual position of the object. Initially intended for use on anti-submarine patrol boats, the technology worked so well that it was soon used by larger ships in the U.S. Navy.

After the end of World War II, Bell Labs resumed its research on semiconduction and other projects that had been interrupted by the war effort. The first experiments on semiconduction were performed in England during the 1930s, and scientists at Bell Labs expanded upon these investigations. Included in the research team, among others, were William Shockley, John Bardeen, and Walter Brittain. The combined research of the team led to the discovery of the ''transistor effect,'' and the origin of the point-contact transistor. This transistor would become an essential component to the radio, television, and computer industries. Shockley, Bardeen, and Brittain received the 1956 Nobel Prize in Physics in recognition of their research, which ushered in the beginning of the microelectronic age.

In 1951 William G. Pfann discovered a technique for purifying germanium. This ultrapurifying method, known as ''zone refining,'' solved the inherent problem of melting materials such as germanium and silicon at extremely high temperatures. Pfann's method brought the purity of materials under control to the extent that it could then be applied to manufacturing semiconductors. During the latter half of the 1950s, two scientists at Bell Labs, C.H. Townes and A.L. Schawlow, collaborated on experiments that ultimately led to the discovery of the laser (light amplification by stimulated emission of radiation) and its principles. Later, additional research in this field led to the invention of the first helium-neon laser and the first continuous wave solid-state laser.

Bell Labs scientists were involved in three major technological developments during the 1960s: electronic switching, satellite communications, and computer operating systems. Before the war, the research laboratory made significant advances in discovering what implications electronic technology had for telephone switching capabilities. In 1953 a research group was given the task of designing an electronic switching system. By 1963 AT&T had installed the first such switching system in Cocoa Beach, Florida. In 1965 AT&T used this technology to install the first commercial office switching system in Succasunna, New Jersey.

The facility was also a leader in investigating satellite communication technology. John R. Pierce, a researcher at Bell Labs, had conducted investigations for years on how to reflect voice signals from a communication satellite. In 1960 his theories were confirmed when voice signals were reflected off a ''passive balloon satellite.'' Two years later, the world's first speech and television transmissions were successfully achieved through a communications satellite named Telstar I. In 1963 a second satellite, Telstar II, was launched into orbit around the earth. The research conducted on this project, and its application, had enormous consequences for world communications. By 1970, less than a decade later, satellite communications systems provided more than 50 percent of all the voice channels between the United States and foreign countries.

The third major technological development to originate at Bell Labs during this time had to do with computer operating systems. Many researchers were unsatisfied with the performance of the operating system on their computers at the lab. They felt that a new system that could run on any type or brand of computer would be more useful to them. Consequently, scientists designed an operating system that was ''open''; a system that could be used by many different computer brands and could also interconnect with other operating systems. This operating system, called UNIX, was first used on a limited basis within AT&T offices and facilities, and among universities and colleges. Before long, however, AT&T realized the vast market potential of the system. By 1989 UNIX was the standard operating system in almost all computers purchased within the United States.

For Bell Labs, the decade of the 1970s was most notable for the awards won by its scientists. In 1973 John W. Tukey was awarded the National Medal of Science for his work in mathematics and theoretical statistics. In 1978 Philip W. Anderson and another scientist received the Nobel Prize in physics for their research into the electronic structure of magnetic and glass materials. Robert W. Wilson and Arno A. Penzias were awarded the Nobel Prize in physics for discovering the almost indiscernible radiation that remained from the ''big bang'' explosion. Their research provided further evidence in support of the ''big bang'' theory, which postulated that a cosmic explosion billions of years ago gave birth to the universe.

The single most important event that affected Bell Labs was the breakup of the Bell System in January 1984. The immediate change involved a reduction of the number of employees from 26,000 down to 19,000. Former Bell Lab employees were transferred to Bell Communications Research (Bellcore) and AT&T Information Systems. But the long-term change was more significant, for the mission of Bell Labs was altered after the breakup. Prior to the divestiture, research and development at the facility focused on the design and improvement of equipment and services in the telecommunications field. Scientists at Bell Labs had been able to choose their own research projects based on their own interests. From the time of the divestiture, however, management at AT&T reorganized Bell Labs in order to reflect the parent company's new focus as a leader in the information age. Instead of concentrating on comprehensive telephone service, Bell Labs' new mission was to develop information systems and services and help AT&T reduce the time between product design and market introduction.

This new orientation for Bell Labs immediately resulted in major achievements. AT&T saved millions of dollars when scientists designed a new dynamic routing system that more efficiently routed phone calls through the company's long-distance telephone network. In 1985 Bell Labs developed an innovative speech processing system, Conversant Systems, that AT&T formed into a new venture. During the same year, Bell Labs became the first company to receive the prestigious National Medal of Technology. In 1986 the research facility assisted Illinois Bell and its parent company in designing and deploying a highly innovative ISDN network that incorporates video, voice, and data signals over the same path of transmission. A year later, Bell Labs discovered a method to increase the current-relaying capacity of ceramic superconductors. In 1988 scientists from the laboratory helped AT&T, along with numerous European and Asian telecommunications firms, install fiber-optic cables under the Atlantic and Pacific Oceans. This technology significantly improved data, voice, and video intercontinental communications. In 1989 scientists from Bell Labs, in collaboration with researchers from Bellcore, developed the world's smallest laser, which AT&T will use to provide more efficient optical communications systems in the future.

During the 1990s, research and development at Bell Labs has focused on three main areas: microelectronics, photonics, and software. These three areas are regarded as cornerstones of the ''Information Age'' and provide the basic technology for practical applications in visual communications, messaging, networked computing, and voice and audio processing. Microelectronics is a fundamental aspect of the rapid development of the fields of computing and telecommunications, and Bell Labs has sought to establish a leadership position in this area. The facility introduced the first million-bit memory chip that could actually be manufactured on a regular basis, as well as the very first 32-bit microprocessor.

The technology that is called photonics involves the use of high-frequency, rapid pulses of light from lasers in order to digitally transmit voice, video, or data over tiny glass fibers. Fiber optic systems designed by scientists at Bell Labs have been used in the United States and incorporated into the intercontinental communications systems under the Atlantic and Pacific Oceans. In 1994 a scientific experiment conducted at Bell Labs resulted in the transmission of 40 billion bits of data per second over one optical fiber. This transmission rate was 10 times the rate of the largest capacity system in commercial use at the time.

The third field of research and development that scientists at Bell Labs focused on in the early 1990s involved software systems. Bell Labs has designed software systems that enable the components within the U.S. telecommunications network to operate smoothly and efficiently. Over 3,000 telephone switching systems across America rely on Bell Labs software. In addition, the UNIX operating system developed at the research facility has grown into one of the most popular systems in the world.

Scientists at Bell Labs continue to work on highly experimental projects that could have an enormous impact on the future of telecommunications. These projects include intelligence machines, machines that operate on voice commands, microelectronic chips with a ten-thousandfold increase in capacity and intelligence, and an affordable global communications system that allows an individual to send or receive information without any technical constraints.

In September 1995, AT&T announced its break up into three separate companies: communications equipment and technology, computer, and communications services. This effected Bell Labs as well. Most of the 26,000 Bell Lab employees became part of the communications equipment and technology business, retaining the Bell Laboratories name. Bell Laboratories also serviced the computer business. About 15 percent of the employees became part of the communications services and assumed the name AT&T Laboratories.

As Bell Laboratories and AT&T raced toward the 21st century, chief scientist, Dr. Arno Penzias, was quoted in the *New York Times* as saying, ''The large-scale mission is still research for fun and profit.''

Further Reading:

Markoff, John, ''Most Employees of Bell Labs Will Join Equipment Business,'' *New York Times,* September 21, 1995, p. C4.

Rapaport, Richard, ''What Does A Nobel Prize For RadiAstronomy Have To Do With Your Telephone?'' *Wired,* April 1995, pp. 124–178.

—Thomas Derdak

Automobili Lamborghini S.p.A.

via Modena
12-40010 Sant'Agata
Bologna
Italy
011 051 956171

Wholly Owned Subsidiary of MedTech, Ltd.
Founded: 1963
Employees: 415
SICs: 5012 Automobiles & Other Motor Vehicles

Automobili Lamborghini S.p.A. is one of the world's most renowned manufacturers of high-performance sports cars; owning a Lamborghini Countach, of which only 1,997 were produced over a period of 25 years, is a dream of every sports car aficionado. The company has fallen on hard times since the mid-1970s, but its recent acquisition by Medtech, Ltd., a conglomerate based in Indonesia, has provided the company with both the financial stability and management acumen to regain its place among the most successful international sports car manufacturers.

The founder of Automobili Lamborghini, Ferruccio Lamborghini, was born in 1916 in the village of Renazzo, near Bologna. As a boy he was fascinated by the mechanics of revolutionary machines such as the automobile and airplane. As soon as he could, he went to Bologna, and he completed studies in mechanics just before the start of World War II. During the war he worked as a supervisor of the Italian Army's vehicle maintenance unit in Rodi, Greece.

Lamborghini's experience in the motor pool prepared him to assume the role of entrepreneur when he returned to Italy after the war. He immediately purchased old military vehicles and collected abandoned German tanks in order to reconfigure them and produce tractors, equipment that was essential for Italy to rebuild itself after the destruction caused by the war. The young businessman was so successful with this enterprise that he purchased a large factory and workshop in Centro during the early part of 1948.

During the 1950s, Lamborghini focused on his tractor business. Sales expanded rapidly, not only in Italy, but soon in other war-ravaged European countries. As revenues increased, he traveled to the United States to acquire technology for the manufacture of heating systems, air conditioners, and automobile parts. During the late 1950s, one of the company's most innovative products was an air-cooled automobile engine. The company's financial stability provided Lamborghini with the opportunity to pursue one of his life-long ambitions: the manufacture of helicopters. Unfortunately, the Italian government refused to grant him a license.

A well-circulated tale describes the genesis of Lamborghini's sports car company during the early 1960s: As he grew more interested in automobiles, Lamborghini purchased a Ferrari, one of the most prestigious, high-performance sports car in the world. One day, while taking a pleasure drive, he noticed a sound in the front of his car and discovered a faulty part. He drove the car to Modena, the headquarters of Ferrari, and asked them to repair or replace the faulty part. He was kept waiting for such a long time that he finally demanded to see Enzo Ferrari, the founder. Ferrari, already a great man in the international race car circuit, also kept Lamborghini waiting. Angry and frustrated with the way he had been treated, Lamborghini decided to establish his own high-performance sports car company.

Situated in Sant'Agata, near Bologna, the Lamborghini car factory began operations in 1963. Lamborghini hired a brilliant automotive engineer by the name of Paolo Stanzani and asked him to establish one of the most technologically advanced car-making facilities in the world. The first Lamborghini sports car was delivered in 1964 and created a sensation in automotive circles. The 350 GT, an aerodynamic sports car with a four-cam V12, five-speed transmission, four-wheel disk brakes, and four-wheel independent suspension, was soon competing for customers that had previously purchased such high-performance cars as Porsche and Jaguar. Especially gratifying to Lamborghini was the fact that his cars were as well received by automobile critics as Enzo Ferrari's.

In 1966 the company produced the 400 GT, while at the same time building its own transmissions. During the same year, Lamborghini S.p.A. produced the Miura P400, which created a buzz in the crowd during the Geneva Motorshow due to its compact 3929 cc transverse V12 powertrain and bare chassis. In 1968 the Islero 400 GT was introduced, featuring a luxury interior, four-wheel independent suspension, disc brakes, and an all-aluminum quad cam V12 engine. Also in 1968, Lamborghini produced the Espada, a four-seater engineered with a one-piece, solid steel body. Within a short time, the Espada became one of the most popular of all the Lamborghini models, and sales of the model remained brisk for years. The company was now known around the world for its sleek, low-slung sports cars, and sold models to celebrities including Grace Kelly and Frank Sinatra, who ordered a custom-made Lamborghini and requested that the interior decoration include genuine leopard skin.

From 1970 to 1972 the company was at the height of its success. A new version of the Miura P400, the Miura P400 SV, was introduced and featured a completely redesigned suspension system and leather interior. Another new prototype, the Countach LP500, had its debut at the Geneva Motor Show in 1971. The design included a handmade aluminum body, aerodynamic contours for high-speed performance, and a dramatic new "wedge" look. In 1972 the company introduced the Urraco P250 at the Turin Motor Show, and later introduced the Jarama 400GTS. With a unique hood scoop, five bolt wheels, and significantly increased horse power, the Jarama was the last Lamborghini sports car to exhibit a front engine. With such new and exciting models, the company seemed destined for even greater financial rewards and international recognition.

Unfortunately, the year 1973 was a turning point for the company. Automobili Lamborghini was hit hard by the oil embargo and by the crisis created by the worldwide recession. The market for high-speed, gas-guzzling sports cars suddenly dried up, and the firm was confronted with rapidly decreasing sales. Disappointed, Ferruccio Lamborghini decided to sell his shares of the company and retire to a 740-acre estate on Lake Trasimeno. Lamborghini Automobili was controlled by the government for a short time, then suffered the indignity of compulsory liquidation.

Yet, due to the determination of the remaining employees, the company continued to manufacture sport cars. In 1974 the Countach LP400 went into production with a 3.9 liter V12 engine and a tubular chassis. In 1975 the Urraco 300 was manufactured and, one year later, the Silhouette was introduced at the Geneva Motor Show. In 1977, in an attempt to revive the company's profitability, production of off-road vehicles for the military was initiated. However, the design of the prototype vehicle was altered when management discovered that the general public was more interested in purchasing the models than was the military.

Despite the seemingly fast-paced production schedule, the companay's fate remained uncertain throughout the decade. In 1980 the Bologna Court sold the firm to the Mimram brothers, young and famous entrepreneurs in the food industry who had a passion for sleek sports cars. They immediately started a comprehensive restructuring program, including the infusion of large amounts of capital to rehabilitate the dilapidated manufacturing facilities in Sant'Agata, and then initiated a worldwide search for highly qualified automotive engineers and designers.

Results from the investment made by the Mimram brothers began to pay off immediately. In 1982 the Countach LP500S was introduced with a new 5-liter, 375-horsepower engine. A brand new model, the Jalpa, was also introduced during the same year. The Jalpa, a two seater, included a 5-speed transmission and a new transverse-mounted V8 engine. In 1985 the Countach underwent its third major redesign and was renamed the LP500S QV. Unfortunately, the rapid production pace did not generate increased income, and the Mimram brothers soon realize that the amount required for capital expenditure was beyond the financial means of individual investors such as themselves. Looking for an experienced and financially stable and partner, they met with representatives of Chrysler Corporation.

Chrysler Corporation was attractive to Lamborghini due to the company's committed management, its ability to introduce new models in a relatively short time and, of course, the mystique of the Lamborghini sports car. Chrysler paid approximately $25 million for Automobili Lamborghini and took control of the company in April 1987. Chrysler management immediately poured $50 million worth of capital into the Italian automobile manufacturer, primarily to increase production and to expand into the United States.

Under Chrysler management, the most popular and successful of all Lamborghini models, the Countach, went out of production after 25 years. The Countach was replaced by the Diablo, the fastest car in the world made on a production line (202 m.p.h.), at a base price of $239,000. In 1990 sales of the car were so brisk that Lamborghini showed a profit of $15,000. During this same time, Chrysler established an American branch to sell Lamborghini's new models. Chrysler developed Lamborghini's U.S. network from a disorganized and loosely connected jumble of private distributors into a highly efficient franchise with support services such as maintenance and service agreements and spare parts distribution. Under Chrysler's direction, Lamborghini also began to manufacture marine engines for the off-shore racing circuit. In addition, a new factory was opened in Modena, Italy, called Lamborghini Engineering, to design and produce Formula One racing cars. For its diligence, Chrysler saw Lamborghini production rise to 673 cars in 1991, and profits increase to $1.32 million.

For all Chrysler's efforts, however, its success with Lamborghini was brief. By 1992 production had dropped to 166 cars, and the company lost nearly $19.3 million. Sales had dropped precipitously, in spite of an expanding franchise network in the United States. Americans just weren't buying the $239,000 Diablo, so plans were initiated to develop an exotic car with a price of $100,000, a range more accessible to American sports car enthusiasts. Yet development of the car lagged, and Chrysler became more and more frustrated with the difficulties involving Lamborghini production methods. Total production for the company amounted to just 215 cars in 1993, a figure that did not satisfy the executives at Chrysler who were used to high-volume car production. As a result, Chrysler began to look for an investor to take Automobili Lamborghini off its hands.

In late 1993, Chrysler reached an agreement with MedTech, Ltd., to sell Lamborghini for approximately $40 million. MedTech Ltd. was a holding company registered in Bermuda and wholly owned by SEDTCO Pty., a large Indonesian conglomerate. SEDTCO, headed by Setiawan Djody and Tommy Suharto, the son of the premier of Indonesia, had extensive worldwide holdings in mining, manufacturing, and shipping. The agreement included the sale of Automobili Lamborghini in Sant'Agata, Lamborghini Engineering, the manufacturer of Formula 1 race cars, and Lamborghini USA. Djody owned a 35 percent stake in Vector Automotive Corporation, a manufacturer of sports cars with an average sticker price of $450,000, and he thought Vector and Lamborghini might collaborate on the design and marketing of new models for the high-performance sports car market.

With Djody acting as chairman, the new owners hired Michael J. Kimberly as president and managing director of the company. Kimberly had worked with Jaguar and Lotus and finally as executive vice-president of General Motors in Malaysia before he was hired for the position at Lamborghini. Kimberly began a comprehensive analysis of the entire Lamborghini operation. He concluded that the company needed more than just one or two models to sell, and he began to make plans for the development of Lamborghini cars at a price accessible to the American ment of Lamborghini cars at a price accessible to the American car enthusiast. At the same time, he implemented a marketing strategy to raise awareness of the attractiveness and mystique the Lamborghini sports car.

By the beginning of 1995, sales of Lamborghini models had jumped 14 percent in the United States and 34 percent worldwide. With an assured flow of investment capital from MedTech, and guided by management with extensive experience in the high-performance sports car market, Automobili Lamborghini was poised for success it has not seen for 25 years.

Principal Subsidiaries: Lamborghini Engineering; Lamborghini USA.

Further Reading:

Automobili Lamborghini News, Number 17, 1994.

Cowell, Alan, "Ferruccio Lamborghini," *New York Times,* February 22, 1993.

Kurylko, Diana T., "Chrysler Sells Lamborghini to Indonesian Group," *Automotive News,* November 22, 1993, p. 18.

Lamborghini: The Man and the Company, Lamborghini USA Company Document, 1995.

Rechtin, Mark, "$100,000 Lamborghini Due in '96," *Automotive News,* June 20, 1994, p. 36.

—Thomas Derdak

Avco Financial Services, Inc.®

Avco Financial Services Inc.

P.O. Box 19701
Irvine, California 92713-9701
U.S.A.
(714) 553-1200

Wholly Owned Subsidiary of Textron Inc.
Incorporated: 1971
Employees: 7,100
Sales: $1.03 billion
SICs: 6141 Personal Credit Institutions

A subsidiary of Textron Inc., Avco Financial Services Inc. is a leading U.S. provider of consumer loans for real estate and personal property. In addition, its insurance division provides life, disability, and casualty insurance. Avco grew primarily through mergers and acquisitions during the mid-1900s before expanding rapidly in the 1980s. Going into the mid-1990s, Avco was operating about 1,200 offices throughout the United States and in parts of Australia, New Zealand, the United Kingdom, and Spain.

Incorporated in 1971, Avco Financial Services was the culmination of several decades of mergers and acquisitions involving various companies. Delta Acceptance Corporation Limited, one of the progenitors, was founded in 1954 in London by Reginald Palmer and Ninian Sanderson to finance the receivables of Palmer's appliance store. A group of U.S. investors who were associated with the Paul Revere Life Company soon became interested in Delta and made an equity investment. That cash injection spurred Delta's growth in the United Kingdom, which prompted the U.S. investors to purchase the company in 1956.

Delta's new owners installed an experienced management team which devised an ambitious plan to turn the company into a coast-to-coast North American provider of diversified financial services. To that end, Delta acquired the Canada-based Crescent Finance Corporation in 1957 and Consolidated Finance Corporation in 1958. It opened several new branches throughout Canada and began making consumer loans for major purchases like cars, appliances, and furniture. In 1960, Delta formed an insurance division called Adanac General Insurance Company. The aim of this subsidiary was to provide credit-related insurance services. Two years later, Delta expanded this enterprise with the purchase of the London and Midland General Insurance Company.

Delta continued to expand in North America during the mid-1960s with the purchase of a group of industrial banks, a home improvement finance company, and other finance-related companies. Delta was operating 212 branches and generating annual sales of about $250 million by 1964, when it became an acquisition target. In December of 1964, Delta was purchased by Avco Corporation, a New York-based firm active in the aerospace industry. Avco renamed the new subsidiary Avco Delta Corp. and continued to expand its financial network throughout North America. In 1965, for example, Avco Delta acquired the Iowa Finance Company and the Citizens Finance Company. This financial arm of the Avco Corp. continued to flourish through the late 1960s.

In 1969, Avco Delta acquired the Seaboard Finance Company. Seaboard was a leading west coast consumer finance institution which had opened its first office in Los Angeles in 1927. Although still based in Los Angeles at the time of its acquisition by Avco Delta, Seaboard was expanding internationally. The merger between Seaboard and Avco Delta was completed in 1971, at which time Avco Corp. named the resulting division Avco Financial Services Inc. During the 1970s, Avco Financial's ongoing global expansion efforts included a renewed emphasis on the United Kingdom market, where Delta had commenced operations in the 1950s. Meanwhile, Avco's loan volume in North America continued to swell. By the end of the decade, Avco Financial was boasting more than $2 billion in receivables from its consumer loans.

During the economic downturn of the early 1980s, several of Avco Financial's operations languished. In 1984, the subsidiary's parent organization, Avco Corp., became the acquisition target of Textron Inc., a $3.2 billion conglomerate active in textile and defense industries, among other businesses. The buyout was not surprising given Textron's history of diversification. In fact, the founder of the company, Royal Little, is credited with pioneering the concept of the diversified conglomerate in the United States. Little began broadening Textron's corporate scope in 1952, buying up companies in unrelated industries in an effort to counter the boom-and-bust cycles that plagued his textiles business. Chief among his acquisitions was Bell Aircraft Corporation, for which he paid $32 million in 1962.

The Avco Corp. purchase was a significant accomplishment for Textron in that it nearly doubled Textron's size and guided the conglomerate into the growing financial services industry. The merger was engineered by Beverly F. Dolan, who had joined Textron years earlier as a result of an acquisition. Dolan and his brother, natives of Augusta, Georgia, had started the golf cart manufacturing company E-Z-Go in 1956. Six years later, Little bought their company for $1 million, although Dolan stayed on board as president of the division. By the 1980s, Dolan had worked his way through the ranks to a top-level executive slot at Textron. Following the Avco buyout he was named chief executive of Textron Inc.

Under Dolan's leadership, Textron continued to acquire new companies and jettison some ailing divisions. However, not all of the acquisitions proved to be profitable for the conglomerate. In fact, the aerospace arm of Avco Corp. faltered after it was taken over by the Textron corporate umbrella. Previously,

Textron (formerly Avco) Aerostructures had prospered under Avco's direction by building wings for the B-1B bomber. Textron managers hoped to replace the expiring B-1B contract in 1986 with another contract to build wings for a military transport plane. Unfortunately, the new contract never materialized. Although Textron was able to keep the company afloat with some civilian contracts, it had to slash the division's work force from 7,100 to just 2,600 between 1986 and 1988.

While Textron endured setbacks caused by Avco's military contract division, the company nevertheless validated its diversification strategy by achieving significant gains with Avco Financial Services. During this period, Textron brought in Charles Rinehart to head up Avco Financial. Rinehart was a California native who had worked his way through the ranks at San Francisco-based Fireman's Fund Insurance Co. before joining Avco at its Irvine headquarters. During the mid-1980s, Rinehart and other executives labored to revive Avco Financial from the effects of the recent recession. Importantly, they reduced the amount of nonperforming and high-risk loans and initiated an aggressive quality campaign to improve operations. "They [Textron] did a good job of cleaning up the finance company," surmised analyst Howard A. Rubel in 1989 in the *Providence Journal-Bulletin.*

A symbol of the changes taking place at Avco was the adoption of a new company logo. In 1987, Avco discarded its old emblem—a Delta sign—and replaced it with a heart-shaped symbol that was intended to convey a sense of caring. Although critics derided the logo as inappropriate for a finance company, favorable consumer test results convinced Avco executives to adopt it. Apparently, the new logo did not damage Avco's financial performance during the late 1980s. In fact, by the end of the decade Avco Financial was ringing up record sales of $1.15 billion, about $108 million of which was netted as income. Those figures represented steady gains during much of the mid-1980s of more than 10 percent annually.

Going into the 1990s, Avco Financial was accounting for roughly 27 percent of Textron's revenues. The bulk of Avco Financial's profits was derived from its core consumer finance businesses, whereas about 15 percent was coming from unrelated sales of life, disability, and casualty insurance. Indeed, as Textron's military contracting divisions faced cutbacks in defense spending, Avco Financial was engaged in a growing and lucrative industry. Most of the company's consumer loans, for example, were bringing in a lofty effective interest of around 20 percent, compared to the rate of roughly 10 percent that Avco was paying for the money to finance the loans.

Although Avco Financial's success during the late 1980s was largely attributable to its improved balance sheet and loan portfolios, gains were also a corollary of management's efforts to instill a culture of quality. The positive impact of quality efforts was evidenced most clearly at Avco's surging Canada division. In 1985, Avco executives in the United States pressed the head of the Canada division to adopt a formal quality initiative. Canadian executives, after visiting Japan to study companies with quality programs, implemented what they called the Quality Improvement Process (QIP). In essence, QIP discarded authoritarian management styles in favor of a team-based decision-making process that involved employees in every level of the company. Although the transition was somewhat turbulent, the end results were impressive. Avco's Canadian division achieved a growth rate of 11 percent annually between 1985 and 1989, in contrast to just five percent growth throughout the early 1980s. Furthermore, operating costs declined and profit margins improved. Because of its quality drive, Avco Canada was awarded the Canada Award for Business Excellence in 1990.

Also bolstering Avco Financial's sales and profits during the late 1980s and early 1990s was its ongoing program of global diversification. By 1989, only 64 percent of Avco's sales and 50 percent of its pre-tax income was coming from its U.S. division. About 20 percent of revenues were attributable to Canada, 7.5 percent to the United Kingdom, and 11 percent to Australia and New Zealand. During the early 1990s, international sales growth continued to outpace Avco's gains in the United States. Most importantly, Avco's British division realized sales and income gains of 40 percent and 30 percent respectively between 1989 and 1993. Avco also commenced a consumer finance division in Spain in 1992 and was operating four offices in that country by 1994.

By the early 1990s, both Rinehart and Dolan had left their posts at Avco and Textron—Dolan retired and Rinehart accepted a position at H.F. Ahmanson & Co., the nation's largest savings and loan institution. Rinehart handed off leadership of Avco Financial to Warren R. Lyons. Under Lyons's direction, Avco's financial performance continued to improve steadily. Sales increased from $1.28 billion in 1990 to $1.36 billion in 1992. Although revenue dipped to $1.35 billion in 1993, Avco's income rose to a record $225 million—a 20 percent increase over 1990. Likewise, Avco's global asset base swelled from $5.09 billion in 1990 to $6.12 billion in 1993. Those gains occurred despite the stagnant performance of Avco's insurance-related business, which accounted for about 10 percent of revenues. Avco attempted to sell some of the poorly performing insurance businesses in 1992, but was still running them by the middle of the decade.

Going into the mid-1990s, Avco was one of the largest consumer finance companies in the United States. It was primarily engaged in providing relatively high-interest rate loans of usually short duration for purchases of cars, consumer goods, and real estate. Avco boosted sales and net income by about 2.8 percent and 14 percent, respectively, in 1994. By that time, the company was employing more than 7,000 workers in 1,200 offices, about 750 of which were located in the United States. International operations included Canada (215 branch offices), Australia (122), the United Kingdom (92), New Zealand (10), and Spain (4). In February of 1994, Avco opened an office in Hong Kong, reflecting the management's intent to penetrate the burgeoning Pacific Rim market for consumer finance services. Avco's long-term prospects were positive given projected growth rates for the financial services industry, Avco's market diversity, and the company's healthy balance sheet in comparison to industry averages.

Principal Subsidiaries: Avco Financial Services Group; Avco Insurance Services Group.

Further Reading:

Caine, Raymond W., Jr., ''Textron's Avco Financial Services Subsidiary Plans to Sell Its Independent Insurance Lines,'' *PR Newswire,* August 28, 1992.

Cox, Tony, ''Avco Moves to Raise $500 Million in Bond Market,'' *Orange County Business Journal,* June 11, 1990, p. 8.

Fortin, Frank, ''Textron Diversification Route Not for Everyone,'' *Providence Business News,* February 3, 1992, p. 1.

Gardner, Jim, ''Avco Seeks Buyer for Weakest Insurance Units,'' *Orange County Business Journal,* September 7, 1992, p. 3.

Harrop, Froma, ''Textron Faces Prospect of . . . No Defense,'' *Providence Journal-Bulletin,* December 24, 1989, p. F1.

Maver, Ken, ''Closing the Gap,'' *London Business Monthly,* January 1990, p. 8.

Mullen, Liz, ''Guts, Smarts and People Skills: Those Qualities Got Charles Rinehart His Job as Thrift Giant H.F. Ahmanson's CEO,'' *Los Angeles Business Journal,* June 6, 1994, p. 14.

Simon, Jane, ''The Instinctive Chief Executive: 'It's Just Like Those Damn Bird Dogs,' '' *New England Business,* June 3, 1985, p. 100.

Swope, Genilee, ''Avco Chooses a Symbol of Caring,'' *Credit,* January–February 1987, p. 28.

—Dave Mote

AZTAR

Aztar Corporation

2390 East Camelback Road, Suite 400
Phoenix, Arizona 85016-3452
U.S.A.
(602) 381-4100
Fax: (602) 381-4107

Public Company
Incorporated: 1989
Employees: 8,200
Sales: $541.4 million
Stock Exchanges: New York
SICs: 6719 Holding Companies Nec; 7011 Hotels & Motels

Aztar Corporation, a spinoff from the late 1980s restructuring of Ramada Inc., is one of the ten largest casino companies in the United States. Aztar operates three major casino hotels: the Tropicana Resort and Casino in Las Vegas; the Ramada Express Hotel and Casino in Laughlin, Nevada; and the TropWorld Casino and Entertainment Resort in Atlantic City. In the early 1990s, the company began to develop riverboat casino projects in Indiana, Missouri, and elsewhere as more and more states viewed gambling as an attractive addition to their economies.

The late 1980s were difficult years for Ramada Inc. as increased competition in the hotel industry led to declining profits and, ultimately, losses. The company posted profits of $17.2 million in 1985, $10.3 million in 1986, and $4.9 million in 1987. On the way to posting a $5.1 million loss in 1988, the company decided in October of that year to restructure by selling its restaurant and hotel groups and retaining only its gaming operations, deemed by company officials as the Ramada assets with the best future. The restructuring was also undertaken to prevent a hostile takeover that the company felt was "grossly inadequate from a financial standpoint." Ramada sold its 152-restaurant Marie Callender chain early in 1989 to the Wilshire Restaurant Group Inc. for $54.5 million. It then reached agreement with New World Hotel (Holdings) Ltd. of Hong Kong to sell all of its hotel operations, including more than 800 hotels and motor inns worldwide, and the Ramada name for $540 million. New World's price included $280 million to be paid to Ramada shareholders and the assumption of approximately $260 million of Ramada's debt.

Before the New World deal could be consummated, a complicated restructuring had to occur, including a new financing plan, and approvals had to be granted by Ramada's shareholders and the gaming regulators of New Jersey and Nevada. The approval process occurred twice because the initial restructuring arrangement was changed due to a downturn in the junk bond market. The original plan had Aztar raising $400 million through the issuance of $230 million in junk bonds and $170 million in first-mortgage notes backed by the company's TropWorld Casino in Atlantic City. The revised plan dropped the junk bonds altogether. It also reduced the amount paid to Ramada shareholders from $7 per share to $1 (but the shareholders would receive one share of Aztar stock for each share of Ramada stock instead of a half-share) and Aztar's initial debt load from $423 million to $189 million. Experts on gaming companies viewed the revised plan as a much healthier one for the new company since they believed $423 million was too great of an initial debt for the company to handle through casino revenues.

The restructured company was to be run by former senior managers of Ramada and its gaming division, including Richard Snell (who was chairman, president, and chief executive of Ramada and became chairman and chief executive of Aztar), Paul E. Rubeli (executive vice-president and head of Ramada's gaming division, who became president and chief operating officer of Aztar), and Robert M. Haddock (who retained the same title with Aztar that he held with Ramada—executive vice president and chief financial officer). Aztar's board was initially composed of nine former Ramada directors, with Haddock filling in the tenth slot that had been vacated. In December 1989 the revised plan was approved overwhelmingly by Ramada shareholders. The gaming regulators of Nevada and New Jersey also approved the plan that month, leading to the closing of the hotel sale. The new Aztar Corporation was born, with a name coined to play on the word "star" combined with the beginning of the word "Aztec," a reference to the gold- and silver-rich Aztec Empire, whose wealth the new gaming company wished to strive for. Aztar's headquarters remained in Ramada's main office in Phoenix. (The first two initials of the new company name were said to be only coincidentally the same as the two-letter postal abbreviation for Arizona.)

Following the completed restructuring, Aztar's assets consisted of three of the four gaming properties that had been owned by Ramada (in July 1989, in the midst of the restructuring, Ramada closed Eddie's Fabulous 50s Casino, a stand-alone casino in Reno, Nevada, because of declining revenues). In 1989 the TropWorld Casino and Entertainment Resort was the largest casino in Atlantic City with 1,014 rooms. Located on the famous boardwalk, it also boasted 80,000 square feet of exhibit and meeting space and a casino area of 88,000 square feet. Previously called the Tropicana, it had just been reopened in September 1988 after the completion of a two-year, $200 million expansion. As part of a company strategy to develop "megafacilities," the expansion featured the addition of a two-acre indoor entertainment venue called Tivoli Pier, an attraction that aimed to replicate the turn-of-the-century peak of the Atlantic City boardwalk. It included various high-tech attractions and games, strolling performers, and a Ferris wheel four stories high. Other TropWorld amenities included the 1,700-seat TropWorld Showroom (at the time the largest in Atlantic City), 18 restaurants and bars, a health club, a miniature golf course, a comedy club, and retail shops. In the face of this major expansion, Aztar would need to absorb the TropWorld's start-up costs and also await major improvements in Atlantic City's infrastructure that were scheduled to be completed over the next several years, including expansion of highway, rail, and airport access and the construction of a new convention center. Company officials believed that the TropWorld was well positioned to take advantage of the increased tourism and convention business that these improvements promised to bring.

In Las Vegas, Aztar had inherited the Tropicana Resort and Casino, which was located on the southeast corner of Las Vegas Boulevard and Tropicana Avenue. Following the completion of a major expansion in 1986, Ramada had introduced a tropical island theme to the casino, calling it "The Island of Las Vegas." The Tropicana featured 1,910 rooms, 100,000 square feet of exhibit and meeting space, and 45,000 square feet of casino space (with 993 slot machines and 72 table games). The facility also featured several other attractions, including the famous "Folies Bergère" show, more than a dozen restaurants and bars, and a five-acre water park. With water one of its major themes, the Tropicana was the first casino to offer swim-up slot machines and blackjack. While 1988 had been the casino's best year ever, company officials believed it was ready for further growth, in particular with the expected mid-1990 opening of the Excalibur Hotel & Casino directly across Las Vegas Boulevard. They believed the new 4,000-room facility would bring additional people to the southern end of the "Strip," where the Tropicana stood alone, unable to attract the many gamblers who like to move from casino to casino.

The third casino in the original Aztar threesome was the Ramada Express Hotel and Casino in Laughlin, Nevada, a fast-growing gambling mecca located in extreme southeastern Nevada near both the California and Arizona borders. Construction of the Ramada Express, the newest but smallest of the three casinos, was completed in 1988. A Victorian-era railroad theme was established in 406 rooms and 30,000 square feet of casino space, with "The Gambling Train of Laughlin" transporting guests from the parking lot to the front door. Although it featured fewer facilities than the larger Aztar properties, the casino enjoyed a significant share of this much-smaller market and had an ideal location in the middle of Laughlin's gambling district.

The initial few years after the restructuring were difficult ones for Aztar. Revenues fell from $522.3 million in 1989 to $508.2 million in 1990 to $481.3 million in 1991. Following an operating profit of $67.4 million in 1990, Aztar managed only a $61.4 million profit in 1991. Many factors contributed to the company's struggles. In 1990 a breach of contract case, which was originally brought against Ramada in the early 1980s and assumed by Aztar following the restructuring, cost the company $34.3 million. Competition was increased with a casino building boom in 1989 and 1990, which saw the completion of the 3,000-room Mirage and 4,000-room Excalibur in Las Vegas, a 2,000-room Hilton in Laughlin, and Atlantic City's 1,250-room Taj Mahal (which made TropWorld the second-largest casino in Atlantic City). This increased capacity greatly exceeded demand with the onset of economic recession, and in particular when the Persian Gulf crisis of late 1990 and the war in early 1991 greatly decreased travel and tourism traffic. Adding to the difficulties for the Nevada casinos was California's severe recession, while TropWorld felt the impact of the deep recession in the northeastern United States.

Aztar's management adopted several strategies to address the difficult environment. While many casinos battled each other for customers through such bargains as reduced room rates, package deals that included transportation, and cheap buffet-style meals, Aztar decided not to chase after people lured by these bargains since they did not tend to spend much money gambling. Rather than trying to attract all potential gamblers, the company decided to take a niche approach to its marketing by concentrating on what they called the "high end of the middle market." Such customers spend between $100 and $400 gambling during an average day. In Las Vegas, for example, this placed the Tropicana between such lower-end casinos as Circus Circus, whose guests spend less than $100 per day, and upscale casinos such as Caesars Palace, a facility for high rollers. In essence, the company sought to attract fewer people who would spend more in their casinos than to seek a high volume of gamblers. To this end, Aztar eliminated many of the bargains it offered. One strategy to reach its desired clientele and to encourage repeat visitors was the initiation of a program modeled after airline frequent-flier programs. Another tactic was to de-emphasize baccarat, favored by high rollers, and concentrate on slot machines.

While the company pursued its new marketing strategy in Atlantic City and Las Vegas, it decided in 1991 to expand its Ramada Express casino in Laughlin. Laughlin had also seen a huge increase in hotel rooms in 1990–1991 (nearly doubling to more than 8,000 rooms), but Aztar management saw a window of opportunity for expansion during the next two years based on the limited capacity of Laughlin's water and sewer system. Since the Ramada Express had been designed to accommodate 1,200 rooms (at the time it was built, Ramada lacked sufficient capital to build it to its capacity), it could be expanded with its current water and sewer allocations. Aztar calculated that other casinos could only add an additional 1,500 rooms in Laughlin based on their water and sewer capacities. In late 1992, the $75 million expansion began. Upon its completion in September 1993, Aztar had increased the hotel space of the Ramada Express to 1,500 rooms with the addition of a 1,100-room tower, and also added 20,000 square feet of additional casino space (for a total of 50,000 square feet), a new parking garage, and additional meeting space and restaurants.

The company's strategies began to pay off with revenues beginning to turn around in 1992. That year Aztar realized a six percent increase in revenues over the previous year, from $481.3 million to $512 million. The slow but steady growth continued the next two years with revenues of $518.8 million in 1993 and $541.4 million in 1994. Evidence that the company's marketing strategy was working came in the form of increased revenue from slot machines, up 19 percent in 1992. Aztar was also able to solidify its financial position during this period. Late in 1992 the company refinanced $171 million in high-yield notes, reducing its debt payments in the process. In 1993 it bought out the limited partners that had owned a majority interest in the TropWorld property for approximately $62 million in cash, gaining complete control over Aztar's largest asset.

Having cleaned up its finances and showing improved results, in the mid-1990s Aztar management turned its attention to expansion, while continuing to vigilantly protect its solid trio of original casinos. With the Tropicana in the weakest position in the increasingly competitive Las Vegas market, the company undertook a minor renovation project in 1993. Where it once stood alone on the southern end of the Strip, the Tropicana now shared a corner with both the 4,000-room Excalibur and the newly opened 5,000-room MGM Grand, with another new neighbor, the 2,500-room Luxor, nearby. While this boom in what became known as ''The New Four Corners of Las Vegas'' promised to bring increasing numbers of people to the vicinity of the Tropicana, company officials felt they needed to redesign the casino's front entrance and facade to entice additional walk-in business from the surrounding resorts. With a ''Caribbean Island'' theme highlighting the design, the renovations were completed in early 1994. These included new stores accessible from the street, a ''Wildlife Walk'' connecting the casino's two towers and featuring natural displays of live birds and other tropical wildlife, and other improvements. At about the same time, the state of Nevada completed construction of a skywalk system connecting ''The New Four Corners of Las Vegas,'' an improvement that promised to increase traffic among the Tropicana and its neighboring casinos.

Aztar was beginning to feel the effects of competition from outside the cities in which its casinos operated, and decided that its first new developments should occur in these nascent gambling areas. By 1993, 14 states had legalized casino gambling and additional states had approved or were considering legalized gambling on riverboats or Indian reservations. The company's first target would be riverboat gambling operations in the Midwest. The riverboat strategy followed closely Aztar's increasing emphasis on slot machine players, since this type of gambling venue is typically dominated by slot machines. In early 1995 the Indiana Gaming Commission approved Aztar's plan for a riverboat casino in downtown Evansville. The $100 million project would include a 310-foot, 2,500-passenger riverboat, a casino on board with 1,250 slot machines and 70 gaming tables, a hotel with 250 rooms, a pavilion entertainment complex, and parking for 1,600 vehicles. The company estimated that the casino could draw 2.3 million visitors each year, provided competition did not arise within nearby Louisville.

Meanwhile, a smaller $55 million riverboat project opened in the spring of 1995 in Caruthersville, Missouri, a town in southeastern Missouri on the Mississippi River about 90 miles north of Memphis, Tennessee. This facility featured a 600-passenger riverboat with a casino of 500 slot machines and 30 gaming tables, an entertainment and ticketing pavilion, parking for 1,000 vehicles, and a recreational vehicle park. At the same time, Aztar was also pursuing several other riverboat facilities. In early 1995 Newport News, Virginia, selected the company to develop a riverboat casino, but Aztar had to await legislative consideration of the legalization of gambling in the state before proceeding. For these and future operations, Aztar decided to use a brand-name marketing strategy to connect the riverboat casinos. ''Casino Aztar'' was tied to the particular site, as in ''Casino Aztar Caruthersville.''

The company also undertook a major addition to the TropWorld casino in Atlantic City, including a new hotel tower with 628 rooms, additional restaurants, and other new facilities. Following completion of the project, scheduled for the summer of 1996, the casino would include more than 1,600 hotel rooms, making it the largest hotel in New Jersey. The budget for the project was $75 million. In order to finance the TropWorld addition and the new riverboat casinos, Aztar secured a financing package from a group of ten banks late in 1994. The package totaled $280 million, the fourth-largest such package ever made within the gambling industry, with $73 million to refinance debt on the Tropicana and $207 million in revolving credit secured by the TropWorld and Ramada Express properties.

With this financing in place, Aztar had sufficient capital to embark on its expansion plan for the mid- to late-1990s. Analysts considered the company's position in Atlantic City to be particularly strong with the expansion of the TropWorld. The completed expansion of the Ramada Express was beginning to pay dividends even with the tremendous growth of Laughlin casinos. The Tropicana continued to face an uncertain future as the addition of several nearby mega-resorts could either hurt or help the Aztar property in Las Vegas. The company's plans for expansion outside Atlantic City and Nevada through riverboat casinos were an ambitious, though unproven, undertaking. As states and cities throughout the United States and Canada expanded or added gambling to their local economies, many observers were wondering when the market would be become glutted with gambling properties and how this would affect such major operators as Aztar.

Principal Subsidiaries: Adamar of Nevada; New Jersey Holdings Corporation.

Further Reading:

Giblin, Paul, ''Aztar Dives into Three Riverboat Casino Ventures,'' *Business Journal: Serving Phoenix & the Valley of the Sun,* December 3, 1993, p. 3.

Gilbertson, Dawn, ''Improving Its Hand: Phoenix Casino Operator Poised for Rebound,'' *Phoenix Gazette,* May 14, 1992.

Jarman, Max, ''Aztar's Fortunes Coming Up 7s,'' *Arizona Business Gazette,* July 15, 1993, p. 5.

Novotny, Jean, ''Ramada to be 'Aztar' after Hotel Sale,'' *Arizona Republic,* July 4, 1989.

Reich, Peter, ''Aztar Is Born: Ramada to Give Up Hotel Biz, *Phoenix Gazette,* December 13, 1989.

——, ''Ramada's New Name Reflects Changes,'' *Phoenix Gazette,* July 4, 1989.

''$280 Million Package for Gaming Company,'' *Arizona Republic,* October 7, 1994, p. E1.

Whaley, Sean, ''Gamers OK Ramada Restructuring,'' *Las Vegas Review Journal,* December 13, 1989.

—David E. Salamie

Banco Bradesco S.A.

Avenida Ipiranga, 282, 10 Andar
Apartodo Postal 8250
01046-010 Osasco, São Paulo
Brazil
(11) 259-2822
Fax: (11) 256-8742

Public Company
Incorporated: 1943
Employees: 71,781
Net Income: US$526.85 million
Stock Exchanges: São Paulo Rio de Janeiro
SICs: 6029 Commercial Banks, Not Elsewhere Classified; 6211 Security Brokers and Dealers; 6411 Insurance Agents, Brokers, and Service

Headquartered in a suburb of São Paulo, Brazil, Banco Bradesco S.A. is Brazil's largest private bank. The firm is a powerhouse by virtually any standard: it ranks as the largest bank employer in the world, the largest private employer in Brazil, and the third-largest banking organization in Latin America. Under the guidance of founder Amador Aguiar for most of its half-century in business, Bradesco revolutionized Brazil's banking industry through a combination of technological foresight and dedication to service. In the mid-1990s, the bank boasted over 1,800 branch offices, over 500 special banking service posts, and 1,800 automatic teller machines (ATMs). The company also managed insurance and travel services, stock brokerages, and credit card administration offices. In addition, Bradesco collects taxes and distributes tax refunds for the Brazilian government, and provides collection services to many of the country's major utilities. International offices in New York, Grand Cayman, and London handle overseas banking services.

The history of Bradesco is a "rags to riches" tale in the tradition of Horatio Alger's uniquely-American success stories, which typically feature a resourceful country boy who creates a bright future for himself in the big city. Indeed, Bradesco founder Amador Aguiar moved in similar fashion from the farmlands of Brazil's Ribeirão Preto region to the cosmopolitan city of São Paulo. Born in 1904, the third of thirteen children of farm workers, Aguiar went to work in a printer's shop at the age of 14. But after losing a finger in a printing machine six years later, the young Brazilian started work as a bank clerk at Banco Noroeste.

Brazilian banks of the early twentieth century paralleled American banks of the late nineteenth century. They restricted their services to the wealthy upper classes and therefore placed themselves in competition for a very limited clientele. Middle and lower class citizens did not use banks, and were not welcome at most financial institutions. This situation was especially pronounced in Brazil, where the gap between the classes was even wider than in the United States.

Aguiar's humble beginnings probably sensitized him to the inequity of Brazil's banking system. After nearly two decades as an employee, in 1943 the industrious Aguiar assumed control of Casa Bancária Almeida e Companhia (Almeida Banking House), a bank with six branches, headquarters in Marília, and a capital stock of ten million cruzeiros. He renamed the institution Banco Brasileiro de Descontos S.A., which was later shortened to Bradesco. (The name translates to "ten-conto bank," a self-effacing reference to an outdated form of currency. Comparable to "dime savings bank," the name emphasized the institution's appeal to small-scale savers.)

Aguiar's approach to banking has been compared to that of Amadeo Peter Giannini, who created the Bank of America (now BankAmerica Corporation) to serve the financial needs of "the little fellows" such as area coffee growers. In order to make his target clientele feel welcome, Aguiar made a number of changes in typical banking services. He expanded office hours so that coffee growers and ranchers could do their banking before their work day began. In order to reduce the "intimidation factor" common to many financial institutions, Aguiar moved his managers and loan officers from "cages" at the rear of the bank to more approachable desks near the front doors. The bank even helped its clients learn to write checks; if an incorrectly endorsed note arrived, Bradesco would call the customer in to correct the document so that the bank could honor it.

Aguiar reformed Bradesco's corporate culture as well, making piety and company loyalty fundamental requirements for hiring and promotion. The work environment was replete with religious references. The company letterhead, for example, featured Bible verses and the phrase "Nos confiamos em Deus," Portugese for "We trust in God." New hires endorsed a "declaration of principles" that described the setting aside of personal interests in favor of the good of the country and the company. A corporate publication emphasized three essential requirements for employees: "punctuality, simplicity and availability."

According to Lynda Schuster's 1985 interview with Aguiar for the *Wall Street Journal,* promotions in the company were made from within and based on what Aguiar described as "superior moral behavior." In the 1990s all of Bradesco's directors had started out at the company in minor office and clerical positions and all had at least 15 years of experience at the bank.

The high moral expectations instituted by Aguiar had a legitimate business function. As one top executive commented in the bank's 50th anniversary publication, "a clear ethics code, strictly enforced, neutralizes any conflict potential that the decentralization of the decision-making process might activate." In other words, the company's policies freed branch managers to make the difficult judgments about extension of loans, mortgages, and lines of business credit, while simultaneously releasing upper-level executives from having to oversee those day-to-day transactions.

Bradesco's mass appeal helped it grow quickly. By 1946 it had expanded sufficiently to warrant the relocation of its headquarters to São Paulo, Brazil's economic capital. The country—and Bradesco—enjoyed a period of brisk economic expansion based in large part on burgeoning coffee exports during the 1950s. Bradesco's confidence in its clientele paid off in a big way during this period, as deposits at the bank doubled every month. Less than a decade after its reformation by Aguiar, Bradesco had become Brazil's largest private financial institution.

The bank also diversified into trading during this period, using its growing number of branch offices to distribute products from the more industrialized areas of the country to more isolated regions. This strategy not only endeared Bradesco to the recipients of medicine, fuel, and other benefits of modernization, but also to the industrialists and manufacturers whose sales were boosted by these efforts. The bank also began processing utility payments at this time.

When Aguiar moved the bank's corporate headquarters to the outskirts of São Paulo in 1953, he named the new location "Cidade de Deus," or "City of God," after a book by the evangelist Saint Augustine. The complex not only featured the standard office buildings, but housing, recreation facilities, hospitals, and schools for the 9,000 employees who worked there. Construction of the compound and support of its inhabitants fostered the growth of a thriving suburb around Cidade de Deus.

Aguiar extended his magnanimity beyond the needs of his employees as well. In 1956 he established The Fundação Bradesco (Bradesco Foundation) to combat illiteracy. Boosted by profits from Bradesco's insurance operations, the program was later expanded to include social services, vocational training, computer equipment, and educational materials. By the early 1990s, the Foundation included 39 schools, 85,000 enrollees, and an annual budget of US$30 million. Aguiar's philanthropy earned him the oft-used title "seu," a rural contraction of the honorific "Señor."

In 1962 Bradesco became the first bank in Brazil to make computer automation part of its daily operations, ignoring the Brazilian banking industry's well-established prejudice against new technologies. Notwithstanding the conventional wisdom, automation proved invaluable in the tumultuous Brazilian economy, which endured triple-digit inflation, rapid currency devaluation, and stagnant gross domestic product growth in the early 1960s. Like other Brazilian banks, Bradesco adapted to this "hyperinflationary" environment, adopting indexing (characterized by Robert M. Bleiberg of *Barron's* as "the widespread use of escalator clauses in financial transactions to minimize the impact of inflation") and issuing daily bank statements so that clients could track their holdings. As one executive reflected in the company history, the daily statement was "an extravagance that impressed people. Some clients considered it an excess but even so understood that the daily statement represented superior service."

A military coup d'etat in Brazil in the mid-1960s ushered in a period of government-led economic planning that brought about "the Brazilian miracle" of the late 1960s and early 1970s. The country enjoyed an unprecedented period of prosperity, low inflation, and economic expansion. Bradesco more than doubled its 326-branch system through acquisitions during this period. The two largest of Bradesco's 17 purchases were INCO-Banco Indústria e Comércio de Santa Catarina's 105-branch system in 1967 and Banco da Bahia's 200 branches in 1973. The bank also launched its first credit card, the Cartão Bradesco, during this period. By 1978, the institution claimed over 1,000 branches.

Aguiar stepped down from Bradesco's executive chairmanship in 1981. He remained true to the Spartan work ethic he imposed on his employees, however, and maintained a daily work schedule. The venerable leader retired in 1990 at the age of 86 and died less than a year later.

Aguiar was succeeded as chief executive by Lázaro de Mello Brandão, who had started his career with Bradesco in 1942 at the age of 15, when the institution was still the Almeida Banking House. Brandão was as hard-working as his predecessor: he put in 12-hour days and was on call "Dia e Noite" (Day and Night, also a slogan for Bradesco's ATM system). He had been a driving force behind the bank's computerization in the 1960s and its internationalization in the early 1980s.

Triple-digit annual inflation once again raged in Brazil in the early 1980s. Banking customers tried to adapt to the situation with daily transfers of funds to accounts with ever-higher yields. Bradesco and other Brazilian banks branches increased their services to accommodate this activity. Bradesco's branch system, for example, increased from 1,400 in 1983 to over 1,900 in 1986. In 1985 alone, the bank opened more than one new branch per day. In order to keep its clients informed of events in the fast-moving Brazilian economy, the bank launched "Alô Bradesco," a free, 24-hour consumer complaint, suggestion, and information line, in 1985. As of 1993, the system had logged 475,000 calls. The bank proudly pointed out that less than ten percent of those calls were complaints.

In 1986 the Sarney administration ratified the "Cruzado Plan," a strategy that purported to halt inflation and simultaneously boost the economy in Brazil. The country adopted a new fixed-rate currency called the cruzado; instituted price and wage freezes; and even limited banking hours to just five midday hours in order to limit activity. Having reconciled themselves to hyperinflation, many Brazilian banks faced a painful readjustment. Milton Moskowitz noted in *The Global Marketplace* that at Bradesco, which had a bank work force of 750,000 people, "some 80,000 lost their jobs early in 1986, and hundreds of branches were closed."

In order to gradually adapt to the artificially-curbed economy, CEO Brandão focused on enhancing productivity through ever-increasing automation. The proliferation of automatic teller machines that offer the full range of traditional bank services diminished the need for employees to work as tellers. In addition, the installation in the early 1990s of a state-of-the-art satellite-based data communications network helped revolutionize the collection of daily transaction records from 200 of Bradesco's branches on the Amazonian frontier. Up to the late 1980s, this information was transmitted through a fleet of boats that traversed the region's estuaries several times each business day.

The bank also ''outsourced'' several peripheral businesses during this period, including operations as diverse as a cabinet-making division, corporate food service, and medical service. The company history commented that ''self-sufficiency was necessary at a time when services in Brazil were incipient and lacked the means to operate on a large scale.'' Bradesco did, however, retain ownership of its printing operations, perhaps in homage to the founder's first profession. Through these and other measures, employment at Bradesco was halved, from 146,000 in 1986 to 81,000 in 1994, but assets climbed from US$13.6 billion to US$15.8 billion during the same period.

The late 1980s and early 1990s also brought a revolution in Bradesco's corporate culture and a deviation from some of Aguiar's strict standards. For example, the board of directors of the company had traditionally worked out in the open. As with the bank's branch managers and teller, these executives had neither private offices nor even a desk drawer to themselves. The president often personally handled many customer and employee issues. But during this period of reform, top executives at the home office and in the branches moved into new quarters with private meeting rooms for confidential consultations with clients.

Although the Brazilian economy was still in turmoil in the early 1990s, Brandão pointed to several positive portents for the economy overall and Bradesco in particular: ''For the first time in the Republic's 103 years an elected president was removed from office without the least infringement of the Constitution. [In addition,] Europe and the United States, important partners for Brazil, are experiencing positive developments. . . . Furthermore, European unification may produce positive developments, especially if the agricultural subsidies are eliminated.''

Brazil is a country of contradictions. It has Latin America's biggest—and most indebted—economy. It has enjoyed periods of exhilarating growth and equally devastating depths of recession. The country boasts some of the world's richest natural resources, but has earned a reputation for squandering those treasures. Its government has been plagued by instability and scandal, yet its citizens have registered popular approval of the ''strong executive system'' that has engendered abuse of power. Bradesco has thrived in this challenging, ever-changing environment, remaining profitable through both hyperinflation and economic controls. Although some analysts questioned the bank's ability to adjust to economic stabilization programs enacted in 1994, Bradesco continued to prosper. In 1993 and 1994, it was the top-rated of Brazil's banks, according to Euromoney, IBCA Limited (London), and Thomson BankWatch Inc. (New York).

Principal Subsidiaries: Bradesco Insurance Group; Bradesco Leasing S.A.; Bradesco S.A. Corretora de Títulos e Valores Mobiliários; Bradesco Turismo S.A. Administração e Serviços; Bradesplan Reflorestamento e Agropecuária Ltda.; ABS-Empreendimentos Imobiliários, Participações e Serviços S.A.; Allianz-Ultramar Companhia Brasileira de Seguros; Alphaville Factoring-Fomento Comercial Ltda.; Atlântica-Prudential Participações S.A.; Baloise-Atlântica Companhia Brasileira de Seguros; Bradescor Corretora de Seguros Ltda.; Gráfica Bradesco Ltda.; Prudential-Atlântica Companhia Brasileira de Seguros; União de Comércio e Participações Ltda.; Vibra-Formação de Vigilantes S.C. Ltda.; Vibra-Vigilância e Transportes de Valores Ltda.

Further Reading:

Bleibert, Robert M., ''Distant Early Warning—Brazil's 'Economic Miracle' Has Lost its Lustre,'' *Barron's,* September 18, 1978, p. 7.

Filho, Armando Trivelate, ''Banco Bradesco Implements Extensive VSAT Network,'' *Communications News,* March 1993, p. 11.

The History of Bradesco's 50 Years, São Paulo, Brazil: Bradesco, S.A., [1993].

McCurry, Patrick, ''Small is Beautiful,'' *Euromoney,* December 1994, pp. 18–20.

Moskowitz, Milton, *The Global Marketplace,* New York: Macmillan, 1987.

—April D. Gasbarre

Barnes Group Inc.

123 Main Street
Bristol, Connecticut 06010
U.S.A.
(203) 583-7070
Fax: (203) 589-3507

Public Company
Incorporated: 1922 as Associated Spring Co.
Employees: 4200
Sales: $569 million
Stock Exchanges: New York
SICs: 3469 Metal Stampings, Not Elsewhere Classified; 3493 Steel Springs Except Wire; 6719 Holding Companies, Not Elsewhere Classified

Barnes Group Inc. serves diversified industrial markets throughout the world. It is the largest manufacturer of springs in North America, for example, and is a leading distributor of maintenance, repair, and overhaul parts and services in the United States. Barnes also sells specialized aerospace parts and services. The company's rich history is illustrative of the Yankee ingenuity that built the American industrial machine.

The founder of what would eventually become a Forbes 500 company was Wallace Barnes. Wallace, nicknamed ''Bub,'' was born on Christmas day in 1827 and grew up in Bristol, Connecticut, where his ancestors had settled in the mid-1600s after arriving from England in 1630. Wallace's ancestor Thomas Barns (the name was later changed to Barnes), the original settler who arrived from England, fought in the Pequot War. After bearing three children, his wife Mary was put to death by hanging in 1662 for ''entertaining familiarity with Satan.'' One of Thomas Barns' children became the first settler of Bristol and that town's first tavern keeper. Succeeding Barnes family members became war heroes, political figures, and noted businessmen.

Wallace Barnes began working for both his father Alphonso and grandfather Thomas in the family hotel and general store. The general store specialized in clocks, but it also sold drugs and general merchandise. Wallace eventually became skilled as a druggist. Partly because he and his father didn't get along, however, he left to start his own druggist shop in a nearby town. Lackluster returns from that venture prompted him to try his hand at a new business, clockmaking. Wallace started out contracting to supply cut glass, doors, and parts to different clockmakers who were part of the bustling clock trade that had developed in Bristol; in fact, Bristol was known as the clockmaking capital of America at the time. Unfortunately, the local clock industry fell on hard times when the Panic of 1857 caused a severe depression.

At the time of the Panic, Wallace was working for clockmaker A.S. Platt. Platt, for whom Wallace had been working at the rate of $1.25 per day, became unable to pay him for his services. Instead of cash, Barnes accepted some hoop-skirt wire as compensation. In a move that demonstrated his dealmaking savvy, Wallace hauled the wire in a wagon to nearby Albany. There, he traded the wire for a financially troubled haberdashery store. Rather than stay to run the store himself, Wallace turned around and traded it for a Missouri farm that he had never seen. Upon returning to Bristol, he managed to trade the farm for a blacksmith shop, which he sold for the handsome sum of $1,600. Incredibly, Wallace used the money to purchase the troubled A.S. Platt, the company that had given him the wire in the first place.

Barnes's new purchase included a bevy of equipment and raw materials. Importantly, Barnes also received the rights to a secret method of tempering steel springs that involved heating the springs and then quenching them in oil. Wallace wisely partnered with E.L. Dunbar, a more experienced manufacturer who was also Wallace's long-time friend. They each contributed $2,000 to the venture and set up shop in a two-story building in Bristol. They started with a handful of employees making springs and hoops for skirts, but their work force quickly expanded when the demand for hoops exploded in the wake of a fashion craze. Wallace and his partner scrambled to relocate in a bigger shop, and by the end of the year had 150 workers manning three eight-hour shifts six days a week. Although the hoopskirt fad died out before the start of the Civil War in 1861, Barnes and Dunbar managed to reap profits of about $225,000 in 1859 alone.

When the Civil War started, Wallace and Dunbar switched to making musket springs and powder horns, among other items. Although the company was still making money, the two partners split in 1863; political differences may have forced the departure of Dunbar, a ''Copperhead'' who sympathized with the South and differed from the staunchly Republican Barnes. Barnes continued to operate the business during the next several years, expanding into new product lines and even patenting several new springs and production techniques. Despite a discouraging fire that destroyed his factory in 1866, Wallace persevered with his springmaking operations and was employing a work force of 35 by the mid-1870s.

Interestingly, the intense and optimistic Wallace Barnes was known in his community during this time more as a trader of Jersey cattle than as a manufacturer. In fact, Wallace was much more of a tinkerer, trader, and venturer than he was a businessman. During the 1880s, when his spring business was faltering, Wallace was probably making more money from the new livestock drug that he had developed and patented and was selling throughout the world. Thus, the success of his spring business was not necessarily paramount. Other interests included a theater that he built in downtown Bristol and coon hunting, a favorite hobby to which he devoted significant energy. When Wallace died in 1893 at the age of 65, he left an estate appraised at about $70,000—not as much as one might expect from such an active businessman, but reflective of his varied interests.

Carlyle Fuller (C.F.) Barnes, the eldest of five of Wallace's sons, had become active in the spring business in the 1880s. He and his brothers changed the name (and focus) of the business, in fact, to the Barnes Brothers Clock Company, although that venture lasted only four years and the brothers returned to making springs instead of clocks. Part of the problem had been that their father had a habit of taking money from that business to cover debts related to other ventures. In any event, C.F. was credited with saving the company from bankruptcy following Wallace's death. Despite economic turbulence at the time, he was able to get his creditors to back his foray into manufacturing bicycle wheels and related parts. The Barnes Company, as it had become known, cashed in on the bicycle fad and generated much needed profits in the late 1890s. That put the company in good financial shape going into the 1900s.

The fading bicycle boom was replaced in the early 1900s by the emerging automobile industry. Barnes benefited from strong demand for motorcar springs for valves, clutches, starters, suspensions, and hundreds of other items. At the same time, Americans were increasingly purchasing other items, introduced in mass during the industrial revolution, that required springs, such as typewriters, telephones, ice-cream makers, electric sewing machines, and more. As demand for Barnes's various springs grew, the company expanded, adding new production facilities and even building its own steel mill. By 1910, when C.F. Barnes's son Fuller joined the company, Barnes was employing a work force of about 200. Fuller's younger brother Harry also started working for the company in 1913. The two brothers helped steer the company through its biggest expansion wave during the next few years, as demand for springs spiraled during World War I, and the company's work force temporarily soared to 1,400. Barnes churned out an estimated 90 million springs for the U.S. government during that war.

Although sales slowed after the war, they were soon supplanted by demand unleashed during the Roaring Twenties. Barnes was reaping about $2 million in revenues annually by the early 1920s and was rapidly expanding its product lines and production facilities. Barnes's primary area of interest, however, was still the automobile industry. Still, the brothers felt that their company lacked the size needed to take a leadership role as a supplier of springs to that industry. To that end, the Barnes brothers engineered the November 1922 merger of three companies to form Associated Spring Co., with Fuller Barnes as president. The new company grew rapidly during the 1920s, increasing sales 85 percent and broadening its scope to include all types of appliance and aviation industries. Associated Spring also purchased other competitors, including the descendant of a springmaking firm created by E.L. Dunbar after he had split from Wallace Barnes.

The stock market crash of 1929 and the resulting Great Depression battered Associated Spring. After nearly a decade of success, the company posted a crushing $43,585 loss in 1931 and then a $482,925 shortfall in 1932. Salary cuts, layoffs, and restructuring allowed the company to survive the Depression. During that period, Barnes was separated from the other two companies with which it had merged, although all three subsidiaries were still under the same corporate umbrella.

By the late 1930s the Barnes factories were humming once again as the United States geared up for World War II. Throughout the war, Barnes delivered millions of springs for airplanes, tanks, trucks, and jeeps. In addition, its steel mill cranked out products ranging from band saws to machine-gun ammunition clips. Associated's total payroll jumped to 6,000 in 1943, when shipments hit an all-time high of $31 million.

When the war ended, Associated Spring and its Barnes subsidiary enjoyed steady demand as peace-time markets surged. Sales in 1946 hit $22.6 million and the company was still employing more than 4,000 workers. To fund growth, Associated went public and sold its shares over-the-counter. It used the cash to expand its factories, open new sales and distribution offices, and to buy other companies. By 1953 the company was capturing about $50 million in annual sales. In that year, Carlyle F. (''Hap'') Barnes, Fuller's son, was made president of Associated; he would become CEO in 1964. Under his direction, the company expanded internationally, first into Puerto Rico and then into Argentina, England, Japan, and Mexico by the early 1960s. Throughout the 1950s and 1960s, Barnes sustained its legacy of innovation in the spring industry. By 1963, in fact, the company was employing 5,200 workers and was selling its shares on the New York Stock Exchange.

Hap Barnes, who had been joined at the executive level by his cousin Wallace (Wally), was satisfied with Associated's performance by the early 1960s. But he also realized that it was time for a change, mostly because the company had become overly dependent on the automotive industry. To reduce the dependency, he decided that the organization should diversify into distribution, which was more closely tied to the countercyclical replacement and overhaul market. To that end, Associated purchased Bowman Products Company in 1964, giving it an instant and significant stature as a distributor of repair and replacement parts. Several acquisitions followed during the mid- and late 1960s, but Bowman proved to be among the most successful. By 1968 Associated was doing $100 million in sales annually, and by the early 1970s was employing 6,000 workers in 41 locations in the United States and abroad. It was even listed on the London Stock Exchange.

During the 1970s Associated stepped up its global expansion efforts. It purchased major spring producers in England and Sweden in the early 1970s, for example, that added about 1,500 workers and more than $11 million in new sales to its portfolio. In the mid-1970s, moreover, Barnes bought companies in South America, Germany, and India. Because of the widened scope of the organization, its name was changed in 1976 from Associated Spring to Barnes Group Inc. One year later, Hap Barnes stepped aside as chief executive and handed the reigns to his cousin, Wally Barnes; Hap remained a senior officer at the company until 1989, his 41st year at Barnes. Wally oversaw the opening of a new $3 million international headquarters in downtown Bristol in 1979.

Under Wally Barnes' direction, Barnes Group continued to expand and acquire companies. In 1979, in fact, Barnes achieved record sales of $432 million, making that its eight consecutive annual rise in both sales and earnings. The sales figure placed Barnes on the Fortune 500 list for the first time. Although Barnes' growth was impressive to many, critics were concerned that the company had expanded too rapidly. Their concerns were confirmed in 1981, when net income plunged from $24 million to just $5 million. One year later that figure dipped to an embarrassing deficit of $5.5 million. Although a recession was partly to blame, Barnes' executives realized that changes were needed. Barnes shuttered several poorly performing plants and divisions in 1983 and sold off several interests that no longer complemented its corporate goals. After showing a loss of $2.6 million in 1983, Barnes enjoyed a profit recovery in 1984 as net income increased to $15.7 million.

Barnes continued to make acquisitions and expand certain operations, particularly those related to aerospace, in the mid- and late 1980s. But it also sustained a concerted effort to cut costs, focus on customer service, and jettison badly performing businesses. It sold a major portion of its distribution business, for example, and got completely out of the steelmaking industry. The end result of restructuring was steady sales growth and healthy profits during most of the 1980s. Revenues increased from about $420 million in 1984 to about $545 million in 1990, while net income hovered between about $13 million and $18 million. Wally Barnes announced his retirement as chief executive in 1990, to become effective in 1991, leaving leadership of the company to someone outside of the Barnes family.

Barnes Group Inc. was hurt by the global economic downturn of the early 1990s. Sales slipped to about $500 million by 1993, and Barnes was forced to post a loss in 1992 as a result of restructuring charges and accounting changes. Barnes stepped up cost-cutting efforts during the period and closed some operations, among other reactions to the downturn. Total Barnes employment fell from about 4,500 to 4,200 during the period. In 1994, however, Barnes rebounded and managed to record its highest profit since 1980. After a few years of turbulence in the executive ranks, Barnes's board named Theodore E. Martin president and chief executive in 1995. Martin had served stints with several manufacturers before joining Barnes in 1990.

Going into the mid-1990s, Barnes was still a global leader in the spring business, which had been its mainstay for most of its 138-year history. Its Associated Spring division, which operated 11 plants in five countries and served a wide range of industries, was accounting for roughly half of corporate revenues in 1995 and the large majority of profit. Through its Bowman division, Barnes was also a top distributor of repair and maintenance parts. Bowman was contributing about 40 percent of Barnes' sales and about one-third of its income. Meanwhile, Barnes' aerospace division was a leading producer of titanium and precision parts for jet engines, and also provided jet-engine refurbishing services. That struggling division lost money during the defense industry downturn in the early 1990s, but was rapidly improving going into the mid-1990s.

Further Reading:

Bullard, Stan, ''Bowman Leaving City for Valley View Site,'' *Crain's Cleveland Business,* February 8, 1993, p. 3.

French, Howard, ''Navy Raids Local Factory: Agents Search Through Windsor Manufacturing's Records,'' *Journal Inquirer,* April 13, 1994, p. A24.

Khermouch, Gerry, ''Barnes' Jet Die Unit Cleans Up its Act; Tough Transition Nears End,'' *Metalworking News,* November 20, 1989, p. 1.

Sand, J. F., Jr., ''Barnes Group Selects Theodore E. Martin Chief Executive,'' *Business Wire,* April 5, 1995.

Tanner, Ogden, *Barnes: An American Enterprise,* East Haven, Conn.: Eastern Press, Inc.

—David Wentz

Bayer A.G.

Bayerwerk
51368 Leverkusen
Germany
0214-301
Fax: 0214-303-620

Public Company
Incorporated: 1952 as Farbenfabriken Bayer A.G.
Employees: 153,866
Sales: DM 41 billion
Stock Exchanges: Munich Bonn Hamburg Frankfurt Paris Luxembourg Vienna Zurich Basle Geneva London Brussels Antwerp
SICs: Industrial Organic Chemicals; 2834 Pharmaceutical Preparations; 2851 Paints, Varnishes, Lacquers, Enamels; 6719 Holding Companies

Bayer A.G., along with BASF and Hoechst, is heir to the German chemical cartel known as I.G. Farben, which the Allies disbanded in 1952 for its close association with the Nazi Party and active participation in war crimes. Rising above its checkered past, Bayer has again assumed a commanding position in the world chemical industry. The diversified company now operates in six broad areas: health care (pharmaceuticals and self-medication), industrial products (including polyurethane), polymers (fibers, plastics, and rubber), imaging technologies (including photographic products), organic products (dyes, pigments, and organic chemicals), and agrochemicals.

Bayer A.G. was founded in Elberfield by Friedrich Bayer in 1865. Bayer's first product of note was a synthetic magenta dye. The works at Elberfield were followed by additional production facilities in Leverkusen (1891), Uerdingen (1907), and Dormagen (1913).

Although Bayer was a world leader in dyestuffs, its place in the history of early twentieth-century chemistry was secured by its contributions to pharmacology. A Bayer chemist, Felix Hoffman, discovered aspirin at the turn of the century. In 1908 the basic compound for sulfa drugs was synthesized in Bayer laboratories. The immediate application of the compound was a reddish orange dye, but it was soon discovered to be effective against pneumonia, a major health hazard of the early twentieth century. Despite the lives that could have been saved if the sulfa drug had been released immediately, Bayer held on to the formula. Frustrated French chemists were forced to duplicate the drug in their own laboratories in order to introduce it to the market.

Bayer chemists regularly tested dye compounds for their effectiveness against bacteria. In 1921 they discovered a cure for African sleeping sickness, an infectious disease that had made parts of Africa uninhabitable. Aware of the political, as well as the pharmacological, implications of its compound, Bayer offered the British the formula to the drug, known as Germanin, in exchange for African colonies. Britain declined the offer. This led to a policy during World War I whereby Bayer deprived the Allies of drugs and anesthetics whenever possible.

In 1925 the president of Bayer, Carl Duisberg, organized a merger of the major German chemical companies into a single entity known as the Interessen Gemeinschaft Farbenwerke, or I.G. Farben. From their inception, the German chemical companies had been organized into a series of progressively more powerful trusts, but with I.G. Farben the last vestiges of competition in the chemical industry were extinguished. Other industries, such as steel, were undergoing a similar process in Germany.

In addition to setting quotas and pooling profits, I.G. Farben pursued political aims, working to prevent any possibility of a leftist uprising that would establish worker control over industry. In order to prevent such an uprising, I.G. Farben financed right-wing politicians and attempted to influence domestic policy in secret meetings with German leaders. The trust also exercised its influence abroad, with Bayer and other companies contributing an estimated ten million marks to Nazi Party associations in other countries. Money was also designated for propaganda: in 1938 Bayer forced an American affiliate, Sterling Drug, to write its advertising contracts in such a way that they would be immediately canceled if the publication in which the advertising appeared presented Germany in an unflattering light.

Bayer and I.G. Farben profited handsomely from their support of Adolf Hitler. By 1942 the I.G. Farben was making a yearly profit of 800 million marks more than its entire combined capitalization in 1925, the year the cartel was formalized. Not only was the I.G. Farben given possession of chemical companies in foreign lands (the I.G. Farben had control of Czechoslovakian dye works a week after the Nazi invasion), but the captured lands provided its factories in Germany with slave labor. In order to take full advantage of slave labor, I.G. Farben plants were built next to Maidanek and Auschwitz.

Many of the I. G. Farben plants contracted during the war were built in remote areas, often with camouflage. These factories did not sustain much physical damage, in contrast to the many German cities that were completely destroyed. By I.G.'s account, only 15 percent of its productive capacity was destroyed by the Allies. The worst damage was sustained by the extensive BASF works and factories in eastern Germany, which were destroyed by I.G. Farben employees so that the buildings would not fall under Russian control.

Immediately after the war many members of I.G. Farben's Vorstand, or board of directors, were arrested and indicted for war crimes. I.G. Farben executives were in the habit of keeping copious records, not only of meetings and phone calls, but also of their private thoughts on I.G. Farben's dealings with the government; as a result, there was extensive written evidence incriminating the Vorstand. Despite this evidence and testimony from concentration camp survivors, the Vorstand was dealt with leniently by the judges at Nuremberg. Journalists covering the 1947 proceedings attributed the light sentences, none of which was longer than four years, to the fact that all the sentences handed down at the end of the trials were less severe, as well as to the judges' unwillingness to expand their definition of war criminals to include businessmen.

I.G. Farben plants operated under Allied supervision from 1947 until 1952, when the organization was dismantled in the interests of ''peace and democracy.'' The division of I.G. Farben generally adhered to the boundaries of the original companies; for example, the works at Leverkusen and Elberfield reverted to Bayer. Bayer also received the AGFA photographic works.

In the first five years of its independence from I.G. Farben, Bayer concentrated on replacing outdated equipment and on supplying Germany's need for chemicals. By 1957 Bayer had developed new insecticides and fibers, as well as new raw and plastic finished materials. Bayer's resiliency in recovering from the war impressed U.S. investors, who held 12 percent of the company's stock.

During the late 1950s Bayer began to expand overseas and by 1962 was manufacturing chemicals in eight countries, including India and Pakistan. Most of the work done abroad was ''final stage processing,'' whereby active ingredients were sent from Germany and mixed with locally obtained inert ingredients that would be expensive to transport overseas. Final stage processing arrangements allowed Bayer to manufacture products, mostly farm chemicals and drugs, in developing countries more profitably.

High tariffs in the United States and high labor costs in Germany also provided incentives for Bayer to acquire production facilities in America. In 1954 Bayer and Monsanto formed a chemical company known as Mobay to manufacture engineering plastics and dyestuffs. Because Bayer did not have sufficient funds to build a plant in the United States, it provided technical expertise while Monsanto provided financial resources. Although Bayer had part and eventually full interest in Mobay, Mobay's promotional material was never allowed to mention Bayer's name, because the American rights to the Bayer trademark were given to Sterling Drug after World War I in retaliation for Bayer's suppression of American dye companies during the early years of the twentieth century.

Realizing that West Germany offered only limited opportunity for growth, Bayer worked to develop products for the U.S. chemical market, emphasizing value-added products for which Bayer held the patents, including pesticides, polyurethane, dye stuffs, and engineering plastics. Technical innovations that allowed Bayer to penetrate the U.S. market included the urethane compound that forms the familiar ''crust'' on urethane used in auto dashboards; before Bayer's discovery, the porous quality of urethane limited its usefulness. During this period Bayer consolidated and slowly expanded its international operations, especially in the United States. Overall, the decade of the 1960s was a good one for Bayer as domestic production increased 350 percent while foreign production increased 700 percent.

In the early 1970s, Bayer began to increase its already substantial investment in the United States. Between 1973 and 1977 its investment rose from $300 to $500 million, which went to expand production capacity and develop its product line, which included dyes, drugs, plastics, and synthetic rubber. Although all patents held by Bayer before 1952 had been taken away as war retribution, by the mid-1970s Bayer had expanded its product line to include 6,000 items, many of them patented by the company.

Bayer increased its capacity by expanding existing plants and purchasing new ones. In 1974 Bayer purchased Cutter Laboratories, a manufacturer of nutritional products and ethical drugs which had financial difficulties until 1977. Later, Allied Chemical sold its organic pigments division to Bayer. In 1977 a U.S. antitrust suit forced Bayer to buy Monsanto's share of Mobay, which generated $540 million in sales. The following year Bayer purchased Miles Laboratories, manufacturers of Alka-Seltzer and Flintstones vitamins.

Bayer had strong incentives to expand its U.S. operations. Due to the prevalence of strikes in Europe which interrupted product shipments, U.S. retailers were wary of contracting with European suppliers who did not have large stockpiles of their products in the United States. Lower energy and labor costs made the United States even more attractive to Bayer. U.S. holdings also cushioned the negative effects of the strong deutsche mark on imports into the United States. By the mid-1970s 65 percent of Bayer's sales came from outside of Germany, making it critical that Bayer protect itself against currency fluctuations.

In the early 1980s Bayer's worldwide holdings expanded to the point that its corporate structure needed to be reorganized. German law mandates a two-tier structure for corporations, with a management board similar in function to the board of directors of an American corporation reporting to a supervisory board made up of major stockholders, labor representatives, and outside interests. This board serves in a supervisory capacity, approves major decisions, and appoints board members. In 1982 Bayer created a third tier below the management board. This board consisted of senior managers and corporate staff members who took over management of specific product lines that had previously been the responsibility of board members.

The late 1980s and early 1990s were a time of stagnant revenues, cost containment efforts, and an increasing emphasis on non-European markets for Bayer. From 1988 through 1993, sales fluctuated between DM 40 billion and DM 43.3 billion, while profits leveled off. Business was affected by a serious recession in Western Europe, political changes in Eastern Europe, a cyclical downturn in the chemical industry, and government reforms in health care and agriculture. In 1993 Bayer's sales of pharmaceuticals in Germany fell 20 percent as a result of government efforts to cut expenditures on pharmaceuticals: doctors, facing reduced drug budgets, began to prescribe more generic drugs in place of the expensive, proprietary drugs developed by Bayer. Agrochemical sales were dampened by the Common Agricultural Policy reform effort that reduced the amount of farm land in Europe and the amount of chemicals used in farming.

Part of Bayer's response to this crisis was to drastically cut costs—$1.6 billion in expenditures were eliminated between 1991 and early 1995. Its worldwide workforce was slashed by 14 percent, and unprofitable operations were shed, including its polyphenylene sulfide unit. In 1992 Bayer integrated all of its U.S. holdings under its Miles Inc. subsidiary, based in Pittsburgh. The following year, under the leadership of a new chairman of the board of management, Manfred Schneider, Bayer committed to enlarging its Asian and North American operations in order to reduce its dependence on the European market. In Asia, Bayer focused its expansion efforts on joint ventures with firms in Japan, Hong Kong, Taiwan, and China. In 1993 Bayer signed an agreement with the Eisai Company of Japan to sell nonprescription drugs, and the following year several joint ventures were signed in China to set up Bayer and Agfa Gevaert production operations there.

In North America, Bayer began a drive not only to bolster its operations but also to fully regain the use of its name. After securing the rights to the Bayer name in the United States after World War I, Sterling Drugs went on to establish Bayer aspirin as a household name. In 1986, for $25 million, Bayer secured from Sterling partial rights to use its name in North America outside the pharmaceutical area. In 1994 Eastman Kodak sold Sterling to the British firm SmithKline Beecham PLC, and only a few weeks later SmithKline sold the North American side of Sterling to Bayer for $1 billion. With the purchase, Bayer not only won back the full rights to its name in North America, but also gained Sterling's $366 million North American over-the-counter (OTC) drug business. In addition to the Bayer aspirin line, the Sterling acquisition included such familiar products as Midol analgesics and NeoSynephrine decongestant. The acquisition pushed Bayer into the top five producers of OTC products worldwide.

After the purchase of Sterling, Bayer changed the name of its Miles Inc. subsidiary to Bayer Corporation. The OTC operations of Miles and Sterling were integrated into a single Bayer Corporation consumer care division. Another strategic step in North America, and one that brought added diversification to Bayer's health care operations, was the 1994 purchase of a 29.3 percent stake in Denver-based Schein Pharmaceutical Inc., a maker of generic drugs. Bayer planned to expand Schein's operations outside North America.

Bayer also beefed up its R&D budget, particularly in health care. Its drug research efforts were already beginning to pay off in the mid-1990s, especially in North America. Bayer's anti-infective drug Ciprobay had generated $1.3 billion in sales by early 1995, with the firm's patent in effect until 2002. In 1993 the company introduced a hemophilia treatment called Kogenate, Bayer's first genetically engineered drug. Other major drugs under development included a cholesterol reducer and treatments for asthma and Alzheimer's disease.

As a result of its increasing diversification within its core businesses and its aggressive program of worldwide expansion, Bayer seemed well positioned in the mid-1990s to continue to operate as one of the leading chemical and pharmaceutical companies in the world.

Principal Subsidiaries: Agfa AG; Agfa Gevaert S.A.; Bayer Capital Corporation N.V.; Bayer Finance S.A.; Bayer-Kaufhaus GmbH; Bayer-Wohnungen GmbH; BeCom Video- und Audio-Communikationsmittel GmbH; Compur-Electronic GmbH; Correcta GmbH; Desowag-Bayer Holzschutz GmbH; EC Erdolchemie GmbH; Flubb- und Schwerspatwerke Pforzheim GmbH; GEFIL Gesellschaft fur Internationalen Laborservice mbH; Gemeinnutzige Wohnungs-Ges. mbH; Hansa Beteiligungsgesellschaft mbH; Maschinenfabrik Hennecke GmbH; Pallas Versicherung AG; Schelde Chemie Brunsbuttel GmbH; Bayer Corporation (U.S.); Chemdesign Corporation (U.S.); Deerfield Urethane, Inc. (U.S.); Haarmann & Reimer Corporation (U.S.); H. C. Starck, Inc. (U.S.); Rhein Chemie Corporation (U.S.); Wolff Walsrode (U.S.).

Further Reading:

"Bayer Regains U.S. Rights to Name with OTC Buy," *Chemical Marketing Reporter,* September 19, 1994, p. 3.

Hasell, Nick, "The View from Bayer," *Management Today,* November 1993, pp. 60–64.

Hayes, Peter, *Industry and Ideology: IG Farben in the Nazi Era,* New York: Cambridge University Press, 1987, 411 p.

Jackson, Debbie, "Bayer: Deals in the Pipeline as Decline Continues," *Chemical Week,* December 8, 1993, p. 18.

——, "Bayer Mobilizes Resources to Counter Crisis at Home," *Chemical Week,* April 21, 1993, pp. 24–31.

——, "Bayer under Pressure," *Chemical Week,* March 24, 1993, p. 19.

——, and Emma Chynoweth, "Recession Reaches German Majors: Turnaround in 1991 Is Still Elusive," *Chemical Week,* April 15, 1992, pp. 22–23.

Kuntz, Mary, "Extra-Strength Aspiration: Can Bayer's New Owners Expand the Market?," *Business Week,* May 1, 1995, p. 46.

Mann, Charles C., and Mark L. Plummer, *The Aspirin Wars: Money, Medicine, and 100 Years of Rampant Competition,* New York: Alfred A. Knopf, 1991, 420 p.

Miller, Karen Lowry, and Joseph Weber, "Bayer Group Eyes a Lost Continent: America," *Business Week International Editions,* June 6, 1994.

Reier, Sharon, "Elephant Walk," *Financial World,* February 28, 1995, pp. 38–39.

Rosendahl, Iris, "Out Miles, in Bayer," *Drug Topics,* February 6, 1995, p. 54.

—updated by David E. Salamie

Bearings, Inc.

3600 Euclid Avenue
Cleveland, Ohio 44115-2515
U.S.A.
(216) 881-8900
Fax: (216) 881-8988

Public Company
Incorporated: 1928 as Ohio Ball Bearing Co.
Employees: 4,000
Sales: $936.25 million
Stock Exchanges: New York
SICs: 5085 Industrial Supplies

With over 340 stocking branches, seven distribution centers, and 20 service shops in 40 states, Bearings, Inc. ranks as one of America's leading independent distributors of specialty replacement bearings, power transmission components, fluid power products, rubber products, and specialty parts. The bulk of the company's sales are in the maintenance, repair, and operations (MRO) market, but Bearings also services original equipment manufacturers (OEM). Although the company diversified its offerings in the early 1990s, bearings still contributed the largest share of annual sales (49.7 percent) and Bearings, Inc. still controlled about one-fourth of the industrial bearings aftermarket. The firm expected to cross the $1 billion annual sales mark in fiscal 1995 (ending June 30, 1995).

The company does not manufacture a single product. Instead, it carries over 900,000 parts produced by more than 2,500 manufacturers. Over the course of its seven decades in business, Bearings, Inc.'s inventory has grown from about $24,000 in the 1920s to about $200 million in the early 1990s. In addition to moving products from their producers to their consumers, Bearings offers its customers services ranging from inventory management to just-in-time delivery to refurbishment and machining. The company's branches are on call 24 hours a day, seven days a week, ready to service the 25,000 customer emergency calls received each year.

Bearings, Inc. was founded by Joseph M. Bruening in 1928. Orphaned as a toddler, Bruening was raised by an uncle and two aunts in early twentieth-century Cincinnati. He took engineering courses at the University of Cincinnati as a young man, but decided that he needed money more than schooling and dropped out. Bruening took his first job with Standard Parts' Cincinnati division and started a practical education in the area of automotive axles and springs. Dissatisfied with Standard Parts' progress, the young entrepreneur went to work for a customer, Tom Moore, in 1922. Moore's business, called Detroit Ball Bearing Co., had begun selling replacement bearings to auto and truck dealers that year.

Later in 1922, after Detroit Ball Bearing established a Cleveland office, Bruening was assigned to run it. His first few days in the city on the shores of Lake Erie were not pleasant ones. Since he was new in town, Bruening secured a room at the downtown YMCA. While showering that first night, all his clothes and money were stolen. Undaunted, he borrowed some clothes from the "Y" and went to work.

Less than a year after his transfer, Bruening was surprised when Moore offered to sell him the profitable Cleveland office. Aware that Bruening had virtually no capital to invest, Moore proposed to give him half of the profits that the Cleveland branch had brought in up to that point: $2,600. Bruening borrowed thousands of dollars from his uncle and landlady as well, and he was able to pay off the entire purchase price of $26,000 within about eighteen months. The company, renamed Ohio Ball Bearing, made $82,000 in its first year of selling replacement parts for cars and trucks.

Bruening established his first branch outlet in Youngstown, Ohio, in 1927. From that point on, the company's geographic reach grew in an ever-widening circle to include such other major Ohio cities as Akron, Columbus, and Cincinnati. Ohio Ball Bearing established its first out-of-state branch—in Indianapolis, Indiana—in 1937.

From its earliest years, the company positioned itself as a vital link in the distribution chain by cultivating a reputation for unparalleled inventory and service. As Bruening stated in a 1973 company history, "our reason for being is that neither manufacturer nor customer can efficiently stock a full line of replacement bearings or other parts. So we stock hundreds of thousands. . . . And when needed, we get them to the customer first." In the early days, that emphasis on service sometimes meant hiring a local motorcycle dealer to deliver parts. By the 1990s, it meant chartering jets in the middle of the night, if necessary.

Ohio Ball Bearing began offering its services to industrial customers after World War II. The company grew quickly as a result of a string of acquisitions in the 1950s and 1960s that culminated in 1971. In 1952 Ohio Ball Bearing merged with Pennsylvania Bearings, Inc., Indiana Bearings, Inc., and West Virginia Bearings, Inc. The new entity was known as Bearings Specialists, Inc. The company name was shortened to just Bearings, Inc. after a 1953 merger with the Pennsylvania company of the same name. The 1957 acquisition of Dixie Bearings, Inc., Southern Bearings Co., and Bearings Service Co. expanded the distributor's reach as far south as Florida.

Growth through acquisition continued in the next decade. Neiman Bearings Co. and its subsidiaries in Missouri and Illinois, as well as Southern Bearings Service of Kentucky and Southern Bearings Co. of Arkansas, were all added to the firm in 1960. In the late 1960s and early 1970s Bearings, Inc. acquired five companies in the Pacific Northwest. This final series of purchases rounded out Bearings' lengthy acquisition spree and brought it nearly nationwide coverage.

Throughout this period of activity, Bearings sales continued to grow. The company's sales doubled from 1963 to 1973, income tripled over that period, and its number of branches grew nearly twofold. Bruening was still president when Bearings celebrated its 50th anniversary in 1973. By that time, the distributor boasted operations in 25 states.

Although it took Bearings 49 years to achieve $100 million in annual sales, that figure tripled over the course of the ensuing decade, to over $350 million in 1982. Bearings underwent a transformation in the late 1980s, however, that started at the highest levels of management. Struggling under the burdens of recession, competition from imports, stagnant growth in the market for bearings, and entrenched administration, the company's chairmanship changed hands three times in the space of two years. John R. Cunin, who served as chief executive officer from 1982 to 1988 and chairman from 1983 to 1990, retired after a 44-year career with Bearings. He was succeeded by George L. LaMore, a 50-year veteran of the company.

In 1984 Cunin had set a goal of crossing the $1 billion mark in sales within four years. Instead, the company's sales flattened out around the $490 million level from 1985 through 1987, and profits plummeted from $11 million in 1985 to $2.2 million in 1986, rebounding slightly to $6.2 million in 1987. The company resumed its pattern of growth after 1988, when a newcomer, John C. "Jack" Dannemiller, was brought on board. Although Cunin and LaMore had engineered a near-doubling of Bearings' annual revenues from $351 million in 1982 to $630 million in 1989, undeniable changes in the marketplace called for a fresh new face. In 1991 the board of directors elected Dannemiller, a 53-year-old with just over three years at Bearings, as chairman and chief executive officer. A number of analysts praised Dannemiller as a good choice.

Dannemiller immediately embarked on a course intended to revitalize the company. Recognizing that Bearings needed to evolve to meet its customers' changing needs, he instituted a reorganization that included acquisitions, consolidation, diversification, and a transformation of the corporate culture. The company had already added King Bearing, Inc., a California-based industrial distributor, to its roster in a $70.5 million acquisition in 1990. Although the purchase proved a bit difficult to integrate and increased Bearings' debt level in the midst of a recession, it nearly quadrupled the parent company's presence in the western United States and increased overall annual revenues by one-third. The addition of Baldwin Rubber Industries in 1993 augmented Bearings' interests in fluid power control and other rubber products. In 1994 the company traded 196,000 shares of stock for ownership of Mainline Industrial Distributors, Inc. With that acquisition came an extra $34 million in annual sales and additional product lines. Bearings further bolstered its standing in the metropolitan Chicago area with the purchase of five more distribution centers later that year. As a result, the firm's proportion of non-bearings sales increased from about 35 percent to over 50 percent during the early 1990s, and its range of products more than tripled. In light of this variety, Dannemiller considered changing the company's name in 1995. This rapid diversification not only made Bearings a more valuable supplier to its customers, but also gave it a stable of higher-margin products and reduced its exposure to unpredictable business cycles. The acquisitions provided Bearings with the critical mass to win and retain major accounts with Miller Brewing Company, Chrysler Corp., Milliken & Co., and Motorola Inc., all of whom were limiting their rosters of suppliers to those who provided the most comprehensive products and services.

Measures to increase productivity and efficiency included the consolidation of Bearings' distribution centers from 15 in the late 1980s to seven by 1994. Bearings also instituted OMNEX 2.0, an advanced management information system, in 1990. This inventory control software provided instantaneous access to the company's national inventory, and was used in conjunction with an electronic data interchange to facilitate faster, more accurate, and more efficient ordering and billing. Automation not only increased internal productivity, but also helped cut customers' costs and thereby make Bearings that much more indispensable to its customers.

As part of the total quality management (TQM) plan the company adopted under the direction of Dannemiller, Bearings' organizational structure was dramatically slimmed. Regional divisions were reduced from 13 to five, and middle managers were given more authority to operate their territories as they saw fit. The company also created over 1,200 quality improvement teams. Employees logged 200,000 hours of skill training in 1994 alone.

In 1995 Robert Damron of McDonald & Co. Investments Inc. told the *Cleveland Plain Dealer* that the CEO of Bearings "does not just want customers to be satisfied. He wants them to feel so jubilant that they would never think of buying anywhere else." The efforts to improve quality paid off in a variety of ways. Bearings' customer billing process was recognized as a "Best Practice" and became a standard imitated by other companies. Customers ranging from Chrysler Corp. to PPG Industries also recognized the distributor's progress with quality awards. But perhaps the most satisfying rewards appeared at the "bottom line." Sales per employee grew from $204,000 in 1992 to $228,000 in 1994, a 5.8 percent annual increase. Dannemiller set a goal of achieving $300,000 in sales per associate by 1999, an ambitious goal that will demand annual increases in sales per employee of over six percent over five years.

Other financial figures for the company were equally encouraging. Fiscal 1994 profits increased 42 percent over the previous year on a mere 13 percent increase in sales. The company marked its seventh consecutive year of revenue increases and its 30th consecutive year of quarterly dividend payments in 1994. Wall Street recognized this sterling fiscal performance by driving Bearings' stock up from a low of about $18 in 1992 to a high of $37.50 in the third quarter of 1994.

Early in 1995, Dannemiller consummated a joint venture with two other distributors. The three companies proposed to offer industrial customers "one-stop shopping." The International Supply Consortium made Cameron & Barkley Co.'s electrical components, Mcjunkin Corp.'s pipes, valves, and fittings, and Bearings' industrial components available to customers under a unified ordering and billing scheme. Dannemiller told Andrew Osterland of *Financial World* that the cooperative could provide ''90 percent of the repair and maintenance products that most manufacturers need.''

Analysts noted that Bearings' strategy meshed well with economic trends in the mid-1990s. Richard Henderson, an industry observer with Pershing in New Jersey, commented to the *Cleveland Plain Dealer* that the ''strong wind blowing at [Bearings'] back'' was powered by stable prices, industrial productivity initiatives, and burgeoning economic growth. But Robert Damron of McDonald & Co. Investments Inc. warned that pending increases in the price of parts could interrupt the distributor's momentum. Dannemiller, however, clearly did not agree with the latter hypothesis. He contended that he expected Bearings to exceed $1 billion in sales in 1994, and predicted that the company would achieve $2 billion in annual revenues by the year 2000.

Principal Subsidiaries: Dixie Bearings, Inc.; Bruening Bearings, Inc.; King Bearing, Inc.; Mainline Industrial Distributors.

Further Reading:

Bruening, Joseph M., *Keeping Industry In Motion for Fifty Years: The Story of Bearings, Inc.* New York: Newcomen Society, 1973.

Gerdel, Thomas W., ''Bearings Inc. Moving to Faster Track,'' *Cleveland Plain Dealer,* September 13, 1991, p. F1.

Gleisser, Marcus, ''Bearings Sets Sales Target of $1 Billion,'' *Cleveland Plain Dealer,* October 17, 1984, p. B6.

Machan, Dyan, ''Paperwork Slayer,'' *Forbes,* April 24, 1995, p. 128.

Osterland, Andrew, ''What Every Foreman Knows,'' *Financial World,* March 28, 1995.

Sabath, Donald, ''Bearings Inc. Joining 3-Firm Consortium,'' *Cleveland Plain Dealer,* August 2, 1994, p. 3C.

''Taking a New Bearing,'' *Cleveland Plain Dealer,* May 21, 1995, p. I1.

—April D. Gasbarre

Bed Bath & Beyond Inc.

715 Morris Avenue
Springfield, New Jersey 07081
U.S.A.
(201) 379–1520
Fax: (201) 379–9057

Public Company
Incorporated: 1971 as Bed 'n Bath Inc.
Employees: 3,200
Sales: $305.8 million
Stock Exchanges: NASDAQ
SICs: 5719 Miscellaneous Homefurnishings Stores

Bed Bath & Beyond Inc. is one of the largest home furnishing specialty stores in the United States. The company operates a chain of approximately 61 stores that sell such domestic merchandise as bed linens, bath accessories, cookware, dinnerware, kitchen utensils, and small electric appliances. Throughout the company's short history, bigger has proven to be better. In the mid–1980s, Bed Bath & Beyond was a pioneer in the concept of superstores: large, well-stocked specialty shops with prices allegedly comparable to, or lower than, department store sale prices. Some Bed Bath & Beyond stores have over 80,000 square feet of selling floor and offer more than 300,000 different items, stacked literally from floor to ceiling. The company expanded rapidly in the early 1990s on the strength of the superstore concept. It doubled the number of stores under the Bed Bath & Beyond banner and tripled annual sales to $306 million by 1993. More than 60 Bed Bath & Beyond stores were located in 16 states entering the mid-1990s; most of these were located in large metropolitan regions. The company has announced plans to open 40 more stores by 1998.

The driving force behind Bed Bath & Beyond is the partnership between founders Leonard Feinstein and Warren Eisenberg. Both men possessed over a decade of retail experience in 1971 when they formed Bed 'n Bath, a small chain of specialty linen and bath shops in suburban New York. As employees in management positions at Arlan's, a discount chain that fell on hard times during the early 1970s, the two sensed an essential change in retailing trends. ''We had witnessed the department store shakeout, and knew that specialty stores were going to be the next wave of retailing,'' Feinstein told *Chain Store Executive* in 1993. ''It was the beginning of the designer approach to linens and housewares and we saw a real window of opportunity.'' Bed 'n Bath's first two 2,000-square-foot stores were located in high-traffic strip malls and carried such brand–names as Cannon, Wamsutta, and Fieldcrest, as well as a line of lower–priced linens and bath towels.

During the 1970s Bed 'n Bath expanded at a healthy but unremarkable pace, and by 1985 the chain had grown to 17 stores located in New York, New Jersey, Connecticut, and California. During this time, however, a number of similar bath and bed specialty shops had opened. What had begun as a niche market was growing increasingly competitive as retailers sensed a ''cocooning trend'' among baby boomers. Specialty chains such as Linens 'n Things, Pacific Linens, and Luxury Linens sprang up to tap into this new market. Feinstein and Eisenberg opened their first superstore in 1985 in an effort to set themselves apart from the sudden wave of competition that had appeared.

The new superstore was revolutionary in a number of ways. Over ten times the size of Bed 'n Bath's original shop, this 20,000-square-foot outlet offered a comprehensive line of home furnishings in addition to Bed 'n Bath's traditional linens and bath products. While most department stores and specialty shops offered only a few select brands, Bed 'n Bath's superstore offered seemingly every possible color, style, and size of each product. Until this time, most independent home textile retailers either copied department store merchandising techniques or followed the mundane merchandising style used by discount retailers. Eisenberg and Feinstein did neither. Bed 'n Bath, along with chains such as Toys ''R'' Us and Blockbuster Video, became pioneering ''category killers'': large specialty retail outlets that beat their competition by offering virtually every possible product in their specific category at everyday low prices. Other than semi–annual clearances to reduce inventory, the company never held sales. They claimed that their prices were already lower than other stores' sale prices.

In 1987 Eisenberg and Feinstein changed the name of their organization to Bed Bath & Beyond in order to more accurately reflect their superstore format. By 1991 Bed Bath & Beyond had opened seven new superstores in New Jersey, California, Virginia, Illinois, Maryland, and Florida, and expanded two existing stores into the superstore format. Sales reached $134 million that year, generating earnings of $10.4 million. Eisenberg and Feinstein funneled the revenue back into the company.

The company's success was considered unusual for the home products industry. As one analyst said, Bed Bath & Beyond ''took a less than strong category and made it important.'' It did so by making ordinary household products seem exciting, even romantic. Customer service was an essential part of this marketing strategy. The company strove to build word–of–mouth advertising through a unique combination of family atmosphere and attentive customer service. Both management and sales personnel worked the floor, arranging merchandise displays, helping shoppers carry products, and otherwise making themselves useful. According to *Fortune,* even Feinstein and Eisenberg would gather on the floor on Saturday, to ''tidy merchandise and . . . pick up bits of litter.'' Check–out waiting time was reduced by increasing the number of cash registers, and the company developed a policy wherein, if the store was out of a desired product, Bed Bath & Beyond would deliver it to the customer's home, free of charge. Due to this strategy, Bed Bath & Beyond was able to keep paid advertising to a minimum. The company often saturated the market with advertising when a new store opened, then successfully relied on word–of–mouth to keep customers coming in.

Another important aspect of Bed Bath & Beyond's success was its merchandise layout. Related product lines were grouped together, giving the impression that the store was "comprised of several individual specialty stores for different product lines," according to company literature. To encourage impulse buying, seasonal products and other impulse items were arranged up front; further back, products were grouped on enormous vertical displays that reached to the ceiling. Such arrangements were designed to make it easier for customers to locate product and also to reinforced the perception that Bed Bath & Beyond offered an enormous assortment of goods.

Feinstein and Eisenberg also took an unusual hands–off approach to management. Bed Bath & Beyond employed no vice presidents. Instead, store managers were given autonomy to cut prices to meet local competition or to try new marketing plans with the consent of the district manager. Within each store, new departments could be created and existing departments could be expanded or reduced as needed to respond to marketing trends.

This decentralization approach permeated all aspects of Bed Bath & Beyond's management. The company had no central warehouses. Goods were delivered directly to stores, where they either entered on-site inventory areas or went directly to the floor. This greatly reduced inventory costs and also gave store managers greater control over the flow of goods through the store.

These management strategies provided Bed Bath & Beyond with one of the retail trade's strongest return on sales during the early 1990s. Out of every $100 in sales, Bed Bath & Beyond retained $7.36. The company's growth soared in the early 1990s, fueled by its ability to tap into hot marketing trends. Between 1989 and 1993 Bed Bath & Beyond increased its number of stores from 24 to 38 in 11 states.

Bed Bath & Beyond went public on the NASDAQ exchange in June 1992, trading at $17 per share. The company immediately became a Wall Street favorite, fueled by a rush of media coverage and the successful launch of a new Manhattan store. Analysts noted that, given the popularity of the merchandising concept that the company was championing, the timing to go public was ideal. By May 1993, shares were trading around $32 as the company announced record sales for the year: $216.7 million in sales, with earnings of $15.9 million.

As proof of Bed Bath & Beyond's status as a trendsetter, one need only examine the success of its Manhattan store. The store opened in November 1992 in what had been an abandoned, graffiti–covered department store at the heart of a dismal section of the city known as Ladies Mile. At the beginning of the twentieth century, Ladies Mile had been a booming retail center, revered as the place where upscale, fashionable ladies bought their clothing. By 1990, despite its desirable location in the center of Manhattan, the district was a mess. When Bed Bath & Beyond opened, however, it kindled a renaissance of the neighborhood. Within a year, a number of other superstores, including Barnes & Noble books, Today's Man menswear, and Staples, a discount office–supply chain, had also renovated boarded–up old emporiums. Bed Bath & Beyond added 30,000 more square feet to the store and it became the company's flagship store, a site where new merchandising concepts (such as a cafe and the introduction of gourmet food products) are given trial runs.

While Bed Bath & Beyond enjoyed tremendous success during this period in the home furnishings business, competitors sought to erode the company's standing. In the early 1990s, its primary rival, Linens 'n Things, began blatantly imitating its merchandising format. Supported by Melville Corp., a large conglomerate whose financial resources far outstrip Bed Bath & Beyond's, Linens 'n Things operated a chain of 144 stores by 1993 with annual sales around $290 million.

Linens 'n Things, which had utilized an integrated computer system since the late 1980s, enjoyed a tremendous advantage over Bed Bath & Beyond in the inventory management area. In 1993, however, Bed Bath & Beyond installed integrated computer systems in all stores that allowed managers to track inventory, sales, and receivables more efficiently. The new automated system also enabled the company to develop a chain–wide bridal registry that analysts estimated would add another 15 percent to annual sales.

Luxury Linens and Pacific Linens also posed a threat to Bed Bath & Beyond's attempts to venture into new markets. Still, the company enjoyed a 37 percent increase in sales in 1992 as it continued to grow without benefit of acquisitions. Most competitors, on the other hand, relied on expansion through acquisitions to a much greater degree. Sales in the first six months of 1993 increased 43 percent and earnings improved by 47 percent, garnering Bed Bath & Beyond first place recognition in *Chain Store Executive*'s survey of high performance retailers.

In 1994 the company began offering such small electric appliances as coffee makers, hair dryers, toaster ovens, and vacuum cleaners. Other home accessories like gourmet foods, clocks, and lamps were added to the product line as well. This further broadened its customer base and fortified the chain's edge in the retail market.

Entering the mid-1990s, Bed Bath & Beyond notes that none of its competition offers the diversity of products it sells. Moreover, no competitors have been able to achieve the profit margins registered by Bed Bath & Beyond. By 1997 Bed Bath & Beyond hopes to have approximately 100 stores across the United States, and Feinstein predicts that company sales will rise by 30 to 35 percent by that time.

The proliferating number of imitators, however, has created what *Barron's* called "a treacherous environment requiring astute management." Analysts fear that the market will be saturated by the year 2000 and that perhaps Bed Bath & Beyond's impressive earnings have already peaked. They note that by 1994, Feinstein, Eisenberg, and members of their respective families had sold almost five million shares. Nevertheless, Feinstein and Eisenberg remain the driving force behind this company, and together they control over 40 percent of company shares. In addition, the two signed an employment agreement that guarantees their continued management of the company until mid–1997.

Further Reading:

"Bigger Stores, Bigger Profits Boost Bed Bath & Beyond," *Chain Store Executive,* November 1993, p. 21.

Norton, Leslie P., "One Step Beyond," *Barron's,* August 8, 1994, p. 17.

Shoulberg, Warren, "Way Beyond," *Home Textiles Today,* September 6, 1993, p. 1.

Slesin, Suzanne, "It's Fun. It's Romantic. It's Soap and Dish Towels," *New York Times,* November 16, 1992, p. C1.

—Maura Troester

Benjamin Moore and Co.

51 Chestnut Ridge Road
Montvale, New Jersey 07645
U.S.A.
(201) 573-9600
Fax: (201) 573-0048

Private Company
Incorporated: 1883
Employees: 1,700
Sales: $440 million
SICs: 2851 Paints & Allied Products

Benjamin Moore and Co. is a leading manufacturer of high-quality paints, stains, and protective coatings, with operations in both the United States and Canada. From its origins as a family-run paint business, the firm grew into an industry leader, ranking as the fourth largest U.S. paint company and seventh top brand, with a seven percent market share by 1992, according to *Chemical Business,* an industry periodical. By the early 1990s, approximately 3,500 independent dealers in the United States and 1,500 in Canada distributed Benjamin Moore products, ranging from interior and exterior latex and oil-based paints to industrial maintenance coatings, safety-coated industrial enamels, porch and floor enamels, wood stains and finishes, and swimming pool paint, in a broad spectrum of colors.

The company's origins date back to 1883, when Benjamin Moore and his brother, Robert Moore, started up a family-run paint business in Brooklyn, New York. At the time, the paint and coatings industry was still in its infancy; not until the mid-1880s did paint producers move decisively toward bulk production and distribution of their products. Chemical advances in such areas as film-forming compounds, emulsions, and inorganic pigment production helped the growing industry cover more and more ground—and surface area—with increasingly durable and adhesive products. Benjamin Moore rode the wave, growing rapidly beyond the regional market of New York and, within years, across the border into Canada and beyond.

From the outset, the Moore brothers distinguished themselves from the competition by stringently adhering to their slogan: "quality, start to finish." Most other paint manufacturers laid claim to products of comparable quality, but the Moores were unique in their willingness to risk market share by charging premium dollar for truly premium paints. This strategy would eventually pay off; once the company had cornered the market niche that was willing and able to distinguish truly premium quality paints—by such criteria as greater durability, broader color spectrums and pigment quality, and easier application—they could depend on their reputation for continued success. Indeed, into the 1990s, Benjamin Moore paints were typically sold at higher prices than other brands. But they were typically considered top-shelf products, and the numbers continued to show that consumers were willing to pay top dollar to invest in truly protective—and beautifying—coatings for their homes and equipment.

From the outset, Benjamin Moore implemented a distribution strategy that helped maintain its niche appeal to premium-quality paint users and helped separate it from the competition. Into the 1990s, the company sold its products only through independent Benjamin Moore paint dealers. Generally, paint reaches the consumer in one of three main ways. Companies can make private-label paints for retailers; they can sell their own brands in hardware stores, home centers, and decorating stores; or they can operate their own retail stores, selling to consumers and painting contractors. While most companies employ a combination of these methods, Benjamin Moore has adhered to its strict system of certifying specific dealers and selling its products only through them.

Benjamin Moore's other characteristic trademark was the closely guarded nature of its business operations. Two generations after its founding brothers plied their trade, the company continued to guard the details of its internal workings and history. In a 1983 celebration of its centennial anniversary, Benjamin Moore made exception to its administrative secrecy, compiling an in-house brochure titled "100 Years of Progress," which included biographical information on the founders and accounts of the company's early history. Unfortunately, by the 1990s, the company was no longer making this brochure available to the public. Nevertheless, the success of Moore products has delineated a historical narrative for itself.

That narrative described continued growth for the company through the First World War, the difficult Depression years, and into the World War II era. In the mid-1940s, the research and development of latex-based paint products proved beneficial to the paint industry in general. As legislation in various states increasingly controlled solvent-thinned paint products, water-based latex paints became more attractive and more environmentally welcome. Moreover, they were noted for ease of application (and cleanup), a beautiful finish, durability, and outstanding protective qualities. Benjamin Moore capitalized on consumer demand for the new product by introducing its own latex line, which grew into several more specialized lines in the decades that followed. By the 1990s, Benjamin Moore offered a latex product for virtually every application. For exterior finishing, the products included: MoorGlo Latex House & Trim Paint, MoorGard Latex House Paint, Moore's Flat Exterior Latex House Paint, Moore's Latex Floor & Patio Enamel, Moore's Latex Exterior Primer, Impervex Enamel, and Moorwood Vinyl Acrylic Latex Stain. The Moore line of interior latex products included: Regal Wall Stain, Regal AquaGlo, Impervex Enamel, Latex Enamel Underbody, Latex Quick Dry Prime Seal, Latex Urethane Acrylic Finish High Gloss, and Latex Urethane Acrylic Finish Low Lustre.

Having focused efforts on numerous industrial coatings for the war effort, Benjamin Moore was positioned to market related products for civilian and industrial use in the postwar era. In 1948, the company founded its Technical Coatings Co. to formulate and manufacture a complete line of primers and topcoats for general industrial coatings as well as coatings used for both rigid and flexible packaging, vacuum metallizing, wood finishing, and coil stock. Five decades later, that division retained its high standing in the industry and continued to grow, acquiring the general industrial coating business of Cook Paint and Varnish Co. of Kansas City, Missouri, in late 1991.

Moore's move into industrial coatings was just one example of how the company accommodated new trends with its marketing strategies and product lines. The passage of the Occupational Safety and Health Act (OSHA) in 1971 helped set up a whole new niche market of industrial operations seeking quality color-coded coatings to meet the new safety standards. OSHA required that all industries color mark physical hazards, safety equipment locations, and fire and other protective equipment, according to the American National Standards Institute (ANSI) code. Moore transformed those legal restrictions into business opportunities, including OSHA/ANSI-compatible colors in its IronClad Quick Dry Industrial Enamel line of paints.

With the rise of computer technology in the everyday affairs of the 1980s, Benjamin Moore once again adapted to the times, introducing computerized color analysis systems to help its dealers match precise pigments to customers' needs. Previously, dealers had depended on the company's proprietary Moor-O-Matic color matching system, using charts, gradation sheets, and a good measure of eye expertise to match up to 1,600 colors to particular projects. The new computerized system, introduced in the early 1980s, analyzed color specimens to provide a formula indicating the base and the precise types and amounts of colorants to match the sample. The system could match virtually any color, with the exception of certain intense or fluorescent colors beyond the paint pigment spectrum. The computerized system was developed over a seven-year period by Benjamin Moore and Digital Equipment Corp. and consisted of a spectrophotometer (color analyzer) and a minicomputer loaded with color-matching software fine-tuned to Moore's paint products.

In 1985, Benjamin Moore also organized a financing plan that would bring the $24,900 computerized system within the budgets of interested dealers. After making an initial ten percent deposit on a system, Benjamin Moore dealers were offered a four-year payment plan by the company. Maurice Workman, Moore's president at the time, told the *Business Journal of New Jersey* on June 13, 1985 that the computer sales were not income producing for the paint company, but were offered as a means of increasing paint sales for its dealers. The bottom line, however, was beneficial to both Benjamin Moore and those dealers that saw improved sales from the technological sales assistant.

Financial assistance to its certified dealers was nothing new to Benjamin Moore. In the 1960s, the company initiated its Temporary Co-Ownership (TCO) program, which provided minority entrepreneurs with the initial funding needed to open a neighborhood paint store—usually approximately $200,000. As the budding businesses turned profitable, the plan called for them to begin buying back their stock, until they fully owned the operation. After the 1992 Los Angeles riots and the media focus on neighborhood reinvestment projects, Benjamin Moore's long-standing program drew considerable attention—and praise. Moreover, in mid-1992, the company announced that Triad Systems Corp. would provide automated business and inventory management systems for the outlets participating in its TCO program. The system would permit maximum efficiency and productivity at the store level and would also use a telecommunications package to transmit data—inventory, sales figures, etc.—to a centralized collection point. Still, the main objective remained the bottom line: "This is not an altruistic move on our part; this is good business for Benjamin Moore," said Billy Sutton, western division vice-president for the company, in an August 31, 1993 *Lost Angeles Times* article.

Benjamin Moore had expanded its coverage through thousands of independent dealers in the United States and Canada from the 1950s onward. In the late 1980s and early 1990s, however, the company took more aggressive steps to not only expand its national market share, but to position itself for international growth potential. In 1985, the company opened a new plant in Pell City, Alabama, followed in 1991 by another in Johnstown, New York. In order to develop markets in British Columbia and eventually the northwestern United States, the company opened its facility in Aldergrove's Gloucester Industrial Estates (western Canada), replacing the plant it opened in Burnaby in 1964. The plant, outfitted for production of both latex and alkyd trade sales paints, nearly doubled the company's production capacity on the west coast. "The plant is designed as a completely closed loop system, for both water-bornes and solvent-bornes. Nothing will be released to either the sewers or the air," said Ron Hoare, senior vice-president of the plant, in a November, 1991 *Coatings* article.

Such environmental conscientiousness, though not new the Benjamin Moore, saw more stringent implementation in response to new Volatile Organic Compounds (VOC) rules and regulations issued by the Environmental Protection Agency and other agencies since the 1980s. As such rules shifted according to region, Benjamin Moore and other paint producers tailored paint formulations to fit VOC standards for the various jurisdictions, making compliance more difficult, though no less prioritized, for the company. "Paint is really a very small part of the emissions problem," Walt Gozden, technical director of Rohm & Haas' Paint Quality Institute, told *Building Supply Home Centers* in a July 1990 article. "But whether that is fair or not, paint manufacturers and retailers are going to have to comply with existing laws," he added.

Benjamin Moore not only complied with environmental laws, but continued to stand out as a particularly "environmentally friendly" paint manufacturer. When the Technical Coatings subsidiary set up a new facility at its Burlington, Canada site in 1992, for example, VOC considerations were a top consideration. Alastair MacDonald, the plant's technical director, explained in a May 1992 *Coatings* article that the entire industry had moved in the direction of high solids, waterborne and powder coatings to meet environmental regulations. And in mid-1995, Benjamin Moore received a Pollution Prevention Award for its Milford, Massachusetts, facility's source reduction and recycling activities, which had been in operation since the 1970s.

Along with moves toward environmental efficiency, Benjamin Moore prepared for the 21st century by implementing state-of-the-art computerized management tools at all its facilities. In August 1992, the company began a transition from mainframe-based data processing to client-server computing by installing a nationwide network of 17 IBM AS/400s and 150 PCs. The company began using the software to automate its entire manufacturing operations, from order entry and inventory management to formula management and invoicing.

That same year, Benjamin Moore invested approximately $3.5 million in a state-of-the art technical and administrative center in Flanders, New Jersey. The facility housed the company's central laboratories and data processing and engineering departments, as well as a model store for sales training and a "paint farm" for rigorous testing of paint products. "The growth of these organizations, along with our desire to create a corporate training center called for a central facility which could accommodate several interrelated departments," Benjamin Belcher Jr., executive vice-president, noted in *The New York Times* on July 5, 1992.

As both consumers and retailers started looking at painting as a system and not just a product, Benjamin Moore developed increasingly sophisticated marketing solutions into the 1990s. One particularly resourceful marketing tool was a 1993 company publication entitled *A Stroke of Brilliance,* a book packed with information and tips on how consumers could apply color and paints to their decorating needs. Interior designer Leslie Harrington presented her expertise in a readable and, not surprisingly, colorful format. The book addressed common questions about how colors match or complement one another, as well as suggestions for painting projects, which ranged from applying matching paint to shower curtains and bathroom walls, to making painted rugs, decorated stairs, stenciled floors, and achieving specialty wall finishes. The book was distributed nationwide at all authorized Benjamin Moore dealers at a cover price of $11.95.

The company also produced "Fantasy Finishes and Beyond," a video tape, also featuring Leslie Harrington, providing step-by-step instructions and lists of tools, techniques, and types of paint for various finishes and design projects. Video technology was also used to develop the Video Color Planner, a color visualization video system that allowed consumers to experiment with the entire selection of Benjamin Moore paints on a video screen. After selecting from a wide variety of pre-programmed interiors or exteriors—or even scanning in images of their own homes—consumers could use a trackball and mouse to apply test colors and finishes on screen before actually rolling up their sleeves on site.

Benjamin Moore also moved into aggressive television advertising, airing the 1993 "Stroke of Brilliance" campaign comprised of spots featuring Myrna Loy in a scene from "Mr. Blandings Builds His Dreamhouse." The following year, the company adopted a new theme, "We Decorate Your Life," with ads featuring the popular Kenny Rogers tune, "You Decorated My Life." Print ads reflecting the TV spots also appeared in national lifestyle publications including *Better Homes & Gardens.*

Realigning its expanding advertising program, the company discontinued all regional agencies—such as an estimated $2 million to $2.5 million account with Chicago-based Keroff & Rosenberg, which closed in late 1994—and consolidated its advertising with Gianettino & Meredith, in New Jersey. Though Keroff & Rosenberg had helped make Chicago the No. 1 market for the paintmaker, Benjamin Moore preferred to centralize its advertising efforts as much as possible into the 1990s.

In a similar vein, the company's Canadian subsidiary launched an aggressive customized flier campaign to aid in the development of a database and a centralized marketing program. Following up on a similar campaign the previous year, in April 1994 Benjamin Moore Canada mailed four-million customized sweepstakes-promotion fliers to retailers for customer distribution on-site or through the mail. It marked the first step toward collecting names for loyalty programs planned for 1995, according to president Charles deGruchy of Salter deGruchy Christenson, the agency in charge of the campaign. In addition, the data compiles by the campaign was used for profiling the for the creation of models for prospecting, according to deGruchy in an April 18, 1994 *DM News* article.

In the mid-1990s, Benjamin Moore continued to expand its global coverage as well. In April 1994, the company announced the formation of a joint venture with Southern Cross Paints, a paint manufacturer headquartered in Auckland, New Zealand, and its existing subsidiary, Benjamin Moore & Co. (NZ) Ltd. The new company, Benjamin Moore Pacific Limited, manufactured both decorative and industrial maintenance coatings. "This joint venture will enable us to meet the growing demands of our existing customer base as well as provide the newest technologies being developed in the coatings industry," stated David Arnold, sales and marketing of Southern Cross Paints, in *American Paint & Coatings Journal* on May 9, 1994. For Benjamin Moore, the venture extended the company's growing global presence and added to the list of manufacturing locations that it already boasted in the early 1990s: Newark, Boston, Richmond, Jacksonville, Johnstown, Cleveland, Chicago, St. Louis, Houston, Dallas, Birmingham, Denver, Los Angeles, Santa Clara, Toronto, Montreal, and Vancouver, as well as thousands of dealers across North America.

As it approached the 21st Century, Benjamin Moore had positioned itself as one of the leading paint manufacturers in North America and one of the top 500 private companies. While the company remained extremely private in disclosure of its business affairs, its products revealed themselves in full color—and quality—virtually everywhere a consumer might look across the United States and Canada.

Principal Subsidiaries: Benjamin Moore & Co., Ltd (Canada); Benjamin Moore Pacific Limited; Technical Coatings, Inc.

Further Reading:

Applegate, Jane, "Moore's Program Lays the Base Coat For Minority-Owned Paint Stores," *Los Angeles Times,* August 31, 1993, p. D3.

Ballinger, Jerrold, "Benjamin Moore Moves Into Retail Loyalty Programs Via Sweeps Mail," *DM News,* April 18, 1994, p. 21.

''Benjamin Moore and Co. Celebrating Success,'' *BC Business,* July 1993, p. 51.

Berger, Amy, ''Benjamin Moore Uses Computers to Analyze Colors,'' *Business Journal of New Jersey,* June 13, 1985, p. 20.

Casson, Clarence, ''Environmental Issues Cloud Paint Strategies,'' *Building Supply Home Centers,* July 1990, p. 138.

Harrington, Leslie, *Color: A Stroke of Brilliance; A Guide to Color & Decorating with Paint,* Montvale, N.J.: Benjamin Moore & Co., 1993, 125 pp.

Larson, Mark, ''Benjamin Moore to Build Paint Factory in Dixon,'' *The Business Journal-Sacramento,* February 4, 1991, p. 3.

McComb, Eileen, ''Technical Coatings Announces Acquisition of Cook Paint and Varnish of Kansas City, Mo.,'' *Business Wire,* December 12, 1991, p. 1.

''Moore Enters Joint Venture with New Zealand Producer,'' *American Paint & Coatings Journal,* May 9, 1994, p. 9.

Moran, Robert, ''Benjamin Moore: A New Coat of IS—Paint Maker Moves Away From Traditional DP Model,'' *Information Week,* June 8, 1992.

''New B.C. Plant Might Sell Paint to Northwest United States; Benjamin Moore and Co.; British Columbia,'' *Coatings,* November 1991, p. 25.

Randel, Susan, ''The Countertrend of House Paints; Chemical Focus,'' *Chemical Business,* October 1992, p. 6.

Scianna, Mary, ''MacDonald: Thirty-Five Year Veteran Proud of Company He's Grown With,'' *Coatings,* May 1992, p. 35.

Wedlock, Sara, ''Paint and Coatings Manufacturers Go for the Green,'' *Modern Paint and Coatings,* March 1995, p. 8.

—Kerstan Cohen

Bergen Brunswig Corporation

4000 Metropolitan Drive
Orange, California 92668
U.S.A.
(714) 3854000
Fax: (714) 9787415

Public Company
Incorporated: 1969
Employees: 4,243
Sales: $7.5 billion
Stock Exchanges: New York
SICs: 5122 Drugs, Proprietaries & Sundries

Bergen Brunswig Corporation is the nation's largest supplier of pharmaceuticals to the managed care market and the second largest wholesaler to the retail pharmacy market. In addition, Bergen Brunswig is the only pharmaceutical distributor that also supplies medical and surgical products on a national basis. Since its incorporation in 1969, it has been on the leading edge of technological advances in electronic data interchange (EDI).

Lucien Napoleon Brunswig, the founder of Bergen Brunswig, was born in 1854 in France, the son of a country doctor. While Lucien felt little inclination to pursue the healing art of his father, he did develop an interest in some day providing the drugs that were vital to patients' treatment. When political turmoil in France in the 1870s prompted Lucien, and many other young French people, to emigrate, he arrived in the United States unemployed and nearly penniless. In 1871 the 17-year-old Lucien was accepted as an apprentice to a U.S. druggist.

Apprenticeship meant more than learning the drug trade; it also entailed sweeping floors, cleaning out the cages of the druggist's pets, and attending to other menial tasks. Despite his meager income, Lucien Brunswig's hard work and thrift helped him save enough to open a retail drug store in Atchison, Kansas, when he was 21 years old. His drugstore was such a success that he sold it profitably and took the train as far southwest as it would go, to a few miles outside of Fort Worth, Texas, then a small, dusty town of a few hundred people.

Brunswig's Fort Worth drugstore, serving both retail and wholesale, flourished. By 1883, less than five years after he had opened the store, his business reported $350,000 in annual sales. In 1882, George R. Finlay, the owner of a well-established wholesale drug firm in New Orleans, invited Brunswig to join him as a partner. Lucien Brunswig readily agreed to sell his own drug business and become Finlay's business partner in New Orleans. Finlay's firm, Wheelock-Finlay, became Finlay and Brunswig. Upon Finlay's death in 1885, Lucien Brunswig took over the entire wholesale drug operation and settled into New Orleans, where he served as a police commissioner of the city for four years. In 1887 Brunswig took on a partner, F.W. Braun.

The following year, Brunswig became interested in expanding West, setting his sights on faraway Los Angeles, California, a growing town of 30,000. Brunswig dispatched Braun to Los Angeles to open one of the few wholesale drug companies in the area, the F.W. Braun Company. Business opened in Los Angeles on the first floor of a two-story adobe house. Pharmaceuticals were not only sold over the counter, but a few salesmen also ventured out to visit druggists and procure their orders, which could be filled within two or three weeks. After a year, F.W. Braun Company was flourishing and moved into the Old Post Office Building next-door, the first of a series of major expansions.

In 1890, while Lucien Brunswig remained in New Orleans, he ordered the opening of what would become a prosperous branch of F.W. Braun in San Diego, California, a city even smaller, dustier, and with fewer drugstores than Los Angeles. The coming of the Spanish-American War was a boost for the drug business nationwide, and Lucien Brunswig's profits continued to soar. In 1903, deciding that the future of his company lay in the West, Brunswig sold his profitable New Orleans establishment and moved with his family to Los Angeles to preside over the continued expansion of his business. In 1907, he bought out Braun, and his business was renamed Brunswig Drug Company.

With headquarters in Los Angeles, the wholesale drug enterprise was soon expanded to include branches in Phoenix and Tucson, Arizona, as well as a short-lived store in Guaymas, Mexico. As a result of World War I, Pacific Coast business boomed, far beyond Brunswig's wildest dreams. In 1922 when other U.S. businesses were experiencing a slump, Brunswig's sale of drugs as well as cosmetics, a recent and lucrative addition to the drug line, reached a record high level. In that same year, Brunswig decided the company needed a manufacturing plant that would house a laboratory and produce cosmetics. Goods that were manufactured in the Brunswig labs eventually made their way to the Philippines, Japan, and the Hawaiian Islands.

A wealthy businessman, Lucien Brunswig had also become an ardent bibliophile, art collector, and philanthropist. In 1927 he presented to the University of California at Los Angeles more than 1,000 books for its library of French language and literature. Moreover, with the onset of the Great Depression, Brunswig's company opened soup kitchens to feed the desperately poor; his own business did not suffer significantly during this time. Brunswig died in 1943, two years after his retirement; he did not live to see his kingdom expand tremendously, as it did in the years following World War II.

Roy V. Schwab succeeded Lucien Brunswig as president of the Brunswig Drug Corporation, moving the company's headquarters in 1947 to Vernon, California. By then, the Brunswig Drug Corporation had divested itself of its manufacturing plant and laboratories, concentrating solely on the wholesale distribution of pharmaceuticals. In fact, Brunswig was considered the most advanced wholesale drug operation in the United States, although by no means the largest. It was, for example, the first wholesale drug company in the United States to introduce computerized punchcards for keeping track of inventories.

In 1949, the 61-year-old Brunswig Drug Corporation merged with the Coffin Redington Company of San Francisco, the first of numerous significant mergers. The company expanded rapidly in California. In 1950 it opened its San Jose division; in 1951, its Sacramento division; and in 1954, its San Bernardino division. In 1952, it acquired the Smith-Faus Drug Company, and by 1960, it had 14 divisions in the southwestern United States.

In the eastern United States, another drug company benefited from the postwar economic boom. In 1947 Emil P. Martini founded and became the first president of the Bergen Drug Company based in Hackensack, New Jersey. A graduate of the New Jersey College of Pharmacy in 1923, Martini opened his first retail pharmacy in Hackensack five years later. A second pharmacy was acquired at the height of the Depression, and a third was acquired in 1937. A well-established member of the community and president of the New Jersey State Board of Pharmacy, Martini helped establish a wholesale drug distribution company in 1947 named after the county of Bergen in which they lived. The success of the Bergen Drug Company was phenomenal, in part because of the insatiable demand for the wonder drugs of World War II, including such antibiotics as penicillin. Despite the growing sales volume, the company continued to offer same-day service.

With the 1955 death of Emil P. Martini, Sr., leadership of the company was turned over to Martini's son, Emil P. Martini Jr. The Bergen Drug Company then began rapidly expanding and acquiring other wholesale drug companies. In 1956, Bergen acquired Drug Service Inc. of Bridgeport, Connecticut. Between 1957 and 1958, Bergen operations were started in three California cities, Fresno, San Francisco, and Covina. In 1959, it became the first company in the nation to use computers for inventory control and accounting purposes. By the 1960s, Bergen Drug Company was among the largest wholesale drug distributors in the United States, supplying 5,000 pharmacists and hospitals.

In May 1969 Martini successfully negotiated the purchase of Brunswig Drug Corporation. The latter had sought to buy the former until Brunswig Drug managers realized that financially it made more sense to have Bergen buy their company, as the price-earnings figures of Bergen's stocks were more advantageous. The name of the new company would be the Bergen Brunswig Corporation.

Several acquisitions followed. In 1970 alone, the Bergen Brunswig Corporation added 12 drug companies and laboratories to its fold, transforming itself into a truly national drug distribution business. Head of the Bergen Drug Company since 1956, Martini, who had graduated with a degree in pharmacy from Purdue University, was given his original job in his father's firm with the understanding that he was to learn the drug distribution business from the bottom up, which he did. Under his direction and that of his younger brother, Robert E. Martini, also a pharmacist and vice-president of the company, the Bergen Brunswig Corporation became in the 1970s one of the most modern drug distribution companies in the United States.

Bergen Brunswig revolutionized the trade in 1971 when it pioneered the electronic transmission of purchase orders to Eli Lilly & Co. In the early 1970s, Bergen Brunswig introduced the handheld computer scanner, with which pharmacists could scan the barcodes on merchandise. Stock was then reordered on the basis of the information collected by the scanner. The inauguration in the late 1970s of an advanced computer system automated the prescription department still further, connecting hospitals and chain pharmacies electronically to Bergen Brunswig's distribution centers. Soon the majority of orders could be transmitted to Bergen Brunswig via telephone lines, and in the 1980s, satellite communication replaced conventional telephone lines. One hundred years after the opening of the F.W. Braun Company wholesale drug store in Los Angeles, the distribution time of drug orders was down from two to three weeks to less than 24 hours.

The 1980s saw the explosion of pharmaceutical and health care product demand, contributing significantly to Bergen Brunswig's phenomenal growth. In 1981 the president of the National Wholesale Drug Association noted a 17 percent increase in the sales of pharmaceuticals in the first half of that year. The stock value of Bergen Brunswig Corporation increased between 1977 and 1981 by 50 percent, while its net earnings in the three-year period of 1987 to 1990 increased 316 percent, with an average annual growth rate of 25 percent. The aging of the U.S. population had something to do with this success, as did the popularity of its two biggest selling drugs, Zantac, for the treatment of ulcers, and Epogen, used in kidney dialysis treatment.

Despite the considerable increase in the number of its customers—10,000 by 1990—Bergen Brunswig could still guarantee next day service by means of its computer system. Bergen Brunswig supplied software to some 300 hospitals, thereby linking them to the company's computer-driven distribution and pricing system. This equipment helped Bergen Brunswig become the largest supplier in the United States of pharmaceuticals to hospitals. In addition, the company attracted customers through its Good Neighbor Pharmacy plan, which catered to the particular needs of independent pharmacies.

The development in the 1980s of a new generation of automated distribution centers speeded up service and delivery to the point where Bergen Brunswig had become the model for drug distribution companies nationwide, although it was second-largest in the drug distribution industry. The corporation's new distribution facility in Corona, California, processed an order every three seconds—with 100 percent accuracy—of any of the 2,500 most popular pharmaceuticals or health care products. The company then focussed on getting closer to the customer—the pharmacist or store manager—in order to anticipate needs to such a degree that the customer might never have to place an order. Toward that end, Bergen Brunswig monitored the customer's stocks and automatically replenished supplies. The automated distribution system enabled Bergen Brunswig and all other wholesale drug companies to process three times as many orders as previously.

The 1980s also saw the development of another line of products, which resulted from Bergen Brunswig's acquisition in 1982 of Commtron, Inc., a national distributor of home videos as well as 4,000 consumer electronic products. By 1990 Commtron, a 79 percent owned subsidiary of the Bergen Brunswig Corporation, became the nation's number-one distributor of videos, with distribution centers and headquarters in Des Moines, Salt Lake City, and Chicago. With 1,000 employees, Commtron's sales in 1990 increased 17 percent over the previous year. However, in June 1992, Bergen Brunswig sold Commtron, in an effort to return its focus to its core pharmaceutical operations. Number two video distributor Ingram Entertainment acquired Commtron for $78.3 million.

Leading the company into the 1990s was Robert Martini, company president and CEO, and Emil Martini Jr., the chairman of the board. Later, Robert Martini took over the position of chairman, and Dwight A. Steffensen became president and chief operating officer. In addition, pharmacists occupied many of the company's top management positions.

In the early 1990s, Bergen Brunswig, like many pharmaceutical and health-care wholesalers, was caught in a margin squeeze, as the public outcry over soaring health-care costs kept drug prices from increasing. In fact, according to industry statistics, gross profit margins declined every year since 1989 because the drug wholesaling industry continued to be very competitive on pricing, and there were reductions in the rate of drug price inflation over recent years. During this time, Bergen Brunswig went through some restructuring including staff reductions, a move to more efficient warehouse facilities, and the elimination of duplicate operating systems resulting from mergers. The company indicated that it saved in excess of $20 million annually from its restructuring. In spite of industry trends, Bergen Brunswig was the only company in the drug wholesaling industry to post an increase in gross profit margins in the December 1994 quarter.

Analysts attributed Bergen Brunswig's success during this critical time to careful management decisions and smart acquisition moves. In 1992, Bergen acquired pharmaceutical distributor Durr-Fillauer Medical Inc. for $484 million. Durr-Fillauer was a national supplier of medical surgical products to hospitals, clinics, and alternate site healthcare facilities. In addition, the company acquired Southeastern Hospital Supply Company and Professional Medical Supply Company. In July 1995 Bergen signed an agreement to acquire Colonial Healthcare Supply Co., one of the ten largest full-line distributors of medical and surgical products in the country. Each of these acquisitions complemented the Durr Medical operations and expanded their presence nationally in this area. Durr Medical became the fourth largest medical-surgical distributor in the United States.

Joint ventures and agreements during the early and mid-1990s made Bergen Brunswig a more visible force in the worldwide pharmaceutical industry. In December 1994, Bergen Brunswig signed a five-year, sole source pharmaceutical distribution agreement with Columbia/HCA Healthcare Corporation, the nation's largest healthcare services provider, operating 195 hospitals and 125 outpatient centers in 34 U.S. states, England, and Switzerland. The total contract was expected to generate $2 billion in revenues for Bergen Brunswig over the life of the agreement. In addition, the company signed a five-year agreement with Safeway Stores Inc. to be its primary supplier of pharmaceuticals, pharmacy-related items, and selected over-the-counter products. The contract was expected to generate over $1 billion in revenue for Bergen over five years. Safeway operated 1,068 stores in the United States and Canada at the time and was the third largest retail grocery chain in North America.

Also known as a technology leader in the distribution industry, Bergen Brunswig focused on offering value-added services to its customers. In July 1994, the company introduced AccuSource, a multimedia communication, product information, and electronic ordering system for retail pharmacy customers. Developed in conjunction with Apple Computer, the program allowed pharmacies to look up items by category, list substitutions available for products, see special pricing, or communicate with a local Bergen Brunswig division through e-mail. The service also provided personalized information so pharmacies could view statistics such as their own net sales, prescription volume, or product mix. In just four months, Bergen received over 2,000 signed contracts for AccuSource, and it represented Apple's largest multimedia project for a single company. Other state-of-the-art services included OnCall*EDI, a fully-integrated on-line ordering system for the institutional pharmacy, and QuikNet, a fully functional electronic system for ordering, managing, and tracking compliance of medical and surgical products for clinics and hospitals. Moreover, the Bergen Brunswig Drug Company, a wholly owned subsidiary of the Bergen Brunswig Corporation, had converted to paperless billing several years before and was constantly refining its funds transfer and information management systems.

Expressing confidence and optimism in their letter to shareholders in the company's 1994 annual report, Martini and Steffensen attributed much of the company's success to its work force, noting that employee "resourcefulness, efficiency and innovation" resulted in "listening to our customers and creating programs and services to help them stay ahead of the competition and better manage their bottom line." Judging by the company's progress over the years, Bergen Brunswig Corporation was ready to face the new century as a leader in the competitive pharmaceutical supply and wholesale markets.

Principal Subsidiaries: Bergen Brunswig Drug Company; Alternate Site Distributors, Inc.; Durr Medical Corporation.

Further Reading:

Barrett, Amy, "Bergen Brunswig: Time to Climb on Board?," *FW,* April 14, 1992, p. 14.

"Bergen Brunswig Begins to Heal," *Forbes,* November 22, 1993, p. 212.

Fay, John T., *NWDA 1876–1986: Centennial Plus Ten,* Alexandria, Vir.: National Wholesale Druggists' Association, 1987.

Meilach, Dona Z., "At Home & On the Road, Pharmaceutical Distributor Uses Variety of Large-Screen Devices," *Computer Pictures,* May/June 1993, p. 14.

Wiley, Karen, ed., *Centennial Sampler: 1888–1988,* Orange: Calif.: Bergen Brunswig Corporation, 1988.

—Sina Dubovoj
—updated by Beth Watson Highman

Berlitz®

Berlitz International, Inc.

293 Wall Street
Princeton, New Jersey 08540
U.S.A.
(609) 924-8500
Fax: (609) 683-9138

Public Subsidiary of Benesse Corporation
Incorporated: 1989
Employees: 3,885
Sales: $300.2 million
Stock Exchanges: New York
SICs: 8299 Schools & Educational; 7389 Business Services Not Elsewhere Classified; 2741 Miscellaneous Publishing

Berlitz International, Inc. is a languages services firm providing language instruction, cross-cultural training, translation services, and publishing products in 33 countries throughout the world. For language instruction, the company employs its proprietary Berlitz Method, which avoids tedious memorization exercises and grammar drills in favor of a conversational, usage-driven approach to virtually all living languages. Berlitz's publishing division produces pocket-size travel guides and language phrase books, as well as bilingual dictionaries, trade paperback travel guides, and self-teaching language guides from audio cassettes to interactive compact discs. The company's translation services provide technical translation, interpretation, software localization, electronic publishing, and other foreign-language-related services. In 1989, Berlitz Languages, Inc. and related divisions were acquired by Macmillan Co.—a leading publisher and subsidiary of the media magnate, Maxwell Communication Corp. plc (MCC)—and renamed Berlitz International, Inc. When MCC began to falter at the end of 1991, MCC sold a majority stake of Berlitz to Fukutake Publishing Co., Ltd., a leading Japanese publisher specializing in correspondence classes. Under the parentage of Fukutake, Berlitz underwent a major restructuring, designed to "ensure consistent, profitable growth for the long term . . . and meet the growing, worldwide demand for language services," according to company chairman Soichiro Fukutake in his 1993 Letter to Shareholders. Soon thereafter, Fukutake changed its name to the Benesse Corporation. Though the company's parent shifted abruptly in the early 1990s, Berlitz stuck firmly to its own corporate identity—and language specialty—as it prepared for the 21st century.

Berlitz origins date back to 1878, when Maximilian D. Berlitz (1852–1921) founded his own language school in Providence, Rhode Island. Fluent in Greek, Latin, and six European languages, Berlitz was teaching at a small local college when he hired an assistant, Nicholas Joly, from France. According to one account, the assistant spoke virtually no English when he arrived. When Berlitz fell ill and was unable to provide classroom supervision over a period of several weeks, Mr. Joly conducted class strictly in French. When Berlitz recovered, he discovered that the students had made remarkable progress in French. Berlitz's main tenet of language instruction—the transfer of usage by actually using nothing other than the language in question—thus gained credibility, providing the impetus for development and fine-tuning of the young school's trademark pedagogy, the Berlitz Method.

Though Berlitz was convinced that his "direct" method of language instruction was the most effective available, it was initially regarded suspiciously by the public and the academic community. Starting with the first greeting by the instructor, the Berlitz Method dictated that only the target language was to be spoken in class. Emphasis was placed on the spoken word, with students learning to read and write only what they had already learned to say and understand. In the place of formal grammar instruction, students absorbed a grammatical system naturally, by using it. Above all, to develop fluency, students learned to think in the new language, not to translate—to associate new words with objects and ideas, rather than with the distractingly familiar words of their mother tongue. In order to encourage students in the use of the target language, instructors typically employed question-and-answer techniques to prompt dialogue while expanding vocabulary.

However unconventional, the young company, known as the Berlitz School of Languages, produced results that simply couldn't be ignored; as the growing number of Berlitz-trained students continued to learn languages in an efficient and enjoyable manner, the school expanded. By the turn of the century, an explosive tourist industry prompted Berlitz to develop travel guides, self-teaching materials, and interpretation services to meet this growing demand. Through both world wars, the number of Berlitz schools multiplied with growing demand for language skills.

After World War II, Berlitz seized emerging opportunities in language training and translation services brought on by multinational companies expanding their business around the world. Such expansion was catapulted by the rise of computer information systems starting in the 1970s. With the advent of digitized communication networks, increasing amounts of information could be conveyed almost instantaneously between virtually any points on the globe, intensifying the need—and the market—for effective cross-cultural and cross-linguistic communication. Moreover, the 1980s saw the crumbling of key international trade barriers, as markets in the former Soviet Union, China, and various developing nations increasingly moved toward free trade. Indeed, the company's 1993 annual report described cutbacks in Western European nations that were experiencing economic stagnation. Meanwhile, the company aggressively moved into rapidly growing markets in Central and Eastern European countries, establishing new facilities in the Czech Republic, Slovakia, Poland, and Eastern Germany. A

December 5, 1993 article in *The Warsaw Voice* heralded the arrival of a new Berlitz school in Warsaw and plans for another in February, as well as other schools in cities like Poznan, Cracow, and Gdansk. To exploit global markets in the 1990s, Berlitz also opened new language centers in Brazil, Colombia, and Venezuela, as well as Mexico, which saw new language-training needs with the passage of NAFTA.

From the 1980s onward, Berlitz's language instruction division increasingly developed options and additions to its classroom instruction facilities. The Berlitz Study Abroad (BSA) Program offered students a complete travel package and the opportunity to study their new language in its country of origin. The Berlitz Jr. program provided special foreign language teaching service for U.S. elementary, middle, and high school students both ''on site'' at schools or camps and at the Berlitz Language Centers. For slightly older students, Berlitz acquired the Language Institute for English (L.I.F.E.) in 1988, providing intensive English instruction, recreational opportunities, and accommodations to foreign students on campuses in Boston, New York, Miami, Orlando, San Diego, San Francisco, and Chicago.

Berlitz developed several products and programs to combine both language and social skills in tandem. The company also expanded on its popular Cross-Cultural Division, designed to instruct students in business and social etiquette and day-to-day activities to supplement language skills. In 1994, the company acquired Cross-Cultural Consultants of Brooklyn, New York, to ensure a stronger future in that growing market. Led by noted author and lecturer Dean Foster, the division held seminars and briefings designed to sensitize businesses to the intricate social, political, and cultural issues that can determine a company's effectiveness in foreign markets.

In the spirit of a skilled language teacher, the company itself listened to the talk around it and continued to develop linguistic solutions to accommodate changing market trends. Joining forces with the University of Phoenix in 1991, for example, Berlitz put together a custom-designed language program for McDonnell Douglas Helicopter Co., which wanted the program to enhance its employees global competitiveness.

In 1995, Berlitz's language instruction division responded to the lifestyle needs of contemporary language enthusiasts by introducing Club Berlitz, a network of groups that enabled members to speak the foreign language of their choice with groups of people at similar proficiency levels. Participants honed their language skills while engaging in activities ranging from international dinner parties to cultural evenings, theme events like plays and movies, and study abroad programs. ''Club Berlitz reflects the growing interest in the study of language and culture for both business and personal use,'' said Hiromasa Yokoi, vice-chairman, chief executive officer, and president of Berlitz International in a March 20, 1995 *Business Wire* article.

Berlitz's dedication to world languages for ''both business and personal use'' spurred the development of two other business segments: publishing and translation. Since the early 1970s, Berlitz Publishing produced language and travel-related publications recognized internationally for their accuracy and user friendliness. By the 1990s, the division was responsible for more than 1,000 titles, ranging from a European Menu Reader to inexpensive pocket paperbacks and state-of-the-art interactive CD-ROMs.

In order to maintain its stature as a premier, single source provider of language services, Berlitz Publishing continued to develop innovative products into the 1990s. A 1991 joint venture with Sphere Inc. (doing business as Spectrum Holobyte), resulted in the co-development of a language learning game based on CD-ROM technology. The game ''El Grito del Jaguar,'' or ''The Cry of the Jaguar,'' taught users Spanish language and Mexican culture through an adventurous computer-driven challenge, setting the ground for similar projects in other languages. That same year, Berlitz's parent company, Maxwell Communications Corp., in conjunction with the European industrial and electronics giant, N.V. Philips, announced a joint venture publishing company, Maxwell Multi Media. The new company planned to produce and sell self-teaching language courses for the home, office, and school using interactive Compact Discs (CD-I) as well as other new media formats.

Though Berlitz would leave the Maxwell empire within a year, some of the strategy from the Philips venture would contribute to later developments. In 1993, for example, Berlitz Publishing Co. signed a licensing agreement with Sierra On-Line Inc., through which Bright Star Technology, a wholly-owned Sierra subsidiary, would develop, manufacture, and market a new CD-ROM-based foreign language and culture series called ''Berlitz Alive!'' Using patented lip-synching technology and animated personal tutors, as well as Berlitz's teaching methodology, Bright Star launched its first foreign-language educational series, ''Japanese Alive!,'' in September 1993. ''Combining Sierra's interactive multimedia technology with Berlitz's language content, name recognition and proven learning methodology opens new markets for our educational products, expanding into adult education and foreign language,'' said Alan J. Higginson, president of Bright Star Technology, in an August 4, 1993 *PR Newswire* article.

Riding the growing wave of digital media, Berlitz also moved onto the internet in 1995, as it assumed management of Prodigy, Inc.'s Foreign Languages bulletin board. On-line customers could gain information about a foreign land, talk in a native tongue, secure translation services, and obtain instant information on all Berlitz products and services.

Into the 1990s, the company's translation segment, Berlitz Translation Services (BTS) maintained its reputation as a world leader in technical documentation translation and software/multimedia localization, as well as full production capabilities in desktop publishing and graphics, audio visual services, and simultaneous and consecutive interpretation.

Founded in 1984, BTS quickly gained a top reputation for its accuracy and its ability to integrate linguistic services and versatile project management. Starting in the late 1980s, the translation segment greatly expanded its international scope through a series of acquisitions, including: the Institute for Fagspneg in Copenhagen (June 1989), Able Translations Ltd. in Baldock, England (Fall 1990), Kayer Coll. Technical Translators in Sindelfingen, Germany (December 1990), Nordoc A/S (1991), and Softrans International Limited (1991). By the mid-1990s, the

BTS International Network provided translation-related services in more than 37 locations across 16 countries.

In the late 1980s and early 1990s, Berlitz underwent several dramatic reorganizations that seemed to threaten the company's stability but that ultimately left it in a strong position to enter the 21st century. In 1989, Berlitz's main business divisions—Berlitz Languages, Inc., Editions Berlitz, S.A., Berlitz Publications, Inc., and other affiliates—were acquired by Macmillan Co., a U.S. based publishing house and subsidiary of the global media magnate, Maxwell Communication Corp. plc (MCC). The new entity was renamed Berlitz International, Inc. With the unexpected death of Robert Maxwell in late 1991, much of his media empire crumbled and fell into the hands of bankruptcy courts, casting doubt over Berlitz's future. Berlitz, however, insisted that it maintained control of its assets and operated independently of the Maxwell chaos. Two days after Maxwell's death, MCC sold its 56 percent stake in Berlitz for $265 million to Fukutake Publishing Co., Ltd., a leading Japanese publisher specializing in correspondence classes, which had already purchased a 20 percent stake in Berlitz Japan in 1990. By 1992, Fukutake's share in Berlitz had grown to 67 percent, with the remaining stock held by public shareholders. Fukutake, a leading Japanese publisher of correspondence courses and other educational materials, combined its resources with those of Berlitz to provide optimal language services worldwide.

Fukutake planned to boost its services throughout the world, with special emphasis on regions of Asia where Berlitz was not as well positioned. With services in Taiwan (since 1989) and South Korea (since 1991), Fukutake announced plans to begin test marketing in China in the mid 1990s. "Economic development and a rise in willingness to learn supplement each other," the company's president said in a November 21, 1994 article in *The Nikkei Weekly.*

Under the management of Mr. Soichiro Fukutake, chairman, and Mr. Hiromasa Yokoi, vice-chairman, CEO, and president, Fukutake took aggressive steps to expand its services in tandem with those of Berlitz, as well as to streamline operations while leveraging the use of technology in the classroom toward greater customer satisfaction. In 1995, the company launched a campaign to maximize its customer services across the board. As part of that effort, in 1995 Fukutake changed its name to the Benesse Corporation. The new name combined the Latin words "bene" and "esse," meaning well-being, to drive home the company's commitment to support customers' personal aspirations for a better life, according to company materials.

In 1995, Berlitz launched an identity-refreshing campaign of its own. The company introduced a new, clean-lined logo and a new, company-wide tagline, "Helping the World Communicate." Berlitz's identity-building efforts intended to reinforce not only its position as the world's premier provider of language services in general, but its tendency to set world standards in those services.

Indeed, with its new Japanese parent, Berlitz would apply some of its own lessons in language instruction and cross-cultural skills to continue its impressive trajectory of growth. Whether Professor Maximilian D. Berlitz's trademark methods were good, bon, bueno—or any other derivation thereof—their merit continued to bolster the success of this well-spoken company.

Principal Subsidiaries: Berlitz Language Instruction, Berlitz Translation Services, Berlitz Publishing.

Further Reading:

"Berlitz & Prodigy Team On Foreign Languages," *Newsbytes News Network,* February 9, 1995.

"Berlitz International Announces Launch of Club Berlitz, First Worldwide Language-Culture Club," *Business Wire,* March 20, 1995.

Berlitz International Inc., "Corporate Backgrounder," Princeton: Berlitz International Inc., 1995.

"Berlitz International Reports Results For Fourth Quarter," *Business Wire,* March 8, 1995.

"Berlitz Reaches Accord to Split From Macmillan," *The New York Times,* December 23, 1992, p. D4.

Bragg, Rebecca, "How The Berlitz Language Empire Came Into Being," *The Toronto Star,* February 8, 1992, p. F2.

Cox, James, "Berlitz Won't Hear of Bankruptcy Talk," *USA Today,* December 31, 1991, p. 3B

Diemniewska, Ewa Kielak, "The Language Revolution: Berlitz Leading the Charge," *The Warsaw Voice,* December 5, 1995.

Fay, Natalie, "Berlitz Japanese; Bright Star Technology's Berlitz For Business Japanese CD-ROM Training Program; Software Review," *MacWeek,* August 1, 1994, p. 45.

Imada, Toshihiko, "Education Firm Burnishes Global Image; Berlitz Parent Fukutake to Adopt New Name," *The Nikkei Weekly,* November 21, 1994, p. 10.

"Maxwell Communications and Berlitz Form Multimedia Publishing Joint Venture with Philips For Language Learning," *PR Newswire,* March 25, 1991.

"McDonnell Douglas to Improve Global Competitiveness Through Second Language Program," *Business Wire,* May 13, 1991.

Sears, David, "Berlitz Interpreter; Data Base of Foreign Words; Software Review," *Compute!,* March 1993, p. 122.

"Sierra On-Line Signs Licensing Agreement With Berlitz Publishing Co.," *PR Newswire,* August 4, 1993.

—Kerstan Cohen

Big Bear Stores Co.

770 W. Goodale Boulevard
Columbus, Ohio 43212
U.S.A.
(614) 464-6500
Fax: (614) 464-6780

Wholly Owned Subsidiary of Penn Traffic Co.
Incorporated: 1933
Employees: 11,500
Sales: $1.39 billion
SIC: 5411 Grocery Stores

Big Bear Stores Co., a wholly owned subsidiary of Penn Traffic Co., is a regional grocery chain operating 65 supermarkets, principally in Ohio, but also in West Virginia. The company also operates 17 department stores and 12 Big Bear Plus stores, which are combination department/grocery stores.

Shortly after King Kullen launched the supermarket idea in New York, Wayne E. Brown founded Big Bear Stores in Columbus, Ohio. The first supermarket in the Midwest, Big Bear was located in a former skating rink. At 47,000 square feet, it was huge by contemporary standards. Shoppers liked the variety such a store could offer, with the butcher, baker and grocer located in one place. Big Bear likely pioneered the idea of one-stop shopping: its premiere store included a drugstore, restaurant, candy department and shoe repair store in addition to foodstuffs.

In the heart of the depression, homemakers welcomed the low-prices made possible by the store's bulk purchases. Moreover, items were attractively displayed so that the customer could pick them off the shelves without the help of a clerk. Traditional store owners disparaged the supermarket concept, believing that customers would steal more than they would buy if given free access to the shelves. Although shoplifting did become a significant problem for supermarkets, the concept of do-it-yourself shopping was here to stay. Big Bear drew 200,000 people on its opening day; and the company opened up its second store in a Columbus piano factory just one year later.

From the start, Big Bear utilized print and radio advertising as well as in-store promotions. In 1936, shoppers could win $5 to $25 by mixing six words with "Big Bear" and "low prices" to create a store slogan. In 1937, Brown and other supermarket owners formed The Supermarket Institute, a professional association for supermarket operators. Through the association, the stores were able to develop and share concepts and conveniences such as motorized check out counters, wire shopping carts, automatic exit doors, fluorescent lighting, bakeries, and other in-store departments.

During the 1940s, the company went public and continued to grow by building new stores. It also bought out and merged with Miller Stores Co., in 1943. In 1948, Big Bear joined with other supermarkets to form Topco Associates. Located in Skokie, Illinois, the corporation employed scientists and researchers to develop and acquire products for distribution.

In 1954, Big Bear purchased Harts discount stores, which operated stores in Lexington, Kentucky, and Evansville, Indiana. In addition to operating the chain, the company drew upon the Harts merchandise to increase the mix of non-grocery items in the Big Bear stores.

By 1956, Big Bear operated 21 supermarkets in Ohio cities with sales of over $50 million, and became a trend-setter in supermarket design. The chain introduced a widely imitated layout in which the perishable departments were located in the middle of the store, with low display fixtures to highlight them, while the store overall was painted in a spectrum of pastel colors. Big Bear was also the first in the nation to use the new IBM 305 Ramac accounting machine.

In 1957, Big Bear built its first stores outside of Ohio, in West Virginia. The company also operated a trading stamp subsidiary. Like most grocery stores, Big Bear awarded customers a number of stamps depending on how much money they spent; the stamps could then be redeemed for a variety of items. The popularity of the stamps declined throughout the industry, however, dropping off sharply in the late 1960s until the practice disappeared altogether by the late 1970s.

Keeping in step with the industry, Big Bear continued to grow steadily. During the 1960s, the chain increased by a few stores per year, doubling its size by the end of the decade. The company was taken private in 1973, the same year its founder Brown retired. Brown, who was ill, owned 20 percent of the company's shares and held voting control through another class of stock. With his cooperation, the chain was purchased through a leveraged buyout by Oppenheimer Partners, New York, which then became Odyssey Partners. Approximately $50 million in equity was purchased from shareholders. A great deal of debt was assumed, but no holdings were sold to pay it off; all debt was scheduled to be repaid by 1991. The company remained intact and management was not changed. At that time, Michael Knilans, who had joined the company as a bag boy in 1942, assumed the presidency.

Larger chains such as A&P, Pick and Pay, and Fisher Foods opened in Columbus during the 1970s and early 1980s, but were driven out while Big Bear maintained its hold on 30 percent of the Columbus market. Continuing its pattern of slow and steady growth, from 1976 to 1981, Big Bear built ten Big Bear stores and one warehouse market. It opened three warehouse stores and two limited assortment outlets in existing buildings. By 1981, the chain consisted of 58 Big Bear supermarkets, four Grocery Warehouses, and two Box Stores.

By the 1980s, the chain had developed a variety of store styles suited to various communities. For scattered populations, there was the combination Harts Family Center/Big Bear Stores. Warehouse stores fared better in small cities, while middle-income areas still required conventional supermarkets. The conventional stores ranged from 32,000 to 42,000 feet and included scratch bakeries and complete delis, with stock varying according to the needs of the community where the unit was located; this size unit continued to make up the majority of Big Bear stores built since the 1980s.

In 1981, in response to the growing white collar suburbs north of Columbus, the company introduced the more cosmopolitan Great Big Bear. At 42,000 feet, it carried almost 20,000 items and was aimed at the upper-middle-class consumer, offering such specialty products as fresh scallops, imported cheeses and a natural food boutique. The first unit's opening day—featuring a Miss America runner up, a talking robot, and 110 year-old lobster—attracted 5,000 people. The store quickly became one of the highest-volume markets in the Columbus area, reaching $300,000 a week in sales, and cutting into the sales of area natural food stores.

With 63 stores and 27 Harts discount department stores, the company had earned $8.6 million in fiscal year 1982 on sales of $652 million. In 1983, the company went public for the second time. In order to fund expansion and the remodeling of older units, Big Bear offered 1.75 million common shares, with the current holders offering about 25 percent of their stock for sale.

In 1985, Big Bear had sales of $650 million and Forbes ranked it number one among 27 regional supermarkets chains in return on equity and important factor in profitability. The next year, Cub Foods entered the Columbus market. That store had pushed under competitors in other markets with its low prices and warehouse style. Instead of trying to beat Cub at its own game, Big Bear capitalized on its competitor's weaknesses. The company stepped up customer services at the store which would compete with the Cub unit, doubling employees there to 155. The newly remodeled store was able to maintain its sales, and Big Bear maintained its hold on one-third of the Columbus grocery market with its 27 area stores. The chain also operated 35 stores outside the Columbus area, including seven in West Virginia and over 30 discount department stores. In fiscal 1988, the company had a net income of $16.3 million on sales of $930 million.

With no national competitors in their market areas, Big Bear was fiscally healthy and well-managed when Penn Traffic Co., which already operated several regional grocery chains, moved in on it. In December 1988, Penn had acquired a 14.5 percent stake in the coming, for about $45 million through a privately negotiated transaction with Value Equity Associates I L.P. of New York. With the financial backing of Salomon Brothers, Penn offered to purchase the remaining shares at $35 a share, or about $296 million altogether. Big Bear rejected the offer and adopted a shareholder rights plan in an effort to deter the unwanted take over, which could cause loss to the company's current stockholders. The company retained Goldman, Sachs & Co. as a financial adviser, in order to buy time to review the situation and develop alternatives. Despite the company's efforts, Penn was able to purchase the chain in 1989. However, the price was raised to $38.60 a share, or a total of $290 million. At that time, Knilans retired and John E. Josephson, formerly senior vice-president of finance and CFO of Penn Traffic, stepped into the presidency.

Heading into the 1990s, Big Bear continued its time-tested strategy of slow expansion through stores tailored to the surrounding community. The newest trend was toward larger stores with even more mixture between general merchandise and traditional supermarket fare. In 1992, there were 11 Big Bear Plus stores, a format created by tearing down the wall in complexes where a Harts and Big Bear had operated side by side.

In 1993, Big Bear built a store in Grove City, Ohio, which was their largest to date at 52,000 square feet of selling floor. Yet the company planned to build a store twice that size, around 120,000 square feet. The new design clustered perishable goods in the front of the store, hoping to tempt shoppers as soon as they entered. This "power aisle" included a service deli, bakery, and produce, seafood and meat departments. The new bakery included a $20,000 machine which scanned photographs and reproduced them on cake with food coloring. The rest of the perimeter included dairy, soft drinks, a walk-through beer cooler, frozen food, a full service band and a flower shop.

As for the rest of the store, groceries and the pharmacy were located in the center, along with a huge variety of non-food items, including clothing, stationary, craft items and picture frames, calculators, cameras, compact discs, sporting goods, toys and appliances such as coffee makers, toasters and hand-held vacuums. The non-food items were integrated with food items. For instance, toys were possibly placed next to cold cereal. Altogether, the new store offered 80,000 different items.

In 1993, after 30 stores participated in a year-long Nielsen study on the effectiveness of the system, Big Bear decided to extend the Vision Value Network to all 71 of its stores. The network provided a touch-sensitive screen offering instant discounts, and terminals were placed at the check-writing stand of check-out counters. The machine also produced paper coupons and handled credit and debit card transactions. Big Bear planned to use the system to promote its private label goods and in-store departments, as well as promote the major brands which were already hooked into the network.

In 1993, Big Bear Stores, along with P&C Food Markets of Syracuse were merged into Penn Traffic's other retail division, RDQ. The move was made in order to give the parent flexibility; at that time, loans could be made for a single entity instead of for three separate ones and legal and accounting functions were consolidated. Big Bear continued its slow but steady expansion strategy and maintained its strong regional standing heading into the late 1990s.

Further Reading:

"The Anatomy of a Successful LBO," *Progressive Grocer,* July 1987, p. 24.

Bennett, Stephen, "Big Bear Sharpens Its Claws," *Progressive Grocer,* December 1992, pp. 34–43.

"Big Bear, P&C Merged into Penn Traffic," *Supermarket News,* April 26, 1993.

''Big Bear to Go Public For the Second Time in Its 49-Year History,'' *Wall Street Journal,* June 16, 1983.

Nannery, Matt, ''Big Bear Set to Expand Vision Value Chainwide,'' *Supermarket News,* March 22, 1993.

Schaeffer, Larry, ''There's Plenty of Spunk in the Old Big Bear,'' *Progressive Grocer,* May 1986, pp. 199–200.

Tanner, Ronald, ''Columbus Discovers the Great Big Bear,'' *Progressive Grocer,* October 1981, pp. 111–15.

Wartzman, Rick, ''Big Bear Rejects Penn Traffic Bid, Adopts Rights Plan,'' *Wall Street Journal,* December 27, 1988.

—Elaine Belsito

Birmingham Steel Corporation

Suite 300
1000 Urban Center Parkway
Birmingham, Alabama 35242-2516
U.S.A.
(205) 970-1200
Fax: (205) 444-3352

Public Company
Incorporated: 1983
Employees: 1,554
Stock Exchanges: New York
Sales: $702 million
SICs: 3312 Blast Furnaces & Steel Mills

Birmingham Steel Corporation is the second-largest publicly held minimill in the United States. The company operates more than a dozen steel production facilities across the United States including four steel minimills, two rod and wire plants, and two steel distribution centers. Birmingham Steel's four minimills rank among the most efficient in the nation, producing a ton of steel in 1.4 worker-hours. Its mill products are made from recycled scrap metal and include reinforcement bars (used in the construction of concrete buildings and highways) and steel rounds, flats, squares, angles, strips and channels (used in the manufacture of a variety of products including farm equipment, safety walks, ornamental furniture, and fences). Birmingham Steel also produces high-quality steel used to manufacture components for the automobile, welding, aerospace, and fastener industries through a subsidiary, the American Steel and Wire Corp.

Birmingham Steel was incorporated in 1983 by the New York-based venture capital group AEA Investors Inc. At that time, the U.S. steel industry was suffering financially from declining construction start-ups and intense competition from newer, more efficient European and Japanese mills. Encumbered by outdated technology, many mills were unable to compete. Throughout the 1970s and into the 1980s, both large and smaller mills eliminated jobs and many mills closed. Birmingham Steel was founded on the belief that some of these smaller mills were greatly undervalued, and if they were purchased and renovated, they could turn a profit. Birmingham Steel was to operate under the ''market mill'' concept, a manufacturing and marketing strategy developed as an alternative to that of the large U.S. steel mills. Also known as mini-mills, these new operations were smaller, more efficient and more specialized than traditional U.S. mills, and were designed to be flexible and responsive to changing market demands.

Birmingham Steel's first acquisition was the Birmingham Bolt Co., which operated a pair of rebar and merchant product minimills in Birmingham, Alabama, and Kankakee, Illinois. The investment was risky, saddling the company with $45 million in debt and two mills that were outdated and inefficient. ''We had two of the oldest, meanest, most terrible mills in the nation,'' Birmingham's chairman and chief executive officer James A. Todd told *Iron Age* in 1993. But Todd, former chief of Birmingham Bolt, knew how to gain the confidence of investors. He met regularly with Wall Street analysts to apprise them of the progress of his company, and in early 1985 he negotiated a deal in which AEA Investors converted Birmingham Steel's $4 million in bonds to equity and put up another $12 million to fund the acquisition of the Mississippi Steel division of Magna Corp. With the acquisition of Mississippi Steel, Birmingham Steel was able to close its environmentally unsound melt shop in Kankakee and supply the mill with billets from its Alabama and Mississippi plants. Several months later, Birmingham Steel went public on the New York Stock Exchange, raising $28 million which was used to pay down debt from the Mississippi Steel and Birmingham Bolt purchases and to upgrade existing facilities. In May 1986 the company made a convertible debenture offering which netted another $30 million.

Within three years, Birmingham Steel found itself in a comfortable position to further pay down debt, renovate existing minimills, and begin shopping for others. In the summer of 1986, the company acquired Intercostal Steel Corp., a privately held minimill located in Chesapeake, Virginia, for $6.5 million in cash. Birmingham Steel began operating the company under the name Norfolk Steel Corp. and announced its intent to capture some of the Northeastern rebar market segment that opened when industry giant Bethlehem Steel Corp. decided to close its Pennsylvania rebar plants. The market looked promising. The new Norfolk Steel had already captured two former Bethlehem accounts, and Birmingham Steel planned to renovate the facilities to increase production fourfold.

Not content to remain a regional producer, Birmingham Steel began searching for other minimills to acquire. ''We're still hungry and we still have money,'' Todd told to *American Metals Market* after the Norfolk purchase. Birmingham Steel next acquired Northwest Steel Rolling Mills Inc. of Seattle, a minimill with a 150,000 ton capacity and annual sales of $40 million. Less than two weeks later, Birmingham Steel purchased Judson Steel Corp. of Emeryville, California. The two mills provided Birmingham Steel with a foothold in the West Coast rebar and merchant markets, generating a total capacity of 300,000 tons per year. The Judson purchase was solidly in keeping with Birmingham Steel's strategy of purchasing undervalued mills: the entire operation had been slated for demolition by its Australian parent company, Peko-Wallsend Ltd., and the land had been earmarked for commercial development.

In the two years after it went public, Birmingham Steel's sales increased fivefold, reaching $218 million in 1987. Its annual steel output hit 648,000 tons, up 49 percent from the 436,000 tons shipped in 1986. Sales of roof support systems also grew at steady rate, and Birmingham Steel held over 50 percent of the market.

Modernization of its milling equipment was essential to maintain Birmingham Steel's competitiveness in an industry plagued by overproduction, and the company strove to continuously upgrade its production facilities. A new melt shop furnace was installed in its Birmingham plant that increased billet capacity to 275,000 tons; new casters and reheat furnaces in the company's Kankakee plant greatly improved productivity there; and the addition of more efficient rolling equipment at the company's Jackson plant led that operation to ship a record 1,100 tons per employee. More troublesome was Birmingham Steel's Norfolk operation. Production was expanded from 80 hours per week to a full 24-hour cycle in 1987, and management soon realized that the plant's efficiency was greatly in need of improvement. The company made some initial improvements that year and allocated $5 million for new rolling mill equipment in 1988.

Shipments, sales, and earnings reached record levels in 1988, fueled primarily by efficient operation of the Seattle, Jackson, and Birmingham plants. Over one million tons of steel were shipped in 1988, sales grew by 59 percent to $344 million, and earnings reached $24.7 million. The company streamlined operations by selling outdated steel fabricating facilities at its Seattle and Norfolk plants and a rebar coating facility that was part of its Kankakee operations. Capital improvements begun at its Kankakee and Norfolk mills were also completed.

1989 was a difficult year for Birmingham Steel. Share prices rose to 29⅝ on the strength of plans to take the company private through a merger with Harbert Corp., then plummeted to 14½ when the merger fell through. Per-share earnings dropped by 58 percent as steel prices slipped and scrap prices remained high. Earnings were further deteriorated by losses due to the troublesome start-up of a new melt shop at the Kankakee plant, costly repairs at the Norfolk plant, and an aborted joint venture to manufacture flat-rolled steel with Proler International Corp. and Danieli & C. Officine Meccaniche of Italy. Regarding the decision to terminate the proposed joint venture (which cost Birmingham Steel $1.5 million), Todd reported to *Financial World* in 1990, "We better take care of what we know how to run before we try to run something that is a new business for us."

Management regrouped in 1990 and focused on expanding existing facilities. Its Jackson melt shop received a $40 million expansion, and plans were made to relocate Salmon Bay's downtown Seattle rolling mill to the site of its suburban melt shop, making the property under the mill free for sale or development. Birmingham Steel began planning the construction of a $125 million minimill near Phoenix. The Phoenix plant would replace the company's aging Emeryville minimill, the land under the Emeryville plant would be sold, and profits from the sales would go toward the construction of the new minimill.

For the first time in Birmingham Steel's history, net sales declined over the previous year, from $442.5 million in 1990 to $407.6 in 1991. The sales drop was caused by recessions in both the West Coast and Northeast markets. This led to a two percent decline in steel shipments and a five percent drop in the selling price of steel. Earnings were eroded as the company closed its Emeryville and Norfolk plants and a melt shop near Seattle. "We probably made a mistake when we bought the mill at Norfolk," Todd conceded to *Iron Age* in 1993. The Northeastern rebar market remained slow throughout the late 1980s, and this factor, combined with ongoing mechanical problems, squeezed profits. "Economic conditions dictated that the company could not tolerate unprofitable operations," Todd reported in the company's 1991 Letter to Stockholders.

Birmingham Steel boosted production at its four remaining minimills and opened steel distribution centers on both the East and West coasts to serve clients who had previously been served by the closed operations. The company also purchased Seattle Steel Inc. and by late 1993 had consolidated its Seattle operations in a new $50 million mill. Plans continued for the new minimill to be built near Phoenix, but a site had not been chosen.

Despite strong competition in the steel market, per share earnings improved greatly in 1992 as Birmingham Steel's continuous modernization program substantially lowered operating costs. The company netted $133 million in a common stock offering, invested $56 million in capital improvements, and reduced its debt by $51 million. By 1992 Birmingham Steel had also begun to sell steel abroad, exporting $24 million worth of steel overseas. In 1993 the company shipped a record 1.6 million tons of steel, 233,000 of which was exported overseas, and sales grew to $442.3 million, but earnings dropped 43 percent from the previous year.

In November 1993, Birmingham Steel purchased American Steel and Wire Corp., an Ohio-based producer of wire and steel rods, for $134 million. American Steel and Wire (ASW), which enjoyed a reputation as the nation's highest-quality producer of steel rods and wire products, provided Birmingham Steel with an entry into the coiled rod and wire markets of the automotive, appliance, and aerospace industries and also greatly reduced its dependency on the highly competitive rebar market. Birmingham Steel began construction of a $110 million, state-of-the-art rolling mill which would boost ASW's annual output from 500,000 tons to approximately 1.1 million tons upon its completion in late 1996.

Birmingham Steel had much to celebrate as it entered its second decade of operation. Sales in 1994 jumped by 59 percent to $702.8 million. Common equity stood at $439 million, and its debt-to-capital ratio was lower than at any time in its history. In early 1995, Birmingham Steel sold its mine roof support business to Excel Mining Systems, Inc., a move that permitted the company focus exclusively on steel production and sales. Birmingham remained committed to capital improvements, outlining a $650 million renovation program through the year 2000. The company was also well positioned to diversify into other markets and continued to investigate potential joint-ventures into the flat rolled steel segment.

Principal Subsidiaries: American Steel and Wire Corp.

Further Reading:

Barrett, Amy, "Outlasting Murphy's Law," *Financial World,* October 2, 1990, p. 46.

"Birmingham Steel: A Minimill Powerhouse," *Institutional Investor,* January 1995, p. 4.

"Birmingham Steel Plans to Buy Facility from USX Corp.," *Wall Street Journal,* December 29, 1989, p. B5.

McManus, George J., "A Whiz at Marketing," *Iron Age: The Management Magazine for Metal Producers,* August 1993.

"Why a Big Steelmaker is Mimicking the Minimills," *Business Week,* March 27, 1989, p. 92.

—Maura Troester

Bohemia, Inc.

85647 Highway 995
Eugene, Oregon 97405
U.S.A.
(503) 744-4600
Fax: (503) 683-7679

Public Company
Incorporated: 1942 as The Bohemia Lumber Company
Employees: 2,120
Sales: $291.7 million
SICs: 2421 Sawmills & Planning Mills, General; 2436 Softwood Veneer & Plywood; 2493 Reconstituted Wood Products; 5031 Lumber, Plywood & Millwork; 4789 Transportation Services, Not Elsewhere Classified; 4011 Railroads—Line-Haul Operating; 0811 Timber Tracts

Until its assets were acquired by Willamette Industries Inc., Bohemia, Inc. was regarded as one of the more progressive forest products companies in the United States, leading the way in the efficient of use of harvested timber. With facilities in Oregon and northern California, Bohemia was involved in manufacturing laminated beams, lumber, plywood, particleboard, and numerous other wood products. The company also maintained a small presence in the marine construction market.

For L. L. ''Stub'' Stewart and his brother Faye Stewart, 1970 marked a transitional point in their tenure as operators in the U.S. forest products industry. Much had changed since they had assumed control of The Bohemia Lumber Company in 1946 and much would change in the years after 1970. One era would witness the rise of their forest products company, the other its demise; together the two time periods relate a story representative of the roller-coaster ride that many of the country's lumber company owners took during the second half of the 20th century. For the two brothers, the good times came before the bad, beginning with their acquisition of The Bohemia Lumber Company following World War II.

The Stewart brothers purchased Bohemia Lumber at a propitious juncture in the 20th century. The wave of prosperity which followed the war's conclusion rejuvenated many industries, including the construction industry, which was the largest single market for companies like Bohemia Lumber. The demand for new housing, which had remained stagnant during the Depression and World War II, sharply increased during the postwar years, making the harvesting and manufacture of timber a lucrative business. To meet this demand, the number of lumber mills in operation soared; however, as more and more new lumber companies entered the business, competition within the industry became increasingly severe.

Small, under-capitalized lumber companies were forced to shut down, causing a precipitous drop in the number of mills in operation throughout the country. From 1950 to 1970, the number of lumber mills in the United States plunged from more than 50,000 to less than 35,000 as the lumber industry underwent two decades of significant change. In the new business environment that arose during these decades, the logging and manufacture of timber became an industry in which only those companies able to make efficient use of raw materials could effectively compete. Integrated mills which used as much of a log as possible became crucial to the success of a lumber company; as a result, the manufacture of plywood, particleboard, and paper became integral elements of a lumber company's profitability. Well-financed companies which were able to incorporate new logging and manufacturing techniques into their operations flourished, while others dropped by the wayside.

In Oregon, where the Stewarts presided over their business, market conditions were particularly harsh. Although the state ranked as the largest timber producing region in the country from 1950 to 1970, the number of lumber mills plummeted during that same period from 1,455 to a mere 450. Despite operating in the midst of so much economic turmoil, Bohemia Lumber took the necessary steps survive and prosper in the highly competitive wood manufacturing industry.

Taking its name from a nearby mining district where James ''Bohemia'' Johnson had discovered gold in 1863, Bohemia Lumber was established in 1916 near Cottage Grove, Oregon, to produce Douglas fir lumber. Three years after its formation, LaSells Stewart, the father of L.L. and Faye, purchased a one-quarter interest in the company. The company remained in LaSells's partial control until after World War II, when Stewart's sons acquired the lumber concern. Graduates of Oregon State University's prestigious School of Forestry, L. L. and Faye Stewart were well-equipped for the defining developments set to sweep through their industry. While the company posed few economic challenges during the first 15 years of their tenure, the brothers' managerial talents would ultimately be put to the test as the lumber market became more competitive. Together they would diversify Bohemia Lumber's interests, steering the company toward more profitable fields and reducing its dependence on one aspect of business.

In 1956, Bohemia Lumber began making moves to compete in increasingly aggressive lumber markets. The Stewart brothers built a new sawmill in Culp Creek, Oregon, to replace the company's original mill; further, they also began acquiring other timber-related interests to complement their sawmill operations. In the mid-1960s, Bohemia Lumber assumed control of Cascade Fiber—an ailing particleboard manufacturer based in Eugene, Oregon—through a management contract. Eventually, Cascade Fiber became a wholly owned division of Bohemia Lumber, when the company purchased the remaining 50 percent interest. This acquisition quickly became one of Bohemia Lumber's more profitable divisions and it added diversity to the company's range of products where none had existed previously. Bohemia Lumber continued to expand in 1969 when it began constructing a laminated beam plant in Saginaw, Oregon. Completed in 1971, the plant could produce 50,000 board feet a day using wood stock the company had previously supplied to other laminated beam manufacturers. Ultimately, laminated beams became Bohemia Lumber's mainstay product.

The same year that Bohemia Lumber began construction of its laminated beam plant, L. L. and Faye Stewart broadened the scope their operations considerably with the acquisition of The Umpqua River Navigation Company. The Umpqua River Navigation Company was involved in the sand and gravel business, in dredging, and in the construction of marine jetties—which were necessities on the Pacific Coast, where few natural harbors existed along the region's numerous navigable rivers. A passenger and freight hauler earlier in the century, Umpqua River Navigation Co. was primarily engaged in marine construction projects awarded through government agency contracts. The addition of Umpqua River Navigation Co., which was formed into Bohemia Lumber's Umpqua Division, provided an immediate boost to profits and gave the Stewart brothers a well-rounded, vertically integrated company to surmount the obstacles that lay ahead in the 1970s and 1980s.

While these moves toward diversification were being executed during the 1960s, significant ownership changes were being effected as well. In 1960, U.S. Plywood-Champion Papers acquired a 50 percent interest in Bohemia Lumber, which it bought back in 1967 in anticipation of Bohemia becoming a publicly owned company. When Bohemia Lumber finally went public in late 1968, the event also signalled a name change from The Bohemia Lumber Company to Bohemia, Inc.

With its new name and the solid backing of its initial stock offering, Bohemia exited the 1960s propelled by unprecedented financial growth and buoyed by its recent diversification into laminated beams and marine construction. Sales increased 50 percent in 1969, jumping from $20.1 million to $30.3 million, but more impressive was Bohemia's profit growth, which soared 900 percent from $507,000 to $4.5 million. Much of Bohemia's financial growth was attributable to its strategic operating philosophy during the 1960s, which elevated the company's stature in the lumber industry from a basic sawmill operator to that of a more sophisticated forest products company with diversified interests in profitable lines of business. By incorporating innovative technologies, such as hauling logs by helium balloons and adopting advanced manufacturing techniques, L. L. and Faye Stewart had created a company able to compete in the lumber industry's new arena.

By the beginning of the 1970s, Bohemia was regarded as one of the more progressive manufacturers of lumber, plywood, and particleboard in the country. The company did much of its own logging, primarily from publicly owned stands of old growth Douglas fir, and operated four plants within Oregon that produced products sold domestically to wholesalers, distributors, retail yards, industrial users, and government agencies. Bohemia also enjoyed a sizeable international demand for its harvested lumber, shipping its softwood lumber to such countries as England, Italy, Switzerland, Germany, Canada, Holland, Belgium, and Australia.

Annual sales, which had hovered around $10 million before the company's diversification and expansion program during the 1960s, approached $60 million annually during the early 1970s and amounted to $130 million annually by the end of the decade. Fueling this growth was a continued commitment to expansion and to using as much of each log as possible. When L.L. and Faye Stewart had acquired the company, using 40 percent of a log was considered efficient. As competition intensified and new technologies emerged, such a percentage could no longer sustain a lumber company's profitability. As one lumber industry official observed, the drive for efficient and total use of harvested timber was analogous to using every part of a hog except its squeal, a goal that Bohemia had demonstrated considerable success in achieving. During the late 1970s, Bohemia stunned the logging industry when it achieved 100 percent log usage by developing a patented extraction process to obtain commercially marketable products from material formerly regarded as waste—Douglas fir bark. From bark, the company was able to produce a wide range of products, including vegetable wax, cork, and extenders for plywood adhesives.

With pioneering manufacturing techniques such as its bark by-product extraction process, Bohemia was able to secure an enviable position in the lumber industry, a position that was bolstered by its steady expansion. By 1974 Bohemia's expansion included the purchase of a 50 percent interest in the Oregon Pacific and Eastern Railway, the construction of a planning mill, and the acquisition of a sawmill in Dexter, Oregon. Concurrent with the completion of its bark conversion plant in 1976, Bohemia constructed a mill designed to process small logs harvested from second growth timber and acquired Yuba River Lumber Company and Brunswick Timber Products, which gave the company three additional sawmills and more than 26,000 acres of timberland.

Despite such impressive gains in the 1970s, Bohemia suffered three years of debilitating losses in the early 1980s when the lumber industry experienced an economic downturn. Between 1982 and 1985, the company racked up operating losses of more than $16 million, while long-term debt rose an alarming 150 percent to $47 million. Chiefly to blame were rising interest rates, which crippled the construction market, and cheap timber from Canada and the southern United States; but even more deleterious to Bohemia's long-term stability was its reliance on publicly owned timber stands. At this time, Bohemia obtained about 70 percent of its timber from public land. This practice proved catastrophic during the recession, for the company had to honor long-term contracts with state and federal agencies even though the markets for its timber products had dwindled. Bohemia continued to be plagued financially by this miscalculation long after economic conditions improved.

In an effort to combat its financial slide during the early 1980s, Bohemia contracted out its logging operations—a move that saved the company $3.5 million a year—and renegotiated its labor contract with employees. In addition, Bohemia sold two inefficient sawmills and a plywood plant, helping the company to recover from its financial malaise. However, as time progressed and environmental concerns intensified, Bohemia's future profitability came into question. Those same public lands which had caused Bohemia so much trouble in the early 1980s now presented a new problem, in that they were becoming the subject of a contentious debate between environmentalists and federal legislators.

The environmental debate surrounding the harvesting of government-owned timber created a new business climate in which two types of lumber companies emerged: large forest product companies owning sizeable private timberlands, and small forest product companies that could operate in an entrepreneurial fashion. Although Bohemia was Oregon's eighth largest forest products company and the state's 13th largest public company, it did not own enough private land or capital to compete with the country's largest forest products producers; likewise, Bohemia was too large and owned too much to be run like an entrepreneurial organization. Acknowledging the company's precarious and vulnerable position, Bohemia's management announced in late 1990 that the company's assets would be liquidated. Less than a year later, Willamette Industries Inc., a $2 billion forest products company also based in Oregon, purchased Bohemia's assets for $122 million, ending its 75-year existence as a lumber company.

Further Reading:

Astman, Fred, "Bohemia Inc.," *Wall Street Transcript,* September 19, 1977.

Beauchamp, Marc, "Almost Out of the Woods," *Forbes,* October 5, 1987, p. 198.

"Bohemia Enters Discussions," *Wall Street Journal,* March 13, 1989, p. A4.

"Bohemia Inc.," *Wall Street Journal,* July 2, 1990, p. C14.

"Bohemia Inc. Completes Purchase," *Wall Street Journal,* December 9, 1980, p. 44.

"Bohemia Inc. Terminates Talks," *Wall Street Journal,* April 10, 1989, p. B5C.

"Bohemia Plans to Sell All Assets in 18 Months," *Forest Industries,* March 1991, p. 8.

"Boise to Sell 11 Plants to Willamette," *New York Times,* May 16, 1992, p. 40.

Brown, Craig, "Drive to Survive," *Oregon Business,* August 1991, p. 29.

Fisher, Roger V., "Bohemia, Inc.," *Wall Street Transcript,* April 30, 1973, p. 32,760.

Mayhew, Harold D., "Bohemia Inc.," *Wall Street Transcript,* November 21, 1983, p. 71,919.

"1969 Will Be Tough to Beat for Bohemia Lumber Co.," *Investment Dealers' Digest,* December 2, 1969, p. 34.

Raphael, Marvin S., "The Bohemia Lumber Company," *Wall Street Transcript,* January 12, 1970, p. 19,176.

Stewart, L.L., "Bohemia Inc.," *Wall Street Transcript,* October 14, 1974, p. 38,419.

Taylor, John H., "The Ducks Are Flying," *Forbes,* July 20, 1992, p. 124.

"Two Buyers Found for Bohemia Assets," *Forest Industries,* September 1991, p. 6.

"Unloading Ships by Balloon May Be More Than Hot Air," *Wall Street Journal,* March 15, 1973, p. 10.

"Willamette to Buy Bohemia," *Wall Street Journal,* August 15, 1991, p. C12.

"Willamette Industries Gets 94.5 Percent of Shares in Offer for Bohemia," *Wall Street Journal,* September 27, 1991, p. B10.

—Jeffrey L. Covell

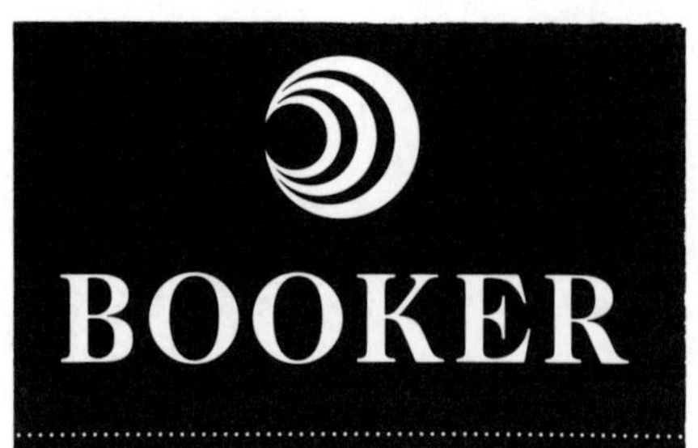

Booker PLC

Portland House
Stag Place
London SW1E 5AY
United Kingdom
(0171) 411 5500
Fax: (0171) 411 5555

Public Company
Incorporated: 1900 as Booker Brothers, McConnell & Co. Ltd.
Employees: 21,049
Sales: £3.72 billion (US$5.94 billion)
Stock Exchanges: London
SICs: 5140 Groceries & Related Products

Chairman Jonathan Taylor has called Booker PLC ''one of very few British companies to have achieved a successful metamorphosis from a colonial plantations company to a modern international business.'' One constant, however, has characterized the company's nearly 200-year evolution: a focus on food products and their distribution. In the early 1990s Booker managed the United Kingdom's biggest food wholesaler, a leading food processor, and the world's largest breeder of broiler poultry. The company also maintained a small book royalties division that awards the annual Booker-McConnell Prize for fiction. Booker's products and services are sold in more than 70 countries in Europe, the Americas, Africa, and the Far East, but the vast majority (82.3 percent) of its 1994 operating income was generated in the United Kingdom.

Booker's history is inextricably linked to Europe's imperialist past. When the Congress of Vienna divided the northeast coast of South America among Great Britain, the Netherlands, and France in 1815, enterprising merchants from those countries moved quickly to exploit the region's natural resources. The Booker brothers—Josias, George, and Richard—were among these entrepreneurs. Josias was first to make the trip overseas. He arrived in the British colony of Demerara (later British Guyana) in 1815 and obtained employment as a manager of a cotton plantation. Over the course of the next two decades, Josias and his brothers set up several merchant trading houses in Liverpool in anticipation of a flourishing sugar and rum trade. They capped their preparatory activities with the 1834 establishment of Booker Brothers & Co. in British Guyana and the acquisition of their first transport ship the following year. After Richard Booker died in 1838, Josias and George consolidated vertically, purchasing sugar plantations throughout British Guyana.

As is often the case in family firms, generational changes precipitated a dramatic transformation of Booker Brothers. In 1854 Josias Booker II (eldest son of Josias I) and John McConnell (who had worked as a clerk for the Bookers since 1846) created a separate new partnership called the Demerara Company. Upon the deaths of Josias I and George in 1865 and 1866, respectively, Josias II and John McConnell assumed control of all the Booker properties, including the sugar plantations and trading companies in Britain and South America. According to a 1987 essay in Milton Moskowitz's *The Global Marketplace*, the new generation ''became the principal shopkeepers of the colony,'' building a formidable trade during the late nineteenth century. Their ''Liverpool Line,'' established in 1887, became one of the top shipping links between South America and Europe.

After Josias II died in the early 1880s, John McConnell inherited control of Booker Bros. & Co., George Booker & Co., and his own John McConnell & Co. McConnell's sons, A.J. and F.V., took possession of the three businesses in 1890 and merged them in 1900 as Booker Brothers, McConnell & Co. Ltd. Guyanan operations had by this time expanded to include sales of food and general merchandise at the retail and wholesale levels.

The company prospered throughout the early twentieth century by maintaining its concentration on the sugar and rum trade and limiting its acquisition activities to the Caribbean region. Booker McConnell made its first public stock offering in 1920 and was listed on the London Stock Exchange that same year. The company name was shortened to Booker, McConnell Ltd. in 1968; in 1986 it was renamed Booker PLC.

Political unrest in Guyana during the early 1950s prompted John ''Jock'' Campbell, chairman of Booker from 1952 to 1967, to diversify both geographically and commercially. Diversification became imperative after Guyana won its independence from Great Britain in 1966 and elected a Communist government. Booker was eventually compelled to sell its sugar plantations and other businesses in that country to the government. Ironically, Guyanan and other Caribbean officials asked Booker and other British sugar moguls to help manage their struggling operations in the early 1990s. Their request for management advice prompted the formation of Booker Tate, a joint venture with Tate & Lyle, in the early 1990s.

Campbell's ''hedge-building'' investments in the United Kingdom, Canada, and central Africa varied widely, from engineering to supermarketing to agricultural consulting. One of the most unusual diversifications made during this era was a division the company called ''Authors.'' This highly unusual sideline developed after the discovery of a loophole in the British tax code that allowed the conglomerate to purchase an author's copyrights, pay him or her a fat fee partly at the expense of the taxpayer, and then collect the royalties. Agatha Christie and Ian Fleming are just two of the bestselling authors in Booker's stable.

The Authors venture soon spawned another celebrated aside. According to Booker's 1994 annual report, Fleming suggested to Campbell over a game of golf that the company pump some of the millions it was earning on the backs of writers back into the literary community. Although Booker is reluctant to give the creator of the James Bond character full credit for the idea, his suggestion influenced the 1969 presentation of the first Booker McConnell Prize for Fiction, which is bestowed upon the best novel published in Britain by a writer from the British Commonwealth. P.H. Newby's *Something to Answer For* won the first Booker Prize, which has become the most coveted and highly esteemed award in British book publishing. The recipient of the honor receives a cash award, and the status of the prize is so great that novels that are short-listed for the award often see dramatic jumps in sales. In 1993 the company bestowed its first Russian Booker McConnell Prize to Mark Kharitonov for his *Lines of Fate*. In 1994 Scottish author James Kelman won the British Booker—and a £20,000 (US$31,600) check—for his novel *How Late It Was, How Late*.

Booker's business focus shifted in the late 1970s and early 1980s. The company divested itself of its money-losing engineering interests, sold its last remaining import/export subsidiary, and made several acquisitions in agribusiness and food distribution. Perhaps anticipating increasing demand for low-fat, relatively low-cost sources of protein, the firm's acquisitions included poultry breeding operations and fish breeding and processing businesses in the late 1970s and early 1980s.

One of the company's first transitional moves came with the 1978 purchase of ten percent of International Basic Economy Corporation (IBEC). IBEC had been founded by Nelson Rockefeller and his brothers in 1947 in the hopes of profitably boosting developing countries' economies. Arbor Acres, an American producer of broiler breeder stock that had been operating since before World War II, became part of the IBEC in 1959. Arbor Acres hoped to expand its chicken breeding network from the United States to Latin America, Europe, the Middle East, and Asia. But when IBEC's sales dropped precipitously in the late 1970s, the Rockefellers elected to liquidate. Booker helped that process along, increasing its share of IBEC to 45 percent in 1980 and a majority interest by 1985. Rodman C. Rockefeller, Nelson's son, served as chairman of Arbor Acres Farms and on Booker's board of directors into the early 1990s.

Infrequent acquisitions of fish breeders and processors in the late 1970s, 1980s, and early 1990s slowly evolved into a significant sector of Booker's business. The company bought W&F Fish Products in 1978, Atlantic Sea Products in 1987, and Marine Harvest International in 1994. By that time, Booker's annual report boasted that it was the largest specialist seafood group in the United Kingdom.

Booker also invested heavily in health foods during the 1980s. The company made at least four acquisitions in this industry in 1986 alone, and continued its buying spree in ensuing years. Health food holdings during this period included Britain's largest health food chain, Holland & Barrett; La Vie Claire, a prominent health food company in France; vitamin and nutritional supplement manufacturers in the United States and Great Britain; and several organic food producers.

During the last half of the 1980s, Booker acquired several wholesale food distributors, including E.C. Steed (1986); Copeman Ridley (1987); J. Evershed & Son (1988); Linfood Cash & Carry (1988); and County Catering Co. (1988). By the end of the decade, the company had amassed Britain's largest food wholesaling business. Its customers, which numbered in the hundreds of thousands, included independent grocers, convenience stores, and caterers. It was around this time that the company shifted its business strategy to concentrate primarily on food wholesaling and distribution to the catering trade. Booker sealed its leading position in that industry with the 1990 acquisition of Fitch Lovell PLC, a leading processor and distributor of fish and other food products, for £279.7 million.

In keeping with its new focus, Booker divested several peripheral businesses during this period. The company sold its chain of Budgen convenience stores, which had been purchased during the 1950s-era diversification, in 1986. The French health food interests were divested in 1989, and those in the United Kingdom were sold in 1990 and 1991.

Booker purchased the balance of Arbor Acres' equity (ten percent) from the Rockefellers in 1991 for $22 million. Under its new management, Arbor Acres had grown to become the world's largest broiler breeding company, with customers in over 70 countries worldwide. It had emerged as the cornerstone of Booker's American agribusiness division, which also included North America's leading turkey breeder, Nicholas Turkey Breeding Farms, and CWT Farms International Inc., a producer of broiler hatching eggs.

Booker adjusted its organizational structure in the early 1990s by establishing four primary divisions: food distribution, which included wholesaling and food service; food processing, which incorporated operations producing fish and prepared foods; U.S. agribusiness, comprised of the poultry breeding operations; and U.K. agribusiness, which included salmon farming, plant breeding, sugar industry services, and forestry. Food distribution contributed about half of the company's net income in the early 1990s, while the international agribusiness and fish processing chipped in about 20 percent each.

Booker has been characterized as a ''dull but worthy'' company. Hectic competition in the British supermarket industry, however, may drag the distributor into the limelight. In 1992, for example, Booker launched its first consumer advertising campaign in support of the ''Family Choice'' branded products it distributed to thousands of independent grocers. These Booker clients were experiencing increased price competition from deep discounters that had entered the market to take advantage of recession-weary Brits.

Booker's sales increased steadily in the early 1990s, from £2.93 billion in 1990 to £3.72 billion in 1994. Net income increased from £49.9 million in 1990 to £59.7 million in 1993, then declined to £45.8 million in 1994. The company blamed the earnings slide on expenses related to the reorganization of the food wholesaling and food service divisions, as well as the acquisition and rationalization of Marine Harvest International, the Scotland-based salmon farming firm. Predictably, Booker Chairman, Jonathan Taylor, expressed confidence that the company's reorganization would begin to pay increased dividends as Great Britain cycled out of recession in the latter part of the 1990s.

Principal Subsidiaries: Booker Belmont Wholesale Limited; Booker Fitch Food Services Limited; Pullman Foods Limited; Blue Cap Logistics Limited; Arctic Seafare Limited; Booker Countryside Limited; Booker Overseas Trading Limited; Booker Tate Limited (50%); Fletcher Smith Limited (65%); L Daehnfeldt A/S (Denmark); McConnell Salmon Limited; Agatha Christie Limited (64%); Glidrose Publications Limited (51%).

Further Reading:

Bidlake, Suzanne, "Booker Boosts Small Stores in Price War," *Marketing,* January 23, 1992, p. 6.

Bykov, Dimitry, Andrei Nemzer, and Alla Latynina, "First Booker Russian Novel Prize Awarded," *Current Digest of the Post-Soviet Press,* January 13, 1993, p. 16.

"Caribbean Sugar: Come Back, Slavemasters," *Economist,* January 23, 1993, p. 83.

Moskowitz, Milton, *The Global Marketplace,* New York: Macmillan Publishing Company, 1987.

"So Far, So Good," *Investors Chronicle,* February 12, 1993, 21.

—April D. Gasbarre

Book-of-the-Month Club, Inc.

1271 Avenue of the Americas
New York, New York 10020
U.S.A.
(212) 522-4200
Fax: (212) 522-7125

Wholly Owned subsidiary of Time Warner Inc.
Incorporated: 1926
Employees: 750
Sales: $250 million
SICs: 5961 Catalog and Mail-Order Houses

Book-of-the-Month Club, Inc. (BOMC) is probably the most famous name in the history of book clubs. Since it was founded in 1926, the company has distributed over 570 million books to members across the United States. In addition to its flagship club of the same name, BOMC operates several other book clubs, including the Quality Paperback Book Club (QPB), the History Book Club, and the Children's Book-of-the-Month Club. BOMC also offers less structured arrangements called continuity programs. These include the Stephen King Library, Books of My Very Own, and The Great Commanders. The BOMC clubs had a total of well over three million members in 1993, a year in which the company shipped 22 million books. BOMC also operates its own publishing division, which specializes in re-issues of classics, out-of-print works, and other books not generally available at bookstores. BOMC is a subsidiary of multimedia giant Time Warner Inc.

The founder and driving force behind the Book-of-the-Month Club during its first few decades of operation was Harry Scherman. Scherman, who was born in Montreal and raised in Philadelphia, began his career as an advertising copywriter. Working for the J. Walter Thompson advertising agency, Scherman learned the essentials of mail-order promotion. His mail-order expertise, combined with his love of literature, led Scherman to co-found a mail-order book firm called the Little Leather Library with colleagues Robert Haas and Maxwell Sackheim in 1916. After a handful of prosperous years, the Little Leather Library fizzled. Scherman and his partners were nevertheless convinced that the idea of selling books through the mail was a winner, and in 1926 they tried again with BOMC. In April of that year, the club's first selection was sent to 4,750 original members. By the end of that year, the club's membership ranks had swollen to 46,539. Because much of the American population did not enjoy easy access to bookstores in the 1920s, BOMC grew quickly, as did many of the imitators that sprang up in the late 1920s and 1930s.

The company's operating premise was that most book lovers do not read as many books as they intend to. By agreeing to purchase at least four books a year, club members could choose a hand-picked group of books that they would receive by mail. The concept was immediately popular. By December 1926 the company had net sales of over half a million dollars. Membership approached 100,000 by 1928. The club held its own during the worst years of the Depression, then soared again in the second half of the 1930s.

In the early years of the company, convenience was the main advantage the club offered to its members; books were sold at full price, with postage costs added. Eventually, however, books selected by BOMC took on a certain prestige, and books offered by the club saw their bookstore sales rise as well. Soon BMOC was ordering books in sufficient quantities to persuade many publishers to give the company price breaks. The discounts were then passed on to club members, who were targeted through advertisements in magazines and weekly book review sections of newspapers. Readers were encouraged to send for further information. BOMC did not begin soliciting memberships directly on a regular basis until about 1939.

During World War II, with other commodities in short supply and cash in abundance, Americans bought more books than they ever had before. Between 1939 and 1946, BOMC's circulation grew from 363,000 to 889,000. Although the world was at war, peace was established between BOMC and the nation's booksellers, who had been harsh critics of book clubs and their role in the industry. An arrangement was forged in which booksellers became intermediaries between the club and its members.

The company also experimented with providing other services outside of its core book business to its customers during the 1940s. In 1943 BOMC made its first Christmas card offer. Reproductions of famous works of art became an occasional club item the same year. In 1948 magazine subscription offers were initiated. BOMC also purchased the Non-Fiction Book Club from Henry Holt & Co. that year and integrated it into its own operation. Other new services added around this time included the Travelers Book Club and a subsidiary called Practical and Educational Books. Some of these trial services were failures. One that was particularly successful, however, was Metropolitan Miniatures. These sets of art reproductions were offered in conjunction with the Metropolitan Museum of Art. By 1951, circulation for Metropolitan Miniatures had exceeded 100,000; 500,000 sets of the miniatures had been distributed by 1956.

BOMC shipped out its 100 millionth book in 1949. During the first half of the 1950s the company continued to try out new services. The Children's Record Guild was launched in 1950, and Music-Appreciation Records, a classical music club for adults, was added in 1954. In 1952 BOMC established Young Readers of America, its first book club specifically designed for children. Young Readers was an instant success. Its first mailing generated over 70,000 subscribers. BOMC's Christmas card service also flourished around this time. In 1954 BOMC became involved in Books Abridged, a monthly digest of four condensations. Books Abridged did not prove to be profitable, however, and it was sold off a year later.

By the middle of the 1950s, BOMC was selling nearly five million books a year. The club's selections had included ten Pulitzer Prize-winning books and works from five Nobel Prize-winning authors. There were about 800,000 members of the company's various clubs by this time, slightly fewer than its 1946 peak total. In 1956 BOMC's 30th birthday was celebrated with the publication of a 40-page booklet by the *New York Times* that outlined the club's history. The booklet pointed out, among other impressive facts, that the number of books BOMC had placed in private homes exceeded by far the number of books in all public libraries and major universities in the United States put together.

BOMC launched yet another music project in 1958, a joint venture called the RCA Victor Society of Great Music. In 1961 Axel Rosin, Scherman's son-in-law, was named president of BOMC; Scherman stayed on as chairman of the board. Rosin had fled Nazi Germany in 1934, and later married Scherman's only daughter, Katharine. By the early 1960s the Scherman family controlled just under half of BOMC's stock, which was traded publicly on the New York Stock Exchange.

Although BOMC's membership continued to grow in the first half of the 1960s, the company's sales began to stagnate as the impact of increased numbers of retail book stores—many of which sold bestsellers at discount prices—was felt. Another important factor was the rise of paperback books. The proliferation of book clubs and the resulting competition was yet another cause for the slump. Between 1962 and 1963, BOMC saw its sales slip from $19.8 million to $17.6 million. To compensate for the shrinking number of books purchased by members, the company spent more money on promotion to beef up membership. As it dug deeper for subscribers, the company encountered a higher percentage of deadbeats, yet another drain on profits.

BOMC rebounded strongly in 1966. The company earned a profit of $1.7 million on $26 million in sales, and the club's membership count passed the one million mark for the first time. By 1967, 35 BOMC selections had won Pulitzers, including *The Caine Mutiny* by Herman Wouk (1952), *Profiles in Courage* by John F. Kennedy (1957), and *The Guns of August* by Barbara W. Tuchman (1963). BOMC maintained its book clubs, record clubs, Christmas cards, and art miniatures, and also introduced a couple of educational programs: Art Seminars in the Home, which consisted of two art appreciation courses developed by the Metropolitan Museum of Art; and two Reading Improvement Programs.

Rosin helped fuel the company's comeback with two bold moves in 1967. First, he created a stir by guaranteeing $250,000 for the right to make William Manchester's *Death of a President* a monthly club selection. The move paid off when the book sold 400,000 copies in the first month alone. Rosin hit another jackpot later in the year when he guaranteed $320,000 for the memoirs of Svetlana Aliluyeva, Josef Stalin's daughter. That deal represented the first time BOMC had paid for the right to distribute a book before its editorial board had even seen the manuscript.

Scherman died in 1969. The chairman of the board position at BOMC remained vacant until 1973, when a realignment of the company's executive positions put Rosin in that post. He also retained his position as chief executive officer, while he was replaced as president by Edward Fitzgerald, formerly a vice-president. Meanwhile, BOMC continued to make slow but steady progress through the first half of the 1970s. Sales grew from $43 million in 1971 to nearly $63 million in 1975. By the mid-1970s, the core book club had about a million members, while the company's seven other clubs had a combined enrollment of about another 500,000. Although the main book club generated about 85 percent of the company's revenue, a number of new clubs were initiated during the early 1970s. The Cookbook Club was purchased from McCall's in 1971. A few years later the club's subject matter was expanded to include crafts, and it was appropriately renamed the Cooking and Crafts Club. In 1972 BOMC acquired the Dolphin Book Club, which covered boating and other nautical subjects. By 1976 Dolphin membership had grown ten-fold to 50,000. Other new programs included Fine Arts 260, which offered graphic arts and sculptures in limited editions, and The Meanings of Modern Art, a home study course begun in 1975. One of the most successful new clubs introduced around this time was the Quality Paperback Book Service (QPB), which featured large, high-quality volumes of popular titles in an array of genres. QPB has remained an important part of BOMC's operations ever since.

In 1977 BOMC was acquired by publishing and forest products company Time Inc. in a deal valued at $63 million. Because Time sold books by mail through its Time-Life Books, Inc. subsidiary, the merger was scrutinized closely by the Federal Trade Commission (FTC) for possible antitrust violations. Nothing came of the FTC's interest in the case, however, and BOMC continued to operate as a subsidiary of Time, which later became Time Warner Inc. as the result of another merger.

As part of Time, BOMC continued to look for ways to wring additional sales from its growing base of club members. In the early 1980s the company determined that there was money to be made by publishing books on its own or in cooperation with publishers, rather than only buying the rights from publishers to sell BOMC editions of their books. In 1982 BOMC established its own original publishing division. Its first publishing projects were reprints of such classics as *All the King's Men* by Robert Penn Warren (published by BOMC in 1982), William Shirer's *Berlin Diary* (published in 1987), and the *Revised English Bible* (published in 1989). The publishing division then moved on to anthologies and multivolume sets. BOMC also sought to grow through acquisition. The company purchased Harcourt Brace Jovanovich Inc.'s History Book Club and two smaller clubs for $25 million in 1987.

BOMC struggled during the early 1990s. Large bookstores operated by chains like Barnes & Noble and B. Dalton were able to consistently undercut BOMC on price, a significant reason for the downturn in the club's performance. In 1992 the company restructured its managing units. Under the new arrangement, control over the different clubs, which had previously enjoyed a high degree of autonomy, was centralized under a new layer of management headed by senior vice-president Neal Goff. The role of the editorial department, led by Brigitte Weeks, was changed to more of an advisory one. The editorial department would no longer make the actual decisions regarding club selections.

Another key change was the appointment of Juanita James to oversee the Book-of-the-Month Club and the Quality Paperback Book Club. James' expertise was in marketing, and as her influence in the company grew, new emphasis was placed on updating BOMC's use of membership information. Instead of treating all members the same, BOMC increasingly based its marketing on specific information about readers' tastes and buying histories. In September 1993, Weeks was fired as editor-in-chief of the club, a development that was interpreted by some industry observers as a clash between literary and marketing considerations. Although the existence of such a battle within the company was denied by president and CEO George Artandi, the trend toward a more commercially-oriented approach was clear. Weeks was replaced by Tracy Brown, the director of trade paperbacks at Little, Brown and Company. Soon after, James was promoted to senior vice-president of club management.

As the pressure to compete with bookstore chains increased, Brown announced in 1994 that BOMC's editorial board, a decades-old group that included respected authors and other literary figures, would be disbanded altogether. In explaining the decision, Brown noted that the pace of decision-making on book selection was accelerating so quickly that the company could no longer afford the luxury of soliciting an editorial board's opinions. Meanwhile, the publishing industry continues to undergo continuous transformations in the 1990s. It remains to be seen how this upheaval will eventually effect the roles of BOMC and the remaining handful of its book club rivals.

Principal Subsidiaries: Book-of-the-Month Customer Services, Inc.; Booksellers By Mail, Inc.; History Book Club, Inc.

Further Reading:

''Axel Rosin: Successful Son-in-Law,'' *Forbes,* August 1, 1967, p. 53.

''Book-of-the-Month Club Ads Pull, Says N. Y. Times' History,'' *Editor & Publisher,* May 19, 1956, p. 17.

''Book-of-the-Month and Time Inc. Merger is Cleared by Holders,'' *Wall Street Journal,* December 1, 1977, p. 35.

''Book-of-the-Month Club Rebound in the Works,'' *Barron's,* April 17, 1967, p. 26.

Campanella, Frank, ''Results Make Good Reading at Book-of-the-Month Club,'' *Barron's,* March 8, 1976, p. 61.

Evans, David, ''Too Late?'' *Forbes,* June 7, 1993, p. 106.

Fein, Esther B., ''Lucrative Republishing,'' *New York Times,* October 28, 1992, p. C19.

Hatch, Dennis, ''Anatomy of a Six-Year Control,'' *Target Marketing,* January 1993, p. 10.

''James New BOMC Chief; Bernard Named Exec. Ed.'' *Publishers Weekly,* October 25, 1993, p. 9.

Lee, Charles, *The Hidden Public,* New York: Doubleday & Company, Inc., 1958.

Lyall, Sarah, ''An Editor's Dismissal Raises Talk of a Clash of Art and Commerce,'' *New York Times,* September 15, 1993, p. C15.

——, ''Book-of-the-Month Club to Dissolve Editorial Board,'' *Chicago Tribune,* July 7, 1994, p. C4.

McDougall, A. Kent, ''Book Club Blues,'' *Wall Street Journal,* May 13, 1964, p. 1.

Reid, Calvin, ''BOMC Restructures Managing Units; Weeks's Role Changed,'' *Publishers Weekly,* January 20, 1992, p. 10.

Sapinsley, B. C., ''Book-of-the-Month Club,'' *Barron's,* November 14, 1955, p. 13.

''Time Inc. Agrees to Merger Plan for $63 Million,'' *Wall Street Journal,* July 6, 1977, p. 5.

''Vox Pops,'' *Forbes,* March 15, 1961, p. 16.

—Robert R. Jacobson

Bose Corporation

The Mountain
Framingham, Massachusetts 01701
U.S.A.
(508) 879-7330
Fax: (508) 872-6541

Private Company
Founded: 1964
Employees: 3,300
Sales: $500 million
SICs: 3651 House Audio and Video Equipment; 3663 Radio and TV Communications Equipment

Ranking 488 on *Ward's* list of the "1000 Largest Privately Held Companies" in the mid-1990s, Bose Corporation is engaged in the development, manufacture, and marketing of loudspeakers, consumer and professional audio systems, automobile sound systems, television sound systems, noise cancellation technology for the defense and aviation sectors, and computer simulation software to analyze auditorium sounds. Initially producing amplifiers for the U.S. Defense Department, Bose later introduced the Bose 901 Direct/Reflecting speaker, which, with modifications, would remain the company's flagship speaker well into the 1990s. Known for its industry innovations and the high quality of its products, Bose markets a wide variety of sound equipment popular among consumers and corporate clients, most notably automobile manufacturers Ford, General Motors, Chrysler, Honda, Nissan, and Audi. The company maintains production facilities and subsidiaries worldwide.

The Bose Corporation's founder, Dr. Amar Bose, was born in 1929 to a political refugee from India and his wife, a Philadelphia school teacher. Bose would later suggest, in an interview in *USA Today,* that defending himself as young boy in a racially prejudiced America equipped him with the fighting spirit important to his success. When his father's import business suffered during World War II, the teenaged Amar Bose convinced his father to begin a radio repair facility in the family business. There, the self-taught Amar did the repair work. Following this early experience in the electronics field, Bose attended the Massachusetts Institute of Technology (MIT), where he earned a doctoral degree in electrical engineering in 1956.

The Bose Corporation arose in part from Dr. Bose's dissatisfaction when he attempted to buy speakers for his home stereo system in 1956. As an engineer, he had expected that laboratory measurements would indicate sound quality. To his dismay, however, he realized that measured sound and perceived sound differed. Dr. Bose directed his research efforts into psychoacoustics, the study of sound as humans perceive it, and psychophysics, the study of the relationship between measurement and perception. His research led to numerous patents and the creation of Bose Corporation in 1964 to develop and market products using those patents. Despite the later financial success of his company, Dr. Bose, professor of electrical engineering and computer science, remained on the staff at MIT into the 1990s, teaching and mentoring undergraduate and graduate thesis students.

Bose started his company at the suggestion of MIT professor Y.W. Lee, who provided Bose with $10,000 in start-up capital. That investment would later be worth an estimated $250,000, when the company repurchased Lee's stock in 1972. So that he could continue his teaching career, Bose hired one of his students, Sherwin Greenblatt, to help develop and market a product. During their first year of business, according to a company publication, Greenblatt was the company's only employee, and "Bose, who was [still] teaching, was paying Greenblatt more than he, himself, was earning as a professor at MIT." Greenblatt would later become president of the company.

Bose produced its first 901 direct/reflecting loudspeaker in 1968, and its first customers were secured through contracts with the military and NASA. The 901 was based on Bose's earlier research, which indicated that in excess of 80 percent of what audiences heard at a concert, for example, was reflected sound; sound bouncing off walls, floors, and ceilings apparently contributed to the quality of the listening experience. Bose determined that his disappointment in speakers then on the market resulted from the fact that speakers only directed sound straight forward. To achieve a better spatial distribution of sound, therefore, Bose developed the 901, which aimed eight of the nine transducers in the speaker to the rear of the speaker where the sound could bounce before it reached the listener. The 901 employed an active equalizer to allow the speaker to reproduce the audio spectrum.

Bose's 901 series was not an immediate success. In fact, *Consumer Reports* dismissed the product, alleging that "individual instruments heard through the 901 . . . tended to wander about the room." Wounded by such criticism, Dr. Bose filed a lawsuit against the magazine, claiming that it had unfairly disparaged his speaker system. Litigation continued for nearly 13 years, and although Dr. Bose ultimately lost his case at the Supreme Court level, the 901 series had long since gained a reputation as one of the finer products on the market.

Critical to Bose's success was the company philosophy, itself a reflection of its founder. Company literature stated: "Bose believes that audio products exist to provide music for everyone, everywhere—that music, not equipment, is the ultimate benefit. The Bose goal is to create products that combine high technology with simplicity and small size, to create the best possible sound systems that are easy to use and accessible to all consumers." From the beginning, Bose directed all profits back into research and development, avowing a greater interest in producing excellent speakers than in money and keeping his company privately held, and therefore not responsible to stockholders, through the 1990s. Dr. Bose and company officials also stressed the importance of creativity at the company. In *Operations* magazine, for example, Greenblatt stated "Our challenge is to prod people into being innovative and using their creativity to do something that's better. In the long run, this is the source of sustainable advantage over our competition."

Since its introduction in 1968, the 901 speaker series underwent several revisions in which sound quality was improved and the speakers were made suitable for the digital age. Bose also applied the direct/reflecting concept to lower priced speakers in the company line and began marketing speakers to the general public for use in home stereo systems.

In the 1970s, Dr. Bose became interested in developing sound reproduction systems for automobiles, having noted that consumers, dissatisfied with the stereo equipment then standard in American cars, were purchasing Japanese systems for installation. The project seemed to present particular challenges given the glass, upholstery, and plastic surfaces in a car's interior. Bose, however, was optimistic, later recalling in a 1990 *Electronic Business* article: "I thought I could actually create better sound in a car than in a room, [since] we can control where the sound goes in a car."

Bose's auto sound system ideas were presented to General Motors Corp. in 1979, and a verbal agreement was reached between Dr. Bose and Edward Czapor, GM's Delco Electronics president, which resulted in four years of Bose research at an estimated $13 million to adapt car audio systems to the acoustic environment of the automobile. At the conclusion of the successful research, Bose formed a joint venture with GM to design and manufacture car audio systems for certain Cadillac, Buick, and Oldsmobile models.

Although initially slow to realize profits, Bose's car stereos and the Original Equipment Manufacturer (OEM) division they necessitated at the company, eventually became highly successful, leading to partnerships with Honda, Acura, Nissan, Infiniti, Audi, Mercedes Benz, and Mazda. In many cases, Bose was able to design products not only for a specific model of car but also for specific options packages offered by the automakers. Bose was even able to meet Honda's requirement that product failure rate not exceed 30 parts per million, an exacting standard. By 1995, Bose's car audio systems would represent about one-fourth of its total sales.

Also in the 1970s, Bose began efforts to introduce its products to the Japanese consumer audio market, an effort begun with much frustration. Bose's initial efforts in the Japanese market were failures; in fact, the company lost money its first eight years in Japan. Then, Dr. Bose recognized the problem as one in which Bose market representatives had failed to establish close human relationships with Japanese distributors. Bose decided to hire a native Japanese to head the company's sales efforts in Japan. After interviewing several unsuitable American candidates, Bose made a few trips to Japan, during which he established social and business contacts. Eventually he hired someone who would have great success introducing Bose products to Japan and would later become a vice-president in the corporation.

Further Bose innovations involved acoustic waveguide technology, through which Bose engineers eventually developed smaller, portable speakers and sound systems capable of producing "big sound." Specifically, acoustic waveguide technology showed that bass notes could be reproduced through a small tube or pipe, similar to that employed in a pipe organ, instead of the much larger "moving cones" used by traditional stereo manufacturers. Amplifying the bass notes via an 80-inch tube folded into less than one cubic foot of space, Bose's Acoustic Wave Music System was introduced in 1984. The stereo system won praise for its compact, simple design as well as sound that many reviewers found rivalled that of larger and more costly stereo speakers and components.

In 1985, Bose began investigating the market for its products in television. As he had with General Motors, Dr. Bose approached a major television manufacturer, Zenith, and proposed that his engineers design a sound system, incorporating their acoustic waveguide technology to produce high fidelity sound in Zenith televisions. Zenith agreed, and the two companies entered into a joint venture which resulted in the deluxe Zenith/Bose television, a set that featured rich sound and, since its tube was folded inside, was only about an inch larger than Zenith's earlier 27-inch screen model.

Also during this time, Bose introduced its Acoustic Noise Canceling headset, a sealed headset designed to cancel out unwanted sound. Remarking on the need for the headset, one writer for *New Scientist* magazine quoted Dr. Bose "The US government pays out $200 million a year in compensation for hearing loss caused by military service. . . . Hearing loss is a common reason for early retirement of pilots, second only to psychological stress." Indeed, the headset proved valuable in military use, particularly among pilots and tank drivers. The headset also had civilian applications and could be used by small aircraft and helicopter pilots. Bose donated two of these headsets to Dick Rutan and Jeanna Yeager, who piloted their light plane the *Voyager* on a nonstop around the world flight in 1986. Moreover, the technology Bose developed could be tailored to cancel out noise in several environments, such as airline passenger compartments or city streets.

By 1989 Bose's sales were estimated at $300 million, a figure that some analysts suggested was conservative. Also at this time, nearly half of Bose's sales were derived from foreign markets; indeed, Bose speakers were outselling all other brands in Japan, including those of the Japanese manufacturers. The early 1990s would see steady gains for Bose, with net revenues increasing to $424 million by 1992.

The acoustiwave technology in Bose speakers and stereo systems made Bose products popular in the 1990s at concerts, theaters, and nightclubs. A Bose loudspeaker was even used at the 1992 Winter Olympics in Albertville, France. Consumers were also introduced to the Bose Wave radio, a small remote-controlled clock radio suited for use in the home. The Wave boasted rich, full sound not found in other portable radios and could also be hooked up to a television or CD player, enhancing the sound capabilities of the user's existing stereo components.

At its manufacturing facilities, Bose became a subscriber to the Total Quality Management concept, introduced by W. Edwards

Deming. Toward that end, Bose assembly line workers were cross-trained and promoted based on performance. Moreover, Bose sought to build teams based upon mutual trust and respect, operating according to principles of responsibility and quality consciousness. Describing the company's management style in a 1993 *Production* article, Bose's vice-president of manufacturing, Tom Beeson, asserted: "Communicate. Spend a lot of time on the factory floor. Micromanage every aspect. Involve all of the people. Foolproof the system so mistakes can't be made. Find the root cause of problems. Operate manufacturing with the fundamental principle: Do it right the first time."

In a 1994 interview with Kathleen Lander of *HPR* magazine, Dr. Amar Bose indicated that Bose Corporation headquarters, known only as The Mountain for its commanding view of the countryside, was scheduled for expansion. The facility would be dedicated to engineering only, and expansion plans called for construction of a concert hall and landscaping to recreate the atmosphere of a college campus.

Innovative product development and streamlined manufacturing and delivery made Bose Corporation the world's leading speaker manufacturer in the 1990s. The company maintained U.S. manufacturing in Massachusetts, Michigan, and Arizona, as well as foreign plants in Canada, Mexico, and Ireland. With subsidiaries throughout Europe, Australia, Canada, Italy, Japan, and Russia, foreign market represented 60 percent of Bose Corporation sales in 1995.

Principal Subsidiaries: Bose AG (Switzerland); Bose A/S (Denmark); Bose Australia; Bose B.V. (Netherlands); Bose Canada, Inc.; Bose GmbH (Germany); Bose K.K. (Japan); Bose Ltd. (Canada); Bose N.V. (Belgium); Stereo Advertising Corp.

Further Reading:

Amemeson, Jane, "Sound is Golden for Dr. Bose," *Compass Readings,* February 1991.

Bradley, Peter, "Global Sourcing Takes Split-Second," *Purchasing,* July 20, 1989, pp. 53–58.

Bulkeley, William M, "Sound Program Lets User Mimic Site's Acoustics," *Wall Street Journal,* October 19, 1994, p. B1.

DeJong, Jennifer, "Redesigning Design," *Computerworld,* November 22, 1993, pp. 87–90.

Fox, Barry, "Antisound Makes it All Quiet on the Western Front," *New Scientist,* December 5, 1992, p. 20.

Greenblatt, Sherwin, "Continuous Improvement In Supply Chain Management," *Chief Executive,* June 1993, pp 40–43.

Hirsch, Julian, "Bose Lifestyle 12 Home Theater System," *Stereo Review,* March 1995, pp. 34–38.

"Hotels Move to a New Beat" *Lodging Hospitality,* April 1994, p. 84.

Lander, Kathleen, "*HPR* Interview: Amar Bose," *HPR: High Performance Review,* June 2, 1994, pp. 51–53.

O'Connor, Leo, "Putting a Lid on Noise Pollution," *Mechanical Engineering,* June 1991, pp. 46–51.

MacNeil, Wayne, "Bar Coding Brings Benefits for Product Distribution," *Automation,* January 1991, p. 40.

McClenahen, John S., "So Long, Salespeople," *Industry Week,* February 18, 1991, pp. 48–51.

Radding, Alan, "Quality is Job #1," *Datamation,* October 1, 1992, pp. 98–100.

Reed, J. D., "Beating Japan Loud and Clear," *Fortune,* October 26, 1987, pp. 65–72.

Rosenbloom, Bert, "Motivating Your International Channel Partners," *Business Horizons,* March/April 1990, pp. 53–57.

"Taking Control of Noise," *Occupational Hazards,* July 1993, p. 34.

Vannan, Thomas, "Of Science and Stereos," *New England Business,* January 1990, p. 80.

Vasilash, Gary, "Bose Manufacturing Audiophiles Extraordinaire," *Production,* September 1993, pp. 64–67.

—Terry W. Hughes

Bozzuto's, Inc.

275 Schoolhouse Road
Cheshire, Connecticut 06410-0340
U.S.A.
(203) 272-3511
Fax: (203) 250-8005

Public Company
Incorporated: 1945 as John Bozzuto & Sons, Inc.
Sales: $319.13 million
Employees: 400
Stock Exchanges: NASDAQ OTC
SICs: 5122 Drugs, Drug Proprietaries and Druggists Sundries; 5141 Groceries, General Line; 6159 Miscellaneous Business Credit Institutions; 7358 Equipment Rental and Leasing; 8721 Accounting, Auditing and Bookkeeping Services

Bozzuto's, Inc. is a wholesale distributor of groceries and nonfood items to independent retail supermarkets and grocery and convenience stores in northern New Jersey, southeastern New York (including Long Island), and southern New England. A subsidiary, AB Small Business Investment Co., Inc., offers secured business loans to qualified independent small businesses; in many cases, loans are granted to Bozzuto's retail grocery-store customers so that they can open new stores or expand existing facilities. Another subsidiary, A.B. Leasing Corp., leases data-processing and delivery equipment. Under the direction of Adam M. Bozzuto, its founder, Bozzuto's, Inc. celebrated its 50th anniversary in 1995.

A native of Waterbury, Connecticut, Bozzuto founded his wholesale company in 1945. However, Bozzuto's remained relatively obscure until 1970, when 190,000 shares of the company's common stock (about one-third of the total) were offered to the public. By 1970, there were some 1,930 grocery wholesalers in the United States, of which 469 were of the type called "voluntaries"—food jobbers selling largely to affiliated retailers. Voluntary grocery wholesaling began in the 1920s as a means of meeting competition from chain stores. Such wholesalers were usually privately owned, and they sold their wares to a select group of independent supermarket owners with whom they had developed close relationships. Typically, voluntary wholesalers also provided additional services on a fee basis such as site selection, financing, training, advertising, and accounting. Voluntaries accounted for nearly half of all wholesale grocery sales in 1970.

Voluntary wholesale grocers provided retailers with goods at warehouse cost plus a small fee, based on volume, freight charges, and other relevant service fees. In addition, they received a two percent discount from their suppliers for prompt payment. Often they provided financial aid to retailers as well. While the profit margin for voluntaries usually was less than one percent of volume, the return on volume could be augmented in a number of ways, such as by packaging and manufacturing. The sale of nonfood items also helped boost revenue so that by the end of 1966 voluntary wholesale grocers were carrying as many as 7,205 different items.

Like many other wholesalers, Bozzuto's established an affiliation with IGA (Independent Grocers' Alliance), a group of about 4,000 retailers, in 1970. Through this alliance, food and other products were typically sold to affiliated retailers on a cost-plus-commission basis. By entering this association, Bozzuto's began serving as many as 184 stores, and its sales and revenues increased from $17 million in 1965 to $46.8 million in 1970. Furthermore, net income rose from $104,503 to $620,131 over this period, while long-term debt shrank from $299,909 to $42,765.

During this period of prosperity, Bozzuto's bought leases on six supermarket locations which it in turn subleased to retailers for a profit; in addition, the company rented a 183,860-square-foot warehouse in Cheshire, Connecticut, which provided customers with 45 percent of their product requirements. Bozzuto's then went on to construct a 42,000-square-foot distribution center for perishable food products in 1971, enabling the company to expand service to its customers in frozen foods, meats, ice cream, fruits and vegetables, and dairy products. Ultimately, this investment markedly increased Bozzuto's capacity to provide the product requirements of its customers to the level of 61 percent. During this period, Bozzuto's also employed a lucrative method of distributing its nonfood items; called drop-shipping, this practice gave customers the option of purchasing products for delivery directly from Bozzuto's suppliers rather than from Bozzuto's own warehouses. Drop shipments represented 30 percent of company sales in 1970. By early 1972, Bozzuto's managed a group of 196 customers, 62 of which were affiliated with IGA and accounted for about two-thirds of the company's total sales and revenues.

This period of strong financial growth also afforded Bozzuto's the opportunity to acquire other businesses. In 1971, the company bought Gordon Fruit and Produce Co., a wholesaler, to provide an entry into the produce business. That same year, Bozzuto's purchased another wholesaler, J. Daren and Sons, Inc. of Norwich, Connecticut, for $757,500 in cash and notes. This acquisition brought Bozzuto's into the institutional-food field for the first time. In 1973, Bozzuto's bought Wayco Foods of Elk Grove Village, Illinois, but sold its controlling interest three years later. The company then sold J. Daren and Sons in 1978. These acquisitions helped raise Bozzuto's consolidated sales to $132 million in 1974, while net earnings rose to $612,494. In addition to its food-service operations, Bozzuto's had by this time developed 10 new supermarkets and remodeled many others for its customers. Moreover, it was engaged in advising independent businessmen in all phases of investing in a supermarket, from raw site analysis to store planning, equipment, and labor supply. This venture led to the creation of a department of advertising and sales promotion in 1974; two years later, Bozzuto established a loan subsidiary called AB Small Business Investment.

Net sales rose from $86.9 million in 1974 to $116.4 million the following year, but dipped slightly during the next three years due to the sales of Wayco and Daren. Similarly, net earnings rose from $612,494 to $942,596 in 1977 during this period, before falling to $528,258 in 1978, largely due to a $133,438 loss posted by Daren. By 1981, Bozzuto's had become the exclusive distributor of products under the IGA label in its marketing area, even though its number of retail grocery customers had fallen to about 150. The company continued to expand operations by buying food and nonfood items from hundreds of suppliers, some of them manufacturers and processors and others food brokers. Furthermore, in 1980 Bozzuto's opened an experimental warehouse-style retail grocery store in New York called Buy-N-Save Cash & Carry.

Bozzuto's also continued to expand its existing operations. Additions to the Cheshire warehouse had brought its capacity up to 245,000 square feet by 1981. In addition, the company's fleet of vehicles now consisted of 45 cargo trailers, 27 refrigerated trailers, 39 tractors, and 27 automobiles. Continuing its rise in profitability, Bozzuto's posted net sales which rose from $148.4 million in 1979 to $179.5 million in 1983. Net income, $717,000 in 1979, dipped as low as $434,000 in 1981 but recovered to $702,000 in 1982 and $757,000 in 1983.

By 1988, Bozzuto's was distributing products to about 245 supermarkets and superettes and 500 convenience stores, although the latter represented only 4 percent of sales. The majority of Bozzuto's customers remained in small- or medium-sized cities. Food products distributed included canned goods, cereals, dairy products, delicatessen items, meats, poultry, seafood, fresh fruits and vegetables, and frozen foods. Nonfood items included cigarettes and tobacco products, health and beauty aids, paper products, cleaning supplies, and small household items. Most products distributed bore the brands of the manufacturers or processors from which Bozzuto's purchased the products, including many nationally advertised brands.

Also during this period, Bozzuto's convenience-store distribution warehouse was moved into a separate facility for greater flexibility and increased production. The fleet of tractors and trailers was being continuously upgraded to preserve the company's record for on-time deliveries. In addition, the company invested in a computerized purchasing system, which was specifically designed to balance inventories and included a "forward buy" feature to maximize the return on investments. Bozzuto's also offered a complement of advertising, merchandising, accounting, and store-design and development services to independent retail grocery operations. Promotional aids included a "Monopoly" game intended to raise spending by retail customers.

In late 1986, Bozzuto's acquired a new subsidiary called A.B. Leasing Corp. for about $1.2 million. This company leased data-processing and delivery equipment. During this period, the company enjoyed steady growth from $220.8 million in 1984 to $233.9 million in 1988; but net earnings fell every year, from $852,000 in 1984 to $450,000 in 1988. Furthermore, long-term debt amounted to about $2.8 million at the end of 1986. However, Bozzuto's fortunes began turning around in 1989, when revenues rose to $259.8 million and net income to $511,000. Two years later, net income passed the $1 million mark for the first time and revenues totalled $260.7 million. 1992 proved even more successful, with $1.65 million earned on revenues of $289.5 million.

In 1993, revenues reached a record $319.13 million and net income a record $1.84 million. Long-term debt was about $13.5 million at the end of the fiscal year. By that time, Bozzuto's offerings included its own Shur Valu private-label line. About 20 Shur Valu items were being offered in bulk to warehouse clubs, as well as nationally branded club packs like 20-pound Meow Mix from Ralston Purina, 35-ounce Cheerios twin pack, 12-pack Scott paper towels, and 256-ounce Tide detergent. Joel Sebastian, Bozzuto's vice president of merchandising and advertising, told *Progressive Grocer* that the company priced club items to make an 8 to 14 percent profit margin. In 1994, Bozzuto's was conducting quarterly IGA-brand promotions. Brian McColgan, a private-label buyer for Bozzuto's, told *Progressive Grocer* that in a single promotion the company "moved close to 50,000 cases, including 6,000 cases of apple juice, 4,000 of paper towels, and 4,000 of bleach."

The 1970 public offering of Bozzuto's stock was priced at $9.75 a share. By 1986, shares were trading over-the-counter at a range between $14 and $22 on the NASDAQ exchange. In subsequent years, the value of the stock fell, although trading was always thin; in 1990 and 1991, for example, there were no bids at all. In 1992, Bozzuto's stock traded in a range of only $8 to $10 a share, well below its book value of $24.50. Interviewed by a reporter for *Barron's* in 1993, Ed McLaughin, an investor in closely held and inactively traded securities, said the stock was grossly undervalued. As of 1994, there were only 210 stockholders. Adam Bozzuto controlled about 44 percent of the stock, his son Michael A. Bozzuto about 10 percent, and his daughter Jayne A. Bozzuto about 10 percent.

Michael Bozzuto, who had been serving as executive vice-president and treasurer of the company since 1981, was named president and chief executive officer in 1994. He also continued in his former posts. Adam Bozzuto, who had been president and chief executive officer, remained chairman of the company at the age of 78, and his son continued to report to him. Jayne Bozzuto continued to serve as a vice-president, a position she assumed in 1982.

Principal Subsidiaries: A.B. Leasing Corp; AB Small Business Investment Co., Inc.; Boz-White Hills, Inc.; Fresh-Line Distributors, Inc.; Tolland Supermarket, Inc.

Further Reading:

Russell, John B., "Bozzuto's Inc.," *Wall Street Transcript,* May 8, 1972, p. 28,280.

Slatter, John, "Independents' Day," *Barron's,* December 29, 1971, pp. 11, 13.

Weinstein, Steve, "Looking Beyond Price," *Progressive Grocer,* September 1994, pp. 56, 58.

Welling, Kathryn M., "World's Second Most Patient Investor," *Barron's,* March 22, 1993, p. 28.

—Robert Halasz

Broderbund®

Broderbund Software, Inc.

500 Redwood Blvd.
P.O. Box 6121
Novato, California 94948-6121
U.S.A.
(415) 382-4400
Fax: (415) 382-4582

Public Company
Incorporated: 1981
Employees: 450
Sales: $111.77 million
Stock Exchanges: NASDAQ
SICs: 7372 Prepackaged Software

Broderbund Software, Inc. develops, publishes and markets consumer software for home, school, and small business use. The company is recognized as a pioneer and leading producer of educational software that has entertainment qualities. In addition to its educational software, the company offers software in two other consumer categories, personal productivity and entertainment. The company's product strategy focuses on developing software for the entire family that is engaging and easy to use and has lasting market appeal.

Since the early 1990s Broderbund has embraced CD-ROM technology as its major software format and has become a leader in interactive children's storybooks through its Living Books joint venture with Random House, Inc. Broderbund's leading products include *The Print Shop* (and descendent programs), one of the all-time best-selling consumer software programs with more than eight million units sold since debuting in 1984; the Carmen Sandiego line of educational games, which has sold more than four million units since premiering in 1985; and Broderbund's entertainment blockbuster *Myst,* which has sold more than one million units since its initial release in 1993. In addition to producing its own software, Broderbund also publishes the works of independent developers through an affiliated-label program. The company sells its software to distributors and directly to schools, end-users, and retail outlets; Broderbund products are available in more than 16,000 stores nationwide. The company's distribution and sales network includes seven national sales offices, a European sales and marketing office in London, and distribution arrangements in Australia and Japan.

Broderbund Software, Inc. traces its heritage to two brothers, Douglas and Gary Carlston, who founded the company during the computer software industry's infancy in 1980 in order to market computer game programs the older Douglas had created. Douglas Carlston was first exposed to computers during the 1960s. As a college student he worked as a part-time programmer in Harvard's Aiken Computation Laboratory. Carlston's interests were myriad, however. During the 1960s and 1970s he also spent a year in Botswana teaching geography and math, returned to the United States to write *Beginning Swahili,* graduated magna cum laude from Harvard, wrote language texts for American Express, studied economics at Johns Hopkins School of Advanced International Studies, returned to Harvard and earned a law degree, and started a two-partner law firm in Maine where he resumed computer programming in his spare time. Utilizing a Radio Shack computer, Carlston developed his first two software games, *Galactic Empire* and *Galactic Trader,* which found commercial success after being published by outside companies.

By 1979 Douglas Carlston was earning more as a programmer than as an attorney. He left his law practice and drove a ten-year-old car across country to Eugene, Oregon, where his younger brother Gary lived. The cross-country trip was apparently too much for the vehicle, given what Douglas Carlston later told *Forbes*: ''We started the company because I was stuck without a car and didn't have the money to buy a new one.'' The name for the Carlston brothers' new company was derived by adding the contrived word ''broder'' (a blend of Swedish and Danish words meaning ''brothers'') to the German word ''bund'' (which in English means ''alliance'').

With working capital of $7,000, all obtained from family members, the ''brothers alliance'' was thus formed to market Douglas Carlston's computer game software directly to retailers rather than through other publishers. By mid-1980, after establishing an alliance with StarCraft, a Japanese software house, the company began marketing home entertainment software. In 1981 Broderbund Software, Inc. was incorporated as a California company.

Douglas Carlston became Broderbund's first president and Gary Carlston was named chief executive officer. In 1981 the brothers were joined by a sister, Cathy Carlston, who became vice-president of educational market planning and was later instrumental in marketing software to schools. The company quickly grew to include more than 40 employees and sell millions of dollars worth of software annually. Broderbund relocated its operations from Eugene to California's Marin County in 1982.

During the early 1980s Broderbund published and distributed what was principally entertainment software, developed in conjunction with freelance programmers. Concerned that the company have adequate back-up capital on hand during its infancy, Douglas Carlston courted a number of outside investors between 1982 and 1984. He raised $3 million, and while the funds were never needed, these investors later played a role in Broderbund's initial public offering.

In 1984 Broderbund diversified, adding productivity and educational programs that the Carlstons believed consumers would want after computers gained widespread acceptance. In 1984

Broderbund scored its first major hit in the category of personal productivity with the release of *The Print Shop,* a pioneering "home creativity" program that enabled users with little computer knowledge to create calendars, greeting cards, fliers, posters, and signs.

Broderbund's first educational software success came after the Carlstons observed increasing numbers of schools purchasing computers despite the limited availability of educational software. The company responded by developing and releasing *Where in the World is Carmen Sandiego?* in 1985. The program, the first of many Carmen Sandiego titles destined to become hits, was credited as the industry's first "edutainment" software, blending both education and entertainment qualities. Based on a geography game the Carlston brothers had invented and played as children, the program was created in conjunction with Broderbund's in-house developers. It soon gained widespread admiration and acceptance from parents and teachers. The educational value of the game was found in its entertaining goal: to piece together geographical and historical clues in order to track Carmen Sandiego, an international jewel thief travelling through time and around the world.

The early 1980s was a largely unregulated period for software developers. Recognizing that upstart companies sometimes created computer versions of arcade games without great consideration for royalties and copyrights, Broderbund utilized a private investigator to seek out those pirating the company's software. The company's efforts to protect its programs translated into several copyright infringement lawsuits during the mid-1980s, and in 1986 Broderbund won a groundbreaking suit that found that software maker Unison World Inc. had infringed on Broderbund's copyright of *The Print Shop.* A federal court ruled that Unison had copied the "overall appearance, structure, and sequence" of Broderbund's software. Broderbund won an undisclosed settlement, and the decision was later cited by other software companies claiming copyright law covered the appearance of a software program as well as a program's basic computer code.

In 1987 Broderbund was reincorporated in Delaware and announced intentions for an initial public offering of stock. But a mid-year industry concern regarding the impact of a new IBM "personal computer" on the then-dominant "microcomputer" industry resulted in a major sell-off of computer stocks. About the same time, Broderbund earnings came in below projections and the public offering was postponed.

In 1989 Broderbund released a software program called *The Playroom.* This program, which later became part of the company's Early Learning Products group, featured two mice that taught preschoolers reading and math fundamentals. That same year Gary Carlston and Cathy Carlston left the company, and Douglas Carlston assumed his brother's former titles of chairman and chief executive. Ed Auer, who had joined Broderbund in 1987 after 23 years at CBS, Inc., was promoted from chief operating officer and senior vice-president to president.

In 1990 Broderbund surpassed the $50 million mark in annual revenues, earning $6.2 million on sales of $50.4 million. In 1991 Broderbund flirted with the idea of merging with Sierra On-Line Inc. in a deal that would have made Broderbund a wholly owned subsidiary of Sierra, an entertainment software publisher. In March of that year the two companies signed a merger agreement for a stock swap worth nearly $90 million, but soon afterwards the deal was called off.

In 1991 Broderbund debuted *Kid Pix,* a children's drawing and painting program initially developed by an Oregon art professor for his son. The program proved to be an affiliated-label hit for Broderbund, which had identified a market need for such a product. For Broderbund's 1991 fiscal year (ending August 31, 1991), sales climbed to $55.7 million as earnings inched up to $7 million. With some of Broderbund's venture capitalists seeking to cash in their investments, in November 1991 the company went public. Investors sold a 36 percent stake in Broderbund for $11 a share. One month later the stock was selling for nearly twice its initial offering price.

In the early 1990s Broderbund benefitted from widespread interest in Carmen Sandiego in the form of numerous licensing agreements and marketing opportunities. In 1991 the company signed an agreement with Western Publishing Company, Inc. to use the Carmen Sandiego adventures to market various printed materials, including books and puzzles. That same year PBS premiered a weekday quiz show that, while it did not garner any licensing fees, exposed a daily audience of one million viewers to the Carmen chase. In 1992 Broderbund sold the live-action film rights for Carmen Sandiego and began discussions with the California company University Games to develop a board game based on the exploits of Carmen Sandiego. A year later, the Fox network debuted an animated Carmen Sandiego show. Video games, clothing, albums, and a calendar also joined the growing list of licensed Carmen Sandiego merchandise.

Broderbund's programs continued to demonstrate their staying power through sales records. In 1992 Carmen Sandiego titles surpassed 2.5 million in sales, while sales of *The Print Shop* titles eclipsed the four-million-unit mark. Conversely, the products offered by most of Broderbund's competitors had a shelf life of less than a year,

In 1992 Broderbund made several moves to expand its product line and marketing opportunities. In July 1992 Broderbund acquired PC Globe, Inc., an Arizona-based manufacturer of electronic maps and atlases, for $1.5 million. As a Broderbund subsidiary, PC Globe went on to publish *Maps 'n' Facts,* a family atlas and geographical information program. The company also added mainstream retailers like Wal-Mart to its established retail base of computer specialty stores, and the expansion of merchandising channels helped accelerate sales; for the 1992 fiscal year Broderbund's revenues rose to $75 million while earnings climbed to $9.65 million. Broderbund's success was noticed by the nation's leading business periodicals. Both *Fortune* and *Forbes* lauded the company, and the latter labeled Broderbund "the country's most successful maker of educational software."

Gambling on the belief that CD-ROM drives would become commonplace on computer drives, Broderbund committed its future product line to CD-ROM platforms in the early 1990s. In February 1992 Broderbund released its first CD-ROM title, *Where in the World is Carmen Sandiego? CD-ROM.* In the spring of 1992, Broderbund released another product that reflected their belief that parents would pay in the neighborhood of $50 for an interactive storybook. *Just Grandma and Me,* Broderbund's second CD-ROM product, was its first interactive children's storybook designed to be read on computers.

For the 1992 holiday season, Broderbund's titles dominated the computer software charts. Five of its programs claimed spots in the list of the top ten best-selling software programs. Broderbund's holiday hits included three of the company's six Carmen Sandiego titles as well as *Kid Pix* and *The Playroom.*

In March 1993 Broderbund's affiliated-label program was dealt a blow when its largest affiliated label, the California developer Maxis Software, went independent after recording more than $10 million in annual sales. Maxis had been with Broderbund since 1988, Broderbund's own revenues for the 1993 fiscal year mushroomed to $95.6 million, garnering the company $13.6 million in earnings.

Broderbund took strides to expand beyond its traditional market of 10- to 14-year-olds in 1993. Targeting an older teenage audience, Broderbund debuted *Myst,* a non-violent adventure-exploration game that encourages players to employ puzzle-solving skills in a surrealistic world; and *3D Home Architect,* a program designed to assist amateur home designers and remodelers in creating rooms or houses. The company also adopted the moniker Early Learning Products for its growing line of educational software programs for children aged three to ten.

Between 1991 and 1993 the number of CD-ROM software titles in the nation grew from about 20 to 400 and CD-ROM software grew to claim about a ten percent stake in the $750 million consumer software market. Broderbund's gamble on CD-ROM technology began yielding concrete dividends in 1993. By the latter part of that year, the company's first two CD-ROM interactive storybooks—*Just Grandma and Me* and *Arthur's Teacher Trouble*—were among the top ten best-selling CD-ROM titles nationally.

To further expand on and accelerate its publication of interactive storybooks, Broderbund agreed in September 1993 to a joint venture with Random House, Inc. to create interactive multimedia storybooks. The storybook series, called Living Books, represented one of the first ventures between a leading consumer software publisher of interactive children's books and a large print publishing house. Living Books was designed to expand existing distribution networks for both companies, capitalize on the growing market for interactive software for children, and accelerate development of each company's electronic book plans. In attempting to captivate young readers while at the same time allowing for an interactive multimedia experience, Living Books titles adopted such features as animated illustrations, multimedia sound effects, and options for the reader. Objects on the screen could be activated through use of a mouse or stories could be narrated, with text simultaneously displayed in English, Spanish, or Japanese.

In December 1993 Broderbund stock—along with the stock of a handful of other software makers—dropped $6 to $34.50 after the company announced it was taking a cautious view towards future growth. The announcement came at a time when the personal computer software market as a whole was making a transition from floppy disk to CD-ROM format. Concerns about Broderbund's future stemmed from a decline in sales of Broderbund's older software titles on floppy disks as well as the entrance of Microsoft Corporation into the home software market with programs similar to Broderbund's *Kid Pix* and *The Print Shop.* During the 1993 holiday season, Broderbund's sales of CD-ROM products rose while sales of floppy disk products and affiliated-label programs fell.

The company's stock eventually rebounded into the $41 range. In February 1994 Broderbund agreed to be acquired in a $400 million stock swap by one of its largest competitors, Electronic Arts Inc., which had three times the sales of Broderbund. The merger was expected to create one of the nation's largest consumer software production companies. The company would serve the home entertainment-education market for both computers and video game players by combining Broderbund's high technology and expertise in interactive software with Electronic Arts Hollywood productions skills and experience providing entertainment and video games for such companies as Sega, Nintendo, and 3DO. The merger also aimed to bolster each company's durability against growing competitive threats: Microsoft, which was impinging on Broderbund's turf, and Acclaim Entertainment, a video game manufacturer and Electronic Arts competitor. Broderbund also hoped that the merger would encourage international expansion opportunities and additional hardware platforms for its software.

In 1994 Ed Auer retired and was replaced by William McDonagh, who had joined the company in 1982 as controller. He advanced through the ranks to the positions of chief financial officer and senior vice president before becoming president. That same year Broderbund created a new business development department to pursue alliances with other companies and increase international sales, which at the time represented less than ten percent of all revenues. During an internal reorganization in 1994, Broderbund also partitioned its program development operations into three separate segments designed to address the company's principal market categories: early learning, entertainment and education, and personal productivity.

In the spring of 1994 the joint-venture Living Books took substantial steps to expand its available titles. It outmaneuvered its competition to acquire the multimedia rights to the books of Dr. Seuss (Theodore Geisel) from the author's widow. Random House, Broderbund's partner in Living Books, had been the exclusive publisher of the 48 Dr. Seuss print books, which had sold over a total of 200 million copies. That same month Living Books also acquired world multimedia rights to the "First Time" series of The Berenstain Bears preschooler stories, which had sold over 165 million copies since debuting in 1982.

In May 1994 Broderbund pulled out of its merger agreement with Electronic Arts after the stock value of both companies took a sizable drop. The devalued Electronic Arts stock reduced Broderbund's take in the deal by nearly $100 million. Broderbund agreed to pay Electronic Arts $10 million to terminate the merger; nonetheless, Broderbund stockholders welcomed the move and the Broderbund's stock value rose $6.50 to $41.25, approximately the level it had been trading at prior to the merger announcement.

During the 1994 fiscal year, Broderbund published 68 new products—50 percent more than the previous year—in part because of the need to address the diverse platform needs of its customers. Broderbund's revenues for the year rose to $111.7 million while profits slid to $11 million. The company's bottom line suffered from the more than $10 million in charges related to the terminated merger with Electronic Arts. Earnings were bolstered by sales of CD-ROM software, which proved less expensive to produce and yielded a higher profit margin than floppy disk programs.

By the beginning of its 1995 fiscal year (September 1994), Broderbund had released a full line of CD-ROM software. A CD-ROM version of *Myst* that featured 2,500 original 3-D graphics and an original soundtrack became the company's most popular product that year. Broderbund hailed it as the first ever blockbuster CD-ROM entertainment software program. By October 1994 the company's stock had risen to $57.50 on the strength of the popularity of CD-ROM-driven computers and Broderbund's Living Books, Early Learning, and *Myst* programs. *Myst* was credited by some analysts as an important reason for the substantial increase in sales of CD-ROM-based computers during the 1994 holiday season.

Broderbund entered 1995 with new generations of popular software, including *The Print Shop Deluxe CD Ensemble* and *3D Home Architect.* The company also announced plans to release its first Berenstain Bears interactive storybook and other new entertainment titles. Its *Myst II* sequel to the original *Myst* program was targeted for release in 1996. For the first six months of fiscal 1995, Broderbund posted revenues of $98 million—better than all of 1993's sales—and earnings of $21.9 million—better than earnings from any preceding full year. Named a *Business Week* ''Hot Growth'' company back in 1993, the magazine noted that by early 1995 Broderbund had brought investors a two-year return of better than 180 percent.

As Broderbund moved towards the conclusion of its 1995 fiscal year, the company continued to benefit from a number of market factors: rapid acceptance of CD-ROM-based computer drives (shipments jumped from 16.5 million in 1993 to 53.9 million in 1994), growing company name recognition, and the sustained popularity of *Myst,* which maintained its place as the country's top consumer software program during the first three months of 1995. Broderbund expected to increasingly benefit from a more cost-effective market environment as hardware platforms consolidated, rendering unnecessary various program versions for DOS, Windows, Macintosh, floppy, and CD-ROM platforms. Most future Broderbund products were expected to be released for CD-ROM-based Macintosh or CD-ROM Windows platforms.

As Broderbund looked to 1996 and beyond, the company expected to continue to capitalize on its historic strengths: its ability to identify emerging consumer interests, utilize emerging technology, and develop software that can make learning fun, appeal to third parties like parents and teachers, and sustain popularity. In its drive to publish popular software, the company also expected program development to continue to focus on interactivity and ease-of-use design ingredients.

In terms of its growth prospects for the remainder of the 1990s, Broderbund appeared well positioned to benefit from several continuing trends: the growth of CD-ROM-based computers; the increasing affordability of high-powered home computers; and the company's expanding merchandising network. With both history and newer trends on its side, there was strong reason to believe that if the education and entertainment software industry continued to meet its projected annual growth rates of 25 to 30 percent for the late 1990s, Broderbund's growth could at least follow suit.

Principal Subsidiaries: PC Globe, Inc.

Further Reading:

Adelson, Andrea, ''Random House Children's Books Headed for PC's,'' *New York Times,* September 11, 1993, p. 39.

Bulkeley, William M., ''Courts Expand the Copyright Protection Of Software, but Many Questions Remain, *Wall Street Journal,* November 18, 1986, p. 35.

The Corporate Backgrounder and Consumer Software Market Update, Broderbund Software, Inc., March 1995.

Cox, Meg, ''Living Books Receives Rights To Seuss Books,'' *Wall Street Journal,* April 21, 1994, p. B7.

Dolan, Carrie, and Don Clark, ''Electronic Arts Sets Acquisition of Broderbund,'' *Wall Street Journal,* February 10, 1994, p. 5.

——, ''Small Software Companies Crack the Educational Market: Childish Pursuits Pay at Broderbund, Home Of Carmen Sandiego,'' *Wall Street Journal,* March 10, 1993, pp. B1–B2.

Fisher, Lawrence M., ''Broderbund Stock Tumbles on Growth Concerns,'' *New York Times,* December 24, 1993, p. D3.

——, ''CD-ROM Sales Propel Profit At Broderbund,'' *New York Times,* March 23, 1995, p. C6.

——, ''Demand for CD-ROM Titles Lifts Broderbund Earnings,'' *New York Times,* October 8, 1994, pp. 39, 41.

——, ''2 Companies In Software Drop Merger: No Broderbund Deal With Electronic Arts,'' *New York Times,* May 4, 1994, p. D5.

Giltenan, Edward, ''Who in the World is Doug Carlston?'' *Forbes,* April 27, 1992, pp. 100–102.

King, Ralph T., Jr., ''Broderbund Jilts Electronic Arts; Scraps Agreement to Be Acquired,'' *Wall Street Journal,* May 4, 1994, p. B5.

Kupfer, Andrew, ''Identify a Need, Turn a Profit,'' *Fortune,* November 30, 1992, pp. 78–79.

Markoff, John, ''Electronic Arts' Move Reflects Industry Trend,'' *New York Times,* February 11, 1994.

—Roger W. Rouland

Brown & Root, Inc.

P.O. Box 3
Houston, Texas 77001
U.S.A.
(713) 676-3011
Fax: (713) 676-7799

Wholly Owned Subsidiary of Halliburton Company
Incorporated: 1929 as Brown & Root, Inc.
Employees: 52,000
Sales: $3.14 billion
Stock Exchanges: New York London Zurich Geneva Basel Lausanne Toronto
SICs: 1541 Industrial Buildings & Warehouses; 8711 Engineering Services; 7349 Building Maintenance Services, Not Elsewhere Classified

One of the largest construction and engineering companies in the world, Brown & Root, Inc. provided a diverse line of services to industrial and government customers in numerous countries. With offices and construction projects scattered across the globe, the company represented a genuine multinational force in the construction industry, earning an enviable reputation as a premier designer and builder of onshore and offshore oil platforms, petrochemical plants, and electric power generators.

With the financial backing of his brother-in-law Dan Root, Herman Brown started a road building company named Brown & Root in 1919 with mortgaged wagons and mules. Indeed, it was a meager beginning for a man who would ultimately spearhead some of the largest and most difficult construction projects in modern history and create one of the world's largest construction and engineering firms.

In considerable debt from setting up his business, Brown found work where he could before landing his first road building job in Freestone, Texas. This opportunity led to other road building and earth-moving work elsewhere as Brown gradually tried to make enough money to pay for the mules and wagons which he later described as a "worn-out . . . three-fresno and plow outfit." Despite Brown's modest equipment, three years after commencing business he was able to win the contracts to rebuild four bridges that had been washed out by a flood in Central Texas. This project represented the fledgling company's first big break, but it also posed a formidable challenge. One of the bridges would require underwater blasting to set its piers, a task for which Brown had no experience; nevertheless, he was commissioned with superintending its execution. This project proved to be the first of many such challenges for Herman Brown and his company.

At many times in Brown & Root's history, the company's employees and management would find themselves either initially lacking the experience to complete a task or being the first group to undertake a certain endeavor. However, cast in the role of pioneer Brown & Root rose to the occasion in an overwhelming majority of these situations, successfully navigating through uncharted waters and completing what theretofore had been considered improbable. For Brown, the solution to this first problem came from his younger brother George.

Possessing a degree in mining from the Colorado School of Mines, George Brown was home convalescing from a mining accident when his brother approached him about Brown & Root's contracts to rebuild the four bridges. The elder Brown convinced his brother to head the project, thereby resolving the underwater blasting issue and bringing George Brown into the Brown & Root fold. Beginning in 1922, the two brothers would work together for the next 40 years, taking Brown & Root to new heights in each succeeding decade and using their contrasting personalities to steward the company through the many challenges that lay waiting ahead. In meeting these challenges, Herman Brown would be remembered as a "working man's man," personally visiting job sites throughout the year, wherever they were, often more inclined to spend time with his employees than with his fellow executives. His brother George was just the opposite, despite his practical experience in mining. George Brown functioned best as Brown & Root's salesman, able to negotiate over the telephone and influence others with his outgoing personality, talents that were best applied to pursuing Brown & Root's business opportunities. With these two complementary styles, George and Herman Brown successfully concluded the reconstruction of the four bridges in Central Texas, opened an office in Houston in 1926, and then spent the remainder of the decade slowly expanding their business largely through work obtained from building contracts awarded by the State of Texas.

Despite the promising beginning that Brown & Root had shown during the 1920s, two calamities struck at the end of the decade which had a profound effect on the company. In 1929, Dan Root, Herman and George Brown's brother-in-law, died, the same year that the stock market crash precipitated the Great Depression, sending the country into a deleterious decade-long economic slide. The death of Root, who had been instrumental in the formation of the company ten years earlier, caused the company to take stock of its situation. The Brown brothers purchased Root's interest in the company and then incorporated as Brown & Root, Inc. that same year, marking a new beginning for the company on the eve of the devastating economic climate of the 1930s.

With the onset of the Depression, the number of state-funded construction projects slowed to a trickle, forcing the two brothers to pursue other work, including hauling garbage for the city of Houston. However, Brown & Root was able to escape from the grip of the Depression in a relatively short time, securing a contract in 1934 for the construction of a board road for Humble Oil Company in Roanoke, Louisiana. The contract was significant for two reasons: first, it extended the company's geographic presence from Texas into Louisiana, and second, it formed the first connection with a company that 30 years later would purchase Brown & Root. Humble Oil, the client for Brown & Root's board road contract, was one of seven major oil companies that owned a company then known as Halliburton Oil Well Cementing Company. This business was later renamed the Halliburton Company, and it would eventually become the parent company of Brown & Root in the 1960s.

Of more immediate significance to the two brothers, though, was a project awarded to the company in 1936, when Brown & Root secured the construction contract for the Marshall Ford Dam. This venture marked the company's entry into heavy construction and the power industry and proved to be a defining moment in the company's history. Located west of Austin, the Marshall Ford Dam, later renamed the Mansfield Dam, would become the largest structure of its kind in Texas, measuring nearly a mile wide and standing 25 stories high. This project, which lasted five years and took two million tons of concrete to complete, elevated Brown & Root's status from that of a constructor of moderately sized projects to a company capable of taking on the largest types of construction projects in the world.

The success of the Marshall Dam project led to more large-scale, government-funded work four years later, when Brown & Root was awarded a contract to help build a $90-million naval air station at Corpus Christi, Texas, in 1940. The construction of the Corpus Christi Naval Air Station was prompted by the looming threat of World War II, and as the United States took steps toward entering the conflict, Brown & Root unexpectedly found itself at the center of the government's plans for armament. In addition to the Corpus Christi project, the U.S. Navy approached George Brown in 1941 about taking over the contract to build four submarine chasers, a venture that would pay the company $640,000 for each vessel. Similar to the company's early years, Brown & Root was faced with a project that called for skills that it did not possess, although this task called for much more sophisticated talents.

With no previous experience in ship building, the Brown brothers formed Brown Shipbuilding Company and began work on the four submarine chasers stipulated in the Navy contract. Their marked success with the first four led to a contract for four additional submarine chasers, then 12 more, finally resulting in an order in early 1942 for a medium-sized fleet of destroyer escorts which yielded Brown & Root $3.3 million for each ship. By the end of the war, George and Herman Brown's uncertain foray into ship building had resulted in 359 combat ships, 12 pursuit craft, 307 landing craft, 36 rocket-firing boats, and four salvage boats being constructed for the U.S. Navy, a production total worth $500 million.

Brown & Root emerged from the war as a major U.S. construction company. Its success with the Marshall Ford Dam, the Corpus Christi Naval Station, and its impressive wartime work had propelled the company into the upper echelon of the country's construction firms, a remarkable achievement for a business that as recently as 20 years earlier was subsisting on constructing wooden roads to support oil field work.

During the postwar period, Brown & Root continued to increase the magnitude and scope of its construction and engineering projects, pioneering a string of industry firsts. In 1946, Brown & Root received its first overseas assignment when it was selected as managing partner for the reconstruction of Guam, which had incurred severe damage during World War II. Also that year, Brown & Root began work on its first major engineering project, a contract for a chlorine caustic plant on the Houston Ship Canal for Diamond Alkali, and was awarded its first paper-mill construction contract from Southland Paper in Lufkin, Texas. The following year, Brown & Root secured a contract from Kerr-McGee to design and build the world's first commercial out-of-sight-of-land oil drilling platform, a pivotal and historic step for a company that would become heavily involved in enabling the off-shore development of oil and gas.

During the 1950s, Brown & Root began to increase its presence outside the United States, laying a foundation for international expansion that would become an integral component of the company's future growth. In 1951, Brown & Root opened an office near Edmonton, Alberta, to facilitate the construction of a petrochemical and synthetic fiber plant. One year later, the company expanded to the southern hemisphere when it began building a series of gas injection plants on Lake Maracaibo, Venezuela. After extending its presence into Canada and Venezuela, Brown & Root tackled two enormous projects in 1958, building the Bhumiphol Dam in Thailand and the Tantangara Dam and Tunnel for the Snowy Mountains Hydroelectric Authority in Australia. The company ended its first decade of international expansion by opening an office in London with the expectation of gaining contracts from anticipated oil and gas exploration in the North Sea.

In the meantime, Brown & Root also continued to augment the scope of its domestic operations. In 1951, the company designed and built a major petrochemical facility for the Celanese Corporation; one year later, it was awarded its first $100-million contract when it constructed a polyethylene plant in Seadrift, Texas, for Union Carbide. This venture expanded Brown & Root's diversification into petroleum and chemical activities and added customers such as Ciba Giegy and Du Pont to the company's growing list of clients.

Going into the 1960s, Brown & Root had gained the reputation of an engineering and construction firm able to take on the largest of construction projects. As the company prepared for the challenges of the 1960s, it would enhance this reputation by becoming highly regarded for its technical expertise. Two projects in particular greatly contributed to this perspective. In 1960, the company became involved in a government project for the National Science Foundation dubbed Project Mohole, the objective of which was to drill in 14,000-foot deep water and penetrate 21,000 feet below the earth's crust. The following year, Brown & Root followed up this ambitious foray into marine engineering technology by being selected by the National Aeronautics and Space Administration (NASA) as architect-engineer for the Manned Spacecraft Center in Houston.

While Brown & Root was taking on these two signal projects, the company's founder was suffering from serious health problems. Herman Brown had undergone heart surgery in 1960, and in its aftermath his prognosis grew increasingly bleak, causing concern over the company's future. A tightly held private firm up to this point, executives resolved to find a company to purchase a controlling interest in Brown & Root as Brown's health worsened in 1961 and 1962. Against this backdrop, Brown & Root was approached by Halliburton Company, an oil field services concern that brought companies with expertise in the oil and gas industry under its corporate umbrella. Since Brown & Root fit Halliburton's acquisition criteria and the company itself was agreeable to becoming part of Halliburton, acquisition negotiations between the two companies commenced in autumn 1962. The deal was completed in November, shortly after Brown's death, with Halliburton paying $32.6 million for roughly 95 percent of Brown & Root up front, then acquiring the remaining five percent in June 1963.

George Brown was elected to Halliburton's board of directors concurrent with Brown & Root's sale, and he continued as the company's president and chief executive officer for another year. In this new era, the company fared as well as it had during its past, becoming, like its parent company, increasingly involved in construction and engineering projects for the oil and gas industry. In 1966, Brown & Root laid the first marine pipeline in the North Sea; two years later, the company laid and buried the world's first 48-inch pipeline in offshore Kuwait.

During the 1970s, Brown & Root would use the talents it had first gained during the construction of the Marshall Ford Dam between 1936 and 1941 to build power generating plants. In 1977 alone, the company placed five electric plants into operation, part of Brown & Root's decade-long effort to meet the rising demand for electric power. Among the decade's other highlights were the design and construction in 1972 of two fabrication facilities, Highland Fabricators in Nigg, Scotland, and Sunda Straits Fabrication Yard in Indonesia. These projects positioned Brown & Root for offshore platform work and the design of Chahbahar Baval Port for the Iranian Imperial Navy in 1975.

After decades of remarkable success, Brown & Root's fortunes began to change in the late 1970s. In January 1977, Brown & Root announced that company documents pertaining to offshore oil platform activities had been subpoenaed by a Federal grand jury to investigate possible antitrust charges. Nine days after the announcement, Foster Parker, George Brown's hand-picked successor to the post of president and chief executive officer of Brown & Root, was discovered dead in his bedroom with a bullet wound in his right temple. No confirmed connection between the grand jury's inquiry and Parker's apparent suicide was immediately made, but nearly two years later, in December 1978, Brown & Root pleaded no contest to antitrust charges and paid $90 million to settle related civil claims. The allegations of price fixing, led, a short time later, to a protracted legal battle with the proprietors of the South Texas Nuclear Project, ending in a $750 million settlement paid by Brown & Root in 1985.

While it was embroiled in legal turmoil, Brown & Root continued to benefit from large construction and engineering projects, completing the Eisenhower Tunnel at Loveland Pass, Colorado, in 1979 and installing the world's first guyed tower platform in 1,200 feet of water in the Gulf of Mexico in 1984. In 1986, Brown & Root completed a $475 million joint-venture project to build a military base for the U.S. Navy and Air Force on the island of Diego Garcia in the Indian Ocean. The same year, it formed Brown & Root Services Corporation to obtain government operations and maintenance work.

As Brown & Root maneuvered through the late 1980s, it strengthened its construction and engineering abilities with the acquisition of two companies: Howard Humphreys, a civil consulting company with expertise in water, dams, roads, bridges, buildings, and tunneling, in 1987, and CF Braun, a process engineering firm, in 1989. Entering the 1990s, Brown & Root extended its presence into Eastern Europe, completed its first major project off the shore of China, and participated in the reconstruction of Kuwait following the Persian Gulf War.

After strengthening its position in Eastern Europe in 1993 by forming Brown & Root Skoda in the Czech Republic through a joint venture, Brown & Root entered the mid-1990s with plans to increase its operations in the region, where opportunities for the company in oil and gas development abounded. The company's future, however, called for Brown & Root personnel to engage in large-sale, sophisticated construction and engineering projects across the globe, where the company had achieved historic success since the 1950s. As Brown & Root moved toward this future, its remarkable rise from a small company boasting no more than mortgaged mules and wagons to one of the largest construction and engineering concerns in the world instilled confidence that the years ahead would represent a continuation of its storied past.

Principal Subsidiaries: Enterprise Building Corporation; Brown & Root Industrial Services, Inc.; Brown & Root Technical Services, Inc.; Brown & Root Services Corporation; Brown & Root International, Inc.; Brown & Root International, Inc. (Panama); Brown & Root (Gulf) E.C. (Bahrain); Brown & Root Offshore Ltd. (Antilles); Brown & Root (Overseas) Limited (United Kingdom).

Further Reading:

Brown & Root, Inc., *Brownbuilder* (75th anniversary edition), 1994.

"Brown & Root Settles," *New York Times,* May 31, 1985, p. D3.

"B&R Executive Sees Busy Future for Marine Work," *Oil and Gas Journal,* November 16, 1970, pp. 217–8.

"Halliburton to Buy Brown & Root from Foundation," *Wall Street Journal,* December 13, 1962, p. 32.

"Halliburton Is Said to Discuss Merger with Brown & Root," *Wall Street Journal,* December 11, 1962, p. 16.

"Halliburton Unit Plans Venture," *Wall Street Journal,* October 26, 1994, p. B5.

Lindsey, Robert, "Puzzle of Executive's Death Stuns Texas," *New York Times,* February 7, 1977, p. 35.

—Jeffrey L. Covell

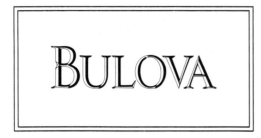

Bulova Corporation

1 Bulova Avenue
Woodside, New York 11377-7874
U.S.A.
(718) 204-3300
Fax: (718) 204-3546

Wholly Owned Subsidiary of Loews Corporation
Incorporated: 1911 as J. Bulova Co.
Employees: 1,150
Sales: $154 million
SICs: 5094 Jewelry, Watches & Precious Stones; 3613 Switchgear & Switchboard Apparatus; 3679 Electronic Components, Not Elsewhere Classified

Bulova Corporation is one of the largest and most venerable watch companies in the world. Among the most widely recognized brand names in its industry, Bulova produces watches in a wide variety of styles and is represented in every price range. At the upper end, the company's offerings include the Bulova Signature Group, the 14-karat gold Ultimé, and the famous Accutron line of luxury watches. In the lower price bracket, Bulova is represented by the Caravelle, a popular line originally introduced in the early 1960s. The company also makes specialty watches featuring other well-known logos. One example is the company's Sportstime line, which features watches representing teams in all of America's major sports leagues. Through its Bulova Technologies, Inc. subsidiary, Bulova is also active in the defense industry. Bulova Technologies specializes in making fuses and other components for military use. In the mid-1990s, it was diversifying into medical equipment and other areas to compensate for decreasing sales to the military. Loews Corporation, which has holdings in the hotel, tobacco, and insurance industries, owns 97 percent of Bulova Corporation's stock.

Joseph Bulova, a Czech immigrant, founded the company that bears his name in 1875. Only 23 years old at the time, Bulova opened a modest jewelry shop in New York City. Initially, Bulova sold mainly pocket watches and other jewelry, but over time he expanded his line of products. He was manufacturing and selling his own desk clocks and other timepieces by 1911, the year he incorporated the operation as J. Bulova Company. By that time, Bulova's pocket watches had already attained a reputation for excellence, and New Yorkers bought them as fast as he could make them.

Although wristwatches existed before World War I, it was returning veterans who made them fashionable. Once Americans became aware of their convenience, the market for wristwatches in the U.S. expanded quickly. In 1919, Bulova introduced the first full line of jeweled wristwatches for men. Over the next several years, Bulova added several other industry firsts, including the first ladies wristwatch line and the first line of diamond wristwatches. In 1926, the company sponsored the first nationally broadcast radio spot commercials, featuring the immortal ''At the tone, it's 8 p.m., B-U-L-O-V-A Bulova watch time'' tag line. Bulova began selling the world's first clock radio two years later. Meanwhile, the company's name was changed to Bulova Watch Company, Inc., reflecting the growing role of Arde Bulova, Joseph's son, in the firm's management.

Bulova continued to innovate in the areas of marketing and advertising over the decades that followed. The company launched the first million-dollar advertising campaign the watch industry had seen in 1931. Ten years later, Bulova aired the world's first television commercial. Broadcast just before a 1941 Brooklyn Dodgers baseball game, the advertisement showed a simple picture of a clock superimposed on a map of the United States. The message was simply ''America runs on Bulova time.''

The entry of the U.S. into World War II led to Bulova's large-scale involvement into military manufacturing. In addition to producing precision timepieces for military equipment, Bulova's mass production facilities also began turning out fuses, aircraft instruments, and other mechanisms for use in the war effort. Toward the end of the war, Bulova opened the Joseph Bulova School of Watchmaking. Its main mission was to help disabled veterans learn a trade upon their return from the war.

By this time, Arde Bulova was firmly in charge of the company, and he ran it very much as a one-man show. Under Arde, Bulova grew to become one of the market leaders among U.S. watchmakers. By the mid-1950s, the company's annual sales had reached $80 million. In 1954, Arde Bulova hired Gen. Omar Bradley, a World War II hero, as chairman of Bulova Research & Development Labs, Inc., a wholly owned subsidiary involved in developing the company's defense product business. Bradley was a close war-time friend of Harry D. Henshel, Arde Bulova's brother-in-law and one of the company's largest shareholders. When Arde Bulova died in 1958, Bradley was the logical choice to take over the chairmanship of Bulova, although it took a committee of 14 department heads to cover the huge range of responsibilities that Arde had refused to delegate in the past.

Meanwhile, a new contender had risen to challenge Bulova's dominant position in the watch industry. Throughout the second half of the 1950s, Bulova faced stiff competition from the Timex watch, made by U.S. Time Corporation. Priced far lower than Bulova products, Timex eroded Bulova's market share enough to cause the company's revenue to slip to $62.8 million by 1961. Under Bradley and CEO Harry B. Henshel, Bulova began to fight back. First, they began to institute modern management practices, replacing the old-fashioned methods of the autocratic Arde Bulova. More importantly, the company developed Accutron, the world's first electronic watch.

Accutron represented the first major revolution in clock technology in three centuries. Before it was available in commercial products, the Accutron timer mechanism saw important action in the space program. When the Accutron watch finally became available to consumers in late 1960, it was a huge success. Far more accurate than any other watch commercially available, the Accutron was the first to be sold with a written guarantee of accuracy to within one minute a month. Accutron technology became the standard for the next decade both on human wrists and in orbiting satellites.

In 1963, Bulova introduced another line of watches, the Caravelle. The Caravelle was the company's answer to Timex and the other cheaper watch lines that had been eating away at Bulova's customer base for several years. Caravelle was priced much lower than the company's other watches, and it was hoped that the line would catch on among younger buyers who would later graduate to more expensive models. With the addition of Accutron and Caravelle, Bulova was able to regain much of the momentum it had lost to Timex and the many nameless brands of cheap watches that had hit the market over the previous decade. The company also eliminated outlets that were selling Bulova watches at discount prices, a practice company officials felt tarnished the Bulova name and reputation for excellence. By fiscal 1964, the year the company shipped its 250,000th Accutron watch, Bulova's revenue finally surpassed its pre-slump level, reaching a new high of $73 million.

The next several years were good ones for Bulova. By 1965, sales had grown to $84 million, about 20 percent of which was generated by defense and industrial products, including timing mechanisms and fuses. There were 58 different Accutron models for the wrist and 11 Accutron desk and table clocks by that time. Bulova controlled an estimated 15 percent of the market for high-priced men's watches. Throughout this period, the company also worked hard to increase its sales abroad. By 1967, 20 percent of Bulova's sales were generated in foreign lands. Bulova watches were being sold in 89 countries by that year, up from 19 in 1961. The fact that most of Bulova's watch movements were assembled in Switzerland added to its international flavor, and in 1967 the company acquired Universal Genève, a Swiss manufacturer of upper-end clocks and watches. Company sales leaped to $124 million for that year. Meanwhile, Bulova remained NASA's timekeeper of choice. Timing devices built by Bulova saw action during the first moon walk in 1969, as well as on subsequent missions.

By the beginning of the 1970s, Bulova had sold nearly 1.5 million Accutrons, and the company's watches could be bought in 110 markets around the world. The company was operating 20 plants, 12 of them in the United States. Even at that time, Bulova was still the only manufacturer of jeweled-movement watches in the United States. In 1971, the company launched a joint venture with a Japanese outfit, Citizen Watch Co., to make Accutrons for sale in Asia. Bulova was offering four basic lines of watches by 1973, covering every price range: the low-priced Caravelle, starting at $10.95; the Bulova line, which cost $35 and up; the still booming Accutron, whose bottom price had dropped to $95; and the Accuquartz, introduced in 1970 as the first quartz watch sold in the United States.

In 1973, Bulova's status as a fiercely independent company came to an end when Gulf & Western Industries, Inc. bought a stake in the company. That interest eventually grew to 29 percent ownership. Bulova's hot streak began to run out about the same time. One reason for the turnaround was that the company seemed to have miscalculated the popularity of digital watches. Bulova stood by idly while competitors were churning out and selling new quartz digital models in huge numbers. The company eventually started selling solid-state digital watches under the name Computron, but not before falling far behind in the battle for that market. Another problem was a dramatic inflation of the Swiss franc in relation to the U.S. dollar. This development made it difficult for Bulova to compete cost-wise, since so much of its manufacturing was done in Switzerland. For 1975, the company lost $25 million on sales of $204 million.

With losses mounting in 1976, Gulf & Western sold its 26.8 percent interest in Bulova to Stelux Manufacturing Company, a watch components maker based in Hong Kong. With Stelux in control of the company, Henshel was replaced as chief executive by C. P. Wong, managing director of Stelux. It was hoped that Bulova would give Stelux a U.S. outlet for its goods, while Stelux would provide the impetus for Bulova's full-scale assault on the digital market. Unfortunately, the purchase of controlling interest by a foreign-owned company made Bulova ineligible for defense contracts, which had accounted for about 10 percent of sales the year before and were one of its few profitable areas. In order to circumvent those regulations, the company formed a subsidiary, Bulova Systems & Instruments Corporation, to perform its defense work under the management of a team of trustees.

The relationship with Stelux did not prove to be as mutually beneficial as had been hoped, and by 1977 Wong had resigned as CEO of Bulova. He gave up his spot as a director the following year. Between fiscal years 1976 and 1978, Bulova's losses totaled $48 million. In 1979, the 30 percent of Bulova's stock owned by Stelux was bought by Loews Corporation, the holding company run by Laurence Tisch, a close friend of Henshel's. Andrew Tisch, Laurence's 30-year-old son, was named president of Bulova, while Henshel stayed on as chairman.

Under the influence of Loews, Bulova gradually began to claw its way back into competitive form. However, the transition was not seamless. In 1982 the company spent $36 million to take some of its less viable watches off the market, and this move contributed to a $27 million loss for the year. Realizing that the company had cut back on quality control, many retailers had given up on Bulova by this time. Under Loews's management, renewed emphasis was placed on quality inspection. Loews also sold off a number of Bulova's assets between 1981 and 1987, including its electronics division, its main building in Queens, and facilities in Italy and Switzerland. By 1984, Loews owned 95 percent of Bulova's common stock, and Bulova turned an operating profit of over $7 million.

During the late 1980s, Bulova worked hard to revamp its image and regain the respect its name once commanded. In order to attract younger customers, the company began making watches under licensing agreements with such firms as Benetton and Harley-Davidson, and with the National Football League. To appeal to the more highbrow market, Bulova began offering watches based on famous works of art. In 1989, Andrew Tisch took over the leadership of another Loews subsidiary, and was replaced at Bulova by Herbert Hofmann. That year, sales of fuses to the government generated 30 percent of the company's revenue.

By 1990, Bulova was the only major American-owned watch maker left in the business, and its $182 million in sales was dwarfed by the $2.6 billion in revenue generated by industry leader Seiko of Japan. Remaining in the black continued to be a struggle for the company. Bulova posted net losses in 1989 and 1990, as trendy watches such as the popular Swatch stole more market share from old-timers like Bulova. Convinced that classic models were finding their way back into fashion, Bulova reintroduced the Accutron in 1991 after seven years out of circulation. The new Accutron line included 26 different styles, and ranged in price from $395 to $1095.

As the 1990s moved on, the company continued to seek ways to restore its former luster through daring marketing and advertising initiatives, though its budget could not match those of its giant foreign competitors Citizen and Seiko. In 1993, Bulova launched a highly publicized advertising campaign featuring nude celebrities wearing Bulova watches. The theme of the campaign was "I'd feel naked without my Bulova." Meanwhile, the company's defense-oriented subsidiary, now called Bulova Technologies, Inc., began diversifying into commercial areas in the face of shrinking military spending. Non-defense business was scheduled to account for a quarter of the subsidiaries revenue for fiscal 1994.

Several years have passed since Bulova existed as a self-supporting company. For some time, it has relied on an inflow of capital from its parent Loews Corporation to meet its annual financial needs. Nevertheless, going into the mid-1990s the Bulova name and reputation continued to hold sway with a significant number of consumers. Watch fashions come and go quickly, but there always seems to be at least a little room in the market for the company that put the first timepiece on the moon.

Principal Subsidiaries: Bulova Technologies, Inc.

Further Reading:

Barmash, Isadore, "Bulova Tries to Make Up Lost Time," *New York Times,* June 13, 1976, p. F3.

——, "Bulova Seeking to Take the Watch Beyond Time," *New York Times,* October 5, 1989, p. D1.

"Bring on the Revolution," *Forbes,* December 1, 1972, p. 72.

"Bulova Earnings Likely to Wind Up at New Peak," *Barron's,* October 30, 1967, p. 38.

"Bulova Fights for its Contracts," *Business Week,* August 30, 1976, p. 28.

"Bulova—Industry Leader," *Financial World,* August 9, 1967, p. 5.

The Bulova Story, Woodside, New York: Bulova Corporation.

"Bulova Watch Gets a Hong Kong Partner," *Business Week,* June 14, 1976, p. 29.

"Bulova Watch Gets a Tisch as President," *New York Times,* October 18, 1979, p. D2.

"Bulova Watch Ticks Off Smart Advance in Profits," *Barron's,* March 1, 1965, p. 20.

"Bulova's Henshel Goes Against the Trend," *Business Week,* July 14, 1973, p. 60.

"Crucial Hours for the Swiss Watch Industry," *Fortune,* August 15, 1969, p. 116.

Finch, Camilla, "Traditional Watch May Wind Bulova Into Better Future," *Crain's New York Business,* December 24, 1990, p. 13.

"Good Time," *Time,* June 16, 1967, p. 85.

"Multinational Approach Helps Bulova Beat Competitors' Time," *Industry Week,* March 22, 1971, p. 19.

"Successor to a One-Man Regime," *Business Week,* November 21, 1959, p. 104.

Tisch, Andrew H., "Why Marketing Ticks at Bulova," *Marketing Communications,* June 1982, p. 26.

"A Troubled Bulova Bides its Time," *Business Week,* June 16, 1975, p. 22.

Underwood, Elaine, "Bulova 'Buffs' up its Image," *Brandweek,* November 29, 1993, p. 6.

"The Watch That Saved Bulova," *Forbes,* November 15, 1964, p. 42.

"Wong Moves in at Bulova," *Business Week,* June 28, 1976, p. 98.

—Robert R. Jacobson

Burns International Security Services

2 Campus Drive
Parsippany, New Jersey 07054
U.S.A.
(201) 267-5300
Fax: (201) 397-2493

Division of Borg-Warner Security Corporation
Incorporated: 1909
Employees: 40,000
Sales: $920 million
SICs: 7381 Detective, Guard, and Armored Car Services

Burns International Security Services, formerly a subsidiary of the Borg-Warner Security Corporation, became a division within its parent company in the mid-1990s. Along with its own security branch divisions and Burns, Borg-Warner Security also held under its corporate umbrella the Wells Fargo Guard Service Division and operated under the familiar Pony Express, Wells Fargo, and Burns names. In complementary tandem, these Borg-Warner divisions and subsidiaries offered a full array of security and protection services designed to meet an ever increasing private-sector security need in a nation that has seen its crime rate grow at an alarming rate. As a Borg-Warner subsidiary, Burns had to weather some difficult years while the parent company repaid a large leveraged buyout debt that had forced it to go private and downsize in the late 1980s before again emerging as a public corporation in 1993. Burns, restricted to providing guards and related security services, benefited from the restructuring and in the mid-1990s was faring well in an industry in which the demand continued to expand.

The base company from which Burns International Security Services evolved, the William J. Burns National Detective Agency, was established in New York in 1909 by the son of Irish immigrant parents. Burns was born in Baltimore, Maryland, in 1861 and raised in Columbus, Ohio. He attended business college, and then joined his father in a tailoring enterprise, but became an amateur sleuth when, in 1878, his father began serving as police commissioner in Columbus. Although he had no official position with the police department, young William earned a reputation for detective work in forgery cases. For a brief period he worked for the Furlong Detective Agency in St. Louis, Missouri, then, in 1889, entered the U.S. Secret Service, where he had considerable success in tracking down counterfeiting operations, both in the United States and Costa Rica. He also uncovered bribery and land fraud by government employees, leading to the conviction of several federal, state, and municipal officials.

Burns left government service in 1906, with a growing reputation for incorruptibility and excellent detective work. For a time he continued to track down dishonest administrators, including the entire board of supervisors of San Francisco, California, and that city's political boss, Abraham Ruef. Burns and his associates had tough going, having to fight corrupt money interests, including, among others, a national trolley car trust and newspaper magnate William Randolph Hearst, who employed the cartoonist Ed Fisher to caricature them in what would later develop into the "Mutt and Jeff" comic strip.

In 1909, the by then celebrated detective organized the William J. Burns National Detective Agency, and within a year convinced the American Bankers' Association to terminate its association with the agency's chief competitor, the long established and renowned Pinkerton Agency. The move gave the new Burns agency the job of protecting the 12,000 member banks. Somewhat later the agency also gained the responsibility of protecting the holdings of the American Hotel Association. Initially, however, the agency was engaged as much in detective and investigative work as in protection services.

William Burns, from time to time returning to government service, left interim control of the agency to his two sons, Raymond J. Burns, president, and William Sherman Burns, secretary and treasurer. In 1913, the agency changed its name to the Burns International Detective Agency. By this time, the company was becoming famous for innovative detective methods, which, in 1916, involved Burns himself in something of a scandal and began the tarnishing of his image. Hired by the millionaire, J. P. Morgan, Burns led a midnight raid on the law offices of Seymour and Seymour, a firm that, like Morgan, was handling the sale of munitions to France and Great Britain, soon to be the allies of the United States in World War I. The firm was suspected of stealing trade secrets from Morgan, and Burns was trying to obtain evidence of its crime. Burns installed a Detectophone in the offices, a primitive listening device and the ancestor of the modern day "bug." Also, with the aid of New York City police, he wire tapped the firm's telephones. The operation came to light when a disgruntled former employee of the Burns Agency disclosed it to the authorities. When the smoke created by newspaper coverage cleared, Burns was fined $100 for illegal entry.

In 1921, William J. Burns took the directorship of the Justice Department's Bureau of Investigation, the forerunner of the FBI. However, his three-year service in that office did nothing to enhance his reputation, since during that time the Bureau became involved in the scandals that plagued the administration of President Warren G. Harding. Burns resigned in 1924, leaving the directorship to his chief assistant, J. Edgar Hoover. By that time he was a fallen idol, a "distinguished sinner," under virulent attack as an agent provocateur whose anti-union and anti-Communist crime-fighting methods played havoc with civil liberties. Burns went into full retirement, moving to Sarasota, Florida, where he died on April 14, 1932.

When Burns died, his agency was the second largest such business in the United States. His sons, Raymond J. and W. Sherman, always more cautious than their controversial father, began the process of transforming the business from a general detective firm to one specializing in guard services. During the Great Depression the agency's guards were used by industrialists, several of whom were under siege by desperate strikers. Some were also used to infiltrate unions as labor spies. In addition, Pinkerton and Burns both provided scabs during strikes, as a subcommittee of the Senate Committee on Education and Labor, chaired by Robert M. LaFollette, Jr., revealed in its investigations. When the practice came to public notice, both agencies ended it. Pinkerton even went so far as to refuse industrial guard services during strikes, but not Burns, which filled the need for some of Pinkerton's former clients. Between 1933 and 1936, the company made almost $330,000 from providing security guards, and in 1936 alone netted close to $156,000 from the operation, an increase of 266 percent over the previous year. However, the notoriety surrounding labor espionage and charges of civil liberty abuse lodged against both Pinkerton and Burns left both companies publicity shy and much more circumspect in their policies.

Raymond J. and W. Sherman Burns remained at the company's helm through the Great Depression, World War II, and into the 1960s. In fact, the agency remained under direct family control into the late 1970s, when George E. B. King, the grandson of William J. Burns, became CEO. During that time the company had shifted its focus from crime investigation to protection service and continued to expand. By the end of the 1950s, Burns was grossing more than $20 million. Among its clients were General Motors, General Electric, Standard Oil of New Jersey, du Pont, A&P, and the American Bankers Association, the organization that had given the agency its first big contract back in 1909.

In 1959, in its 50th year, the company had 30 regional offices and close to 12,000 employees, about one-fourth of whom were either former FBI agents or policemen. Although it took on most protection and detective jobs, except divorce investigations, Burns declined to engage in labor espionage and cases involving politics, the areas in which it had previously been publicly embarrassed. The agency continued to use infiltration methods, and its Undercover Department remained at the core of the organization. Claiming to have the personnel and resources to take on an assignment ''of any size, any time and place a client wants it,'' Burns employees masqueraded undercover as everything from janitors to college professors, at rates of up to $25 per hour, depending on the assignment. Moreover, the company maintained enviable crime analysis laboratories and massive identification files, using an impressive array of state-of-the-art scientific equipment. By that time, supported by these resources, Burns was taking on about 5,000 assignments per year, some with considerable public fanfare, as when, in 1959, it was hired by the former Soviet Union to protect visiting Russian dignitaries, including Premier Khrushchev, and provide security at the Soviet trade fair in New York.

The business of Burns often necessitated clandestine or covert operations, which, as in the 1930s, subjected it to exposure and negative publicity. For example, in 1961 the agency went head to head with the American Association of University Professors (AAUP) when it circulated a letter indicating that it was ready to provide agents to infiltrate college student bodies in order to spy on faculty members. Burns apologized for what it maintained was the misguided scheme of a single operative in Houston and promised that academic espionage would be added to its list of taboo assignments.

As Burns continued to change its essential focus from criminal investigation to protection services, it led the way in what was a rapidly expanding industry. Undertaking some unique assignments, the agency agreed to protect the canine guards of the Dog Owners Guidance Service of New York against dog nappers. That company's watchdogs came equipped with collars announcing that they were under the protection of Burns. It was that sort of service that helped Burns improve its sometimes tarnished image.

In the 1970s, Pinkerton's and Burns International Security Services were the two largest contract security companies in the United States but were being pushed hard by the Wackenhut Corporation, a relatively new player in the security service game. There was undoubtedly room for competition, though, for it was in that decade, fired by drug trafficking, that the crime rate began a rapid upwards spiral. In 1974, analysts estimated that a full two percent of the GNP was being lost to crime.

By 1978, Burns had 99 branch offices in North and South America. Both Pinkerton and Burns were grossing about $200 million in business, and both employed about 40,000 people. With emphasis on security rather than detective work, Burns and Pinkerton became known colloquially as rent-a-cop businesses. Although Burns continued to provide alarm installation and monitoring systems, by 1979 about 86 percent of its total sales came from its guard services.

Despite the industry's growth, even the 1970s proved challenging for Burns. In 1971, a New York detective was convicted of selling police records to private businesses, including Pinkerton, Wackenhut, and Burns, and the security firms were fined for ''giving unlawful gratuities'' and ''rewarding official misconduct.'' Burns also came under scrutiny for its practice of hiring ex-FBI agents, although it was hardly alone in doing so. Competition was also growing, and Burns, Pinkerton, and Wackenhut saw their combined share of the guard-service market drop from 39 percent in 1972 to about 23 percent by 1982. Of the three giants, Burns reportedly fared the worst. Still under the nominal control of the Burns family, its high net earning mark of about $8 million dropped to about $4 million in 1981. It then altered its market strategy somewhat, going after the business of large national and international firms, even using the equipment of its rivals to meet its customers' demands.

In 1982, Burns International Security Services became a subsidiary of Baker Industries and moved its operation from its Briar Cliff Manor headquarters in Westchester County, New York, to Parsippany, New Jersey. Baker had itself been acquired by the Borg-Warner Security Corporation in 1978, a division of Borg-Warner that was originally created as part of a continuing diversification and expansion program begun in the 1950s. Baker, operating under the Wells Fargo name, was a provider of armored car services, and Burns added new investigative and security services, providing additional diversification within the security service arena.

The security business, still dominated by Burns, Pinkerton, and Wackenhut, picked up and boomed throughout the 1980s. By 1982, it had become a $3.3 billion industry, of which Burns had a $250 million share, second only to Pinkerton's $300 million. With crime rapidly becoming the number one problem in the United States, the number of persons employed by private security firms grew from about 1.05 million in 1980 to 1.6 million by 1993. Many companies that had formerly hired their own security guards changed to using services that Burns and other firms offered.

However, the period proved difficult for Burns's parent company. Straddled with a large debt, Borg-Warner had to take steps to downsize and restrict its operations. In 1986, it spun off York, one of its holdings, to its shareholders. The next year it was threatened with a hostile takeover from corporate raiders Irwin Jacobs and Samuel Heyman. It was saved when Merrill Lynch Capital Partners organized a leveraged buyout and converted Borg-Warner to a private company. Burdened with a $4.5 billion debt, Borg-Warner sold off all its holdings except its automotive and security divisions, including Burns. The company went public again in 1993, as Borg-Warner Security, and spun off Borg-Warner Automotive to its shareholders. With the restructuring, Burns initially remained a publicly traded subsidiary but was later converted to a division within the corporate infrastructure of Borg-Warner. Nevertheless, the Burns Agency has remained at the old Baker corporate headquarters in Parsippany with a major branch operating in Hartford, Connecticut.

According to a 1993 study by industry analyst William Cunningham, growth in protection and security services would continue into the 21st century. In fact, in the mid-1990s, there were over twice as many private-sector security personnel as there were public-sector law enforcement agents, and with a relative decline in public law-enforcement funding, the demand on the private sector would likely continue to increase. Such projections boded well for Burns International.

Further Reading:

Caesar, Gene, *The Incredible Detective: The Biography of William J. Burns,* Englewood Cliffs, N.J.: Prentice-Hall, 1968.

"The Dog Watch," *Newsweek,* September 12, 1962, p. 104.

Dorfman, John R., "Caught Flat-Footed," *Forbes,* April 12, 1982, pp. 74, 78.

"George E. B. King Elected Top Executive of Burns International," *Wall Street Journal,* May 4, 1979.

"The History of William J. Burns," *The Nation,* November 23, 1927, p. 561.

"Junior Burns Man," *Newsweek,* May 22, 1961, p. 60.

Kerber, Ross, "Policing the Growing Security Business," *Washington Post,* September 6, 1993, p. 5E.

Lipson, Milton, *On Guard: The Business of Private Security,* New York: Quadrangle/New York Times Book Co., 1975.

O'Toole, George, *The Private Sector: Private Spies, Rent-a-Cops, and the Police-Industrial Complex,* New York: W.W. Norton, 1978.

Rackham, Anne, "Bad Times Mean Good Times for Security Guard Firms," *Los Angeles Business Journal,* February 15, 1993, p. 23.

"Crime: The Super Sleuths," *Newsweek,* August 31, 1959, p. 67–68.

"Notes from the Capital: W. J. Burns," *The Nation,* July 13, 1916, p. 32.

Youmans, Sabrina, "Private Security Firms Locking Up Varied Services," *San Diego Business Journal,* October 11, 1993, p. 21.

—John W. Fiero

CalComp Inc.

2411 W. La Palma Avenue
Anaheim, California 92803
U.S.A.
(714) 821-2000
Fax: (714) 821-2228

Wholly Owned Subsidiary of Lockheed Corp.
Incorporated: 1958
Employees: 1,125
Sales: $230 million
SICs: 3577 Computer Peripheral Equipment, Not Elsewhere Classified

CalComp Inc. designs, manufacturers, and markets a broad line of computer graphics equipment used by architects, engineers, graphic designers, mapmakers, and electronic publishers. Known for its invention in 1959 of the digital plotter (a device that translates mathematical data from a computer into maps, architectural renderings, and engineering mock-ups), CalComp has grown to offer equipment for virtually all computer graphics applications. Its Plotter Division designs and manufactures over ten models of pen and electrostatic plotters, while the company's Printer Division produces laser and color printers, color thermal transfer printers, and large-format film imaging systems. Its Digitizer Division manufactures small- and large-format graphic tablets, large-format scanners, and components supplied to manufacturers of pen-based computers. With annual revenues of over $230 million, CalComp has 50 sales and service offices through North America. It also maintains 11 offices in Europe, one in Hong Kong, one in Australia, and a distribution network that covers Africa and the Middle East. It is a wholly owned subsidiary of Lockheed Corp., a major supplier of military, aeronautical, missile, and satellite systems.

When CalComp was incorporated in 1958, it was one of the first companies in the United States to market peripheral products designed specifically to work with digital computers. Prior to that time, computers were utilized for high-tech, military applications. CalComp's appearance, however, coincided with the first wave of acceptance of computers by such mainstream businesses as banks and insurance companies. The military industry remained a major player in the development and use of computer systems, however, and CalComp survived in its early years as a result of this military research.

Incorporated as California Computer Products, Inc., the company's origins can be traced as far back as 1953 when Gene Seid and Robert Morton, two engineers who were involved in the burgeoning field of digital computers, created a prototype of one of the world's first digital plotters. Working out of a converted Firestone tire store in Los Angeles, the two attempted to form a company to manufacture and market the plotter. When they failed to secure the initial contract that would have launched the company, Seid took a job with the Autonetics Division at the North American Aviation Company and, according to company documents, Morton "kept plugging away alone in a tiny Los Angeles shop."

At North American Aviation, Seid met engineers Lester L. Kilpatrick and Ron Cone, and a lawyer named Gene Beckman. The four discussed the prospects of joining Morton and devised a strong marketing plan for the plotter. In 1958 they resigned from their jobs and incorporated California Computer Products. Kilpatrick was named president and chairman of the company. With only a lathe, a mill, some machine tools, and $20,000 in financing, the five set up shop in a garage in Downey, California. They were able to secure a number of small military research and development contracts. In its first year, the company posted earnings of $27,000 on sales of $370,000. CalComp never posted a loss at any time during its first decade of operation. At the same time, though, it barely posted profits sufficient to support its growth. According to company documents, "every time the company needed more help, it would pay employees in shares of stock in order to overcome the constant, nagging lack of capital."

In its early years, CalComp devoted most of its energies to military research. The company expanded slowly, garnering new contracts and adding new personnel to meet the demands. Work on Morton and Seid's plotter was relegated to weekends. In 1959 the company developed the world's first drum plotter, but few expected the instrument to grow into CalComp's strongest product line. As one early employee recalled, "nobody ever thought about making a living selling plotters." By 1961, however, sales of CalComp's Model 565 drum plotter were so promising that the company went public with a $300,000 Regulation A stock issue. The company introduced a complete line of drum plotters a year later, and by 1963, income from sales of CalComp's plotters was beginning to outpace income from military research.

Earnings tripled in 1964 to $459,000 on sales of $5.2 million, and in 1965 the company was listed on the American and Pacific Coast stock exchanges. During the mid-1960s computers continued to advance and become more user-friendly through the addition of peripheral products such as keyboards, monitors, printers, and plotters such as those designed by CalComp. CalComp remained an innovator in the burgeoning computer graphics industry during this period. It introduced new products such as devices to transfer data from the computers to the plotters, interface components, magnetic tape units, and supplies such as spare parts and specially treated printout paper. In 1967 CalComp ventured into the then-young market for proprietary software, hiring a staff of 60 to write programs "oriented to the solutions of problems which, when solved, could be plotted on CalComp equipment," Kilpatrick said in 1968. The programs, which ran on IBM computers, were developed because CalComp's sales force noticed that a number of potential clients often lacked the software programs necessary to run CalComp's plotters. Armed with its own programs and a marketing deal with IBM, CalComp was able to sell an integrated plotter package.

By 1968 between 80 percent and 90 percent of all plotters in existence were manufactured by CalComp. Sales had grown to $16 million, supported by 26 sales and service operations in the United States and 11 in Europe. CalComp's profits were lower than some of its competitors, however. Observers cited the low profit margin of its equipment, which sold at prices between $3,500 and $50,000. Seventy-eight percent of CalComp's equipment was sold directly to end-users; the remaining percentage of equipment was sold to original equipment manufacturers such as IBM and Digital Equipment Corp., who used the plotters as components in larger integrated systems. In 1968 the company purchased a 65 percent interest in Century Data Systems, Inc., a manufacturer of computer memory disc drives, for $1.3 million. The move proved to be a dangerous one for the fledgling company. Century Data Systems' main competitor, IBM, controlled 90 percent of the memory disk drive market and had a much stronger balance sheet than CalComp.

CalComp's sales in 1970 were up 35 percent to $27.5 million, although profits continued to lag as the company sought to refine its marketing operations and strengthen its sales force. CalComp was by then the largest producer of computer graphics equipment in the United States. Century Data Systems, while still a small player in the disk drive market, also experienced strong sales growth. Century and similar small concerns proved adept at chopping away at IBM's share of the $1 billion disk drive market. Fueled by the success of its own plotters and Century Data's disk drives, CalComp announced that it expected to double sales by 1972.

The company underestimated the marketing power of IBM. In 1972 CalComp posted a loss of $12.9 million, although sales had almost doubled to $53.8 million. According to *Electronics Business,* IBM was "apparently stung by the inroads into its customer base . . . and struck back with some faster and cheaper equipment of its own." The move created a price war that threatened to cripple smaller manufacturers like CalComp. For their part, smaller manufacturers banded together under the banner of the Computer Peripheral Manufacturers Association and filed an injunction against IBM with the U.S. Justice Department.

In 1973 Telex Corporation won a landmark suit in which it charged that IBM deliberately cut its prices and designed equipment so it would not easily interface with products made by its competitors. When Telex was awarded $352 million in damages, other peripheral manufacturers began to believe they too had a chance of settling against IBM. Shortly after the Telex announcement (which IBM appealed), CalComp filed a $300 million antitrust suit of its own in 1973, charging IBM with "monopolizing the peripheral business for IBM computers." Primary equipment mentioned in the suit included Century Data's tape drives, tape drive controllers, disk drives, disk drive controllers, and plug-compatible peripherals such as CalComp's plotters. "There is no way in the long run [that] we can compete if an outfit of IBM's size can selectively change their profit margins on those products on which we compete and make up for it in other areas where competition is not so fierce," Kilpatrick told *Financial World* in 1973. For its part, IBM filed a countersuit in which it charged CalComp with monopolizing the plotter market. The two companies thus entered into a long, protracted, legal battle.

Alarmed that its was losing market share to IBM, and virtually certain that conditions would not change quickly, CalComp enlarged its peripherals business through a series of acquisitions. In 1973 CalComp purchased Signal Galaxies, Xytek Corp., and Braegen Corp., three companies that manufactured equipment that "goes with and extends sales of disc and tape drives." Signal and Braegen were merged into Century Data and Xytek, a manufacturer of automated tape libraries, became a wholly-owned subsidiary of CalComp under the name XTX Corp. But while CalComp registered increased sales in 1975, the company posted a $12.4 million loss.

Discovery proceedings for the IBM suit lasted three years. CalComp combined its suit with six other West Coast companies for this initial phase. In 1976 CalComp's suit entered the trial phase before a standing-room-only crowd in the U.S. Circuit Court in Los Angeles. The trial lasted one year and produced a verdict against CalComp. CalComp immediately appealed the decision, but in 1979 the Circuit Court of Appeals upheld the earlier ruling , saying IBM "was under no obligation to help CalComp or other peripheral equipment manufacturers to survive or expand." That year, the perhaps battle-weary company sold Century Data Systems to Xerox Corp. and entered into talks to be purchased by Sanders Associates, Inc., a military electronics company that also designed and manufactured graphics terminals.

In February 1980 Sanders offered to buy CalComp. Kilpatrick was against the merger and had attempted an earlier proxy battle to take control of the board, but Sanders managed to obtain the majority share of voting stock and thus secured the deal. Shortly after the merger Kilpatrick resigned from his post as president and chairman.

Throughout the 1970s, CalComp's growth was erratic. In 1978 the company reported a profit of $1.5 million on sales of $120 million, but by the time Sanders offered to purchase the company in 1980, CalComp was suffering from a six-month deficit of $2.7 million as a result of the divestment of Century Data and the ensuing loss of sales. During the merger negotiations, Sanders gave the company a $7.6 million loan, half of which CalComp used to purchase a successful line of electrostatic plotter and interfaces from Gould Inc. The other half was used to develop CalComp's marketing for the new product line. (Gould held 27 percent of the electrostatic plotter market, which was expected to grow by 30 percent annually.)

According to Jack Bowers, the president and chief executive officer of Sanders at the time, the company's objective in purchasing CalComp was to improve its footing in the computer graphics market. CalComp had several product lines that served this objective well. The company had quietly founded a division in the early 1970s to manufacture interactive graphics systems; by 1979 sales of these systems had grown to account for a significant percentage of CalComp's $44 million in revenues. In

1978 the company introduced a line of pen plotters capable of producing line drawings of such intricate things as circuit boards. This product line, coupled with its recent electrostatic plotter purchase, positioned CalComp as one of three companies to offer both electrostatic and pen plotters under the same brand name.

M. Joel Kosheff was appointed president of CalComp after the Sanders purchase. The company was then reorganized into four divisions (plotters, digitizers, displays, and computer-aided design and computer-aided manufacturing (CAD/CAM) systems), each of which gave CalComp a strong foothold in the computer graphics market. In 1983 Kosheff was replaced by William P. Conlin, a former executive at Burroughs Corp. Conlin reorganized CalComp from top to bottom, restructuring the manufacturing process in each division and implementing the innovative techniques of just-in-time manufacturing and inventory management. Conlin also instructed virtually every employee in the company to read Richard Schonberger's *World Class Manufacturing: The Lessons of Simplicity Applied.*

Conlin's changes proved fruitful. By 1988 CalComp's plotter division had reduced inventory by 65 percent, shortened cycle times, and cut the number of suppliers by 40 percent. These improvements contributed to a 62 percent increase in revenues. Similarly, CalComp's display division was able to reduce the time necessary to assemble a circuit board from 12 weeks to three weeks. When the process was transferred to CalComp's digitizer division, it reduced costs to such an extent that the company was able to move its assembly facilities in Singapore back to the United States.

Under Conlin, CalComp also revamped its marketing strategy. In 1983 the company began selling through Entre Computer centers, a value-added reseller of computer components. By 1988 sales through Entre accounted for 40 percent of total revenues. CalComp's distribution channels also became better balanced during this time. In the company's early years, 55 percent of CalComp's sales went directly to end-users, while 45 percent went to original equipment manufacturers. By 1988 this ratio had changed. Twenty percent of CalComp's sales went directly to end-users; the other 80 percent were sold to original equipment manufacturers, distributors, and other alternative channels. The company also sought to capture a segment of the growing personal computer market, cutting prices by as much as 38 percent on products such as its new 5800 series of electrostatic plotters. These maneuvers resulted in a doubling of all plotter sales within six months.

In 1986 Sanders Associates was purchased by Lockheed Corporation, and CalComp was merged into Lockheed's Information Systems Group. Lockheed took a hands-off management approach, however. It allowed Conlin to continue his transformation of the company. His new manufacturing and management strategy enabled CalComp to seriously challenge Hewlett Packard Co.'s number one ranking in the worldwide pen plotter market and Versatec Inc.'s leadership of the electrostatic plotter market. In 1988 CalComp edged out Hewlett Packard and Versatec for a $3 million contract to supply Mentor Graphics Corp. with electrostatic, pen, and thermal-transfer plotters. Mentor president Gerard Langeler told *Electronics Business* that the company desired "quality and breadth of product line, so we could deal with one supplier. CalComp not only won the evaluation but it was a reasonably clear win. It was not a nail biter." He cited CalComp's new focus on producing high-quality products as an important factor in the decision. "Their quality approach to manufacturing is particularly important in electromagnetic type devices. . . . CalComp appears to have done a very good job."

CalComp did have some failures during the 1980s, though. In 1984 the company established a separate division to sell peripheral products in the burgeoning personal computers market. Amid much fanfare, the company predicted the division would boost company sales to $1 billion by 1990. Although the division successfully established a presence for CalComp in the personal computers market, sales never really took off. The division was merged back into CalComp's other divisions by 1988.

By 1990 CalComp was firmly established as an international computer graphics peripheral company. It had manufacturing operations in the United States and sales and distribution subsidiaries in over 50 U.S. cities, Canada, Mexico, South America, Europe, Africa, the Middle East, Asia, Southeast Asia, New Zealand, and Australia. The company produced over 100 different versions of plotters, display systems, and digitizers and posted sales of $450 million.

Due to the growing complexity of CalComp's operations, Conlin reorganized the company once more in 1990. Each division was established as a separate company, with a separate president given sole responsibility for operations. These executives were given the autonomy to alter marketing or manufacturing as needed to respond to changes in the marketplace. Larry Sanders was named president of CalComp Plotter Co., Gary Long was named president of CalComp Digitizer Co., and Roger Damphousse was appointed president of CalComp Display Co. In addition, two sales and service companies were formed: CalComp Europe, with Theo Eering as president, and CalComp Asia/Pacific, with Doug May as president.

CalComp grew steadily in the early 1990s as the company introduced major new products in each of its divisions at a rate of about five products per year. In 1991 the company strengthened its presence in the CAD/CAM market with the purchase of Access Graphics Technology Inc., a leading distributor of computer aided design equipment. The company also entered into a number of strategic alliances. It signed a distribution agreement with Microsoft Corporation to bundle Microsoft Pen Extensions with CalComp digitizer tablets for use with Microsoft's Windows 3.1 software, and joined with Canon Corp. to enter the ink jet plotter market in 1993. In addition, CalComp broadened its distribution network, signing distribution agreements with Merisel and Tech Data in 1990 and another with Budde International in 1993. These agreements made CalComp's products available in over 120 countries. Gary Long was named president of CalComp in 1994, a year marked by continuing company efforts to refine its manufacturing techniques and revamp its cost structure.

As it nears its 30th anniversary of existence, CalComp seems to be on stronger financial ground than it has been during most of its history. Although sales continued to fluctuate (dipping to

$230 million in 1993), the company is better equipped to ride out these downturns because of the relatively strong financial status of its parent company. The early years of the computer industry were difficult for small manufacturers like CalComp, and many similar operations failed to survive. CalComp's strong position today is testimony to its solid product line and tenacious management. These characteristics, combined with Lockheed's support, should keep the company financially healthy for years to come.

Principal Subsidiaries: Access Graphics Technology Inc.; CalComp Inc. Display Products Division; CalComp Inc. Plotter Products Division; CalComp Inc. Computer Graphics Group; CalComp Europe; CalComp Asia/Pacific.

Further Reading:

''CalComp's Bet on Smart Plotters,'' *Business Week,* May 19, 1980, p. 124B.

''The IBM-Telex Fallout,'' *Financial World,* October 31, 1973, p. 54.

Moad, Jeff, ''Appeals Court Upholds IBM in CalComp Suit,'' *Electronic News,* June 25, 1979, p. 1.

Rayner, Bruce C.P., ''Made in America: CalComp Plots a World-Class Future,'' *Electronic Business,* August 1, 1988, p. 29.

—Maura Troester

Canadian Utilities Limited

10035-105 Street
Edmonton, Alberta T5J 2V6
Canada
(403) 420-7400
Fax: (403) 420-7400

Public Company
Incorporated: 1911 as the Canadian Western Natural Gas, Light, Heat, and Power Company Limited
Employees: 4,795
Sales: C$3 billion
Stock Exchanges: Montreal Toronto
SICs: 4900 Electric, Gas & Sanitary Services; 1300 Oil & Gas Extraction; 3600 Electronic & Other Electrical Equipment

Canadian Utilities Limited supplies gas and electricity to a broad base of customers in the province of Alberta, through its subsidiaries Northwestern Utilities Limited, Canadian Western Natural Gas Company Limited, and Alberta Power Limited. In addition, the company provides electricity to some of the country's far northern lands and also conducts other activities related to its core utilities operations. The company was founded in the early days of Canada's natural gas industry and has continued to grow in tandem with the area that it serves.

The earliest enterprise of the Canadian Utilities group was Canadian Western Natural Gas Company, Ltd., which was founded in the early 1900s by geological engineer Eugene Coste. According to company historian Len Stahl, Coste had become known as "the father of the natural gas industry in Canada, having . . . brought in the first commercial discovery of natural gas in Ontario in 1889." While employed by the Canadian Pacific Railway (CPR) in 1909, Coste discovered a large natural gas reserve on a bank of the South Saskatchewan River in southern Alberta. He acquired rights to this field, dubbed Bow Island field, from the CPR and then went to England to raise capital, selling $4.5 million worth of stock slated for building a pipeline from the Bow Island site to the cities of Calgary and Lethbridge.

On July 19, 1911, Coste incorporated his company under the name Canadian Western Natural Gas, Light, Heat, and Power Company. In addition to planning the construction of the Bow Island pipeline, the company acquired two established Calgary franchises: a coal gas plant consisting of 30 miles of pipe serving 2,200 customers and a pipeline serving about 50 customers, including the Calgary Brewing & Malting Company. On April 12, 1912, the company began construction of its 170 mile Bow Island pipeline. Eighty-six days later, the completed pipeline was the third-largest gas pipeline in North America and the most northerly gas transmission line in the world.

Although the public initially greeted the transition from coal to gas fuel with some skepticism, residents of Lethbridge began using Canadian Western gas for lighting purposes by the fall of 1912, and thereafter the demand for gas increased dramatically. Soon the nearby towns of Nanton, Okotoks, and Brooks were linked to the system, and in 1913, Fort Macleod, Granum, and Claresholm also gained the option of gas lighting. Over the year, Canadian Western gained a client base of 3,400, whom it served from 20 wells yielding gas in the Bow Island field. By 1914 Canadian Western's revenues topped $1 million for the first time.

Although the years immediately following its establishment presented some challenges for the company, Canadian Western continued to gain customers. The company suffered a temporary setback in 1915, when torrential rainfall wiped out its main pipeline to Calgary; the city was without gas service for two days while the company's repair crew worked to get supplies and repair the break in the face of severe weather conditions that had washed out railroad tracks and bridges. This time also marked the beginning of a legal dispute between the company and the city of Calgary, whose officials maintained that the company's franchise did not cover the entire city of Calgary. Canadian Western prevailed in 1917, when the Supreme Court of Alberta ruled that it did have the right to provide gas to all parts of the city.

By 1920, supplies of gas in Canadian Western's Bow Island field had begun to wane. Because of the shortage of gas, the company was forced to limit its service to some industrial customers, in order to supply residential sites. Operators at regulator stations in the city communicated by phone in order to move supplies of gas around quickly and maintain high pressure in the lines. As a result of these measures, Canadian Western's revenues dropped by ten percent.

To alleviate this shortage, Canadian Western began an effort to develop new supplies of gas. The company expanded its gas supply beyond Bow Island in 1921, when it opened the Chin Coulee well 40 miles east of Lethbridge. To cover the costs of this expansion, the company requested its first rate increase from its customers. This increase was grudgingly granted by the city, on the conditions that the company also construct a second ten-inch gas line from a site in the Turner Valley, as well as begin a drilling program at two other sites.

Two years later, in 1923, another gas company, called Northwestern Utilities Limited, was established in Edmonton. This company was a successor to a corporation formed in 1914 to develop the resources of the Viking Field, a deposit of natural gas in northern Alberta. During the summer and fall of 1923, a pipeline was constructed from the Viking Field to Edmonton under tense conditions, as the company raced to beat the winter freeze.

During this time, a controlling interest in Northwestern Utilities was held by the International Utilities Corporation, a company based in the United States, which financed, engineered, and managed a variety of public utilities. In 1925, this company also began to buy up shares in Alberta's Canadian Western, and the two utilities became sister companies, linked by ownership and shared expertise in management.

In the late 1920s, other non-gas utilities companies were established in Canada, which would later become linked to Northwestern and Canadian Western. The electric company known as Northern Power and Light Ltd., was established in Indian Head, Saskatchewan; Mid-West Utilities Limited, which, in turn, owned the Vegreville Utilities Ltd., operator of a coal-fired, hand-fed steam engine and two generating units that supplied power to 380 customers; and plants in Hanna, Stettler, Lloydminster, Grande Prairie, and Raymond. During this time, Mid-West Utilities changed its name to Canadian Utilities Limited, hoping to avoid confusion with another American utility company of the same name.

Northwestern suffered a major setback in January 1928, when shifting ice in a farmer's ditch broke the Viking pipeline, cutting off gas to Edmonton in minus 20 degree weather. Although gas was restored as quickly as possible, this event, and other concerns, prompted the company to begin an effort to duplicate this pipeline, increasing its capacity. Other safety measures were installed as well.

At the same time, Canadian Utilities was working to set up an electrical grid system in the areas where it served customers. The company purchased additional power plants in key locations, and then ran transmission lines between them. In this way, new communities were brought into the system, and antiquated equipment was gradually retired. In 1930, the network of Canadian Utilities companies was purchased by the Dominion Gas and Electric Company, a subsidiary of the American Commonwealths Power Corporation.

With the advent of the Great Depression in 1929, Northwestern found that demand for its products dropped significantly, as many industrial customers went out of business, and residential customers were forced to resume use of coal. Northwestern Utilities also faced a spectacular misfortune in 1932, when the leak of a Northwestern gas main in downtown Edmonton caused the destruction of a leading hotel in the city and several surrounding structures. The fire broke out in the basement of the Corona Hotel on a February evening, and firemen fought it throughout the night before they were able to bring it under control. The resulting lawsuits from this event threatened to put Northwestern into bankruptcy. In an effort to ensure that no such conflagration ever took place again, the company instituted a program of odorization of its gas for safety purposes. In 1934, Northwestern was handed a legal defeat in cases resulting from the hotel fire. This blow came on top of the generally bleak economic picture in Alberta at that time.

Northwestern's sister company, Canadian Western, fared better during the 1930s, adding customers in new communities, and new features to its gas distribution system. One innovation involved the storing of excess gas resulting from oil extraction at Turner Valley, gas that had previously been burned off as a waste product. P.D. Mellon, Canadian Western's vice-president, worked with geologists on his idea for storing the gas via pipes at the Bow Island site. The resulting piping system was reversible and could therefore accept gas for storage in the summer and make it available again during peak winter months.

In the mid-1930s, the electric utility company, Canadian Utilities, was merged with the Union Power company in an effort to stem the tide of losses that Canadian Utilities had suffered every year since 1928. Canadian Utilities was thereafter able to benefit from the proceeds of Union Power's coal holdings.

At the end of the 1930s, Canada, as part of the British Empire, became embroiled in World War II, after Britain declared war on Germany in 1939. Many employees of the gas and electric utilities of Alberta left their jobs to join the armed forces, and materials and supplies were also diverted to the war effort. In 1940, Northwestern installed heating, cooking, and water heating equipment at two air training schools being constructed in the area. Canadian Western also began serving air force training centers.

The war time economy provided opportunities for some utilities and challenges for others. For example, Canadian Utilities was able to expand into the far northern territories of Canada, via the newly constructed Alaska Highway, and began supplying electric power to the booming town of Fort St. John, British Columbia. And while Canadian Western was reporting record sales, Northwestern's efforts to meet increasing demand for gas were thwarted by the rationing of steel, which was needed to lay additional pipe.

In 1944, the Dominion Gas and Electric Company merged with the International Utilities Company, the old American partner of the Alberta companies. In doing so, International Utilities provided additional capital to the Canadian operations. The company used a portion of these funds to push forward with efforts at rural electrification. Test lines were run out to Vegreville in February 1945, and to Melfort, Saskatchewan. Moreover, International began investing in Northwestern and Canadian Utilities.

After the war's end in 1945, the utility companies resumed their normal operations and rate of growth. Alberta saw the formation of another new gas and electric company, Northland Utilities Limited, which served customers in the Peace River area. Moreover, Canadian Utilities' operations were soon focused solely in Alberta, when the Saskatchewan Power Commission began buying up all the smaller utilities with a vision of nationalizing the industry in that province. A similar trend soon took Canadian Utilities out of British Columbia as well.

In 1947, Alberta's demand for gas began increasing rapidly due to a population boom and an accident at an oil well. Canada's oil boom began in February of that year with the discovery of oil near the town of Leduc, Alberta, and increasing numbers of people began moving to the area to share in the wealth. One year later, another well at this site, the Atlantic No. 3, went out of control, spilling oil onto the countryside for six months before igniting in September, and finally being subdued. Northwestern was soon struggling to meet the demand for gas.

In 1954 the first step to uniting Alberta's gas and electric companies was taken, when one man, F. Austin Brownie, president of Northwestern and Canadian Western, was also appointed head of Canadian Utilities. Under Brownie, Canadian Utilities began expanding its Alberta holdings, purchasing the McMurray Light and Power Company Limited and Slave Lake Utilities.

In 1961, International Utilities, the corporate owner of the three linked Alberta companies, also purchased Northland Utilities Limited, and merged this company into the group. At that time, due to changes in the Canadian tax structure, International Utilities also established itself as a United States corporation resident in Canada, hoping to blunt criticism of foreign ownership of the Alberta properties.

Later in the 1960s, International Utilities nearly doubled in size through the purchase of the General Waterworks Corporation. This move helped to pave the way for a major restructuring of the companies in the early 1970s, when Canadian Utilities became the corporate parent of Canadian Western, Northwestern, Northland, and Alberta Power Limited, which was formed to take over the electrical operations previously run by Canadian Utilities. Northland was then merged into Northwestern. The resulting company, known as CU, became one of the largest investor-owned utilities in Canada. At this time, International Utilities also returned to residence in the United States.

In the early 1970s, a unified CU began to devote more of its attention to conservation and environmental awareness. In addition, the company began to branch out to other areas related to the utilities industry. In 1973, CU Engineering Limited was formed to provide consulting services; in 1975, CU Ethane Limited was formed to build and operate an ethane extraction plant in Edmonton as a joint venture; and in 1976, CU Resources Limited was created to develop non-utility resource properties.

One of CU's missions during the 1970s was to respond to environmental issues. Canadians were becoming increasingly aware of the need to conserve energy, and also sought to enact laws for keeping their air and waters clean and protecting wildlife. Toward that end, the company formed an environmental planning commission, headed by Gordon R. Cameron, which worked to ensure that CU was respecting the environment by modernizing facilities to emit fewer pollutants. Moreover, the company investigated such novel ideas as using natural gas to power automobiles.

At the start of the 1980s, majority ownership of CU was transferred from International Utilities to ATCO Limited, a Canadian-based conglomerate that had started as a vendor of trailer homes in 1946. In the spring of 1980, ATCO paid $325 million for International's 58 percent share in the company, and installed its chairman as the chief executive officer of CU. In the wake of this purchase, the Calgary Power company (which then changed its name to the Transalta Utilities Corporation) offered to buy up the 42 percent of CU's shares that ATCO did not own. This offer led to a standoff between CU and TransAlta, with legal entanglements that reached all the way to the Canadian Supreme Court. In 1982, the two companies agreed to withdraw from the dispute and gradually dispose of each other's shares.

In the early 1980s, CU also suffered from the effects of a recession which hit Alberta. The company attempted to reduce operating costs, and also applied for a rate increase to offset the financial downturn. In the spring of 1982, CU also restructured its subsidiaries, creating ATCOR Resources Limited. This group was formed from the ATCO Gas & Oil operations and the non-utility branches of CU. Shortly after this merger, CU discontinued the engineering consulting branch, after demand for these services dropped.

In the mid-1980s, ATCOR became increasingly involved in frontier exploration. In 1986, the division was reorganized again, taking the name CU Enterprises, Inc. This entity specialized in oil and gas exploration and production, and the processing and marketing of natural gas. By 1987, it had become the largest direct marketer of natural gas to final users in Canada.

By the late 1980s, CU served more than 600,000 natural gas customers and 150,000 electric customers. The company continued to turn a profit, despite a sharp drop in growth for its main area of operation, Alberta. These earnings continued throughout the early 1990s. By the end of 1994, CU was servicing nearly 900,000 utility customers. Under the leadership of R.D. Southern, chairman and CEO, and J.D. Wood, president and CEO, the company also became involved in some new complementary operations, including the acquisition from ATCO of Frontec, a leading Canadian contractor of technical services with over $3 billion in assets and facilities. CU was also pursuing acquisitions of independent power plants in western Europe, Australia, and the United States. As CU moved into the latter part of the decade, it appeared well-positioned to continue the success of its earlier decades.

Principal Subsidiaries: Alberta Power Ltd.; Canadian Western Natural Gas Company Ltd.; Northwestern Utilities Ltd.; ATCOR Resources Ltd.; Northland Utilities Enterprises Ltd; CU Power International Ltd.; CU Water Limited; CU Gas Limited.

Further Reading:

Atkinson, Pat, "Ten Top Shops: Canadian Utilities Automates Computer Operations," *Canadian Datasystems,* Spetember 1990, pp. 40, 42.

Sherman, Kevin, "Local-Area Networks: The Canadian Utilities Experience," *Computing Canada,* March 16, 1989, p. 40.

Stahl, Len, *A Record of Service: The History of Western Canada's Pioneer Gas and Electric Utilities,* Edmonton: Canadian Utilities Limited, 1987, 333 p.

—Elizabeth Rourke

Canandaigua Wine Company, Inc.

116 Buffalo Street
Canandaigua, New York 14424
U.S.A.
(716) 394-7900

Public Company
Founded: 1945
Sales: $861 million
Employees: 900
Stock Exchanges: NASDAQ
SICs: 2084 Wines, Brandy & Brandy Spirits; 0172 Grapes

Canandaigua Wine Company is one of the largest and most successful producers of wines, beers, and distilled spirits in the United States. The company produces and markets more than 125 brands of alcohol through 1000 wholesale distributors. Canandaigua is the second largest domestic producer of wines, the fourth largest importer of foreign beers, and the eighth largest distributor of distilled spirits within the United States. The company's brands of table wine, sparkling wines, dessert wines, foreign and domestic beers, and hard liquor are famous, including such well-known names as Almaden Golden Chardonnay, Inglenook Napa Valley, Cook's Champagne, J. Roget Champagne, Corona Extra, St. Pauli Girl, Point Special, Peroni, Cribari Vermouth, Richard's Wild Irish Rose Dessert Wine, Italian Swiss Colony Dessert Wine, Widmer Port, and Manischewitz Concord Grape Table Wine.

In 1935, some years after the repeal of the Volstead Act and the end of prohibition, Mack Sands opened the Car-Cal Winery. Located in North Carolina, Car-Cal Winery produced varietal table wines for limited distribution. Mack's son, Marvin, learned about the wine industry from his father, and was soon determined to open a winery of his own. In 1945, Marvin's dream materialized, and he established Canandaigua Industries. Sands hired eight workers to produce and sell bulk wine in wooden barrels to companies which would bottle them on the East Coast.

In just two years, business was so good that Sands decided to significantly change the direction of his company. With a steady flow of cash to deal with unforeseen emergencies, the head of Canandaigua Industries was determined to produce and sell wine using his own name brands. In 1948, the Car-Cal operation run by Mack Sands was closed, and all wine production was transferred to the facility in Canandaigua. In the same year, Marvin Sands purchased the Mother Vineyard Wine Company, located in Manteo, North Carolina, the first in a long line of strategic acquisitions designed to expand Canandaigua's market position.

Primarily concentrating on regional markets, Canandaigua's new brand of wines were moderately successful. In 1951, the younger Sands opened Richards Wine Cellars in Petersburg, Virginia, and asked his father to assume control of the operation. Not long afterwards, the Onslow Wine Company was added to the growing list of regional wine producers owned and operated by Canandaigua. Both Richards Wine Cellars and Onslow Wine Company produced a wine called Scuppernong, made from varietal grapes grown primarily in the southern United States which serve as a popular source of wines throughout the region. In spite of this expansion, sales remained relatively slow and the company's business did not grow rapidly.

In 1954, however, Sands was lucky enough to come across something most entrepreneurs only dream about—a widely successful product that catapults a company into a future of rapid growth and high profits. This product became known as the Wild Irish Rose brand of dessert wines, and spearheaded Canandaigua's development for years and years. Quickly realizing the potential of his new product, Sands implemented an extremely innovative franchising system, the very first in the wine industry. The franchising network included an agreement between Canandaigua and five independent bottling companies located in various parts of the United States. These bottlers were given the franchise rights to bottle and distribute Wild Irish Rose brands in their areas. With a minimum capital investment, Sands reaped the rewards of seeing his hot-selling Wild Irish Rose gain a larger and larger part of the dessert wine market.

During the late 1950s, revenues generated from the widespread sale of Wild Irish Rose allowed Canandaigua to concentrate on increasing its own production facilities. As sales of the dessert wine brand continued to grow, the company expanded to meet the explosive demands of the marketplace. People were hired to help extend the company's sales network, and a wholesale distributor operation was also established. During the early and mid-1960s, both the sales staff and the wholesale distributor network was strengthened to meet the ever-growing demand for Wild Irish Rose brands. As sales increased, Sands continued his policy of strategic acquisition by purchasing the Tenner Brothers Winery, located in South Carolina, in 1965, and adding Hammondsport Wine Company in 1969. The acquisition of Hammondsport gave Canandaigua an entry into the sparkling wine market, a direction that Sands had wanted his company to take for years.

During the early 1970s, Canandaigua became a public corporation and issued an initial sale of company stock on the NASDAQ stock exchange. Several important brands of wine were produced at Richards Wine Cellars, but it was the acquisitions strategy that continued to shape the company. The most significant acquisition was made in 1974 when Canandaigua purchased the Bisceglia Brothers Winery in Madera, California. This gave the company access to a large varietal wine market in the western United States. Another milestone in the firm's history was the production of its own brand of champagne, J.

Roget, in 1979. This champagne was an immediate triumph, and contributed to Canandaigua's seemingly endless string of successful product introductions.

The 1980s were boom years for the company. In 1984, Canandaigua introduced Sun Country Wine Cooler, a concoction of wine, spritzer, and fruit flavorings. The cooler caught like wildfire across the United States and revenues for the product skyrocketed. During the early 1980s, the firm purchased Robin et Cie, a French producer of high-quality table wine, and renamed it the Batavia Wine Company. Batavia soon began to create different brands of sparkling wines, including champagne. In 1987, Canandaigua purchased a plant in McFarland, California, in order to produce grape juice concentrate and grape spirits.

The two most important acquisitions in 1987, however, included Widmer's Wine Cellars, and the Manischewitz brands from Monarch Wine Company. Widmer's Wine Cellars, located in Naples, New York, was one of the most successful and popular producers of table wine on the East Coast. Producing a wide range of table wines, from Dry Riesling to California varietals, Widmer had won a host of awards in wine competitions. In the late 1980s, Manischewitz was the best-selling brand name in Kosher wines. When Canandaigua purchased the Manischewitz assets, all the production facilities were relocated to the Widmer plant in Naples, New York. Canandaigua's commitment to the production of the Manischewitz brands involves a separate facility which maintains strict supervision for the making of Kosher wine under the auspices of the Union of Orthodox Jewish Congregations of America.

In 1988, the company added Cal-Products in order to produce grape spirits. During the same year, the company purchased the Cisco brand name products from Guild Wineries, a maker of table wines, dessert wines, and champagnes. Canandaigua was so pleased with the revenue generated by these products that it acquired Guild Wineries in 1991. This purchase brought with it the popular brands of Dunnewood wines, Cribari vermouth, and Cook's champagne. Italian Swiss Colony brand dessert wines were also bought at this time. During the late 1980s and early 1990s, in addition to the acquisition of domestic firms which produced wines, champagnes and juices, the company began to import the Marcus James brand of table wines from Brazil, the popular Mateus brand from Portugal, the Keller Geister brand of table wines from Germany, and Mondoro Asti Spumante from Italy.

During the decade of the 1990s, with Sands heading the company as chairman of the board of directors, Canandaigua continued to expand. One of the most significant acquisitions included Barton Incorporated. Barton, Inc., located in Chicago, Illinois, was one of the largest producers of distiller spirits and also one of the largest importers of foreign beers. A firm with additional facilities in Carson, California, and Atlanta, Georgia, Barton was in the midst of its own expansion program when acquired by Canandaigua. This purchase provided Canandaigua with an entry into the lucrative distilled spirits market. Barton's brands were already selling well, including Scotch whiskeys like House of Stuart and Speyburn single malt, Canadian whiskeys such as Canadian Host and Northern Light, and American whiskeys named Corby's Reserve and Kentucky Gentleman. At the time of the acquisition, Barton Vodka was one of the largest selling domestically made vodkas in the United States. The Barton Beer division was just beginning to reap the rewards of importing such popular items as Corona Light from Mexico and Tsingtao from the People's Republic of China.

In October 1993, Canandaigua purchased the Vintners brands, including Paul Masson and Taylor California Cellars. The Paul Masson brand, one of the most popular and respected in the wine industry, was given a new label with a heavy television advertising campaign that included the familiar phrase, "We will sell no wine before its time." Taylor California Cellars brand of table wines, one of the best-selling brands in America, was given a new price structure. Less than one year after the purchase of the Vintners brands, wholesale orders began to exceed company estimates, and sales steadily increased. In July 1994, Canandaigua became the sole American importer and distributor of Codorniu sparkling wines. Established in 1972 by the Codorniu family in Barcelona, Spain, the winery was the first to produce Methode Champernoise sparking wines on the Iberian peninsula. In 1992, Cordorniu built a facility in Napa Valley where it began to produce the popular Codorniu Napa Valley Brut Cuvee.

A very significant acquisition for Canandaigua occurred in 1994 when the company purchased both Almaden Vineyards and Inglenook Vineyards. Inglenook Vineyards, founded in 1879 by a sea captain from Finland—Gustave Niebaum—and Almaden Vineyards, established by Etienne Thee and Charles LeFranc in 1852, were two of the oldest and most well-respected wineries in the United States. Together the two companies sold approximately 15 million cases of wines in 1993, and Almaden ranked fifth while Inglenook ranked sixth in table wine sales within the United States. Almaden alone, before its acquisition by Canandaigua, had captured over six percent of the American table wine market. Inglenook had cornered over five percent of the domestic table wine market.

With these acquisitions, Canandaigua owned and operated four of the five GAMIT brands (GAMIT is the acronym for the five major wine brands in the United States: Gallo, Almaden, Paul Masson, Inglenook, and Taylor California Cellars). These wineries produced significant amounts of varietal wines, and Canandaigua positioned itself to take advantage of the growing varietal wine market through its acquisition strategy. At the same time, the company also improved upon its ranking as the second leading wine producer in America. Under new marketing techniques implemented by management at Canandaigua, Almaden wines such as Mountain Burgundy and Golden Chardonnay grew in popularity and increasing company revenues. A new pricing structure for Inglenook varietal wines, such as Premium Select, Estate Cellars, and Napa Valley, also led to increasing sales.

Double-digit sales growth during the early 1990s catapulted Canandaigua into one of the largest and most popular of the alcoholic beverage producers and importers in the United States. From 1990 to 1994, the company's gross sales shot up from $201 million to $861 million, nearly a fourfold increase. In 1994, net income was recorded at $26 million, a 71 percent increase over the previous year. The acquisition of Barton resulted in a sales increase of $211 million for 1994, while the purchase of Vintners generated $119 million for the same fiscal year. In just one month of sales, the Almaden and Inglenook acquisition added an impressive $17 million to the 1994 year in sales.

In 1994, the company announced a comprehensive restructuring program that was estimated to save approximately $1.7 million in 1995 and over $13.3 million by 1996. The acquisition of Barton and Vintners gave rise to an integration of sales staff, improvement of customer services, a more focused marketing campaign, more efficient production techniques, an implementation of up-to-date information systems, and more effective finance and administrative operations. During the mid-1990s, Canandaigua planned to consolidate all its facilities already located in California, which would enable the company to group three separate bottling operations in one location. The new facility, the Mission Bell plant in Madera, California, was expected to bottle more than 22 million cases annually.

Under the leadership of Marvin Sands, Canandaigua appeared to be headed for even greater profitability in the future. The company had captured 32 percent of the domestic champagne market, the largest in the industry. By the mid-1990s, the company's Barton Beer Division held 10 percent of the total market share for imported beers in the United States. In 1994, the division's domestic brand, Point Special, increased sales by an astounding 25 percent. And the company's Dunnewood brand, a California varietal wine, also increased its sales by 25 percent in 1994. With such popular brands, and astute management that foresaw opportunities and took advantage of trends in the marketplace, it was no surprise that the company's stock price increased by a record 37 percent for fiscal 1994.

Further Reading:

"A 47-Year History of Canandaigua Wine Company," *The Cellar Echo* (Canandaigua Wine Co., Inc. Employee Newsletter), November 1992.

Kimelman, John, "Canandaigua Wine: Grape Expectations," *Financial World,* February 2, 1993, p. 16.

Lane, Randall, "Who's Afraid of Big, Bad Gallo?" *Forbes,* February 13, 1995, p. 180.

Reflecting On Success, Canandaigua, N.Y.: Canandaigua Wine Co. Inc., 1995.

—Thomas Derdak

Cargill Inc.

P.O. Box 9300
Minneapolis, Minnesota 55440-9300
U.S.A.
(612) 742-7575
Fax: (612) 742-7899

Private Company
Incorporated: 1930
Employees: 70,500
Sales: $47.1 billion
SICs: 5153 Grain & Field Beans; 4424 Deep Sea Domestic Transportation of Freight; 6221 Commodity Contracts Brokers & Dealers; 2041 Flour & Other Grain Mill Products

Cargill Inc. is the largest private corporation in the United States. Long known as a merchant of commodities, by the early 1990s Cargill had become one of the largest diversified services companies in the country. In addition to merchandising grains and oilseeds, Cargill operates as a transporter of commodities; a supplier of feed, seed, fertilizer, and other products to agricultural producers; a processor of food ingredients (such as corn syrup and flour) and of brand name products (such as meat and poultry products); an industrial producer of steel, salt, and other products; and a financial and technical services provider. Its diversified operations became increasingly important when the trade in commodities suffered a prolonged downturn beginning in 1980.

Cargill's corporate philosophy, shaped by its participation in the grain trade, emphasizes secrecy and an intricate worldwide intelligence network. Robert Bergland, former secretary of agriculture, told the *Minneapolis Star and Tribune* that "they probably have the best crop-marketing intelligence available anywhere, and that includes the CIA." While secrecy provides an enormous operational advantage to Cargill, it creates problems as well. One frustrated journalist summarized Cargill as a "secretive, inbred and suspicious" company. Cargill's low profile has created no reservoir of favorable public opinion in difficult times. After becoming president of Cargill in 1957, an exasperated Cargill MacMillan complained that the company only received public attention when it was involved in a court case. As late as 1977, a company survey revealed that while 94 percent of farmers had heard of Cargill, only 49 percent knew what the company did.

William Wallace Cargill began his career in the grain business in 1865 in Conover, Iowa. The business grew as it followed the expansion of the railroad into northern Iowa after the Civil War. In 1875 William Cargill moved the headquarters of his company to La Crosse, Wisconsin. He formed several different partnerships with his brothers, Samuel and James. With Samuel he formed W. W. Cargill and Brother in 1867, which became the W. W. Cargill Company in 1892. James Cargill operated in the Red River Valley in North Dakota and Minnesota with a partner, John D. McMillan. In 1882 the partners sold their Red River Valley grain elevators to William Cargill in order to raise more capital. Then in 1888, James, William, and Sam Cargill formed Cargill Brothers. In 1890 this firm became the Cargill Elevator Company, headquartered in Minneapolis, Minnesota.

In 1895 William W. Cargill's daughter married John Hugh MacMillan, and later his son William S. Cargill also married a MacMillan. When the elder Cargill died in 1909, John Hugh MacMillan forced out William S. Cargill and took control of the company. An ensuing feud simmered for decades, but control of the company now rests firmly in the hands of the MacMillan family, although some Cargills still hold stock.

John MacMillan ran the company until 1936, leading the company through a difficult period after the struggle for power; not until 1916 was its financial situation completely secure. MacMillan was a cautious manager who established the rule that the company would not speculate in commodities, a careful policy that helped establish the company's reputation in banking circles—an important consideration since the large deals that became Cargill's mainstay required huge lines of credit.

After World War I, MacMillan took two steps that helped lay the foundation for the future growth of the company. Since its beginnings in 1865, Cargill had been based entirely in the Midwest, selling to eastern brokers. When brokers from Albany, New York, began to open offices in the Midwest, bypassing Cargill as a middleman, Cargill opened an office in New York in 1922. In 1929 Cargill opened a permanent office in Argentina to secure immediate information on Latin American wheat prices. In 1930 the Cargill Elevator Company became Cargill Inc.

John MacMillan, Jr., became president of Cargill in 1936. While maintaining many of his father's cautious policies, he also brought an imaginative and visionary quality to the company. During the Depression, Cargill invested heavily in the storage and transportation of grain, secure in the knowledge that a recovering economy would find Cargill prepared to reap maximum benefit. He also left his mark on grain transportation. Unsatisfied with the standard barge design, he and some associates designed a new type of articulated barge and submitted the design to shipyards. When no company would build the barges, Cargill established its own unit to construct them. Soon Cargill built barges at half the typical cost and with twice the capacity of standard barges.

At the same time, the aggressive nature of MacMillan's management style also created problems for the company, most notably in the September Corn Case of 1937. The 1936 corn crop had been poor, and the 1937 crop would not be available until October. The Chicago Board of Trade and the United States Commodity Exchange Authority accused Cargill of trying to corner the corn market. When Cargill refused a Board of Trade order to sell some of its corn, the board suspended Cargill Grain Company, the subsidiary that conducted trading, from membership. When the board eventually lifted its suspension, Cargill refused to rejoin. For decades, Cargill carried on its trading through independent traders and proclaimed its satisfaction with the greater security this method afforded. Nevertheless, it did rejoin in 1962.

By 1940, 60 percent of Cargill's business involved foreign markets, and World War II had a crippling effect on business. While Cargill did build ships for the Navy, this enterprise could not replace its lost international business, so the company began a major diversification program, entering into vegetable oil and animal feed. The two activities are closely related: pressing oil leaves high-protein meal, which is then used in animal feed. In 1945 Cargill purchased Nutrena, an animal-feed producer, thereby doubling its capacity in poultry and animal feeds. Corn and soybean processing were two of the most rapidly expanding agricultural areas in the 20 years after World War II, however, and oil processing soon outstripped the value of animal feeds. By 1949, Cargill had made a major entry into soybean processing, and its researchers were already exploring the value of safflower and sunflower oil.

John MacMillan, Jr., and his brother Cargill were determined to expand the company after the war, but in a cautious manner that minimized risk. Cargill took the lead among the major grain companies in efforts to combine a network of inland grain elevators with the ability to export large quantities of grain. Two developments in the 1950s helped to establish Cargill in world trade. In 1955 Cargill opened a Swiss subsidiary, Tradax, to sell grain in Europe. Eventually, Tradax grew into one of the largest grain companies in the world. And in 1960, Cargill opened a 13-million-bushel grain elevator in Baie Comeau, Quebec. This facility allowed Cargill to store grain for shipment during the months that winter weather closed the Great Lakes to traffic. The grain elevator also cut the cost of midwestern grain bound for Europe by 15¢ a bushel. In order to maximize profit, the barges that took grain to Baie Comeau hauled back iron ore. Also in the 1950s, barges that carried grain to New Orleans began to backhaul salt. Both practices would lead to profitable new enterprises for Cargill. Before the end of the decade, Cargill's sales topped the $1 billion mark.

Cargill became involved in grain sales to communist countries at an early date. In the early 1960s, Cargill began to sell grain to Hungary and the Soviet Union, while its Canadian subsidiary also played a significant role in trade with the Soviets. After a lapse in trade of several years during the late 1960s, Soviet leader Leonid Brezhnev resumed grain deals as part of his effort to improve the Soviet standard of living. At the same time, the United States, anxious to improve relations with the Soviet Union, eased trade restrictions. These developments set the stage for the famous grain purchase of 1972. The U.S.S.R. purchased 20 million tons of wheat—roughly one-fourth of the American harvest—of which Cargill sold one million tons.

While Cargill actually lost money on the sale, the ensuing change in the market was more important. The massive sale of wheat, combined with a worldwide drought, drove up agricultural prices and increased Cargill's profits in all areas of operations. Sales increased from $2.2 billion in 1971 to $28.5 billion in 1981. Together with Cargill's success in high-fructose corn syrup and animal feed, this boom financed a significant expansion: during that decade Cargill purchased 137 grain elevators; coal, steel, and flour companies; and Ralston Purina's turkey processing and marketing division.

The 1980s brought economic problems that slowed Cargill's growth. A 1980 U.S. government embargo on grain sales to the Soviet Union left Cargill long on grain. While the government provided support for companies that were damaged by the embargo, a rise in the value of the dollar and a debt crisis in developing countries further burdened American agriculture firms. Cargill continued to search for opportunities in the depressed business cycle. Typical of its approach was the purchase of Ralston Purina's soybean-crushing plants in 1985. Overcapacity in the soybean industry did not dissuade Cargill. Whitney MacMillan pointed out that when a business is not doing well there is more room for improvement, and Cargill remained confident that investment during hard times would reap major rewards during the next rise in the business cycle.

Despite periodic downturns, Cargill had exhibited an impressive compound annual growth rate of 15.8 percent sustained over a 25-year period, based on net worth (from $95 million in 1966 to $3.7 billion in 1991). Part of this success has been credited to its consistently strong management. Early in the 1930s, Cargill began one of the first management-trainee programs in the country. Cargill did not rely on business-school graduates but took trainees from a wide range of backgrounds and introduced them to the company's system. Cargill placed young executives in responsible positions quickly and groomed those who succeeded. This system proved its worth in 1960 when John MacMillan, Jr., died. For 16 years nonfamily employees ran the company under the leadership of Erwin Kelm. When Kelm retired in 1976, Whitney MacMillan, great-grandson of founder W. W. Cargill, became chairman. Most upper-level administrators at the company were graduates of Cargill's training program, and these officers, like family members, took the long view in planning for the welfare of the company.

As Cargill increasingly depended upon nonfamily members to run it, the company faced several challenges starting in the mid-1980s that would force it to undergo its most dramatic transformation to date. From the mid-1980s through the early 1990s, Cargill consistently failed to meet its company-wide sales targets primarily because of continued difficulties in grain merchandising, a sector that had never recovered from the 1980 embargo. Cargill's successes had also led to a bloated operation in which ConAgra Inc., its biggest customer, had to purchase products from 18 different Cargill divisions. Chairman Whitney MacMillan and most of the other senior leaders were nearing retirement age with no clear successor from the younger ranks in sight. Finally, some of the family members were lobbying for the opportunity to cash in on Cargill's success through more than the relatively modest annual dividends they received from their stock.

With the help of consultants McKinsey & Company, MacMillan initiated a major reorganization of Cargill's North American operations in 1990. The previous organization along product lines was replaced with a "soft matrix" type of structure, which intermixed product line and geographical area management. In order to bring fresh ideas into the organization, Cargill's board of directors was overhauled to include five members from management, five family shareholders, and five outside directors (the first outsiders in 40 years). The structure was also intended to allow the board to mediate between family members and Cargill management.

Such mediation would become more and more critical since Cargill faced the prospect of its first nonfamily CEO since the Erwin Kelm era of 1960–76. Only two fifth-generation family members worked for the firm, and neither had enough experience to take over when MacMillan retired. Eventually MacMillan selected Ernest S. Micek, former president of Cargill's food sector, as his successor. Micek was named president and chief operating officer in 1994 before taking over as CEO in August 1995. Still, at age 59, Micek was anticipating a short tenure (especially by Cargill standards), since company rules mandated retirement at age 65. MacMillan remained chairman of the board.

Meanwhile, and amid false rumors that Cargill would finally go public, the issue of company ownership was at least temporarily settled through the implementation of an employee stock ownership plan in 1991. Family members were given the opportunity to cash in as much as 30 percent of their ownership stake in Cargill. It turned out that only 17 percent was sold, for a total of $730 million, funded through borrowing. About 20,000 Cargill employees in the United States were eligible to receive the resulting stock, ending a long history of ownership exclusively by Cargills and MacMillans.

To reduce Cargill's dependence on the perpetually fickle grain business, the company committed to a program of radical diversification. One aspect of this program was to no longer simply be a commodity merchandiser, but to process the commodities as well—what many call "moving up the food chain." Already an established meatpacker in the United States through its Excel subsidiary, which was acquired in 1979, Cargill opened a new plant in Alberta, Canada, in 1989 in the midst of a downturn in meat sales and became the top meat packer in Canada by 1992. The company also began producing brand-name products for sale to consumers, such as its Sun Valley Poultry chickens and turkeys in England and its Honeysuckle White and Riverside turkeys in the United States. Through these efforts, Cargill was attempting to gain ground on competitors like ConAgra, which had moved heavily into branded products throughout the 1980s. By 1993 Cargill was the third-largest U.S. food company, behind only Philip Morris and ConAgra, and its annual food sales had reached as high as $22 billion.

A second area of diversification was the development of Cargill's Financial Markets Division. Based on knowledge gained through decades of trading in the world markets, this operation supported the efforts of the parent company and its subsidiaries through a full spectrum of financial services. Started in the mid-1980s and expanded rapidly in the early 1990s, the division generated almost $100 million in earnings for the 1992–93 fiscal year out of the company total of $358 million.

By the mid-1990s, Cargill had surprised many observers by its diversity in both operations and the locations of those operations. In addition to being the top grain company in the world and the number three food company in the United States, the company also boasted the eighth-largest U.S. steel producer in its North Star Steel subsidiary, the top position in European cocoa processing, and the number one ranking among pet food processors in Argentina. No longer the family-dominated firm of previous decades, the company nevertheless seemed certain to remain one of the most powerful companies in the world.

Principal Subsidiaries: Cargill Citro-America, Inc.; Cargill Investor Services Inc.; Cargill Leasing Corporation; Cargill Marine and Terminal, Inc.; Cargill Petroleum, Inc.; Excel Corp.; Ladish Malting Co.; North Star Steel Co.; Wilbur Chocolate Co., Inc.; Seminole Fertilizer; Cargill NV (Belgium); Cargill Agricola S.A. (Brazil); Cargill Ltd. (Canada); Cargill Trading Ltd. (Korea); Cargill International S.A. (Switzerland); Cargill UK Ltd.

Further Reading:

Berss, Marcia, "End of an Era," *Forbes,* April 29, 1991, pp. 41–42.

Broehl, Wayne G., Jr., *Cargill: Trading the World's Grain,* Hanover, New Hampshire: University Press of New England, 1992, 1,007 p.

"Cargill Inc. Names Ernest Micek to Post of Chief Executive," *Wall Street Journal,* March 29, 1995, p. B12.

Davies, Michael, "Reaping the Harvest?," *Corporate Location,* November/December 1994, pp. 26–29.

Greising, David; William C. Symonds; and Karen Lowry Miller, "At Cargill, the Ties that Bind Aren't Binding Anymore," *Business Week,* November 18, 1991, pp. 92–93, 96.

Henkoff, Ronald, "Cargill's Heir-Raising Future," *Fortune,* July 1, 1991, p. 70.

——, "Inside America's Biggest Private Company," *Fortune,* July 13, 1992, pp. 83–90.

The History of Cargill, Incorporated, 1865–1945, Minneapolis: Cargill, 1945.

Kneen, Brewster, *Invisible Giant: Cargill and Its Transnational Strategies,* Boulder, Colorado: Pluto Press, 1995.

——, *Trading Up: How Cargill, the World's Largest Grain Trading Company, Is Changing Canadian Agriculture,* Toronto: NC Press, 1990, 136 p.

Morgan, Dan, *Merchants of Grain,* New York: Viking Press, 1979, 387 p.

Pehanich, Mike, "The Quiet Giant Climbs the Value Chain," *Prepared Foods,* October 1993, p. 22.

Schafer, Lee, "Cargill and the Ultimate Commodity," *Corporate Report-Minnesota,* April, 1994, pp. 52ff.

——, "Executive of the Year," *Corporate Report-Minnesota,* January 1993, pp. 46ff.

Schmitz, Andrew, *Grain Export Cartels,* Cambridge, Massachusetts: Ballinger Publishing Company, 1981, 298 p.

Work, John L., *Cargill Beginnings: An Account of Early Years,* Minnetonka, Minnesota: Cargill, 1965, 154 p.

—updated by David E. Salamie

Carpenter Technology Corporation

P.O. Box 14662
Reading, Pennsylvania 19612-4662
U.S.A.
(610) 208-2000
Fax: (610) 208-3242

Public Company
Incorporated: 1889 as Carpenter Steel Company
Employees: 4,200
Sales: $628.8 million
Stock Exchanges: New York
SICs: 3441 Fabricated Structural Steel

Carpenter Technology Corporation produces and distributes specialty steel and structural ceramics worldwide for consumer and industrial applications. The company's products are part of every Pentagon weapons system and comprise approximately six pounds of every American automobile. In 1995, Carpenter employed 4,200 workers throughout the world, including a core force of 2,600 at its Reading, Pennsylvania, headquarters.

The man whose name the present company bears, James Henry Carpenter, served in the Navy during the Civil War, then embarked on a career as a construction engineer, developing an interest in metallurgy and the manufacture of tool steel. A New Yorker, Carpenter was encouraged to found a steel-making enterprise in Reading, Pennsylvania, by a visionary city councilman who, realizing that the region's bustling iron industry would naturally support such a venture, foresaw a boon to the city's economy. Incorporated in New Jersey on June 7, 1889, Carpenter Steel Company leased a rail-making plant in Reading and soon received its first order for 3,000 tons of steel. Within five months, the fledgling company had outgrown the rail-making plant and acquired a facility known as Union Foundry, which over 100 years later still functioned as company headquarters and a specialty steel mill.

Carpenter's branching into specialty steel operations began with a May 1890 contract with the U.S. Secretary of the Navy. Having found Carpenter's tool steels to be of superior quality, the Navy was betting, correctly as it turned out, that the company could develop armor-piercing projectiles. The fulfillment of the Navy contract was enabled by a patent granted to James Carpenter for an "air-hardening steel" manufacturing process. In November 1896, the Navy informed Congress that Carpenter's projectiles had tested successfully, calling them "the first made that would pierce improved armor plate." In the Spanish-American War of 1898, the routing of the Spanish fleet at Manila Bay was credited in part to Carpenter projectiles.

Unfortunately, the preeminence Carpenter achieved through its wartime armaments proved to be a curse when the Spanish-American War, and the contracts it fostered, ended. Complicating the decline in business was the death, in March 1898, of founder James Carpenter. By 1903, the company had fallen into receivership. However, the court-appointed receiver, Robert E. Jennings, was a former vice-president of a rival steel company and would soon oversee a dramatic resurgence at Carpenter. Elected president of a reorganized Carpenter Steel Company the following year, Jennings's expertise was in marketing; for the remainder of the decade he presided over innovations resulting in a variety of steel grades broad enough for almost every extant tooling application, including heavy-duty cutting tools, high-speed cutting tools, and hot heading.

Early in the 20th century, the nascent automobile industry afforded the single most auspicious market for Carpenter's innovations in specialty steel. In 1905, the company developed a prime grade chrome-nickel steel; by 1908 it had created ten other steels that were used to make automobile chassis. Most of the "runabout" vehicles of the day ran on Carpenter steel, and "Old 16," the racer that won the Vanderbilt Cup in 1908, comprised front and rear axles, crankshaft, gears, and other parts fabricated from Carpenter steel. Affinity with automobile manufacturers gave rise to a hallmark of Carpenter's distribution system: maintaining service centers where its customers were based. The beginnings of its modern regional service center system began with the opening of branch warehouses in Cleveland and Hartford, then the centers of automobile production, in 1907 and 1909.

With the 1917 entrance of the United States into World War I, wartime munitions and supplies overtook automotive steel as Carpenter's principal product. The Reading plant operated on around-the-clock shifts, producing everything from tool steels to soldiers' safety razor blades. Accelerated production levels, however, did not distract Carpenter from technical and metallurgical innovation. During the war, the company put into operation four new electric-arc furnaces, which allowed greater control over the melting process than had the old crucible furnaces. It also turned out its first batch, in December 1917, of what would become its principal product: stainless steel. The first applications of this new high-strength, chemical-resistant steel were airplane engine components, cutlery, and spark plugs.

Continuing its quest to improve what was already a successful product line, Carpenter unveiled its "rustless steel," an alloy of .3 percent carbon, 20 percent chromium, and one percent copper, in December 1920. Throughout the 1920s, Carpenter spent much effort in improving the fabricability, into parts, of its stainless steel. In 1928, it brought out the first free-machining, "antifriction" stainless steel, sulfur being the component responsible for the breakthrough. The introduction of stainless steel strip in the mid-1920s reestablished Carpenter as an important supplier to the automobile industry; in 1929, the company trumpeted the statistic of 24 pounds of automotive trim on each Pierce Arrow car. Strip also began to be welded into tubing, and in 1927, Carpenter's Welded Alloy Tube Division became the earliest commercial supplier of stainless tubing, with applications in chemical processing, oil refining, generation of electricity, and food and beverage processing.

Another historical milestone that demonstrated Carpenter's preeminence was Charles Lindbergh's pioneering nonstop flight from New York to Paris in May 1927. The gears, shafts, and fasteners of the engine of the "Spirit of St. Louis," Lindbergh's legendary plane, were all made from Carpenter steel. An identical engine had powered Richard Byrd's flight to the North Pole the previous year. Even the Wright Brothers' maiden flight in 1903 had been achieved with Carpenter steel-based engine components. The aircraft industry, like the earthbound automobile industry, owed much of its success to Carpenter.

The Great Depression, particularly during the early 1930s, caused Carpenter to operate at a loss for three consecutive years and forced it to downsize. Still, the company's penchant for new product development continued virtually unabated. The Depression years saw the introduction of new stainless steels with additives of selenium, tellurium, and chrome and nickel. For the first time, Carpenter began licensing other manufacturers to produce some of its stainless steels. Also during the 1930s, increasingly high wear-resisting varieties of tool steel were introduced, and in 1937 Carpenter brought out *Tool Steel Simplified,* a book of diagrams to assist customers in choosing the proper tool steel for a specific application, depending on toughness and hardening properties. The book would remain a standard industry reference work through the 1970s. In June 1937, Carpenter Steel Company went public.

The most obvious challenge to Carpenter in the 1940s, as to the country as a whole, was World War II. In March 1941, with U.S. entrance into the war looking increasingly probable, the U.S. Office of Production Management summoned Carpenter's president to Washington, D.C., to discuss expanding the company's production capacity on an urgent basis. Carpenter's board of directors responded by voting an immediate capital investment program of nearly $1 million. During the course of the war, the company's numerous varieties of stainless steel found their way into virtually every conceivable wartime application: engine parts, steel fasteners, and cockpit instruments for fighter planes and bombers; components of Sherman tanks and submarines; radio masts for PT boats and radio equipment for battle fronts; and medical supplies such as hypodermic needles and surgical implements.

After the war, Carpenter returned to stable, profitable operations. The 1950s brought significant technological advances in melting, particularly with the process of vacuum arc remelting in a consumable-electrode furnace, which allowed unprecedented high purity in steel alloys—and none too soon, since applications in the embryonic aerospace field required immaculate degrees of purity. During the same decade, Carpenter introduced "Stainless 20," an alloy which by virtue of rare earth element additives could withstand harsh, corrosive chemicals. Expansion of infrastructure and capacity continued apace. In 1951, Carpenter bought a wire redrawing plant in New Jersey, thus acquiring the capability to produce extremely fine wire for applications such as surgical sutures and knitting machines. The year 1954 saw the addition of a new mill in Reading which allowed Carpenter to become extremely competitive in the manufacture of specialty alloy wire. When, in the mid-1950s, the company found itself having to turn down orders despite operating at full capacity, it purchased Northeastern Steel Corporation in Bridgeport, Connecticut, enabling a 100 percent increase in the production of ingots.

Research and development (R&D) and technology were the dominant themes of the 1960s; the company changed its name in 1968 to reflect this, becoming Carpenter Technology Corporation and reincorporating in the state of Delaware. The company also announced that it was spending five times as much on R&D as were other steel manufacturers, and proudly opened a new $3 million R&D center in Reading in 1967. Carpenter began to cast a wide technological net through three strategic acquisitions: NTH Products, Inc., of El Cajon, California, in 1961; a 50 percent share in Gardner Cryogenics Corporation, Bethlehem, Pennsylvania, in 1969; and a 50 percent share in Titanium Technology Corporation, Pomona, California, also in 1969.

NTH Products eventually became Carpenter's special products division, responsible for making metal and specialty steel products such as tubular components, precision-rolled solid shapes, and photoetch sheets. It also made fuel channels for nuclear reactor cores. Gardner Cryogenics (taking its name from the science of low-temperature phenomena) facilitated the company's entrance into making storage and transport equipment. Titanium Technology Corporation supplied the aerospace and other industries with titanium castings.

Infrastructure enhancements in the 1960s included the installation of a 15,000-pound vacuum induction furnace, which permitted the melting of alloys of unprecedented purity, and of a mill capable of rolling thin electronic alloy strip used in transistors and semiconductors. Then, in the early 1970s, installation of two varieties of increasingly sophisticated furnaces enabled additional improvements to the product line. First, two 25-ton ElectroSlag Remelting furnaces, which had their world premiere at Carpenter, allowed ingots to be remelted in molten slag, reducing overall amounts of microscopic impurities. Then the Argon-Oxygen Decarburizing unit accomplished, as its name implied, efficient removal of carbon through a process of blowing argon and oxygen through the steel bath.

Carpenter managed to ride out the two national recessions of the 1970s, with sales and profit figures consistently breaking records throughout the decade. Separate multi-million dollar capital expansion plans were put into action in 1976 and 1979. Beginning in 1970, the company had implemented a pollution control plan, installing ducts, exhaust fans, and 2,400 filter bags to trap exhaust fumes and iron oxide dust that would otherwise escape into the atmosphere.

The 1970s also saw Carpenter reverse course after its earlier aggressive pursuit of diversification. Many previously acquired enterprises were sold during the decade, including the New Jersey wire redrawing plant, Titanium Technology Corporation, Gardner Cryogenics, and affiliates in Brazil and Mexico. According to Howard O. Beaver, Jr., who was then president, the divested enterprises "did not fit Carpenter's long-range goals and objectives," and the proceeds from the sales would be "more effectively employed" in enhancements to the stainless steel product line.

The recession of 1981–82 was one of the deepest ever to afflict the U.S. economy, and steel companies were especially hard-hit due to fierce competition and price undercutting from foreign producers. To combat such severe economic buffetings, the bulk of the domestic industry began selling off tangential operations and trying to diversify by branching into insurance or retail—but not Carpenter. Even though its fiscal year 1982 earnings fell significantly below the previous year, the company was proceeding unflinchingly with its 1979 capital investment plan. The new president, Paul Roedel, conceded that Carpenter's previous efforts in diversification had caused return on capital to plummet and vowed the same mistake would not be repeated.

Factors that tended to immunize Carpenter better than most steel producers against recession were noted in a 1982 *Forbes* magazine article. Its highly specialized steels were selling at ten times the average price per ton of the rest of the industry, and its share of the specialty steel market was 25 percent. Company philosophy was to broaden the market base, which it had done successfully, rather than diversify the product line. Its nationwide warehouse and service center system, begun in 1907, now numbered 21 facilities, and had put Carpenter in the unique position of hearing its customers' conundrums first-hand; this allowed the company to develop custom markets for itself.

By fiscal year 1989, when Carpenter marked its 100th anniversary, the 1982 recession was just a memory as net sales reached an all-time high of $634.3 million, and net income was 19 percent higher than in the previous year. Market forces had reduced the number of publicly traded specialty steel companies to four at this point, but these entities, Carpenter included, were regarded by financial analysts as highly efficient and high in quality. Consumer demand for specialty steel had risen faster than the economy in general since the early 1960s, and over the same period, the amount of specialty steel in cars had risen from ten to 70 pounds.

Carpenter had made two significant acquisitions during the 1980s—Eagle Precision Metals Corporation of Fryeburg, Maine, and AMAX Specialty Metals Corporation of Orangeburg, South Carolina—and had sold the Bridgeport, Connecticut, steel-making facility after market growth rate had slowed. Eagle, a precision drilling facility, beefed up Carpenter's ability to produce high quality hollow steel bars, while AMAX was a wire-finishing plant, capable of redrawing steel wire to extremely fine sizes.

Economic cycles continued to affect Carpenter's balance sheet; the 1991 recession once again forced restructuring and downsizing, and as with many basic-industry companies, recovery seemed more elusive than with the economy as a whole. However, at the end of fiscal year 1994, Carpenter president Robert W. Cardy exulted that net sales had been second only to 1989 and observed that the company was operating virtually at full capacity. The dual goals of the year—"to strengthen and grow specialty metal operations worldwide, and to expand strategic business opportunities worldwide"—had been achieved.

Especially important during 1994 were two acquisitions destined to fulfill Carpenter's aspirations as a worldwide steel distributor. First, a joint venture with Walsin-Lihwa, a Taiwanese cable and wire manufacturer, resulted in the company's first presence in Asia. Second, the acquisition of Aceros Fortuna, Mexico's number one specialty steel distributor, resulted in the bulk of Carpenter's increased 1994 sales. On the domestic front, Carpenter bought Certech, Inc., a Woodridge, New Jersey, maker of structural ceramics. According to a senior vice-president, "Some customers who traditionally bought steel had switched to structural ceramics for some applications. To keep its customers, Carpenter decided to broaden its product line."

According to *American Metal Market,* structural ceramics had high temperature properties and high corrosion resistance, and were "used to make precision valves, components for electrical and fiber optic connectors, special wear inserts, and critical application components for the plasma spray industry." Carpenter accelerated its push into this new field in 1995 with the acquisition of Technical Ceramics Laboratories, Inc. (TCL) of Alpharetta, Georgia. TCL's specialty, ceramics research, was expected to complement the ceramics manufacturing capability provided by Certech.

As its second century of operation unfolded, Carpenter was poised to become increasingly influential as a global supplier of specialty steels, structural ceramics, and specialty materials complementing applications that were formerly the exclusive domain of metals. This emphasis, together with its far-reaching warehouse and service center system, indicated that Carpenter planned to bolster and broaden its market niches and customer bases.

Principal Subsidiaries: Carpenter Technology International Corporation (U.S. Virgin Islands); CRS Holdings Inc.; Carpenter Investments, Inc.; Eagle (CRS) Investments Inc.; Certech, Inc.; Certech International Ltd. (U.K.); Certech Incorporated; Carpenter Technology Limited (Canada); Carpenter Technology GmbH (Germany); Carpenter Technology (Europe) S.A. (Belgium); Carpenter Technology SARL (France); Carpenter Technology Corporation (Taiwan); Carpenter Technology s.r.l. (Italy); Aceros Fortuna, S.A. de C.V. (Mexico); Movilidad Moderna, S.A. de C.V. (Mexico); Temple y Forja Fortuna, S.A. de C.V. (Mexico).

Further Reading:

Building a New Growth Model for Carpenter, Reading: Carpenter Technology Corporation, 1994.

Building on 100 years of Progress, Reading: Carpenter Technology Corporation.

Byrne, John A., "Three Numbers," *Forbes,* April 12, 1982, p. 121.

"Carpenter Meets Financial Goals, Continues Expansion in FY94," *Business Wire,* October 25, 1994.

"Carpenter Reports Record Sales and Higher Earnings for the Year Ended June 30, 1989," *PR Newswire,* July 28, 1989.

"Carpenter Sales Rise 21 Percent," *PR Newswire,* April 24, 1980.

"From Carrier Decks to Off-Road Biking," *Machine Design,* April 6, 1995, p. 36.

Hershey, Robert D., "In One City, Signs of an Upturn," *New York Times,* June 13, 1991, p. D1.

Ozanian, Michael K., "Today's Steals," *Financial World,* September 5, 1989, p. 49.

Welch, David T., "Carpenter Inks Deal to Buy Ceramic Firm," *American Metal Market,* March 6, 1995, p. 4.

—Val Holley

Chaparral Steel Co.

300 Ward Road
Midlothian, Texas 76065-9651
U.S.A.
(214) 775-8241
Fax: (214) 775-6262

Public Subsidiary of Texas Industries, Inc.
Incorporated: 1973
Employees: 1,000
Stock Exchanges: New York
Sales: $462.3 million
SICs: 3312 Blast Furnaces & Steel Mills

Named after the roadrunner that darts over the rolling hills of central Texas, Chaparral Steel Co. was one of the original mini-mills that revolutionized the U.S. steel industry in the 1970s. The company is known for its innovative management practices which, among other things, allows workers to set their own pay rate. This flexible management style—combined with an ongoing commitment to improved technology—made Chaparral the world's lowest-cost producer of steel in 1992. Products are made from recycled scrap metal (Chaparral can shred an automobile in 18 seconds) and include large structural beams, reinforcing rods, special bar quality rounds, channels, and merchant quality rounds. Chaparral is considered a small- to mid-size steel producer, shipping over 1.4 tons annually to customers in the construction, defense, energy, automotive, railroad, and mobile home industries. Sales are primarily in North America, although they had begun expanding to Europe and Asia in the mid-1990s. Chaparral is 81 percent owned by Texas Industries Inc., a cement and construction concern, and is traded on the New York Stock Exchange.

Chaparral was incorporated in 1973 as a 50–50 joint venture between Texas Industries Inc. and Co-Steel International, of Canada. At that time, analysts were predicting the demise of the U.S. steel industry as European and Japanese mills began flooding the U.S. market shares with inexpensive steel. Encumbered by oversized operations and outdated technology, U.S. manufacturers were virtually unable to compete with the newer and more efficient foreign mills. One by one, factories began closing across the Northeast and Midwest.

Chaparral was founded under the "market mill" concept, a manufacturing/marketing strategy developed in the late 1960s as an alternative to large U.S. steel mills. Also known as mini-mills, these new operations were smaller, more efficient, and more specialized than traditional U.S. mills and were also quite flexible in responding to changing market demands.

Under the direction of chief executive officer Gordon Forward, a Canadian with a Ph.D. in metallurgy, Chaparral's first steel beams rolled off the line in 1975. One of the major technological advancements at the new company was the continuous casting of all steel products, a process which greatly reduced the amount of power necessary to produce a ton of steel. Equally important to Chaparral's low costs, however, was its innovative management philosophy. Operating, according to company literature, as a "classless corporation, [with] universal education and freedom to act," Chaparral sought to make its employees, as well as the machinery, efficient.

Chaparral was founded without the traditional trappings of corporate hierarchies. Time cards, rigid lunch hours, and breaks were eliminated; employees took breaks when they felt it was necessary. Coffee was free, management dressed casually, and such executive perks as reserved parking spots were abolished, as were separate entrances for employee locker rooms and executive offices. In return for this freedom, workers were expected to become intellectually as well as physically involved with their jobs. "We figured if we could tap the egos of everyone in the company, we could move mountains," Forward told *Fortune* magazine in 1992. Chaparral provided all employees with the opportunity for training in such varied subjects as electronics, credit history, and metallurgy. Bonuses and pay raises were commensurate with the skills an employee had acquired and the contributions he or she had made to the company.

During its first five years of operation, the company shipped about 2,500 tons of products (primarily reinforcement bars, carbon and alloy quality bars, and structural shapes) to customers within a 200-mile radius of its plant in Midlothian, Texas. Raw material was initially purchased pre-shredded from local scrap yards. However, by the late 1970s, the company had purchased its own automobile shredder, and in 1981 it acquired the Schwartz Iron & Metal Co., a local scrap metal concern, capable of processing 10,000 tons per year. That year, the company also underwent a $180 million expansion, boosting its production volume of billet (steel in intermediate stage of production) from 400,000 tons to one million tons annually, and of finished steel from 600,000 to 1.5 million tons. In addition, the company began manufacturing its core products in a wider variety of sizes, a move which allowed it to begin competing with major mills.

Chaparral's product line, however, was still not as diversified as the product lines of major mills. "We're not trying to be all things to all people," Jeffrey A. Werner, vice-president of marketing, told *American Metals Market* in 1982. "We're still producing the same products. But with more sizes available, that gives us the ability to reach further. To what extent we'll be a major factor [in the national steel market] is yet to be determined," Werner observed, adding that the diversity of Chaparral's new products took "some of the peaks and valleys out of the marketplace."

With its improved capacity in place, the company began expanding its marketing efforts, opening regional offices in Kansas City, Detroit, Atlanta, Houston, and Los Angeles. Northwestern and Northeastern states were excluded from the expansion due to the high costs of shipping to these regions. Despite the company's expansion, sales were down in 1982. High interest rates had created a depression in the building industry which in turn severely affected the steel industry and forced many steel makers to lay off thousands of employees. In mid-1982 Chaparral cut back steel production by 30 percent for several months, yet laid off no employees.

Chaparral's marketing strategy during this economic downturn was to lower the overall cost of its products by eliminating freight charges from its bill. ''Nobody can get a premium in this market today,'' Werner told *American Metals Market.* ''In this kind of market, people do all sorts of things they wouldn't normally do,'' he noted. In addition, the company reduced prices on reinforced bars from $250 a ton to $240 a ton, and merchant and structural steel prices by $15 per ton. Competition heated up as steel merchants continued to cut prices in order to get a greater share of the dwindling market. When Chaparral attempted to raise prices on merchant hot-rolled steel bars, competitors lowered theirs, so Chaparral had no choice but to follow suit.

By 1983, mini-mills like Chaparral accounted for one-fifth of the output of steel in the United States. Chaparral was the price leader in reinforced bars and one of the lowest-priced producers of steel in the world. The company could produce a (short) ton of steel in two man hours—slightly less that the 2.4 man hours required to produce the same amount at the most efficient Japanese steel mills and far less than the eight man hours required at most major U.S. steel mills.

Prices on the U.S. market remained depressed, however. In early 1984 the company filed a suit with the Office of the U.S. Trade Representative, accusing Polish and Norwegian manufacturers of selling their products in the United States at prices below cost. In response to the market, Chaparral lowered its prices again in October. Then in December 1984, Chaparral filed another dumping suit against Japan, Mexico, and several unnamed members of the European Economic Community.

In 1985, parent company Texas Industries bought Co-Steel's 50 percent share in Chaparral for $42 million in cash, plus a contingent payment based on Chaparral's performance due in 1990. Under Texas Industries, Chaparral began investigating the possibility of further expansion, believing that a diversified product base was essential to its survival. A section mill which had been under construction since 1983 was soon to be completed and was expected to increase production capacity by 700,000 tons. Caught between the need to expand further while simultaneously keeping costs low, Chaparral began a feasibility study into production of large structural beams. Its closest rival, Nucor Corporation, which operated four mini-mills across the United States, had recently entered into a joint venture with a Japanese firm to produce large flange beams, and Chaparral did not want to be left behind.

The company survived the recession due to its ability to keep costs low, and when the market picked up, Chaparral was on top. It sold 1.09 million tons of steel in 1986, earning a gross profit of $67 million on sales of $297 million. Fifty-five percent of products sold were medium and heavy structural steel, 30 percent were reinforcement bars, and 15 percent were carbon and alloy bars. Labor costs were reduced to between nine and ten percent of sales, far below the ''traditional'' industry figures of 40 percent. Energy costs were also reduced that year when the company installed a bottom-tapped furnace, designed to burn fuel more efficiently.

By 1987 Chaparral was the tenth largest steel producer in the United States, with a market that encompassed the United States and parts of Canada. In July of that year, the company made its first shipment to Western Europe, and by the end of 1988 Chaparral products were sold in most Western European countries. Capacity was boosted from 1.3 million tons to 1.5 million tons per year with the addition of a new horizontal continuous caster (said to be the only one in the United States at the time) and a ladle furnace, which allowed the company to produce a wider variety of steel grades.

Sales in 1987 rose 7.3 percent to $318 million, and operating profits jumped to $42.5 million. According to Robert D. Rogers, president of Texas Industries, these results were achieved in a market that was only average for structural products and declining for bar products. Productivity increased slightly that year, to 1.6 man hours per ton of steel, compared to an international industry average of six man hours per ton.

In June 1988, Chaparral made an initial public offering of 5.4 million shares. Securities analysts applauded Chaparral's timing, noting that prices of stocks in the steel industry were climbing while the rest of the market remained sluggish. Proceeds were used to pay a $75 million debt owed to Texas Industries. With its ever-expanding product line, Chaparral sought to expand its market base as well. In 1989 it began marketing large structural beams to the booming Mexican construction industry and also began selling products in Japan. Sales leapt from $376 million in 1988 to $451 million the following year. That year the company also obtained financing to begin construction of a $60 million large section mill which would allow it to produce a 24-inch structural beam. The company's flexible management policy was also beginning to pay off during this time; several Chaparral employees developed a modified caster which allowed Chaparral to produce large structural beams five times faster than traditional methods, and at a cost believed to be the lowest in the world.

The U.S. construction industry entered a lull in the early 1990s. Despite Chaparral's attempt to offset its low domestic demand by doubling its overseas shipments, net income in 1990 plummeted over 50 percent to $24 million on sales of $404 million. The company continued to push for a greater share of the U.S. market and became the first domestic mill to introduce a new grade of wide-flange steel beams that met the specifications set by the construction industry. While the introduction allowed Chaparral to significantly undercut market prices, it also raised the ire of its competitors who accused Chaparral of ''disrupting an industry-wide effort to introduce the product in an orderly manner,'' when engineers and construction companies voiced their confusion about the strength of dual-certified beams.

By 1992 Chaparral was profitable again, with net income of $7 million on $416 million in sales. The following year, however, the company posted a $2 million loss due to an unusual combination of adverse market conditions. Both the domestic and overseas markets remained sluggish while prices of natural gas, scrap metal, and electrode reached an unprecedented high. In an effort to control costs, the company cut its on-site contract work force by 250. Sales that year grew 3.8 percent to $420.2 million, but the company was not able to turn a profit.

Another way Chaparral cut costs was to reduce shipping expenses by focusing on markets closer to its manufacturing operations. In December 1993, the company entered a marketing agreement with the Mexican steel company Altos Hornos de Mexico SA de CV (Ahmas). Under the agreement, Ahmas would serve as the sole representative for Chaparral's small and mid-size steel beams in Mexico and Chaparral would serve as the exclusive U.S. agent for Ahmas's wide-flange beams. The agreement placed Chaparral in a strong position to benefit from Mexico's then-booming construction industry and also set the groundwork for a potential increase in sales once the North American Free Trade Agreement revoked the ten percent tariff on goods flowing between the United States and Mexico. Due to this and other cost-cutting measures, Chaparral fared considerably better in 1994, posting a net income of $11.9 million on record sales of $462 million.

In its first 20 years of production, Chaparral earned a reputation as one of the most efficient steel mills in the world. The steel market was a highly cyclical one, yet Chaparral survived its storms through a combination of innovative management and aggressive marketing. Its flexible management style combined with such cost-saving innovations as a $60,000 employee-developed machine that does a better job than a similar $250,000 machine, resulted in a highly efficient and motivated work force. In the mid-1990s Chaparral was a lean, efficient mill well poised to weather almost any downturn in the turbulent U.S. steel industry.

Further Reading:

"American Steel: Resurrection," *The Economist,* April 2, 1983, p. 75.

Dumaine, Brian, "Chaparral Steel: Unleash Workers and Cut Costs," *Fortune,* May 18, 1992, p. 88.

Kantrow, Alan M., "Wide-Open Management at Chaparral Steel," *Harvard Business Review,* May 1986, p. 96.

—Maura Troester

The Chase Manhattan Corporation

1 Chase Manhattan Plaza
New York, New York 10081-0001
U.S.A.
(212) 552-2222
Fax: (212) 552-5928

Public Company
Incorporated: 1969
Employees: 35,774
Total Assets: $123.9 billion
Stock Exchanges: New York London Paris Düsseldorf Frankfurt
SICs: 6712 Bank Holding Companies; 6021 National Commercial Banks; 6022 State Commercial Banks; 6211 Security Brokers & Dealers; 6162 Mortgage Bankers & Correspondents

Following its 1995 merger with Chemical Banking Corporation, the Chase Manhattan Corporation rose from sixth to first largest bank in the United States. Shifting the direction of its operations in a restructuring initiated in 1990, Chase no longer aims to be a full-service global bank but focuses instead on three areas: regional retail banking, national consumer products, and global commercial banking. Long one of the most widely recognized names in banking, Chase suffered a market decline in the 1980s and early 1990s, making it a continuing object of takeover speculation, in particular in the frenzy of banking consolidation of the mid-1990s. In August 1995, the speculation ended.

Chase Manhattan's earliest predecessor, The Manhattan Company, was formed in 1799, ostensibly to supply New York with clean water to fight a yellow fever epidemic. Its real purpose, however, was to establish a bank. Organized by Aaron Burr to challenge the supremacy of the Bank of New York and the Bank of the United States, the company had a charter in which Burr had surreptitiously inserted a clause authorizing it to engage in other businesses with any leftover capital. To no one's surprise, the company soon discovered that the water-supply operation would not require all of its resources, so the Bank of Manhattan Company was opened in 1799 at 40 Wall Street. The bank's first president was Daniel Ludlow.

In 1808, the year Daniel Ludlow resigned, the company was allowed to sell the water operation to the City of New York and devote its energy to banking. From that time onward, the Bank of Manhattan flourished. The bank introduced several innovative banking practices, among them, the method by which it had gained a charter. Its example spawned corruption among other groups who sought incorporation; the construction of canals during the 1820s and 1830s or the building of railroads in the 1850s and 1860s often became the pretext for procuring a bank charter that might not otherwise have been granted.

Since the bank had virtually no restrictions in its charter, it was able to loan money to a wide variety of patrons, including tradespeople, land speculators, and manufacturers as well as the New York state government. This open banking policy provided a great impetus for westward expansion in the United States during the mid- and late 19th century. By the turn of the century the Bank of Manhattan had established itself as one of the largest holders of individual depositor accounts. Its policy of providing personal banking services worked so well that, at the time of its merger with Chase in 1955, the Bank of Manhattan operated 67 branches throughout New York City and was widely regarded as one of the most successful and prestigious regional banks in America.

The other part of Chase Manhattan, the Chase National Bank, was established in New York in 1877 and named after Salmon P. Chase, Secretary of the Treasury under Abraham Lincoln. It was not until 1911, however, when Albert Henry Wiggin took over the leadership of the bank, that Chase developed into a power on Wall Street. In 1905, at the age of 36, Wiggin became the youngest vice-president in the company's history. By 1911 he was president of the bank and by 1917 the chairman of its board of directors.

Chase was a relatively small bank when Wiggin took over, but he soon began to transform it into one of the largest in the world. He did this by expanding the bank's list of corporate accounts through the offer of more banking services, especially trust services. Wiggin helped to found Mercantile Trust in 1917 and in the same year organized Chase Securities Corporation to distribute and underwrite stocks and bonds. This affiliate soon became a major force in the equities markets. In addition, Wiggin established strong ties to big business by recruiting the bank's directors from the most influential companies in the United States.

Wiggin's greatest contribution to the bank was his arrangement of a series of mergers during the 1920s and early 1930s in which Chase absorbed seven major banks in New York City. The largest of those, the Equitable Trust Company, had more than $1 billion in resources when it was acquired in 1930. The eighth largest bank in the United States at the time, it was owned by John D. Rockefeller and led by Rockefeller's brother-in-law Winthrop Aldrich. Not long after the merger, Wiggin assumed the chairmanship of what was then the largest bank in the world.

In 1932, however, the leadership at Chase changed dramatically. Wiggin had used not only his own funds, but also those of the bank to engage in stock speculation, and that year was forced to resign. In the following years, Wiggin and several of his close associates were disgraced by a congressional investigation that uncovered, among other transgressions, the use of affiliated companies to circumvent the laws restricting stock market transactions. Moreover, it was learned that during the stock market crash of 1929, Wiggin had made $4 million selling Chase stock short—and using bank funds to do so.

Winthrop Aldrich directed the bank's operations from the mid-1930s to the end of World War II, a period when Chase continued to expand and develop, becoming the first bank to open branches in both Germany and Japan after World War II. However, Aldrich knew that Chase was hampered in its domestic development by the fact that all of its consumer branches were located in Manhattan. The bank had always concentrated on corporate and foreign business and ignored innovations such as branch banking, leaving it in a weak position to capitalize on the prosperity of middle-income Americans during the postwar boom. In 1955, Aldrich arranged a merger between Chase and the Bank of Manhattan, at the time the nation's 15th largest bank, but more importantly one with an extensive branch network throughout New York City.

From the time of the merger between Chase and the Bank of Manhattan, there was a new driving force behind the bank's activities: David Rockefeller. Rockefeller had joined Chase as the assistant manager of its foreign department after the war, becoming vice-president by 1949. In the early 1950s, he was head of the bank's metropolitan department; it was actually Rockefeller who advised Aldrich on the benefits of the merger with the Bank of Manhattan. With the merger complete, he was named executive vice-president and given the task of developing the largest bank in New York City. At the same time he was also appointed vice-chairman of the executive committee. In 1969, he became chairman of the board of directors, the same year the Chase Manhattan Corporation was incorporated and the Chase Manhattan Bank N.A. became its wholly-owned subsidiary.

As the head of Chase Manhattan, David Rockefeller soon became a major international power broker. Never really interested in the day-to-day operations of the bank, he began to travel extensively, meeting with political and business leaders around the world. This high international profile led Rockefeller to use the bank in the service of what he regarded as desirable American foreign policy; by becoming one of the pillars of the U.S. foreign policy establishment, his influence on the Council of Foreign Relations and Trilateral Commission was very strong.

This close association between Chase and the prevailing U.S. political establishment inevitably drew the bank into controversy. In 1965, Chase's decision to purchase a major share in the second largest bank in South Africa provoked an intense campaign by civil rights groups to persuade institutions and individuals to withdraw their money from a firm that clearly supported the apartheid regime. In 1966, widespread protests were directed against the bank following Rockefeller's decision to open a Chase branch in Saigon. A strong supporter of U.S. involvement in the Vietnam War, Rockefeller traveled to the capital of South Vietnam to open the building personally; a sandstone fortress, it was designed to withstand mortar attacks and mine explosions.

David Rockefeller and Chase's foreign controversies continued into the 1970s. During this time, the shah of Iran had been the bank's best customer in the Middle East. Iran's $2.5 billion in deposits from oil profits amounted to approximately eight percent of Chase's total deposits in 1975. When the shah fell from power in 1979, it was Rockefeller who, along with Henry Kissinger—at that time the chairman of the firm's international advisory committee—persuaded the Carter administration to allow the shah into the United States. When Iran tried to retaliate by withdrawing its funds from Chase, Rockefeller succeeded in convincing the government to freeze all Iranian assets in U.S. banks, a move that led to the seizure of hostages at the American Embassy in Teheran.

The 1970s were a difficult time for the bank. Chase lost significant domestic business as regional banks lessened their dependence on Chase Manhattan for their own growth and expansion; their burgeoning resources made it less important that they go to the ''banker's banker'' for loans. In addition, Chase lost millions of dollars in bad loans to Latin American countries, which resulted in its being placed on the Federal Reserve's list of ''problem banks''—ones that needed constant supervision. Although the company's foreign income increased from one-half to two-thirds of its total income during this time—to nearly $4 billion—the bank had a hard time competing with Citibank's aggressive expansion. Nevertheless, Chase remained the country's third largest bank, with 226 branches in New York City and 105 branches and 34 subsidiaries around the globe.

The 1980s ushered in a period of significant acquisitions for Chase. In 1984, the bank purchased Nederlandse Credietbank N.V., a Dutch bank headquartered in Amsterdam. The same year it purchased the Lincoln First Bank in Rochester, New York. In 1985, the bank bought six Ohio savings and loan institutions. In 1986, Chase acquired Continental Bancor.

In 1981, David Rockefeller retired from his position at Chase. Willard C. Butcher, his hand-picked replacement, had been president and CEO of Chase, and succeeded him as chairman of the board. Butcher took up where his predecessor left off; Chase maintained a very high profile in international finance, continuing to view itself as a worldwide power broker.

But the most important problem for Chase Manhattan in the 1980s was a series of bad loans that had no equal in quantity or in magnitude in the bank's history. It started when Drysdale Government Securities defaulted early in 1982 on $160 million in interest payments to brokerage firms. Chase had acted as an intermediary for these deals, and thus was forced to pay $117 million of the interest Drysdale owed. Only a few months later, Penn Square Bank, N.A. collapsed after $2.5 billion in unsecured loans that it had made to oil and natural gas interests in Oklahoma went sour. Chase purchased some of those loans, but moved quickly to write off $161 million of them to prevent further financial damage. Chase had also been one of the most heavily exposed banks lending money to Third World countries. On February 20, 1987 Brazil announced that it would suspend payment on its foreign debt and threw the money-center banks into a panic. In May, Chase added $1.6 billion to its loan loss reserves. As a result, it posted a loss of $894.5 million for 1987—the worst year for American banking since the Great Depression.

Battered by the Third World debt crisis and faced with strong competition from insurgent regional banks, Chase Manhattan faltered in the late 1980s. Between 1986 and 1988, it reduced its work force by ten percent, or about 6,000 employees. In 1988 the *New York Times* speculated that the venerable banking giant might be a takeover candidate because of its depressed stock price and prestigious name. Then, in 1989 and 1990 Chase suffered huge losses from commercial real estate loans, sinking the bank's finances to new lows. Reflecting the seriousness of the situation, the bank's board asked Butcher to retire a year early so that a new team could deal with the crisis.

Butcher's heir apparent during the turbulent late 1980s was his president and chief operating officer, Thomas G. Labrecque. Following a stint in the Navy, Labrecque had joined Chase in 1964 as a trainee, moving up the ranks until 1970 when he started working directly for Rockefeller on various trouble-shooting assignments. He made his mark at Chase in 1975 with his work on the Municipal Assistance Corp. which helped bail New York City out of a financial crisis. Labrecque was also credited with convincing Chase's board in 1978 that the bank should expand its retail business—which by the 1990s would generate nearly half of the bank's revenues. In 1981 he was named president.

Industry observers noted that Labrecque's more well-known predecessors had emphasized Chase's worldwide position at the expense of a domestic operation which, with its various problems and scandals of the 1980s, seemed out of control. When Labrecque—virtually unknown outside of banking circles—took over as CEO in late 1990, his immediate task was to implement a restructuring plan intended to rein in control of Chase's operations and turn the bank's fortunes around. Like other banks struggling through those industry-wide difficult years, Chase cut costs, trimmed staff (another 6,000 by the end of 1991), and reduced operations. Labrecque also scaled back the bank's international presence by beginning to jettison its foreign retail banking subsidiaries; no longer would Chase aim to be a full-service world bank, such as its long-time rival Citicorp. Branch banking operations outside the New York area—in Arizona, Florida, and Ohio—were eliminated. Successful consumer lending operations were shorn up through such moves as the 1993 acquisition of consumer mortgage company Troy & Nichols, Inc. Overall, Chase intended to concentrate on three areas: regional banking in the New York tri-state region; national consumer operations in credit cards, mortgages, and automobile loans; and international investment banking.

Chase also began at this time to focus more on technology, a particular strength of the man Labrecque chose as his president, Arthur F. Ryan, who had been in charge of the firm's consumer bank. The company initiated a $500 million program to upgrade its information processing systems. It also entered into the on-line home banking arena through alliances with Microsoft Corp., Intuit Inc., America Online, and CompuServe.

Perhaps most importantly, Labrecque and Ryan embarked in 1992 on a program to transform Chase's corporate culture. In addition to efforts to bolster quality control and customer service, perhaps the most important addition to Chase's operations was that of teamwork; the bank had historically suffered from turf wars. As a result of these efforts, by 1994, cost-containment efforts had translated into an improvement in the bank's overhead efficiency ratio (noninterest expenses divided by revenues) from 75 percent to 60 percent. Following a net loss of $334 million in 1990, Chase enjoyed four successive years healthily in the black; 1991 showed $520 million in net income on net revenues of $3.35 billion, while 1994 showed $1.08 billion in net income on net revenues of $3.69 billion.

The question for Chase in the mid-1990s was whether all of Labrecque and Ryan's efforts had come soon enough to save the bank's independence. In the fiercely competitive environment of the times, Chase had actually lost ground; increasing consolidation engendered through a mind-boggling series of bank mergers from 1993 through 1995 had caused Chase's ranking among U.S. banks to fall from second to seventh in terms of total assets. Weakness in the price of its stock, reflecting ongoing investor skepticism, not only prevented Chase from strengthening itself through further acquisitions but also made the bank itself vulnerable to takeover. Moreover, the company's June 1995 announcement to lay off an additional 3,000 to 6,000 workers (or 8.5 to 17 percent of its work force) by early 1996, further fueled takeover speculation.

Finally, on August 28, 1995, the wait was over. Chemical Banking Corporation announced a merger with Chase Manhattan. The $10 billion stock swap transformed sixth-largest Chase and fourth-largest Chemical into the largest banking company on the United States with assets of nearly $300 billion. Although it was termed a merger of equals, it was regarded by the market as an acquisition of Chase by Chemical even though the combined corporation would use the more prestigious Chase name.

In September 1995, the first round of executive positions was announced with more than half the positions going to Chemical executives. As the year closed, Chase was adjusting to the merger and to its new position as the largest banking concern in the U.S.

Principal Subsidiaries: Chase Manhattan Bank, N.A. (Argentina); Chase Manhattan Trading S.A. (Argentina); Chase Manhattan Bank (Austria), A.G.; Chase Manhattan Trust Cayman Ltd. (Bahamas); Chase Manhattan Trust Corporation Limited (Bahamas); Chase Manhattan Bank, N.A. (Bahrain); Chase Manhattan Bank, N.A. (Belgium); Banco Chase Manhattan S.A. (Brazil); Chase Manhattan Administracao E Servicios, S.A. (Brazil); Chase Manhattan, S.A. Credito Financiamento Investimento (Brazil); Chase Manhattan, S.A. Distribuidora de Titulos E Valores Mobiliarios (Brazil); Chase Manhattan Bank of Canada; Chase Manhattan Leasing Canada Limited; Chase Bank & Trust Co. (Channel Islands), Ltd. (Channel Islands); Chase Manhattan Bank, N.A. (Channel Islands); Chase Manhattan Trust Corporation Limited (Chile); Inversiones Chase Manhattan Limitada (Chile); Chase Manhattan Bank, N.A. (China); Chase Manhattan Bank, N.A. (Colombia); Chase Invest A/S (Denmark); Chase Manhattan Bank, N.A. (Denmark); Chase Manhattan Bank, N.A. (Dominican Republic); Chase Manhattan Bank, N.A. (France); Chase Manhattan, S.A. (France); Chase Bank, A.G. (Germany); Chase Manhattan Bank, N.A. (Greece); Chase Manhattan Bank, N.A. (Hong Kong); Chase Manhattan Financial Services (Hong Kong) Ltd.;

Chase Manhattan Investment Services (Hong Kong) Ltd.; Chase Manhattan Trust Company (Hong Kong) Ltd.; Chase Manhattan Bank, N.A. (India); Chase Manhattan Bank, N.A. (Indonesia); P.T. Chase Leasing Indonesia; Chase Bank (Ireland) PLC; Chasefin-Chase Finanziara, S.p.A. (Italy); Chase Investmenti Mobiliari S.p.A. (Italy); Chase Manhattan Bank, N.A. (Italy); Chase Leasing (Japan) Limited; Chase Manhattan Bank, N.A. (Japan); Chase Manhattan Securities (Japan); Chase Manhattan Trust and Banking Company (Japan) Limited; Chase Manhattan Bank, N.A. (Korea); Chase Manhattan Bank Luxembourg, S.A.; Chase Manhattan Bank, N.A. (Malaysia); Chase Manhattan Bank, N.A. (Mexico); Chase Bank NV (Netherlands); Chase Manhattan Bank, N.A. (Netherlands); Chase Manhattan Overseas Finance Corporation, N.V. (Netherlands); Chase Manhattan Bank, N.A. (Pakistan); Chase Manhattan Bank, N.A. (Panama); Chase Manhattan Bank, N.A. (Philippines); Chase Manhattan Bank, N.A. (Portugal); Chase Manhattan Bank, N.A. (Russia); Chase Investment Bank Limited (Singapore); Chase Manhattan Bank, N.A. (Singapore); Chase Manhattan Futures Corp. (Singapore); Chase Manhattan Bank Espana S.A.; Chase Manhattan Bank, S.A. (Spain); Chase Manhattan Securities S.A. (Spain); Chase Leasing (S.A.E.) (Spain); Chase Manhattan Overseas Corporation (Sweden); Chase Manhattan Bank, N.A. (Switzerland); Chase Manhattan Bank (Switzerland); Chase Manhattan Bank, N.A. (Taiwan); Chase Manhattan Bank, N.A. (Thailand); Chase Manhattan Bank, N.A. (Turkey); Chase Investment Bank Holdings Limited (U.K.); Chase Investment Bank Limited (U.K.); Chase Leasing Limited (U.K.); Chase Manhattan Capital Markets (U.K.) Ltd.; Chase Manhattan Equities Limited; Chase Manhattan Futures (U.K.) Ltd.; Chase Manhattan Gilts Ltd. (U.K.); Chase Manhattan Milbank, Ltd. (U.K.); Chase Manhattan Trustees, Ltd. (U.K.); Chase Trade Finance, Ltd. (U.K.); Chase Home Mortgage Corporation; Chase Manhattan of California Thrift Corp.; The Chase Manhattan Bank (USA), N.A.; Chase Bank of Maryland; Chase National Corporate Services, Inc.; Chase Trade, Inc.; Chase Auto Finance Corp.; Chase Education Finance; Chase Manhattan Futures Corp.; Chase Manhattan Trust Co. of California, N.A.; Chase Access Services Corp.; Chase Automated Clearing House, Inc.; Chase U.S. Consumer Services.

Further Reading:

Hansell, Saul, "Chemical Wins Most Top Posts In Chase Merger," *New York Times,* September 29, 1995, p. C1, C6.

Holland, Kelley, "A Chastened Chase: The Humbled Bank Starts to Revive—by Transforming Its Culture," *Business Week,* pp. 106–109.

Lipin, Steven, "Joining Fortunes: Chemical and Chase Set $10 Billion Merger, Forming Biggest Bank," *Wall Street Journal,* August 28, 1995, p. A1, A4.

Meehan, John, and Leah J. Nathans, "Agony at Chase Manhattan: Can Incoming CEO Labrecque Keep the Bank Independent?," *Business Week,* October 8, 1990, pp. 32–36.

O'Brien, Timothy L., and Steven Lipin, "In Latest Round of Banking Mergers, Even Big Institutions Become Targets," *Wall Street Journal,* July 14, 1995, pp. A3, A4.

O'Brien, Timothy L., "Chase Manhattan Planning to Lay Off 8.5% to 17% of Work Force by Early '96," *Wall Street Journal,* June 27, 1995, p. A3.

——, "Intuit to Unveil On-Line Pact with 20 Firms," *Wall Street Journal,* July 14, 1995, pp. A2, A5.

Rogers, David, *The Future of American Banking: Managing for Change,* New York: McGraw-Hill, 1993, 346 p.

Schifrin, Matthew, "Chase Manhattan's Unsung Turnaround," *Forbes,* October 25, 1993, pp. 141–146.

Wilson, John Donald, *The Chase: The Chase Manhattan Bank, N.A., 1945–1985,* Boston: Harvard Business School Press, 1986, 432 p.

—updated by David E. Salamie

Chemed Corporation

255 East 5th Street
Cincinnati, Ohio 45282
U.S.A.
(513) 762-6900

Public Company
Founded: 1970
Employees: 4834
Sales: $525.1 million
Stock Exchanges: New York
SICs: 7699 Repair Services, Not Elsewhere Classified; 5113 Industrial & Personal Service Paper

Chemed Corporation, headquartered in Cincinnati, Ohio, is a highly successful, diversified firm with large market shares in a variety of different areas. Areas of involvement include medical and dental supplies for the private-practice market, hospice care, and home healthcare services; commercial drain cleaning, plumbing, air-conditioning repair, pipe-cleaning, and appliance maintenance services; janitorial products and services; and pharmacy management for the long-term patient care market. The company's Veratex Group, which provides products for the disposable dental and medical supplies market, serves over 30 percent of all private-practice dentists across the United States.

Chemed Corporation's long history dates back to the founding of the DuBois Soap Company. In June 1920 a confident and ambitious salesman named T.V. DuBois decided to open his own business. DuBois established the DuBois Soap Company in a rented building, a small, four-story structure adjacent to the Ohio River. The fledgling operation made soap chips and powders for the city's growing restaurant trade. Within a few short years, the firm was selling its products all over the state. As revenues increased, additional employees were added to the payroll.

DuBois Soap Company survived the bleak years of the Great Depression in good financial condition. During the late 1930s and early 1940s the company expanded its restaurant dishwashing product line to encompass a whole range of different items, including industrial cleaning and maintenance products for other industries. Soon DuBois was servicing restaurants, steel companies, heavy manufacturing firms, and food processing plants. With the rapid expansion of its product line, the company decided to increase the amount of space for its administrative and manufacturing facilities in Cincinnati. By the end of World War II, the company was producing a huge variety of cleaning and maintenance products and had developed a reputation as one of the leaders in the specialty chemical industry.

During the late 1940s and throughout the 1950s, DuBois developed its sales network and expanded its manufacturing plants. Three new facilities were built in California, New Jersey, and Texas. As DuBois's revenues increased, the company came to the attention of W.R. Grace, a large conglomerate with holdings in the chemical, manufacturing, retail, fertilizer, food products, and restaurant industries. In 1964 Grace acquired DuBois and incorporated the company into its Specialty Products Group, renaming the firm the DuBois Chemicals Division. In 1971 Grace management transformed its specialty chemicals group, which included the DuBois Chemicals Division, into the Chemed Corporation. DuBois Chemicals developed and manufactured professional cleaning and maintenance chemicals, dispensing equipment, and processing compounds. It served as the single largest area of operation within Chemed. While Grace maintained ownership of the majority of Chemed stock, the company was given autonomy to develop its own products.

Another firm that remained an important part of Chemed Corporation in the mid-1990s was the National Sanitary Supply Company. Founded in 1929, National developed in much the same manner as DuBois. The company offered a variety of chemical products used to clean and maintain industrial, commercial, and institutional facilities. Goods produced by National over the years included floor finishes, trash liners, mops, buckets, brushes, paper and packaging products, and cleaning chemicals and equipment. By the time the company was purchased by Chemed in 1983, National had become the largest distributor of sanitary maintenance supplies in America.

The third major company to shape Chemed Corporation was Roto-Rooter, Inc. Founded in 1936, Roto-Rooter provided sewer and drain cleaning services. After a time it expanded its range of service to include plumbing repair and maintenance. The firm grew at such a rapid pace that management decided to establish a network of independent franchises that could conduct business throughout the United States. By the time Chemed purchased the company in 1980, Roto-Rooter has become the leading supplier of sewer and drain cleaning services across America. The company, which claimed that it had serviced more than two million customers, boasted that it had cleaned one out of every six clogged drains or sewers in the country.

Armed with the thriving DuBois and Roto-Rooter businesses, and with plans to acquire National Sanitary Supply already in motion, Chemed management decided to buy the remainder of W.R. Grace's 16.7 million shares of Chemed stock. This transaction allowed Chemed to become a totally autonomous, independent corporation. It was listed on the New York Stock Exchange in 1982.

Even as Chemed developed into a successful independent organization, DuBois remained the cornerstone of its operations. Throughout the 1980s, Chemed grew as DuBois grew. DuBois manufactured and marketed hundreds of specialty chemical products—including paint strippers, cutting fluids, specialty lubricants, sanitation chemicals, and water treatment chemicals—for use as industrial cleaning and maintenance compounds. The company sold its product line to customers in a number of diverse industries. Public utilities, mining organizations, airlines, meat packers, breweries, dairy plants, railroads, metal finishers, publishing companies, hospitals, and retail establishments all purchased materials from DuBois. In the mid-1980s the company expanded its services to include laundry and linen supplies and uniform rentals. During this time DuBois expanded its product line to major overseas markets. By the end of the 1980s, the company had opened offices in Australia, England, France, Germany, Holland, Japan, Mexico, Saudi Arabia, Singapore, South Africa, Sweden, and Venezuela.

Chemed also established several new businesses during the 1980s. In 1981 Chemed established Omnicare, Inc., a company designed to supply pharmacy management services and distribute dental and medical supplies. Omnicare was divided into two operating divisions, the Sequoia Pharmacy Group and the Veratex Group. Sequoia provided services for more than 200 nursing homes, and by 1990 it represented over 20 percent of Omnicare revenues. The Veratex Group, a supplier of medical and dental products, grew even more rapidly. By 1990 the Veratex Group ranked third in America's dressings and sponge market on the strength of its sales of over 800 different kinds of proprietary disposable paper, gauze, and cotton products to professionals working in the veterinary, medical, and dental fields.

National Sanitary Supply Company and Roto-Rooter also helped Chemed increase its revenues during the 1980s. By the early 1990s, National reported over 150,000 standing accounts across the country, with 22 distribution centers in 14 states. The performance of Roto-Rooter was even better. In 1990, a year when revenues from the company's plumbing services increased 26 percent, the firm introduced a revolutionary drain and sewer cleaning product that broke down organic waste by biological means and converted it into water and harmless carbon dioxide. Roto-Rooter also made significant inroads toward expanding its base of operations through a franchising agreement that allowed the company to distribute products in Japan.

In the early 1990s, management at Chemed decided to concentrate on marketing and service-oriented businesses, rather than capital or production-intensive manufacturing. Although DuBois was the largest revenue and profit-generating division within Chemed, with sales of $275 million in 1990 and 2,800 employees, management thought it best to sell its flagship operation in order to refocus the company's priorities. As a result, DuBois was sold for $243 million to Molson Companies, Ltd., the largest brewery in Canada and the sixth leading beer maker in the United States. Molson immediately combined DuBois with its Diversey Corporation subsidiary.

Chemed implemented a comprehensive restructuring program with the money garnered from the sale of DuBois. The revenue was immediately reinvested in the company's growing healthcare business. Money was also funneled into Chemed's appliance repair service interests. Chemed sold off Omnicare as well, but retained its highly profitable Veratex Group. Sales for Veratex amounted to over $95 million in 1994, but growing competition within the industry and significant changes in the healthcare industry forced the Veratex Group to reduce its work force and cut operating expenses. One development of interest in the industry, for example, was the decision by Tidi Wholesale, a leader in the manufacture of disposable medical and dental products, to merge its product line with Erving Healthcare, a producer of environmentally safe, recycled paper products.

National Sanitary Supply Company had offices in 71 locations across the United States in the mid-1990s. The company, which touts itself as a ''one-stop shop'' for its customers, is one of the largest distributors of sanitary maintenance supply products in the country. In 1995 the company offered more than 10,000 products used to clean and maintain all types of commercial, industrial, and institutional facilities.

Roto-Rooter is the largest supplier of drain cleaning and plumbing services in America. The company also maintains the country's largest service contract business for the appliance, heating, and air conditioning repair markets. Roto-Rooter has increased its overseas operations as well. Entering the mid-1990s the company was an industry leader in Canada and operated 17 franchises in Japan. In 1994 the company expanded the number of its service technicians by 15 percent. All this activity contributed to greater revenues for Roto-Rooter. From 1993 to 1994, the company reported a 20 percent growth in plumbing revenues. But Roto-Rooter has enjoyed steady growth for a number of years. From 1984 to 1994, for instance, revenues exploded from $28.2 million to $171.9 million.

In addition to the Veratex Group, National Sanitary Supply Company, and Roto-Rooter, Chemed had one other major subsidiary in the mid-1990s: Patient Care, Inc. Founded in 1974 to provide comprehensive home-healthcare services in the New York, New Jersey, and Connecticut areas, Patient Care was acquired by Chemed in 1993. In the mid-1990s Patient Care's work force included more than 4,500 nurses, home health care aides, speech therapists, physical therapists, occupational therapists, medical social workers, nutritionists, and other healthcare workers. Regarded by many as one of the anticipated solutions to the ever-increasing costs of in-patient health services, the $20 billion homecare industry has grown rapidly in the 1990s. Mindful that the homecare market is extremely fragmented, Patient Care claims that its own comprehensive line of healthcare services offers better resources and is more cost-effective than smaller home health agencies. In its first year with Chemed, Patient Care proved to be a valuable acquisition. From 1993 to 1994 Patient Care's revenues grew from $53.5 million to $69 million.

Led by chairman and chief executive officer Edward L. Hutton, president Kevin J. McNamara, and Board of Directors chairman J. Peter Grace, Chemed seemed poised to take advantage of growing market trends in service-oriented industries such as home healthcare and plumbing and drain cleaning in the mid-1990s. Dividends continue to increase from its core interests, and management has seen further financial gains from investments in other firms like Vital Health Corporation and Exel Ltd.

Principal Subsidiaries: Veratex Group; National Sanitary Supply Company; Roto-Rooter, Inc.; Patient Care, Inc.

Further Reading:

Bastian, Lisa, and Jeffrey Waddle, ''Corporate Profiles,'' *Cincinnati: City of Charm,* 1992, pp. 308–309.

Chemed Annual Report, Cincinnati: Chemed Corporation, 1994.

—Thomas Derdak

Chi-Chi's Inc.

10200 Linn Station Road
Louisville, Kentucky 40223
U.S.A.
(502) 426-3900
Fax: (502) 339-4204

Wholly Owned Subsidiary of Family Restaurants Inc.
Incorporated: 1975
Employees: 20,000
Sales: $433.1 million
SICs: 5812 Eating Places; 6794 Patent Owners and Lessors

Chi-Chi's, Inc., owned by Family Restaurants Inc., is a chain of 206 Mexican dinner houses which operates principally in the Midwest. In addition to company-owned stores, there are three licensed franchisees, in Europe, Canada, and South Carolina, which operate approximately 20 stores altogether. After a booming start in the late 1970s, and a growth spurt in the early 1980s, Chi-Chi's sales began to decline. While still a leader in their segment, the company has continued to face increasing competition from Mexican and other restaurants, leveling off their sales and growth.

Established in 1975 by Mexican restaurant magnate Marno McDermott and investor Max Gee, Chi-Chi's specialty was Sonoran-style Mexican food. Starting in the early 1980s, Chairman and CEO Shelly Frank drove rapid expansion of company-owned stores. Spurred on by stores which frequently opened to sales of $70,000 or $80,000 a week, Chi-Chi's spread throughout the Midwest, where they had virtually no competition.

From 1981 to 1983, company-owned restaurants soared from one to 46, and profits multiplied elevenfold from the beginning of the decade to $9.1 million in 1983. In 1985 alone, 42 new Chi-Chi's opened, with 27 company-owned and 15 franchised. This increased total units by more than one-third, and company-owned units by 50 percent. In 1984, Chi-Chi's net income peaked at 16.7 million. By 1986, Chi-Chi's operated 200 restaurants.

From 1984 to 1987, however, the chain's profitability began to slide. This coincided with an overall decline in the industry due to lowered alcohol consumption, saturated restaurant markets, maturing baby boomers, and the growing popularity of at-home food and entertainment options. Chi-Chi's was also showing weakness created by the stress of rapid expansion.

During its growth spurt, the chain had built 10,000 to 12,000 square foot restaurants which were too large to operate profitably as the economy flattened out in the mid-1980s. In addition, Chi-Chi's had clustered restaurants in order to seize high market share in a given area, cutting average sales for individual units. There were also several failed attempts to penetrate new markets: nine company-owned units choked in New York City, as did three in New England. Franchises in Atlanta, Texas, New Mexico, and San Diego also failed to take root.

While Chi-Chi's had grown, it had neglected to create an effective corporate communication network. The corporate management was not in touch with the needs of field managers and franchisees, so that team spirit and confidence in the company was ebbing low. Franchisees were feeling uneasy, particularly after the Chapter 11 bankruptcy of Chi-Chi's Food Services Inc., an Oklahoma City-based franchise that was a subsidiary of Kelly Johnston Enterprises. But even in company-owned stores, management turnover had reach as high as 80 percent. Inconsistency in management translated to the customer as unreliable service and food. After their peak year in 1984, sales began to decline and by 1986, total revenues had dropped from $269.3 million to $206 million, while net income bottomed at $9.1 million from $15.6 million.

When Shelly Frank retired in 1986, Hal Smith came on board as Chi-Chi's leader, leaving his position as president and CEO of the Chili's restaurant chain. Smith identified three major problems in the company: declining store sales, poor unit profitability, and high management turnover. His recovery strategy focused on opening the lines of corporate communication and streamlining the bureaucracy. Smith gained the support of the corporate officers, all of whom had been hired by Frank, by having tete-a-tetes with every middle and upper-level manager in order to get the lay of the land. He reduced corporate staff by 18 percent and redefined certain jobs.

Chi-Chi's held its first management conference in September 1987, bringing together over 200 general managers, area supervisors, regional directors, and executives to galvanize the team. Further, Smith encouraged direct communication between field managers and the home offices in Louisville. Franchisees were pleased to find Smith, who would personally return phone calls, far more accessible than his predecessor.

A former franchise owner was brought on as vice-president of franchise relations in 1987, and the independent operators were encouraged to develop and share ideas with the company. Consul Corp, which operated 40 restaurants, had pioneered the idea of the El Pronto walk-up units, which featured selections from the full Chi-Chi's menu. The company tested two small El-Prontos in midwest malls. In turn, the company helped smaller franchisees cover the $45,000 costs of refurbishing units and stepped up communications and visits.

In company-owned stores, Smith cut paper work for store managers so that they could turn their attention to the customers. Managers' schedules, which had frequently ballooned to 80 hours and six days a week, were cut back to 50 to 55 hours a week with two consecutive days off. Managers' salaries were also made more competitive. New bonus plans, health and life insurance plans and a stock ownership program were instituted. Training was improved for managers, and employees and servers were encouraged to show their personality within the parameters of quality service. Within a year, management turnover was reduced to 35 percent.

Within two years, Smith had created a team of employees—from executives, to managers and wait staff—that felt committed to working at Chi-Chi's. Financial benefits began to appear early in 1987, when same-store average volumes were up slightly for the first time in more than a year, and the second time in four years. Instead of expansion, Chi-Chi's had disposed of 21 marginal stores by April of 1988, taking a $20 million write-off against earnings. The chain planned to build only eight to ten new restaurants in fiscal 1988, down from the previous rate of 20 to 30 a year. Only five new stores were franchised.

Chi-Chi's also opened three new conceptual restaurants in the winter of 1987–88: Papanda's Border Cafe, Chajita's Mexican Cafe, and G.W. Sharkey's. Papanda's was a Mexican restaurant aimed at the Southeast and south central U.S., where Chi-Chi's had previously failed; Chajita's was a fast food restaurant with touches of dining house atmosphere; and G.W. Sharkey's Oyster Bar and Grill was a fresh seafood restaurant. All three restaurants featured display mesquite grilling, informality, and a good price/value ratio.

By 1988, all the refurbishment attracted an unwanted take-over bid from the Carlyle Group, a limited partnership that had recently become Chi-Chi's largest stockholder with 7.5 percent outstanding shares. Chi-Chi's commissioned First Boston Corp. to locate an investor to outbid Carlyle's offer of $200 million. Carlyle removed its bid in February of 1988, but in April, the company was purchased by San Diego-based Foodmaker, Inc., the owner of Jack in the Box restaurants, currently the country's fifth largest fast food chain. It purchased the 129 company operated Chi-Chi's (there were also 77 franchises) for about $235 million in April of 1988. Chi-Chi's retained its own corporate staff and Hal Smith continued to head the company as a division of Foodmaker.

The chain did well for a period, hitting its best year to date in 1990 with sales of $450 million; things held steady in fiscal 1991, with pretax profits of $57.3 million on about the same amount of sales. Despite continued good management, the tight economy began taking a toll on the chain once again. In 1992, Chi-Chi's was still second in its segment, but sales had dropped to $445 million and guest counts were on the decline yet again throughout the 160 company-owned and 65 franchised restaurants. Segment leader Taco Bell threatened Chi-Chi's with its cheap eats and 4,000 outlets racking up sales of $3.3 billion. The competition proliferated as McDonalds offered a breakfast burrito, and restaurants of every stripe added Mexican food to their menus. In addition, non-Mexican restaurants were outstripping Chi-Chi's at the low-cost, fun atmosphere game. Dinner house chains like the Olive Garden, Cookers, and Macaroni Grills, were stealing customers from Chi-Chi's with their appealing image of fresh food and hospitality.

To combat the slump in sales, Chi-Chi's introduced value-priced entrees at $3.99 and $4.99, and freshly prepared rice, beans and beef. Smith felt that customers were not aware of the amount of "scratch" cooking that went on in Chi-Chi's kitchens, and the chain began emphasizing the fresh food in their advertising. Tortilla making machines were brought in to the lobbies of company-owned stores to give customers an immediate message of freshness.

The restaurant's original menu of Sonoran cuisine was all but replaced by Tex-Mex and grilled items. The menu thrust was to take popular American foods and "mexicanize" them; the chain was experimenting with items such as Mexican pasta with blue-corn fettucine, and Mexican pizza as an entree, and Mexican stir fry.

In June 1992, Smith quit Chi-Chi's unexpectedly, citing personal reasons. A year earlier, Mike Fiori, Smith's vice-president, had left the chain after ten years of service to head competitor On The Border. Thus, Smith's departure left only two senior executives with extensive Chi-Chi's experience. Kenneth R. Williams, executive vice-president of Jack in the Box, was named to replace him.

In the summer of 1992, Chi-Chi's and its parent, Foodmaker, took over Consul Restaurant Corp., a major franchisee operating in Chapter 11 bankruptcy. Although Consul aligned with a group of unsecured creditors to counter the takeover bid, Chi-Chi's was able to purchase the publicly traded Consul's assets for 8.7 million in cash, taking over its operations and debt.

Consul owed 17 million in debt, most of which stemmed from the company's failed expansion into Texas and the western markets in the mid-1980s, where fourteen units went under. Chi-Chi's kept only 22 of the 26 Chi-Chi's units Consul operated, liquidating the remaining assets in order to pay consul's creditors at 80 cents on the dollar. The Consul units, located in Minnesota, Wisconsin, Nebraska, and North and South Dakota, were refurbished and upgraded, and new menu items were introduced, along with new uniforms, table wear and Tortilla machines. Most of the field employees were retained, although CEO William D. Etter and chief financial officer Bob Lamp were replaced. Williams was tapped to be senior vice-president of Foodmaker just six months after taking the presidency of Chi-Chi's and was succeeded by long-time Chi-Chi's employee Joe Micatrotto.

In 1993, the chain continued to see same-store sales slip. Store makeovers that ran to $200,000 per unit and featured a festive color scheme with banners, striped neon lighting, new tiling and wood, a sun room and a display cart featuring an array of fresh fruit were continued. Spinach quesadillas were introduced, while advertising featured "Fiesta for Two," a complete dinner package for $14.99.

Early in 1994, Chi-Chi's was acquired by Family Restaurants Inc. Family Restaurants was formed after the Chapter 11 bankruptcy reorganization of Restaurant Enterprises Group, which already owned Chi-Chi's top competitor El Torito. The chains were brought together under one parent, newly named Family Restaurants. Although each retained its individual name and style, the marriage created the first coast-to-coast chain of full-service Mexican restaurants, comprising 315 units, including some Casa Gallardo establishments as well as other divisions.

The merger also made Family Restaurants one of the five or six largest operators of full-service restaurants, with a total of 680 units in all.

Foodmaker exchanged the 237 unit chain for a 40 percent stake in the new venture and approximately $200 million in cash. They shared ownership of Family Restaurants with Apollo Advisers L.P., and Green Equity Investors L.P. Micatrotto was brought on to lead the restructured Family Restaurants. Barry Krantz assumed leadership of Family's Mexican division in February of 1995. By the mid-1990s, Chi-Chi's was strengthened by its merger with El Torito, but the chain continued to face the stiff competition that characterized the early 1990s.

Further Reading:

Carlino, Bill, "Chi-Chi's, El Torito Preen for Marriage," *Nation's Restaurant News,* August 9, 1993, p. 3, 73.
——, "Micatrotto Steps Up, Fills Chi-Chi's Top Spot," *Nation's Restaurant News,* January 4, 1993, pp. 3, 80.
"The Changing Face of Chi-Chi's," *Restaurant Business,* March 1, 1988, pp. 146–63.
"Chi-Chi's: The Newest Challenge," *Restaurant Business,* August 10, 1988, p. 116–17.
Martin, Richard, "REGI Finalizes Deal to Acquire Chi-Chi's," *Nation's Restaurant News,* November 8, 1993, p. 1, 101.
O'Keegan, Peter O., "Chi-Chi's Prexy Smith Quits," *Nation's Restaurant News,* June 8, 1992, pp. 1, 49.
——, "Consul, Creditors Team Up to Oppose Chi-Chi's Takeover," *Nation's Restaurant News,* April 27, 1992, pp. 1, 58.

—Elaine Belsito

Clayton Homes Incorporated

P.O. Box 15169
Knoxville, Tennessee 37901
U.S.A.
(615) 970-7200
Fax: (615) 970-1238

Public Company
Incorporated: 1968
Employees: 4,000
Sales: $628 million
Stock Exchanges: New York
SICs: 2451 Mobile Homes

Clayton Homes Incorporated is the largest retailer of manufactured homes in the United States, and its manufacturing division is the nation's fourth-largest. Clayton is one of two vertically integrated manufactured housing companies in the country. It makes and sells manufactured homes, provides related financial services and insurance, and also owns communities in nine states. These four levels of operations have enabled it to ride smoothly through a wildly fluctuating market.

To a great extent, the company reflects the image of its fascinating founder. James L. Clayton was born in a tin-roofed home, with no plumbing or electricity, on a sharecropper's farm in 1934. By the age of five, he was making cotton rows with a log pulled by a farm mule and getting paid 25 cents a day. He had his own cotton patch by age 12. After finishing high school, Clayton left for Memphis with his guitar. He went to school, sold vacuum cleaners, and played in honky-tonks three nights a week.

After transferring to the University of Tennessee at Knoxville, Clayton earned a degree in engineering and then a radio broadcast engineer's license. He got a job with WATE-TV, and from 1960 to 1976 he was a part-time host on "Star Time," a weekly variety show on Knoxville TV. While Clayton was singing duets with Dolly Parton and strumming guitar, he was also buying and selling cars. He first entered the car business in college, when he sold his own car through the classifieds and realized that it might be a good way to make some spending money. As an undergraduate, Clayton opened a small used-car lot in North Knoxville. Before long, he was joined in the business by his younger brother Joe. By the time he earned his degree, Clayton was making more by selling cars as a hobby than he was by working at the TV station.

The Clayton brothers obtained a Volvo franchise in 1958, one of the first in the area. They bought other import franchises the following year, and in 1960 they purchased an American Motors franchise. After the variety show started, Clayton's visibility and duets with Parton did not hurt business on his car lot. He even made his own commercials, with the guitar. The young businessman experienced a slight setback in 1961, however. A Knoxville bank called in a loan, and Clayton's lot went into bankruptcy. After the bank dissolved the fledgling company, Clayton decided to pursue a law degree. He and his brother soon opened their second used-car business on the same lot.

Clayton received his law degree in 1964. Two years later, he borrowed $25,000 from a local bank and launched Clayton Homes—a mobile homes retail outlet—just over the highway from the car lot. Clayton entered this business, too, as a result of a college lark: he sold his first two mobile homes on behalf of his law school classmates who were leaving Knoxville after graduating.

Clayton soon discovered that selling mobile homes was similar to selling cars, except that the margins and markups were much higher. He also found himself well-situated for this business, since his regular TV appearances made him a local celebrity, while the Southeast was the country's largest market for mobile homes. By 1970, Clayton was moving about 700 units a year off the lot. He built his first manufacturing plant a year earlier. Clayton became absorbed in this new arena immediately, and before long he sold his half of the car business to his brother.

The ingredients of success were there from the start for Clayton Homes. Clayton quickly learned that high turnover was key. Even early on, he would forfeit margins to move units. Because of his rapid turnover, his inventory financing—often a heavy burden in this industry—was modest in relation to how many homes he sold.

Another key strategy was vertical integration. By 1970, Clayton was manufacturing as well as selling mobile homes. Four years later, he started a mortgage subsidiary to finance the company's sales, Vanderbilt Mortgage and Finance. Eventually, Clayton's vertical integration meant that the company built the homes, sold them, insured them, financed the sales, and provided communities in which the homes could be parked. A customer could walk onto a Clayton Homes lot, and the company could make money from that customer in four different ways. The financing division helped Clayton survive the squeeze when recession hit during the late 1980s. To counterbalance the incentives for salesmen to move units off the lot—even at the risk of making unstable loans—Clayton introduced accountability by holding the sales manager responsible for half of a bad loan. That policy kept Clayton's charge-offs due to bad loans at around 0.4 percent of sales, a third of what its main competitors faced.

By June 1983, Clayton Homes was ready to go public. Less than two years later, the stock was traded on the New York Stock Exchange. Clayton's timing was sterling. Overall industry shipments dipped 40 percent in 1984, and this downturn continued through 1991. During that period, however, earnings per share at Clayton Homes grew at a compounded annual rate of 23 percent, while its share of the market in mobile home sales shot from 1.8 percent to 7.4 percent. Meanwhile, the company's close competitors—Oakwood Homes and Fleetwood Enterprises—suffered significant declines, in large part due to depressed conditions in their previously reliable Texas markets. The collapse of oil prices during the early 1980s hit these key markets hard, but Clayton had yet to enter Texas.

Through the 1980s, Clayton thrived in its no-nonsense way. When the market dipped along with the economy from the mid-1980s to the early 1990s, Clayton responded by calculating the level of payment its basic customer base could afford, $200 per month. The company then worked backwards, designing homes that could be made and sold within that budget. As a result, Clayton's revenues rose during the economic downturn from $122 million in 1985 to $476 million in 1993.

Clayton Homes opened its first manufactured-home community in Texas in 1987. By 1989, it had made *Forbes*'s list of the "200 Best Small Companies in America" for four years in a row. *Financial World* included Clayton Homes among its list of 500 companies on the "fast track." In 1991, James Clayton received a Horatio Alger Award, sharing the honor that year with Phil Gramm and Colin Powell, among others. By that time, Clayton was chairman of the country's largest retailer of mobile homes, overseeing 10 manufacturing plants, 125 company-owned dealers, and 325 independent dealers in 24 states. Clayton had communities in Tennessee, North Carolina, Michigan, and Missouri by 1991. These communities resembled subdivisions, and some included amenities such as tennis and basketball courts, fish-stocked ponds, and clubhouses. Sales reached $371 million by 1992 and kept climbing. Nearly half of the company's profits that year came from its financial services division.

In the early 1990s, the industry was revived as lower mortgage interest rates stimulated sales. The recovery was subdued, but manufactured homes fared better than multi-family housing, and the South and South-Central regions of the United States led the housing rebound. About three-quarters of Clayton's market was within a day's trip of one of its plants in Tennessee. Sales in 1993 topped $476 million.

In August of that year, there was a flurry of concern as tax problems surfaced. Evidently, Clayton Homes had failed to pay sales tax on units sold at five mobile home parks it owned in Tennessee. Clayton and other company officials blamed the mistake on the comptroller of the company's retail division. That individual had been moonlighting as Clayton's personal accountant, and Clayton filed suit against him for allegedly embezzling more than $3 million of the chief executive's personal funds. Tennessee's commissioner of revenue stated that his agency was not investigating Clayton Homes's officers, but only this individual, who was fired. Two board members resigned around the same time. Clayton Homes paid Tennessee $163,000 for the back sales taxes. The incident ultimately proved to be a blip on the screen for Clayton, which remained highly lucrative for investors.

One reason mobile homes have fared well in the past decade, while housing in general fared poorly, was that they tended to be much more affordable. In the winter of 1995, the industry received another boost when the government abolished tax incentives for multi-family apartment construction, which is the main alternative for blue-collar and retiree housing. Mobile home manufacturers also were cheered by greater diversity in the economic base of the Southwest and Southeast, where half of all mobile home sales took place. As the region reduced its dependence on the oil industry, mobile home retailers became better insulated against foreclosures caused by economic fluctuations. Also, the overall trend that saw low-paying service positions replacing high-paying manufacturing jobs helped Clayton, since a $20,000 mobile home was feasible for a service worker.

The homes being manufactured at Clayton's 14 factories by February of 1995 had many of the charms and amenities of a site-built home, including cathedral ceilings, fireplaces, walk-in closets, and whirlpool tubs. And they took only days, instead of months or years, to build. Such product improvements, along with favorable conditions in the general economy, led to a 20 percent annual growth rate in the manufactured housing and recreational vehicle industries between 1992 and 1994. Clayton Homes, which had withstood shifting industry winds with its strategy of vertical integration, appeared well-positioned to continue its success in the future.

Principal Subsidiaries: CMH Manufacturing, Inc.; CMH Homes, Inc.; Vanderbilt Mortgage & Finance, Inc.; Clayton-Vanderbilt, Inc.; Vanderbilt Property and Casualty Insurance Co., Ltd.; CMH Insurance Agency, Inc.; CABS, Inc.; CMH Parks, Inc.; JH Properties, Inc.; CMH Capital, Inc.; Blevins Mobile Homes, Inc.; Clayton's-Tullahoma, Inc.; Vanderbilt Life and Casualty Insurance Co., Ltd.

Further Reading:

Babej, Marc, "House Party," *Forbes,* January 3, 1994, p. 122.

"Clayton Homes," *Wall Street Journal,* July 7, 1994, p. B4.

"Clayton Homes Plans Buyback," *Wall Street Journal,* February 25, 1994, p. B6.

Haines, Thomas, "Profile: James L. Clayton," *AOPA Pilot,* November 1991, pp. 3–6.

Kelley, Kristopher, "Manufactured Housing," *Value Line Investment Survey,* August 20, 1993, p. 1538; November 19, 1993, p. 1540.

Kimelman, John, "Clayton Homes: Tempest in a Teapot?" *Financial World,* September 28, 1993, p. 22.

——, "Clayton Homes: There's no Place Like . . . ," *Financial World,* July 20, 1993, p. 16.

——, "Guilt by Association," *Financial World,* February 21, 1995, p. 34.

Marcial, Gene, "Looking for the Main Chance in the Mainstream," *Business Week,* March 28, 1994, p. 156.

Olszewski, Paul, "Manufactured Housing/Rec Vehicle," *Value Line Investment Survey,* August 19, 1994, p. 1543; February 18, 1994, p. 1540; November 18, 1994, p. 1541.

Perricone, Laura, "The Herald, Rock Hill, S.C., People on the Move Column," *Knight-Ridder/Tribune Business News,* October 27, 1994.

"Shares of Clayton Homes Take Another Tumble," *New York Times,* August 20, 1993, p. C3.

Stern, William, "The Singing Mobile Home Salesman," *Forbes,* October 26, 1992, pp. 240–242.

—Carol I. Keeley

Cleveland-Cliffs

Cleveland-Cliffs Inc.

1100 Superior Avenue
Cleveland, Ohio 44114-2589
U.S.A.
(216) 694-5700
Fax: (216) 694-4880

Public Company
Incorporated: 1850 as The Cleveland Iron Mining Company
Employees: 6,309
Sales: $379.8 million
Stock Exchanges: New York Chicago
SICs: 1011 Iron Ores

With seven iron ore mines in the United States, Canada, and Australia, Cleveland-Cliffs Inc. is the Western world's leading producer of iron ore pellets. As North America's only full-service iron ore firm, the company manages 47 percent of the continent's total capacity for production of iron ore pellets. Cleveland-Cliffs has been faced with competition from imports, takeover attempts, shareholder revolts, an ill-advised diversification, and the vagaries of the cyclical steel industry over the years, but as it entered the mid-1990s, the company had established a position of strength at the top of its field. Some industry observers hold that Cleveland-Cliffs reached the pinnacle of its industry by holding to one essential objective first promulgated by William G. Mather in the 1930s and summed up in 1974 by then-CEO H. Stuart Harrison: "No matter what may happen, don't part with domestic iron ore reserves."

Cleveland-Cliffs' predecessor, the Cleveland Iron Mining Company, was established in 1846 by a group of investors led by Samuel L. Mather. Mather, an attorney, had moved to Cleveland, Ohio, in 1843, just two years after iron ore was discovered in the Marquette Range of Michigan's Upper Peninsula. Although Mather was confident that, given time, the venture would prove profitable, it was for many years a losing proposition. Transportation costs were prohibitive until 1855, when the Sault Ste. Marie shipping canal was completed. A 1974 company history noted that "it cost $200 a ton to smelt the ore and ship it down to Pittsburgh where [it] was selling at $80 per ton." Cleveland Iron Mining was only able to survive these difficult formative years through a "unique financial device" concocted by then-treasurer Mather and company President W.J. Gordon. They printed up scrip known as "Iron Money" in one-, two-, three-, and five-dollar denominations and met their financial commitments with these "IOUs" until the company's cash flow stabilized.

As the years went by and surface mines in the region were depleted, firms like Cleveland Iron Mining were forced to seek underground sources. Up to this time, mining was a fairly simple, but extremely labor-intensive, process. Below-ground mining necessitated the development of such specialized devices as power drills, hoisting and conveying machinery, pumps, and ventilation equipment. Cleveland Iron Mining in 1877 became one of the first firms to use these types of equipment to locate ore bodies. The company also pioneered the used of electricity at its mines, often establishing its own on-site hydroelectric and coal-fired generators. These one-time necessities grew into a profitable sideline in the early twentieth century.

During the late nineteenth century, Cleveland Iron Mining diversified into timber harvesting as a predictable adjunct to its mining efforts, for timber was used to support mine shafts and as fuel for blast furnaces. At its zenith, the mining company's lumber output topped 80 million feet of timber, and its timberland holdings peaked at 750,000 acres. As this property was cleared, it was often sold. After the turn of the century, the company formed a joint venture in paper production with the Munising Paper Company. It also acquired an interest in the Munising Woodenware Company, a manufacturer of wooden bowls, clothespins, and rolling pins. The company divested itself of these timber sidelines in the 1930s.

The discovery of high-grade iron ore deposits at open-pit sites in Minnesota's Mesabi Range in the 1890s—and the new competitive front it opened—accelerated changes already underway in the Michigan-based segment of the iron mining industry. Between 1893 and 1905, many steel companies consolidated vertically through the acquisition of iron ore properties in the Lake Superior district. In order to protect their interests, several large mining companies merged and/or acquired their smaller competitors. This early shakeout formed the enduring structure of the industry.

A major transition at Cleveland Iron Mining reflected this change. In 1891 the company merged with the Iron Cliffs Mining Company to form the Cleveland-Cliffs Iron Company. Organized in 1864 by Samuel Tilden, the Iron Cliffs Company held broad mining interests, but suffered from an aging and disinterested management.

The merger was spurred by Jeptha H. Wade, Sr., former cofounder and president of Western Union Telegraph Company, who purchased a controlling interest in Iron Cliffs in the late 1880s. He entered negotiations with Samuel Mather to unify the two mining companies, but before the merger could be concluded, both Wade and Mather died. Their sons, Jeptha Wade, Jr., and William G. Mather, consummated the deal, which gave the new business entity the fiscal wherewithal to be an effective competitor. Using their unified resources, Cleveland-Cliffs joined the Pittsburgh & Lake Angeline Iron Company to build a railroad from the mines to docks at Presque Isle in the late 1890s. (By the mid-1970s, the railroad transported over seven million tons of ore and one million tons of general freight each year.)

William Mather was elected president of Cleveland-Cliffs. Mather, who had started his career with Cleveland Iron Mining as a clerk in 1878, served as president for 42 years. Perhaps inspired by social reforms of the turn-of-the-century Progressive Era, the second-generation leader established a department that provided disability and death benefits to miners and their families, as well as educational assistance, a pension fund, and a worker safety program.

The ever-growing capital requirements of mining made it an increasingly venturesome proposition in the early twentieth century. In order to distribute the risk, Cleveland-Cliffs formed partnerships with steel companies to own and operate mines. The company established its first joint venture of this type in 1903 when it leased the Negaunee Mine to a company it co-owned with Bethlehem Steel Corporation. Cleveland-Cliffs' customer relationships were often strengthened through the exchange of ore for stock and equity positions in steel companies.

This policy developed into a more coherent program in 1929, when Cleveland financier Cyrus Eaton hatched a plan to form a top-ranking steel company through the union of several mid-sized competitors. In exchange for financing part of the venture, Cleveland-Cliffs would become its preferred supplier. The scheme called for Cleveland-Cliffs to establish a new entity, Cliffs Corporation, that would be jointly owned by Eaton and a group of steel magnates. For his part, Eaton traded a $40-million portfolio of dividend-paying steel stocks in Republic Steel Corporation, Inland Steel Co., and Youngstown Sheet and Tube. Meanwhile, Cleveland-Cliffs acquired a controlling interest in Corrigan-McKinney Steel Company, a Cleveland steelmaker, for $23 million in borrowed funds. The industrialists intended to merge these four steel companies into a new business called Midwest Steel Corporation. The onset of the Great Depression, however, squelched the plan. Cleveland-Cliffs was left with a heavy debt load in the midst of the world's deepest economic downturn. The company recorded a loss in 1932.

A company history published in 1974 called this low point "William G. Mather's finest hour." It was at this desperate time that he established Cleveland-Cliffs' policy of sacrificing all but domestic iron ore reserves to keep the mining concern alive. Despite his efforts, Cleveland-Cliff's financial condition continued to deteriorate. In 1933 local banker Edward B. Greene, an in-law of the Wade family, replaced Mather as president, who assumed the position of chairman. Greene reduced Cleveland-Cliff's debt through sale of some timberlands and steel stocks, and the 1935 divestment of Corrigan-McKinney to Republic Steel. The financial reorganization brought about the 1947 reunion of Cleveland-Cliffs and the practically purposeless Cliffs Corporation. Mather retired in 1952 and was replaced by Greene. The position of president was briefly filled by Alexander C. Brown.

In the meantime, three forces converged on the iron industry and Cleveland-Cliffs to bring about fundamental changes in the business. World War II's military requirements had driven seemingly insatiable demand for high-quality iron ore. Given the high costs (and unpredictable payoff) of domestic underground exploration, iron and steel producers looked for alternative sources of high-grade ore through overseas exploration. Cleveland-Cliffs thus pursued options in eastern Canada, Venezuela, Colombia, Chile, and Peru, although it later scaled back its international operations to Canada and Australia.

At the same time, the U.S. steel market was inundated with high-grade, yet cheap, foreign ore. From 1953 to 1963, imports increased from eight percent of domestic consumption to 36 percent. The combination of high costs, competition, and exhaustion of higher-grade domestic ore sources forced hundreds of American mines out of business in the postwar era.

Walter A. Sterling, who was elected president of Cleveland-Cliffs in 1953 and chief executive officer in 1955, instigated the company's transition to an emphasis on upgrading abundant low-quality ores into material useful to the steel industry. Over the course of the decade, Cleveland-Cliffs adopted the pelletizing process that later became the standard for the American steel industry. First developed in Europe in the early twentieth century, pelletization is a method of iron processing that upgrades low-quality iron ores through concentration (grinding and separating the unwanted materials from the desirable ore) and pelletization (moistening, forming, and firing the ore into spheres suitable for use in a blast furnace). By the time Sterling retired in 1961, Cleveland-Cliffs was poised for a decade of growth. Sterling was succeeded as president and chief executive officer by H. Stuart Harrison, a Cleveland-Cliffs veteran of 24 years.

Cleveland-Cliffs was not exempt from merger overtures during this era of heavy industry activity. By the late 1960s, Detroit Steel had accumulated nearly one-third of Cleveland-Cliffs' stock. Although heirs of the Mather, Wade, and Greene families owned a similar-sized stake in the company, many feared that a firm interested in acquiring Cleveland-Cliffs could launch a strong offensive through Detroit Steel. That apprehension came to fruition in 1970, when Cyclops Corporation, a steel company, bought 19 percent of Detroit Steel. In order to diffuse the situation, Cleveland-Cliffs essentially repurchased its own stock from Detroit Steel by acquiring the remaining shares of the latter company for $50 million, recovering its own 1.1 million shares, and turning over its majority interest in Detroit Steel to Cyclops.

Having repulsed this threat to its independence, Cleveland-Cliffs undertook a diversification program in the early 1970s in hopes of reducing its reliance on the cyclical steel industry. The strategy included re-entry into the timber market, as well as investment in shale oil, uranium, and copper mining. This tactic soon proved disastrous. In 1982, Cleveland-Cliffs experienced its first loss since the Great Depression. Cliffs executives blamed a 51 percent reduction in North American iron ore production and a 44 percent decline in iron ore shipments. Indeed, the U.S. iron mining industry took a beating throughout the 1980s, as increasing imports and two severe recessions forced the closure of one third of America's iron ore mines. But notwithstanding these inherent problems, analysts—and significantly, some Cleveland-Cliffs shareholders—blamed the company's difficulties on its oil and gas operations, which experienced an 85 percent plummet in earnings in 1982. In recognition of this dreadful performance, *Fortune* indicated in 1991 that some Wall Street pundits dubbed the company's acquisition plan "de-worse-ification."

A second loss in 1986 brought the company perilously close to bankruptcy. By the end of 1987, Cleveland-Cliffs had $126 million in past due loans. As the company's stock declined, management instituted several anti-takeover measures, including a "poison pill" plan and "golden parachutes" that secured their own financial futures. The crisis—and the board's reaction to it—precipitated a battle with shareholders over the best way to restructure the company's debt. CEO M. Thomas Moore wanted to pay off the liability with the proceeds of a new stock issue, but dissident shareholders led by David Bolger, who held 6.8 percent of the company's stock, favored a more creative plan. According to a January 1988 *Forbes* article, Bolger proposed to "raise $144 million in new bank debt, toss in $221 million cash from the company treasury and the sale of a Michigan power plant, call in $53 million in preferred [stock] and make a hefty $168 million cash distribution to shareholders."

Moore tried his plan and floated four million shares in the fall of 1987. The company, however, was only able to earn $62.4 million on the $68 million offering. Within days of the scheme's failure, Bolger called for a special vote on the composition of Cleveland-Cliffs' upper echelon. The majority of shareholders elected to retain Moore and the board of directors, but only after the corporate leaders announced that they had adopted a plan to either recapitalize or sell the company.

The reorganization that ensued involved divesting the firm's peripheral holdings, closing two mines, paying down debt with the proceeds, and renegotiating contracts with customers, unions, and utilities. The restructuring culminated with a $175.9 million repurchase of over one-third of the company's stock.

Cleveland-Cliffs acquired a major rival, Pickands Mather, just in time for a late 1980s steel industry revival. Voluntary restraint agreements with importers also helped, giving U.S. iron miners time to retool. By the end of the decade, Cleveland-Cliffs was again garnering commendations. A 1990 article in the *Engineering & Mining Journal* asserted that "perhaps no mining company has been as successful as Cleveland-Cliffs." Indeed, from 1986 to 1992, the firm's stock rose 500 percent. In 1991 the company gave shareholders a special $4 cash dividend.

Although Cleveland-Cliffs had recovered from its stumbling performance in the mid-1980s, in 1991 management again faced a shareholder revolt. This battle was initiated by Julian H. Robertson of Tiger Management Associates, which held ten percent of Cleveland-Cliffs' stock. Robertson, who was characterized in a 1991 *Fortune* article as "one of Wall Street's hottest money managers," worried that Cleveland-Cliffs would use the over $115 million in cash and marketable securities it had built up to launch another "de-worse-ification." Robertson fomented a proxy vote and won the right to seat five directors (a minority) on an expanded board.

Even these new leaders, however, were powerless to prevent the problems that plagued Cleveland-Cliffs in the early 1990s. In 1992 two of Cliffs' major customers—Sharon Steel, which contributed 11 percent of annual operating revenues, and McLouth Steel Products, which chipped in an estimated 25 percent—encountered significant financial difficulties. Sharon Steel sought Chapter 11 bankruptcy protection that year, and McLouth stopped payments on its shipments. Cliffs was cited as the largest creditor of each of these two businesses. Fearful that it might never recover revenues lost to these two causes, Cleveland-Cliffs set aside $17.5 million in a contingency fund. This precaution contributed to the company's net loss of $7.9 million in 1992. A year later, in August 1993, labor problems bruised third quarter earnings. Finally, Cleveland-Cliffs faced threats from ever-present imports and new competition from "minimills," which utilized electric arc furnaces to turn scrap metal into usable steel. By 1993, this new technology had captured 43 percent of total steelmaking.

Nonetheless, several industry observers expressed confidence that Cleveland-Cliffs' strengths would enable it to meet the challenges of the 1990s. They cited the company's position of dominance in the iron ore mining industry, its strong balance sheet, and its research into alternative production methods (including iron carbide and scrap metal substitutes) as evidence of its vigor. Industry factors, including the close accord of supply and demand, also boded well for the mining concern.

In the fall of 1994, Cliffs bolstered its top-ranking position with the acquisition of Cypress Amax Minerals Co.'s iron ore mine and power plant in Minnesota for $66 million. The addition increased Cleveland-Cliffs annual production capacity by 69 percent, from 5.8 million tons to 9.8 million tons of standard pellets. The company netted $42.8 million on sales of $344.8 million that year, their highest levels for both figures since 1990.

Principal Subsidiaries: The Cleveland-Cliffs Iron Company; Cliffs Mining Company; Cliffs Mining Services Company; Cliffs Reduced Iron Corporation; Northshore Mining Company; Pickands Mather & Co. International.

Further Reading:

Bradley, Hassell, "Cleveland-Cliffs' Moore Challenges Status Quo," *American Metal Market,* September 24, 1990, p. 24A.

Caney, Derek J., "Cliffs Completes Buy of Northshore Assets," *American Metal Market,* October 7, 1994, p. 3.

"Cleveland-Cliffs: 1st Loss in 50 Years, $30.2M Deficit," *American Metal Market,* February 4, 1993, p. 3.

Furukawa, Tsukasa, "Mitsubishi, Cliffs Eye Plant for Iron Carbide," *American Metal Market,* June 4, 1993, p. 5.

Harrison, H. Stuart, *The Cleveland-Cliffs Iron Company,* New York: Newcomen Society, 1974.

Hohl, Paul, "Cliffs Bolger Claims Victory After Vote," *American Metal Market,* December 17, 1987, p. 2.

——, "Cliffs Plans Stock Buy-back to Further its Restructuring," *American Metal Market,* March 18, 1988, p. 3.

Lappen, Alyssa A., "Dilution Control," *Forbes,* January 11, 1988, p. 10.

McGough, Robert, "High Iron," *Financial World,* April 14, 1992, p. 26.

Norton, Rob, "Who Owns This Company, Anyhow?" *Fortune,* July 29, 1991, p. 131.

Reingold, Jennifer, "Cleveland-Cliffs: A Bet on Upgrading Minimills," *Financial World,* March 29, 1994, p. 22.

Zaburunov, Steven A., "Cost Reduction at Cleveland-Cliffs," *EMJ—Engineering & Mining Journal,* September 1990, p. 29.

—April Dougal Gasbarre

COBE®

COBE Laboratories, Inc.

1185 Oak Street
Lakewood, Colorado 80215-4498
U.S.A.
(303) 232-6800
Fax: (303) 231-4545

Wholly Owned Subsidiary of Gambro AB
Incorporated: 1964
Employees: 2,000
Sales: $500 million
SICs: 2835 In Vitro & In Vivo Diagnostic Agents; 2836 Biological Products Except Diagnostic; 3841 Surgical & Medical Instruments; 8092 Kidney Dialysis Centers

COBE Laboratories, Inc. is a leading developer of medical devices and systems for handling blood outside the body, focusing on three major areas: renal care, cardiovascular products, and blood component technology. Its renal care business is a market leader in the manufacture of dialyzers, dialysis machines, and other equipment needed by patients with chronic kidney failure. COBE's cardiovascular units sustain the functions of the heart and lungs while a patient undergoes heart surgery. The company has also pioneered blood component technology products used to divide blood into its separate components for the treatment of various illnesses. During its first 25 years, COBE succeeded in creating marketing channels in more than 50 countries. Since being acquired by the Swedish medical technology company Gambro AB in 1990, COBE has been able to take advantage of its parent's larger non-U.S. presence to solidify its worldwide marketing efforts and has had additional capital for acquisitions and alliances that have strengthened and expanded its activities in health care services.

COBE was founded in 1964 by Robert Collins and Randall Bellows, both of whom had worked at a major hospital supplier near San Francisco called Pharmaseal. COBE's name was derived from the first two letters of the founders' last names. Working out of a garage in Los Angeles, the two men made custom heart-lung tubing packs used to connect patients to heart-lung machines. In 1965, COBE merged with Medical Marketing, a Seattle firm owned by Collins's and Bellows's friend Ted Dale, who had persuaded the Seattle Artificial Kidney Center to use COBE's custom tubing packs. The merger increased the young company's ability to market its products and initiated its venture into the dialysis industry, which would eventually become the core of its business.

Dialysis products introduced in the company's first five years included hemodialysis blood tubing sets and the Kiil dialyzer (a dialyzer is an artificial kidney—essentially a specialized filter—used in dialysis to cleanse the patient's blood). In 1967 Collins and Bellows relocated the company to Lakewood, Colorado, a suburb of Denver, in part because they felt they needed a more centralized location for distribution purposes.

During the early 1970s, COBE expanded its presence in the dialysis market. COBE replaced the Kiil dialyzer (weighing 75 pounds) with a less bulky one called the Mini-D. It also developed the Centry dialysis monitoring system, at 78 pounds also more portable than earlier models. Together, these introductions began to make home dialysis more practical—a boon for the patient in terms of improved chances of rehabilitation, the elimination of thrice-weekly trips to the hospital, and much lower costs. The Centry system also had some advantages over existing systems: it was compatible with elements of dialysis machinery manufactured by other firms and used tap water in its mixture of cleansing solution. Added to the COBE line in 1971 was an Automated Peritoneal Dialysis unit for patients not able to tolerate hemodialysis, a system designed to complement the Centry system.

Such product introductions, particularly those involving COBE's dialysis products, were bolstered in 1972 when Medicare was expanded to cover end-stage renal disease. As a result, many more people could be supported with dialysis treatments and the market for dialysis equipment grew. That same year, COBE became a public company.

Very early in its history, COBE executives recognized the international market as a key to the company's growth. In 1967, the company's first international distributor, AMCO, Inc., was appointed in Japan. The company established its first international subsidiary in Brussels, Belgium, in 1973, followed by additional subsidiaries in West Germany, Canada, France, and the United Kingdom over the next four years.

Domestic sales efforts were facilitated through the establishment of three regional distribution centers covering the West (Fremont, California), Midwest (Chicago), and East (Glen Burnie, Maryland). COBE's new product development and marketing efforts resulted in sales of $16.8 million by its tenth anniversary in 1974 and its first $10 million sales quarter in 1977.

In 1975, with the introduction of its next dialysis machine—the Centry 2—COBE could offer a complete dialysis system, the first in the industry, and one designed for portability and ideal for home use. The system was also attractive to hospitals and dialysis centers because the dialysis process was faster than in older models, cutting costs by allowing staff to handle more patients in the same amount of time. The Centry 2 controlled the complete dialysis process, which involved transporting blood through tubing to an artificial kidney (dialyzer) which cleansed the blood and removed excess fluid. A monitor kept track of the complete process. COBE manufactured all components of the system, including dialyzers, blood tubing, chemicals, and other supplies necessary to the hemodialysis process. This first application of a system approach to renal care helped COBE become a market leader in the United States over the next several years. By 1978, renal care accounted for 76 percent of the company's revenues, and COBE posted a one-year increase of 49 percent in renal care sales from $32.1 million in 1977 to $47.7 million in 1978.

COBE also secured a place in the cardiovascular field with the acquisition of Galen Laboratories in 1973. The key product acquired thereby was the Optiflo Oxygenator. During heart surgery when blood flow to the heart and lungs was halted, the function of the lungs was replaced by the oxygenator, which supplied the patient's blood with oxygen as the lung normally would, while the blood-pumping function of the heart was replaced by an artificial pump. Having thus entered the oxygenator market, COBE introduced the second-generation Optiflo II Oxygenator in 1978. With the development of the COBE Stockert Perfusion Pump, the company could offer a complete life support system for the increasingly common open heart surgery procedures of the time. Further innovation occurred in 1982 with the development of the COBE Membrane Lung (CML) Oxygenator. This membrane oxygenator significantly advanced the safety of cardiovascular surgery; virtually made obsolete the commonly-used bubble oxygenator; and propelled COBE to a market leadership position in the cardiovascular field, eventually to a 20 percent worldwide market share by the end of the 1980s.

After more than a dozen years of healthy growth (net sales more than doubled in a four-year span alone from $45.6 million in 1977 to $92.6 million in 1980), COBE experienced some difficult years in the early 1980s. Net sales growth in 1981 slowed to less than five percent over 1980, while in 1982 it only improved to 8.5 percent. And although the sales increases were higher during the next three years (due in part to several acquisitions), profits fell from $6 million in 1982 to $5.6 million in 1983 and to $3.2 million in 1984, again due in part to acquisitions, notably that of IBM Biomedical Systems, but also attributable to the failure of a new product, a hollow fiber dialyzer.

Moreover, separate sales figures for the Medical Systems Division (primarily the renal care products) indicated that during the first five years of the 1980s that concern had grown only 11 percent, while the Cardiovascular Division grew by an impressive 126 percent. Indeed, the dialysis market had stagnated because of increased competition initiated by cost-containment efforts by doctors and hospitals affected by changes in government-sponsored health coverage. The company sought to offset these troubles by renewing its emphasis on new product development, aggressively pursuing strategic acquisitions, and broadening its product line with the expansion into a third major product area: blood component technology.

During this time, COBE's Centry dialysis systems held about 40 percent of the U.S. market in single-patient machines. In 1981, the company introduced two new renal care products to the Centry line. The Centry 2 Rx system was designed to provide patients with prescription hemodialysis by allowing a doctor to vary the amount of sodium and sodium bicarbonate delivered to the patient during dialysis depending on individual needs. The Centry 2000 was a more sophisticated microprocessor giving a doctor greater control over the dialysis process and featuring additional safety features. The company's commitment in the 1980s to new product development was particularly evident in its introduction of the Centrysystem 3 in 1986, its first new dialysis system in 11 years. In designing its third-generation system, COBE kept firmly in mind the increasing cost-consciousness of physicians and hospitals. The major advantage of the Centrysystem 3 was its ability to safely cut the treatment time for a dialysis session in half, thus allowing hospitals and dialysis centers to handle twice as many patients in the same amount of time. The company promised further cost savings from the system's ease of use and lower maintenance costs due to its increased reliability. Complementing this new product development activity was the acquisition also in 1989 of Secon GmbH, a German medical technology company that manufactured a compact hollow fiber dialyzer that worked perfectly with the Centrysystem 3 and could be readily marketed with it.

With the goal of decreasing the company's reliance on its renal care products, COBE expanded into its third major area of research and development in the early 1980s by introducing the Therapeutic Plasma Exchange System, or Centry TPE System. Blood component technology had become increasingly important during this period for the treatment of cancer and immune system diseases. Treatments for these ailments involved transfusions of individual blood components, such as platelets, stem cells, bone marrow, and plasma. In some treatments certain components were extracted from the patient's blood, treated, and then reinfused. After Centry TPE was introduced in 1981, COBE delved further into this area with its 1984 acquisition of IBM's Biomedical Systems division. The acquisition brought products that became known as the COBE 2991 Cell Processor and the COBE 2997 Blood Cell Separator, both used for blood component therapy. It also led to the development and 1988 introduction of the COBE Spectra Apheresis System used to collect from donors very pure blood components (such as platelets) primarily for cancer therapy treatments. That same year a related acquisition of Kardiothor brought the BRAT Intraoperative Blood Salvage System to the COBE cardiovascular line. The BRAT system was used during surgery to clean and recycle the patient's blood for reinfusion, reducing the need for transfusions from donors. All of these blood banking technologies became increasingly important as the purity of the world's blood supply came into question with the discovery of the HIV virus and AIDs.

By 1989 COBE had grown to net sales of $237.9 million with a profit of $9.8 million, up from sales of $92.6 million in 1980. Besides its overall growth and profitability, the company successfully diversified its product line and eliminated its over-reliance on the inconsistent dialysis market. At the end of the decade, sales were almost evenly divided between the Medical Systems Division (51.6 percent) and the Cardiovascular Division (48.4 percent). Significant too was the company's impressive increase in sales outside the United States. Since establishing an International Division in 1985 for marketing its products overseas, COBE increased its foreign sales from $39.5 million to $82.1 million, a 108 percent increase. Further, the International Division accounted in 1989 for 45 percent of the company's sales, compared to only 26 percent in 1985. Particularly given COBE's increasing success outside the United States, many observers were surprised to learn in 1990 that COBE was to be acquired by Sweden-based Gambro AB. Having fended off several hostile takeover bids over the course of the

1980s, however, COBE officials agreed to sell the company to Gambro AB.

The terms of the sale were an offer to buy all outstanding shares of COBE stock for $37 per share, or a total of approximately $253 million. The deal was announced in March and consummated in June after a detailed antitrust examination by the U.S. Federal Trade Commission. At the time of the acquisition, Gambro was based in Lund, Sweden, was partly owned by the Swedish automobile manufacturer Volvo, and had sales of about $500 million (or twice that of COBE). The two companies were both leaders in the renal care field, and in the year of the acquisition renal care sales accounted for 74 percent of Gambro's sales. Although they were competitors, their dialysis products and marketing efforts were considered complementary. For instance, while COBE's dialysis machines were considered market leaders, the company lacked certain components of dialysis systems that Gambro excelled in, particularly dialysis membranes. In terms of marketing, Gambro could take advantage of COBE's dominant presence in the U.S. market, while COBE products could now be more easily sold worldwide. The acquisition also significantly diversified Gambro, which had been limited to the renal care and intensive care/anesthesia fields. It now gained a significant foothold in the cardiovascular and blood component technology fields. The primary reason given by COBE's co-founders for the sale was to "assist COBE in expanding the marketing of its products in countries outside the U.S."

Following the acquisition, COBE's operations were divided into several subsidiaries under COBE Laboratories, Inc. The dialysis products were organized as COBE Renal Care, Inc.; the cardiovascular products as COBE Cardiovascular, Inc.; the international marketing division as COBE International Division; and the blood component technology products as COBE BCT, Inc. (separated for the first time). Robert Collins and Randall Bellows, the company founders, both retired following the sale, but continued to be involved in the operations as members of COBE's board of directors. Observers estimated that Collins's share of the sale amounted to $30 million, while Bellows reaped $10.1 million. Gambro then brought in Mats Wahlström to become the new president of COBE.

The benefits to COBE from the merger became readily apparent over the next two years as the company began to get involved in major acquisitions it would have been unable to afford on its own. The largest involved a series of 1991 and 1992 investments (the final one totaling $53.6 million) in REN Corp. USA, Inc., giving COBE a majority interest in the company and control of its board. Based in Nashville, Tennessee, REN owned the fourth largest chain of dialysis clinics in the United States, with 51 clinics, about 4,000 patients, and potential for growth based on the increasing privatization of health-care services. The acquisition of REN not only moved the company into the field of health-care services for the first time but also changed its renal care activities into a more vertically integrated operation. In 1994 the COBE Renal Care subsidiary acquired the Florida-based Dial Medical for an undisclosed sum. This deal further broadened COBE's renal care assets by giving it a much stronger presence in the market for dialysis concentrates, which Dial Medical produced and distributed.

Meanwhile, COBE BCT was busy making alliances with other medical firms. In September 1993 an agreement was reached between the subsidiary and Cryopharm Corporation of Pasadena, California. Under the terms, COBE invested $4.6 million over two years for the development and marketing of a cryogenic preservation technology patented by Cryopharm. While blood components stored at room temperature were only viable for five days, using the new freezing method meant that platelets, red blood cells, bone marrow, and blood stem cells could be successfully stored in freezers for several months. The agreement called for the companies to co-develop the technology and for COBE to market it, having obtained worldwide rights. Two months later a second alliance was announced between COBE BCT and Aastrom Biosciences, Inc., based in Ann Arbor, Michigan. COBE invested $20 million in Aastrom's Stem Cell Expansion System, which used a bioreactor to multiply stem cells 75-100 times. The technology would allow many more patients to receive cancer treatment at reduced costs. COBE gained worldwide rights to the bioreactor technology for such treatments using stem cells.

In a little more than 30 years, COBE Laboratories had grown from a $40,000 one-product business to a diversified, multinational corporation with annual revenues of more than half a billion dollars. As it approached the end of the century, it had the security of being owned by a global leader in health technology and could afford to solidify its position through major acquisitions and alliances. COBE's activities in the early 1990s suggested that it would continue to pursue innovations in its areas of expertise and to further diversify its operations.

Principal Subsidiaries: COBE BCT, Inc.; COBE Cardiovascular, Inc.; COBE International Division; COBE Renal Care, Inc.; REN Corporation (53.5%).

Further Reading:

Bettelheim, Andriel, "Swedish Company Buys Cobe Labs," *Denver Post,* March 17, 1990, pp. 1C, 6C.

Bulman, Philip, "Cobe Pumps Profits into Pioneering Blood Research," *Denver Post,* October 6, 1986, p. 3D.

"COBE Seeks Higher Share of Cardiovascular Market," *Rocky Mountain News,* June 30, 1976, pp. 74, 77.

"Cryopharm Corp. Announces First Corporate Partnership," *Business Wire,* September 16, 1993.

Day, Janet, "Merger, Acquisition Beef Up Medical Equipment Industry," *Denver Post,* July 8, 1992, p. 2C.

"Gambro's COBE BCT Commits $20 Million to Stem Cell Therapy Alliance with Aastrom Biosciences, Inc.," *Business Wire,* November 5, 1993.

Kaplan, Howard M., "While Waiting for a Kidney . . . : A Fast-Growing Colorado Firm Builds—and Exports to Scores of Countries—the Remarkable Dialyzers that Save Lives," *Denver Post Empire Magazine,* June 25, 1972, pp. 16–20.

Margolin, Morton L., "Cobe Labs a Star in Chamber Campaign," *Rocky Mountain News,* August 22, 1977, pp. 69, 71.

Printz, Carrie, "COBE Hopes Merger Will Inject New Blood into Its Foreign Sales," *Denver Business Journal,* May 28, 1990, p. 20.

Weber, Joe, "COBE Chiefs' Business Savvy Pays Off in Product Success," *Rocky Mountain News,* July 13, 1986, pp. 76–77.

—David E. Salamie

Coca-Cola Enterprises, Inc.

1 Coca-Cola Plaza Northwest
Atlanta, Georgia 30313
U.S.A.
(404) 676-6792
Fax: (404) 676-6792

Public Company
Incorporated: 1986
Employees: 26,000
Sales: $5.46 billion
Stock Exchanges: New York Pacific Boston Midwest Cincinnati Philadelphia
SICs: 2086 Bottled & Canned Soft Drinks

The largest bottling group owned by The Coca-Cola Company, Coca-Cola Enterprises, Inc. produces, markets, and distributes the carbonated soft drinks of its 49 percent owner, The Coca-Cola Company. During the mid-1990s, Coca-Cola Enterprises sold beverages in 38 states, the District of Columbia, the U.S. Virgin Islands, and the Netherlands.

Among the collection of bottling operations composing Coca-Cola Enterprises during the 1990s, the oldest traced its roots back to 1889, when one of the most incredible and profitable transactions in U.S. business history occurred. That year, three years after the first Coca-Cola drink mixture was concocted, two lawyers from Chattanooga, Tennessee, bought the exclusive rights to sell America's newest beverage, Coca-Cola, in bottles. For what retrospectively ranks as one of the biggest bargains in the annals of business history, the two lawyers together paid $1 for Coca-Cola's exclusive bottling rights, giving the investors what would a century later evolve into a multi-billion dollar enterprise for having paid two quarters apiece.

Based on the actions the two entrepreneurs took immediately after investing their $1, they did have some idea of the fortune they had just acquired. With the help of financier John T. Lupton, the two lawyers divided the country into small territories and sold regional rights of the sale of Coca-Cola to other entrepreneurs, thus beginning the development of an intricate and massive network of Coca-Cola bottlers.

The franchising of Coca-Cola bottling operations, superintended by John T. Lupton, made fortunes for many independent bottlers, most notably for Lupton himself and his heirs, as the web of bottling operations spread across the country, embracing every corner of the nation. For The Coca-Cola Company, the relationship with its bottlers was a profitable one: The company marketed its product, then sold Coca-Cola concentrate to bottlers who performed the less profitable task of sweetening and carbonating the syrup, packaging it, then distributing it to retailers. Working as such, the process of making and selling Coca-Cola grew into an enormous business, profiting The Coca-Cola Company and, to a lesser extent, the independent, regionally-based Coca-Cola bottlers. The Coca-Cola empire functioned in this manner for nearly the next century.

Although The Coca-Cola Company maintained some ownership of the bottling of its product, an overwhelming majority of the bottling of Coca-Cola was performed by the independent bottlers who were first ceded bottling rights by Lupton and the two Chattanooga lawyers. In 1944, the predecessor to the Coca-Cola Enterprises company that operated during the 1990s was formed as a wholly owned subsidiary of The Coca-Cola Company to manage the small portion of bottling operations directly owned by its parent company. This company was deactivated in 1970, then reactivated 16 years later, in 1986, when almost coincidental developments forced The Coca-Cola Company to jump into the bottling business in an aggressive manner. The result was Coca-Cola Enterprises, Inc., a nearly $3 billion bottling operation comprising a majority of the independent bottling companies that had packaged and distributed Coca-Cola in cans and bottles for more than the previous half century.

Truly a modern creation despite its links to 1944 and 1899, Coca-Cola Enterprises was formed as more of solution to developments in the soft drink industry that begged a response than as a strategic maneuver effected by The Coca-Cola Company. The origins of Coca-Cola Enterprises may be traced to early 1986, when the descendants of John T. Lupton, lead by an ancestor of the same name, initiated negotiations with The Coca-Cola Company about selling their bottling operations which were the largest of the soft drink company's sundry independent bottlers.

The company, headed by the latest John T. Lupton, and aptly named JTL Corporation, began negotiating with The Coca-Cola Company in January 1986 about selling its bottling operations to the diversified soft drink giant. The Coca-Cola Company at this point owned bottling operations that constituted roughly 11 percent of its domestic sales volume, to which the addition of JTL's bottling operations, located in Texas, Florida, Colorado, and Arizona, would add another 14 percent, giving the Coca-Cola Company direct control over one quarter of its domestic sales volume. JTL, with $1 billion in estimated 1985 sales, represented a significant acquisition for The Coca-Cola Company; it would bring the company's bottling ownership more in line with rival PepsiCo Inc., which had always owned a sizeable portion of its bottling operations.

Negotiations between JTL and The Coca-Cola Company continued throughout January, 1986 with an agreement to merge reached before the end of the month. As negotiations to complete the merger carried into February, another large Coca-Cola bottling operation became available when Beatrice Companies, Inc., a Chicago-based food concern and owner of the second largest collection of Coca-Cola bottling operations, began looking to sell its stake in bottling Coca-Cola. Beatrice was in the process of being acquired by Kohlberg Kravis Roberts & Company, a $6.2 billion leveraged buyout that forced Beatrice to divest a wealth of assets before mid-1987. Slated for divestiture was the company's most profitable major segment—Coca-Cola bottling facilities stretching across nine states, including one of the country's most lucrative regions, California.

Faced with either letting the two largest bottling operations in the country fall into potentially hostile hands or acquiring them, The Coca-Cola Company's management opted for the latter, quickly finding themselves in the midst of purchasing two companies with combined annual revenues of more than $2 billion. The potential consolidation of these two enormous bottling organizations was reflective of an industry-wide pattern that had developed during the previous ten years, as small independent bottlers merged and became large independent bottlers, winnowing the ranks of the bottling industry to more effectively compete in the new era of the "cola wars." In 1975, there were an estimated 2,400 soft drink bottling plants in the United States; ten years later, when JTL's and Beatrice's bottling groups were up for sale, the number of plants had dropped to 1,400 and by 1990 the number whittled to 730.

As The Coca-Cola Company's negotiations with JTL and Beatrice dragged on through the spring and into the summer, speculations abounded that The Coca-Cola Company would form a separate bottling entity with the two acquisitions and the bottling operations it already owned. Although purchasing JTL's and Beatrice's bottling operations would give the soft drink company more control over its bottlers than it had in the past, the addition of the two heavyweight bottlers would also give the soft drink company considerable debt. A solution to this problem would come later, but as the summer wore on, the agreement to acquire the largest of the two companies, JTL Corp., fell apart, making The Coca-Cola Company's worries about assuming debilitating debt appear moot.

Some members of the Lupton family had decided in late June against selling the source of their family's fortune, wishing instead to remain independent, as they had for nearly a century. At about the same time JTL withdrew from negotiations with The Coca-Cola Company, however, an agreement between The Coca-Cola Company and Beatrice was reached, stipulating that the soft drink company would purchase Beatrice's bottling group for $1 billion. Two weeks later, the directors of JTL made an about-face, deciding again to sell their bottling operations to the Coca-Cola Company for $1.4 billion.

The two transactions were completed in the fall, forming the foundation for a new prodigious force in the soft drink bottling industry, Coca-Cola Enterprises, Inc., a company that would become known throughout the industry as CCE. The Coca-Cola Company borrowed $2.4 billion to buy JTL and Beatrice's bottling group, incurring enough debt to dilute its earnings. To avoid this drain on its finances, the soft drink company's management decided to sell 51 percent of CCE's ownership to the public, the largest initial stock offering in the history of the United States at that point. By doing so, the debt accumulated from its bottling acquisitions was wiped off The Coca-Cola Company's financial books, while the stock-buying public was relied upon to invest $1.5 billion to get CCE up and running. Several days after filing the prospectus for its CCE public offering, The Coca-Cola Company signed an agreement to buy Coca-Cola Bottling Company of Southern Florida with the intention of turning around and selling the bottling group to CCE. This, the soft drink company did and would continue to do, building up its control over its domestic bottlers located in regions contiguous to the bottling operations it already owned through its 49 percent stake in CCE. Donald Keough, chief operating officer of The Coca-Cola Company and CCE's chairman, superintended over this expansion of CCE's operating territory, but the bottling company was essentially stewarded during its first years by Brian Dyson, who was described by the *Wall Street Journal* as a "professorial Argentine who runs marathons." Dyson was selected as CCE's chief executive officer after earning much praise as the president of Coca-Cola USA, the domestic soft drink arm of The Coca-Cola Company; in that capacity, Dyson had spearheaded the soft drink company's marketing forays into the sale of diet Coke and the company's reformulated "new" Coke.

In his new position, Dyson faced the formidable task of satisfying CCE's shareholders in a business essentially foreign to The Coca-Cola Company. In contrast to the company he left to lead CCE, Dyson found himself in the less profitable, more capital-intensive business of carbonating Coca-Cola concentrate, bottling it, and selling it to stores, where the contentious pricing battle between The Coca-Cola Company and PepsiCo reached its most palpable point. Ironically, in this battle, The Coca-Cola Company and CCE fought for divergent goals: The Coca-Cola Company was concerned primarily with the volume of concentrate it sold, which generally increased when the retail price of Coke dropped, while CCE was concerned primarily with keeping its production and distribution costs as far below the retail price of Coke as possible. Thrust into this new, somewhat alien segment of the soft drink industry, Dyson went about bottling and selling a very familiar product, increasing the scope of CCE operations throughout the late 1980s.

In July 1987, CCE acquired the group of bottling companies The Coca-Cola Company had acquired in the fall of 1986, paying its 49 percent owners $173 million for bottling properties in Florida, Alabama, and Texas. Six months later, in January 1988, CCE agreed to pay $500 million to acquire additional bottlers from The Coca-Cola Company, this time for operations serving Miami, Memphis, Delaware, and Maryland. This set of acquisitions gave The Coca-Cola Company control over 45 percent of its domestic volume.

Other minor acquisitions followed, including the absorption of West Georgia Coca-Cola Bottlers, Inc., Coca-Cola Bottling Co. of West Point-LaGrange, Palestine Coca-Cola Bottling Co., and Coca-Cola Bottling Co. of Greenville, Inc., all purchased in 1989. As CCE entered the 1990s, it purchased another large bottler from The Coca-Cola Company, Coca-Cola Bottling Company of Arkansas, for an estimated $250 million, leading the way to an acquisition the following year that signalled significant changes at CCE. Available for acquisition was Johnston Coca-Cola Bottling Company of Chattanooga, of which The Coca-Cola Company already owned 20 percent. Johnston represented roughly 11 percent of national Coca-Cola volume, second in size only to CCE itself. Serving a population base of 27.5 million spread across 15 states, Johnston's operations would place 55 percent of total domestic Coca-Cola bottle-and-can volume under one operational and financial structure—the ever-widening corporate umbrella of CCE—but perhaps as equally beneficial for CCE was the managerial expertise the company would obtain through its purchase of Johnston. This infusion of new management was needed because CCE, in the four years since its formation, had demonstrated lackluster performance by executing its role as a Coca-Cola bottler in 26 states with disappointing results.

During CCE's first four years of existence, much of Coca-Cola's domestic volume growth was derived not from CCE's bottling operations but from The Coca-Cola Company's independent franchised bottlers. Much of the blame for CCE's woes, which in addition to flat sales included low employee morale, was placed on the shoulders of the company's chief executive, Dyson. Critics charged that Dyson lacked the "street smarts" and the proper personality to deal with retailers. Whatever the cause of CCE's ails, the effect was clear: CCE needed to substantially ameliorate its performance. Johnston's president and chief operating officer, Henry Schimberg, and its 45 percent owner, Summerfield K. Johnston were perceived as the managers to effect such a turnaround.

Summerfield Johnston, whose grandfather purchased the first Coca-cola bottling franchise in 1901, and Schimberg, who was slated to occupy the same positions at CCE as he did at Johnston, were respected as skilled bottling managers—something Dyson, despite his success at Coca-Cola USA, was not. Under Schimberg's stewardship, Johnston Bottling had recorded eight percent annual growth in sales volume—twice the industry rate—and nearly quintupled its operating profit during the same span that Dyson had overseen CCE's flat growth. Dyson, it readily became apparent, was on his way out, a prediction made by the business press when it was learned that Dyson was not even informed of the pending Johnston acquisition until a deal had already been struck.

In December 1991, CCE acquired Johnston and with it, the talents of Schimberg, who took over the day-to-day operations of CCE. In his new post, Schimberg successfully achieved a profitable balance between the opposing goals of price and volume. Between 1991 and 1993, operating profit rose from $538 million to $804 million, while bottle-and-can case growth jumped from 0 percent to four percent. More important to CCE's shareholders, who held a 51 percent stake in the company, CCE's stock price climbed from $12.25 to $19.00 by 1994, giving both CCE shareholders and CCE management hope that the company would continue to record encouraging growth in the future.

As CCE entered the mid-1990s, Schimberg's strategic maneuvers continued to work their magic. By reorganizing the company, Schimberg had laid a new foundation for its future, decentralizing CCE's management to drive decision-making down as close to the point of retail sale as possible. In this manner, with close attention paid to the point of sale, Schimberg hoped to create a legacy of success for The Coca-Cola Company's largest bottling group.

Principal Subsidiaries: BCI Coca-Cola Bottling Co. of Los Angeles; Bottling Holdings (International) Inc.; CCT Acquisition Corporation, Inc.; The Coca-Cola Bottling Company of Memphis; Delaware Coca-Cola Bottling Company; Enterprises Consulting, Inc.; Florida Coca-Cola Bottling Company; Johnston Coca-Cola Bottling Group, Inc.; The Louisiana Coca-Cola Bottling Company, Ltd.; Valley Coca-Cola Bottling Company, Inc.; Vending Holding Company; The Wave Insurance Company.

Further Reading:

"Coca-Cola Completes $1 Billion Acquisition of Beatrice Cos. Line," *Wall Street Journal,* September 24, 1986, p. 40.
"Coca-Cola Is Selling Firms to Bottler for $173 Million," *Wall Street Journal,* July 7, 1987, p. 5.
"Coke Buys Another Big Bottler," *Business Week,* July 14, 1986, p. 34.
"Coke's Fizzy Deal," *Fortune,* November 24, 1986, p. 9.
"Coke's Linkup with Its No. 1 Bottler," *Business Week,* February 10, 1986, p. 36.
Jabbonsky, Larry, "Coca-Cola Enterprises Up Close," *Beverage World,* November 1991, pp. 23–6.
——, "Resurrecting CCE," *Beverage World,* November 1994, pp. 24–35.
——, "Talking Bottling," *Beverage World,* January 1992, pp. 6, 28–33.
Johnson, Robert, "Beatrice Is Said to Discuss Sale of Coke Line to Coke," *Wall Street Journal,* June 16, 1986, p. 2.
Kleiner, Kurt, "Howard Knows Things Go Better with Coke," *Baltimore Business Journal,* November 20, 1992, p. 6.
Morris, Betsy, "Coca-Cola Enterprises Agrees to Acquire Big Bottlers From Coke for $500 Million," *Wall Street Journal,* January 29, 1988, p. 22.
Oman, Bruce, "From the Bottom Up," *Beverage World,* January 1993, p. 48.
Sellers, Patricia, "Coke's Plan To Pump Up the Volume," *Fortune,* November 18, 1991, p. 157.
Smith, Timothy K., "Coca-Cola Co. Agrees to Buy JTL Corp., Its Largest U.S. Bottler, for $1.4 Billion," *Wall Street Journal,* July 2, 1986, p. 3.
——, "Coca-Cola Plans to Sell 51% of Bottling Group Publicly for $1.5 Billion," *Wall Street Journal,* October 15, 1986, p. 1.
Ticer, Scott, "Coke's Monster Stock Offering Could Go Flat," *Business Week,* October 27, 1986, p. 45.

—Jeffrey L. Covell

Cole National Corporation

5915 Landerbrook Drive
Mayfield Heights, Ohio 44124
U.S.A.
(216) 449-4100
Fax: (216) 461-3489

Public Company
Founded: 1930 as National Key Company
Sales: $528.04 million
Stock Exchanges: New York
SICs: 5995 Optical Goods Stores; 5947 Gift, Novelty & Souvenir Shops; 7699 Repair Services, Not Elsewhere Classified

Over the course of its more than 50 years in business, Cole National Corporation (CNC) has dabbled in specialty retail ventures ranging from children's toys to cookie-baking to shoe repair and watchbands. Key-cutting services, however, remained a continued aspect of Cole's offerings throughout the decades. Although the company's key-cutting business has diminished in importance over the years (and was downplayed in the mid-1990s), it long formed the backbone of the retail firm operated by the Cole family.

Based in a suburb of Cleveland, Cole National Corporation boasted over 2,200 stores in the early 1990s. the company's retail businesses were about evenly split between the eyewear and giftware markets at that time. The Cole Vision division, which operated under the Sears Optical and Montgomery Ward Vision Center names in the early 1990s, was America's third-largest optical retailer. CNC started marketing managed vision care to large group accounts in the early 1990s. By 1994, this fast-growing operation listed 15.6 million members. CNC's other major retail holding, the Cole Gift division, operated over 1,300 stores in two formats. Its Things Remembered stores were usually located within malls, while Cole Gift Centers were leased shops within department stores. In 1994 CNC emerged from a ten-year period in which it was privately-held with a $60 million initial public offering.

Company namesake and guiding light Joseph E. Cole was born in Cleveland in 1915, the youngest of nine children. He started his retail career with Cleveland's National Key Company in 1935 at the age of twenty. He left National Key nine years later to establish the key division of Curtis Industries, another Cleveland business.

Cole's first key shop was set up in the parking lot of a local Sears, Roebuck & Co. store that same year. By the end of the decade, Cole had built his little sideline into America's second-largest key retailer. The self-made entrepreneur was coronated "king of keys" in 1950, when he acquired National Key and Curtis' key division, the industry's two top players. The newly unified firm took the name of its larger constituent, National Key. (Although National Key was founded in 1932, Cole National claimed 1944 as its inaugural year.)

Joe Cole's key-selling concept was predicated on the idea that keymaking was a highly specialized, service-oriented business. While mass retailers wanted a share of this segment's high profit margins, they did not want to deal with the equally high level of training, service, and inventory control it demanded. Cole leased space from such leading department stores as Sears, Roebuck and Co., Montgomery Ward, and Kresge's. He then installed key-making machines, trained store employees to cut keys, and oversaw the operations' complex 3,000-unit inventory. While Cole neither manufactured keys nor owned stores, Cole found a profitable niche in providing its services to customers and retailers.

A company executive would later characterize Cole's counters as "an oasis of service in a sea of self-service." The tiny selling areas emerged as the most productive areas—in terms of profits per square foot—in some stores. During the 1950s, the company expanded into the manufacture and sale of key chains and jewelry, and launched a while-you-wait shoe repair division.

The explosion of automotive and home sales in the postwar era made expansion of the replacement key industry virtually inevitable. Less than a decade after assuming the helm of National Key, Joe Cole increased sales fourfold, from $2.33 million in 1950 to $10.52 million in 1959. When the firm went public that year, it sold out its entire offering in one day. The Cole family retained a 25 percent stake in their company, which by that time was netting over $635,000 annually.

The company used the proceeds of its initial public offering to fund an acquisition spree in 1960. Over the course of that single year, the firm purchased Fairfield Publishing, a greeting-card company; Shore Manufacturing, a novelty business; and Masco Optical. Having thus diversified from its base in keys—and in recognition of its leader—the company was renamed Cole National Corp. in 1960.

That same year, Cole tested a new concept in optical retailing, establishing an eyewear counter within space leased from a Detroit Montgomery Ward store. This venture was based on the same concept as the company's key business. Company strategists recognized that mass retailers had the traffic, but not the expertise, to run such an operation. Masco Optical became the foundation of a chain of optical counters that numbered over 150 locations by the end of the 1960s. Optical centers had become Cole National's largest division by 1964, contributing about half of annual sales.

Although CNC retained a focus on retailing, it also diversified into manufacturing during the 1960s. It acquired Sterling Industries, a Cleveland manufacturer of aluminum, steel and plastic products in 1961, thereby winning an exclusive contract with Welcome Wagon. In 1966 Cole National merged with Susan Crane, producers of giftwrap, and acquired the Gene Upton Co., manufacturers of self-adhesive metal letters and numbers. Two years later it acquired Manco, Inc., a manufacturer of Topps and Everbest brand watchbands. The Manco purchase included Canadian, British, and Japanese retail outlets. Griffon Cutlery Corp., a marketer of manicure tools, was added to the roster in 1969. These acquisitions more than quadrupled Cole National's sales to over $40 million, but also invited speculation from analysts that the company had over-extended itself. In 1970, in fact, the retail conglomerate's profits declined by half.

The company's acquisitive push also got it into trouble with the Federal Trade Commission in the mid-1960s. Cole National had purchased Independent Lock Co., a 45-year-old manufacturer of locks and key blanks with about $14 million in annual sales, early in 1964. In 1967, however, the government compelled Cole to sell the business, which would have nearly doubled CNC's annual sales.

Although Joseph Cole brought in new presidents to help him run the company beginning in the 1960s, he retained *defacto* control of his firm as its chairman and chief executive officer. In the face of declining profits in the 1970s, son Jeffrey A. Cole convinced his father to bring a group of young MBAs like himself into upper management. According to a 1980 article in *Forbes,* the "young turks . . . managed to rid the company of its poorer diversifications, prevent Joe Cole from making any more bad moves and get the company back to its special service orientation." Both the Canadian retail operations and a distribution business were put on the auction block. In spite of (or perhaps because of) the divestments, annual revenues rose by nearly 50 percent, from $106 million in 1976 to $158 million in 1980. One survivor of the cutbacks was Things Remembered, the chain of mall-based gift shops that specialized in monogrammed and engraved items. Established in 1967 by Cole National, the chain had expanded to 280 shops in 38 states by 1980.

In 1984 Kohlberg Kravis Roberts and Co., an investment firm, took Cole National Corp. private through a leveraged buyout. The outsiders took a managerial approach typical of the investment-house "reorganizations" of the 1980s. They sold off Cole's Craft Showcase chain in 1984 and the Original Cookie Co. stores in 1985. In 1987 a group led by Jeffrey Cole took on more debt to regain control of the retail conglomerate. They created a holding company, CNC Holding Corp., and kept the firm private until 1994.

During the early 1980s, CNC had made what has been called "its highest-profile deal" with the 1981 acquisition of Child World Inc., which then ranked second only to Toys-R-Us among toy supermarket chains. By 1985, when the parent sold 18 percent of the Child World subsidiary to the public, the chain boasted over 100 stores in 21 states under the Child World and Children's Palace names. But a late 1980s retail slump, combined with intense competition from Toys-R-Us and a $300 million-plus debt load, crippled the subsidiary chain. While Jeffrey Cole struggled to sell off the business—in 1990 a potential acquirer failed to secure financing—Child World incurred a massive $192 million loss on sales of $830 million.

Cole's woes concerning Child World were compounded when the chain was one of seven toy stores named in a 1990 federal lawsuit brought by the Consumer Product Safety Commission. Nonetheless, CNC was finally able to sell the subsidiary to a coalition of former Toys-R-Us executives. Instead of cash, Cole traded $60 million in long-term debt for $30 million in short-term debt. While Cole had been able to negotiate a $157 million price tag for the stores in 1990, it was clearly not in a strong bargaining position by this time. The divestment slashed Cole's annual sales from over $1.25 billion in 1990 to $425 million in 1991. Within a year of the exchange, Child World's new owners were forced to file for bankruptcy and liquidate the entire chain.

That deal left CNC with three retail divisions: Things Remembered gift shops; Cole Key; and Cole Vision. Cole's Vision group, along with much of the eyewear industry, had enjoyed double-digit annual growth in the 1980s. By the early 1990s Cole Vision ranked third among the United States' largest eyewear chains, and its more than 750 outlets contributed about half of the company's sales. Although annual increases in eyewear sales fizzled to just one percent by that time, CNC expressed confidence that aging baby boomers would be buying many pairs of glasses and contacts after the dreary economy reheated in the mid-1990s. In fact, the company expanded its eyecare business into the managed healthcare market in the early years of the decade, establishing benefits contracts with labor unions, insurance companies, health management organizations, and other large groups.

CNC also converted hundreds of its Cole key counters in department stores into "Gift Centers" that resembled the successful Things Remembered shops. The growing emphasis on giftware prompted expansion of the concept into a "superstore" format and the addition of personalized soft goods such as shirts on a test basis.

After incurring back-to-back net losses in 1990 and 1991, Cole National's profits multiplied steadily, from $5.5 million in 1992 to $24.7 million in 1994. Sales increased as well, from $428.1 million to $528.1 million over the same period. Most of that increase came from expansion; same-store sales increased by 8.2 percent in 1993 and 3.5 percent in 1994. An aggressive growth plan fueled the acquisition or establishment of 235 new retail locations in 1994.

That same year, Cole National returned to the public arena with a 6.5 million share offer, the proceeds of which were used to reduce persistent leveraged buyout (LBO) debt. The reborn firm's "first" annual report enumerated several corporate goals, including debt reduction, increased earnings growth, and (re)doubling sales to over $1 billion by 2001.

Further Reading:

Cochran, Thomas N., "Offerings in the Offing: Cole National," *Barron's,* April 4, 1994, p. 46.

Fisher, Christy, "Eyewear Sales Slow," *Advertising Age,* March 9, 1992, p. 46.

Funk, Nancy M., "Cole Unit Struggles in Tough Climate for Retailing," *Cleveland Plain Dealer,* December 9, 1990, pp. E1, E3.

——, ''Child World Posts Huge Loss,'' *Cleveland Plain Dealer,* March 30, 1991, p. E1.

Gleisser, Marcus, ''Cole National Reports Lower Retail Sales,'' *Cleveland Plain Dealer,* January 10, 1995, p. C4.

Hagan, John F., ''Area Firm Linked to Hazardous-Toys Suit,'' *Cleveland Plain Dealer,* August 21, 1990, p. B1.

''Key Maker Cole Sharpens Its Vision,'' *Business Week,* January 15, 1966, pp. 84, 86.

Koff, Stephen, ''Child World Closing All Toy Stores,'' *Cleveland Plain Dealer,* July 14, 1992, p. G1.

Rose, William Ganson, *Cleveland: The Making of a City,* Cleveland: World Publishing Co., 1950.

''Service at a (Stiff) Price,'' *Forbes,* February 4, 1980, p. 84.

Van Tassel, David D., and John J. Grabowski, *The Encyclopedia of Cleveland History,* Bloomington, Ind.: Indiana University Press, 1987.

—April D. Gasbarre

Collins & Aikman Corporation

701 McCullough Drive
Charlotte, North Carolina 28262
U.S.A.
(704) 547-8500
Fax: (704) 548-2360

Public Company
Incorporated: 1988
Employees: 12,000
Sales: $1.5 billion
Stock Exchanges: New York
SICs: 2221 Broadwoven Fabric Mills—Manmade; 2231 Broadwoven Fabric Mills—Wool; 2273 Carpets & Rugs

Founded as a supplier of window shades in the mid-nineteenth century, Collins & Aikman Corporation has survived a century and a half of corporate maneuvering to become a leading supplier of automotive trim, upholstery fabrics, and wallpaper.

The business that was to become Collins & Aikman was founded in 1843 on the lower East side of New York. Sensing that the rapid growth of the increasingly crowded city would spur the market for privacy products, 21-year-old Gibbons L. Kelty opened a window shade shop on Catherine Street. Kelty's business prospered, and he gradually added various home furnishings lines and began to import upholstery fabrics. Kelty also opened a textile factory across the East River in Astoria.

By 1870 G. L. Kelty & Co. was operating several downtown stores, selling furniture, curtains, and upholstery. That year, Gibbons Kelty admitted his nephew, Charles M. Aikman, into partnership, and in 1871 they were joined by Gibbons's son, William Kelty. A year later Kelty became the first U.S. weaver of satin damask, and it won a gold medal for these fabrics at an American Centennial exhibition a few years later.

After Gibbons Kelty died in 1889, Charles Aikman formed C. M. Aikman & Co. and bought out the principal Kelty interests. The Kelty holdings included a half interest in a weave plant in the Manayunk section of Philadelphia. The other half was owned by William G. Collins. In 1891 they incorporated Collins & Aikman (C&A), with Aikman as president and Collins as secretary and treasurer. C&A continued its expansion as a specialist in heavy, upholstery-type fabrics. In 1898 it became the first American producer of jacquard velvet. About the same time the company got out of its original window shade business.

Charles Aikman retired in 1909 and sold his C. M. Aikman & Co. (which he may have used primarily as a holding company for his C&A and other interests) to C&A. A few years later, William Collins also retired, turning the presidency over to his son Kenneth. Tragically, Kenneth Collins was killed in early 1916 in a fire, after he had rescued two women who were trapped. His cousin, Dr. William M. Collins, who had held the title of treasurer in the company, took over as interim president, but by July 1916 the Collins family sold its holdings to Thomas Doody and Melville Curtis, who had first bought a stake in the firm in 1911 and had been directors and assistant treasurers.

Early in their tenure, Doody and Curtis brought in Willis G. McCullough, whose family was to play a major role in C&A for 70 years. Hired as a salesman, McCullough was promoted to sales manager within a year and also named treasurer and elected to the board. By 1929 he was president (with Melville Curtis stepping up to chairman), a job he held until his death in 1948.

In the early 1920s, McCullough was instrumental in steering C&A into what was quickly to become its largest business—and has remained so much of the time since. For a producer of upholstery fabrics, auto seat materials seemed a natural outlet, and soon C&A also provided fabrics for headlining, sidewalls, and other automotive uses. McCullough persuaded the company to build a new plant for auto and furniture fabrics in West Philadelphia.

In 1926 Collins & Aikman Company went public and was listed on the New York Stock Exchange. The next year it reincorporated as Collins & Aikman Corp. while absorbing three other companies, including its long-time mohair yarn supplier, Cranston Mills of Rhode Island, and a velvet weaver which gave it a plant in North Carolina. More plants were built over the years. In 1929 C&A established a Canadian subsidiary with a plant in Farnham, Quebec, to supply the auto and furniture industries. By 1937 C&A moved into supplying the infant airline industry with specially developed fabrics that were light and durable. The company later supplied fabric for President Roosevelt's plane.

C&A managed to stay in the black for all but one year during the Depression. With the advent of World War II, civilian auto production, which by then accounted for about 75 percent of C&A's volume, came to a halt. The company switched to duck, alpaca linings, and upholstery fabrics for war uses, but it took time to adapt to new machinery, techniques, and employees. Profits collapsed from $3.1 million in the February 1941 fiscal year to $123,000 in fiscal 1943 before rebounding partway to $2.0 million in fiscal 1945.

Throughout his presidency, Willis McCullough emphasized C&A's tradition of research and development. For instance, the company developed techniques for back-coating auto and furniture fabrics and for large-scale range dyeing of pile fabrics. Even during the war, research efforts continued. In 1943 C&A patented a double-faced thermal cloth, initially used for cold-weather uniforms, and it worked with nylon originator duPont to adapt this first synthetic "miracle fiber" for upholstery fabrics. Also during the war, C&A expanded its presence in North Carolina by acquiring Norwood Company, a cotton spinner, in 1943, then modernizing its plant with the C&A-developed Bird spinning system.

McCullough also made C&A an early provider of health insurance and the 40-hour week. McCullough himself was very reticent. He kept published information about the company at a minimum and never permitted his photo to be released to the press. *Fortune,* with its army of indefatigable researchers, long tried to gather enough material for an article on C&A, but finally gave up in frustration.

After McCullough's death in 1948, general counsel Albert Jube stepped in as what a company history describes as ''caretaker president.'' Whitworth Bird, who had developed the Bird spinning system for the company, took over in 1953. But despite the general economic prosperity in the United States, the first decade after the war was difficult for many textile companies, including C&A. It was saddled with many obsolete, high-cost plants in the Northeast and undertook a painful process of relocating to the South, especially North Carolina. C&A continued as a major supplier to the auto companies, but the shift away from pile and plush upholstery and greater use of plastics in seats and body linings cut C&A's contribution per car. C&A's efforts to compete with large, mass-volume textilers in ''flat fabrics'' for men's and women's clothing incurred substantial losses, until the Rhode Island plant producing them was finally closed in 1956. C&A ran three deficits in the four years ending February 1957.

In December 1956, C&A hired 49-year-old textile veteran Ellis Leach as president. With automotive products dropping as a percentage of C&A's sales, Leach stressed flexibility and emphasis on more specialized and stylish products. A prime goal was ''getting away from staple items'' where fierce competition permitted little if any profit, while ''putting emphasis on style'' where ''our forte lies in the finish of a product.'' Aided by Stead & Miller, a subsidiary acquired in 1952 that emphasized furniture damasks and novelty weaves, C&A increased furniture upholstery fabrics to a quarter of total business by the late 1950s, much of it to better-quality furniture makers. For the apparel market, C&A developed synthetic fur-like fabrics, mainly for use as liners that could also be reversed for use as outerwear, and trim. It also came out with periodic novelty items like Bear Hug shaggy-pile coats, and supplied plush ''fur'' for the toy market.

In 1961 Leach stepped up to the position of chairman and the presidency was assumed by 36-year-old Donald McCullough, the younger son of Willis, a Yale-trained engineer who had been persuaded by his father to turn down a job at Republic Steel to start as a C&A trainee in 1946. When Leach retired in 1966, Don McCullough also became chairman and CEO. Don McCullough shared Leach's faith in ''mobility and flexibility.'' Their policy was not only to replace plants and machinery as they became outmoded, but also to replace products that had outworn their welcome with new, market-pleasing varieties. They also believed in frequent acquisitions to expand C&A's market niches.

The 1960 acquisition of Pennsylvania-based Bangor Mills gave C&A an entry into tricot knitting. In less than a decade C&A tripled its tricot capacity and developed Certifab tricot for bonding to other fabrics. Another new field was entered in 1965 through Painter Carpet Mills, a specialist in commercial and institutional carpeting. C&A acquired wall coverings producer Imperial Paper in 1971 and Tennessee Trifting, which made scatter rugs, in 1972. By then, 42 percent of C&A's business was in apparel fabrics, while the home furnishing market (which comprised both furniture fabrics and wallpaper) accounted for 36 percent. Although the auto business was bringing in more revenues than it had in the past and was extended to such important new products as molded carpet flooring, C&A's transportation business (which also included airline sales) was down to about 20 percent of its revenues.

Leach and McCullough's policies paid off financially, with C&A returning to the black in Leach's first year and growing steadily for the next quarter century. Acquisitions and internal growth increased sales from $45 million in the year ending February 1959 to more than $200 million in 1969 and $1 billion in 1985. Earnings over the same period rose from $1.7 million (which was still below the nearly $2 million netted in mid-Depression 1937) to more than $60 million in 1985. Five stock splits between 1961 and 1985 turned each pre-1961 share into 24 new shares. Thus, the $22 market price of the stock in June 1985 compared with a split-adjusted trading range of $.50 to $1 during most of the 1950s and a 1937 high of $2.60.

The price nearly doubled again over the next twelve months, but by then C&A was beginning to get caught up in the market excitement that made most any company, whether ill or well managed, small or large, a potential buyout target. In particular, C&A attracted the attention of Sanford Sigoloff, CEO of The Wickes Companies.

Like C&A, Wickes traced its origin to family businesses started in the mid-1800s. By the 1960s it was an important supplier of building materials and operated the Builders Emporium chain and other outlets. In 1980 it merged with Gamble-Skogmo, which operated a variety of merchandising units. However, the resultant Wickes Companies was burdened by $2 billion in debt and many run-down operating units. In March 1982 it turned for help to Sigoloff, who had a reputation as a turnaround specialist. Sigoloff, whose self-adopted nickname was ''Ming the Merciless,'' derived from a villain in Flash Gordon comic strips, prided himself on ruthless cost-cutting and efficiency. He promptly threw Wickes into Chapter 11 bankruptcy and managed to bring the reorganized company out again by January 1985, winning wide admiration for the speed and effectiveness of his moves.

Wickes was barely four months out of bankruptcy when Sigoloff announced his intention of making a $1 billion acquisition within a year. He handily beat that timetable when in September 1985 he completed the $1 billion purchase of Gulf & Western's Consumer and Industrial Products Group, doubling Wickes's size.

He amassed a new $1.2 billion war chest in 1986, but hostile efforts to capture National Gypsum and Owens-Corning Fiberglas both failed. He was more successful in quiet negotiations with C&A, and won the board's assent in November with a ''can't-refuse'' offer of $1.16 billion. That meant $53 a C&A share, a 50 percent premium over the market price two days earlier and double the price 12 months before. At almost the same time Wickes struck a $1.62 billion deal for Lear Siegler, but the takeover market had peaked and Wickes's investment bank Drexel Burnham Lambert was beginning to have problems of its own. The Lear deal was dropped by ''mutual consent'' in

December, but the C&A transaction was pushed through. It formally took effect in January 1987.

In April came a shocker. It was discovered that for nearly a decade C&A had produced $360 million in carpeting that didn't meet flammability tests, although Wickes noted that it thought the products were safe. In early May the head of the Floor Coverings division was removed. Then the news improved. Government-ordered tests indicated the problem might not be as severe as first feared. That summer Wickes established an $11.2 million after-tax reserve, which, as the *Wall Street Journal* noted, "surprised analysts who initially estimated liability in the hundreds of millions." For the year ended January 1988, C&A contributed $83 million in operating profits to the Wickes total.

Even so, Wickes, again burdened with heavy debt, never managed to gain momentum. Corporate-wide profits were down substantially for the year ending January 1988, and the company was in the red for the next two quarters, burdened by losses from units slated for disposal. In August 1988 Sigoloff tried a new tack. He proposed a buyout by his management team at $12 a Wickes share, well below what stockholders had been led to believe was the company's true value (the theoretical and admittedly unrealistic book value had been $25). Many Wall Street analysts reasoned that "Ming" really wanted to put the company "in play," hoping to attract higher bids by outsiders. But with Wickes having to admit that earnings would be below projections (a falloff in C&A results was given much of the blame), no other bids were generated, and Sigoloff himself was unable to get the needed financing.

In November, Wickes settled for a buyout offer by prominent Wall Street investors Blackstone Group and Wasserstein Perella at $11.25 a share through a newly formed company named WCI Holdings Corp. The transaction, through which WCI also inherited some $2 billion of Wickes debt, was completed in December 1988. Representatives of Blackstone and Wasserstein took over as the 58-year-old Sigoloff departed.

In contrast to the highly centralized, detailed control practiced by Sigoloff, the new group allowed considerable operational autonomy, stating, "We plan to establish a sense of ownership among the executives at each of the businesses." But by then the former senior executives at C&A were gone. Don McCullough retired at the end of 1987. He was succeeded as the unit's CEO by Alfred Crimmins, who had been president since 1984, but within five months Crimmins and a score of other executives also departed and Sigoloff had divisional C&A executives report directly to him.

In February 1989 the new owners brought in Thomas Hannah, an executive from the Milliken textile firm, to head C&A. In 1994 he was also named Chief Executive Officer of the restructured parent corporation.

WCI was determined to quickly implement a restructuring plan that slashed corporate overhead and focused on "businesses in which it enjoyed a competitive advantage"—which turned out to be primarily the old C&A activities. This was emphasized by the 1992 name change from WCI to Collins & Aikman and the move of corporate headquarters from Southern California to Charlotte, North Carolina, in the heartland of C&A operations. During the restructuring process, some 27 business units, which had contributed 73 percent of 1988 sales, were divested (some to groups headed by division management). When no buyers could be found, some units were closed, as was the case with the Builders Emporium chain. One unit from the Wickes Manufacturing side originally slated for divesting—Dura Convertible Systems, the largest producer of top systems for convertibles—won a last-minute reprieve and was shifted to the C&A automotive group.

In the new C&A, automotive products were once again the dominant segment, accounting for 59 percent of the $1.5 billion in sales for fiscal 1994, with at least some C&A product in 86 percent of all North American cars. Customers included not only the Big Three but also U.S. plants of foreign producers. C&A claimed to be the largest supplier of seat fabrics, floor mats, and convertible tops, and ranked number two in molded floor carpets and luggage compartment trim. C&A moved abroad with plants in Mexico and Austria, primarily to serve local Chrysler plants. The company's other market segments included interior furnishings (27 percent), in which the company ranked first in both flat-woven upholstery fabric and commercial-type carpets, and wallcoverings (14 percent) in which C&A also claimed first place with its Imperial label.

By July 1994 C&A was ready to go public again, with an offering of 15 million shares at $10.50 each, followed by listing on the New York Stock Exchange. However, Blackstone and Wasserstein Perella still retained 76 percent of outstanding stock. Proceeds of the offering permitted substantial lowering of outstanding debt and refinancing of much of the rest on more favorable terms. CEO Tom Hannah noted that C&A was prepared "to grow in businesses we know and understand. . . . We will invest in [our] existing businesses and [also] seek to expand into related product lines and in international markets to service our customers."

Principal Subsidiaries: Collins & Aikman Products Co.; Ack-Ti-Lining, Inc.; The Akro Corporation; Cepco Incorporated; Collins & Aikman Automotive International, Inc.; Collins & Aikman Floor Coverings, Inc.; Collins & Aikman Holdings Canada, Inc.; Collins & Aikman Products GmbH (Austria); Carcorp, Inc.; Collins & Aikman United Kingdom, Ltd.; Dura Convertible Systems, Inc.; Imperial Wallcoverings, Inc.; Collins & Aikman de Mexico, S.A. de C.V.; Greeff Fabrics, Inc.

Further Reading:

"At 150, Collins & Aikman Is Dedicated to Its Markets," *Textile World,* June 1993, pp. 38–47.

Collins & Aikman: A Continuing Story, Charlotte, North Carolina: Collins & Aikman Corp., 1995.

Sanger, Elizabeth, "Snappy Threads: Textile Maker Collins & Aikman Thrives," *Barron's,* July 7, 1986, pp. 35–36.

Sansweet, Stephen J., "Investment Firms Agree to Buy Wickes," *Wall Street Journal,* October 27, 1988.

"Textiles: Collins & Aikman's Specialty Fabrics Find More Market Areas," *Investor's Reader,* June 2, 1971, pp. 6–9.

"Textile Specialist Collins & Aikman," *Investor's Reader,* September 16, 1959, pp. 19–21.

—Henry R. Hecht

Comair Holdings Inc.

P.O. Box 75201
Cincinnati, Ohio 45275
U.S.A.
(513) 525-2550
Fax: (513) 525-3716

Public Company
Incorporated: 1977
Employees: 2,200
Sales: $297 million
Stock Exchanges: NASDAQ
SICs: 4512 Air Transportation, Scheduled; 6719 Holding Companies, Not Elsewhere Classified; 8249 Vocational Schools, Not Elsewhere Classified

Comair Holdings Inc. is the parent firm of subsidiary Comair Inc., a regional airline which makes up 96 percent of the company's business. Through a partnership with Delta Airlines, Comair Inc. provides connecting flights between 78 cities in 27 states. In addition to its U.S. flights, Comair provides service to the Bahamas and Canada. Comair Holdings also oversees the operations of several other subsidiaries, including Comair Aviation Academy Inc. (a flight training service), Comair Investment Co., Comair Services Inc. (a noncommercial charter service), and CVG Aviation Inc. (which owns and operates the airline's hub at the Cincinnati/Northern Kentucky International Airport).

Comair was established in Cincinnati in April 1977 by the father and son team of Raymond and David Mueller. A couple of years earlier, David Mueller had been working as a corporate pilot for a Cincinnati bank, when he first observed the inadequacy of flight service in the area. He and his father decided to found a company that would provide higher frequency flights between cities lacking efficient, reliable air service. Raymond Mueller was the company's first president and David Mueller, aged 25, was the executive vice-president.

From their base at the Greater Cincinnati International Airport, David Mueller also served as pilot, reservationist, and baggage clerk at the fledgling company. With a fleet of three Piper-Navajo aircraft, the company's first scheduled flights offered transportation between Cincinnati, Cleveland, Detroit, and Akron-Canton, all within a 500-mile radius. As the company grew, larger nine passenger Piper-Chieftain aircraft were added to the fleet.

The company had only been in business for two years when tragedy struck. In 1979, a Comair plane crashed at the Greater Cincinnati International Airport, killing eight people. The settlements and fines cost Comair approximately $500,000. Moreover, the company garnered considerable negative national publicity, as increasing numbers of Americans began to question the safety of the smaller planes used by regional airlines. In 1980, the company reported an earnings loss and faced what the younger Mueller would later refer to as "the company's darkest moment."

Describing the company's plans to overcome the setback, in a March 1984 interview in *The Cincinnati Post,* Mueller asserted that he and his father "decided to bet the family jewels" on their ability to turn Comair around, noting that they eventually were just "plain lucky." Specifically, Comair focused on keeping costs low, increasing the frequency of flights to selected cities, and providing comfortable seating in planes carrying 50 or fewer travellers. The strategy paid off. Comair not only overcame the crash, but also secured a solid place among regional air carriers in the Midwest. The company also benefited from the deregulation of the airline industry in the early 1980s. As the major airlines dropped unprofitable routes in the face of intensified competition, Comair and other regional fliers were quick to fill the gap in service.

In 1981, Comair began a major enhancement program, upgrading its fleet with more modern turbo-prop aircraft and doubling the size of its fleet with the addition of ten Brazilian-made Embraer Bandeirante twin-engine airplanes. The following year, Comair added SB3-30s to its fleet; with a capacity of 30 passengers, these were the first Comair aircraft to feature flight attendants, lavatories, and in-flight food and beverage service. With plans for a $1 million expansion of its home base, Comair was taken public in 1981, trading on the NASDAQ National Market System for the first time in July of that year.

With continued investments in new aircraft, Comair was able to increase the frequency of its flights. While most regional airlines were focusing on hooking up passengers with major airline flights, 70 percent of Comair's passengers (the vast majority of which were business people) were reaching their final destination on Comair. Although this meant that the smaller Comair was competing directly with industry giants, Comair had the advantage of offering more frequent flights.

Nevertheless, Comair recognized the value of linking its service to that of the major airlines and in December 1981 began its relationship with Delta Air Lines, becoming part of the Deltamatic computerized reservation system. Within three years, Delta and Comair had entered into a marketing agreement under which Comair became an official Delta Connection carrier. Comair's Cincinnati departures were thereafter coordinated to help customers catch Delta flights at other airports in 15 cities located in seven states. With the expansion of Delta Airline's Cincinnati operations and the growth of the Greater Cincinnati area, the two companies oversaw more than 100 daily departures from the Cincinnati Airport in 1984.

Comair's fleet at this time consisted of approximately 21 jet-prop aircraft, having been augmented by the September 1984 addition of a Saab-Fairchild 340 airliner, the first airplane designed specifically for regional service. Designed through a joint venture between manufacturers Fairchild Industries and Saab-Scania AB, this craft could travel at faster speeds and offered increased passenger comfort, and Comair had soon ordered 12 more of the same model. Such growth prompted the company to expand its facilities at the Cincinnati Airport with the construction of a $1.8 million corporate office building as well as a new hangar.

Remarking on the success of Comair's relationship with Delta in a December 1984 *Cincinnati Enquirer* article, Charles Curran, Comair's senior vice-president for marketing, noted that since becoming the Delta Connection, Comair had tripled its business. The following year found Comair reporting considerable increases in all areas used by the industry to measure an airline's vitality.

Indeed, in a 12-month period beginning in August 1984, the company increased the number of passengers it flew from the Cincinnati Airport by 200 percent, making Comair the airport's busiest airline, with more daily departures (93) than any other airline. Moreover, the company ranked second only to Delta at the airport for the number of passengers carried. During this time, the company served 23 markets from Cincinnati and flew as far north as Toronto, as far east as Richmond, Virginia, and as far south as Chattanooga, Tennessee. Comair ranked seventh in size among national regional carriers.

Because the airline now carried a wider variety of passengers seeking connections with Delta flights, rather than Cincinnati-based business travelers only, it began to broaden its scope in the mid-1980s. Tapping Delta's diverse customer base, Comair eventually expanded its services to include limited weekend flights, as well as flights to tourist destinations and smaller cities of as few as 150,000 people.

A series of unfortunate events, however, contributed to Comair's first quarterly loss as a public company in March 1986. One factor in this loss was a March 10th tornado that hit two Comair hangars, severely damaging four planes and the airline's offices. Although the loss was insured, business for March was disrupted while repairs were made; March was usually the company's busiest month of the quarter. In addition, in December 1985, the Federal Aviation Administration (FAA) grounded all ten of Comair's Saab-Fairchild 340s, citing problems with their twin turbo prop engines that could cause the planes to catch fire in icy weather. In order for the 340s to resume flying, they had to be fitted with a system for continuous engine ignition, and this was not completed at Comair until January 5. A final factor in the company's depressed earnings, one that industry analysts regarded as perhaps the most crucial, was that Comair had operated with excess seating capacity over the year. Preparing for a proposed expansion of Delta's flight service from Cincinnati, Comair had purchased several new planes and was having a hard time filling seats as it waited for Delta to complete the expansion project.

Delta's expanded hub did materialize the following year, and the two companies were soon overseeing over 125 Cincinnati departures daily. Moreover, the company's fortunes brightened in the second period of 1986, when the company was able to battle fierce fare competitions by reducing unit costs per available seat-mile to under 17 cents for the first time in history. Despite the early quarterly loss, Comair showed a profit for the 1986 fiscal year. Charles Curran reminded the public, in a September 1986 *Cincinnati Post* article, that Comair had "never had an unprofitable year since [its] inception on April 1, 1977."

In May 1986, Comair issued 1.85 million new shares of common stock to Delta, generating $16.9 million for Comair. Delta thus emerged with a 20 percent interest in the regional airline and a new seat on Comair's board of directors. Commenting on the transaction in the *Cincinnati Post,* a Delta official stated that the company had made the investment "to solidify and enhance the Delta Connection program in which the two companies have successfully engaged the past two years." Comair used the increase in capital to replace its lost hangars and office, and to continue upgrading its fleet of 37 aircraft. By July 1987, Comair was flying to 29 cities and had plans to add other locations at a rate of four or five per year.

During this time, Comair began flying to Florida at the request of Delta, which had recently become the official airline for Disney World in Orlando and needed the regional carrier to feed its airliners bound for larger cities. Comair joined with Delta to open hubs in Orlando and Ft. Lauderdale, and its success was immediate; the Florida market was profitable by the fifth month of operation. The number of daily Florida flights steadily increased until the figure rivaled that reported at the home base of Cincinnati.

Not surprisingly, David Mueller, who had replaced his father as company president, announced at the company's September 1988 annual shareholder meeting that Comair would be looking for "any and all aviation related business in which we can be successful." Preparing for acquisitions, Comair Inc. was soon reorganized into a subsidiary of a new Kentucky parent firm, Comair Holdings Inc. The regional airline, along with CVG Aviation, a jet charter service concern that provided services for non-commercial planes at the Cincinnati Airport, were both now subsidiaries of the new Comair Holdings. Eventual acquisitions included a flight training company, an investment company, and an aircraft leasing company.

Comair's flight service was expanded to include routes between Cincinnati and Chicago's Midway Airport as well as routes between Florida and the Bahamas. And, as Delta announced plans in 1990 for a $319 million expansion, Comair officials expected to almost double the company's operations over the next few years. Comair placed orders for more than 100 planes, 60 of which were Brazilian jets that would enable Comair to more than double its flying radius from its current hubs. Comair also set its sights on moving from its one-gate operation to a separate facility with a minimum of 25 to 30 gates.

In October 1990, David A. Siebenburgen succeeded David Mueller as president of Comair Holdings Inc. Siebenburgen remained in his previous capacity as chief operating officer as well, while Mueller retained his roles as chairman and chief executive officer. Over the next two years, Comair focused on adding flights both in frequency and to new locations. By 1991, Comair's aircraft fleet had grown to 75, including five new 340s for the Cincinnati market and 20 Embraer Brasilias for the Florida market. Naturally, the company's work force grew in accordance, surpassing 2,000 by the spring of 1990. In spring of 1992, Comair began seasonal flights to vacation sites such as Myrtle Beach.

In April 1992, American Airlines announced rate changes that would affect the entire airline industry. While American simplified and lowered their fares, other major airlines moved to match these rates, hoping that increased passenger volume would offset losses from lower fares. While some industry analysts warned that the regional airlines affiliated with major airlines would suffer from the fare war, Comair was nevertheless able to utilize cost containment strategies to come out ahead. In addition, one company official stated in a May 1992 *Cincinnati Business Courier* that "a major financial blow to Delta would not necessarily have an equal impact on Comair. Unlike other regional carriers that are totally dependent on a major airline, Comair connects only 45 to 50 percent of its business with Delta. And the break-even load factor—the percentage of seats that must be sold for a flight to break even—is 39 percent for Comair vs. about 70 percent for major carriers." Indeed, in the early 1990s, while the major airlines reported a collective loss of $10 billion, Comair was one of the few airlines to remain profitable. Comair's combination of good planning for future growth and a tight rein on costs had once again seen it through a rough time.

In the spring of 1993, Comair announced the acquisition of its first 50-passenger Canadair jet. Known as the world's quietest jet airplane, the Canadair had a top cruising speed of 530 miles per hour, and it's range was 1,500 miles—three times the range of Comair's then-current fleet and well beyond the typical two-hour flight limit of most regional airlines with turboprops. Comair ordered 20 of these jets and planned to enter markets in 36 new cities through 1995.

On September 3, 1994, Comair began leasing and operating from a new $50 million terminal built by the Greater Cincinnati International Airport. With 53 gates, the 170,000 square-foot facility enabled Comair to double its passenger capacity. Amenities in the terminal included automated teller machines, a combination newsstand and gift shop, and a food court, with McDonald's, PizzaHut Express, and other fast-food restaurants commonly found in larger airline terminals, but not as prevalent in a regional airline terminal. Another unique item was the "Kid's Corner," a space filled with large, bright plastic toys and a play yard for children.

Commuter airlines began a shaky few months in October 1994, when an American Eagle plane crashed in Indiana. As Federal regulators investigated the matter, suggesting that commuter airline restrictions and safety regulations were perhaps inadequate, the public lost some confidence in their commuter flights. In addition, Comair felt specific pressure from new cost-cutting measures implemented by the major airlines and new low fare competition. As a result, Comair's stock fell to $17 a share in December of that year, down from a high of $34.50 in late 1993.

Referring to the volatility of Comair's stock price, in an August 1994 article in the *Cincinnati Enquirer,* CEO Mueller suggested to shareholders that Comair was being unfairly associated with other commuter air link-ups. "While the carrier continues to make money, investors lump Comair together with other regional airlines—even those that haven't performed as well," he noted.

Comair sustained the bad publicity generated by the American Eagle crash; in 1994 the company reported record revenues of $297 million, posted record profits of $28.5 million and carried a record 2.7 million passengers over the course of the year. Moreover, Comair's expansion continued. In January 1995, the company reached an agreement with Canada's Bombardier Inc. to acquire five more Canadair Jet aircraft, with conditional orders and available options to purchase 35 more. Once a formal purchase agreement was completed, delivery was expected to continue through fiscal 1999. Fulfillment of the order would give Comair 70 Canadair jets, which would help the company continue to enhance its Cincinnati and Orlando hubs.

Principal Subsidiaries: Comair, Inc.; Comair Services, Inc.; Comair Aviation Academy, Inc.; CVG Aviation, Inc.; Comair Investment Company; Comair Aircraft, Inc.

Further Reading:

Agnew, Ronnie, "Comair Wants to Be Top Gun in Fla.," *The Cincinnati Enquirer,* October 24, 1988, p. F5.

Boyer, Mike, "Following a Year of Turbulence, Comair May See Brighter Skies," *The Cincinnati Enquirer,* January 5, 1987, p. E4.

——, "Profitable Comair Takes off on Major Expansion," *The Cincinnati Enquirer,* March 14, 1993, pp. H1, H10.

Bryant, Adam, "Commuter Airlines like Comair Expect Growth Despite Problems," *The New York Times,* December 7, 1994, p. C6.

Gleason, Mark, "Cost-Cutting Helps Comair Fly High Again," *Cincinnati Business Courier,* November 9, 1992, pp. 3, 39.

Harrington, Jeff, "Analysts Rate Comair as High Flier Even with Flat Earnings," *The Cincinnati Enquirer,* July 1, 1991, p. C6.

Heidenreich, Rob, "Comair Successful By Many Measures," *The Cincinnati Enquirer,* September 12, 1985, p. D9.

Kennedy, Rick, "Piloting Comair Higher," *The Cincinnati Post,* March 6, 1984, p. B1.

Lewis, Arnold, "The New Standard for Regional Terminals," *Business & Commercial Aviation,* January 1995, pp. C2–C6.

Marino, Jacqueline, "Comair's Business Soars," *The Cincinnati Enquirer,* June 26, 1994, pp. E1, E3.

Olson, Thomas, "Comair Takes Off into New Markets," *Cincinnati Business Courier,* June 18–24, 1990, pp. 1, 18.

Ott, James, "Cincinnati Expansion Project Key to Delta, Comair Future," *Aviation Week & Space Technology,* October 18, 1993, p. 51.

——, "RJ Fuels Growth in Comair's Traffic," *Aviation Week & Space Technology,* December 12, 1994, pp. 40, 42.

Prendergast, Jane, "Comair Gets New Home at Airport," *The Cincinnati Enquirer,* August 31, 1994, pp. B1, B4.

Rawe, Dick, "Comair Enjoys the Sun," *The Cincinnati Post,* February 11, 1988, p. C7.

——, "Comair Growing in New Ways," *The Cincinnati Post,* March 12, 1993, p. A5.

——, "Stock Deal, Links with Delta Air to Thrust Comair to New Heights," *The Cincinnati Post,* May 30, 1986, p. A7.

Rhodes, Gary, "Comair Unveils New Jet," *The Cincinnati Post,* May 14, 1993, p. C10.

Schaber, Greg, "For Comair, Rate Game Means Wait Game," *Cincinnati Business Courier,* May 11–17, 1992, pp. 1, 8.

Turner, Patrick, "The Public File: Comair Holdings, Inc.," *The Business Record,* August 15, 1994, p. 10.

Weathers, William A., "Comair to Build $1.8 Million Office at Airport," *The Cincinnati Enquirer,* December 22, 1984, p. B5.

—Jennifer Voskuhl Canipe

Computerland Corp.

200 Continental Blvd.
El Segundo, California 90245
U.S.A.
(510) 734-4000
Fax: (510) 734-4802

Wholly Owned Subsidiary of Merisel, Inc.
Incorporated: 1976
Employees: 8,000
Sales: $1.1 billion
SICs: 5734 Computer & Software Stores; 7378 Computer Maintenance & Repair

ComputerLand Corp., a wholly owned subsidiary of Merisel, Inc. is a leading retailer of computer systems and related products. The company distributes computer products from major microcomputer manufacturers to a network of approximately 750 independently owned computer outlets in the United States. The principal computer manufacturers, including IBM, Apple, Compaq, Hewlett-Packard, and others, have historically required retailers to purchase their products from selected affiliated distributors such as ComputerLand rather than from wholesalers. Despite a troubled history, ComputerLand currently operates as a profitable subsidiary of Merisel.

Computerland was created in 1976 just as the market for personal computers was beginning to take off. The company's founder, William H. Millard, was a rags-to-riches entrepreneur. Millard was raised in Oakland, California, the oldest of six children from a blue-collar family. While growing up, Millard delivered newspapers until he was a high school senior. He also worked as a drugstore clerk and held several summer jobs to earn additional money for his family. At parochial school, he developed an interest in science, technology, and mathematics. Upon graduating from high school, Millard held several odd jobs, including a Southern Pacific switchman, an assembly line worker, a truck driver, and a welder's helper. He attended the University of San Francisco but a lack of funds caused him to drop out after three semesters. He then became a loan officer for a finance company in Oakland, eventually becoming branch manager.

In 1958, Millard moved into computer operations after the finance company established an electronic data-processing facility in Los Angeles to facilitate transactions from branch offices across the country. Millard's first experience with a computer was the Univac I, a huge piece of machinery the size of a room and with a tangled array of vacuum tubes and wires that would eventually be replaced by the silicon chip. Millard's subsequent experience as programmer, systems analyst, and supervisor of data processing earned him jobs throughout the 1960s overseeing computerization projects for county governments in Oakland and San Francisco. He also briefly worked as an IBM salesman.

Millard took advantage of this experience in 1969, forming a company called Systems Dynamics to sell custom software to businesses using IBM computers. Unfortunately, the company failed after three years leaving Millard bankrupt and $25,000 in debt. Another bank loan enabled him to form a software consulting business, Information Management Science Associates, Inc., or IMS. During this time, Millard began experimenting with the relatively new microprocessor technology, and in 1975 he invented one of the first personal computers, the IMSAI 8080. To market the computer, Millard, his wife, and their three children ran a rudimentary mail order business from their kitchen. This procedure included hand sorting the microprocessor parts from muffin tins to plastic bags and, with assembly and soldering instructions, selling them to hobbyists for $399. The price was later raised to $499.

In 1976, when personal computers began to appear in stores, IMS attempted to produce and sell the IMSAI 8080 as a finished product. For a brief period, the IMSAI 8080 stood at the forefront of the PC revolution, but problems with production and quality ultimately doomed the venture. Similar homemade products—including the Apple computer, made by Steve Jobs and Stephen Wozniak out of a garage—far surpassed IMS in innovation and quality. In 1979, after amassing debts totalling $1.9 million, the IMSAI manufacturing subsidiary of the parent firm IMS Associates went bankrupt. Millard's debt's included a $250,000 promissory note owed to the Marriner venture capital group, which had provided funds to keep the 8080 computer afloat.

Despite IMSAI's collapse, Millard still saw an opportunity to sell computers manufactured by others. In September 1976, he formed Computer Shack with $10,000. The company rapidly became a profitable franchise chain, selling personal computers to hobbyists and small businesses. A legal challenge from Tandy, owner of Radio Shack, compelled Millard to change the company's name to Computerland. Millard aggressively set up franchises in malls and downtown areas throughout the country. As a result, the company went from 24 stores and $1.5 million in sales in 1977 to 147 stores and $75 million in sales in 1980. Computerland's profits exploded after IBM introduced their PC in the early 1980s and the corporate giant decided to sell the product solely through IBM stores, Sears Business Systems Centers, and Computerland. Company sales skyrocketed from $151 million in 1981 to $1.4 billion in 1984, making ComputerLand the world's largest chain of retail stores for computers. By 1985, the company operated more than 820 outlets in 24 countries, including China.

Although Millard had achieved millionaire status with ComputerLand, his good fortune quickly dissolved. One cause was a long running legal dispute over a promissory note he signed in

1976 when his computer firm IMSAI was having financial troubles. The note involved a $250,000 debt to the Marriner venture capital group, a small firm based in Lynnfield, Massachusetts, which had rescued Millard's foundering company. Millard made the scheduled interest payments, planning to pay off the promissory note in full by the expiration date in May 1981. The note was originally convertible solely into shares of IMS stock. But after Millard began diverting capital from the failing IMSAI to establish ComputerLand, the Marriner Group contended that the note should also be convertible into shares of the new company, as well as those of Millard's other holdings. Millard eventually signed an agreement to this effect.

An acrimonious court battle erupted after the Marriner Group sold the note to a third party, John Martin-Musumeci of Micro/Vest, an investment partnership. A former employee of Millard's, Martin-Musumeci had sold ComputerLand franchises before being fired in May 1977. In December 1980, he privately sold his 1.05 percent stake in ComputerLand to Bruno Andrighetto, a Bay Area produce magnate and stock investor who had an interest in the computer industry. Martin-Musumeci also conferred with Andrighetto on the Marriner note and the potential rewards of its conversion rights. The two formed Micro/Vest and brought in another former IMS associate, Philip L. Reed III, who had once been a close friend of the Millard family and who had left IMSAI before it folded. The partners purchased Millard's $250,000 note from Mariner for $300,000 plus the prospect of another $100,000 contingent on its conversion into 20 percent of ComputerLand's equity. Micro/Vest's claim for 20 percent of the shares ignited a contentious legal fight amid charges and countercharges of betrayal, fraud, and violations of the security laws. Millard's accusations of security violations stemmed from Micro/Vest selling speculative shares in the note to dozens of outsiders based on the outcome of the suit. For its part, Micro/Vest stated that such a move was necessary to help raise the $1.3 million to pay for the years of litigation.

Finally, on March 11, 1985, a California Superior Court jury handed Millard a serious defeat, ruling that the promissory note was convertible into 20 percent of ComputerLand stock and requiring Millard to transfer 20 percent of his other holdings to Micro/Vest as well. The court also hit Millard and IMS, his holding company, with $115 million in punitive damages and ordered ComputerLand to pay another $10 million as punishment for Millard's delaying court tactics. Millard could appeal by posting a $238 million bond, 10 percent of that in cash. However, the banks severed ComputerLand's credit line after Millard failed to raise the necessary funds and announced that he might file for Chapter 11 bankruptcy protection.

In addition to the litigation matter with Micro/Vest, many of ComputerLand's franchises openly rebelled against Millard's autocratic management style. What originally began as Millard's refusal to take the company public, soon involved charges that the owner extracted severely high royalty fees. In 1984, most of the franchises' competitors were publicly owned chains. Although growing at a robust 30 percent a year, the franchises feared losing out to competitors. The dealers demanded access to expansion capital to fuel growth, but Millard's franchise agreement strictly prohibited them from going public and therefore kept them comparatively small, fragmented, and easy to control. Millard feared that to take ComputerLand public would cause consolidation among his franchises as some bought out or acquired others, resulting in the domination of a few large dealers. This possibility would not only weaken his control over the company, but it would also destroy what Millard considered to be ComputerLand's key to success—individual entrepreneurs serving a local community. The agreement also provided Millard with the option of raising public capital to open his own ComputerLand stores which could compete with his franchises. This prospect, coupled with fierce competition from other computer retailers including Entre and BusinessLand, aroused considerable concern among the ComputerLand dealers.

To assuage dealer concerns and still maintain control, Millard tried to engineer a complicated compromise. He planned to create a subsidiary, ComputerLand Stores Inc. (CSI), which would trade shares with the franchises before turning public. Under this arrangement, CSI would issue common stock to the franchises for a percentage of their stores. The franchises would also give CSI participating preferred stock, paying a dividend based on gross sales. Following the transaction, Millard planned to take CSI public leaving him firmly in control. However, the dealers vetoed his proposal and continued their demands for expansion capital.

By 1985, intense competition and sagging sales were causing hard times for computer retailers, a development which exacerbated the open revolt against Millard. A number of dealers, especially those on the verge of bankruptcy, demanded relief from Millard's royalty and advertising fees, which ranged from 5 percent to 8 percent of their monthly income. Franchises also claimed that Millard was failing to honor pledges to sell them computers at cost. When Millard ignored their pleas, a group of 350 franchises threatened to file suit. Already besieged by the Micro/Vest litigation, Millard settled with the franchises and stepped down as head of ComputerLand. He and his family still remained the company's major stockholders, however, owning some 96 percent of the shares.

After his ouster, Millard invited his former partner, Edward E. Faber, to take over as chairman of the company. A former marketing manager for IBM, Faber had helped Millard found and develop the ComputerLand chain in 1976, serving as company president until 1983. Importantly, Faber's work over the years with the hundreds of ComputerLand franchises had earned him their respect and trust. Among his most important changes, Faber shifted the company's legal troubles from ComputerLand to the Millard family. He also negotiated a deal with Micro/Vest to have ComputerLand dropped from the suit, which Millard was appealing, in return for removing the Millard family from the management of the company. As a result, the stock and voting rights became subject to an extraordinary arrangement. While the Millard family held 96 percent of the company's shares, they now had no voting rights. Faber himself controlled 99 percent of the voting rights with just 3 percent of ComputerLand's stock. In the Micro/Vest settlement, Faber also agreed to expand the board to include two ComputerLand franchises and to take the company public.

In 1987, following Faber's sweeping changes, Millard exiled himself to the tax haven of Saipan, the capital of the Northern

Mariana islands, and sold his remaining 52 percent stake in the company for $80 million. The principle buyers were E. M. Warburg Pincus & Co. and William Y. Tauscher, a takeover specialist. Tauscher's diverse portfolio included major holdings in CoastAmerica Corp., a hardware store chain run by close friend Richard H. Bard, and in Vons Cos., a Southern California supermarket chain. He also headed FoxMeyer Corp., the wholesale drug distributor he developed and sold to National Intergroup, Inc. At the age of 38, Tauscher saw a great opportunity in ComputerLand and joined with Bard and the investment bank E. M. Warburg Pincus & Co. to buy a controlling stake in the company. The partners planned to take the company public as quickly as possible to double the value of their shares.

This scheme took a peculiar turn in 1988 when Wall Street showed little interest in ComputerLand's first public offering. Then the company's veteran president and chief executive officer, Kenneth R. Waters, unexpectedly quit over ComputerLand's continued turmoil. Tauscher, who had not planned on directly managing the firm, took over as chief executive officer. At the time, the PC business had reached new heights in fierce competition. Mail-order sellers and discounters were taking an enormous share of the market, hitting the retailers especially hard. ComputerLand lost money in both 1987 and 1989. Further, its chain of 609 stores in 1985 had shrunk to 481 three years later. By this time, the company's retail sales were only a small percentage of the total business, the bulk instead coming from sales to corporations. But even in this lucrative market sales began to spiral downward and profit margins decreased.

In an effort to prevent further losses for ComputerLand, Tauscher implemented an aggressive campaign to cut costs and consolidate stores. As part of this initiative, he laid off 40 of 600 staff, combined two offices into a new building in Pleasanton, California, and forced financially weak stores to merge or be sold to stronger operations. Tauscher also hired Edward R. Anderson away from rival computer retailer Computer Factory, Inc. to serve as his new chief operating officer. At the same time, Tauscher continued to shift the core business away from the crowded middle retail market to focus on small business customers. He also bought many of ComputerLand's big-city franchises catering to large corporate customers. To win more corporate clients, he improved the company's service and support network and set up a direct electronic link which allowed customers to shop by computer. In addition to his emphasis on large markets, Tauscher also retained franchises in smaller cities to handle the low end of the retail market.

By 1991, Tauscher's survival strategy began to pay off. While rival BusinessLand sank to near bankruptcy before being acquired by JWP Inc., and Compucom Systems Inc., the nation's seventh largest computer seller, left the retail business altogether, ComputerLand embarked on greater expansion. In June 1991, the company acquired Nynex's chain of 79 computer stores, including its sales force and sophisticated service and support center. In the fall, Tauscher opened a trial superstore in Atlanta called ComputerLand Express, with the aim of opening superstores nationwide. ComputerLand's major competitors arose primarily from mergers and acquisitions, including JWP's purchase of BusinessLand; Intelligent Electronics's buyout of the Bizmark superstores; Valcom's merger with Inacomp Computer Centers, resulting in Inacom; and Compucom's acquisition of the Computer Factory, primarily to move into corporate sales. To confront increasing cost competition, Tauscher began relying primarily on producers of low price IBM-compatible clones, such as AST Research and NEC.

Despite Tauscher's increasingly successful business strategy, ComputerLand faced renewed anger from franchises over having to compete with company-owned stores stemming from the Nynex acquisition. The most bitter case involved dealer D&W Computer stores of Florida, which sued ComputerLand contending that it was being forced out of business. In November 1991, Tauscher told the *New York Times* that most of the territorial disputes with the franchises were already resolved.

By 1994, Tauscher had largely succeeded in repositioning ComputerLand, shedding its retail operations to focus on supplying system integration and services to Fortune 1000 companies. The ComputerLand name and all franchise holdings were sold to Merisel, Inc., the largest publicly held wholesaler distributor of microcomputer hardware and software products. Tauscher renamed his company Vanstar following the sale of ComputerLand for approximately $80 million in cash. With the ComputerLand acquisition, completed on January 31, 1994, Merisel became the industry's leading retailer of computer systems and related products. Through ComputerLand, Merisel now distributes computer systems to about 750 independently owned product resellers comprising both ComputerLand franchisees and resellers purchasing under the ComputerLand Business' Datago Program. The latter customers consist of independent dealers and value-added resellers who purchase products from ComputerLand on a cost-plus basis but without licensing the ComputerLand name. In addition to the ComputerLand purchase, Merisel bought all of ComputerLand's franchise and third-party reseller agreements, as well as all U.S. rights to the ComputerLand trademarks, trade names, service marks, copyrights, patents, and logos.

Further Reading:

Brody, Michael, "ComputerLand's Suddenly Poorer Boss," *Fortune*, April 15, 1985.

Clark, Tim, "Fresh Start for Vanstar," *Business Marketing*, April 1994.

Hafner, Katherine M., "Ed Faber's Victorious Return to ComputerLand," *Business Week*, April 7, 1986.

Littman, Jonathan, "A Script Worthy of Hemingway," *Forbes*, August 6, 1990.

Markoff, John, "ComputerLand's Survival Strategy," *The New York Times*, November 13, 1991.

Rudolph, Barbara, "All in the Family," *Time*, October 14, 1985.

Shao, Maria, "How a Quick Fix Backfired at ComputerLand," *Business Week*, October 10, 1988.

Weigner, Kathleen K., "Bill Millard's Private War," *Forbes*, July 2, 1984.

——, "The Beleaguered Billionaire," *Forbes*, August 26, 1985.

—Bruce Montgomery

The Condé Nast Publications Inc.

350 Madison Avenue
New York, New York 10017
U.S.A
(212) 880-8800
Fax: (212) 880-8086

Wholly Owned Subsidiary of S. I. Newhouse, Inc.
Incorporated: 1922
Employees: 2,000
Sales: $330 million (estimated)
SICs: 2721 Periodicals Publishing & Printing

The Condé Nast Publications Inc. (CNP) is one of the world's foremost publishers of specialized magazines, spanning topics as diverse as high fashion, home decoration, travel, sports, literature, social life and commentary, gourmet cuisine, architecture, and popular culture. Building on the success of his flagship *Vogue* magazine, which he bought in 1909, founder Condé Nast (1873–1942) established a virtual magazine empire that helped shape the opinions and tastes of readers around the globe. By the mid-1990s, the company boasted more than thirteen high-profile publications, including *Vogue, House & Garden, Architectural Digest, Glamour, Mademoiselle, Bride's, Self, Gentlemen's Quarterly, Vanity Fair, Gourmet, Bon Appétit, Condé Nast's Traveler, Details, Allure,* and *Street and Smith's Sports Group,* and planned to introduce several online publications.

The energy that allowed Condé Nast to launch such a wide variety of magazines also helped him pioneer the magazine industry in general. He combined innovative publishing theories with a flair for nurturing both readers and advertisers. Condé Nast's most enduring contribution to the publishing industry was his development of the concept of specialized, or "class," publications directed at particular groups of people with common interests. Through careful marketing and selective editorial management, such publications shunned attempts to gain bulk readership in favor of attracting select, and ultimately more devoted, readers of a given persuasion or social profile. As Condé Nast pointed out in his 1913 essay "Class Publications," the population of the United States—90 million at the time—"divides not only along the lines of wealth, education, and refinement, but classifies itself even more strongly along lines of interest. . . . A 'class' publication is nothing more nor less than a publication that looks for its circulation *only* to those having in common a certain characteristic marked enough to group them into a class."

For Condé Nast, a specialized publication required absolute determination of purpose. "It takes the farsightedness and *the utmost fixity of purpose,*" he continued in his landmark essay, "to prevent any really good class publication from growing into a general magazine and thereby diluting its circulation enough to defeat its own ends." As the science of marketing research advanced—aided by improvements in survey techniques and communication technology—and allowed publishers to identify and target special-interest groups, Condé Nast's unconventional recipe became the undisputed norm in magazine publishing.

The success of Condé Nast's fashion-driven publications was mirrored—and partly secured—by the charm and polish of the man himself. His family, of mixed French and German stock, had settled for several generations in the United States. Condé Nast was strongly influenced by his aristocratic French mother, who infused him with the calculated manners and social restraint of high social circles. His father lived mostly abroad and died young, leaving much less, if any, influence on his son. As an adult, Condé Nast was noted for his urbane persona. He was always exquisitely groomed and well-mannered and seemed in total command of his faculties. Allegedly, he never raised his voice or used angry words. "If situations became too fraught, Condé would become surprisingly difficult to find," according to Madge Garland, fashion editor of *Vogue* in the 1930s, in a 1982 book review for *Financial Times.*

Such honorable charm was at odds with some of Nast's other reputed trademarks, including manipulative or discriminatory treatment of his staff and an ostentatious lifestyle. Though in debt millions of dollars, for example, he maintained a 30-room apartment and held stylish parties for the rich and famous, while at the same time he cut staff salaries and positions. Still, Condé Nast's determination to produce near-perfect magazines and to capitalize on the money-making potential of fashion remained constant. "If one had to choose one individual who has had more influence than any other on the way women in the Western world dress and arrange their homes, it would be hard to find a rival to Condé Nast," Madge Garland declared in the *Financial Times.*

Vogue magazine served as the early testing ground for Condé Nast's "class publication" theories and his business savvy. *Vogue* was first published in 1892 as a weekly journal of society and fashion news interspersed with verse and lightly humorous drawings. Condé Nast bought the magazine in 1909 with the intention of upgrading it, and he became its active owner-manager. He stuck to his "fixity of purpose" doctrine in order to secure the magazine's "pure class" standing. Fiction, for example, was not welcome in early *Vogue,* even though Condé Nast admitted that it would help maintain a larger circulation. "That those who became readers of *Vogue* because of its news of the so-called 'smart' world would be equally interested in the fashions and in all the rest of *Vogue*'s contents, we were fairly certain; but that all those who might be attracted to *Vogue* through fiction would be *seriously* interested in the rest of its contents or in its advertisements, we had every reason to doubt,'' he explained in ''Class Publications.'' By extension, Condé Nast argued that advertisers were also best served by his strategy: advertisements could be tailored to the specific readership of a ''class publication'' rather than thrown out to the more random, quantity-driven readership of general publications.

Adding to the success of his *Vogue* acquisition, Condé Nast bought an interest in *House & Garden* in 1911 and four years later took it over completely. Nast transformed the magazine from an architectural journal into an interior-design authority. In 1914, Condé Nast introduced *Vanity Fair,* a magazine that quickly set publishing standards in arts, politics, sports, and society. Under the editorship of Frank Crowninshield, *Vanity Fair* gained a reputation as a sophisticated and glamorous magazine infused with a lighthearted and often acerbic wit. In 1936, the magazine was merged with *Vogue*—an idea that ''stank,'' Crowninshield reportedly told Condé Nast—only to re-emerge on its own in 1983.

While publications like *Vanity Fair* worked to broaden the publisher's readership at home, Condé Nast was using the popularity of *Vogue* to lay the groundwork for overseas business. With the introduction of British *Vogue* in 1916, Nast became the first person to publish international editions of magazines. A French company was established a few years later, followed by the Italian *Vogue* in the early 1960s. By the 1990s, CNP's foreign operations included publishing subsidiaries in England, France, Italy, Germany, Australia, and Spain, with licensee arrangements in Mexico, Brazil, and Japan.

Nast also took steps to ensure quality production of his growing family of magazines. In 1921, he bought a small interest in the Arbor Press of Greenwich, Connecticut. That facility eventually became The Condé Nast Press, and was expanded and completely modernized to become one of the finest magazine manufacturing plants in the country. The press closed in 1964, to make way for more centrally located sites capable of producing higher volume.

Despite the rigors of the Depression, CNP forged ahead with innovations in design and quality in the 1930s. Color photographs appeared within the pages of *Vogue, Vanity Fair,* and *House & Garden,* and in 1932 the first color photograph appeared on the cover of Vogue. To crown these advances, Nast introduced *Glamour* magazine in 1939, the last publication that he would personally develop in the CNP collection. By the 1990s, *Glamour* had become the largest-selling fashion/beauty/lifestyle magazine in the world. It also gained its share of critical recognition, winning the National Magazine Award for General Excellence in 1981 and 1992, among other distinctions. Few other women's magazines matched its scope, from politics to personal issues.

The year 1959 marked a threshold in CNP's growth and diversification, as S. I. Newhouse, the renowned newspaper and media giant, purchased a controlling interest in the company and instituted a changing of the guard in senior administrative positions. With the death of S. I. Newhouse, Sr. in 1979, management of the privately held empire, Advance Publications Inc., was passed on to his two sons. S. I. Newhouse, Jr. (known as ''Si'') ran the magazine and book operations, while Donald Newhouse took charge of the newspaper and cable television operations. The magazines belonged either to Condé Nast Publications, Inc. or to Advance Magazine Publisher Inc., which published the *New Yorker* and the Sunday newspaper supplement *Parade.* The books fell under Random House Inc. and its subsidiaries.

While Si's abrupt dismissals of numerous magazine editors won him a fearsome reputation within the industry, he later became known for his relaxed style. By 1992, this intensely private man—who was the boss, brains, and banker of CNP—was ''so unprepossessing in appearance that a new executive once mistook him for the office carpenter . . . wearing a sweater, no tie and in all probability no shoes,'' according to Deirdre Carmody of the *New York Times.*

The Newhouse leadership of CNP initiated a period marked by acquisitions and overhauls of existing publications, rather than the founding of new publications, in the highly competitive—and uncertain—publishing industry. The same year that S. I. Newhouse acquired CNP, for example, Condé Nast acquired Street & Smith Publications, Inc., which included titles such as *Mademoiselle* and the Street & Smith's sports annuals (*College Football, Pro Football, Baseball, Pro and College/Prep Basketball*).

Two decades later, in 1979, that pattern of Newhouse-style acquisitions continued, as the publisher purchased *Gentlemen's Quarterly* (*GQ*) from Esquire Inc. Founded in 1928 as a fashion booklet distributed in men's clothing stores, that magazine grew into a preeminent source for probing magazine journalism, fiction, essays, and eclectic coverage of subjects from food to financial planning for the 25-to-39-year-old male audience.

That same year, CNP revisited its old ways by introducing *Self* magazine, the first publication started from scratch since 1939. *Self* became a popular sourcebook for women who ''are reinventing almost every aspect of their lives from a health-aware, issue-oriented point of view,'' according to a CNP brochure. Offering information-packed, fast-read journalism to busy women, *Self*'s circulation was no less fast-paced: within 30 months of its launch, the magazine reached over one million readers.

From the early 1980s to the 1990s, CNP continued to control an impressive range of magazines, reinforcing its image as a diverse, top-notch publisher. In 1982, the company added to its historical prestige by buying the *Tatler,* a British monthly magazine devoted to social news, the arts, features, and fashion. (CNP had no plans to issue the magazine in the United States.) The first *Tatler* was produced in 1709 by the essayist Richard Steele, who distributed issues free in coffee houses. Though that venture closed down within two years, intermittent publishers resumed Steele's enterprise until a monthly *Tatler* finally took hold in 1901.

Less than a year after taking on the impressive history of Steele's *Tatler,* CNP made a comparable move in the United States by reviving *Vanity Fair* in March 1983. That venerable magazine had been merged with *Vogue* since 1936. Though the undertaking was widely criticized, CNP invested roughly $10 million toward strengthening the magazine editorially and getting it off to a powerful new start. Building on Cleveland Amory's 1960 declaration that *Vanity Fair* had been ''America's most memorable magazine,'' CNP packed the lavish first re-issue with an entire short novel by Gabriel Garcia Marquez, winner of the 1982 Nobel Prize for Literature. Its 290 glossy pages also included lively articles by the likes of Gore Vidal reporting from the Gobi Desert, paleontologist Stephen Jay Gould speculating on why .400 hitters have disappeared from baseball, and other gems. That same year, CNP also acquired *Gourmet* magazine, the oldest and second-largest of the four major American epicurean magazines.

CNP's appetite for growth was hardly sated with the acquisition of *Gourmet,* as the company continued to launch new, premium magazines in the late 1980s. In September 1987, for example, Condé Nast's *Traveler,* a monthly travel magazine for the affluent, incurred an introductory cost of approximately $40 million. *Traveler* built on the foundation—but went far beyond the scope—of Citicorp's *Signature.* Harold Evans, *Traveler*'s editor-in-chief, told *Advertising Age* that CNP would bring to *Signature* ''real journalists'' from newspapers like the *New York Times.* Additionally, *Traveler* joined the Condé Nast Ltd. advertising sales package, which also included *Gourmet* and *House & Garden.*

Travel was not the only domain into which CNP ventured in the late 1980s. In January 1988, the publisher acquired *Details* magazine, an irreverent chronicle of Manhattan's downtown art, fashion, and club scene, and transformed it into a young men's fashion and lifestyle magazine for the 1990s. Later that year, CNP also acquired *Woman* magazine, an eight-year-old bimonthly with a circulation of 525,000, from Harris Publications. Less sophisticated than CNP's other women's magazines, the new magazine would steer into a previously uncharted niche market. And even as the magazine publishing industry continued to reel from economic malaise, CNP started yet another glossy spread, *Allure* magazine, in March 1991. Devoted entirely to beauty, *Allure* jumped from a starting circulation of 200,000 to reach 625,000 before its second anniversary, making it one of the fastest-growing magazines of its time. With its unusual combination of high fashion and piquant journalism, *Allure* was nominated for a National Magazine Award in its first year.

In addition to the editorial quality of its publications, CNP maintained its place atop the magazine publishing industry through shrewd marketing strategies. Building upon Condé Nast's theories of ''class'' publications, the company traditionally offered few, if any, cut rates for advertisers. The company believed that its magazines were put together in such a way that little advertising waste was accrued. Appropriate ads could be targeted to the magazines' select readerships, so ad discounts were not only unnecessary, but counterproductive. Describing the ''circulation man'' of a ''class publication'' in his famous essay, Nast wrote: ''If allowed to offer premiums at all, he must see that they are very closely akin to the editorial nature of the publication; if he gets into clubbing offers, he must choose his company with the greatest care; he must not offer commissions that will tempt magazine agencies to force his circulation; he must not on any account cut his rates.''

As late as 1990, CNP upheld its rule of never cutting rates. In 1991, the company began offering advertising buying combinations that provided added value to advertisers, such as the Package of Women and the Ltd. Package. ''With an overall marketing partnership they're doing something more creative, it makes doing business with them easier for us, and they can increase business without cutting rates,'' George Hayes, director of the Comcord Group at McCann-Erickson, explained in *Mediaweek.*

CNP's policy was not without its controversies, however. In fact, CNP engaged in a highly visible conflict with General Motors Corp. regarding advertising rates in late 1989. GM began a boycott of CNP magazines when the publisher refused to restructure its rates at a discount as demanded by GM. With an advertising budget amounting to approximately $266.2 million for magazines alone, the standoff represented a substantial amount of money for both parties. In March 1993, however, CNP announced its Condé Nast Select package, which set new discounts for multi-title and multi-package buys. Though Phil Guarascio, GM's general manager of marketing and advertising, allegedly wanted special treatment beyond that package, the companies resumed negotiations. After a five-year boycott of CNP, GM returned to the books in August 1994 with fall advertising pages and planned an extensive schedule for 1995. *Mediaweek* stated that CNP would receive some $20 million in advertising business from the car company.

Also in 1994, CNP overcame its long-standing aversion to such deals and launched four custom publishing projects for outside clients, with plans to develop even more revenue-producing projects. Custom publishing was part of a big push, initiated by CNP president Steven T. Florio, to develop a new corporate franchise for the privately held company, including event marketing, group sales, and minority investment in magazines. Such a strategy marked a notable reversal of the publisher's traditional adherence to ''the sanctity of its core products,'' according to Melanie Warner of *Inside Media.*

Custom publishing was one of numerous initiatives at CNP to secure its image, circulation, and ad revenue. In June 1994, for example, the company started an aggressive $1 million-plus corporate image TV campaign—followed by trade and consumer print ads—to promote its stable of glossy monthlies. Berlin, Wright & Cameron produced the 60-second spot that broke during the NBA finals. ''It will attempt to position Condé Nast as the quality publisher in America,'' Florio told *Advertising Age.* ''The whole theme is the quality of our content, and with all the noise about the information superhighway and the technology age, ultimately what it all comes down to is content.''

The company invested in other marketing and distribution solutions, as well. As early as 1990, CNP and Time Distribution Services (TDS) reached an agreement whereby TDS provided retail sales and merchandising services for a number of Condé Nast magazines. In 1992, CNP also collaborated with Spiegel, Inc., the retail giant, to develop automatic subscription renewals, by which a subscription is automatically renewed each year until the subscriber cancels. The process was intended to increase circulation profits by reducing expensive renewal and new-subscriber acquisition costs. Theoretically, it also permitted higher subscription prices by deferring payment to consumers' credit cards.

In 1995, CNP began prepping the market for new products, including its 1996 relaunch of the company's original title, *House & Garden,* which would be formally flagged as *Condé Nast's House & Garden.* Indeed, the company had already laid the groundwork for continued growth with several impressive magazine acquisitions and launches in the early 1990s. In March 1993, for example, CNP acquired Knapp Communications, which published *Architectural Digest* and *Bon Appétit. Architectural Digest* boasted sumptuous spreads on the homes of the rich and famous and was the number one magazine in terms of advertising pages in the home-decoration field. *Bon Appétit*'s circulation of 1.2 million placed it in the top ranks of food magazines.

In addition, with its acquisition of the sports-oriented Street & Smith's subsidiary, in 1995 CNP planned to produce a 610,000-circulation annual aimed at high school basketball players, followed by a similar publication aimed at football players. In January 1994, CNP reacted to the "information highway" hype and bought a 15 percent interest in *Wired,* the self-anointed "house organ of the digital revolution." CNP chairman S. I. Newhouse hoped to use *Wired* as a "media lab" to explore possibilities in new technologies and help evaluate the future of magazines.

The results of that exploration began to manifest themselves in April 1995, when Advance Publications (Condé Nast's parent) and seven other major newspaper publishers formed a new company to create a national network of local on-line newspapers and periodicals. The new company, New Century Network, would help the member publishers provide local on-line services to their communities. The alliance was yet another step in Condé Nast's search for technological solutions in the growing information age.

As CNP publications joined the digital age, the legendary Condé Nast culture—of high-brow literati and urbane tea-sippers—was undergoing changes of its own. Despite some fundamental changes in character, CNP maintained its reputation as a "turbulent glamorland of magazines," according to Paul D. Colford *Newsday.* Colford went on to describe a "Madison Avenue kingdom where princes and princesses (editors and publishers) come and go at the bidding of the impetuous king (chairman), S. I. (Si) Newhouse Jr." And Veronique Vienne, writing in the *Columbia Journalism Review,* added: "It is change for the sake of change. Condé Nast management philosophy mirrors the industry it serves, the world of fashion where the only certainty is the knowledge that the present fad will soon be outmoded."

Into the 1990s, however, CNP's game of managerial musical chairs became more serious, as several key directors stepped down from their long-held thrones. At the top of the hierarchy sat Alexander Liberman, who for more than fifty years had been the creative force—as editorial director—behind the entire group of magazines. "Liberman knows how to underplay stylishness for the benefit of style and emphasize immediacy rather than fads," Vienne noted.

In April 1994, the 81-year-old Liberman was succeeded by 36-year-old James Truman, former editor of *Details* magazine, giving the media cause for lively speculation. "Painter, sculptor, pragmatist, the Russian-born Liberman was the job.... Writer, wit, and Brit, now Truman is the job," quipped the *Los Angeles Times.* Media consensus was that Truman would help Newhouse appeal to the youth market and carry the magazines—along with new publications—into the information age. Describing his job in the *Los Angeles Times,* Truman said "it's kind of like a magazine doctor, but in the broader sense, you know, Alex made it more than that and I would like to make it more than that."

New, young blood also found its way into the other key CNP post, as Steven T. Florio was named president effective June 1, 1994. Florio—who had served nine years as president and six years as CEO of the *New Yorker*—succeeded Bernard Leser, 68, a 34-year veteran of CNP and president since 1987. "This is a generational move which is very important for Condé Nast," Leser stated in *Advertising Age.* "We're all in our 60s at the corporate level, so it's right for us to get a younger man in here." Florio said he hoped to bring a high energy level and an interest in technology to the company. Approaching the 21st century, CNP remained a company on the move. With a new set of young executives at the helm, the renowned publisher was positioned to take its shifting groups of "class" or specialized readers into the information age.

Further Reading:

A Brief History of The Condé Nast Publications, New York: CNP, 1993.

Carmody, Deirdre, "At Condé Nast, Newhouse Maintains Loose Reins with a Tight Grip," *New York Times,* July 27, 1992, p. D6.

——, "Food and Design Magazines Are Bought by Condé Nast," *New York Times,* March 31, 1993, p. D1.

——, "New President of Condé Nast Predicts Clear Sailing Ahead," *New York Times,* December 19, 1994, p. D1.

Clark, Tim, "Year-old 'Wired' So Cool, It's Hot," *Advertising Age,* March 7, 1994, p. 10S.

Colford, Paul D., "Condé Nast Excels at Musical Chairs," *Newsday,* July 21, 1994, p. BO2.

"Condé Nast Acquires the Tatler," *New York Times,* April 6, 1982, p. D3.

Donaton, Scott, and Kate Fitzgerald, "Automatic Renewal Tests at Condé Nast," *Advertising Age,* February 3, 1992, p. 10.

——, and Pat Sloan, "Florio Takes Charge at Condé Nast; New Generation Rises to Power," *Advertising Age,* January 17, 1994, p. 1.

——, "Condé Nast TV Ad Touts Image," *Advertising Age,* May 16, 1994, p. 2.

"Eight Major U.S. Newspaper Companies Form National Network of Online Services," *Business Wire,* April 19, 1995.

Elliott, Stuart J., "First-class Traveler; Condé Nast Hopes 'Signature' Serves as Foundation for Upscale Monthly," *Advertising Age,* April 13, 1987, p. 86.

Garland, Madge, review of *The Man Who Was Vogue: The Life and Times of Condé Nast, Financial Times,* September 11, 1982.

Huhn, Mary, "GM Returns to Condé Nast," *Mediaweek,* August 8, 1994, p. 3.

——, "Si Wired for New Media," *Mediaweek,* January 24, 1994, p. 5.

Kelly, Keith J., "Advance, Condé Nast Romance GM," *Advertising Age,* December 19, 1994, p. 34.

——, "Condé Nast Old Guard Is Marching Out," *Advertising Age,* February 6, 1995, p. 40E.

——, "Hearst, Condé Nast Flexing Interest in Sports/Fitness," *Advertising Age,* March 20, 1995, p. 34.

——, and Pat Sloan, "Brand Move by Condé Nast," *Advertising Age,* April 17, 1995, p. 8.

''King James; At 36, James Truman Rules the Condé Nast Magazine Empire,'' *Los Angeles Times,* May 10, 1994, p. E1.

Lorne, Manly, ''Condé Nast Buys into Group Marketing,'' *Mediaweek,* September 9, 1991, p. 3.

''Resurrecting a Legend; Condé Nast Brings Back Vanity Fair—But Not Entirely to Life,'' *Time,* February 21, 1983, p. 62.

Salmans, Sandra, ''Condé Nast Buying Gourmet Magazine,'' *New York Times,* September 28, 1983, p. D15.

Seebohm, Caroline, *The Man Who Was Vogue: The Life and Times of Condé Nast,* London: Weidenfeld and Nicolson, 1982.

Smith, Liz, ''Condé Nast's Hot Seat,'' *Newsday,* December 4, 1994, p. A11.

''Time Distribution Services to Handle Retail Marketing of Condé Nast Titles,'' *PR Newswire,* October 5, 1990.

Vienne, Veronique, ''Make It Right Then Toss It Away; An Inside View of Corporate Culture at Condé Nast,'' *Columbia Journalism Review,* July–August 1991, p. 28.

—Kerstan Cohen

Connecticut Light and Power Co.

107 Selden St.
Berlin, Connecticut 06037-1616
U.S.A.
(203) 665-5000
Fax: (203) 665-3599

Wholly Owned Subsidiary of Northeast Utilities
Incorporated: 1905 as Rocky River Power Co.
Sales: $2.37 billion
Employees: 2,697
SICs: 4911 Electric Services

Going into the mid-1990s, Connecticut Light and Power Co. (CL&P) had been the largest utility in that state since 1927. At the end of 1993, the company was providing electric service to over one million customers in 149 Connecticut cities and towns. Its generating capacity of 5.292 megawatts came from a combination of steam, internal-combustion, hydro, gas-turbine, nuclear, and pumped-storage plants. Connecticut Light and Power became a wholly owned subsidiary of newly formed Northeast Utilities in 1966.

J. Henry Roraback, a lawyer, laid the foundations of the future company, when he lobbied the state legislature to pass a special act chartering the Rocky River Power Co. in 1905. This charter gave Roraback sole power rights to the Rocky River, a tributary of the Housatonic River. A 1909 amendment gave Roraback permission to distribute power wholesale throughout the state, to construct dams on a stretch of the Housatonic in northwestern Connecticut, and to build mills and manufacturing plants in the same area. Roraback's political influence grew even greater when he became chairman of the state Republican party in 1912, a position he held until his death in 1937. Between 1915 and 1931, the party controlled both the legislature and governorship and virtually every Republican candidacy had to be cleared with "J. Henry." A big, forceful, mustachioed man who resembled the popular depiction of a political boss, Roraback actually denied the renomination of two Connecticut governors.

Roraback's power company was inactive until 1917, when he secured financial backing from a large Philadelphia-based utility holding company, the United Gas and Improvement Co. (UGI). UGI bought the Housatonic Power Co. from the New York, New Haven & Hartford Railroad Co. After this acquisition, the Rocky River Power Co. purchased all franchises, leases, and properties of the Housatonic Power Co., the United Electric Light and Water Co., and the Seymour Electric Light Co., changing the name of the combined companies to the Connecticut Light and Power Co. Roraback's financial backer UGI held a controlling interest in the new company. Roraback, originally a vice-president as well as a stockholder and director, became president of the company in 1925.

CL&P's first development project was to build the Stevenson dam and hydroelectric plant on the Housatonic. Completed in 1919, it impounded what came to be called Lake Zoar. That same year, the Connecticut legislature gave CL&P the right to divert water from the Housatonic back into the Rocky River, where it could be dammed and stored for release in periods of low water flow. The subsequent reservoir was named Lake Candlewood and became the state's largest body of water.

By 1918, CL&P had already established itself as the second largest utility in Connecticut. In succeeding years, the utility sought to expand its markets, which resulted in the construction of an enormous new steam plant in Devon, about three miles from the Housatonic's mouth, in 1924. After three years had passed, CL&P became the leading utility in Connecticut, with $8.3 million in operating revenues, compared to $2.6 million in 1918. Part of this growth was due to acquisitions or mergers with smaller power companies, which ultimately enabled CL&P to broaden its scope from the western part of the state into central and eastern Connecticut. A holding company, the Connecticut Electric Service Co., was created in 1925 to separate the retail aspects of the business from the power generation and wholesale elements of the business.

By the end of 1929, CL&P was supplying electricity to 60 cities and towns in Connecticut with an estimated population of 481,651. The utility also furnished electric current to other public utilities for sale in 26 towns with an estimated population of over 193,000. Also by this time, gas service had become possible after the company received sweeping authority from the state legislature to lay mains and pipelines for this purpose. Eventually, CL&P provided gas directly to 10 towns with a population of about 161,000 and supplied gas to other utilities. In all, the company owned 12 plants by the end of the 1920s. Dividends which were first paid out in 1927 continued from that date without a break.

Operating revenues of $14.6 million in 1929 continued to grow steadily even during the Depression, reaching $19.7 million in 1939. Net income, which was $3.8 million in 1929, gradually rose to $4.2 million in 1939. Electric output rose from 580.4 million kilowatt hours in 1919 to 625.9 million in 1939, while gas output rose from 3.1 billion cubic feet to 4.8 billion during the same ten-year period. The number of electricity customers increased during this period from 112,965 to 168,351, and the number of gas customers from 32,192 to 69,688. Through the course of this decade, CL&P owned and operated 11 electric generating plants and five manufactured-gas plants.

CL&P became an independent company in 1941 when UGI was forced by federal legislators to divest itself of its holdings outside Pennsylvania. By 1948, the utility was serving a population of about 715,000 over an area of about 3,455 square miles. It owned and operated 24 electric generating plants as well as its five gas plants. In that year CP&L applied for and received its first rate increase since 1920. Between 1918 and 1949, the electricity rate per kilowatt hour had fallen from an average of 10.04 cents to an average of 3.3 cents. In the meantime, the average annual household consumption of electricity increased more than ninefold during this period.

Construction of a new CP&L headquarters building was completed in 1952, replacing offices in Hartford and Waterbury. Three years later, the company opened Shepaug, its largest electricity generating plant to date. Lake Lillinonah was created from water backing up behind the plant's dam and, like Zoar and Candlewood, became an area for public recreation. In 1956 the company became the first utility to order an IBM 7070 ''electronic brain,'' using this early computer as the heart of its newly created data-processing department.

In 1958, CL&P owned and operated 36 electric generating units. By this time, manufactured gas had been replaced largely by natural gas, leading to the development of production plants for reforming natural gas in Norwalk and Waterbury and propane-air standby plants in five other communities. The utility continued to thrive in the mid-1950s, serving 853,000 people and taking in nearly $75 million, with a net income of $11.3 million. Having joined 11 other New England utilities in 1956 to build an experimental 134,000-kilowatt nuclear power plant in Rowe, Massachusetts, CP&L received 15 percent of its output when operations began in 1961.

In 1966, CL&P was serving a population in excess of 1,382,000 over an area of about 3,641 square miles. It owned and operated 39 electricity generating plants and was part of a consortium constructing Connecticut Yankee, a 490,000-kilowatt nuclear power plant in Haddam, Connecticut. A wholly owned subsidiary, Connecticut Gas Co., was providing natural gas in 12 service areas, while a mixture of natural and manufactured gas was being distributed in five communities and propane-air standby plants in eight others. During this period, operating revenues rose to a healthy $122.8 million, and net income stood at $20.5 million.

1966 witnessed the creation of Northeast Utilities to serve as a utility holding company consisting of Western Massachusetts Co., Connecticut Light and Power, and Hartford Electric Light Co. This consolidation was the latest step in a history of cooperation between these companies dating back to 1925, when the three utilities first engaged in joint power-pooling and long-range planning. CL&P's chairman and chief executive officer, Sherman R. Knapp, became president and chief executive officer of Northeast Utilities. Of the three original companies in Northeast Utilities (NU), CL&P was by far the senior partner. At the beginning of the 1980s, for example, its common stock was valued at $478.9 million, 51 percent of the nearly $931-million value of the NU common stock held by all of NU's subsidiaries.

The Connecticut Yankee project was completed in 1968, with CL&P holding 34.5-percent ownership in the nuclear power plant. A second nuclear plant completed in 1970 at Millstone Point, on Long Island Sound near Waterford, Connecticut, was entirely owned by NU and 81 percent by CL&P. These plants made NU the world's largest producer of nuclear-generated electric power.

In 1972, about 74 percent of Connecticut's area and 50 percent of its population was being served by NU. Four years later, 81 percent of NU's revenue and a larger part of its income was coming from Connecticut. Relations between the holding company—especially its CL&P subsidiary—and the state's regulatory authorities became of prime importance as energy costs rose worldwide in the wake of the 1973–74 Arab oil embargo. In all, CL&P filed eight rate-increase requests during the 1970s, which generated a tremendous political controversy.

While running for governor in 1974, Democratic party candidate Ella T. Grasso contended that CL&P had overcharged customers by more than $4 million in the last year. Grasso and state consumer groups brought an action blocking the state's Public Utilities Commission from granting CL&P a rate increase of 8.8 percent. After she was elected, the commission was replaced by a Public Utilities Control Authority that appeared to be more consumer-oriented. In December 1976, the authority ordered CL&P (and Hartford) to cut their gas and electricity rates to 1974 levels—a $22 million reduction in place of their request for a $56 million increase.

Under the impact of increased costs, CL&P's net income fell from $73.5 million in 1974 to $57.7 million in 1975, even though electric operating revenues increased from $338.3 million to $364.8 million (compared to only $139.1 million in 1969). In 1979 operating revenues were up to $591.6 million, but net income, at $57.8 million, was barely higher than the 1975 figure.

At the same time that the utility was facing a profit squeeze from being denied a rate increase, CL&P was confronted with heavy expenses from its overreliance on nuclear power. Before high costs arising from the energy crisis encouraged conservation, NU had projected an increase in electricity demand of about seven percent a year until the end of the century. Accordingly, by 1976 NU had sunk more than $1.3 billion—over half of its assets—into nuclear power. This investment included work at Millstone Point on two more nuclear power plants. Millstone II, which like Millstone I was 81-percent owned by CL&P, was completed in 1974. By 1981, NU was obtaining 54 percent of its energy from nuclear power, the highest ratio for a company of its size in the nation.

From a consumer standpoint, NU's heavy reliance on nuclear power made the company's electricity rates the lowest in the Northeast. But the long-range costs for the NU system, and especially for CL&P, threatened to make ''Millstone'' an apt name. CL&P started paying fees to the U.S. Department of Energy for the disposal of spent fuel in 1983. Through the end of 1993, the company had paid the department $134.5 million for assuming responsibility for this high-level-radiation nuclear waste. A 1992 study estimated that CL&P's share of decommissioning costs for nuclear power plants totalled $801.4 million.

CL&P absorbed Hartford Electric Light Co. in 1982, assuming Hartford's outstanding bonds and other obligations. This acquisition raised the number of CL&P electric generating units to 65. Net income rose almost 50 percent the next year and another 25 percent in 1984, when the company earned $284.2 million—

five times the 1979 figure—on operating revenues of $1.76 billion, under three times the 1979 figure. Further, the utility registered a 20.7 percent return on equity that year. However, state regulators, who had authorized only a 15.9 percent return, witnessed this prosperity and subsequently proposed to block the company from billing customers for at least $40 million to $50 million in fuel costs. In 1986, the regulators rejected CL&P's request for a $147-million rate increase and froze rates until the beginning of 1988.

Millstone III, Connecticut's fourth and largest nuclear power plant, was completed in 1986 at a cost of more than $3.8 billion, compared to its original estimate of $400 million. CL&P's stake in this facility was 53 percent. During the same year, CL&P was allowed to increase rates over five years to recover costs. As a result, Moody's Investor Service Inc. upgraded about $1.5 billion of the utility's securities, consisting of first and refunding mortgage bonds, unsecured pollution-control revenue bonds, and preferred stock. CL&P got another break in 1990, when state regulators gave it permission to charge ratepayers for $167 million, or about 60 percent, of its $276.5-million investment in construction of the Seabrook, New Hampshire, nuclear power plant. CL&P held a four percent stake in that facility, which opened in 1990. CL&P also held a 12 percent stake in Maine Yankee's nuclear plant and a 9.5 percent stake in Vermont Yankee's nuclear plant. The Yankee plant in Rowe, Massachusetts, was closed in 1992.

In June 1987, the federal Securities and Exchange Commission ordered NU to divest itself of its natural gas business. As a result, CL&P's Connecticut Gas Co. unit was transferred in mid-1989 to a new holding company formed by NU, Yankee Energy Gas System, Inc. NU distributed to shareholders of record one share of Yankee Energy Gas System for each 20 shares of NU stock. The next year, government regulators again focused their attention on CL&P, this time ruling that the company must greatly expand its conservation efforts. One of the most successful environmental programs that the utility implemented was the free collection of old refrigerators and freezers which consumed extremely high quantities of power. In the period between 1990 and 1994, more than 49,000 refrigerators and almost 11,000 freezers were collected in Connecticut and western Massachusetts, resulting in the recycling of almost 11 million pounds of metals and several thousands of pounds of refrigerants.

An issue of concern among Connecticut residents in the 1990s was the possible harmful effects of electromagnetic radiation from power lines which emanated from CL&P's 243 distribution substations. For example, some residents of Guilford, Connecticut, charged that the utility's substation in their town was responsible for several cases of cancer. This allegation was given significant publicity in a 1990 *New Yorker* article. However, after an in-depth investigation state officials concluded that there was no correlation between the incidences of cancer and the utility's power lines. Nevertheless, in 1993 when CL&P proposed to make good on a 21-year-old promise to move its Lodge Avenue substation in New Canaan, some residents opposed a planned relocation to a site only 700 feet from a school.

In 1993, CL&P delivered electricity to an average of 1,078,925 customers. Of this total, 39 percent were residential customers, 33 percent commercial, 14 percent industrial, and 11 percent wholesale. Sales, in kilowatt hours, came to $26.1 million, operating revenues to $2.37 billion, and net income to $191.4 million. Long-term debt stood at $1.74 billion. Of CL&P's total generating capacity at the end of that year, 49 percent came from steam, internal-combustion, hydropower, and gas-turbine plants, 37.5 percent from nuclear plants, and 13.5 percent from pumped storage, with most of its storage power deriving from the utility's 81-percent share in a project at Northfield Mountain, Massachusetts.

Further Reading:

Bingham, Harold J., *History of Connecticut,* Vol. 3, New York: Lewis Historical Publishing Co., 1962, pp. 26–32.

Campanella, Frank W., ''Balmier Climate: Regulatory Outlook Has Turned Favorable for Northeast Utilities,'' *Barron's,* August 16, 1982, p. 40.

Campbell, Charles L., *Progress and Change: A Brief History of Connecticut's Largest Electric & Gas Company,* New York: The Newcomen Society in North America, 1950.

Dahill, Edwin McNeil, Jr., *Connecticut's J. Henry Roraback,* Ph.D. diss., New York: Columbia University Teachers College, 1971.

Donnelly, J. Louis, ''Economies of Scale,'' *Barron's,* April 15, 1968, pp. 11, 27.

Nicholson, Sy, ''CL&P Co. Prepares for Expanded Power Needs in the 60s,'' *Investment Dealers' Digest,* May 8, 1961, p. 32.

Pierce, Neal R., *The New England States.* New York: W.W. Norton, 1976, pp. 189–190.

Shenon, Philip W., ''Excess Energy: Many Electric Utilities Suffer as Conservation Holds Down Demand,'' *Wall Street Journal,* October 8, 1980, pp. 1, 17.

Wessel, David, ''Northeast Utilities Unit's 20.7 Percent Return Fuels Regulatory Interest and Investor Nervousness,'' *Wall Street Journal,* March 27, 1985, p. 63.

—Robert Halasz

Continental Grain Company

277 Park Avenue
New York, New York 10172
U.S.A.
(212) 207-5100
Fax: (212) 207-5043

Private Company
Incorporated: 1921
Employees: 14,500
Sales: $15 billion
SICs: 5153 Grain & Field Beans; 2048 Prepared Feeds Not Elsewhere Classified

The second largest grain and related commodities company in the world, Continental Grain Company also represented one of the largest private companies in the world and one of the most secretive. Starting as a commodity trading business in Belgium in 1813, Continental Grain developed simultaneously with the modern industrial and agricultural age. Indeed, the company evolved from a humble European trading house to become a diversified commodity trading company with operations in livestock, shipping, food processing, oil, and financial services.

In 1994, Paul J. Fribourg was named president and chief operating officer of Continental Grain, representing the sixth generation of the Fribourg family to enter the company's highest echelon of management. Concurrent with Paul Fribourg's promotion, his father, Michel Fribourg, made room for his second-born son in Continental's executive management hierarchy by moving aside to become the company's chairman emeritus. This event marked the gradual transfer of power from one Fribourg to another in a chain of command that stretched back nearly two centuries. It was Michel Fribourg's great-great-grandfather, Simon Fribourg, who founded the commodity trading business in his native Belgium in 1813. Fribourg's business was nearly two decades old when the industrial revolution commenced, forever changing the face of Europe and creating fertile ground for Simon Fribourg's commodity business.

That Simon Fribourg founded his business before this monumental shift from an agrarian Europe to an industrial one was propitious. In the coming half century, Europe would experience unprecedented scientific progress and social change, engendering significant and wide-ranging developments in industry, commerce, and trade that brought vast new wealth to western European countries. Before the century was through, an extensive system of railways, under construction in Belgium by the 1850s, would not only significantly increase the speed of shipping goods, but it would also cut the cost of transportation in half. The methods by which these goods were produced changed as well, as small-scale craft industries and guilds gave way to the age of mechanization and full-fledged manufacturing plants. With the proliferation of these modern, heavy industries came large towns and cities and the emergence of a new class of citizens able to survive and prosper through the manipulation of capital rather than by owning land or tending to it.

As the effects of this industrial revolution spread, a society and marketplace for Fribourg and his business were made immeasurably stronger, buttressed by the advent of a middle class, the development of railroads, and the emergence of large urban and industrial centers. The effects of the forces that created this new Europe would enable Fribourg and his descendants to flourish in a world of commerce that, as the industrial revolution took firm root in Europe then spread elsewhere, witnessed the rise of merchants, manufacturers, bankers, and commodity traders like Fribourg.

Before Europe was transformed by the industrial revolution, Fribourg operated exclusively in Belgium, maintaining his company as a domestic commodity trading business. Simon then gave control of the company to his son, Michel Fribourg. Under Michel Fribourg's watch, the family business would make a significant move beyond Belgium's borders, as the currents of the industrial revolution reverberated from their origin in Britain to reshape three continental countries in particular: Germany, France, and Belgium.

Although many of the changes taking place during the century pointed toward industrial progress, rapid advances in agricultural methods occurred as well, leading to more abundant crops and occasional surpluses of food. Steam-plows and steam-threshers were becoming more and more common by the 1840s, replacing the tedious and millennia-old method of tilling and harvesting by hand. By the time these new agricultural implements were emerging in substantial numbers, investments by the Belgian aristocracy stimulated the growth of heavy industries in the valleys of the Meuse and Sambre.

Despite these early technological gains, the Irish potato disease of 1845 and 1846 had repercussive effects on the European mainland, leading to a grave shortage of wheat that doubled prices in western Europe in the late 1840s. Food riots erupted in Italy, France, Germany, and Belgium, and a financial crisis erupted after banks exhausted stocks of gold to pay for wheat. To exacerbate the situation, a severe drought crippled Belgian agriculture in 1848. In the midst of this tumult, Michel Fribourg made a fateful decision that forever changed the future course of his family's business. In 1848, Fribourg traded several trunks of gold for the as yet untapped market of Ukrainian wheat, which he in turn sold to his hungry fellow Belgians. This event signalled the beginning of the rise of the Fribourg family fortune.

In the coming years, the tides of change moved in a favorable direction for the Fribourg family, particularly as it began to operate as an import and export commodity trading business. Although industrial output had doubled in Europe in the 35 years spanning Simon Fribourg's founding of the business and the decision by his son to purchase Ukrainian wheat, free trade in the region continued to be stymied by a complicated web of tariffs and import restrictions. However, this web began to unravel slowly, just prior to Michel Fribourg's foray into Ukrainian wheat, making the second half of the 19th century a much more hospitable environment for the family business. As with the industrial revolution itself, Britain led the way toward the easing of tariffs and import restrictions, repealing the Corn Laws in 1846 and removing regulations which hampered wheat imports. Other European countries followed suit, enabling the Fribourg enterprise to expand and prosper; by the end of the century it had become a grain trading empire.

Nearly all of the changes that made the 19th century a signal era in modern history also made countries highly dependent on traded grain. As the 20th century approached, the company's position as a premier commodity trader put the Fribourg empire at the crest of the remarkable period of commercial growth that would affect the entire world. The same industrial, social, and scientific advances which had swept through Europe were, by the turn of the century, raging in the United States, a country with tremendously vast agricultural potential. Accompanying this shift from east to west, particularly in terms of agricultural production, Russia, which had become Europe's primary grain supplier in the 19th century, ceased to serve as such after World War I, creating a new market for the Fribourg family to broker their commodity services.

To capitalize on this limitless new market, the Fribourg family business, at that time led by Jules and Rene Fribourg, established its first U.S. office in Chicago in 1921. That same year, the company was reorganized as Continental Grain Company. Continental Grain strengthened its U.S. presence in 1930, when it leased a Galveston terminal from Southern Pacific Railroad. Interestingly, the Great Depression served Continental Grain well, for it enabled the company to purchase existing U.S. grain facilities at bargain prices. During the decade-long financial slide, Continental Grain purchased U.S. grain elevators across the country, obtaining facilities in such key locations as Kansas City, Nashville, and Toledo, Ohio. By the end of the decade and after less than twenty years in the United States, the company had established both a sophisticated grain network and a stable and growing business in North America.

The outbreak of World War II in 1939 not only signalled the coming of hostilities that would stretch across the globe, but it also portended flight from Belgium for the Fribourg family. When the Germans captured Belgium in 1940, the Fribourgs were forced to flee their homeland and emigrate to the United States, where they continued to run their successful agricultural commodities business. Among the family members in this abrupt emigration was Michel Fribourg, named after his great-grandfather who had established the firm foundation for Continental Grain's subsequent success.

After his father's death in 1944, Michel Fribourg, then 31 years old, assumed control of what had become a $300-million family enterprise. Ultimately, Michel would prove to be one of the company's most capable leaders, preparing Continental Grain for a modern global economy most notably through the diversification of the company's business network into the production of beef, pork, and poultry products and the broadening of their business scope to include feed and flour milling and financial services. Michel Fribourg also achieved considerable success in geographically increasing the scope of Continental Grain's operations by expanding them into more than 50 countries, which served customers in more than 100 countries.

The strides achieved by Michel Fribourg during the postwar period were momentous, particularly through two of his most noteworthy achievements, one of which bore a striking resemblance to the greatest achievement recorded by his great-grandfather and namesake. Through the negotiating efforts of Michel Fribourg in the 1960s, Continental Grain hammered out a historic grain trade agreement with the Soviet Union, becoming the first company to export American grain to the United States' cold war adversary. This lucrative trade agreement was followed a decade later by a similar deal with China, and Continental Grain became the first company to export American grain to that country.

Against the backdrop of these two significant trade agreements, Continental Grain embarked on an aggressive acquisition program during the 1960s and 1970s, purchasing Allied Mills, Inc., a feed mill concern, in 1965, and absorbing numerous agricultural and transport businesses. These acquisitions, part of Michel Fribourg's diversification drive, brought together several notable properties under Continental Grain's corporate umbrella, including feedlots in Texas, an English soybean producer, a bakery, and Quaker Oats's agricultural products unit.

Entering the 1980s, Continental Grain narrowed the scope of its operations, divesting itself of its banking units and its commodities brokerage house. By the middle of the decade, the company was generating an estimated $14 billion in annual sales, up from roughly $5 billion a decade earlier, a prodigious sales volume recorded as the company underwent managerial changes of an unprecedented nature. One of the architects of the company's success during this period was Donald Staheli, who had joined the Allied Mills unit in 1969 and who eventually became president of Continental Grain in 1984. Four years later, when Michel Fribourg relinquished his chief executive post, Staheli became Continental Grain's chief executive, the first non-Fribourg to hold such a position in the company's 175-year history.

However, this historic shift in power only lasted a few years before a new Fribourg embraced the family legacy. Paul Fribourg, son of Michel, had spent his entire career at Continental Grain after his graduation from Amherst College in 1976. He joined the company's Chicago office in the mid-1970s, beginning as a grain merchandiser and then climbing up the corporate ladder as so many Fribourg's had done before him. By the late 1980s, Paul Fribourg was exercising his own influence on the company, realigning its international grain and oilseeds operations to create Continental Grain's World Grain and Oilseeds Processing Group, a division which he headed. Paul assumed his place in the Fribourg family legacy in 1994 when he was named chief executive of Continental Grain.

As it had for decades, Continental Grain operated during the 1990s as the second largest grain and related commodities company in the world, trailing only Minneapolis-based Cargill Inc.

Although sales were essentially flat during the first half of the decade, remaining static at an estimated $15 billion, the company maintained its firm economic foundation. Indeed, given the company's pervasive presence in the worldwide grain trading market and its nearly two centuries of success, Continental Grain enjoyed an enviable position as a steadfast leader in the international grain commodities market. As the company planned for the future with Paul Fribourg at the helm and the Fribourg family controlling 100 percent of Continental Grain's stock, the company was poised to thrive in the coming decades just as it had for nearly two centuries.

Principal Subsidiaries: Continental Grain Company Dutch Quality House; Continental Grain Company Fall River Feedlots Division; Continental Grain Company Grant County Feeders.

Further Reading:

Byrne, Harlan S., ''Land of Plenty,'' *Wall Street Journal,* October 18, 1973, p. 1.

''Continental Grain Company Loads Historic Corn Shipment,'' *Milling & Baking News,* May 18, 1993, p. 29.

''Continental Grain Lumbers through Market,'' *Bank Loan Report,* September 14, 1992.

''Continental's Coup,'' *Newsweek,* February 3, 1964, p. 65.

Lavinia, Robert J., ''Continental Grain-Tosco Joint Venture Launched,'' *PR Newswire,* October 30, 1992, p. 1.

''Michel Fribourg,'' *Forbes,* October 26, 1987, p. 154.

''Shh . . . Hedging Going On!,'' *Forbes,* November 1, 1976, p. 47.

Vail, Bruce, ''Continental Grain Realigns Shipping Units,'' *American Shipper,* September 1994, p. 23.

Zuckerman, Laurence, ''Executive-Suite Shifts at Continental Grain,'' *New York Times,* July 1, 1994, p. D3.

—Jeffrey L. Covell

Crown Cork & Seal Company, Inc.

Crown, Cork & Seal Company, Inc.

9300 Ashton Road
Philadelphia, Pennsylvania 19136
U.S.A.
(215) 6985100
Fax: (215) 6987050

Public Company
Incorporated: 1927
Employees: 22,373
Sales: $4.45 billion
Stock Exchanges: New York
SICs: 3411 Metal Cans; 3089 Plastics Products Nec; 3466 Crowns & Closures; 3569 General Industrial Machinery Nec

Once considered a sleepy producer of metal beverage crowns, Crown Cork & Seal Company, Inc., has grown to become a leading multinational corporation engaged in the manufacture of crowns and closures, a variety of food and beverage packages, and packaging machinery. In just three years Crown doubled its global sales and grew to 152 plants in 42 countries; the company now ranks as the world's second-largest aluminum can maker and the number one company in the packaging business.

Crown Cork's origins date back to 1927 when it was incorporated in New York City as a consolidation of New Process Cork Company Inc. and New York Improved Patents Corporation. The following year the company expanded its operation to include plants overseas. It formed the Crown Cork International Corporation as a holding company for subsidiaries engaged in bottle crown and other cork business outside the United States. This early entry into the foreign market gave Crown Cork an advantage over its competitors in the container and closure fields, an edge that it still holds today.

Crown Cork did not even venture into the can making business until 1936 when it purchased the Acme Can Company and began building its first large can plant in Philadelphia under the name Crown Can. While the middle of the Depression would seem to be the worst possible time to enter a capital-intensive industry, Crown's can operation was successful right from the start. Processed canning was quickly taking the place of home canning as the preferred way to preserve and store perishable goods. For this reason the container industry, until very recently, has been immune to the economic cycles that plague most other types of businesses, industrial or otherwise.

Crown Cork & Seal was an enigma within the container business because it had achieved financial results that contradicted industry logic. Profit margins in can manufacturing had been small and shrinking for decades, and can makers like American and Continental had been relying on diversification and economies of scale to create profits. Crown Cork & Seal, on the other hand, had neither expanded into noncontainer fields nor sought to augment its own can making program by purchasing other small can operations. Yet it managed to maintain an earnings growth rate of 20 percent a year. How did it do this?

The answer can be traced back to 1957, when an Irishman named John F. Connelly became its president. At that time Crown Cork lacked strong leadership and was dangerously close to bankruptcy. It suffered a first-quarter loss of over $600,000, and Bankers Trust was calling in a $2.5 million loan, with an additional $4.5 million due by the end of the year.

Connelly took dramatic measures. He halted can production altogether and filled the company's remaining orders with a large stockpile of unpurchased cans that had been allowed to accumulate. The customers did not object, and the money saved by selling old inventory instead of producing new cans brought Crown Cork close to solvency. In addition, unprofitable and unpromising product lines, such as icecube trays, were immediately discontinued.

Connelly also reduced overhead costs, particularly those incurred by redundant labor. In one 20 month span the payroll was cut by 25 percent, with pink slips issued to managers and unskilled workers alike. The moves were drastic but necessary. By the end of 1957 the company was making both cans and profits.

Once the initial bankruptcy crisis had passed, Connelly directed Crown Cork & Seal with renewed energy into two areas within which Crown had traditionally held an advantage: aerosol cans and foreign container markets. In the years immediately preceding Connelly's tenure, the company, while not neglecting these markets, had not pursued them with the vigor they warranted.

Crown Cork & Seal had pioneered the aerosol can in 1946 and Connelly was shrewd enough to recognize its potential. Hair spray, bathroom cleaning supplies, insecticides, and many other household products would come to be staples for the American consumer and would be marketed in aerosol dispensers.

In 1963, for example, Crown installed two aerosol can product lines in its Toronto factory, thinking that it would take the market five years to absorb the output. Within a year, however, another plant was required to handle the orders. A decade later, the same situation was repeated in Mexico. Only in the late 1970s and 1980s, when the negative environmental impact of aerosol cans became widely known (it was discovered that aerosol containers expel fluorocarbons which destroy the earth's fragile ozone layer), did Crown begin to reexamine this sector of its business. The company was among the first to develop an aerosol can that did not propel fluorocarbons into the atmosphere.

Connelly invested considerable capital to reclaim Crown's preeminence overseas in closures and cans. Between 1955 and 1960 the company received what were called "pioneer rights" from many foreign governments seeking to build up their industrial sectors. These "rights" gave Crown first chance at any new can or closure business being introduced into these developing nations. This kind of leverage permitted the company to make large profits while using industrial equipment that was, by American standards, obsolete. Moreover, the pioneer rights allowed Crown to pay no taxes for up to ten years.

Crown's international operations were managed and staffed only by nationals of each country, with no Americans on Crown's payroll outside the United States. Connelly sent the foreign plants outdated but still-functioning equipment and let them begin. Crown profited from its disposal of antiquated machinery and created a far-ranging network of semiautonomous subsidiaries in the process.

In the early 1960s, the can industry was losing more and more ground to the nonreturnable bottle. It appeared that cans would never be able to capture the lion's share of the beverage container market. For this reason American Can and Continental began experimenting with large-scale diversification into noncontainer fields. Crown Cork, however, did not follow the example; in fact, Connelly went against the prevailing wisdom and entrenched Crown Cork still further into the consumer product can business, spending $121 million on a capital improvement program initiated in 1962.

In 1963, just as the can making industry was experiencing its first recession in decades, the pulltab poptop was introduced. In the words of one can maker at the time, the new and seemingly simple innovation made opening a can "as easy as pulling the ring off a grenade, and a lot safer." The new pulltab opener revolutionized the industry while helping to dramatically increase canned beverage consumption. At the same time, Americans began drinking more beer and soft drinks than ever before, and the can industry experienced a seven-year period of unprecedented growth. Crown Cork, an early entrant in the pulltab can market, performed even better than American Can and Continental, and its year-to-year profits increased by double digit percentage points.

In the early 1970s the beverage can market leveled out, with many of the major brewers and soft drink producers developing facilities to manufacture their own cans. A number of can companies, particularly American and Continental, did not adjust well to the diminishing growth in beverage can demand. They were overextended and operating at a greater capacity than necessary. Crown Cork, which did not rely as heavily on can customers like Schlitz and Pepsi, was not as severely affected when beverage companies began manufacturing their own cans. Furthermore, Crown's foreign enterprises, which were accounting for close to 40 percent of total sales, were expanding rapidly. They more than compensated for any domestic decrease in revenues. Crown also became involved in the printing aspect of the industry by acquiring the R. Hoe & Company metal decorating firm in 1970. With this addition to its operation, Crown had the equipment necessary for imprinting color lithography upon its cans and bottle caps. By 1974 Crown had a consolidated net profit of over $39 million—double that of its 1967 results.

The first widespread production of two-piece aluminum cans began in the mid-1970s. Aluminum was relatively expensive, but simpler to manufacture, lighter for the consumer, and recyclable. Connelly, however, once again went against industry trends. Just as he had refused to participate in the diversification trend years before, he steered Crown Cork clear of the aluminum two-piece can. He decided instead to concentrate on the old-style three-piece steel can that had been the mainstay of the industry for years. Many industry analysts regarded this strategy as particularly risky since the Food and Drug Administration had indicated that it might outlaw the three-piece can because the lead used to solder the three seams of the can was considered a health hazard. To circumvent this problem Crown began welding rather than soldering its cans.

Connelly was against switching from steel to aluminum for two reasons. First, by relying on the steel can the company was relieved of the high research and development costs necessary for changing to aluminum can manufacturing. Second, Connelly realized that there were only a handful of corporations selling aluminum in bulk. This meant that the can makers would be paying a premium price for their raw materials. Crown, by using steel, could play the various steel producers off one another and drive the price of its materials down. The strategy worked, and Crown's company was making profits while his larger and more progressive competitors spent hundreds of millions of dollars on retooling for aluminum cans.

Connelly, it seemed, made very few mistakes. In all of his years as president, the company never suffered a quarterly loss and was virtually debt-free. During the 1980s, when competitors were spending and buying themselves into debt, Crown sat conservatively waiting. By the 1990s the company was ready to position itself as a major player in the industry, taking advantage of weak economies and buying competitors' assets at low prices.

The man that lead Crown's amazing growth in the 1990s was not Connelly, but his protégé, William Avery. Avery joined Crown in 1959 as a management trainee and then worked in manufacturing and marketing. Connelly watched Avery's potential grow and groomed him to take over the company. One day, Connelly who was described as an "ultraconservative, tight-lipped, and tightfisted boss," called Avery into his office and told him to stop being intimidated. Said Avery in a 1993 article in *Financial World,* "He told me, 'Bill, I am very disappointed in you. You have to set your sights higher. You have to think of taking my job.' " In 1989, after a period of diminishing health, Connelly died, and Avery took over the company.

Avery remarked in *Financial World,* "When I became president in 1989, I had to light a fire and get the company going again. [The company's growth] had slowed down in the 1980s. John Connelly's health was not good, the company had no debt and we were very vulnerable to a takeover." Avery began acquiring companies at a rapid pace. In fact, in five years he purchased 20 businesses with combined sales in the billions.

Under Avery, Crown's revenues doubled to $3.8 billion in 1993 and reached almost $4.5 billion in 1994.

Avery approached newer markets in developing countries cautiously through joint ventures. The acquisition of Continental Can's U.S., Canadian, and overseas plants where done in three deals from 1990 to 1991. It cost Crown $791 million, but gave it several foreign joint ventures and put the company in Korea, Saudi Arabia, Hong Kong, Venezuela, and China, where many of its U.S. competitors were not. This purchase brought in $2 billion in new sales, almost doubling Crown's size. Along with this purchase came Continental's technical center located outside of Chicago. Under Connelly, spending for research and development was almost nonexistent. But by the late 1980s, Crown's customers wanted more than just lower prices; they also wanted new products like lighter weight, custom-designed cans and specific metal coatings. Continental's research center gave Crown the ability to develop new cans to meet their specific needs.

In January 1993, Crown paid $519 million for Constar International, Inc., a leading maker of plastic containers for beverages, food, household items, and chemicals. That same day, Crown acquired the Cleveland-based Van Dorn Company, a $314 million maker of metal, plastic, and composite containers for a variety of industries. The total merger was valued at $175 million and enabled Crown to improve its economies of scale, as well as add to its technological and marketing expertise.

Other ventures during this time included an agreement in China with Shanghai Crown Maling Packaging Co. Ltd. to manufacture aluminum beverage cans and a joint venture with a Vietnamese company to produce two-piece aluminum beverage cans. In 1994 Crown Cork ranked as the world's second-largest aluminum can maker with the expansion of its Aluplata facility near Buenos Aires, which included the addition of a second can line capable of producing 1,600 cans a minute, for a total of more than 800 million cans a year. Through a 1995 acquisition of France's CarnaudMetalbox, Crown became number one in packaging, with more than $10 billion in sales. That same year, Crown announced that it was building a new $21.3 million corporate headquarters in Philadelphia.

Crown's aggressive acquisition strategy virtually doubled sales and capacity in the food and beverage areas. It also made Crown a national presence with the ability to serve U.S. customers from coast to coast while simultaneously establishing a very strong global position. Even with the recent growth that has catapulted Crown into the ranks of the world's leading multinational corporations, under the leadership of Avery Crown still follows the homespun teaching of Connelly, who maintained that "success breeds success": when managers work for the benefit of the stockholders, everyone is going to be successful, including the employees, suppliers, and customers.

Principal Subsidiaries: Crown Cork & Seal Company (PA.) Inc.; H-V Industries, Inc.; Northern Engineering and Machine Corp.; Volstro Manufacturing Co., Inc.; Wissota Enterprises, Inc.; Midway Tool Engineering Company, Inc.; Nationwide Recyclers, Inc.; Nationwide Coil Coating Company, Inc.; CONSTAR International, Inc.; Van Dorn Company; Crown Financial Corporation; Foreign Manufacturers Finance Corporation; Crown Cork & Seal Foreign Sales Corporation (Virgin Islands); Crown Beverage Packaging, Inc.; Automated Containers Corporation; Crown-LaWarre Precision Technologies, Inc.; Central States Can Company of Puerto Rico, Inc.

Further Reading:

"Crown Cork & Seal," *Beverage World,* February 1992, p. 18.
"Crown Gets Its Company," *Beverage World,* January 1993, p. 22.
"Crown Launches Steel Can Unit," *American Metal Market,* August 16, 1994, p. 5.
Davis, Tim, "Crowning Achievement: Embarking on Its Second Century in Business This Year, Crown Cork & Seal Is Well Poised to Meet Its Mission of Becoming a World-Class Manufacturer," *Beverage World,* February 1992, pp. 66 (2).
Halbfinger, David M., "Metals Companies All Made Critical '92 Acquisitions," *Philadelphia Business Journal,* May 31, 1993, p. B11.
Khalaf, Roula, "New Era," *Forbes,* April 26, 1993, pp. 158 (3).
Panchapakasen, Meena, "Indecent Expansion," *Financial World,* July 6, 1993, pp. 34 (2).
Regan, Bob, "Crown Cork Bids $5.2B for French Aluminum Can Firm," *American Metal Market,* May 24, 1995, p. 2.
——, "Crown Cork in Third China Swing," *American Metal Market,* November 13, 1992, p. 2.
——, "Crown Cork Plans to Expand Argentine Can Production," *American Metal Market,* December 22, 1994, p. 12.
——, "Crown Plans $21M HQ," *American Metal Market,* May 31, 1995, p. 2
"Vietnamese Venture," *Beverage World,* September 1994, p. 16.

—updated by Beth Watson Highman

DALLAS
SEMICONDUCTOR

Dallas Semiconductor Corp.

4401 South Beltwood Parkway
Dallas, Texas 75244-3292
U.S.A.
(214) 450-0400
Fax: (214) 450-0958

Public Company
Incorporated: 1984
Employees: 696
Stock Exchanges: New York
Sales: $181.4 million
SICs: 3674 Semiconductors & Related Devices

Dallas Semiconductor Corp. designs, manufactures, and markets a wide variety of semiconductors and semiconductor-based subsystems used in computers and other electronic equipment. Its product mix is considered one of the most diversified in the market, with 215 base products and over 1,000 variations. The company sells its components directly to manufacturers of personal computers, industrial controls, automatic identification devices, telecommunications equipment, and scientific and medical equipment, among others. With over 8,000 customers worldwide—including Compaq, Digital Equipment, Hewlett Packard, IBM, Matsushita, Motorola, and Samsung—Dallas Semiconductor enjoys one of the more balanced customer mixes in the semiconductor industry. These factors have helped it successfully navigate the volatile semiconductor market, posting over five straight years of record sales. In 1994 sales totaled $181.4 million, with a net income of $29.7 million.

The continued success of Dallas Semiconductor is perhaps the product of a lesson well learned. Dallas Semiconductor was established in 1984 by C. Vincent Prothro (chairman, chief executive officer, and president) and several of his former colleagues from the Mostek Corp. From 1977 to 1982, Prothro had served as president and then chief executive of Mostek, a subsidiary of United Technologies, a company which pioneered the development of random-access memory chips. In 1980, Mostek was an incredibly profitable firm. It was one of the few manufacturers of a random access memory chip, known as a DRAM, that had quickly become a standard component in personal computers and other electronic products. In 1981, Mostek enjoyed 55 percent of the world market and $360 million in sales. The following year, however, shipments increased by 20 percent yet sales plummeted by $160 million to $200 million. One year later, sales were even more dismal.

During the early 1980s, a number of competitors in Asia and the United States had developed less expensive ways of making a chip capable of performing the same function as Mostek's. ''With almost no warning, we went from having a wonderful time to being in great jeopardy,'' Prothro told *Investor's Business Daily* in 1993. The semiconductor war was on, and the market became treacherous. One of Mostek's problems was that it hadn't diversified either its product line or its customer base: 70 percent of its sales were of the same product, split between five customers.

In 1983, Prothro left Mostek and with a number of partners formed Southwest Enterprise Associates, a high-technology venture capital fund. The following year, Dallas Semiconductor was established as Prothro and Southwest Enterprise joined forces with Dr. Chao C. Mai and Michael L. Bolan, former Mostek executives, and John W. Smith, Jr., a venture capitalist who assumed the duties of president, chief executive officer, and chief operating officer.

The men recognized the need for a strategy that would prevent the company from relying on a single market, product, customer, or technology. ''The semiconductor industry long ago learned to make the same product cheaply,'' Bolan told *Fortune* in 1985. ''Our goal is to make unique products cheaply.'' Its strategy was to address specific client needs, develop a solution, and then later adapt the solution to fit other client needs.

One of the primary ways Dallas Semiconductor sought to do this was to allow clients to customize chips at a very late stage in the production process. Known as ''late definition technology'' the process used ion implants, lasers, or embedded lithium to etch chips according to precise customer specifications. This process gave Dallas Semiconductor a great deal of flexibility in adapting to changes in the marketplace and also provided the foundation for the company's versatile product mix. ''All the major developments in the industry have been decided by the marketplace, not by planning,'' Bolan said in 1985, adding that ''Our cardinal promise is not to fall in love with any one product.''

Another innovation was a product whose origins could be traced to Mostek: the pairing of lithium batteries—a small, long-lasting battery found in wristwatches—with a random access memory chip called a complementary metal oxide semiconductor or CMOS. CMOS were used to power individual software programs and were popular because data could be added to or erased from them at will. Their main drawback, however, was that whenever the power supply was cut from the chip, all stored data was erased from the chip's memory. With this new product, known as non-volatile RAM, the lithium battery would continue to supply power when electricity failed, allowing the chip to be powered continuously for over ten years. The development was essential for life-saving medical equipment and even for more prosaic uses such as cash registers or banking systems that keep running totals of deposits and other transactions.

By March 1995, Dallas Semiconductor had regional sales offices in Philadelphia, Indianapolis, and Phoenix, and had begun filling orders for a series of non-volatile RAM it had developed based on the above lithium battery technology. The company also introduced a line of electronic chips to prevent software theft based on the same technology. The product consisted of a key containing an integrated circuit coupled with a lithium battery and a corresponding socket inserted into the computer. Software manufacturers could encode the key's circuit to match a code in the software package, and only when the user inserted the key in the socket could he or she use the program. Although theft was one of the primary concerns of software manufacturers, this product was not as successful as the non-volatile RAM, most likely because end-use software buyers were reluctant to purchase and install the socket.

In its first year of operation, Dallas Semiconductor posted sales of approximately $3 million, slightly below its projected figure of $3.5 million. In 1986, the company received $10.8 million in a second round of capitalization, a move which increased its total capitalization to $32.2 million. Construction continued on the company's fabrication plant, which had already grown to 65,000 square feet. By late 1986, the company had introduced a line of application-specific telecommunications products, primarily T1 circuits capable of supporting a high volume of voice and data transmission.

In 1987, the three-year old Dallas Semiconductor went public on the New York Stock Exchange at $9 per share. The initial public offering brought in an estimated $30 million which was funneled into research and development. This led to the creation of ''one-conductor semiconductor technology'' which, when coupled with the company's other technologies, formed the basis of Dallas Semiconductor's automatic identification systems and Touch Memory chips. In 1987 the company also introduced a line of highly successful computer clocks, a simple self-powered component added to computers which could keep time for ten years, regardless of whether the machine was turned on. One version was even capable of ''waking a computer up'' to perform a specific task and then shutting it down after the task was completed. Dallas Semiconductor quickly became the market leader in computer clocks, a position it continued to hold in the mid-1990s.

In its first four years of business, Dallas Semiconductor's annual sales increased almost tenfold to $30.6 million, and net income grew to $2.6 million. Sales jumped in 1989 to $58 million; net income grew to $9.9 million. All income was fueled back into operations under the conservative directorship of Prothro who had begun assuming many of the executive duties held by Smith. In 1989, Smith retired and Prothro assumed position of chairman, chief executive officer, and president of the company.

In 1991 Dallas Semiconductor borrowed a concept from Post-It Notes and introduced an innovative line of data storage and retrieval systems called Touch Memory. The system consisted of a memory chip stored in a stainless steel case about the size of a nickel. On the back of the case was a band of adhesive that allowed the chip to be attached to anything from goods moving through a factory to employee identification tags. Data could be stored in and retrieved from the chip using a simple metal probe linked to a hand-held computing device, personal computer, or factory controller. Because the chips could be updated at will, they were more flexible than bar codes or printed tags; because they were small, they could be placed just about anywhere.

Dallas Semiconductor soon began customizing this system for a variety of different applications. In 1993 the U.S. Postal Service purchased the system to monitor drop box mail collection and to provide carriers with an efficient means of reporting on the condition of the postal box. Ryder Systems Inc., operator of nation-wide truck rental service, purchased over 1,000 systems of Touch Memory in 1994 which it attached to rental trucks and used to store maintenance records. Another variation of the system was used to replace punch cards that had been used by farm workers to count the number of bushels each farmer picked. This system allowed farm owners to track each worker's daily harvest more efficiently and simplified payroll procedures. However, according to the *Wall Street Journal,* it also caused concern among farm workers unions, due to the possibility that the ''system would allow [farm] owners to track [workers] from job to job, in effect keeping a record of their employment history.''

By 1993 Dallas Semiconductor had developed over 170 base products in 14 different categories. Its core products included telecommunications and time-keeping systems, non-volatile RAM, automatic identification systems, and microcontrollers. ''Individually none of the products are show-stoppers,'' an analyst told *Investor's Business Daily* that year, ''but collectively they provide nice growth and better than average earnings.'' Net sales totaled $156.8 million and were divided between over 8,000 customers. For 75 percent of these customers, Dallas Semiconductor was the product's sole supplier.

The company continued to pour its earnings into research and development, creating novel applications for existing technology and building a new wafer fabrication facility that doubled the company's production capacity in 1994. In 1993 Dallas Semiconductor was nominated for *EDN Magazine*'s ''Innovation of the Year'' award when it launched a high-speed microcontroller that was three times faster than existing micros. Touch Memory continued to show promise as the company introduced an Emissions Memory Tag which allowed chemical companies to monitor emissions for compliance with the 1994 Clean Air Act. The company also successfully transferred its digital technology to create the first digital thermometer that could be read directly by a computer. And in 1994 the company introduced a microchip said to prevent even the best computer hacker from entering corporate systems. Called Dallas SignOn, the chip uses the same technology as hotel security cards and is allegedly 100 percent tamper-proof. In 1994, although sales in some core products began to slow due to mature markets, company-wide sales grew for the fifth consecutive year to $181.4 million.

In just ten years, Dallas Semiconductor's sales grew from $3 million to over $180 million. In the mid-1990s, the company made the *Forbes* list of the 200 best small companies in America, and its future seemed healthy. This was largely attributable to Prothro, known as a ''cost-conscious manager who is focused on the bottom line and gets by with moderate resources.'' Prothro's management style was perhaps best characterized by the company's efficient use of existing technology and its steady, measured growth. The company had $75 million in reserve that would serve it well if the semiconductor market were to take a sudden turn for the worse. But more importantly, it had a diversified line of products which it sold to an equally diverse clientele in a variety of markets.

As further proof of its growing financial strength, Dallas Semiconductor declared its first dividend ($0.025 per share) in the first quarter of 1995. Future plans included efforts to expand its markets in Europe and Asia, and to grow through various acquisitions. In 1994 the company considered a merger with RF Monolithics Inc., a manufacturer of remote and wireless technologies; however, the deal seemed to have fallen through. Most likely this was due to Prothro's concern with the bottom line. ''When we put this company together, we wanted it to be self-funding, not a giant consumer of cash,'' Prothro told *Investor's Business Daily* in 1994, adding that ''We'll take the slower growth path if we can become more profitable as a result.''

Further Reading:

Deagon, Brian, ''Dallas Semiconductor's Prothro: Making a Mark With Lots of Products, A Little Humor,'' *Investor's Business Daily,* July 8, 1993.

Hayes, Thomas C., ''A Chip Maker Shuns Big Markets and Finds Growth in Small Places,'' *The New York Times,* February 5, 1993, p. 4C.

Newport, John Paul, Jr. ''A Maker of Chips That Won't Forget,'' *Fortune,* June 10, 1985, p. 106.

—Maura Troester

Dynatech Corporation

3 New England Executive Park
Burlington, Massachusetts 01803-5087
U.S.A.
(617) 272-6100
Fax: (617) 272-2304

Public Company
Employees: 2,600
Sales: $458.4 million
Stock Exchanges: NASDAQ
SICs: 3825 Instruments to Measure Electricity; 3663 Radio & T.V. Equipment; 3845 Electromedical Equipment; 3674 Semiconductors & Related Devices

Dynatech Corporation is one of the world's leading suppliers of products that support voice, video, and data communications. From its headquarters in Burlington, Massachusetts, the highly decentralized company oversees more than 30 subsidiaries located throughout North America, Europe, and Asia that make and sell a diversified line of high-tech electronic and microprocessor-based equipment, instruments, and systems used to support the generation, transmission, and presentation of information. More than two-thirds of its annual revenue is derived from the sale of information support products, while the remainder is generated by the diversified instrumentation segment of the company—a variety of medical and diagnostic products used in laboratories and health care facilities, including laboratory diagnostic equipment and computer software for the pharmaceuticals industry. A pioneer in developing hardware and software for the information superhighway, Dynatech is a top competitor in a number of niche markets. Some of its leading product lines include portable test instruments for telecommunications networks, packet switches used to break up data into "packets" for efficient transmission over public or private data networks, and airplane passenger cabin information systems, which display position defining maps, airport terminal charts, and in-flight information.

Like many of the high-tech companies that have flourished in the 1990s, Dynatech can trace its origin to a university laboratory. In the late 1950s, years before the advent of the Information Age, Dr. Warren M. Rohsenow, then a professor at the Massachusetts Institute of Technology, and J. P. Barger, one of his graduate students who later joined him on the school's engineering faculty, began providing research and development services in the field of heat-transfer technology to a number of government and industrial clients. Discovering the potential for a lucrative business, the two incorporated their company in 1959.

During the early 1960s the company made the transition from being primarily a consulting firm to a manufacturer of high-tech electronics products. While Rohsenow and Barger's academic colleagues and the investors in their company encouraged the founders to develop a strong, single product line, they opted for a different strategy: growth through diversification. "When we started we had an uphill sell," Barger stated in Michael O'Connell's profile of the company in the Massachusetts *Sun.* "People kept telling us, 'You gotta remember the good old American sayings—that you have to stick to your guns . . . you can't juggle all these balls in the air at once.' " In an industry where research and development usually renders new products obsolete in a relatively short time, having only one or two product lines on the market, the founders believed, would make the company more vulnerable. A variety of products, on the other hand, would protect the company from the sharp downturns associated with the short product cycles. The company channelled its energy and resources in three general directions: data communications, medical products, and scientific instruments/research and development.

During the 1960s Dynatech began manufacturing breakthrough products in each of these three fields, enabling the company to build a sound financial base. In the early 1960s Dynatech made a name for itself in the field of data communications by developing a multi-circuit jack for the U.S. government. This pioneering data communications network management product, which later became known as the Dyna-Patch when it was commercialized in the 1970s, was used to redirect the "traffic flow" of data by breaking up information into smaller units, or "patches," that could be transmitted more efficiently. The mid-1960s saw the company's medical products division revolutionize the field of immunological testing with the introduction of the Microliter System—a miniaturized fluid handling system that dilutes a patient's blood serum with reagents in minute, precisely measured amounts, enabling simple immunological and biological tests to be performed with greater precision. Meanwhile the company continued providing research, development, and consulting services in the fields of chemical and mechanical engineering to various industrial and governmental clients, while developing a number of testing instruments. By the end of the decade, Dynatech had grown to become almost a $5 million company.

Having made its first major acquisition of a public company in 1968 with the purchase of Cooke Engineering Company, Dynatech continued to expand its operations through the 1970s by taking over a number of niche companies. In 1977, for example, the company purchased a controlling interest in Artek Systems Corporation, a New York manufacturer of medical electronic instruments that automatically count bacteria and cells using television scanning techniques. The medical instrument segment of the company overtook the scientific instrument/research and development division as the company's leading generator of revenue, accounting for nearly half of the company's $27.5 million in sales by the end of the decade, with such products as the MIC-2000, a highly sophisticated and cost-effective test system used to provide proper antibiotic dosage information to physicians. The data communications division made up a third of the company's revenues.

By sticking close to its policy of operating multiple business units, Dynatech was able to continue breaking performance records throughout the early 1980s, despite a recession in the U.S. economy and the introduction of unfavorable legislation. In 1982 the Reagan administration's dismantling of the Department of Energy brought about the dissolution of several contracts with Dynatech, stalling the growth of the company's research and development unit. Moreover, the relaxation of certain Occupational Safety and Health Administration (OSHA) standards caused a significant decline in sales of the company's industrial respiratory devices. The sluggish performance of these areas of the company, however, only served to illustrate the efficacy of the company's philosophy of decentralization and diversity: between 1980 and 1983 total revenue jumped to $27.5 million, an increase of more than 260 percent, as the company's data communications and medical instruments divisions made substantial gains.

As Dynatech celebrated its twenty-fifth anniversary in 1984, its business mix continued to shift toward communications. A decline in the company's medical diagnostics business, coupled with the acquisition of Controlonics Corporation, a leading manufacturer of radar detectors and other microwave-based products, and exceptional growth in data and video communications products, bumped communication product sales to $98 million—two-thirds of the company's $147 million in total sales. The fastest-growing segment of the company was bolstered by the success of such products as the CTM-1000, an electronic matrix system used by network managers to reroute signals to numerous pieces of communications equipment electronically, without having to shut down operations or rewire the hardware manually.

By staying clear of billion-dollar markets dominated by industry giants and attacking the niche markets they neglected, Dynatech continued to separate itself from the growing field of electronics companies. Recording annual sales increases of between 25 and 50 percent during the mid-1980s, Dynatech outperformed the vast majority of the nation's top electronics companies: during the same period, the companies listed in the *Electronic Business* 200 averaged only 4.5 percent sales growth.

Averaging between six and seven acquisitions a year during the 1980s—53 between 1977 and 1987—Dynatech took the lead in a number of smaller markets, capturing a number one or two share in the following: asynchronous packet assemblers/disassemblers (equipment that packages data signals for transmission); patch panels (network management equipment used to detect faults when a communications system goes down); and matrix switches (equipment used to tow switch actual circuits rather than switching packets of information).

The company's success during the 1980s can be attributed not only to the diversity in its product line, but also by the decentralized management style developed by Rohsenow and Barger. The companies under the Dynatech umbrella were given the freedom to handle their own research and development, manufacturing, and sales, while being closely monitored by the president and management team at corporate headquarters. As long as profits met corporate standards, subsidiaries retained their autonomy, though according to Ronald O. Bub, president of Dynatech subsidiary Trigon Industries Inc., "if you don't perform, they'll divest your company!" Nevertheless, Bub praised Dynatech's management style in dealing with struggling companies: "Instead of shooting me," he explained, the management team offered solutions to help improve his company's bottom line, leaving him with control over his business.

This collaborative approach has also been developed among the various subsidiaries. Dynatech espouses organizational learning, or what John Reno, who took over as president in the fall of 1992, has called "leveraging ideas." The company brings people together from a variety of its businesses whose daily jobs are related to similar issues. Meeting three or four times a year for a few days, the representatives exchange views on marketing, health care, and various other subjects likely to apply to almost all of the Dynatech companies. Providing a forum for a wide variety of perspectives on common issues, Reno explained to *Institutional Investor,* has generated new ideas that have yielded quantifiable results. For example, by implementing an improved quality control system and building to orders, rather than carrying a large amount of inventory, the company has been able to lower its defective product ratio by as much as 25 percent and save millions of dollars along the way.

Nevertheless, a brief period of slowed growth during the early 1990s forced the company to rethink some of its fundamental operating principles. Although sales continued to increase at a steady rate, enabling the company to approach the half-billion dollar mark, profits were on the decline, and in 1993, for the first time in its history, the company lost money, recording a net loss of nearly $30 million. According to some market analysts—and some disappointed stockholders who attempted to force a sale of the firm—the company's long-held strategy of diversification had gone too far: Dynatech had too many product lines spread across too many markets.

In an effort to satisfy the long-term interests of its stockholders, the company implemented a major restructuring program in April 1994 that was designed to strengthen its focus on markets supporting voice, data, and video communications. First, the company separated its businesses into two segments, each with its own marketing strategy: the businesses that supported voice, video, and data communications were grouped under the Information Support Products segment, while a much smaller group of electronics and software businesses were placed under the heading Diversified Instrumentation. Second, the company identified and made plans to sell 13 product lines and businesses representing approximately $140 million in annual revenues that did not fit into its long-term strategy. By July of that year, Dynatech sold five companies, including one of its largest subsidiaries, Whistler Corporation, a car alarm/radar detector manufacturer. Finally, the company consolidated a number of its operations in an attempt to streamline and reduce operating expenses.

Although the expenses that accompanied these actions brought about an initial downturn in profits, by the time the transition was near completion in February 1995, the positive effects of the restructuring were apparent. Total sales during the first three quarters of the fiscal year had increased by 12 percent over the previous year; more importantly, net income was up 77 percent. By tightening its focus on the information support products industry, the company was able to take advantage of the ever-increasing demand for communications products brought on by the rapid growth of the personal computer, fax, and modem markets. In addition, the deregulation of the communications industry, combined with the increased affordability of more and more powerful computers began to blur the line between traditional suppliers of communications and entertainment products, providing increased opportunities.

In an attempt to take full advantage of these growing markets, Dynatech has introduced a number of new technologies that promise to play a fundamental role in the generation, transmission, and presentation of information. For instance, in 1994 the company added an Emmy award-winning, nonlinear editing system, designed to greatly reduce film and video editing time and expense, to its video product line. In the field of information transmission, the company introduced a new Synchronous Optical Network (SONET), a series of standards for testing high-speed, fiber-optic-based communications, such as those used by telephone companies, banks, and airlines. In the field of information presentation, which includes video-related applications such as video conferencing, the company secured a partnership with computer giant Hewlett-Packard to develop and manufacture video boards for their workstation platforms, with the result that Dynatech products will now be compatible with the majority of the computer workstation market.

Perhaps the most exciting and revolutionary development for Dynatech in the 1990s and beyond can be found in its use of Asynchronous Transfer Mode (ATM) technology. Considered one of the most effective means of transmitting video, audio, and data because it can send video data to specific addresses instead of broadcasting everywhere on the network, this technology has the capability to perform a variety of interactive video functions and has been used to conduct interactive computer video tours of residential real estate. By investing heavily in such technologies and continuing to streamline its operations, Dynatech has placed itself in position to be a key player in the development of the information superhighway. As multimedia computers become more commonplace, Dynatech has promised to be a major supplier of the equipment necessary to ensure the smooth flow of information.

Principal Subsidiaries: Dynatech Laboratories Inc.; Utah Scientific Inc.; Dynatech Nevada Inc.; Trigon-Adcotech; Digital Technology Inc.; Qualimetrics Inc.; Dynatech Microwave Technology Inc.; Parallax Graphics Inc.; Dynatech Computer Systems Inc.; ComCoTec Inc.; U.S. Computer Systems Inc.; Innovative Electronics Inc.; Lighting Location and Protection Inc.; Threshold Corp.; H.K. Microwave Inc.; ALTA Group; L.E.A. Dynatech; UNEX Corp.; Dynatech Communications Inc.; Telecommunication Techniques Corp.

Further Reading:

Knell, Michael E., ''Diverse Dynatech Poised for Growth,'' *Boston Herald,* December 28, 1992.

Kuhn, Robert Lawrence Kuhn, ''Creative Strategic Management,'' *Journal of Business Strategy,* March/April 1988, pp. 62–64.

McCright, John S. ''Power Grab at Dynatech,'' *Boston Business Journal,* July 22, 1994.

O'Connell, Michael, ''Burlington Firm's Consistent Growth Reflects Its Strategic Diversification,'' *Lowell Sun,* February 8, 1987.

''Philanthropy and Philosophy,'' *New England Business,* December 1, 1989.

Reno, John, ''Leveraging Ideas,'' *Institutional Investor,* July 1993, pp. 27–28.

Suby, Carol, ''Dynatech Profits by Shying Away from Big Markets,'' *Electronic Business,* February 15, 1987, pp. 66–69.

—Jason Gallman

Ecolab Inc.

370 Wabasha Street
Ecolab Center
Saint Paul, Minnesota 55102-1390
U.S.A.
(612) 293-2233
Fax: (612) 293-2814

Public Company
Incorporated: 1924 as Economics Laboratory
Employees: 8,206
Sales: $1.21 billion
Stock Exchanges: New York Pacific Boston Cincinnati Midwest Philadelphia
SICs: 2841 Soap & Other Detergents; 2842 Polishes & Sanitation Goods; 7342 Disinfecting & Pest Control Services

Ecolab Inc. is the world's leading supplier of cleaning, sanitizing, and maintenance products and services for the institutional, hospitality, and industrial markets. The company operates in virtually every country in the world either directly, or through distribution and licensing agreements, or via its Henkel-Ecolab joint venture with the German firm Henkel KGaA. Ecolab aims not only to be a worldwide operator but also to offer a full range of products and services to its core customers.

For the first 60 years of its existence Ecolab was managed by members of the Osborn family. Merrit J. Osborn, founder of the original Economics Laboratory, abandoned his occupation as a Michigan salesman and organized a specialty chemical manufacturer in 1924. The company's first product was a rug cleaner for hotels. While the Osborns no longer held management positions at Ecolab in the mid-1990s, many of the company's products remain directed toward institutional markets.

In the 1950s the company's product line grew to include consumer detergents and institutional cleaning specialties for restaurants, food processors, and dairies. This area of business came to represent the cornerstone of the company's success; between the years 1970 and 1980 the chemical specialties business quadrupled, generating $640 million by the end of the ten-year period. Yet early in its history the company actively pursued customers outside of the consumer and institutional markets.

By purchasing the Magnus Company in the early 1950s, Economics Laboratory gained access to the industrial specialty market. Magnus's primary business, the selling of cleaning and specialty formulas to numerous industries, including pulp and paper, metalworking, transportation, and petrochemical processing, contributed $12.1 million in sales during 1973.

The company grew large enough by 1957 to become a public corporation. Earnings per share rose higher than an average 15 percent annually for the next 20 years. The mid-1960s marked a high point in the company's history as earnings grew 16 percent every year. This was exceeded only by a three-year performance between 1974 and 1977, in which profits eventually reached a 19 percent growth rate. By 1973 Economics Laboratory was divided into five divisions. The Magnus division produced items for the industrial market, while the institutional division manufactured dishwasher products and sanitation formulas. In the consumer division, home dishwasher detergent as well as coffee filters, floor cleaners, and laundry aids were produced. The Klenzade division provided specialty detergents to the food processing industry. Overseas sales were controlled by the international division, founded by future chairman and chief executive officer Fred T. Lanners, Jr. who, it was said, paid his first employees out of his own expense account.

Of all the company's products, detergents for household dishwashers became its bestseller. Second only to Procter & Gamble's automatic dishwasher detergent in domestic sales, Economics Laboratory's detergents were preeminent in overseas markets. In the early 1970s, despite the fine company performance, Economics Laboratory attempted to expand its business by offering several new service and equipment packages. One such package offered on-premise laundry services for hospitals and hotels. This business was strengthened by the purchase of three subsidiaries all engaged in the laundry industry. Another package offered sanitation and cleaning service to the food industry. The company's dishwashing operation service, for example, addressed every aspect of the procedure from selecting the detergent to training the employees.

This trend toward offering services to supplement specialty chemical products represented Economics Laboratory's new market strategy. According to Fred Lanners, then president of the firm, service activity was indispensable to building markets and the single most important asset to offer customers. Prospective company employees were hired according to whether they had the ability to give an impression of total commitment to the needs of clients. Aside from laundry and sanitation, future plans included offering a comprehensive cleaning service to food establishments and a chemical surveillance service to food manufacturers and handlers. The ideas for the structure and implementation of these service packages emerged from Economics Laboratory's research and development department. The increasing importance of this department resulted in a staff of 200 by 1973.

In 1978 the company underwent a number of changes as the profit margin dipped to ten percent. Sales of dishwashing detergent had slowed and the expansion of international operations had a temporary adverse effect on profits. Both causes for the reduced profit gains appeared easily correctable and no major reorganization was in order. Yet the disappointing figures happened to occur at the same time new executives filled positions in Economics Laboratory's management.

E. B. Osborn, son of the founder Merrit J. Osborn, ended his long tenure as chief executive officer so that Lanners, the first nonfamily member to achieve such high executive status, could assume the new title. Lanners began at Economics Laboratory in the research and development department, becoming first the chief scientist and then the assistant to the research and development director. At the time of the management shift, E. B. Osborn's experience at the company covered 50 years. The third-generation descendant, S. Bartlett Osborn, stepped up to the positions of executive vice-president and chief operating officer.

By 1979 business had resumed at an accelerated pace. Sales increased 16 percent and earnings per share rose 16.6 percent over the previous year. International sales now increased at a faster pace than domestic sales. Profits, however, did not substantially increase; the unimpressive 6.6 percent was traceable to the effects of a large hiring campaign. The 130 new employees in marketing represented the firm's largest sales personnel increase ever in the course of one year.

The hiring of new staff marked only one tactic in management's strategy for growth. In addition to a larger sales force and continued expansion into foreign markets, Economics Laboratory announced plans to use some of its supply of cash to acquire Apollo Technologies for $71.2 million. This manufacturer of chemicals and pollution-control equipment was purchased to improve the company's industrial market share. As the company's traditional lines of business in consumer and institutional products neared the limits of market penetration, Economics Laboratory looked for ways to supplement the operations of the Magnus division. Company management hoped that the acquisition of Apollo could offer that supplement.

At first the subsidiary served this function well, and both companies found the relationship mutually beneficial. Apollo gained the financial backing necessary to enter new markets, particularly overseas, and Economics Laboratory broadened its business in the industrial sector. The Apollo subsidiary now held the responsibility for selling all Economics Laboratory's industrial chemical specialties. In addition to marketing coal additives, catalysts, and dust-control products to the electrical utility and mining industries, Apollo's sales staff was given the added task of selling lubricants, pulp-processing compounds, and temperature reducers to the metal processing and paper industries.

The major advantage Apollo's business activities held for its parent company was the ability to raise the industrial service operations to the same level of success as the Economics Laboratory's institutional services. Prior to the acquisition, Economics Laboratory's industrial business suffered from an inability to offer comprehensive services to its customers. With the purchase, Economics Laboratory acquired not only a company, but also technical service engineers to supervise product implementation.

In 1981 Philip T. Perkins assumed the title of president and chief operating officer. The new top executive had joined Economics Laboratory in 1968 as vice-president of the company's consumer division. As a graduate of Michigan State University, Perkins used his self-created bachelor's degree in food distribution to assume a number of positions in consumer operations both at Economics Laboratory and other companies. His experience in Economics Laboratory's consumer division attracted the attention of his colleagues; after three years of employment he was chosen as the company's most valuable employee. Prior to becoming president and chief operating officer, Perkins held the position of executive vice-president and chief operating officer of the international division.

As a new top executive, Perkins was considered particularly useful in overseeing the international operations. Before assuming his new title he had developed a plan to consolidate the program into a highly efficient network. His plan was credited with helping to maintain the division's impressive growth rate. Aside from continuing to expand international operations, Perkins planned to increase research and development spending by 25 percent.

The last remaining promotion entitled to Perkins was the advancement to chairman and chief executive officer. Although it was generally assumed that Perkins was being prepared for this final promotion, tradition at the company protected the incumbency of its older chairmen. For this reason, no one expected the 62-year-old Lanners, then chairman and chief executive officer, to be relinquishing his duties in the near future.

Perkins's promotion, however, never materialized. In a surprise move Economics Laboratory recruited and hired its new top executive from outside the company. This abrupt shift in 1982 is said to have been management's response to a sharp decline in sales of pollution-control chemicals. In attempting to remedy the situation, operating units were restructured and a new leader was sought with a strong background in chemistry and experience in the industrial sector. The recruitment process singled out Richard C. Ashley, former president of Allied Chemical and a group vice-president of the parent company. Ashley's degree in chemistry and his successful experience in the chemical field met the company's qualifications.

Ashley's talents were expected to be particularly useful in addressing the ailing Apollo subsidiary. Sales, dropping precipitously to $5 million, had been adversely affected by the depressed industrial sector and by revisions in the Clean Air Act. The move to realign operating units represented the first in a series of steps devised to increase Apollo's business. Soon after assuming his new position, however, Ashley was tragically killed in a car accident.

Once again Economics Laboratory recruited outside the company for a new chairman and chief executive officer. Early in 1983 Pierson M. "Sandy" Grieve, a 55-year-old executive from the consumer goods company Questor, filled the position. Grieve's experience in acquisitions and corporate planning, as well as his aggressive and articulate management style, were his most valuable assets.

Just a week after assuming his new title, Grieve displayed his talent for decisive strategic planning; the Apollo subsidiary was to be shut down. The closing of the operation caused a $43 million write-off but eliminated the possibility of continuing adverse effects on profits. Grieve's next strategic move involved reorganizing the Magnus division, issuing ultimatums on sales performance for certain foreign markets not up to standards, and hiring 100 new salespeople to market expanded product lines. Although sales had reached $670 million, ranking the company fourth among the top manufacturers of domestic cleaning products, debts over the past years had accumulated, and the institutional market, representing Economics Laboratory's largest customer base, had shrunk.

Grieve's decision to close Apollo was just one major of the many decisions required early in his tenure. Only months later, a significant attempt by an industry competitor to replace the nation's top dishwashing detergents caused Economics Laboratory's product to slip from second to third place. Lever Brothers, a large consumer product company, released its Sunlight brand detergent and captured a sizeable portion of the market. To prevent any further erosion of the company's market share, Grieve issued a plan to develop new products internally. Moreover, for the first time in ten years, he increased allocations for product promotion by adding $5 million to the soap products' advertising budget.

A final cause for concern emerged with the aggressive maneuvers of the Molson Companies Ltd., a Canadian brewing concern. In an attempt to capture a share of Economics Laboratory's U.S. institutional and industrial markets, Molson purchased the Diversey Corporation, a specialty chemical company. Diversey successfully increased Molson's presence in the United States and in five years the company tripled its sales.

Despite these concerns, Grieve's strategy to regain certain markets appeared effective. By 1986 $55 million in assets had been sold, including the pulp and paper division, the domestic portion of Magnus, the coffee filter business, and several plants. Other consolidation measures involved the laying off of employees and the implementation of new packaging processes. Long-term debt was reduced by an equivalent of $10 million and the company once again controlled a comfortable amount of cash. With the acquisition of Lystads, an exterminating service, and ICE, a pest control operation, Economics Laboratory attempted to broaden its customer base in its institutional division. Similarly, with the purchase of Foussard Associates, a laundry product and service operation, the company sought to augment growth in its institutional division. In 1986, the company also changed its name to Ecolab Inc.

Although its institutional and industrial customers had always comprised Ecolab's core markets, the consumer market had also figured into the product mix. In 1987, Grieve would take the company in two directions at the same time in regard to the consumer market. The firm abandoned its battle with Procter & Gamble and other dishwashing detergent makers, selling its dishwashing unit because it simply could no longer compete. About the same time, Ecolab purchased the lawn care servicer ChemLawn, a move that would prove to be the biggest disappointment of Grieve's years at the company's helm.

Industry analysts contended that Ecolab paid too much to acquire ChemLawn, which set off an unfortunate chain of events. In its initial couple of years under Ecolab, ChemLawn was unable to generate enough revenue to pay back the costs of the acquisition. Ecolab management decided to increase revenue through price increases, hoping its focus on delivering a quality service would mitigate any negative effects. But ChemLawn's customers turned out to be much more price-sensitive than expected. Grieve later noted that part of this sensitivity stemmed from consumers considering lawn care a discretionary purchase. Moreover, he observed, an increase in environmental awareness in the late 1980s hit the industry just after Ecolab acquired ChemLawn. Overall, the ChemLawn acquisition was eventually regarded simply a matter of an ill-fit. In fact, after losing money under Ecolab, ChemLawn bounced back to profitability under Service Master L.P., who purchased ChemLawn in 1992 for $103 million. With the sale, Ecolab had to take a $263 million write-off against 1991 earnings.

Ecolab was able to recover from its ChemLawn disaster through a program that Grieve began in the late 1980s during the initial stages of the ChemLawn debacle. This strategy, now known as "Circle the Customer—Circle the Globe," brought the firm to its strong position of the mid-1990s. The "Circle the Globe" part of the program emphasized Ecolab's intention to become a worldwide leader in its core businesses. Initially the firm concentrated on the Asia-Pacific region, moving into the area in the late 1980s—one of the first U.S. firms to do so in a concerted way. Ecolab also significantly increased its presence in Latin America, Africa, and the Middle East, particularly in the early 1990s. Growth was achieved through setting up operations in those countries, or via distribution and licensing agreements.

Ecolab then entered into a joint venture with the German firm Henkel KGaA. Called Henkel-Ecolab, the 50–50 joint venture, although experiencing some difficulties as a result of a poor European economy, had in a few short years become the leader in Europe in institutional and hospitality cleaning, sanitizing, and maintenance. The joint venture operated in both Western and Eastern Europe, including Russia and other former republics of the Soviet Union. By 1994, 22 percent of Ecolab's net sales originated outside the United States.

Ecolab's "Circle the Customer" strategy was intended to maximize its investment in its core businesses by broadening the range of products and services it offered its customers. By concentrating on the institutional, industrial, and hospitality industries, which it knew best, Ecolab extended its base of core customers in an incremental fashion, most notably with its late 1994 acquisition of Kay Chemical. Ecolab was already a leader in cleaning and sanitizing products for the full-service restaurant industry and added, through this acquisition, the leader in this area for fast-food restaurants—an industry experiencing rapid worldwide growth.

Since its sale of ChemLawn in 1992, Ecolab has enjoyed steady growth in net sales and net income, culminating in 1994 sales of $1.21 billion and $90.46 million in net income—evidence that Grieve's focus on the firm's core businesses and worldwide expansion had begun to pay off. The health of the firm was also evidenced by the smooth transition to new leadership in 1994 and 1995 brought on by Grieve's retirement after 12 years in charge. Allan L. Schuman—who had been president and chief operating officer—became president and chief executive early in 1995. Michael E. Shannon—who had served as vice-chairman and chief financial officer—became chairman of the board at the beginning of 1996. The two essentially acted as dual leaders, an arrangement that evolved more by accident than by design, based on Schuman and Shannon's strong achievements in their previous positions, complementary personalities and skills, and ability to work as a team. Ecolab thus appeared to be poised for even greater achievements in the later 1990s.

Principal Subsidiaries: Ecolab Pty. Ltd. (Australia); Ecolab Canada; Soilax S.A. (France); Soilax de Mexico S.A.; Ecolab New Zealand Ltd.; Ecolab Pte. Ltd. (Singapore); Soilax AB (Sweden); Soilax Benelux N.V. (Sweden); Ecolab Ltd. (U.K.); Ecolab Institutional Group; Ecolab Manufacturing Inc.; Klenzade; Pest Elimination.

Further Reading:

''Cleaning-Products Company Set to Acquire Kay Chemical,'' *Wall Street Journal,* November 4, 1994, p. A6.

Davis, Riccardo A., ''St. Paul, Minn.-Based Ecolab Acquires Industrial Cleaning Products Maker,'' *Saint Paul Pioneer Press,* November 4, 1994.

Fredrickson, Tom, ''ChemLawn Blooms under New Owners,'' *Minneapolis St. Paul Citybusiness,* July 22, 1994.

——, ''Ecolab to Have One CEO in Name, Two in Practice,'' *Minneapolis St. Paul Citybusiness,* October 15, 1993.

Kapner, Suzanne, ''Allan Schuman: President, Ecolab, St. Paul, Minnesota,'' *Nation's Restaurant News,* January 1995, pp. 189–190.

Peterson, Susan E., ''Ecolab to Buy Manufacturer of Fast-Food Cleaning Supplies: Kay Chemical Will Be Acquired in $95 Million Deal,'' *Star Tribune: Newspaper of the Twin Cities,* November 4, 1994, p. 1D.

Schafer, Lee, ''An Interview with Ecolab's Sandy Grieve,'' *Corporate Report* (Minneapolis), July 1, 1994, pp. 44+.

—updated by David E. Salamie

Encore Computer Corporation

6901 West Sunrise Boulevard
Fort Lauderdale, Florida 33313
U.S.A.
(305) 587-2900
Fax: (305) 797-5793

Public Company
Founded: 1983
Employees: 1,330
Revenues: $130 million
Stock Exchanges: NASDAQ
SICs: 3571 Electronic Computers

Encore Computer Corporation is one of the leading American manufacturers of open, scalable computer and storage systems for data centers and mission-critical applications. The company's highly innovative Memory Channel technology, coupled with its sophisticated Infinity 90 Series commercial parallel processing systems for mainframe computers, place it at the forefront of the ever-changing computer systems industry. Yet from the very beginning of its existence, Encore has struggled with financial problems, and its survival as an independent company is not yet assured.

Encore Computer Corporation began its life under the most auspicious of circumstances. Kenneth G. Fisher, who had built the Prime Computer Company from a fledgling $7 million operation into a $350 million giant in just six short years, combined with C. Gordon Bell and Henry Burkhardt III to form Encore in 1983. Bell had previously worked as an engineering vice-president at Digital Equipment Corporation, and Burkhardt had co-founded Data General Corporation. These three luminaries from the computer industry joined together to raise nearly $50 million to fund the startup of the new company. The trio intended to develop and market an extremely broad range of products, including desktop computers and large mainframes. With the market for computers worth over $31 billion at the time, Fisher and his colleagues felt certain they could secure a healthy portion of it for Encore.

At first, everything went according to plan. A technical staff was hired from the research laboratories at Carnegie-Mellon University in Pittsburgh, and a headquarters was established in Wellesley Hills, Massachusetts. Bell undertook the supervision of the engineering and design department, while Fisher and Burkhardt concentrated on finance, sales, and marketing. Encore acquired Hydra Computer Systems, Inc. to develop processors, Foundation Computer Systems, Inc. to write software, and Resolution Systems, Inc. to produce the terminals. The number of employees shot up to 110, and management projected early 1985 as the date for the initial models to roll out of the company's plant.

By January 1984, however, the company had lost $1.2 million. Undeterred by the costs incurred during the initial setup of Encore, Fisher, Bell, and Burkhardt forged ahead. During 1984 and 1985, the company concentrated on designing and marketing UNIX-based computers and terminal servers. During the same time, Encore developed a reputation as a leader in early symmetric and parallel multiprocessing designs for computers. Both the Defense Advanced Research Projects Agency, an office of the United States government, and the academic community became interested in the company's innovative software and architectural hardware. Members of these communities agreed to fund additional multiprocessing research conducted by Encore engineers. Armed with this ready financial backing, by 1988 Encore was able to build and deploy its own revolutionary design for a 32-way UNIX symmetrical multiprocessor with unprecedented computational abilities.

In order to build upon this technology, in 1989 Encore purchased the assets of the Computer Systems Division (CDS) of Gould Electronics. The Computer Systems Division of Gould dates back to 1961, a period when the competition between the United States and the Soviet Union for space technology encouraged numerous American firms to pursue contracts with the National Aeronautical and Space Administration (NASA). One of those companies, Systems Engineering Labs (SEL), targeted the field of data acquisition. SEL manufactured the industry's first 32-bit minicomputer, a development that spurred the explosion of the telemetry, energy, and vehicle simulation markets. SEL grew accordingly as it designed high technology products for its customers in power utilities and aerospace.

In 1981 Gould recognized the leadership role Systems Engineering was playing in the superminicomputer industry. It purchased SEL and reorganized it under the name Computer Systems Division (CDS). As part of Gould, the new Computer Systems Division continued to design and manufacture computer systems for the simulation, energy, and telemetry markets. In 1985 CDS created a distributed shared memory system that became known as the Reflective Memory System. This system not only provided a simple memory model, but also solved failure obstacles. The reflective memory system passively "reflected" memory updates to the memory boards on every one of the computers on the participating system. Each individual computer in a system possessed a reflective memory adapter and functioned as a repository for shared data. Armed with its own adapter, each computer was therefore protected from the failure of any other computer.

The strategy behind Encore's acquisition of Gould's Computer Systems Division was simple. Encore combined its own high technology symmetrical multiprocessing research and design advances with CSD's microprocessor-based systems and high-speed reflective memory system. The combination of high technology laid the groundwork for the development of Encore's Infinity 90 Series.

Infinity 90 is an open systems mainframe that provides I/O bandwidth and massive storage capacity. The topology of the system is designed to solve any single failure within a network without disrupting the entire system. Encore felt that the mainframe was a significant advance over traditional mainframe solutions to systems failures and storage capacity. Encore management believed the development of the Infinity 90 Series was the answer to their financial difficulties.

During the late 1980s and early 1990s, there was a detectable trend within the computer industry away from traditional proprietary computer technologies toward a more open systems technology. Nonetheless, the market for such technology remained very small. Encore committed over $76 million to develop a new generation of computer systems (the Infinity 90 Series and the Encore 90 Families) based on the open systems architecture, but demand for its products remained weak. Encore's new open systems technology did not generate the level of demand and income that management initially anticipated. At the same time, the company's older technology reached the final stages of its marketability and began to experience declining sales. The increasingly precarious financial position of the company began to affect the working relations of the founders, and Bell and Burkhardt decided to resign. Fisher remained chief executive officer and chairman of the board, but was confronted with what seemed to be intractable financial problems. Sales of $215 million in 1990 dropped to $153 million by 1991.

Faced with declining revenues and a smaller customer base than originally projected, Fisher responded aggressively by implementing a complete restructuring of the company. He reduced Encore's number of employees, consolidated manufacturing and warehousing facilities, and devoted even more money to research and development. Pinched to generate a sufficient cash flow to pay for operating expenses, Fisher looked for help from the outside.

In 1991 Encore entered into an agreement with Japan Energy Corporation and a number of its subsidiaries to provide working capital for the financially-strapped high-tech firm. The agreement included a revolving loan program amounting to $50 million and a refinanced loan amounting to $80 million. Fisher also agreed to a large exchange of stock for help in paying off Encore's growing debts.

With the assistance of Japan Energy, Fisher was able to obtain Encore additional time to prepare the Infinity 90 Series for market. When the Infinity 90 product line was introduced, however, the overall market conditions and the demand for open systems products did not increase significantly. Sales for 1992 dropped to $130 million. That year the company was suspended from participation in the NASDAQ Stock Exchange because it was unable to meet minimum trading requirements.

To guard against anticipated future developments in the marketplace, Fisher reduced the level of sales to U.S. government agencies. With the end of the cold war in Europe, Fisher correctly perceived that the U.S. government, and especially the Department of Defense, would reduce its expenditures for computers and computer-related services. In 1992 and 1993, sales to various departments of the U.S. government amounted to 29 percent and 37 percent of the company's total net sales, respectively. To offset the potential damage that could be inflicted on Encore if the source of these revenues was reduced, he concentrated on expanding the Infinity 90 Series product line, still convinced of the application and high growth potentiality of non-traditional computer markets.

Encore, however, endured another disappointing year in 1993. The declining demand for open systems technology exceeded the projections of company management and, as a result, revenues continued to spiral downward. Estimates for international sales and growth of non-traditional computer markets were also significantly higher than actual sales and growth rates. At the end of fiscal 1993, the company reported sales of $93 million, a $35 million decrease from the previous year, and an operating loss of over $69 million. In light of these problems, Fisher was forced to reduce Encore's work force by ten percent in June and an additional eight percent in December of the same year. The company's European work force was reduced by approximately 20 percent. It marked the third straight year that the company had cut the number of workers it employed. Other cost-cutting measures included the elimination of excess sales and service offices.

With Fisher in firm control of Encore and a comprehensive restructuring program completed, the company's fortunes suddenly turned around. In late 1993 and early 1994, Encore management negotiated a major contract with Digital Equipment Corporation to license the company's connectivity technology for use in DEC's product line. This move, expected to produce a large amount of revenue through royalties, started to show results in early 1995. Encore also won a contract with the U.S. Department of Defense to replace and upgrade already employed IBM mainframes with its Infinity 90 Series at certain centers operated around the world. The first system was installed in January 1994. The Department of Defense was so pleased with the performance of this equipment that it concluded an agreement to install $20 million worth of Encore systems during the remainder of 1994.

Throughout 1994, Encore succeeded in winning additional contracts. The company reached an agreement with Amdahl Corporation to distribute an IBM-compatible storage system using a modified Infinity 90 mainframe computer. This was the first product designed and manufactured by Encore to be compatible with IBM's product environment, and the introduction of this system marked Encore's first foray into a $13 billion market. Encore noted that the product was the first in the industry with the ability to connect to an IBM system and provide storage functions, while at the same time perform as an open systems mainframe computer. The result was a five-year distribution partnership that amounted to over $1 billion. Finally, in early 1994, the company was recapitalized and began to sell its stock once again on the NASDAQ Exchange. By the end of fiscal 1994, Encore sales had rebounded to $130 million on the strength of Fisher's reconfiguration of Encore into an alternative mainframe and storage systems company.

Further Reading:

Baatz, E.B., "How To Win The Hearts (And Cash) Of Fickle Venture Capitalists," *Electronic Business*, June 1992, p. 96.

"Can Three Hotshots Make Encore Take Off?" *Business Week*, August 27, 1984, p. 93.

—Thomas Derdak

Euro RSCG Worldwide S.A.

84, Rue de Villiers
92683 Levallois-Perret Cedex
France
(331) 41 34 30 00
Fax: (331) 41 34 31 51

Public Company
Employees: 6,800
Gross Billings: Ffr 27.11 billion
Stock Exchanges: Paris London
SICs: 7311 Advertising Agencies; 7319 Advertising, Not Elsewhere Classified; 7331 Direct Mail Advertising Services; 8732 Commercial Nonphysical Research; 8740 Management and Public Relations

Euro RSCG Worldwide S.A. is the leading advertising agency in Europe. With full-service operations in 30 countries and just over two percent of the US$300 billion global advertising market, France-based Euro RSCG ranks seventh among the world's largest agency networks. The firm is the only one of the industry's leading agencies that is not American, Japanese, or British, and the company has worn its distinctly European mantle with pride. Euro RSCG is part-owned by French media giant Havas Agence S.A. In the early 1990s, Banque Nationale de Paris (BNP), a French bank, held 6.2 percent of the agency's equity, and another French financial institution, Societe General, owned another 1.9 percent.

Euro RSCG is a ''mega-agency'' that formed as a result of the rather surprising 1991 merger of Eurocom S.A., France's top advertising agency, and Roux Séguéla Cayzac & Goudard, the country's third-ranked advertising firm. The billion-franc union was spurred by global industry consolidation as well as factors specific to the French advertising market. A spate of mergers and acquisitions in the late 1980s had transformed the structure of the global advertising industry. Marketing conglomerates (comprised of a holding company and several individual advertising agencies) that could offer their international clients comprehensive services proliferated throughout this period.

Eurocom evolved from Univas, the international advertising division of French media giant Havas S.A. Havas, which shared ownership of Univas with the French government, was itself majority-government-owned. The agency formed a system of cross-ownerships and old-boy networks that permitted it to capture the advertising business of several companies in such state-controlled industries as banking and insurance without engendering outright conflicts of interest. Early clients included Air France, Berlitz, and L'Oreal. By the late 1970s, Univas' annual billings totaled an estimated US$230 million.

Around this time, the firm made its first acquisitive move toward the United States, a market that had long been regarded as a key to internationalization. These efforts, though, resulted in failed affiliations with Needham, Harper & Steers and Kelly Nason, Inc. The latter was characterized as a ''fiasco:'' Kelly Nason ''literally disintegrate[d] within a year of the purchase,'' and Univas lost an estimated US$2.5 million on the deal.

Although Univas' billings continued to multiply to the point that it ranked in the global top twenty by 1980, the agency network was widely denigrated as a bureaucratic bastion of perks, privileges, and corruption. Corporate leadership changed with each federal administration, and individual agencies within the system were said by Debra Goldman of *ADWEEK* to be ''filled with faceless civil servants and sons of clients who got their jobs through the elite who-you-know circuit.''

In the late 1960s and early 1970s, several independent agencies were founded as alternatives to the government ad regime. Roux Séguéla Cayzac & Goudard was one of these upstarts, created in 1972 under the creative leadership of Jacques Séguéla. Advertising was Séguéla's third career; he had previously tried pharmacy and journalism, then turned to media in his thirties. Under this ''mercurial'' leader, RSCG quickly earned a reputation for brash, unfettered creativity. One of the agency's first ads featured an unauthorized image of then-French President Georges Pompidou. Although all copies of the piece were ordered to be confiscated, the resulting publicity more than made up for the loss. A groundbreaking campaign for automaker Citroen won several awards for its use of slang, as opposed to ''official'' French. Within less than a decade of its inception, RSCG's estimated US$80.5 million in annual billings ranked it among France's top three advertising houses.

Séguéla and his partners created their independent agency as a foil to the government-owned Havas/Univas. Ironically, the agency made its name in political advertising. In 1975 RSCG handled three concurrent, but unrelated, political campaigns. The apex of the company's work in this area came in 1981, when the firm was awarded responsibility for Socialist François Mitterrand's campaign for the presidency. The campaign's theme, ''La Force Tranquille'' (''Man of Tranquil Force''), was given much credit for Mitterrand's upset victory.

It appeared to many in the industry that RSCG, which was already known as ''France's most creative and controversial agency,'' had found its own patron in the government, but when Mitterrand reportedly shunned Séguéla's subsequent public relations plans, their relationship fell apart. RSCG resumed its contrarian position, and Séguéla ensured that it became one of the country's most vocal opponents of government-sponsored advertising in general and Eurocom in particular.

Despite its rather poor reputation, Eurocom's expanding sphere of influence won it several major accounts. In 1982, for example, French automaker Peugeot awarded Eurocom virtually all its European business. This move was Europe's largest account transfer to that date.

By the late 1980s, Eurocom's international network included Australie and Synergie in France, Ata Tonic in Italy, Ruiz-Nicoli in Madrid, and V und B II Warbargentur in Germany. In 1987 (the same year that the French government divested its stake in Havas) Eurocom joined two other major global advertising groups—America's Young & Rubicam and Japan's Dentsu—in a multi-cultural joint venture known as HDM Worldwide Direct. (The acronym indicated the enterprise's primary investors, Havas Conseil, Dentsu, and Marstellar.) It was hoped that the cooperation between Asian, European, and American agencies would provide them with competitive advantages over their rivals. Although HDM soon ranked among the top ten agency networks in both Europe and Asia, by the end of the decade Eurocom had grown increasingly dissatisfied with what it perceived as an unequal partnership.

Alain de Pouzilhac, who had joined Eurocom in 1976, succeeded Bernard Brochand as president of the four-agency group in 1989. Described in a 1991 *ADWEEK* as ''fiercely competitive,'' he was the driving force behind Eurocom's transformation from a primarily French bureaucracy into a vital global competitor. Early 1990s acquisitions (which *Marketing* characterized as a ''merger orgy'') increased international revenues from only one percent of Eurocom's total to 60 percent from 1985 to 1990. Late in 1990, Eurocom paid an estimated US$55 million for its partners' equity in HDM's US$1.5 billion (annual billings) European operations. Double-digit annual increases in French advertising spending throughout the 1980s also helped boost Eurocom's status.

Meanwhile, Roux Séquéla Cayzac & Goudard also rode the tide of French industry growth, borrowing heavily to finance acquisitions that propelled it into the global top 15. But an advertising drought in the early 1990s stranded RSCG with more than Ffr 1 billion (US$200 million) in debt, and the company neared default. The firm lost Ffr 280 million in 1991 before selling out to ''arch-enemy'' Eurocom for Ffr 500 million. In a statement to *Marketing* magazine's Dilip Subramanian, Séguéla brushed off two decades of outwardly vociferous rivalry as mere sport: ''one year you play for one club, the next year against it.''

The new partners spent the next two years reconciling client and management conflicts before finalizing their merger in 1993. The union was mutually beneficial: Eurocom got a badly-needed influx of fresh creative talent and two new American agencies (as well as a US$100 million Procter & Gamble account), while RSCG got the financial backing it desperately needed. Four RSCG partners stayed on to take leading roles in the unified company. Alain Cayzac assumed the role of chairman of French operations, Jean-Michel Goudard became CEO of international operations, and Jacques Séguéla took worldwide creative responsibilities. Bernard Roux left the group to form his own agency with Christophe Lambert and Thierry Consigovy. De Pouzilhac, who became chairman of the new mega-agency, announced that the distinctly French group would prove a formidable opponent for American and Japanese firms. Indeed, the new advertising powerhouse boasted nearly twice as much in annual revenues as its closest Euro-competitor, France's Publicis FCB.

Realizing that globalization necessitated establishing a foothold in the United States, the world's largest advertising market, de Pouzilhac focused his attention on that country in the early 1990s. Eurocom's 1989 acquisition of Della Femina, McNamee had fared only slightly better than its 1970s-era missteps. Agency namesake Jerry Della Femina proved reluctant to put aside his desire to control the holding company's U.S. properties. The merger with RSCG had added two new American shops—Tatham/RSCG and Messner, Vetere, Berger, Carey, Schmetterer—and therefore compounded difficulties with Della Femina. After months of well-publicized and reportedly rancorous conflict, Euro RSCG bought out Della Femina's contract for US$30 million in 1992. His agency was subsequently merged with Messner, Vetere, Berger, Carey, Schmetterer.

An industry observer with *The Economist* noted that, despite its advance in world rankings and expansionist efforts in the United States, Euro RSCG's extra-European revenues still amounted to less than one-third of gross income in 1992. In order to become more truly global, the agency began establishing offices in the Pacific Rim, which was expected to experience double-digit revenue growth in the 1990s. The group created or acquired offices in Australia, China, Hong Kong, Malaysia, Singapore, Taiwan, and Thailand.

Advertising industry legislation in the early 1990s also compelled Euro RSCG's efforts at international expansion. *Loi Evin,* a 1991 dictum that banned all tobacco and alcohol ads, was the first major strike. The truly painful *loi Sapin,* which regulated billing practices, went into effect in 1993. Sapin outlawed the ''sur-commissions,'' derisively called kickbacks by some, that many French ad agencies previously received from media companies. The new legislation mandated direct, precise client billing. Several trade journals denounced the rule, which had the effect of slashing admittedly generous profit margins. Layoffs and wage freezes erupted throughout the country's ad houses. Euro RSCG's French staffing levels were reduced by more than 30 percent in 1993 and 1994.

A 1994 stock analysis by B. Lacordaire of the Thompson Financial Networks attributed Ffr 130 million of Euro RSCG's 1993–1994 Ffr 250 million revenue decline to the effects of the loi Sapin. Jean-Michel Goudard characterized the loi Sapin as ''a disaster'' to *ADWEEK*'s Daniel Tilles, although he acknowledged in the same interview that ''France [had] been tarnished by the media practices of the past 20 years.'' Although a new governmental administration launched an investigation of the law's effects, the loi Sapin remained in effect in 1995.

The combination of recession, legislative constraints, and ongoing merger-related restructuring (including some client-conflict fallout) had slashed Euro RSCG's net revenues by 33 percent from 1992 to 1993. In an effort to compensate, the agency network issued Ffr 1 billion in bonds, Ffr 150 million of which were subscribed by Havas, thereby raising the latter company's stake in Euro RSCG to 38 percent. The proceeds were put toward reduction of Euro RSCG's billion-franc debt.

Notwithstanding Euro RSCG's difficulties in the mid-1990s, CEO Alain de Pouzilhac was confident that the year 2000 would mark the beginning of Europe's ascendancy, and that his agency network was well-positioned for the new era. Euro RSCG's leader has set a goal of "ranking among the world's top five by the beginning of the next century." At least two industry analysts agreed with his estimation. Thomson Financial Networks analyst B. Lacordaire predicted a 29 percent increase in the company's net income for 1995 on the strength of cost-cutting measures. A separate analysis predicted income growth of 45 percent for 1994 and another 52 percent in 1995.

Principal Subsidiaries: Euro RSCG France (99%); Euro RSCG (Germany); V & B (Germany; 60%); Euro RSCG (Austria; 86%); Garbarski Euro RSCG (Belgium; 70%); Palmares (Belgium; 88%); Equator (Belgium; 87%); Euro RSCG Denmark; Euro RSCG (Spain; 63%); Vizeversa (Spain; 66%); Unitros (Spain; 51%); EWDB Espana (50%); Euro RSCG Finland (96%); Euro RSCG Athens (51%); HDM Hellas; Benjamens Van Doors Euro RSCG (Netherlands); Anema & Hageman (Netherlands; 85%); Euro RSCG Havasi (Hungary; 67%); Eurocom Advertising Italia; Equipe (Italy; 51%); BGS (Italy; 79%); RSCG Mezzano Constantini Mignani (Italy; 59%); Ata Tonic (Italy; 75%); Klem RSCG (Morocco; 50%); Euro RSCG (Norway; 75%); Euro RSCG (Poland; 60%); Euro RSCG Publicidade (Portugal; 71%); Euro RSCG (Czech Republic); Evelink (United Kingdom); Eurscg Holding (Sweden); Euro RSCG (Sweden); Eurad (Switzerland; 51%); EWDB North America (United States); MVBMS (United States; 60.8%); Euro RSCG Holdings (United States); The Ball Partnership Investments (Bermuda); Euro RSCG Ball Partnership (Australia); Euro RSCG Ball Partnership (Hong Kong); Euro RSCG Ball Partnership (Singapore); Euro RSCG Ball Partnership (Malaysia); Euro RSCG Ball Partnership (Taiwan; 80%); Euro RSCG Ball Partnership (Thailand).

Further Reading:

Burton, Patrick, "Loi Sapin's Threat," *Marketing,* March 25, 1993, p. 19.

Crumley, Bruce, "Fiat Quits Euro RSCG," *Advertising Age,* October 21, 1991, pp. 1, 56.

Emmrich, Stuart, "Alain de Pouzilhac: Eurocom Chairman Sets Acquisition Course for America," *ADWEEK Eastern Edition,* April 8, 1991, p. 16.

"Eurover There," *The Economist,* July 4, 1992, pp. 58, 60.

Goldman, Debra, "The French Connection," *ADWEEK Eastern Edition,* December 16, 1991, p. 18.

Hill, Philip, "Jacques Séguéla is Alive and Well," *Advertising Age,* November 19, 1984, pp. 56, 60.

Lacordaire, B., "Euro RSCG - Company Report," Thomson Financial Networks Inc., 1994.

Lafayette, Jon, "HDM Doomed? Eurocom Nears Buyout, Merger," *Advertising Age,* November 12, 1990, pp. 1, 78.

McCormack, Kevin, "Will Eurocom Divorce Partners in HDM Venture?" *ADWEEK Eastern Edition,* September 17, 1990, p. 1.

Pfaff, Carolyn, "Vuitton Taps Séguéla for Forgery Fight," *Advertising Age,* April 23, 1979, p. 84.

——, "Peugeot Puts All at Univas," *Advertising Age,* June 14, 1982, pp. 1, 68.

Pfaff, Carolyn, and Anika Mechalowska, "New French Regime Shakes Up Marketers," *Advertising Age,* May 18, 1981, pp. 1, 113.

Subramanian, Dilip, "The Ad Party is Over in Paris; Double-Digit Growth has Given Way to Sub-Inflation Rates," *Marketing,* December 9, 1991.

——, "Renegades Sell to Former Foe," *Marketing,* January 6, 1992, p. 18.

Tilles, Daniel, "French Agency Heads Sound Off on 'Sapin;' " *ADWEEK Eastern Edition,* August 23, 1993, p. 12.

Wilson, Claire, "Eurocom Unruffled by Sale," *Advertising Age,* May 25, 1987, p. 48.

—April D. Gasbarre

Eurotunnel PLC

Victoria Plaza
Buckingham Palace Road
London SW1W OST
United Kingdom
(71) 8347575
Fax: (71) 8215242

Public Company
Incorporated: 1985 as Eurotunnel Ltd.
Employees: 1,300
Sales: $7.36 billion
Stock Exchanges: London
SICs: 1622 Bridge, Tunnel, & Elevated Highway Construction; 4011 Railroads, Line-Haul Operating; 4013 Switching and Terminal Services; 4789 Transportation Services Not Elsewhere Classified

Eurotunnel PLC, through its Eurotunnel subsidiaries, was established to design, finance, construct, and operate a 31-mile tunnel that links France and England beneath the English Channel. The tunnel, or ''chunnel,'' was completed in 1993 and opened to passenger traffic in 1994. Although the ambitious tunnel project was beset from the start with cost overruns, construction problems, and delays, the finished product stands as an impressive monument to mankind's technological and engineering prowess.

On June 20, 1993, the first passenger train traveled through the tunnel beneath the English Channel, marking the completion of the largest private engineering project in history. The 31-mile tunnel, 23.5 miles of which is under 150 feet of water, linked for the first time the countries of England and France. The completed tunnel was the culmination of seven years of business problems, controversial political disputes, and engineering setbacks. For example, many U.K. citizens resented the fact that England would no longer be an island. Further, investors and contractors argued about who would pay for the major cost overruns even as the chunnel opened for business. Nevertheless, many Eurotunnel employees, contractors, and associates involved in building and financing the tunnel looked back on the project as the achievement of a lifetime.

While Eurotunnel was incorporated in 1985 for the purpose of building a ''fixed link'' between England and France, the concept of bridging the English channel was an old one. In 1751, for example, the Amiens Academy in France conducted a competition which awarded participants for offering innovative ways to cross the English Channel. Since that time, engineers and politicians presented numerous alternatives to the traditional ferry system, but none of the ideas ever progressed to the construction phase due to enormous financial and complicated engineering hurdles. One ambitious construction program actually advanced to the tunneling stage in 1974, but the initiative was abandoned soon after it had begun.

Despite the failure of this construction program, support for the idea continued to mount. In 1978, a group of British and French contractors revisited the 1974 effort to see where the project had failed. Further, in September of 1981 English Prime Minister Margaret Thatcher and French President Mitterand announced that they would join forces to finance new studies for a fixed link across the English Channel. Subsequently, a consortium of five French and five British contractors, along with five banks, proposed a scheme to finance and construct a tunnel connecting Paris and London. That group, which was initially headed by former diplomat Sir Nicholas Henderson, was the start of Eurotunnel. The French contractors involved in the project included Bouygues SA, Dumes SA, Societe, Auxiliaire d'Entrepreses SA, Societe Generale d'Entrepreses, and Spie Batignolles SA. The English contractors included Balfour Beatty Construction Ltd., Costain Civil Engineering Ltd., Tarmac Construction Ltd., Taylor Woodrow Construction Ltd., and Wimpey International Ltd.

While the original Channel Tunnel Group, as it called itself, was not the only consortium interested in building the tunnel across the English Channel, they were perhaps the most organized. Because the consortium comprised an experienced team of contractors and financiers, such as National Westminister Bank, they easily won the contract when the French and British governments invited groups to bid on the massive project in April 1985. The Channel Tunnel Group was selected to head the project the following January; in addition, the two governments signed an agreement that authorized the company to operate the tunnel for 55 years. After the Channel Tunnel Group was awarded the project, the contractors joined to form Transmanche-Link (TML), the company that would actually build the tunnel. Likewise, the group that would oversee the completion and operation of the chunnel formed Eurotunnel PLC, which became a public company in July of 1986. Lord Pennock served as chairman of Eurotunnel until February of 1987, when Alastair Morton assumed control of the consortium.

The chief purpose of separating the construction from the management aspects of the chunnel project was to restrict the contractors' access to the bank's financial resources, forming a sort of checks and balances arrangement designed to avoid conflicts of interest. Unfortunately, this effort was less than successful. Before the arrangement was finalized, all members agreed on the terms of a contract which effectively allowed TML—which constituted the contractors—to circumvent the restrictions imposed by its financiers. Further, the agreement failed to provide Eurotunnel—which was supposed to oversee the operations—representation by independent management. ''In the files of the French Treasury is a memorandum that argues with passion . . . that in no circumstances should the contract for the construction . . . be signed while the contractors were still majority shareholders and Eurotunnel did not have independent management,'' Morton explained in the May 2, 1994, *Engineering News Record.* ''But it did happen, and there was trouble ever after that.''

One of the high points of the chunnel project came in July 1987, when England and France signed an historic treaty approving the connection between the two countries. Despite this diplomatic triumph, Eurotunnel lacked the cash necessary to fund the massive US $7-billion-plus project. In fact, the group of financiers involved in the project had only raised about US $500 million in 1986 and they had planned to make a second public stock offering in November of 1987. To their dismay, the U.S. stock market crashed in October of that year; nevertheless, they went ahead with the offering. In what one Eurotunnel executive called a miracle, the project collected more than 100,000 shareholders almost overnight and boosted Eurotunnel's coffers by about US $1.5 billion.

Once the investment capital had been secured, TML began boring the tunnel from an existing service tunnel in the United Kingdom. About three months later a French tunnel-boring machine began grinding its way toward England. The concept was to bore a 31-mile link 150 feet below the English Channel that consisted of three tunnels—two rail tunnels and a smaller service tunnel. When completed, passenger shuttles and trains would be able to travel through the tunnels at speeds of 90 miles per hour and higher. Instead of boarding a ferry for a one-and-one-half-hour ride across the channel, passengers could make the trip in about 30 minutes. The project would offer new opportunities to commuters living in either England or France. For example, a sales representative in Britain could also cover a territory in France. Similarly, a resident of Calais, where the tunnel emerges in France, could go to dinner and a movie in London and return home by late evening. Further, freight carriers, including over-the-road trucking companies, could benefit from the underwater tunnel.

Despite all of these high hopes for the completed project, fundamental construction problems arose early. As a result, tunneling fell behind schedule, particularly from the United Kingdom's end, and bitter disputes over money and project control erupted between several different parties. Most early differences were eventually smoothed out through renegotiation of contract payments and management changes. In May of 1989, American Jack Lemley was hired as the chief executive of TML. When he arrived in Europe, he was surprised to find virtually independent construction teams operating on each side of the channel. Under his direction, TML gradually unified its contractors on either side of the English Channel, reduced several unnecessary project costs, and reaffirmed their plan to meet the original construction schedule. Despite these significant gains in management, setbacks continued to plague Eurotunnel throughout the construction phase.

A particularly disastrous setback involved the complications caused by a 5.4-meter-wide tunnel boring machine striking bad ground, in spite of the fact that decades of soil studies found the area stable. The state-of-the-art, computer-controlled machine, which was specially designed for the tunnel project, was only capable of boring through compact chalk. The bad patch of ground into which it drilled caused moisture to seep into the machine's electrical systems and devastated its specialized concrete lining system. Eurotunnel was forced to invest heavily to compensate for the mishap, and this and other setbacks contributed to another major dispute regarding the method of payment that Eurotunnel had agreed to use to compensate TML contractors who fixed equipment. The end result was a US $2.5 billion lawsuit filed by TML against Eurotunnel and a lengthy court battle that raged through most of the construction phase in the late 1980s and early 1990s.

In addition to disputes with its sister company, Eurotunnel was also burdened by frustrating intervention from government agencies. Leading the bureaucratic assault was the Intergovernmental Commission (IGC), an oversight body focusing on safety requirements made up of civil servants from both France and the United Kingdom. In one instance, early in the project TML had asked for the IGC's approval to install standard 600-millimeter doors in the passenger car trains. The request became mired in red tape at the IGC, so TML went ahead and ordered the doors in an effort to keep up with its construction schedule. After the doors had been built, the IGC decided to mandate 700-millimeter doors. This changed caused a nearly nine-month delay in the project and cost Eurotunnel a staggering US $70 million to rectify. Similarly, although the chunnel was designed using seismic criteria used for nuclear power plants, the IGC decided midway through construction process to increase the relevant design factor fourfold. Furthermore, the IGC decided in the final stages of the project to require the installation of an advanced electronic anti-terrorist system.

Such poorly executed mandates contributed to huge cost overruns and construction delays on the tunnel project. Whereas in 1988 Eurotunnel had set a target opening date of May 1993, one year later the completion date was pushed back to June. By February 1992, TML, mired in uncontrollable delays, abandoned the May projection altogether. Later that year, TML estimated that the tunnel would be in operation by December, although that date was eventually postponed as well. As bureaucratic and engineering setbacks proliferated, the relationship between TML and Eurotunnel became more strained. For its part, Eurotunnel was in a double bind because it was trying to facilitate cooperation between a demanding consortium of contractors at TML on one side and a powerful group of financiers on the other, while at the same time struggling to overcome bureaucratic hurdles. Suspicion and mistrust gradually permeated the entire business relationship, to the point that Eurotunnel unsuccessfully sought an injunction to stop TML's work on the tunnel.

In Morton's estimation, much of the problem stemmed from TML's heavy influence that it had negotiated in the original agreement with Eurotunnel. ''[Eurotunnel] had to wrest control of the project from the contractor [TML] . . . without intervening in its responsibility . . . for the design-build commission and guarantee,'' Morton recalled in the May 2, 1994, *Engineering News Record.* ''The continuous dilemma of what exactly was the contractor's position [relating to] the client . . . and what exactly was both the capability and responsibility of the client has been the drama of the tunnel.'' While Eurotunnel took exception to TML's grab for power, TML executives blamed construction difficulties in part on Eurotunnel's inexperience in overseeing large construction projects. Despite these internal disputes, Eurotunnel and TML rose to the challenge of finding the money to pay for cost overruns and completing the tunnel on a reasonable time table.

Indeed, as construction costs escalated, Eurotunnel scrambled to amass the world's largest syndicate of investors and financial institutions, which included 220 banks throughout the world. Using virtually no public funds, Eurotunnel had raised US $13.5 billion in capital by 1994 and was working to secure at least another US $1.5 billion. Meanwhile, TML shifted into high gear during the early 1990s in an effort to overcome bureaucratic and engineering hurdles and meet its ambitious construction schedule. TML eventually broke tunnel-boring speed records, advancing more than 1,400 feet in just one week. TML and Eurotunnel celebrated the official breakthrough of the service tunnel on December 1, 1990. The historic event—French and English workmen punching through a rock wall to join hands below the English Channel—was televised throughout the world. The celebration was repeated in May of 1991 when the north tunnel was completed, and again in June when the south shafts were joined.

TML and Eurotunnel spent 1992 and 1993 getting the tunnels and related amenities finished. That effort entailed, among other activities, installing electrical and communications equipment, finishing 150 cross passages between the service and rail tunnels, and constructing terminals on each side of the channel. The first passenger train traveled through the tunnel in May of 1993, and the official opening was slated for May 6, 1994. As TML put the finishing touches on the chunnel and Eurotunnel scrambled to raise more funds, the two groups nevertheless continued to battle each other in the courts. Initially, TML was hesitant to give up full control of the chunnel to its sister company, but after a series of negotiations involving TML, Eurotunnel, and major investors, an agreement to transfer control from TML to Eurotunnel was reached. Eurotunnel took full control of the project beginning late in 1993 and conducted final tests on the system with the help of TML in 1994. Overall, the project had taken 99 months from start to finish, 15,000 workers were involved, and 11 giant tunnel boring machines were used.

The chunnel was officially inaugurated on May 8, 1994. It soon began providing limited passenger service and was almost fully operational after several months. The system was designed to accommodate 2,500-foot-long shuttle trains that traveled at 90 miles per hour. Cars and buses pulled onto large wagons on the train, and passengers were allowed to move about on the wagons during the ride through the chunnel. Truck drivers pulled their rigs onto more rudimentary wagons and traveled separately from their vehicles. Interspersed with those shuttles, moreover, were high-speed trains that could also run on Britain's and continental Europe's railway systems. The train system lived up to its promise of moving passengers between London and Paris in three hours, and between the continents in about 35 minutes. Partly because of cost overruns, Eurotunnel began charging rates of US $240 to US $460 per passenger, depending on the time of year, for a round trip. That compared to about US $90 for a one-and-one-half-hour ferry trip.

When the chunnel opened in 1994, critics condemned Eurotunnel and the other parties involved in the project for creating an expensive, undesirable, and unnecessary transport system. The project was indeed expensive; originally expected to cost US$ 7.5 billion, expenditures had mushroomed to US $15 billion by 1994 and then to a staggering US $23 billion by early 1995. Eurotunnel was left grappling with a cash crunch, and angry creditors began pressuring the company to pay its bills. Fortunately for Eurotunnel, by 1995 the chunnel was beginning to live up to its originators' claims of being a viable system of transportation. In fact, by February of that year the chunnel had snapped up an impressive 20 to 25 percent of the cross-channel freight market. Furthermore, the service was competing aggressively with airlines serving the London/Paris and London/Belgium routes. Although the chunnel's profit potential remained unproven going into the mid-1990s, its status as an engineering marvel of the 20th century was undeniable.

Principal Subsidiaries: The Channel Tunnel Group Ltd.; Eurotunnel Finance Ltd.; Eurotunnel Developments Ltd.; Eurotunnel Services Ltd.

Further Reading:

"The Channel Battle," *Corporate Location,* Channel Tunnel Region Supplement, 1994, pp. 25–31.

"The Chunnel's Chances," *Fortune,* December 21, 1987, p. 9.

Davidson, Andrew, "Sir Alastair Morton," *Management Today,* October 1994, pp. 50–54.

Downer, Stephen, "So Far, Eurotunnel a Ferry Good Thing," *Advertising Age,* May 2, 1994, p. 39.

"EDMS Helps Channel Chunnel Project," *IMC Journal,* November/December 1994, pp. 8–11.

Fairweather, Virginia, "The Channel Tunnel: Larger than Life, and Late," *Civil Engineering,* May 1994, pp. 42–46.

Ferrabee, James, "Confident Chunnel Man," *Gazette,* February 8, 1995, p. D7.

Healy, Tim, "Kent Firm Sees Light at End of Tunnel," *Seattle Times,* October 31, 1990, p. 1D.

Laushway, Ester, "Paris: Chunnel Vision," *Europe: Magazine of the European Community,* May 1994, pp. 43–45.

Levine, Joshua, "Chunnel Vision," *Forbes,* February 14, 1990, p. 146.

Lincoln, Lori, " 'Chunnel' to Open in Late Summer '93: Tunnel Rail Service Will Link Britain, Continent," *Travel Weekly,* April 9, 1992, p. E3.

Nankivell, Neville, "Channel Tunnel Facing Contract Dateline," *Financial Post,* March 27, 1993, p. 18.

Reina, Peter, "After 99 Months' Work Channel Tunnel Prepares for Trains," *Engineering News Record,* May 2, 1994, pp. 22–26.

Stewart, Toy, "Luxury, Calm, and Speed: It's the Chunnel Train," *Business Week,* November 14, 1994, p. 143.

—Dave Mote

Evergreen Marine Corporation Taiwan Ltd.

330 Minsheng East Road
Taipei 10444
Taiwan
88625057766
Fax: 88625055255

Subsidiary of Evergreen Group
Founded: 1968
Employees: 3,900
Sales: $1.2 billion
Stock Exchanges: Taiwan Taipei
SICs: 4731 Freight Transportation Arrangement

Evergreen Marine Corporation Taiwan Ltd. is the largest container shipping company in the world and one of the most successful companies in Taiwan. Although it was only 25 years old in 1994—young compared to many major shipping companies—Evergreen had risen quickly to the top of the shipping industry by focusing on innovation, quality, customer service, and global expansion. Evergreen also expanded into other industries—including construction, trucking, hotel operation, and air transportation—through an umbrella organization called Evergreen Group.

Evergreen Marine Corp. was founded by Y. F. Chang, a Taiwanese visionary whose success has made him one of the wealthiest entrepreneurs in the world and a celebrity in his home country. Chang, the son of a ship's carpenter, grew up in the shipping industry. In fact, before he started Evergreen in 1968, the 41-year-old Chang had worked his way up from a lowly shipping clerk, to sailor, and eventually to captain of a ship. The hard work and leadership skills that had helped him attain that position would prove to be essential to the future success of his fledgling company. Chang started Evergreen with one small ship—a 20-year-old cargo vessel named the *Central Trust*—and 50 employees, 32 of whom worked at sea. He began by offering ship-anywhere service to Taiwanese exporters.

During his first year of business, one of Chang's customers paid him handsomely to make a delivery to the Persian Gulf. From this experience, the opportunistic Chang realized that the potentially lucrative shipping route between East Asia and the Persian Gulf was being neglected by his competitors, many of whom were focusing on the giant North American market. At the time, several oil-rich Middle Eastern countries were just becoming familiar with 20th century technology and modern culture. They were spending billions of dollars on massive modernization projects involving the construction of schools, communication infrastructure, hospitals, airports, and power plants, to name a few. Chang quickly zeroed in on that route. He purchased a second ship in 1969, and initiated regularly scheduled service to the Middle East. Despite early losses, Chang was able to secure enough capital to purchase several more vessels during the early 1970s.

As his Middle East service expanded, Chang searched for other untapped market niches. In 1972, he began offering service between East Asia and Central America, a region that most shipping companies had dismissed as highly unprofitable. Then, in 1974, Evergreen began offering service between East Asia and the U.S. East Coast—Evergreen opened a New York office in cooperation with a U.S. company and purchased four new vessels from a Japanese shipbuilder. The new ships were relatively small S-class vessels, and many observers believed that they were too small to be profitable considering the extreme competition in the U.S. East Coast market. Despite these predictions, Evergreen succeeded in carving out a market; in fact, Chang further developed the company's American market opportunities, ordering more ships and launching new service routes to California in 1976 and then to Seattle in 1977. Due to these heavy investments, Evergreen posted a string of early losses throughout the late 1960s and early 1970s; further, the company was affected along with the rest of the shipping industry by the energy crises of 1974 and 1975. Eventually, though, business improved in the late 1970s and Evergreen began to show profits.

Evergreen's survival and growth during the industry downturn of the mid-1970s was the result of savvy business management, sheer tenacity, and Chang's willingness to take risks. Chang's gains were particularly impressive considering that his competition largely comprised containerized shippers. Indeed, prior to the late 1960s most freight was shipped loose on bulk carriers. Goods were trucked or sent by rail to a port, unloaded, and then reloaded onto a ship. The system was slow and inefficient, and the open goods were vulnerable to spoilage and pilferage. In 1956, American Malcolm McLean, the operator of a trucking company, conceived the idea of containerized shipping, in which goods were loaded into a container at the factory, taken to port, and loaded directly onto a ship. By the late 1960s, established shipping companies had either converted to the new system or had been trammeled by their competitors.

Unfortunately for Chang, Evergreen lacked the resources necessary to convert older ships to containerized haulers. It was largely because of that disadvantage that he attacked the smaller, neglected routes during the late 1960s and early 1970s, and concentrated on efficiency and customer satisfaction. When Evergreen finally did convert to containerized shipping, the company took the industry by storm. Evergreen began offering containerized shipping in its U.S. markets in 1975. Throughout the late 1970s, Chang invested aggressively to update existing ships and expand its line of freighters. As part of Chang's plan to develop a worldwide network of containerized shipping routes, Evergreen initiated new routes serving Europe, the Red

Sea, and the East Mediterranean. At the same time, he augmented the expansion effort with Evergreen Transport Corp., a trucking company that he started in 1973 to support Evergreen Marine's shipping operations.

Evergreen's willingness and ability to penetrate competitive global markets was evidenced by its North European initiative. At the time, that lucrative market was largely managed by the well-established Far Eastern Freight Conference (FEFC). The FEFC was dominated by established shipping companies, and outsiders like Evergreen were not encouraged to compete. Nevertheless, Evergreen executives began an in-depth analyses of the North Europe market, as they did for all of the regions that they considered servicing. Although they were hesitant to tap the market because of the entrenched competition, Evergreen officials commenced service in Northern Europe in 1979. The gamble paid off and Evergreen quickly developed a profitable operation in the region. Going into the early 1980s, Evergreen was serving all three major markets: Asia, North America, and Europe.

By the early 1980s, Evergreen had established itself as an emerging force in the global shipping industry. The company's green shipping containers were becoming an increasingly common sight in ports throughout the world, and Evergreen was aggressively investing for future growth. Indeed, Evergreen assumed full control of its New York operation early in the decade and quickly opened more than 20 offices in the United States and three more in Canada. Importantly, Evergreen launched its prosperous "round-the-world" service in 1984. This ambitious scheme linked Evergreen's fleet of vessels, as well as ships owned by other carriers in some instances, to offer through service around the globe. Evergreen began regularly sending eastbound ships from Singapore to Pusan and Tokyo, through the Panama Canal, to New York, across the Atlantic, through the Suez Canal, and back to Singapore. A similar westbound service departed regularly from Tokyo and made stops in Korca, Singapore, Europe, and New York, among other ports. The round-the-world voyages typically required about 75 days and were coordinated with the help of satellite systems.

Partly to help finance the round-the-world service, Evergreen invested more than $1.5 billion in new ships, terminals, trucks, and containers between 1983 and 1986. The heavy investments surprised other members of the shipping industry, most of whom were suffering from a severe industry downturn. They watched curiously as Evergreen expanded, while at the same time excess shipping capacity was suppressing prices and reducing industry profits. Furthermore, competitors wondered where the tight-lipped Chang found the money to expand: some analysts speculated that Japanese trading house Marubeni was financing Evergreen under-the-table, while others suspected various Japanese or American banks. Regardless of who fronted the investment capital, Evergreen's operations swelled during the mid-1980s as its reach stretched to every corner of the globe. While many of its competitors reduced services or failed, Evergreen's share of major East-West shipping routes ballooned to a dominating 10 percent. Amazingly, Evergreen was still a private company—75 percent owned by Chang and 25 percent owned by his employees.

Evergreen's stunning gains during the shipping industry recession of the mid-1980s were largely attributable to the company's innovative and disciplined workers. The company's philosophy was reflected by its name, Evergreen, which symbolized Chang's goal of constant growth. That growth was achieved by an incessant preoccupation with customer service, which drove the company to become constantly more proficient and productive. Evergreen's heavy investments in cutting edge technology, for example, had made it the most cost-effective carrier in the world. Evergreen ships were outfitted with microcomputers and satellite tracking systems that allowed the company to pinpoint the exact location of each of its containers at all times. As a result, Evergreen's large ships were staffed by just 17 crew members in comparison to an industry average of about 30. A 1986 study showed that Evergreen's cost of delivering a 20-foot container was only $835, compared to $1320 for the average major U.S. carrier. Furthermore, Evergreen was generating a profit of about $80 per container while the industry average was less than $10.

Chang gave the credit for Evergreen's success to its top-notch employees. In contrast to most other shipping lines, Evergreen staffed its ships with highly trained crew members, many of whom had college degrees. Chang personally interviewed every employee that joined the Taiwan office, and once applicants were invited to join Evergreen they were treated well. The company paid higher salaries than most of its competitors and fringe benefits were plentiful. For example, Chang motivated workers by compensating them with ownership shares in the company. The result was an intense loyalty toward, and respect for, the company, which translated indirectly into customer loyalty. Evergreen's Taiwan headquarters was quiet and efficient. The highly dedicated employees arrived early and departed late, and their desks were devoid of personal effects. Furthermore, no one smoked, sipped tea, read newspapers, or used telephones for personal calls during business hours.

By late 1986, Evergreen was operating 52 ships and managing 160,000 containers. Moreover, in addition to Evergreen Marine, Chang's privately held enterprise had branched out to include 14 different companies, most of which were engaged in the manufacturer, storage, and transportation of containers. All of the divisions had names beginning with "Ever." For example, Chang owned Everlaurel, a Japanese trading company, and Evergenius, a software supplier. Those two companies mirrored Chang's intent to diversify out of the shipping industry into a range of new businesses. Indeed, Chang felt that he had achieved his goal of permeating the shipping industry and that the only challenge remaining was to increase Evergreen's market share. To raise expansion capital for more growth, Chang took Evergreen public in September 1987 with a listing on the Taiwan Stock Exchange. Financials released in that year showed that Evergreen's diversified operations had garnered $1.2 billion in revenues in 1986, $50 million of which was netted as profit.

Beginning in 1988, Evergreen Marine Corp. entered a period of consolidation. During that time, the company worked to reorganize its existing operations, cut unnecessary overhead, and reevaluate its presence in foreign markets. Meanwhile, Chang pursued new ventures through Evergreen Marine Corp.'s parent company, Evergreen Group. In 1989, Evergreen started Taiwan's first private international airline, EVA Airways Corporation. The start-up was the result of months of intensive research by Evergreen managers. Using the same customer orientation that had made Evergreen Marine successful, company employees soon turned the fledgling EVA into a small but successful international airline. EVA's planes even reflected the technology focus of Evergreen's ships. Televisions were mounted on the backs of seats, for example, and satellite telephones were available. Furthermore, EVA's technologically advanced planes averaged less than one year in age by 1994, giving the company a significant long-term advantage over competitors with aging fleets. By 1994, EVA was operating 20 aircraft and serving cities in Asia, North America, Europe, and Australia.

Another of Evergreen Group's major ventures in the early 1990s was its hotel business, which represented Chang's efforts to become active in travel and leisure industries. Evergreen's first hotel was the Evergreen Plaza Hotel, which opened in Hong Kong in 1991. The hotel featured 22 floors with 360 rooms and offered a full range of amenities for business travelers. Evergreen opened a second hotel, the 400-room Evergreen Laurel Hotel, in Taiwan in 1992. In 1993, moreover, the company began operating a second Evergreen Laurel Hotel in Bangkok. Other Evergreen hotels were slated to open during the mid-1990s. Evergreen's hotels offered luxury accommodations, Western cuisine, and full recreational and conference amenities.

While the Evergreen Group expanded, the core Evergreen Marine Corp.—the company was renamed Evergreen Marine Corp. Taiwan Ltd.—renewed its global expansion effort. It was aided by its smaller sister company Uniglory, which was started in 1984 and was 50-percent-owned by Evergreen going into 1995. The number of ships operated by Evergreen Marine declined between 1986 and 1993, but Evergreen's shipping capacity increased. Indeed, in 1993 Evergreen Marine launched its first ship with more than 4,000 TEUs (an indicator of carrying capacity). In 1994, moreover, Evergreen ordered 10 new giant ships; five with 4,229 TEU capacity and five with 4,900 TEU capacity. That brought the total number of ships operating in Evergreen Marine's fleet to 56 by 1995.

On Evergreen's 25th anniversary in 1993, the company was displaying healthy revenues of $1.2 billion and profits of $106 million. During that short time, Chang had built the largest shipping company in the world and had become a world-renowned entrepreneur with companies involved in a vast array of industries. Furthermore, at the age of 66 and still firmly in control of the company he started, Chang showed no signs of slowing down. When asked to give advice to shipping industry newcomers in the 1994 *Journal of Commerce and Commercial,* Chang suggested: "they must better themselves with all-round shipping experience and a strong willingness to serve customer's needs. There also has to be a commitment to taking some risks in life because not everything turns out successful. And finally, one must possess a spirit of adventure."

Further Reading:

Canna, Elizabeth, "What's Next for Evergreen?" *American Shipper,* October 1994, p. 38.

"Chairman Chang's Vision," *Journal of Commerce and Commercial,* September 22, 1993, p. S3.

"Evergreen Celebrates 25 Years of Service and Success," *Journal of Commerce and Commercial,* September 22, 1993, pp. S1–S2.

"Hotels and Resorts Prove Natural Extension," *Journal of Commerce and Commercial,* September 22, 1993, p. S9.

Kilgore, Margaret A., "Evergreen Marine . . . Sails Into Leadership," *Southern California,* May 1986, Section 1, p. 7.

Moskowitz, Milton, *The Global Marketplace,* New York: Macmillan, 1987.

Sauder, Rick, "Quiet Event Will Have Port Shaking with Four-year-long Repercussions," *Richmond Times-Dispatch,* March 1993.

"The Secret to Evergreen's Success," *Journal of Commerce and Commercial,* September 22, 1993, p. S2(2).

"Worldwide Aviation Success Built on Transportation Heritage," *Journal of Commerce and Commercial,* September 22, 1993, p. S10.

—Dave Mote

EXECUTONE®

Executone Information Systems, Inc.

478 Wheelers Farms Road
Milford, Connecticut 06460
U.S.A.
(203) 876-7600

Public Company
Incorporated: 1988 as Executone Information Systems
Employees: 2,400
Sales: $292 million
Stock Exchanges: NASDAQ
SICs: 3661 Telephone & Telegraph Apparatus

Executone Information Systems, Inc. is the third largest supplier of telephone systems to the under 300 desktop voice processing market in the United States. The company designs, manufactures, sells, installs, and supports voice processing systems and healthcare communications systems, while also providing long distance telephone service. Its products, which are used by more than 250,000 businesses across the country, are sold under the Executone, Infostar, IDS, Lifesaver, and Infostar/ILS brand names through a worldwide network of nearly 200 direct sales and service offices and independent distributors. The only vendor that supplies inbound, outbound, and administrative call processing within an integrated system, Executone has continued to survive and flourish in an intensely competitive deregulated market through its ability to offer customers a complete line of telecommunication services. The company is also believed to be the only telecommunications company other than AT&T to be vertically integrated, controlling all the major elements of its business, including manufacturing, marketing, distribution, installation, service, and support.

In the later decades of the 1900s, Executone's broad line of services focused on seven product areas. More than two-thirds of the company's 1994 revenue was derived from the sale, maintenance, and upgrading of the company's three types of voice processing equipment: traditional telephone systems, which included a number of software applications that supported services ranging from automatic dialing to video display; call center management products, which identified incoming callers and provided outbound callers with a detailed record of contacts; and voice messaging products, which furnish businesses with automated handling of both external and internal callers. A fourth division of the company's communication products was designed specifically to serve the needs of the healthcare industry, linking patients, nurses, and doctors through microprocessor based systems, intercoms, paging and sound equipment, and room status indicators. During this period, Executone also manufactured locator systems that used infrared transmitter badges to communicate location data to sensors installed throughout a facility, a wide range of videoconferencing systems and services, and a variety of cost-effective telephone services.

What began as a manufacturer of boss-to-secretary intercom systems in 1937, a small business known at the time as Executone, Inc., and grew to become a leading producer of paging devices and intercom systems during the 1950s, represented only one strand of the communications conglomerate's heritage. Although the Executone name survived throughout the decades, three separate companies were responsible for the formation of the firm as it stood in the 1990s: Executone, Inc., Isotec Communications, Inc., and Vodavi Technology Corporation. As was the case with many companies within the industry that managed to survive both the long era of monopolized telephone service and the deregulation period initiated in the early 1980s, the history of Executone Information Systems, Inc. was marked by legislation, acquisition, merger, and reorganization.

Since the invention of the telephone by Alexander Graham Bell in 1876, AT&T, which owned the Bell Telephone System, dominated the telecommunications industry. As early as 1930, though, the United States Justice Department made attempts to dissolve the mammoth monopoly. Four decades later, they finally brought an antitrust suit against the company. In 1982, rather than face a trial, the world's largest and richest monopoly agreed to divest itself of its Bell companies and relinquish its control of the local telephone service industry. Two years later, AT&T, the division responsible for long distance phone service, was officially separated from the local Bell companies. Under the terms of the agreement, Bell, which was divided into seven independent companies, could furnish long distance service for a limited time and local service to the customer; however, it could not provide equipment. For the first time, customers not only had the option to pick and choose their benefits and control pricing on their service, but they were also given the freedom to purchase the telephone equipment of their choice.

In an attempt to capture a profitable share of the deregulated market, hundreds of new and existing companies began manufacturing communications equipment. Executone, a subsidiary of Atlanta-based telecommunications conglomerate Contel Corporation since 1979, found its niche as a distributor of telephone systems to small businesses. With annual revenues of $200 million during the mid-1980s, the company grew to become the nation's largest independent supplier of telephone systems to businesses with less than 200 phone stations. A number of factors, however, brought about a decline in profits that made the company a liability to Contel.

First, increased competition from a more efficient AT&T and a host of others, combined with the strong performance of the dollar overseas, which in turn inflated the price of Japanese electronic components upon which Executone depended, hampered sales and depleted profits. According to some analysts, the movement of company headquarters from Long Island, New

York to Atlanta, Georgia in 1985, also contributed to the poor performance of the company. Not only was the transfer expensive, but it resulted in the loss of around 80 percent of its personnel, including many of its senior employees. As well, a rapid turnover in top level management positions, signified by the replacement of six presidents in nine years, prevented the company from developing a coherent management philosophy. Although the company continued to record strong yearly sales increases, it failed to turn a profit for the parent company, losing an estimated $14.7 million in 1987.

As Executone fell deeper into the red, one of its major suppliers, Vodavi Technology Corporation—a $73 million Arizona-based designer and seller of telecommunications equipment founded by Steven Sherman in 1983—and Isotec Communications Incorporated—a newly public $101 million Connecticut-based designer, manufacturer, and marketer of microprocessor-based communications systems for small businesses—joined forces in December 1987 to purchase Executone for a reported $60 million. Under the terms of the agreement, Vodavi and Isotec each acquired 50 percent of Executone with the intention to merge their respective businesses in mid-1988. On July 7, 1988, the shareholders of both Isotec and Vodavi approved the reorganization and merger of Isotec with and into Vodavi. As the only surviving company, if only in a legal sense, Vodavi was renamed Executone Information Systems, Inc.

The management, philosophy, and business strategy of what instantly became the nation's second largest distributor of small to medium-sized business telephone systems, was supplied by Isotec and its leader, Allen Kessman, who took over as the new corporation's first chief executive officer. Under his direction, Executone Information Systems followed the course of Isotec's vertical integration strategy of complete control over product design, manufacturing, marketing, and service, while at the same time intensifying the company's efforts to diversify its product line and establish and expand its end-user base for post-sales activities. With the merger also came a number of additional benefits: reduced competition through consolidation; increased operating efficiencies from the elimination of duplicate resources; a substantial increase in installed base from combining Isotec's and Executone's product lines; a more focused marketing strategy; and a broadening of manufacturing capabilities.

Despite these advantages, the Darien, Connecticut-based Executone, failed to turn a profit in 1989, its first complete year of operation, and continued to struggle as it entered the new decade. In addition to having to contend with the costs and internal reorganizational issues that followed the company's formation, Executone was further distracted by the United States Commerce Department, which, in response to an AT&T petition, established dumping duties as high as 158 percent for several Far East Asian multiline business communications equipment manufacturers, including Korea's Goldstar Telecommunications and Oriental Precision Company, two of Executone's major subcontractors. While the new tariffs significantly increased production costs, market forces prevented the company from raising prices high enough to make a profit in new systems installations.

To offset losses in this area, the company looked to divert its resources from new systems sales to selling additional services to its existing customer base. To that end, in July 1990, the company made long distance service available to its customers on a national basis through its Infostar LD+ program, offering its small business customers the added efficiency of a one-stop telecommunications provider and a single point of contact and billing for equipment and long distance service. That same year, the company introduced a new line of PC-based software products, including enhanced automatic call distribution (ACD), predictive of power dialing (also known as out-bound ACD), and integrated voice mail. Finally, the company revitalized its nurse communications product line, which was being used in 60 percent of the nation's hospitals, and placed more emphasis on its telecommunications contracts with various prisons, especially in California.

In addition to making these technological advancements, the company directed its attention to making its sales force more productive, a necessity in the ultracompetitive telecommunications equipment industry. In April 1991, the company launched a pilot project known as Sales Navigation, designed both to increase the amount of time salespeople would spend in actual face-to-face selling and to "qualify" customers, that is, learning whom to call on and knowing what questions to ask individuals. The new program essentially replaced the time-intensive initial stages of the sales process—those involving the location and evaluation of prospective customers—with a more efficient system. The new system used direct mail, telemarketing, lead-tracking software, and a "sales navigator"—someone who uses the telephone to respond to prospects—guiding them through the complications of investing in phone equipment and providing them with the appropriate follow-up material specific to the needs of their business. At that point, the traditional sales force would take over the "smart lead," armed with detailed information: what prospects needed, the size of their business, the equipment they were currently using, and who the key decision makers were at the company.

In addition, Executone's 400 field reps were equipped with laptop computers that not only provided the necessary information, but, through a custom-designed sales information system called Computer-Aided Selling (CAS), they could generate error-free proposals, complete with pricing and profit margin figures. According to *Success* magazine's Jenny C. McCune, the new system "transformed selling from an artistic endeavor into a scientific discipline." CAS also significantly reduced turnover in its sales force: the stress involved in selling big-ticket items in such an intensely competitive market had led many salespeople to quit during their training program, but the new system enabled the company to retain nearly all of its salespeople and even recruit sales personnel from other companies. The effect of automation on the company's bottom line was also dramatic. While revenues increased only eight percent during the first four years of the program's use, net income more than tripled, reaching a level of $5.2 million in 1993.

Behind the strength of its fully automated sales force and a number of technological improvements to its diverse product lines, Executone registered its third consecutive year of record-breaking performance, turning in revenues of nearly $292 million and profits of $7.5 million in 1994. Much of the seven percent gain in total revenue was generated through the expansion of the Infostar-LD+ program and increased sales of systems upgraded and voice-processing products. One of the company's most significant and potentially profitable developments during the year was the introduction of the TeleSearch feature to its locator systems. A product designed to improve productivity and efficiency in the office, TeleSearch integrated locating and telephone systems, providing customers with the ability to find personnel immediately and have them return calls quickly from any phone anywhere in the world. Another new product, Care/Com II-E, a nurse call system, was introduced in the company's healthcare division, furnishing non-acute care hospitals with a less expensive and smaller version of the company's more comprehensive LifeSaver system.

To accommodate the growth of the company during the 1990s and to prepare for the future, Executone made a number of organizational changes in 1994. The company moved its corporate headquarters from Darien to Milford, Connecticut, taking over a 150,000 square-foot building formerly leased by IBM, while selling its Vodavi Communications Systems Division to Va Technology Acquisition Corporation for an estimated $10.9 million. Finally, the company added four regional presidents to its management team in an attempt to facilitate more high-level contacts with prospects and customers throughout the country.

Having reduced its debt by almost $80 million between 1989 and 1994, Executone positioned itself well for continued growth through the rest of the decade. Although the telecommunications market remained one of the world's most competitive, Executone's commitment to acquiring and developing new technology promised to keep the company near the top of the field. In April 1995, for instance, the company signed a distribution contract with Dialogic Communications Corporation (DCC), the nation's leading provider of Automated Callout Solutions, for a personal computer-based software application known as "The Communicator," which was designed to notify personnel via telephone, pager, and facsimile during emergencies. Executone planned to introduce the product—which had been used successfully in nuclear plants, government buildings, military bases, and major corporations—to healthcare providers and correctional facilities. The alliance with DCC also enabled Executone to add the latest in Audio Response Unit (ARU) technology to its cable television and wireless products. With the new ARU II Voice Processing Solution, the company had the capability to usher in a new era the cable television industry, offering customers door-to-door local access and service in nearly any location in America.

Principal Subsidiaries: Infostar, Inc.; Executone Europe Ltd.; Executone Network Services, Inc.; Blaser Industries, Inc. (80.5%)

Further Reading:

Albrecht, Susan C., "Loss Report Imminent: Purchase, Merger Aimed at Returning Vodavi to Success," *Arizona Business Gazette,* March 21, 1988, p. 14.

——, "New Company Ready to Dial Up Success," *Arizona Business Gazette,* July 18, 1988, p. 19.

Andrew, Meg, "The Dialing Dilemma: The Telephone Industry and Consumers Are Reeling From the Effects of Deregulation," *Business View,* August 1986, p. 8.

Beel, Susan, "Interconnect Firms Cut Back as Sales Slow," *San Diego Business Journal,* March 8, 1993, p. 22.

Cavanaugh, Tim, "Albany Executone Unperturbed by Sale of Parent," *Capital District Business Review,* December 14, 1987, p. 7.

Everett, Martin, "Instead of Fishing for Leads, Executone Navigates," *Sales and Marketing Management,* October 1991, pp. 86–89.

Feingold, Jeff, "Phone Wars Start to Take Their Toll," *New Hampshire Business Review,* October 15, 1986, p. 1.

Jordan, John, "Executone Information Systems Moving Its HQ to Milford," *Fairfield County Business Journal,* November 1, 1993, p. 1.

Larson, Mark, "Executone Rings Up Profit as Staffers Dial a Bonus," *Business Journal—Sacramento,* March 11, 1991, p. 5.

Mason, Michael, "Contel Keeps Reorganizing as It Adds New Companies," *Atlanta Business Chronicle,* October 20, 1986, p. 48.

McCune, Jenny C., "Empower with Technology," *Success,* May 1993, pp. 41–43.

Rodrian, Scott, "Vodavi Deals to Become $350 Million Giant," *Business Journal—Phoenix & the Valley of the Sun,* December 21, 1987, p. 1.

——, "Vodavi's Founder Sherman Resigns to Pursue 'Creation of New Entities,' " *Business Journal—Phoenix & the Valley of the Sun,* June 27, 1988, p. 7.

Thorne, Linda, "The Interconnect Wars," *New Mexico Business Journal,* January 1987, p. 26.

Troxell, Tom, "Isotec-Vodavi-Executone Marriage Bears Hope, Risk," *Intercorp,* May 27, 1988, p. 40.

—Jason Gallman

FAMILY DOLLAR®

Family Dollar Stores, Inc.

P.O. Box 1017
Charlotte, North Carolina 28201
U.S.A.
(704) 847-6961
Fax: (704) 847-5534

Public Company
Incorporated: 1959
Employees: 14,700
Sales: $1.4 billion
Stock Exchanges: New York
SICs: 5331 Variety Stores

Family Dollar Stores, Inc. is a chain of discount stores that offer inexpensive merchandise for family and home needs to customers in the Midwest, the South, and the Northeast. Since opening the first Family Dollar store in Charlotte, North Carolina, founder Leon Levine has seen a lot of changes. The stores rose rapidly in profitability and presence until the mid-1980s national superstore boom led by such companies as Wal-Mart. Since then, Family Dollar has retrenched and reworked its basic strengths, while also expanding its network of over 2,000 stores.

Company founder, Leon Levine, learned the retail business from his father. In fact, when his father Harry Levine died in 1947, Leon and his brother Al took over the store their father began; Leon was 13 years old at the time. The store, in Rockingham, North Carolina, billed itself as a department store, but was really more closely allied to the old-fashioned general store. By 1959, Leon was ready to strike out on his own, and he opened the first Family Dollar store in Charlotte. His target customer was the lower-middle income family who couldn't afford fancy name brands and wasn't a slave to high fashion, but did need good clothing and durable shoes.

The Family Dollar store proved popular among value shoppers, and soon new outlets were opened. By the early 1970s, the company had gone public and had opened its 100th store in Brevard, North Carolina. Although it was not the first in the self-service, discount variety field, Family Dollar secured a leading spot.

One difficulty in targeting lower income consumers was that they were often the first hit during bad economic weathers—whether due to inflation or recession—and were quickly forced to cut back on spending. Thus, while Family Dollar expanded and achieved record sales in the early 1970s, the mid-1970s presented a particular challenge. Clustered in the southern states, the chain was hard hit by fallout from the traumatized textile industry in 1974. Many of Family Dollar's customers in that region were textile workers; many others worked in the tobacco and furniture industries, and were similarly hard-hit. Family Dollar saw its profits fall by as much as 50 percent in 1974 and 1975, which was especially shocking given the company's growth rate in the years before; earnings in the early 1970s had shot up 24 percent annually, on average.

To offset the effects of this economic downturn, the company began targeting some of its weaknesses, seeking to improve marketing and merchandising, as well as to diversify geographically. It also dropped its policy of pricing all merchandising at $3 or less, which, while it had appealed to shoppers, had proved too hard on store margins. Family Dollar also tightened inventory controls, adding an electronic data processing system. Though the economy continued to be volatile in the late 1970s, Family Dollar was able to exceed $100 million in sales in fiscal year 1978, and hit a record $151 million in sales in 1979. Same-store sales remained fairly flat around that time, however.

Family Dollar was operating about 400 outlets in eight states, all in the South, by 1980. Most of the sales gains over the next few years were from additional stores. In 1979, Family Dollar acquired 40 Top Dollar stores from Sav-A-Stop. That same year, it also opened 36 new units of its own, putting it ahead of its own expansion schedule.

Family Dollar's draw at the time was its bargain-priced goods—such items as toys, automotive equipment, and school supplies—all displayed within 6,000 to 8,000 square feet of store. Much of the company's merchandise had come from vendors or suppliers who had overbought, so the company's savings on those underpriced goods could be passed on to its customers. Another winning strategy was to gather up manufacturer's overruns. Size and strategy helped as well. When Procter & Gamble refused to give Levine a deal on Pampers disposable diapers, figuring he would have to stock them anyway, Levine stocked more Kleenex disposable diapers, as well as a Family Dollar brand, and soon Pampers became less necessary.

Another ingredient in Family Dollar's success was its efficient distribution system, handled entirely out of Charlotte, from which the company was able to make bulk deliveries to its stores. In 1980, the size of the distribution center was doubled so that the company could take further advantage of discounts on single, bulk deliveries, as well as open new stores without concern about stock shortages.

Although Family Dollar was branching out geographically at this time, with 70 to 80 outlets in Georgia, it was still primarily a Carolina chain. Soon, the company began investigating further opportunities in Alabama, Tennessee, the Virginias, Florida, Kentucky, and Mississippi. Because the company had no long-term debt—despite the recent Top Dollar stores acquisition—the cash flow freed Family Dollar to expand without too much risk in borrowing. In fact, it opened 33 new stores between September 1979 and September 1980, and was boasting a growth of about 30 percent per year since 1975. Family Dollar stores generally operated in leased buildings, which saved the company on capital investment. In March 1982, the company's 500th store opened, in Brunswick, Georgia.

Family Dollar continued to thrive through the early 1980s, ringing up more record profits—in fact, it had a nine-year streak of them—and opening more than 100 new stores a year between 1982 and 1987. But while the company was becoming a more national presence, it failed to keep a close eye on increasing competition from Wal-Mart Stores. Suddenly, sales growth in recently opened stores tripped from nine percent in 1984, to a dull two percent in 1985, then came to a dead halt the following year, and dropped ten percent in 1987.

At the time, and, indeed, since the company's inception, Family Dollar shoppers were families making less than $25,000 a year. Most stores were rooted in rural areas, usually in towns of less than 15,000, often within walking distance or a very short drive from home. The average Family Dollar customer shopped there at least once a week, spending about $8 on average. The stores were about one-tenth the size of a Wal-Mart or Kmart, so product lines had to be meticulously selected and limited. Even though the bigger stores could offer more merchandise, the draw of Family Dollar stores was often location. Wal-Marts were typically planted outside or on the edge of town, while Family Dollars were downtown. The real problem arose when Family Dollar management, preoccupied with expansion, stopped checking on the competition's pricings. When it did check, only after sales slipped enough to cause alarm, it found that Wal-Mart was pricing sometimes as much as ten percent below Family Dollar—often on such things as health and beauty products that Family Dollar was advertising heavily as on sale.

Thus, in 1987, Family Dollar instituted a new pricing policy: they would not be undersold. Within two months, same-store sales were up ten percent. Clearly, the lower prices wounded margins somewhat, but the company compensated by scaling back its expansion. It had been expanding as far north as Michigan, and as far west as Texas, and right into Sam Walton's Wal-Mart territory. In 1986, there were 1,107 Family Dollar stores in 23 states. At the same time, Wal-Marts were infiltrating Family Dollar's stronghold, the rural southeast. Wal-Mart was using its buying power to plunge prices while Family Dollar was using its profits to open more stores.

After catching itself and lowering prices to boost sales, the company faced another challenge in the form of a management shake up. In the mid-1980s, Leon Levine was the company's chairman and chief executive; Leon's first cousin, Lewis E. Levine, served as president and chief operating officer; and Leon's son Howard Levine was senior vice-president of merchandising. In September of 1987, just as Family Dollar reported its fourth consecutive quarter of lower earnings, Lewis Levine abruptly resigned, and Howard Levine left as well. Lewis had been with the company for 17 years and was reportedly upset by salary differentials (CEO Leon Levine made an estimated $1.84 million in 1986, while Lewis made just over $260,040). Moreover, the cousins had disagreed over strategy; Lewis felt that Leon wasn't responding quickly enough to changes necessary to defend against the encroaching Wal-Mart. Essentially, it come down to stand-off, in which Lewis asked for more control and the board asked for Lewis's resignation. Leon served as president until a successor was named, capping his own salary at $350,000 for 1987 and 1988. Leon's son, Howard Levine, the heir-apparent, seemed to have left the company for more personal reasons.

Meanwhile, the battle with Wal-Mart grew heated. Family Dollar's new "everyday-low-price" strategy was still hard on the margins. In 1987, the company was spending $2 million to renovate its 1,272 stores, to make the most of their compact size. When Family Dollar first began matching or beating Wal-Mart on prices for items like health and beauty aids and automotive supplies, same-store sales rose nine percent for a few months, but then fell back to the levels of the year prior. Still, Family Dollar felt that it had two advantages: it could squeeze into urban store spaces without fear of a large Wal-Mart moving in next door, and Family Dollar was still virtually debt-free.

After an intense headhunting mission, Levine appointed Ralph Dillon the new president and CEO of Family Dollar. Formerly the head of Coast American Corporation, Denver's retail franchise, Dillon joined Family Dollar in summer of 1987. Faced with rising sales, given the new store expansions, but essentially flat earnings, Dillon's strategy was simple: return to the basics that built Family Dollar in the first place, particularly in regards to pricing. The previous management's efforts at aggressive markdowns were pushed even further; a policy was now instituted requiring that any item tagged at more than $15 gain approval first from top management.

To assist margins, the company began stocking more of its own labeled products, as well as manufacturer's overruns and close-outs, practices that had been scaled back in the 1980s when the stores had tried to upscale merchandise. Also stocked were irregular brand-name goods, meaning jeans and sweaters that were slightly flawed. Other high-margin goods such as seasonal candies and costume jewelry were pushed. Coupled with an ad-blitz stressing the chain's return to "everyday low prices," Family Dollar felt confident of a comeback. The cuts would bite into the company's overall margin for a couple of years. Still, because of its healthy cash flow and minimal debt, the company had the equipment to ride out a recession and get through its own changes.

And indeed, despite the tough economic weathers of the late 1980s, Family Dollar was thriving again and, by 1991, was reporting another record year. Importantly, same-store sales were up, overall sales exceeded the $1 billion mark for the first time, and revenues increased 18 percent in 1992 alone. That same year, the company planned to open 150 new stores, concentrating in New England, where existing store sales were above average. By year-end, Family Dollar had opened 175 new stores and closed 25.

Meanwhile, the management concentrated on improving gross margins. A new point-of-sale (POS) system was installed, which gave detailed information on apparel styles, colors, and sizes selling well in each store. The POS system also helped stores track regional competition on certain products. During this time, Peter Hayes became the new president of Family Dollar.

By 1992, as Wal-Mart captured 26 percent of the discount store market and many smaller discounters were sent into bankruptcy, Family Dollar seemed to have survived by concentrating on its core strengths of convenience, solid stock, and low prices. Family Dollar stores were on average within three miles of shopper's homes, and were still about one-tenth the size of Wal-Mart stores. Moreover, because its stocks were smaller per store, the price of staples such as toothpaste and laundry detergent at Family Dollar were often slightly more than one might pay at Wal-Mart. Nevertheless, many customers seemed willing to pay slightly higher prices in exchange for convenience of location and getting around more quickly in a smaller store. Family Dollar had faced the superstore threat head-on, and was, by 1992, even posting a better net margin than Wal-Mart.

Apparel represented about 45 percent of the Family Dollar stock in 1993, while "hard" goods made up the remainder. The company spread out its search for merchandise, and took advantage of downtime in factories—contracting them to manufacture merchandise at cut rates during times they would usually be fallow. About ten percent of the company's overall business was attributable to private label sales, and most store merchandise was priced lower than $18. The company was also sprucing up its distribution system, installing a building in Memphis, Arkansas, of more than 550,000 square feet, which when combined with the North Carolina center, totaled about 1.3 million square feet of space. Both centers were fully automated.

In 1994, having regained its sales strength, Family Dollar focused on fine-tuning its strategy of centering itself as a neighborhood convenience store with low prices. It began phasing out low-margin items like tools, paints, and motor oils, replacing them with more popular, higher priced items like toys and portable stereos. The pricing policy began allowing for items up to $25. Expansion was also a focus; 165 new units were added to the Family Dollar chain in 1993, and the same number was planned for 1994. Indeed, the rash of bankruptcies among regional discount chains provided Family Dollar with opportunities for growth.

In the spring of 1994, Hayes resigned as president and chief operating officer of Family Dollar Stores, taking a position as president of a Florida-based jewelry company. He was replaced by John Reier, who had been with the company since 1987, having been senior vice-president in charge of Family Dollar's merchandising and advertising. Leon Levine remained board chair and CEO. Given the highly competitive nature of the industry, Family Dollar sales and earnings failed to meet expectations in 1994. In the 1994 annual report to shareholders, Levine remained optimistic, however, noting that the company would continue its aggressive expansion plans and continue to pursue price reductions at Family Dollar stores.

Further Reading:

Clune, Ray, "Family Dollar Sticks to Its Niche," *Daily News Record,* December 6, 1993, pp.4,5.

D'Innocenzio, Anne, "Building the Family Image," *Women's Wear Daily,* January 26, 1994, p. 18.

"Family Dollar Quietly Invades Northeast," *Discount Store News,* December 7, 1992, pp. 4, 5.

Foust, Dean, "The Family Feud at Family Dollar Stores," *Business Week,* September 21, 1987, pp. 32, 33.

Greene, Richard, "The Leon and Al Show," *Forbes,* September 29, 1980, pp. 52–54.

Grover, Mary Beth, "Tornado Watch," *Forbes,* June 22, 1992, pp. 66–69.

Keefe, Lisa, "Guess Who Lost," *Forbes,* September 7, 1987, pp. 60,61.

Palmer, Jay, "Back to Basics," *Barron's,* August 29, 1988, pp. 20, 21.

Tronell, Thomas, "Bucking a Slump," *Barron's,* January 21, 1980, pp. 39,41.

—Carol I. Keeley

Ferrari S.p.A.

Corso Marconi 10
Turin
Italy
011 39 11 65651
Ferrari North America Inc.
250 Sylvan Ave.
Englewood Cliffs, New Jersey 07632
U.S.A.
(201) 816-2600

Wholly Owned Subsidiary of Fiat S.p.A.
Sales:
Incorporated: 1960
Employees: 80
SICs: 5012 Automobiles & Other Motor Vehicles; 5013 Motor Vehicle Supplies & New Parts

Synonymous with speed and performance, Ferrari sports cars are among the most prestigious automobiles in the world, along with Porsche, Maserati, Alfa Romeo, Jaguar, and Lamborghini. The name Ferrari is still venerated on the international racing circuit, and many automotive experts regard the Ferrari GTO as one of the most exotic sports cars ever made. Only 35 Ferrari GTOs were built, and some of them have been sold as collectors' items for more than $10 million.

The company's founder, Enzo Ferrari, was born in 1898 in Modena, Italy, to a lower-middle-class family. Lacking a formal education, he was given the job of shoeing horses for the Italian Army during World War I. After the war, he traveled to Turin and applied for work at Fiat, already one of the most prominent automobile manufacturers in Europe. Unceremoniously rejected, Ferrari nurtured a grudge against Fiat that developed into a driving ambition. Determined to break into the automotive industry, Ferrari began to frequent the bars and cafes around Turin where famous race car drivers sought their entertainment. In one of these bars Ferrari met Ugo Sivocci, a test driver for a new automobile manufacturer named Costruzioni Meccaniche Nazionalia (CMN). Sivocci hired Ferrari as his assistant and the young man competed in his first race in October 1919.

Ferrari did not remain with CMN for very long, and soon joined Alfa Romeo, located in Portello on the outskirts of Milan. Founded in 1909 by Cavaliere Ugo Stella, Alfa manufactured a line of automobiles and sponsored cars for the racing circuit. Ferrari was hired by Alfa Romeo as a test driver, and was also contracted by the company to sell its cars. During the early 1920s Ferrari crisscrossed the Italian roads between Milan and Turin selling automobiles, buying parts, delivering new cars to wealthy customers, spying on Fiat, and racing Alfas.

During these years Ferrari earned his laurels as a race car driver. In 1923 he won the Chilometro Lanciato at Geneva, the Circuito del Polesine at Robigo, and the annual race at Ravenna. In 1924 he won the Pescara, run on the Adriatic coast. The death in 1925 of popular Antonio Ascari, Alfa Romeo's premier driver, led the company to cancel all racing competition out of respect for the fallen employee. Disappointed that his own racing career was interrupted, Ferrari redirected his energy and focused on developing his distributorship for Alfa Romeo. By the end of 1925, Ferrari had expanding his holdings into a large dealership and service center. By 1927 he was behind the wheel of a racing car once again, and won the Modena race and the Circuito di Alessandria that year. In 1928 Ferrari repeated as champion in both of these races.

As Alfa Romeo's fortunes declined during the late 1920s and early 1930s, it was taken over by the Istituto di Ricostruzione Industriale (IRI), a government organization formed to assist companies experiencing financial difficulties. As a consequence of this takeover, Alfa Romeo withdrew its direct involvement from the racing car circuit, except for the international Grand Prix races. Ferrari, however, was not to be denied, and, parlaying his contacts with the Americans at Shell Oil, the Germans at Bosch ignition systems, and his fellow Italians at Pirelli tires, he formed the Societa Anonima Scuderia Ferrari, a stable of racing cars and drivers dedicated to furthering the sport of competitive racing. Ferrari promised his fellow investors that his operation would not only buy and race cars, but also build high-performance automobiles for the sports car enthusiast some time in the future. Alfa Romeo contracted the new Scuderia to act as its official representative in some races.

With the increasing strength of the Facist Party under the leadership of Benito Mussolini during the 1930s, Ferrari decided to become a member of the Facist Party. His association with the Fascists dovetailed with his ambition to run Alfa Romeo's racing program, which, of course, was operating under the auspices of the government-controlled IRI. Ferrari's ambitions were frustrated, however, with the arrival of Wifredo Ricart, a Spanish engineer hired by IRI to revitalize Alfa Romeo and return the company to the winner's circle on the competitive race car circuit. Ferrari's personal dislike of Ricart was evident from the beginning, but increased dramatically when he discovered that Ricart was behind Alfa Romeo's decision to buy 80 percent of the Scuderia Ferrari and return administration of the racing program to the company's office in Portello. With acrimony and bitterness compounded during every meeting between the two men, and after a particularly unpleasant exchange in which Ricart likened himself to a genius, Ferrari decided it was best to end his association with the Spanish engineer and Alfa Romeo.

Ferrari's parting agreement with Alfa Romeo stipulated that he could neither use the name of Scuderia Ferrari nor engage in racing for four years. For this, he received a generous severance package, and wasted no time in establishing Auto Avio Costruzione, a custom machine shop that initially manufactured small aircraft engines for planes. The famous Ferrari symbol of the prancing horse first appeared during this time on company letterhead and marketing brochures. With Italy's entry into World War II in 1940, Ferrari's factory was soon producing machine tools for the Axis armies, including sophisticated hydraulic grinders. Although his company profited from its association with the Axis Powers, Ferrari was impatient because the war years interrupted international motor racing.

After the war, Ferrari was approached by a group of car enthusiasts who convinced him to manufacture the 125, a new car for the racing circuit. In March 1947, the prototype 125 took its initial test drive, and later in the year entered and won the Circuito del Valentino in Turin before the wealthy and elite of Italian society. Soon after the race, such dignitaries as Count Bruno Sterzi and Count Soave Besana of Milan and the Russian Prince Igor Troubetzkoy (husband of Barbara Hutton, the heiress to the Woolworth fortune) were knocking on Ferrari's door in Modena to purchase his cars. By December, Enzo Ferrari was manufacturing a limited number of high-performance sports cars. Ferrari's first cars, such as the Tipo 166 Spider Corsa, were triple-purpose vehicles. They could be used as sports cars on the public road, as competitive sports cars in races such as the Mille Miglia, and as entries in Formula Two racing events (with fenders and other equipment removed).

By the summer of 1948, Ferrari's automobile designers had completed work on a non-racing car. This *gran turismo* automobile would be made with windows, heaters, a top, and leather upholstery. Each car body was to be hand-made by artisans with traditionally exquisite Italian styling and craftsmanship, and delivered to distributors in batches of less than ten automobiles at a time. When the car was finally delivered, the customer would have the final decision regarding paint color, upholstery, and external trim. Until Ferrari was taken over by Fiat in 1969, all cars made by the company were manufactured by this method and, hence, no two cars were identical.

During the early 1950s, Ferrari cars were ordered by the international elite, including the Aga Khan, King Leopold of Belgium, the Shah of Iran, Juan Peron, Crown Prince Faisal of Saudi Arabia, and members of both the Dulles and Du Pont families. The company listed dealer franchises in London, Rome, Zurich, Algiers, Casablanca, Melbourne, Florence, Brussels, Montevideo, Sao Paulo, Paris, and New York. Although Ferrari engines were temperamental and frequently overheated, the combination of their nastiness with their brilliant body work and designs created an unparalleled mystique. Alfa Romeos, Maseratis, and Jaguars seemed to pale in comparison.

Despite the growing success of his commercial enterprise, Ferrari remained obsessed with racing, with most of the money he earned from selling sports cars in Europe and America used to fund the annual Grand Prix and Formula One races. The fortunes of race car sponsors are volatile, however: in 1952 cars designed and manufactured by Ferrari won 16 of the 17 races the company had entered; in 1957, Ferrari won only a few of the numerous races on the international circuit. Nevertheless, by the end of the 1950s Enzo Ferrari had become a national institution in motor racing, a kind of quasi-official representative of the Italian nation in every race. Ferrari began to believe the press reports about his responsibility in carrying Italy's banner in international racing, and devoted more and more time to his racing team. While most Italians celebrated Christmas and Easter Sunday, Ferrari was conducting business to improve his chances of winning the next race.

In 1960 the firm was restructured as a public corporation under the name Societa Esercizio Fabbriche Automobili e Corse Ferrari. Approximately 40 percent of all Ferrari cars were exported to North America, primarily for the American market. The cars were stripped down and detuned versions of the company's racers, and even though the money made from selling these automobiles to wealthy Americans allowed Ferrari to pursue his motor racing dreams, Ferrari was indifferent to almost every aspect of the manufacturing process.

Ferrari made it known in the industry that he wanted a large firm to take over the administration and management of his factories so he could devote all his energy to racing, and in the early 1960s, Ford Motor Company made overtures to the Italian car maker. In return for rights to the Ferrari name, trademark, patents, future technical developments, and 90 percent of the company's stock, Ford agreed to purchase the sports car manufacturer for $18 million. The acquisition of Ferrari by Ford developed into a national issue, with the Italian press leading the opposition to the deal as a matter of national honor. Negotiations proceeded smoothly until Ferrari insisted on maintaining complete control over the racing operation. Ford executives balked and could not accept a completely independent operation working within the organization. The deal between Ford and Ferrari, which appeared so promising, was suddenly canceled.

Sports car manufacturers such as Porsche, Jaguar, and the brand new Lamborghini began to chip away at Ferrari's market in both Europe and America, and the grand master's continued indifference to passenger-car production at his own firm finally took its toll: the designs of 330GTs, 275GTBs, and other models were downright ugly, and production was shoddy. Car bodies were inclined to rust easily and component parts were badly or cheaply tooled. American distributors soon discovered that the Ferrari sports cars of the late 1960s were almost impossible to sell. Between 1968 and 1969, car sales dropped from 729 to 619 units. Lacking funds for expansion, and with Ferrari's insistence on competing in many races at once rather than concentrating his limited resources on, for example, the Formula One competition, the company began to suffer financially. Yet Ferrari himself was a prisoner of his own public image—he was the focal point, the icon, of a nation hungry for respect in the international community. Ferrari realized that massive amounts of money were required for the company to survive, so he turned to Fiat for help. Since Ferrari had harbored such a lifelong dislike of Fiat, it was an ironic turn of events.

On June 21, 1969, Fiat purchased Ferrari for $11 million. According to the terms of the agreement, Fiat gained 40 percent of Ferrari stock and would manage the passenger car operation, while Ferrari himself retained 49 percent of the stock and complete control over the motor racing operation. Fiat immediately took over the daily administration of designing, manufacturing, marketing, and selling Ferrari's road cars, and invested millions in modernizing the company's factory and expanding its production. By 1970, under the new Fiat management, production of Ferrari passenger cars had increased to over 1,000, and by the end of the decade production has reached the 2,000 mark. Fiat doubled the size of the Ferrari factory and was committed to making Ferrari cars the focus of its international marketing.

During the 1970s and 1980s, the collection of Ferrari automobiles by car enthusiasts reached the intensity of a quasi-religious experience. Americans and Europeans alike paid enormous sums of money for the older Ferrari racing machines, and one Frenchman even converted his entire 375-acre estate outside Paris into a shine for Ferrari automobiles. Enzo Ferrari was not the slightest bit interested in the deification of his cars and, more often than not, displayed contempt for the individuals who bought Ferrari cars as a status symbol. After selling the passenger car operation to Fiat, for nearly two decades the old man remained engrossed by the fortunes of his racing team. When Enzo Ferrari died on August 15, 1988, the Italian population went into mourning. The last of the automotive giants had passed away. Shortly after his death, Fiat management announced that the Ferrari factory works would increase production, and that the last remnants of handcrafted car production would be gradually phased out.

With the financial backing of Fiat, Ferrari had attempted to increase its presence in the American market during the early and mid-1990s, in part by sponsoring races for owners of Ferrari 348 sports cars. Reviving Ferrari's image as a racing machine has been effective, with many new customers willing to invest the money needed to modify their cars for the racing circuit. In 1994 sales of Ferrari cars in the United States alone shot up 20 percent. As the company unveiled its new Spider convertible on fashionable Rodeo Drive in Beverly Hills, California—in the first premier of a Ferrari car in the United States—Fiat had high expectations that American customers would once again be captivated by the mystique of Ferrari sports cars.

Further Reading:

Henry, Jim, "Car Sales Are the Big Prize in Ferrari Race Series," *Automotive News,* July 11, 1994, p. 34.

——, "Fiat Gives U.S. More Attention," *Automotive News,* March 15, 1993, p. 6.

Yates, Brock, *Enzo Ferrari: The Man, the Cars, the Races, the Machine,* New York: Doubleday, 1991.

—Thomas Derdak

Fifth Third Bancorp

Fifth Third Center
Cincinnati, Ohio 45263
U.S.A.
(513) 579-5300
Fax: (513) 744-6701

Public Company
Incorporated: 1904
Employees: 5,644
Total Assets: $14.95 billion
Stock Exchanges: NASDAQ
SICs: 6712 Bank Holding Companies; 6021 National Commercial Banks; 6022 State Commercial Banks

Over the course of its more than 125-year history, Fifth Third Bancorp has grown from a small local institution with a capital stock of just $25,000 into a leading regional bank with $15 billion in assets. Although Fifth Third has pursued growth through acquisition in an era of intense bank industry consolidation, its highest priorities have clearly been safety and profitability. While Fifth Third does not rank among the United States' biggest banks, the company has topped analysts' lists of the country's best financial institutions. Among other honors, Fifth Third has earned the highest ranking among *United States Banker*'s index of the country's top-performing banks in 1993 and 1994. The Salomon Brothers investment house ranked Fifth Third tops in overall profitability, productivity, capital, and asset quality every year from 1989 through 1994. As of early 1995, the company had increased earnings for over 20 consecutive years.

Fifth Third's success has been credited to an endemic sales culture, strict expense controls (it costs the bank less than 50¢ to generate each dollar of income), a cautious approach to lending, and a high level of fee income. Industry observers have also cited its geographic situation in the comparatively stable Midwest—Fifth Third has operations in Ohio, Kentucky, Indiana, and Florida—as an important element of its success. CEO George A. Schaefer, Jr., who was named ''1994 Banker of the Year'' by *American Banker,* told *U.S. Banker* that an enterprising corporate culture was also a significant contributor to the institution's progress. ''In the service business, you have to out-hustle the competition to survive.''

The firm traces its history to the mid-nineteenth century formulation of America's national banking system. Although national banks had existed in the United States since the late eighteenth century, a lack of consensus on the advantages of a national currency prevented the federal government from establishing a unified currency structure. Rampant inflation during the Civil War, however, prompted the 1863 ratification of the Federal Banking Act, thereby creating a uniform, government-backed national currency to replace the divers currencies issued by state banks and other firms. That same year, a group of influential Cincinnati businessmen led by A.L. Mowry applied for and received one of the first national bank charters. Their institution, Cincinnati's Third National Bank, opened in a Masonic Temple later that year under a 20-year charter.

The firm that would become Fifth Third Bancorp evolved and grew through dozens of mergers over the ensuing decades. When the Third National Bank acquired the Bank of the Ohio Valley in 1871, the *Cincinnati Enquirer* hailed the union as ''one of the best managed [banks] in Ohio.'' The superlative descriptions continued when Third National was recapitalized in 1882 at $1.6 million, the highest-asset bank in the state.

The Panic of 1907 brought a run on banks and the first substantial banking and currency reform since the Civil War. Fearful of widespread bank failures, the federal government ordered the consolidation of several big-city banks to shore up weaker institutions. As a result, Third National merged with Fifth National to form The Fifth Third National Bank of Cincinnati, with a capitalization of $2.5 million and $12.1 million in deposits, in 1908. Fifth Third's 1910 acquisition of two other local banks—American National Bank and S. Kuhn & Sons—increased its capital to $3 million.

The Federal Reserve Act of 1913 organized a regional system of 12 Federal Reserve banks that were capitalized with contributions from national banks in each region. The legislation required each national bank to deposit three percent of its capital and surplus into its regional Federal Reserve bank. These moves helped inspire confidence in the national banks, thus preventing panics and runs on banks. The Federal Reserve Act also gave the federal government more control over the United States' money supply, made commercial credit available, and discouraged venturesome banking practices. Although bankers initially resisted its creation, the Federal Reserve laid the groundwork for America's modern banking system.

Another bank industry consolidation followed World War I. The 1919 affiliation with Union Savings Bank and Trust Company, a state-chartered bank, brought several changes to Fifth Third's operations. Affiliation with a state bank permitted Fifth Third to circumvent the stricture against national banks' establishment of branches. Before the end of the year, Fifth Third assumed control of the assets of several local banks, including Market National Bank, Security Savings Bank and Safe Deposit Company, Mohawk State Bank, and Walnut Hills Savings Bank. It operated these institutions as branch offices.

Although the 1920s were marked by increased governmental supervision and general economic prosperity, many American banks remained weak. The situation gave Fifth Third the opportunity to continue to grow through the acquisition of four local banks. Fifth Third consolidated with the Union Trust Company to form the Fifth Third Union Trust Company in 1927. The advent of the Great Depression in 1929 intensified this activity somewhat, because Fifth Third was one of the stronger banks in the Cincinnati area. Fifth Third assumed control of three banks from 1930 to 1933.

The Great Depression also brought increased regulation of the banking industry, including expansion of the Federal Reserve Board's powers and the establishment of the Federal Deposit Insurance Corporation (FDIC). The economic crisis also spawned a plethora of federal and state legislation restricting interstate retail banking. Strong popular and governmental reaction to the Great Depression helped make banking one of the most regulated segments of American industry (and inspired *The Economist* to call the American system "one of the world's wackiest banking systems" in 1988). These barriers effectively restricted Fifth Third's growth through acquisition until after World War II.

Distanced from the Great Depression by the trauma of global war, U.S. banks began to cautiously expand their operations to include a broader range of financial services, especially in the field of retail or personal banking, in the postwar era. Under the direction of G. Carlton Hill from 1955 to 1963, Fifth Third began to formulate its focus on retail or consumer banking. For example, the company established a travel department to issue travelers checks and plan tours. These activities intensified during the presidency of Bill Rowe, who was the son of 1930s-era Fifth Third leader John J. Rowe. Over the course of the 1960s, the bank instituted a program of internal expansion with an emphasis on convenience and personal service. Advertising featuring the company's 5/3 shield logo promoted Fifth Third's many suburban locations and extended hours.

During the 1970s, the bank moved to shift its lending emphasis from commercial or business loans to consumer credit. In 1973, Fifth Third hired Johnny Bench, famed catcher for the Cincinnati Reds baseball team, as spokesman. It adopted the long-running slogan "The only bank you'll ever need" the same year.

"Back office" changes supported the bank's growth and profitability. Fifth Third, which had booted up its first computer in 1960, initiated home banking services and JEANIE automated teller machines (ATMs) in the 1970s. The institution's home banking system, which could be accessed via the average touch-tone phone, was uniquely user-friendly. These electronic services formed the basis of what would become Fifth Third's Midwest Payment Services department. Later in the decade, the bank offered its automated services to other banks and corporate clients. By the early 1990s, Midwest Payment Services maintained automated teller machines and electronic cash registers for over 1,000 clients. This lucrative business niche contributed one-third of the bank's annual income in the early 1990s.

The 1975 creation of a bank holding company, Fifth Third Bancorp, enabled the institution to sidestep some of the most rigorous state banking regulations. This new corporate entity was not technically a bank and thus was exempt from laws that prohibited cross-county branching. By 1976 Fifth Third included 37 banking offices.

The further liberalization of Ohio banking laws in the early 1980s expanded both the types of products banks were permitted to offer and the geographic reach they were allowed to attain. Strictures against growth outside the home bank's county were first to fall. Barriers to interstate branching continued to deteriorate in the early 1980s. In September 1985, federal and state banking regulations changed dramatically, freeing Ohio's banks to enter into agreements with banking organizations outside the state. Fifth Third became Ohio's first holding company to take advantage of the new legislation when it acquired American National Bank in Newport, Kentucky, just across the Ohio River, later that year. Fifth Third's roster of branches increased by 125 percent over the course of the 1980s, and it expanded its reach from a single Ohio county to an interstate bank.

Much of this vigorous growth was inspired by a new corporate leader, Clement L. Buenger, who took the helm of Fifth Third in 1981. Buenger, who was called "one of the best acts in the business" in a 1991 *Fortune* article, brought his background in life insurance sales to the bank. The new president transformed the bank's corporate culture through innovative incentive programs and personal example. Whereas some Fifth Third offices were only open from 10:00 a.m. to 2:00 p.m., Buenger worked 10- to 12-hour days and expected many of his managers to do the same. The president (who later became CEO and chairman) even made cold calls on prospective clients. One incentive program, the "Shoe Leather Award" evolved from his passion for earning new business. A new pair of designer shoes was awarded to each month's best cold caller. In fact, all employees could earn sales incentives: *Fortune* noted in 1991 that the bank "already [had] several secretaries worth $500,000."

Fifth Third's focus on consumer banking and safe lending helped the bank avoid the real estate loans, Third World debt, and leveraged-buyout problems that troubled many financial institutions during the 1980s. The "banking bust" that followed led *Fortune* to call the early 1990s "the hardest times for [bankers] since the Great Depression" in November 1991.

George Schaefer, Jr., took Fifth Third's reins in 1989 at the age of 44. Schaefer was trained in engineering, but when a hoped-for job designing a nuclear power plant fell through in 1969, he entered the bank's management trainee program. Some industry observers predicted that the new leader would be stymied, both by the shadow of his predecessor and by the difficult banking environment. But while literally hundreds of banks failed each year in the late 1980s and early 1990s, Fifth Third continued its outstanding performance, and was even able to benefit from the misfortune of others by inexpensively acquiring dozens of new outlets. This allowed the bank to slowly expand its sphere of influence, yet maintain shareholder value.

In 1992 Fifth Third proposed a merger with Star Banc Corp. that would have unified the two largest Cincinnati-based financial institutions. Star had not grown as fast as Fifth Third, but its recent record of continued growth made it an enticing acquisition target. The alliance was viewed by many analysts and investors as a good deal for both banks—Fifth Third made a generous offer of $42 per share, which amounted to more than twice Star's book value. But when CEO Schaefer prematurely publicized the heretofore private proposition, Star's long-time president, Oliver Waddell balked, and the target's board unanimously rejected the offer.

Shunned by Star, Schaefer returned to Fifth Third's previous course of growth through relatively small acquisitions. Then, in 1994, the bank made two significant purchases: the 45-office Cumberland Federal Bancorporation in Kentucky, which had $1.1 billion in assets; and Falls Financial Inc. in northeastern Ohio, a company with $581 million in assets. According to the company's 1994 annual report, these two acquisitions contributed to the largest one-year increase in assets—22 percent—in the institution's history. The purchases also made Fifth Third America's preeminent operator of supermarket bank locations, with 81 full-service locations.

From 1989 through 1994, the bank's return on assets (ROA) ranged from 1.62 percent to 1.74 percent, triple the average for *Fortune*'s top 100 commercial banks. During that same period, the institution's non-interest and interest income, as well as its assets base, virtually doubled. This superlative performance kept Fifth Third's stock trading at high multiples—14 times earnings and more than twice book value. The stock tripled from 1989 to 1994.

With a young, yet experienced chief executive, firm fundamentals, and a promising economic environment, Fifth Third appears to have the necessary ingredients for continued success.

Principal Subsidiaries: Fifth Third Bank of Central Indiana; Fifth Third Bank of Central Kentucky, Inc.; Fifth Third Bank of Northern Kentucky, Inc.; Fifth Third Company; Fifth Third Trust Co. & Savings Bank, FSB; Midwest Payment Systems, Inc.; Fifth Third Community Development Company; Fifth Third Investment Company; Fifth Third Bank, Cincinnati; Fifth Third Bank of Columbus; Fifth Third Leasing Company; Fifth Third Securities Inc.; Fifth Third Bank of Southern Ohio; Fifth Third Bank of Northwestern Ohio, N.A.; Fifth Third Bank of Western Ohio, N.A.; Fifth Third Bank of Southeastern Indiana.

Further Reading:

Bennett, Robert A., "How to Earn 1.6% on Assets," *United States Banker,* January 1992, pp. 20–27.

Buenger, Clement L., *Fifth Third Bank: "The Only Bank You'll Ever Need,* New York: Newcomen Society of the United States, 1991.

"Fifth Third Drops Offer to Buy Star Banc Corp.," *American Banker,* July 1, 1992, p. 1.

"Fifth Third, the 'Charlie Hustle' of Banking," *United States Banker,* April 1995, p. 24.

Fraust, Bart, "Fifth Third to Enter Kentucky: Becomes 1st Ohio Holding Company to Acquire Out-of-State Bank," *American Banker,* July 31, 1985, p. 3.

Klinkermann, Steve, et al. "Fifth Third's Schaefer: Hard Work, Expense Control and the Secrets to Success," *American Banker,* December 19, 1994, p. 16.

Pare, Terence P., "Bankers Who Beat the Bust," *Fortune,* November 4, 1991, p. 159.

Peale, Cliff, "Merger Proposal Came Too Quickly for Star," *Cincinnati Business Courier,* May 4, 1992, p. 3.

Piggott, Charles, "The World's Best Banks: The Americans Bounce Back," *Euromoney,* August 1994, p. 68–72.

"The Safest and Soundest of the Big Banks," *United States Banker,* July 1992, pp. 19–25.

Slater, Robert Bruce, "Banking's Cincinnati Kid," *Bankers Monthly,* January 1993, p. 14.

—April D. Gasbarre

Fisher Controls International, Inc.

8000 Maryland Avenue 1300
St. Louis, Missouri 63105
U.S.A.
(314) 746-9900
Fax: (314) 754-3457

Wholly Owned Subsidiary of Emerson Electric Co.
Incorporated: 1888 as Fisher Governor Company
Employees: 9,600
Sales: $928 million
SICs: 3492 Fluid Power Valves & Hose Fittings; 3823 Process Control Instruments

A global supplier of control valves and regulators, Fisher Controls International, Inc. is one of the largest and oldest process control companies. Fisher's Type 1 pump governor was invented by the founder in 1880 and remains—virtually unchanged—part of the company's product line today.

Those unfamiliar with the work of control valves and regulators might dismiss them as simple hardware store items, but they are more vital than their modest names imply. They help to maintain steady pressure in the pipes that carry gases, fluids, or steam to keep those pipes from exploding.

Company founder William Fisher was first inspired to create a control devise after he and others spent hours trying to keep a city from being engulfed in flames. Fisher had moved to the United States from England at the age of 14. Once they reached America, his family settled in Iowa. Working in a small engine shop, Fisher became well-versed in the major power source of the era: steam. After he helped to install new water facilities in two other Iowa cities, Fisher was invited to apply his knowledge of water and steam to the waterworks system in a third city.

As a fire raged all night in Marshalltown, Iowa, Fisher throttled the city's steam-driven pumps by hand in order to keep the pressure in the city's mains steady. It seemed to him that a device could be made that would control the pumps and maintain them at a constant pressure. After months of experiments, the young man designed the Fisher Type 1 constant pressure pump governor.

Joining with a town machinist, Fisher pooled $600 to buy a manufacturing building. The pumps were in production in 1880, although Fisher didn't receive a patent for another four years. In order to keep the company afloat, Fisher also repaired machines and sold bicycles and Kodak cameras. In fact, Fisher was an exclusive sales representative for Eastman Kodak cameras and supplies in 1898.

The company scraped together $30,000 by 1888 and was incorporated as the Fisher Governor Company. Fisher spread the gospel of his new invention through his membership in the power plant engineering association and, soon enough, word of mouth kicked in. Company sales reached $44,000 by 1905. Only two years later, Fisher's invention was laboring away in power plants throughout the United States, Canada, and Great Britain.

As demand for the product increased, so did the need for variations of the pump. A vertical-type reducing valve became the first of a series of controls that were added to the Type 1. Not long afterward, lever valves, exhaust relief valves, back pressure valves, and steam trap valves were added.

Business boomed, but the company lost its founder in 1905. His widow, Martha, took Fisher's place as president, while their son Jasper traveled the country as a cigar salesman. Jasper Fisher came home and took the company's reins in 1912, when annual sales were about $60,000. At that time the company had nine machinists and assemblers and five office employees.

Knowledgeable about sales, Jasper Fisher knew that quality products were not always enough to be successful. A sales agency was established in 1913, and Fisher traveled the continent himself as the company launched its first nationwide advertising campaign. As World War I unfolded, demand for Fisher's products in various industries rose dramatically, particularly in the petroleum industry. The company soon employed 60 workers. By the end of World War I, Fisher was on more solid financial ground. It had also developed new technologies and products.

Fisher enjoyed substantial profits from the growth in the steel, petroleum, power, and gas industries in the early 1920s. The company's automated valves were indispensable in each of these burgeoning industries, so Fisher grew with them. This was fortunate, because the Great Depression of the early 1930s devastated the nation's economy. Half of the factories in the United States were forced to close their doors during the Great Depression, but Fisher managed to stay open. Sales were limp and production was minimal, but the plants stayed alive. As soon as business began to grow stronger in the late 1930s, Fisher updated machinery and added new products to its line. The company even finished an addition to its manufacturing plant in 1940.

During this time, the company lost another helmsman. Jasper Fisher died in 1938. Like his father, he was well-loved by employees and colleagues. Jasper's son, J.W. "Bill" Fisher, joined the company's finance department in 1940. Jasper's widow, Edna, became president and her son Bill became vice-president in 1944. Although this succession seemed a continuance of Fisher tradition, the company had in fact shifted its management style. A strong board now led Fisher. The two Fishers were elected to their positions.

Although the company had enjoyed growth spurts earlier in its history, nothing in its past matched the surge of growth experienced by the company during World War II. The appetite for the company's automatic control valve equipment was huge, as valves were used in the production of ships, planes, tanks, and guns. Fisher also supplied valves that were used in the manufacturing of life-saving drugs, as well as valves used in oil refineries and gas production, and chemical and synthetic rubber manufacturing.

Despite a shortage of materials and men, the company built new plants and machines and operated 24 hours a day to meet demand. The shortage of manpower put a premium on automation, and any ideas that reduced labor were lauded. In light of its wartime achievements, the company received an Army-Navy "E" flag in 1943, given in recognition of "superior production achievements of vital war materials."

The technological advances spawned by World War II continued after the conclusion of the conflict. Although Fisher was faced with labor problems, a new manufacturing addition was installed in 1948 to help meet rising sales. Edna Fisher retired in May 1954 and was succeeded by her son, Bill. At this point, Fisher was very alert to expanding markets in Europe, but international growth was set back by currency exchanges and export fees.

Fisher addressed this dilemma by entering into a licensing agreement with Elliott Automation of the United Kingdom in 1950. Under the terms of the agreement, the two companies would jointly manufacture Fisher valves and controllers. In 1955 Fisher opened a factory in Ontario, Canada, to meet the demands of that country's expanding oil and natural gas industries.

By the late 1950s, Fisher's expansion was swift. The company moved into a new office building designed to house its research, engineering, sales, and administrative departments, which had been cramped because of the growing need for factory space. In 1957 Fisher purchased the Pennsylvania-based Continental Equipment Company. Continental was known for its superior butterfly control valves, which were used by process industries. In the late 1950s process industries, like so many other industries, were being revolutionized by electronics. Fisher, which was determined to flow with the changes, established electronic design and assembly departments. Assemblers acquired a new technical language and tool skills in these departments, and soon they were generating such new products as electronic level controllers and transducers.

This emphasis on new products and technologies remained throughout the 1960s. Overseas growth continued at the same time. Fisher entered into a new licensing agreement to manufacture in Japan in 1960. This allowed the company to use manufacturing facilities in Japan to produce all Fisher products sold in that market. The following year, Fisher opened a temporary factory in Monterrey, Mexico, until a permanent plant was opened near Mexico City in 1965. In order to be closer to its LP-gas customers, the gas regulator division of Fisher moved to Texas that same year. Manufacturing capacity continued to explode in 1967, when Fisher enlarged two more plants and opened a new eight-acre facility in Marshalltown, birthplace of the founder's inspiration. A joint venture named Nippon-Fisher was launched in 1969, whereby Fisher manufactured and sold its products in Japan and the Far East.

Fisher also merged with Monsanto Company, the country's fourth largest chemical company. Monsanto purchased 67 percent of Fisher in 1969; the remaining 33 percent was purchased in 1983. At that time, Monsanto was determined to diversify. Upon joining the company, Fisher began manufacturing a line of electronic instrumentation that Monsanto had developed. Fisher's name, to reflect its own diversification, was changed to Fisher Controls Company. Bill Fisher resigned as president in 1969, but stayed on as chairman of the board until 1974. Tom Shive became Fisher's president in 1969.

Electronic instrumentation was Fisher's theme for the 1970s. The line of analog instrumentation developed by Monsanto for process control was the progenitor of the PROVOX distributed control system, which Fisher introduced in 1980. The company invested heavily in product development and the buildings needed to make them. Fisher opened its first European manufacturing facility in 1970, in Cornwall, England. The plant made electronic instrumentation. Two years later, the company's engineering team moved to a new facility large enough to accommodate its expanding needs. Repair facilities were added to the company's services in the early 1970s and proved popular enough to be quickly expanded, with representatives in Louisiana, Texas, New Jersey, Ohio, and Alberta, Canada. These facilities repaired control valves and instruments.

Marshall Die Casting joined Fisher in 1975, after supplying aluminum and zinc die castings to the company for more than 30 years. A new line of rotary-shaft valves was unveiled in the 1970s. The product line was immediately successful, and a new plant was opened in 1976 just to manufacture this popular line. Fisher Brazil, a facility that produced both control valve and instrumentation products for South American countries, opened its doors in 1977. Two years later, portions of the General Electric Company of the United Kingdom united with Fisher to form Fisher Controls Corporation of Delaware, a manufacturing, sales and service system poised to install Fisher's products worldwide.

In 1981 Fisher's sales reached $650 million. North and South American customers made up 60 percent of those sales. New service centers were opened in the United Kingdom, followed by a new valve manufacturing plant in Medway, England. Fisher also acquired Posi-Seal in 1985.

Fisher's place within Monsanto began to chafe both companies, however. Monsanto, which had decided to focus its operations on agricultural products, pharmaceuticals, chemicals, and food ingredients, sold Fisher to Emerson Electric Company in 1992 for $1.28 billion. Fisher experienced an increase in its 1991 operating income when Monsanto decided to sell it, but sales for that year were $928 million. The wedding to Emerson seemed to be a sensible one. Emerson produced electrical, electronic and other products for consumer, commercial and industrial markets. Its sales for 1991 were $7.4 billion. The purchase made Emerson the largest provider of process control equipment. Fisher also entered into a joint venture with Tianjin Fourth Automation Instrumentation Factory in China in 1992.

The arrangement was made to produce control valves for Asian markets.

Emerson orchestrated the blending of Fisher's strengths with those of Rosemount Incorporated, a much younger company with innovative products used in the aeronautics and space industries, as well as control and instrumentation product lines and temperature and pressure transmitters. The Fisher-Rosemount family of companies dominated the global market of process management in the early 1990s. It offered the widest line of process automation products, including process management systems, control valves, regulators, transmitters, and analyzers. The combined companies have operations—including sales, service and manufacturing—in more than 80 countries and serve a range of process industries. Few industries are not touched by Fisher: Fisher-Rosemount supplies companies in such diverse areas as chemical processing, plastics, glass, refining, oil and gas production, natural gas distribution, power, pulp and paper, food and beverages, pharmaceuticals, and metals and mining.

Principal Subsidiaries: Xomox Corporation; H.D. Baumann, Inc.

Further Reading:

"Advanced Control Systems," *Pulp & Paper,* February 1992, p. 101.

" 'Cascaded' Pilot Regulators Help Reduce LPG loss in Hot Weather," *Oil and Gas Journal,* August 8, 1994, p. 63.

"Emerson to Buy Monsanto Subsidiary," *Journal of Commerce and Commercial,* August 5, 1992, p. 7A.

Feder, Barnaby, "Emerson to Buy Fisher for Nearly $1.28 Billion," *New York Times,* August 5, 1992, p. D3.

"Fisher Controls Flow with Software," *Design News,* July 19, 1993, p. 34.

"Fisher Controls International," *Oil and Gas Journal,* February 10, 1992, p. 67.

"Fisher Controls International, Inc.," *Pulp & Paper,* September 1992, p. 195.

"Fisher Controls International Inc.," *Prepared Foods,* August 1992, p. 146.

"Monsanto Surprises with Fisher Sell-Off," *ECN-European Chemical News,* August 10, 1992, p. 8.

Mullin, Rick, "Computers and Process Control," *Chemical Week,* November 25, 1992, p. 30.

Storck, William, "Monsanto to Sell Fisher Controls Subsidiary," *Chemical & Engineering News,* August 10, 1992, p. 5.

—Carol I. Keeley

Flint Ink Corporation

25111 Glendale Avenue
Detroit, Michigan 48239
U.S.A.
(313) 538-6800
Fax: (313) 538-6800

Private Company
Incorporated: 1920 as Howard Flint Ink Company
Employees: 2,600
Sales: $550 million
SICs: 2893 Printing Ink

Flint Ink Corporation is the largest American-owned manufacturer of printing inks for newspaper, magazine packaging, commercial, and screen printing applications. The company is the third-largest ink producer in the world and the tenth-largest privately held corporation in Michigan. The corporation's CDR Pigments and Dispersions unit and David M Company are leading manufacturers of pigments/dispersions and offset printing blankets, respectively. Flint Ink operates 69 facilities in the United States, Canada, and Mexico, employing nearly 2,500 people. The Flint Ink Research Center in Ann Arbor, Michigan, provides state-of-the-art product research, environmental testing, and support.

Flint Ink Corporation was founded in 1920 in Detroit by H. Howard Flint as the Howard Flint Ink Company. From its earliest years, the company utilized quality control methods to test raw materials and finished products, and was the first ink company to do so. The year 1922 saw the company's first tanker truck delivery of letterpress news ink. In 1926 Flint Ink opened its first branch in Indianapolis, which was followed by the opening of four additional branches over the next decade. The company acquired Temple Inks Company of Denver in 1936—the same year its sales hit the $1 million mark.

By the 1940s, Flint Ink had equipped all of its branches with full quality control and formulation labs and established rigid product specifications. One of its subsidiaries, California Ink Company (Cal/Ink), became the first U.S. company to make and market lithol red pigments. In 1950 Cal/Ink developed the nation's first magnetic inks for check imprinting. Seven years later, the company changed its name to Flint Ink Corporation. Within three years, the company had expanded into the publication gravure business, a process used by publishers desiring the highest quality color reproductions for long run applications.

In 1966 H. Howard Flint's son, Edgar B. Flint, succeeded his father as chief operating officer. Two years later, Flint Ink made the first tanker delivery of offset news ink, and in 1969 the company introduced the use of alkaline fountain solutions for newspaper printing. In 1975 Flint Ink acquired Cal/Ink and opened a state-of-the-art gravure facility in New Albany, Indiana. A joint venture between Flint Ink and Sun-Fast Color in 1977 made Flint Mexicana, S.A., de C.V. the second-largest ink manufacturer in Mexico. The next year Flint Ink pioneered the use of conductivity to monitor the concentration of fountain solution, and in 1979 the company made its first tanker delivery of offset color news inks.

Chromatic Color, another subsidiary, was incorporated in 1980 and began producing dry and flushed color. Two years later, Robert H. Flint succeeded his brother Edgar as president and CEO. Flint Ink acquired Drew Graphics, Inc., a manufacturer of water dispersions for the ink, paper, paint, and coatings industries in 1984. The following year marked the completion of the company's second varnish plant, furthering Flint Ink's move toward vertical integration. Flint Ink acquired Capitol Printing Ink Company in 1986, providing a larger presence on the East Coast. In 1987 Robert H. Flint was elected chairman and CEO and H. Howard Flint II was elected president and COO, ushering in the third generation of managerial Flints. That same year Flint Ink was a majority participant in a leveraged buyout of the Sinclair & Valentine Division of Allied-Signal. The acquisition provided Flint Ink with ownership of the fourth-largest manufacturer in the commercial and packaging printing ink segments. The Sinclair & Valentine Division included David M, Ridgway Color, the S & V Canadian unit, and S & V Screen Inks.

Another important milestone reached in 1987 was the completion of the Flint Ink Research Center, a 72,000-square-foot research facility in Ann Arbor, Michigan. The research center was established to develop new technology to confront the challenges faced by the printing industry, including the availability and cost of raw materials, environmental protection, and the computerization of press-side and pre-press operations. Researchers are seeking to develop proprietary raw materials that offer greater performance as well as environmental and economic value. Chemists at the center are investigating new inks with the characteristics necessary for optimum performance on new substrates, on higher-speed computerized presses, and with developing press and plate chemistry. Extensive research has led to "environmentally friendly" alternatives in ink technology, utilizing vegetable oils or water in place of traditional petroleum or solvent ingredients.

Building upon the company's history of quality control and quality assurance methods, Flint Ink embarked on "The Flint Ink Quality Journey" in 1987. The journey employed the principles and techniques of continuous quality improvement, and re-emphasized long-term quality partnerships with customers and suppliers. A comprehensive training program was begun to provide managers and employees alike with problem-solving techniques, testing procedures, and statistical methods. Milestones along the journey have included the following: statistical methods were used to monitor ink batch specifications; product quality certification procedures were put in place; computerized color matching in branch sites insured that every custom match was completed quickly and accurately; improvements in delivery methods and scheduling permitted just-in-time delivery to minimize inventories; and quality partnerships were established with both customers and suppliers to increase awareness of needs, define common goals, set specifications, improve communications, and resolve problems.

Flint Ink was reorganized in 1991, consolidating several subsidiary firms under the Flint Ink umbrella. S & V Printing Ink, Capitol Printing Ink, and Cal/Ink began operating under the Flint Ink Corporation name. Chromatic Color, Ridgway Color, and Drew Graphics began operating as CDR Pigments & Dispersions. S & V Screen of Canada became Flint Ink Corporation of Canada, and S & V Screen Inks became Summit Screen Inks. In addition, LeMaster Litho Supply was acquired.

Flint Ink continued to be a leader in the area of environmentally friendly products, including low-rub, soy oil-based newspaper inks. In 1991 the firm introduced AGRI-TEK vegetable-oil based inks for commercial sheetfed and folding carton applications. The company by that time had a fully staffed Environmental Services Department that evaluated and addressed regulatory issues as they affected Flint Ink products and customer applications. A 1992 article in *Crain's Detroit Business,* ''Flint Ink's Future Is Printed in Soybeans,'' reported that the company was producing soy- and water-based inks in anticipation that the use of traditional petroleum-based inks would diminish under environmental pressures. Chairman/CEO Robert Flint predicted that mounting environmental regulations for air quality, pollution, and hazardous waste would spur the shift away from petroleum toward alternative materials, noting, ''I think, maybe, by the turn of the century, we're going to see the end of petroleum inks.''

H. Howard Flint II was named chairman and CEO in 1992, while four directors were added to the board from outside the family. Two years later a fifth non-family-member was elected to the board, bringing the membership to 11. In 1994 Flint Ink opened its first offices overseas, including a sales office in Singapore to explore entry into Pacific Rim markets. CDR Pigments & Dispersions established CDR International and opened a sales office in Brussels to expand into the European market. The company also acquired outstanding shares of Flint Mexicana, assuming full ownership.

In 1994 the corporation also acquired Rendic International, a Miami-based distributor of graphic arts supplies, in order to strengthen the ink manufacturer's position in South America and the Far East. Rendic International had marketed printing inks, blankets, and printing presses outside of the United States for Flint Ink Corporation and Rockwell International for more than a decade. The company's president, Jerko E. Rendik, was asked to stay on to help Flint Ink continue to expand its export business. Rendic noted that he believed his company's familiarity with South America and the Pacific Rim made it a good fit with Flint Ink's plan for growth in the world market.

In another major initiative, Flint Ink completed the purchase of North American Printing Ink Company, with plants in Elgin and Salem, Illinois. According to Flint Ink Chairman Howard Flint II, the move was expected to enhance the company's ability to service large heatset publication printers. NAPIC had specialized in the manufacture of heatset inks for use in magazine printing. Since its founding in 1978, the company had achieved a major position as a supplier to publication printing plants throughout the United States. Under the terms of the agreement, NAPIC remained a separate business unit, operating within Flint Ink's Publication Ink Group.

Flint Ink of Canada purchased Lester Ink and Coatings Company in 1994 to provide Flint Ink with much-needed sheetfed manufacturing capacity. Flint Ink of Canada president Dan Keough stated that Lester's well-established reputation for excellent quality in the products it manufactures and the company's leadership in the commercial sheetfed market will give Flint Ink added presence in that important market segment. Lester Inks and Coatings had sales offices in Montreal, Vancouver, and Calgary, in addition to its 60,000-square-foot manufacturing site in Toronto.

Flint Ink was named the winner of the 1994 Distribution/Nasstrac LTL Shipper of the Year Award, according to an article in *Distribution* magazine. ''By helping its more than 70 LTL carriers improve their operations, the Detroit-based manufacturer of printing inks has actively spread the quality message among carrier and shipper channels,'' the article stated. ''Flint Ink has simplified its shipping process for field supervisors by creating a routing software package; centralized its traffic function to coordinate transportation operations for its manufacturing locations; hired certified hazardous materials instructors to train staff; developed its own rate base to insure fair bidding; implemented contracts with all its TL and LTL carriers; and developed quality programs that are compatible with ISO 9000 standards.''

In the company's ongoing quest to develop environmentally friendly processes, Flint Ink announced in 1995 an exclusive distribution agreement with Unichema International to market Unichema's PRIFER 3303+ low-VOC, non-volatile roller and blanket wash for sheetfed lithographic inks. The agreement was reached after testing by Flint Ink showed the vegetable-based wash to combine environmental benefits, commercial practicality, and effective cleaning capabilities. According to Leonard Walle, Flink Ink's director of marketing, pressure has increased to reduce emissions in order to avoid operating permit requirements. ''One of the most significant areas for potential reduction is the chemicals used for cleaning press rollers and blankets—chemicals which have traditionally been petroleum-based and very high in VOCs,'' he stated. Walle noted that control technique guidelines for offset lithographic printers set forth by the EPA in September 1993 recommended the use of cleaning solutions that do not contain any hazardous air pollutants and have less than 30 percent VOC by weight in their useable form.

In an effort to help customers achieve lower emissions, Flint Ink tested a number of environmentally friendly press washes to determine which offered reduced VOCs while at the same time giving cleaning results comparable to conventional cleaners. Extensive testing settled upon a product that was cost-effective, safe, and non-volatile. With Flint Ink's continued leadership in promoting environmental awareness, investment in research, commitment to quality, and steady growth, the company was well positioned for success into the 21st century.

Further Reading:

King, Angela, ''Flint Ink's Future Is Printed in Soybeans,'' *Crain's Detroit Business,* August 31, 1992, p. 3 (2).

Thomas, Jim, ''The Color of Excellence,'' *Distribution,* September 1994, pp. 42ff.

—Pamela Berry

Formica Corporation

1680 Route 23 North
Wayne, New Jersey 07474
U.S.A.
(201) 305-9400
Fax: (201) 305-1095

Private Company
Incorporated: 1913 as Formica Insulation Company
Employees: 3,200
Sales: $560 million
SICs: 2891 Adhesives and Sealants; 3083 Laminated Plastics Plate and Sheet

Perhaps best known for its kitchen counter surfaces, Formica Corporation is the world's largest manufacturer of high-pressure laminate for use in residential and commercial building. In fact, the name Formica has become virtually synonymous with decorative laminate, and the company's products, available in a wide variety of colors, textures, and patterns, are used extensively on countertops, cabinets, and furniture, not only in the United States, but increasingly in other countries. The company maintains factories in England, France, Germany, Spain, Canada, and Taiwan.

Daniel J. O'Conor and Herbert A. Faber, the founders of Formica, were two engineers who met in 1907, their first year of employment at Westinghouse Electric in Pittsburgh. Westinghouse was one of many manufacturers experimenting with the developing field of synthetics manufacture, with each scrambling to find applied uses for the new materials. O'Conor and Faber rose through the ranks of the company, with O'Conor in the research engineering department and Faber in sales. Westinghouse and others soon began to experiment with several new laminate processes that had been patented by renowned inventor Dr. Leo Baekeland. In 1907, Baekeland had created Bakelite—the first totally synthetic plastic—which proved to be the heat- and moisture-resistant material that prompted a revolution in American industry. After Baekeland had made his invention known and received the patents for it in 1910, many manufacturers rushed to take advantage of the new material's properties. Bakelite in liquid form could impregnate materials such as canvas or paper to them give insulating properties. In that year O'Conor at Westinghouse manufactured the first sheet of laminate by coating kraft paper with liquid Bakelite and then pressing it flat. Westinghouse applied for the patent for the process in 1913, and it was granted in 1918.

Faber and O'Conor left Westinghouse in 1913, convinced that this new laminated material was an important one and that it was underappreciated and underdeveloped at Westinghouse. In search of capital, they found a partner in J.G. Tomlin, a lawyer and banker from Kentucky who gave them $2,500, for which he received a one-third stake in the new venture. They made Cincinnati, Faber's home town, its headquarters. The company's first plant was a rented two-story space, and it held a 35-horsepower boiler and a gas stove. It opened its doors in 1913 with an order to be filled: commutator V-rings for the Chalmers Motor Company. Other early clients were Ideal (later Delco) Electronics and Bell Electric Motor.

O'Conor and Faber saw the future of this new product as an insulating material, especially suited in electrical processes. Mica had been popular as just such an insulator but had grown expensive and hard to come by. Faber called the new material Formica, at it could be used "for mica." Thus the first applications for the material were almost exclusively industrial. This early Formica was dark in color and without the surface layer that was to be added later. During the first year the company made only rings and tubes.

The company incorporated on October 15, 1913 as the Formica Insulation Company. The new corporation was listed on the Cincinnati stock exchange, and 600 shares were issued at $25. Faber was president and treasurer, and O'Conor was vice-president and secretary.

In July 1914, a new flat-sheet press arrived at the factory, which allowed the company to produce laminate. Formica produced laminate on order only, buying the resin that was necessary to the process from the Bakelite Company; from the beginning, it had been operating under license from Baekeland. However, that year Bakelite—under pressure from its biggest client, Westinghouse—informed O'Conor that it would no longer sell resin to the company (except for the manufacture of commutator rings) and that Westinghouse was going to start to manufacture laminate. O'Conor and Faber immediately found an alternative in the resin known as Redmanol, developed by L.V. Redman. Redman was a chemist who had previously worked for Adolph and Sam Karpen, Chicago-based furniture manufacturers, to find ways to improve their furniture's varnish.

The first years were lean ones for the new company, and for much of its early existence it owed everyone. Nevertheless, the list of clients grew to include Kellogg Switchboard, Cutler-Hammer, and Allis-Chalmers Manufacturing. Sales in 1917 reached $75,000. By 1919, the company had taken advantage of contracts with the military and its sales had grown to $175,000.

The newly emergent field of plastics manufacture was predictably riven by claims and counterclaims of patent infringement. On June 11, 1919, Westinghouse sued Formica for infringing on its patent for laminated phenolic canvas. The district court in Cincinnati eventually ruled in favor of Formica. Westinghouse then brought two more lawsuits against it—one regarding rods, tubes, and molded parts, the second concerning the patent that Westinghouse had acquired in 1913 for the process that O'Conor had developed while working there. Formica won those suits, also. The company was then sued by Continental Fibre; again, Formica prevailed. Then, Baekeland took actions to sue users of Formica and Redmanol. Interestingly, the Karpen brothers bought a majority interest in Condensite Corporation, which carried numerous laminate patents; then, in 1922, Condensite Corporation, Redmanol Company, and Bakelite Company merged to form the Bakelite Corporation. From that point forward Formica was able to again have access to Bakelite's products.

In the early 1920s, radios grew popular, and Formica was able to take advantage of this boon as its laminate was not only used as a mounting table to insulate the interior's parts from one another but also as paneling on the exterior of the radio. Many of those sets were do-it-yourself models. Although home-manufacture radios were a short-lived fad, the process brought the company much-needed capital and the company found itself solvent for the first time since its inception. Company sales were $400,000 in 1920; $1.9 million in 1923; and $3 million by 1924. Also, the company started to make brown as well as the standard black so as to better match household furniture. Formica was moving beyond its early uses for electrical insulation as well as for electronic and automobile parts to take advantage of the popularity of the new consumer appliances; beside radios, these included washing machines, vacuum cleaners, and refrigerators.

In the mid-1920s, the company pushed further to discover new decorative applications for their product. It soon hired Jack Cochrane, an MIT graduate, to develop the technology to make Formica more consumer-friendly by becoming more appealing and colorful. The company also brought in new capital by a new stock offering so as to extend its research and facilities. Expansion was important at this time as Bakelite's patents expired in 1926 and 1927, and many competitors—including Monsanto and Spaulding Fibre Company—eagerly entered the laminate business. In 1927, Formica jumped ahead of the pack with two important patents that spelled out the production of a multilayer lithographed woodgrain laminate on a flat-bed press. These patents were the starting point for Formica's lead in decorative laminate. In 1931, the company received three more patents, which concerned an all-paper laminate, as well as a process by which the laminates were made cigarette burn-resistant. These changes also made the product more appealing to the consumer.

In the early 1930s, Jack Cochrane, who was to become the director of research, developed a laminate that used urea instead of phenol to coat the top layer of kraft paper, and which was then laminated under pressure to the phenol-impregnated pages underneath. This change made Formica laminate easy-to-clean, fire-resistant, durable, and available in dozens of colors. Formica won several major commissions; for wall panels in the *HMS Queen Mary* and reading tables in the Library of Congress in Washington, D.C. However, the urea-formaldehyde laminate was expensive to produce. The company continued to search for ways to add color to the laminate as well as to lower its cost; only dark colors were able to hide the resin that formed the core of a sheet of Formica.

Finally, in 1938, those qualities became possible when Formica replaced its urea-formaldehyde resin with melamine, which allowed for greater durability and improved appearance. (Melamine had been popularized in the durable dishes that were marketed in the United States by American Cyanamid.) In this configuration, which was to become the standard Formica laminate that became so well-known in the 1950s and 1960s, the seven layers of kraft paper were still impregnated with phenol-formaldehyde resin; the difference was that the top decorative layer was coated with melamine and then topped with an opaque sheet melamine, which, when cured in the press, became transparent. This innovation allowed light colors to be used, and melamine was less costly and easier to cure. Formica could then became a product that was widely available and more affordable. With this important innovation, Formica was soon incorporated into furniture manufacturing, especially kitchen counter tops and dinettes.

Formica endeavored to interest the big furniture manufacturers of its laminate's functionality and appeal but did not stir much interest. It also sought to excite store-fixture makers, especially those that made soda fountains, of Formica's advantages. Failing that, the company went into the furniture business itself—the company began to produce whole dinette tops that were then shipped to furniture manufacturers, who added legs and chairs. The product proved popular and moved briskly, and its increasing sales were only interrupted by the war, during which the company was given over completely to war goods.

During World War II, only industrial-grade Formica was produced, and it found many uses in the war effort. Sales, which in 1940 had been $4.25 million, grew to $15.74 million in 1943. After the war, Formica, like so many other companies, sought to take advantage of the consumer-goods explosion. It began to direct its efforts into placing its products in homes, schools, and other public buildings. Hundreds of colors and patterns of its laminate were available. Dinette production exploded; in mid-1948, the company produced 28,000 dinette sheets (table tops) weekly, and this number grew to 55,000 in 1950. The company's sales of decorative laminate reached approximately $15 million; its industrial laminates brought in about $5 million. As a mark of the change in direction of the company, the name was changed from the Formica Insulation Company to the Formica Company. By 1951, sales had reached $24 million. Demand for Formica laminate consistently outpaced supply, a problem that was aggravated by Formica's policy of producing laminate on order only. Many dealers got around this by ordering material in bulk.

In 1956, the company was bought by American Cyanamid, and its name was changed to Formica Corporation as it became a subsidiary of that huge conglomerate. Many felt that American Cyanamid did not invest the energy or resources to keep Formica in the vanguard, instead relying on its brand name to earn income. ''Cyanamid didn't invest as much as entrepreneurs would, and they began to rely on the strength of the brand when competitors were saying, 'That's the guy to get','' said Vincent Langone, who joined Cyanamid in 1967 and who later became Formica's president. In 1966, the company opened a new plant in Sacramento, California, and for the first time since World War II, the company was able to keep up demand for its laminate.

In the 1970s, Formica was unseated as the dominant force in U.S. laminate manufacture by Ralph Wilson Plastics of Tempe,

Texas. Ralph Wilson and its Wilsonart products were able to take advantage of the perception that Formica, having grown to number one, had become sluggish and arrogant, often taking weeks to deliver product.

In the early 1980s, Formica tried to update its image, which for many had passed from being synonymous with American ingenuity to the worst excess of American consumerism—man-made, synthetic, and tacky. Formica unveiled a new product, ColorCore, which was a laminate that gave the appearance of solidity. In other words, an object covered with ColorCore laminate seemed as though it was made of that product's color throughout; that is, it was not as apparently artificial as standard laminate. Formica also sponsored an exhibition, which traveled to various galleries and museums, and many leading designers and artists responded to its call for entries, and that show produced some well-received pieces. Despite these and other efforts, Formica was unable to make its laminate a hip, post-modern decorating tool.

In May 1984, American Cyanamid decided to divest itself of Formica, believing that the company did not fit into its strategy of focusing upon high-growth potential and high-technology businesses. The company, which earned about $335 million in sales, was purchased by a group of senior managers and Shearson Lehman in a leveraged buyout that became effective in May 1985 for a reported $200 million in cash and preferred stock. The sale involved all of Formica's U.S. and overseas operations except for those in Latin America. The company quickly acquired Design Plus of York, Pennsylvania, a company that used computers to aid in kitchen remodeling, and Wildon Industries of Mount Bethel, Pennsylvania, which produced synthetic marble. The company saw its future in higher-margin products.

In 1987 Formica went public. Sales had grown since the divestiture from American Cyanamid, and the company had sought to aggressively make itself more competitive, but the company needed capital as the leveraged buyout of 1985 had brought with it a heavy debt and burdensome interest payments. The stock offering went for $11.75 a share and raised about $50 million.

In May 1989, after various suitors expressed an interest in gaining control of Formica, the company was again taken private after it was sold to FM Acquisition Corporation, a group led by company president Vincent Langone. Sales that year reached $410 million. The company again suffered the burden of heavy debt payments, however, requiring an estimated $40 million annually to pay the interest alone.

Nevertheless, analysts noted that the company was focusing effectively on customer service and support in the 1990s. Moreover, Formica continued to improve upon its product line, introducing new surface materials under the brand names of Nuvel, Surell, Granulon, and Formica Ligna, a wood veneer product. Although du Pont, manufacturer of the popular Corian counter surface, had gained the greatest market share for laminates in the United States, Formica ran a strong second. With over 50 percent of its sales derived from international operations in the mid-1990s, Formica seemed likely to maintain its position as the world's leading laminate producer.

Further Reading:

Feder, Barnaby J., "Formica: When a Household Name Becomes an 'Also-Ran'," *The New York Times,* August 12, 1990, p. 12F.

"Formica Is on Top," *Fortune,* October 1951, pp. 116–118, 150–156.

Grant Lewin, Susan, ed., *Formica & Design: From the Counter Top to High Art,* New York: Rizzoli, 1991, p. 191.

Schiff, David, "Special Interests: Management Proposes LBO for Formica," *Barron's,* April 10, 1989, p. 60.

Trachtenberg, Jeffrey A., "Even the Kitchen Sink," *Forbes,* February 24, 1986, pp. 110–111.

—Cheryl Collins

Foxboro Company

33 Commercial Street
Foxboro, Massachusetts 02035
U.S.A.
(508) 543-8750
Fax: (508) 549-6770

Wholly Owned Subsidiary of Siebe, P.L.C.
Incorporated: 1908 as the Industrial Instrument Company
Employees: 6,000
Sales: $600 million
SICs: 3823 Process Control Instruments

The Foxboro Company is a leading manufacturer of industrial controls. The company supplies devices for monitoring and automating manufacturing processes to the chemical, oil and gas, paper, food, pharmaceutical, mining, electric, water, and scientific industries. Founded in New England in the early years of the twentieth century, Foxboro grew as a result of continuous innovation in the products that it offered.

Foxboro was founded by the Bristol brothers. Edgar Hiel Bristol and Bennet Beri Bristol were heirs to a company run by their father and based in Waterbury, Connecticut. They withdrew from the family business, though, and set up the Industrial Instrument Company in 1908. As part of their effort to launch a company capable of producing instrument controls, the Bristol brothers purchased two companies in this industry: the Standard Gauge Manufacturing Company, of Syracuse, New York; and the Standard Electric Time Company, a clock manufacturer in Waterbury.

The Bristols then set out to find a suitable site for their new business. They settled on Foxboro, Massachusetts, a town of 3,500 people that had an unused set of 12 sturdy brick industrial buildings. The fledgling company bought these Neponset Avenue buildings, originally built in 1894 by the Van Choate Electric Company, in the summer of 1908. Industrial Instrument began the process of transferring the operations of the Standard Gauge company from Syracuse to Massachusetts. In December 1908 the first set of Standard Gauge employees arrived from New York, and much of the firm's equipment later followed in wooden crates.

Industrial Equipment also bought another firm, the Shepherd Plating and Finishing Company, based in Waterbury. It moved that company to Foxboro as well. By the end of the year, the company had 53 employees who earned about 13 cents an hour turning out gauges for use in steam boilers, refrigeration units, and automobiles.

In 1909 Industrial Instrument bought the American Instrument Company of Newark, New Jersey, a subdivision of the Western Electric Company. This company specialized in precision instruments, and Industrial benefitted from the purchase of its lathes, presses, and automatic screw machines. In March 1910 the company closed its Waterbury head office after the Bristols determined that its distance from the Foxboro plant made management of the company difficult.

Throughout the second decade of the new century, Industrial Instrument struggled to stay afloat. The company even rented out extra space in its plant to other manufacturers in an effort to raise revenue. Industrial marketed low pressure automobile gauges, high pressure gauges, and temperature monitors. By 1911 the company had introduced the first multiple-pen recorder and sold its first long-distance recording psychrometer. As time passed, Industrial began to market flow instruments and devices to measure differential pressure. The company's primary clients for these instruments were gas companies, utilities, and the process industries.

In 1912 Industrial Instrument sold its Standard Time division back to its original owner after determining that its operations did not fit in well with the rest of its activities. The company also established branch offices in major industrial cities across the United States, including New York, Chicago, and Cleveland, and kept in touch with customers through a publication called *The Foxboro Recorder.*

In 1912 Industrial Instrument adopted a trademark featuring Foxboro, the name of the company's hometown, in order to clear up confusion about the company's identity. On January 1, 1914, Industrial Instrument also changed its name to the Foxboro Company. The following year, the company mounted an exhibition at the World's Fair in San Francisco in an effort to market its goods to a wider variety of national manufacturers.

Foxboro continued its record of innovation in recording devices in the mid-1910s. The company entered the field of automatic controls and introduced a recorder-controller contained in a single case. In addition, the company adapted its automobile temperature gauge for use in airplanes after winning a large contract from the British military, which was fighting the Germans in World War I. Bolstered by this agreement, the Foxboro Company left its state of financial jeopardy behind.

In the wake of World War I, Foxboro continued to market its products for measuring manufacturing processes. The company's pneumatic controller and mercury flow meters were installed in many different process plants. After Foxboro attached an electric motor to its chart drives, the company's products became even more popular.

The company's fortunes improved in other respects as well. Foxboro had previously established an outpost in Tulsa, Oklahoma, to serve the natural gas industry. As a result of innovations in this office, Foxboro altered the way the proper size of a gauge was determined. In addition, the company's Oklahoma employees experimented with modifications to its controllers. Spurred by these innovations, Foxboro created the Model 10 Stabilog Controller, the industry's first proportional plus reset controller. This popular product allowed the company to survive the difficult years of the 1930s.

Foxboro also relied on sales to the oil industry in the 1930s. This market was growing rapidly, driven by the country's industrial expansion and the increasing number of cars on the road. Foxboro sold gauges for use in oil refineries, and also moved into the metal treating, ceramic, and glass industries. To expand its product offerings, Foxboro bought the Wilson-Maeulen Company in 1932. This acquisition became the core of the company's pyrometer department, which made electrical high temperature controls.

In 1933 Foxboro expanded its operations to Canada with a three-man office in Montreal that did business under the name Foxboro Company, Limited. In the following year, the company expanded to Britain, merging the British Gauge and Instrument Company and the Yoxall Instrument Company into Foxboro-Yoxall, Limited. Foxboro also continued its expansion in the United States. By 1935 the company had 14 sales offices distributed around every region of the country. In 1936 Foxboro added to its product line again when it bought the Atlantic Precision Instrument Company of Malden, Massachusetts. With this move, the company entered the market for electronic instruments.

Foxboro's ties to British industry helped the company win contracts for war-related work even before the United States entered World War II. In June 1941 the company began to manufacture torpedo mechanisms for the British Admiralty. Later, the company took on a number of projects for the U.S. Defense Department, including an effort to improve mechanisms to chart the course of U.S. torpedoes. Foxboro's payroll doubled during the war, and the company hired a large number of women for the first time. The company's British unit doubled its personnel as well. Both of Foxboro's founders died in the early 1940s, and leadership of the company was assumed by two Bristol sons. Benjamin became president and Rexford was named treasurer.

After the conclusion of World War II, Foxboro returned to its peacetime production levels. The company rolled out a new controller in 1946, the Model 40, which significantly updated the pre-war Model 30. Foxboro also introduced all-electronic Dynalog instruments; a CycleLog Controller for use by textile firms who were dying fabric; the Dynatherm temperature bulb; and a large number of other innovative products.

By 1950 Foxboro had grown to include 1,550 employees. The company embarked on a building program in the early 1950s in recognition of the ever-increasing number of orders that Foxboro's facilities were being asked to fill. In addition to a new warehouse and a new assembly building, Foxboro also constructed a ''House in the Pines'' for the use of its training school at that time. In 1952 the company built a new print shop that also doubled as a home for its New England sales office. Four years later, Foxboro expanded its physical plant again.

Throughout the 1950s Foxboro continued its program of product innovation. In 1951 the company rolled out its Consotrol series of indicating receiver controllers. This new model was followed by other instruments, both pneumatic and electric, to transmit measurements.

Foxboro expanded its geographic reach as its product line grew and its production capacity was bolstered. In 1952 the company added a Mexican company, Graficas e Instrumentos S.A., which provided instrument supplies and repair services to customers in Mexico. Three years later Foxboro completed an agreement with Yokogawa Electric Works, Limited, based in Tokyo. Under this arrangement, Yokogawa manufactured and distributed Foxboro instruments in the Far East. In addition to these alliances, Foxboro established ties with a number of companies in other areas of the globe. The company typically selected well-regarded engineering firms that were able to provide service and engineering support to foreign users of its instruments. Foxboro partnerships were set up in South Africa, Cuba, the Philippines, Saudi Arabia, and the East Indies, among other locations.

Foxboro also strengthened its operations in the United States during the mid-1950s. Branch shop operations in San Leandro, California; Dallas, Texas; and Pittsburgh, Pennsylvania, were moved into new buildings. Foxboro also established new branches in Skokie, Illinois; Houston, Texas; Corpus Christi, Texas; and Atlanta, Georgia.

By 1958 Foxboro employed more than 2,100 workers and the company's physical plant had expanded to encompass 490,000 square feet. That year the company sold shares on the stock market for the first time, becoming a publicly-owned company. Benjamin and Rexford Bristol, along with a third investor, retained control of a third of Foxboro's shares.

In the 1960s, Foxboro continued its record of product innovation. After introducing its first solid state electronic control system in the late 1950s, the company came out with a direct digital process control system in 1964, and an intrinsically safe electronic control system certified by the Underwriter's Laboratories two years later. Foxboro finished out the decade by rolling out its first computerized batch process.

In the 1970s Foxboro continued to update its products. This practice contributed to the company's steady 15 percent growth rate during this period. In 1972 Foxboro introduced its first distributed control system, which it dubbed the SPEC 200, with an INTERSPEC serial digital data highway. Three years later, the company introduced its first pneumatic composition transmitter. This was followed by the 1976 roll-out of VIDEOSPEC, Foxboro's first CRT-based shared video display system with variable function keys.

By the end of the decade, Foxboro's sales had grown to $471 million a year. While the company competed with another firm, Honeywell, for the leading position in the process controls market, it dominated the field in serving the chemical, petrochemical, and oil markets. Sales in these three areas accounted for nearly half of Foxboro's orders.

In 1979 Foxboro introduced its Spectrum series of systems for electronic control. This line allowed the company to combine newer digital control devices with standard analog measures and computerized communications equipment into one process control system. The analog devices measured, while the digital mechanisms counted. Mixing these two modes represented an important advance for Foxboro. On the strength of the Spectrum line, Foxboro reported a 20 percent surge in orders over the first half of 1980.

Foxboro also got a boost in July 1980 when the federal government decided to promote the development of synthetic fuels. Plants built to manufacture these substances relied heavily on Foxboro controls, and this development pushed the company's stock up ten points, lending fuel to rumors about a potential takeover by partial-owner Schlumberger, Limited.

Despite this good news for the company, some industry observers faulted Foxboro's tradition-minded management for not wringing the maximum profit from their operations. "It's all so paternalistic. They don't lay off people when they should, and that's why the upper management is pretty lackluster," one New York analyst told the *Wall Street Journal.*

Nevertheless, Foxboro's sales rose to $484 million in 1980. A year later, the company formed a joint venture to manufacture electronic instrumentation with two Chinese firms. This project, called Shanghai-Foxboro, was launched in 1982. In October of that year, Foxboro also bought a significant portion of the Microprocessor Systems company, a manufacturer of small computers. In November, however, the company announced a freeze of all salaries for the next six months; earnings had dropped 28 percent in one quarter. In December 1982 the company made a further effort to cut costs when it shut down all U.S. operations for a week. Despite these measures, the company's fortunes continued to worsen in the following year, as Foxboro reported that its net income dropped 83 percent in the first half of the year. In August the company announced that it would again shut down for a week in an effort to conserve costs.

In 1984 Foxboro added to its product line by acquiring two other companies. The company paid $8 million for Octek, a maker of machine vision devices, then purchased Systronics, a manufacturer of flow monitoring and control equipment. Despite these acquisitions, Foxboro was forced to lay off 150 people in mid-1985 in response to a slowing economy. The company ended the year in the red.

Foxboro's troubles continued throughout the late 1980s. In 1987 the company suffered yet another loss, and in December of that year Foxboro's management announced that the company would take a $45 million charge, allowing it to reduce its work force by more than ten percent. Although many of Foxboro's longtime employees took early retirement at this time, the company was again in financial trouble in 1989. It posted losses of $4.5 million, largely as a result of miscalculated costs for big European contracts.

By the spring of 1990, Foxboro's five-year record of financial difficulties had aroused the ire of the company's stockholders, which included members of the Bristol family, who still owned 22 percent of the firm, and high-profile investor George Soros, owner of 4.8 percent of Foxboro's shares. In response to this investor dissatisfaction, Foxboro announced in March 1990 that it was seeking an outside buyer. By June of that year the company reached an agreement with Siebe P.L.C. The British company paid $656 million for Foxboro and announced that it planned to "bury" the company's closest competitor.

Essential to this effort was Foxboro's new process control automation system. With open architecture and object-based communications features, it was called the Intelligent Automation (I/A) Series. This system, one of the most advanced available, cost Foxboro $250 million to create. When the I/A Series developed software problems, Foxboro's profits took a nosedive, and the company was forced to cut back on research and development spending in other areas. Siebe hoped that a retooled I/A Series would contribute strongly to a return to robust profits. Under its new corporate leadership, Foxboro continued to update its products to remain competitive in the 1990s. It became the cornerstone of its parent's Siebe Control Systems Division.

Further Reading:

A Little of Ourselves, Foxboro, Massachusetts: The Foxboro Company, 1958.

Melcher, Richard A., and Gary McWilliams, "Shakeup On The Factory Floor," *Business Week,* July 9, 1990.

Shenon, Philip, "Eyes of Investors Turn to Shy Foxboro As Synthetic Fuel Future Looks Good," *Wall Street Journal,* July 31, 1980.

—Elizabeth Rourke

The Fred W. Albrecht Grocery Co.

P.O. Box 1910
Akron, Ohio 44309
U.S.A.
(216) 733-2861
Fax: (216) 733-8782

Private Company
Incorporated: 1920
Employees: 3,000
Sales: $480 million
SICs: 5411 Grocery Stores

With its chain of 11 Acme supermarkets, nine Acme SuperCenters (which combine general merchandise and grocery items), and 14 Y-Mart convenience pharmacies, The Fred W. Albrecht Grocery Co. is a leading player in the 19-county northeast Ohio retail food market. Founded before the turn of the twentieth century, the family owned and operated firm has used a strategy of acquisition and adaptation to capture and maintain a dominant position in the Akron market.

Ironically, company namesake Fred W. Albrecht was a reluctant grocer. As a youth, he had hoped to avoid ''all [the business's] hardships, all its long hours and its unpleasantness.'' Nonetheless, he took over his older brother's store in the small town of Massillon, Ohio, in the late nineteenth century. A family dispute may have compelled his 1891 move to nearby Akron, where he bought a storefront at a sheriff's sale and founded his own grocery. Later characterized as a ''paternalistic'' manager, Albrecht juggled the dual roles of patriarch and businessman in the early days of the enterprise. His wife Mary handled the accounting, their three children learned to clerk and deliver goods in their after-school hours, and brother-in-law Edward Buehl hired on as resident pharmacist.

In those days, grocery stores were very different from the megamarkets common in the 1990s. For most of the late 19th and early 20th centuries, small neighborhood groceries offered a limited selection of bulk dry goods, including tea, coffee, spices, sugar, and flour. Homemakers bought produce, meat, and fish elsewhere. Customers dropped off (and later phoned in) their orders, which were filled by white-aproned clerks behind high counters and then hand delivered. Grocers typically extended credit to all their customers.

Albrecht's early disdain for the grocery business may have aroused his desire to reform it. By the end of his first decade in business, he had already abandoned the industry's widespread—and admittedly ''promiscuous''—credit practices. Just two years after he founded his store, the Panic of 1893 plunged the country into the worst economic depression to date. High unemployment throughout the 1890s exacerbated endemic problems with late payment and nonpayment of bills in the grocery industry's indiscriminate credit system.

After enduring several years of unpredictable cash flow and what Albrecht called the ''unpleasantness'' of collecting past-due accounts, the grocer decided to convert his store to a cash basis. In an effort to retain as many customers as possible, Albrecht closed shop and circulated a flyer announcing a comprehensive remodeling. Mimicking strategies he had observed at a Philadelphia grocery chain, Albrecht painted his store an outrageously bright—and incidentally eye-catching—yellow. Black lettering proclaimed the store's new name, The Acme Grocery, which had also been appropriated from the eastern store. The announcement of the new payment policy was almost an aside, but Albrecht assured his customers that his store's lower cash prices would offset any inconvenience.

Although some consumers balked at the new policy and the rather garish color scheme, Albrecht's cash flow must have benefited; by 1909, he owned a chain of 13 stores. Four years and seven more groceries later, he had started warehousing goods on his own. The fast-growing chain surpassed $1 million in annual sales for the first time in 1914. It was around this time that Albrecht made a second significant business innovation. Upon returning from a trip to California, an employee told Albrecht of a chain in Pasadena that had cut its costs significantly by eliminating delivery service. Lower retail prices kept the customers coming in spite of the reduced service. After a test market quintupled its sales, Albrecht decided to convert his entire chain to cash-and-carry, renaming them Acme Cash Basket Stores.

With the local tire industry booming, the Acme chain grew to 40 stores by 1918 and incorporated two years later. A limited number of shares were offered to customers and employees, the proceeds of which were used to finance construction of a bakery and cracker factory.

By the 1920s, Albrecht had built Akron's largest grocery chain. When the city celebrated its 100th anniversary in 1925, Acme established its 100th store. With this significant milestone to his credit, the founder went into semi-retirement and sons Hurl and Ivan took the reins. The business continued to grow during this prosperous decade; by the early 1930s, the chain boasted 125 stores in and around Akron. The Great Depression, however, brought Acme's four decades of fantastic growth to an abrupt halt and ushered in a slump that was not truly surmounted until after World War II. The end of the war lifted a 20-year veil of consumer restraint and heralded what *Fortune* magazine called ''The Great American Boom.'' The Acme chain, and the grocery industry in general, underwent a profound transformation during this period of rapidly increasing consumer demand.

Unfortunately, Acme found itself slightly behind the times. While other grocers in the region had begun the switch to the supermarket format, the vast majority of Acme stores were old-fashioned corner groceries, where clerks still fetched goods from floor-to-ceiling shelves for waiting customers. The Albrechts had tested supermarketing in the 1930s and early 1940s, but had had little luck with the format. Then, in 1949, the company tested a radically new idea: the Food-O-Mat. The Food-O-Mat concept featured a single, long display of specially-designed automatic shelves that were stocked from behind. One competitor compared the appearance of the distinctly 1950s-era gimmick to that of a bowling alley. Although the Food-O-Mats failed because they were too standardized for the burgeoning variety of consumer goods that were coming to market, they signaled the end of an overly-conservative period in Acme's history.

The early 1950s were a period of rapid change for the Acme chain. Ivan ''Ike'' Albrecht succeeded his brother as company president in 1950, when Hurl became chairman. Upon Hurl's death just three years later, Ike moved up to chairman. Fred C. Pockrandt—who, although not a member of the Albrecht family, had worked at Acme since he was in high school—assumed the presidency.

Upon realizing that large-scale, self-service stores were the wave of the future, the chain's management began closing its vast network of neighborhood groceries and opening regionally-focused supermarkets. The new shops were often referred to as ''double stores'' because they were literally twice as large as the old ones. New features included expansive parking lots, meat and produce departments, and health and beauty aids. The chain opened its first store in a suburban shopping center in 1952.

Acme underwent what company historian Priscilla M. Harding called ''a major management realignment'' when Pockrandt retired in 1959. It seems apparent that, under increasingly intense competitive pressures, the non-family executive favored a strategic merger or a profit-generating sell-out. But that was a proposition to which his successor, Fred I. Albrecht, was adamantly opposed. The third-generation leader vehemently stated his position in a company newsletter: ''Acme has no intention of selling. This is our chain. We have made it what it is today . . . kept it strong and healthy. One and all, we are proud of it, for it means more to us than just another business enterprise. It is part of us—it is our reputation—it is our life as well as our livelihood.'' Fred I. Albrecht continued the chain's postwar modernization program in the 1960s. Acme's 75th anniversary in 1966 coincided with the closure of the chain's last corner grocery.

Ever-intensifying (and sometimes self-defeating) competition characterized the supermarket industry in the last half of the 20th century. Northeast Ohio was an especially hard-fought market; increasing expenditures for promotions (such as trading stamps, couponing, contests, and preferred customer cards), print and television advertising, overhead, and labor combined with a shrinking consumer base, the encroachment of strong national chains, and the general economic malaise that gripped the once-prosperous Rust Belt to squeeze profit margins and virtually eliminate growth.

As a result, supermarketers looked for ways to cut costs and boost margins. In the 1970s, Acme used automation, cooperation, and diversification to enhance its competitiveness. The company installed its first mainframe computers and barcode scanners during the decade, helping to streamline operations from the warehouse to the checkout line. Acme also cut its wholesale food costs by joining a national food cooperative, Topco, in 1971. This move enabled the chain to offer its own private label line and thereby retain more of the profits on those items. Diversification into pharmacies and one-stop superstores also helped raise Acme's profit margins. In 1970, Acme acquired the six-store Youngfellow Drug chain through an exchange of stock and began converting old Acme Cash Baskets into ''Y-Marts.'' The company hoped to make the Y-Mart ''the ultimate convenience store'' by combining drugstore and grocery items. Acme launched five new Click general merchandise outlets (later renamed Acme SuperCenters) over the course of the decade as well.

Albrecht's annual revenues increased by over 160 percent from 1970 to 1978, to $202 million. In spite of formidable competition from The Great Atlantic and Pacific Tea Company (A&P), the Acme chain claimed over half of the Akron grocery market at the end of the decade. Although A&P deserted the cut-throat northeast Ohio market, the home team faced a parade of national and regional opponents in the 1980s and early 1990s.

In 1983, longtime rival Kroger Company launched the first salvo in an especially bitter price war with a triple coupon campaign. Acme returned fire with an everyday low price (EDLP) campaign, marking down prices on over 8,000 grocery items. The battle heated up in 1984, when Pittsburgh-based Giant Eagle Inc. entered the Akron market. Although Acme suffered a significant loss that year, it was able to withstand the onslaught. Kroger abandoned the northeast Ohio market in 1985, blaming high labor costs for its closure of 27 area stores and a regional distribution center. Steven Albrecht, the fourth generation of the family to lead the company, called Acme's acquisition of four locations formerly owned by Kroger ''exhilarating.''

In the wake of price-fixing charges against three Cleveland supermarket chains as well as its victory over Kroger, Acme went on the offensive in the mid-1980s, establishing its first store in the metropolitan Cleveland market. Billed as Ohio's largest supermarket, the suburban store cost $8 million to build, occupied 72,000 square feet, and featured a bake shop, deli, floral center, and areas leased to other merchants. Albrecht was able to launch at least one other store in the Cleveland area in the early 1990s. As the underdog, however, Acme faced what one rival called ''very active and aggressive efforts by all the competition'' in its new haunts. In 1987, Cleveland's three largest grocery chains—Fisher Foods, Inc., Rini Supermarkets, and Rego Supermarkets and American Seaway Foods, Inc.—merged to form northeast Ohio's largest grocery chain, Riser Foods, Inc.

The supermarket industry's ongoing problems of decreasing population, market saturation, and some of the lowest profit margins in the United States were exacerbated by competition on new fronts. Some of these challengers, including Food 4 Less and Minneapolis-based Twin-Valu, used nonunion labor to lower their costs and pull Acme's attention back to its home market. Supermarkets also began to feel the pressure of intra-industry competition from alternative-format stores including wholesale clubs, mass merchandisers, and supercenters launched by Wal-Mart Stores, Inc. (Sam's Club), and Kmart Corporation (Super Kmart), for example. A recession that started in the late 1980s and continued into the early 1990s compelled cash-strapped consumers to shop around for bargains. These low-cost outlets helped fuel a 3.3 percent decline in food prices in the first few years of the decade. The Food Marketing Institute warned grocers that these new rivals would increase their share of the grocery business from six to 13 percent by the turn of the century. Acme responded with general merchandise/supermarkets of its own known as Acme SuperCenters. One industry analyst predicted that this ''battle of the supercenters . . . promises to be long and bitter.'' Some observers noted societal shifts that hurt traditional groceries as well. For example, changing household and work patterns favored more convenience store shopping and fast food dining.

The combined competitive forces exerted by a large new opponent in Cleveland (Riser Foods), poor economic conditions, and new superstore rivals compelled Acme's 1994 retrenchment. That year, the company sold its Cleveland locations to Rini-Rego Supermarkets Inc. One of the few remaining privately- and family-owned supermarket chains in the area, the Fred W. Albrecht Grocery Co. worked to continually update and expand its merchandise offerings, remodel stores, and gain economies through computerization in order to compete in this ever-challenging industry.

Further Reading:

Crispens, Jonna, ''Albrecht is Rolling Out Updated POS Systems,'' *Supermarket News,* April 25, 1994, p. 11.

Garry, Michael, ''Showdown! Standing Up to Supercenters,'' *Progressive Grocer,* February 1993, pp. 44–50.

Harding, Priscilla M., *The Highest Point: A Centennial History of The Fred W. Albrecht Grocery Company,* Akron, Ohio: Summit County Historical Society, 1991.

Jordan, George E., ''Biggest Supermarket Ever Planned in South Euclid,'' *Cleveland Plain Dealer,* March 13, 1984, p. 9C.

Karle, Delinda, and George E. Jordan, ''Supermarts Here Face Akron Challenger,'' *Cleveland Plain Dealer,* May 12, 1985, p. 2D.

Karle, Delinda, ''After Dark: Bid for Bucks Lights Up Night,'' *Cleveland Plain Dealer,* May 12, 1985, pp. 1D, 2D.

'' 'We Can Outmerchandise Them',*'' Progressive Grocer,* May 1994, p. 35.

—April Dougal Gasbarre

genzyme

Genzyme Corporation

One Kendall Square
Cambridge, Massachusetts 02139-1562
U.S.A.
(617) 252-7500
Fax: (617) 252-7600

Public Company
Incorporated: 1981
Employees: 1,724
Sales: $ 295 million
Stock Exchanges: NASDAQ
SICs: 2836 Biological Products Except Diagnostic; 3841 Surgical & Medical Instruments; 2834 Pharmaceutical Preparations; 8071 Medical Laboratories

Genzyme Corporation is a leading biotechnology company that focuses on five business areas: therapeutics, diagnostic services, diagnostic products, pharmaceutical and fine chemicals, and tissue repair. Headquartered in Boston, Massachusetts, Genzyme has production facilities, research laboratories, and sales and marketing offices throughout the world.

In 1981, Henry Blair founded Genzyme to produce products based on enzyme technologies. With the help of venture capital funding, Blair acquired Whatman Biochemicals Ltd, which became Genzyme Biochemicals. In 1982, Blair acquired a British catalog business, Kock Light Laboratories, a supplier of chemicals to the pharmaceutical industry. The pharmaceutical manufacturing arm of Kock Laboratories in 1986 became Genzyme Pharmaceutical and Fine Chemicals based in Haverill, England.

Despite these developments, Genzyme struggled until 1983, when Dutch-born Henri Termeer left Baxter Travenol (now Baxter International) to become company chairman at Genzyme. Termeer had studied economics at the University of Rotterdam and had earned an MBA at the University of Virginia before joining Baxter in 1973. After undergoing two years of training in Chicago, Baxter assigned him to run its largest overseas sales organization in Germany. The position gave him valuable experience in managing a major business operation. By the time he joined Genzyme, Termeer was one of Baxter's executive vice-presidents. He was recruited to Genzyme by the venture capital firm, Oak Investment Partners, which had substantial investments in the start-up company.

Termeer took a personal risk in moving to Genzyme, sacrificing half his salary and a comfortable lifestyle in southern California for forbidding office space in Boston's notorious Combat Zone—the city's red light district. The company had just 11 people. On assuming the chairmanship, Termeer immediately began a search for investment capital. He also formed an advisory board, comprising a group of eminent MIT scientists to identify promising new areas for product development. While many biotechnology companies worked to develop huge blockbuster drugs, Genzyme crafted a niche strategy focusing on less glamorous products that could be readily sold. This strategy proved to position the company well, even as it developed longer term products.

Genzyme aggressively pursued its strategy first through developing expertise in engineering and modifying enzymes and carbohydrates. Enzymes are proteins that essentially act as catalysts for many cellular processes, while carbohydrates often coat proteins and govern their interactions with other substances or chemicals. The company's expertise in these areas yielded readily marketable products. Genzyme developed and marketed a product called cholesterol oxidase including an enzyme that worked as the active agent in cholesterol tests.

In 1983, Termeer became president of Genzyme and in 1985 he was named chief executive officer. In 1986, Genzyme became a public company with an initial public offering that raised $28.2 million. In the same year, the company opened a Japanese subsidiary financed by Japanese sales, and built a manufacturing facility in Cambridge, Massachusetts for the production of medical grade hyaluronic acid. Genzyme also raised $10 million to finance the development of Ceredase through a research and development limited partnership. Genzyme divested Koch-Light Laboratories in 1987. In 1988, the company, with partial funding from the Department of Trade & Industry, opened a pharmaceutical chemical plant in Haverville, United Kingdom, doubling Genzyme's manufacturing capacity. In addition, the company received U.S. Food and Drug Administration approval to market the antibiotic Clindamycin Phosphate for the treatment of serious hospital infections.

In 1989, Termeer acquired Integrated Genetics (IG) of Framingham, Massachusetts, a move that industry observers termed a masterstroke. Termeer's successful negotiations for the company stemmed from a coincidental meeting with IG Chairman Robert Carpenter. Both attended a reunion of Baxter alumni in Chicago, and the two alums accompanied one another on the return flight to Boston. Although mired in financial difficulty, IG possessed superior technology. In 1988, Termeer unsuccessfully bid for IG when its stock hovered at $5 per share. But Carpenter was willing to deal in 1989 after trying to sell out to a large pharmaceutical company. Several weeks after the airplane flight, Carpenter accepted Genzyme's offer for less than $3 a share in Genzyme stock, amounting to $31.5 million. The acquisition considerably strengthened Genzyme's expertise in molecular biology, protein chemistry, carbohydrate engineering, nucleic acid chemistry, and enzymology.

In the same year, Genzyme raised $39.1 million in a public stock offering and another $36.8 million through a research and development limited partnership to develop four hyaluronic-acid (HA) based drugs to reduce the formation of postoperative adhesions. The company also formed its Genzyme Diagnostics Division. By the end of 1989, Genzyme reported revenues of $34.1 million.

By far, Genzyme's most lucrative, if not controversial, product was the drug Ceredase, approved by the U.S. Food and Drug Administration in 1991. The drug was the first effective treatment for Gaucher's disease, a rare but previously untreatable and potentially fatal genetic disorder. The illness, which afflicted about 20,000 people worldwide in the early 1990s, most commonly strikes Jews of East European descent. The victims of the disease lack a natural enzyme that metabolizes fats, causing lipids, or fatty substances, to mass in the liver, spleen, and bone marrow causing a variety of crippling conditions and years of painful physical deterioration. Genzyme's scientists successfully produced the missing enzyme which could be infused interveneously and consequently reverse the lipid buildup allowing patients to live normal and active lives with few side affects.

While Ceredase won praise as a life-saving treatment, it also drew criticism for being the most expensive drug ever sold, running on average $150,000 per patient a year. As a result, the drug became a vehicle for criticism of high drug prices. In 1992, the Office of Technology Assessment, a nonpartisan Congressional research agency, issued a report accusing Genzyme of pricing the drug so high that patients would have to exhaust their lifetime insurance to buy Ceredase for two or three years. The report noted that the real costs and risks of developing the drug were low because most of work was done by government researchers. The federal agency stated the pricing also raised serious questions concerning whether the government should participate in developing drugs with little or no control over their final pricing. Company chairman and president, Henri Termeer, said the agency's report was flawed and that the high cost stemmed from the enormous expense of producing the product. To assuage criticism, Genzyme agreed to give Ceredase to patients whose insurance benefits ran out. Nevertheless, others also voiced complaints. Speaking on behalf of the National Organization for Rare Disorders, Abbey S. Meyers, the organization's president, stated in *The Wall Street Journal* on May 20, 1994 that ''we were appalled'' at Genzyme's pricing of Ceredase. This criticism was the latest in complaints about the exorbitant cost of biotechnology drugs. In Congressional hearings, patients had complained about the cost of the anemia drug erythropoietin, or EPO, from Amgen Inc., which cost between $4,000 and $6,000 a year; and Genentech Inc.'s human growth hormone at $12,000 to $18,000 a year. But Ceredase's price far surpassed either of these two drugs and quickly drove the issue onto the legislative agenda.

These criticisms aside, Ceredase was enormously expensive to make, relying on enzyme extraction from placenta, or afterbirth from hospitals around the world. The harvesting of the material was done by a unit of the Institut Merieux of Paris. The production of a year's supply for the average patient required approximately 20,000 placentas equaling about 27 tons of material. In 1994, Genzyme supplied Ceredase to 1,100 patients. The drug's high price stemmed also from its applicability to only a small number of patients, placing the primary burden for paying the research costs and a return to investors on those being treated. Genzyme argued, moreover, that Ceredase differed from other drugs in a critical respect that influenced its price. Typically, drug prices were set to be competitive with existing treatments, including surgery and hospitalization, in spite of production costs. But since Ceredase was the only existing treatment for Gaucher's disease, the price reflected the drug's full production and marketing costs.

Genzyme's monopoly on Ceredase was protected under the Orphan Drug Act, passed in 1983 to give seven year exclusive rights to drug companies which produce drugs for rare diseases (those afflicting under 200,000 people). According to Termeer, the Act attracted the capital investment needed to research and develop the drug. In 1994, Genzyme received FDA approval to market Cerezyme, a genetically engineered replacement for Ceredase. The company also hoped to benefit from Orphan Act designation for various projects concerning cystic fibrosis, Fabry's disease, and severe burns.

By 1991, Genzyme raised nearly $100 million for research and development while retaining control over its equity and production rights, a stark contrast to many young biotechnology firms which had to sacrifice these assets to finance themselves. Nearly half the funds, $47.3 million, came from a public offering of Neozyme I Corp., formed by Genzyme in 1990 to research and develop six health care products. In 1992, the company formed Neozyme II to fund other Genzyme projects. The companies largely operated as paper businesses to finance research and development projects and retain rights to the products. If the projects proved successful, Genzyme could buy the rights back.

In 1991, Genzyme also took IG laboratories—the genetic testing services business—public, raising another $14.1 million. Genzyme reported revenues of $121.7 million, more than double 1990 revenues of $54.8 million. In addition, Genzyme announced that it would build new corporate headquarters and manufacturing facilities in Boston in a 51-acre site along the Charles river. The company looked at sites in more than a dozen states, narrowing its choice to two in Massachusetts—Boston and Cambridge—both with international scientific reputations. These sites were close to Genzyme's current headquarters in Cambridge and close to large clusters of biotechnology companies. Boston's offer of a sizeable state-owned parcel that could be quickly developed, plus many inducements, including breaks on city and state taxes and government assistance with site planning, road construction, utility rates, and others, clinched the deal. Regional economists hoped that Genzyme's $110 million facility would be one anchor of a thriving regional biotechnology industry, bringing thousands of new research and manufacturing jobs to raise the city and Massachusetts out of recession. Genzyme also ran a pilot production facility in Framingham, Massachusetts, and operations in the Netherlands, Japan, and England.

Genzyme's other corporate moves in 1991 included the selling of its interest in GENE-TRAK systems for $10 million and the acquisition of Genecore International's diagnostic enzyme business. The acquisition gave Genzyme worldwide diagnostic sales, production capacity, inventory, as well as related patent and distribution rights. The company also established Genzyme, B.V., a European subsidiary in Naardan Holland to manage the development and regulatory approval of Genzyme's biotherapeutic products.

Genzyme's research achievements for 1991 included beginning clinical development of Thyrogen, a thyroid stimulating human hormone for use in the diagnosis and treatment of thyroid cancer. Genzyme also initiated clinical development of HAL-S synovial fluid replacement, a treatment for tissue damage resulting from arthroscopic surgery. In addition, Genzyme and Tufts University scientists jointly performed breakthrough analysis concerning the role of a key protein responsible for cystic fibrosis, a lung disease. In 1992, the researchers innovated a method to mass produce this protein for the treatment of the disease by genetically altering mice with a human gene governing production of the protein and then harvesting it from fat globules in mouse's milk. The discovery marked the first time that animal milk was used to produce proteins of this type.

In 1992, Genzyme developed technology to make purer and stronger pharmaceuticals and to simplify the pharmaceutical preparation process. Genzyme won FDA orphan drug designation for several treatments, covering Cystic Fibrosis Transmembrane Conductance Regulation (r-CFTR), Cystic Fibrosis Gene Therapy (CFGT), Thyrogen Cancer Agent, and Vianain Enzymatic Debridement Agent for treating severe burn patients. In 1994, the company received FDA approval to sell Cerezyme, the genetically engineered replacement for Ceredase.

By the early 1990s, Genzyme had become a large and thriving diversified company, contrary to many biotechnology firms plagued by clinical failures, cuts in research, layoffs, and funding troubles. In 1994, Repligen Inc. of Cambridge, Massachusetts announced layoffs of one-third of its staff after failing to find financial backing. Synergen Inc.'s stock plunged on news that its leading drug failed in clinical trials, compelling the Boulder, Colorado, firm to cut more than half of its payroll. Glycomed Inc. of Alameda, California, eliminated 30 percent of its workforce to conserve cash. Cambridge Biotech Corp. of Worcester, Massachussets, a once-leading biotech firm, filed for Chapter 11 protection. And signaling the industry's poor health, Oppenheimer Global Bio-Tech Fund, a specialty mutual fund for stock investors, announced that it was shifting investment strategy to focus on ''emerging growth'' stocks. With these reversals, investor confidence plummeted, causing financing to dry up, research projects to be dropped, and leaving many smaller firms vulnerable if their flagship drugs failed to pay off. To raise cash, several companies licensed their main products at minimal sale prices. Other companies canceled plans to add manufacturing capacity and sold facilities and leased them back. The main culprit for the industry's woes was a string of clinical failures, as some biotech firms prematurely initiated clinical studies to gain the broadest possible market exposure for their products. Still, in 1994 over 100 biotechnology products were either in final Phase III clinical tests or awaiting FDA marketing approval.

Genzyme and other large biotechnology companies capitalized on the industry fall out by buying financially troubled firms and products at low prices. Genzyme aggressively began acquiring companies in the late 1980s as part of a broad strategy to minimize risk. Besides the acquisitions of Integrated Genetics and Gencore International, in 1992, Genzyme acquired Medix Biotech, Inc., a producer and supplier of monoclonal and polyclonal antibodies, immunoassay components, and immunodiagnostic services. In the same year, the company's U.K. subsidiary, Genzyme Limited, bought Enzymatix Limited of Cambridge, United Kingdom, which was integrated into Genzyme's Pharmaceutical and Fine Chemicals division. Genzyme also acquired Vivigen, a genetics testing laboratory in Sante Fe, New Mexico. In 1993, Genzyme acquired both Virotech of Russelsheim, Germany, a producer and distributor of in-vitro diagnostic kits, and Omni Res srl of Milan, Italy, a producer and seller of immunobiological products. Acquisitions in 1994 included a Swiss pharmaceutical concern, Sygena Ltd.; BioSurface Technology Inc., a developer of wound healing products; and TSI Inc., a former high flying drug testing company that expanded too rapidly and posted major financial losses. The TSI acquisition was made by Genzyme Transgenics Corp., created by Genzyme in 1993 to promote and develop technology combining recombinant microbiology and experimental embryology to produce specialized proteins from animal milk. The TSI purchase made Genzyme Transgenics, 73 percent owned by Genzyme—the largest player in the emerging biotechnology market called ''pharming,'' the use of genetically altered farm animals to produce pharmaceuticals.

Genzyme's diversification moves generally received praise, but they also raised speculation that the company would face difficulty integrating the various operations. Moreover, despite the company's numerous acquisitions, its major revenue producer was still just one product, Ceredase/Cerezyme. Beyond this product, Genzyme's line of future drugs contained no blockbuster moneymakers, a strategy originally crafted by Termeer to minimize risk. Unlike many of its competitors, Genzyme had yet to experience any major disappointments in clinical trials on near-term drug development projects. In 1995, Genzyme's next project, a range of hyaluronic acid (HA) products, also looked promising. Hyaluronic acid comprises a polysaccharide found in a variety of human tissues that can be used to prevent post-operative adhesions following abdominal, gynecological, cardiac, and orthopedic surgery. Noting that hyaluronic acid could be used by virtually all surgeons, Genzyme predicted that the market for the drug would be about $1.3 billion, four times that for Ceredase. Unlike the Ceredase market, however, Genzyme faced several competitors for hyaluronic acid, including major pharmaceutical companies. Other products were also being developed to serve the same purpose. In addition, concerns arose that the product was unlikely to be universally effective in preventing postoperative adhesions, and thus the marketing of the drug would be split with competing products. Nevertheless, Termeer expressed confidence in the drug and said that Genzyme would beat competitors to the market by at least five years.

Genzyme's diversification also included a move into gene therapy. While its leading product, Ceredase, and its genetically engineered successor, Cerezyme, proved highly effective, the company began working with scientists at the University of Pittsburgh and at IntroGene B.V., a biotech firm in Rijswijk, the Netherlands, to develop a gene therapuetic treatment to replace the drugs. The new therapy, if successful, would correct the enduring genetic defects responsible for Gaucher's disease. In addition, in 1995 Genzyme planned to spend $400 million to research and develop gene therapy to treat cystic fibrosis, the most common fatal hereditary disease in the United States. These moves partly stemmed from attempts to avoid obsolescence as the revolutionary developments in gene therapy, still mostly in the exploratory stage, threatened to bypasss biotechnology developments.

By the mid-1990s, Genzyme continued to be well positioned to capitalize on emerging technologies and to minimize risk if several of its products failed. The company arose in 1981 to become one of the top five biotechnology companies in terms of sales. Nevertheless the biotechnology field remained highly competitive, comprising numerous rivals in the United States and elsewhere, many of which had greater resources than Genzyme. With large pharmaceutical and biotechnology companies as competitors, the prospect loomed that these companies would develop more effective products and marketing strategies. Indeed, Genzyme's competitive pressures were most acute in the therapeutics field. Although no alternatives existed for Ceredase and Cerezyme, another company was attempting to make an alternative product using an enzyme in insect cells. Genzyme's hyaluronic acid products for postoperative adhesions faced competition from both HA-based and non HA-based products. The company anticipated that the chief competitive factor would be the measure of acceptance by surgeons depending on product performance and price. Several academic and commercial enterprises were engaged in developing therapies to treat either the symptoms or the cause of cystic fibrosis. A number of groups were developing gene therapy approaches to the disease and received government approval to conduct limited human trials. Other organizations were investigating pharmacological and biological agents that would alleviate the symptoms of the disease. A leading biotech firm, Genentech Inc., had already received FDA marketing approval for its product Pulmozyme. With these competitive elements, anyone of these groups could develop gene therapy products or drug therapies before Genzyme, or obtain patent protection that would effectively bar the company from commercializing its technology. Nevertheless, Genzyme's aggressive strategy had paid off in the past and appeared to position the company well for future developments.

Principal Subsidiaries: Genzyme Trnasgenics Corporation (73%); IG Laboratories, Inc. (69%).

Further Reading:

Alster, Norm, ''Henri Termeer's Orphan Drug Strategy,'' *Forbes,* May 27, 1991, pp. 202–205.

Diesenhouse, Susan, ''Boston Over Cambridge In a Biotechnology Race,'' *The New York Times,* December 25, 1991.

Hilts, Philip J., ''U.S. Agency Criticizes High Price of Drug,'' *The New York Times,* October 6, 1992.

Rosenberg, Ronald, ''Genzyme's Plan to Beat Obsolescence,'' *The Boston Globe,* January 8, 1995.

Schwartz, John, and Carolyn Friday, ''Beating The Odds in Biotech,'' *Newsweek,* October 12, 1992, p. 63.

Stecklow, Steve ''Genzyme Receives FDA Approval To Sell Cerezyme'' *The Wall Street Journal,* May 25, 1994.

Stipp, David, ''Biotechnology Firms Find Themselves in Cash Crunch,'' *The Wall Street Journal,* July 26, 1994, p. B10.

——, ''Genzyme to Buy BioSurface, Merge It Into a New Unit With Separate Stock,'' *The Wall Street Journal,* July 26, 1994, p. B4.

——, ''Stock Swap for TSI Set By Genzyme Transgenics Corp.,'' *The Wall Street Journal,* June 16, 1994, p. B7.

Tanouye, Elyse, ''What's Fair?: Critics Say Many New Drugs Are Priced Far Too High,'' *The Wall Street Journal,* May 20, 1994, p. R11.

—Bruce P. Montgomery

Gorton's

88 Roger Street
Gloucester, Massachusetts 01930
U.S.A.
(508) 283-3000
Fax: (508) 281-8295

Wholly Owned Subsidiary of Unilever United States, Inc.
Incorporated: 1906 as Gorton-Pew Fisheries Co.
Employees: 850
Sales: $400 million
SICs: 2092 Fresh Frozen Packaged Fish & Seafoods

A company with roots as old as the fishing industry itself, Gorton's, a wholly owned subsidiary of Unilever United States, Inc., is a perennial leader in the seafood industry. Gorton's, which at one time hauled fish over the sides of its own ships and cured them on board, has been a pioneer in the frozen convenience seafood industry. It has remained a leader in the frozen fish market in the mid-1990s.

One of the earliest settlements in New England, Gloucester is the cradle of America's fishing industry. Long before the official birthdate of Gorton's, its parent companies were building their own reputations. John Pew & Company was the oldest fish packer in the city, established in 1849. Slade Gorton & Company, founded in 1868, was the first to package salt-dried fish in barrels. Both establishments sailed the Atlantic with company-owned schooners, pulling in cod and mackerel and salt-curing them on board. Gorton also dealt in pickled fish.

Gorton's became a registered trademark in 1875. Business was good enough for Slade Gorton that by 1889 he'd expanded to two buildings and 40 employees. Gorton's cod became the first nationally advertised fish; its billboards lined railways and roads across the continent. Fish was not a common staple of the American diet in those days, but Gorton's emphasized its innovative preparation of its product. Billed as "Absolutely Boneless Codfish" in 1901, the fish—which sold for nine cents a pound—was dried, salted, wrapped, and packed. After the fish was purchased, it needed to be soaked before preparing. It was only the first of many industry innovations for the company.

In 1906 Slade Gorton and John Pew merged their businesses with Reed & Gamage and David B. Smith & Company, owner of the largest fleet of vessels of any port on the Atlantic seaboard at that time. It was a marriage of Gloucester's top fishing businesses. The company that was created, Gorton-Pew Fisheries Company, is considered Gorton's predecessor.

Soon, Gorton's codfish cakes were a household item. While the rest of the world was becoming mechanized by steam-powered engines and automated production lines, the fishing industry continued to operate as it had in years past. Fish were still caught in hand-made nets, dried in the open air, and filleted by hand. It was labor-intensive work.

By 1912 Gorton's was offering boneless herring and smoked halibut, as well as Gorton's Cod Liver Oil Cough Candy. Shortly after World War I, however, the company shipped an ill-fated load of fish to Italy. The government had changed hands by the time the boat docked. The fish were taken, but no payment was made. Gorton-Pew went into bankruptcy as a result of the confiscation and several other company problems. According to a judge's statements at a hearing on the company's solvency in 1922, there had been some gross mismanagement as well. Gorton's owed various banks more than $1.3 million.

The company was reorganized in 1923 by a Boston lawyer named William Putnam, who went on to become Gorton's president. Putnam steered the company toward refrigeration, the key to the industry's future. The frozen food revolution impacted Gorton's more than any other historical event. The company recognized the opportunities that refrigeration offered early on, entering the fish-freezing business in the early 1930s. In fact, the company purchased the Gloucester Cold Storage and Warehouse Company in 1929, an indication that the company was looking ahead even at that early date.

World War II brought an increase in demand for fish products for those in the armed services, but it also brought government restrictions on the use of tin. The ultimate industry boost came from the meat shortage that was in place during the war. The shortage forced consumers to pursue alternative food choices, and fish producers were a primary beneficiary.

In 1944 Gorton's introduced the first frozen fish steak, a forerunner of what has become a company staple. Five years later, Gorton-Pew made national headlines when it made the first refrigerator trailer truck shipment of frozen fish across the continent, from Gloucester, Massachusetts, to San Francisco, California. The trip took eight days.

Until the mid-1900s, fish had little appeal to Americans, especially to those further inland from both coasts. Fish's main advantage over meat products was its low price. The health benefits associated with fish had not yet been discovered. More homes tried fish during the war's meat shortage, but it wasn't until seafood merged with the era of super convenience that it became a household essential. Gorton's Fried and Frozen Codfish, the first modern convenience frozen seafood, was introduced in 1952 and became a huge hit with housewives.

Shortly before that time, E. Robert Kinney's company, North Atlantic Packing, had been tapped by Gorton's for a joint enterprise—canned sardines. Kinney became a director of Gorton's in 1953, where he dealt with company problems in Canada. Gorton's net sales reached eight figures for the first time in

1955 on the strength of a 27 percent increase over the prior year. A $1 million modern seafood processing plant was opened in 1956 in Gloucester. A year later, the company changed its name to Gorton's of Gloucester. At that time, the company's product lines included main courses; fried and frozen specialties; frozen portion-controlled fish for institutional use; canned fish; and the company's first staple—salted and pickled fish.

In the latter part of the 1950s, the volume of fish that Gorton's was able to sell exceeded the supply available from domestic fishermen. Gorton's used foreign sources of fish for the first time during this period. Kinney became company president in 1958 and ushered the company through a period of major acquisitions and corporate growth.

Gorton's made a whirlwind of purchases during the 1960s. The company started with Florida Frozen Foods, a purchase that brought a Miami-based shrimp processing plant and other brands of breaded shrimp to Gorton's. Another food service market notable, Blue Water Seafoods of Cleveland, was acquired in 1961. The following year, Gorton's helped form Trans World Seafood, Inc., a trading company for seafood commodities. It acquired Riggin & Robbins and Red L Foods in the same year. The year 1962 was notable for another reason as well: Gorton's began supplying McDonald's with fillet of fish for its sandwiches. (Gorton's remained the largest supplier of fish to McDonald's in the mid-1990s.)

Gorton's purchased Blue Water Sea Foods of Montreal, Canada, in 1963, then added Fulham Brothers, a west coast marketer of seafoods. With its purchase of Connecticut's Freeborn Farms in 1966, Gorton's made its first foray outside seafoods. Freeborn produced frozen hors d'oeuvres. Items like frozen deviled crab and stuffed flounder were the specialty of Bayou Foods of Mobile, Alabama, which joined Gorton's in 1966. Point Chehalis Packers of Westport, Washington, a crab and salmon producer, came aboard in 1967. Another shrimp producer, the Africa-based Crevettes du Cameroun, was acquired by Gorton's in 1968, as was B.B. Foods of Kentucky. This was also the year that Gorton's became a wholly owned subsidiary of General Mills, Inc.

When Gorton's joined General Mills, Kinney became a General Mills vice-president and Ross Clouston succeeded him as president of Gorton's. Clouston had been president and general manager of Gorton's seafood division. He steered Gorton's into research and development of seafood products, doubling the company's research and development labs in 1969. By 1971 the company was offering such new products for retail as single-serving shrimp and chips; ocean snacks; seven fish-shaped fillets, for children; and new heat-and-serve entrees. In the food service industry, Gorton's concentrated on total convenience and created new frozen prepared entrees; seafood combination dinners; and crab-stuffed fish and shrimp.

The company had sixteen plants in the early 1970s in such diverse locations as Gloucester, Los Angeles, Florida, and Alaska. The company also maintained international offices in Canada, Peru, and West Africa. Its primary brands at the time were Gorton's of Gloucester, Blue Water Seafoods, Tropic-Fair, Four Fishermen, and Bayou. A specialty products division was created in 1979 to sell batter to other food companies.

In the early 1980s, Gorton's sold Blue Water Food Service, although it still owned Blue Water's retail business in the early 1990s. The Miama-based shrimp plant was closed and the company's shrimp operations were moved to Mobile, Alabama.

Clouston became chairman in 1986, making way for Steven Warhover to become Gorton's president, a position he continued to hold in 1995. Bayou Foods was sold in 1987, a divestment that marked an end to Gorton's active acquisition and divestment philosophy. From that time through mid-1995, Gorton's has not bought or sold any other operations.

Gorton's retained its lead in 1990 in the frozen seafood category by introducing new products such as the only marinated breaded flavored shrimps on the market. In 1993 Gorton's revamped its fish offerings with its introduction of various special-flavored breaded fillets. The company expanded this line with lemon pepper fillets and southern fried country style fillets. In 1994 it offered the first non-breaded pre-grilled fish.

Gorton's was acquired by Unilever in May 1995. One of the world's largest consumer goods companies, Unilever maintained joint headquarters in London and Rotterdam in the mid-1990s. It had virtually no frozen food sales in the United States other than ice cream until it purchased Gorton's. Unilever, though, has worldwide sales of $45 billion in other markets, and was the world's largest producer of tea, ice cream, margarine, and spreads in the early 1990s. Gorton's is expected to increase Unilever's U.S. sales figures considerably.

Further Reading:

Jones, Syl, "A Gorton's Family Album: More Than a Century of Memories," *Family: Published for the Men and Women of General Mills Family of Fine Companies,* 1977, pp. 9–17.

Lingle, Rick, "Vacuum-Sealed Frozen Seafood," *Prepared Foods,* September 1992, p. 96.

—Carol I. Keeley

Grinnell Corp.

3 Tyco Park
Exeter, New Hampshire 03833-1114
U.S.A.
(603) 778-9200
Fax: (603) 778-9260

Wholly Owned Subsidiary of Tyco International Ltd.
Founded: 1850 as the Providence Steam and Gas Pipe Co.
Sales: $1.2 billion
Employees: 12,000
SICS: 3317 Steel Pipe and Tubes; 3491 Industrial Valves; 3494 Valves and Pipe Fittings; 3498 Fabricated Pipe and Fittings; 3569 General Industrial Machinery and Equipment; 3824 Totalizing Fluid Meters and Counting Devices

Grinnell Corp., a subsidiary of Tyco International Ltd., became the largest fire protection company in the world when it acquired Wormald International Ltd. in 1990. Prior to that date, Grinnell had achieved a reputation as the largest installer, manufacturer, and supplier of automatic sprinkler and fire protection and detection systems in North America since the 1880s. By the 1990s, Grinnell was also manufacturing a wide variety of valves, pipes, couplings, fittings, meters, and tubing for flow control (the movement of any type of gas or liquid). In all, Grinnell offered more than 5,000 fire protection products and devices.

The ancestor of the Grinnell Corp. was the Providence Steam and Gas Pipe Co., founded in Providence, Rhode Island, in 1850. Although its initial task was to install Providence's original gas mains, the company also acted as a plumbing supplier. Soon enough, the business was engaged largely in the manufacture and installation of fire-extinguishing apparatus for factories, especially textile mills. Providence Steam and Gas also provided heating service with exhaust steam from Corliss engines, supplied water, and constructed plants for making gas from resin, crude oil, and coal.

In 1869, Frederick Grinnell, a Massachusetts-born engineer, purchased a controlling interest in Providence Steam and Gas and became its president. At this time, fire-extinguishing apparatus in factories consisted mainly of perforated pipes connected to a water-supply system and installed along the ceilings. Providence Steam and Gas Pipe began installing such pipes in New England mills in 1873. However, these systems had to be turned on manually, by which time a fire might have blazed out of control. In 1874, Henry S. Parmelee of New Haven, Connecticut, patented an automatic sprinkling device, and four years later the Providence Steam and Gas Pipe Co. secured the right to manufacture and install it, paying royalties to the inventor. In 1881, Grinnell patented an improved, more sensitive sprinkling system, which featured a valve sprinkler with deflectors that was activated by the melting of solder.

During the next 10 years, Grinnell sprinklers were installed in more than 10,000 buildings and were credited with putting out more than 1,000 incipient fires. Over the next two decades, Grinnell perfected four types of metal-disc sprinklers; by 1890, Grinnell had invented the glass-disc sprinkler which became the industry standard for the next 50 years. He took out some 40 patents for improvements and also invented a dry-pipe valve and automatic fire-alarm system. Grinnell also expanded his business operations in 1892 when Providence Steam and Gas Pipe and two other sprinkler manufacturers were consolidated as the General Fire Extinguisher Co. To improve the quality of its iron castings, General Fire Extinguisher established its own foundry and shops in Cranston, Rhode Island, opening the operation in 1909. Later, the company also began meeting the casting needs of other manufacturers as well.

Grinnell died in 1905 and was succeeded by his former executive assistant, Frank H. Maynard. The Canadian General Fire Extinguisher Co., Ltd. (later Grinnell Co. of Canada, Ltd.), was incorporated in 1914. Five years later, Grinnell Co., Inc. was chartered to act as a sales agency for General Fire Extinguisher, and Grinnell Co. of the Pacific was formed to consolidate and expand West Coast operations. In 1921, General Fire Extinguisher purchased the American Moistening Co., which provided artificial humidification systems for textile manufacturers.

Grinnell's son Russell succeeded Maynard as president of General Fire Extinguisher in 1925. At this time, the company operated nine manufacturing plants in the U.S. and Canada, which produced sprinkler systems, industrial piping systems, heating equipment, drying machinery, humidifying equipment, cast-iron fittings, and brass goods. The company's assets between 1921 and 1926 fluctuated between $15 million and $17 million. Dividends, in 1923, had been paid for more than 20 years at the rate of 10 percent a year and sometimes more.

General Fire Extinguisher continued to expand its operations in the 1920s and 1930s, purchasing the Ontario Malleable Iron Co. in 1928 and the Columbia (Pennsylvania) Malleable Castings Corp. in 1931 to produce iron and aluminum fittings and hangers. Nevertheless, company assets fell to under $12 million in 1933. About 2,650 persons were employed by the company in 1935, down from 4,000 on the eve of the Depression. The value of the General Fire Extinguisher stock which had been sold over the counter throughout the company's independent history dropped from $45 a share in 1930 to $7 a share in 1934.

During World War II, the bulk of General Fire Extinguisher's production was aimed at the war effort. By 1944, when the company name was changed to the Grinnell Corp., there were 13 factories in the United States and four in Canada. The company's assets came to $20.5 million, and the number of employees stood at about 6,875. In 1949, Grinnell bought a controlling interest in the Automatic Fire Alarm Co., which monitored automatic fire-protection systems in New York, Boston, and Philadelphia. The following year, Grinnell acquired Holmes Electric Protective Co., a supplier of burglar-alarm services to banks in New York, Philadelphia, and Pittsburgh.

By 1953, Grinnell's net sales had reached nearly $150 million, while its net profit surpassed $6.6 million and its assets were almost $100 million. Its stock traded for almost triple the average value in 1949. In addition, the number of Grinnell Corp. employees had grown to 9,000. That same year, Grinnell acquired a controlling interest in American District Telegraph Co. (ADT), manufacturer of electrical supervisory and alarm systems for protection against fire, burglary, holdup, and other hazards. Grinnell's annual net sales reached $200 million in 1959, when its net profit was $8.6 million, its assets nearly $127 million, and the number of employees, 9,800. Further, Grinnell stock was trading at nearly triple the 1953 value.

In 1958, Grinnell and three other companies agreed to dissolve what the federal government charged was an illegal conspiracy to lock out the competition from prospective customers for the sale of special-hazard sprinkler systems. The companies also agreed not to fix prices or agree on bids for work. Six years later, Grinnell and the three subsidiary companies it had acquired from 1949 to 1953 were found guilty in Boston's federal district court of violating antitrust laws by monopolizing the central-station fire- and burglar-alarm protective business. Grinnell was ordered to file a plan to divest its controlling interest in Holmes, ADT, and the Automatic Fire Alarm Co. by April 1, 1966. Judge Charles E. Wyzanski, Jr., also ordered the four concerns to cease to employ James Douglas Fleming, Grinnell's president since 1948, after April 1, 1966.

At this time, Grinnell and its acquired subsidiaries held more than 87 percent of the central-station fire and burglar alarm business in the United States, according to the U.S. Justice Department. However, this field of business accounted for only about 20 percent of Grinnell's annual sales volume and profits, with plumbing supplies and fixtures being responsible for most of the rest. "We are major manufacturers of the valves and fittings that go into sprinkling systems, but that is not our biggest business," Fleming told a *Forbes* interviewer in 1965. "We also make industrial piping systems and humidifying systems. We are strictly an industrial supplier."

Wyzanski's verdict was upheld in 1966 by the Supreme Court, and the following year the judge ordered Grinnell to rid itself of the stock it held in its three subsidiary companies. This divestiture was completed in 1968, with Grinnell distributing to stockholders all of its shares in the companies. Meanwhile, some 35 damage suits were filed against Grinnell alleging that the company had engaged in monopolistic practices. The plaintiffs were mostly comprised of customers who claimed that they had been overcharged by Grinnell and competitors who claimed they had been unfairly deprived of business. Despite $45 million cost of settling these suits, Grinnell emerged from these legal battles as financially sound as ever. In fact, per-share earnings climbed from $7.82 in 1966 to $10.06 in 1967. Further, the three divested subsidiaries, rather than Grinnell, were ordered to pay two-thirds of damages assessed in lawsuits.

By 1969, Grinnell operated 12 manufacturing plants in the United States and Canada and 42 warehouses in the United States, Canada, Mexico, and Germany. The Supply & Sales Division contributed nearly two-thirds of the company's sales volume. Of this total, fabricated pipe fittings, valves, and hangers accounted for half of the sales, with the rest chiefly coming from custom bending and shaping pipe made by other manufacturers to customer specifications. Fire protection constituted another 22 percent of sales. The Industrial Piping Division, producers of piping systems for utility power plants and pipe process networks for chemical companies, accounted for about 10 percent of sales. The remaining 2.5 percent came from industrial humidification. Grinnell also owned 45 percent of Hajoca Corp., a wholesaler of plumbing supplies. Net sales came to a record $341.3 million in 1968, and the company held $50 million in cash and equivalents.

Grinnell's bottom line was so attractive that in December 1968 the giant conglomerate International Telephone & Telegraph (ITT) offered to acquire Grinnell for an exchange of stock valued at almost $250 million. Grinnell shareholders backed the merger in August 1969, despite the Justice Department's decision to oppose it on antitrust grounds. In 1971, a consent judgment required ITT to divest itself of Grinnell's fire-protection division and Grinnell's share in Hajoca by September 24, 1973.

When ITT was unable to receive what it considered an acceptable bid for the fire-protection unit, which had annual sales of about $75 million by that date, the concern was turned over to a court-appointed trustee. Operating as Grinnell Fire Protection Systems Co., the unit, whose annual turnover had risen to $107 million, was purchased by Tyco Laboratories in 1976. As part of the deal with ITT, Tyco agreed to pay ITT $14 million and 40 percent of Grinnell's net earnings for the next ten years, with a minimum total payment of $28.5 million guaranteed; in return, Tyco gained two manufacturing plants, plus other facilities, tools, equipment, patent rights, and trademarks.

With this acquisition, Grinnell Fire Protection became Tyco's leading manufacturing unit and accounted for the bulk of its business. Tyco's sales for fire protection and safety grew from nearly $103 million in 1977 to $179.1 million in 1980, and its income from these operations increased from nearly $7 million to $18.9 million. Between 1981 and 1985, Tyco's sales of fire-protection equipment rose from $193.6 million to $211.3 million, but its income from fire-protection equipment fell from $17.8 million to $11.4 million. In 1981, Grinnell Fire Protection patented the Fast Response sprinkler head, which operates up to ten times faster than standard response sprinklers.

The rest of the former Grinnell was known as the ITT Grinnell Corp. In 1977, its valve division was formed into a new subsidiary called ITT Grinnell Valve Co. Inc. The following year, the valve company's headquarters was moved from Elmira, New York, to ITT Grinnell corporate headquarters in Providence. In 1986, Tyco bought 48 U.S. and Canadian production and distribution operations of ITT Grinnell for about $220 million. ITT

Grinnell had sales of about $460 million in 1984 for its valves and related products.

Under Tyco's management, Grinnell expanded measurably in the 1980s and 1990s. In 1986, the subsidiary bought Hersey Products, Inc., a manufacturer of meters and backflow preventers, for $12.4 million in cash. The following year, it acquired Allied Tube and Conduit Corp., a manufacturer of piping products, fence posts and rails, and electrical conduits. In 1988, Grinnell also purchased Mueller Co., a manufacturer of brass and flow-control products, water meters, backflow preventers, specialty valves, and high-quality products for the gas industry. During fiscal 1990, the company acquired three fire-protection and flow-control companies for $27.6 million. One of these concerns was National Pipe & Tube Co., a specialist in oil field casing and tubing. The other acquisitions were N & O Distribution in the Netherlands and Chubb Firekill, an English fire-protection contractor.

In the early 1990s, Grinnell continued to expanded its international operations, acquiring Wormald International Ltd.—the largest fire-protection company in Europe, Asia, and Australia—for $358.7 million in cash, 5 million shares of Tyco common stock, and five-year warrants to purchase 5 million additional shares of Tyco common stock at $70 per share. This purchase included Ansul, a Wisconsin-based company making a vast array of products, including fire extinguishers, fire protection systems, mining vehicles, offshore oil rigs, and spill-control products for neutralizing and solidifying hazardous waste accidents.

During this period, Grinnell benefitted significantly from local and state legislation which required the installation of fire-protection systems throughout the public service sector. In addition, the retrofitting, servicing, and maintenance of fire-protection systems in existing buildings accounted for about 60 percent of Grinnell's North American contracting sales in fiscal 1992, 1993, and 1994. At this time, Grinnell's North American distribution network was also selling fire-protection sprinklers, gray-iron pipe fittings, malleable iron fittings, and other flow-control products, as well as Allied steel pipe. With regard to flow control, Grinnell was an industry leader in Europe, Asia, and the Pacific, as well as in the Americas.

During early 1994, Grinnell became embroiled in a labor dispute when the company attempted to negotiate a contract seeking the reduction of wages and fringe benefits for its unionized fire-protection employees and the elimination of unproductive working conditions. When negotiations with the United Association Sprinklerfitters "Road Local" 669 ended in an impasse, Grinnell replaced the striking workers and joined the American Fire Sprinkler Association, a group oriented toward the open shop approach to manufacturing.

In that same year, Grinnell continued its program of acquiring competitors in the pipe-fitting and fire prevention industries. The company purchased Preferred Pipe Products, Inc.—a St. Louis-based manufacturer of specialty pipefitting products for the oil field and petrochemical industries—for $17.6 million. In addition, Grinnell bought the malleable ironfitting assets of the Stanley Flagg division of the American Cast Iron Pipe Co. (Amcast). Grinnell's tremendous success with acquisitions led to remarkably high profits for their parent company. Of Tyco's 1994 sales of $3.26 billion, $2.44 billion, or nearly 75 percent, came from fire protection or flow control managed largely by Grinnell. Moreover, of Tyco's operating income of $263.9 million, $139.2 million, or nearly 53 percent, came from the same unit.

Going into the mid-1990s, Grinnell Corp. was actually a family of companies that included Grinnell Manufacturing, Grinnell Fire Protection, Grinnell Supply Sales, Ansul, Wormald, Mueller, Hersey, Allied, and Total Walther. Through its long history of sound management decisions and strategic acquisitions, the Grinnell Corp. had established the solid financial footing necessary to sustain the company well into the 21st century.

Principal Subsidiaries: Grinnell Building Products Pty. Ltd. (Australia); G.F.P.S. Pty. Ltd. (Australia); Grinnell Asia Pacific Pty. Ltd. (Australia); Tyco Grinnell Asia Pacific Pty. Ltd. (Australia); Grinnell Hoffmann Sprinkler GMBH (Germany); Mexico Grinnell Sistemas de Protecion Contra Incendio Mexico S.A. de C.V. (Mexico); Grinnell Sales and Distribution B.V. (Netherlands); Grinnell Supply Sales Asia Pte. Ltd. (Singapore); Tyco Grinnell Asia Pacific (Thailand) Ltd. (Thailand); Grinnell (UK) Ltd. (U.K.).

Further Reading:

"Get Rid of That Man," *Forbes,* June 1, 1965, p. 39.
Green, Leslie, and Richard Elliott, Jr., "Cause for Alarm," *Barron's,* May 30, 1966, pp. 3, 13, 16, 18, 20–21.
——, "Security at a Discount?" *Barron's,* June 6, 1966, pp. 9–10, 12–13.
Grinnell: 1850 to 1950, Providence, R.I.: Grinnell Corp., n.d.
Hoddeson, David, "After the Break-Up," *Barron's,* May 27, 1968, pp. 5, 26–27.
"ITT Plans to Buy Grinnell Corp. in Stock Swap," *Wall Street Journal,* December 2, 1968, p. 36.
Kohlmeier, Louis, "ITT Agrees on Record Divestiture in Move to End Antitrust Disputes," *Wall Street Journal,* August 2, 1971, p. 2.
Mader, Robert P., "Grinnell Moves Toward Open Shop," *Contractor,* September 1994, pp. 1, 53.
Mendell, Clarence W., "Frederick Grinnell," *Dictionary of American Biography,* Vol. 8, New York: Scribner's, 1943.
"Tyco Labs Is Named Successful Bidder for ITT's Grinnell," *Wall Street Journal,* September 23, 1975, p. 16.
"Tyco to Reunite Group with Grinnell for $195 Million," *American Metal Market,* November 18, 1985, pp. 5, 15.

—Robert Halasz

Grossman's Inc.

200 Union Street
Braintree, Massachusetts 02184-5761
U.S.A.
(617) 848-0100
Fax: (617) 848-8173

Public Company
Incorporated: 1919
Employees: 5,000
Sales: $833 million
Stock Exchanges: New York
SICs: 5211 Lumber & Other Building Materials

Grossman's Inc. is a leading retailer of building materials in the northeastern United States. In the early 1990s the company operated four chains of stores that provided a wide variety of home improvement supplies to customers throughout New England and surrounding states, as well as selected locations in the Midwest and West. Founded in Massachusetts before the turn of the century, Grossman's remained a family-owned firm through the 1960s. It then joined a larger conglomerate, which was subsequently taken over and driven into bankruptcy in the 1980s. Grossman's emerged from the bankruptcy with a semblance of its original business, a chain of lumber and construction supply stores, intact.

Grossman's was founded by Louis Grossman, who emigrated to the United States from Podeski, Russia, paying $17 to travel in steerage to Ellis Island. From New York, Grossman made his way to the Boston metropolitan area, where he first made a living as a peddler, subsisting on $1.50 per week for room and board. After saving enough to purchase a horse and wagon, Grossman became a traveling junk dealer, collecting and selling items on a route that ran between the Boston satellites of Quincy, to the south, and Walpole, to the north. He eventually added the imperfect products of a roofing firm to his line of items.

In 1900 Grossman brought his two oldest sons, Reuben and Jacob, aged 14 and 12, respectively, into his business. In recognition of their involvement, he renamed his business L. Grossman and Sons. He expanded his business, branching out into used furniture. In 1907 the Grossmans bought their first piece of property, acquiring an old monument manufacturing plant in Quincy. The sale of the materials left in the plant at auction netted the Grossmans their first significant profit.

Throughout the end of that decade, and into the first half of the next, the Grossmans gradually expanded their trade in building materials, which had begun with roofing seconds and been boosted by their purchase of the monument site. In 1915, as a result of this expansion, the company purchased a new supply yard. The Grossmans distributed building supplies from this site, although they continued with their junk business as well. Five years later the company bought another parcel of land in Quincy.

In 1922 the Grossmans entered a new business. In the wake of World War I, which had come to a close in 1918, the U.S. government had amassed a large stockpile of equipment that they sought to sell. The Grossmans first entered the war surplus market with a purchase of goods from the Hingham Naval Ammunition Depot. Later, the company purchased army camps, naval installations, and war plants. The Grossmans dismantled buildings and sold off everything salvageable.

In 1923 Sidney Grossman, the youngest of Louis Grossman's sons, joined the family firm. With his arrival, all four of the founder's sons had become involved in the business. By this time the company's first site was used only for storage. Its dwindling junk business was still in operation, but the Grossmans devoted the bulk of their attention to their large and thriving lumber and building materials operation.

Another major war surplus purchase of the 1920s was the Coddington Point section of the Newport Naval Training Station, in Rhode Island. This site became known as the "Deserted City," as the Grossmans sold off 75 different buildings and their contents.

In the midst of disassembling the Deserted City, the Grossmans changed their policy in salvaging such properties. The company decided to preserve and maintain buildings in future projects, rather than break them up for salvage. This was the practice the company followed in taking over the Simon Lake Torpedo Station in Bridgeport, Connecticut.

In 1927 L. Grossman and Son's purchased the wreck of a large five-masted schooner, the *Nancy,* that had run up on the beach at Nantasket. The company dismantled the boat on the spot and sold the ship's five great masts to a granite producer in the area. Louis Grossman retired the following year, and the company he had founded changed its name to L. Grossman Sons, Incorporated. His four sons took full control of the company, assuming various titles in accordance with their age; Reuben became president, Jacob served as vice-president, Joseph assumed the position of treasurer, and Sidney served as the secretary.

The following year Grossman's opened its first branch lumber yard in Billerica, Massachusetts. This expansion testified to the success of the company's retail concept, which extended the traditional lumber yard to include almost anything needed for home construction or repair. In this way, Grossman's set up a "one stop" store where contractors, carpenters, or home owners could buy "everything to build with, under one roof," as the company advertised. In addition, Grossman's offered generous credit arrangements for many of its customers, a policy that further promoted the company's growth.

With the collapse of the stock market in 1929 and the onset of the Great Depression, many of New England's industries were badly shaken. As companies failed, Grossman's took over their old buildings, maintaining them until new industrial tenants could be found. The company handled textile mills, foundries, chemical plants, shoe factories, furniture factories, and other derelict sites.

Grossman's continued to sell building materials and salvage abandoned properties throughout the 1930s. In 1938 an enormous hurricane struck New England, felling vast numbers of trees. The federal government purchased the timber in an effort to bail out devastated landowners, then contracted with Grossman's to turn the fallen trees into usable lumber. The company created the Eastern Pine Sales Corporation to handle this task. The new firm sold 800 million feet of lumber—enough to circle the earth six times—before the supply of storm-downed trees was exhausted.

In the following decade, Grossman's repeated its war surplus endeavors in the wake of World War II, only on a much larger scale. The company formed the Grossman Surplus Company in 1946 and purchased a one-hundred acre site in Braintree, Massachusetts, to store unused war supplies. The company took possession of the contents of dismantled army camps, naval bases, and shipyards. The vast array of goods stored at the site in Braintree soon attracted tourists as well as potential buyers.

Grossman's also profited from the explosion in demand for housing in the wake of the war. The company purchased surplus Quonset huts and army barracks and encouraged young couples to turn the structures into temporary homes. Grossman's sold them for no down payment and a monthly fee that was less than the usual rent on a space of the same size.

When a wider variety of building materials became available, Grossman's developed the "Build-It-Yourself" home. The company sold blueprints, instructions, and materials for building a house to customers who owned land. This program eventually grew into an entire Grossman Homes Division.

Grossman's expanded its core areas of business throughout the 1950s. In 1950 the company bought the 240 buildings of Passamaquoddy, an abandoned Seabee camp, which it attempted to restore to usefulness. In 1954 the company took over the abandoned mill property of the Goodall-Sanford textile mills in Sanford, Maine, and found new tenants for the space within a year, thus ensuring the town's economic stability. The following year, the company took over the facilities of the Bigelow-Sanford Carpet Company in Amsterdam, New York. Six years passed before Grossman's was able to lease all the space in the company's 40 buildings.

In 1958 Grossman's embarked on a new campaign to expand the market for home improvement supplies, coining the slogan, "Do It Yourself—Or We'll Do It For You." The company hoped to entice those novice homeowners who were uncomfortable with tools and projects to turn to Grossman's for assistance. For customers with greater proficiency, Grossman's marketed the "We Start It—You Finish It," concept, in which free plans, advice, and competent workmen helped homeowners upgrade their property. Throughout the post-war era, the company's enormous full-service lumberyard and hardware store operations consolidated their share of the building materials market. They drove many smaller hardware store operations across New England out of business.

In addition, Grossman's began to manufacture prefabricated component homes in a plant in Braintree, Massachusetts. The company also made office buildings, vacation cottages, garden houses, and garages. The various pieces of these structures were shipped up and down the east coast on flatbed trucks that bore the legend, "Here Comes Grossman's," the company's longtime logo.

In the 1960s Grossman's continued with its efforts to broaden the available market for its products. In 1962 the company inaugurated a pilot "cash and carry" home improvement store in Wallingford, Connecticut. Instead of a full-service lumberyard, this outlet offered low prices to customers who were able to serve themselves. The store carried only lumber, lumber products, building materials, and high volume plumbing, heating, and electrical supplies. Buyers brought their own cars and trucks to the railroad sidings where supplies were delivered, and loaded up the products they wanted themselves.

When the first test store proved successful, the company expanded the cash and carry concept throughout New England, opening stores in Springfield and Wellesley, Massachusetts; Woonsockey, Rhode Island; and other locations. By this time, a third generation of Grossmans had entered the family business. Six of Louis Grossman's grandsons—Nissie, Maurice ("Mike"), Bernard, Everett, John, and Morton—joined the company. The enterprise they ran operated throughout six northeastern states.

Grossman's remained a regional, family-owned business throughout the 1960s. By the end of the decade, the company operated 81 building materials stores in New England, New York, and Pennsylvania. In 1969, however, Grossman's was purchased by the Evans Products Company of Portland, Oregon, for $801,000 in cash and 572,000 shares of stock. Evans was a forest products company that had diversified into related fields of home building, household items, transportation, and retail building products (the division in which Grossman's operations were placed). Despite the new ownership, Grossman's management, made up primarily of Grossman family members, remained in place.

Grossman's experienced continued financial growth in the 1970s, despite the parent company's remote ownership. By 1980 the company's corporate parent had attracted the attention of corporate raider Victor Posner, who began to purchase stock in Evans through Sharon Steel, a company that he controlled. In March 1980 Sharon Steel purchased a 5.3 percent interest in Evans; by the beginning of 1982 he controlled 42 percent of the company's stock. In February 1982 Sharon and Evans tentatively agreed to merge. By this time, Maurice Grossman had become president of Evans' retail division, its biggest and most profitable unit.

Evans posted losses of $12 million in the first six months of 1982, and the company decided to sell its most profitable unit, the 340-store retail building products division, in order to raise funds. Grossman's, a unit of the retail building products division, tracked the efforts closely. By the end of the year the company was still seeking a buyer for these operations. In the meantime, its losses continued to mount. ''We haven't had a buyer offer what we consider a fair price,'' an Evans spokesman told the *Wall Street Journal.*

In April 1983 the banks to which Evans owed money refused to allow the company to merge with Posner's Sharon Steel. Unable to sell Evans' retail products division, Posner, who took the title of chairman of Evans in June 1983, decided to raise money to reduce debt by spinning off the division as a public company. Following this announcement, Posner moved to solidify his control of Evans, installing family members and other close associates in key positions.

In January 1984 Posner himself took over as chief executive officer. He announced that the company's headquarters would be moved to a heavily guarded residential hotel where Posner lived in Miami in April 1984. Upon hearing this news, a number of Evans' upper level executives resigned their positions. In April 1984 four more directors of Evans, including Maurice Grossman, quit their jobs. These moves followed grim financial performances the previous two years. The company posted 1982 losses of $64.8 million and a 1983 deficit of $63.9 million. The plan to spin off the retail products division had fallen by the wayside as the company struggled for survival.

By March 11, 1985, that effort had largely failed. Evans filed for bankruptcy, but the company's creditors charged that Posner had stripped the company of cash. This move came after Posner rejected two offers for the retail buildings products division, one from outside his company and one from within, despite the fact that Evans was unable to win investment capital from banks to finance the profitable unit's further growth. After major vendors cut off shipments to the retail group because of uncertainty about Evans' financial condition, the company as a whole was forced into insolvency.

Throughout 1986 Evans struggled to emerge from bankruptcy. In July the company's creditors rejected a plan that would have enabled Posner to maintain some stake in the company. Finally, in November, a re-structured Evans emerged from bankruptcy. The company's lenders had dissolved the company and made Grossman's the umbrella company for all of Evans' retail properties. Maurice Grossman returned to take control of the company. Evans' bank lenders and vendor creditors were paid, in part, with Grossman's stock. The company was saddled with a heavy debt load, although this debt was partially offset by tax loss carry-forwards that promised to exempt it from taxes for years to come. With 7,800 employees, the new Grossman's included 273 retail outlets, including separate chains of building products stores in the Northeast, the mid-Atlantic region, the South, and northwestern California. The company also owned warehouse stores in the Pacific Southwest.

Grossman's first priority after its re-establishment as an independent company was to upgrade its stores, which had been allowed to languish while Evans was in its financial death throes. In 1987 Grossman's benefitted from a robust economy in the mid-Atlantic and Northeast regions, its primary stronghold. In July 1987 the company offered stock to the public. By 1988 the company had established a prototype store in Hanover, Massachusetts, for its $75 million remodeling plan, which included a much wider array of merchandise and features designed to attract female shoppers.

Despite success in remodeling stores and reducing its debt, Grossman's stock price remained low. In February 1989 the company announced that it might sell off all or part of its operations. Seven months later, Grossman's completed one part of this effort when it sold its 59 Moore's Division stores, located in the mid-Atlantic and South, to Harcros Lumber and Building Supplies, Inc. Stores in the Northwest and in the East were also sold or closed, and the proceeds from these transactions lessened the company's debt load. When the divestment was completed, the company had reduced its number of stores by more than 100, to 156. Most of the company's remaining outlets were located in the Northeast.

By 1990 Grossman's effort to refinance had attracted the interest of a Hawaii real estate investor. The investor acquired 4.7 percent of the company's shares and made an offer to acquire the rest. When this offer was rejected in April 1990, the stockholder launched an attempt to take over the company by replacing Grossman's corporate board. The Hawaiian investors charged that Grossman's had not taken sufficient steps to meet the challenge of nationwide hardware giant Home Depot, which was moving into the Northeast. They noted that Grossman's returns had faltered as the overall economy in the Northeast went into a tailspin. The effort to unseat Grossman's management failed, though, and the company undertook a study to determine how best to remain competitive.

In the first half of the 1990s, Grossman's moved to implement the new plan that resulted from that analysis. The company repositioned its eastern stores and expanded operations once again in the West. In 1993 the company announced that it would expand its Contractor's Warehouse concept to the Midwest. By the mid-1990s, Grossman's had further reduced its eastern operations and launched an international venture with a joint partner in Mexico as part of its effort to thrive in the coming years.

Further Reading:

Bellew, Patricia A., ''Four Directors Resign From Evans Products Under Posner's Sway,'' *Wall Street Journal,* April 19, 1984.

Bianco, Anthony, ''Victor Posner Isn't Sitting Pretty Now,'' *Business Week,* March 25, 1985.

Chase, Marilyn, ''Evans Products Says 3 Executives Quit, Citing Victor Posner's Role as Chairman,'' *Wall Street Journal,* February 13, 1984.

''Evans Products' 'Empty Nest,' '' *Business Week,* January 18, 1982.

Laderman, Jeffrey M., ''Grossman's New Look May Be More Than Just A Facade,'' *Business Week,* June 15, 1987.

Tanouye, Elyse T., ''What Are They Fighting Over?'' *Barron's,* October 8, 1990.

''Victor Posner's Problem Child: Evans Products,'' *Business Week,* December 5, 1983.

''When It Makes Sense to Sell a Winner,'' *Business Week,* September 27, 1982.

—Elizabeth Rourke

H.E. Butt Grocery Co.

646 South Main
San Antonio, Texas 78204
U.S.A.
(210) 246-8000
Fax: (210) 246-8067

Private Company
Incorporated: 1905 as C.C. Butt Grocery Store
Employees: 38,000
Sales: $3.2 billion
SICs: 5411 Grocery Stores

H.E. Butt Grocery Co. (HEB) is a leading Texas grocery store chain. HEB operated more than 200 grocery stores in more than 100 Texas cities in the early 1990s, and was expanding into Houston and other markets going into the mid-1990s. In addition, HEB was innovating new types of stores that were creating entirely new markets for the 90-year-old enterprise. HEB's story is one of hard work and perseverance.

HEB started out as a single store in Kerrville, a small town in the Texas Hill Country. Charles C. and Florence Butt moved to Kerrville from Memphis, Tennessee. Charles was suffering from tuberculosis, and they hoped that the drier climate would improve his condition. Once the family was settled in Kerrville, Florence was faced with supporting the family herself. She decided to open a grocery store. The family purchased a two-story house, planning to live upstairs and operate the store downstairs. With investment capital of $60, the family opened the C.C. Butt Grocery Store on November 26, 1905. They began selling food in bulk as a charge and delivery operation. Florence's young sons delivered the food via baby carriage until they could afford to buy a little red wagon.

By 1908 the Butt store had established itself within the local community as "dealers in staples, fancy groceries and fresh meats." The boys had even been able to buy a horse and wagon to make deliveries. Also, Florence was building a profitable fresh-baked bread business as a sideline. She arranged for bread to be delivered by train from San Antonio and then immediately delivered to residences by her sons. The market for fresh bread was relatively new at the time because many women were hesitant to buy bread for fear of being considered too lazy to bake their own. Nevertheless, bread deliveries increased, initiating what would become a legacy of innovation at Butt Grocery.

All three of the Butt brothers—Charles, Eugene, and Howard E.—worked in the family business while they were growing up. But it was Howard who took an early liking to the business, and was even described in company annals as a "grocery man" from the beginning. At the age of 22, in 1917, Howard was still working in the grocery store. Shortly after the United States entered World War I, however, Howard joined the Navy. After a two-year tour he returned to Kerrville to take over the store. He had a lot of ideas and was eager to implement them. His first move was to relocate the store to a busier corner in the burgeoning downtown Kerrville. In the new location, Butt installed the first in-store meat market and delicatessen. He also began a policy of constantly offering new and different items to patrons.

Importantly, Butt also tried a risky new experiment. Traditionally, customers had delivered or phoned in their orders, and the grocer had gathered and delivered the groceries along with a bill due at the end of the month. By the early 1920s, though, a growing number of people had their own cars and were able to more easily transport their own groceries. Butt believed that those customers, and maybe many others, would be willing to wait on themselves, pay cash, and transport their own groceries if they could save money. The savings would come from reduced labor and equipment costs at the store, and from the elimination of unpaid grocery bills. In December 1921 Butt sent out handwritten penny postcards to his customers, explaining the change. On New Years day the store opened under the name of C.C. Butt Cash and Carry.

The cash-and-carry experiment was an instant hit. In fact, Butt decided in 1924 that it was time to expand. He opened a new store about 60 miles from Kerrville in a town called Junction. Although other stores were already established there, Butt's innovative cash-and-carry system and superior inventory allowed his store to thrive. Meanwhile, Butt continued to tweak his formula by experimenting with new services and products. Most importantly, he began to question why a housewife shouldn't be able to get common household items other than food and staples from a grocery store. Throughout the 1920s he slowly began adding to his inventory: everything from pots and pans to tools and textiles.

In 1926 Butt discovered a new avenue to growth. Piggly-Wiggly, a grocery store chain that had become well-known in the region by utilizing many of the same tactics that Butt was using, began selling franchises. Butt purchased some of the franchise rights, reasoning that he could successfully combine his views about customer service, as well as his experience with cash-and-carry, with the recognized Piggly-Wiggly name. Butt opened his first Piggly-Wiggly in Del Rio in 1926. The success of that venture lead him to open two more stores in 1927 in Brady and Gonzales, purchase three additional Piggly-Wiggly's in 1928, and to build two more new outlets in San Benito and Harlingen. After roaring through the 1920s, Howard moved the company's headquarters to Harlingen to get closer to his Piggly-Wiggly stores. He also changed the name of the company to H.E. Butt Grocery Co. By that time, Butt's first Piggly-Wiggly store in Del Rio was serving 5,000 customers each day.

The stock market crashed in 1929, spawning the Great Depression. Fortunately, Butt was relatively well positioned for the downturn in comparison to many other businesses at the time.

His stores were geared for value, and grocery items were among the last goods that people stopped buying during the Depression. In fact, rather than slowing down, Butt continued to grow during the late 1920s and early 1930s, opening stores throughout the Rio Grande Valley and remodeling existing stores. By 1931 Butt Grocery was operating a total of 24 stores, and plans were being made for new outlets.

Butt suffered a major setback in 1933, when a hurricane swept from the coast into the Rio Grande Valley and damaged many of Butt's stores and warehouses. Interestingly, Butt's Piggly-Wiggly in Harlingen was the only grocery store in its area to open immediately after the hurricane. Despite the bad luck, Butt quickly restored his businesses and even managed to pursue a charitable venture. In 1934, when he was still in his 30s, Howard filed the H.E. Butt Foundation charter, a charitable organization created to aid the community. That effort was the first of many charitable acts that would earn Butt a reputation as a dedicated philanthropist.

H.E. Butt began to integrate vertically when it opened its own bakery and purchased a canning company in 1936. By that year, Butt was generating about $2 million worth of business annually from 31 stores. A new outlet built in Kerrville sported a parking lot with 100 spaces—quite a step up from the horse hitching post stationed in front of the original Kerrville store. In 1938, moreover, Butt expanded into the 75,000-person Austin market, the largest metropolitan area that it had entered. The company was also doing business in San Antonio by 1942 and was increasing its presence in its established markets.

Butt's contributed to the World War II effort during the 1940s by supplying canned vegetables and fruits from its canning facility to troops overseas. In addition, many company employees served in the armed forces. At the same time, the company continued to progress. It opened the first air-conditioned grocery store and also began offering frozen foods, which were considered a novelty at the time. Shortages of many food items continued after the war, but by the late 1940s Butt's business was back to normal. Encouraged by the success of the air-conditioned store, Howard opened one of the first truly large grocery stores in Texas in 1949. The Corpus Christi store had 22,500 square feet of space and was the first to have a separate drug department, cosmetic area, and lunch counter.

The large grocery store was a hit, and Butt's focused on the concept from that point forward. In 1950 the company opened a large store in Waco—the company's 53rd outlet—that featured an unheard of 12 checkout stands, two parking lots, and a self-service meat counter. Within two years several similar stores had been built and H.E. Butt's chain had swelled to 58. The company continued to push for more growth. To increase sales at existing stores, it began operating the Texas Gold Stamp Company as a subsidiary in 1955; the promotion gave customers stamps for each purchase, which they could then exchange for household items. Howard continued to add new stores during the late 1950s and early 1960s. One store even featured spectacular ''magic carpets'' (automatic doors), parking for 300 cars, and 12 separate departments.

By the end of the 1960s, HEB, as it had become known, was ready for a change. The dynamic and innovative Howard Butt officially passed the torch to his sons, Howard E. Jr. and the younger Charles. Charles Butt, a Wharton graduate, assumed the helm. He restructured the company's management and recruited several experienced grocery executives to help him make HEB a force in the 1970s and 1980s. To that end, HEB opened its own ice cream plant, a new bread bakery, a large pastry bakery, and new offices and warehouses during the early and mid-1970s. Butt also began designing the company's first ''Futuremarket,'' which would incorporate a gourmet deli, flower market, and in-store bakery among other features. Meanwhile, Howard E. Butt, Sr., fulfilled a long-time dream when, in 1974, he opened the H.E. Butt Camp, an 1,800-acre camp in the Texas Hill Country where nonprofit and Christian groups could retreat.

HEB opened its first superstore, or Futuremarket, in 1981. The then-massive store had 56,000 square feet and was considered a one-stop shopping center. Also in the early 1980s, HEB began selling generic goods and added a photo-processing plant to support in-store photo departments. Going into the mid-1980s, HEB was operating nearly 150 stores throughout central and south Texas and serving more than one million families. And it continued to expand its store offerings with an array of new departments ranging from seafood shops and salad bars to nutrition centers and fast-food, take-home departments. Furthermore, Charles Butt was branching into new markets outside of the grocery store industry. Most notably, HEB opened its first H-E-B Video Central/HEB Video Superstore outlet in 1987 to capitalize on the booming home video industry; within a few years, HEB would tag more than 20 additional video stores onto that division.

A secondary benefit of HEB's foray into the video store business was that it gave the company an in-road into the massive Houston and surrounding East Texas markets, which it still had not entered by the late 1980s. Indeed, in 1988 HEB entered the East Texas market with a new store concept called HEB Pantry Foods. These stores were smaller than the superstores and featured only four departments: grocery, meat, produce, and health and beauty. They also focused on value, attempting to minimize operating costs by eliminating nonessential, low-profit departments. HEB quickly added to the chain and by 1991 was working to build 22 more Pantrys in Houston within a year. Also in 1991, H. E. Butt Sr. died. Among his legacies was the successful Howard E. Butt Foundation that he had established in 1934. By the time he died, the foundation had built libraries, swimming pools, charitable food centers, and other amenities in the communities in which Butt stores operated. It had also reached out to the needy in other parts of Texas and even Mexico, among other initiatives.

At the same time that HEB was expanding with smaller stores, it was also engaged in the development of a new venture that would lead to the chain's biggest-ever store. In the late 1980s, the innovative Charles Butt dispatched a team to study the great food merchandisers of the world in London, New York, Atlanta, and other places. He used the ideas they brought back to create the unique Central Market, a superstore that threw out the concept of one-stop shopping and emphasized perishable goods. The company opened the first Central Market in Austin in 1993. The store boasted 60,800 square feet and a large, tree-shaded parking lot. In contrast to conventional superstores, the

Central Market offered a plethora of fresh foods and flowers, including many exotic goods, while it shunned common items like detergent, packaged baked goods, and ordinary sodas, and cereals. Although the store still emphasized value, it was geared more toward upscale buyers with a greater amount of disposable income.

Initial success at the H-E-B Central Market was accompanied going into the mid-1990s by ongoing gains at HEB's Central superstore, as well as HEB Pantry Foods, H-E-B Video Central, and other divisions. The still privately-held company was opening additional Central markets and was working to secure its position as a major force in the grocery industry throughout Texas by the turn of the century. At the same time, Charles Butt sustained the grocer's legacy of charitable giving, as evidenced by an ambitious program to install 1,000 satellite systems in Texas schools by the year 2,000; by 1994, HEB had already installed 450 of the systems.

Principal Subsidiaries: Central Market; H-E-B Pantry Foods; H-E-B Video Central; H-E-B Rx Express

Further Reading:

Douglas, Michael, ''H-E-B Bites Into Houston Market With Discount Grocery Stores,'' *Houston Business Journal,* November 4, 1991, p. 12.

Dunlap, Lisa, ''HEB Cracks Houston Market With Videos Instead of Groceries,'' *San Antonio Business Journal,* January 9, 1989, p. 3.

The History of H.E. Butt Grocery Company, San Antonio: H.E. Butt Grocery Company, 1994.

Sharpe, Patricia, ''Central Marketing: H.E.B.'s Research Said Austinites Would Rush to a Huge Gourmet Grocery. It was Right,'' *Texas Monthly,* May 1994, p. 98.

Sultenfuss, Diana, ''H-E-B Processes 130,000 Gallons of AMPI Milk Daily,'' *San Antonio Light,* March 28, 1992, Bus. Sec.

—Dave Mote

Heekin Can Inc.

11310 Cornell Park Drive
Cincinnati, Ohio 45242
U.S.A.
(513) 388-2200

Wholly Owned Division of Ball Corporation
Founded: 1901
Employees: 1,500
Sales: $375 million (est. 1994)
SICs: 3411 Metal Cans

In the early 1990s, Heekin Can Inc. ranked as one of America's largest regional metal can producers. The company had started out as a sideline to James Heekin's nineteenth-century coffee and spice business, but soon evolved into the most important of the family's enterprises. In 1965, after three generations under family ownership and management, Heekin Can was sold to Diamond International Corp., a public packaging conglomerate. When Diamond was acquired in a 1982 hostile takeover, Heekin was spun off in a heavily-leveraged buyout orchestrated by its management and a group of outside investors. Heekin went public for the first time in 1985, and subsequently became a darling of Wall Street. In 1992 the can company agreed to be acquired by Ball Corp., a Fortune 500 manufacturer of glass and metal containers for the food and beverage industries. At that time, Heekin boasted 11 plants in Arkansas, Illinois, Indiana, Ohio, Pennsylvania, Tennessee, West Virginia, and Wisconsin. After the acquisition, Heekin was merged into Ball's Metal Food Container and Specialty Products Group, and the Heekin name was dropped. The $89.1 million exchange of stock consummated in 1993 helped establish Ball as North America's third-largest manufacturer of food containers.

Company founder James Heekin was born December 8, 1843, the eldest son of Irish immigrants who had emigrated to the United States during the mid-nineteenth century potato famine. During the 1850s, the family moved to Cincinnati, where James' father peddled Irish linens along the Ohio River. When the patriarch died on one of these long business trips, 14-year-old James was left to support his family. Although he was "discouraged and disheartened at the prospect" (as he wrote in his diary on his 15th birthday), the youngster did all he could to earn money to support his widowed mother and seven siblings. James first worked in a bakery, then trained as a barrel cooper, and eventually sold clothes and linens in the same manner as his father.

During the Civil War it was a common practice for wealthier draftees to hire unenlisted men as "stand-ins." In 1863 James Heekin accepted $300 in exchange for enlisting in the Union Army in another man's place. It was the only "job" he could find at the time. At war's end in 1865, Heekin took a job as a salesman with a local coffee, tea, and spice dealer.

After gaining five years' experience in the field, Heekin established a partnership with Barney Corbett to acquire a failed coffee brokerage owned by Charles Lewis. The transaction would have been characterized as a leveraged buyout in the 1990s—Heekin and Corbett borrowed the entire purchase price. Heekin later bought out his partner's interest and paid off all the company's liabilities. Unfettered from debt and strategically located in the city that was known as the gateway to the West, James Heekin and Company soon grew into one of the country's largest, most well-known coffee dealers.

By the turn of the century Heekin had established the Heekin Spice Company to sell tea, spice, baking powder, and extracts. He bought packaging—tin cans—from a southern Ohio can company. When the supplier hiked his prices in 1900, Heekin decided to produce his own cans. He subsequently founded the Heekin Can Company. Within a few years, the can company's product lines included packaging for baking powder, tea, extracts, and other foods.

When the founder died in 1904, son James J. Heekin took the helm of the business. The second-generation leader oversaw the adoption of several technological advances, including lithography, which was used to decorate the cans. Heekin also introduced the open-top cylinder can, also known as the "sanitary" or "packers" can, in the early 1900s. This new design soon became an industry standard.

Heavy demand from a fast-growing customer, R.J. Reynolds Company (which sold its then-popular Prince Albert tobacco in tin cans), combined with new technological imperatives, pushed the company to purchase a second manufacturing site in 1915. According to a company history, volume at this new plant grew so much that at one point it was "the largest metal lithographing plant under one roof in the nation."

When James J. Heekin retired in 1928, Albert Heekin, another son of the founder, assumed the presidency. Daniel M. Heekin, yet another of the founder's 15 children, advanced to Heekin Can's presidency in 1948. He had served as president of the Can Manufacturing Institute during World War II, when widespread shortages made production difficult. But pent-up demand for consumer goods drove rapid expansion in the late 1940s and early 1950s, and the company established four new plants in Arkansas and Tennessee.

Management finally shifted to the third generation of Heekins in 1954, when Albert E. Heekin, Jr., succeeded his uncle as president of Heekin Can. Albert guided the company's acquisition of a modern plant in Newtown, near Cincinnati. The factory soon boasted coating and decorating equipment, coil-cutting (or sheet-metal cutting) lines, two-piece aluminum beverage lines (also known as draw-and-iron lines), welded aerosol lines, and three-piece packer lines. The new plant would long stand as Heekin's flagship factory. In 1962 Heekin commenced construction of a satellite plant in Augusta, Wisconsin, near Bush Brothers & Co., an important Heekin customer.

The Heekins established an emphasis on research and development that would endure long after the family ceased its involvement in the company. Albert, Jr., for example, boosted the company's research budget to an annual sum of over $50 million during the 1950s. Three years of research culminated in the 1959 patent of a plastic embossing process that allowed Heekin to mimic virtually any texture on its cans. This innovation gave Heekin an edge on its larger competitors, American Can Co. and Continental Can Co., for it was able to add plastic caps, closures, and other injection molded products to its offerings during this period.

By 1964 Heekin was America's fifth-largest producer of metal containers, with annual sales of about $30 million and eight Midwestern plants. Faced with intensifying competition and the prospect of a hostile takeover in the midst of industry consolidation, Albert Heekin, Jr., decided to sell the family business on his terms. He began negotiations with Diamond International Corp. Heekin Can was just one of many acquisitions that expanded Diamond International Corp. from a $200 million matchmaker in the late 1950s to a $500 million diversified packaging conglomerate by 1970. Diamond exchanged 480,000 of its own shares, worth about $18 million, for ownership of the can company in 1965.

Heekin was first organized as a division in Diamond's organizational structure, but was later converted to subsidiary status. Business tripled during Heekin's two decades under Diamond's management, as the subsidiary diversified into P.E.T. (polyethylene plastic) bottles and other containers.

British takeover artist Sir James Goldsmith pulled off a leveraged buyout of Diamond in 1982. As one of the conglomerate's healthiest components, Heekin was quickly spun off to raise funds to reduce Goldsmith's leveraged buyout debt. A coalition of private investors—including former U.S. Treasury Secretary William Simon of Wesray Holdings Corp. and Heekin executives—engineered the $108.8 million deal. Wesray, which accumulated about three-fourths of Heekin's stock, only brought $250,000 in equity to the table. The remaining $108.55 million of the purchase price came from a creative patchwork of sources backed primarily by Heekin's own resources (not Wesray's). A $39.8 million revolving line of credit from Citicorp Industrial Credit was secured by first claim on Heekin's receivables and inventory and second claim on its equipment. A $20 million loan from Manufacturers Hanover Leasing Corp. was guaranteed by first claim to Heekin's equipment and second claim to its receivables and inventory. The can company itself chipped in $14.9 million cash and paid $24.1 million for the sale/leaseback of its own plants and offices. A $9 million note from Heekin to Diamond and a $750,000 loan from Wesray to Heekin completed the financing. Interest expenses on the weighty debt load cut Heekin's pre-tax margins in half, from eight percent in 1982 to four percent in 1984. Nonetheless, the can company's sales increased from $173 million in 1973 to $215 million in 1984, and its profits more than doubled during that time, from $3.1 million to $7.3 million.

In order to pay down its debt, Heekin went public in 1985 with a $44-million offering of 3.25 million shares. The offering included about half of Wesray's holdings. The sale helped reduce the company's debt-to-equity ratio from 24.7 to 1 in 1983 to 2.5 to 1 in 1987. John Haas, who had been with Heekin since the pre-Diamond days, was elected president.

Heekin wasn't the only can manufacturer to experience sweeping change in the 1980s. Within a span of just five years, all three of the industry's top firms—American Can Co., National Can Co., and Continental Packaging Inc.—had been taken over at least once.

In light of its new ownership status and the changed industry imperatives, Heekin's management reorganized its capital and research strategy. In a late 1980s "back to basics" movement, the company sold its aluminum can interests to Reynolds Metal Co. and returned its emphasis to food cans. But this was not a regressive action; the company also boosted its research and development efforts in order to stay ahead of competitors in the food can and plastic container industries. By 1987 nearly three-fourths of Heekin's revenues were generated by food-can sales—triple the industry standard. Five years later this share had increased to about 90 percent, with the remainder in aerosol and metal decorating. President Haas felt that concentrating on a specialized niche would bolster Heekin's position as the country's largest regional can manufacturer. He asserted in a 1988 interview with the *Cincinnati Business Courier* that "its the only way a company like ours can survive."

But while Heekin Can was strong in the realm of food-can manufacturing, observers noted that the vast majority of Heekin's sales were concentrated in just 20 accounts. In fact, the company's three largest customers—Kal Kan Foods, Bush Brothers & Co., and Allen Canning—accounted for at least 50 percent of Heekin's annual revenues by the mid-1980s. That dependency was considered a serious vulnerability during this period.

Another major industry transition in the late 1980s afforded Heekin Can the opportunity to embark upon the most ambitious acquisition program in the company's history. Prior to this time, approximately half of America's food manufacturers made their own cans, just as Heekin Tea and Spice had at the turn of the century. But in the late 1980s, several major food producers began divesting their can-making subsidiaries. As Heekin President John Haas noted in the *Cincinnati Business Courier* in 1987, "can-making was a sideline for the food makers. They are starting to sell plants and leave the business because of the capital and the risk involved." Heekin was an active buyer of these facilities. The company acquired plants from Stokley USA Inc., Quaker Oats Co., and Pittsburgh Metal Lithographing Co., and opened a new Ohio factory in 1987, thereby increasing its manufacturing capacity by well over 20 percent. The deals with Stokley and Quaker Oats also gave Heekin "instant customers," for the contracts included multi-year supply agreements with the food companies.

Those acquisitions also shifted Heekin's customer base from Cincinnati to Indianapolis. When two of three unions representing workers at the company's Newtown factory rejected the company's demands for concessions that would bring costs in line with their new business imperatives, management simply began moving jobs and equipment to the new plants. Employment at Newtown dropped from 720 to 380 in 1988.

Heekin's annual sales increased from $207.5 million in 1986 to $336 million in 1989, and net income nearly doubled, from $7 million to $13 million. Called "a sleepy survivor in a tumultuous industry" in a 1990 *Cincinnati Business Courier* feature, Heekin's performance and its management were extolled by several industry observers. H. Edward Schollmeyer, a top analyst with PaineWebber Inc., praised Heekin's management as "topnotch" in a 1987 *Cincinnati Business Courier* piece. John Doss, an executive of Thomson McKinnon Securities, concurred, pointing to Heekin's administration and its niche in the industry as keys to its success. In 1987 the *Wall Street Transcript* named Haas one of the container industry's three best executives. The combination of praise and performance promoted Heekin's stock price from less than $14 in 1985 to $40 early in 1990. Despite its speedy appreciation, however, Heekin's stock was considered undervalued. The stock price was viewed by some as an invitation to attempt a takeover of the company.

In fact, Julian H. Robertson of Tiger Management Associates took a 5.5 percent equity position in Heekin "for investment purposes" in 1989. Soon afterward, the can company's management adopted a poison-pill provision and "supermajority" clause during this period to deter any hostile raiders.

Nonetheless, in 1992 Heekin agreed to be acquired by Ball Corp., a $2.3-billion manufacturer of glass and metal containers for the food and beverage industries. Ball's William A. Lincoln praised Heekin as "probably one of the lowest-cost producers of metal food containers" in a 1993 corporate publication. The $89.1 million exchange of stock, consummated in 1993, made Ball, which already has significant food container operations in Canada, the third-largest manufacturer of food containers in North America.

John Haas was appointed president of Ball's metal food container and specialty products group in 1993. (Ironically, Haas had worked at Ball for a short time in the late 1970s, but returned to Heekin by the early 1980s.) The new parent hoped that Heekin, which became part of Ball's Metal Food Container and Specialty Products Group, would be a catalyst for international expansion in the years to come.

Further Reading:

Autry, Ret, "Companies to Watch: Heekin Can," *Fortune,* December 3, 1990, p. 144.

Bolan, Shawn, "James Heekin and the Heekin Can Company," Cincinnati: Heekin Can Company, 1982.

Brammer, Rhonda, "The Simonizing Process, Or, How to Buy a Company for Nothing Down," *Barron's,* November 11, 1985, p. 16.

"Bright Prospects for Packager," *Financial World,* April 16, 1969, pp. 10–11.

Crisafulli, Tricia, "Reynolds Expanding Can Operations," *American Metal Market,* August 26, 1985, p. 18.

Daumeyer, Rob, "Heekin Can on Acquisition Spree; Wall Street Rated Stock a 'Buy,' " *Cincinnati Business Courier,* November 30, 1987, p. 1.

McCarty, S. Scott, "Going Global," *Ball Line Quarterly,* May 1993.

Norton, Rob, "Who Owns This Company, Anyhow?" *Fortune,* July 29, 1991, p. 131.

Olson, Thomas, "Heekin Restructures To Grow, Cans Raiders' Plans," *Cincinnati Business Courier,* January 22, 1990, p. 9.

Paton, Huntley, "Piece by Piece, Heekin Reduces Newtown Plant," *Cincinnati Business Courier,* October 17, 1988, p. 4.

—April D. Gasbarre

Heineken N.V.

P.O. Box 28
1000 AA Amsterdam, Netherlands
The Netherlands
(20) 5 239 239
Fax: (20) 6 263 503

Public Company
Incorporated: 1873
Employees: 23,997
Sales: $5.65 billion
Stock Exchanges: Amsterdam Brussels Luxembourg
SICs: 2082 Malt Beverages; 2086 Bottled and Canned Soft Drinks & Carbonated Waters; 5181 Beer and Ale; 5149 Groceries & Related Products, Not Elsewhere Classified

Heineken N.V. owns and operates one of the largest and most respected network of breweries in the world, producing the popular Heineken and Amstel Light brands of beer, as well as Murphy's Irish Stout and Buckler nonalcoholic beer, all of which the company markets worldwide. In 1995, Heineken ranked second in the world beer market, selling beer in more than 150 countries and brewing beer in 90 of those countries. The family-run business built a solid reputation early in its history for maintaining high standards for its beer, standards the company continued to adhere to over a century later. Moreover, Heineken was also the single largest exporter of beer in the world. The company had operations in many countries outside its base in The Netherlands, though in the mid-1990s it had no brewing facilities in the United States, by far the company's largest export market.

In 1864 Gerard Adriaan Heineken convinced his mother that there would be fewer problems with alcoholism in Holland if the Dutch could be induced to drink beer instead of gin, and, moreover, that beer brewed in Holland was of such poor quality that he felt a personal obligation to produce a high-quality beer. Heineken's mother bought him an Amsterdam brewery known as De Hooiberg (The Haystack) which had been established almost 300 years before. Heineken was only 22 when he assumed control of De Hooiberg, one of Amsterdam's largest breweries. He was so successful that after four years he built a new, larger brewery and closed the original facility. His business continued to grow rapidly, and after six more years, in 1874, he purchased a Rotterdam brewery to add to his operation.

During this time, using a new cooling technique developed by Carl von Linde, Heineken gained the ability to brew year round at a consistent quality level. Heineken was thus one of the first breweries in the world to eliminate the brewer's traditional dependence on seasonal natural ice. In 1879 Heineken hired Dr. Elion, a former student of Louis Pasteur, to research yeast. Over the next 13 years Elion systematically bred and selected a specific yeast cell for Heineken, which came to be known as the "Heineken Ayeast" (yeast being the source of alcohol and carbon dioxide in beer). The Heineken Ayeast would continue in use into the 20th century and would eventually be shipped from Holland to all breweries owned or operated by the company, providing for a uniformity in taste among Heineken products, regardless of the different climates in which they were produced or consumed.

Heineken began to export just 12 years after the De Hooiberg purchase. Exporting to the United States began soon after the founder's son, Dr. H. P. Heineken, assumed control of the company in 1914. Traveling on the Dutch liner Nieuw Amsterdam to New York, he met Leo van Munching, the liner's bartender. Impressed by van Munching's knowledge of beer, Heineken offered him a position as the company's importer in New York. The bartender quickly accepted.

Van Munching distributed Heineken beer to the finer restaurants, taverns, and hotels in the New York area until Prohibition forced him to stop in 1920. After the repeal of Prohibition in 1933, Heineken was the first beer imported into the United States. World War II once again brought importing to a temporary halt while van Munching served in the U.S. Navy. When he returned in 1945, he formed Van Munching and Company, Inc. and established a nationwide distribution system to expand the beer's market beyond the New York area.

Beginning in the 1940s, the U.S. market became extremely important to Heineken, eventually becoming the beer's largest market outside the Netherlands. Through Van Munching's distribution system, Heineken became the dominant beer import in most of the United States. While many imports were available only in metropolitan areas or other limited geographical regions, by the 1980s Heineken was available in 70 percent of the nation's retail outlets handling alcoholic beverages. The majority of Heineken beer destined for America was brewed at the company's Hertogenbosch brewery, where special production lines accommodated the varied labeling requirements of the different states. Heineken beer also became the leading import in Japan, Canada, and Australia. Moreover, currency fluctuations had little effect on the company itself, largely because Heineken sold its beer to Van Munching, which paid the brewer in guilders and thereby assumed all currency risks.

In 1930 the company entered the first of many joint brewing ventures in countries to which it had previously exported. That year Malayan Breweries was formed in Singapore in association with a local partner. This was followed closely by participation in a brewery in Indonesia. In 1949 the company built the first of four breweries in Nigeria; the fourth opened in 1982. Between 1958 and 1972 the company also built four breweries and two soft drink plants in Zaire. Heineken had breweries in Rwanda, Chad, Angola, the People's Republic of Congo, Ghana, Madagascar, and Sierra Leone as well.

During the late 1940s H. P. Heineken sent his son Alfred to New York to learn about Van Munching's marketing operation. The young Heineken took advertising and business courses in the evening and spent his days canvassing New York on foot with Van Munching's sales staff. His return to Holland in 1948 marked the beginning of a new era in the company's marketing strategy. Alfred Heineken had been impressed with the changes in the American lifestyle brought about by electrical refrigerators and modern supermarkets, and he foresaw the eventual impact of modern conveniences on the Dutch way of life. He prompted the company to implement marketing techniques that capitalized on these habits. Recognizing the importance of the take-home market, for instance, the company began selling beer in grocery stores (with store displays designed by Alfred Heineken). In addition, Heineken began advertising its beer on the radio. Previously, advertising had been considered unnecessary because tavern owners were tied to specific breweries.

In the 1960s the company institutionalized its meticulous quality control efforts under its technical services group, Heineken Technisch Beheer, or H.T.B. High quality was always the company's hallmark. The brewing process of medium-quality beers usually took three days and aging lasted a week at most. Heineken, however, brewed its beer for eight days and aged it for six weeks. The H.T.B. unit operated out of the company's laboratory at Zoeterwoude in The Netherlands and provided laboratory services, research on raw materials, project engineering, and other services for all breweries associated with the company. There was also a tasting center at the Zoeterwoude laboratory. Samples of all beers brewed under Heineken supervision were shipped there each month to be tested by panels of taste experts. The tests at Zoeterwoude augmented the taste testing that was carried out at each individual brewery.

Product diversification began relatively late in Heineken's history, because the company's emphasis had been on expanding its markets. However, in 1968 the company purchased the Amstel Brewery, Holland's second largest, founded by Jonkheer C. A. de Pesters and J. H. van Marwijk Kooy in 1870 and the first in Holland to brew lager beers. Amstel's export market was firmly established by the time Heineken purchased the operation. Heineken eventually entered the low calorie beer market with Amstel Light, and Amstel beers were sold in more than 60 countries.

Shortly after the Amstel purchase, the company changed its name from Heineken's Beer Brewery Company to Heineken. The company's remarkable success outside The Netherlands led management to emphasize Heineken's international presence rather than casting it as a Dutch company with significant international operations. In fact, the company looked upon all of Europe as its domestic market. Heineken Holland had headquarters at the Zoeterwoude brewery. Its various breweries contracted with Heineken World to supply worldwide beer shipments. Heineken World headquarters remained in Amsterdam and were housed in an addition to the Heineken family home.

In 1970 Heineken entered the stout market by buying the failing James J. Murphy brewery in Cork, Ireland. In addition to Murphy's Irish Stout, the brewery produced Heineken light lager brew under license. Wines, spirits, and soft drinks were also becoming increasingly important Heineken products. Soft drinks were made at Bunnik by Vrumona B.V., and the company bottled PepsiCola and 7Up under license. Heineken and its affiliates also sold Royal Club, Sisi, Sourcy, and B3 soft drinks; Royal Club and Green Sands shandies; and nonalcoholic beers such as Amstel Brew. Spirits and wines included Bologna, Hoppe, Coebergh, Glenmark, Grand Monarque, and Jagermeister brands. In 1971 Heineken purchased the Bokma distillery. Bokma Genever was Holland's most popular gin. The distillery at Zoetermeer was the headquarters of Heineken's Netherlands Wine and Spirits Group B.V.

The French market proved the most challenging to Heineken, and since entering France in 1972, Heineken had only one profitable year there by the mid-1980s. The situation was considered so bleak that in 1986 the company and its French partner cut 500 jobs and closed down three breweries and a bottling plant in France, offering displaced employees retraining and outplacement. From 1983 to 1986 Heineken invested significantly in Sogebra S.A. (Société Générale de Brasserie), trying to sustain the company's French activities.

In the 1980s the company was a victim of a series of criminal incidents. In 1982 two unsuccessful blackmail attempts were made against the brewery, followed the next year by an extortion attempt. The most serious incident was the November 1983 kidnapping of the company chief, Alfred Heineken, and his chauffeur. The two were held for 21 days and released after the company paid out an estimated 30 million guilders for their return (though the actual amount was never made public).

Heineken spent tens of millions of guilders each year to bolster its image as a prestigious import. The company's refusal to brew in the United States, even though its beer is brewed under license in many other countries, was in part attributable to a need to maintain the image. Löwenbräu's experience was not lost on Heineken; when Miller began brewing Löwenbräu under license in the United States the German brand lost a major portion of its market share. It appeared that Americans enjoyed the exclusivity of an import. The premium price they paid for Heineken beer lent credence to the image.

Heineken was unquestionably a powerful force in the brewing industry in the 1980s. In revenues it ranked fifth in the world behind AnheuserBusch, Miller, Britain's Allied, and Japan's Kirin. Its share of the world beer market increased from 2.61 to 2.82 percent between 1977 and 1981.

Management policies at Heineken changed little over the years. The family retained control over virtually all aspects of the company, which was managed by a small team selected by the head of the family. The group was kept small in order to prevent factions from developing. However, as in the past, the family head of the company was involved in Heineken's day-to-day functions. Alfred Heineken, grandson of the founder and owner of 50 percent of the shares in the company, directly supervised research and development, finance, and public relations in the mid-1980s. Though Alfred Heineken officially retired in 1989, he kept close ties with the company well into the 1990s, serving as chairman and delegate member of the board of directors.

As the company entered the 1990s, Gerard Van Schaik took over as chairman. When Van Schaik joined the company in

1959, he was responsible for export sales to the United States, which then, as in the 1990s, was the most important source of profits for Heineken. U.S. sales represented just 2.6 percent of the company's total, but contributed 23 percent of the company's $435 million in pretax profits in 1991; a 24-bottle case of Heineken sold on average for about 50 percent more than a case of the domestic favorite Budweiser.

Van Schaik focused on expanding the company's presence in Germany, by far the world's top consumer of beer. Emphasizing Heineken as a premium beer, the company invested in costly advertising, targeting in particular young Germans who, it was hoped, might find a foreign, imported beer appealing. Also during this time, Van Schaik oversaw an important American acquisition, when Heineken purchased Van Munching & Company, the U.S. operation that had handled the Heineken import business in the United States for six decades. This business then became officially known as Heineken USA, the American arm of subsidiary Heineken Worldwide.

In the 1990s specialty beers remained very strong among the American beer-drinking public as many consumers began drinking less and drinking better beers. Heineken was able to take advantage of this trend, offering a more full-bodied, European beer that many consumers desired. In fact, Heineken became the leading imported beer in the United States and brought the entire Heineken USA portfolio double digit growth in 1994. During this time, more than one out of every five imports in the United States was a Heineken.

According to a 1992 *Forbes* magazine article, worldwide annual beer consumption had increased to about 30 billion gallons, equivalent to more than ten six-packs of beer per person per year, with especially strong volume in Latin American and Asia. In accordance with this trend, Heineken announced in 1992 that it had signed a joint agreement to become the first foreign beer producer in Vietnam. A $42.5 million brewery located near HoChi Minh City began producing beer under the Heineken and Tiger labels. Heineken also moved into China, which in 1994 represented the world's second largest beer market, after the United States. By 1994, Heineken had three export offices and three breweries in China. Later, Heineken and Fraser & Neave joined forces to build a brewery in Cambodia, producing about 17 million liters of Tiger and ABC stout annually.

Karel Vuursteen became Heineken's chairman in 1993 and continued to expand the company's international presence focusing on Latin America, the Far East, Scandinavia, and Middle Europe. To facilitate the introduction of Heineken in Poland, Heineken paid $40 million for a 25 percent stake in Poland's Zywiec Brewing. Moreover, in April 1995 Heineken acquired Interbrew Italia SpA from Interbrew of Belgium, increasing Heineken's Italian market share from 25 to 30 percent.

When asked by a company publication, *The World of Heineken,* what position the company would occupy in ten years, Vuursteen responded, ''We are going to consolidate and expand our leading position as a brewer in Europe. . . . Essential in that drive for growth is a true understanding of the three C's: customers, consumers and competitors.'' Following this principle, Heineken would likely remain a major force in the world's brewing industry for many years to come.

Principal Subsidiaries: Heineken Nederlands Beheer BV; Heineken Brouwerijen BV; Heineken Nederland BV; Heineken Internationaal Beheer BV; Heineken Technical Services B.V.; Inverba Holland BV; Amstel Brouwerij BV; Amstel Internationaal BV; Vrumona BV; Brouwerij De Ridder B.V.; Limba B.V.; Brand Bierbrouwerij B.V.; Gemeenschappelijk Bezit Brand B.V.; Beheer- en Exploitatiemaatschappij Brand B.V.; Sogebra S.A. (France); El Aguila S.A. (Spain; 64.8%); Calanda Haldengut AG (Switzerland; 89.3%); Amstel Sörgyár RT (Hungary); Mouterij Albert NV (Belgium); Ibecor S.A. (Belgium); Atheniean Brewery S.A. (Greece), 98.8%; Murphy Brewery Ireland Ltd. (Ireland); Heineken Finance N.V.; Heineken USA Inc.; Brasseries, Limonaderies et Malteries du Zaire 'Bralima' S.A.R.L. (71.8%); Brasseries et Limonaderies du Rwanda 'Bralirwa' S.A. (70%); Brasseries et Limonaderies du Burundi 'Brarudi' S.A.R.L. (59.3%); Brasseries de Bourbon S.A. (Reunion; 52.4%); P.T. Multi Bintang Indonesia (77.2%).

Further Reading:

Brown, Andrew C., ''A Dutch Challenge to the King of Stout; Heineken, the Masterly European Marketer of Light Lagers, Has Moved Boldly into Guinness's Backyard,'' *Fortune,* February 3, 1986, p. 75.

''Empire Builder,'' *Beverage World,* April 1995, p. 20.

Fuhrman, Peter, ''Make Haste Slowly,'' *Forbes,* November 9, 1992, p. 44.

''Heineken Buys into Polish Brewer,'' *Advertising Age,* March 14, 1994, p. 41.

''Heineken's Gift to Cambodia,'' *Beverage World,* December 1994, p. 20.

''Heineken Three Ways,'' *Beverage World,* May 1992, p. 16.

''Heineken to Open Vietnam Brewery,'' *Nation's Restaurant News,* January 6, 1992, p. 54.

Prince, Greg W., ''The Green Standard,'' *Beverage World,* February 1995, p. 30.

The World of Heineken, Amsterdam: Heineken International Beheer, May 1995, 34 p.

—updated by Beth Watson Highman

Hills Stores Company

15 Dan Road
Canton, Massachusetts 02021
U.S.A.
(617) 821-1000

Public Company
Incorporated: 1957, as Hills Department Stores Inc.
Employees: 18,650
Sales: $1.856 billion
Stock Exchanges: New York
SICs: 5311 Department Stores

A pioneer in the discount store industry, Hills Stores Company is the eighth-largest general merchandise discount retailer in the United States. Most of its stores are located in the Midwest and mid-Atlantic states. The company filed for Chapter 11 bankruptcy protection in 1991, as it faced large debt service from a leveraged buyout and aggressive competition from Wal-Mart and Kmart. It has since achieved a noteworthy recovery and is facing its competitors head-on.

The first Hills department store opened up in Youngstown, Ohio, in 1957. Founder Herbert H. Goldberger had operated hosiery stores before starting what quickly became a chain of discount stores. There were seven Hills stores by 1964, when the chain was sold to SCOA Industries, Inc. By the mid-1960s, there were 12 Hills stores sprinkled through Pennsylvania, Ohio, and West Virginia. Goldberger saw the company grow to 99 stores during his tenure as president, which ended when he turned the reins over to his son, Stephen A. Goldberger, in 1981. The chain grew to about 125 stores by the mid-1980s.

A Boston-based takeover pro, Thomas H. Lee, helped Goldberger acquire SCOA through a leveraged buyout in 1985. All of the company's subsidiaries but Hills were sold off, but the $642 million deal left the discount retailer with substantial debt. Hills took on even more debt four years later, when it bought 33 Gold Circle stores from Federated Department Stores. Those stores formed part of the 41 new stores Hills opened in 1989. The expansion gamble did not prove to be a good one, however. The economy took a plunge, sales suffered, and Hills's efforts to restructure its balance sheet failed. To complicate matters further, many of its stores were in the heart of Wal-Mart and Kmart territory. Carrying more than $900 million debt during a retailing recession, Hills could not afford to tune up its stores to take on its hefty competitors. The company filed a petition for relief under Chapter 11 of the U.S. Bankruptcy Code in February 1991.

After becoming the chairman of Hills, Lee began looking for someone to resuscitate the company. Michael Bozic had spent 27 years at Sears, Roebuck & Company, rising to become head of the Sears Merchandise Group, one of the company's main divisions. As Hills's new president and CEO, Bozic took swift action. The company closed 63 unprofitable stores and withdrew from some markets altogether—such as Nashville and the states of Georgia and Michigan. It concentrated instead on the locations that were already strong: Pittsburgh, Buffalo, and Ohio towns like Cleveland, Akron, and Youngstown.

A central distribution center was set up in a former Sears building in Columbus, Ohio. Virtually all merchandise would flow through this facility. This cut the costs of inventory control and overhead, as vendors could deliver merchandise to this site instead of to each of Hills's stores. Cashiers were cut back to a transactions-per-hour standard. Hills also undertook a major remodeling program, though it did so on a budget. In 1992, Hills was spending about $650,000 per store, compared with the $2 million that Kmart was spending that same year. One of the shortcuts Hills took during remodeling was painting its stores white with modest-color trim. This cut the expense of warehousing a rainbow of paints, and helped to highlight the merchandise.

Another facet of Hills's strategy was to target its primary customers: women shopping for values for themselves and their families. The merchandise mix at Hills was already tipped toward these customers, with an emphasis on apparel and toys. Instead of changing this mix, Hills decided to punch up its presentation. For example, the chain invested in new fixtures that displayed items so shoppers could see the fronts of sweaters, jackets, and blouses, rather than seeing long racks of clothes with only the sleeves showing. While the economies of scale available to larger companies like Wal-Mart meant that they could undercut Hills on the prices of many items, Hills had an advantage in that it mostly stocked soft goods and apparel, which generally commanded higher margins. In 1992, about half of Hills's sales came from apparel and soft goods, compared to about 30 percent at Wal-Mart. Hills also launched a line of private-label apparel—basics for children and adults—called American Spirit. The line emphasized its U.S. origins by featuring shots of the factories where the apparel was made in the Labor Day advertising circular that introduced it.

Toys were also a Hills trademark. Most bigger discounters stocked up on toys near the holidays, then trimmed back again. Hills's large year-round toy selection accounted for more than 10 percent of its sales. To make room, the company left items like sporting goods, appliances, automotive products, and lawn and garden supplies to its competitors. Hills's strongest lines were apparel and soft items, like towels and sheets. Bozic summed up the company's strategy in dealing with its giant retail competitors: "The trick is to dance with them and not fight with them." By the end of 1992, Hills was the top performer in the discount retail store market.

By the end of 1993, 78 of Hills's 151 stores had been remodeled and sales were a stunning $1.76 billion. In October 1993, the company emerged from bankruptcy, having won court approval for its reorganization plan a month earlier. That plan included the distribution of more than $540 million in cash, bonds, and company stock to creditors. To reflect its rebirth, the company changed its name from Hills Department Stores Inc. to Hills Stores Company. A banking syndicate headed up by Chemical Banking Corporation granted the chain an unsecured three-year working capital facility of $225 million. Hills gained confidence with its robust 1993 sales, but it was nonetheless sobering that two other discount chains filed for bankruptcy around this time: Rose's Stores Inc. and Jamesway Corporation. Regional chains experienced great difficulty competing with the giant national chains like Wal-Mart, Kmart, and Target Stores.

Hills's recovery was solid enough that it opened a new store in Reading, Pennsylvania, in 1994—its first since 1990. The new store—formerly a Kmart—competed directly with two Wal-Marts and a new Kmart nearby. Considered a prototype, the new store featured further improvements in its displays of women's apparel as well as bar-code scanning and new department graphics. By this time, Hills had a total of 151 units, including six stores in Virginia and one apiece in Kentucky, Massachusetts, and Maryland. Sales in its midwestern and eastern states stores were steady, and Bozic was pursuing concessionaires for the stores that were more than 100,000 square feet.

Just as it seemed as though the company's recovery was on track, a fight broke out among shareholders. An investment fund that owned just under 10 percent of Hills's common shares, Dickstein Partners, L.P., pitched a stock-repurchase plan. Mark Dickstein argued that the company's stock was undervalued and the board was not acting aggressively enough. Dickstein made his fortune by investing in bankrupt companies such as First Republic Bank in Texas and the retailer Carson, Pirie, Scott & Company. What worried Bozic and other Hills executives was that Dickstein's plan would tack $150 million in debt onto the company's balance sheet. Thomas Lee, who had led the leveraged buyout and amassed the debt that had contributed to the company's bankruptcy in 1991, was still Hills's chairman and his memory was fresh. Dickstein approached the shareholders for formal support for his plan. The battle had reached such a pitch by the fall that Dickstein made a bid to replace half of the company's directors. But a truce was reached at the end of September, and Hills announced a $75 million stock buyback.

Hills closed 1994 with new optimism and announced an "aggressive growth plan" that included opening 15 new stores in 1995 and up to 20 stores a year for several years after that. Notably, the company opened two stores in Richmond, Virginia—considered Wal-Mart territory—in fall of 1994 and was stampeded by holiday shoppers headed for the Power Rangers aisle. This marked Hills's furthest southeastern expansion. The stores included wider aisles for stroller-pushing shoppers, and Hills's first newborn section. It also sold special-sized women's apparel. By that time, Hills had remodeled all but 37 of its existing stores, leaving its weakest stores for last. Sales for 1994 topped $1.8 billion. The entire chain expected to have its new look in place by spring 1995, one year ahead of schedule.

Principal Subsidiaries: Canton Advertising, Inc.

Further Reading:

"A Familiar Story—with a Few Lessons for the Future," *Discount Store News,* October 17, 1994, p. 12.

Andreoli, Teresa, "Hills Wows Richmond Shoppers," *Discount Store News,* November 21, 1994, p. 1.

Bailey, Steve, "Life after Bankruptcy," *Boston Globe,* September 22, 1994.

Berss, Marcia, "A Turnaround Is the Best Revenge," *Forbes,* August 3, 1992, p. 83.

Emert, Carol, "Heine Security Makes a Bid for Hills," *WWD,* August 23, 1994, p. 2.

"Hills Back in Black in Fourth Quarter," *Daily News Record,* March 20, 1992, p. 10.

"Hills's Bozic Named Discounter of the Year," *Discount Store News,* June 20, 1994.

"Hills Department Stores Out of Chapter 11," *New York Times,* October 6, 1993, p. 10.

"Hills Gets Court Approval on Chapter 11 Reorganization," *WWD,* September 13, 1993, p. 35.

"Hills Has Net Loss after Charges," *Daily News Record,* August 20, 1992, p. 8.

"Hills Puts Emphasis on Cost Containment," *MMR,* April 18, 1994, p. 24.

Liebeck, Laura, "After Merry Christmas, Hills Sees Happy New Year," *Discount Store News,* February 1, 1993, p. 3.

——, "Hills Bounces Back with Expansion, Remodeling," *Discount Store News,* April 4, 1994.

——, "Hills Files Plan to Emerge from Chapter 11 by September," *Discount Store News,* June 21, 1993, p. 1.

——, "Hills Looks to Greener Pastures," *Discount Store News,* May 3, 1993, p. 1.

——, "Hills New Prototype Redefines the Chain," *Discount Store News,* May 18, 1992. p. 1.

——, "Hills Rolls Out American Spirit Apparel with Patriotic Theme," *Discount Store News,* October 5, 1992, p. 3.

——, "Reorganized Hills Starts Expanding," *Discount Store News,* November 1, 1993, p. 1.

Nordby, Neil, "Hills, Stein Mart Fuel Rise in DSN Stock Index," *Discount Store News,* December 7, 1992, p. 26.

Strom, Stephanie, "Hills Stores, in Comeback, Seeks Life after Wal-Mart," *New York Times,* September 26, 1994.

—Carol I. Keeley

Hoechst Celanese Corporation

1041 Route 202-206
Bridgewater, New Jersey 08807
U.S.A.
(908) 231-2000
Fax: (908) 231-3225

Wholly Owned Subsidiary of Hoechst A.G.
Incorporated: 1987
Employees: 29,900
Sales: $6.89 billion
Stock Exchanges: New York
SICs: 2821 Plastics Materials & Resins; 2824 Organic Fibers Noncellulosic; 2834 Pharmaceutical Preparations; 0711 Soil Preparation Services

A subsidiary of the enormous German chemical company Hoechst A.G., Hoechst Celanese Corporation manufactured and sold a diversified line of products that included textile and technical fibers, specialty and bulk chemicals, and pharmaceuticals produced from manufacturing facilities scattered throughout the United States, Mexico, and Canada. Hoechst Celanese was formed when two companies, American Hoechst Corporation and Celanese Corporation, merged in 1987, creating a more than $4 billion company involved in the production and sale of specialty and basic chemicals and textile fibers.

The true origins of Hoechst Celanese stretch back considerably further than 1987, when the diversified chemical, fiber, and pharmaceutical company was formed through the absorption of Celanese Corporation into Germany-based Hoechst A.G. Although the company technically came into being early that year, its emergence was an inorganic one, representing the consolidation of one foreign-based company's U.S. operations with those of a smaller U.S.-based company. In fact, the foundation for the Hoechst Celanese Corp. dates back more than a century before its creation in the late 1980s, back to a modest manufacturing site along the banks of the Main River near Frankfurt, Germany, in 1863 and to a small shed in Basel, Switzerland, in 1904. From these two locations, 230 miles and 41 years apart, Meister, Lucious and Company, the predecessor to Hoechst A.G., and Celanese Corporation were born.

With a three-horsepower steam engine and a small boiler, Meister, Lucious and Company began operations in 1863 in the village of Hoechst, near Frankfurt on the banks of the Main River. Inside the boiler, aniline oil and arsenic acid were cooked together, producing a synthetic fuchsia dye, the first of more than 10,000 different dyes the company would develop and manufacture over the next twenty years. By the early 1880s, after recording its initial success with dye production, the enterprise had expanded into other business lines, most notably the discovery and development of analgesics and other drugs. With these new products, Meister, Lucious and Company quickly became a leader in the pharmaceutical industry.

From the outset, producing chemicals was an integral component of the company's business, and in this area Hoechst's predecessor distinguished itself, becoming the core of one of two large chemical cartels formed in Germany after the turn of the century. In 1925, the two cartels merged, forming a single company called Interessen Gemeinschaft Farbenwerke, or IG Farben. With its position as the largest representative of one of Germany's most important industries, IG Farben wielded much power during the years between World War I and World War II. In fact, the company was instrumental in placing company officials in the German senate who became vocal proponents of German rearmament. As the 1933 elections neared, the natural candidate for IG Farben to support was the vituperative and caustic leader of the National Socialist Workers' party, Adolph Hitler.

With Hitler's rise to power and the outbreak of World War II six years later, IG Farben benefitted immeasurably, producing gun powder, chemical weapons, and synthetic materials to fuel Hitler's martial expansion in Europe. By the end of the war, however, IG Farben's support for Hitler and the Nazi cause lead to the prosecution of its directors at Nuremburg and to its dissolution by the Allies in 1952. From this breakup, Farbwerke Hoechst A.G. emerged—acquiring a fiber manufacturer, Bobingen AG, during its exit from the old chemical cartel—and began the slow process of rebuilding its position in the worldwide chemical market.

During the postwar period, Hoechst's rebuilding process occurred rapidly. In 1953, the company gained the worldwide rights, exclusive of the United States, to manufacture polyester; that same year it formed a U.S. subsidiary, American Hoechst Corporation, based in Somerville, New Jersey. One year later, Hoechst began to work with polyethylene and polyolefins. In 1956, the company began manufacturing petrochemicals, elevating itself into the upper echelons of the chemical industry to become, once again, one of the leading chemical companies in the world by the 1960s. Expansion continued during the decade, including the acquisition of a Dutch plastic molding manufacturer, the construction of a polyester plant in Austria, a foray into oxo-alcohols in France, and, most important to the future formation of Hoechst Celanese, a joint venture in Europe with Celanese Corporation in 1962.

Celanese Corporation had spent the previous half century primarily manufacturing cellulose acetate products, including cellulose acetate yarn, which was sold as "artificial silk." The company was founded by two Swiss brothers, Dr. Camille E. Dreyfus and Dr. Henri Dreyfus, who, in 1904, began their research in a small shed located in their father's garden in Basel, Switzerland. The two chemists opened their first factory in Switzerland in 1910, initially producing cellulose acetate as a non-flammable motion picture film base, a welcome alternative to highly volatile cellulose nitrate base film. Later, the Dreyfus brothers began producing acetate fiber yarn on an experimental basis, then were invited to the United States by the country's government in 1917 to produce acetate lacquer coat for U.S. military aviation needs. A factory was opened the following year in Cumberland, Maryland, to accomplish this task, marking the beginning of the company's presence in the United States.

After World War I, the two brothers resumed their prewar work, producing at a plant in England the first commercial cellulose acetate yarn in 1921. Referred to as "artificial silk," cellulose acetate yarn production boosted the company's profits, with the first spool manufactured from the Maryland plant completed on Christmas Day, 1924.

After experiencing initial resistance from consumers in the United States, artificial silk production ultimately invigorated the company's fortunes and fueled its expansion into the production of plastics and industrial chemicals by the late 1930s. From the diversification into plastics and industrial chemicals, Celanese was forced to expand into a broad range of business lines during the 1950s and 1960s, when new synthetic fibers such as nylon, polyester, and acrylic introduced after World War II crippled the market for cellulose fiber. Searching for new business ventures related to the expertise that the company had gained over the previous five decades, Celanese moved into the production of polyester, nylon, triacetate, chemicals, plastics, paint, petroleum, and forest products. It was during this diversification during the 1950s and 1960s that Celanese entered into a joint agreement with Hoechst in 1962, linking together for the first time the Hoechst and Celanese names.

Hoechst's rebirth after World War II led to significant diversification and expansion during the 1950s and 1960s, when the company, including its U.S. subsidiary, American Hoechst Corporation, recorded enviable success. However, the 1970s engendered highly disappointing results, when the company suffered debilitating losses in the fibers market. By the beginning of the 1980s, Hoechst was looking for economic relief and a return to greater profitability by eschewing further involvement in man-made fibers and basic chemicals, and instead concentrating on building its interests in specialty chemicals.

In order to achieve this new objective, American Hoechst needed to arrest its financial slide by streamlining its operations and reducing rising costs. In 1981, the producer of chemicals, pharmaceuticals, cosmetics, and other products collected $1.6 billion in sales and earned $24 million. The following year, sales slipped to $1.51 billion and, despite more optimistic projections, earnings suffered a precipitous plunge to $3 million. A company-wide reorganization was effected that year, breaking American Hoechst's business lines into four operating groups—fibers and film, petrochemicals and plastics, specialty products, and health care and agricultural chemicals—which resulted in more encouraging growth in 1983 and 1984. Sales increased from $1.6 billion in 1983 to $1.76 billion in 1984, while earnings rebounded from their debilitating fall in 1982 to $35.5 million in 1983 and then to $53.2 million in 1984.

After these changes had been made, American Hoechst surprised industry analysts with its $2.8 billion friendly bid for Celanese in late 1986. As one observer related to *Business Week* with regard to American Hoechst's puzzling tender offer for Celanese, "They [American Hoechst] spent 10 years getting out of commodity fibers, and here they are buying one of the biggest," an assessment that, in large measure, was accurate. Roughly half of Celanese's $2.5 billion in sales was derived from man-made fibers, which, once the transaction was approved by governing regulatory bodies, would increase American Hoechst's reliance on commodity-based products. From American Hoechst's perspective, however, the acquisition of Celanese made good sense. The addition of Celanese, with its core businesses in polyester fibers and commodity-based chemicals, would make American Hoechst's parent company, Hoechst A.G., a major player in the U.S. market and one of the largest chemical producers in the world, collecting a combined $17.5 billion in annual sales. For American Hoechst, Celanese's marketing clout and extensive sales network would enable the company to distribute a broad range of new products, as well as significantly increase its annual sales volume from $1.7 billion to $4.2 billion. With these benefits fueling American Hoechst's interest in acquiring Celanese, the proposed merger was submitted for Federal Trade Commission (FTC) approval, while befuddled onlookers cast their doubts as to the prudence of such a merger.

FTC approval was slow in coming, delayed by two requests for further information regarding the merger; by the end of February 1987, though, the FTC had given its assent, ordering American Hoechst to divest certain assets totaling more than $300 million before final approval would be granted. This action was done and the merger was completed, with the new company's senior management selected in March. Slated to head the new chemicals, pharmaceuticals, and fibers company was Jeurgen Dormann, American Hoechst's former chairman, who was named Hoechst Celanese's chairman and chief executive officer. Named to Hoechst Celanese's other most senior positions were Dieter zur Loye, former president and chief executive officer of American Hoechst, who was selected as the new company's vice chairman, and Ernest H. Drew, a former Celanese group vice president, who became Hoechst Celanese's president and chief operating officer. Hoechst Celanese's senior management remained as such until late in the company's first year of operation, when Dormann relinquished his posts as chairman and chief executive officer in December 1987, focusing his talents instead on serving as chairman and chief executive of Hoechst Corporation, Hoechst Celanese's holding company. Drew and zur Loye filled the void created by Dormann's absence, with the former adding the title of chief executive officer to his name and the latter ascending to the chairmanship of the company.

Led by these managers, Hoechst Celanese proved its detractors wrong during its first several years of existence. Annual sales reached $4.61 billion in Hoechst Celanese's inaugural year, then jumped by more than $1 billion the following year, when the company recorded $5.67 billion in sales. Following the company's success in 1988, it recorded $6.01 billion in sales in 1989, a year during which substantial operational changes were effected. Hoechst Celanese reorganized into five major business groups that year, each group structured to comprise the five distinct segments of the company's business. Completed in July 1989, the reorganization left Hoechst Celanese with an Advanced Materials division, which constituted the company's involvement in engineering plastics and other advanced materials that the company expected to become involved with in the future. Through its Advanced Technology business group, Hoechst Celanese conducted its research and development of specialty products, the exploration of certain new business development activities, and the execution of the company's major technical efforts. Rounding off the list of the company's new business groups was its Chemicals division, which comprised specialty and commodity chemicals, its Fibers and Film division, and its Life Sciences division, which focused on pharmaceuticals, animal health, and agricultural crop protection businesses. Concurrent with these operational changes, zur Loye announced his retirement from the company after 34 years of service.

Restructured in this manner, Hoechst Celanese entered the 1990s after registering great success in its previous three years of operation. A $550 million investment program was launched in 1991 to satisfy Environmental Protection Agency regulations and to expand the company's capacity in chemical and fiber production, but the first signal development in the new decade unfolded two years later in 1993, when Hoechst Celanese once again furrowed the brows of industry analysts with the announcement of another acquisition.

Slated for acquisition this time was Copley Pharmaceuticals Inc., a Canton, Massachusetts-based manufacturer of generic and over-the-counter drugs with $52 million in 1992 sales and $12.3 million in earnings. Reacting to the acquisition, the *Wall Street Journal* remarked, ''The transaction brings together two unremarkable drug companies struggling to cope in an industry roiled by the specter of health-care reform and the emergence of powerful managed-care buyers.'' What alarmed observers most, however, was the price Hoechst Celanese was offering for a 51 percent stake in Copley, an enormous $546 million for a company that collected $53 million in sales a year. Typically, in similar transactions, the acquiring company paid three or four times the annual sales of the company to be acquired, but the price Hoechst Celanese offered was roughly 20 times greater than Copley's sales volume, considering that Hoechst Celanese was acquiring just over half of the company, and 90 times greater than Copley's earnings.

To be sure, the price for Copley was exceedingly high, but there were several mitigating factors that suggested Copley's worth to Hoechst Celanese could not be reckoned in the manner typical of such transactions. In the year before Hoechst Celanese's offer, Copley had recorded a stunning 80 percent sales gain and, as the deal was being negotiated in late 1993, Copley was expected to record an additional 73 percent sales increase, which accounted, in part, for Hoechst Celanese's prodigious offer. Perhaps more important and of more worth to Hoechst Celanese was Copley's solid presence in the generic and over-the-counter drug market, which was expected to grow immeasurably once impending health-care reform occurred and managed-care buyers began looking for less expensive drugs. In the 23 months leading up to Hoechst Celanese's offer, Copley had gained 23 approvals for new products, which promised to augment significantly the company's already sizeable product portfolio of roughly 90 generic, prescription, and over-the-counter drugs. Furthermore, with Hoechst Celanese's ability to obtain bulk chemical supplies, supplies critical to a generic drug company's success, the complementary nature of the acquisition provided a potentially profitable, synergistic relationship between the two, convincing Hoechst Celanese's management that the acquisition was worth the price.

The deal was concluded in November 1993, when Hoechst Celanese obtained a nearly 53 percent stake in Copley for $546 million. The addition of Copley immediately broadened the product line of Hoechst Celanese's pharmaceutical subsidiary, Hoechst-Roussel Pharmaceuticals Inc., making the unit which the *Wall Street Journal* had characterized as ''unremarkable'' a burgeoning force in the U.S. drug market.

Hoechst Celanese generated $6.9 billion in sales in 1993, then entered 1994 hoping to begin benefitting from its acquisition of Copley. The company realigned its management team in May 1994, with Drew becoming chairman in addition to the chief executive position he had held since 1988. Karl G. Engels, Hoechst Celanese's vice president, succeeded Drew as president of the company.

As Hoechst Celanese entered the mid-1990s, speculations surfaced that the company would be spun off from Hoechst A.G. to create a separate, publicly held company as early as 1996. Whether or not this public offering occurred, Drew was formulating ambitious plans for the company's growth into the next century, plans that focused on increasing Hoechst Celanese's presence in the U.S. generic and over-the-counter drug market. Although sweeping health-care reform had become less imminent by the mid-1990s, Drew was hoping to increase Hoechst Celanese's sales in health care to $1.5 billion by the end of the decade, largely through expanding the company's position as a supplier in the generic drugs segment and through bolstering its position as a prescription drug supplier in North America. With these objectives driving the company forward, Hoechst Celanese geared itself for the 21st century and beyond, intent on maintaining and increasing its role as a formidable force in the U.S. chemical, fiber, and pharmaceutical markets.

Principal Subsidiaries: Hoechst CelMex Performance Products; Hoechst-Roussel Pharmaceuticals Inc.; Hoechst Celanese Chemical Group, Inc.; Celanese Fibers, Inc.; Amcel International Company, Inc.; Celanese Canada Inc. (56 percent); Celanese S.A.; Corporate Class Software, Inc. (82 percent); Cape Industries Affiliates (74 percent); Interactive Radiation Inc. (20 percent); Celanese Mexicana, S.A. (40 percent); Celgene Corp. (32 percent); Endotronics, Inc. (36 percent); Codon (18 percent); Nova Pharmaceuticals Corp. (3 percent); Codenoll Technology Corp. (16 percent); Ceramics Process System Corp. (7 percent); China National Tobacco Corp.; Polyplastics Co., Ltd. (45 percent); Ticona (41 percent); IB Chemicals Co. (50 percent); RV Chemicals Ltd. (40 percent); Virchen SA/NV (51 percent).

Further Reading:

Alexander, Suzanne, ''Jane Hirsh Saw the Future, and It Was Generic,'' *Wall Street Journal,* October 12, 1993, p. B1.

''American Hoechst Plans New Corporate Structure,'' *Chemical Marketing Reporter,* December 2, 1974, p. 26.

''American Hoechst's '82 Sales Seen Up 15 Percent to $1.8 Billion,'' *Chemical Marketing Reporter,* March 29, 1982, p. 9.

''American Hoechst's Celanese Tender Offer Extended Until Jan. 9,'' *Wall Street Journal,* December 30, 1986, p. 2.

Brockington, Langdon, ''FTC Calls For a Sell-Off of Assets,'' *Chemical Week,* March 4, 1987, p. 12.

Bryant, Adam, ''Plastic Pipe Makers Plan to Settle Lawsuit,'' *New York Times,* October 25, 1994, p. D4.

Cowan, Alison Leigh, ''Hoechst's Puzzling Return to Commodity Chemicals,'' *Business Week,* November 17, 1986, p. 65.

''Fina Agrees to Buy Polyethylene Plant in Texas From Hoechst Celanese Corp.,'' *Wall Street Journal,* July 7, 1992, p. B8.

''Hoechst Celanese Picks Top Managers; Dormann Is Chairman,'' *Wall Street Journal,* March 5, 1987, p. 20.

''Hoechst Celanese Realigns Staff; Drew Is Named Chairman,'' *Wall Street Journal,* May 6, 1994, p. B6.

''Hoechst Celanese Regroups As Zur Loye Steps Down,'' *Chemical Marketing Reporter,* June 12, 1989, p. 5.

''Hoechst Celanese Restructures, Names Four to New Post,'' *Wall Street Journal,* February 10, 1992, p. B2.

''Hoechst Sees Moderation in Growth of Sales This Year,'' *Chemical Marketing Reporter,* March 18, 1985, p. 9.

''Hoechst's U.S. Unit Appoints Zur Loye Chairman, Drew Chief,'' *Wall Street Journal,* December 29, 1987, p. 20.

''Hoechst Unit Clears Hurdle That Held Up Its Offer for Celanese,'' *Wall Street Journal,* January 12, 1987, p. 28.

Hunter, David, ''Hoechst Celanese: Betting On Managed Care,'' *Chemical Week,* June 15, 1994, p. 40.

Jackson, Debbie, ''Hoechst Revamps for the Future,'' *Chemical Week,* June 26, 1991, pp. 65–7.

Pazstor, Andy, ''Hoechst Unit Wins a Round in Celanese Bid,'' *Wall Street Journal,* February 25, 1987, p. 26.

Plishner, Emily S., ''Hoechst Repositions in U.S. Pharmaceuticals Market,'' *Chemical Week,* October 20, 1993, p. 12.

Schmitt, Richard B., ''Shell, DuPont, Hoechst Are Said to Near Polybutylene Settlement of $750 Million,'' *Wall Street Journal,* October 21, 1994, p. A4.

Shurman, Joseph V., ''Born to the Purple,'' *Barron's,* July 10, 1972, p. 11.

Storck, William, ''American Hoechst Putting More Emphasis on Profitability,'' *Chemical & Engineering News,* November 28, 1983, p. 9.

Tanouye, Elyse, ''Generic Drug Firms Step Into Limelight with Rich Offer for Stake in Copley,'' *Wall Street Journal,* October 12, 1993, p. 42.

——, ''Hoechst Unit Plans to Acquire Stake in Copley,'' *Wall Street Journal,* October 11, 1993, p. A3.

—Jeffrey L. Covell

HON INDUSTRIES

HON INDUSTRIES Inc.

414 East Third Street
Muscatine, Iowa 52761-7109
U.S.A.
(319) 264-7400
Fax: (319) 264-7217

Public Company
Incorporated: 1944 as Home-O-Nize Co.
Employees: 6,250
Sales: $846 million
Stock Exchanges: NASDAQ
SICs: 2521 Wood Office Furniture; 2522 Office Furniture Except Wood; 3272 Concrete Products, Not Elsewhere Classified; 3433 Heating Equipment Except Electric

HON INDUSTRIES Inc. is one of America's leading manufacturers and marketers of business furniture, work space accessories, and fireplaces. From small beginnings, the company developed into a thriving business with offices, showrooms, and distribution and manufacturing centers nationwide and annual sales reaching toward the billion dollar mark.

HON was conceived in a backyard in Iowa on a Sunday afternoon in 1943 by C. Maxwell Stanley and Clement T. Hanson. The two long-time friends were discussing the war, politics, and business, when Stanley proposed that he and Hanson start a manufacturing business after the war, one in which they could put into practice their common beliefs. Specifically, Stanley and Hanson agreed that good personal relations between management and workers were crucial to a company's success, but that American business, focusing only on making a profit, had ceased to treat employees with fairness and respect. Moreover, they believed that when the war was over, the United States would see large unemployment figures. Their idea, therefore, was to build a successful company that would not only provide work for returning veterans, but would distinguish itself for its enlightened employee-management relations. Hanson thought it was a good idea and suggested inviting a mutual friend, H. Wood Miller, to join the business venture. Combined, the three had a variety of different attributes and experience to bring to their new business.

Stanley had earned a bachelor's degree in general engineering and a master's degree in hydraulic engineering, both from the University of Iowa, and had worked several years for engineering firms in Chicago and in Dubuque before arriving in Muscatine, Iowa, in 1932 at the depth of the Great Depression. There, he became a partner in a small engineering firm and built the business, which eventually became Stanley Consultants, Inc. A leader in the profession, Stanley authored *The Consulting Engineer,* a definitive text on private consulting.

Clement T. Hanson was a graduate of the College of Commerce at the University of Iowa. He had worked as advertising executive for a firm in Iowa and as head of sales at a company in Illinois, developing along the way a keen interest and expertise in the areas of communications, public relations, and marketing. H. Wood Miller had spent several years studying design at the Art Institute of Chicago, eventually establishing his own design firm, the H. Wood Miller Company, which served several industrial clients.

Welcoming the challenge of creating and managing a new business, the three men began making plans. They were very confident in their abilities and eager to use them in a new venture. But as Max Stanley stated in *The HON Story,* "Our confident enthusiasm was matched only by our considerable naiveté. Little did we understand the difficult problems and obstacles that new enterprises usually encounter. But this was as it should be. Had we foreseen the hurdles, we might never have ventured."

Predicting the huge postwar construction boom, Stanley, Hanson, and Miller decided to target the home market, and, from there, narrowed down their ideas to focus on products for the kitchen. They eventually decided to enter the home appliance field with the manufacture of home freezers, followed by steel kitchen cabinets.

While considering what their company should be called, Hanson proposed Home-O-Nize. His colleagues liked the sound of it; the first syllable suggested the ultimate destination of their products, while the third syllable would be useful in creating future advertising slogans, such as "Economize with Home-O-Nize" or "Modernize with Home-O-Nize." Since Hanson, Miller, and Stanley had no actual production experience, they brought in Albert F. Uchtorff, president and owner of a sheet metal products manufacturing company, who offered his facilities for manufacture of the company's first product. On January 6, 1944, the four signed the Articles of Incorporation for the Home-O-Nize Company; offices were set up in Davenport, Iowa, and each of the four directors contributed $1,000 for ten shares of stock to the start-up project.

That year, product development began. Miller made sketches for a deep freeze unit, as well as for some unique kitchen cabinets that could be quickly erected in a variety of configurations to custom fit a kitchen. He and Miller began setting up a prototype shop, while Stanley began working with compressors. The company hired its first employee, who worked with the sheet metal on a part-time basis. Soon, the men opted to focus solely on realizing Miller's kitchen cabinet idea, rather than on freezer production.

Before actually introducing a product, however, the company met with adversity. Several disagreements between Uchtorff and the three company founders, over the direction and scope of Home-O-Nize, eventually prompted Uchtorff to sell his stock and resign from the fledgling board of directors. Uchtorff left what would become a successful project, and the company was left without a manufacturing plan and facilities.

Nevertheless, the three persevered, deciding that they would eventually establish their own manufacturing plant. First, however, they went ahead with their official presentation of the kitchen cabinet prototype, and distributors reacted with enthusiasm. Financing during this time was obtained through a $100,000 loan from a federal agency as well as a successful stock sale; by the spring of 1947, 988 shares of Home-O-Nize had been sold to investors, and the three founders increased their shares as well.

After finding a suitable plant location in Muscatine, Iowa, hiring workers, investing in the necessary machinery, and securing a contract from Stampings Inc., the Home-O-Nize company manufactured its first product in April 1947; ironically, it was neither a freezer nor a kitchen cabinet that first left the plant, but instead an aluminum hood used in installing commercial gas at farms, residences, and businesses. A steel shortage in 1947 and 1948 prevented the company from ever realizing its original plans; as the founders waited out the shortage, they took on contract work that would eventually lead them into the office supply business.

The cutting of aluminum hoods for Stampings left a considerable amount of metal scraps, and the company soon found a use for them: the company began making anodized aluminum coasters for beverage glasses. Stamping the coasters with a company logo or a sailboat motif, Home-O-Nize marketed the coasters to businesses, which used them as gifts. They also began manufacturing aluminum ground markers to identify garden plants and recipe file boxes.

The development and sale of such 3″ × 5″ and 4″ × 6″ file boxes changed the direction of the company. Disappointed with its continuing inability to purchase steel for kitchen cabinets, and pleased with the market reception of the card file boxes, the company decided to direct its focus on office products. Green card files were produced for office use, red and white recipe files were made for the home, and red and black versions were sold to the Sunbeam Company in large quantities for use as premiums. Sales from the products made from scrap in 1947 amounted to almost $20,000.

During this time the group also developed programs and policies to support their continued belief that a company's success was based on good employee relations. While developing an employee manual, Hanson suggested that they refer to all employees as "members," a word that suggested, according to Stanley, "a greater sense of belonging and participation." Also, at the onset, the company established an automatic cost-of-living adjustment keyed to the cost-of-living index. The company was among the first to establish such a program; most large corporations adopted this practice only under union pressure.

With the help of a contract for farm equipment from John Deere's Harvester Works, 1948 became Home-O-Nize's first profitable year. However, the company was still under-financed and sought additional contracts to keep its manufacturing plant busy. In 1949, Home-O-Nize signed a contract worth $450,000 with Associated Manufacturers, Inc. to produce a newly designed corn picker that attached directly to the front of a tractor. However, what seemed like a promising job turned into "the greatest fiasco in the history of Home-O-Nize," according to Stanley. Home-O-Nize produced the corn picker, with designs provided by Associated that proved full of bugs; at its first field test, the corn picker failed after just one pass. Months of costly redesign ensued, for which, as it turned out, Associated was unable to pay. Litigation ensued, and Associated eventually defaulted on the contract, entering into bankruptcy.

As a result, Home-O-Nize was forced to reduce costs and that meant making some considerable staff reductions. The company salvaged what they could from inventory and wrote off a loss of $52,541 on the corn pickers. Moreover, with additional write-offs from their unrealized kitchen cabinet project, Home-O-Nize's cash position diminished by more than $100,000 during 1949. The company's financial position was at the worst level ever experienced.

The company survived, though, through loans, stock purchases, and a contract with the Bell Aircraft Company. On March 2, 1950, Home-O-Nize bought Bell's manufacturing rights to the Prime-Mover, an engine-powered wheelbarrow with a capacity of 1,000 pounds, and incorporated its subsidiary as The Prime-Mover Co. This purchase meant steady income and ultimately saved the company. The combined sales of Home-O-Nize and Prime-Mover totaled more than $600,000 at year end 1950.

The period from 1951–1955 was known as Operation Independence Home-O-Nize, with a goal of expanding the Prime-Mover and office product businesses, and to decrease dependence on contract work. During the four-year period of Operation Independence, the company saw their basic objectives realized. By 1953, total consolidated sales passed the $1 million milestone and two years later exceeded $2 million. Profitability resumed in 1952, to start more than four decades of uninterrupted profits.

Office products were becoming the chief product line for Home-O-Nize during this time. In addition to its non-suspension card files, the company began developing combination cabinets in 1953. One such product was the Unifile, which featured a unique one key handle that operated plungers to lock all doors and drawers, and incorporated an optional interior security compartment. The Unifile was a steady seller from its introduction and would remain in the HON product line into the 1990s. Other products during this period were full suspension filing cabinets, coat racks, and single pedestal desks with hairpin legs and matching tables. The company also began its name transition. Although the corporate name remained Home-O-Nize, the office products were branded H-O-N and given their own division within the company.

In the mid-1950s, the company strove for a greater market penetration through expanding sales of its office products and Prime-Movers, while raising productivity, improving the quality of products, and strengthening its financial position. The result was a decade of explosive growth. Annual sales passed $5 million in 1961 and surpassed $10 million in 1965. The number of members working at the company more than tripled, from less than 200 in 1956 to over 500 by the end of 1965. During this period, H. Wood Miller left Home-O-Nize to focus more closely on his industrial design work. He remained a shareholder, however, and, on occasion, assisted the company's engineers with design projects.

The HON line of office equipment during this time grew to include such products as steel drawer card cabinets, steel cash boxes, the HONOR line of products for the schoolroom, and the VS (standing for Very Special) line of higher end office products. The company also acquired Luxco Company of La Crosse, Wisconsin, a manufacturer of chairs, stools, and machine stands, introducing HON to the seating industry.

But the major marketing breakthrough of the time was HON's entry into the wholesale marketplace. By 1965, the company was serving about 75 wholesalers located throughout the United States, with about 35 percent of its furniture reaching dealers through this channel. Home-O-Nize also began selling HON products to Sears, Roebuck & Co., for retail to small businesses or consumers who maintained offices in their home. Continuing efficiency and expansion into new plant locations helped with growth during this period.

The 1960s also brought changes in management and in the company name. Stanley M. Howe was appointed executive vice-president of the company in 1961, and became president in 1964. Howe had joined Home-O-Nize in 1948, as the assistant to the head of the planning division. Proving himself a manufacturing genius and a shrewd administrative leader, Howe shared the founders' vision of growth and had become vice-president of production by 1954. He would later become chairman of HON after the death of Max Stanley in 1984. Having long ago shifted its focus away from manufacturing products for the kitchen and home, the company changed its name in 1968 to HON INDUSTRIES, Inc.

Geographic expansion and acquisitions characterized the late 1960s and 1970s at HON. In 1967, the company purchased a plant site in Cedartown, Georgia, marking its first move out of Iowa on the way to becoming a national manufacturer. The introduction of computers in 1968, helped in the management and control of operations of the growing company. By 1969, net sales were $25 million. During this time, cofounder Clement Hanson retired from HON.

Under the leadership of CEO Stanley, the company continued to add to its holdings. Holga Metal Products of Van Nuys, California, was acquired in 1971, giving the company a manufacturing facility in the rapidly growing southern California region. Corry Jamestown of Corry, Pennsylvania, was acquired in 1972, HON's first venture into the higher priced segment of the office furniture market. HON then bought Norman Bates Inc. of Anaheim, California, their first venture into wood manufacturing. To serve the East Coast markets, HON opened a plant in Virginia. The acquisition of Murphy-Miller of Owensboro, Kentucky, put HON into the wood seating business in 1977. By 1979, net sales surpassed $198 million, an eight-fold increase since 1969.

HON INDUSTRIES expansion continued in the 1980s. Heibert Inc. of Carson, California, brought HON into high quality wood furniture and wood office systems furniture. Heatilator, the leading name in prefabricated fireplaces became part of HON INDUSTRIES in 1981. J.K. Rischel Company, manufacturers of traditional wood office furniture, was purchased in 1982, and the next year, HON acquired 35 percent of Ring King Visibles, a rapidly growing office products company. In 1986, they acquired Budget Panels, Inc. of Kent, Washington.

In the spring of 1986, two years after the death of Maxwell Stanley, and after nearly a tenfold increase in sales from 1972 to 1985, HON was notified that it had become a Fortune 500 company. The company had a record of making 124 consecutive quarterly common stock dividends by 1985. In fact, cash dividends from a single share of stock issued by Home-O-Nize in its first public offering in 1946 totaled more than $10,600 by 1985.

By 1987, under the leadership of chairman and president Stanley Howe, HON had become known as the most efficient producer in the industry worldwide, capable of producing a desk every minute, a file every 40 seconds, and a chair every 20 seconds. Company sales reached $555 million that year, which also marked HON's 40th year in operation.

The XLM Company was established during this time to manufacture a unique new design of budget file cabinets to be sold through mass merchandisers, and the company consolidated its Corry Jamestown and Hiebert divisions into a new operation known as the CorryHiebert Corporation. After a difficult decision, HON sold Prime-Mover to BT Industries, a worldwide materials handling equipment company; the sale benefited shareholders, as the company received a $8.3 million after-tax gain. In 1989, HON acquired The Gunlocke Company, of Wayland, New York, an established architectural and design firm for office furniture. Moreover, the remaining shares of Ring King Visibles were purchased and the company became a wholly owned subsidiary of HON.

The 1990s saw the rise to prominence of the home office, as estimates suggested that 26 million Americans did some part-time work at home and another 25 percent worked full time at home. This trend gave way to the emergence of two new major outlets of office furniture: warehouse clubs and office product superstores, such as Office Depot. HON moved quickly to become a major supplier to these retailers.

In March 1990, Jack D. Michaels, formerly the president and CEO of Hussmann Corp., was named president of HON INDUSTRIES. Michaels was eventually given the position of CEO as well, while Howe remained on as chairman of the board. Under Michaels, HON made a long-term commitment to explore and develop international opportunities with the formation of HON Export Limited. In 1991, the company had its first decline in sales in four decades, caused by a flat growth in the office furniture industry and the lowest level of housing starts since World War II.

But in following years, sales increased again. In 1993, the company made record investments in new product development, new capital equipment, new business ventures, and member development. Although HON was forced to close its

CorryHiebert Corporation office, it entered a new market through the acquisition of the DOVRE brand of cast iron fireplaces and wood stoves, which were manufactured and marketed through Heatilator. According to a 1995 *Fortune* article, HON was one of America's most admired companies in the furniture industry in the mid-1990s. Moreover, the company had positioned itself for continued growth and success into the 21st century. With a corporate goal of doubling its profit by the year 2000, HON was maintaining its leadership position nationally and was expanding its presence internationally.

Principal Subsidiaries: BPI Inc.; Chandler Attwood Limited; The Gunlocke Company; Heatilator Inc.; Holga, Inc.; HON Export Limited; Ring King Visibles, Inc.

Further Reading:

Driscoll, Lisa, "Compensating for Workers' Comp Costs," *Business Week,* February 3, 1992, p. 72.

Francett, Barbara, "Using Price to Change Buying Patterns," *Computerworld,* October 29, 1990, p. 116.

Jacob, Rahul, "Corporate Reputation," *Fortune,* March 6, 1995, pp. 54–90.

LaBar, Gregg, "Getting Work Off Employees' Backs," *Occupational Hazards,* April 1991, pp. 27–31.

Stanley, C. Maxwell, and James H. Soltow, *The HON Story,* Ames, Iowa: Iowa State University Press, 1991, 197 p.

Welsh, Tricia, "Best and Worst Corporate Reputations," *Fortune,* February 7, 1994, pp. 58–69.

—Beth Watson Highman

Hudson Foods Inc.

1225 Hudson Road
Rogers, Arkansas 72756
U.S.A.
(501) 636-1100
Fax: (501) 621-5192

Public Company
Incorporated: 1972
Employees: 9,000
Sales: $1.04 billion
Stock Exchanges: New York
SICs: 2015 Poultry Slaughtering and Processing; 2013 Sausages and Other Prepared Meats

Hudson Foods, Inc., is one of the largest producers of poultry and prepared meats in the United States. The company's client base includes grocery chains, wholesalers, and the food service industry. It is a wholly integrated producer of poultry products, capable of breeding, hatching, feeding, raising, slaughtering, processing, and marketing chicken and turkey. Hudson also produces eggs and egg products through its NEPCO division and frozen prepared foods through its subsidiary Pierre Frozen Foods Inc. Prepared meats, such as bologna, sliced turkey and sausage links are sold under the company's Ohse, Schweigert, and Roegelein brands; poultry is sold under the Hudson brand name. Entering the mid-1990s, the company operated processing and sales operations in 11 states, a sales and distribution center in Poland, and a sales office in Russia. In 1994 company sales topped $1 billion for the first time.

Hudson Foods was incorporated in 1972 when Ralston Purina Co. sought to divest itself of its poultry business. Its nationwide facilities were bought by approximately seven different buyers, among them James T. "Red" Hudson, a long-time employee of Ralston Purina who purchased the company's poultry processing and broiler operation in Springdale, Arkansas, as well as five distribution centers located throughout the South. According to Hudson, few changes were made at the new company. "We essentially took down one sign and put up another, changed bank accounts and went forward with people that had experience of 20 to 25 years in a lot of areas," he said in a May 1989 *Wall Street Transcript* article.

The company grew quietly in its early years, adding breeder flocks, hatcheries, and growout farms to its operations. It also entered into a joint venture with Armour Food Co. to supply all the live chicken needed for its ice-pack chicken processing plant in Murfreesboro, Arkansas plant. In 1977 the company built a $1.4 million plant to turn offal and chicken feathers into high-protein meal used in animal feel. The addition of the feed plant, which was capable of producing 35 tons of feel pellets per hour, made Hudson a fully-integrated poultry operation and provided greater control over the cost and quality of its chicken feed.

By 1979 Hudson's processing capacity had grown to 1.25 million birds per week. That year it diversified into the turkey business, purchasing a processing plant from North Star Foods and another from Empire Foods, both of Missouri. The acquisitions provided Hudson with an annual output of over three million turkeys, and served to strengthen the company's position in grocery store freezers and foodservice operations. Hudson continued with internal expansion efforts that year as well. It broke ground for a new chicken feed-mill-hatchery-broiler processing plant that would boost annual capacity to almost two million birds per week upon its completion in 1982.

In 1982 Hudson bought Armour Food's Murfreesboro boiler processing plant, a move that increased its ice pack chicken processing capacity by 1.3 million per year. Boosted by strong demand and Hudson's timely acquisitions, sales grew steadily, reaching $184.6 million in 1985. The following year, the company went public on the American Stock Exchange. Soon after its initial public offering, Hudson nearly doubled its capacity with the purchase of Corbett Enterprises Inc., a chicken, turkey, eggs, and egg product operation with sales of $142.7 million. The $61.7 million acquisition, funded by an earlier sale of eight percent debentures due in the year 2006, made Hudson the seventh largest producer of chicken in the United States.

In 1987 Hudson expanded into the prepared beef and pork market with the purchase of Thies Companies, a luncheon meats manufacturer and distributor. The $12 million purchase gave Hudson rights to the Ohse brand, which had been founded in 1932 and was well-established in about five southern states. Sales in 1987 hit a record $430 million.

The following year, however, Hudson's sales slipped by $27 million as a nationwide salmonella scare caused many consumers to avoid chicken purchases. Given Hudson's high debt-to-equity ratio brought on by its earlier acquisitions, the loss of sales could have had drastic effects on the company's financial health. Due to a favorable combination of tax regulations and debt classifications, though, the company survived virtually unscathed.

In 1989 company sales topped $549 million and net earnings totaled $14.8 million. Consumer demand for chicken was on the rise as fast-food chains and other foodservice operations initiated intensive campaigns to market chicken as a low-fat, low cholesterol alternative to beef. Hudson had also diversified its product base by this time. Approximately one-eighth of the company's output came from the Ohse meat lines, while another one-eighth was in turkey. Chicken, eggs, and egg products accounted for 75 percent of output. Half of the company's production in these areas was sold under the Hudson brand name; the other half was sold to restaurants and fast-food chains.

Hudson maintained operations in Arkansas, Georgia, Alabama, Maryland, Indiana, Missouri, and Oklahoma, and although its market primarily covered the Midwest, it expanded north to Canada and west to California. Chairman and CEO James T. Hudson summarized his company's position in the *Wall Street Transcript:* "Our company is a food company and we intend to stay in the food area. . . . We definitely see ourselves increasing market share in our poultry area but we also see the opportunity to increase in various lunch meats, some of which have a base raw material of poultry, but with some beef and pork. With the trend, which has been in the development stage for a number of years where more families eat out, we're seeing an awful lot of our products going into the fast food segment and into the prepared food section in the retail stores."

Hudson further increased its presence in the northern market in 1989 when it purchased a turkey processing plant and the Schweigert line of luncheon meats from Land O'Lakes Inc. for a stock exchange valued at about $10.6 million, plus a future payment in cash or stock. The exchange gave Hudson the rights to the Schweigert brand name. The agreement also gave Hudson temporary rights to market turkey and turkey products under the Land O'Lakes brand while it merged the Land O'Lakes operations with its own.

During the 1980s Hudson's growth followed an industry-wide trend in which the small, independent processing plants that once dotted the country were absorbed by approximately ten companies. These industry giants grew to control over 80 percent of national poultry production by 1990. As Hudson approached its third decade of operation, the company entered a new phase of development. It began its first regional advertising campaign, utilizing television, radio, and local newspapers; built a research and development center to create further-processed food products; and began marketing its new products overseas.

Hudson continued its acquisitions of small companies as it moved towards its goal of becoming a complete food company. In February 1990 it purchased Pierre Frozen Foods, a supplier of prepared frozen foods to the foodservice industry, for approximately $10 million in stock and cash. Two months later it acquired the Roegelein Co., a manufacturer and marketer of luncheon meats under the Roegelein brand name. A short time after that acquisition, Hudson purchased a major chain of wholesale club stores to provide a retail outlet for its products. The company also began construction of a plant to produce highly processed convenience food items from turkey; such a facility would complement the Land O'Lakes line of turkey products it had recently acquired.

Sales grew to $666.7 million in 1990, but earnings plummeted to $8.7 million from $22.8 million the previous year. The sharp drop in earnings was primarily due to an industry-wide glut of chicken and turkey that spurred dramatic reductions in prices. Turkey sales were further eroded that year by construction delays and start-up troubles at Hudson's new turkey-processing plant. Armed with a ten-fold increase in research and development funding, Hudson began an aggressive campaign to create convenience items for the grocery and foodservice market. Its goal was to minimize the company's vulnerability to the commodity-driven poultry market by developing value-added items from its pre-existing product lines.

By the end of 1991, Hudson had organized its businesses into five divisions (chicken, luncheon meats, portioned entrees, turkey, and egg products) and was taking measures to consolidate and coordinate the production and sales of its brands. Chicken sales continued to be the company's major source of revenue, accounting for 55 percent of output from its chicken division. Other significant sources included turkey (12 percent of output), Ohse, Roegelein and Schweigert luncheon meats lines (19 percent), and Hudson's new Pierre Frozen Foods division (14 percent).

Overproduction of turkey and turkey products continued to plague the industry in 1992. Hudson responded to the market by streamlining operations, dropping unprofitable product lines, and focusing on marketing through club stores. The company also emphasized efforts to reach the food service market, where demand was strongest. By centralizing financial operations, coordinating sales, and making capital improvement at almost all its plants, Hudson was able to cut operating expenditures in its luncheon meats division by 15 percent in 1992.

That year the company also transformed its turkey division to develop other processed turkey products such as turkey pastrami and turkey ham. Marketed through grocery store delicatessens and foodservice distributors under the Deli Mesiter brand, sales of Hudson's turkey products soon began to rival sales of its whole birds. Sales in its Pierre Frozen Foods division grew by 50 percent in 1992, fueled by sales into new Canadian and Mexican markets and the popularity of its Rib-B-Q boneless barbecue-flavored pork, Micro-Wiches pre-wrapped microwaveable sandwiches, and school cafeteria lunch programs.

Despite these successes, Hudson faced a number of difficulties in 1992. Profits in its chicken division continued to lag, burdened by industry overproduction and unfavorable events in the local and international economies. Hudson continued to develop new chicken product lines, though, including a line of spiced and breaded individually frozen chicken portions that allowed the company to market to grocery delicatessens as well as foodservice companies and club stores.

Sales in Hudson's egg division, which had posted strong earnings through the late 1980s, also slumped in 1992 as the industry faced a glut of eggs on the market. As with its other divisions, Hudson sought to reduce its vulnerability to commodity prices by developing a number of low-cholesterol egg-based products at its NEPCO egg further-processing plant.

Annual sales in 1992 reached a record high of $809 million, yet net income plummeted again to $2.1 million, down from $8.7 million in 1991. To further reduce its vulnerability to the American poultry market, Hudson embarked on an international sales drive, acquiring new clients in Central America, Eastern Europe, the Middle East, and the Pacific Rim.

By 1993 Hudson's focus on research and development and division integration began to pay off. Its Complete Meal Kits, a line of chicken fajitas, beef stir fry, and breakfast sandwiches was launched in 1993. Marketed through Hudson's its portioned foods (Pierre) division, the product line showed a profit in its first year. Sales of its further-processed turkey products also improved, while sales of Hudson's eggs and egg products to snack food, pasta, and baked goods manufacturers rose as well. Sales grew by 400 percent between 1990 and 1993, and although profits slumped, the company was positioning itself for growth. In 1993 sales reached $920.5 million and net income leapt to $15 million, buoyed by the stabilization of the poultry market and improved operating efficiencies in all Hudson's divisions.

In 1994 Hudson's enjoyed a record $1.04 billion in sales. Net income grew to $27.0 million, up 69.7 percent from 1993. The company landed a multi-year contract to produce beef patties for Burger King, while its chicken and portioned entree divisions posted their best years in the history of the company on the strength of a contract to supply poultry to Boston Chicken, a rapidly expanding national restaurant chain. Hudson's Pierre Frozen Foods division experienced growth as well, supported by an innovative marketing program that won a National Frozen Food Manufacturers Association award for best frozen food merchandising.

After 30 years of growth through acquisition, Hudson has successfully expanded its sales in recent years through innovative product development and marketing. It has a well-balanced portfolio of product lines and a diverse array of customers—from shoppers at warehouse clubs, delicatessens, and grocery store chains to restaurants, school cafeterias, and national fast food chains. Entering the mid-1990s, Hudson, armed with a strong balance sheet, planned to continue expansion efforts through acquisitions and internal growth.

Further Reading:

Byrne, Harlan S., ''Hudson Foods: Poultry Processor Has a Lot to Crow About,'' *Barron's,* January 10, 1994, p. 33.

Cochran, Thomas N., ''Hudson Foods Inc.: If Chicken is a Winner, Can Turkey be Far Behind?,'' *Barron's,* October 10, 1988, pp. 45–46.

''Hudson Foods Adds Feed Mill to Poultry Complex,'' *Feedstuffs,* May 22, 1978, p. 7.

''Hudson Foods, Inc.,'' *The Wall Street Transcript,* May 22, 1989, p. 93,720.

Smith, Rod, ''Hudson Foods Achieves Goal of Becoming Complete Food Company,'' *Feedstuff,* February 4, 1991, p. 6.

—Maura Troester

Hunter Fan Company

P.O. Box 14775
Memphis, Tennessee 38114
U.S.A.
(901) 743-1360
Fax: (901) 745-9265

Private Company
Incorporated: 1901 as Hunter Fan and Ventilating Company
Employees: 450
Sales: $200 million (est.)
SICs: 3634 Electronic Housewares & Fans; 3822 Environmental Controls

Hunter Fan Company is the world's oldest and largest ceiling fan manufacturer. The Memphis-based company produces more than 300 residential, commercial, and industrial ceiling fan models under such names as the 1886 Limited Edition, the Hunter Original, the Seville, and the Fantasy Flier. Recognized throughout North America and the world for its unparalleled commitment to quality, the result of a 500-step inspection process, Hunter has earned a reputation for producing powerful but quiet, wobble-free ceiling fans and is believed to offer the most extensive service and warranty program in the industry. Although the company is best known for its wide variety of ceiling fans that are sold through home centers, discount stores, fan shops, and lighting showrooms, it also manufactures more than 100 decorative and mounting accessories as well as a line of programmable thermostats, highly energy-efficient room air conditioners, and decorative indoor/outdoor residential lighting products. Accounting for nearly one percent of the room air conditioner market, Hunter has manufacturing operations in Memphis as well as in Mexico and the Far East.

The Hunter Fan Company was founded in 1886 in Syracuse, New York, by James C. Hunter and his father, John Hunter, immigrants from Ireland. Originally known as the Hunter Fan and Ventilating Company, the fledgling business first engaged in the manufacture of water motors and meters. The founders expanded their operations to include the production of belt-driven fans, the power for which was first provided by water motors and later by the Tuerk Electric Motor, which they developed. The Hunter reputation for quality was established early in the company's history: some of these earliest belt-driven fans are still in use today after more than a century.

In 1889 the growing company moved its operations to Fulton, New York, where it would spend the next fifty years at a plant located at Front Street, extending from Huling Street to Tolbot Street. Twelve years later, upon the death of John Hunter, his six sons incorporated the company and focused their attention on expanding the production of ceiling fans. By the early 1920s, the company was widely known for its high-quality electric fans. The early models featured natural wood blades with ornate hardware and came with only two blades; however, for two dollars more, customers could purchase a four-bladed model. Noted for their elaborate ''Dragon'' design, the electric fans were best suited for ceilings from ten feet and up and were advertised as ''ready for electric lights.'' By the early 1920s the Hunter name was widely known throughout the United States and the world. The fans were especially popular in India and China, and throughout the Far East, where thousands were exported each year.

By the mid-1920s, desk oscillating fans had been added to the Hunter product line. In 1936, after purchasing the fan division of Century Electric Company, Hunter began manufacturing large pedestal air circulating fans and direct exhaust fans as well, which were used by many of the finest hotels and stores. Two years later, the company began producing attic fans as well. With the onset of World War II, the company suspended the manufacturing of ventilating equipment for consumer use and concentrated its efforts on aiding the war effort, producing belt fans for government use in Army hospitals and barracks, and portable ventilators and oscillators for the Navy.

With the postwar boom in the U.S. economy, Hunter expanded its operations to keep up with the growing need for commercial and industrial ventilating equipment. In 1946 the company moved its plant from Fulton to its present location in Memphis in order to take advantage of the rapid industrial expansion of the South. Three years later, Hunter was acquired by Robbins & Meyers, Inc., a fan manufacturer based in Springfield, Illinois. For the next 45 years, Hunter operated as a wholly owned subsidiary of Robbins & Meyers, producing a complete line of residential, commercial, and industrial fans.

Although Hunter performed consistently well throughout the 1960s and 1970s, by the mid-1980s the company's limited line of ventilating products, combined with the entrance of a number of new competitors into the market, brought on financial crisis. In 1984, following two consecutive years of losses, the struggling company was purchased from Robbins & Meyers by a group of senior managers led by William C. Clouspy, who took over as company chairman and chief executive officer. Clouspy, who explained to the *Memphis Business Journal* that the parent company sold Hunter because ''they thought we were going down the tubes,'' accepted the risk and took the firm private, rather than see the century-old company fail.

During the two years following the takeover, the management team guided the company through the financial crisis, developing a strategy of product diversification that made Hunter profitable once again. By broadening the ceiling fan line and adding air conditioners, dehumidifiers, programmable thermostats, and lighting, Clouspy and his fellow managers were able to pay off 85 percent of the initial acquisition debt in just two years, while increasing total revenue to an estimated $123 million, an improvement of 23 percent from the previous year.

Solidifying its financial base by refinancing its remaining debt, Hunter was now in position to expand its operations through acquisition. The management team purchased Melnor Industries, a leading designer and manufacturer of lawn and garden watering equipment, and Kenroy International, Inc., a designer and importer of residential lighting products. In June 1987, the company went public under the name Hunter-Melnor, Inc., with an initial offering of 1.05 million shares at $9 per share.

The company's renewed success was attributed in part to the management style of Clouspy and his colleagues, who opted for a highly decentralized team of four presidents, each responsible for one division of the company. Practicing ''participative management,'' the officers were given the freedom to exchange ideas while retaining the flexibility needed to lead the company in creative directions.

As Hunter was expanding its operations during this period, the company again underwent an organizational change. In 1988, just a year after it had gone public, the company was privatized through a leveraged buyout led by the investment firm Leach McMicking. The transition, however, did not impede the turnaround of the company. Boosted by the strong performance of the Melnor group and its line of garden chemical products, the Hunter group was able to take advantage of the expanding fan market, landing four new major customers: Payless Cashways, Kmart, Wal-Mart, and Target. Fan sales, once limited primarily to the South, had extended throughout the nation. While Miami, for instance, represented Hunter's top sales city in 1984, Phoenix headed the list in 1987, followed by Philadelphia and Chicago. At least three factors contributed to this geographical expansion: a significant decline in prices, enabling more customers to purchase fans; the discovery of multiple applications for ceiling fans for different rooms of a home; and a general move in the replacement market toward the higher-priced, higher-quality fans for which Hunter has been known. Driven by these forces, fan sales jumped from 1.2 million units in 1980 to 16 million in 1987, the company's one-hundredth year of operation.

As Hunter-Melnor, led by president and chief executive officer G. Douglas Lingren, entered the new decade, sales had grown to more than $100 million on the strength of the company's ability to keep abreast with market trends and develop new products. Competing in a market driven by such volatile factors as the weather, new home construction, and remodeling, Hunter and the rest of the industry were especially vulnerable to the recessionary economy of the late 1980s and early 1990s. Nevertheless, Hunter continued its pattern of growth by focusing on the remodelling segment of the industry, where the demand for its upscale units represented the greatest potential for profit. To take full advantage of this market, the company—having acquired Ronel, a New Jersey-based manufacturer of decorative lighting fixtures, in July 1989—became the first in the industry to define the ceiling fan as a primary source of light, adapting halogen lights to its units. The company also began selling units with wall-mounted and hand-held remote controls designed for ease of operation, while adding new models designed and painted specifically for use in the kitchen and outdoors.

While these strategies kept Hunter-Melnor at the forefront of the industry, the company's profitable Hunter division was weighted down by debt affecting the entire company. To alleviate this problem and make each division bear the responsibility for its own debt, Hunter-Melnor was divided into two corporations in September 1991. Under the reorganization plan, Robert Beasely took over as the new president and chief executive officer of Hunter Fan. Kenroy International was placed under its control as a subsidiary. Less encumbered by debt, Hunter Fan was able to direct its attention and resources to advertising and product development.

While continuing to emphasize the home fashion aspect of its ceiling fans, adding such models as the Fantasy Flier—a fan replica derived from a naval archival drawing of an F4U fighter plane—to its product line, Hunter Fan launched the largest advertising campaign in the history of the industry. The company set the stage for its aggressive strategy in the summer of 1992 by reformatting its logo across all of its product lines, incorporating a new Hunter green color and introducing upscale packaging graphics. Starting in May 1993, the company began advertising a wide variety of its ceiling fans in 30-second prime time television spots and in such popular magazines as *Newsweek* and *Sports Illustrated,* in which two-page, four-color spreads appeared. The unprecedented advertisements emphasized both the multipurpose dimension of ceiling fans, showing their effectiveness in areas as diverse as the bathroom and the porch, and the economical advantages of the product, making the case that fans are a cost-effective alternative to air conditioning.

In the summer of 1993, the company introduced more than a hundred new lighting fixtures, including models featuring weathered metal, colored glass, and textured finishes, strengthening its reputation as the leading supplier of upscale decorative fans. In October of that same year, the company added another potentially profitable market to its repertoire when the United States Food and Drug Administration approved its air purifiers as Class II medical devices. This marked only the second time that an air purifier manufacturer had received this certification, and the decision made it possible for Hunter Fan to market its products to hospitals, nursing homes, and allergists. Accordingly, the company launched a national print ad campaign targeting consumers with ads in magazines such as *Ladies Home Journal, Reader's Digest,* and *Modern Maturity.*

Perhaps the company's most innovative and publicized campaign began in February 1995, seven months into a major league baseball strike. Going against conventional wisdom, Hunter Fan unveiled a baseball-themed ceiling fan and introduced a nationwide ''Why I Love Baseball'' program, calling for baseball fans to write letters explaining why they cherish the national pastime. As an added incentive to the fans, the company awarded trips to the Baseball Hall of Fame in Cooperstown, New York, and ceiling fans to winners of the contest, which was judged by such well-known baseball fans as filmmaker Ken Burns, *Sporting News* editor John Rawlings, and the ''Clown Prince of Baseball,'' Max Patkin. Instead of proving a liability, the strike actually succeeded in generating widespread interest in the contest and in the novelty item. With more than 225 U.S. radio stations and a host of television stations and major publications covering the campaign, Hunter Fan was able to reap benefits from what may have first appeared to be a marketing disaster: in just the first few weeks of the campaign, the baseball fan became one of the company's leading sellers.

Behind the strength of its bold marketing strategy, Hunter Fan has entered its second century of operation well positioned for continued expansion. With a wide range of ceiling fans, lighting fixtures, and other cooling products in its repertoire, and its long history of excellence in quality and service, the company is expected to move well beyond the $200 million mark. How far past this level the company will go depends largely on the state of the U.S. construction market, the success of new competitors to the industry, and the height of the mercury on the thermometer.

Principal Subsidiaries: Kenroy International.

Further Reading:

Borowsky, Mark, "Hunter-Melnor Splits into Separate Divisions for Fan, Sprinkler Operations," *Memphis Business Journal,* September 2, 1991, p. 8.

"Ceiling Fans Grow Broader in Features, Functions, and Light up at Higher End," *HFD,* August 27, 1990, p. 32.

"Ceiling Fans Propel Profits," *HFD,* March 9, 1992, p. 19.

Elstrom, Peter J. W., "Meet Peter Smith, Quiet Buyout Ace," *Crain's Chicago Business,* August 9, 1992, p. 3.

Hunter Fan Company History/Heritage, Hunter Fan Company: Memphis, Tennessee, 1995.

"Hunter Fans Out, Adds 131 Lighting Fixtures," *HFD,* August 30, 1993, p. 22.

"Hunter Fan Wins FDA Class II Rating," *HFD,* October 18, 1993, p. 93.

"Hunter-Melnor to Split Operations," *HFD,* September 9, 1991, p. 30.

"Hunter's Ad Campaign Begins," *HFD,* June 14, 1993, p. 26.

"Hunter's Small-Room Air Purifier," *HFD,* December 27, 1993, p. 45.

"Lighting Floods Juvenile Niche," *HFD,* September 21, 1992, p. 21.

"Revised Image Sells Ceiling Fans Despite Cool Temps," *National Home Center News,* January 18, 1993, p. 28.

Sewell, Tim, "Hunter Counts on Baseball Fans for Latest Product," *Memphis Business Journal,* March 20, 1995.

Wellborn, Bill, "Winds of Profit Blow Hunter-Melnor's Way Since Acquisitions Tap New Markets," *Memphis Business Journal,* January 25, 1988, p. 1.

—Jason Gallman

inacom™

InaCom Corporation

10810 Farnam Drive
Omaha, Nebraska 68154
U.S.A.
(402) 392-3900
Fax: (402) 392-7214

Public Company
Incorporated: 1991
Employees: 1,883
Sales: $1.54 billion
Stock Exchanges: NASDAQ
SICs: 5045 Computers, Peripherals & Software; 6794 Patent Owners & Lessors

The third-largest and most profitable computer distributor in the United States, InaCom Corporation was formed in 1991, when ValCom Inc. and Inacomp Computer Centers Inc. merged. The resulting company represented an immediate force in the retail computer services industry. In a few short years, InaCom became considerably larger, negotiating several pivotal deals that positioned it as one of the most successful, high-growth companies in the country. During the mid-1990s, InaCom marketed and distributed information technology products and services through a network of more than 1,500 business locations for a wide range of manufacturers.

When William L. Fairfield started selling computer systems for Valmont Industries, Inc. in 1982, he hoped to bring the agricultural community surrounding Valley, Nebraska, into the computer age. Valmont Industries, a manufacturer of electric power transmission and irrigation equipment based in Nebraska, had created a subsidiary named ValCom Inc. to market a unique line of computer software tailored to the needs of local farmers; it was Fairfield's job to convince these farmers that they too could benefit from the rapid advancements being achieved by the computer industry. A Nebraska native with an M.B.A. from Harvard, Fairfield unfortunately discovered that he was pursuing clientele that, as it turned out, did not demonstrate any discernible desire to join the computer age, at least not with ValCom's software. When Fairfield realized the focus of ValCom's business was obscured, the new direction he took quickly turned Valmont Industries' sideline business into one of the largest and most profitable computer distributors in the United States.

Before ValCom's rapid maturation into an industry leader, the subsidiary languished as a developer and marketer of agricultural software, failing to derive any substantial business from the sale of its narrowly focused computer programs. Swine Management and Poultry Farm Management, two of the numerous software programs Fairfield was attempting to sell, proved to be poor performers and rested on dust-gathering retail shelves. Fully aware that ValCom's agricultural software programs were producing lackluster results, Fairfield turned to market research, looking for a solution to ValCom's woes. From such a study, Fairfield made an important discovery. The majority of ValCom's customers were not farmers, but were local bankers, shopkeepers, and lawyers; people with little use for Swine Management software, yet drawn to ValCom's retail outlets by the service and training provided with the personal computers they purchased. Fairfield's findings rerouted ValCom toward the proper and profitable direction. The subsidiary abandoned the market for software products like Swine Management and concentrated instead on selling computer hardware and providing computer services to small businesses, creating the foundation for what would become in less than a decade a billion-dollar computer services and distribution force.

By 1987, ValCom had grown into a successful enterprise, generating $164 million in sales that year, enough to convince Valmont Industries' management that its subsidiary could stand on its own. Valmont Industries spun off ValCom in 1987, selling 1.1 million common shares of its subsidiary for approximately $12.1 million, or 25 percent of ValCom, through an initial public offering in September. Before the year was through, ValCom was an entirely publicly owned company poised to strengthen its presence in the computer distribution industry.

With Fairfield at the helm, serving as the company's president and chief executive officer, ValCom generated $231.8 million in sales after its first year of operation as a separate corporate entity and recorded $5 million in earnings, a 38 percent increase from 1987's total. During the year, ValCom began its climb toward becoming one of the largest chain of retail computer stores by acquiring a New Jersey-based chain named Clancy Paul Inc. The $3.8 million acquisition gave ValCom six Clancy Paul computer centers and five new centers in the southwestern United States, setting the tone for the years ahead when ValCom would strengthen its geographic network of retail locations through acquisition and affiliations.

By 1989, ValCom was the fourth-largest chain of retail computer stores in the nation, collecting $359 million in sales and supported by 181 ValCom business centers spread across 16 states. By selling hardware manufactured by IBM, Compaq, NEC, and AT&T, as well as computer equipment produced by other manufacturers, ValCom was fast becoming a giant retailing competitor, relying on the service and technical assistance it provided to outdistance the competition. In the years ahead, its concentration on service coupled with a shift toward selling large computer systems less vulnerable to competition from low-priced computer clones would enable the company to withstand the damaging affects of a nationwide recession. In the economic downturn set to unfold, the retail computer industry would become increasingly competitive, a development that compelled ValCom to intensify its efforts toward growth. It was either acquire or be acquired in the coming decade, years during which the retail industry consolidated in the face of growing competition and declining sales. Against this backdrop, ValCom moved forward, intent on becoming one of the consolidators rather than a target for some other retail chain.

In 1990, ValCom resumed its acquisitional approach toward growth, purchasing the computer division of The Office Works, Inc. for $8 million in July and the communications division of Terra International, Inc. in December. However, these events were overshadowed by what occurred in 1991, when ValCom became part of a new, much larger corporate organization called InaCom Corporation. In April 1991, ValCom and Inacomp Computer Centers Inc., a Troy, Michigan-based computer retailer and service provider, announced they had signed a definitive agreement to merge—a partnership that would combine ValCom's $428 million in 1990 sales with Inacomp's $500 million sales total. In August the merger was concluded, creating a nearly billion-dollar computer retailer that ranked in sales just behind Intelligent Electronics Inc., ComputerLand Corp., and then-struggling Businessland Inc. With 685 company-owned stores, franchise branches, and affiliated dealers across the country, ValCom, now known as InaCom, had made a tremendous leap toward attaining the geographic presence necessary to compete in the fiercely competitive 1990s. Importantly, ValCom gained Inacomp's network of *Fortune* 1000 oriented dealers and superstores as a complementary addition to its own stalwart presence in smaller markets. Together, the two companies increased their ability to attract corporate customers by virtue of the full-range of services that they could provide and their greater presence nationwide, giving InaCom a solid and broad base upon which to grow.

Fairfield was named the new company's president and chief executive officer, retaining the same corporate titles he had held at ValCom, while Richard Inatome, Inacomp's president and chief executive officer, was selected as InaCom's chairman. Under the stewardship of these two leaders, InaCom reorganized one month after the merger was concluded in an effort to orchestrate an efficient integration of ValCom's and Inacomp's resources. Mid-level administrative positions that became superfluous once the two companies merged were eliminated, resulting in a loss of 125 jobs, or seven percent of InaCom's work force, and certain branch locations were consolidated. Retail and service outlets that competed in the same markets were combined, as were some of the smaller, non-competing branches, which were consolidated into larger, more efficient locations.

By the end of InaCom's first full year of operation, sales had eclipsed the billion-dollar mark, rising to a robust $1.01 billion from the $680 million recorded in 1991. Net income shot up as well, bounding from just over $2 million to nearly $12 million; further, income levels promised to rise considerably higher after InaCom entered into a pivotal arrangement with another computer retail chain in December 1992. Whereas the merger of ValCom and Inacomp had extended the company's geographic reach in the United States, its alliance with Paris-based International Group (ICG) gave InaCom a commensurate boost to its international presence. The December 1992 alliance with ICG, one of the largest computer services companies in Europe, allowed InaCom to provide its U.S.-based multinational clients with a valuable service—the coordination of the design, purchase, installation, and support of their global information systems through one source. Instead of having to search for a computer supplier overseas and then spending time to acquaint the foreign supplier with the company's business and its particular needs, InaCom's corporate clients could arrange all details through InaCom. In turn, ICG's European and Asian corporate customers could use InaCom's numerous U.S. locations for service and support to their U.S.-based businesses.

The alliance with ICG was perceived as an excellent strategic move on the part of Inatome and Fairfield, but before the praise became monotonous, InaCom made another signal move a month after linking forces with ICG. In January 1993, InaCom announced its intentions to acquire the majority of Sears Business Centers operated by Sears, Roebuck & Company through the retail giant's Sears Merchandising Group. Sears, over the course of the previous few years, had been divesting properties deemed inconsistent with its core retailing business; among the properties slated to go were the company's computer retail and services centers, launched in 1981 to sell computers and provide computer network integration services to large corporations. By 1993, the number of Sears Business Centers had grown to 49, and their inclusion in the InaCom empire represented an ideal opportunity to advance Inatome and Fairfield's strategy to increase its national presence in marketing services and the telecommunications field.

In February 1993, the transaction with Sears was completed. InaCom paid $5.8 million and assumed certain liabilities for 44 of 49 Sears Business Centers, properties that generated $436 million in 1992 sales. Twenty of the branches acquired were located in markets where InaCom did not maintain a presence, which increased the number of InaCom's affiliated locations to more than 1,200, while the remainder were merged into existing franchises. Summing up InaCom's rapid expansion over the previous three years, Fairfield declared to *PC Week* after the acquisition of the 44 Sears Business Centers, "What we have now is true national coverage." Aside from gaining a greater national presence, InaCom also gained an entirely new type of client with its Sears Business Centers acquisition, inheriting a $400 million U.S. Department of Defense contract to supply 75,000 notebook and laptop computers. Sears Business Centers had been awarded the contract a year prior to InaCom's acquisition.

The addition of the 44 Sears Business Centers were expected to increase InaCom's sales 50 percent once the properties were fully absorbed into the InaCom organization, a prodigious leap in sales for a company that had recorded several revenue increases of a similar magnitude. Perhaps more impressive, the company's vigorous rate of expansion was achieved alongside equally prolific increases in its net income, making InaCom the most profitable computer distributor and retailer in the country. As InaCom entered the mid-1990s, buoyed by its strong international presence through its affiliation with ICG and its enviable market position throughout the United States, it figured to be one of the leading companies of its kind for the remainder of the decade and into the 21st century.

Principal Subsidiaries: ValCom Computer Centers, Inc.; Clancy-Paul, Inc.; ValCom Southwest, Inc.; Business Technology Group, Inc.; Strategic Products and Services, Inc.; ValCom Mid-Atlantic, Inc.; VTC, Inc.; Inacomp America, Inc.; Inacomp Computer Centers of Georgia, Inc.; Inacomp Financial Services, Inc.; I.C.C. of Florida, Inc.; Inacomp Computer Centers of California, Inc.; Inacomp Computer Centers, Inc.; Inacomp Southwest, Inc.; InaCom Business Centers, Inc.

Further Reading:

Clash, James M., ''From Swine to RAMs,'' *Forbes,* June 7, 1993, p. 126.

Dostert, Michele, ''Global Integration Alliance Formed,'' *Computerworld,* December 14, 1992, p. 15.

Fisher, Susan E., ''Reseller InaCom Streamlines Its Operations,'' *PC Week,* September 9, 1991, p. 122.

——, ''ValCom, Inacomp to Merge,'' *PC Week,* April 22, 1991, p. 119.

''Inacom Buys Computer Business,'' *Wall Street Journal,* October 17, 1994, p. B5.

''Inacom Completes Acquisition of Sears Business Centers,'' *PC Week,* March 1, 1993, p. 118.

Moore, Mark, ''InaCom Acquires Sears Division,'' *PC Week,* January 25, 1993, p. 154.

Ringer, Richard, ''Sears Unit Being Sold to Inacom,'' *New York Times,* January 14, 1993, p. D5.

''ValCom Inc.,'' *Barron's,* February 6, 1989, p. 59.

''Valmont Industries Inc.,'' *Wall Street Journal,* September 4, 1987, p. 21.

—Jeffrey L. Covell

International Family Entertainment Inc.

2877 Guardian Lane
Virginia Beach, Virginia 23452
U.S.A.
(804) 459-6000
Fax: (804) 459-6427

Public Company
Incorporated: 1977
Employees: 280
Sales: $208 million
Stock Exchanges: New York
SICs: 4833 Television Broadcasting Stations

Founded in the late 1970s by televangelist and one-time presidential hopeful Pat Robertson, International Family Entertainment, Inc. (IFE) owns and operates a number of ''family-oriented'' entertainment companies. Its flagship operation, the Family Channel, is the fifth largest cable television network in the U.S., with over 60 million subscribers and a television household penetration rate of 63 percent. IFE also owns and operates two related networks, the Family Channel (UK) and the Cable Health Club, as well as MTM Entertainment Inc., the television production company founded by actress Mary Tyler Moore. Further, IFE operates a smaller live entertainment division, comprised of the Great American Entertainment Company, a producer of live country music variety shows in South Carolina, and Dorothy Hamill International, parent of Dorothy Hamill's Ice Capades, a popular live figure skating show that tours North America.

IFE is an outgrowth of the Christian Broadcasting Network (CBN), Robertson's not-for-profit television ministry. In 1960, the Yale Law School graduate and son of a former U.S. Senator purchased a failing television station in Portsmouth, Virginia, for $37,000. With only one camera and virtually no operating capital, Robertson began preaching to local residents via television. Success was slow until 1963, when Robertson created the *700 Club,* an evangelical program once described as ''a hybrid of telethon, talk show and Sunday school class'' by *Time* magazine. The idea behind Robertson's *700 Club* was to find 700 viewers willing to support the program by donating $10 a month to cover basic operating expenses. Ultimately, more than 700 people donated to the operation, and by the mid-1970s the network was able to purchase two more television stations, one in Atlanta, Georgia, and the other in Dallas, Texas.

The popularity of the Christian Broadcasting Network did not soar until 1977 when CBN changed its name to CBN Satellite Services and became the first satellite-launched network on cable television, as well as the first network devoted entirely to religious programming. Financed primarily by viewer donations, CBN Satellite Services was considered by industry analysts to be a hazardous venture. The cable industry was still in its infant stages and there were no precedents on which Robertson could judge the success of a station devoted solely to Christian programming. At the same time, says *TV Communications,* ''the company's move to join Home Box Office and WTGC-Atlanta . . . served as a political 'plus' for the cable industry. Religious programming provided a comforting addition to pay cable's ''R''-rated movies, [which were] just new enough to have the public curious but still skeptical.'' Few in the industry expected the network's success to come as quickly as it did. Within its first year, CBN had signed on 3 million subscribers, and could boast more potential viewers than all satellite services combined. By 1979, CBN's subscription rate had grown to 5 million. The network's religious format was so popular it spawned its own competition: People That Love (PTL) Television and Trinity Broadcasting, both of which broadcast via the same satellite system as CBN.

CBN's initial cable television format consisted of one eight-hour programming block run three times daily. The network's cornerstone remained Robertson's *700 Club,* but programming also expanded to include a number of Christian-oriented children's programs, educational shows, concerts, and news updates. Although CBN began soliciting advertisers in 1977 (when it landed a $5 million advertising contract with Richardson-Vicks), the organization remained entirely non-profit, receiving about $5 million in viewer donations per year.

By 1981, CBN had 10.7 million subscribers and annual revenues of approximately $60 million. That year, the network underwent a second transformation, changing its name to CBN Cable Network and broadening its format to offer mainstream fare such as game shows, soap operas, and docu-dramas. Led by Robertson's son Tim—who got his start in the company at age 16 and worked his way up the ranks after graduating with a B.A. from Columbia University—CBN sought to become ''the place where everybody would turn for family programming.'' The younger Robertson chose to imitate the format of the three major networks—soap operas in the afternoon, news at five, movies in the evening—based on the assumption that most viewers were already accustomed to that format.

The fundamental way in which CBN sought to distinguish itself was through content. ''There's a yearning inside of people for the ultimate meaning in life,'' the elder Robertson told *Time* magazine in 1982. ''We hope to come up with programs that provide answers to that yearning. The problem is not just sex and violence on the major networks, it's the banality.'' To that end, CBN aired *Another Life,* a soap opera starring, as Robertson said: ''a mean, despicable, female J.R.,'' based on the famous character from the television series *Dallas*; ''a crazed person'' who courts her; and ''a nice Christian couple, around whom all this swirls.'' In addition, CBN began airing *The*

Waltons, a television series about a wholesome country family during the Great Depression, and a 26-week special on people who have had "miraculous encounters with God."

In 1982, CBN built a $38 million headquarters in Virginia Beach, complete with a state-of-the art studio, a university, and an executive office center built in the shape of a cross. CBN signed contracts with Tele-Communications, Inc. (TCI), and ATC, two of the nation's largest cable service providers, and by 1984 the network was beginning to turn a profit. As co-host of the *700 Club,* Pat Robertson was becoming a nationally known figure, using his daily "sermonettes" to comment on everything from the busing issue to U.S. trade with Taiwan, and blasting Hollywood entertainment industry for what he perceived as its active contribution to the moral decline of society. In 1988, Robertson unsuccessfully ran for President of the United States on the Republican ticket, using his platform to continue his attack on Hollywood and to trumpet the "traditional family values" that he shared with the network.

Throughout the early 1980s, the general public identified CBN primarily with Robertson and its religious programs; however, about 78 percent of its programming was devoted to entertainment. As the network grew under the direction of the younger Robertson, it sharpened its image as a family-oriented network by offering the so-called "golden oldies" of American television: family situation comedies such as *Father Knows Best* and *Hazel*; Westerns such as *Gunsmoke* and *Bonanza*; and detective series like *Remington Steele*. By 1988, CBN had taken on the name "The Family Channel" in a move to position itself as more than a religious network. That year, it also began developing original programming. One of its first ventures, *Bordertown,* an innovative rendering of the traditional Western series, became the number one original series on cable within a year of its introduction.

The network inaugurated yet another transformation in 1989 as CBN management became concerned that The Family Channel was growing too profitable to meet IRS requirements for a non-profit corporation. In order to protect CBN's non-profit status, the Robertsons joined forces with TCI Development Corp., a subsidiary of Tele-Communications Inc., to form International Family Entertainment Inc. (IFE), a holding company that would serve as parent organization for The Family Channel. In 1990, International Family Entertainment bought The Family Channel from CBN for $250 million in convertible securities. The Robertsons paid $150,000 for 4.5 million shares and a controlling interest in the company. Soon after the purchase, the two awarded themselves an additional 1.5 million shares. Tim Robertson became president. His father took on other executive duties, while continuing to host the *700 Club,* which remained in CBN's hands as a non-profit entity and was guaranteed a prime-time spot in the network. Initially, because The Family Channel was spun-off through convertible securities, CBN held 64.3 percent of IFE stock. It held no voting rights, however, and was thus able to retain its non-profit status.

By this time, The Family Channel was indisputably the top family-oriented network on the cable television system. Its subscriber rate of 48.5 million households far surpassed the 5 million or so subscribers to the Disney Channel, IFE's nearest competitor. Its original programs, *Rin Tin Tin—Canine Cop* and *T and T,* were moderately successful. A fourth original series, *Zorro,* debuted in 1990 and quickly took second place behind *Bordertown* as the most popular original series on basic cable. Robertson's conservative philosophy stood firmly behind every show that aired on The Family Channel. "You won't see Murder on Elm Street on the Family Channel," IFE's programming executive announced in 1990 in the *Christian Science Monitor*. The younger Robertson echoed that sentiment: "At 'fam' we say let's have programs that celebrate love and life. Let's talk about values between husbands and wives and children, where they can have loving, caring relationships in which children aren't smart alecks and the parents aren't buffoons." He added, "We feel there is very clearly an identifiable niche that exists there both for viewers and cable operators alike." If the elder Robertson can be credited with giving a voice to the thoughts of the conservative, religious right, his son deserves credit for marketing it with incredible business savvy.

The Family Channel was not without its detractors, however. Many media analysts argued that programs such as *Father Knows Best* and *Hazel* presented an overly idealized version of American families. Others stated that the profusion of violent war movies and Westerns did not conform to the network's declared intent of providing wholesome family-oriented programming. In defense, one Family Channel executive told the *Christian Science Monitor,* "We make exceptions for Westerns and movies because the violence is part of what actually went on and is far from most people's daily lives. They don't put fear in you of walking down a dark street at night or make you afraid to go camping."

Less than a year after The Family Channel became a for-profit entity, it began a $4 million marketing campaign entitled "Accentuate the Positive." The campaign ran for five weeks on ABC and CBS, as well as on a number of cable stations including TBS SuperStation, CNN, and ESPN. As a result of the new campaign, marketing costs jumped 27 percent in 1992. Programming and production costs grew by a similar percentage, as IFE continued to develop original programming, including three successful new series, *Big Brother Jake, The New Zorro* and *Maniac Mansion.* That year, IFE also began testing international markets when it entered into an agreement with Hyundai Corp. of South Korea, in which the automobile manufacturer advertised on The Family Channel and persuaded the South Korean government to authorize a "cable test run" of The Family Channel in its country.

In 1992, IFE made an initial public offering on the New York Stock Exchange which raised $46.2 million. According to the *Washington Post,* the Robertsons continued to hold 6 million voting shares, or 61 percent of the company, by then worth an estimated $96 million. Of the 3 million shares, the younger Robertson held 2.1 million and the elder held 900,000. In addition, Pat Robertson controlled the remaining 3 million shares through a charitable trust of which he was a beneficiary and the trustee. Although the trust produced no income in its early years, it could legally pay a beneficiary $2.4 million per year. Upon Robertson's death, the remaining trust would revert to CBN.

After the initial public offering, the Robertsons encountered some public criticism for earning large profits off the sale of an organization that, essentially, was founded through religious donations. "It may be as legal as can be," James Dunn of the Baptist Joint Committee on Public Affairs told *Newsweek* in 1994. "But to me it's immoral to build your business empire based on tax deductible gifts to a ministry." CBN remains Robertson's ministry and its officials believe differently, stating that Robertson's "business skills have enabled CBN to thrive in an environment that has crippled other ministries."

As CBN has thrived, so has IFE. In 1993, it acquired London-based TVS Entertainment PLC, parent company of MTM Entertainment for $94 million. The acquisition gave IFE an extensive library of family-friendly television programs, including *Hill Street Blues, The Bob Newhart Show* and *The Mary Tyler Moore Show.* It also provided IFE with a platform from which it could launch an entry into the British cable television market. Within a year of the TVS purchase, a United Kingdom version of The Family Channel was established. Initial success was slow, as subscribers complained that the channel did not air enough British programs, but within a year the network was making a concerted effort to deliver programs that reflected its traditional family values and also appealed to British tastes.

In 1992, IFE also began a trial run of programs for two potential new channels: Cable Health Club and the Game Channel. The following year, IFE launched Cable Health Club, a 24-hour health and fitness club. The Family Channel continued to air new programs in the U.S. which were well received by viewers, especially the six-part animated children's series *The World of Peter Rabbit and Friends.* In 1993, IFE ventured into live entertainment with the purchase of three theaters in Myrtle Beach, South Carolina, that showcase country music acts. Within the year, IFE added more clout to its live entertainment division with the purchase of Dorothy Hamill International, producer of Dorothy Hamill's Ice Capades, one of the stronger touring shows in the volatile live entertainment industry. Revenues in the company's first year after going public totaled $208 million.

In less than ten years, IFE transformed itself from a non-profit television ministry into an international entertainment company. Although the company remained committed to the principles on which The Family Channel was founded, it was now free to grow in fields that were previously off limits. Going into the mid-1990s, expansion seemed inevitable, given that the company held $140 million in cash reserves and had minimal debt. Further, the younger Robertson announced plans to establish The Family Channel throughout Europe on a country-by-country basis, and he believed that someday The Family Channel's international audience would outnumber its U.S. audience. However, there were a number of obstacles to overcome in the process of establishing networks across Europe—among them different regulations concerning cable systems, as well as the more delicate matter of cultural preferences, which ultimately dictate the success of any entertainment venture. During this period, the company sought to expand in the U.S. as well. In 1994, it made an unsuccessful $40-million bid for the Nostalgia Network Inc., and most likely will consider other acquisitions. Given its already strong position in the cable television market and the Robertsons' uncanny ability to turn a profit, IFE's future success seems certain.

Principal Subsidiaries: MTM Entertainment Inc.

Further Reading:

Fromson, Brett D., "Stock Sale to Multiply Robertsons' Riches," *Washington Post,* April 14, 1992, p. D1.

Gannan, Lynne, "Spreading the Gospel by Satellite," *TV Communications,* April 1, 1979, p. 35.

"Mr. Robertson's Global Family, *World Screen News,* February 1994, p. 38.

—Maura Troester

J Sainsbury plc

Stamford House
Stamford Street
London SE1 9LL
United Kingdom
(44) 1 71 921-6000
Fax: (44) 1 71 921-6132

Public Company
Incorporated: 1922 as J. Sainsbury Ltd.
Employees: 141,000
Sales: £10.6 billion ($18 billion)
Stock Exchanges: London
SICs: 5411 Grocery Stores; 5210 Lumber and Other Building Materials; 5261 Retail Nurseries and Garden Stores; 6552 Subdividers and Developers, Not Elsewhere Classified; 2030 Preserved Fruits and Vegetables

Supermarkets, hypermarkets, and other grocery outlets clustered tightly in the south of England form the nucleus of Britain's largest food and wine retailer: J Sainsbury plc, or Sainsbury's, as it is widely known. The company's expansion over a period of 125 years has been cautious but inexorable, accelerating in the latter decades of the century, and reaching overseas in the late 1980s. Unlike many of its competitors—which diversified into other business areas to counter the slow growth expected in the retail food industry—Sainsbury's continued to build the retailing businesses in which it excelled.

By the mid-1990s, that empire encompassed over 1,100 retail locations, including the namesake chain of over 340 supermarkets; a controlling stake in the Homebase chain of 76 do-it-yourself retail centers; ten Savacentre hypermarket stores; and Shaw's Supermarkets, a chain of 87 supermarkets in the northeast United States. Late in 1994, Sainsbury's increased its overseas presence with the purchase of a 50 percent stake in Washington, D.C.'s Giant Food Inc., a 159-store supermarket chain.

Sainsbury's is not only Britain's largest retailer of food and wine but also its most respected, according to nationwide surveys of industry analysts and company directors. The company has earned top or near-top ratings for product and service quality, successful development, profitable pricing, overall financial performance, advertising and marketing, and superior management, as well as recruitment, training, and retention of high-caliber employees. More than one-third of Sainsbury's employees own shares in the company.

Sainsbury's was off to a romantic but practical start in 1869 when two young employees of neighboring London shops met, married, and started a small dairy store in their three-story Drury Lane home. Mary Ann Staples, 19, had grown up in her father's dairy business. John James Sainsbury, 25, had worked for a hardware merchant and grocer. Their shop was a success from the start, as both John and Mary Ann had the business knowledge and capacity for hard work that it took to win the loyalty of the local trade. Their passion for order, cleanliness, and high-quality merchandise made the shop an inviting place, in contrast to the prevalent clutter of many tiny family-owned shops and the insanitary conditions of the street vendors' stalls and carts.

Seven years later the Sainsburys opened a second shop in a newly developed section of town and moved into the upper portion of the building. Within a few years, they had opened several similar branches, planning to have a shop for each of their sons to manage when he grew up. By the time their six sons were adults, the branches far outnumbered them. Yet caution has always been characteristic of Sainsbury expansion; they regularly passed up opportunities to buy groups or chains of stores, preferring to develop each new store independently.

The passion for high quality led them to a turning point in 1882, when they opened a branch in Croydon. They used advanced design and materials that had an elegance not attempted in the other shops and made the store easy to keep clean. The walls, floor, and counter fronts were tiled, the countertops were marble slabs. Customers were seated on bentwood chairs. The store's cleanliness—still a rarity in food shops of that time—and elaborate decor helped attract more prosperous customers; it was an instant success. Several similar shops were added during that decade, while Sainsbury's also developed a less elaborate design for suburban branches opened during those years. In these, business could be done through open windows, as in the common market areas, but the design also attracted customers to come into the store to see a greater variety of food.

In 1891, Sainsbury's moved its headquarters to Blackfriars, where it remained throughout the 20th century. The location provided easy access to wholesale markets and transportation. To obtain the best quality in food, Sainsbury's always kept in close touch with suppliers, and it controlled and distributed stock from a central depot until the 1960s.

By the turn of the century sons John Benjamin, George, and Arthur were working in the family business; they and other company employees were trained with equal care and attention to detail. Alfred and Paul went through the same training when they joined the company in 1906 and 1921 respectively. Frank, the third son, took up poultry and pork farming in 1902 and became a major supplier.

During this time, in terms of numbers, rivals seemed to be outdistancing Sainsbury's. Lipton's, the largest, had 500 stores. It took Sainsbury's another 14 years to open its 115th branch. But Sainsbury's continued to place the highest priority on quality, taking the time to weigh each decision, whether it meant researching suppliers for a new product, assessing the reliability of a new supplier, or measuring the business potential of a new site.

The outbreak of World War I slowed expansion plans even further. Rationing and shortages of food, particularly fresh produce, led to the creation of grocery departments selling jams, spices, potted meat, and flour—all bearing Sainsbury's own label. Women began attending the training classes at the Blackfriars headquarters, to replace the male employees who had left for military service. Some worked in the packing plant for Sainsbury-label foods; others served as salespeople in the stores.

Eldest son John Benjamin took much of the initiative in the interwar years, adding new grocery lines while retaining his father's insistence on high quality. By 1922 there were 136 branches, many of them along the new suburban rail lines, and the firm was incorporated. Mary Ann died in 1927 and her husband in 1928, leaving John Benjamin in charge. By this time, so much public attention accompanied branch openings that when Sainsbury's opened a branch in Cambridge, it published an apology in the local newspaper for the impact of a huge opening day crowd. Altogether, 57 new branches were opened between 1919 and 1929, and the gilded glass Sainsbury sign had become a universal symbol of a spacious, orderly interior displaying foods of the finest quality.

There was an apparent break with tradition in 1936 when Sainsbury's bought the Thoroughgood stores, a chain of nine shops in Britain's Midlands. But the purchase was made with the same care and emphasis on quality that had distinguished all other Sainsbury branches. Stamford House, which had been built in 1912 as an extension of the headquarters at Blackfriars, was extended to provide more space for the centralized supply procurement and distribution that maintained quality control for all branches, which by this time numbered 244. Specially designed lightweight vans had replaced horse-drawn vehicles, further speeding deliveries.

World War II not only slowed Sainsbury's growth, through shortages of food and labor, but also brought the stores into the line of fire. Some branches were totally destroyed; others were extensively damaged. Vehicles carrying mobile shops carried on trade as far as possible in the areas affected by the Blitz. But the evacuation of bomb-damaged areas made it impossible to carry on the centralized procurement and distribution operation that had provided efficiency, economy, and standardization of products and services. Along with other wartime restrictions, this caused sales to dwindle to half the prewar level.

John Benjamin's sons Alan and Robert, who had shared the general manager's post since their father's retirement in 1938, became aware of the crucial role of communications during the trying days of this wartime decentralization. The *JS Journal,* begun in 1946 (and its sister publication, the *Employee Report,* begun in the late 1970s) exemplified the thorough job of reporting that kept staff members abreast of company developments and business conditions. Both publications have won national awards for excellence.

Long before the last of the wartime restrictions were lifted in 1954, the brothers had begun an aggressive recovery program. Basic operations were recentralized to regain the economies of scale that kept prices down while retaining a substantial profit margin. Alan studied America's burgeoning supermarkets and opened the first self-service Sainsbury's in June, 1950 in Croydon, where his grandfather had opened his "turning point" store nearly 70 years earlier.

Expansion in the 1950s often meant converting existing stores to supermarkets in addition to adding new outlets. In 1955, the 7,500-square-foot Sainsbury's at Lewisham was considered the largest supermarket in Europe. By 1969, Sainsbury supermarkets had an average of 10,000 square feet of space. Supermarkets and hypermarkets in the 1980s would triple that amount.

John Benjamin and Arthur were the only two of the founders' sons whose own sons joined the family business. Arthur's son James, who had joined the company in 1926, was named Commander of the Order of the British Empire for his accomplishments. He created new factory facilities at Sainsbury's headquarters in 1936 and also set up the Haverhill line of meat products.

John Benjamin's sons Alan and Robert, and Alan's son John, were also honored for their work. Alan was made Baron Sainsbury of Drury Lane in 1962, and his son John was made Baron Sainsbury of Preston Candover in 1989. Robert was knighted in 1967. Alan and Robert shared the presidency of Sainsbury's, John was chairman, and Robert's son David was deputy chairman through the 1980s.

With typical caution, Sainsbury's did not actually use the word supermarket in its own communications until the late 1960s, even though it owned almost 100. Nonetheless, the company was at the forefront of new technology. In 1961, for example, Sainsbury's became Britain's first food retailer to computerize its distribution system. In the late 1980s, electronic cash registers at the checkout counter were replaced by scanners. Multibuy, a special feature of the scanning system, automatically applied a discount to multiple purchases of certain designated items. Spaceman, a microcomputer planning system, used on-screen graphics to plot the allocation of merchandise to specific shelf space in the stores. Electric funds transferred at the point of sale (EFTPOS), allowed customers to use debit cards to make purchases.

Sainsbury's centenary, 1969, sparked a series of rapid changes. Alan's son, John, became chairman of a new management tier, which reported directly to the board of directors. Departmental directors were given greater responsibility for operating functions to strengthen the centralized control that had always been company policy. With ordering, warehousing, and distribution computerized, strict controls on the speeded-up activity were vital. Sainsbury's became a public company in 1973, two years after making a name change: the period after the initial J was dropped.

Personnel policies at Sainsbury's adhered closely to the principles established at its founding: thorough training, open communication, and continuing training on the job. The company recruited actively at schools and universities, preferring to "grow its own talent," but holding employees to high standards of performance. Along with other leading companies and the City University Business School, Sainsbury's conducted a practical management course, the Management MBA. Sainsbury's employees participated in profit sharing and share option schemes.

The company's community involvement was also active, taking many forms. John Sainsbury addressed the London Conference on saving the ozone layer early in 1989. The only retailer invited to take part in the conference and the associated exhibition, he presented details of the technological changes made in Sainsbury's aerosol products and plant operations to eliminate chlorofluorocarbons from their operations. Incubation of small start-up businesses, arts sponsorships, and grand-scale charity drives were other ongoing projects.

Forces within the grocery industry compelled Sainsbury's to begin a program of diversification within the retail category. Increased competition from discounters threatened to squeeze profit margins. Creeping market saturation and flat population growth combined to intensify competition as well. Sainsbury's began to make significant additions to its nonfood merchandise for the first time. The company's first petrol station, a convenience for shoppers, was opened in 1974 at a Cambridge store. To gain the economies of direct supplier-to-store deliveries, Sainsbury's formed a joint venture with British Home Stores in 1975, launching a chain of hypermarkets—huge stores combining grocery items and hard goods—called Savacentre. Sainsbury's retained control of all food-related operations, leaving nonfood lines to its partner until 1988, when Savacentre became a wholly owned subsidiary of Sainsbury's.

Homebase, a chain of upscale do-it-yourself stores, was in the planning stage by 1979. Sainsbury's owned 75 percent of this joint venture, and Grand Bazaar Innovations Bon Marché, Belgium's largest retailer, owned the remaining 25 percent. The partners opened their first Homebase home and garden center in 1981, and had expanded the chain to 76 locations by the mid-1990s.

Sainsbury's looked to overseas markets for growth opportunities as well. In 1983, the company began to amass shares in Shaw's Supermarkets, a New England supermarket chain. Founded in 1860, Shaw's heritage of carrying high-quality food at the lowest prices meshed well with the ideals of the British firm. And like Sainsbury's, Shaw's has also been at the forefront of computer technology. By 1987, Sainsbury's had completed the purchase of 100 percent of the 60 stores in Massachusetts, Maine, and New Hampshire, and had plans to open additional stores in that area. The company boosted its holdings in the United States with the 1994 acquisition of 50 percent of Giant Food Inc., a Washington, D.C.-area chain. Sainsbury's was expected to purchase the remaining shares of the 159-store chain by the end of the decade. Closer to home, Sainsbury's opened a Savacentre hypermarket in Scotland in 1984.

Sainsbury's also developed a powerful private-label program. By the mid-1990s, its own-label products generated 66 percent of total sales. Three of the company's proprietary products in particular made headlines in the early 1990s. Novon, a laundry detergent introduced in 1992, marked Sainsbury's move into head-to-head competition with national brands. Within just six weeks of Novon's launch, the company's share of the detergents market doubled to 20 percent. In 1994, Sainsbury's changed the formulation and packaging of its own cola beverage, reintroducing it as "Classic Cola." The budget-priced cola featured red cans with italicized letters and a stripe; ads promoted the drink's "Original American Taste." Within just a few weeks, Classic Cola won 13 percent of Britain's total cola market, while sales of both Coca-Cola and Pepsi at Sainsbury stores plummeted. Not surprisingly, an incensed Coca-Cola demanded that Sainsbury's modify its packaging, claiming that the brands' similarity prevented customers from discerning between them. The supermarket chain acquiesced, but significantly decreased the rival brand's share of shelf space in stores.

Another highly successful, but less confrontational, private-label product also broke new ground for the category. In 1993, the company launched its own periodical, *Sainsbury's: The Magazine*. Like the publications it competed with, *Sainsbury's: The Magazine* featured illustrated pieces on fashion, health, and cooking, as well as national brand advertising. Sold only in Sainsbury's supermarkets, the magazine became "the most successful new magazine venture in Britain in many years," according to a November 1994 *Forbes* article.

While other family-run firms have encountered problems with succession or overly conservative management, Sainsbury's innovative marketing, aggressive international expansion, and cautious borrowing seemed to portend a promising future for the company. Under the leadership of Chairman, CEO, and great grandson of the founders David Sainsbury in the early 1990s, sales had tripled from £3 billion in 1985 to £10.6 billion in 1994. Net income more than quintupled from £108 million in 1985 to £503 million in 1993, then plunged to £142 million the following year.

Principal Subsidiaries: Homebase Ltd. (75%); J Sainsbury Developments Ltd.; J Sainsbury (Channel Islands) Ltd.; Savacentre Ltd.; Shaw's Supermarkets, Inc. (U.S.); Giant Foods Inc. (50%) (U.S.).

Further Reading:

The First 120 Years of Sainsbury's, 1869–1989, London: Sainsbury's, 1989.

JS 100: The Story of Sainsbury's, London: Sainsbury's, 1969.

Nicholas, Ruth, "Sainsbury Cola Gives in to Coke," *Marketing,* May 12, 1994. p. 1.

Rogers, David, "Britain's Supermarkets: An Industry in Turmoil," *Supermarket Business,* August 1989, p. 37.

Stogel, Chuck, "The Once and Future King?," *Brandweek,* May 8, 1995, p. 34.

Williams, B. R., *The Best Butter in the World: A History of Sainsbury's,* London: Ebury, 1994.

Wilsher, Peer. "Housekeeping?," *Management Today,* December 1993, p. 38.

Zwiebach, Elliot, "Sainsbury to Buy 50 percent of Giant's Voting Stock," *Supermarket News,* October 10, 1994, p. 1.

—updated by April Dougal Gasbarre

Jaguar Cars, Ltd.

Brown's Lane
Allesley
Coventry CV5 9DR
England
(011) 44 12 03402121

Wholly Owned Subsidiary of Ford Motor Company
Founded: 1922 as Swallow Sidecar Company
Employees: 250
Sales: $2 billion
SICs: 5013 Motor Vehicle Supplies & New Parts

Jaguar Cars, Ltd., is one of the most famous luxury automobile manufacturers in the world. With its sleek lines, leather interiors, and smooth engines, Jaguar is the car of choice for wealthy brokers who work on Wall Street in New York and the *nouveau riche* in Japan who shop on Tokyo's Ginza. However, like many other luxury car and sports car producers, Jaguar experienced many financial difficulties during the 1980s. Although the company was purchased by Ford Motor Company in 1990 for $2.6 billion, sales remain far lower than those posted by competitors like Mercedes Benz and Rolls Royce.

The driving force behind Jaguar, William Lyons, was born on September 4, 1901, in Blackpool, a town in the county of Lancashire, England. Uninterested in academics as a teenager, he was on the verge of entering the shipbuilding industry when his father encouraged him to work at Crossley Motors, Ltd., and attend engineering classes during the evening. Crossley was a distinguished automobile manufacturer during the early twentieth century. By the time Lyons went to work at its factory in Manchester, near the end of World War I, Crossley's chassis were used by the British government for military ambulances, staff cars, and small trucks. The success of the war years carried into the early 1920s, and sales of Crossley cars increased. Lyons was unhappy at Crossley, however, and he soon left the company to work for Brown and Mallalieu, an automobile distributor, as a junior salesman.

In the early 1920s Lyons met William Walmsley, a veteran of World War I whose hobby was building sidecars for motorcycles. Lyons approached Walmsley, a neighbor of his parents in Blackpool, about setting up a joint effort to manufacture and sell sidecars. Walmsley was reluctant at first, but was finally overwhelmed by Lyons' enthusiasm. The two men procured a loan of 1,000 pounds from a local bank and established the Swallow Sidecar Company in 1922. While Walmsley focused on building the company's sidecars, Lyons concentrated on hiring labor, renting a working place, and advertising. Soon the company was garnering a reputation for its sidecars, which were used during motorcycling competitions. By 1926 the rapidly expanding firm was operating from three different locations in Blackpool and had hired numerous employees. The company's rapid growth prompted Lyons and Walmsley to leave Blackpool and relocate in Coventry, where there was more than enough space to accommodate further expansion. In 1928 about 50 employees moved to Coventry to continue working at the renamed Swallow Sidecar and Coach Building Company.

With the move to Coventry, Swallow began to produce coachwork for chassis provided by Fiat, Austin, and Alvis. The Fiat-Swallow, with its two-door salon coachwork, impressive radiator, and two-tone coloring, was an immediate success, and soon the company was manufacturing 50 cars per week. In 1929 the company unveiled its Standard-Swallow; two years later, brand new cars such as the SS1 and the SS2 (which could cruise at 50 mph) were introduced. The SS1 was a low-built, two-door, sports coupe that featured two passenger seats and room in the back of the body for a large luggage box. In order to increase sales, Lyons encouraged owners of Swallow cars to enter motoring competitions. The first SS1 made its racing debut in the 1932 Torquay 1,000-mile rally.

The decade of the 1930s was a watershed period for the company. Sales of Swallow cars were increasing at such a fast pace that by 1933 the company counted 18 distributors worldwide. Continental agents included those in The Netherlands, Denmark, Austria, Portugal, Belgium, and Switzerland; non-European agents were located in Calcutta, Delhi, Cape Town, and Johannesburg. In the spring of the same year, Swallow manufactured its first touring sedan, a car that featured coachwork on a SS1 chassis. The new sedan sold well from the start. During the mid-1930s, the SS product line offered four engine sizes, two chassis, and a choice of sport coupe, salon or touring coachwork. Comfort in the car's interior design, the elegance of the car's body lines, and its reliable engine performance began to garner the company a reputation in such prestigious auto publications as *The Standard Car Review, The Autocar, The Motor, Motorsport,* and *The Motorist.*

The success of Swallow convinced Lyons to exercise his purchase option agreement with Walmsley. The partnership was dissolved, Walmsley resigned, and a new company, SS Cars, Ltd., was formed. The company was incorporated in 1933, and soon afterwards offered the sale of its stock to the public on the London Exchange. Lyons become the chairman and managing director of SS Cars. He assumed total control of all its operations. Although the sidecar business remained lucrative, Lyons kept careful watch over this portion of the firm, and thought it best to organize its operations as an entirely separate entity, called the Swallow Coachbuilding Company, in 1935. With the administrative duties out of the way, and a reorganization of the company complete, Lyons turned his attention to advertising. He wanted a brand new name for his cars that would capture the imagination of the motoring enthusiast. The Nelson advertising agency, hired by Lyons to create a new image for his automobiles, selected the name Jaguar.

The first SS Jaguar 100 was introduced in 1935 and, as the company dropped the SS1 and SS2 product lines, sales for its new unit increased dramatically. The firm's first all-steel car was brought out in 1937. It featured a broader body, overhead valves, and a choice of 3.5, 2.7, or 1.8 litre engines. The 3.5-litre model was the company's first car to reach 100 mph. Armed with a work force of over 1,500 in Coventry, by August of 1938 SS Cars, Ltd. was producing more than 5,000 cars per year. Profits continued to rise, and the company's success seemed unlimited.

Unfortunately, the onset of World War II abruptly halted production at SS Cars, Ltd. All of the company's factories and plants were reconfigured for military use by the British government. Within a very short time, SS Cars, Ltd., was the official repair company for the Whitley bomber. It also was contracted to make parts for airplanes such as the Stirling, the Mosquito, the Spitfire, and the Lancaster bomber. One bright spot during the wartime era was the purchase of up-to-date equipment by the Ministry of War for the company's use in its factories. The only portion of the company that maintained its pre-war level of production was the sidecar shop, which manufactured over 10,000 units for the British army's motor corps.

Management at SS Cars, Ltd., announced in early 1945 that it intended to change its name to Jaguar Cars, Ltd. A short time later, the symbol of the SS hexagon was replaced with the new ''J'' and Jaguar symbols. Jaguar was now a completely independent British-operated and managed company—the fulfillment of William Lyons' dream. Without wasting a moment, Lyons decided that Jaguar could increase sales and improve its engine design by engaging in even more racing competitions than before the war. This decision resulted in the formation of a Jaguar racing team that competed in all the major car races. The SS Jaguar 100 was the winning car in the Palos Verdes road trials in the United States in 1947. Other racing competitions, such as the *Concours d'Elegance,* run in the city of Brussels were also won by drivers in Jaguar 100s. The additional publicity helped the company export its first cars to the United States and Australia, an indication that the company's reputation had reached international proportions. By the end of the decade, Jaguar's name was synonymous with the British export business.

During the decade of the 1950s, Jaguar experienced unprecedented success. Back in 1928, when the company moved from Blackpool to Coventry, there had been only 40,000 square feet of floor space for employees to build cars; by 1950, expansion at the Coventry assembly plant had surpassed 600,000 square feet. In 1934 the company reported that exports amounted to less than ten percent of total sales; by 1951 exports amounted to 84 percent of total sales.

In 1952 over 20 constabularies throughout Britain were using Jaguars as police cars, and arrangements were made for police mechanics to attend the company's repair school in Coventry. The Jaguar racing team won the prestigious 24-hour LeMans race in 1953 as growing numbers of drivers competing in international races began to use Jaguar engines in their own vehicles. As Jaguar team drivers earned plaudits and laurels for Coventry, export sales continued to increase, particularly in the United States. By 1954 management decided to form Jaguar Cars North American Corporation in recognition of Jaguar's large share of the sports car market. In 1956 the British government formally recognized William Lyons for building the company and developing such a remarkably successful export business by naming him a Knight Bachelor. But just as gratifying to Sir William were reports published in both *Road & Track* and *Popular Mechanics* magazines in which readers selected Jaguar as the world's most popular sports car, with Porsche a distant second in both polls. Jaguar had become a household word in the automotive industry.

During the 1960s Jaguar implemented a comprehensive ''expansion through acquisition'' strategy. In May 1960 the company doubled its size with the purchase of Daimler Company, Ltd., of Coventry. Unrelated to the famous German car company Daimler-Benz, the British firm was an old and distinguished manufacturer of automobiles, bus and coach chassis, and armored vehicles for the military. With this acquisition, the number of Jaguar employees doubled to 8,000. Guy Motors, a small manufacturer of trucks and trolleybuses, was purchased in 1961. Within a few years, Jaguar management had revitalized the company and re-engineered its factory to produce a new line of trucks and farm tractors.

The most important acquisition during this time, however, involved the takeover of Coventry Climax Engines, Ltd., a small but world-famous producer of racing and passenger car engines. Other acquisitions made by the Jaguar Group during these years included Lanchester Motor Company, Ltd., Barker and Company, Ltd., Henry Meadows, Ltd., and Newtherm Oil Burners, Ltd.

As Sir William Lyons grew older and realized that retirement was drawing near, he became increasingly concerned about the survival of his company. He felt that trade unionism, and the effects of its wage demands, contributed to rampant inflation and harmed the automobile industry in Britain. With these concerns uppermost in his mind, in 1966 Sir William decided—perhaps unwisely—to merge Jaguar Cars, Ltd., with the British Motor Corporation, an organization that controlled and operated a growing number of British car manufacturers. Lyons retained his title of chairman and managing director, and appointed Raymond England and Robert Grice as joint deputy managing directors to coordinate administration and manufacturing during the early months of the merger. In 1968 Lyons relinquished his managing director title, although he remained chairman and chief executive; England and Grice were appointed joint managing directors. But the year ended on a sour note when British Motor Corporation announced its merger with British Leyland. The new British Leyland Motor Corporation opened for business in May 1968.

By 1972, when Jaguar Cars, Ltd., celebrated the 50th anniversary of its founding, the company had almost ceased to exist as an independent manufacturer. Although the brand new XJ series of Jaguar cars were designed and produced during this time, British Leyland was in the throes of severe financial difficulties. With all the old management team from Jaguar gone, the company's departments were incorporated into the Leyland administrative structure. When a government report revealed that Leyland was in debt, management responded by implementing a comprehensive reorganization that eliminated Jaguar as an operating entity and replaced it with a division called Leyland Cars. Jaguar Cars, Ltd., was now a ''committee'' within the administrative hierarchy of British Leyland. By 1980 Jaguar workers were still engaged in car manufacturing, but were without management power. Morale among Jaguar employees in Coventry was at its lowest ebb.

A change in management at British Leyland, coupled with a desire to reinvigorate Jaguar so that it could sell more cars, led to the appointment of John Egan as the company's new chief executive. Egan immediately assumed greater control over Jaguar's marketing and exporting plans. He also revived Jaguar's role in international racing competitions. In the United States, the name Jaguar Cars, Ltd. was used once again, while Jaguar Deutschland GmbH was formed in West Germany. The XJ-S sports coupes and XJ salons began to sell in significantly larger quantities than any time in the previous 10 years. By 1983 sales of Jaguar cars in the United States amounted to over 15,000, and sales in other countries registered rapid improvement. Under Egan's leadership, the company regained its name, Jaguar Cars, Ltd., and in 1985 the firm was given its freedom—Jaguar Cars, Ltd., was spun-off and became an independent company.

Despite its successful push for independence, quality control problems plagued many of Jaguar's final products. Problems with complicated and unreliable cooling and electrical systems in the XJ models began to drive away customers. Sales dropped from a high of 50,000 units in 1989 to 30,000 in 1990; pre-tax profits decreased from $150 million in 1988 to a loss of approximately $25 million by 1990.

In 1990, as a result of these problems, Ford Motor Company acquired Jaguar for $2.6 billion. Ford removed Egan and appointed its own man, Nicholas V. Scheele, as the company chairman and chief executive officer. With the unlimited purse of Ford, the new chairman began a comprehensive reorganization of Jaguar, including a cost-cutting strategy that eliminated half of the company's employees (from 12,000 down to 6,000), the improvement of the fragile electrical system in all XJ models, and the overhaul of the assembly line in Coventry.

In 1994 sales of Jaguar cars rebounded to 40,000 units and sales increased to $2 billion. It is Jaguar's hope that new management and Ford's financial backing will enable the company to regain the reputation that it had for years as one of the world's preeminent luxury car manufacturers.

Further Reading:

Flynn, Julia, ''Is the Jinx Finally Off Jaguar?'' *Business Week,* October 10, 1994, p. 62.

''Leather, Luxury, and Losses: Jaguar and SAAB,'' *Economist,* July 17, 1993, p. 65.

Taylor, Alex, ''Shaking Up Jaguar,'' *Fortune,* September 6, 1993, pp. 65–68.

Whyte, Andrew, *Jaguar: The Definitive History of a Great British Car,* Somerset: Patrick Stevens Ltd., 1985.

—Thomas Derdak

Jayco Inc.

P.O. Box 460
Middlebury, Indiana 46540
U.S.A.
(219) 825-5861
Fax: (219) 825-7354

Private Company
Incorporated: 1967
Employees: 1,287
Sales: $205 million
SICs: 3716 Motor Homes

Jayco, Inc. is a leading manufacturer of recreation vehicles (RVs), including travel trailers, truck campers, and motorhomes, and is the second largest producer of towable RVs in the world. The company also performs van conversions and is active in Australia through an affiliated company, Jayco Caravan Manufacturing, Inc. Jayco grew rapidly during the late 1980s and early 1990s, more than tripling in size.

Jayco is the progeny of inventor and entrepreneur Lloyd J. Bontrager. Bontrager was working for a recreational vehicle manufacturer in northern Indiana in the mid-1960s. The burgeoning RV industry was growing rapidly at the time as America's baby-boom families took to the highways with campers in tow. The innovative Bontrager had made important contributions to his employer, including the development of new camping trailers and the creation of the company's sewing department. He had also set up and managed an RV manufacturing plant for the company. Importantly, Bontrager invented a lifter system for fold-down camping trailers that made the campers much easier to pop up and close.

Despite his success at the company, Bontrager was frustrated. He believed that he could build a better trailer if given the freedom to do so by his employer. At the urging of his wife, Bertha, Lloyd decided to strike out on his own. He began experimenting with new fold-down trailer designs at his family farm in the northern Indiana town of Middlebury. Working out of two chicken houses and a barn, Bontrager managed to develop and patent a lifter system for fold-down trailers that was much easier to use than any other mechanism on the market. He quit his job late in 1967 and started his own company, Jayco Inc., a name he derived from his own middle name. Bontrager was joined in the venture by two partners: Clarence Lambright, who was put in charge of purchasing, and Bud Copsey, an investor. Bertha Bontrager did the bookkeeping, and Lloyd's sons helped with design and production.

Bontrager hired Glen Riegsecker early in 1968 as his first salaried employee at a wage of $2 per hour. Riegsecker helped to transform the barn and chicken houses into assembly-line RV production facilities. In those buildings, the Bontragers developed three prototype campers; the JayEagle, JayHawk, and JayRobin. Orders began rolling in for the innovative fold-down campers, which could be pulled behind a vehicle and easily popped up at a campsite. The fledgling company managed to sell, primarily through local dealers, 132 fold-down campers in its first year of operation. By the end of 1968 the company had a work force of 15 and was beginning to outgrow its farm production plant.

Early in 1969 Bontrager hired his neighbor, Allen Yoder, Jr., to become the company's national sales manager. Yoder was working as a mortgage lender at a local bank at the time but was enthused about the opportunity to join the growing Jayco. With Yoder exploiting the spiraling nationwide demand for campers, Jayco's output soared during 1969 and 1970. Jayco left its farm factory in 1969 and moved to a newly constructed plant nearby. Then, in 1970, the company added another plant in Harper, Kansas, to serve Jayco's surging customer base in the western United States. Incredibly, Jayco shipped more than 2,000 of its easy-to-use, high-quality, fold-down campers in 1970 to both U.S. and Canadian dealers. To keep workers inspired, Lloyd and Bertha promised an all-you-can-eat chicken dinner for the entire staff every time that the company met its production quotas; that effort gave birth to the annual company family picnic, replete with food, games, and a greased pig contest.

Besides its successful fold-down camper line, Jayco also experimented with other projects during its first few years. Among them was the short-lived Camp-n-Cruise, a fold-down style camper built on a pontoon boat. A more successful innovation was the JayThrush, an extension to the Jay product line and the largest Jayco camper. Subsequently, Jayco introduced the hefty JayKing, which was the first fold-down camper ever to offer full-height countertops and a three-cubic-foot refrigerator.

Just as important to the company's success as its new products, however, was its management style. Bontrager placed a special emphasis on developing good relations with his dealers, and even began inviting them to the company's picnics. He also believed that all of the employees should work together with the trust and respect shared by a family.

Jayco bought out another camper manufacturer in 1971, which helped it to produce 3,500 campers that year. Jayco's sales continued to increase in 1972 and 1973. Meanwhile, the energetic Bontrager became involved in other pursuits. He became an avid pilot, for example, and was hospitalized for several months following a nearly fatal crash. Prior to the crash, the Bontragers ventured to Australia to meet a friend, Charles Motely, who had started an RV business there. They struck a deal with Motley that lead to a partnership lasting into the 1990s. Within a year Jayco was shipping components to Motley's plant in Australia. While Bontrager was in the hospital, moreover, Yoder and other Jayco employees developed the

Sportster, a slide-in camper designed to fit a pick-up truck bed. Also in 1972, Jayco bought the Pioneer Boat Company and began manufacturing fishing boats.

Among Jayco's most successful products during the early 1970s was the JayWren travel trailer, its first camper that was not a fold-down. The trailer was unique in that it was only seven feet high—small enough to fit in a standard garage—yet still allowed plenty of head room for the average consumer. As with other Jayco products, Lloyd Bontrager played an important role in the hands-on development of the JayWren. The introduction of the JayWren, combined with fat sales gains for other Jayco products, pushed the company's shipments to $11 million during 1972. Jayco brought out its first mini-motorhome early in 1973 and later that year introduced the first fold-down camper with dual axles. Jayco also expanded into Canada when it purchased Ontario-based Aero Leisure Products. By the end of 1973 Jayco was supplying a network of 235 dealers in Canada and the United States.

Jayco's success during the late 1960s and early 1970s was largely a result of its management philosophy, which fostered innovation, quality, and service. But it was also a corollary of the red-hot North American RV fad, which resulted in annual RV sales of more than 500,000 annually by 1993. Thus, when the energy crises of the mid-1970s dawned, Jayco and many other RV manufacturers suffered. Indeed, by 1974 the U.S. RV industry was shipping little more than half the number units ordered one year earlier. Jayco was forced to shutter its Kansas and Canadian plants and to temporarily discontinue production of minimotorhomes. Work force reductions and cost-cutting measures were enacted as part of an effort to keep the company afloat.

As they would in future recessions, Jayco managers refused to acknowledge the energy crunch as a setback. Instead, they used the slowdown as an opportunity to diversify into other markets. Jayco increased its boat-building activity, for example, and built and sold some experimental products. But the company also continued to invent new fold-down camper products. It started selling the Flipper in 1975, for example, which was effectively a sideways (vertical) fold-down, designed to be pulled behind subcompact cars; the product failed to gain acceptance in the marketplace, however, and was discontinued in 1976. Jayco also started building campers for full-size truck beds, which would particularly appeal to the hunting market.

The energy crunch subsided in 1977 and 1978, and Jayco's revenues climbed back to early 1970s levels. Jayco resumed the manufacture of mini-motorhomes, and new production facilities were added to allow Jayco to produce its own cushions, drapes, seats, tents, and other parts and accessories for its campers. Lloyd Bontrager's son, Wilbur, began assuming a greater leadership role in the company during that period. Like his father, he made contributions to product design. In 1977, for instance, he helped develop a domed roof for fold-down campers that would shed water and proved stronger than conventional roofs. He also helped to develop overhead cabinets for campers.

The respite from the mid-1970s downturn was fleeting. A second energy crunch hit the RV industry in 1979 and through the early 1980s. Total industry shipments plunged to a ten-year low of just 181,400. Jayco's shipments plummeted by about 50 percent and many of its competitors threw in the towel. Jayco itself exited some of its markets, including the mini-motorhome segment. It was able to survive, though, by focusing on its traditional core business of fold-down trailers. In that slice of the industry, Jayco managed to boost its status during the late 1970s to become the third largest manufacturer of fold-downs in the country. Jayco also managed to gain by penetrating the European market in a partnership with British-based Conway Campers, which produced the tent-like camping product called the Conway Cottage Camper. Importantly, Jayco developed a line of light-weight economy travel trailers—the Featherlite I and II—that were designed with fuel efficiency in mind.

Jayco was rewarded after the early 1980s slowdown by surging RV markets and significantly reduced industry competition. Jayco became determined to capitalize on the recovery by becoming more marketing-oriented with efforts to learn exactly what customers wanted. To that end, Jayco introduced a new line of travel and fold-down campers targeted at the budget-conscious consumer. These campers were referred to as the ''J'' line (and, later, the Jay Series). Jayco also innovated new products, some of which eventually failed, including a four-wheeled travel trailer that resembled a motorhome without a cab, and the JayTiki fold-down camper from which part of the living area flipped out of the trailer and onto the ground. Finally, Jayco began to cull customer loyalty during the mid-1980s with its ''Safari Club'' for Jayco RV owners.

By 1985 Jayco had not only left the recession behind but was enjoying its greatest growth spurt ever. Indeed, sales of Jayco's diversified product line were skyrocketing throughout North America. Unfortunately, the optimism that permeated the company's work force was quelled by a tragic accident. On Easter Sunday of that year, Lloyd Bontrager, sons Wendell and Marcus, and a research and development worker named Nelson Hershberger were killed when the plane Lloyd was piloting went down in a storm. Bontrager's wishes for Jayco were summed up in a letter he addressed to employees shortly before his death: ''Here at Jayco we try to provide a pleasant Christian atmosphere where we can all work together in harmony. We believe we are all God's children, and as such we deserve mutual respect, honor, and fair treatment. This is as true for our dealers and customers as it is for those of us who work in the offices or the manufacturing plants.''

One month after Bontrager's death, Jayco's board appointed Al Yoder, Jr., to serve as president of the still privately held company; Bertha Bontrager became chairman of the board. The 57-year-old Yoder had been a key contributor to Jayco since he joined the company in 1969. He was also very active as a leader in major RV industry associations and had helped to develop the first television program devoted entirely to the RV lifestyle. Jayco continued to prosper. In fact, its growth pace quickened for a number of reasons. Among other trends benefiting the industry, fuel prices were low, baby boomers were beginning to buy campers to take their kids camping, and outdoor activities were becoming more popular.

As demand increased, Jayco's financial performance improved. Those gains were largely the result of initiatives pushed by Yoder. For example, Yoder commenced an aggressive drive to improve quality, which included informing workers about all other phases of production with which they were not personally involved. He also oversaw the complete redesign of many Jayco products to appeal more to baby-boom consumers. In addition, Jayco launched a lauded advertising campaign that utilized artwork styled after Norman Rockwell's paintings. Jayco also introduced several new products, including a large trailer that sported a stand-up bedroom as well as a streamlined front end.

Jayco's sales boomed during the mid-1980s. Indeed, by 1987—Jayco's 20th anniversary—the company was the fourth largest manufacturer of towable RVs in the United States. Besides its core fold-down, travel trailers, and motorhomes, Jayco offered van conversions and pop-up and hardwall truck campers. Those products were sold through a network of 260 dealers in every state (except Hawaii), most Canadian provinces, Puerto Rico, and Japan. By that time, the Jayco "family" had grown to more than 600 employees. During the 1980s, moreover, Jayco realized unprecedented growth. The number of units shipped bolted to a high of 223,000 in 1988 as the company's work force surpassed 700 and the dealer network swelled to about 300.

The RV industry suffered from another downturn during the late 1980s and early 1990s, though it was not as serious as previous slowdowns. Again, Yoder refused to recognize the downturn as a negative, claiming that a recession was a mind set that was worsened by the media dwelling on it and by businesses that were scared to move forward. Supporting that assertion, in 1990, Yoder, in the midst of the U.S. recession, initiated a two-stage expansion program. Following that plan, Jayco purchased new manufacturing facilities in Middlebury and nearby LaGrange. That effort nearly doubled the company's total acreage to more than 100, about 500,000 square feet of which was covered by manufacturing facilities. As production capacity increased, the recession waned. Indeed, after recording $142 million in sales in 1992, Jayco's revenues rose 42 percent in 1993 to $202 million.

In April 1993 the 65-year-old Yoder announced his retirement from Jayco. After 25 years of service he was stepping down to pursue other interests; he was very active in the Mennonite Church, for example, and was also involved in other business interests including a small furniture company. Yoder was succeeded as president by Bernard G. Lambright, while Wilbur Bontrager remained at the company as chairman of the board. Jayco continued to post healthy gains in 1994. By 1995, in fact, Jayco's work force had grown to 1,300 and Jayco had become the second largest manufacturer of towable products in the nation.

Principal Subsidiaries: Starcraft R.V., Inc.

Further Reading:

Cipriano, Gil, "Attitude as Recession-Beater Works at Jayco," *Tribune Business Weekly* (South Bend, Ind.), July 22, 1992, p. 10.

Family: The Story of Jayco, Middlebury, Ind.: Jayco, Inc., 1988.

"Jayco's Dramatic Redesign of 1993 Lines Marks 25th Anniversary," *RV Business,* September 1992, p. 9.

"Jayco President Announces Retirement," *Tribune Business Weekly* (South Bend, Ind.), April 21, 1993, p. 3.

Kurowski, Jeff, "Jayco's Yoder Retiring After 25 Years," *South Bend Tribune,* April 25, 1993.

Overton, Dave, "Jayco's Cutting Back on Waste," *Elkhart (Indiana) Truth,* February 9, 1992.

—Dave Mote

Kellogg's®

Kellogg Company

One Kellogg Square
Battle Creek, Michigan 49016-3599
U.S.A.
(616) 961-2000
Fax: (616) 961-2871

Public Company
Incorporated: 1906 as Battle Creek Toasted Corn Flake Company
Employees: 15,657
Sales: $6.56 billion
Stock Exchanges: New York Boston Cincinnati Midwest Philadelphia
SICs: 2043 Cereal Breakfast Foods; 2038 Frozen Specialties Nec; 2099 Food Preparations Nec; 2051 Bread, Cake, & Related Products

Will Keith Kellogg once estimated that 42 cereal companies were launched in the breakfast-food boom during the early years of the twentieth century. His own venture, founded as the Battle Creek Toasted Corn Flake Company, was among the last, but it outlasted most of its early competitors and has dominated the ready-to-eat cereal industry every since. The Kellogg Company, as it was ultimately named, followed a straight and profitable path, avoiding takeovers and diversification, relying heavily on advertising and promotion, and posting profits nearly every year of its existence.

By the time Kellogg launched his cereal company in 1906 he had already been in the cereal business for more than ten years, as an employee of the Adventist Battle Creek Sanitarium run by his brother, Dr. John Harvey Kellogg. Dr. Kellogg, a strict vegetarian and the sanitarium's internationally celebrated director, also invented and marketed various health foods. One of the foods sold by Dr. Kellogg's Sanitas Food Company was called Granose, a wheat flake the Kellogg brothers had stumbled upon while trying to develop a more digestible form of bread. The wheat flake was produced one night in 1894 following a long series of unsuccessful experiments. The men were running boiled wheat dough through a pair of rollers in the sanitarium basement. The dough had always come out sticky and gummy, until by accident the experiments were interrupted long enough for the boiled dough to dry out. When the dry dough was run through the rollers, it broke into thin flakes, one for each wheat berry, and flaked cereals were born.

Commercial production of the Granose flakes began in 1895 with improvised machinery in a barn on the sanitarium grounds. The factory was soon in continuous production, turning out more than 100,000 pounds of flakes in its first year. A ten-ounce box sold for 15 cents, which meant that the Kelloggs collected $12 for each 60-cent bushel of wheat processed, a feat that did not go unnoticed around Battle Creek, Michigan.

In 1900 production was moved to a new $50,000 facility. When the new factory building was completed, Dr. Kellogg insisted that he had not authorized it, forcing W. K. to pay for it himself.

Meanwhile, other companies were growing quickly, but Dr. Kellogg refused to invest in the company's expansion. Its most notable competitor was the Postum Cereal Company, launched by a former sanitarium patient, C. W. Post. Post added Grape-Nuts to his line in 1898 and by 1900 was netting $3 million a year, an accomplishment that inspired dozens of imitators and turned Battle Creek into the cereal-making capital of the United States.

In 1902 Sanitas improved the corn flake it had first introduced in 1898. The new product had better flavor and a longer shelf life than the 1898 version. By the following year the company was advertising in newspapers and on billboards, sending salesmen into the wholesale market, and introducing an ambitious door-to-door sampling program. By late 1905, Sanitas was producing 150 cases of corn flakes a day with sales of $100,000 a year.

The next year W. K. Kellogg launched the Battle Creek Toasted Corn Flake Company with the help of another enthusiastic former sanitarium patient. Kellogg recognized that advertising and promotion were key to success in a market flooded with look-alike products—the company spent a third of its initial working capital on an ad in *Ladies Home Journal.*

Orders, fueled by early advertising efforts, continually outstripped production, even after the company leased factory space at two additional locations. In 1907 output had reached 2,900 cases a day, with a net profit of about a dollar per case. In May 1907 the company became the Toasted Corn Flake Company. That July a fire destroyed the main factory building. On the spot, W. K. Kellogg began making plans for a new fireproof factory, and within a week he had purchased land at a site strategically located between two competing railroad lines. Kellogg had the new plant, with a capacity of 4,200 cases a day, in full operation six months after the fire. ''That's all the business I ever want,'' he is said to have told his son, John L. Kellogg, at the time.

By the time of the fire, the company had already spent $300,000 on advertising but the advertising barrage continued. One anonymous campaign told newspaper readers to ''wink at your grocer and see what your get.'' Winkers got a free sample of Kellogg's Corn Flakes. In New York City, the ad helped boost Corn Flake sales fifteenfold. In 1911 the advertising budget reached $1 million.

By that time, W. K. Kellogg had finally managed to buy out the last of his brother's share of the company, giving him more than

50 percent of its stock. W. K. Kellogg's company had become the Kellogg Toasted Corn Flake Company in 1909, but Dr. Kellogg's Sanitas Food Company had been renamed the Kellogg Food Company and used similar slogans and packaging. W. K. sued his brother for rights to the family name and was finally successful in 1921.

In 1922 the company reincorporated as the Kellogg Company because it had lost its trademark claim to the name "Toasted Corn Flakes," and had expanded its product line so much that the name no longer accurately described the company. Kellogg introduced Krumbles in 1912, followed by 40% Bran Flakes in 1915 and All-Bran in 1916.

Kellogg also made other changes, improving his product, packaging, and processing methods. Many of those developments came from W. K.'s son John L. Kellogg, who began working for the company in its earliest days. J. L. Kellogg developed a malting process to give the corn flakes a more nut-like flavor, saved $250,000 a year by switching from a waxed paper wrapper on the outside of the box to a waxed paper liner inside, and invented All-Bran by adding a malt flavoring to the bran cereal. His father credited him with more than 200 patents and trademarks.

Sales and profits continued to climb, financing several additions to the Battle Creek plant and the addition of a plant in Canada, opened in 1914, as well as an ever-increasing advertising budget. The one exception came just after World War I, when shortages of raw materials and rail cars crippled the once-thriving business. W. K. Kellogg returned from a world tour and canceled advertising contracts and sampling operations, and, for six months, he and his son worked without pay. The company issued $500,000 in gold notes in 1919 and in 1920 posted the only loss in its history. Still, Kellogg rejected a competitor's buyout offer.

At that point the Battle Creek plant had 15 acres of floor space, production capacity of 30,000 cases a day, and a shipping capacity of 50 rail cars a day. Each day it converted 15,000 bushels of white southern corn into Corn Flakes. The company had 20 branch offices and employed as many as 400 salesmen. During the next decade the Kellogg Company more than doubled the floor space at its Battle Creek factory and opened another overseas plant in Sydney, Australia, in 1924.

Also during that period, W. K. Kellogg began looking for a successor since in 1925 he had forced his son, who served briefly as president, out of the company after John Kellogg bought an oat-milling plant and divorced his wife to marry an office employee. W. K. Kellogg objected both to his son's moral lapse and to his preference for oats. Several other presidents followed, but none could manage well enough to keep W. K. Kellogg away. During the Great Depression the company's directors decided to cut advertising, premiums, and other expenses. When Kellogg heard of it, he returned from his California home, called a meeting, and told the officers to press ahead. They voted again, this time adding $1 million to the advertising budget. The company's upward sales curve continued right through the Depression, and profits improved from around $4.3 million a year in the late 1920s to $5.7 million in the early 1930s.

In 1930 W. K. Kellogg established the W. K. Kellogg Foundation to support agricultural, health, and educational institutions. Kellogg eventually gave the foundation his majority interest in Kellogg Company. The company, under W. K.'s control, also did its part to fight unemployment, hiring a crew to landscape a ten-acre park on the Battle Creek plant grounds and introducing a six-hour, four-shift day.

In 1939 Kellogg finally found a permanent president, Watson H. Vanderploeg, who was hired away from a Chicago bank. Vanderploeg led the company from 1939 until his death in 1957.

Vanderploeg expanded Kellogg's successful advertise-and-grow policy, adding new products and taking them into new markets. In 1941 the company began a $1 million modernization program, updating old steam-generation equipment and adding new bins and processing equipment. The company also added new plants in the United States and abroad. Domestic plants were established in Omaha, Nebraska; Lockport, Illinois; San Leandro, California; and Memphis, Tennessee. Additional foreign operations were established in Manchester, England, in 1938, followed by plants in South Africa, Mexico, Ireland, Sweden, the Netherlands, Denmark, New Zealand, Norway, Venezuela, Colombia, Brazil, Switzerland, and Finland. During the five years after World War II, Kellogg expanded net fixed assets from $6.6 million to $20.6 million. As always, this expansion was financed entirely out of earnings.

The company also continued to add new products, but it never strayed far from the ready-to-eat cereal business. In 1952 more than 85 percent of sales came from ten breakfast cereals, although the company also sold a line of dog food, some poultry and animal feeds, and Gold Medal pasta. *Barron's* noted that Kellogg's profit margins, consistently between six and seven percent of sales, were more than double those of other food companies. The company produced 35 percent of the nation's ready-to-eat cereal and was the world's largest manufacturer of cold cereal. Kellogg's success came from its emphasis on quality products; high-speed automated equipment, which kept labor costs to about 15 percent of sales; and substantial foreign earnings that were exempt from the excess-profits tax. Dividends tended to be generous and had been paid every year since 1908; sales, which had been $33 million in 1939, began to top $100 million in 1948. By the early 1950s an estimated one-third of those sales were outside the United States.

In the early 1950s Kellogg's continued success was tied to two outside developments: the postwar baby boom, and television advertising. To appeal to the new younger market Kellogg and other cereal makers brought out new lines of presweetened cereals and unabashedly made the key ingredient part of the name. Kellogg's entries included Sugar Frosted Flakes, Sugar Smacks, Sugar Corn Pops, Sugar All-Stars, and Cocoa Crispies. The company created Tony the Tiger and other cartoon pitchmen to sell the products on Saturday-morning television. Sales and profits doubled over the decade. In 1960 Kellogg earned $21.5 million on sales of $256.2 million and boosted its market share to 40 percent.

The company continued adding new cereals, aiming some at adolescent baby boomers and others, like Special K and Product

19 at their parents. Kellogg's Corn Flakes still led the cereal market and got more advertising support than any other cereal on grocers' shelves. Kellogg poured nearly $10 million into Corn Flakes advertising in both 1964 and 1965, putting more than two-thirds of those dollars into television.

In 1969 Kellogg finally made a significant move away from the ready-to-eat breakfast-food business, acquiring Salada Foods, a tea company. The following year Kellogg bought Fearn International, which sold soups, sauces, and desserts to restaurants. Kellogg added Mrs. Smith's Pie Company in 1976 and Pure Packed Foods, a maker of non-dairy frozen foods for institutional customers, in 1977. Kellogg also bought several small foreign food companies.

The diversification may have been motivated in part by increasing attacks on Kellogg's cereal business. Criticism boiled over in 1972 when the Federal Trade Commission (FTC) accused Kellogg and its leading rivals General Mills and General Foods of holding a shared monopoly and overcharging consumers more than $1 billion during the previous 15 years. The FTC said the companies used massive advertising (12 percent of sales), brand proliferation, and allocation of shelf space to keep out competitors and maintain high prices and profit margins. There was no disputing the profit margins, but the companies argued that the advertising and product proliferation were the result of competition, not monopoly. The cereal companies won their point following a lengthy hearing. During the same period, the industry's presweetened cereals and related advertising also took a beating. The American Dental Association accused the industry of obscuring the sugar content of those cereals and Action for Children's Television lodged a complaint with the FTC, saying that the mostly sugar cereals were equivalent to candy. Kellogg flooded consumer groups and the FTC with data playing down the sugar content by showing that only three percent of a child's sugar consumption comes from presweetened cereals. This publicity caused sugared-cereal sales to fall five percent in 1978, the first decline since their introduction in the 1950s.

The biggest threat to Kellogg's continued growth wasn't criticism, but rather the aging of its market. By the end of the 1970s growth slowed dramatically as the baby boom generation passed from the under-25 group, which consumes an average of 11 pounds of cereal a year, to the 25–50 age group, which eats less than half as much cereal. Cereal-market growth dropped, and Kellogg lost the most. Its market share fell from 43 percent in 1972 to 37 percent in 1983.

While Wall Street urged the company to shift its growth targets into anything but the stagnating cereal market, Kellogg continued to put its biggest efforts into its cereal business, emphasizing some of the same nutritional concepts that had given birth to the ready-to-eat breakfast business. And Kellogg was less unwilling to diversify than unable. It made three unsuccessful bids for the Tropicana Products orange juice company and another for Binney & Smith, makers of Crayola Crayons. Despite its problems, Kellogg believed the cereal business still represented its best investment opportunity. "When you average 28 percent return on equity in your own business, it's pretty hard to find impressive acquisitions," said Chairman William E. LaMothe, a onetime salesman who became CEO in 1979.

In 1984 Kellogg bought about 20 percent of its own stock back from the W. K. Kellogg Foundation, a move that increased profits and helped defend the company against future takeover attempts while satisfying a legal requirement limiting the holdings of foundations without giving potential raiders access to the stock.

Meanwhile, the company's response to generally sagging markets in the late 1970s was much like Will Kellogg's during the Depression: more advertising. Kellogg also boosted product research and stepped up new-product introductions. In 1979 the company rolled out five new products and had three more in test markets. By 1983 Kellogg's research-and-development budget was $20 million, triple the 1978 allotment. Targeting a more health-conscious market, Kellogg spent $50 million to bring three varieties of Nutri-Grain cereal to market in 1982. Kellogg added almost as many products in the next two years as it had in the previous four. And in 1984 Kellogg sparked a fiber fad when it began adding a health message from the National Cancer Institute to its All-Bran cereal.

By the mid-1980s the results of Kellogg's renewed assault on the cereal market were mixed. The company's hopes of raising per capita cereal consumption to 12 pounds by 1985 fell flat. But Kellogg did regain much of its lost market share, claiming 40 percent in 1985, and it continued to outperform itself year after year. In 1986 Kellogg posted its 30th consecutive dividend increase, its 35th consecutive earnings increase, and its 42nd consecutive sales increase.

In 1988 the company sold its U.S. and Canadian tea operations, in a demonstration of Kellogg's renewed commitment to the cereal market. In the early 1990s, however, Kellogg failed to move fast enough to profit from the oat bran craze and lost market share in the United States, primarily to General Mills Inc.'s oat-heavy brands such as Cheerios and Honey Nut Cheerios. Further erosion resulted from an upsurge in sales of private-label store brands, notably those produced by Ralston Purina Co. spin-off Ralcorp Holdings Inc. By developing knockoffs of such Kellogg standbys as Corn Flakes and Apple Jacks and selling them for as much as a dollar less per box, Ralcorp and other companies increased private-label cereal market share to six percent by 1994 at the expense of Kellogg and other makers of brand-name cereals. Sales of branded cereals increased only three percent in 1994 over 1993; in this flat market, Kellogg's U.S. market share fell to as low as 33.8 percent in 1994.

In order to hold on to as much of its market share as it could, Kellogg management once again turned to increased marketing and advertising in 1990. Even in the face of the pressure from lower-priced private-label products, the company also continued to raise its prices in the early 1990s to generate sufficient revenue. This trend was finally reversed in 1994, however, when General Mills lowered its prices, forcing Kellogg to do the same.

In the midst of these difficulties, LaMothe retired in 1992 and was replaced as chairman and CEO by the president of Kellogg, Arnold G. Langbo. Under Langbo's direction, the company underwent a reengineering effort in 1993 that committed the company to concentrate its efforts on its core business of breakfast cereal. That year and the next, Kellogg divested itself of such noncore assets as its Mrs. Smith's Frozen Foods pie business, Cereal Packaging, Ltd., based in England, and its Argentine snack food business.

Its emphasis on its core business was also extended to its operations outside the United States, where company officials saw the greatest potential for future growth. By 1991 Kellogg held 50 percent of the non-U.S. cereal market, and 34 percent of its profits were generated outside the United States. In most of the markets in which it operated, it had at least six of the top ten cereal brands. Looking to the future, Kellogg's primary target markets of Europe, Asia, and Latin America had not yet reached the more mature levels of the United States. While per capita cereal consumption in the United States was ten pounds per year, in most other markets it was less than two pounds. After expanding into Italy in the early 1990s, Kellogg became the first major cereal company to open plants in three markets: the former Soviet Union with a plant in Riga, Latvia, in 1993; India with a plant in Taloja, in 1994; and China with a plant in Guangzhou, in 1995. With these new operations, Kellogg had 29 plants operating in 19 countries and could reach consumers in almost 160 countries.

Although Kellogg had a commanding position internationally, it faced a new and more formidable international competitor starting in 1989. General Mills and the Swiss food titan Nestlé S.A. established a joint venture called Cereal Partners Worldwide (CPW), which essentially combined General Mills's cereal brands and cereal-making equipment with Nestlé's name recognition in numerous markets and vast experience with retailers there. By 1994, CPW was already beginning to eat into Kellogg's market share in various countries.

Overall, Kellogg's 1990s difficulties had only slowed—not stopped—the firm's tradition of continual growth. Net sales increased at the modest rates of seven percent, two percent, and four percent in 1992, 1993, and 1994, respectively (1994 was Kellogg's 50th consecutive year of sales growth). With U.S. sales still accounting for 59 percent of the overall total, however, and competition heating up overseas, Kellogg faced its most challenging environment since the early 1920s. In addition to its aggressive expansion into overseas markets with huge potential for growth, another promising sign for a bright future for Kellogg was a revitalized new product development program. More disciplined than the scattershot approach of the 1980s, the program was beginning to produce such winners as Low Fat Granola, Rice Krispies Treats, and a line of cereal developed in partnership with ConAgra, Inc., under the food conglomerate's Healthy Choice brand.

Principal Subsidiaries: Kellogg USA Inc.; Kellogg Company Argentina S.A.C.I.F.; Kellogg (Aust.) Proprietary Ltd. (Australia); Kellogg Brasil & CIA; Kellogg Canada Inc.; Kellogg de Colombia S.A.; Nordisk Kelloggs A/S (Denmark); Kellogg's Produits Alimentaires, S.A. (France); Kellogg (Deutschland) Gesellschaft mit beschrankter Haftung (GmbH); Kellogg de Centro America S.A. (Guatemala); Kellogg (Japan) K.K.; Nhong Shim Kellogg Co. Ltd. (Korea); Kellogg de Mexico S.A. de C.V.; Kellogg Company of South Africa (Proprietary) Limited; Kellogg Espana, S.A.; Kellogg Company of Great Britain, Ltd.; Alimentos Kellogg S.A. (Venezuela).

Further Reading:

Carson, Gerald, *Cornflake Crusade,* Salem, New Hampshire: Ayer, 1976, 305 p.

The History of Kellogg Company, Battle Creek, Michigan: Kellogg Company, 1986.

Knowlton, Christopher, "Europe Cooks up a Cereal Brawl," *Fortune,* June 3, 1991, pp. 175–78.

Powell, Horace B., *The Original Has This Signature: W. K. Kellogg,* Englewood Cliffs, New Jersey: Prentice-Hall, 1956, 358 p.

Serwer, Andrew E., "What Price Brand Loyalty?," *Fortune,* January 10, 1994, pp. 103–04.

Treece, James B., and Greg Burns, "The Nervous Faces around Kellogg's Breakfast Table," *Business Week,* July 18, 1994, p. 33.

Woodruff, David, "Winning the War of Battle Creek," *Business Week,* May 13, 1991, p. 80.

—updated by David E. Salamie

KENNAMETAL®

Kennametal, Inc.

P.O. Box 231
Latrobe, Pennsylvania 15650
U.S.A.
(412) 539-5000

Public Company
Founded: 1938
Sales: $881 million
Employees: 5,000
Stock Exchanges: New York
SICs: 3541 Machine Tools Metal Cutting Types; 3545 Machine Tools Accessories; 3532 Mining Machinery

Kennametal, Inc., is one of the world's largest and most successful manufacturers of cutting tools for the metalworking industry. The company has three main areas of concentration: metalworking products, including cutting tools and related accessories for the metal cutting industry; mining and construction products, including mining tools such as drums, blocks, bits and compacts, and construction tools such as grader blades and snowplow blades; and metallurgical products, including the production of proprietary metallurgical powders for manufacturing its products. With plants in Canada, France, Germany, The Netherlands, and England, Kennametal is the recognized leader in technical developments for tools that cut steel and other hard metals.

In 1832 a coppersmith named Robert McKenna traveled from Ireland to Pittsburgh, Pennsylvania. McKenna established his own copperworks and, after he died in 1852, the business was reorganized by his three sons—Alexander, John, and Thomas—as A. & J. McKenna. The name was later changed to the A. and T. McKenna Brass and Copper Works. By 1899 all the brothers had died, and the firm was once again reorganized, this time under the name McKenna Brothers Brass Company. The seven sons of Thomas McKenna continued the brass and copper works, and also struck an agreement with Firth Sterling Steel Company to become its sole agent for selling cutting tools in the cities of Pittsburgh and Cincinnati, Ohio.

In 1900 one of the seven brothers, A.G. McKenna, developed an alloy tool steel that contained about 18 percent tungsten. A.G.'s development was a milestone in cutting medium steel. Prior to that time, the cutting speed of steel had been only about 16 feet per minute in 1800 and 26 feet per minute in 1860. The 18 percent tungsten alloy, however, increased the cutting speed to 99 feet per minute. Yet this was not the final development. When A.G. added one percent vanadium, the cutting speed nearly doubled. As a result, in 1910 the McKenna clan organized a new company. The offices for the new venture, Vanadium Alloys Steel Company (VASCO), were established in Latrobe, Pennsylvania. The McKenna family was the majority stockholder, and McKenna Brothers Brass Company became the new firm's sales agent in the United States.

A.G. McKenna was the single largest stockholder and the impetus behind the firm's metallurgical developments, although he was never officially an officer of the company. Men of A.G.'s acquaintance at Firth Sterling ran the company until brother Roy McKenna became president in 1915. VASCO grew rapidly under the able management of Roy, especially during World War I. The company manufactured most of the ferro-tungsten alloy needed for the American war effort. Near the end of the war, VASCO was producing half as much ferro-tungsten as tool steel sales. It is at this point in the history of Kennametal that Philip M. McKenna begins to play a prominent role.

Philip was exposed to the finer points of metallurgy at a very young age by his father, A.G. McKenna. Born in 1897, by the age of seven Philip was given the responsibility of stoking the fire for his father's blacksmith forge, where he carefully watched the heating of drill steels. In 1907 Philip learned how to operate a lathe and, when he later entered high school, was knowledgeable enough to manufacture a true-tempered hunting knife on his own. Trained in pattern-making, drafting, and mechanical drawing in high school, in 1914 he worked as an assistant in the Iron Division of the U.S. Bureau of Standards. His duties there included cleaning electroplating and other equipment. By 1915 Philip was employed as a professional chemist and had secured two registered patents, one for an efficient process to extract tungsten values from ores, the other for a method of separating cobalt from nickel.

An ambitious young man, Philip convinced his father to help him start Chemical Products Company in order to market some of his patents. Chemical Products began to provide cobalt, based on the process patented by Philip, for VASCO to use. When the supply of tungsten became more urgent with the advent of World War I, Philip patented a highly efficient method of producing ferro-tungsten. This process was not only used by his own company but also employed by VASCO. After the war, Philip engaged in a number of activities. He attended Columbia University, searched for tantalum and niobium ores in the American west, closed down the Chemical Products Company, and started an analytic laboratory in San Leandro, California, for the purpose of conducting more intense research on tooling materials.

In 1928 Philip moved to Latrobe, Pennsylvania, to become research director at VASCO. At VASCO, Philip began to work with tantalum alloys in order to produce better steel-cutting tools than the tungsten carbide tools manufactured by other companies. In 1936 an agreement was reached to create a new company, Vascoloy-Ramet, for the manufacture of tantalum carbide tools. Participants in the venture included Ramet Corporation of America, General Electric Company, Carboloy Company, and Fansteel Metallurgical Corporation. Sales in 1936 amounted to $450,000, but the new company was plagued with mismanagement and complaints from customers about tools that were poorly made. At one point, Chevrolet Auto Body rejected 1,200 tools made by Vascoloy-Ramet. Dissatisfied with the direction of the new company, Philip resigned from Vanadium Alloys in early 1938.

Just a few months later, Philip was busy forming a new company based on the tungsten-titanium carbide composition he had patented while working for VASCO. The denseness of this metal, known by its trade name Kennametal, led to an easier machining process. As a result, tools could be made more quickly than ever before. Although the firm was initially set up as a sole proprietorship to develop and manufacture tool materials, in 1940 Philip convinced his cousin Alex, his brother Donald, and other McKenna family members to join him as partners in the new company. Philip's development of hard carbide tools produced results immediately—tools manufactured by the new McKenna Metals Company were soon recognized as the highest quality products in the entire metal cutting industry. During the first year of operations, the company's sales amounted to $30,000. By the end of fiscal 1941, however, sales had skyrocketed to $999,000.

The coming of World War II provided McKenna Metals Company with just the outlet it needed to market its tools. In 1941 the firm received its first order based on the Lend-Lease agreement between the United States and Britain. Orders also arrived from United States Steel Export Company and Chrysler Tank Arsenal. Due to the rapid growth of the firm and the burgeoning administrative responsibilities, in 1943 Philip decided to conclude the partnership and incorporate under the name of Kennametal, Inc. Throughout the war, the company helped machine the enormous quantities of steel required to produce war materials for the U.S. armed forces. It improved tooling for shell production at the same time that it developed a process that increased the production of tungsten carbine penetrators (the outer core of a shell casing made to pierce German tank armor). Kennametal's revenues increased to $7.55 million by the end of fiscal 1943.

The end of the war in 1945 triggered a decrease in orders from the U.S. government, and Kennametal's revenues suddenly dropped. To compensate for this loss of business, Philip McKenna began to develop tools for the mining industry. A new plant was built in Bedford, Pennsylvania, for the production of these mining tools.

In 1946 the company started a virtual revolution in the metal cutting industry. Philip and the men working for him at Kennametal developed indexable carbide insert systems (which included thermal strain-free assemblies and precision-ground "throw-away" inserts) and a carbide designed specifically for all-purpose, high-speed tooling. It was not long, however, before the company was once again in the employ of the U.S. government.

When the Korean War started in 1950, the U.S. Department of Defense contracted Kennametal to manufacture the anti-tank penetrators that it had become famous for producing during the second World War. With 190,000 of these items produced for use in Korea, sales increased to $24 million by the end of 1954.

The mid- and late 1950s were a period of expansion and growth for the company. Kennametal opened a tungsten mining venture in Nevada, with the accumulated stockpile sold to the American government. When mining was halted in 1957, the company patented an original process to reduce tungsten ore concentrates into tungsten carbide. This revolutionary process formed the basis of Kennametal's tungsten powder business for the future. In 1958 the company expanded overseas with the creation of Kennametal Overseas Corporation. It also established an affiliation with an Italian firm to sinter Kennametal's carbide in Europe. A joint venture was established in Britain just a few years later.

During the 1960s, revenues for the company continued to increase. In 1962 sales were 31 percent higher than the previous year, while net income was up 58 percent; 1963 revenues increased more than 12 percent, while net profits rose 29 percent. Major technological developments were also introduced by Kennametal during the decade, including the production of high-purity tantalum powders for electronic applications and tool materials, the production of heavy tungsten alloy materials under the trade name "Kennertium," and the manufacture of Kengrip tire studs. Three rock bit firms were purchased, new warehouses were opened in Illinois and West Virginia, a powder preparation plant was built in Fallon, Nevada, and sales offices were established in West Germany and Australia. Sales over the period from 1961 to 1969 more than doubled, and net income was five times greater at the end of the decade than it had been at the beginning. Philip McKenna died in 1969, but the company remained under the management of family members. Alex McKenna retained his position as president and chief executive officer, and Donald McKenna assumed the position of chairman of the board.

Kennametal's success continued into the 1970s as the new generation of family members supervised the development of innovative products and manufacturing techniques. In collaboration with its Italian affiliate, the company developed a clamping system that provided more stable and accurate holding of metal cutting tools. Kennametal also introduced a revolutionary line of ceramic tooling materials, such as ceramic inserts and holders. By the end of the decade, Kennametal was the undisputed leader in metal cutting tooling throughout the United States. The company had grown into the largest producer of cemented carbide products, bypassing such industry giants as General Electric.

Kennametal made its first public stock offering in 1977, a move that triggered a dramatic surge in interest in the company. By the end of fiscal 1979, sales had more than tripled, net income and earnings per share had quadrupled, and dividends had more than doubled. With the influx of new capital, management expanded the company's West German and Australian operations and acquired the oldest carbide producer in Canada, A.C. Wickman.

The 1980s began auspiciously for the company, with record sales of $389.9 million by 1982. In 1983, however, sales dropped 31 percent due to the worst recession since World War II. Nonetheless, management initiated a comprehensive expansion and acquisition strategy. Two new plants were built in North Carolina, and construction was completed on a new headquarters near Latrobe Airport, in Pennsylvania. Consolidation of operations in Ohio led to the construction of a new steel products plant in Cleveland. A new plant was also built in Neunkirchen, West Germany. In addition, Kennametal purchased all the holdings of Lempereur (Belgium, The Netherlands, and France), Craig Bit Company (Canada), and Bristol-Erickson (England). During this time, a joint venture was started with Kobe Steel in Japan to market the company's metalworking and construction products in that country. By the late 1980s, the company had completely recovered from the recession of the early and mid-1980s; it posted record sales of $420 million in 1988.

With a revitalized cash flow, Kennametal entered the 1990s determined to surpass its previous success. Management's first move was the acquisition of J&L Industrial Supply, a catalog supplier of metalwork tooling located in Detroit, Michigan. Kennametal's purchase of J&L provided the company with the ability to respond more quickly than ever before to satisfy customer needs for metalwork equipment and supplies. In 1993 Kennametal purchased an 81-percent interest in Hertel AG, a German manufacturer of tooling systems. This acquisition was made to give Kennametal greater access to the growing Eastern European markets. In 1994 Kennametal purchased W.W. Grainger (an American distributor of industrial equipment and supplies), thus improving upon its fast-growing marketing base already established with J&L. These acquisitions boosted Kennametal to a position as the second largest metalworking products manufacturer in the world, and the leader in mining and construction tooling. Nearly 35 percent of the company's total sales are from outside the United States.

In 1991 Kennametal created a $27 million Corporate Technology Center in order to remain at the forefront of technological developments in the metalcutting industry. New products and manufacturing techniques in metalcutting inserts, toolholding systems, carbide-tipped bits for mining machines and road planers, and other metalcutting tooling applications of carbides, ceramics, and artificial diamonds are the focus of engineers at the center. The center, located near company headquarters at Latrobe, Pennsylvania, also provides consulting services in tooling management and productivity to meet the unique and rapidly changing needs of Kennametal customers.

The McKenna family still owns a significant portion of the company's stock, and Quentin C. McKenna, a distant relative of Philip, acts as chairman of the board. But the first non-family member, Robert L. McGeehan, has been appointed president and chief executive officer. Management changes, however, will not derail Kennametal's continuing success provided the company maintains its tradition of innovative metalcutting tool production.

Further Reading:

''Head To Head With Robert McGeehan, President, Kennametal, Inc.,'' *Cutting Tool Engineering,* October 1991, pp. 21–24.

McKenna, Donald C., *The Roots of Kennametal, or Philip McKenna and How He Grew,* Latrobe: Kennametal, Inc., 1974.

''The Shopper's Edge: Kennametal's Changing Marketing Strategy,'' *Pittsburgh High Technology,* Pittsburgh High Technology Council, reprint.

—Thomas Derdak

KinderCare Learning Centers, Inc.

2400 Presidents Drive
Montgomery, Alabama 36116
U.S.A.
(334) 277-5090
Fax: (334) 271-1210

Public Company
Incorporated: 1970
Employees: 21,000
Total Assets: $456.9 million
Stock Exchanges: NASDAQ
SICs: 8351 Child Day Care Services

KinderCare Learning Centers, Inc. is the largest chain of child-care facilities in the United States, based upon number of centers, children served, and revenues. Following a rapid rise to prominence in the 1970s, the company began to diversify, incurring significant debt along the way that prompted its 1992 filing for bankruptcy. In April 1993, however, KinderCare emerged from bankruptcy and looked forward to renewed success, focusing on filling the specific needs of niche markets, including infant care and facilities for older children of working parents. By the end of the year, 1,165 KinderCare centers were operating in 39 states.

The company traces its history to the late 1960s, when Perry Mendel, a real estate developer from Montgomery, Alabama, speculated that the increasing numbers of women entering the work force might prompt a rise in demand for preschool child care. Remarking on his inspiration, Mendel later recalled in a *Management Review* article that one morning as he breakfasted with a group of associates, he noticed a man "not in our group, who drove a Lincoln Continental and read *The Wall Street* Journal. . . . I asked my friends what he did for a living. They replied, 'Nothing, but his wife has two daycare centers for children.' That set off bells in my head." Mendel reportedly began talking with the man and eventually purchased one of the two centers. New to the business, Mendel spent about a year researching the industry, touring child care centers across the country and reading up on state regulations.

Mendel discovered that many working parents insisted on more than just babysitters. Specifically, they wanted centers that provided individual attention, nutritious foods, exercise, and education. Thus, Mendel planned to open a facility in which children would not only be safe and loved, but would also learn. Prior to the opening of the first center, Mendel spent many months drawing up a detailed plan of how the corporation should function. His plan covered such details as classroom size and required length of naps. Moreover, Mendel sought out the advice of experts; nutrition experts from Vanderbilt University planned hot-meal menus, and education specialists developed learning programs. Tight quality-control measures were planned to ensure programs would be carried out as prescribed.

The company began as Kinder-Care Nursery Schools, and the first facility was opened on July 14, 1969. Accommodating 70 children, the center featured a distinctive exterior decorated with a Humpty-Dumpty motif and a red bell tower that would eventually be incorporated as the company's logo. Future centers would adopt the readily identifiable exterior design, helping to create brand name recognition along the same principles developed by McDonald's restaurants and Holiday Inn hotels. Unlike such popular chains, however, Kinder-Care discontinued the idea of franchising in 1970, when Mendel determined that most people interested in the child care business lacked the expertise or were unable to arrange the financing.

Nevertheless, the success of Kinder-Care was just as Mendel had envisioned; the demand was there and the company began to flourish. A second facility was opened within the year, and in 1970 the company changed its name to Kinder-Care Learning Centers, Inc. to better reflect its emphasis on education. By 1971, 19 centers were in operation, the first infant care was offered, and the company had extended its services to include transportation for those school-aged who needed it, via rented Volkswagen vans.

Expansion of the centers continued apace, as the company went public in 1972. Soon thereafter Kinder-Care established a new corporate headquarters in Montgomery and began to invest in television advertising. To help with the mass marketing of the concept, Mendel employed Richard Grassgreen, an IRS attorney and tax expert, whose financial knowledge and experience complemented Mendel's marketing strengths. By 1974 there were 60 centers located in 17 states and over 500 employees nationwide. Growth prompted the company to divide its operations into six geographical regions, managed by regional directors, in 1975.

Continuing to expand the scope of their operations, Mendel began acquiring other child care center companies in the late 1970s. The company's first major acquisition came in 1977, when it purchased the 15 facilities of Playcare. In 1979, as Kinder-Care celebrated its tenth anniversary, three more major acquisitions took place: Mini-Skools, Living and Learning, and American Pre-Schools. Moreover, the company opened its 300th center that year. Such activity prompted the national media to take notice of Kinder-Care; business periodicals began to feature coverage of the company's rapid rise and founder Mendel even made an appearance on NBC's *Today Show*.

While increasing its national presence, the company also focused on providing valuable programs for the children entrusted to their care as well as their employees. Kinder-Care began publishing activity books and calendars for children. Moreover, the centers established health and safety coordinators, an educational assistance program for employees, and Quality Focus, a program emphasizing quality and professionalism in child care. The KinderCare Kindustry centers, a child care concept first established at Walt Disney World and later renamed Kinder-Care at Work, were established either near companies or within companies to cater specifically to working parents. In 1985, Kinder-Care opened its 1,000th center. Competition in the industry was comprised chiefly of La Petite Academy and Daybridge/Children's World, but neither approached Kinder-Care's size.

In 1987, Kinder-Care was reporting annual revenues of $900 million, and analysts were remarking on the company's rapid growth, observing that stock had soared from 12 cents a share to $20 at its high in mid-1987. *Management Review* magazine stated in a 1988 article that the investment community watched a $100 investment in the company's stock in 1972 grow into $7,000 in 1987. In fact, during this time, Kinder-Care was expanding at the rate of one new center every three days.

This trend was soon to sour, however, as Mendel and Grassgreen begun widening the scope of their plans for the company. Years before, the men had been approached by Michael Milken, an investor from the firm of Drexel Burnham Lambert, who suggested that the company begin diversifying its equity and building an investment portfolio. Toward that end, Kinder-Care acquired a wide variety of companies in the 1980s, including chains of photo studios, shoe stores, other retail operations, and two savings and loan associations. Late in 1987, Kinder-Care acquired Sylvan Learning Centers, a provider of supplemental instruction to children and adults, and the largest franchiser of its kind. The company also made a $10 million investment in Trans-Resources Inc., an Israel-based chemical and fertilizer manufacturer.

In a 1989 article in *Business Week,* one reporter noted, ''Kinder-Care Learning Centers Inc., once a successful pioneer in day care, has become one of the most confused stock investments of the decade.'' By this time, Kinder-Care stockholders and the banks that had lent it money were also sharply criticizing the diversification program, complaining that they had intended to invest in a day care operation and not the repository of other interests that now comprised the company. In fact, according to a 1988 *Forbes* article, less than half of Kinder-Care's sales and profits for the year were expected to come from its child care centers. Moreover, investors now found that they held stock in a new company all together: the Enstar Group Inc., which was formed as a holding company during this time for Kinder-Care and the myriad other companies now associated with it.

With guidance from Drexel, Enstar had financed expansion by diluting its stock through public offerings and purchasing junk bonds. As a result, the company's debt load increased from $10 million to about $620 million in 1988. While some of the money was used to expand the child care centers, much of it was used to make further investments, and following some initial payoffs from the plan, the company found itself in deep financial trouble, particularly after the stock market crash in October 1987.

With declining stock prices and desperate for cash, Mendel and Grassgreen set up Enstar's Kinder-Care division as a subsidiary and sold stock in Kinder-Care at $7 per share. Although the offering raised $42 million, Enstar's debts remained exceedingly high. Next, Mendel and Grassgreen accepted a 1989 offer from the Lodestar Group, a New York investment banking firm, for a rights offering, in which shareholders would generate new equity capital through their purchase of Kinder-Care stock from Enstar at a discount price.

As a result, Kinder-Care was finally disassociated from Enstar, and 63 percent of its stock was held by Lodestar. Unfortunately however, the company was still $400 million in debt and, moreover, was entangled in several lawsuits involving Mendel, Grassgreen, Michael Milken, and angry stockholders.

During this difficult period, Tull Gearreald took command of the company as president and CEO. Gearreald, an investment banker, was a founder of Lodestar and had served on the board of directors at Kinder-Care. He promptly declared the company would remain focused on what it was originally established to do: care for children.

In the early 1990s, Gearreald oversaw a program focusing on ''Helping America's Busiest Families,'' which offered additional services for parents of Kinder-Care kids. Specifically, Kinder-Care centers began extending their hours and also stocked their centers with hairdressers for children, as well as dry-cleaning drop-off and pick-up stations, shoe repair services, and postal facilities for their busy parents. During this time, the company also established a computer network so that each of its 1,196 centers was directly linked to a central computer in Montgomery.

Curriculum during this time was bolstered through the development of programs designed to reestablish Kinder-Care's focus on social, physical, emotional, and intellectual growth for the child. For example, the ''Let Me Do It!'' program focused on teaching two-year olds to learn at their own pace and through play; preschoolers were taught through a program called ''One Upon a Time,'' built around motivational and interesting stories from children's literature; and ''Your Big Backyard'' used the National Wildlife Federation magazine for preschooler curriculum activities. In 1992, the company updated its bell tower logo and removed the hyphen in the spelling of Kinder-Care.

However, still faltering under its high debt load, KinderCare filed for Chapter 11 bankruptcy protection on November 10, 1992. The company continued operating, and in January 1993, in a move that may have helped bring new life to their balance sheet, KinderCare sold off Sylvan Learning Centers for $8 million. Five months later, KinderCare emerged from bankruptcy, when its creditors took on a portion of its debt in exchange for an 86.5 percent share in the company and three positions on the board of directors. Thereafter, the company followed a strict reorganization plan, adopted a new stock policy, and elected a new board of directors, with Gearreald continuing as CEO and director and Philip Maslowe, formerly of Thrifty Corporation, serving as chief financial officer. The company was also given new life as several national demographic trends led to an increased demand for KinderCare's services; while the number of babies born to American households was on the rise, the demand for child care was also increasing rapidly.

KinderCare focused on niche markets to help it recover. Kid's Choice Centers were developed to cater to those parents with older children in need of supervision after school. Moreover, the KinderCare at Work on-site corporate centers were thriving, gaining patronage by parents employed by Citicorp, Delco Electronics, Ford Motor Company, Lego Systems, and The Walt Disney Company, as well as at several universities and hospitals.

By 1994, KinderCare was preparing to open its first center in the United Kingdom and expected to open five to seven more centers within the next two years. At mid-year the company operated 1,132 child care centers in 38 states and had enrollment of approximately 114,000 full-time and part-time children. The company was also continuing its tradition of fund-raising for the Muscular Dystrophy Association, for which it become a national corporate sponsor in 1985. With a new focus and enthusiasm for the future, Gearreald declared in the company newsletter, *CenterLine,* on occasion of the company's 25th anniversary: "Twenty-five years old is the beginning of a new Golden Age for KinderCare. . . . We're mature but youthful, energetic yet self-controlled—self-sufficient, productive and caring. We are a Family with lots of children!" He predicted that KinderCare would expand to include 2,000, or perhaps 3,000, centers with over 300,000 children over the next ten years, with further expansion in the United Kingdom, Scandinavia, and the Far East. By remaining focused on day care and providing innovated programs for children, KinderCare was likely to continue as the industry leader.

Principal Subsidiaries: Mini-Skools Limited; KinderCare Development Corporation; KinderCare Real Estate; KinderCare Learning Centres, Limited.

Further Reading:

Caminiti, Susan, "KinderCare Learning Centers: New Lessons in Customer Service," *Fortune,* September 20, 1993, pp. 79–80.

Cohan, Joy, "KinderCare Goes to Work with Hospital Employees," *Personnel Journal, Marketplace Supplement,* March 1993, p. 4.

Dubashi, Jagannath, "Once Burned . . . ," *Financial World,* June 8, 1993, pp. 432–433.

Englade, Kenneth F., "The Bottom Line on Kinder-Care," *Across the Board,* April 1988, pp. 44–53.

Fisher, Christy, "Extra Frills Pay Dividends for Child Centers," *Advertising Age,* July 27, 1992, pp. 28–30.

Fitzgerald, Nora, "Child's Play," *Adweek,* July 25, 1994, pp. 1, 5.

Hawkins, Chuck, "Ring Around the Rosie at Kinder-Care," *Business Week,* December 18, 1989, pp. 45–46.

Jakubovics, Jerry, "Perry Mendel: Turning Childcare into a Cash Business," *Management Review,* June 1988, pp. 11–13.

"Kinder-Care Takes Charge of Its Development," *Corporate Design,* May/June 1987, pp. 76–81.

Quinn, Lawrence R., "S&L Buyers: A Mixed Bag," *United States Banker,* October 1988, pp. 37–44.

Samper, J. Phillip, "Rocking the Cradle to Compete in the Job Market," *Journal of Compensation & Benefits,* January/February 1991, pp. 34–36.

Schifrin, Matthew, "The Little Nursery that Lost Its Way," *Forbes,* May 16, 1988, pp. 34–35.

—Beth Watson Highman

AMERICAN MADE
Starrett®

L.S. Starrett Co.

121 Crescent Street
Athol, Massachusetts 01331-1915
U.S.A.
(508) 249-3551
Fax: (508) 249-8495

Public Company
Incorporated: 1900
Employees: 2,563
Sales: $180.2 million
Stock Exchanges: New York Boston Chicago
SICs: 3423 Hand and Edge Tools, Except Machine Tools and Handsaws; 3425 Saw Blades and Handsaws; 3545 Cutting Tools, Machine Tool Accessories and Machinists' Precision Measuring Devices; 3823 Industrial Instruments for Measurement, Display and Control of Process Variables and Related Products; 3827 Optical Instruments and Lenses

Founded in 1880, the L.S. Starrett Co. manufactures more than 5,000 industrial, professional, and consumer products, but is perhaps best known for its precision hand tools, some of which are considered virtual works of art. Although Starrett was a public company, the conservatively managed business remained, after more than 100 years in operation, a family-run operation. In fact, Starrett's president in the mid-1990s was the great-grandson of the founder.

The founder, Laroy Sunderland Starrett, one of 12 children of a Maine farmer, rented a 600-acre Newburyport, Massachusetts, farm in 1861. Mechanically inclined, he also patented a number of inventions, including a meat chopper, a washing machine, and a butter working machine. In 1868, Starrett became general agent and superintendent of the Athol Machine Co. of Athol, Massachusetts, incorporated with the purpose of manufacturing his inventions. He eventually took out about 100 patents.

Among Starrett's inventions were a number of hand tools useful in the building trades. The first of these devices, patented in 1879, was a combination square that contained a steel rule with a sliding head. With the aid of the head, it could be used as a square or mitre, a bevel, or a plumb bob. Starrett established a shop on Athol's Crescent Street in 1880 to manufacture the popular hand tool. Ambitiously seeking out new markets for his inventions, he made his name known worldwide by establishing agencies in London and Paris in 1882. Also during the 1880s, Starrett manufactured steel rules and tapes, micrometers, calipers, and dividers.

As business increased, Starrett established a larger factory on the other side of Crescent Street. In 1894, the compound was expanded to span Millers River, and it occupied some 60,000 square feet in 1901. A year later, a new building of more than twice the floor space was erected on an adjoining site. The enterprise was incorporated in 1900, with Starrett as president and treasurer; along with him, four other members constituted the stockholders and directors. By 1906, Starrett was employing about 1,000 workers in the Athol factory and a caliper-manufacturing plant in Springfield, Massachusetts.

L.S. Starrett Co. reported assets of $8.6 million in 1918. By the time its founder died in 1922, the Athol factory was being hailed as the largest plant in the world wholly devoted to making fine mechanical tools. These products included micrometer gauges of more than 30 different styles and nearly 200 types of calipers and dividers. In addition, L.S. Starrett maintained offices and stores in New York, Chicago, and London, and special agencies in England, Germany, France, Belgium, Italy, Switzerland, Sweden, Denmark, Austria, Argentina, Australia, and Japan.

When L.S. Starrett was reincorporated in 1929, its assets had fallen to $4.8 million and the number of employees to about 720. In 1934, as the nation was slowly emerging from the depths of the Great Depression, assets were down to $3.8 million and employment to 402. However, following deficits in both 1932 and 1933, the company had earned a net income of $190,134 on sales of over $1.3 million, a distinct improvement over the $734,110 in sales registered in 1932 and $856,845 in 1933. At the end of the year, Starrett was able to resume dividends, which had not been paid in 1932 or 1933. In 1935, Starrett acquired the ''Last Word'' indicator business of Henry A. Lowe Co. in Cleveland, Ohio, and moved its equipment to the Athol factory. Throughout the remainder of the decade, Starrett gradually recovered from the Depression despite damage to the company's facilities from river floods in 1936 and 1938.

In fiscal year 1941 (ending June 30, 1940) L.S. Starrett's net income was $740,978 on record sales of more than $3.6 million. The number of employees had grown to 1,300 and the number of stockholders to 1,742. During World War II, Starrett increased its output eightfold, operating around the clock. Net sales advanced to a peak of $12.9 million in fiscal 1943. During this period of prosperity, Arthur H. Starrett, the founder's grandson, assumed the presidency. Starrett took control of the company in 1946, only to watch postwar sales slump to $6.9 million in 1950. As a result, net income declined from $1.4 million in 1943 to $486,129 in 1950, and by 1950 employment fell to 1,135 from the 1943 high of 2,034.

The advent of the Korean War in the early 1950s created a new surge in business for Starrett, which the company was able to sustain after the 1953 armistice. In fiscal year 1957—Starrett's best year of the decade—the company earned $1.5 million on net sales of $16.2 million. Shortly thereafter, Starrett began a modest program of acquisitions. In 1959, the company purchased Bristol Engineering & Manufacturing Co. based in Rehoboth, Massachusetts. Further, Starrett acquired Rhode Island Tool Co. of Providence for shares of common stock in 1962. That same year, Starrett acquired Webber Gage Co. of Cleveland, Ohio, for 20,000 shares of stock and $840,000 in cash. The acquisition of Webber, a manufacturer of precision gage blocks and certain types of optical measuring tools, enabled Starrett to begin manufacturing extremely high precision products.

Meanwhile, Transue & Williams Steel Forging Corp. of Alliance, Ohio, a maker of forgings and stampings for the automotive, truck, and tractor industries, was buying significant amounts of Starrett stock. Together with stock purchases by Russell McPhail, chairman of Transue & Williams, and his McPhail Candy Corp., these holdings represented about 30 percent of Starrett's outstanding stock in 1964, with a value of $6.8 million. At the 1963 annual meeting, McPhail unsuccessfully proposed a cumulative-voting proposal that would have made it easier for him and other minority stockholders to win seats on the company's board of directors. This challenge to Starrett's family management ended in October 1964, when the company purchased and retired the McPhail-Transue & Williams stock holdings for $31 a share, or about $6.8 million.

In the 1960s, Starrett's fortunes were favorably tied to war once again—this time the conflict was in Vietnam. Net sales, only $12.8 million in fiscal 1959, surged to $33.1 million in 1968, while net income grew from $886,588 to $4.2 million during this period. By the end of the decade, the company had major branches in Chicago, Cleveland, Los Angeles, Providence, and Springfield, New Jersey, and a warehouse in Toronto. Further, Starrett established subsidiaries in Brazil and Scotland in 1958 to manufacture products for foreign markets, and a Canadian subsidiary was established in 1962. Starrett also owned Herramientas de Precision—a Mexican subsidiary—from 1972 to 1985.

During this period, Starrett was also making its presence known in nonmilitary markets. While it would seem that hand-operated tools should have been rendered obsolete with the advent of power machinery and automation, the reality was that a growing number of do-it-yourself property owners were in the market for affordable and easy-to-use hand tools for repair and maintenance. At the other end of the spectrum, the increasing complexity of modern industry stimulated demand for all kinds of specialized hardware, some of which Starrett was manufacturing.

In fiscal 1970, Starrett bought Herman Stone Co., a Dayton, Ohio, producer of granite slabs for measuring tables, for $308,000 worth of stock. It was made a division of Starrett and moved to Mount Airy, North Carolina, in 1972. During the 1970s, Starrett's net sales grew from $28.7 million in 1971 to $92.9 million in 1979, while net income rose from $2.7 million to $10.8 million over that period. By this time, Starrett tools and instruments were being sold in over 100 countries through a network of industrial distributors. By far, the largest consumer of Starrett's products was the metalworking industry—which constituted about 65 percent of the company's revenue—but other important costumers were automotive, aviation, marine, and farm equipment shops, as well as tradesmen such as builders, carpenters, plumbers, and electricians.

Douglas R. Starrett, who had joined the company as an apprentice tool-and-die maker in 1941, succeeded his father as president in 1962. By 1985, the Starrett headquarters was a little-changed four-story brick factory and the company's inventory of little metal parts was piled haphazardly into wooden boxes. Despite its outmoded appearance, Starrett's profit margin of 10.7 percent was three times that of the rest of the machine-tool industry. Even in the face of Japanese competition and its own high prices, Starrett's tools were selling because they were so finely made. Ground to within two-thousands of an inch and sometimes triple-plated, these tools were valued by machinists as the equivalent of works of art.

Half the company's shares were being held by present and retired employees under a retirement-benefits plan adopted in 1946. In fact, the Starrett family held only slightly more than 2 percent of the stock. However, after the employee stock-ownership plan purchased 400,000 shares in the Starrett treasury in 1984, the company bought 341,514 shares from stockholders at $30 a share to avoid dilution of the existing shareholders' voting power. As added protection against any future takeover attempts of the company, Starrett adopted a "poison pill" defense in 1990.

After a sharp slide in fiscal 1983 due to a severe recession, Starrett's sales resumed steady growth later in the decade, reaching $169.9 million in 1988, when net income came to $15.8 million. In 1986, the company bought Evans Rule Co. of North Charleston, South Carolina, for between $20 million and $30 million. A subsidiary of Masco Corp., Evans was producing measuring tapes and associated items.

Interviewed for *New England Business* in 1987, Douglas Starrett reaffirmed his company's commitment to manufacturing. "We could have reduced ourselves to a selling organization," he said, citing companies that had abandoned domestic manufacturing in favor of foreign-made goods. While expressing confidence that Starrett could compete with Japanese and German competitors, Starrett admitted that he was troubled by potential low-wage rivals from China, Taiwan, or South Korea, subsidized production overseas, and product dumping in U.S. markets.

During the 1980s, L.S. Starrett began manufacturing coordinate measuring machines, which combine the functions of several tools and allow for faster and more efficient measuring. A new division for this purpose was established in Mount Airy. To complement this investment, Starrett acquired Sigma Optical, a British firm designing and manufacturing optical measuring projectors, in 1990, establishing a new division for this purpose in Farmington Hills, Michigan.

As Starrett entered the 1990s, net sales, which had reached a peak of $201.6 million during fiscal 1990, fell to $174.8 million three years later. Net earnings dropped from $18.8 million to $8.7 million over this period. In the 1993 annual report, Douglas Starrett deemed 1990 "the year of the largest federal tax increase in history" and went on to say that "because of that tax increase, the economy has gone downhill ever since." Sales increased slightly to $180.2 million and earnings to $9 million in fiscal 1994. The mid-1990s held even more promise for Starrett; during the first nine months of 1995, sales rose from

$133 million to $156.2 million and net income from $5.7 million to $8.8 million.

Among the products being manufactured by Starrett in the 1990s were precision tools, tape measures, levels, electronic gages, dial indicators, gage blocks, digital readout measuring tools, granite surface plants, optical measuring projectors, coordinate measuring machines, vices, M1 lubricant, hacksaw blades, hole saws, band saw blades, jigsaw blades, reciprocating saw blades, and precision ground flat stock. Subsidiaries in Brazil and Scotland were making hacksaw and band saw blades and a limited line of precision tools and measuring tapes. These foreign operations accounted for 26 percent of the company's sales in 1994. One retailer, Sears, accounted for about 11 percent of the company's sales.

The factory in Athol, on about 15 acres of company-owned land, remained Starrett's principal plant, with 25 buildings and about 535,000 square feet of production and storage area. The Granite Surface Plate Division and Coordinate Measuring Machine Division resided in the Mount Airy facility. The Webber Gage Division owned and occupied two buildings in Cleveland. The Evans Rule Division owned and occupied a building in North Charleston, South Carolina, and leased manufacturing space in Mayaguez, Puerto Rico. The Level Division owned and occupied a building in Alum Bank, Pennsylvania. The Advanced Technology Division occupied leased facilities in Gardner, Massachusetts.

Starrett's Brazilian subsidiary owned and occupied a facility in Itu, Brazil. The Scottish subsidiary owned a manufacturing plant in Jedburgh, Scotland, and also leased manufacturing space in Skipton, England. The Canadian subsidiary owned and occupied a building in Toronto. There were also Starrett-owned warehouse/sales offices in Atlanta, Georgia; Buena Park, California; Elmhurst, Illinois; and Farmington Hills, Michigan. Two granite quarries owned by Starrett in North Carolina were sold during fiscal 1994.

Owners and directors of L.S. Starrett Co. controlled 6.9 percent of the voting power in 1994. The president's son Douglas A. Starrett, 42 in 1994, became executive vice-president of the company in 1985. Employee benefit plans accounted for about 17 percent of Starrett's shares of common stock in 1994, according to a Standard & Poor's report; however, the company's annual report declared that present and former employees held about one-half of the outstanding stock. Starrett's long-term debt was $10.8 million.

Principal Subsidiaries: Evans Rule Co., Inc.; Level Industries, Inc.; The L.S. Starrett Co. Ltd. (Scotland); The L.S. Starrett Co. of Canada Ltd; The L.S. Starrett International Co. (Barbados); Starrett Industria e Commercio Ltda. (Brazil); Starrett Securities Corp.

Further Reading:

Baldwin, William, "The Antique Shop in Athol," *Forbes,* November 4, 1985, pp. 54, 58.

Crane, Ellery Bicknell, ed., *History of Worcester County Massachusetts,* Vol. 2, New York and Chicago: Lewis Historical Publishing Co., 1924, pp. 79–80, 829, 845–846.

McLaughlin, Mark, "The Tales of Two Survivors," *New England Business,* September 21, 1987, pp. 11, 13, 15–16.

Mitman, Carl W., "Starrett, Laroy S." in *Dictionary of American Biography,* Vol. 17, New York: Scribner's, 1943, pp. 535–536.

The Starrett Story, Athol, Mass.: L.S. Starrett Co., 1991.

—Robert Halasz

LAMSON & SESSIONS

Lamson & Sessions Co.

25701 Science Park Drive
Beachwood, Ohio 44122-9803
U.S.A.
(216) 464-3400
Fax: (216) 464-1455

Public Company
Incorporated: 1883
Employees: 1,325
Sales: $287.65 million
Stock Exchanges: New York Pacific
SICs: 3644 Noncurrent-Carrying Wiring Devices; 3661 Telephone & Telegraph Apparatus; 3084 Plastics Pipe; 3782 Aircraft Parts and Equipment, Not Elsewhere Classified.

For the vast majority of its over 125 years in business, Lamson & Sessions Co. was a top manufacturer of industrial fasteners—including nuts, bolts, screws, and some exclusive parts—for original equipment manufacturers. But when inexpensive imports infiltrated the company's traditional markets beginning in the late 1960s, Lamson & Sessions made an ill-advised diversification into the manufacture of railroad freight cars. The utter collapse of that market in the early 1980s nearly caused the company's demise. After a series of debt restructurings and strategic acquisitions, the reformed company was primarily involved in the production of industrial and construction products. Spearheaded by its Carlon division, Lamson & Sessions ranked as America's top manufacturer of thermoplastic (i.e., polyvinyl chloride or PVC) pipe, conduit, enclosures, wiring devices, and accessories for the construction, consumer, power, and communications markets. The manufacture of aircraft parts—the result of another 1960s-era diversification—contributed 6 percent of annual sales into the mid-1990s. At that time, the company boasted operations in Ohio, Iowa, California, Florida, Pennsylvania, Texas, Oklahoma, Wisconsin, and Canada.

Lamson & Sessions was founded as a partnership among three men—brothers Thomas H. and Isaac P. Lamson, and Samuel W. Sessions. Their Connecticut business hand-forged nuts and bolts for carriages and wheels using a technique developed during the Civil War. Each of the partners contributed his own expertise to the company: Sam was the office manager, Isaac managed the seven employees on the shop floor, and Thomas was in charge of packing and shipping. The company's 30-product line generated $20,000 in annual sales by 1867.

Growing markets, little competition, and plentiful sources of raw materials, fuel, labor, and transportation drew Lamson & Sessions to the banks of northeast Ohio's Cuyahoga River in 1869. Lamson & Sessions moved to a larger plant in 1882 and was incorporated in Cleveland in 1883. By the turn of the century, the company had begun producing standardized fasteners for the automotive industry. Production for the U.S. effort in World War I drove sales over the $1 million mark in 1916 and past the $2 million level in 1918.

Under a plan devised by George S. Case Jr. and Roy Smith in the 1920s, the company grew through acquisition and internal expansion to become a leading producer of industrial fasteners. Lamson & Sessions acquired Falls Rivet Company in 1921, merged with the Kirk-Latty Manufacturing Company five years later, and added Foster Nut & Bolt Company, Lake Erie Bolt & Nut Company, and American Bolt Company in 1929. A new plant was constructed in Birmingham, Alabama, during this period as well. These additions not only expanded Lamson & Sessions' geographic reach, but also broadened its line of fasteners to include parts for the railroad and auto industries, among others. The company made an initial public stock offering of 20,000 shares and earned a listing on the Cleveland Stock Exchange in 1928. Having achieved a successful expansion, George Case Jr. was elected president of Lamson & Sessions in 1929.

In spite of the stock market crash in 1929 and the ensuing Depression that gripped the economy, Lamson & Sessions boasted eight plants and $11 million in annual revenues by 1930. But as the economic crisis deepened, the company's cash flow dried up. A $750,000 Reconstruction Finance Corporation loan kept the company afloat in 1935. Following the company's emergence from the Great Depression, Case added chairman of the board to his title. He would serve in that capacity through the late 1960s, overseeing an eight-fold increase in annual revenues, from $11 million in 1930 to $89 million in 1969.

World War II-driven demand helped fuel another upturn at Lamson & Sessions in the 1940s, and the company was able to resume its growth through acquisition in the 1950s. The purchase of Stoker Locknut and Machinery Corporation (Pennsylvania) in 1954 was followed by Lamson & Sessions' first foray outside the fastener industry with its 1955 acquisition of Kent Machine Company, a job machine shop. The firm constructed new plants in Chicago and Cleveland and consolidated several operations in those cities over the course of the next two years. Lamson & Sessions closed the decade with the 1959 acquisition of a majority interest in Industria de Parafasos Mapri, S.A., a Brazilian company that ranked as South America's pre-eminent producer of nuts and bolts. The corporation ventured across the Atlantic Ocean to acquire a controlling interest in a West German fastener maker, Fastenrath-Lamson & Sessions GmbH, in 1964.

The growing company undertook a more deliberate diversification in the mid- to late 1960s. In 1966, the firm acquired Angell Manufacturing Company (Kentucky), manufacturer of decorative metal trim and brand identification plates for appliances.

Lamson & Sessions also established a Canadian subsidiary that year, in Toronto, to make and distribute all its products in that country. The purchase two years later of Standard Mirror Company (New York) added a leading producer of automotive mirrors to Lamson & Sessions' roster of businesses. Seeking a high-margin niche in the fastener industry, Lamson & Sessions acquired Valley Bolt Corporation, a California manufacturer of specialized fasteners for the aerospace and aircraft industries, in the mid-1960s. Lamson & Sessions bought Todeco, Inc., another California producer of bearings and other engineered machine components for the same field, and merged the two as the Valley-Todeco, Inc. subsidiary. The 1970 purchase of Expert, Inc. (Michigan) expanded machining operations to include manufacture of machinery for automated assembly systems.

Harold F. Nunn succeeded George Case as president and CEO in 1968. When Nunn was sidelined just two years later with an illness, the board selected George Grabner to lead Lamson & Sessions. Although the company sold its Brazilian fastener subsidiary to U.S. Steel in 1970, it bolstered its domestic fastener business with the acquisition of Zimmer Manufacturing Industries, Inc. (Michigan) and American Screw Products Company (Ohio) in 1973 and 1974, respectively. But when cheap imports began to infiltrate the industry in the 1960s and competition intensified in the 1970s, the firm's management began to question their dedication to the fastener industry.

In the late 1970s, Lamson & Sessions began a new program of diversification that focused on transportation. Specifically, the company acquired Youngstown Steel Door Company, the leading manufacturer of railroad freight cars and components in the United States, in 1976, and added United-American Car, another company in that field, in 1979. Lamson & Sessions merged with Midsco, Incorporated in 1979 as well. Midsco's lead company was Midland Steel Products Co., the country's preeminent producer of mid-sized truck frames.

The entry into railcar manufacture could not have been more poorly timed. Lamson's two primary businesses, industrial fasteners and railcars, were in swift and irreversible decline. Worse, a recession bruised the company's truck frame business. Lamson & Sessions suffered a $15.5 million loss that year.

Grabner brought in Russel B. Every, who had been chairman and president of Midsco, to be president of Lamson & Sessions in 1980. The two men struggled mightily to stop the company's downward spiral. From 1981 through 1985, they divested the fastener interests, sold several losing divisions, and shut down foundry and die casting operations. The divestments and layoffs slashed employment by 78 percent, from 6,000 to 1,300. The company also reduced its selling and administrative expenses by more than half, from $31 million in 1980 to $14 million by 1986, and cut its debt from $100 million to $52 million through belt-tightening measures. Nonetheless, Lamson & Sessions' losses continued to mount, while annual revenues dropped. Sales declined from $215.98 million in 1981 to $130 million in 1982, while losses increased from $9 million to $18.8 million during the same period. The company's net worth plummeted from nearly $88 million in 1979 to just $300,000 in 1983, when net losses peaked at $44 million. Investors balked after Lamson & Sessions eliminated its dividend, depreciating the stock from $19 in 1980 to $1.75 per share in 1983.

According to an April 1983 article in the *Plain Dealer,* Grabner continued to express confidence in the doomed railcar industry, asserting that the market "may be dormant right now, but demand for railroad cars and trucks will return." Unfortunately, he was wrong. Railroad car orders overall plummeted from 119,000 in 1979 to only 6,300 in 1982 and box car orders plunged from 4,200 to 250 over the same period.

In 1987, Russel B. Every told the Cleveland chapter of the Association for Corporate Growth, in a speech reprinted in the *Journal of Corporate Growth,* that "the sale of United-American Car in early 1984 saved Lamson & Sessions." That February, Emery and Grabner cut a hand-written, midnight deal for the divestment of United-American Car, thereby bringing in $10 million cash. According to Every, "That sale gave [Lamson & Sessions] the cash infusion we needed to make our massive debt restructuring program viable."

The executives had started bargaining with the company's 24 debt-holders, mostly insurance companies and banks, to restructure Lamson & Sessions' debt in 1983. Early in 1984, they used $15 million borrowed from Congress Financial Corp. to retire about $13 million of its $54 million debt. New, two-year notes for the remaining $41 million of the obligations were issued as interim financing. That July, Lamson & Sessions exchanged $12 million of the short-term notes for $12 million in newly created preferred stock that could be converted into about one-third of Lamson's common shares. The company completed the first phase of its financial restructuring by converting the remaining $29 million debt into low- and no-interest notes. These efforts helped lower annual debt service, free up operating capital, and thereby allowed the company to avoid Chapter 11 bankruptcy.

Every succeeded Grabner as CEO that same year and was elected chairman early in 1985 upon his predecessor's retirement. Every soon realized that Lamson & Sessions's contraction had positioned it primarily in "mature and possibly shrinking markets," as he noted in the *Journal of Corporate Growth.* The new CEO was convinced that his company would not be able to achieve "real health without a major acquisition of a company serving a growing market." The firm's creditors, however, had made strictures against the company assuming more debt part of their restructuring agreement, and they were extremely reluctant to abandon that safety valve. Over six months of what Every called "lengthy and very difficult negotiations," Lamson & Sessions talked its creditors into taking $17.5 million in cash (part of which was again borrowed from Congress Financial) in exchange for the $31.4 million in securities and interest owed them. The lenders also surrendered part of their preferred stock in exchange for warrants to purchase 500,000 common shares. The restructuring gave Lamson & Sessions an extraordinary gain of $13.3 million and made possible the financing of a sizable acquisition.

Although Lamson & Sessions thought it had the wherewithal to make a major purchase, some industry observers disagreed. In 1986, the company targeted the Carlon division of TBG Inc. (New York), which ranked as a top American manufacturer of thermoplastic accessories for electrical applications. But neither Carlon's European owners nor their financiers, Salomon Brothers, believed that Lamson & Sessions would be able to garner the financing commitments necessary to acquire Carlon. According to December 1987 coverage in the *Plain Dealer,* Carlon was over twice the size of Lamson & Sessions. Every, however, had earned the confidence of Congress Financial Corp., which increased the company's $20 million credit line more than fivefold, to $110 million, in order to enable Lamson & Sessions to make the purchase. At the time, it was Congress Financial's largest-ever acquisition line of credit. The company completed its $85 million leveraged buyout of Carlon late in 1986.

Transformed over the space of a few years from a company with 78 percent of its sales in the railroad and fastener businesses to one with 62 percent of its annual revenues in industrial construction, Lamson & Sessions was reorganized around its new subsidiary. It even moved its headquarters to the east Cleveland suburb of Beachwood, where Carlon was based. After the 1988 divestments of the Youngstown Steel Door Company (spun off to a management group) and a couple of other unrelated businesses, Lamson & Sessions was reorganized around its two remaining businesses. Midland Steel Products Co. and Valley-Todeco were organized as the Transportation Equipment Products division, while Carlon formed the Industrial/Construction Products division.

As it turned out, the Carlon acquisition was infinitely better timed than Lamson & Session's railroad fiasco. The division, which contributed 65 percent of the parent's 1987 sales of $340.4 million, prospered in the burgeoning construction environment of the late 1980s, posting a record-high net income of $9.4 million in fiscal 1988. Lamson & Sessions quickly became a darling of Wall Street investors. A 1987 stock offering raised about $58 million for debt reduction, and from January to October 1988 the shares appreciated 243.3 percent to almost $19. By mid-1988, Lamson & Sessions' net worth had rebounded to $56 million.

Although he had barely served a year with Lamson & Sessions, president and chief operating officer John B. Schulze was selected to succeed Russel B. Every as chief executive officer in January 1989. Schulze advanced to chairman upon Every's retirement one year later.

Unfortunately, the early 1990s brought a recession that hit Lamson & Sessions's chief markets, construction and trucking, especially hard. The company's annual sales declined slightly in 1991 and continued to slip in 1992. And although revenues started to climb in 1993 and 1994, the company was unable to record a profit in any of these fiscal years. Losses totaled over $70 million and the stock dropped to just under $5 in early 1994.

It was around that time that Lamson & Sessions elected to exit the truck business. Midland Steel Products was sold to a subsidiary of Iochpe-Maxion S.A., a Brazilian firm, in mid-1994. The proceeds of the divestment were used to lower the company's debt service. In a seeming vindication of the decision, Lamson & Sessions reported that the year's fourth quarter was the company's first profitable quarter in five years.

Although Carlon has also been characterized as a cyclical business, CEO Schulze hoped that expanding its markets to include the consumer "do-it-yourself" segment would help to smooth the ups and downs. By 1994, that segment contributed 17 percent of annual revenues. Research and development outlays averaging just over $3 million per year were expected to add new proprietary products to the mix. In an early 1995 press release, Schulze cited "strengthening our balance sheet performance and reducing the cost of our debt" as primary corporate goals."

Principal Subsidiaries: Carlon Canada Ltd.; Carlon Chimes Co.

Further Reading:

Every, Russel B., "The Rebuilding of Lamson & Session: An American Success Story," *Journal for Corporate Growth,* June 1988, pp. 99–105.

Gerdel, Thomas W., "Lamson Revamps Debt Structure, Looks to Future," *Plain Dealer* (Cleveland), March 31, 1984, p. C1.

Gleisser, Marcus, "Lamson & Sessions Chief Is Optimistic," *Plain Dealer,* April 23, 1983, p. C7.

History of the Lamson & Sessions Co., Cleveland: Lamson & Sessions Co., 1975.

Karle, Delinda, "Lamson & Sessions Continues Growth," *Plain Dealer,* December 10, 1987, p. F9.

——, "Lamson Rebounds from Deep Plunge," *Plain Dealer,* July 25, 1988, p. C9.

"Lamson Buys Back All Its Debt at a Discount," *Plain Dealer,* June 7, 1985, p. B18.

Rose, William Ganson, *Cleveland: The Making of a City,* Cleveland: World Publishing Co., 1950.

Sabath, Donald, "Lamson Meeting Hears Good News," *Plain Dealer,* June 29, 1984, p. C8.

Sabath, "Weakness in Two Markets Leads to Loss at Lamson," *Plain Dealer,* April 27, 1991, p. D3.

Van Tassel, David D., and John J. Grabowski, *The Encyclopedia of Cleveland History,* Bloomington: Indiana University Press, 1987.

—April D. Gasbarre

Laura Ashley Holdings plc

150 Bath Road
Maidenhead
Berkshire SL6 4YS
United Kingdom
(01628) 39151
Fax: (01628) 71122

Public Company
Incorporated: 1954
Employees: 4,697
Sales: £300 million
Stock Exchanges: London
SICs: 6711 Holding Companies; 2331 Women's and Girls' Blouses; 2335 Women's and Girls' Dresses; 2399 Fabricated Textile Products, Nec; 2649 Converted Paper & Paperboard Products, Nec; 2851 Paints, Varnishes, Lacquers, Enamels, & Allied Products

Laura Ashley Holdings plc is an international designer and retailer of clothing and home furnishings. Invariably described as "quintessentially English," the Laura Ashley name conjures up images of pretty, romantic women (or rooms) draped in tasteful, gracious dresses (or soft furnishings). Laura Ashley markets a dream of English gentility and elegance, as well as countryside wholesomeness and purity that can be purchased in the urban centers of Britain and around the world. To financial analysts and shareholders, however, the Laura Ashley name conjures up another, less pleasing image: that of a company which seems strangely unable to translate its popularity into profits.

"I trust my feelings implicitly in my work. I look at fabrics and I need to feel they've got life and animation—they've got to have character to work for me." Thus Laura Ashley's eponymous founder described the inspiration for her work. Laura and her husband Bernard started their business in 1953. Working from the kitchen table in their London home, the two used the hand silk screen method to print textiles. Laura designed small items such as linen napkins and tablemats while Bernard's specialty was furnishing prints. Design inspiration came from many sources, particularly nature and nineteenth-century prints by artists such as William Morris. So favorable was the initial reaction to the Ashleys' work that within a year they had formed a private limited company and hired more employees. Laura Ashley products were sold in London in the stores John Lewis, Heal's, and Liberty's, and almost from the beginning, were shipped to Paris, Amsterdam, the United States, and Australia. Operations continued to grow, and by 1957, when the first Laura Ashley showroom was opened in London's Burlington Street, domestic and overseas customers numbered about 500.

In 1961 the company introduced its first item of apparel—gardening overalls—and within five years clothing accounted for a significant proportion of Laura Ashley's revenues. Another, larger, London showroom was opened in 1966, and two years later the first Laura Ashley shop debuted, in Pelham Street, Kensington, London. A year later a second shop opened, in Fulham Road, London, and it became apparent that the company was moving firmly from being a design-based business to becoming a retailer in its own right. From this juncture the company grew very quickly, with profits recycled back into research, design, more factories, and a rapidly increasingly number of Laura Ashley outlets.

Along with domestic expansion came overseas growth: the first foreign shop opened in Geneva in 1972, followed two years later by stores in Paris, Dusseldorf, and San Francisco. Success followed success, and it seemed that the global appeal of Laura Ashley's pretty floral designs would result in a retail empire. Until 1985.

In that watershed year, with 30 years of steady, solid success to their credit, and every expectation that expansion would continue, Laura and Bernard Ashley decided to float the company on the stock market. Sadly, Laura died in an accident just weeks before the flotation. The validity of the somewhat melodramatic conclusion later reached by the *Sunday Times*—"with her death, the company lost its essence"—is arguable, but it is certainly true that the new plc was soon engulfed in severe difficulties.

The flotation itself was an undeniable triumph, with shares oversubscribed 34 times. Yet only five years later, in 1990, the company had plummeted sharply into the red and was at serious risk from a takeover bid.

What had gone wrong? Part of the trouble arose from the general economic situation—many British companies suffered in the economic recession of the late 1980s—and part from the prevailing fashions of the times: Laura Ashley's trademark of graceful, floral, feminine apparel was at odds with the vogue for sharp-suited power dressing.

Probably much more damaging than the recession or contrary fashion trends, however, was what the *Independent on Sunday* understatedly labeled Laura Ashley's "rather naive management." Flushed with success (and plenty of capital) after the flotation, Laura Ashley plunged into enthusiastic expansion. By 1987 the company was operating in thirteen different countries but not operating all that well in most of them. The company's performance in the North American market was particularly troubled, bedeviled as it was by an unneccesarily complicated, top-heavy structure, excessive overhead and inventory costs, and an inadequate allocation and distribution system that was exacerbated by deficient communications methods.

Laura Ashley's management team appeared to have little control over a decentralized, haphazard, and inefficient corporate structure. Further, rather than reining back when it began to find itself in financial trouble, the company spent even more; borrowing reached unmanageable proportions, and profits first dwindled, then disappeared. Perhaps the *Economist* described it best: "For decades Laura Ashley made money by selling a vision of Englishness: flowing, flowery frocks and furnishing fabrics in polite, pastel tones. But it also came to indulge in a very English failing—mismanaging the transition from a successful family business to an international retail chain." In 1990 Laura Ashley posted a loss of £11.5 million and was saved only by the intervention of the Japanese retailer Aeon, whose welcome infusion of cash, in exchange for a 15 percent stake, bailed the company out.

For thirteen months during this crucial time, to the amazement of financial analysts, the company operated without a chief executive. Finally in 1991 an American manager, Jim Maxmin, was brought to the position. Maxmin, who later stated starkly that the company had been "heinously mismanaged," embarked on a program of cutbacks, reorganization, and realignment. Believing that Laura Ashley's real strength lay in its quality as a brand, rather than its status as a retailer, Maxmin sought to concentrate on the company's strengths—creating popular designs in clothing and furnishing—and extricate it from those activities in which its record was less favorable. To this end, most manufacturing and distribution operations were contracted out. The latter was achieved via an alliance with Federal Express, in a move to reduce expensive inventories and improve stock movement (a perennial problem area for Laura Ashley, which had on one occasion shipped its winter stock to the United States two months late.) Staffing levels were cut and managers were encouraged to take a more hands-on approach to retailing operations. They were required, for instance, to periodically visit shop floors and endure stints on the customer complaints line. Maxmin's strategies were successful, and Laura Ashley worked its way back to a slight profit in 1992–93 after several years of losses. Recovery continued steadily, though it was slowed by lingering difficulties in the American market.

It came as something as a surprise, then, when it was announced in 1994 that Maxmin was to leave the company after a boardroom "disagreement over investment levels." No further explanation was forthcoming and no new chief executive was actively sought to replace Maxmin. He left with a compensation package of £1.8 million in a year when the company's entire profits totaled £3 million.

After Maxmin's departure, Laura Ashley continued its course of rationalization. Laura Ashley, commented *The Times,* still retained "an absurdly large infrastructure plagued with overmanning." Further jobs were cut, particularly in senior management and administration, in which employee numbers were slashed by a quarter. From 1990 to 1995 some 1,500 jobs were eliminated and six factories closed. "Non-core" products were axed from the Laura Ashley line, and renewed efforts were made to reduce overheads. The head offices in North America and Europe were pared down, bringing them under the jurisdiction of the U.K. head office. In the United States, the company closed down some stores and amalgamated others, and the firm began pulling out of Australia completely. The company also focused on improving its information systems to help alleviate the self-confessed "dysfunction and confusion which has inhibited our past development and held back profitability." Most significantly, Laura Ashley continued to concentrate on its strengths: creative design, a popular brand, a readily identifiable and appreciated image. Laura Ashley undoubtedly serves a niche market but its customers tend to be very loyal. According to the company's former marketing director, the typical Laura Ashley shopper is "romantic, feminine . . . caring, environmentally aware . . . , family orientated, cultured, well-travelled and educated." She is also in the higher socioeconomic brackets and spans all age groups. She is worth wooing, and the company has done so through strategies ranging from special promotional activities such as "tea and Pimm's" parties in its stores, to a personalized interior design service offering customers home visits by "home stylists."

Laura Ashley remains an irony of British business. The quality and desirability of the product it sells are not—and never have been—in doubt. Promoted as a "lifestyle" brand, Laura Ashley scores consistently high in terms of customer recognition and appreciation. "Life," as Laura Ashley's lyrical annual report notes, "is often an assault on the mind." Laura Ashley aims to soften the blow for its customers by offering products that are "unselfconsciously graceful and soothing" and evoke "a timeless mood of peace and serenity." The concept clearly appeals. Somehow, though, while Laura Ashley's creative philosophy may be globally popular, the company's bottom line remains strangely depressing: on a 1994 turnover figure of £300 million, Laura Ashley's profits were a disappointing £3 million. Only time can answer the question posed by the *Economist:* "Will Laura Ashley always remain a business best known for its potential rather than its profits?"

Principal Subsidiaries: Ashley Shops (Ireland) Ltd.; Laura Ashley B.V. (Netherlands); Laura Ashley Espana S.A. (Spain); Laura Ashley GesmbH (Austria); Laura Ashley GmbH (Germany); Laura Ashley, Inc. (U.S.A.); Laura Ashley Ltd.; Laura Ashley N.V. (Belgium); Laura Ashley S.A. (France); Laura Ashley S.A. (Switzerland); Laura Ashley Shops Ltd. (Canada); Laura Ashley Srl (Italy).

Further Reading:

Bain, Sally, "Life Begins at 40 for Laura Ashley," *Marketing,* May 13, 1993, pp. 18–21.

"Chief's Design Out of Style at Laura Ashley," *Sunday Times,* April 17, 1994.

Gilchrist, Susan, "Followers Need Faith in Fashion of Laura Ashley," *The Times,* February 7, 1995, p. 27.

——, "Laura Ashley Cuts Jobs," *The Times,* February 7, 1995, p. 23.

Hollinger, Peggy, "UK Company News: Minimum Reasons Maximise Puzzle," *Financial Times,* April 15, 1994.

"Knifework in the Shrubbery," *Economist,* April 16, 1994.

"Laura Ashley," *The Times,* February 7, 1995, p. 26.

"Laura Ashley Axe Falls on Managers," *Daily Telegraph,* February 7, 1995.

"Laura Ashley Draped in the Colour of Money," *Daily Telegraph,* June 8, 1994.

"Laura Ashley Fails to Bloom," *Independent,* September 23, 1994.

"Laura Ashley Follows the Same Old Pattern," *Independent on Sunday,* April 17, 1994.

Laura Ashley: History, Maidenhead: Laura Ashley Holdings plc, n.d., 5 p.

"Laura Ashley Needs a Heavyweight," *Independent,* April 13, 1994.
"Laura Ashley on Course with Pounds 3m," *Daily Telegraph,* April 15, 1994.
"The New Pattern for Laura Ashley," *Sunday Express,* April 17, 1994.
"Out of Fashion," *The Times,* April 15, 1994.
"Shears Snip Away at Cumbersome Laura Ashley," *Guardian,* February 7, 1995.
Snowdon, Ros, "Fashion Retailers Dress to Impress," *Marketing Week,* February 11, 1994, p. 24.
Stevens, Larry, "A Perfect Fit," *Bobbin,* November 1992, pp. 88–91.
"UK Company News: Further Cuts at Laura Ashley," *Financial Times,* February 7, 1995.

—Robin DuBlanc

Lego A/S

DK-7190 Billund
Denmark
75 33 11 88
Fax: 75 35 33 60

Private Company
Incorporated: 1944
Employees: 8,800
Sales: $2 billion
SICs: 3944 Games, Toys, and Children's Vehicles

Managed by the founding company, Lego A/S of Billund, Denmark, the Lego Group consisted of 45 companies which distributed Lego toys in 133 countries around the world in the mid-1990s. Owned exclusively by the Kristiansen family of Denmark, this intensely private company has never released sales figures for public review. However, industry analysts have estimated annual revenues at about $2 billion, making Lego the fifth largest toy company in the world. The tremendous global success of Lego can be attributed both to the ingenuity of the Lego System toys and to the integrated marketing approach of this one-brand corporate group. Lego products, including the Duplo line for preschoolers and the Lego Technic line for older children, can be found in about 75 percent of American and 80 percent of European households with children.

The Lego brand of toys was created in 1932 when Ole Kirk Kristiansen, a Danish carpenter, decided to extend his carpentry business by manufacturing a line of simple, hand-carved, wooden toys. He called his new toy business "Lego" as a contraction of two Danish words "leg godt" meaning "play well." Years later when Lego construction toys became immensely popular in Europe, people pointed out that Lego also means "I assemble" in latin, but Kristiansen always claimed that this double meaning was purely serendipitous. During the bleak years of the 1930s, Kristiansen sold his simple wooden toys door to door in the tiny farming community of Billund, Denmark, where he lived. After facing near bankruptcy in 1932, Ole Kirk managed to survive by combining the production of his wooden toys with more mundane household implements such as ladders and milking stools. In one memorable year, the small woodworking firm became involved with the international yo-yo craze. Lego began large scale production of the toy only to discover that, like most toy fads, the yo-yo boom died as suddenly as it had begun. His storerooms crammed with thousands of the unwanted wooden discs, Kristiansen converted yo-yo halves into wheels for a new toy truck that became very popular with Danish children.

After the turmoil of World War II and a disastrous fire that destroyed the toy factory in 1942, Ole Kirk Kristiansen decided to rebuild his enterprise. A larger and more modern factory was built near the site of the old warehouse in Billund and the company was converted from a sole-trading firm to a private limited toy manufacturing company named Legetojsfabrikken LEGO Billund A/S (The LEGO Billund Toy Factory Ltd.). Ole Kirk took the title of senior manager and appointed his son Godtfred as junior manager. By 1947, the Lego company had matured into a prosperous family enterprise which manufactured almost 150 different kinds of carved wooden toys and employed about 40 people.

In the postwar period, good quality plastic became widely available for the first time, prompting Lego to add plastic toys to its line of merchandise. Initially, these plastic toys were coolly received by Danish consumers, with one journalist pointing out that "plastics will never take the place of good, solid wooden toys." Despite this early setback, Lego continued to experiment with plastic toys; in 1949, Lego made its first tentative step into toy history when the company introduced Automatic Binding Bricks, a plastic building toy in which the blocks could grip together to prevent block towers from toppling on little children. These blocks had studs on top, like today's Lego bricks, but their undersides were hollow, allowing the blocks to grip only when they were placed directly on top of one another. These bricks were not well received by toy consumers and many were returned from retailers unsold.

The concept for the Lego System was born in 1954 when Ole Kirk Kristiansen's son Godtfred visited a local toy fair. One of the buyers at the fair complained to Godtfred that all of the toys being offered at the exposition were alike and that no toy company offered a comprehensive toy system that would encourage creativity in children. Godtfred felt challenged by this complaint and returned to the Lego toy factory determined to come up with an original toy system. He drew up a list of ten requirements that he felt were essential for a quality line of toys. Among the more obvious criteria, like high quality and good play value, were some particular qualities that would distinguish the future Lego brick system. These criteria included the requirement that the toy line be enjoyable for either sex, that it cover a wide age group, that the system include a large number of components, and that compatible pieces be available for adding on to the parts already purchased. Upon reviewing more than 200 toys already being produced by the Lego company, Godtfred decided that the Automatic Binding Bricks, which at this time accounted for only about 5 percent of sales, held the most promise as the basis for an integrated toy system.

In 1955, the building bricks, manufactured in bright red, yellow, white, and blue, were renamed the "Lego System of Play" and marketed not just as building blocks but as an integrated toy system. Packaged with model street signs, cars and trucks, the construction set encouraged children to create whole city blocks instead of just one building. The great virtue of the Lego System was that it was infinitely expandable; a parent could purchase a set with bricks and accessories and then be encouraged to buy limitless numbers of add-on sets. In succeeding years, the small Billund toy factory was deluged with orders for the Lego System of Play, due in large measure to Godtfred's insistence on extensive advertising and personal sales meetings with the major Danish toy retailers.

Although sales of the new toy system exceeded expectations, the company continued to experiment with the design of the product. A major breakthrough came in 1957 when, after testing a variety of models with local children, the company introduced the now-famous Lego brick with studs on top and tubes underneath. This new design not only held the bricks together more firmly, but it allowed a child to place the bricks together in any configuration. Three eight-studded bricks could now be combined in 1,060 ways. A child could build tall structures of practically any shape or size, limited only by the number of Lego bricks at his or her disposal.

With the new and improved bricks, soaring Danish sales, and a newly renovated and expanded factory, Lego executives felt that it was time to make a serious effort at marketing their toy system internationally. Initially, Lego had exported their products on only a limited basis by means of wholesale agents in other European countries; however, by the late 1950s they began to set up their own foreign sales subsidiaries. In 1956, the first foreign sales office was opened in Germany, to be followed quickly by offices in Switzerland, Belgium, France, Sweden, and Great Britain. Through these subsidiaries, the Lego company began to consider the whole of Europe as their home market for the Lego product and to use this base to extend sales overseas. By the early 1960s, licenses for the North American production and distribution of the plastic toy had been sold to the Samsonite Corporation; further, the Lego Overseas division recruited sales agents to sell the plastic bricks in Africa, Asia, Australia and South America.

From the start of this international expansion, Lego executives had decided that only the Lego construction system would be marketed internationally. This decision would mark the first step in Lego's move to become a one product company as the small plastic bricks began to account for larger and larger shares of sales. The fate of the wooden toys that had been the mainstay of the business for more than 20 years was finally sealed in 1960 when a fire destroyed the portion of the factory in which they were produced. Lego managers decided not to rebuild the wooden toy division, but instead to concentrate all production facilities on the Lego construction toy system.

American distribution of Lego products began in 1961 when the giant Samsonite Corporation acquired the American and Canadian license to manufacture and distribute the popular Danish construction toy. Samsonite was looking to diversify its growing company and felt that its experience in plastics and retailing corresponded well with the plastic toy industry. Samsonite opened plants in Stratford, Ontario, and Loveland, Colorado, to manufacture Lego bricks and established a separate sales force to market the product. Although Samsonite managed to sell a respectable $5 million in Lego products annually in North America, the sales figures never matched the huge success that Lego was having in the European market. As a result, Samsonite relinquished its Lego System license in 1973. "Our managerial expertise was better suited to consumer durables than to toys, so we eased out of the toy business" a Samsonite executive stated in a 1976 article in *Business Week.* The Lego Group moved in immediately, establishing an American sales company, Lego Systems, Inc., in Brookfield, Connecticut. In only two years, through heavy investment in advertising and promotion, the subsidiary was able to raise sales levels by more than 10 times; to meet this enormous increase in demand, the Lego Group set up a huge 143 acre site in Enfield, Connecticut, in 1975 for the manufacture and sales of Lego products. By 1976, annual retail sales in the U.S. had reached $100 million, accounting for almost one third of Lego sales worldwide.

By the early 1970s, the Lego company employed 1,000 workers at its Billund headquarters, was earning $50 million annually, and was responsible for nearly 1 percent of Denmark's industrial exports, according to toy historian Marvin Kaye. As the sales of the Lego construction toy system grew and new foreign sales subsidiaries were opened, it became imperative for Lego A/S to reorganize its administrative structure. Under the directorship of Godtfred Kristiansen, who had assumed control of the company after his father's retirement in 1956, Lego began to transform itself from a small family business into a multinational corporation. Although this evolution was begun in the 1960s, with the creation of separate divisions to handle product development, technological development, and sales and promotion, the pace and scale of these changes increased dramatically in the mid 1970s. In 1976, partly at the urging of Godtfred's son Kjeld Kirk Kristiansen, the Lego company was split into five sister companies.

International management and coordination was transferred to a new company called Interlego A/S (later to be renamed Lego A/S) and for the first time an outsider, Vagn Holck Andersen, was appointed to head overall operations. Lego System A/S would retain responsibility for the manufacture and direct supervision of European sales companies, Lego Systems Inc. would oversee North American sales and production, Lego Overseas A/S would coordinate sales in those countries without their own sales companies, and Lego Futura ApS would be responsible for product development. According to a 1974 article in *International Management,* Godtfred was reluctant to give up direct control over the day to day management of Lego, but he eventually agreed to create a more efficient management system. However, Godtfred was firm in his determination to keep the company private in spite of suggestions that going public would provide the capital for a more rapid expansion. In 1979, the Kristiansen family regained direct administrative control of the company with the appointment of Godtfred's son Kjeld Kristiansen as president of Interlego A/S.

The basic Lego brick remained virtually unchanged since its introduction in 1958. The mechanical properties and raw material of the bricks were improved so that they fit together more easily, but a brick made in 1958 would still join with one made in the mid-1990s. However, many new components were added to the Lego system with the basic requirement that all new products be compatible with all other elements of the system. In the 1960s, the Lego System sets began to be organized around specific themes, including trains, space, and airplanes. By the 1990s, these theme-related sets had evolved into ten product lines: Freestyle, Belville, Town, Space, Castle, Pirates, Ships,

Trains, Aquazone, and Model Team. Each product line included many different sets with components geared to each specific theme, but nonetheless compatible with the components of all the other product lines.

One of Godtfred Kristiansen's original principles for his toy system was that it be attractive to both boys and girls. Although girls had always formed a share of the Lego market, market research revealed that the majority of Lego sets were being bought for boys. Over the years, Lego has attempted to broaden its appeal to girls. In 1979, the company introduced a Lego block based jewelry set, but it failed to capture the imagination of the five- to seven-year-old girls for which it was designed; the line was discontinued after a couple of years of mediocre sales. Undaunted, Lego introduced a new segment of their Basic product line oriented specifically for girls. Called Paradisa, the principal feature of the new line was its color. Pale pink, pastel, purple, and turquoise blocks were considered more attractive to girls than the traditional primary colors of the Lego System products. According to David Lafrennie, Lego's American PR director, the Paradisa line was very successful, and Belville, a girl-oriented set with a "role-playing" theme, was launched in 1994.

Another of Godtfred Kristiansen's principles was that the toy system be fun for all ages. From its introduction, Lego System was designed for a fairly broad age range of three to 16 years, but the Kristiansens felt that they could strengthen either extreme of this range by adding lines specifically developed for pre-schoolers and the older child. In 1969, Duplo Toys were introduced. Using the same principle of the interlocking brick as the Lego System, Duplo bricks were larger and easier to manipulate with small hands; further, they could also be combined with the smaller Lego bricks as the child grew. Lego Technic, introduced in 1977, was designed to bolster the other end of the age range and bring Lego play into the teen years. With Lego Technic the older child could build technically realistic models using the gears, pulleys, beams and other special pieces found in Lego Technic sets.

By the early 1980s, Lego had amassed an enormous share of the worldwide construction toy segment. Sales grew at an average rate of about 10 percent a year through the 1980s and early 1990s in spite of overall slow growth in the toy industry. In the late 1980s, total sales had soared to about $600 million, much of the increase due to the huge gains made in the United States and Canada. This steady growth was capped by an astounding 18 percent increase in 1991, at a time when overall toy industry sales rose by only 4 percent. In 1992, Lego controlled about 80 percent of the construction toy market, according to *Advertising Age.* By the mid-1990s, the small Billund carpentry business had grown into a group of 45 companies on six continents employing almost 9,000 people.

The largest threat to Lego's dominance of the construction toy market in the 1980s and 1990s did not come from competing construction toys but from Lego imitators. One of the great virtues of the Lego System was the simplicity of its basic building blocks, but this simplicity has also proved to be a liability in which other companies could easily reproduce the basic design. Compounding this problem was the fact that the patent on the design for the Lego brick expired in 1981, forcing Lego to enter lawsuits with other companies involving trademark infringement on packaging, logos, and accessories but not on the brick design itself. Although a number of small companies produced cheap imitations of Lego using names like Rego, Dalu, or even Leggo, these small-scale unpromoted brands proved to be little more than an irritant to the giant Lego Group. A much greater threat came from the established toy company Tyco Toys, Inc., which in 1984 launched its Super Blocks series featuring plastic building blocks that were interchangeable with Lego bricks. Lego Systems sued Tyco in both the U.S. and Hong Kong courts but, after four years of litigation, they were unsuccessful in stopping sales of Super Blocks. Tyco's copy-cat product, while never approaching Lego sales volumes in the U.S., nonetheless managed to capture some 10 percent of U.S. sales of construction toys in the late 1980s. Even more importantly, the lower price of Super Blocks put pressure on Lego to keep their prices at a competitive level.

Although Lego had essentially been a single brand company since the early 1960s, the 1990s witnessed growth in the non-toy segment of the Lego Group. This new market included the extension of Lego licenses to a variety of children's items including clothing, children's room decor, and books. Since 1968, an invaluable part of the Lego marketing campaign in Europe had been the Legoland Park in Billund, Denmark. Built from some 42 million Lego bricks, the theme park attracted more than 20 million visitors, all of whom went home with a new vision of the potential of Lego toys. A new Lego theme park was scheduled to open outside London in 1996 and plans for an American park in Carlsbad, California, were also underway.

Lego marketers attributed the tremendous success of their construction system to their integrated marketing approach and their emphasis on brand building. "We put all our eggs in one basket, and we market that basket," Dick Garvey, vice-president of marketing, stated in a 1992 article in *Advertising Age.* However, a toy analyst with Kidder, Peabody & Co. told *Advertising Age*'s Kate Fitzgerald in 1991 that Lego's phenomenal growth could not last: "Lego's been allowed to grow by leaps and bounds for the past decade mainly because they had a lot of catching up to do. The construction-toy market in the U.S. was wide open . . . Lego is only now reaching the saturation point in the U.S. and they're going to have a hard time keeping up their momentum." In spite of these predictions, Lego sales have continued to grow in the 1990s, largely due to increases in sales of Lego Technic and the popular new lines for girls. With its stable base and continually evolving new product lines, Lego Systems remains poised to dominate the plastic construction toy segment of the industry well into the 21st century.

Principal Subsidiaries: Lego Futura ApS (Denmark); Lego Dacta (Denmark and Germany); Lego World (Denmark, Great Britain, and United States); Lego System A/S (Denmark); Lego Systems Inc. (United States); Lego Overseas A/S (Denmark); Lego Produktion AG (Switzerland).

Further Reading:

"A Danish Toymaker Puts It Together in the U.S.," *Business Week,* September 6, 1976, pp. 80, 83.

50 Years of Play, Billund, Denmark: The Lego Group, 1982.

Fitzgerald, Kate, ''Lego: Dick Garvey. (The Marketing 100),'' *Advertising Age,* July 8, 1992, p. S20.

——, ''Toyland's Elusive Goal—Win Over Both Sexes,'' *Advertising Age,* February 8, 1993, pp. S2, S18.

Kaye, Marvin, *The Story of Monopoly, Silly Putty, Bingo, Twister, Scrabble, Frisbee et cetera,* New York: Stein and Day, 1973, pp. 155–159.

Kestin, Hesh, ''Nothing Like a Dane,'' *Forbes,* November 3, 1986, pp. 145, 148.

''Lego and Tyco Blocks,'' *New York Times,* November 15, 1988, p. D13.

''Lego Taps New Markets, but Keeps an Eye on Its Image,'' *Brandweek,* February 8, 1993, p.28.

Meeks, Fleming, ''So Sue Me,'' *Forbes,* November 28, 1988, pp. 72, 74.

Morais, Richard C., ''Babes in Toyland?,'' *Forbes,* January 3, 1994, pp. 70–71.

Oates, David, ''The King of the Lego Castle,'' *International Management,* January 1974, pp. 32–36.

—Hilary Gopnik

Lincoln Electric Co.

22801 St. Clair Avenue
Cleveland, Ohio 44117
U.S.A.
(216) 481-8100
Fax: (216) 486-1751

Public Company
Incorporated: 1906
Employees: 2,000
Sales: $906.6 million
Stock Exchanges: New York
SICs: 3548 Welding Apparatus; 3621 Motors & Generators

Lincoln Electric Co., a leading producer of industrial electric motors and high-tech cutting equipment, is the world's largest manufacturer of arc-welding products. Although the majority of the company's equity remained in the hands of Lincoln family members in the early 1990s, the firm commemorated its 1995 centenary with a $100-million public stock offering, the first such stock offering in the company's history. The mid-1990s were also marked by a return to business profitability for the company. After suffering back-to-back net losses in 1992 and 1993, the company scored record sales and earnings in 1994. Many industry analysts attribute the company's long-term success and resiliency to its methods of managing and rewarding its workers, who rank among the world's highest-paid and most productive.

Lincoln Electric is perhaps best known for its unique strategy for handling employee relations, known as the Lincoln Incentive Management System. This program evolved during the first half of the twentieth century, and has remained virtually intact during the second half of the century. It focuses on six themes that are interwoven throughout the company's history: people as assets, Christian ethics, principles, simplicity, competition, and customer satisfaction.

Although Lincoln Electric Co. was founded by John C. Lincoln in 1895, it is his younger brother, James, who is most identified with the firm and its unique management system. Both were sons of an unordained minister. James Finney Lincoln was born in 1883 in Painesville, Ohio, about 25 miles northeast of Cleveland. His middle name refers to Charles Grandison Finney, a well-known nineteenth-century revivalist who also served as president of Oberlin College.

Lincoln's Congregationalist upbringing undoubtedly contributed one of the fundamental tenets of the Incentive Management System: Christian ethics. He based this precept on a simple exhortation from the Sermon on the Mount: "Do unto others as you would have them do unto you." In his 1961 book, *A New Approach to Industrial Economics,* Lincoln called this "program" (widely known as the Golden Rule), "the complete answer to all problems that can arise between people."

James grew up on a farm, then traced his elder brother's footsteps to Ohio State University and the study of electrical engineering. In the preface to *A New Approach,* biographer Charles G. Herbruck noted Lincoln's athletic prowess over his academic performance. "One of Ohio State's outstanding fullbacks," according to Herbruck, Lincoln led the school's football team to an undefeated season in the fall of 1906. In 1907, however, Lincoln was struck with typhoid fever. The illness so debilitated him that he was compelled to drop out of school.

Rather than finish out the year and earn his degree, Lincoln elected to go to work for his older brother, John, who had founded the Lincoln Electric Company in 1895 to manufacture and repair electric motors. By the time he was joined by his younger sibling, John had expanded into the new field of rechargeable batteries for electric automobiles and begun research in arc welding.

James became the firm's first and only salesman, working for $50 per month and a two percent commission on sales. John, who was more interested in new product development than corporate operations, soon abdicated the management of the company to his younger brother. James advanced to vice-president within four years, and became general manager of the entire operation in 1914 at the age of 31.

One of James Lincoln's first moves as head of the company reflected his acknowledgement that he was relatively inexperienced, but eventually became a fundamental feature of the company's Incentive Management System. He formed an advisory board comprised of elected representatives from each department within the firm. Although no authority was delegated to the group, its members could bring literally any issue, large or small, to the floor for discussion. This management technique was one practical outgrowth of Lincoln's goal to treat people as assets deserving respect.

This body's twice-monthly meetings became a permanent facet of Lincoln Electric's management scheme. The board's continued existence has also been cited as a factor in the company's non-union and strike-free history. One longtime employee interviewed for Robert Levering and Milton Moskowitz's 1993 book, *The 100 Best Companies to Work for in America,* commented that, "you tell them [the Advisory Board] everything you want to tell them. It's just like if you had a union, but you tell it to the top management, the chairman and the president."

Freed from the constraints of management to concentrate on his craft, John Lincoln developed the electric arc welding machine that would become his company's primary product. Arc welding had originated in the late nineteenth century, but early methods resulted in brittle, unreliable joints. The introduction of a new electrode in 1907 resulted in stronger welds and convinced James Lincoln that the arc welder was the manufacturing tool of the future. Up to that time, welding was used primarily for repairs, but Lincoln envisioned its application at virtually all stages of manufacturing and construction. Still, he found it difficult to convince potential customers that welding was a viable—or even superior—method of joining materials. According to biographer Herbruck, one dubious observer told Lincoln that he would "kick off with his toe any weld Mr. Lincoln could make."

In order to promote the concept, Lincoln started a welding school (which would become America's oldest and most reputable), sponsored design competitions, published books, conducted seminars, and wrote articles in trade journals. He also began applying the techniques to his own products. The use of arc welding during the manufacturing process helped Lincoln Electric gain up to 50 percent cost reductions on the production of electric motors and the welding machines themselves. His efforts finally paid off. During the period between the two world wars, Lincoln was able to convince an engineering and construction firm—the Austin Company—to use welding techniques on a building. Although expensive, the resulting structure helped launch a new era in commercial construction.

In the meantime, Lincoln had begun implementation of some of the practical aspects of the Incentive Management System. The piecework pay system was adopted in 1915. Under this system, periodic evaluations of the time required, difficulty of, and "going rate" for each job set the per-piece rate. Some have criticized piecework as a high-pressure method of recognizing a worker's contribution, but supporters claim that studies have shown that Lincoln's workers are often twice as productive as their counterparts in competitors' shops. They also argue that Lincoln workers earn more than their counterparts elsewhere, with some workers' annual pay exceeding $100,000.

Lincoln added employee benefits during this period as well. The company added an employee stock option plan in 1925 (workers owned an estimated 30 percent of the company in the early 1990s), offered life insurance in 1915, and started the company's suggestion system in 1929.

The hardships of the Great Depression precipitated Lincoln Electric's famous "bonus plan." In 1934 Lincoln employees responded to depression-era cuts in hours and pay by offering—through their advisory board—to work longer hours in exchange for a share of the company's profits. That first year's payout, which was distributed from profits after taxes and dividends had been paid, averaged 30 percent of each worker's regular annual pay. Although a discretionary item, the annual bonus (with some modification) has remained in place throughout the rest of the company's history.

The addition of the bonus plan necessitated the implementation of a merit evaluation program that assigned equal weight to four areas: production, quality, cooperation and ideas, and supervision required. In the Lincoln evaluation program, each employee starts the year with 100 points. Points are added or subtracted in the course of semi-annual reviews. For the most part, its a zero-sum game: workers compete for a limited number of points in all areas but quality. If one loses a point, another has a chance to earn it. Moskowitz and Levering contend in *The 100 Best Companies to Work for in America,* however, that "Lincoln's competitive incentive system has not fostered a dog-eat-dog environment, but rather one where people seem to be working harmoniously." The bonus system and evaluation process embodied two of Lincoln's cherished precepts: decision-making based on unwavering principles and "the universal benefits of competition." The institution of these and other programs supported continued growth for Lincoln. By the mid-1930s James Lincoln had turned his company into what a 1993 *Compensation and Benefits Review* article called "one of the first companies in the United States to install a successful productivity-based incentive system for all employees."

By the early 1940s Lincoln had grown to become the world's largest manufacturer of arc welding equipment, with subsidiaries in Canada, the United Kingdom, and Australia, and licensees in Mexico, Brazil, and Argentina. By 1944 Lincoln Electric's benefits package included a company-funded pension plan. An internal promotion program that bolstered already-strong company loyalty was also launched.

Lincoln experimented with a "guaranteed employment" policy in the post-World War II era. This arrangement was designed to preserve a skilled work force and encourage employee suggestions for increased efficiency. According to the policy, anyone who worked at the company for two years—later increased to three years—would not be laid off (although the work week could be shortened to 30 hours and workers could be reassigned, possibly to lower-paying jobs). The program was made permanent in 1958, but management retained the right to institute a layoff as long as it gave workers six months' notice.

Unlike many companies in other manufacturing sectors, Lincoln staved off foreign competitors by maintaining high productivity and quality, yet offering their goods at low prices. Although material costs multiplied in the postwar era, James Lincoln set a goal of reducing costs by ten percent annually. With money- and time-saving ideas from the employee suggestion plan, the company was able to hold prices at 1933 levels until runaway inflation in the 1970s compelled price hikes.

Lincoln was able to incorporate his management theories into the 1951 design and construction of a new 30-acre plant in Euclid. The building, which did not include windows, carpeting, or executive quarters, embodied his belief that simplicity in design contributes to organization management.

James Lincoln acted as the company's president until 1954, when he advanced to chairman of the board. He was succeeded as president by William Irrgang, a German engineer with 26 years of experience at Lincoln Electric. Irrgang, who advanced to chairman in 1965 and assumed the new title of CEO in 1972, essentially carried on the conservative policies of his mentor throughout his 14-year tenure. For example, Lincoln had a capital investment policy that prohibited spending on projects with a payback of over one year. Although this policy was effective for the essentially domestic business of James Lincoln's era, it did not account for the increasingly global economy that emerged in later decades.

George "Ted" Willis, a graduate of Harvard Business School, became president in 1972. He had first heard James Lincoln speak about the Incentive Management System in the 1940s, and decided to join the company in 1947 upon earning an MBA.

During the early 1980s, Willis was constrained from aggressively expanding the company's interests by Irrgang's conservatism and an overall economic recession. Lincoln Electric's revenues dropped 40 percent, from $450 million in 1981 to $220 million in 1982, as all of the company's traditional markets declined. The economic crisis put the manufacturer's no-layoff policy to the test. About 15 percent of Lincoln's employees were reassigned; production workers did plant maintenance, took clerical assignments, and even went on the road as salesmen. Average pay was halved, from $44,000 to $22,000. The salaries of top executives were trimmed as well, although not as severely. George Willis' pay dropped 20 percent, and Donald Hastings' compensation was cut by over 11 percent.

Still, no one was laid off, and the company (which remained profitable) even managed to pay a bonus. In order to boost sales, Lincoln introduced the industry's first five-year warranty on motors, expanded its distributor network by 71 percent, and guaranteed cost savings to its customers.

Lincoln emerged from the early 1980s downturn debt-free and profitable. It also retained its leadership of the welding industry. It was poised for growth, and when ultimate leadership of the company passed to Willis upon Irrgang's death in 1986, Willis wasted no time in expanding the company, both in terms of product offerings and geography. New welding and cutting products, including flux wire, robotic, and gas-based welding systems, helped expand Lincoln's product offerings to a full line of welding equipment.

The company maintained solid relationships with its employees in the 1980s and early 1990s. Employee turnover at the company in the first 90 days ran high, at 25 percent, but remained remarkably low (three percent) overall. A rewarding retirement plan (called "the best . . . in the land," by Moskowitz and Levering) probably contributed to this outstanding statistic as well. After 40 years' service, employees receive an annuity that allows them to retire at age 65 with full pay. Lincoln has no mandatory retirement age, though, so if an employee continued to work after age 65, he would receive his regular earnings in addition to the pension.

A total of 19 acquisitions from 1986 to 1991 helped boost annual sales by 87.3 percent, from $445.31 million to $833.89 million. The first of these was close to home; in 1986 Lincoln acquired Cleveland's Airco Electrode plant from BOC Group. A second transfer of property from the United Kingdom's BOC to Lincoln Electric, a Montreal electrode plant, occurred that same year. In 1987 Lincoln purchased an Australian electrode plant from France's Air Liquide. A 1988 joint venture with Norweld Holding A.A., a Norwegian company with $100 million in annual sales, quadrupled Lincoln's business in Northern Europe to $135 million annually. That same year saw the acquisition of two welding factories in Mexico and two more in Brazil.

Upon his 1992 retirement, Willis was praised for doubling Lincoln Electric's sales, expanding its international presence from four to 15 countries, and securing a spot for the company on the "Forbes 500." That dramatic growth, however, came at a cost. The repercussions were felt during Donald Hastings' term as CEO and chairman. The fast-paced expansion had increased long-term debt from $17.5 million in 1988 to $221.5 million in 1993. Unanticipated difficulties in transplanting the incentive system to operations in such countries as Brazil, Mexico, and Germany, coupled with a 40 percent drop in the European market, contributed to a $46 million loss in 1992. Although orders in the United States were so high that Lincoln stayed open through its usual summer shutdown in 1993, the company still suffered its worst quarter ever. The company saw an overall loss of $38 million in 1993.

Early in 1994, the company closed factories in Europe, Latin America, and South America, thereby eliminating 770 jobs. In the United States, however, where demand continued to run high, the company added 600 jobs. The company's decision to shed itself of those international operations resulted in a complete turnaround: 1994 sales and earnings reached record levels of $907 million and $48 million, respectively. The company hoped to mark its centenary year, 1995, by surpassing $1 billion in annual sales.

Principal Subsidiaries: Lincoln Electric Co. Seal-Seat Co.; Lincoln Big-Three, Inc.; Lincoln Electric Co. Harris Calorific.

Further Reading:

Bendix, Jeffrey, "A Day's Pay for a Day's Work," *Cleveland Enterprise,* December 1992–January 1993.

Bredin, James, "Don Hastings Sparks Success," *Industry Week,* December 6, 1993, p. 21.

Chilton, Kenneth, "Lincoln Electric's Incentive System," *Compensation and Benefits Review,* November–December 1993, p. 21.

Gerdel, Thomas W., "Lincoln Electric of Euclid Tells Secret of Productivity," *Cleveland Plain Dealer,* February 18, 1983, p. C7.

——, "Experts Debate Copying Lincoln's Incentive Plan," *Cleveland Plain Dealer,* February 22, 1983, p. C1.

——, "Lincoln Electric Will Expand in Europe," *Cleveland Plain Dealer,* May 31, 1988, p. C1.

——, "Lincoln Electric Incentive System Sometimes Suffers in Translation," *Cleveland Plain Dealer,* December 20, 1992, p. F4.

——, "Quality Pays Off, and How," *Cleveland Plain Dealer,* December 20, 1992, pp. F1, F4.

——, "Workers Asked to Skip Vacations," *Cleveland Plain Dealer,* June 18, 1993, p. F1.

Leinert, Anita, "A Dinosaur of a Different Color," *Management Review,* February 1995, p. 24.

Levering, Robert, and Milton Moskowitz, *The 100 Best Companies to Work for in America,* New York: Doubleday/Currency, 1993.

Lincoln, James F., *A New Approach to Industrial Economics,* New York: Devin-Adair Co., 1961.

Modic, Stanley J., "Fine-Tuning a Classic," *Industry Week,* March 6, 1989, p. 15.

Moley, Raymond, *The American Century of John C. Lincoln,* New York: Duell, Sloan & Pearce, 1962.

Posner, Bruce, "Right From the Start," *Inc.,* August 1988, p. 95.

Sabath, Donald, "Lincoln Electric Closing Some Foreign Factories, Eliminating 770 Jobs," *Cleveland Plain Dealer,* March 29, 1994, p. 4C.

——, "Lincoln Electric Going Public," *Cleveland Plain Dealer,* March 31, 1995, p. 1C.

——, "Spinoffs Turn Lincoln Electric Losses to Profits," *Cleveland Plain Dealer,* March 7, 1995, p. C4.

Seifullah, Alan A. A., "Lincoln Electric's No-Layoff Plan," *Cleveland Plain Dealer,* May 3, 1987, p. E4.

Weiss, Barbara, "Lincoln Electric Expands Worldwide," *Metalworking News,* June 6, 1988, p. 6.

—April D. Gasbarre

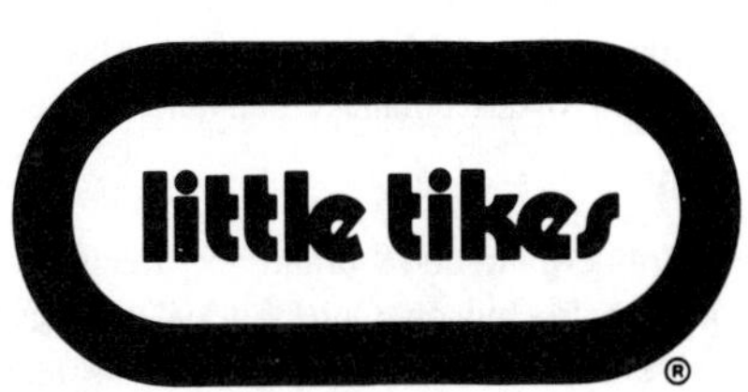

Little Tikes Co.

2180 Barlow Road
Hudson, Ohio 44236
U.S.A.
(216) 650-3000
Fax: (216) 650-3109

Wholly Owned Subsidiary of Rubbermaid Inc.
Incorporated: 1970
Employees: 3,500
Sales: $444 million (estimate)
SICs: 3944 Games, Toys & Children's Vehicles; 2512 Upholstered Household Furniture.

The distinctive, brightly colored plastic toys produced by the Little Tikes Co. have become a staple for American children under the age of five. Little Tikes is the fourth-largest American toy manufacturer and one of the top three toy makers for the pre-school market. A wholly owned subsidiary of Rubbermaid Inc., Little Tikes has enjoyed meteoric growth over the past decade. From annual sales of about $50 million in 1984, Little Tikes sales rose to over $400 million by 1995. These enormous gains have occurred despite the company's steadfast refusal to advertise its products to kids. With the exception of a few print ads in parenting magazines, the company's promotional activities consist exclusively of catalogue distribution, very visible customer support services, and word of mouth.

The Little Tikes Co. was founded in 1970 by Thomas G. Murdough. Murdough became interested in the toy business in 1968 when his then-employer, Wilson Sporting Goods, asked him to run marketing for its Wonder Products subsidiary. The late 1960s saw the toy industry undergo a period of intense transformation, as smaller companies and distributors found themselves being swallowed up by the big manufacturers. Murdough was reportedly appalled by the increasing shoddiness of toys. According to an article in *Fortune,* Murdough felt that the toy manufacturers' sole aim was to bring toys to market at ever-cheaper prices. This trend was exacerbated by the huge new discount retailers who often sold popular toys at a loss in order to bring people into their stores. Murdough was determined to buck this trend. He quit his marketing job at Wilson and set out to start his own company. Murdough saw a need for well-made plastic toys, as only the cheapest fabrication processes and forms of plastic raw materials were being used in toy manufacture at that time. In 1970 he formed the Little Tikes Co. and, with nine employees, began to manufacture large plastic outdoor play equipment, toyboxes, and children's furniture in an old barn in Aurora, Ohio.

Little Tikes pioneered the use of rotational molding, an industrial process for molding plastic that had formerly been used mainly to produce large products like agricultural tanks and chemical containers. Rotational molding could produce larger, more durable products than the traditional blow molding that had been widely used in the toy industry. By allowing for a large variety of shapes with large surface areas, fewer parts were needed to create each large toy. Fewer parts meant not only less assembly time on the factory floor, but also a more durable final product. In addition, the new process permitted the production of a variety of colors at the same time, adding versatility to the production process.

From the start Murdough insisted on maintaining his own personal approach towards toy marketing. He was convinced that by restricting distribution of his products to independent toy stores and toy supermarkets he could avoid the deep discounting that had eventually forced other toy manufacturers to lower production costs and quality. Large discount stores like Kmart tended to "cherry-pick" the hottest items out of a given manufacturer's line and then sell them at or under cost in order to draw parents in. Small retailers were then faced with lowering their prices in order to compete. As their profit margins shrunk to unmanageable levels, they then put pressure on manufacturers to further lower wholesale costs. Murdough avoided this pattern by simply declining to distribute through large discount stores. "Murdough had a good understanding of how not to go to market. He was very careful not to flood the market with merchandise," said one retailing executive in a 1989 *Business Week* article. Murdough carefully nurtured his relationship with the small toy retailers. By discouraging deep discounting of its most popular toys, Little Tikes kept profit margins high for all its retailers. In exchange, the company insisted that retailers stock the full range of the Little Tikes line.

In addition to keeping retailers happy, Murdough's approach to marketing allowed Little Tikes to create an up-scale, "boutique" image for its products. This was important because Little Tikes relied almost exclusively on word of mouth to promote its large, and often pricey, plastic play equipment. Murdough was convinced that advertising to kids was not only morally questionable, but was also not good business sense. Little Tikes toys were almost exclusively designed for pre-schoolers, an age when pressure to conform to fads is at a minimum. The pre-school market had always shown much more brand loyalty than other segments of the toy industry. Parents tended to choose toys they felt would be durable and safe for the younger child, and they relied on a manufacturer's reputation to ensure this kind of quality.

The giants of the pre-school toy industry, Fisher-Price and Playskool, had relied heavily on building brand equity to achieve their dominance of this sector, and it was clear that Little Tikes had to build a stellar reputation if it wanted to succeed. Advertising on television was a very expensive and not particularly effective way of communicating a message of reliability to new parents. For this reason, Murdough chose to forego all television advertising and concentrate instead on creating a reputation for superb customer service. Little Tikes became one of the first companies to mold an 800 number into all its products and to hire and train specialized staff to respond promptly to customer queries and complaints. The company enclosed a catalogue displaying the whole Little Tikes line with all its toys in order to encourage a feeling of buying into a brand instead of just a single toy. With much lower advertising costs, Little Tikes could also afford to charge less for its products than the heavily advertised competition, which further encouraged parents to try the Little Tikes plastic play equipment.

Murdough's approach to the internal management of Little Tikes was as unconventional as his marketing philosophy. From the start, when all the employees of Little Tikes could easily fit into his office, Murdough held monthly no-holds-barred meetings to discuss company strategy. As the company grew Murdough retained this open style of management. He introduced profit-sharing, subsidized on-site child-care, and offered tuition reimbursement for employees furthering their education. In an industry that was known for a cutthroat approach to personnel management, Little Tikes commanded impressive staff loyalty. Murdough was also committed to keeping jobs in the United States. When most toy makers were transferring the bulk of their manufacturing overseas, 99 percent of Little Tikes products sold in the United States were made and assembled there.

The Little Tikes product marketing approach was an overwhelming success. As the baby-boom generation began to have kids of their own, the pre-school toy industry boomed. Little Tikes's image as a sort of parents' toy club encouraged word-of-mouth advertising, and sales soared. The company quickly outgrew the old barn that had served as its headquarters and manufacturing plant, and in the mid-1970s moved its operations to a much larger plant in Macedonia, Ohio. Within the next decade Little Tikes would also open manufacturing plants in Ireland and Canada and begin distribution of its toys outside the United States. By the end of the 1970s Little Tikes's sales had grown to about $15 million and its product line had expanded to include ride-on toys. In 1979 the company introduced its first major hit toy, the Cozy Coupe ride-in car. This red and yellow foot-powered vehicle was enclosed, unlike the time-honored tricycle, and seemed to give kids a sense of security about venturing forth in the world. By the early 1990s the Cozy Coupe was the best-selling car in North America, beating both Ford's Taurus and Honda's Accord, which prompted Ford's marketing director to quip that they'd "have to give those kids a good trade-in on a Taurus."

With its Cozy Coupe and a variety of very popular playhouses and outdoor play equipment, Little Tikes entered the 1980s in a position to begin competing seriously with the large, established pre-school toy manufacturers. In 1982, during a period of decline for the toy industry as a whole, Little Tikes sales increased by 28 percent to $23.1 million, which was followed by an astounding 73 percent rise to $42.9 million in 1983. It was clear that Little Tikes toys were more than just a passing fad. During the same period the giant housewares company Rubbermaid Inc. was undergoing a major restructuring and was searching for new acquisitions. The fledgling toy company, with its emphasis on plastic and its family image, was a good match for Rubbermaid and an offer was made. Murdough was reluctant to give up control of Little Tikes, but he felt that the company needed Rubbermaid's capital if it was to continue to expand. Rubbermaid acknowledged that Murdough and his management team had been fundamental to the success of the toy company. In 1984 Rubbermaid bought Little Tikes for about $50 million, with the agreement that Murdough would stay on as president and his approach towards management and marketing would be retained.

With new capital from Rubbermaid and a brand new manufacturing plant and headquarters in Hudson, Ohio, Little Tikes was set to begin an intensive expansion of its product line and distribution. It added a "spring-summer" line of outdoor play equipment that included climbing and sliding sets as well as plastic sports equipment. The company also began to depart from its exclusive reliance on rotational molding by having a line of small injection-molded toys manufactured for it at other facilities. With its new products and increased manufacturing capabilities, Little Tikes sales grew at a rate that far exceeded the toy industry as a whole. By 1987 the company's sales had topped $100 million, and then they more than doubled in the following two years to reach about $270 million in 1989. Little Tikes accounted for 28 percent of its parent company's profits by the late 1980s, prompting one analyst to comment in the *Wall Street Journal* that Little Tikes was the "star" of Rubbermaid's stable of companies.

Throughout the growth period of the 1980s Murdough managed to retain the approach to marketing that had been so successful for the toy company. Only 6 percent of sales was spent on advertising, compared to an industry average of about 20 percent. Little Tikes also continued to resist television advertising or any ads directed at children. In 1985 Murdough even canceled Little Tikes's membership in the Toy Manufacturers of America because of the trade association's support of marketing to children. The customer service branch of the company was expanded and catalogue mailings continued to grow.

In spite of this seemingly steady course, friction began to develop between the managers of Little Tikes and Rubbermaid over the retail distribution of Little Tikes toys. Large discounters like Kmart and Ames were the linchpin of Rubbermaid's approach to selling its popular housewares, and senior management at Rubbermaid began to put pressure on Little Tikes to end its policy of selling only through toy and specialty stores. Murdough felt that to allow discounters to carry only the best-selling Little Tikes products would be unfair to Little Tikes's full-line retailers, who had to make considerable commitments of floor and stockroom space to accommodate the large playsets. Murdough insisted that selling through discount chains would lead to short product life spans. "You saturate the marketplace," Murdough told the *Wall Street Journal* in 1989. "That's a big part of the reason the toy industry is flat on its back."

By the fall of 1989, it became clear that Murdough and parent Rubbermaid's positions on marketing could not be reconciled, and Murdough resigned his position with the company. "It turns out we never needed Rubbermaid's money," said a frustrated Murdough in a 1993 *Forbes* article. "I was spending all my time just keeping them [Rubbermaid executives] out of my hair.'' Rubbermaid chairman Stanley C. Gault, however, insisted that the dispute was not so much about retail relationships as Murdough's management style. ''[Murdough] is unable to work for a boss, regardless of the autonomy he has. He won't take criticism,'' Gault told the *Wall Street Journal* after the resignation.

Rubbermaid quickly appointed Gary Baughman, who had headed up its Evenflo division, as the new president of Little Tikes. Under Baughman, Little Tikes began to experiment with broader advertising, even conducting an ad agency review, but test marketing surveys revealed that 30-second television spots were ineffective at conveying the Little Tikes message and the campaign was dropped. Instead, the course that Murdough had set was strengthened and a new 6,000-square-foot center was built to house the company's growing customer service department. Baughman chose to concentrate on increasing the efficiency of the production end of the company, and five additional manufacturing plants were opened in the United States over the course of the following five years.

The early 1990s saw Rubbermaid making intensive efforts to increase its international presence, which at that time accounted for only about 15 percent of total sales. To this end, Little Tikes manufacturing and distribution centers were built in Luxembourg and Korea to serve the European and Asian markets. In spite of increased foreign manufacturing, about 80 percent of Little Tikes toys sold in the United States were still manufactured in North America.

Little Tikes's policy of growth took on a new direction in the 1990s as the company acquired three small commercial playground equipment companies: Iron Mountain Forge (Missouri), Ausplay (Australia), and Paris Playground Equipment (Canada). In conjunction with these companies, Little Tikes began to produce large commercial playground equipment suitable for child care centers and community playgrounds. The large plastic and steel PlayCenters were designed to sell at about $3,000, some two to five times less than the more traditional wood and steel structures. Although the longevity of these plastic play systems was only one-third that of the more traditional steel playgrounds, Little Tikes felt that the significantly lower cost would be attractive to child care centers, which tended to replace equipment every few years. In spite of president Baughman's 1994 defection to rival toy company Tyco, Little Tikes seemed poised to continue its rapid growth in the last half of the 1990s.

Further Reading:

Fitzgerald, Kate, ''Disney Aids Mattel Surge in Two-Legged Toy Race,'' *Advertising Age,* September 28, 1994, p. 41.

Flax, Steven, ''The Christmas Zing in Zapless Toys,'' *Fortune,* December 26, 1983, pp. 98–103.

Grimm, Matthew, ''Little Tikes with a Grown-Up Dilemma,'' *Adweek's Marketing Week,* September 10, 1990, p. 18.

Lavin, Douglas, ''Ford's Taurus No. 1? That's Bull Says Car Maker with Cozy Niche,'' *Wall Street Journal,* January 11, 1993, p. B1.

Mallory, Maria, ''Why Little Tikes Managers Picked Up Their Toys and Left,'' *Business Week,* November 27, 1989, p. 33.

Palmeri, Christopher, ''Back in Charge,'' *Forbes,* January 18, 1993, pp. 102–103.

Pierson, John, ''Form and Function,'' *Wall Street Journal,* August 5, 1994, p. B1.

Rakoczy, Christine, ''Quality Isn't Kid Stuff,'' *Quality in Manufacturing,* November/December 1992.

Swasy, Alecia, ''Corporate Focus: Rubbermaid Moves beyond the Kitchen,'' *Wall Street Journal,* February 3, 1989.

Verespej, Michael, ''A New Age for Little Tikes,'' *Industry Week,* April 16, 1990, pp. 11–13.

''Who's News: Rubbermaid Names Evenflo's Baughman President of Its Little Tikes Co. Toy Unit,'' *Wall Street Journal,* December 5, 1989.

Zapanta, Melissa, ''Little Tikes Sells Product with Reputation, Few Ads,'' *Crain's Cleveland Business,* August 31, 1992, p. 17.

—Hilary Gopnik

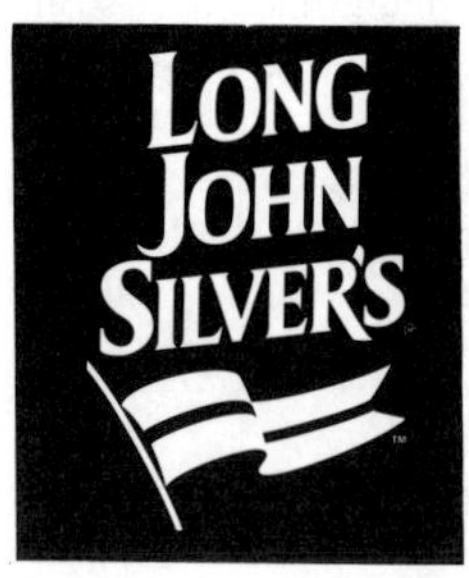

Long John Silver's Restaurants Inc.

101 Jerrico Drive
Lexington, Kentucky 40509
U.S.A.
(606) 263-6000
Fax: (606) 263-6680

Private Company
Incorporated: 1946 as Jerrico Inc.
Employees: 26,000
Sales: $923 million
SICs: 5812 Eating Places; 6794 Patent Owners and Lessors

Long John Silver's Restaurants Inc. is the country's largest quick-service seafood restaurant chain, with around 71 percent of the estimated $1.3 billion market. With headquarters in Kentucky and divisional offices Atlanta, Dallas, and Kansas City, the company oversees a network of over 1,400 restaurants, 480 of which are franchises, in the United States, Canada, Saudi Arabia, and Singapore. Until the late 1980s, Long John Silver's was one of a group of restaurants held by Jerrico Inc., a food service group that included Jerry's Restaurants and the Fazoli's pasta chains. Jerry's and Fazoli's were divested, however, and the company's focus shifted to its seafood establishment, Long John Silver's.

The history of Long John Silver's (LJS) can be traced to 1929, when Jerome Lederer, the company founder, opened a six-seat hamburger stand he called the White Tavern Shoppe in Shelbyville, Kentucky. The concept proved popular and thrived throughout the Great Depression. Altogether, 13 White Tavern Shoppes were in existence when World War II came along and claimed ten of them due to shortages of meat, sugar, and manpower.

Lederer regrouped in 1946, establishing his company as Jerrico Inc. and introducing a new restaurant in Lexington, called Jerry's Five and Dime, reflecting the new establishment's focus on promoting 15-cent roast beef sandwiches. In 1947, realizing that people weren't willing to pay that much for a roast beef sandwich, Lederer converted Jerry's menu to focus on hamburgers.

As he rebuilt his company, Lederer hired Warren W. Rosenthal to manage his restaurants in 1948. The two men reportedly met when Rosenthal rented a room from Lederer while attending the University of Kentucky. Although Rosenthal initially considered careers in retailing and in life insurance, he eventually accepted Lederer's invitation to join him in the restaurant business. Soon the two men were looking for a restaurant concept they could duplicate across the country. They tried new menu concepts at Jerry's by adapting food service ideas borrowed from restaurants in other locations.

The popularity of eating away from home and the growth of the restaurant business in general was just beginning; Jerrico's timing was perfect. By 1957, Jerrico was operating seven Jerry's Restaurants and was one of the first companies to use the franchise concept as a means of stimulating growth. Rosenthal, who had been made chief executive officer of Jerrico, eventually served as president and gained ownership of the company as well when Lederer died in 1963.

Jerrico's success in the food service industry has been credited to the company's willingness to generate ideas and take risks. Indeed, the company tested a variety of restaurant concepts during the 1960s, including: Lott's (roast beef and other sandwiches); Davy's Dock (full service seafood); Don Q's (Spanish food); and The Governor's Table (full service dining).

Then, in 1969, Rosenthal was inspired to try out a new market for quick-service seafood as competition for the standard American favorites of hamburger, pizza, and fried chicken. Rosenthal studied the competition, particularly the menu at the H. Salt Fish and Chips chain, and then convinced James Patterson, a Jerry's Restaurant franchisee, to join him at Jerrico to help develop the notion of an expanded version of fast food fish-n-chips. Patterson became the first president of Long John Silver's.

Shortly after taking Jerrico public in 1969, Rosenthal launched Long John Silver's Fish & Chips, a name inspired by Robert Louis Stevenson's novel *Treasure Island.* Located on Southland Drive in Lexington, the first restaurant was a success; LJS developed into a chain and soon became Jerrico's most successful endeavor. By the end of 1971, there were more than 200 LJS units in operation.

Designed to provide the atmosphere of a seafood establishment along a wharf, the outlets' interiors were decked out with brass lanterns, signal flags, and boat oars. The original menu featured battered fish, chicken, french fries, and hushpuppies. However, noting that competitor H. Salt had a relatively limited menu and was experiencing financial difficulties, Rosenthal quickly moved to expand LJS's offerings, implementing a more comprehensive line of seafood to augment its batter-dipped fillets. By 1973, the chain's name was changed to Long John Silver's Seafood Shoppes to reflect this expanded menu. During this time, Ernest E. Renaud, Jerrico's executive vice-president since 1971, became the second president in LJS history.

By June 1976, there were 621 LJS restaurants in operation. Of these, 262 were owned directly by Jerrico and another 359 were franchised to independent operators, who paid a fee to Jerrico for the concept and covered construction and business costs themselves. Within two years, the total number of shops had grown to 1,000, of which 464 were company-owned. In May 1978, Jerrico consolidated its operations from four buildings scattered around Lexington to a new $7 million headquarters.

Changes in LJS leadership took place in the early and mid-1980s. In 1982, Renaud was named president of parent company Jerrico in addition to his duties as LJS president, while Rosenthal retained a role as chairman of the board. In 1984, John E. Tobe, who had been LJS's chief financial officer since the early 1970s, succeeded Renaud.

Growth at LJS continued apace in the 1980s, as company-owned development increased significantly. By 1984, Jerrico owned 812 of a total 1,355 LJS restaurants, and by 1987 LJS accounted for approximately 75 percent of Jerrico's total revenues and 80 percent of its operating profits. That year, the chain boasted 1,421 outlets with reported sales of $451 million, roughly 65 percent of the "fast fish" category. Although LJS was not considered a truly national chain at the time, it was gaining enough ground to warrant an investment in regional network television advertising time. Jerrico's intent was to have stores in all areas of the country by 1990, and to have LJS become a full network television advertiser.

During this time, Jerrico's other business interests included a chain of Jerry's Restaurants and other new restaurant concepts the company was testing, including a full service Italian restaurant called Florenz, established in Ohio. Jerrico also opened its first fast-food Italian restaurant—called Gratzi's—in 1988. Such diversification was prompted in part by the continually rising prices of Icelandic cod, LJS's staple menu item; hoping not to become overly dependent on the LJS chain, with its rising operating costs, Jerrico continued to expand its holdings. Moreover, LJS was facing increasing competition from outside the industry, particularly from grocers and their suppliers, who were quick to take advantage of market demand for fast food that could be microwaved at home. In 1989, Jerrico premiered Fazoli's, a quick-service Italian pasta restaurant modeled after the Florenz established.

However, national economic recession and the high price of fish brought some problems for Jerrico in the late 1980s, and the company would soon undergo dramatic changes. When the company's stock value began to waver as investors grew concerned over reduced profits, talk of taking the company private through a management-led buyout surfaced. In September 1989, Jerrico was acquired for $620 million in a leveraged buy out by a company called Pisces Inc., made up of a group of senior Jerrico executives and a joint force of Castle Harlan and DJS-Inverness, both New York-based investment firms. Warren Rosenthal, having been with the company 41 years, retired as chairman of the board at the age of 67. He was reportedly well compensated for his role in developing the company, receiving an executive severance payment of $1.275 million in addition to the $57.4 million he received from cashing in related stock interests. LJS, which reported sales of $826 million in 1989, became a subsidiary of Pisces Inc.

Clinton A. Clark, a partner at Castle Harlan, joined the board of LJS during the buy out and became the company's president in 1990. Clark was charged with bringing the company safely through the immediate post buyout, debt laden years. During his tenure, Clark began an effective turnaround of the company. He created an LJS mission statement centered on providing superior products, guest satisfaction, mutual respect among team members, and "a vision of excellence" for the future.

As part of Clark's refocusing efforts, the new parent company decided to dedicate all of its resources to the operations of LJS in 1990. Toward that end, the company's other three restaurant concepts—Jerry's, Fazoli's, and Florenz—were put on the block. The 46 Jerry's restaurants were purchased by Atlanta-based Great American Restaurants, the country's largest franchisee of Denny's Family Restaurants. Fazoli's, a particularly promising start-up, was bought by the Japanese-owned firm Seed Restaurant Group Inc. Jerrico attempted to sell its seven Florenz restaurants as a chain, but was unsuccessful, and by 1991, all seven sites were closed. Jerrico Inc., as it was, ceased to function, and the company that emerged was known by a more recognized name, Long John Silver's Restaurants Inc.

In the early 1990s, LJS began to tailor its menu to answer the growing nutrition concerns of its health-conscious customers. Broiled and grilled items were introduced and represented the fastest-growing of the restaurant's product lines. In 1991, the company introduced three hot meals, baked rather than fried and all priced at around $4, during Lent season. According to a February 1992 article in *Restaurants & Institutions,* Mary Roseman, director of nutrition and consumer information at LJS, asserted that "the baked program provides good sales when we can support it with marketing. Unfortunately, though, when you're not on TV or not really pounding the message, it's hard to keep the interest there." Advertising on a national scale was still two years away for LJS.

Market trends were not favorable for LJS during this time. According to one Illinois-based market research firm, the share of industry traffic at fish and seafood specialty restaurants slipped from 2.8 percent in 1986 to 2.5 percent in 1991. The quick service growth area in 1991 came from other nonseafood chains, which were adding some seafood items to their menus.

This additional competition as well as increased prices of some staple menu items put seafood restaurants at a disadvantage in the quick-service industry. Value had to be improved if consumers were expected to eat a seafood dinner instead of a lower priced hamburger and fries meal. In October, LJS revealed a new value menu chainwide. The Add-a-Piece menu enabled the purchase of any basic meal with additional individual pieces of fried fish, shrimp or chicken for 69 cents or less. With the price of a basic meal at around $1.99, the new menu allowed increased flexibility for the customer and the elimination of redundant items from the menu.

After guiding the company successfully through its move from public to private status, Clark, who had become chairman in February 1992, announced his resignation in July 1993. In October 1993, Clyde E. Culp, a member of the company's board, was named president and chief executive officer. Culp's vision for the company was to "reinvigorate the quick-service seafood category" through LJS's dominant position within the segment.

In the spring of 1993, the company's first kiosk was opened at the Louisville General Electric plant in Louisville, Kentucky. The kiosk, called Long John Silver's Express, was a smaller version of the restaurant and was franchised by Canteen Corp., a large contract food service provider owned by TW Services. The kiosk offered a limited menu with four meal choices.

During the first three weeks of operation, Canteen's lunch participation increased by approximately 1,200 customers.

That summer, LJS reported that drive-through service, among those LJS outlets that had it, was increasing sales by almost 30 percent. Recognizing the needs of an expanded customer base, Bruce Cotton, LJS vice-president of public relations, explained in a July 1993 *Restaurants & Institutions* article that "at first, we didn't feel fish would transport very well, so we worked on better carryout containers and holding times for fish. We also changed our french fries to an extra-crispy type that holds heat really well."

In August 1994, in a rare advertising move, LJS unveiled its "America's Favorite Shrimp Game" tie-in with the premier of the Universal Pictures film "Little Rascals." Jobie Dixon, LJS vice-president of marketing and creative media explained in the August 1994 *Nation's Restaurant News* that the company was aware of movie/fast-food promotions being run by McDonald's and Burger King, and that "research shows that if you get a good, interesting tie-in, it can add some magic for the consumer that translates into extra visits." Scheduled to run through mid-September, both the movie and "America's Favorite Shrimp Game" exceeded expectations.

Because of its earlier success with kiosks, LJS continued to add these nontraditional sites, expanding primarily on university campuses. In September 1994, the company opened a store front unit at California Polytechnic State University, its first West Coast kiosk. John Ramsey, vice-president of franchise development, stated in a September 1994 *Nation's Restaurant News* that the company believed college students would "look for branded food names that they recognize from home. . . . Students know our food will taste the same at Cal-Poly as it does in their home towns."

Also during this time, Triarc Cos., a diversified holding company and the parent of Arby's Inc., announced plans to acquire LJS for $75 million in cash and $450 million in assumed debt. Triarc's plan was to dual-brand its stores, housing its lunch-oriented Arby's restaurants under the same roofs as dinner-oriented LJS restaurants. However, in December, with rising interest rates and unfavorable capital markets looming, Triarc declared that it was canceling the debt-heavy deal. Both companies, however, said they would continue to pursue the possibility of joint housing.

LJS continued to enhance its menu, presenting its Flavorbaked line in the fall of 1994. This line included chicken breast and fish sandwiches, light-portion items, meals, and combination deals. LJS promoted the introduction with a $5.5 million marketing campaign, using network/cable television advertisements and couponing to support the new products.

LJS reported systemwide sales of $923 million for fiscal 1994 from its 1,456 company-owned and franchised locations in 38 states, Canada, Singapore, and Saudi Arabia. The company had 70 participating franchise groups ranging in size from 1 to 89 units. The company saw record sales in early 1995 and also experienced record annual franchise growth, as the new franchise projects in development at the time outnumbered those of fiscal years 1993 and 1994 combined. Although Long John Silver's remained $292.6 million in debt, incurred during the 1989 buyout, the company appeared prepared for continued growth and success, planning to add 100 franchise units and 50 company-owned units annually through the 1990s.

Further Reading:

Allen, Robin Lee, "Long John, Rascals 'Gang' Up for Shrimp Promo," *Nation's Restaurant News,* August 22, 1994, p. 12.

——, "Long John's Sails on in Wake of Clark's Exit," *Nation's Restaurant News,* July 26, 1993, p.3.

Chaudhry, Rajan, "Fast-Food Seafood Chains Sell Health, Variety," *Restaurants & Institutions,* February 26, 1992, pp. 12–13.

Daykin, Tom, "Jerrico Will Sell Jerry's, Fazoli's," *Lexington (Kentucky) Herald-Leader,* May 2, 1990, pp. A1, A5.

"Jerrico Inc.," *Advertising Age,* November 23, 1987, p. S31.

Jordan, Jim, "From Humble Start, Jerrico Tinkered Its Way to Success," *Lexington (Kentucky) Herald-Leader,* August 14, 1989, pp. D1, D8–9.

——, "Little by Little, Jerrico Chief Maps Future," *Lexington (Kentucky) Herald-Leader,* August 14, 1989, pp. D1, D9.

"LJS Franchisee Spawns Fast-Fish Double Drive-Thru," *Nation's Restaurant News,* August 17, 1992, p. 2.

"LJS Opens Cal-Poly Kiosk," *Nation's Restaurant News,* September 5, 1994, p. 11.

"LJS Rolls Out New Flavorbaked Line," *Nation's Restaurant News,* November 7, 1994, p. 2.

"Long John Silver's Chairman Resigns," *Nation's Restaurant News,* July 19, 1993, p. 2.

Pack, Todd, "Ex-Jerrico Restaurants: Where Are They Now?," *Lexington (Kentucky) Herald-Leader,* March 26, 1995, Bus. Sec. p. 14.

"Patrons Don't Live by Fish Alone," *Restaurants & Institutions,* July 15, 1993, pp. 161, 164, 168.

Pearce, Bette, "Jerrico is Packing Up and Heading for a New Home," *Lexington (Kentucky) Herald-Leader,* January 15, 1978, p. B5.

Prather, Paul, "Rosenthal: 'Happy To Step Out'," *Lexington (Kentucky) Herald-Leader,* October 8, 1990, p. A8.

"Triarc Cos. Cancel Its Plan to Acquire Long John Silver's," *The Wall Street Journal,* December 13, 1994, p. B4.

Walkup, Carolyn, "Long John Silver's Teams with Canteen to Open First Kiosk," *Nation's Restaurant News,* March 22, 1993, pp. 3, 67.

—Jennifer Voskuhl Canipe

LSI Logic Corporation

1551 McCarthy Boulevard
Milpitas, California 95035
U.S.A.
(408) 433-8000
Fax: (408) 434-6457

Public Company
Incorporated: 1980 as LSI Logic, Inc.
Employees: 3,370
Sales: $902 million
Stock Exchanges: New York
SICs: 3674 Semiconductors & Related Devices; 3577 Computer Peripheral Equipment Not Elsewhere Classified

A leading competitor in the customized semiconductor market, LSI Logic Corporation represents a defining force in a segment of the semiconductor industry that was recording robust growth during the mid-1990s. Formed in 1980, LSI Logic emerged during the nascence of the industry it dominated during the 1990s, helping to create and shape a market that was predicted to represent more than $5 billion by the beginning of the 21st century.

During the early 1980s, the global semiconductor industry was neither a fertile nor a hospitable market for U.S. companies to enter. By 1991, Japanese manufacturers had gained an early and sizeable lead over the rest of world, controlling 70 percent of the worldwide market for 64K DRAM chips—key components in computers, video games, and telecommunications systems and the most widely-sought products on the market. The few U.S. semiconductor manufacturers mustering any appreciable opposition against the Japanese during the period were large corporations based in California's Silicon Valley. These manufacturers—even those with sufficient financial clout—struggled to catch up in an expensive high-technology race most especially against the Japanese, who held considerable market share and ample funding for the expensive endeavor of designing and producing memory chips.

Such was the climate pervading the semiconductor industry during the formation of LSI Logic. Despite the overwhelming odds against a small entrepreneurial company successfully competing in a market where much larger corporations were floundering, Wilfred J. Corrigan, the founder of LSI Logic, was intent on carving a niche in the industry, and in defying what he later called the "conventional wisdom that the semiconductor industry was only for major corporations." To accomplish this formidable task, Corrigan positioned LSI Logic in a small segment of the semiconductor industry, focusing on a branch that offered tremendous growth potential and the opportunity for a small, fledgling enterprise to survive. By doing this, Corrigan gave LSI Logic a viable niche in which to begin business. No matter the strength of his idea, however, Corrigan needed money to get his venture started. The money would need to come from investors willing to take a high-risk gamble with their dollars on the slim hope that a small company could effectively compete in the combative semiconductor industry. Much, then, would depend on Corrigan's ability to convince the financial community that his company was worth investing in, a task made even more difficult by his recent, less-than-illustrious track record as the leader of another company involved in the semiconductor industry. The high risk of financing such a small, entrepreneurial company, combined with Corrigan's unfavorable record in the years leading up to his new venture with LSI Logic, presented investors with an opportunity they presumably would avoid.

Roughly six years prior to LSI Logic's formation, Corrigan, son of a Liverpool, England dock worker and a graduate in chemical engineering from the Imperial College of Science, had gained control over a prominent semiconductor company, Fairchild Camera and Instrument Company. Serving as Fairchild's chairman, chief executive, and president, Corrigan led the company through an overambitious and disastrous diversification into video games and digital watches while losing market share and falling behind in the technological race in the semiconductor business. Against this backdrop of disappointing results, Corrigan gained the reputation as a somewhat dictatorial leader who liked to show the opening scene of the movie "Patton" during sales meetings. Corrigan's troubled tenure as Fairchild's top executive ended approximately five years after it began, precipitated by Fairchild's acquisition by another company, Schlumberger Ltd., in 1979. Less than a year later, Corrigan left Fairchild to embark on a short stint as a private investor, then began effecting plans to launch his own business, LSI Logic.

With LSI Logic, Corrigan planned to enter a small segment of the semiconductor industry that produced relatively small batches of semi-finished microelectronic chips, which were then customized for each customer. As opposed to the major segment of the semiconductor industry contested by large manufacturers in Silicon Valley and in Japan, the customized chip industry produced chips that enabled its customers to differentiate their products from those of their competitors, while the major semiconductor companies manufactured standard chips in bulk. Corrigan intended to focus on one technique in the customized chip business known as gate arrays, in which the basic logic elements, or "gates," were laid out on a chip and then connected in a particular customized order during the last stages of production.

During the early 1980s, this field of the semiconductor industry was quite small, yet Corrigan believed the demand for customized chips, or application-specific integrated circuits (ASICs), would grow immensely in the coming decade. Corrigan convinced a group of venture capitalists, based chiefly in the Bay Area, to provide his company with the $6 million necessary to begin business. The company was incorporated in November 1980 and began operating in early 1981 using leased facilities in Santa Clara, California. Corrigan occupied the same executive positions he had held at Fairchild, serving as LSI Logic's chairman, chief executive officer, and president, ready to steward the company in a market that represented under $100 million at the time but was expected to become a $1 billion industry by 1986.

Although Corrigan held the same senior management titles at LSI Logic as he had at Fairchild, there the similarities ended. At LSI Logic, Corrigan shed the unsavory image he had developed at Fairchild and astutely led his small company through its formative first years. In August 1981, less than a year after beginning business, LSI Logic entered what company officials described as the "first fully cooperative semiconductor development program involving U.S. and Japanese companies" when it formed a joint venture with Toshiba Corporation to develop a line of advanced semi-custom circuits. The joint venture represented a connection that would grow stronger and deeper as the company sought to take the lead in a burgeoning market. To secure a commanding position in the market, however, LSI Logic needed ample funding for developmental programs intrinsic to success in a high-technology business. Corrigan was repeatedly able to obtain the necessary capital for development which consequently enabled LSI Logic to expand and capture market share in a field other semiconductor companies were slow to enter. Another major infusion of capital arrived in March 1982, this time totaling more than $16 million, the bulk of which came from the same venture capitalists that had provided the money to get LSI Logic started. A group of investment bankers in the United Kingdom and First Interstate Bank supplied the rest of the money, which was used for capital equipment purchases and plant expansion.

Despite the arrival of the needed funding, the year-end finances were disappointing. By the end of 1982, LSI Logic had collected $5 million in sales, but recorded a loss of $3.7 million, making Corrigan's plan of reaping profits in the customized chip market still a dream. The following year, however, the company recorded the first of many prodigious leaps in its sales volume, when revenues shot up seven-fold to $35 million. Perhaps more encouraging, LSI Logic also demonstrated its profitability, registering $12.5 million in net income for the year—an enormous sum given the company's revenue total. During the next few years, however, LSI Logic's profit total fell considerably short of the sales-to-profit ratio recorded in 1983; revenues rose vigorously throughout the decade, but profits remained comparatively low.

As before, the drive to become the leader in its market required the infusion of capital, something LSI Logic needed in 1981, 1982, and again in 1983. In May 1983, while LSI Logic was recording its first year of undeniable financial strength, Corrigan orchestrated his company's first public offering, which the Japanese investors readily accepted. Japanese investors acquired a considerable portion of LSI Logic's stock, demonstrating a willingness to invest in the company. Corrigan then allowed Japanese investors to take part in LSI Logic's growth the following year with the formation of LSI Logic's Japanese affiliate, Nihon LSI Logic Corporation. The venture financing of Nihon LSI Logic was completed in April 1984 through a private offering in Japan that raised $20 million and ceded a group of 28 Japanese investors a 33 percent stake in the newly formed affiliate. Corrigan raised an additional $20 million by employing the same strategy two months later through a private placement for LSI Logic's British subsidiary, LSI Logic Ltd.

The creation of Nihon LSI Logic and the strengthening of the British subsidiary, LSI Logic Ltd., which had been in existence since 1982, were part of Corrigan's strategy to expand internationally. Corrigan envisioned the establishment of largely autonomous operations in three major markets: Japan, the United States, and Europe. Corrigan referred to this blueprint for expansion as his "global triad strategy," a plan that would firmly root LSI Logic's presence in three critical regions and, according to Corrigan, insulate each autonomous division from downturns peculiar to each continent while enabling each part of the "triad" to take advantage of changing market conditions in its region.

By the beginning of 1985, Corrigan could claim overwhelming success in one market of his global triad strategy, when LSI Logic ranked as the number one company in the U.S. market for ASICs. LSI Logic controlled 40 percent of the market by this time and its sales volume reflected its quick rise in the industry. Sales had soared from the $35 million generated in 1983 to $84.4 million by 1984, then shot past the $100 million mark the following year, reaching $140 million. The company's net income, in contrast, did not record a commensurate meteoric rise, falling, in fact, from $15.4 million in 1984 to $10.1 million in 1985. In comparison to other U.S. semiconductor companies, however, LSI Logic at least remained profitable, a rare occurrence among other domestic rivals who were suffering debilitating losses from unrelenting Japanese competition.

To actualize his global triad strategy and help invigorate laggard profits, Corrigan moved resolutely toward the eye of storm, increasing LSI Logic's presence where the most powerful semiconductor companies existed—in Japan. In 1985, LSI Logic extended its joint development program through a multiyear agreement with Toshiba. During that same year, LSI Logic entered into a joint venture with Kawasaki Steel—Japan's third largest steel manufacturer—to build a $100 million wafer fabrication plant near Tokyo.

By 1986, LSI Logic controlled 45 percent of the U.S. ASICs market and 25 percent of the worldwide market. Although the company had secured an enviable position in the customized chip market, the increasing growth of the industry's sales volume had drawn numerous competitors attracted by the enormous growth potential in the business. By the mid-1980s, LSI Logic was competing in a crowded field and one that, as the decade progressed, became increasingly unprofitable. Much attention had been paid to revenue growth in the customized chip market, but little could be said of parallel profit growth, a phenomenon borne out in the annual revenue and net income totals recorded by LSI Logic, an industry leader. LSI Logic could claim enviable victories in revenue growth, market share, and consistent advancement in technological sophistication, but these victories came with a price: alarmingly low profits. In 1986, LSI Logic generated nearly $200 million in revenues, yet recorded a paltry $3.8 million in net income. Two years later, revenues surged to $379 million, while the company's net income climbed to $23.8 million, which was a considerable increase to be sure, but it was merely a prelude to two years of consecutive losses totaling nearly $60 million. By 1991, after halting its two-year net income slide into the red, LSI Logic, still an industry leader, was a $700 million company with net income amounting to $8.3 million, or $4 million less than it had earned when it was a $35 million company in 1982. Significant changes were needed to lift LSI Logic's profitability, but the company's transformation was costly, leading to another year of what industry pundits termed LSI Logic's "profitless prosperity."

In 1992, the company instituted sweeping cost-cutting measures to reduce overhead expenses and to embark on a new path toward increased profitability. Employment was trimmed by 1,000, falling to 4,500; a test and assembly plant in Braunschweig, Germany was closed; and several operations deemed inconsistent with the company's new future were eliminated. The company-wide downsizing program reduced LSI Logic's operating expenses as a percentage of revenues from 36 percent to 27 percent, but it also resulted in an enormous $102 million restructuring charge and a $110 million loss for the year, making 1992 the third of the previous four years that LSI Logic lost money.

The changes effected in 1992 sought to propel the company back into the black and end its near decade-long inability to produce profits commensurate with its leading position in the customized chip market. Reducing overhead was not sufficient by itself to eliminate LSI Logic's ails. To more resolutely transform the company's fortunes, Corrigan also implemented LSI Logic's CoreWare program in 1992. This program offered customers access to a library of system-level building blocks and design tools. The company had always distinguished itself with its ability to provide a high level of customer service through computer software and other means, one of the chief reasons Corrigan believed back in 1980 that a small company could fare better in the customized chip market than a large company. CoreWare represented a significant leap in LSI Logic's ability to provide responsive service and, perhaps most importantly, CoreWare represented a sophisticated service that would yield higher profit margins, something the company desperately needed.

With the changes implemented in 1992, including its centerpiece CoreWare program, LSI Logic moved forward, invigorated and redirected toward a more positive future. By the end of the company's first fiscal quarter in 1995, it had recorded increases in its revenues for ten consecutive quarters. The company had also recorded consecutive quarterly improvements in its net income total during the same time span, a feat without rival in the company's history. In the first quarter of 1995 alone, LSI Logic recorded $45.3 million net income, twice the amount it had generated during its most profitable year before the implementation of its cost-cutting measures and the CoreWare program. With this encouraging financial growth fueling optimism, Corrigan and the management of LSI Logic planned for a future beyond the mid-1990s that promised to be decidedly more profitable than the company's past.

Principal Subsidiaries: Nihon Semiconductor, Inc.; Headland Technology Ltd.; Headland Technology GmbH; LSI Logic Europe (United Kingdom) plc (97%); LSI Logic Corporation of Canada, Inc. (55%); LSI Logic K.K. (Japan) (64%); LSI Logic Foreign Sales Corporation (U.S. Virgin Islands); LSI Logic Asia, Inc.; LSI Logic International Services, Inc.

Further Reading:

"Cash Backing for LSI," *Electronics Weekly,* March 31, 1982, p. 4.
"LSI Corp.," *Business Week,* August 24, 1981, p. 42L.
"LSI Logic to Build Fast Chip in Venture with 2 Other Firms," *Wall Street Journal,* March 27, 1990, p. 4B.
"LSI to Buy All of Chip Venture," *Wall Street Journal,* January 27, 1995, p. 7A.
McCarthy, Vance, "LSI Logic Steps Away from Chip Consortium," *PC Week,* January 13, 1992, p. 120.
Pollack, Andrew, "A Computer Chip Maker in the Black," *New York Times,* November 5, 1985, p. 1D.
——, "Big Goals and Hurdles for New Chip Maker," *New York Times,* July 13, 1989, p. 1D.
Ristelhueber, Robert, "LSI Logic Is Turning Around Its 'Nonprofit Personality,'" *Electronic Business,* October 1993, p. 29.
——, "Profitless Prosperity Hits the Gate Array Market, *Electronic Business,* March 1993, pp. 108–09.
Russel, W. Sabin, "Ex-FC&I Chairman Starts Array Firm," *Electronic News,* January 19, 1981, p. 8.
Tharp, Mike, "LSI Logic Corp. Does as the Japanese Do," *Wall Street Journal,* April 17, 1986, p. 6.
"Try It in Japan," *Forbes,* June 18, 1984, p. 176.
Wilson, John W., "Selling Chips to the Japanese: LSI Logic Has an Ace Up Its Sleeve," *Business Week,* January 28, 1985, pp. 133–34.

—Jeffrey L. Covell

Marquette Electronics, Inc.

8200 West Tower Avenue
Milwaukee, Wisconsin 53223
U.S.A.
(414) 355-5000
Fax: (414) 355-3790

Public Company
Incorporated: 1965
Employees: 1,498
Sales: $253.8 million
Stock Exchanges: NASDAQ
SICs: 3845 Electromedical Equipment

Founded in 1965, Marquette Electronics, Inc., has grown in harmony with the rise of computer technology to become a leading manufacturer of medical electronic equipment and systems for the diagnosis and monitoring of patients requiring critical care. The company is a world market leader in sales of computerized electrocardiographic equipment and related supplies, and is also one of the market leaders in sales of systems used for monitoring vital patient physiological parameters.

When Michael J. Cudahy and Warren B. Cozzens set out to establish an electronics company in 1965, they initially explored the manufacture of a wide range of electronic equipment. Even while their main product line remained sketchy, the two entrepreneurs, who had been manufacturers' representatives, had agreed on a name for their fledgling company: ''I'd had some consulting work done from a professor at Marquette [University], and I thought it would be a nice thing to do,'' Cudahy told the *Business Journal-Milwaukee.*

Determining a product line took a little more deliberation, as the entrepreneurs had to feel out the market. In late 1965 Marquette delivered its first successful product: a centralized electrocardiograph (ECG) system, to Northwestern University Medical School in Chicago. The system, developed in collaboration with 3M, Hewlett-Packard Co., and a division of American Telephone & Telegraph Co., centralized the records of patient heart performance, a breakthrough in information storage and retrieval capabilities for the medical industry. Thus, Marquette derived its first business pulse through the marketing and distribution of a heart-monitoring device, setting the groundwork for a long line of innovative and use-friendly devices for medical professionals.

The success of its first electrocardiograph system prompted the young company to sell similar systems to dozens of other medical institutions in the United States and Canada, and before long Marquette was developing ECG's of its own. The company established ties with major medical players, such as the Mayo Clinic in Rochester, Minnesota, and with technology firms including the data processing giant IBM. As computer technology and artificial intelligence evolved through the 1960s and 1970s, these alliances proved fundamental to Marquette's role in solving medical problems with innovative technological tools and solutions.

By exploiting both technology and insight into medical needs, Marquette worked its way into a leading position in electrocardiography, stress testing, ambulatory ECG monitoring, critical care monitoring, and cath lab data management, as well as many other segments of medical electronics. Just as the company had pioneered the analysis of ECGs by computer in the 1960s, it introduced the first commercially available computer-based exercise testing system in 1976. Such innovations helped Marquette sustain constant growth into the 1980s. Sales of $15.7 million in 1980 ballooned to $91.9 million by 1986 and $189.3 million by 1990.

These figures largely reflected strategic alliances and acquisitions through which Marquette was able to utilize technologies developed by other companies and enhance the productivity of its core products. In 1982, for example, the company acquired a patient-monitoring equipment line from General Electric Corp. That acquisition served as the basis for the creation of the model 7000 monitor, the industry's first 32-bit microprocessor-based bedside monitor. In 1987 the company gained a new line of defibrillators through the purchase of 89 percent of the shares of TemTech Ltd., of Northern Ireland, which was renamed Marquette N. Ireland Ltd. And in 1988, the company acquired from Perkin-Elmer Corp. a line of equipment that monitored the composition of the breath of patients undergoing surgery. Expansion of that line brought about the formation of Marquette Gas Analysis, a subsidiary based in St. Louis.

Marquette's forays into new technologies would ultimately enable the company to service every major facet of the critical care spectrum, from defibrillators in emergency cardiac care to instruments used to analyze respiratory and anesthetic gases, cardiac catheterization monitoring, fetal/perinatal monitoring, and clinical information systems. Most importantly, Marquette was able to integrate these various systems in the Marquette Unity Network, one body of information accessible throughout a hospital and its satellites. Marquette equipment was designed to share information among the operating room, recovery room, intensive care unit, telemetry step-down area, emergency department, cardiac cath lab, cardiology department, and other patient areas. Such an integrated system enabled medical institutions to improve the quality of health care delivery while increasing productivity and containing costs.

From its earliest days, Marquette's innovative spirit was part and parcel of a progressive and nonconformist corporate character, guided in large part by the company's charismatic president and co-founder, Michael J. Cudahy. Cudahy stressed the importance of a comfortable work environment run on mutual trust between employees and employers and empowering all levels of the workforce to go beyond job descriptions and contribute to Marquette's innovation.

Marquette's relaxed yet efficient corporate culture drew continued praise from the press, and landed the company among other progressive business leaders in *The 100 Best Companies to Work for in America,* by Robert Levering and Milton Moskowitz. As early as 1984, the company opened a child-care center, the first such on-site facility in the state of Wisconsin. Other features reflecting the company's worker-friendly character included small offices for top management; an on-site restaurant, *Le Bistro,* that trusted employees' discretion enough to serve alcohol; refusal to subject employees to drug testing procedures, despite pressure from major accounts and business partners to do so; access to phones for unmonitored local calls; and a marked absence of time clocks.

That atmosphere of familial trust and employee empowerment felt the strain of the company's growth and expansion after the 1980s, however. By 1990, Marquette's more than 1000 employees could hardly approach the accessible president on a regular basis, nor could they be expected to know each other on a first-name basis. Moreover, the need for more space set in motion plans to develop new facilities, further straining Marquette's grow-but-stay-small scheme. In response, Cudahy moved to break the company down into semi-autonomous divisions, which could each maintain many of the qualities that the company had enjoyed in its smaller youth. "It's my answer to the inevitable getting large—and fearfully, bureaucratic," he told the *Business Journal of Milwaukee.*

As Marquette approached the 1990s, additional pressure was placed on the company's independent character by the prospect of its selling shares to the public. For years, the company had offered an employee stock-ownership plan (ESOP), as one fringe benefit to its workers (in addition to a savings plan and profit sharing). After tremendous growth in the 1980s, shares held by employees had grown substantially, but represented no real-world value as long as they couldn't be traded in the marketplace. Cudahy also had a vested interest in redeemable shares; by 1990, he owned 46 percent of the company's Class A stock and 100 percent of its Class C stock, while Marquette's ESOP owned roughly another 20 percent.

Despite the financial attraction of investing Marquette's shares with market value by going public, Cudahy was resistant to the idea. In 1984, he had authored an article for *Fortune* magazine entitled "Going Wrong by Going Public," in which he outlined the difficulty of maintaining corporate integrity and flexibility in a publicly owned business. By the late 1980s, however, he had somewhat tempered his views, maintaining that going public could actually help Marquette preserve its independence.

These deliberations came to a head in the fall of 1991, when Marquette sold 15 percent of its shares to outsiders, making its stock available on the over-the-counter market. Cudahy called the move "the lesser of two evils," and took immediate moves to retain ownership in-house; after Marquette went public, more than 50 percent of its stocks were held by 13 Marquette directors and officers, while Cudahy himself held on to 37.6 percent of the shares. Moreover, in a vigorous drive to avoid what he called "the sell-out syndrome," he turned down numerous offers by outside firms to acquire Marquette. Cudahy said that he would not let Wall Street narrow his vision to short-term goals. "I'm just going to do it the way I have been doing it . . . and if they don't like it, they can lump it," he told the authors of *The 100 Best Companies.*

Despite its increasing size and status as a publicly traded company, Marquette continued to grow in the early 1990s without losing its innovative, progressive character. In mid-1991, the company embarked on a substantial expansion of its Milwaukee headquarters, adding 85,000 square feet as a stopgap construction program before proceeding with plans for additional facilities that growth would mandate within several years. The addition accommodated new robotics systems for production of advanced electronic circuit boards for a new line of monitoring devices in development. The new facility also enabled Marquette to move production of defibrillators from its subsidiary in Northern Ireland to Milwaukee, creating approximately 30 new positions at the headquarters and better servicing the rapidly growing American market.

Marquette also made the most of its expertise and improved production facilities by forging strategic joint ventures in the early 1990s. In July 1992, Marquette and Optical Sensors (OSM) announced an exclusive, worldwide joint manufacturing and distribution agreement for a system combining OSM's fiber optic blood gas sensors with Marquette's patient monitoring hardware and software. Marquette would sell the equipment to its existing customer base, leaving the rest of the market to OSM. In October of that year, Marquette announced another joint project with Gambro Engstrom of Stockholm, the first company to manufacture a critical care, volume-oriented ventilator and a leader in innovative anesthesia equipment. The initial joint project would integrate the Engstrom Anesthesia System, Model 9010 with Marquette products, allowing for a single display for viewing both patient and equipment status in the anesthesia environment, thus paving the way for future anesthesia products for worldwide distribution. With the stars the limit for its innovative products, Marquette was also awarded a contract from Martin-Marietta Corp. to manufacture mass spectrometry units, one of which would help monitor astronauts' vital functions during a NASA mission in which the Space Shuttle would dock aboard the Russian space center, MIR, in June 1995.

Walking the fine line between its entrepreneurial spirit and its drive to become the world's biggest medical electronics company, Marquette moved to strengthen its leadership team in 1993. In September of that year, the board appointed Barry K. Allen as Marquette's new president and chief operating officer, joining Mr. Cudahy, who became chairman and CEO. The succession represented one of many steps toward strengthening the company for the rigors of an increasingly global and competitive marketplace.

By the mid-1990s, that marketplace was being aggressively cultivated: international sales accounted for 28 percent of total revenues in 1994, for example. A particular hot spot was Asia, where booming economies spurred new hospital construction requiring new equipment. In 1994 alone, sales of Marquette's products in Korea doubled, according to that year's annual report. Other Asian markets showed similar promise: growing health care services in Thailand called for construction of more than 30 private hospitals, and the Malaysian government launched a program to construct a cardiothoracic center in every 250-kilometer radius. Marquette also tailored its sales and marketing strategies to develop important markets in South and Central America. And in Europe, a group of international investors called Health Care International began construction of several facilities—including Clydebank Hospital in Glasgow, Scotland—that would bridge the gap between U.S. and European heath care styles. By 1994, nearly $3 million in Marquette products had been ordered for that facility.

Marquette continued to forge strategic partnership agreements with various companies in order to "leverage our established breadth and depth strategies," according to a 1994–95 Interim Report for the third quarter. In September 1994, the company expanded on its joint venture with Gambro Engstrom AB by renewing the development agreement with that company's parent, Instrumentarium Corp., of Helsinki, Finland. Among their expanded cooperative efforts was an anesthesia delivery workstation that Marquette added to its product line. In December 1994 Marquette also concluded an agreement with Nihon Kohden Corporation of Tokyo, Japan to sell and service Marquette products in that country.

Treading with measured steps into the operating room of the future, Marquette also signed a five-year agreement with North American Dräger (NAD), of Telford, Pennsylvania, which held a 50 percent share of the anesthesia delivery machine market. According to the agreement, Marquette would provide signal acquisition circuit boards for use in NAD's anesthesia delivery machines, promising additional penetration into that growing market.

With these alliances and its continued emphasis on research and development, Marquette was well positioned to enjoy excellent health in the medical electronics marketplace of the 21st century. The company faced daunting obstacles, however, as sweeping plans for health care reform helped turn that industry into a roller-coaster ride for investors and manufacturing companies alike. Sharon di Stefano, health care industry analyst at Smith Barney in New York, told Mark Dillon of the *Miami Review* that hospitals—under increasing government and insurer pressure to cut costs—wouldn't have the budgets to buy high-tech devices in the Marquette vein. Cudahy, on the other hand, pointed out that long-term demographics of an aging population were in the company's favor. Moreover, he argued that attention to cost reduction in emergency and routine patient monitoring would actually increase the need for efficient and effective devices like Marquette's.

For Cudahy, the continued success of Marquette depended on the company's innovativeness—an area in which it continued to excel. "We have . . . looked for problems in medicine and the solving of those problems, under the assumption that if we solved a problem, sales would be very easy to come by," he told Pat Foran of the *Business Journal of Milwaukee.* In other words, Cudahy placed the same confidence in his company that he had always placed in its individual employees: given the chance to think creatively and perform to their fullest, he expected nothing but the best.

Principal Subsidiaries: Marquette Electronics, Inc., European Center (France); Marquette Electronics Pty Ltd. (Australia); Marquette Benelux N.V./S.A.(Belgium); Marquette France, S.A.R.L.; Marquette Electronics, Inc., Zweigniederlassung (Germany); Marquette Electronics, Inc., Asia Pacific District (Japan); Marquette Italia, Srl (Italy); Marquette Espana S.A. (Spain); Marquette Scandinavia (Sweden); Marquette Electronics (G.B.) Ltd. (United Kingdom).

Further Reading:

Dillon, Mark, "Is Wall Street Misreading Marquette's Pulse?" *Miami Review,* August 21, 1992, p. A6.

Foran, Pat, "The Inevitable: Marquette Electronics' Michael Cudahy Bows to Change in Considering Stock Offering," *Business Journal-Milwaukee,* January 29, 1990, Vol. 7, No. 16, Sec. 2, p. 10.

Kirchen, Rich, "Marquette Nixes New Plant Plans, Builds Addition, *Business Journal-Milwaukee,* May 27, 1991, Vol. 8, No. 33, Sec. 1, p. 1.

Levering, Robert, and Milton Moskowitz, *The 100 Best Companies to Work For in America,* New York: Currency Doubleday, 1993.

"Marquette and Nihon Kohden Sign Distribution Agreement," *Business Wire,* December 5, 1994.

"Marquette Electronics, Inc. Gets Nod For NASA Contract," *Business Wire,* June 24, 1993.

"Marquette Electronics Moving Its Defibrillator Manufacturing Operations from Ireland to Milwaukee," *Business Wire,* April 10, 1992.

"Optical Sensors for Medicine, Marquette Electronics Sign Manufacturing, Distribution Agreement," *PR Newswire,* July 9, 1992.

—Kerstan Cohen

Marshalls

Marshalls Incorporated

P.O. Box 9030
Andover, Massachusetts 01810
U.S.A.
(508) 474-7000
Fax: (508) 474-7159

Division of Melville Corporation
Incorporated: 1923
Employees: 21,000
Sales: $2.8 billion
SICs: 5651 Family Clothing Stores; 5661 Shoe Stores

Marshall's Incorporated is one of the nation's leading off-price family retailers. Marshall's stores offer a wide range of apparel for men, women, and children, as well as furnishings for the home. Experiencing steady growth since its inception in the 1950s, the company faced intense competition in the 1990s, the effects of which it sought to offset by tailoring its merchandise to suit customer preferences at each store location, stepping up its advertising program, remodeling some stores and expanding others, and broadening the scope of its product lines to include gourmet foods and giftware.

The company traces its history to 1956, when Alfred Marshall gathered together a band of innovative entrepreneurs on the East Coast. Contemplating the dual postwar phenomena of a boom in the economy and growth in the suburbs, Marshall and associates came upon a way to meet it profitably. Together, they opened a self-service department store in Beverly, Massachusetts, offering apparel and homewares at alluringly low prices.

The concept proved extremely successful; ten years later, Marshalls had become the leading off-price retail chain in the nation. Given the volatility of the American economy in the 1970s, with recession affecting the spending habits of most shoppers, the off-price industry gathered speed. By buying up manufacturers' post-season, over-run, and close-out stock, Marshalls was able to offer fashionable, high-quality "designer" items at prices 20 to 60 percent less than those of the department stores.

The problem with the creative and successful plan, however, was that it inspired many imitators. As Marshalls' sales recipe became a favorite, many other retailers created off-price stores of their own. Moreover, department stores were also fighting for their share of consumer interest and began marking down merchandise as well.

By the mid-1970s, it became clear that for Marshalls to survive the off-price wars, it needed to expand aggressively. The company had earned $3.2 million on sales of $77.1 million in fiscal 1975, but its stores were still mostly limited to the New England area. The stores then averaged around 30,000 square feet and were situated in high-traffic areas such as strip malls and shopping centers.

During this time, Marshalls' potential for expansion attracted the attention of the Melville Corporation. Melville had been known mostly for footwear—most notably, its Thom McAn brand—but by the end of 1976, shoes accounted for only 60 percent of Melville's volume as the company underwent an aggressive diversification program. The country's 32nd-largest retail company at the time, Melville was purchasing specialty chains, including Chess King men's clothing outlets, Foxmoor's chain of women's apparel stores, and the CVS drugstore chain. In February 1976, Melville added Marshalls' 32 stores to its holdings, paying about $40 million for the company. Under the parentage of Melville, Marshall's opened seven more stores in 1976; five in the Northeast, one in Los Angeles, and one in Chicago. That year, with assistance from its latest purchase, Melville reached the $1 billion mark in sales.

The needs of consumers shifted considerably during the mercurial 1980s, and the retail industry had to work quickly to accommodate the changes. At some points, status-conscious label hunters dominated the market; at other times, thrift was the driving influence. Marshalls reached its own $1 billion benchmark in 1983. By that time, it was Melville's largest holding. Moreover, Melville's acquisition during this time of Linens 'n Things, an off-price bedding and table goods chain, would complement its Marshalls operations, which eventually focused more on home furnishings. In 1983, Marshalls announced plans to expand at a rate of roughly 40 stores per year over the next five years, starting with 38 new stores in 1983. The number of Marshalls stores by year's end totaled 175.

The plan, however, proved overconfident. Marshalls' store sales became suddenly sluggish in the mid-1980s. By 1985, Marshalls had slowed its store growth accordingly. Part of the problem was its fiercest competitor, T.J. Maxx, the country's second largest off-price chain. Indeed, one analyst, quoted in *Advertising Age,* compared Marshalls and T.J. Maxx to Pepsi and Coke, warring for market share and recognition. Moreover, off-price retailers in general no longer dominated the market. They had taken considerable market share away from department stores in the late 1970s and early 1980s, but department stores had rallied by the mid-1980s, and were fighting back with slashed prices on comparable merchandise.

At the same time, discounters were wooing the consumers more interested in bargains than brand names. By 1987, discounters had become the fastest-growing retail segment. For a brief time, Marshalls was caught between the two conflicting strategies to lure in consumers: lower prices or offer more recognizable, and pricier, brands? If its customers were driven equally by a desire for quality, value, and selection, Marshalls had to find a way to balance the three without compromising. Some critics suggested that the company had been compromising on quality for some time.

In 1986, Michael Friedheim took over the direction of Marshalls, when president Gerald Kanter left the company. Friedheim, formerly executive vice-president of Melville, brought merchandising expertise to the drifting company and soon made a decision regarding Marshalls' future. Beginning in 1987, Friedheim and Marshalls opted to eschew the discount route and upgrade its goods. New merchandise was brought in, with higher prices and more recognizable brand names, including clothing of the premium Liz Claiborne brand. Cinching this marketing decision was the realization that Marshalls customers were mostly people with good taste and moderate incomes between $25,000 and $50,000; in short, Marshalls customers sought top brands that often didn't fit their budgets.

This turnaround continued in 1987, when Francis (Frank) Arnone became president and CEO of Marshalls. Arnone had previously served as CEO of two Carter Hawley Hale divisions and brought with him a wealth of executive merchandising experience.

While Marshalls was restocking with slightly higher grade goods, it was also enhancing its misses' apparel category. Women's apparel represented about 60 percent of the stores' volume in 1988. Monthly comparative store sales, an industry measurement of a chain's health, picked up 6.5 percent in 1987, and by the end of 1988 comparative store sales were four percent ahead. The company's plans for expanding its store openings were realized during this time, as about 25 new Marshalls stores were being opening annually.

Also during this time, Arnone noted that Marshalls was selling high volumes of non-apparel items, such as pillows and bedding. To gain the expertise and valuable store space needed to offer full lines of home furnishings, Marshalls purchased all ten of Branden's home-oriented stores from the Dayton Hudson Corporation. Parent Melville sold four of the ten stores to Levitz Furniture Company, but all of Branden's units in Florida and one in Atlanta, Georgia, were retained.

Marshalls set about converting the 50,000 square foot Branden's units to fit a new concept: superstores in which the giftwares and home furnishings departments occupied considerable space. Moreover, the company planned to open 50 additional Marshall's stores in 1989. Facilitating such growth was the acquisition of 12 Channel Home Center sites in 1989. Eight of the sites were on Long Island and the rest were in Connecticut and Massachusetts. The Centers loaned themselves well to Marshalls new superstores.

That same year, Marshalls' war with T.J. Maxx was reaching a boiling point. By summer of 1989, Marshalls had 317 stores in 40 states and intended to open 40 outlets a year for the next five years. T.J. Maxx had 328 stores in 40 states, planned 45 additions annually, and was rapidly closing the gap between itself and the off-price retailing leader. The war was especially visible in competing ad campaigns, as both stores vied for consumers being bombarded with "everyday low price" marketing messages. Marshalls total sales had inched up 9.3 percent in 1988, reaching $1.75 billion. The numbers were slightly misleading, however, as same-store sales increased only slightly more than two percent. Due in part to aggressive advertising, those numbers improved in 1989. But that wasn't enough.

Marshalls accelerated its efforts in the early 1990s through subtle shifts on earlier elected directions: remodeling its stores to attract more upscale customers, through merchandise, size and design. In addition to new superstores, Marshalls began remodeling existing stores. The prototype for the stores featured bright colors, improved signage, new fixtures—an array of measures intended to attract upscale customers through a more fashionable atmosphere.

The new superstores were nearly double the size of Marshalls' regular stores, and the extra room accommodated expanded specialty areas, including departments that had never appeared in some of the original stores. Marshalls traditional departments included misses and junior sportswear, dresses, larger sizes, petites, lingerie, accessories, infants' and children's apparel, a range of men's wear, footwear, domestics, jewelry, and giftware. In the new superstores, however, domestic areas were expanded, and broader clothes lines for women and men were added, including the addition of maternity clothing and men's suits. In addition, there were new departments for boys' wear, fine jewelry, luggage, and health and beauty aids.

The new Marshalls had a layout similar to that employed in department stores. Moreover, the Designers Back Room was inaugurated in a Newton, Massachusetts, Marshalls in 1990. Considered stores-within-a-store, the Designers Back Room was a separate room of about 1,000 square feet, stocked with higher-end designer and bridge label merchandise.

Sales for 1990 hit the $2 billion mark, and the following spring Marshalls had 398 stores in 38 states. A new president and CEO joined Marshall at this time; Jerome R. Rossi had joined the company after serving as chairman of the May Company division of Foley's in Houston. Rossi continued piloting the transformation of Marshalls into a store with a larger home section and upscale goods. It was Rossi's intention to sustain Marshalls growth while maintaining its status as a family store that equally emphasized men's, women's, and children's apparel, footwear, and home furnishings. After several rocky years, the off-price apparel industry had a flush year in 1992, with overall annual results up 13.2 percent to $11.7 billion.

Marshalls was still the pack leader in the early 1990s, but T.J. Maxx was still running a close second. In fact, T.J. Maxx had been edging for the number one spot for the past three years. In 1992, sales for Marshalls were $2.6 million; T.J. Maxx's sales were $2.58 million. Throughout 1992, while Marshalls had concentrated on developing its merchandising strategy and controlling spending, T.J. Maxx was aggressively opening 37 new stores. During the same period, Marshalls' new store openings numbered about eight, after factoring in some closings and relocations. Still, Marshalls was a big earner for Melville that year. Moreover, the parent company was divesting itself of poor performers, including Chess King, so that it could concentrate on core performers like Marshalls and CVS.

Marshalls had moved as far as Hawaii by 1993, the same year it was expanding its downtown presence with new stores in Boston and Portland, Oregon. Marshalls opened 40 new stores in

1994, remodeling about 50 others, refining its focus on a broader range of items and plotting to keep its spot as leader.

Further Reading:

Brumback, Nancy, "Marshalls Sees Growth Despite Tough Economy," *HFD*, January 13, 1992, p. 26.

Lettich, Jill, "Marshalls Attracts More Upscale Shoppers with New Larger Stores," *Discount Store News*, April 15, 1991, pp. 46, 60.

Graham, Judith, "Marshalls, T.J. Maxx Duel Over Off-Price Leadership," *Advertising Age*, June 26, 1989, pp. 3, 75.

Moin, David, "Marshalls: Making a Comeback," *Women's Wear Daily*, November 14, 1988, p. 14.

"Off-Price Apparel Booming in a Recovery Year," *Discount Store News*, July 5, 1993, p. 74.

—Carol I. Keeley

McLane Company, Inc.

P.O. Box 6115
Temple, Texas 76503-6115
U.S.A.
(817) 771-7500
Fax: (817) 771-7449

Wholly Owned Subsidiary of Wal-Mart Stores, Inc.
Incorporated: 1964
Employees: 8,200
Sales: $6.7 billion
SICs: 5141 Groceries, General Line; 5142 Packaged Frozen Foods; 5149 Groceries & Related Products, Not Elsewhere Classified; 2099 Food Preparations, Not Elsewhere Classified; 7374 Data Processing Services; 4213 Trucking, Except Local

McLane Company, Inc., is one of the largest wholesale distribution companies in the United States. McLane serves customers in all 50 states, and has a total base of over 44,000 customers. Of that total, 26,000 customers are convenience stores, making McLane the world's largest supplier to that market. In addition, the company is a major importer of gourmet and ethnic foods through its specialty food division. Other McLane divisions are engaged in foodservice, trucking, data processing, and food processing. McLane is owned by Wal-Mart Stores, Inc., the largest retail operation in the world. Since its acquisition by Wal-Mart in 1990, grocery distribution has played a growing role in McLane's business, which had previously focused even more heavily on convenience stores.

The history of McLane Company dates back to 1894, when founder Robert McLane opened his first grocery store in Cameron, Texas, a farming community in the central part of the state. McLane's, as the store was called, was successful from the outset, and by 1895 McLane had doubled the size of his store and added a receiving platform. A few years later he put up another building nearby, which he leased to Rotan Grocery Company, one of his wholesale suppliers. When Rotan was bought out by another company in 1903, the wholesale business in that building was shut down. McLane decided to fill the void himself, and within the year he launched his own wholesale operation. He staffed the new firm, dubbed the Robert McLane Company, with three full-time employees.

The company performed well over the next decade, and by 1912 McLane had 12 people working in his office. In 1913 McLane opened a second warehouse, located in the nearby town of Caldwell. The company bought its first two trucks in 1915. The trucks were used only for local deliveries, while shipments to outlying areas were still made by rail. By this time, McLane had a seven-man sales force that roamed the countryside. This enabled Robert McLane to scale back his traveling and spend more time at the company's Cameron headquarters. A year later, the company erected an adjoining building to the original Cameron warehouse. A third building, a garage for servicing the company's growing fleet of trucks, was added to the complex in 1919. Deliveries by truck to locations outside of Cameron were begun the following year. In 1921 Drayton McLane, Robert's son, joined the company on a full-time basis. He had worked in the business on a part-time basis throughout his childhood.

After more than twenty years of quick and steady growth, the company's fortunes finally began to level off around this time. Central Texas was hit with a series of alternating floods and droughts that devastated its agricultural economy during the 1920s. This in turn had a negative impact on retailers and wholesalers who depended on farmers for most of their business. Nevertheless, McLane was able to emerge from this period relatively unscathed, although the company did not undertake any significant expansion projects.

The 1930s began badly as the effects of the stock market crash of 1929 began to make their way into rural Texas. By 1937, though, with the U.S. economy well on its way to recovery, McLane's annual sales had reached $440,000. World War II, and the rationing that came along with it, made it much easier for wholesalers to turn a profit. McLane and countless other businesses were beneficiaries of the economic boom that followed the conclusion of World War II. By 1945 the nation's highway system had improved to the point where McLane could make all of its deliveries by truck. The company broke the $1 million mark in annual sales for the first time in 1946.

The McLane Company grew steadily throughout the 1950s. By 1951 company sales doubled again to more than $2 million. Robert McLane died in 1952, just short of his 85th birthday. He was succeeded as company president by his son Drayton. At that time the company served stores across an area within a 60-mile radius of Cameron. The $3 million sales barrier was surpassed in 1957, and Drayton McLane became president of the Texas Wholesale Grocers Association the following year. In 1959 a third generation of the McLane family—namely Drayton, Jr.,—went to work full-time in the family business. He secured a masters degree in marketing from Michigan State University prior to joining the company.

In the first half of the 1960s, McLane's sales stagnated, increasing from $3.6 million in 1960 to $3.8 million in 1964. Two major developments, both under the guidance of Drayton McLane, Jr., took place at the company during that span, however. The company's first computer, an IBM punch card tabulator, was installed in 1962. Around the same time, McLane launched its Voluntary Group Program. The Program allowed independent food retailers to band together for joint buying power to purchase private label brands offered by the wholesaler. By 1964 McLane had about 40 stores in its program and had acquired the franchise rights to market products under the Shopworth and Valu-Mart trade names. Meanwhile, Drayton McLane, Sr., was elected president of the United States Wholesale Grocers Association in 1963.

As Drayton, Jr., gained influence in company decisions, McLane made moves to regain its momentum in the second half of the decade. First, Drayton, Jr., convinced his father that the company should build a new distribution center. Unable to secure financing in Cameron for a modern facility, the company found in Temple, Texas, both a bank and a city willing to help make the new facility happen. McLane moved into its new 48,000-square-foot warehouse in Temple Industrial Park in March 1966. By that time, McLane Company had 45 employees and its 15 tractor-trailers were delivering merchandise within an 80-mile radius to about 300 stores.

McLane made its initial move into convenience store distribution in 1967. That year, the company contracted with the Southland Corporation to distribute goods to 67 7-Eleven stores in central Texas. In 1968 McLane achieved another important breakthrough, this time in its supermarket business, when it signed a franchise agreement to distribute merchandise under the Red & White label in 23 Texas counties. McLane's Shopworth and Valu-Mart labels were eliminated. In spite of Red & White's success, it was the convenience store market that proved to be McLane's most important growth area for years to come. The late 1960s were marked by McLane's formation of a non-foods division to distribute health and beauty aids and other general merchandise. This enabled the company to become the sole supplier for many of the convenience stores it serviced. In 1969 McLane's sales surpassed the $10 million mark.

McLane grew at a furious pace during the 1970s. By 1971 the company had 163 employees and sales of $19.5 million. The company expanded its warehouse in Temple by 75 percent and purchased its first big diesel truck that year. Within a few years, McLane was delivering products to customers in three states: Texas, Oklahoma, and New Mexico. By 1974 company sales had skyrocketed to $51 million. Its customers included 800 convenience stores, which accounted for about 40 percent of total sales. Later that year, McLane signed a contract with ABC Grocery to distribute to a handful of Stop 'N' Go, 7-Eleven, and Tenneco convenience stores in Denver. Although this arrangement lost money for the company at first, it led to the eventual buyout of ABC in 1976. ABC was renamed McLane/Western and became the company's first division outside of Temple.

Over the next several years, McLane expanded westward briskly. The fast growth of the company's truck fleet required the addition of a transportation center in Temple. The facility was completed in 1977. McLane's relationship with Southland continued to be profitable during this period. Unhappy with the companies that were supplying 7-Eleven stores in the Pacific Northwest, Southland suggested that McLane might receive a substantial amount of convenience store business very quickly if it decided to establish operations in that region. McLane/Northwest was established in Tacoma, Washington, in 1980. As expected, the division quickly picked up all of the supply business for the region's 7-Eleven stores. It also secured an agreement to serve 52 Circle K stores in Oregon. McLane/Southeast, based in Athens, Georgia, was established the same year.

The arrangement with Southland was so successful in the Northwest that it seemed logical to repeat the process in northern California. To that end, McLane/Pacific was created in 1983 in Merced, California. Two years later, McLane/Sunwest was formed in Arizona. In addition to geographic expansion, the company moved into other areas of business. In 1981 McLane Information Systems, the company's data processing operation, became its own division. The following year, McLane purchased Wholesale Food Supply, Inc. of Abilene, Texas, a company specializing in institutional foodservice, and turned it into the McLane/Foodservice division. To accommodate the company's explosive growth during the first half of the 1980s, McLane/Southwest (the new name for the original Temple branch) moved into a new distribution center in 1983. A second branch of McLane/Foodservice also went into operation in Temple that year. In 1984, the year McLane/Northeast was launched in Syracuse, New York, McLane's sales topped $1 billion.

Merit Distribution Services, the company's trucking division, was set up in 1985 to serve all of McLane's other divisions as well as outside customers. By 1986 company sales had reached $1.5 billion, and new divisions had been opened in Mississippi (McLane/Southern) and Florida (McLane/Suneast). In 1987 the company created McLane/America, an importer and distributor of specialty, gourmet, ethnic, and health foods based in Salt Lake City, Utah. Yet another regional division, McLane/Midwest, was launched in 1989 in Carmi, Illinois. The company posted sales of $2.6 billion that year.

In 1990 McLane was acquired by Wal-Mart, the largest retail chain in the world. Prior to the merger, McLane was already doing about $500 million worth of business with Wal-Mart, and Drayton McLane, Jr., had become close friends with Wal-Mart founder Sam Walton. The acquisition by Wal-Mart brought about a quantum leap in business volume for McLane. This expansion was accelerated even more in 1992, when Southland made its exit from the distribution business to focus on its retail operations. Southland sold two distribution centers and three food processing facilities to McLane. These new businesses added well over $1 billion in sales and 2,000 employees to McLane's totals.

In July 1992, Drayton McLane, Jr., bought major league baseball's Houston Astros. A few months later he stepped down as president and CEO of McLane Company to concentrate on running the team, although he retained his chairmanship of McLane. Joe Hardin, Jr., took over as president and CEO. McLane continued to grow dramatically under Hardin. In 1993 the company recorded sales of $6.3 billion, including $2.5 million in business with parent company Wal-Mart. As the 1990s rolled on, McLane continued to seek new areas in which to expand. With a presence in all 50 states, the company began looking southward. McLane de Mexico, a large distribution center in Mexico City, was opened with an eye toward penetrating the Mexican market.

As McLane celebrated its centennial in 1994, the company showed no signs of slowing down. A distribution center to serve convenience stores and mass merchandisers in Kentucky and Ohio was opened, and the company leased space for a large distribution center for its McLane/Foodservice division. In 1995 Hardin returned to Wal-Mart to become chief operating officer. He was replaced as president and CEO of McLane by W. Grady Rosier, an 11-year veteran of the company.

Principal Subsidiaries: McLane Foods, Inc.; McLane Foodservice/Temple, Inc.; McLane/America, Inc.; McLane/Eastern, Inc.; McLane/High Plains, Inc.; McLane/Midwest, Inc.; McLane/Pacific, Inc.; McLane/Southern, Inc.; McLane/Suneast, Inc.; McLane/Sunwest, Inc.; McLane/Western, Inc.; Merit Distribution Services, Inc.; Professional Data Solutions, Inc.

Further Reading:

Kahler, Martha, and Jeff Hampton, *McLane Company, Inc.: The First One Hundred Years,* Temple, TX: McLane Company, Inc., 1994.

Markowitz, Arthur, ''McLane Helps Wal-Mart Bite into Food Biz,'' *Discount Store News,* November 16, 1992, p. 1.

Simmons, Tim, ''Drayton & Sam,'' *Supermarket News,* October 8, 1990, p. 2.

''Wal-Mart to Acquire McLane, Distributor to Retail Industry,'' *Wall Street Journal,* October 2, 1990, p. C22.

Zwiebach, Elliot, ''Wal-Mart to Acquire McLane Co.,'' *Supermarket News,* October 8, 1990, p. 1.

—Robert R. Jacobson

Megafoods Stores, Inc.

Megafoods Stores Inc.

1455 South Stapley Drive
Mesa, Arizona 85204
U.S.A.
(602) 926-1087
Fax: (602) 926-1237

Public Company
Incorporated: 1987
Employees: 3,500
Sales: $409 million
Stock Exchanges: New York
SICs: 5411 Grocery Stores

Megafoods Stores Inc. operates a chain of 50 grocery stores in Arizona, Nevada, and Texas. Following its inception in 1987, the company expanded at a rapid pace by catering to value-oriented shoppers. Its chain peaked at more than 70 stores before Megafoods filed for Chapter 11 protection from its creditors. The grocer was struggling to emerge from bankruptcy going into the mid-1990s.

Dean Miller founded Megafoods in 1987. Although he was only 30 at the time, Miller had more than 15 years of experience in the industry. In fact, both his father and grandfather had worked in the grocery business, and Miller himself had started to work at age 13 in the back room of a grocery store in Spokane, Washington. Miller gradually worked his way up to store manager before deciding to go into business for himself. At the age of 25, he opened a specialty food store, which developed into a chain of outlets in Lodi, California. After a few years, Miller sold this business and moved to Arizona, where he launched a few other grocery-related ventures before devising the Megafoods concept. Joined in the venture by Jack J. Walker, a 52-year-old associate of Miller's with a background in real estate, Miller opened his first Megafoods store in Phoenix, Arizona, with about 50 employees.

Miller faced an uphill battle with his tiny Megafoods operation. He was entering a hyper-competitive industry which was dominated by giant regional and national grocers. Most of those organizations had either acquired or forced the mom-and-pop and local grocery store operators out of business years earlier. The big grocery chains, aside from having relatively easy access to investment capital, enjoyed wide economies of scale that helped them to keep costs low. For example, they had greater purchasing power over their suppliers than small grocers and they benefitted from efficiencies related to distribution and marketing. Although his venture was thinly financed, Miller believed that he could undercut his competitors and steal market share through savvy management and aggressive cost controls. His basic concept was to create an unusual hybrid grocery store that had the look and feel of a mainstream supermarket but sported warehouse prices.

During its first year of operation, Megafoods captured $33 million in sales and lost about a half million dollars. Despite this inauspicious start, Miller believed that his new concept was viable and he was eager to expand. Further, his financing problem was diminished by Fleming Foods West, a major regional grocery supplier. Besides financing and supplying much of the inventory for Megafoods, Fleming also provided loans to back the chain's expansion, sometimes accepting ownership in the company as compensation. Drawing on Fleming's resources as well as internally generated cash, Miller was able to add three new Megafoods stores to his burgeoning chain by the end of 1988. Megafoods' revenues in that year jumped 52 percent to $50 million while net losses tripled to $1.5 million.

Still confident in his long-term strategy, Miller was unfazed by the 1988 losses. In fact, Megafoods doubled its number of stores to eight and grew its assets to more than $20 million during the next year. Revenues nearly doubled in 1989 and Megafoods netted income of $222,000, it first annual profit. With continued support from Fleming—Megafoods entered into an agreement ensuring that Fleming would be its primary supplier through 1997—Miller tapped cash flow to add six more stores to his growing chain during 1990. In that year, Megafoods' receipts bolted to an impressive $180 million. Miller spent 1991 regrouping and enhancing his existing stores, although he did add one store to the chain. By 1991, Megafoods was operating 15 stores in Arizona and California. Sales soared to nearly $250 million as net income bounded to $627,000. Meanwhile, Megafoods executives were formulating an even more aggressive growth stratagem.

Megafoods' expansion in the midst of heated competition and an economic downturn in the early 1990s was largely attributable to its unique discount strategy. For example, Megafoods offered the lowest prices in its service areas by monitoring competitors' prices, feeding them into a computer on a weekly basis, and then adjusting its own prices accordingly. The overall pricing scheme, which Megafoods referred to as "price impact," was designed to undercut supermarket competitors by an average of five percent. The company made sure that consumers were aware of the low prices by displaying pricing labels that compared the Megafoods' price with the competitors' prices. Furthermore, customers entering Megafoods' stores were greeted by a "Wall of Values," a wide aisleway stacked floor-to-ceiling with shipping cartons full of deeply discounted, national brand, "shocker" items. From there, shoppers entered into an area with bright, fully stocked shelves and produce counters which looked more like a typical supermarket. The effect was designed to reinforce the company's advertising theme of "Shop Us Like a Supermarket. Save Like a Warehouse Club."

While at the same time simulating the look and feel of supermarkets, Megafoods was able to achieve its low-cost advantage by utilizing certain warehouse tactics. For instance, the company carefully analyzed customer service activities to determine which were the most cost effective. In addition, Megafoods offered several inexpensive services not offered by the warehouse clubs, but did not provide others such as bagging groceries. The company also sustained an intense focus on analyzing and managing costs. For example, its warehouse configuration allowed Megafoods to construct new store building shells at capital costs approximately 20 percent lower than typical supermarkets. Likewise, labor costs were minimized by using a high-tech computerized time and attendance system that analyzed chain-wide productivity on a daily basis.

Megafoods also reduced costs by stocking a significant amount of prepackaged bulk merchandise, which eliminated in-store preparation costs on such products as baked goods and meats. Similarly, most goods were displayed on warehouse racking systems or in their shipping containers as a means of lowering costs related to double handling and back-room storage. In contrast to warehouse stores, Megafoods stocked a selection of goods roughly equivalent to the assortment stocked by mainstream supermarkets. Megafoods also differed from club warehouses in that its stores were conveniently located in highly visible shopping areas. The outlets were slightly smaller than warehouse stores, but larger than most supermarkets. In addition, Megafoods stores charged no membership fees and were open 24 hours, seven days a week. One result of Megafoods' overall strategy was that sales per employee-hour stood at nearly $150 in the early 1990s, compared to about $96 for the average supermarket chain.

With its recipe for success seemingly in place by 1991, Megafoods stepped up its expansion initiative in 1992. The company's basic strategy was to boost market share in existing markets and to open new stores in areas where its price impact program would be most effective. To fund the growth effort, Miller took Megafoods public on the over-the-counter market in July of 1992. Another stock sale in December brought additional cash into Megafoods' coffers. The grocery chain used that money to crack into the Las Vegas, Nevada, market with two new stores and to expand in Arizona for a year-end total of 22 outlets, a sum which included the closing of an unprofitable store in California. The Megafoods organization showed healthy growth in 1992, with sales of $292 million and net income of about $300,000. Contributing to this rising profit margin was an innovative venture initiated in one of Megafoods' California stores: an in-store, take-out food court. Miller planned to implement the successful concept throughout the chain through agreements with Kentucky Fried Chicken, Pizza Hut, and Taco Bell.

Although Megafoods' expansion and sales increases in the early 1990s seemed encouraging to many observers, the gains masked serious underlying problems. In fact, by 1992 Megafoods was in heavy debt to Fleming. While the chain used part of the money raised through public offerings to reduce the $10 million bill, Megafoods still owed Fleming well over $5 million going into 1993. For this and other reasons, the relationship between Miller and Fleming executives began to erode. Evidencing the friction was Miller's effort during 1992 and 1993 to reduce Megafoods' dependence on Fleming as a supplier. Although Megafoods had signed an agreement with Fleming to purchase more than 50 percent of its stock from them through 1997, Miller began to pursue a contract with Safeway that would significantly reduce Fleming's role as a supplier. However, the contract was contingent on Fleming releasing Megafoods from their original agreement. In addition, Miller's co-founder, Walker, was relieved of his duties as chief financial officer of Megafoods in August of 1992 when outside accusations arose regarding questionable business dealings. Ultimately, Miller denied that these accusations had anything to do with Walker's demotion to senior vice-president in charge of real estate.

As Megafoods' potential problems were becoming increasingly apparent in 1993, the company continued to push its program for rapid expansion. Indeed, Megafoods outpaced even its own 1992 growth projections, taking over 15 Kroger stores in San Antonio, Texas. Megafoods remodeled the stores and partially converted them to its warehouse format and operated the refurbished outlets under the name "Texans' Supermarkets." Megafoods also added new stores in California, Nevada, and Arizona. By the end of 1993, Megafoods was boasting a chain of 46 stores spread throughout the southwestern region of the United States. The huge expansion boosted Megafoods' work force from 1,950 people in 1992 to more than 5,000 employees, most of whom had to be trained quickly in order to work within the Megafoods organization.

While the 1993 store additions rocketed Megafoods' revenues past $400 million for that year, the company began to show signs that it had overextended itself with acquisitions. In particular, the Kroger buyout proved to be a poor strategic move in that inadequate market research and unexpected competitive response in San Antonio, among other factors, stifled the cash flow that the Megafoods executives were counting on from the deal. To cut costs, Megafoods began pressuring Fleming to renegotiate their supply contract while at the same time reaching a tentative agreement with Safeway to begin buying more than 50 percent of its stock from the supplier. Armed with the Safeway agreement, Megafoods gave Fleming three months to come to terms with them or risk termination of the Megafoods/Fleming contract. While Fleming eventually backed down and agreed to renegotiate the contract, the supplier was less than overjoyed with Megafoods' tactics.

Although Megafoods posted a staggering $19.5 million net loss in 1993, Miller optimistically attributed the sharp decline to temporary setbacks related to the Kroger acquisition and to various one-time costs related to overall expansion expenditures. In the Megafoods annual report, Miller insisted that the losses were the result of an investment in the company's long-term profitability and he urged Megafoods to expand even more aggressively in 1994. In April of that year, Megafoods assumed control of 28 Handy Andy stores in San Antonio. Subsequent acquisitions during the next few months boosted the total number of Megafoods outlets to 71. Even before the Handy Andy takeover was finalized, however, critics were beginning to question Miller's acquisition strategy. "I think its a bad time for Megafoods to be buying anything," related one analyst in the April 8, 1994, *Arizona Republic.*

By late 1994, the Megafoods chain had become so unwieldy that profit margins slipped sharply, the 36-store San Antonio operation noticeably languished, and Megafoods experienced severe cash flow problems. Importantly, the long-running dispute with Fleming came to a head in mid-1994 when Fleming charged that Megafoods was failing to live up to the terms of their contract. Incensed, Fleming's CEO Bob Stauth verbally condemned Miller and Megafoods in a public statement, saying ''I don't want your business.'' Fleming threatened to halt shipments to the company, but Megafoods finally reached a tentative truce with the supplier by promising to pay cash for all deliveries. This resolution was of little comfort to either party, however; two days later, on August 17, Megafoods announced that it was filing for Chapter 11 bankruptcy.

When Megafoods filed for bankruptcy protection from its creditors, it was operating 71 stores in four states and employing a work force of about 5,500. During the next few months, Megafoods executives and directors labored to cut costs and maximize the value of their assets. By November, the Megafoods chain had been pared down to 58 stores and the number of employees on the payroll had been cut to 4,400. Following meetings in which shareholders expressed their displeasure with existing management, both Walker and Miller announced their resignations. By February of 1995, the company was employing 3,500 people and operating 50 stores in Arizona, Nevada, and Texas, having shut down all California operations. Under new management, Megafoods was laboring to develop an official plan of reorganization which would allow the company to pay off its debts and emerge from bankruptcy.

Principal Subsidiaries: Mega Warehouse Foods.

Further Reading:

Creno, Glen, ''Megafoods Posts Loss, as Expected,'' *Phoenix Gazette,* November 10, 1993, p. C1.

——, ''Warehouse or Supermarket? Megafoods Wants to Be Both as It Keeps Growing,'' *Phoenix Gazette,* September 16, 1993, p. C1.

Deters, Barbara, ''Megafoods Files for Chapter 11 Protection,'' *Arizona Republic,* August 18, 1994, p. C1.

——, ''Megafoods Meets Creditors in Court,'' *Arizona Republic,* October 6, 1994, p. C1.

——, ''Megafoods President Resigns,'' *Arizona Republic,* February 2, 1995, p. D1.

Gillespie, Phyllis, ''Megafoods, Smitty's Deal in Rumor Mill,'' *Arizona Republic,* April 8, 1994, p. E1.

——, ''Megafoods Dumps Executive,'' *Arizona Republic,* August 26, 1992, p. C1.

——, ''Megafoods Stock Sells Under Goal,'' *Arizona Republic,* July 25, 1992, p. C1.

Luebke, Cathy, ''Megafoods Stores Inc.,'' *The Business Journal-Serving Phoenix & the Valley of the Sun,* June 25, 1993, p. B42.

Maietta, Vince, ''Megafoods Going Public,'' *Business Journal-Phoenix,* June 12, 1992, p. 1.

Snyder, Jodie, ''Megafoods Eyes Move to Mexico,'' *Phoenix Gazette,* June 11, 1993, p. C1.

——, ''Megafoods Makes Stock Offer,'' *Phoenix Gazette,* June 10, 1992, p. C1.

—Dave Mote

Merillat Industries Inc.

5353 West U.S. Highway 223
P.O. Box 1946
Adrian, Michigan 49221
U.S.A.
(517) 263-0771
Fax: (517) 265-4435

Wholly Owned Subsidiary of Masco Corp.
Incorporated: 1946 as Merillat Woodworking Company
Employees: 3,100
Sales: $250 million (estimated)
SICs: 2434 Wood Kitchen Cabinets

Merillat Industries Inc., a subsidiary of Masco Corp., is the largest manufacturer of cabinetry for the kitchen, bath, and home in the United States. Merillat was launched in 1946 as Merillat Woodworking Company by Orville and Ruth Merillat. In the early days, the company manufactured custom kitchen cabinetry at a 2,400-square-foot plant in Adrian, Michigan. Merillat's original product line, Merillat Kitchens of Birch, was sold mainly to local consumers. It was also available through two modular housing manufacturers based in nearby Toledo, Ohio.

By the mid-1950s, consumer demand for Merillat products was increasing significantly, as was Merillat's market share. To cope with increasing demand, the company moved to a new, 15,000-square-foot, modular kitchen cabinet manufacturing plant, also located in Adrian. The firm also implemented several new marketing strategies, including a two-step distribution system designed to provide more efficient product delivery.

Throughout the years, Merillat continued to position itself as a leader in the manufacture of cabinetry. For example, the company instituted a mechanized assembly line that was able to manufacture its kitchen and bath cabinets—with self-closing hinges, high-pressure laminate construction, and aluminum drawer glides—more quickly. In 1962, Merillat received a patent for its self-closing hinges, leading to a new level of industry awareness of the company's technological advances.

In the mid-1960s, Merillat introduced a product line with reversible doors and drawer fronts, featuring two different wood grain-designed Formica brand laminates. The company also developed a hollow core laminated door, moving away from birch and toward the lightweight, highly durable products that the market was demanding. To stay ahead of increasing demand for its products, Merillat expanded its Adrian plant to 76,000 square feet in 1964, and to 135,000 square feet in 1966.

In 1968, Richard Merillat, son of the company founders, obtained a design patent for the ''Romance'' cabinet line. ''Romance'' was awarded a patent for utilizing injection-molded plastic doors—an industry first. Prestique, a styrene material used in ''Romance'' cabinet production, provided the look and feel of wood, while being resistant to moisture damage.

In 1971, the 25th anniversary of the founding of Merillat Woodworking, the company was renamed Merillat Industries Inc. Soon after, the company introduced cabinets with solid oak, double-doweled front frames and vinyl-laminated particle board end panels. By the mid-1970s, Merillat had expanded its product line with the introduction of an oak raised-panel cabinet called Forest Oak. In 1976, the firm built a manufacturing facility in the town of Jackson, Ohio, for the production of solid oak front frames.

The opening of the Jackson plant signaled a growth period during which Merillat Industries became the nation's largest manufacturer of cabinetry for the kitchen, bath, and home. By the mid-1980s, the firm had more than 2,000 employees in seven plants throughout the country: Adrian, Michigan; Jackson, Ohio; Lakeville, Minnesota; Culpeper, Virginia; Atkins, Virginia; Rapid City, South Dakota; and Las Vegas, Nevada. In 1982, the company moved into a new 21,000-square-foot corporate headquarters in Adrian. Three years later, Richard Merillat assumed the position of president of Merillat Industries, while Orville Merillat was named chairman.

The evolution of the company continued in 1986 with the opening of a door frame and veneering plant in Mt. Jackson, Virginia. In addition, the Jackson, Ohio, and Culpeper, Virginia, plants were expanded that year. In 1988, a 43,000-square-foot addition tripled the size of Merillat's headquarters, enabling the company to better meet the increasing demands of the market.

In 1991, Merillat opened two additional manufacturing plants. The 75,000-square-foot plant in Atkins, Virginia, was opened to manufacture door panels. A new 225,000-square-foot plant in Loudenville, Ohio, was built to manufacture the Amera cabinetry line. Amera was introduced to provide product alternatives in the expanding remodeling market, which was becoming increasingly populated by sophisticated and upscale consumers. The Atkins and Loudenville plants brought Merillat's total manufacturing plant count to 10 facilities and more than 2.5 million square feet. Merillat also had distribution centers in Denver, Colorado; Orlando, Florida; and West Palm Beach, Florida. The company sold its product through a network of 100 distributors and specialists who worked directly with major building contractors and individual remodelers.

In January 1992, Merillat introduced six new oak raised-panel cabinetry styles with full-overlay design into its ready-to-install cabinetry lines. Alexis and Alexis Arch provided a light finish, Bristen and Bristen Arch provided a medium finish, and Cambric and Cambric Arch provided a pickled finish. The products were all available with optional mullion doors with glass inserts.

The following year, Merillat introduced four new frameless maple raised-panel cabinetry styles: Kingsley and Kingsley Arch with natural finishes, and Rockingham and Rockingham Arch with pickled finishes. Also introduced at this time was a new generation of Merillat's traditional overlay light, medium, and pickled-oak cabinetry with the addition of full-concealed hinges, a new edge profile on doors and drawer fronts, and Merillat's own dual captive WhisperGlide drawer and tray system.

In 1994, Merillat introduced the Premium Woods, a line of three new wood species in traditional overlay, raised-panel cabinetry. The Premium Woods included Preston Cherry, which was available in Nutmeg finish and red-toned Paprika; Darlan Hickory, which was available in Nutmeg and honey-colored Cider; and Shetland Maple, which was available in natural finish and oatmeal pickled finish. At that time, Merillat offered more than 40 traditional and contemporary cabinet styles in cherry, maple, hickory, and oak. In addition, Merillat cabinets were offered in three oak finishes, two cherry finishes, two hickory finishes, and two maple finishes. They were also available in one vinyl and four melamine laminate colors. Cabinet doors in the ready-to-install line had a variety of style treatments, including raised center panels with square, arched, and cathedral styling, square recessed panels, mullion doors with glass inserts, and flush contemporary doors, some with sculptured oak pulls and trim.

Merillat also offered more than 100 ''Customizers'' accessories for the kitchen and bath. The Customizers program provided builders or remodelers with a wide range of accessories. For example, the Appliance Garage provided a convenient stow-away area for appliances, and the swing-out pantry helped make the homeowner's kitchen accessible but not cluttered. Other accessories included drawer dividers, tip-out hampers, and a hutch. The program was supported by a full package of marketing materials and trade publication advertising. William H. Ficken, Merillat's vice-president of marketing, told *Professional Builder & Remodeler* that he believed the customized package of accessories was very important to the builder as well as the buyer. ''The Customizers Program addresses the fact that there is a need to properly accessorize the kitchen and other areas of the home,'' he said. ''Builders who upsell will have a good sales margin opportunity in these option packages.''

Amera was another Merillat cabinet product line that offered customization and attention to detail. Amera kitchen products came in more than 50,000 combinations, including traditional framed and European frameless construction, 21 traditional and contemporary door styles, four wood species, six wood finishes, five laminate colors, and a full range of storage features.

By the mid-1990s, Merillat was well-established as an upscale manufacturer and marketer of high-quality products. An article that appeared in the *Detroit News* noted that Merillat kitchen products were used in the 1994 renovation of the Manoogian Mansion, the traditional home of Detroit's mayor. Merillat attributed its success to its focus on brand awareness, according to *Professional Builder & Remodeler.* ''We have the highest brand awareness of other cabinet makers,'' a Merillat representative stated. ''Our customers recognize that our name creates a quality impact and awareness.''

Further Reading:

Colborn, Marge, ''Masco Is Making the Most of the Manoogian Face-lift,'' *Detroit News,* September 24, 1994, p. D20.

Kuhl, Helen, ''Introducing Merillat's First Frameless Line,'' *Wood & Wood Products,* November 1988, p. 68.

Merillat—America's Cabinetmaker Fact Sheet, Adrian, Michigan: Merillat Industries, 1994.

''Merillat Means Cabinets and So Much More,'' *Professional Builder & Remodeler,* November 1, 1991, p. 121.

—Pamela Berry

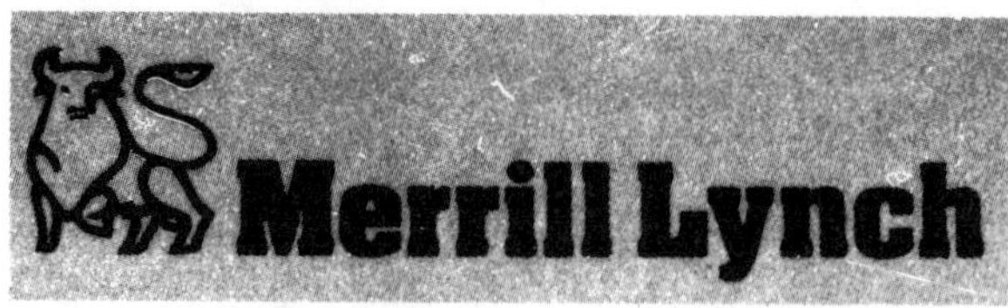

Merrill Lynch & Co., Inc.

World Financial Center
North Tower
New York, New York 10281-1332
U.S.A.
(212) 449-1000
Fax: (212) 449-7357

Public Company
Incorporated: 1959
Employees: 43,800
Total Assets: $163.75 billion
Stock Exchanges: New York Chicago Pacific London Paris Tokyo
SICs: 6211 Security Brokers & Dealers; 6282 Investment Advice; 6311 Life Insurance; 6719 Holding Companies, Nec

Merrill Lynch & Co., Inc. is the largest retail brokerage house in the United States, the leading U.S. investment banker, and a global leader in debt and equity underwriting, bond underwriting, and merchant banking. Long committed to the needs of the small investor, Merrill continually diversified its offerings from the late 1960s through the 1990s. Now a global giant in the industry, increasingly active in a variety of investment fields outside the retail business, Merrill has evolved far from its original concentration on what its founder called ''people's capitalism.''

Merrill Lynch's oldest direct predecessor was the partnership of Burrill & Housman, founded in 1885. In 1890 William Burrill left the firm he had created, and the next year Arthur Housman's brother Clarence joined what was then A. A. Housman & Company. When Arthur Housman died in 1907, he left behind one of Wall Street's leading brokerage houses.

That same year, Charles Merrill and Edmund Lynch arrived in New York, where they met and became friends. The two 22-year-old entrepreneurs had both recently finished college and gravitated to Wall Street to seek their fortune. At that time, the stock market was chiefly the domain of a small number of eastern businessmen, but Merrill quickly realized the vast potential of financial markets funded by a broad spectrum of middle-class Americans. He received his initial training in the bond department of Burr & Company, and then set up his own firm in 1914. The following year he persuaded Edmund Lynch to join him, and Merrill, Lynch & Company was born.

The company prospered and grew quickly, earning a strong reputation in financial circles for financing the newly emerging chain store industry. Merrill himself was a founder of Safeway Stores, and the company underwrote the initial public offering for McCrory Stores. By the late 1920s, Merrill, Lynch was reaping the benefits of that decade's prolonged economic boom, but Charles Merrill gradually became uneasy about the frantic pace of investment. He predicted that bad times were ahead as early as 1928, warning his clients and his own firm to get ready for an economic downturn. When the crash came in 1929, Merrill, Lynch had already streamlined its operations and invested in low-risk concerns. Despite this foresight, in 1930 Merrill and Lynch decided to sell the firm's retail business to E. A. Pierce & Company and concentrate on investment banking.

E. A. Pierce & Company was the direct descendent of A. A. Housman & Company. The company was named for Edward Allen Pierce, who had joined Housman in 1901, become a partner in 1915, and the managing partner in 1921. After World War I, Pierce concentrated on building the firm into a nationwide network of branches connected by telegraph, in order to reach more customers. After a 1926 merger with Gwathmey & Company, the firm was renamed E. A. Pierce & Company the following year.

Like most brokers, Pierce struggled through the depression years, and in 1939 he persuaded Charles Merrill to rejoin him in the retail business. In 1940 Merrill Lynch, E. A. Pierce & Cassatt opened its doors, dropping the comma between Merrill and Lynch for the first time and adding Cassatt, a Philadelphia firm that had sold part of its business to Pierce and part to Merrill, Lynch in 1935.

The new firm was devoted to the radical concept of offering to its investors a ''department store of finance.'' Clients were urged to research their financial options, and Merrill Lynch saw itself as a partner in that process, even providing educational materials. In 1941 the firm merged again; this time it became Merrill Lynch, Pierce, Fenner & Beane when it absorbed Fenner & Beane, a New Orleans company that was the nation's largest commodities house and the second-largest ''wire house'' (an investment firm that, like E. A. Pierce, depended on its private telegraph wires for a broad-based business).

During World War II the company benefited greatly from the economic turnaround brought by increasing military spending. Throughout the bull market of the postwar period and the 1950s, Merrill Lynch continued to be an innovator and a popularizer of financial information. The firm erected a permanent Investment Information Center in Grand Central Station, distributed educational brochures, ran ads with titles like ''What Everybody Ought to Know About This Stock and Bond Business,'' and even sponsored investment seminars for women. These new ideas made Merrill Lynch the best-known investment firm of the day. Charles Merrill's reputation soared to such heights that shortly before his death in 1956 one Wall Street historian referred to him as ''the first authentically great man produced by the financial markets in 50 years.''

In 1958 the firm juggled names again. Alpheus Beane, Jr., dropped out of the firm, and since Winthrop Smith had taken over as directing partner two years earlier, the firm was renamed Merrill Lynch, Pierce, Fenner & Smith (ML). The next year it became the first large Wall Street firm to incorporate, and earnings reached a record high of $13 million.

During the 1960s the company began to diversify and expand internationally. In 1964 Merrill Lynch entered the government-securities business when it acquired C. J. Devine, the nation's largest and most prestigious specialist in that market. Over the course of the decade the firm also entered the fields of real estate financing, asset management, and economic consulting, and added 20 new overseas offices. The company paid special attention to establishing a European presence, which allowed participation in the developing Eurobond market, and by 1964 had succeeded in becoming the first U.S. securities firm in Japan. In that same year ML was named lead underwriter for the $100 million public offering of Comsat, builder of the world's first telecommunications satellite, thus solidifying its position as one of the country's major investment-banking firms. The company underwrote the sale of Howard Hughes's TWA stock in 1965, and in the next ten years added significant new business with firms such as Commonwealth Edison, Fruehauf, and Arco. By the end of the decade Merrill was managing about $2 billion annually in such offerings.

One of these projects, a 1966 debenture issue for Douglas Aircraft, led to an investigation by the Securities and Exchange Commission (SEC) and a substantial rewriting of the regulations governing full-service investment firms like ML. The SEC charged that Merrill had passed on to some of its institutional clients confidential information about Douglas gathered while serving as the latter's investment banker. The company neither admitted nor denied the allegations but did agree to pay some fines, and the SEC took the opportunity to tighten its rules regarding insider trading and the prevention of unwarranted intraoffice disclosures.

Net income in 1967 was a handsome $55 million, representing an increase of 300 percent during the previous eight years. In the following year, Donald T. Regan was named president of Merrill Lynch, and two years later he became chairman and CEO. Regan guided ML in an ambitious program of diversification aimed at making the company a "one-stop investment and estate-planning institution." This included ML's first determined entry into the real estate field with the 1968 acquisition of Hubbard, Westervelt & Motteley, enabling it to offer to customers a range of mortgages, leasebacks, and other options; a major move into the mutual fund markets; and the purchase of Royal Securities Corporation of Canada, significantly strengthening ML's position in that country.

The firm also absorbed the New York Stock Exchange's fifth-largest brokerage house, Goodbody & Company, in 1970 when that company fell victim to Wall Street's so-called "paper crunch disaster." Overextended trading houses were generating more transaction records than their accounting departments could keep up with, resulting, in the case of Goodbody and many others, in massive confusion and eventual collapse. The exchange asked ML to step in and help Goodbody, and ML ended up acquiring the firm at the end of 1970. The bailout cost little and brought ML new expertise in the area of unit trusts and options trading.

In 1971 Merrill Lynch became the second member of the New York Stock Exchange to invite public ownership of its shares, and in July of that year became the first to have its own shares traded there. Shortly thereafter, the company adopted its most recent change of name, forming a holding company called Merrill Lynch & Co., Inc., with Merrill Lynch, Pierce, Fenner & Smith as its principal subsidiary.

Regan's diversification program continued with a 1972 move into international banking. London-based Brown-Shipley Ltd. soon became Merrill Lynch International Bank, and in 1974 ML acquired the Family Life Insurance Company of Seattle, Washington. In 1976 ML formulated a strategy to meet the challenge of the increasingly complex international financial marketplace by offering "a diversified array of securities, insurance, banking, tax, money management, financing, and financial counseling." Formerly clear demarcations between the various money professions were rapidly blurring, as ML demonstrated in 1977 when it announced the creation of the Cash Management Account (CMA). This unique account allowed individual investors to write checks and make Visa charges against their money market funds. Banks did not appreciate this incursion into their territory and mounted a number of legal campaigns to stop it, to no avail. By 1989, fully half of ML's $304 billion in customer accounts were placed in CMAs, and most of the other leading brokerage houses had developed similar integrated-investment vehicles.

Despite its sustained attempt to achieve a steady level of profit through diversification, ML's earnings have reflected the volatile nature of its core securities business. For example, 1971 profit reached a new high of $70 million, but was followed by the difficult oil-embargo years of 1972–74; and while 1975's record $100 million was not equaled for several years afterward, 1980 saw record highs of $218 million in profit and $3 billion in revenues. That year also marked the end of the Regan era at ML, as new U.S. President Ronald Reagan named Donald T. Regan secretary of the treasury and later made him White House chief of staff.

Roger Birk became the company's new chairman and CEO, followed in 1984 by William A. Schreyer. Schreyer, unhappy with ML's failure to match the earnings of some of its more flamboyant competitors, made increased profitability his chief goal. To that end, Schreyer reorganized the vast company, strengthened its trading, underwriting, and merger and acquisition departments, and made a $1 billion move into new offices in the World Financial Center. The firm also cut spiraling operating costs and trimmed 2,500 employees from its ranks.

In 1985 ML met a longstanding goal when it became one of the first six foreign companies to join the Tokyo Stock Exchange. The following year, when the firm became a member of the London Exchange, ML was able to offer round-the-clock trading. Later in 1986 ML sold its real estate brokerage unit as part of Schreyer's plan to unload low-profit concerns so that the company could focus more on using its powerful retail divisions to sell the securities its investment-banking department brought in. The strategy worked; profits increased to a record $453 million during that year.

Also in 1986, scandal hit when Leslie Roberts, a 23-year-old Merrill Lynch broker, was arrested by the FBI for mail fraud. Roberts's complex fraud scheme lost huge sums—as much as $10 million from a single investor's account. The Roberts case typified for many the money fever of pre-crash Wall Street, and the incident attracted international attention.

Then in April 1987, the company was caught speculating in hugely unsuccessful fashion when it lost $377 million trading mortgage-backed securities—the largest one-day, one-company trading loss in Wall Street history. Coupled with the crash of October 1987, profits were sent reeling and ML was forced to freeze salaries, cut bonuses, dismiss employees, and slash commission payouts to its sales force. But profits increased dramatically the next year, reaching a record high of $463 million. During 1988 ML also achieved a long-held goal when it edged out Salomon Brothers to become the largest underwriter in America. The following year ML realized another long-term goal: the firm became the world leader in debt and equity securities, this time besting First Boston Corporation in the race for the top spot. Merrill Lynch remained in the thick of the hot merger-and-acquisition business as well, earning, for example, a tidy $90 million for helping put together the $25 billion leveraged buyout of RJR Nabisco Inc. that year.

Although Merrill Lynch's revenue and assets under management grew steadily from 1988 to 1990, its return on equity continued to lag behind other firms in the industry. Observers in particular cited the company's traditional inability to control costs—according to *Business Week,* it was "powerful but awkward and overweight . . . hobbled by a costly, bloated bureaucracy." Schreyer embarked on an ambitious reorganization which created 18 operating divisions, the managers of which were accountable for all costs therein. ML also downsized, reducing its head count from 48,000 in 1989 to 37,000 in 1991 and eliminating unprofitable subsidiaries such as Merrill Lynch Realty, Inc. and its clearing service Broadcort Capital Corp. It made additional cuts in its non-U.S. operations. Schreyer's overall cost-containment program paid off by reducing costs $400 million dollars from 1989 to 1991.

Perhaps most importantly, however, Schreyer changed the mind-set of the company from an obsession with generating revenue to a focus on earning profits. Compensation programs tied to the production of revenue were scrapped to make room for new schemes based on return on equity (ROE). Schreyer set an overall company goal of 15 percent ROE, but also held ML divisions to this standard as well. As a result, Merrill Lynch's ROE figures improved dramatically in the early 1990s—5.8 percent in 1990, 20.8 percent in 1991, 22 percent in 1992, and 27.3 percent in 1993. This achievement did not, however, come at the expense of growth. From 1990 to 1993, gross revenues increased from $11.15 billion to $16.59 billion, while assets under management increased from $110 billion to $161 billion. In the midst of this success, Schreyer retired in 1993 and was replaced as chairman and CEO by Daniel P. Tully, who had been president and COO.

By 1994 ML had perhaps achieved a long-held goal of diversification to such a degree that it could achieve an average ROE of 15 percent across business cycles. Other firms in the industry struggled in 1994 as a series of U.S. Federal Reserve interest rate hikes battered the bond market and reduced underwriting dramatically. Merrill Lynch—though its profits were down significantly in the second, third, and fourth quarters—still managed a ROE of 18.6 percent for the year on record gross revenues of $18.23 billion. Since the company had the ability to offer its customers a full range of financial services and investment opportunities, it could generate revenues—and profits—in all types of market environments. ML's continuing growth in the global market—highlighted in 1994 by its first-time leadership in Eurobond and global bond underwriting—also promised to help the firm overcome downturns in the economies of individual countries or regions.

1994 did leave a cloud hanging over the otherwise sunny forecast for Merrill Lynch's future. Orange County, California, was forced to file for bankruptcy late in 1994 after losing nearly $2 billion in a $7.6 billion county investment fund. Throughout the 1990s, the Orange County treasurer had leveraged the fund in order to purchase securities that would increase sharply if interest rates fell. The scheme worked very well until the 1994 Federal Reserve rate hikes sent the fund's securities into a tailspin. The county subsequently sued ML for $2 billion, claiming that the firm had advised the treasurer to make investments that exceeded state-mandated limits on risk. Merrill Lynch denied that it had done anything wrong, and claimed that it had not been the treasurer's financial adviser.

In mid-1995 Merrill Lynch became the largest investment bank in the world in terms of equity sales, trading, and research through its acquisition of England's biggest independent securities firm, Smith New Court PLC. With the $842 million purchase, ML not only increased its presence in England but also gained businesses in several countries where it had none, such as South Africa, Malaysia, and Thailand. The acquisition thus brough further geographic diversification to Merrill Lynch's operations.

In the difficult environment of the mid-1990s financial services industry, Merrill Lynch was at the top and nearing its goal of "being the world's preeminent financial management and advisory company." If observers' predictions of an impending shakeout in the industry were to come to pass, the company was well positioned to take advantage of the fallout and strengthen its hold on various segments of the industry.

Principal Subsidiaries: Merrill Lynch, Pierce, Fenner & Smith Inc.; Helmco-Lacy; Merrill Lynch Bank & Trust Co.; Merrill Lynch Business Financial Services Inc.; Merrill Lynch Capital Partners, Inc.; Merrill Lynch Capital Services, Inc.; Merrill Lynch Credit Corporation; Merrill Lynch Derivative Products, Inc.; Merrill Lynch Fiduciary Services, Inc.; Merrill Lynch Futures Investment Partners Inc.; Merrill Lynch Government Securities, Inc.; Merrill Lynch Group, Inc.; Merrill Lynch, Hubbard, Inc.; Merrill Lynch Insurance Group, Inc. (50%); Merrill Lynch Interfunding Inc.; Merrill Lynch International, Inc.; Merrill Lynch Investment Management, Inc.; Merrill Lynch Life Agency Inc.; Merrill Lynch Money Markets Inc.; Merrill Lynch Private Capital Inc.; Merrill Lynch Specialists,

Inc.; Merrill Lynch Trust Company; Star Manufacturing Co.; Wagner Stott Clearing Corp.

Further Reading:

"American Municipalities: Merrill Lynched," *Economist,* December 17, 1994, pp. 76–78.

Byrnes, Nanette, and Leah Nathans Spiro, "Will Merrill Take a Hit in Orange County?," *Business Week,* February 13, 1995, p. 86.

"The Culprits of Orange County," *Fortune,* March 20, 1995, pp. 58–59.

Friedman, Jon, "The Remaking of Merrill Lynch," *Business Week,* July 17, 1989, pp. 122–25.

Hecht, Henry, ed., *A Legacy of Leadership: Merrill Lynch 1885–1985,* New York: Merrill Lynch, 1985, 151 p.

LaPlante, Alice, "Merrill's Wired Stampede," *Forbes,* June 6, 1994, pp. 76–80.

Lenzer, Robert, "Merrill at the Half-Trillion Mark," *Forbes,* April 26, 1993, pp. 42–43.

Michels, Antony J., "Get Lean When the Times Are Fat," *Fortune,* May 17, 1993, pp. 97–100.

Regan, Donald T., *The Merrill Lynch Story,* New York: Newcomen Society in North America, 1981, 22 p.

Savitz, Eric J., "Bull in a China Shop?: Merrill Lynch May Be Getting a Bum Rap from Investors," *Barron's,* September 17, 1990, pp. 10–11, 20.

Spiro, Leah Nathans, "Raging Bull: The Trimmer New Look of Merrill Lynch," *Business Week,* November 25, 1991, pp. 218–21.

—updated by David E. Salamie

Methode Electronics, Inc.

7444 West Wilson Avenue
Chicago, Illinois 60656
U.S.A.
(708) 867-9600
Fax: (708) 867-3288

Public Company
Incorporated: 1946
Employees: 2,500
Sales: $213.3 million
Stock Exchanges: NASDAQ
SICs: 3678 Electronic Connectors; 3679 Electronic Components Not Elsewhere Classified; 3676 Electronic Resistors

Methode Electronics, Inc. produces and sells electronic components used in a variety of manufacturing processes. Most of the company's products are involved in connecting, controlling, or distributing electrical energy, pulse and signal. Methode's devices are commonly found in data processing equipment, instruments, communication products, and automobiles. The company also supplies components for military and aerospace manufacturing. Methode maintains 16 manufacturing facilities and three service centers. The company produces connectors for the electronics industry at four factories in Chicago and two plants each in Singapore and the United Kingdom. In one U.K. plant and four facilities in the midwestern United States, the company produces a wide range of controls, air bag transducers, and wiring harnesses for the automotive industry. The Big Three U.S. automakers together account for about 45 percent of Methode's sales. Methode manufactures printed circuit boards, its staple product until about 1980, at sites on both coasts of the United States.

Methode Electronics, Inc. was founded by William McGinley just after the end of World War II. As of 1995, McGinley remained the only company president in Methode's half-century history. During its first three decades of operation, Methode's bread-and-butter product was the circuit boards it provided to television manufacturers and makers of other consumer electronics. By the 1960s, the company was big enough to begin swallowing up smaller operations. In 1962, Methode acquired Carter Precision Electric Co., Inc., and five years later, the company purchased Technical Components Co., Inc., a manufacturer based in the suburbs of Chicago. In 1969, Methode swapped 5,000 shares of convertible preferred stock for Graphic Research Inc., a maker of printed circuit boards for military applications, based in Chatsworth, California.

During the 1970s, Methode continued to grow steadily. In 1975, the company formed a new subsidiary called Carthage Precision Electric Company, located in Carthage, Illinois. The Carter unit it had acquired 13 years earlier was integrated into the new Carthage subsidiary. Meanwhile, executives at Methode's Graphic Research subsidiary had expressed a need for better printed circuit board testing equipment. To meet this request, another subsidiary, PWR, Inc., was formed. By the beginning of 1976, PWR had set up shop in the Graphic Research building, and manufacturing of printed circuit board testing systems had begun.

Toward the end of the 1970s, McGinley initiated a couple of strategic shifts that paid off handsomely for Methode. Prior to that time, the company was making primary custom-built circuit boards and connectors according to designs supplied by its customers. McGinley decided that these custom-building contracts, while a fairly low-risk proposition, were not profitable enough. Methode began instead to sell products that it had designed itself. While this approach was riskier, since it involved the additional expenses of designing and developing the products, it would lead to much greater profit margins.

McGinley's other change of direction stemmed from his recognition of the fact that most television and other consumer electronics manufacturing were emigrating from the United States to Asia in rapid fashion. To adjust to this phenomenon, he began shifting Methode's product development efforts away from televisions toward a greater emphasis on making connectors for the automobile, computer, and aerospace industries. The shift was in full gear by 1980. By that time, the company had annual sales of $44.7 million, up from $27.5 million only four years earlier. Printed circuit boards still generated the biggest share of sales—35 percent—by 1981. Connectors accounted for 24 percent, while 20 percent came from switches and other transportation controls.

Over the next few years, Methode focused increasingly on producing connectors and controls, and its best customers were the major car companies. For 1984, those two products accounted for 61 percent of the company's $82.4 million in revenue, and one-fifth of Methode's net sales for the year came from one company, General Motors. Windshield wipers, turn signals, and cruise control components were among the hot sellers to the auto manufacturers. By this time, printed circuit boards were accounting for only about 19 percent of the company's total revenue.

By 1985, it was clear that Methode's decision to concentrate on the auto industry was a good one. Homing in on the car companies meant that Methode was largely steering clear of the computer market. Most of its rivals had done the opposite. When a major sales slump hit the personal computer business in the mid-1980s, most electronic component manufacturers suffered along with it. Methode's largest competitor, Amp Inc., for instance, saw its sales shrink by seven percent and its earnings decline by one third in 1985. Methode, on the other hand, remained on a roll. The company was supplying nearly all of Ford Motor Company's cruise-control switches, and all three major American auto makers were buying a large share of their steering-column controls (for headlight intensity, wipers, etc.) from Methode. In addition to its automotive products, Methode's military business was booming as well. The Reagan administration's beefed-up defense budget put large sums of money into the hands of big military contractors like Raytheon Co., Boeing Co., and Hughes Aircraft. Since each of those, and many others, were Methode customers, a healthy share of that defense budget eventually ended up in Methode's till.

In the second half of the 1980s, Methode made moves to place itself in an even more vital position in the automotive chain of production. By 1986, Methode was the only major producer of the electronic components for the new passive restraint systems being built into many new cars. Unfortunately, auto production was slow that year, resulting in flat sales and a small decline in earnings for Methode. Nevertheless, Methode was able to take advantage of the quick proliferation of electronic gizmos appearing in cars. Meanwhile, the company sought to stake out a bit more territory in the computer business. Toward that end, Methode began producing sophisticated connectors for IBM's new generation of personal computers. Having already taken a beating from the consumer electronics industry a decade earlier, the company proceeded somewhat cautiously in the volatile computer market. Methode made one major geographical move in 1986; in order to be closer to manufacturers in the Far East, the company opened a plant in Singapore that year.

Methode's sales grew to $113 million by fiscal 1988. The company's biggest boost during the last few years of the 1980s came from the accelerating use of air bags in automobile manufacturing. With federal regulations requiring incremental increases in the inclusion of air bags, a huge new demand for the necessary electronic elements was created. Methode completed the development of a specialized spring system that connected impact sensors to the air bag's inflation mechanism in 1988. Before the end of the year, contracts for the air bag springs were already signed with Ford and Chrysler, and negotiations with General Motors—which was already coming to Methode for all of its fluid-level sensor switches—were underway.

While Methode's automotive business was cruising along in high gear, its aerospace operations were stuck on the ground. The company's Graphic Research subsidiary was encountering several problems. One obstacle was the slowdown of the space shuttle program, a big source of Graphic Research's revenue, in the wake of the Challenger disaster. An even bigger headache was created by repeated delays in the company's production of multilayer circuit boards for the government's Trident missile system. The situation at Graphic Research eventually got so bad that Methode began looking for somebody to take the subsidiary off its hands. No takers emerged, however, and by the middle of 1989, Graphic's Trident troubles were solved, enabling the subsidiary to begin operating profitably once again.

Just as Graphic Research was righting itself, another of Methode's California subsidiaries was entering a rough period. Trace Laboratories, a manufacturer of circuit board testing equipment, began losing money after experiencing numerous delays in the development of its state-of-the-art Manufacturing Defects Analyzer. Meanwhile, the company's car controls continued to sell like hotcakes, and Methode's overall sales reached $122 million for the fiscal year ending in April of 1989. Even a sickly automobile industry at the start of the 1990s could not slow Methode down. The company's air bag spring mechanism alone generated about $15 million in revenue for 1990. During 1991, the heart of the recession, Methode's sales grew to $149 million, chiefly on the strength of its position as the only domestic supplier of the clockspring air bag sensor connector. By that time, the company had begun to penetrate the Japanese auto market as well, landing deals to supply electronic components to Mazda and Mitsubishi.

By 1992, General Motors, which had previously made its own air bag connectors, finally became the last of the Big Three to sign on with Methode. Automotive controls and electronic connectors for other applications were combining to account for all of Methode's earnings by this time, as the company's aerospace operations remained in a holding pattern. Trace Laboratories' circuit board testing business was still floundering, losing about $1 million a year and failing in its attempts to finish developing its long-awaited Manufacturing Defects Analyzer. After countless delays, false starts, and missed deadlines, Methode finally decided to cut its losses on Trace in 1992. The subsidiary was sold off, and Methode took a big write-off against earnings for its years of unfulfilled investment.

Foreign sales began to receive more and more attention at Methode as the 1990s continued. By 1993 the company had added Volvo as a customer and was negotiating with Honda and Nissan. In addition, it was building a factory in Scotland. Around this time, Methode started to forge a broader presence in the fiber-optics industry. In July of 1993, the company purchased Mikon, Ltd., a manufacturer of fiber-optic cable assemblies, based in Haverhill, England. The acquisition of Mikon gave Methode an instant foothold in the European telecommunications business. Altogether, 1993 was a big year for Methode, with major jumps in both earnings and revenue.

1994 was another record year for Methode, with sales reaching an all-time high of $213 million. Automotive controls, as usual, played a large role in the company's performance, as car makers continued to include more and more electronic gadgetry for safety and comfort on their standard models. 1994 was also a big year for the company's fiber-optics operations, as sales of components for that industry doubled. The increasing importance of fiber optics led Methode to create a new Optoelectronic Products Division. Another new area to receive much attention at Methode was smart connectors. This new line of products was capable of using intelligence to monitor and adjust signal in very little time. Other areas in which Methode began testing the waters included interconnection devices for airplane telephones and thermoplastic connectors capable of withstanding extreme environmental conditions.

In November 1994, Methode expressed a commitment to acquire a plant in China, which was thought to be the world's most important emerging market. The company hoped to initiate production there during the mid-1990s. The company also acquired cable assembly operations in New Haven, Connecticut, and Limerick, Ireland, from ETOS Fujikura International during the latter part of 1994. These moves represented the most logical next step for Methode—to make itself into a truly international company. Methode's record of growth since about 1980 had been extremely impressive, whether through astute planning, or, as company president McGinley suggested to H. Lee Murphy of *Crain's Chicago Business*, "just dumb luck in having the right products at the right time." Methode's lingering growth spurt was expected to continue for some time if that luck extended to its international expansion as well.

Principal Subsidiaries: Graphic Research, Inc.; Intertrace Technology, Inc.; Methode Electronics Europe, Ltd. (U.K.); Methode Development Company; Methode Electronics Far East PTE, Ltd. (Singapore); Trace Laboratories East; Trace Laboratories Central; Methode Electronics, Inc.—East; Methode Mikon Ltd. (U.K.); Methode Technical Components

Further Reading:

"Air Bag Intro May Inflate Methode's Profits," *Crain's Chicago Business,* September 26, 1988, p. 24.

"Auto Biz to Return Methode to Driver's Seat," *Crain's Chicago Business,* September 21, 1987, p. 21.

"Car Components Keep Methode in High Gear," *Crain's Chicago Business,* September 29, 1991, p. 16.

Maturi, Richard J., "Room to Grow," *Barron's,* September 23, 1985, p. 63.

McCormick, Jay, "How Methode Beat the Odds in Sagging Electronic Market," *Crain's Chicago Business,* September 16, 1985, p. 3.

"Methode Electronics Switching Game Plan," *Crain's Chicago Business,* September 21, 1992, p. 52.

"Methode Forms Unit to Produce PCB Testers," *Electronic News,* January 12, 1976, p. 43.

"Methode-Ology," *Forbes,* March 2, 1992, p. 130.

Murphy, H. Lee, "Air Bag Component Biz Inflates Results for Methode Electronics," *Crain's Chicago Business,* September 17, 1990, p. 30.

"New Woes May Slow Methode," *Crain's Chicago Business,* September 18, 1989, p. 24.

"The Right Connection," *Barron's,* January 11, 1982, p. 40.

Vinton, Bob, "Methode to Scrap Chicago PC if No Buyer is Found," *Electronic News,* March 30, 1981, p. 58.

Zipser, Andy, "Methode to His Madness," *Barron's,* October 12, 1992, p. 46.

—Robert R. Jacobson

Metropolitan Financial Corporation

P.O. Box 522
Minneapolis, Minnesota 55480
U.S.A.
(612) 973-1111
Fax: (612) 344-1029

Wholly Owned Subsidiary of First Bank System, Inc.
Incorporated: 1926 as Metropolitan Federal Savings & Loan Association of Fargo, North Dakota
Employees: 2,600
Assets: $8 billion
SICs: 6712 Bank Holding Companies; 6036 Savings Institutions Except Federal

One of the largest savings and loan holding companies in the United States before its acquisition by First Bank System in 1995, Metropolitan Financial Corporation grew from a small building and loan concern incorporated in 1926 into a diversified regional banking giant during its 68 years of independent existence in the upper midwestern United States. Capitalizing on the savings and loan fiasco during the late 1980s, Metropolitan Financial recorded much of its enormous growth during this period and quickly became a stalwart in the savings and loan industry.

When Norman M. Jones joined the family business in 1952, it was a modestly sized building and loan association based in Fargo, North Dakota, where it had operated for the past 26 years. Then known as Metropolitan Federal Savings & Loan Association, the bank had spent its first quarter century accumulating $3.4 million in assets, enough to warrant the employment of seven people, three of whom were Jones, his father, and his grandfather. When the reins of leadership were passed to Norman Jones 15 years later in 1967, Metropolitan Federal's new chief executive officer inherited five branch offices. Over the course of the next 15 years, Jones gradually increased Metropolitan Federal's geographic presence, establishing branch offices primarily in rural settings; in the process, Jones made his family's business a discernible banking force in North Dakota. In the 30 years before Jones assumed leadership of the savings and loan, his father and grandfather had built a respectably sized banking organization comprising five branch offices; in roughly half that time, Jones would open four times as many Metropolitan Federal branches, elevating the family business to the forefront of North Dakotan thrift institutions and creating a stable foundation for the prolific growth to come in the 1980s.

Several important changes in the corporate structure of Metropolitan Federal were effected during the first half of the 1980s which helped the banking organization assume a more aggressive stance toward growth. The first of these changes occurred in 1983 when the bank switched to stock ownership, converting from a federally chartered mutual bank to a federally chartered capital stock association. The following year, the bank's shareholders voted to change from a stock savings and loan to a federal stock savings bank, a conversion that also resulted in a name change from Metropolitan Federal Savings & Loan Association to Metropolitan Federal Bank. Concurrent with this restructuring, shareholders elected to form a bank holding company for the new Metropolitan Federal to be named Metropolitan Financial Corporation. This reorganization allowed Metropolitan Federal to increase the types of services that it could legally offer and gave the financial institution better access to credit markets.

While Jones presided over these significant alterations in Metropolitan's organization, indications of the rapid growth to come were just beginning to surface. In September 1984, two months after Metropolitan Federal Savings & Loan Association became Metropolitan Federal Bank, the institution acquired a failed savings and loan in Mitchell, South Dakota, with the assistance of the Federal Savings and Loan Insurance Corporation (FSLIC), giving Metropolitan its 35th branch office and its first in South Dakota. For Jones and his management team, the absorption of Mitchell Home Savings and Loan added $17 million to Metropolitan's $1.4 billion in assets and extended the company's geographic presence southward into South Dakota. Of greater significance was the nature of the merger itself, however, for it established a model from which Jones and other company officials would predicate Metropolitan's growth later in the decade.

After the acquisition of Mitchell Home Savings, Metropolitan completed two more pivotal acquisitions, the first of which came in 1985. That year, Metropolitan bought out another troubled savings and loan institution, this time in Moorhead, Minnesota, near the North Dakota-Minnesota border, where the company already had an appreciable grip on the area's banking business. Metropolitan had little need to bolster its presence in Moorhead, something Jones later admitted to *American Banker* when he confessed, "We were already serving Moorhead pretty well; we didn't need an office there." Like the acquisition of Mitchell Home Savings the year before, however, the significance of the Moorhead purchase was not the property gained but its implications for the future. For Jones, the move into Moorhead represented "a stepping stone to the Twin Cities." Jones carried out this strategy two years later when Metropolitan purchased Rothschild Financial Corporation, located in the Minneapolis-St. Paul area, for $25 million. Rothschild Financial represented more than a harbinger of the future actions to be undertaken by Metropolitan; the mortgage concern by itself significantly contributed to Metropolitan's operations, marking its entry into mortgage banking and establishing the company as a major regional mortgage banker.

On the heels of Metropolitan's acquisition of Rothschild Financial, conditions began to develop in the U.S. banking industry that portended disaster for many members of the banking community, but signalled a period of exceptional growth for Metropolitan. Savings and loan institutions across the country were failing at an alarming rate, establishing a pattern that would soon build to a nationwide crisis costing the government and taxpayers more than $300 billion. Although an overwhelming majority of the savings and loan industry's failures would occur in Texas, where 114 of the state's 244 thrifts would be declared insolvent by the beginning of 1989, the crisis nevertheless afflicted nearly every state in the nation.

In the midst of this savings and loan disaster, Metropolitan weathered the storm and, at the same time, prepared to embark on a prodigious expansion program. The national banking crisis worsened in 1988, its debilitating effects punctuated by the failure of two California thrifts in June and another in September. The first two failures effectively stripped the FSLIC of its $1.3 billion cash reserves, while the rescue of a third California failure—the fourth billion-dollar failure in a three-week span—cost the government a staggering $2 billion. During this period of financially catastrophic failures, Metropolitan took advantage of its stalwart position in the industry and arranged for the acquisition of six insolvent thrifts, the absorption of which transformed the banking organization into a genuine interstate financial services provider.

On August 26, 1988, all six savings and loans were officially brought under the Metropolitan corporate umbrella. The addition of these thrifts greatly increased the scope of Metropolitan's operations, making it one of the early winners in the race to restructure the country's savings and loan industry. Perhaps the most rewarding aspect of the acquisitions, though, was the low price Metropolitan paid to become one of the early winners; similar to the company's 1984 acquisition of Mitchell Home Savings, this deal was made with the help of the FSLIC, which provided sufficient financial assistance to enable Metropolitan's multiple acquisition. In fact, for the six thrifts purchased in August, combined with another acquisition involving the merger of First Financial Savings Banks in Des Moines, Iowa, Metropolitan paid a mere $40 million, while the government paid $367 million in notes from the FSLIC and contributed $191 million worth of FSLIC-covered non-performing assets. Metropolitan continued to expand later that year, when it acquired the fourth-largest real estate company in the nation, Edina Realty Inc., its subsidiary, Edina Financial Services, Inc., and Equity Title Services Company.

The addition of Edina Realty, with 50 offices and annual sales of $3.5 billion, capped a remarkable year for Metropolitan. Literally overnight, the savings and loan concern transformed itself from a comparatively unknown thrift institution into a banking powerhouse buttressed by major mortgage banking interests and formidable real-estate brokerage concerns. Metropolitan's assets jumped 76 percent from 1987 to 1988, reaching $4.1 billion, and its loan portfolio soared 78 percent to $1.8 billion, making Metropolitan's 62nd year of existence by far its most active.

While Metropolitan's frenetic acquisition pace of 1988 gave way to a period of relative inactivity, discord between Jones and another executive took on its own unique significance. In November 1990, Jones, then 60 years old, stepped down as Metropolitan's chief executive, and Paul A. Lipetzky was promoted to the post of president and chief operating officer. While Jones remained the company's chairman, Lipetzky took over day-to-day operations of Metropolitan, although he was never officially named chief executive officer. Under Lipetzky's leadership, Metropolitan fared well, increasing its earnings from $28.3 million in 1990 to $57.5 million in 1991. Despite this success, Lipetzky was forced to step down in mid-1992, after Jones informed him that he would be returning as Metropolitan's chief executive officer. Jones had vacated the chief executive post in 1990 primarily because Metropolitan was in the process of absorbing its numerous acquisitions into the company's organization and had no immediate plans to expand. Two years later, with dozens of potential properties available for acquisition, Jones decided to return to Metropolitan to undertake the challenging task.

Metropolitan had already begun a push toward acquiring additional banking interests earlier in 1992, purchasing $71 million in deposits from Moneycor Savings Bank in March, the deposits of 12 branches of First Federal Savings Bank in April, and acquiring Security Financial Group, Inc. for $12.8 million in September. With Jones at the helm, Metropolitan continued to increase its assets, acquiring Home Owners Savings Bank and American Charter Federal Savings & Loan in December 1992, additions that raised the company's total assets to $6.6 billion. Metropolitan acquired Western Financial Corporation and its subsidiary, Columbia Savings Association, in June 1993, Eureka Savings Bank in August 1993, then completed a giant acquisition in March 1994, when it obtained Rocky Mountain Financial Corporation and its subsidiary, Rocky Mountain Bank.

At the time, Rocky Mountain Financial ranked as the second largest banking institution in Wyoming, and its addition to the growing Metropolitan empire lifted the corporation's assets to $7.8 billion. Through this acquisition, Metropolitan had become the 11th-largest thrift holding company in the United States, with 211 branches covering nine states from Arizona to Ohio. Four months after Metropolitan acquired Rocky Mountain Financial, Metropolitan signed an agreement to be acquired by First Bank System, Inc., a Minneapolis-based commercial banking company with $26.5 billion in assets. In January 1995, the transaction was completed for $800 million in stock, effectively ending Metropolitan's existence as a distinct corporate entity and giving First Bank System an impressive $8 billion in additional assets, $5 billion in additional deposits, and entry into four new states.

Principal Subsidiaries: Metropolitan Federal Bank; Metropolitan Services Corporation; Equity Title Services, Inc.; American Charter Credit Corporation; Security Consumer Services, Inc.; First Realty Property Management, Ltd.; Columbia Mortgage Corporation; Western Columbia Mortgage Holding, Inc.

Further Reading:

Byrne, Harlan S., "Metropolitan Financial Corp.," *Barron's,* June 12, 1989, pp. 55–6.

Engen, John, "A Big Small-Town Acquirer," *American Banker,* May 5, 1994, p. 4.

''First Bank System Inc.,'' *Wall Street Journal,* January 27, 1995, p. D3.

''Issues of Two Firms Will Begin Trading in the Big Board,'' *Wall Street Journal,* November 18, 1985, p. 53.

''Jones of Metropolitan Financial Will Quit Chief Executive Post,'' *Wall Street Journal,* November 7, 1990, p. B8.

Kapiloff, Howard, ''In Minnesota, Big Thrift Goes to First Bank,'' *American Banker,* July 5, 1994, p. 1.

''Metropolitan Federal Savings & Loan Association of Fargo,'' *Wall Street Journal,* April 23, 1984, p. 46.

''Metropolitan Federal Takes Over Failed S&L,'' *Wall Street Journal,* September 5, 1984, p. 16.

''Metropolitan Financial Appoints Jones President,'' *Wall Street Journal,* August 28, 1986, p. 22.

''Metropolitan Financial Corp.,'' *Wall Street Journal,* March 30, 1987, p. 36.

Miller, James P., ''First Bank System Agrees to Purchase Metropolitan Financial for $863 Million,'' *Wall Street Journal,* July 5, 1994, p. B6.

Schafer, Lee, ''Error Apparent,'' *Corporate Report Minnesota,* December 1992, pp. 52–9.

—Jeffrey L. Covell

Monfort, Inc.

P.O. Box G
Greeley, Colorado 80632
U.S.A.
(303) 353-2311
Fax: (303) 351-0096

Wholly Owned Subsidiary of ConAgra, Inc.
Incorporated: 1930
Employees: 14,976
Sales: $5.59 billion
SICs: 0211 Beef Cattle Feedlots; 2011 Meat Packing Plants; 5147 Meats & Meat Products

Monfort, Inc., as part of its parent's ConAgra Red Meat Companies subsidiary, is one of the leading meat companies in the United States. During its years as an independent company, Monfort developed into a vertically integrated corporation involved in feeding cattle and lambs; meat packing operations; fabrication operations to produce meat products for hotels, restaurants, institutions, and supermarkets; and the transport and distribution of its products to its customers. Monfort suffered through a number of difficult years in the 1970s and early 1980s, in part because of conflicts between Monfort management and workers. ConAgra acquired Monfort in 1987 and then merged the operations of a former Monfort competitor (Swift Independent Packing Company) into the company, an integration that proved difficult. Monfort has since been beset by a number of other problems—additional worker-management conflicts and lawsuits and fines from government agencies over anti-union tactics and other issues—while at the same time it has attempted to improve its operating results in the highly competitive meat industry through innovative processes and products.

Monfort began in 1930 as founder Warren H. Monfort's cattle feedlot north of Greeley, Colorado. Starting with 18 head in the midst of the Great Depression, Monfort began to buy additional range cattle for his feedlot. During this period, many farmers began to use tractors instead of horses in their fields, creating a huge surplus of corn. By taking advantage of the surplus feed, Monfort became a pioneer in providing packing plants with well-fed cattle year-round. The feedlot grew quickly into one of the largest in the country, with a 3,500-head capacity in the midst of World War II, 8,000 by 1950, and 32,000 by 1960.

During the 1960s the feedlot expanded rapidly into the first 100,000-head feedlot by 1968. While Monfort's increased capacity for cattle was impressive, it was the company's extensive vertical expansion and integration efforts during the decade that made it a major player in the meat industry and began its transition into the self-styled "complete meat company." Before the 1960s, cattle typically took the following route in their transformation into meat: pasture for initial feeding, feedlot for final feeding (usually several months), slaughterhouse in large city, butcher shop or supermarket for processing of the carcasses. In 1960 Monfort purchased a slaughterhouse in Greeley from Capitol Pack, Inc., and five years later added processing (or fabrication) capability to the plant, then called the Greeley Beef Plant. Monfort's innovation of slaughtering and processing cattle near where they were fed reduced the overall cost of producing meat through reduced transportation costs (processed carcasses weighed less than cattle) and reduced labor costs (Monfort processing workers were typically paid less and had to work faster than butchers in urban areas). While Monfort's fabrication operation used beef by-products to make dog food, fertilizer, and other products, its boxed beef operation—the first on a large scale—was considered truly innovative. During the fabrication operation the carcass would be divided into various cuts of beef and boxed ready for shipping directly to restaurants and hotels, a streamlined operation. These new approaches were soon adopted by other meat packers and were possible largely because of improvements in refrigeration, transportation, and the U.S. highway system.

Following the addition of fabrication operations to the Greeley plant, Monfort expanded into lamb processing and increased the plant's capacity a number of times. By 1969 it had processed 645,214 lambs and 331,381 cattle in a single year with sales of $157.6 million. That same year, Monfort expanded vertically once again with the acquisition of its major distributor, Mapelli Brothers Food Distribution Co. The company also added a transportation operation, which was incorporated as Monfort Transportation Co. in 1973. With the exception of the pre-feedlot feeding of cattle, some feedlot feeding of cattle, and both pre-feedlot and feedlot feeding of lambs, Monfort now controlled the entire meat production and distribution process. Having established an exceptionally strong, integrated organization, the company embarked on an ambitious expansion program in the early 1970s. Monfort built a second 100,000-head capacity feedlot near Gilcrest in northern Colorado, expanded its plant in Greeley, and added a new line of consumer portion food products to its established boxed beef line. Part of the financing for these projects came from a $16 million stock offering in 1970, which took the company public for the first time under the name Monfort of Colorado, Inc. The following year, the second Monfort generation took over when Warren Monfort retired and his son Kenneth Monfort took over. Annual sales topped $400 million and the company would soon join the Fortune 500.

Monfort then faced its first major crisis starting in 1973, when a combination of factors depressed the meat packing industry, forcing many of Monfort's competitors out of business. With average after-tax returns in the low single digits, the industry can be hit hard by economic difficulties. Monfort and its competitors had to contend with the doubling of grain prices nearly overnight after a massive government grain shipment to the

Soviet Union in 1973; reduced frozen beef prices as a result of the government's inflation-fighting wage and price controls; and increased costs from having to comply with new government regulation of chemical additives. With the overall U.S. market for beef products stabilizing and overseas markets difficult to penetrate, Monfort could only seek to reduce costs in order to stay competitive. One strategy the company employed was to have its cattle suppliers provide larger range-fed animals, thus reducing the amount of time they spent in the feedlot and saving on grain costs. Another, perhaps more important innovation (and one the company would continue to rely on from the early 1970s through the early 1980s), was to reduce its labor costs. According to Carol Andreas in *Meatpackers and Beef Barons,* Monfort brought in efficiency experts to streamline procedures and instituted a gradual speed-up of the slaughtering and processing lines in the 1970s in order to improve its bottom line. Not coincidentally, the company faced its first major labor conflicts during this period with strikes in 1970 and 1974.

Monfort enjoyed a resurgence in 1978 and 1979 that proved to be short-lived. Sales increased from $363.9 million in 1977 to $451.3 million in 1978 to $622.2 million in 1979, but a net loss of $178,000 in 1979 foreshadowed an extremely difficult 1980. That year the company suffered an after-tax loss of $23.9 million on sales of $755.7 million. Company officials reported that a number of factors contributed to poor results. First, three packing plants that the company purchased in 1979 took longer than anticipated to integrate into the Monfort operations. The most important of these, a beef plant in Grand Island, Nebraska, purchased from Swift & Co., was acquired to end the company's sole dependence on the Greeley plant for beef packing and processing. Its poor 1980 results were exacerbated by damage inflicted by tornadoes that hit Grand Island in June. Monfort management, however, considered labor conflicts at its Greeley plant to be the main source of its difficulties.

The company felt that the Greeley plant was increasingly uncompetitive because its workers were better paid than those of Monfort's competitors. Iowa Beef Processors in particular was said by industry experts to be the instigator of the downward trend in labor costs as a result of its successful battle with a union in 1969, as well as through a multi-plant negotiation strategy that allowed it to play one plant against another. Although Monfort denied undertaking a deliberate strategy to break the United Food and Commercial Workers union local at Greeley, Carol Andreas contends that they did just that. Nine hundred workers at the plant went on strike on November 1, 1979, following the expiration of their contract. In early January 1980 the company presented its final offer. While the offer included a modest wage increase (which was far below the then-high inflation rate), the offer reduced benefits and set up a two-tier wage scale that started new hires at a lower base. Although the workers felt the offer was unacceptable, they had few options now that Monfort had a second plant operating in Grand Island. Furthermore, the company announced they would reopen the Greeley plant on January 14th with replacement workers if necessary. The workers decided to go back to work without a contract.

The events that followed have been in dispute ever since. In its 1980 annual report, Monfort management contended that after the workers returned, "problems developed in the plant involving productivity and product quality," and that they faced economic problems, such as high interest rates and concerns from creditors about the company's financial health. Monfort closed the Greeley plant on March 28, 1990, blaming its need to significantly reduce its operating costs and survive as a company. Most of the terminated workers disputed this argument, however, pointing to the company's $46.5 million spent on 1979 plant acquisitions as proof of the company's strength. Illustrating the poor relations between the workers and company management, Andreas described a chaotic two months at the plant, with line speed-ups and company harassment of workers on the one hand and worker slowdowns and sabotage on the other.

Whatever the real reason for the closure, Monfort kept the plant shut for two years, reopening it in March 1982 without union representation. The union local then sued the company for unfair labor practices, claiming that the company refused to rehire some of the former workers. Thus began a 12-year legal battle, which was eventually won by the union in 1994 when Monfort was ordered to pay $10.6 million in back pay to 268 former workers—the fourth-largest such payment in the history of the National Labor Relations Board. Further labor trouble began in 1983 when workers at the Greeley plant voted against labor representation. Accusations of intimidation by company officials led to another lengthy legal battle, which was again won by the union. In 1992 a federal judge ruled that Monfort had violated fair labor laws during the 1983 union vote and ordered a re-vote. In September 1994 Greeley workers not only voted overwhelmingly in favor of union representation but also voted for mandatory union membership at the plant. That year a federal judge also ordered the company to pay a $125,000 fine for its anti-union activities.

When the Greeley plant reopened in 1982, industry observers estimated that labor costs were 25 percent lower than in 1980. In 1981 the company had closed a processing plant in Denver and frozen wages for both hourly and management workers. In general, Monfort aimed to streamline its operations and reduce its operating costs in order to stay competitive. Although the company appeared to enjoy healthy growth and steady earnings over the new few years—sales increased from $996.9 million in 1982 to $1.58 billion in 1986 while after-tax earnings ranged from $14.5 million to $25.1 million—Monfort management was increasingly concerned about consolidation in the meat packing industry. As the two leading companies, Excel Corp.—owned by Cargill Inc.—and Iowa Beef Processors (IBP), continued to grow through the acquisition of smaller packers, company officials feared that the industry was moving toward two-company consolidation and the demise of Monfort.

When Excel, the second-largest U.S. meat packer, announced that it would purchase the third-largest U.S. meat packer, the Spencer Beef Division of Land O'Lakes, Monfort filed suit to stop the acquisition. In essence, the company maintained that Excel was attempting to monopolize the meat packing industry in the Midwest through the purchase of smaller companies and construction of new plants near those of its competitors. Although Monfort won an initial judgment and the first Excel appeal, the U.S. Supreme Court in 1986 overturned the original ruling by a vote of six to two. The court held that rather than creating a monopolistic environment, the acquisition instead fostered ''vigorous competition.''

This ruling played a major role in the company's 1987 decision to agree to a buyout by ConAgra, Inc. In the midst of a spate of takeovers following the 1986 court ruling, ConAgra, a diversified food conglomerate based in Omaha, acquired Monfort in a May 1987 stock swap valued at $295.6 million. ConAgra was an established powerhouse in chicken, had purchased 21 Armour meat-processing facilities in 1984, and now added the vertical meat holdings of Monfort to its food empire. Monfort president Ken Monfort cited three reasons for the sale: a ''fair'' price offered by ConAgra, Inc.; the chance to become part of a diversified organization; and the financial backing to weather an economic slump. With the industry consolidating following the antitrust decision, Monfort would then be in a better position to compete with IBP, Excel, and others as it could draw on ConAgra's vast resources to expand.

In fact, less than one year after the sale, Monfort grew substantially through additional ConAgra acquisition activity. Following the acquisition, ConAgra set up a ConAgra Red Meat Companies subsidiary, which included Monfort. Ken Monfort was named head of the new ConAgra subsidiary, while a third generation of Monforts took over Monfort of Colorado with the ascent of Richard L. Monfort, Ken's son. Later in 1987 a long-planned third 100,000-head cattle feedlot finally opened near Yuma, in eastern Colorado. More significantly, ConAgra made its second major meat company acquisition of the year in October with the purchase of the Swift Independent Packing Company (SIPCO). In March 1988 ConAgra merged some of the SIPCO holdings—including three beef plants, three pork plants, and one lamb plant—into Monfort. This integration proved to be difficult in the short run as management differences between Monfort and Swift had to be reconciled. A major area of conflict was in style—Monfort had always had a fairly loose approach to management, while Swift, a company founded in the mid-1800s, had developed numerous rules for everything over the course of its long history. Two other significant events occurred over the next two years in Monfort's transition from independent to subsidiary: later in 1988 the name of the company was changed from the regional-sounding Monfort of Colorado, Inc., to the more generic Monfort, Inc.; and in July 1989 Ken Monfort retired, Richard Monfort took over the reins of ConAgra Red Meat Companies, and Michael L. Sanem became president of Monfort.

Beginning in 1989, Monfort responded to growing demand from consumers for leaner beef by reducing the amount of exterior fat on its boxed beef to ¼ inch. While this innovation proved successful, many butchers were cutting the fat still further after receiving it from Monfort. In response, in 1992 the company introduced the Super Lite Trim line of products, which reduced the fat to ⅛ inch. To achieve such a close trim cost-effectively, Monfort developed a new trimming method using handheld rotary knives on just-slaughtered carcasses. Such carcasses are still warm, making the trimming easier; the warm fat is also translucent, allowing workers to see the tissue beneath the fat and to maintain the desired close cut. Another advantage of the so-called ''hot'' trimming was that the meat products could be chilled much sooner after slaughter, lengthening their shelf life.

In the early 1990s the issue of tainted meat products, particularly hamburger, received widespread publicity and affected nearly all meatpackers, including Monfort. The company was one of the first in the industry to test for the E. coli 0157:H7 bacteria starting in 1992 at its own laboratory near the Greeley packing plant. Costing more than $3 million to set up, the lab was designed for a multitude of uses, including testing for bacterial and other contamination, sampling for pesticide residue in cattle feeds, and analyzing products for nutritional labeling. The lab also began conducting tests for outside clients. After E. coli-contaminated hamburger caused the death of four children and the illness of hundreds of others in the northwest in 1993, Monfort reacted swiftly when state inspectors in Florida discovered E. coli in a sample of Monfort ground beef in late 1994. The company voluntarily recalled 9,000 pounds of ground beef from the same lot as the contaminated sample. Further tests from the lot all proved negative. At about this same time, the U.S. Department of Agriculture began a controversial nationwide testing program for E. coli that was being challenged in court by meat industry lobbying groups.

As Monfort moved into the final phases of its integration into ConAgra in the early 1990s, a new company emphasis on public relations—not uncommon in newly acquired companies—seemed to point to the company's future. Industry observers believed that the company had finally ended its long-turbulent relationship with organized labor in 1994 when it settled its 12-year-old dispute over the 1980 closing and the 1982 reopening of the Greeley plant. That same year saw the first union contract at the plant in 15 years. Observers credited Richard Monfort with engineering this rapprochement with labor. So, when he announced in June 1995 that he was stepping down from his leadership of ConAgra Red Meat Companies, to be replaced by Kevin LaFleur, many called it the end of an era—the final chapter in a company's long struggle with a determined union and the final chapter in the Monfort family domination of Monfort, Inc.

Further Reading:

Andreas, Carol, *Meatpackers and Beef Barons,* Niwot, Colorado: University Press of Colorado, 1994, 225 p.

Armijo, Patrick, ''Monfort Union: A New Era,'' *Greeley Daily Tribune,* September 18, 1994.

Burcke, James M., Meatpacker's Losses Trimmed Down to Size,'' *Business Insurance,* April 18, 1994, pp. 118–19.

Ivey, Mike, ''How ConAgra Grew Big—and Now, Beefy,'' *Business Week,* May 18, 1987, pp. 87–88.

Jackson, Bill, ''History on the Hoof,'' *Greeley Daily Tribune,* January 23, 1994.

Leib, Jeffrey, ''Meat Giant Monfort under Siege,'' *Denver Post,* July 18, 1993, p. G1.

Murphy, Dan, ''Sky's the Limit,'' *National Provisioner,* August 1993.

Nyberg, Bartell, ''Ken Monfort Is Optimistic: Cattlemen Will Survive,'' *Denver Post Empire Magazine,* March 2, 1975, pp. 8–11.

——, ''Omaha Titan Buys Monfort,'' *Denver Post,* March 6, 1987, p. A1.

Reed, Carson, ''The Baron of Beef,'' *Colorado Business Magazine,* July, 1989, pp. 14–15.

Romano, Michael, ''Beef Baron,'' *Rocky Mountain News,* May 3, 1987, pp. 18–22M.

—David E. Salamie

Montres Rolex S.A.

Rue Francois-Dussaud 3
Case Postale 92
1211 Geneva 24
Switzerland
(22) 308-2200
Fax: (22) 300-2255

Private Company
Incorporated: 1905 as Wilsdorf & Davis
Employees: 2,800
SICs: 3873 Watches, Clocks & Clockwork Operated Devices & Parts; 5094 Jewelry, Watches, Precious Stones & Precious Metals, Wholesale; 6531 Real Estate Agents & Managers; 7631 Watch, Clock & Jewelry Repair

Montres Rolex S.A. is the best known of the premier producers of fine watches in the world. Recognized as an innovator in technology and marketing, the company is credited with establishing the widespread popularity of the wristwatch in the early twentieth century. Rolex watches are prized for their precision time-keeping, durability, functionality, and distinctive design. Rolex's mystique as a closely held private company and its carefully cultivated image continue to strengthen the watch's desirability as a status symbol as well as a precision instrument.

The company's founder, Hans Wilsdorf, was born in Kulmbach, Bavaria, on March 22, 1881. One of three children, Wilsdorf was orphaned at the age of twelve. He was raised by his uncles, who encouraged him to be independent and self-reliant at a very early age. According to Osvaldo Patrizzi, author of *Orologi Da Polso Rolex,* Wilsdorf later attributed his success to that early upbringing. As a teenager, Wilsdorf studied mathematics and languages at school and apprenticed with a prominent exporter of artificial pearls. At nineteen he went to work as an errand boy and English translator for Cuno Kourten, a major clock and watch exporter in La Chaux de Fonds, Switzerland, which, along with Geneva, formed the hub of the high-quality watchmaking industry at the time. There, Wilsdorf was exposed to the most influential people and practices in watchmaking, which would later be an important asset in the founding and success of Rolex.

In 1903 Wilsdorf moved to London, where he worked for a large watch store. Two years later, he borrowed money from his sister and brother-in-law to establish his own company, Wilsdorf & Davis, with his brother-in-law a partner in the venture. Wilsdorf chose London for his new enterprise at least in part because of its position at the time as the world's economic center. Its colonial holdings gave England tremendous wealth as well as a network of trade avenues that would later be advantageous in Rolex's international business.

Wilsdorf soon distinguished his company from its many successful competitors in two essential ways. First, he was tireless and methodical in pursuit of perfection in his products. Second, he specialized in unusual items, most notably the wristwatch. Pocket watches were still the accepted timepiece, with wristwatches considered inelegant and useful only for specialty purposes, such as sporting activities, where it was impractical to consult a pocket watch. The association of the wristwatch with hard physical work gave it a rough connotation that was distasteful to the genteel consumer. In his book *Timeless Elegance—Rolex,* George Gordon noted that men were heard to say they would "sooner wear a skirt than a wristwatch!"

The wristwatch also presented logistical difficulties, including ensuring accuracy in so small a device and avoiding damage in the watch's unprotected position on the outside of the wrist: unlike a pocket watch, a wristwatch was exposed to blows, moisture, and dust. Shipments of wristwatches sent abroad were often found to have rusted by the time they arrived from exposure to dampness.

These obstacles were a galvanizing force for Wilsdorf, who cast a shrewd eye to the future. He calculated that resistance to the wristwatch would wane as its usefulness grew with the changing times. The wristwatch was already becoming more popular with young people and with the fashion world, which appreciated its ornamental value.

The wristwatch was also becoming more suitable for an increasingly active and mobile society. Technological innovations made travel to distant shores available to a significant number of people. It also generated sports requiring rugged, specialized equipment, of which the wristwatch became an indispensable part. Flying expeditions, car racing, mountain climbing, and sea exploration grew in popularity and caught the public imagination. Rough and tumble sports began to take on a romantic and adventurous sheen. Rolex capitalized on these associations and continued to promote this image heavily in its marketing materials.

Early in his venture, Wilsdorf demonstrated his nature as a risk-taker and innovator by making a large investment in small caliber lever escapement wristwatches. He spent several hundred thousand Swiss francs, five times the capital of his firm, on the first order. Wilsdorf purchased the internal mechanisms from the Swiss firm of Herman Aegler, a manufacturer whose reputation for quality Wilsdorf knew from his time as an apprentice. The mechanisms were machine-made and so were available at a reasonable price; they were also durable and precise.

To house the mechanisms, Wilsdorf supplied the cases, which he purchased from well-known English manufacturers. The cases were made in sterling silver and three types of gold in a wide array of styles for dress, casual, or sportswear. The watches sold briskly in England and abroad, including the Far

East. Working in concert with Aegler on logistical aspects of production, Wilsdorf developed a line of immensely popular watches.

The next several years saw many changes and innovations at Wilsdorf & Davis. In 1906 Wilsdorf introduced the expandable metal watch strap. This style of strap, made to match the watch case, would become a signature Rolex look continuing to the present day. The next year, Wilsdorf opened a technical office at La Chaux de Fonds, Switzerland. Wilsdorf delegated the management of that office, obtained British citizenship, and settled in London, marrying a short time later. In 1908 he coined the name ''Rolex'' to establish a signature brand that would distinguish his product from other watches that may even have contained the same parts. Wilsdorf chose the name Rolex because it was easy to pronounce in different languages and short enough to show clearly on a watch face.

This move demonstrated Wilsdorf's far-sightedness. Although it later became common practice to use one brand name for the entire watch, it was a new idea at the time. The different watch parts came from different manufacturers and distributors and it was the retailer's name that appeared on the watch face and internal movements. Wilsdorf justified his desire to use his own trade name by maintaining that the watches he sold had to meet more stringent quality criteria than either the manufacturer or the other suppliers required. Initially, Wilsdorf met with great resistance from retailers. By placing only a small number of watches with the name ''Rolex'' on the face with the other watches in an order, Wilsdorf was able to convince retailers to take the Rolex-brand watches along with the ones stamped with the retailer's name. He gradually introduced the Rolex name in the marketplace by increasing the proportion of Rolex watches in his shipments over time. An intensive marketing campaign later solidified the name recognition of Rolex. By establishing an identity separate from that of the retailer, Wilsdorf had shifted the balance of control in his favor, and retailers came to rely on the Rolex name as a customer draw as much as Wilsdorf relied on the retailers for market exposure.

At the time that Wilsdorf established the Rolex brand name, he began to focus in earnest on the production of wristwatches with the accuracy of a chronometer. Two milestone awards were bestowed on his timepieces in 1910 and 1914. In 1910 Wilsdorf & Davis was given the world's first certificate of a first-class chronometer for a wristwatch from the School of Horology at Bienne, Switzerland. In 1914 a Rolex wristwatch was awarded a Class A certificate by the distinguished Kew Observatory in England, the first given to a wrist chronometer. The certificate required passing a series of tests over 45 days. The watch was tested in five different positions and three different temperatures: ambient (65 degrees Fahrenheit), oven-hot, and refrigerator-cold. From that time on, all Rolex watches were required to meet chronometer standards and none was sold without a certificate. Self-imposed standards were applied to all of the internal mechanisms received from outside suppliers. If the movements did not meet the standards after seven days of rigorous testing, they were rejected. The reputation of the Rolex as a quality instrument continued to grow.

Postwar import tax increases prompted Wilsdorf to move his company headquarters to Switzerland in 1919. He established Montres Rolex S.A. in Geneva and retained the London office as a branch office. In the 1920s, Wilsdorf established Rolex's image as a sportsman's technological tool. He tackled the problems of moisture, dust, and heat resistance and began working toward an automatic winding mechanism. He introduced new styles that were waterproof, lightweight, and durable. He also began a series of innovative marketing events showcasing Rolex watches in real-world action. As he introduced new models, he would link them to events generating new records in sporting and technological achievement. In particular, he focused on sports events requiring considerable daring and, most often, considerable means. The elite sporting associations made Rolex popular not only with sportsmen but also with wealthy spectators as the watch became a status symbol. In 1925 Rolex registered the crown trademark, a symbol of its elite aspirations.

Rolex introduced the Rolex Oyster, the world's first waterproof, airtight wristwatch in 1926. He patented the twinlock and triplock screw-down crown and the waterproof case. The following year marked the first of many record-setting marketing events. Mercedes Gleitz swam the English Channel in the record time of 15 hours and 15 minutes wearing a Rolex watch. When she emerged, the watch had kept perfect time. To capitalize on the event, Rolexes were often displayed in aquariums in jewelers' windows. By 1927, ''Rolex'' was printed on the case, movement, and dial of all Rolex watches. The following year saw the introduction of the Rolex Prince, an elegantly styled timepiece that gained a reputation as a gentleman's watch.

In 1931 Rolex introduced the Rolex Oyster Perpetual, the first waterproof, self-winding wristwatch. The rotor automatic winding mechanism, invented by Rolex's technical chief, was semicircular and able to turn both clockwise and counter-clockwise, so that the movement of a wrist could wind it. The watch was even more accurate than a traditional watch, since the tension put on the mechanism by constant winding was greater than that provided by winding done once a day. In another marketing coup, in 1935 a Rolex Oyster went over 300 miles per hour on the wrist of Sir Malcolm Campbell as he set the world land-speed record in his race car at Salt Lake Flats.

The 1940s were a significant decade for the future of Rolex. In 1944, Wilsdorf's wife died after a four-day illness. The couple had no children, and Wilsdorf was determined to protect the business he had created, even after his death. He set up the Hans Wilsdorf Foundation and transferred his interest in Rolex to the foundation, creating a governing council and detailing precisely how he wanted the funds handled. His specifications included large donations to charity, horological institutions, universities, and professional schools.

Rolex achieved an industry record in 1945 with 50,000 certificates for wrist chronometers. The company introduced four new models over the next few years, introducing the Date Just in 1945, the Rolex Moonphase in 1947, and the Rolex Day/Date/Month and the Oyster Day/Date/Month in 1949.

In 1953 Rolex enjoyed another marketing coup when the British Himalayas Expedition reached the summit of Mount Everest wearing Rolex Oyster Perpetuals—which lost no accuracy in extreme weather and rough handling. A new Day/Date model was introduced in 1956 that had the day written in full in one of

26 languages. The first automatic waterproof watch, the Submariner, was introduced in 1953, with resistance to 100 meters' depth, and the GMT Master, a watch for pilots that tracked time in two different time zones simultaneously, was introduced in 1955.

In early 1960, Rolex performed its most astonishing feat when the bathyscaphe *Trieste* emerged from 35,798 feet with a special Oyster attached to its outside still running perfectly. The watch had been exposed to a pressure of almost seven tons per square inch.

Later that year Hans Wilsdorf died at the age of 78, and in 1963 Andre Heiniger assumed leadership of the company. Heiniger, born in 1921 at La Chaux de Fonds, continued to guide the firm in much same way Wilsdorf had. During Heiniger's tenure, however, tradition became more of a focus than innovation. Rolex continued to do well by keeping quality high and production relatively low, maintaining a steady course through fluctuations in the economy, explosions in the price of components such as gold, and the flood of electronic parts into the watchmaking industry.

In 1971 Rolex introduced the Oyster Perpetual ''Sea Dweller,'' the first diving watch with a helium valve for saturation diving, which was waterproof to 2,000 feet. In 1975 six divers won the world diving record off the Labrador coast in Canada, reaching 350 meters wearing Rolex Sea Dwellers. In 1978 Rolex introduced a quartz movement Oyster waterproof to 165 feet and resistant to magnetic pull up to 1000 Oersted. The same year, a Rolex Oyster Quartz reached the top of Mount Everest as Reinhold Messner made a significant climb without an oxygen mask. In 1973 Tom Shepperd crossed the Sahara wearing a Rolex Oyster GMT Master, which was unimpaired by exposure to extreme heat or sand storms.

During the 1980s, Rolex introduced improved versions of its traditional styles. The Rolex Oyster Perpetual Chronograph Chronometer Daytona with tachometer was introduced in 1988, and by 1989 over half of all the Swiss chronometers certified by the Swiss Institutes for Chronometers had been produced by Rolex. The year 1990 marked the manufacture of 10 million chronometers. New models such as the Oyster Perpetual Yachtmaster built on Rolex's reputation for creating instruments for the elite sporting set, and advertising targeted such upscale magazines as *Gourmet* and *Outside,* showing Rolex watches in action with such elite performers as the U.S Equestrian Team and the U.S. Sailing Team.

From the early 1960s through the mid-1990s, Rolex's sales increased by approximately 20 percent a year, while the production of about 500,000 watches a year, well short of demand, kept the price high. In fact, Rolex was so successful in creating a status icon that counterfeiting became a major issue for the company. To deter counterfeiters, Rolex invested in an anti-counterfeiting device that was not reproducible. Equally inimitable is the quality built into each timepiece: in the 1990s Rolex remained one of only a few Swiss manufacturers still doing a majority of hand building, carefully guarding its niche as a producer of durable luxury chronometers.

Principal Subsidiaries: Rolex Industries, Inc. (U.S.A.); Rolex Watch U.S.A., Inc.; The Rolex Watch Co., Ltd. (U.K.).

Further Reading:

Gordon, George, *Timeless Elegance—Rolex,* Hong Kong: Zie Yongder Co., Ltd., 1989.

Jardine, Cassandra, ''Timeless Mystique of the Rolex,'' *Business-London,* February 1988, pp. 114–17.

Patrizzi, Osvaldo, *Orologi Da Polso Rolex,* Milano: Antiqorum Italia Srl, 1992.

Sasseen, Jane, ''Consumer Products: Stop Thief,'' *International Management,* September 1990, p. 48–51.

Schnorbus, Paula, ''Tick Tock,'' *Marketing & Media Decisions,* October 1988, p. 117–32.

—Katherine Smethurst

MOOG

Moog Inc.

Jamison Road
East Aurora, New York 14502
U.S.A.
(716) 652-2000
Fax: 716-687-4457

Public Company
Incorporated: 1951 as Moog Valve Co. Inc.
Employees: 3,140
Sales: $307.4 million
Stock Exchanges: American
SICs: 3728 Aircraft Parts & Equipment, Not Elsewhere Classified; 3625 Relays & Industrial Controls; 3541 Machine Tools Metal Cutting Types; 3724 Aircraft Engines & Engine Parts; 3764 Guided Missile & Space Vehicle Propulsion Units & Propulsion Unit Parts

Moog Inc. is a worldwide manufacturer of precision control components and systems. Moog actuation devices control high-performance aircraft, satellites and space vehicles, strategic and tactical missiles, and automated industrial machinery. As defense budgets faced dramatic cutbacks starting in the late 1980s, Moog was forced to adapt quickly to new markets by moving into new product lines. By the mid-1990s, the company had greatly enhanced its presence in flight controls, becoming one of the top suppliers to the Boeing Commercial Airplane Group. Responding to the defense cuts and to hard times in the commercial airplane business at large, the company introduced products in such areas as injection molding, entertainment simulation, and industrial hydraulics. Such adaptation shed positive light on a future combining contracts for military hardware with commercial and industrial applications for a wide range of control systems.

Moog's products are flexible enough to fill diverse needs in many different markets. In the domain of aircraft controls, Moog's components include hydraulic actuators and mechanical rotary actuators. In the late 1980s, Moog joined forces with Bendix Corporation, a leader in flight controls for such leading aircraft as the F-14 and F-111 fighter jets, as well as the Boeing 747. Together, the companies provided all the actuators for the RAH-66 Comanche helicopter, among other systems. Other key projects employing Moog actuators have included the F/A-18 Fighter Program; the Taiwanese Indigenous Defense Fighter (IDF); various Boeing aircraft; Airbus planes such as those in the A330/340 family; and McDonnell Douglas commercial aircraft parts such as flight control servovalves, anti-skid brake valves, and hydraulic accumulators.

Moog has also been a leading supplier to the space industry, supplying controls for satellites and a broad line of standard products to companies including Hughes, Martin, and Loral in the United States, Royal Ordnance and Matra Marconi Space in England, and BPD in Italy. Moog's propellant isolation valves were used on the much-publicized Motorola Iridium Satellite system. Its solid rocket boosters were used for the U.S. Space Shuttle orbiter and its cold gas thrusters provided propulsion for NASA astronauts wearing a self-rescue device called Simplified Aid for Extra-Vehicular Rescue (SAFER).

The company has also been a principal supplier of flight control servovalves and seroactuators for use on military and commercial aircraft, helicopters, and the Space Shuttle orbiter. Moog's control systems have been used on U.S. strategic ballistic missiles, including Trident and Peacekeeper (MX), while its thrust vector controls have helped steer those and other tactical missile systems. In tactical missiles, Moog has supplied hydraulic servovalves for the Patriot program. In the mid-1990s, the company delivered a Thrust Vector Control (TVC) System designed for the booster rockets on the Titan IV launch vehicle. Other projects have included a propellant valve for the French launch vehicle, Ariane 5; designs for bipropellant thrusters to be incorporated into the Theater High Altitude Area Defense (THAAD) anti-missile defense system; and on-board systems for thermal management controls for space stations.

Moog has also supplied power actuators, electronics, and commercial controls for diverse applications. Its microprocessor-based products are used in radio controls for underground mining and for custom control equipment. The company's digital process controllers are essential in a variety of injection molding and blow molding machines used to make products out of plastic. These valves are paired with Moog's electronic controls used to manage the servovalve functions as well as the sequence of machine operations and temperatures. Moog also manufactures state-of-the-art brushless electric servomotors and controls for the industrial automation equipment market, robotics, and the aerospace industry.

Another important market for Moog's control components has been power generation equipment, which continued to grow globally as energy producers sought fuel-efficient, environmentally friendly solutions to growing energy needs. Moog control components have been sold to gas and steam turbine manufacturers throughout the world, including European Gas Turbines, Juovo Pignone, Phillips, Volvo, GEC, MHI, Mitsui, Fuji Electric, and other international market leaders. In the 1990s, developing economies in the Pacific Rim opened expansive new markets in those regions.

The story of Moog, Inc., began when Bill Moog, a design engineer at Cornell Aeronautical Laboratories in Buffalo, New York, developed an electro-hydraulic servovalve to control the movement of guided missiles and brought it to market. Short on capital and devoid of manufacturing facilities, Mr. Moog persuaded a local machine shop to produce the parts for his valve on speculation. Payment for their services making the valve parts was contingent on his selling the assembled units. Working from the basement of his East Aurora home, the world headquarters for what he affectionately named the Little Gem Valve Company, Mr. Moog assembled and tested the first units himself.

Moog's first sale of four valves to Bendix Aviation Inc. was quickly followed by larger orders from such companies as Boeing and Convair. With his brother Art and a fellow engineer at Cornell, Lew Geyer, the young entrepreneur formed the Moog Valve Company on July 1, 1951. Long hours were dedicated to the completion of a manufacturing and development facility, which was devastated by a fire in 1952. Unshaken, the partners forged ahead, rebuilding their business far beyond its original limits.

In 1959 the young company went public, and sales from both aerospace and industrial valves surpassed the $10 million mark. Moog's products found markets beyond guided missiles, in military aircraft, commercial airplanes, and eventually nonmilitary systems from mobile opera stages to entertainment simulators. In 1965 the company changed its name to Moog Inc. and was listed on the American Exchange for the first time.

Rapid growth and decentralization marked the next two decades. Starting in the mid-1960s, subsidiaries were established in Europe and Asia, and the domestic company was broken into divisions for maximum efficiency and optimal customer service. Historically, the company would begin with sales and service of imported products and then move to in-country manufacture, assimilating technical personnel from local universities and industries to design products tailored to the preferences of local markets. In 1966 a German subsidiary, Moog GmbH, was established along those lines. A U.K. subsidiary, Moog Controls Ltd, followed. Thereafter, subsidiaries were developed in France, Italy, Spain, Ireland, Sweden, and Finland.

Though the first non-U.S. subsidiaries were established in Europe, Moog quickly moved into all corners of the globe. In 1970 the company established Moog Japan Ltd., with facilities taking root in Korea, Hong Kong, and Australia during subsequent years. In 1985 Moog established a manufacturing operation in the Philippines, with inauguration of another such facility in Banhalore, India, five years later. In addition, the first South American subsidiaries were started up in 1981, in Sao Paulo, Brazil, followed by numerous others over the years. Indeed, by 1994, approximately one third of Moog's revenues were from customers outside the United States.

By 1980, Moog had become a global leader in electrohydraulic controls and a pioneer in pneumatic and electromechanical control applications. That year, *Fortune Magazine* listed the company's servovalve as one of the "100 Best Products America Makes."

In addition to market demand for its top-notch products, Moog gained a reputation as a team-driven work environment distinguished by innovative thinking, individual responsibility, and unusual commitment on the part of employees and employer alike. The company won admiration—and a chapter—in Robert Levering and Milton Moskowitz's 1993 book *The 100 Best Companies to Work for in America,* even after difficult years during which Moog had to lay off workers. "I think it's clear we made the book because we have what I call a sense of community," Robert T. Brady, president, told the *Buffalo News.*

In the early 1980s, Moog made the strategic decision to expand its product range beyond hydraulics and into electric servomotors. The company's industrial motor development required extensive research and development efforts that would take more than a decade to pay for. Still, the investment was well on its way to paying off, with customer applications ranging from robotics with Bosch (Germany), to material handling with ISI (U.S.), and Engel Automation (Austria). In addition, the wide variety of specialty machine applications for the motors ranged from brush-making machines to textile, glass grinding, packaging, weaving, and printing machines.

An important offshoot of Moog's industrial motor development came in the form of electric drives and elevation controls for gun systems in military vehicles. Sophisticated systems had to be designed to manage the electric power in the motors in such a way that precision could be maintained as the vehicles traversed bumpy terrain and handled rapid maneuvers. Customers have included Bofors, which manufactured the Combat Vehicle 90/40 for the Swedish army, and the Norwegian company, Hägglunds, which provided a similar vehicle to its military.

In 1988 Bill Moog resigned from the company he had founded to concentrate on developing new suspension technology for autos. Mr. Moog acquired two of Moog Inc.'s divisions—the domestic industrial controls business and its automotive operations—in exchange for all his equity. The 72-year-old entrepreneur would become the president and chairman of a joint venture with Group Lotus, a British sports car maker owned by General Motors. The venture was formed in 1986 to develop new suspension systems employing hydraulic systems controlled by a computer to sense and correct bumps. According to industry analysts, Moog Inc. was not interested in pursuing those interests. According to Moog Inc.'s 1994 annual report, the company initially intended to buy back the industrial servovalve division it had sold to Bill Moog. When Mr. Moog put his new company up for sale in 1994, however, a bidding war boosted the price beyond what Moog Inc. deemed reasonable. Thereafter, the company worked carefully to regain market share in that domain.

After Mr. Moog's departure, Moog Inc. realigned its management, naming Richard A. Aubrecht chairman, Kenneth J. McIlraith vice chairman, and Robert T. Brady president and chief executive. That new team was quickly put to the test after the company reported losses of $14 million and initiated a restructuring of its domestic operations. The reorganization called for elimination of eight percent of the staff, representing a serious blow to a company that considered job security for its employees a top priority.

Drastic defense cuts worldwide, paired with recessionary world economies, put a damper on Moog's aircraft business, leading to a major realignment of business strategies in the early 1990s. In 1992, the company took it on the chin, as Washington either canceled or severely cut back on programs using Moog's valves, including the B-2 bomber, the F-15 fighter, and the MX,

Midgetman, and Maverick missiles. Moog was forced to scale back operations, cutting 24 percent of its work force and closing a factory in Clearwater, Florida, and two plants in upstate New York. "Like many companies around the world, we've had to re-think, re-define, and re-organize our way of doing business," wrote Robert T. Brady, president and CEO, and Richard A. Aubrecht, chairman of the board, in their 1994 Letter to Shareholders.

Among Moog's steps to strengthen its market share, in late 1994, the company purchased the product lines of AlliedSignal Actuation systems, a company divided between flight control actuation for military aircraft and controls for commercial airplanes. The addition of AlliedSignal greatly strengthened Moog's overall position in flight controls, enhanced its relationship with the Boeing Commercial Airplane Group, and extended its contacts in the general aviation market to Canadair, Gulfstream, and Lear.

Moog also applied its expertise in electric motors to various applications in entertainment simulators. In 1991 the company's business development team identified the need for electrically actuated motion base for the entertainment business. After Moog designers completed several electric actuation projects for NASA, the company development of entertainment simulators continued to grow and attract new clients in that growing market. Projects included four Japanese platforms, including two to Shirahama Earth Adventure and another to Geo-Bio World in Fukuoka. Moog also designed a system for Bill Saleir's Tempus Expeditions, a company that packaged high quality audio-video-kinetic entertainment in megamalls, such as the Mall of America in Minneapolis. Tempus's growing operations, as well as a surge in Asian Pacific theme parks showed great promise for Moog's activity in this domain. By 1994, the same company that manufactured controls for real spacecraft and jets was creating self-contained simulators that gave participants the impression—jolts, sights, sounds, and all—that they were on a flight to Mars, or on a jet fighter mission.

While Moog's strategic defenses against the volatility of defense and aviation markets produced positive results, the company still faced many uncertainties. A case in point was the company's contract to supply actuation systems for the B-2 bomber program. After supplying actuation systems for all but the last four of the 20 aircraft in production, further expectations hinged on Congressional go-ahead for an additional 20 aircraft. "From our point of view, the politics of buying additional B-2's are too speculative to count on." The fate of numerous other projects, such as rotor and tail rotor actuators for the Comanche helicopter, remained contingent on Congressional decisions or other outside forces.

That message was driven home in November 1993, when Congress cut $7.5 million out of Moog's $10 million proposal for a high-tech research project, its "Center for Advanced Control Systems." The project, aiming to convert the defense industry jobs of the past into the jobs of the future, would only be able to sponsor three or four research projects, compared to the eight originally planned. "We're delighted to have the $2.5 million," Aubrecht told the *Buffalo News* on November 12, 1993, adding that once the company demonstrated its capabilities, it hoped to earn larger support in the future.

Into the 21st century, the company hoped to maintain a balance between its domestic business and its international business, which continued to generate one-third of its revenues. Moog also looked for increased opportunities in industrial products, both inside and outside the United States, and expected a substantial increase in business with Boeing, as recovery in international markets was expected to boost production of 747 and 757 aircraft. Regardless of the direction the market might take, Moog was well poised for change and adaptation. From valves for steering guided missiles, the company's product line had, itself, been guided into outer space, Japanese theme parks, mineral mines. . . everywhere a use could be found for its top quality valves and components.

Principal Subsidiaries: Moog Australia Pty., Ltd.; Moog do Brasil Controles Ltda. (Brazil); Mooh Buhl Automation (Denmark); Moog Controls Ltd. (U.K.); Moog OY (Finland); Moog Sarl (France); Moog GmbH (Germany); Moog Controls Hong Kong Ltd.; Moog Controls (India) Pvt. Ltd.; Moog Ltd. (Ireland); Moog Italiana S.r.l. (Italy); Moog Japan Ltd.; Moog Korea Ltd.; Moog Controls Corporation (Philippines); Moog Singapore Pte. Ltd.; Moog Sarl Sucursal en España (Spain); Moog Norden A.B. (Sweden); Esprit Technology, Inc.

Further Reading:

Campbell, Tom, "Investors Want Answers as Moog Founder Leaves," *Business First-Buffalo,* February 8, 1988, Vol. 4, No. 16, Sec. 1, p. 2.

Cuff, Daniel F., "Founder of Moog Starts New Company," *New York Times,* March 2, 1988, p. D4.

DePerro, Don, "Grant Denial Sours Moog on Training Center," *Business First-Buffalo,* December 9, 1985, Vol. 2, No. 7, Sec. 1, p. 1.

——, "Push on to Develop Full-Scale Moog Training Center," February 10, 1986, Vol. 2, No. 16, p. 14.

Hartley, Tom, "Moog Hopes to Generate Sales in Electric Engine Development," *Business First-Buffalo,* August 16, 1993, Vol. 9, No. 44, Sec. 1, p. 1.

Khermouch, Gerry, "Moog's Industrial Controls May Reclaim Spotlight; Seeks to Offset Slack from Slowing Aero Arm," *Metalworking News,* December 28, 1987, Vol. 14, No. 663, p. 5.

Levering, Robert, and Milton Moskowitz, *The 100 Best Companies to Work for in America,* New York: Currency Doubleday, 1993, pp. 302–06.

Robinson, David, "Moog Eliminating 80 Jobs in East Aurora; End of B-2 Stealth Bomber Forces Action . . . " *Buffalo News,* October 3, 1994, p. 11.

Schroeder, Richard, "Entertainment Simulators the Next Big Market for Moog?" *Buffalo News,* February 10, 1994.

Zremski, Jerry, "Congress Cuts $7.5 Million from Moog Project," *Buffalo News,* November 12, 1993.

—Kerstan Cohen

Morse Shoe Inc.

555 Turnpike Street
Canton, Massachusetts 02021
U.S.A.
(617) 828-9300
Fax: (617) 828-5059

Wholly Owned Subsidiary of J. Baker, Inc.
Incorporated: 1922 as Teddy's Shoe Store
Employees: 4,500
Sales: $420 million
SICs: 5661 Shoe Stores; 5139 Footwear

Morse Shoe Inc. is a leading seller of low-priced shoes, which it sells through its Fayva chain of shoe stores and through leased shoe sales operations that it runs in department stores. The company, which was founded by the Morse family in the 1920s, has enjoyed steady growth in the ensuing decades. It first sold stock to the public in the 1960s, was taken private in the late 1980s, and was finally purchased by its largest competitor in the early 1990s.

Morse got its start in 1922, when Lester Morse joined with two partners to open a store called Teddy's Shoe Store in Massachusetts. Shortly after the business was begun, Lester was joined by Alfred Morse, who worked for the company briefly before leaving to strike out on his own in 1925. In March 1927, Alfred returned to the shoe trade, opening a ladies' shoe store in Providence, Rhode Island.

In the late 1920s both Lester and Alfred Morse expanded their operations. Lester opened a chain of shoe stores under the name Morse Shoe Stores Corporation in Massachusetts. To the south, Alfred's group of retail outlets was known as Morse's, Inc. By the start of the 1930s, it had become clear that the Morses could reduce costs if they combined some operations. In 1933 the Morses opened a joint buying office.

Both Morse chains operated under the same principles. The stores sold only women's shoes and were run under similar concepts. The Morses were careful not to open stores in the same cities, and so avoided competition with each other. Eventually, the Morses expanded their line to include some children's shoes. Further cooperation in their activities came when the two established a joint warehouse, with goods for each chain's stores on separate floors.

In the 1940s a third Morse joined the family operation. William joined his older brother Alfred to start a wholesale shoe division. This joint venture sold shoes to department stores. Morse bought moderately priced shoes directly from manufacturers, then resold them to department stores at a profit. Such arrangements enabled the Morse brothers to take care of all of the stores' shoe needs. Sales receipts were sent to the brothers so that they could monitor department stores' stock.

In the early 1950s Morse implemented an electronic data processing system at its warehouse. Each pair of shoes was tagged with a two-part ticket. When a pair of shoes was sold, half of the ticket was removed. The information on the ticket stub was then tabulated at the company's main office, an arrangement that allowed the company to track stock by style, color, heel height, and price.

By 1955 the two Morse shoe operations comprised 45 stores. The company was incorporated in two states, with Lester's operation based in Massachusetts, and Alfred's registered in Rhode Island. In the mid-1950s, the Morses expanded their operations again as they explored the recently-established discount shoe retailing market. Unlike conventional shoe stores, where customers were waited on by salesmen whose salaries and commissions added to the price of the products, discount shoe operations were self-serve. Customers selected and fitted their own shoes, and paid a lower price for them as a result.

Morse opened two discount shoe departments within larger department stores. The first department store to lease such an operation was Arlan's, located in Fall River, Massachusetts. The second Morse discount shoe lessor was placed within the new King's department store, located in Lowell, Massachusetts. Following the success of these two tests, Morse moved aggressively into the discount shoe market. The company leased space within department stores, paying the host store a percentage of sales from the area. Because Morse's discount operations produced a high volume of sales, the company typically was able to pay host department stores a smaller percentage of sales than its competitors.

In the late 1950s Alfred and Lester Morse merged their operations, with each taking half of the stock in the joint corporation. The company was incorporated as Morse Shoe, Inc., in 1961 in preparation for an offering of stock to the public. The Morses structured their company so that each leased shoe department was a separate corporation under the umbrella of the parent company.

In April 1962 the Morses used the over-the-counter market to sell shares in their company for the first time. More than two years later, in November 1964, the company moved to the New York Stock Exchange.

In the mid-1960s Morse split its operations into two separate lines of goods in an effort to avoid the problem of competing with itself in different department stores. As part of its effort to keep the operations separated, the company set up two separate inventories in its warehouse and coded its shoes with different color tickets. Morse eventually established three separate lines of shoes to offer retailers.

In 1968 Morse entered the shoe manufacturing business for the first time. The company bought the Porter Shoe Manufacturing Company, based in Milford, Massachusetts, and the Jonell Shoe Manufacturing Corporation. The following year, Morse bought the Lowell Shoe Company and the Puerto Rico-based Isabela Shoe Corporation. Morse also expanded its operations to Canada. By the end of the 1960s, the company ran 33 discount shoe departments in large stores in Canada. By 1969 Morse operated more than 650 shoe sales outlets that generated sales of more than $160 million.

But while Morse's discount department store operations continued to thrive throughout the 1960s, the company's freestanding retail outlets, located in 47 cities and towns throughout southern New England, began to suffer a decline in sales. In small towns, the company's stores, which typically logged $100,00 to $125,000 in annual sales, found themselves competing for customers with growing numbers of shopping malls, discount department stores, and large national retailers such as Sears, Roebuck & Company. As roads improved in rural areas, people became willing to drive further in order to shop and spend their money. Over time, sales at many of Morse's freestanding stores shrank while wages and costs increased. The operations ceased to be profitable.

When Morse's leases on stores in smaller urban centers expired, the company closed these stores. By the end of the decade, the company had reduced the number of retail outlets it ran to 25, all of which were located in larger cities. The stores that were spared provided a higher volume of sales and profits.

To supply its Canadian operation, Morse opened a warehouse in Montreal. Morse's American operations were served by a 467,000-square-foot warehouse in Canton, Massachusetts. The company filled this facility with shoes made at its own factories in New England and Puerto Rico and shoes purchased from more than 100 other suppliers. Among these sources were Italian manufacturers, who made casual shoes, dress shoes, and other styles for men, and Japanese sources, who manufactured rubber shoes and tennis shoes. In addition, shoes were imported from England, France, Belgium, Holland, Spain, India, and Mexico. Forty percent of the company's products were shipped to North America from overseas.

All of the shoes from Morse's various sources were branded with the company's own trade names, which included "Jewel Tones," "Pretties," "Carousels," and "Jumping Jacks" for children, and a number of different labels for men. These shoes were distributed through 56 different sales regions.

At the start of the 1970s, Morse moved back into the freestanding retail store segment of its market with renewed energy. The company purchased the Fayva chain of self-service shoe stores, which had outlets in three states. Morse also added to its manufacturing capacity with the 1972 purchase of the Jo-Gal Shoe Company, Inc., based in Lawrence, Massachusetts.

Throughout the 1970s, Morse worked to rapidly expand the number of stores in its Fayva chain. Starting in 1978, the Fayva franchise was expanded by more than 100 stores a year. By 1980 Fayva's operations had grown to include 662 stores in 27 states.

In 1981 Morse opened an additional 106 Fayva stores, bringing its total to 768. Expansion of the Fayva concept, slated to take place at the rate of 125 stores per year, constituted Morse's main thrust for growth in the 1980s. The company planned to expand in markets where Fayva was already established. Southern California, Texas, Florida, and big cities east of the Mississippi were thus targeted. Morse hoped that this strategy would enable it to maximize the effectiveness of its advertising dollar.

The company maintained three other freestanding retail outlets in addition to Fayva: 43 Morse full service family shoes stores, located in 22 states; 59 Upstage women's fashion shoe boutiques, spread across 27 states; and six Jack and Jill stores, which sold children's footwear. In addition to its chains of stores, Morse also operated 453 footwear departments in various discount stores across the United States. Overall, Morse boasted 1,329 retail units in 35 states and 10 Canadian provinces.

Morse also maintained two distribution arms that sold shoes to other retailers through the company's factory sales force. The company's Meridian Footwear operation designed, developed, imported, and distributed men's, women's, and children's shoes. Meridian marketed "Disney Pals" children's shoes, athletic shoes, and fashion footwear that was resold in shoe and department stores across the United States, Canada, and Europe. The company's other distribution arm, the Super Shoe division, merchandised shoes to discount stores, drug stores, general retailers, and food stores. Finally, Morse maintained a Lowell Shoe, Inc., subsidiary. Lowell Shoe sold women's work shoes and white shoes for medical personnel.

These combined operations made Morse one of the country's ten largest footwear retailers. In 1981 the company registered sales of $447 million, an increase of $10 million over the previous years' sales. Company management was concerned, however, that earnings for 1981 had been fairly flat. Morse thus scaled back its ambitious plans to roll out the Fayva chain in 1982. The company targeted just 80 new store openings per year instead of its previously planned 125.

In 1982 Morse's earnings continued to be depressed by an overall recession in the economy. In addition, the company's rapid addition of new shoe stores had given it a number of unprofitable locations. By the early 1980s it was clear that Morse had grown stagnant, and that a change in the company's top management was needed. Morse's chairman, who had been with the company for 32 years, was 70 years old and had fallen ill. The company's president had also been with Morse for over three decades.

In July 1982 both of these men resigned. They were replaced by Manuel Rosenberg, an outsider who had been an executive for an upscale department store. Rosenberg moved immediately to review Morse's operations and return them to profitability. In November 1982 Morse announced that it would close 165 unprofitable shoe stores. "These stores have represented significant erosion of our profitability. With a healthier base of stores, we plan to expand the Fayva chain," Rosenberg told the *Wall Street Journal.* Because of write-offs associated with the store closings, Fayva reported a loss for 1982.

In addition to closing unprofitable stores, Rosenberg put in place a general restructuring of Morse's operations. He split off the company's various units into separate divisions and profit centers. Expenses were reduced through a freeze on hiring and salary increases, a cut in headquarters staff, and the elimination of three-quarters of the company's stock dividend. Many of Rosenberg's moves were indicative of an effort to implement better controls over Morse's operations and relieve some of the strain that had accumulated during Morse's period of rapid expansion.

Morse also made a number of changes at its stores in an effort to increase sales. In its Fayva outlets, Morse began to offer more fashionable shoes. The company increased the level of stock available at each location and lowered prices, bringing them back into better alignment with the quality of its shoes. In addition, Morse made deep cuts in the prices of its outmoded stock to clear it out of its stores. The company also began to offer special promotions on popular styles.

By the start of 1983, these efforts had begun to take effect. In the first six months of the year, Morse reported a 19 percent increase in sales, to $249 million in revenues. In the third quarter of the year, sales rose an additional 22 percent. Overall, Morse reported 1983 earnings of $19.1 million.

Morse continued its efforts to strengthen its profitability through the mid-1980s. In January 1984 the company closed its Jo-Gal women's shoe factory in Lawrence, Massachusetts; nine months later it sold its Milford Shoe Division. Although Morse signed agreements to run shoe departments in ShopKo Stores and G.C. Murphy Stores during that year, it lost the right to run such operations in Wal-Mart stores in October 1984.

By the end of 1985, Morse's sales had risen to $541 million, generating earnings of $7.2 million. The company attracted the attention of corporate raiders. A single investor, Asher B. Edelman, acquired 5.9 percent of its stock at the end of 1986. By the middle of 1987, a group led by Edelman had acquired 8.8 percent of Morse's shares. At that time, this group made a bid to purchase the entire company. Morse's management responded by forming a competing group to acquire the company in a leveraged buy-out. By July 1987 this transaction had been completed for $263 million.

In the late 1980s and early 1990s Morse saw its primary group of stores—Fayva—encounter stiff competition from the Payless Shoe Source chain, owned by the May Department Stores. Fayva's market share gradually eroded, and the company was unable to increase sales and make improvements in its stores.

In January 1993 Morse was sold to J. Baker, Inc., its biggest competitor in the licensed shoe department business, for $58 million. In the wake of its acquisition, Morse's new owners embarked on a campaign to return the company's operations to profitability. Baker moved to close Fayva's unprofitable locations and to update its other outlets. By 1994 the chain's number of locations had shrunk to 360, which generated sales of $173 million. "We took the markdowns we had to take and we've spent money remodeling or renovating more than half the units and rolling out new product packaging and displays," Baker's president told *Stores.*

With these steps, Baker hoped to convert Fayva's many browsers to buyers, and to win some market share back from Payless. The Payless chain, however, announced plans for a major expansion into the Northeast, the part of the country where most of Fayva's stores are located. To combat its prime competitor, Fayva planned to customize the product offerings of each store after examining the needs of its location and the demographic profile of its customers. Baker hopes that such moves will rejuvenate its Morse operations and return the company to the state of financial health that it had enjoyed throughout most of its history.

Further Reading:

Kastiel, Diane Lynn, "Direct Mail Gives Shoe Retailers a Leg Up," *Advertising Age,* March 7, 1985.

"Morse Shoe: Rosenberg's Repair Job Puts It Back On Its Feet," *Business Week,* September 26, 1983.

Reda, Susan, "J. Baker Answers Wake-Up Call," *Stores,* November, 1994.

Reingold, Jennifer, "J. Baker: If the Shoe (and the Shirt) Fits," *FW,* October 12, 1993.

Winans, R. Foster, "Morse Shoe, Despite Predicted '82 Loss, Surges As the Company Trims Its Unprofitable Stores," *Wall Street Journal,* November 23, 1982.

—Elizabeth Rourke

Motel 6 Corporation

14651 Dallas Parkway
Dallas, Texas 75240
U.S.A.
(214) 386-6161
Fax: (214) 702-5996

Wholly Owned Subsidiary of Accor S.A.
Incorporated: 1962
Employees: 14,460
Sales: $600 million
SICs: 7011 Hotels & Motels

One of the most successful motel companies in the United States, Motel 6 Corporation operates a chain of budget motels that cover the country, providing affordable accommodations to both recreational and business travelers. Created by two former building contractors, Motel 6 recorded solid growth during the 1960s and early 1970s, propelling the company toward the vanguard of the U.S. budget motel industry—a position the motel chain continued to hold through the mid-1990s.

In the early 1970s a new breed of motel operators began to emerge in the United States: a small group of companies no more than a decade old that promised to reshape an industry dominated by large and entrenched corporate giants. It was not the first time the lodging industry had undergone a radical transformation; years earlier the same large motel companies that stood atop the motel industry during the 1970s had captured an appreciable share of the overall lodging market from hotel operators by charging considerably lower room rates. Now, as these same motel companies reaped the rewards of their successful incursion of decades before, they found themselves vulnerable to attack by newer motel companies employing a similar strategy. In this latest revolution to sweep through the lodging industry, however, the motel industry turned against itself.

Leading this new attack against such larger motel chains as Holiday Inns and Sheraton were Scottish Inns of America, Inc., Chalet Suisse International, Inc., Days Inns of America, Inc., Econo-Travel Corporation, and a motel operator the *Wall Street Journal* referred to as the "grandaddy of budget motel companies," Motel 6, Inc. Although the strategy employed by this relatively new band of budget motel companies was similar to the strategy once utilized by Holiday Inns and other large motel chains—charge lower rates than the competition—their approach was novel. Nearly all of the budget motel companies creating a stir in the lodging industry during the early 1970s were operated by management with professional backgrounds in construction rather than hotel management. Such was the case with Motel 6, one of the discount pack that would force motel industry stalwarts to rethink their marketing strategies.

Though it enjoyed an enviable market position in the early 1970s, Motel 6 was then only a decade old. Formed in 1962 by two Santa Barbara building contractors who specialized in low-cost housing projects, Motel 6 had clearly caught the motel industry by storm with its rapid growth. Mid-way through their careers as contractors, Paul A. Greene and William W. Becker decided to apply their talents to creating a motel that could charge rock-bottom prices yet still generate a profit, something they were aptly suited for given their construction experience. With $800,000 in cash, the two partners began formulating their plan to create a profitable bargain motel in 1960, starting initially with $4 per room per night as their target price. After exploratory research proved that figure too low, Greene and Becker raised their target price to $5 per night, then finally settled on $6 per night two years after beginning their design work. Once all the preliminary work was concluded and it was decided that a $6 nightly charge would cover land leases, mortgages, maid service, managers' salaries, and building costs, Greene and Becker set to work, opening their first Motel 6 in 1962. Their 54-unit complex in Santa Barbara was itself a notable achievement and an exception to the other motels scattered across the country.

While Greene and Becker were constructing their first budget motel, other larger operators, such as Holiday Inns, were creating increasingly luxurious properties, emulating hotels rather than countering them as they had first done. Amid this growing trend toward grander motels with their necessarily higher prices, Greene and Becker offered an alternative: a motel without the amenities of other motels, but one that charged substantially less than its competition. There were numerous factors that enabled the two partners to charge $6 for a night's stay, chief among them the fact that they built the motel themselves. Other motel operators intent on securing a foothold in the budget motel market were, typically, businesspeople with hotel management experience—not construction experience—who set themselves to the task of creating and operating a budget motel after construction of their property was completed.

Not so with Greene and Becker. After spending two years developing a suitable model for their enterprise, Greene and Becker had designed nearly every aspect of their first Motel 6 to reduce costs wherever possible. The Santa Barbara property did not boast a dining facility, as did many large, higher priced motel chains. Beds were built flush to the floor to shorten the time required to clean each room, shower stalls were constructed with rounded edges to eliminate scrubbing in corners, glasses were replaced with Styrofoam cups, sheets were wash-and-wear, dressers were eliminated, television sets were outfitted with coin boxes that required a guest to deposit $.25 for six hours of viewing, and advertising for the motel relied exclusively on billboard announcements.

The first Motel 6 established a pattern for the many other Motel 6's to follow, a pattern that proved to be almost immediately successful. It was also a pattern predicated on ignorance of the motel industry, yet buttressed by expertise in the construction industry. As Becker later remarked to the *Wall Street Journal* regarding his company's genesis, "When we entered the business, we had the advantage of not knowing anything about it, so we weren't burdened by preconceived notions." Freed from the standard philosophy dictating other motel operators' actions, the company expanded. Four years after the first Motel 6 opened, there were 26 motels in operation, each built for 50 percent of the construction costs other motel properties required. The company generated more than $4 million in sales in 1966 and earned more than $750,000, double the figures recorded the previous year. From California, Greene and Becker had moved into Utah, Nevada, and Arizona, and were awaiting the completion of a 12-story motel in Waikiki and two more motels in Iowa, targeting any community that had a population base of at least 50,000.

By this time Motel 6's advertising budget was less than it was at the company's inception four years earlier, declining as Motel 6 billboards were eliminated. But perhaps more remarkable—and more indicative of the chain's growing success—was its occupancy rate, the true measure of a lodging facility's success. In 1962, the company recorded a 53 percent occupancy rate, a figure below the national average, but by 1966 Motel 6 was registering an 84.9 percent occupancy rate, well above the national average of 67 percent. This gave Greene and Becker all the encouragement they needed to continue expanding their motel chain. As Motel 6's successes mounted during the late 1960s, outside investors began paying closer attention to the company's burgeoning growth, attention Greene and Becker welcomed. In a 1967 interview with *Newsweek,* Becker stated as much, auguring Motel 6's future course when he remarked, "We're sort of mavericks in this business, because we've done something that a lot of people said was impossible. Consequently, at times, we haven't had the full confidence of the financial community ... being acquired by a conglomerate would certainly make us accepted members." Shortly thereafter, the company was acquired by City Investing Company, giving it the financial wherewithal to expand at a robust pace.

By the early 1970s, Motel 6 and its group of budget-oriented competitors also had begun to draw the attention of their larger, more luxurious competitors by capturing some of their market share. In 1972, budget motels, the most active of which were companies with construction expertise rather than motel or hotel management expertise, accounted for between 2 percent and 3 percent of the lodging industry's aggregate revenues of $9 billion, up from essentially zero before the decade began. The sudden rise and encroachment of budget motels was sufficient to force larger motel chains to adapt to the changing market conditions. But as Motel 6 had demonstrated a decade earlier, driving overhead costs down was not something to be accomplished administratively; it was something to be realized, first and foremost, by paying assiduous attention to construction costs and design plans.

One of the pioneers of this revolutionary concept, Motel 6 moved forward with optimistic plans, bolstered by the growing presence and acceptance of budget motels across the country, particularly in the southwestern and western United States. The company now had roughly 110 motels stretched across 30 states, with plans to add 570 motels by the end of the decade. Those plans were dashed, however, as growth slowed during the balance of the 1970s, at least in terms of the company's hopeful prognostications. Proposing to operate 680 motels by 1979, Motel 6 only had 378 properties in operation by 1985, the year City Investing Company sold the motel chain to an investor group led by Kohlberg, Kravis, Roberts & Company (KKR) for $881 million. Although City Investing's divestiture of the budget motel chain was not directly related to Motel 6's laggard expansion—City Investing's shareholders had voted to liquidate a majority of the company's assets to focus primarily on selling home insurance—there were clear indications that Motel 6 was suffering from potentially debilitating problems.

More alarming than the motel chain's slower-than-expected expansion was its consistently shrinking occupancy rate, which declined from over 90 percent during the early 1970s, to 81 percent by 1981, and to 59 percent by the time of the sale by City Investing. Chiefly to blame for Motel 6's malaise were the same companies that had grown along with Motel 6 to be prodigious forces in the lodging industry during the 1960s and 1970s. By the 1980s competition among these companies had become intense, heightened after two decades of expansion that had blanketed the country with budget motels. In the drive to lure guests into its rooms, Motel 6 was losing ground and its expansion efforts were losing momentum. Meanwhile, its closest rivals began sprucing up their rooms, making them more hospitable, and consequently robbing Motel 6 of its historically high occupancy rates.

To ameliorate Motel 6's market position, the investor group led by KKR had several solutions in mind. Motel 6's new owners began adding amenities that Greene and Becker had previously eschewed (installing telephones and color television sets throughout the motel chain's properties), placing an emphasis on attracting business travelers to complement the company's primary clientele of weekend pleasure travelers, and accelerating expansion. By far the most important change brought about by the company's new management was a major marketing push, the first advertising campaign put forth in Motel 6's history.

Spearheading the company's entry into the public spotlight was Joseph W. McCarthy, a former employee at Sheraton Corporation and Quality Inns who was hired by KKR in January 1986 to become Motel 6's president. Slated to air in the fall of that year, Motel 6's radio advertising campaign featured National Public Radio announcer Tom Bodett and his signature Motel 6 tag line, "We'll leave the light on for you." The advertisements were immediately successful and were quickly copied by fellow leading budget motel companies. Econo-Lodges hired comedian Tim Conway and Red Roof Inns hired Martin Mull, giving way to a new era in the budget motel industry, an era with a humorous slant. By 1988, thanks largely to the company's advertisements, Motel 6's occupancy rate had stopped its steady decline and climbed to nearly 73 percent, 6 percent higher than the current national average.

Once Motel 6's performance was invigorated by its radio advertising and the changes instituted by KKR, the motel chain stepped up its expansion efforts, hoping to improve upon or at least maintain its number two ranking in the United States. Trailing only Days Inns of America, Motel 6 increased its geographic presence in the late 1980s, expanding from 401 motels in 39 states in 1986 to 554 motels in 42 states by 1990. That year, the motel chain underwent its third change in ownership when Accor S.A.—a $4 billion French conglomerate with holdings in restaurants, hotels, motels, travel agencies, car rental companies, and restaurant voucher firms—purchased Motel 6 from KKR for $1.3 billion.

Accor, which owned a chain of motels in Europe similar to Motel 6 that were called Formule 1, had made its initial move into the United States in 1979 when it opened a hotel in Minneapolis, a move that proved to be only moderately successful. Six years later, the company launched its Formule 1 concept, a motel chain that met with immediate success. By the late 1980s, Accor was ready to make another attempt to enter the U.S. lodging market and the acquisition of Motel 6 provided the means. The addition of Motel 6's more than 550 establishments vaulted Accor to the number two position worldwide and gave Motel 6, which retained its existing management, a new infusion of cash to wage its advertising war and continue expanding. In 1991, Accor purchased 53 Regal Inns and Affordable Inns from RHC Holding Corporation, bolstering the motel chain's market position, while plans were formulated for Motel 6's advertising debut on television. With Tom Bodett continuing to serve as the motel chain's spokesman, Motel 6 began broadcasting its first television commercials in 1992, by which time it had ascended to the country's number one position, supported by the 672 motels that bore the Motel 6 name.

As Motel 6 entered the mid-1990s, it was competing for preeminence in the budget motel market in a decidedly different fashion than it had 30 years earlier, a change that was most discernible in the chain's advertising efforts. The rooms composing the Motel 6 empire had changed as well, becoming slightly more luxurious than the units Greene and Becker had first designed. However, one characteristic remained constant throughout the company's history: Motel 6 rooms were typically the lowest-priced lodging accommodations offered by any regional or national competitor in the country. With this philosophy underpinning the motel chain's success and the financial strength of Accor fueling its expansion, Motel 6 charted its future for the 21st century as a leader in a highly agressive industry.

Further Reading:

''Accor to Close 20 Motels Cites Security Problems,'' *Wall Street Journal,* October 21, 1992, p. A11.
''Bedding Down the Budget-Minded,'' *Business Week,* August 27, 1966, pp. 57–59.
''City Investing Completes Sale,'' *Wall Street Journal,* February 27, 1985, p. 14.
Dunkin, Amy, ''Cheap Dreams: The Budget Inn Boom,'' *Business Week,* July 14, 1986, p. 76.
Fisher, Christy, and Ira Teinowitz, ''Budget Motels Take to Humor Ads,'' *Advertising Age,* November 14, 1988, p. 65.
Hayes, Mary, ''Motels Offer Rock-Bottom Rates to Those Wanting Bare Minimum,'' *Business Journal—San Jose,* February 24, 1992, p. 22.
Lehner, Urban C., ''Economy Motels Lure Travelers with Prices as Low as $6 a Room,'' *Wall Street Journal,* December 26, 1972, p. 1.
''Lodging: The Inn Crowd,'' *Newsweek,* February 19, 1973, pp. 69–70.
''Motel 6 LP Acquires 46 Inns,'' *Wall Street Journal,* February 15, 1989, p. A4.
''Motels: Discount House,'' *Newsweek,* October 9, 1967, p. 85.
Reier, Sharon, ''Bedroom Eyes,'' *FW,* June 9, 1992, pp. 56–59.
Riemer, Blanea, ''This Buy-America Bandwagon Could Hit a Few Potholes,'' *Business Week,* July 30, 1990, p. 34.
Teinowitz, Ira, ''Hotels, Rental Cars Hope for Sonic Boom,'' *Advertising Age,* June 15, 1992, p. 3.
Totty, Michael, ''Motel 6 Radio Ads Credited for Rise in Occupancy Rate,'' *Wall Street Journal,* May 12, 1988, p. 28.
Wade, Betsy, ''Motels Turn Their Attention to Security,'' *New York Times,* May 24, 1992, p. xx3.

—Jeffrey L. Covell

National Patent Development Corporation

9 West 57th Street
New York, New York 10019
U.S.A.
(212) 826-8500

Public Company
Incorporated: 1959
Employees: 2,570
Sales: $204 million
Stock Exchanges: American
SICs:

National Patent Development Corporation (NPD), incorporated in Delaware in 1959, is primarily a holding company, a legal entity separate and distinct from its various operating subsidiaries. NPD's operations comprise three business segments: Physical Science, Distribution, and Optical Plastics. In addition, National Patent has numerous investments in the domestic health care, biopharmaceutical, and environmental technology industries and holds 54 percent of outstanding shares of common stock in a company distributing pharmaceutical products in Russia.

In 1959, three New York City lawyers, Jerome Feldman, Martin M. Pollak, and Jess Larson, began NPD as a scouting service for dormant patents. Their idea originated in 1958 after Feldman and Pollak heard about a new resin plasticizer developed and put on hold by a company unsure about the product's marketability. The partners believed the resin offered a superior base material for the manufacture of lipstick and they offered to arrange a licensing agreement. Although the partners found a major cosmetics manufacturer, problems arose when each company told them to get their fee from the other.

While the deal ultimately fell through, Feldman and Pollak saw profit potential in the patent exchange business and decided to form a company that could act, under contract, as a middleman. They found a third partner in Jess Larson, an attorney with considerable government experience, having formerly served as Administrator of the General Services Administration, War Assets Administrator, and Brigadier General in the Air Force Reserve. Larson also saw the possibility of reaping substantial profits developing new commercial products from forgotten patents.

From the beginning NPD focused on screening and buying patents on various devices, technologies, and materials, and then licensing them to other companies or trying to market the products themselves. To screen the thousands of patents lying idle in corporate files, the partners formed a consulting board consisting of patent lawyers, scientists, and engineers.

National Patent began gaining momentum in 1961, a year before the Cuban Missile Crisis, after Feldman and Pollak wrote a letter to then-Soviet Premier Nikita Khrushchev asking for rights to Soviet inventions. Surprisingly, despite Cold War tensions, the Soviets were willing to deal to obtain American dollars and invited them to visit. After three weeks in Russia, NPD experts screened Soviet developments by conferring with some 250 Russian scientists and technicians and won patent rights to market 14 innovations in the United States. National Patent then signed an agreement with Amtorg, the U.S.-based Soviet trade wing.

While some Soviet-acquired innovations proved profitable, others flopped. A surgical stapling device that replaced needle-and-thread suturing earned enough for Feldman to start a medical instrument business. That venture—U.S. Surgical—was later sold off and grew into a multi-million dollar corporation. Unfortunately, most products were far less successful, like an electric eyepad touted as inducing a blissful nap.

Using their Kremlin link, NPD made inquiries in other Communist bloc countries; in Czechoslovakia they met Otto Wichterle, polymer chemist at the Czechoslovak Academy of Sciences. Wichterle devised a novel application for a new plastic compound called Hema, which turned soft and pliable when infused with a liquid. Hema was originally intended for making artificial veins and body organs, but Wichterle found that spinning a droplet of Hema in a thimble-size dish could produce a soft contact lens.

In the West, contact lenses were still produced of hard plastic. By purchasing the spinning technology and the rights to make and market Hema, NPD found its first important product. Nevertheless, for two years the company experimented with the compound, prevented by scarce capital from marketing its new product. Then in 1966 NPD concluded a licensing agreement with Bausch & Lomb of Rochester, New York, a major player in the optical business and well aware of the potential market for soft lenses. The agreement gave Bausch & Lomb exclusive license to the new lens material and Wichterle's spinning and manufacturing technology. In return, NPD would receive a licensing fee plus half of all Bausch & Lomb's domestic lens profits.

After the Bausch & Lomb agreement, Feldman searched for other uses for Hema, which had been trademarked as Hydron. While National Patent licensed the rights to Hydron for contact lenses, it retained rights to use the compound for other applications and to produce new products. The company's labs produced a range of new Hydron-based products, including nail polish, burn-wound dressings, dental root-canal fillers, artificial breasts, and algae-resistant boat paint.

Most promising of all was a reactive chemical that showed potential for dissolving tooth decay, thus replacing drilling. Feldman found the compound at Tufts University, bought the patent rights, and offered the product to Warner-Lambert, which anticipated a use for the product as a plaque-removal agent in mouthwash. NPD's stock shot up from less than $10 in 1971 to $67 a share in 1972, one year after the Food & Drug Administration (FDA) approved Bausch & Lomb's new soft lens.

NPD shareholders' rising expectations proved false when the company's fortunes turned sour. Bausch & Lomb royalties proved disappointing, prompting National Patent to file suit in a protracted legal battle that threatened to end NPD's royalties entirely. Then Warner-Lambert announced that trial tests on schoolchildren showed their new mouthwash to be a failure as a plaque remover. NPD's stock collapsed to just $4 a share in 1973. Responding to these disappointments, Feldman diversified the company into gardening supplies, sporting equipment, solar energy, medical instruments, and contact lenses, planning to make NPD more independent. He also recruited a Russian professor to train company chemists in the production of interferons, a group of proteins produced by the body's immune system to help combat disease. This erratic strategy proved a dismal failure, causing a decade of poor earnings and a blighted reputation for the company. Feldman later recalled this period as the "dark years."

Through the 1970s, National Patent's fortunes rested on a $14 million settlement from Bausch & Lomb. Charles Allen, a world-class deal-maker and founder of Allen & Co., also figured prominently in the company's survival. Allen took Feldman as a client, arranged private infusions of cash, and bought NPD stock even when times appeared bleakest. He soon controlled one of the largest interests in NPD after the combined holdings of Feldman and Pollak. In spite of Allen's help, NPD continued to be plagued by marketing mishaps and technological failures. For example, a malfunction in an intravenous control system forced an expensive recall, and the company fell more than a year behind schedule in developing and marketing a solar energy cell. As a result, Feldman cut corporate staff and sold off NPD's medical equipment and solar energy ventures.

Pollak had better luck with American Hydron, NPD's contact-lens subsidiary. Established in 1979 as International Hydron Corporation to manufacture and sell contact lenses in the United States, the subsidiary produced its first earnings in 1982. A year later industry leader Bausch & Lomb considered American Hydron its major competitor in the sale of daily-wear soft contacts. Pollak's clever marketing strategy—offering Mercedes-Benzes, videocassette recorders, and gold coins to optometrists who placed large orders—caused the subsidiary's second-year shipments to double.

Despite intense competition, American Hydron fared well in producing high-quality lenses at a low cost. By the end of 1983, the subsidiary unveiled a new, compact, spincast system that could make lenses similar to Bausch & Lomb's most popular line. American Hydron also began testing collagen, a protein produced from cowhide, in an attempt to displace Hydron in low-cost lens production. By 1987, American Hydron was producing contact lenses using three distinct methods—lathing, cast molding, and spincasting, each having its own production and marketing advantages. While lens lathing was labor intensive, it proved superior for specialty lenses and low production. Cast molding maintained high optical lens quality but was more efficient in large-volume production. Spincasting was particularly suited for large-volume manufacture with low labor costs.

At the same time, NPD's Interferon Sciences, Inc. (ISI) subsidiary was moving toward marketing a host of interferon-based treatments for viral diseases. Production problems stemming from inefficiencies in extracting interferon from leukocytes, or white blood cells, were helped by the company's Czech connection. Pollak was vice-chairman of the Czechoslovak-U.S. Economic Council, a bilateral organization formed to promote trade between the two countries. This role introduced him to council chairman Fred Kuhlmann, vice-president of Anheuser-Busch, a St. Louis-based brewery that used Czechoslovakian hops to make beer. Anheuser's advanced fermentation technology for cultivating yeast cells proved to be the solution to the interferon production problem. Through the innovative process of "transformation," DNA molecules containing the genetic code for interferon could be extracted from human white blood cells and inserted into yeast cells, thereby producing interferon on a large scale.

Mutual interest in this process led both companies to embark on a joint production enterprise. ISI would alter individual yeast cells for use by Anheuser to produce billions of offspring. In return for the option of making new interferon products, Anheuser would provide ISI $6 million for research and development. This money aided Interferon Sciences' clinical trials of an interferon ointment for treating genital herpes—which afflicted an estimated 20 million in the United States alone—and allowed the company to begin testing a treatment for genital warts.

Feldman's typical business strategy was to spin off new technological ventures into separate companies while retaining most of their stock. By doing so, he transformed NPD into a holding company benefitted by the rising asset value of satellite companies taken public. In 1981, Feldman spun off ISI into a public company while retaining 75 percent of the shares. Two years later he spun off NPS Waste Technologies, an innovator in particle-glass filtering mechanisms for radioactive waste.

By 1987, NPD essentially operated through various subsidiaries and affiliates as a manufacturer and distributer of a wide array of products and services. The company's operations consisted primarily of four business segments, as well as various research and development programs that were not yet commercially viable. The company's Ophthalmic Products Group produced and marketed soft contact lenses and accessories. The Medical Science Group produced and distributed first aid products, surgical dressings, and various other hospital and medical products primarily through three subsidiaries, Acme Cotton Products, Chaston Medical & Surgical Products, and Abbey Medical, Inc. In addition to its interferon subsidiary, the Medical Group included dental products, such as the Caridex (R) Caries Removal System. An FDA-approved product that showed promise in removing tooth decay without the need for drilling, Caridex was the same failed dental plaque remover that had shown false promise a decade earlier.

NPD's Consumer and Service Group distributed home and garden products, as well as produced paint, paint specialties, coated and molded plastic products, and electronic components through several subsidiaries: J. Levin & Co., Inc., E. Rabinowe & Co., Inc., acquired in 1985, and Interstate Paint Distributors Inc., acquired in 1986. The Physical Science Group provided training, operations, engineering, and maintenance services to the electrical power industry and the U.S. Navy. In addition, this group also developed, manufactured, and marketed products and services used in the clean-up of low-level radioactive material from waste water at utility-operated nuclear power plants.

In 1987, NPD sold its interest in both International Hydron and Abbey Medical, Inc., a renter and seller of durable medical equipment. In 1989, the Medical Group introduced a new quick-opening adhesive bandage, STAT STRIP, to the hospital and medical markets. Interferon Sciences (ISI), received FDA approval of its Alferon N Injection, an alpha interferon product derived from human leukocytes developed for the treatment of recurring genital warts in patients 18 years or older. This achievement essentially transformed ISI from a research and development firm into an operating pharmaceutical company. An agreement was made with the Purdue Fredrick Company, a privately owned multinational drug company, to market Alferon N Injections in the United States and abroad. In addition, ISI acquired the worldwide rights from Amarillo Cell Culture for the oral administration of natural interferon, apparently effective in boosting the immune system. In addition, NPD's consumer and service group, collectively known as the Five Star Group, acquired State Leed, a distributor of various paint items. Together these companies, comprising J. Levin, E. Rabinowe, and Interstate Paint Distributors, had become the largest U.S. distributor of paint specialties, including interior and exterior stains, brushes, rollers, and caulking compounds.

By 1995, NPD had developed into three primary business segments: Physical Science, Distribution, and Optical Plastics. The company also had investments in Hydro Med Sciences (HMS), a health care business, and GTS Duratek, Inc., an environmental technology firm, as well as continuing investments in ISI.

The Physical Science Group consisted of SGLG, Inc. (formerly GPS Technologies), of which NPD had a 91 percent controlling interest; and General Physics Corporation, approximately 51 percent owned. General Physics provided numerous services, including personnel training and engineering, environmental, and technical support, to commercial nuclear and power utilities, the U.S. Departments of Defense and Energy, *Fortune* 500 companies, and other commercial and governmental clients. SGLG was a holding company with a 35 percent interest in GSE Systems, a company specializing in simulator software. In 1995 General Physics acquired Cygna Energy Services, a provider of design engineering, materials management, and safety analysis services to the nuclear power industry. General Physics also acquired all of the assets of SGLG, Inc. for approximately $34 million. In response to federal cutbacks in the Departments of Defense and Energy, General Physics began focusing on expanding its management and technical training services as well as specialized engineering services to manufacturers and federal agencies.

Five Star operated as a wholesale distributor of home decorating, hardware, and finishing products. Through the mid-1990s, Five Star remained the largest distributor in the United States of paint products and accessories, caulking compounds, and other items, despite intense competition from considerably larger hardware franchises, including Servistar and True Value.

The Optical Plastics Group operated through NPD's wholly owned subsidiary MXL Industries, a producer of molded and coated optical and non-optical products. MXL also made state-of-the-art injection molding tools, using polycarbonate resin to make shields, face masks, and lenses for over 55 clients in the safety, recreation, and military industries.

NPD's Hydro Med Sciences subsidiary manufactured medical devices, drugs, and cosmetic polymer products. HMS was established to explore the application of HydronR polymers for biomedical purposes. Since the 1970s HMS was involved in the development of human and veterinary drugs and dental and medical devices. The company developed the Syncro-Mate BR implant for the synchronized breeding of bovine heifers, the first veterinary implant drug to be approved by the FDA. HMS also produced a water-soluble HydronR polymer for commercial applications in cosmetic products, including body lotions, moisturizers, and sunscreens.

ISI, a biopharmaceutical company, continued to be involved principally in the production and sale of Alferon N Injections. In 1995, the product still represented the only FDA-approved drug based on a natural source for the treatment of certain types of genital warts. ISI also explored new applications for its injectable, topical, and oral formulations of natural alpha interferon for the treatment of HIV, hepatitis C, hepatitis B, multiple sclerosis, cancers, and other diseases. In the biomedical industry, various alpha interferon drugs have been approved for 17 different medical uses in more than 60 countries. As a group, sales of these biopharmaceuticals approached $2 billion in 1994. Gaining approval to sell the product in Mexico in the mid-1990s, ISI also sought regulatory approval to market Alferon N Injections in Austria, Canada, Hong Kong, Israel, Singapore, and the United Kingdom.

ISI's other products under development included Alferon N Gel and Alferon LDO. Alferon N Gel, a topical application, had potential for treating cervical dysplasia, recurrent genital herpes, other viral diseases, and cancers. Alferon LDO constituted a low oral dose of liquid alpha interferon, possibly proving beneficial in treating HIV and other viral diseases. These products were undergoing clinical trials during the mid-1990s.

NPD organized its American Drug Company (ADC) subsidiary in 1993 to distribute general pharmaceuticals and medical products in Russia and the Commonwealth of Independent States (CIS), the former Soviet republic. ADC was formed from NPD Trading (USA), Inc., which had been set up in 1990 to provide consulting services to Western businesses in Russia and Eastern Europe. NPD Trading would continue to operate as a subsidiary of the newly formed ADC, providing a broad range of business services to many American and Western corporations. Through NPD Trading, ADC's various activities involved developing and assisting Western businesses to create trading, manufacturing, and investment opportunities in Russia, the Czech and

Slovak Republics, and other countries in Eastern Europe and the CIS. ADC also focused on marketing American-made pharmaceuticals and health care products—antibiotic ointments, pain-relief medication, vitamins, bandages, prescription injectable anti-cancer drugs, antibiotics, and other prescription drugs—under its own label in Russia and the CIS. To distribute these products, ADC initiated marketing ventures with hospitals, pharmacies, and clinics throughout Russia and the CIS.

NPD's interests in environmental technology centered on GTS Duratek, Inc. As of March 1, 1995, NPD decreased its holdings of Duratek's outstanding shares of common stock from 61 to 40 percent. Incorporated in Delaware in December 1982, Duratek's operations comprised two principal groups: the Technology Group converted radioactive and hazardous waste to glass by means of in-furnace vitrification processes, as well as specializing in removing radioactive and hazardous contaminants from waste water through a filtration and ion process. The Services Group provided consulting, engineering, and training services, as well as technical personnel, assistance with nuclear power outages and operations, and Department of Energy environmental restoration projects. As of 1995, major customers for these services included Duke Power Company, Vermont Yankee Nuclear Power Corporation, New York Power Authority, Tennessee Valley Authority, GPU Nuclear Corporation, PECO Energy Company, and FERMCO.

Principal Subsidiaries: GPS Technologies; GTS Duratek, Inc.; General Physics Corporation; Interferon Sciences, Inc.; Five Star Group, Inc.; MXL Industries, Inc.; American Drug Company.

Further Reading:

Curan, John J., ''National Patent Rises Again,'' *Fortune,* August 8, 1983, pp. 98–102.

Marcial, Gene G., and Jeffery M. Laderman, ''Why National Patent Is Feeling No Pain,'' *Business Week,* January 13, 1986.

''National Patent Development Corp: Soft Lenses Now Mean Hard Profits for This Fallen Angel,'' *Financial World,* February 1, 1976, p. 3.

''Russian Grab Bag,'' *Newsweek,* July 31, 1961, pp. 60–63.

''The Riches in Dormant Patents,'' *Business Week,* April 15, 1961, p. 96.

—Bruce Montgomery

NS National-Standard

National Standard Co.

1618 Terminal Road
Niles, Michigan 49120
U.S.A.
(616) 683-8100
Fax: (616) 683-6249

Public Company
Incorporated: 1907
Employees: 1,282
Sales: $217.92 million
Stock Exchanges: New York Midwest
SICs: 3315 Steel Wire and Related Products; 3496 Miscellaneous Fabricated Wire Products

National Standard Co. has been one of the leading manufacturers of wire products in North America for almost 100 years. The company's wire has been used in a huge variety of products ranging from tires to harpsichords. After a period of extensive diversification and growth in the 1970s and 1980s, during which the company produced everything from telephone wire to lithography equipment to medical equipment, the company retreated to its roots as a manufacturer of metal wire products. National Standard is now the major supplier of filters for automobile air bag inflators.

National Standard was founded in 1907 when William Harrah and Charles Anderson, two lifelong friends, decided to take the small wire cloth company they managed in Niles, Michigan, and turn it into a manufacturer of lightning rods. Incorporated as the National Cable & Manufacturing Co., the company assumed its present name in 1913 when it acquired Cook Standard Tool Co. and merged the names of the companies along with their operations. In 1911, after much debate and discussion between the two partners, the small company took what was arguably the most important step in its history when it commissioned a special machine for manufacturing a new kind of wire braid to be used in the budding rubber tire industry. This "bead wire" was needed by automobile tire manufacturers to keep rubber tires from flying off the wheel under centrifugal force. In one form or another, this application would remain the mainstay of National Standard's business for the next 70 years.

In 1926, during the height of the 1920s stock market boom, National Standard went public with an IPO of 110,000 shares. By this time the company was manufacturing not only wire braid and steel cables but such large machinery as wrecking cranes and jacks at their plants in Niles, Michigan, and Akron, Ohio. National Standard had also opened National Standard Co. of Canada, a wholly owned subsidiary based in Guelph, Ontario, in order to serve the growing Canadian tire industry.

The company continued to enjoy domestic and foreign expansion during the 1930s in spite of the Great Depression. A new plant was opened in Los Angeles and a new subsidiary was founded in Worcester County, England. The first major period of diversification and growth for National Standard occurred in the late 1930s when the firm acquired three companies whose products would remain important in the company's business for some 50 years. The acquisition of Worcester Wire Works expanded the company's wire manufacturing to include high grade specialty drawn wire for fine applications such as musical instruments and bobby pins. The Athenia Steel Co. of Clifton, New Jersey, provided flat rolled steel, originally for such diverse uses as razor blades, corsets, and watch springs, then later for manufacturing equipment. Finally, the Wagner Litho Machinery Co. of Hoboken, New Jersey, contributed sales of additional large machinery to be used in the metal lithography that decorated the plethora of tin cans, biscuit boxes, and metal toys that characterized the material culture of that era. Sales soared as a result of the acquisitions, reaching $15 million by 1945.

Sales and earnings continued to grow at a steady rate through the 1940s and 1950s. National Standard assumed the role of a dependable, conservative, American corporation. Annual dividends were paid regularly from 1915 on and—with the exception of an occasional acquisition—National Standard stayed out of the corporate limelight. Annual sales at National Standard, which had increased the number of workers it employed to almost 2,000, reached $52 million by 1960, more than double the figure of a decade earlier.

The 1960s and early 1970s marked the second period of major expansion for National Standard. Over the course of this period the company would acquire eight manufacturing companies and found five foreign subsidiaries and six foreign affiliates. Some of these acquisitions were related to the company's core wire business, but others involved marked departures from the wire industry.

Since its inception, National Standard had maintained strong ties to the rubber industry as a result of its sales of bead wire for the reinforcement of automobile tires. The company had also become one of the leading producers of hose reinforcing wire over the years, further strengthening its relationship to the rubber industry. Although wire remained the cornerstone of National Standard's business, the company began to gear the machinery production that had been a component of the business since 1913 towards the rubber industry as well.

In 1966 the company acquired Rawls Brothers Co. of Lima, Ohio, a manufacturer of machinery used for retreading tires. In 1971 this component of the company's business was strengthened by the acquisition of Fasco Tire Equipment Co., a maker of tire recapping equipment. National Standard's own machinery division in Niles, Michigan, also entered the tire machinery industry. It designed and manufactured equipment used to build the steel belted radial tires that were being aggressively promoted in the early 1970s and for which National Standard was already providing steel cord.

In addition to acquisitions that provided diversification for the growing company, National Standard also built on its core wire business through acquisitions and the development of new products. One important product contribution to come out of the company's research and development department in the early 1960s was Copperply wire, a copper-coated steel wire for the telephone transmission market. Because of Copperply's strength and resiliency, transmission poles could be spaced much farther apart than before, significantly reducing installation costs. With the tremendous growth in communications in the 1960s and 1970s, Copperply proved to be a significant portion of National Standard's non-tire-related wire sales during this period.

National Standard further expanded its involvement in the wire products industry with the acquisition of Cheney Bigelow Wire Works in 1962. Cheney Bigelow produced fourdrinier wire, a specialized wire used in papermaking equipment. Cheney Bigelow's fourdrinier wire accounted for an impressive 15 percent of total sales for the company by 1965. In the early 1970s, however, metallic fourdrinier wire was increasingly replaced in papermaking by synthetic alternatives. This development forced National Standard to close the main Cheney Bigelow plant in 1974.

In the non-wire field, National Standard's established businesses prospered in the 1960s and 1970s. The company's Wagner division, which produced lithography machinery used in decorating tin and aluminum products, was a major factor in the company's continued growth. Although the decorated tin biscuit boxes and toys that had formed the original end product of the Wagner's machinery were no longer fashionable, the 1960s explosion in metal soft drink and beer cans more than compensated for this decline. Not only was this machinery in increasing demand, but the cost of the equipment used to decorate the thin tinplate used for beverage cans was twice as much as the cost of traditional pressed tin. As America's leading producer of this equipment, National Standard's Wagner division thrived.

International sales made up an increasingly large part of National Standard's revenues during the 1960s. The company frequently looked to the overseas market when American sales lagged. National Standard's British subsidiary expanded through acquisitions and new plant openings. By 1970 the company had four divisions in the United Kingdom, each producing products mainly for the European tire industry. The company also opened a South African subsidiary in the late 1950s, and affiliates in India and Australia in the 1960s, through National Standard of England.

National Standard also formed a partnership with FAN of West Germany, a company that operated wire plants in West Germany, Belgium, and Luxembourg to service the European tire industry. These FAN affiliates struggled for profitability from the start. National Standard's 1974 withdrawal from these partnerships would mark the beginning of a period of extensive retraction for the company.

National Standard's sales continued to grow steadily in the 1970s. By 1979 annual sales had reached $331 million, more than double the $116 million in sales that the company had posted in 1969. Earnings were more variable during this period, but after reaching a peak of near $12 million in 1974, net income levelled off in the late 1970s to a respectable $8-$9 million. In a 1980 article in *Industry Week,* National Standard's newly appointed president, Gerald H. Frieling, predicted a 15 percent annual growth rate through the 1980s and speculated that National Standard could be a $1 billion company by 1990. Few corporate predictions have been so devastatingly inaccurate.

When Frieling was appointed to head National Standard it was already apparent that all was not well with the 70-year-old firm. Although sales had reached record levels in 1979, sales for the first three quarters of 1980 were down, and by the end of the fiscal year earnings would be only half those of the previous year. The rubber tire industry, a market on which the company depended heavily, was in a period of stagnant growth. Frieling felt that the company needed to look for new markets while also rationalizing its current operations.

National Standard had responded to industry needs on a case by case basis in the past, producing new products when the need arose. Frieling wanted to create a body of technology that would differentiate the company's products and carve out a distinct segment of the wire market. "Before," Frieling noted in the interview with *Industry Week,* "we looked at each plant as a collection of machines. We'd make a little piece of this and another of that just to keep them busy. . . . [Now] instead of reacting to the market, we're going to go after the market segments in an aggressive way by developing new technologies."

The sheer size of National Standard made an overhaul of the business a daunting proposition. With 22 domestic operations and four foreign concerns involved in the manufacture of a huge variety of products, it was sometimes difficult to determine which products were making money and which were dead weight. Moreover, each facility had its own processes and management techniques, which made quality control and long-term planning difficult. Frieling, however, was determined to create a set of long-range goals for the entire company. In addition to heavy investment in research and development, he planned to sell marginal operations, acquire companies that could provide new technologies, and rationalize the production at existing plants.

In keeping with Frieling's goals, over the course of 1981 and 1982 the number of production facilities producing bead and hose wire was reduced from eight to three, while the number of weld wire plants fell from five to two. The National Standard plant in Mount Joy, Pennsylvania was remodelled to accommodate production of a broad range of products from other facilities that were closed down. Included in these plant closings were facilities in Los Angeles and Worcester, Massachusetts, that had been in operation since the early part of the century. In addition, the Cheney Bigelow and Rawls divisions were sold and foreign operations in Wales and Scotland were closed. National Standard's machinery operations, including Wagner Lithography, Bartell stranding equipment, and the National Standard tire building machinery, had previously been dispersed in a number of divisions across the country. Under the company reorganization they were consolidated into one division, with all production and development transferred to a plant in Rome, New York.

Although Frieling's long-term plans may have been justifiable, the timing of this restructuring could not have been worse. The early 1980s were a period of serious recession for the American automobile industry on which National Standard depended for much of its business. Reduced sales, increased research and development costs, and the reorganization of facilities combined to lower net earnings in 1981 to only $1.2 million, a dramatic decrease from the almost $13 million the company had netted only two years earlier. By 1982 the situation had worsened; the company posted a net loss of $11.5 million. For the first time since going public in 1926, the company failed to pay a dividend. Although much of this loss could be attributed to non-recurring charges resulting from plant closings, sales were also down by 20 percent. The tire industry on which National Standard depended so heavily was going through extremely tough times, buffeted by longer lasting radial tires and foreign competition that permanently changed the structure of that industry. It was clear that National Standard had to find new markets and new products, but investments in research and development would not bear fruit for a number of years. It would be difficult for the company to keep investor confidence up in the meantime.

During the mid-1980s, as the automobile and tire industry experienced a mild upswing, it began to look as if National Standard's restructuring program might have worked. Income returned to around the $8 million mark and sales were up, but by the following year it became apparent that National Standard could no longer depend on rebounding with the car tire industry. Although sales volume increased, foreign competition made it impossible to raise prices to keep up with higher raw material and production costs of traditional National Standard products.

The company knew that its financial woes were not at an end. Research and development was investigating promising new products, including Fibrex (a woven fiber used for battery filters), Archon II (a patented arc-weld process control system), and a line of new medical products developed in the company's new Medical Products facility in Gainesville, Florida, but none of these new products could accumulate large sales quickly. By 1987 National Standard was once again in the red, with a net loss of over $11 million. In addition, the company's early success in keeping long-term debt relatively low during the reorganization had waned. Increased losses resulted in a rise in debt, which further damaged shareholder equity.

By 1989, with net losses of over $12 million, it became clear that National Standard's troubles were more than the temporary result of restructuring. The company had not paid a dividend in three years and debt continued to grow. Gerald Frieling resigned his position with the company in July 1989 and Michael B. Savitske was appointed to replace him.

In the early 1990s, faced with ten years of dismal performances and ever increasing losses, National Standard was forced into a position of major retraction. Although the restructuring of the 1980s had involved the divestment of unprofitable or marginal companies, the company now began to divest itself of all but its core business in order to raise cash. The once revolutionary Copperply product line and the newly developed Archon II weld monitoring system were both sold to competitors in 1989, and the huge "City Complex" facility in Niles was closed. This was quickly followed by divestiture of almost all the company's non-wire related divisions, including the Medical Products Group and specialty steel and wire divisions. In 1991 the entire National Standard Machinery Systems Division was sold, putting an end to what had been a major product line for the company since 1916. This divestiture also extended to foreign subsidiaries, including National Standard South Africa and the Telford and Taydor divisions of National Standard England. The only new product line that was spared was the development of woven wire filters to be used in automotive air bag inflators. This new technology was the one bright point in the company's outlook, for many car makers were making air bags standard equipment in the 1990s. A joint venture with Toyota Tsusho America, Inc., and other Japanese wire makers ensured both a supply of the wire cloth needed for these filters and an entry into the Japanese auto parts industry.

By 1995, the company that at its height had owned 22 manufacturing divisions and four foreign subsidiaries and had employed over 5,000 workers, was reduced to only two major product lines—wire products and air bag filters—and 1,000 employees across the country. In spite of this dramatic reduction, National Standard's troubles were still not over. The company's sales of welding wire increased in the mid-1990s, but other core wire products struggled. A bitter, year-long strike at the company's Columbiana, Alabama, plant caused buyers to look elsewhere for the hose wire produced there. This development eventually forced National Standard to close the facility and end hose wire production in North America. To make matters worse, the closure of this and other manufacturing facilities embroiled National Standard in a series of environmental clean-up operations that would cost the company over $10 million.

In 1993 National Standard incurred a devastating loss of $53 million. The *Value Line Investment Survey,* which had always followed the company, quietly dropped the floundering firm, stating that its "high-risk issue should be of little interest to most investors." Although increased sales of welding wire and air bag filters helped a struggling National Standard to reduce losses in 1994 and return to profitability in 1995, the company's financial position had been so weakened by the mid-1990s that a quick or extensive recovery seemed improbable.

Principal Subsidiaries: National Standard Export Co.; National Standard Co. Ltd., England; National Standard of Canada Ltd., Canada.

Further Reading:

Horovitz, Bruce, "Fixing a Company That Isn't Broken," *Industry Week,* October 27, 1980, pp. 63–65.

"National-Standard Appears Geared for Further Improvement in Net," *Barron's,* January 4, 1965, p. 20.

"New Products Strengthen National-Standard Outlook," *Barron's,* September 4, 1961, p. 22.

Tuttle, Howard C., "Wire Keeps Welding Robots Alive," *Production,* June 1985, pp. 64–65.

—Hilary Gopnik

Newport News Shipbuilding and Dry Dock Co.

4101 Washington Avenue
Newport News, Virginia 23607
U.S.A.
(804) 380-2000
Fax: (804) 380-3114

Wholly Owned Subsidiary of Tenneco Inc.
Incorporated: 1886 as Chesapeake Dry Dock & Construction Co.
Employees: 19,950
Sales: $1.8 billion
SICs: 3731 Ship Building & Repairing

Newport News Shipbuilding and Dry Dock Co., a subsidiary of Tenneco Inc., is the nation's largest privately owned shipyard and the only one in the United States capable of building and servicing a full range of nuclear-powered and conventional ships for both defense and commercial service. The largest employer in Virginia, the company has expanded nationwide, building, over its more than 100-year history, more than 700 vessels, including many that have taken part in the great historical events of 20th-century American history, from the days of President Theodore Roosevelt's Great White Fleet to the battles of World War II and on into the nuclear age. The company's other products have ranged from traffic signals to giant turbines.

Newport News Shipbuilding was founded in 1886 at one of the most favorable shipping locations in the United States. The yard owes its existence to Collis P. Huntington, one of the business partners who founded the Central Pacific Railroad and drove it eastward through the Sierras to form the nation's first transcontinental rail line. After his successes in California, Huntington returned east and was instrumental in building the Chesapeake & Ohio Railroad from Richmond to the town named for him in West Virginia. Then he turned his sights to develop Newport News as the carrier's eastern terminus. He was president of the Old Dominion Land Co. which laid out lots to start the development of the town. Coal and grain facilities were built and Huntington then sought to found a drydock there.

Commenting on the yard's location, Huntington later noted that "It was my original intention to start a shipyard plant in the best location in the world, and I succeeded in my purpose. It is right at the gateway of the sea. There is never any ice in the winter, and it is never so cold but you can hammer metal out of doors."

The drydock was opened April 29, 1889, and the maritime press hailed it as the "wonder of the age." The first shipbuilding job was a reconstruction project, but the contract for Hull No. 1, the tug *Dorothy,* was signed in 1890. After many years of service that tug would eventuall return to the yard in 1974 and be dedicated as a permanent exhibit in 1976.

According to the official history, William Tazewell's *Newport News Shipbuilding The First Century,* Huntington protested to the Secretary of the Navy in 1890 about competition from the Norfolk Navy Yard, a harbinger of many such disputes over government versus private shipbuilding in the future. Newport's first successful bids for construction of naval vessels, three gunboats, followed in 1893. The navy was pleased with the work and the yard was awarded more contracts for battleship construction. In this period the yard was also doing considerable commercial work, including the construction of cargo ships, passenger vessels, bay and river steamers and tugs. In 1899, contracts for new vessels exceeded $10.5 million and 4,500 men were employed at the yard. Dry Dock No. 2 opened in 1901, the first of several expansions that continued into the 1990s.

Newport News was a company town in all respects, and Huntington personally underwrote financial losses in the early days. Huntington was said to be one of the largest, if not the largest, landholders in the country, and ran his vast interests from his New York office until his death in 1900. Ownership of the Newport News company then passed to Collis's son Archer Milton Huntington, a scholar, poet, and philanthropist with little interest in the shipyard.

Thus, after Huntington's death, the man most instrumental in guiding the shipyard was Homer L. Ferguson, a former navy officer and student of naval architecture and marine engineering, who came on board at the yard in 1905 and was made assistant superintendent of hull contruction. Ferguson would become president of the company in 1915, serving in that capacity until 1946, when he was named chairman of the board. During his tenure at Newport News, he successfully steered the company through a long period that included two wars and the Great Depression.

In 1907 President Roosevelt dispatched the Great White Fleet on a round-the-world voyage to demonstrate American sea power. Seven of the fleet's 16 battleships had been built at Newport News. The shipyard was also soon to demonstrate its adaptability, and when all-big-gun ships became the standard for naval warfare, built six of these "dreadnought" ships, most of which saw service as late as World War II. The yard's adaptability was recognized frequently in later years. It built its first five submarines in 1905, and in 1934 the navy turned to the yard for the first aircraft carrier designed for such service. Most construction, however, continued to be for merchant shipping, among which were barges used in construction of the Panama Canal.

There were boom conditions at the yard during World War I, when the company built 25 destroyers and the last battleship launched until World War II. Moreover Newport News reconditioned the liner *Leviathan* for use as a troopship. After wartime projects were completed, there was a period in which no more naval work and few commercial contracts were available. The company took whatever work it could find and diverged into other manufacturing.

The disarmament treaties of the 1920s resulted in scrapping a number of warships, but the gathering war clouds of World War II saw a revival of shipbuilding. According to a *Fortune* magazine article of 1936, although 49 U.S. shipyards had been closed since 1920, Newport News became stronger due to "the ablest management in the business" under Ferguson.

In addition to its shipbuilding in this period, the company repaired locomotives, built an aqueduct, a bridge, and an office building, manufactured traffic lights and transmission towers and 9,000 freight cars, as well as producing a variety of other equipment. Perhaps the most spectacular of all non-shipbuilding work was the fabrication of the largest turbines in the world for the Dnieprostroi Dam in the Soviet Union. After World War II, the company entered the atomic energy field, fabricating assemblies for nuclear reactors.

In 1940, Archer Huntington sold the shipyard to a syndicate of underwriters. Rumors of a sale had been circulating for years, and once the company was again thriving after the Great Depression, Archer regarded the time as right for a sale. The book value of the plant and property was reported at $17.79 million and its replacement value was around $29 million. The group of investors reportedly purchased Newport News for $18 million and the company went public, trading shares on the New York stock exchange.

Also during this time, the navy ordered seven carriers and four cruisers from Newport News, the beginning of a string of orders as a world war again seemed imminent. Newport News set up a subsidiary, North Carolina Shipbuilding Co. in Wilmington, North Carolina, to help handle the crush of wartime business. Vessels built there included 126 "Liberty" cargo ships before it was closed at the end of the war. Employment at Newport News rose to a high of 31,000 in 1943, with more than 50,000 at the Wilmington subsidiary.

However, the exultation felt by management and employees at the close of the war they helped win was tempered by uncertainty of the future. In the lean days that followed, the yard performed ship conversions and repair work. But with the development of jet aircraft, existing carriers were inadequate and the navy began planning supercarriers. After the outbreak of the Korean War the yard was awarded a contract for the first of several new supercarriers, the *Forrestal.*

A memorable day in the yard's history came on February 8, 1950, when the keel assembly for the *United States,* the largest passenger ship ever built in the nation, was laid. Launched in the summer of 1951, it was the world's fastest passenger ship and the first built at the yard in ten years. Also, in the fall of 1950, the yard fabricated the last turbines for the Grand Coulee Dam in the state of Washington.

In 1951 William E. Blewett, Jr., became the shipyard's eighth president. A forceful leader, Blewett decided to shift the company's focus into the field of nuclear power, a move praised more than 30 years later by another company president, Edward J. Campbell, as "easily the most significant of the last 45 years." By 1956, the company's Atomic Power Division had more than 200 employees, and a new subsidiary, the Eastern Idaho Construction Co., was formed to set up a reactor test station near Arco, Idaho. Engineers worked there with the navy's Bureau of Ships, planning for atomic-powered supercarriers. The age of the supertankers had also arrived, and on August 7, 1958, the largest tanker yet built in the United States, the *Sansinena,* was launched at the yard.

The advent of nuclear power brought numerous changes to Newport News Shipbuilding, with new sections devoted to quality inspection, health physics, controlled material handling, and lead shielding. Since its earliest days the yard had an active apprenticeship program, and now it added classes and lectures about the new science of atomic propulsion.

In 1959 the yard launched its first nuclear powered submarine, the *Shark,* the first submarine built by Newport News in more than 50 years. The *Enterprise,* the world's first nuclear-powered carrier, was launched on September 24, 1960. The *Robert E. Lee,* christened December 18, 1959, was the first of 14 Polaris-class subs built at the yard. A new subsidiary, Newport News Industrial Corp., was set up to engage in specialized work on land-based nuclear power plants.

The 1960s brought several challenges to Newport News. The Equal Employment Opportunity Commission charged in 1966 that the company was discriminating against its African American employees. Although the company denied the charge, it entered into an agreement to accelerate promotions of African Americans and also began hiring greater numbers of women for jobs previously held only by men.

Moreover, by the fall of 1967, Newport News faced serious financial problems, as aerospace giants were moving into shipbuilding, leaving Newport News dangerously undercapitalized to compete. The yard reported a loss of nearly $3.5 million in the first half of 1968, a decisive factor in merger negotiations that the company began pursuing. In September 1968, Tenneco Inc., of Houston, Texas, acquired Newport News Shipbuilding for approximately $123 million.

In the course of restructuring Newport News, Tenneco encountered strong opposition from organized labor and the Occupational Health and Safety Administration (OSHA). Eventually, the employees gained representation by the United Steelworkers Union. OSHA levied a fine of $766,190 on the shipyard, citing 617 cases of deficient medical care, unsafe working conditions, and excessive noise. It was reportedly the largest fine OSHA had ever imposed on any company.

In the wake of such problems, Wall Street analysts advised Tenneco to sell Newport News, warning that the division would require costly modernization and reorganization. But Tenneco officials recognized the shipyard's potential, especially after plans for a 600-ship navy were announced in 1981. Indeed, the navy depended on the yard for all kinds of ships; it was chosen as the lead yard in designing the *Los Angeles* class of attack subs, launched on April 6, 1974. Moreover, the company continued to overhaul and refuel Polaris subs on a regular schedule and converted several into improved Poseidon missile systems.

Conversion and repairs remained a staple and the company's manufacturing operations were steady. In fact, the business backlog at Newport News had reached $1.4 billion by the end of 1971, and employment had risen to 27,500 by 1972.

However, while revenues rose year to year, profits failed to keep pace, as the company was faced with a profit squeeze due largely to the costs of plant expansions and labor. Indeed, the building of more modern ships, particularly the nuclear-powered vessels, proved a necessarily time-consuming process, as designs were changed mid-construction, and workers often found themselves idle while their co-workers completed other aspects of construction.

Also a major dispute between the yard and the U.S. Navy developed over the costs of building nuclear ships. The navy's Admiral Rickover continuously disputed costs, accusing Newport News of being unable to do its job properly. Newport News, in turn, accused the navy of being unable to properly finance its fleet. This dispute reached a climax in 1975, when the shipyard temporarily halted work on a cruiser. The yard threatened to get out of the business, but its claims against the navy were finally settled out of court when Deputy Defense Secretary William P. Clements Jr., realizing that the situation had gotten out of hand, sought negotiations. A settlement was reached, and the relationship between shipbuilder and the navy was mended.

During this time, with the navy representing a 93 percent share of the company's operating revenues, Newport News decided to attract more commercial business. The company constructed the new North Yard, where the liquefied natural gas carrier *El Paso Southern* was launched in 1977, followed by other supertankers. While the company enjoyed record revenues in 1975 through 1977, the commercial market for oil tankers declined dramatically in the face of a worldwide oil crisis, and eventually Newport News's revenues declined similarly.

During this time, a new Newport News president, Edward J. Campbell, was named, and he promptly set about turning the company around. Faced with declining profits, outmoded facilities, pending lawsuits, and even a substantial strike by ship designers and production workers, Campbell had his work cut out for him. Lawsuits and strikes were eventually settled, and Campbell focused on a program for improving conditions at the yards.

His efforts paid off; for the first time, company revenues topped the billion dollar mark in 1981 and profits rose to $82 million. In 1983 the company posted record sales and income for the fourth straight year, with profits of $150 million and employment at 29,000. At the end of 1982, the navy awarded Newport News a $3.1 billion contract for the fifth and sixth Nimitz-class carriers, reportedly the biggest contract ever awarded a shipbuilder, and guaranteeing work into the 1990s. Moreover, an improved modular construction method was developed, employing computer technology that cut man hours and eliminated errors. In fact, the Tenneco annual report for 1984 reported that ''Improvements in earnings over the last five years are a direct result of innovative engineering concepts in modular construction and incentive-based contracts with the U.S. Navy.''

Newport News reentered the commercial cargo ship market in a big way in October 1994 when it signed a $150 million tanker contract with Eletson Corp., a major Greek shipping company. Newport News said the contract was the first commercial construction contract from an international ship owner won by an American yard since 1957. ''After almost 40 years of eating the dust of low-cost Korean, Japanese and West German yards, U.S. shipbuilders are suddenly back in world markets with a bang,'' a *Forbes* magazine reporter noted, adding that ''work rule changes, greatly improved modular construction techniques, and a remorseless attack on overhead costs have helped builders like Newport News, long dependent on big navy contracts for their living capitalize on . . . wage differentials.''

Other commercial construction contracts brought so much business that Newport News abandoned a bid to build tankers for a Canadian consortium, citing time and space constraints. At the end of 1994, the company had work under contract extending into 2002. Moreover, a letter of intent between Newport News and the United Arab Emirates was signed in December 1994 to establish a new shipbuilding and repair company in Abu Dhabi. The shipyard was to be an equity investor and manage the Abu Dhabi Ship Building Co., which would construct and repair military and commercial vessels. During this time, W. R. (Pat) Phillips was named chairman and chief executive officer of the shipyard and William P. Fricks was promoted to executive vice-president and chief operating officer.

Navy work still comprised the majority of the yard's business in 1994, when the company was awarded a $3 billion contract to build the Nimitz-class aircraft carrier *Ronald Reagan.* The christening of the last Los Angeles-class vessel *Cheyenne* came in April 1995. Due to cutbacks in the defense budget, however, the yard entered into a bitter contest with Electric Boat Division of General Dynamics Corporation, of Groton, Connnecticut, for the contract to design and build the navy's new attack submarines.

Tenneco approved a $68 million World-Class Shipbuilding Project in December 1994, to upgrade the yard's steel fabrication facilities, a step the company expected would dramatically reduce costs for future ship construction. Newport News also began a $29 million project to extend the yard's largest dry dock, allowing for simultaneous construction of carriers and large commercial ships.

Still, operating income for 1994 was $200 million, compared with $225 million in 1993, and revenues also decreased slightly from $1.9 billion to $1.8 billion. While the *New York Times* reported that several analysts were predicting that Tenneco would divest itself of Newport News, Tenneco chairman and chief executive officer Dana G. Mead maintained that the corporation had no such plans. In its 1994 annual report, company officials stated that the shipyard would continue to pursue additional U.S. Navy contracts in its core business of new ship construction, refueling and overhaul, and nuclear engineering. However, they said the yard also would continue working to diversify through commercial shipbuilding and foreign military sales, and by ''increasing sales of technological expertise.''

Further Reading:

Jones, Kathryn, "Tenneco's Plan May Reap $1 Billion," *New York Times,* December 14, 1994, p. D4.

Phalon, Richard, "Back in the Game," *Forbes,* December 5. 1994, pp. 58–60.

Schmitt, Eric, "Two Submarine Makers Vie for a $60 Billion Project," *New York Times,* May 17, 1995, p. A1.

Shorrock, Tim, "Virginia Yard Homes in on Five-Ship Contract," *Journal of Commerce,* May 17, 1995, p. B8.

Tazewell, William L., *Newport News Shipbuilding The First Century,* Newport News, Va.: The Mariner's Museum, 1986.

"Va. Yard Wins Federal Aid to Design LNG Tanker," *Journal of Commerce,* June 2, 1995, p. B8.

—William O. Craig

Officine Alfieri Maserati S.p.A.

Viale C Menotti 322
I-41100 Modena (MO)
Italy
011 059 230101
Fax: 011 059 222867

Wholly Owned Subsidiary of Fiat S.p.A.
Founded: 1926
Employees: 1,735
SICs: 5013 Motor Vehicle Supplies & Spare Parts

A Maserati sports car is one of the few automobiles in the world that immediately evokes images of wealth and prestige. The original clientele who purchased Maserati cars were part of a European social set that frequented the casinos in Monte Carlo and the beaches on the French Riviera. Although well known for its limited production of high performance sports cars during the 1920s and 1930s, the firm gained its reputation on the racing circuit. Like Porsche, Alfa Romeo, Jaguar, Ferrari, and Lamborghini, the early Maserati touring and racing cars are now expensive collector's items. Unfortunately, due to years of mismanagement and lack of direction, the firm deteriorated until it was purchased by Fiat in the early 1990s. Under Fiat's control, however, Maserati's fortunes are slowly improving.

The roots of Maserati can be traced back to the early years of the 20th century. Five brothers, Carlo, Bindo, Alfieri, Ettore and Ernesto Maserati, lived in Bologna, Italy, with their aging parents. The eldest of the brothers, Carlo, worked as a race car driver for Fiat and Bianchi, but died in 1911. The second-born Bindo, and the third oldest brother, Alfieri, worked in the assembly plant for Italian car manufacturer Isotta Fraschini. The younger brothers, Ettore and Ernesto, shared their siblings fascination with automobiles, and followed them into working for various car manufacturers in the area surrounding Bologna.

When the fortunes of Isotta Fraschini began to decline during World War I, Bindo and Alfieri began to manufacture spark plugs and other engine components for the Italian war effort. By the time the war ended in November of 1918, the two brothers were producing an entire line of engine components under the family name. Soon the two younger brothers joined them, and, by the mid-1920s, the Maserati brothers were designing and building racing machines for Diatto, another Italian car manufacturer. Alfieri was the impetus behind Diatto's racing success, and began to build a reputation within the racing circuit when he designed and produced an impressive straight-eight Grand Prix racer.

When Diatto dropped out of the race car circuit in 1926, the four Maserati brothers acquired the company's racing cars and began to redesign, update, and improve these models. Working in a tiny family garage close to the Ponte Vecchio in Bologna, the brothers formed their own company, Officine Alfieri Maserati S.p.A., and decided to use the ancient symbol of Bologna, Neptune's trident, as the logo for the firm.

The company's first great success occurred in 1929, with the creation of a Formula Libre racing machine. This car, with a pair of 8-cylinder engines mounted next to each other, was capable of dazzling speed. On September 28, 1929, a young driver named Baconin Borzacchini drove this car along a stretch of road near Cremona and reached a speed of 154 mph. When news of this accomplishment spread around the racing circuit, the Bologna Automobile Club arranged an enormous banquet to pay homage to the brothers who built the car and to the man who drove it. Even Enzo Ferrari, one of the most respected men in Italian racing and who would soon see the Maserati firm as his fiercest competitor, was in attendance at this festive event.

Tragedy took the Maserati brothers by surprise in 1932, and the firm was never quite the same again. Alfieri Maserati, well respected by his brothers and clearly the leader of the firm, crashed during a race at Messina in the early part of the year and died under the surgeon's knife from massive internal injuries. At the age of 42, Alfieri was in the prime of life and, with his broad knowledge in the field of automotive engineering, seemed destined to carry the name of Maserati to the highest pinnacle of race car success. Needless to say, his death was devastating to the firm, since the company manufactured only a few sports cars and single-seater automobiles annually.

After the loss of Alfieri, the remaining Maserati brothers attempted to continue manufacturing high-performance sports cars and racing automobiles. However, even though they were hardworking and skilled craftsmen, and able to produce superb machines, none of the brothers possessed the business acumen to develop the firm into an enduring and successful operation. By 1936, the Maserati brothers were able to manufacture only nine cars. One year later, following an intense period of deliberation, the remaining Maserati brothers, Bindo, Ernesto, and Ettore, sold their controlling interest in the firm to the Orsi family of Modena.

The Orsi family, headed by the father, Adolfo, and his son, Omer, had earned a fortune in steel mill production, agricultural equipment manufacturing, and a trolley car system which they operated in Modena. The Orsi family purchased Maserati to continue manufacturing racing cars, and to expand the production of Maserati spark plugs, which was the one part of the firm that had always been profitable. All the Maserati brothers were hired by Adolfo and Omer to a ten year management contract. Under the terms of the agreement, the Maseratis were given the freedom to design and produce high-performance racing cars. But, in spite of its appearance, the contract relegated the Maserati brothers to no more than highly paid employees, without any genuine influence over company policy or decision-making.

Despite these restrictions, with the largesse of the Orsi family funds, the Maserati brothers began to create a number of impressive racing machines. In May of 1939, an American named Wilbur Shaw, driving a supercharged Maserati 8CFT, won the Indianapolis 500. Shaw won the same race in 1940 driving another Maserati car, and was on his way to a third consecutive victory with a Maserati model in 1941, when a rear wire wheel broke near the end of the race. The Indianapolis 500 was the one race in the United States that all the Italians followed with great enthusiasm, and the Maserati victories assured the company of lasting prestige in the automobile industry.

In the fall of 1939, the Orsi family decided to reorganize the Maserati firm, and moved the entire factory, including unfinished cars, tools, spare parts, and management offices to Modena. Adolfo Orsi assumed the position of president of the company, while Alceste Giacomazzi, Adolfo's brother-in-law, become the new general director. Orsi and Giacomazzi were also able to entice Alberto Massimino, the designer of Ferrari automobiles, to leave that company and become chief designer at Maserati. With these changes, the Maserati brothers were left without any real say as to how the company should be developed. Bindo Maserati was appointed head of the Maserati racing operation but marginalized when company policy was decided upon.

Part of the Orsi family strategy to reorganize the Maserati firm involved the perception that war was imminent, and that the company could take advantage of the Italian war effort. Adolfo planned to expand and increase the Maserati business by mass-producing spark plugs, batteries, and electric delivery trucks needed by the Italian Ministry of War. The president also envisaged a lucrative contract with the government to refit and overhaul military trucks and cars during the war. When World War II started in Europe, the Maserati firm was prepared for any manufacturing requests from Benito Mussolini's Fascist government.

When the war came to an end in the spring of 1945, the Maserati operation had not been severely damaged like other automobile manufacturers in Italy. As a result, the firm resumed the production of automobiles almost immediately. In May of 1945, Maserati entered and won the Indianapolis 500, while also placing third and seventh in the overall field. By May of 1946, Massimino had designed a brand new A6 sports car that rivaled the best of the models produced by Ferrari and Alfa Romeo. In 1947, Maserati cars were recording victory after victory on the racetrack, and began to take away some of the customers who had purchased Ferrari cars for years.

In 1947, the Maserati brothers finished their ten-year contract with the Orsi family and decided to form a new automobile company, Officina Specializzata Costruzione Automobili, in their hometown of Bologna. Producing high-performance cars on a limited scale, the brothers garnered a reputation for manufacturing quality automobiles. The end of the Maserati family involvement in car production came in 1967, when the aging and frail brothers sold their interest in OSCA to MV-Agusta.

In February of 1949, the Orsi family suddenly and inexplicably withdrew from racing competition. Rumors of financial problems provided the backdrop for another sudden announcement by Adolfo Orsi that the Maserati firm would close its doors until a comprehensive reorganization was completed. When the company finally reopened for business, Adolfo announced that Maserati would place greater emphasis on the development and production of touring cars. At the same time, the company would also continue its production of machine tools and small electric trucks for the commercial markets. These decisions were to have long-term effects on the direction and prestige of the Maserati firm. No longer competing against Ferrari and Alfa Romeo in the elite sports car market, the Maserati firm began to lose the luster of its honored past.

Throughout the decade of the 1950s, the Orsi family operated Maserati as a diversified manufacturing firm. Emphasis was still placed on the production of machine tools and electric trucks, but the company's involvement in the racing circuit was minimal. As the Orsi family finances began to decline because of mismanagement, and promising ventures in places like Argentina and Western Europe turned sour, it turned more and more to mass-production items. By the late 1950s and early 1960s, Maserati was manufacturing high-volume touring cars and just a smattering of sports cars and racing automobiles. The company's original purpose, and the Maserati brothers' goal, was to build high-performance sports cars. Hopelessly directionless, the Maserati firm began to lose money, and the Orsi family searched for a solution.

In 1966, the Orsi family reached an agreement with Citroen, a French automobile manufacturer, to jointly produce both touring cars and sports cars for the general market. Initially quite promising, the joint venture wasn't able to capture enough of the market to stay financially afloat. With family finances at their lowest, the Orsi family decided to sell the Maserati operation to Alejandro de Tomaso, an Argentina businessman who garnered a reputation for acquiring bankrupt companies. De Tomaso already had taken control of Benelli and Moto Guzzi, two Italian motorcycle manufacturers, and Innocenti, a maker of mini-cars. But de Tomaso's ideas about how to design and manufacture automobiles were not successful, and the Maserati firm suffered as a result. The Maserati BiTurbo was a poorly designed car, and its performance was much less than expected. Sales continued to spiral downward, and the firm's reputation sank lower and lower.

During the 1970s, for many of the American and European car manufacturers, over-capacity resulted in a loss of revenues and profitability. In the United States, Ford, General Motors, and Chrysler reported record-setting losses during the mid-1970s. In Europe, the situation was even worse. British Leyland, Chrysler UK, and Citroen were kept afloat only through government assistance. The European high-performance car manufacturers were also experiencing hard times: Jensen in Britain and Iso in Italy filed for bankruptcy and disappeared from sight, while Jaguar was taken over by British Leyland, Ferrari was acquired by Fiat, and Lamborghini was passed from one owner to the next.

Throughout the 1970s, Maserati's fate was much the same. After numerous but unsuccessful attempts to design and manufacture new models for wealthier clientele in America and

Europe, and ever-larger infusions of cash from de Tomaso, the Argentina businessman soon began to see his fortune slip away. Maserati's production capacity dwindled to almost nothing. In 1984, de Tomaso found a friend in Lee Iacocca, the man serving as chairman of Chrysler and responsible for its remarkable comeback from financial disaster. De Tomaso convinced the head of Chrysler to finance the development of a Maserati luxury sports car, with Chrysler selling the cars through its own dealerships.

Iococca projected sales of between 5,000 to 8,000 of the Maserati-Chrysler sports cars at a minimal price tag of $35,000. Profits would be huge, and the coupe would help to upscale the American car manufacturer's product line. But the joint venture started off on the wrong foot when de Tomaso and Iococca agreed to place a Chrysler engine in a Maserati body. Combining the worst of both cars, the machine was an engineer's nightmare. The car was underpowered, there were gaps between the fenders and the doors, the power windows didn't work well, the chrome trim around the wheel base kept falling away, the car leaked, and the convertible top didn't fit properly. Maserati employees fought with Chrysler employees about everything, including whether the steering wheel should be natural wood or fake wood grain. All the while, de Tomaso requested more and more money from Chrysler.

Projected for sale in 1986 and then in 1987, the Maserati Touring Coupe wasn't close to being finished by the beginning of 1988. Iococca, growing impatient with de Tomaso, sent a team to Milan to assess the situation. The team discovered only 35 of the initial 200 cars manufactured suitable for sale. When the Touring Coupe finally arrived in Chrysler showrooms, it looked very similar to the Chrysler LeBaron coupe—but the LeBaron was less than half the price of the Maserati. When the figures were totaled, Chrysler lost nearly $400 million on the joint project with Maserati, and in 1989, after producing a little more than 7,000 of the cars, Iococca decided to end his partnership with de Tomaso.

With the loss of Chrysler financing, de Tomaso could not continue to underwrite Maserati's operating costs all by himself. As a result, de Tomaso decided to sell Maserati to Fiat, Italy's largest car manufacturer. After lengthy negotiations, in the spring of 1993 Fiat purchased Maserati at a cost of $51 million. Fiat had experienced severe financial losses during the early 1990s, primarily due to a loss of market share in Italy and Europe in general. However, under new management, Fiat rebuilt its position in both the domestic and foreign car markets, and Maserati figured prominently in its owner's resurgence. After a period or incorporation and reorganization, the Maserati division of Fiat began to sell high-performance sports cars once again in the 1990s.

Further Reading:

''Fiat Auto Buys All of Maserati,'' *Automotive News,* May 24, 1993, p. 2.

Rossant, John, ''The Man Who's Driving Fiat Like A Ferrari,'' *Business Week,* January 23, 1995, pp. 82–83.

Yates, Brock W., *Enzo Ferrari: The Man, The Cars, The Races, The Machine,* New York: Doubleday, 1991.

—Thomas Derdak

Olin Corporation

120 Long Ridge Road
Stamford, Connecticut 06904-1355
U.S.A.
(203) 3562000
Fax: (203) 356-3595

Public Company
Incorporated: 1892 as Western Powder Company
Employees: 12,800
Sales: $2.66 billion
Stock Exchanges: New York Pacific Chicago
SICs: 2812 Alkalies & Chlorine; 2842 Polishes & Sanitation Goods; 3351 Copper Rolling & Drawing; 3483 Ammunition except for Small Arms

Olin Corporation is a Fortune 200 company whose businesses are concentrated in chemicals, materials and metals, defense, sporting ammunition, and aerospace. Olin Corporation has been a protean organization throughout its history, with a product list ranging from cigarette papers and cellophane to snow skis and home-building material.

Olin Industries was founded in 1892 as the Western Powder Company by a former baseball player named Franklin Olin. The Du Pont family and their Gunpowder Trust acquired 49 percent of Olin's company in 1909, and they nearly replaced Olin, who scrambled for the remaining 51 percent and retained control.

Western's first acquisition after the incident, Winchester Arms, was a defensive move against Du Pont, which might have purchased the company to deprive Western of a customer for its gunpowder. The Winchester plants, famous for "the guns that won the West," acquitted themselves admirably during the two world wars; for example, they put an important new gun, the M1 Carbine, into production in just 13 days. Besides the gunpowder and munitions factories, Western Powder also operated a brass works at that time.

When Franklin Olin retired, he kept most of the Western Powder Company's stock for himself and divided the rest between his two sons, Spencer and John. They consolidated Western's properties and renamed the new enterprise Olin Industries. Soon Olin Industries began to diversify into paper, fuel, petrochemicals, cellophane, and lumber. The company was managed by John and Spencer Olin along with Bill Hanes. All three were in their sixties, and the lack of a suitable candidate to succeed John, who was president, was the major concern of a company that was otherwise in excellent shape.

The lack of a logical successor was an important factor in John Olin's proposal to Tom Nicholls, the 44-year-old president of Mathieson Chemical Company, which manufactured ammonia and caustic soda, to merge their companies. Starting in 1947 Nicholls, with the help of his friend John Leppart, had transformed Mathieson, a small regional chemical company that concentrated on a few commodity chemicals, into a company with $366 million in sales—a 600 percent increase over Mathieson's performance before Nicholls took over. This dramatic turnaround was accomplished by a diversification into less cyclical products and the acquisition of companies with strong marketing organizations.

John Olin and Tom Nicholls were friends; in fact, they often went hunting together. The idea of a merger was first broached in 1951, but discarded because a satisfactory division of power did not seem possible. Nicholls headed a company almost equal to Olin in size, and neither he nor John Olin wanted to be subordinate to the other. Nevertheless, a merger remained tempting because it would further Olin's new expansion into chemicals and bring Mathieson closer to consumers. The companies had previously cooperated on a rocket fuels venture which proved they could work together.

During the initial discussions of a merger between the two corporations, Mathieson purchased Squibb, a well known manufacturer of pharmaceuticals that was only slightly smaller than itself. In 1953, while on a hunting trip, Olin finally convinced Nicholls that a merger was possible. Within a matter of days Bill Hanes had arrived at a satisfactory division of power. The new Olin-Mathieson would be run by a triumvirate of John Olin, Nicholls, and Hanes. Olin would be chairman, Nicholls president, and Hanes head of finance.

The press offered its congratulations in 1953 when the agreement took place. Many analysts remarked on the compatibility of the Olin and Mathieson operations and the apparent dovetailing of their strategic directions. Mathieson was moving from basic chemicals to consumer goods while Olin, a manufacturer of consumer goods, was moving into basic chemicals. The only indication of trouble came from inside the company. Said an Olin-Mathieson executive soon after the merger, "We'll have to keep Tommy (Nicholls) from expanding for the present; this is a time to digest."

However, the desire to diversify triumphed over prudence. Within 18 months of its incorporation the Olin Mathieson Chemical Company had purchased three new businesses: Marquardt Aircraft, Blockson Chemical, and the Brown Paper Mill Company. This last purchase alone cost $90 million. By 1958 Olin Mathieson was producing one of the widest assortments of products of any company in the United States, yet its strategy was not proving successful. Sales for that year were a disappointing $20 million, although Bill Hanes had said in 1956 that sales would soon be hitting $1 billion. The causes of Olin Mathieson's poor performance were manifold.

The August 1958 issue of Fortune magazine accused the company of allowing itself to be constantly sidetracked. Indeed,

Olin Mathieson seemed to lack direction. Part of the problem lay in its strategy of diversification and part in the structure of the new company itself. *Fortune* called the management of Olin Mathieson "a loose confederation of tribal chieftains." This charge was borne out by a 1958 meeting where the 36 research chiefs met for the first time and two of them discovered that they had been doing identical research on a fuel additive.

The lack of communication and poor diversification strategy led to the 1957 purchase of an aluminum plant. The aluminum industry was an expensive one to enter and the purchase of the aluminum works put Olin Mathieson into debt. In addition, the timing of the purchase could not have been worse, as a soft market was imminent. The business community was surprised at the poor planning of the aluminum operation because Olin Mathieson had not secured a source of bauxite, a principal ingredient in aluminum manufacture and one that was frequently in short supply. For the next two decades Olin Mathieson would find its fortunes rising and falling with the profitability of aluminum.

Nicholls was soon promoted to the board, John Olin became chairman of the executive committee, and Stan Osborne became president. Osborne was a feisty but accessible administrator. He was also a Spanish history buff; in fact, he was engaged in writing a book on that very subject when he was promoted. Determined to avoid the corporate equivalent of the sinking of the Spanish Armada, he began to dispose of unprofitable and incompatible product lines and assure a supply of bauxite. Osborne undertook cost control measures, including a $20,000 cut in his own salary. The business press praised his damage control.

After the two bad years of 1957 and 1958 when sales declined, the balance sheet began to improve. In 1959 profits increased 17 percent over the previous year, but that rate of growth did not continue. Although Osborne's cost-cutting measures kept the company from disaster, he was clearly frustrated by the company's slow progress. He resigned in 1963 for a career in banking.

Throughout the 1960s Olin Mathieson continued to be plagued by the same problems that had come to light in 1958. In 1967 the new president, a man named Grand, initiated a program not unlike Osborne's recovery plan. Unprofitable divisions were ordered to show an eight percent yearly increase in profits. This was not an unattainable figure for most of the divisions. Even Squibb, which was responsible for a quarter of the company's sales, was producing a mediocre five percent return on assets. In 1967 Grand planned a program of expansion into recreation, housing, lumber, and chemicals. In 1969 the company adopted the name Olin Corporation.

In what was developing into a disheartening pattern, Olin celebrated the new decade with a decline in profits. A prolonged strike by American autoworkers decreased the market for aluminum. Furthermore, new environmental regulations were expensive. Two plants, one manufacturing DDT and the other soda ash, had to be shut down because they could not meet environmental protection standards. These closings resulted in a $26 million loss. The timing of Olin's new housing venture recalled its venture into aluminum, since the market went into a downslide soon after Olin entered it. Sporting goods, sold through the Winchester division, became one of the company's priorities. Olin ski equipment was marketed and sold successfully.

Grand died suddenly in 1971. In 1974 the next president of Olin, James Towey, was able to boast an 80 percent jump in earnings, largely due to the sale of the aluminum operations and polyester film factories which had been depressing earnings. The aluminum works had earned $19 million over a ten-year period and had lost $32 million. The chemicals division, always a company mainstay, performed well, and the agricultural products division prospered. Brass and paper, steady sources of income, held their ground. In 1975 the company continued to sell unprofitable product lines, such as a parka business it had bought a few years before.

In the late 1970s housing and Winchester Arms took on the role of the ill-fated aluminum works in suppressing profits. Winchester's operating profits plunged 37 percent in one year, despite the quality of its guns and their name recognition.

Forbes once referred to Olin as the world's longest-running garage sale. Indeed, the company had, and still has, a habit of buying unprofitable businesses and then selling them within a few years, often at a loss. In 1985 the profitable but slow-growing paper division was sold, along with the last of the home-building concerns. The company's most recent round of divestment caused shareholders' equity to drop by 25 percent, although its shares went up three points.

To reinvigorate the company, Olin looked to metal and chemical products, especially chemicals used by the electronics industry. This began with the expansion in electronics and aerospace during 1980. In 1985 Olin acquired Rockcor Inc., which produces rockets, gas generators, and data systems for battlefield intelligence, as well as devices to measure the strength of underground nuclear tests. In 1985 Olin lost twice as much money as it made the previous year.

The leaders of the company, John Johnstone, Jr., and chairman John Henske, cut back programs that cost the company a $330 million pretax charge in 1985, including car and boat flares, cellophane, skis, cigarette paper, and photographic chemicals. In 1991 Johnstone announced another round of streamlining, divesting several under-performing chemical lines and its European sporting ammunition business.

Olin vowed to focus on three core businesses: metals, chemicals and defense, and sporting ammunition. In 1992 the company established a new aliphatic diisocyanate (ADI) unit in Lake Charles, Louisiana, which prepared it for a major push into the area of performance urethanes, used in coatings for products on cars and appliances. The investment built on Olin's $450-million per year position in the urethane-based toluene diisocyanate (TDI) market. In order to expand its supply operations to the microelectronics industry, Olin built a new 211,000-square-foot plant in Mesa, Arizona, to produce a chemical used in the production of semiconductors, which was scheduled to open in the fourth quarter of 1995.

Strategic investments made over several years, combined with reductions in salaried personnel and other operating costs, enabled Olin to increase earnings as the economy strengthened. In early 1994 Olin acquired GenCorp's Aerojet medium caliber ammunition business, making Olin one of only two U.S. producers of medium caliber ammunition. Also during that year, the Brass, Electronic Materials, and Winchester divisions earned record operating profits, while Chlor-Alkali Products, biocides, pool chemicals, Ordnance, and Aerospace showed significant improvements. Under the leadership of Johnstone as chairman and CEO and Donald W. Griffin as president and COO, Olin posted record sales of $2.7 billion and earnings of $91 million, an important increase from 1993 sales of $2.4 billion and earnings of $40 million before a $132 million after tax-charge to income, which resulted in a net loss of $92 million that year.

As the company faced the new century, Olin planned to sharpen its cost-effectiveness, capitalize on global growth opportunities, fine-tune its business mix, and take actions needed to build on its strong market positions. For example, Olin Brass planned investments in 1995 and 1996 at its Indianapolis plant to modernize production equipment, improve efficiency, and broaden product capabilities for seamless copper alloy tubes used in specialized applications. Olin also focused on strengthening its position in pool chemical brands, including HTH, Pace, and Sock It brands. In 1994 Olin sold over 40 percent of its dry sanitizer pool chemical outside the United States as demand increased abroad. Olin's zinc Omadine biocide, used in antidandruff shampoos, held a leading position in the market for a long time, and the company exported a significant amount overseas to meet the increased demand for personal care products in the Far East.

Olin's letter to shareholders in its 1994 annual report stated: "While we were gratified by our progress, we're not at all satisfied with it. Our earnings may now be at respectable levels, but we're still a long way from where we want to be." Focusing on its core businesses and refining corporate objectives, the company continued to position itself for its next 100 years of business.

Principal Subsidiaries: Aegis, Inc. (50%); Bridgeport Brass Corporation; Bryan Metals, Inc.; G.D. International, Ltd.; General Defense Corporation; Hi-Pure Chemicals, Inc.; Hunt Foreign Investment Corp.; Image Technology Corporation; OCG Holdings, Inc. (50%); Olin-Asahi Interconnect Technologies (50%); Olin Export Trading Corporation; Olin Fabricated Metals Products; Olin Far East, Limited; Olin Hunt Specialty Products Inc.; Olin Hunt Sub. I Corp.; Olin Pantex, Inc.; Olin Specialty Metals Corporation; A.J. Oster Company; Pacific Electro-Dynamics, Inc.; Physics International Co.; Ravenna Arsenal, Inc.; Rocket Research Company; Superior Pool Products, Inc.; Niachlor (50%); OCG Microelectric Materials, Inc. (50%); Aquachlor (Proprietary) Limited (South Africa; 50%); Asahi-Olin Ltd. (Japan; 50%); Etoxyl, C.A. (Venezuela; 48.9%); Fuji-Hunt Electronics Technology Co. Ltd. (Japan; 24.5%); Hydrochim, S.A. (France; 63%); Judd-Olin (U.K.) Limited (50%); Kyodo TDI Limited Company (Japan; 40%); Langenberg Kupfer und Messingwerke GmbH (Germany; 49%); Nordesclor S.A. (Brazil; 50%); Nutmeg Insurance Limited (Bermuda); OCG Microelectronic Materials (Switzerland—50%; Germany—50%; United Kingdom—50%; France—50%; Italy—50%); Olin Australia Limited; Olin Brazil Ltda.; Olin Canada Inc.; Olin Chemicals, B.V. (Ireland); Olin Corporation N.Z. Limited (New Zealand); N.V. Olin Europe S.A. (Belgium); N.V. Olin Hunt Specialty Products (Belgium); N.V. Olin Hunt Trading (Belgium); Olin Hunt Specialty Products S.r.i. (Italy); Olin Industrial (Hong Kong) Limited; Olin Japan, Inc.; Olin (Proprietary) Limited (South Africa); Olin Pte., Ltd., Singapore; Olin Quimica, S.A. (Venezuela); Olin Quimica, S.A. de C.V. (Mexico); Olin S.A. (France); Olin UK Ltd.; Olin GmbH (Germany); Productora de Alcoholes Hidratados C.A. (PRALCA) (Venezuela; 25%); Schwermetall Halbzeugwerk, GmbH & Co., KG (Germany; 24.5%); Yamaha-Olin Metal Corporation (Japan; 50%); OCG Microelectronic Materials N.V. (Belgium; 50%).

Further Reading:

Burrough, D. J., "Olin Building $30 Million Mesa Plant," *Business Journal,* October 28, 1994, pp. 1 (2).

Caney, Derek J., "Olin's Plans $132M Corporate Restructuring, Job Cutbacks," *American Metal Market,* December 20, 1993, p. 8.

Highlights in the History of Olin Corporation, Stamford, Connecticut: Olin Corporation, 1992, 21 p.

Hunter, David, "Olin Adds Value with Performance Urethanes Unit," *Chemical Week,* May 20, 1992, p. 8.

Lubove, Seth, "No More Adventurism," *Forbes,* December 7, 1992, pp. 122 (2).

"Olin Draws Black Ink in 1st Qtr. with Earnings of $23.6 Million," *American Metal Market,* April 27, 1992, p. 6.

"Shhh! Olin Plans New Brass Mill but Don't Tell Anyone," *St. Louis Business Journal,* April 5, 1993, p. 4.

Thomas, Jr., Robert M., "Spencer Truman Olin, Executive for Olin Corporation, Dies at 96," *New York Times,* April 17, 1995, p. B9.

—updated by Beth Watson Highman

Ore-Ida Foods Incorporated

P.O. Box 10
Boise, Idaho 83707
U.S.A.
(208) 383-6100
Fax: (208) 383-6100

Wholly Owned Subsidiary of Heinz
Incorporated: 1951 as Oregon Frozen Foods Company
Employees: 4,500
Sales: $1 billion
SICs: 2037 Frozen Foods & Vegetables; 2038 Frozen Specialties Nec

Best known for its Tater Tots, Ore-Ida Foods Incorporated is the leading retail brand of frozen potato products in the United States and the world's largest processor of diversified frozen foods.

The company was founded in the early 1920s by F. Nephi and Golden T. Grigg, brothers in a small town in eastern Oregon who were peddling fresh sweet corn in their early teens. Going door-to-door in a horse-drawn wagon, they learned that people wanted sweet corn fresh from the field, as corn loses its sugar and moisture content quickly. The brothers discovered that by picking the corn around midnight—a cool and dewy hour—they caught the kernels at their peak of freshness. At first they tended their own small plot of produce, but before long they had to buy vegetables from others. They began shipping corn by railroad to other cities, packing their sweet corn in crushed ice to keep it fresh on its way to kitchens up to 600 miles away. Customers as far away as Portland, Salt Lake City, and Butte, Montana, were loyal to the Griggs' sweet corn.

By 1942 growing demand forced the brothers to modernize their packing methods. Corn that had been pre-cooled in ice water was packed into crates, then more ice was loaded on top as the corn traveled in trucks and railroad cars to its destination. In 1943 a new quick-freeze factory was built in their town of Ontario, Oregon, by the Bridgford Company of California. Beginning in 1947 the brothers began sending much of their sweet corn to the factory. Within a year, they were shipping their fresh frozen sweet corn as far away as Washington, D.C., and Los Angeles. Production and sales tripled. They expanded their sweet corn acreage to 2,000 for the 1949 season.

However, problems were brewing at the Bridgford plant, which had evidently been designed without consideration of the area's climate and agricultural conditions—or even its employees: the plant had no heat, parking lots, or lunchroom. The plant closed down in September 1948 and was in bankruptcy court by early 1950. Realizing that frozen foods were the wave of the future, the Grigg brothers—whose operation became the Oregon Frozen Foods Company in 1951—set their sights on purchasing the bankrupt plant. When the foreclosure sale was held in 1952 the Griggs were prepared with money they had raised by mortgaging their homes and property, but the bidding drove the plant's price up to nearly twice what they had expected. The Griggs had inspired much confidence over the years, though, and soon other investors were flocking to join the venture. One man even sold his farm to help secure the plant.

After the purchase, the Griggs realized that their processing season would have to expand to justify the expense of the plant. They initially tried small amounts of seasonal fruits and vegetables, but they needed more volume. In eastern Oregon and southwestern Idaho there was one big money crop that seemed to vie with the brother's sweet corn: potatoes. So in 1952, Ore-Ida Potato Products Incorporated was created as another operating company, leasing the plant for use when season's corn processing was done.

Oregon Frozen Foods still had hurdles ahead. Having mortgaged everything they owned, the Griggs had to make the round of banks to secure operating capital. It soon became clear that not everyone shared their vision. Many lenders balked at the idea of frozen potatoes. Wouldn't the potatoes turn black? Frozen food wouldn't sell. What folks wanted was fresh. The young company ended up using raw potatoes as collateral for the loans it needed. With the loans in place, about 100 employees began running the potatoes through a carrot peeler. The company's first French fried potato was processed in 1952. The following year, Tater Tots were born.

Part of the genius of Tater Tots was the fact that it made a by-product into a top-selling product. Nephi Grigg took the potato slivers left over from shaving potatoes into French fries—which ordinarily were sold for a pittance and used for livestock feed—ground them together, added flour and spices, and pushed the mix through holes cut into plywood. Then he cooked the results in hot oil. The brothers were so enthusiastic about the future of frozen foods that they traveled to woo potential customers themselves, with briefcases filled with samples of their products in dry ice.

The company's main business was soon the processing and sale of frozen potato products. From 1951 to 1960 the company expanded dramatically. It was producing about 300,000 pounds of saleable potatoes a day, which requires twice that amount in raw potatoes, creating a serious storage problem. Plants processing potatoes could only run from August through April until long-haul storage was born in the 1960s, after which the company could receive shipments from California throughout the year to keep the potato processing running year-round. In 1960, with the company's products selling throughout the United States and into parts of Canada, a second factory was built in Burley, Idaho, to meet production demands. The new $3 million plant produced 500,000 pounds of potatoes a day.

Until this point, Ore-Ida had been a web of small companies, many run by friends and family of the Grigg brothers. In 1961 these entities were merged, becoming Ore-Ida Foods, Inc, and the company went public, raising almost $2.5 million. With the fresh funds, another facility was purchased in Burley; later another plant was built in Greenville, Michigan.

In 1962 Ore-Ida began processing and marketing French fried onion rings and fresh frozen chopped onions, made from sweet Spanish onions. These, and fresh frozen corn, quickly became high-volume items. Although depressed potato prices and other factors generated a net operating loss for the six-month period that ended in April, sales were still increasing and a new onion processing addition was completed to meet the demand for French fried onion rings. Sales grew from more than $24 million in 1963 to nearly $31 million in 1964, and the company's plants were transforming one million pounds of raw produce into packaged products every day. Between 1964 and 1965 the company doubled its capacity again, and the Griggs brothers, who found the sudden growth dizzying, decided to sell.

Ore-Ida was purchased by H. J. Heinz Company, which was also going through growing pains in 1965 as it evaluated its potential for becoming a giant in the frozen food industry, which appeared to be poised for explosive growth. Ore-Ida provided a perfect opportunity for Heinz to diversify and to expand its position in frozen foods. In a stock swap worth about $27 million, Ore-Ida became a division of Heinz, under the name Ore-Ida Foods, Inc.

Not long after the acquisition, Ore-Ida began losing money, which was a shock to everyone familiar with the company. When Heinz dispatched a team to investigate, they discovered a system of mismanagement that included contracting from farms that company executives had a stake in at inflated prices. Despite Heinz's reputation for having a hands-off policies with subsidiaries, it axed virtually all of Ore-Ida's senior management in a single bloody Monday in August 1967.

Nephi Grigg, who had been the company's president since 1951 and had served on the Heinz's board of directors since the merger, left Ore-Ida in 1969 to pursue other interests. Grigg went on to spend much time in the service of his Mormon faith, serving as a bishop, a Stake High Council member, and a mission president. Robert K. Pedersen became president and CEO of Ore-Ida. Pedersen invested in new products, new facilities, new packaging, and extensive market research. The company gained market share, moving from a roughly 20 to 50 percent share of the frozen potato business between 1971 and 1982, and plants continued to be built, expanded, and upgraded. In 1975 Ore-Ida unveiled its first national network television campaign, which marked the first time any frozen potato brand had appeared on television.

In 1977 Paul Corddry became president. That year, Ore-Ida purchased Baltino Foods, an Ohio-based company that manufactured frozen and refrigerated pizza products, and changed its name to Massilon. Corddry continued the company's efforts to build brand recognition; in 1978 alone, $15 million was spent for ads on television and in women's magazines.

Heinz acquired Foodways National, Inc., that same year and made Foodways a subsidiary of Ore-Ida. Operating two factories in Connecticut and New York, Foodways produced Weight Watchers frozen entrees. At the time, Foodways was considered "the Listerine of frozen dinners," as Corddry put it, featuring "lousy food, medicinal-looking packaging." Ore-Ida spent more than a year repackaging and improving the product line before developing new products. Competition between Weight Watchers and Lean Cuisine helped build the category, and Foodways eventually overtook Lean Cuisine to bring a steady stream of profits to Ore-Ida.

In 1980 Ore-Ida purchased Gagliardi Brothers, which produced a regional line of Steak-umm products. Although sales of Ore-Ida's frozen potato product line did not increase, profits doubled between 1982 and 1987, largely because of Foodways' success. In 1987 Foodways' momentum dropped, and a huge potato crop depressed prices—in fact, the crop was so huge that supermarkets were giving away free bags of potatoes. Ore-Ida recovered in the following years, though, with market share going from 44 to back up to 50 percent between 1988 and 1991.

Meanwhile, the company continued to expand its product line, both through acquisition and in-house product development. Bavarian Specialty Foods was purchased by Heinz and added to Ore-Ida's family in 1989, as was Celestial Farms in 1990. The following year Heinz formed Weight Watchers Food Company, which included Foodways. Ore-Ida also developed new lines of twice-baked potatoes, microwave potatoes, and battered fries.

In 1991 Heinz also acquired JL Foods, a major supplier of frozen foods to the food-service industry. Three of JL's six subsidiaries—Delicious Foods, Oregon Farms, and Chef Francisco—were integrated into Ore-Ida. At the same time, 1991 was another rough year for the company, as economic recession combined with another boom crop. Ore-Ida lost three to four share points and profits sagged. Between 1992 and 1993 Ore-Ida closed plants, consolidated operations, and sold interests.

Ore-Ida became the number one seller of frozen appetizers overnight through Heinz's $90 million acquisition of Moore's and Domani brands from Clorox's Food Service Products Division. In 1994 Ore-Ida sold its Steak-umm business in order to expand its production of pasta and sandwich lines. Microwaveable mashed potatoes were introduced, as were Fast Fries, the first retail oven-baked product to replicate the taste and texture of fast-food restaurant French fries.

In 1995 Nephi Grigg died. The Tater Tots he invented some forty years earlier still sell like mad.

Further Reading:

Foa Dienstag, Eleanor, *In Good Company: 125 Years at the Heinz Table,* Warner Books, 1994.

"H.J. Heinz Agrees to Buy Ore-Ida for $30 Million," *Wall Street Journal,* May 21, 1965, p. 5.

"The Ore-Ida Story," *Sunday Argus Observer,* June 5, 1983, Sec. E.

—Carol I. Keeley

Otis Elevator Company, Inc.

10 Farm Springs
Farmington, Connecticut 06032
U.S.A.
(203) 676-5400
Fax: (203) 676-6973

Wholly Owned Subsidiary of United Technologies Corporation
Incorporated: 1867 as Otis Brothers & Co.
Employees: 66,000
Sales: $4.64 billion
SICs: 3534 Elevators and Moving Stairways

Otis Elevator Company, Inc. is the world's largest company in the manufacture, maintenance, and service of elevators, escalators, moving walkways, and other horizontal transportation systems. After over a century in business, Otis has more than 1.2 million elevators and escalators in operation throughout the world, including eight of the world's ten tallest buildings and 60 of the tallest 100. By the mid-1990s Otis could boast that its products were available virtually worldwide; in fact, with 25 major manufacturing facilities in 16 countries and 1,700 offices spanning the globe, 85 percent of its business was generated outside the United States. Otis became a subsidiary of United Technologies Corporation in 1975.

Although vertical hoisting devices date back as far as the construction of the pyramids in Egypt, they all contained the same drawback: if the supporting rope or cable snapped, the platform plummeted to the ground. Vermont-born Elisha Graves Otis, a mechanic living in Yonkers, New York, invented the first safety hoist in 1852. He attached saw-toothed rachet bars to each of the four side guide rails and placed a wagon spring on top of the platform. When the lifting cable was attached to the upper bar of the spring, the pull from the heavy platform made the spring taut enough to keep it from touching the rachet bars. If the cable snapped, the tension on the spring would be released, and each end would engage the ratchet bars, locking the platform in place and preventing it from falling.

Armed with two unsolicited $300 elevator orders, Otis opened his own factory in Yonkers on September 20, 1853. The following year he demonstrated his invention at the Crystal Palace Exposition in New York City. By the end of 1856 he had sold more than 40 elevators, all for use in carrying freight. The next year he installed the first passenger elevator—with a completely enclosed car—in a five-storied New York retail building. A classic Yankee tinkerer, Otis developed his elevator design without a drawing board, blueprint, or prototype model, illustrating his invention only to the degree required for a Patent Office application. But his talents did not extend to business. When Otis died in 1861 of "nervous depression and diphtheria," he left an estate of only $5,000, counterbalanced by $8,200 in debts.

Otis's two sons, Charles and Norton, took over the business, which became known as Otis Brothers & Co. Between them they amassed 53 patents for elevator design and safety devices. By 1872 the company had built more than 2,000 steam-powered elevators and taken in more than a million dollars. In 1878 Otis introduced a faster, more economical hydraulic elevator. During 1880–81 the company received orders to install elevators in the Capitol, the White House, and in the Washington Monument. The year 1889 marked the introduction of the first successful direct-connected electric-powered elevator and the exhibition of the first escalator—the term was an Otis trademark until 1950—at the 1900 Paris Exposition. In 1903–04 Otis introduced the gearless-traction electric elevator, a design that remains essentially unchanged today.

The Otis Elevator Co. was formed in 1898 from the $11-million merger of Otis Brothers & Co. and 14 other elevator companies. This proved so powerful a combine that in 1906 the company had to agree to stop collusive bidding and other restraints of trade. Otis started buying established firms overseas as early as 1902. By 1912, when net income came to $883,317, the company owned seven factories in the United States and by 1924 had subsidiaries in Canada, Germany, Italy, and Belgium. To offset slow sales during recessions, Otis began selling contracts to service and maintain its installations in 1922. Net income reached nearly $8.4 million by 1929 before dipping sharply with the advent of the Great Depression. The company lost money for the first time in 1933 and 1934, yet continued to pay out dividends, an unbroken tradition since 1903.

The first third of the century saw constant improvements in Otis elevators. In 1915 the company introduced a self-levelling device that allowed the elevator platform to stop exactly at floor level. A push-button system introduced in 1924 made stops and speed automatic rather than at the option of the operator. When the Empire State Building, the world's tallest building, was completed in 1931, its Otis elevators were capable of a record speed of 1,200 feet per minute. The following year Otis installed the first double-deck elevator in a Wall Street office tower; it featured eight double-decked cars that stopped at two floors at the same time.

During World War II Otis filled military orders. The war generated not only orders for elevators, but also for rangefinders and tank and aircraft-engine components. Defense contracts continued to be important during the Korean War era, accounting for 22 percent of Otis's business in 1953.

Even before World War II push-button elevators were common in apartment houses, private residences, and small office buildings for many years. In 1948 Otis introduced the improved Autotronic system for commercial installations. Electronic controls were sufficient to operate the cars, and a computer directed a bank of cars to handle traffic most efficiently. Two years later Otis introduced Autotronic elevators that could function without an attendant. By 1956 the position of elevator attendant was no longer a job with a rosy future; every major commercial building using Otis elevators wanted Autotronic equipment. Unlike the earlier push-button models, these elevators were large, fast, and could change speeds and adjust their schedules to suit traffic demands, bypassing floors when fully loaded. Moreover, Otis projected an annual saving of $7,000 per car in labor costs. In 1956 it did some $20 million worth of conversion work from manual to automatic.

Despite these developments, the decade following World War II was a period of some stagnation for Otis. Although net sales passed $90 million in 1948 and approached $120 million by 1954, net income fell from $12.1 million to $9.6 million. In 1952 Otis's share of the nation's new elevator business dropped to an unusually low 40 percent due to high prices. The company had to cut its operating margin from 20 to 11 percent in order to regain market share from its competitors. Other problems identified with making elevators were the cyclical nature of the construction industry and growing suburbanization, which in this period was characterized by ranch-style homes and single-story shopping centers.

To jump-start its flagging business, Otis began to diversify. Its first outside acquisition since 1898 was the purchase of Transmitter Equipment Manufacturing Co. (Temco) in 1953. Temco, which held a contract to make electronic pilot trainers, became Otis's defense and industrial division. The following year, Otis bought fork-lift truck manufacturer Baker-Raulang Co., which became its truck division. And toward the end of 1955 Otis began producing automatic bowling pinsetters. None of these ventures would prove profitable over the long run: Temco was a poor performer and actually lost money in 1963; Baker lost money every year but one between 1955 and 1961; and after a strong start the pinsetter operation fell into the red and was sold in 1963. Between 1955 and 1968 Otis's net sales increased fourfold, from $121 million to $481 million, but its net income rose only from $11.9 million to $22.1 million during the same period.

In 1968, a year after Otis installed 255 elevators and 71 escalators in New York City's newly completed World Trade Center, the company held nearly half the U.S. elevator market. It continued to look to other areas for profit, however. In a 1968 *Forbes* article, President Fayette S. Dunn explained: "Elevator prices are down. With everyone trying to increase their market share, we just can't make the money on contracts we should." Between 1967 and 1970 Otis acquired five companies involved in materials handling: York Manufacturing Co., a maker of large lift trucks; Moto-Truc Co., producer of smaller lift trucks; West Coast Machinery, manufacturer of postal and in-plant vehicles, golf carts, and personnel carriers; Euclid Crane & Hoist Co., builder of hoists and cranes; and Saxby, S.A., a French manufacturer of hoists and cranes. In 1969 the company established the Diversified Systems Division to apply elevator and escalator technology to automated automobile-parking, container-handling, and warehouse systems.

The company also was actively engaged in designing and manufacturing automated horizontal moving systems. Otis's "Trav-O-Lator" moving walkways were engineered to carry people, horizontally or on an incline, quickly and comfortably at airline terminals and other points where large numbers of people had to be moved without congestion.

By 1973 Otis had passed $800 million in sales. Maintaining plants in 17 countries, and dependent on overseas operations for 37 percent of its net income, Otis's share of the elevator market in low-rise buildings had increased from 19 percent to 30 percent in five years. Earnings had risen every year since 1968. The backlog of orders in March 1973 was $1.1 billion, an all-time high. Net sales reached a record $1.1 billion in 1974—more than half of which was generated overseas—and net income a record $43.5 million. Among its foreign operations in 1975 were five special glass-walled observation elevators for the world's tallest free-standing structure, Toronto's 1,815-foot-tall CN Tower.

Otis's rapid expansion overseas was not without hazards. In 1976 the company revealed to a federal agency that it estimated it had made between $5 million and $6 million in improper payments during the past five years, some of them to foreign government officials and employees. These payments were made in connection with installations in large buildings where government involvement was substantial and bribery and kickbacks were allegedly normal procedures. In 1975 65 percent of Otis's $752.7 million in new orders had come from foreign sources.

In October 1975 United Technologies Corporation (UTC) made a cash offer of $42 a share for more than 55 percent of Otis's stock, which was trading for $37.63 a share at the time. UTC's motivation was to end its heavy dependence on military contracts at the end of the Vietnam War. Otis's management at first resisted the offer but dropped its opposition in November after UTC agreed to pay an additional $2 per share and buy up all Otis's common stock. The cost was estimated at $276 million. The untendered shares were exchanged for shares of a new convertible preferred United Technologies stock under a 1976 merger.

Otis continued to grow as a UTC subsidiary. Sales volume passed $1.5 billion in 1980, $2 billion in 1986, $3 billion in 1989, and $4 billion in 1990. The flagship Yonkers factory, parts of which dated back to 1868, was deemed obsolete and abandoned in 1983. An elevator test tower and engineering center was completed in Bristol, Connecticut, four years later. This exceptionally slender, 383-foot, 29-story, $20 million structure was just 54 feet across but accommodated 11 elevators and an escalator. The structure, which helped Otis develop models that rode more smoothly, operated more efficiently, and broke down less often, was its first North American test tower; others were located in France, Italy, Japan, Spain, India, and China.

Otis unveiled its "Elevonic 101" system—the first elevator control system using microprocessors to control every aspect of elevator operations—in 1979. The Elevonic 401, introduced in 1981, was the first control system with synthesized speech, information display, and security systems. It dispatched cars in response to variations in building traffic as they occurred. The Elevonic 411 system, introduced in 1990 for gearless elevators, was capable of modifying its software-based dispatching rules for more responsive elevator service. When linked to a new computerized control system, it enabled building managers to coordinate the performance of up to 64 elevators.

New artificial-intelligence software patented by Otis in 1993 used "fuzzy logic" to estimate how many people were waiting for elevators at a given moment in office buildings or hospitals where several elevators were operational and traffic patterns changed throughout the day. The program tracked traffic flow by compiling information about time elapsed between stops at the same floor, the number of buttons pushed by people boarding a car, and the car's changing weight load. It then combined this data to arrive at an estimate of the number waiting and decided which car to send—not necessarily the closest one. The first Otis elevator system incorporating fuzzy-logic modules was installed at the Hyatt Osaka Regency Hotel in Osaka, Japan, which opened in 1994.

OTISLINE, a computerized, 24-hour-a-day dispatch service for mechanics, was introduced in 1983 to aid the world's largest elevator-service work force. In 1985 an Otis people-mover system was introduced to connect Harbour Island and downtown Tampa, Florida. People movers were also installed by Otis in Serfus, Austria, and Sun City, South Africa. In 1992 the company completed a similar "horizontal elevator" in the new Tokyo international airport at Narita, Japan. Like the Florida shuttle, it combined elevator and Hovercraft technology, transporting a total of 9,800 standing passengers and their luggage 900 feet between two terminals each hour. One-car trains moved at 13 miles an hour on a half-inch cushion of air.

In 1984, when Otis accounted for 20,000 of the 100,000 elevators sold in the world each year, the company signed a joint venture to build elevators in China; a decade later, it had three Chinese joint-venture plants. In 1990 Otis renewed a relationship with Russia it had not engaged in since providing Czar Nicholas II with three elevators in the early part of the century. By the end of 1992 Otis had formed four Russian and one Ukrainian joint ventures to manufacture, install, and maintain elevators and was maintaining about 20 percent of the elevators in these two countries by 1994. It opened its first major manufacturing plant in Southeast Asia—in Malaysia—in 1993. The following year, the U.S. government lifted its trade embargo with Vietnam and Otis negotiated two joint ventures with Vietnamese companies to sell, install, service, and maintain elevators throughout that country.

Otis had 24 percent of the world market for elevators and escalators in 1990, twice as large a share as its nearest competitor. By then the company had installed 1.2 million elevators. But it was not resting on its laurels. Its president, Karl Krapek, told a correspondent for the London-based magazine *Business,* "We are one of the few American industries that can compete long-term and successfully against the Japanese. There are very few left: jet engines, helicopters, and elevators. Boy, we have to do that. And we will do that." By late 1992 Otis had raised its market share in Japan to 13 percent, compared to 3 percent 20 years earlier.

With the end of the cold war, Otis replaced aircraft-engine manufacturer Pratt & Whitney as UTC's largest income producer. UTC lost money in 1991 and 1992, mainly because of Pratt & Whitney's problems. To cut costs the company modernized manufacturing techniques. Otis was one of the UTC units to abandon standard assembly-line production in favor of worker teams that assembled products from start to finish. UTC claimed that by giving workers more responsibility it reduced mistakes and eliminated downtime. As an example, the company noted that workers at an Otis plant in France were, in 1993, turning out a top-selling elevator in five days, compared to five weeks in 1991.

In 1994 Otis's revenues of $4.64 billion comprised nearly 22 percent of UTC's total revenue, while its operating profits of $421 million were more than 27 percent of the parent company's total. It held 23 percent of the world market in new elevator equipment in 1994 and was selling about 39,000 elevators and escalators annually. Otis also serviced about 790,000 elevators and escalators. Two-thirds of its approximately 66,000 employees were field installers and mechanics averaging 15 years of company experience. Installation and maintenance accounted for 61 percent of Otis's revenue in 1992 and an even greater proportion of company profits.

By the mid-1990s Otis's major manufacturing facilities were located around the world—in the United States, Mexico, Brazil, Great Britain, France, Germany, Italy, Spain, the Czech Republic, Russia, Japan, China, India, Taiwan, Malaysia, and Australia. With an eye towards the future of transportation system technology, Otis invested more than $100 million during 1994 in engineering and research and development.

Further Reading:

Drain, Sharon Cramer, "A Mechanic Gave the World a Lift," *American History Illustrated,* November 1987, pp. 42–50.

"For Otis: More Electronics," *Business Week,* October 17, 1953, pp. 119–20.

"Going Down, Please," *Time,* November 24, 1975, p. 92.

"How to Make Mistakes and Still Prosper," *Forbes,* May 1, 1964, p. 35.

"How Otis Gets the Business," *Fortune,* July 1954, pp. 100–03, 124, 126.

Jackson, Donald Dale, "Elevating Thoughts from Elisha Otis and Fellow Uplifters," *Smithsonian,* November 1989, pp. 211–18.

Kleinfield, N. R., "Otis's '29 Stories Full of What-Ifs,' " *New York Times,* July 2, 1989, p. III4.

Lawless, John, "Mighty Otis Stays on Top," *Business,* November 1990, pp. 131–32, 134.

"Otis Goes on an Acquisition Ride," *Business Week,* June 6, 1970, pp. 132, 134.

"Otis—Going Up!" *Financial World,* May 9, 1973, p. 12.

Pinder, Jeanne B., "Fuzzy Thinking Has Merits When It Comes to Elevators," *New York Times,* September 22, 1993, pp. D1, D9.

Shipman, Alan, "Otis Seizes the High Ground," *International Management,* November 1992, pp. 50–52.

Smart, Tim, "UTC Gets a Lift from Its Smaller Engines," *Business Week,* December 20, 1993, pp. 109–10.

"Why Go Outside?" *Forbes,* May 15, 1968, p. 82.

—Robert Halasz

Packard Bell Electronics, Inc.

102 Canoga Ave.
Chatsworth, California 91311
U.S.A.
(818) 865-1555
Fax: (818) 865-0176

Private Company
Incorporated: 1986
Employees: 1,200
Sales: $1.25 billion
SICs: 3751 Electronic Computers

Packard Bell Electronics, Inc. was the largest vendor of personal computers (PCs) in the United States in 1995, and the leading seller of PCs through retail establishments. The company has grown explosively since its inception in 1986 through aggressive and innovative marketing strategies. By the mid-1990s, Packard Bell was also in the process of a rapid expansion in the European market.

Although Packard Bell Electronics was officially founded in 1986, the name Packard Bell had its origins in the early 20th century. In the 1920s the name emerged as a popular brand of console radios—then a chief form of electronic entertainment. The Packard Bell name was kept alive during the mid-1900s as a brand name in the television industry. Like most U.S. consumer electronics firms, however, Packard Bell deteriorated during the 1960s and 1970s in the wake of industry consolidation and foreign competition. The struggling Packard Bell Co. was purchased by Teledyne in 1968, but was effectively dead by the middle of the next decade, consisting only of some outdated facilities and trade names.

The company languished until 1985, when it caught the eye of Beny Alagem, a 32-year-old Israeli immigrant and naturalized U.S. citizen. Alagem was intrigued, not by the remnants of the Packard Bell company itself, but rather by the once-venerable Packard Bell brand name. Alagem approached Teledyne, which agreed to sell the rights to the name for less than $100,000. His idea was to use the name to market the latest breed of hot-selling consumer electronics, personal computers. ''The company had a rich history and a good name for quality products,'' Alagem recalled in *Forbes.* ''Buying that name was a stroke of genius,'' George Pursglove, a HQ Office Warehouse executive, stated in the same article. ''Older customers think Packard Bell is the company that made radios and televisions. Younger ones think it's the people who made cars, or telephones, or Hewlett-Packard.''

Joining Alagem in his latest business venture were two long-time business partners, 32-year-old Jason Barzilay and Alex Sandel, then 42. The three Israeli-born partners had moved to southern California in the 1970s because of its thriving Israeli business community and educational institutions. Alagem, then in his 20s, took business and finance courses at California Polytechnic Institute. He later joined with Sandel, an electronics engineer, to start a semiconductor distribution business. Barzilay entered the picture in 1983. He was also operating an electronics distribution business at the time, but had formerly worked at Burroughs and Rockwell International in engineering and sales positions. The three men combined their companies to form Cal Circuit Abco Inc., a Woodland Hills, California-based distributor of semiconductors and computer peripherals. By the mid-1980s the successful enterprise was generating more than $500 million in annual revenues.

When Alagem purchased the Packard Bell name in 1985 the PC industry was beginning to explode. While IBM had pioneered the industry, the number of industry participants offering inexpensive IBM clones was proliferating. Alagem and his partners believed that the PC business was moving away from a high-end retail environment and toward a commodity industry characterized by low margins and high volume. And they wanted to profit from the coming boom in computer sales. Alagem knew that Asian suppliers could produce customized computers and peripheral equipment inexpensively, and he and his partners already had experience in the distribution end of the industry. So, in 1986 the three men formed Packard Bell Electronics Inc., contracting both with their Asian suppliers to design a product line specifically for their company and with several Asian manufacturers, including Tatung Co. of Taiwan and Samsung of Korea, to build the machines.

The first Packard Bell personal computer hit store shelves in 1987. Unfortunately, the product was just one of several IBM clones entering an increasingly crowded market. Because Packard Bell couldn't rely on technological advantages or patent protection, it had to depend primarily on merchandising savvy and low prices to separate its products from those offered by the competition. To that end, the three entrepreneurs developed and executed a cunning and successful stratagem. For starters, they began selling their products under the nostalgic Packard Bell marketing theme, ''America grew up listening to us. It still does.'' That established slogan, along with the recognized Packard Bell name, gave the company's computers instant credibility—a rare asset in the burgeoning personal computer industry.

In addition, Packard Bell's machines proffered numerous innovations that, at the time, represented notable breakthroughs in the personal computer industry. For example, Packard Bell computers were among the first to come equipped with both 3 ½-inch and 5 ¼-inch diskette drives, which smoothed the transition to smaller drives for users replacing older computers. Furthermore, standard Packard Bell's PCs were outfitted with a comparatively large 40-megabyte hard drive, yet were often offered at a lower price than competing brands with a smaller memory capacity. Importantly, Packard Bell became the first company to pre-install software with its computers. This pivotal innovation spared customers the tedious hassle of loading the operating system and application software, and it represented a giant leap toward the industry's goal of delivering a computer that could be used by technologically inexperienced customers straight out of the box.

Even more important to Packard Bell's success during the late 1980s than low cost and unique features was its distribution method. Prior to the late 1980s, almost all PCs were sold in computer stores or through sales representatives. Packard Bell bucked the industry standard when it became one of the first PC manufacturers to focus on mass retail sales channels. It sold its computers almost exclusively through giant retail stores like Sears, as well as discount chains, warehouse stores, and electronics and appliance centers. Major computer makers, clinging to the belief that consumers would continue to value service over price, scoffed at the mass market concept. Thus, as the percentage of PCs sold through mass-market channels increased from four percent in 1987 to 12 percent in 1992, Packard Bell rode at the top of the wave. By 1992, in fact, Packard Bell controlled a leading 26 percent of that distribution channel, and it would boost that share to more than 45 percent by the mid-1990s.

As Packard Bell's market share surged, so did sales and profits. By 1989, only two years after starting up, Packard Bell generated an estimated $600 million in annual sales. That figure jumped to $700 million in 1991, despite a U.S. economic downturn in 1990 and 1991. Meanwhile, Packard Bell continued to penetrate markets with new products, low prices, and unconventional distribution channels. In 1992, for example, the company unveiled a local area network (LAN) system that, in contrast to the competition, was ready to hook up and use straight out of the box. Simultaneously, Packard Bell introduced a new version of its top-of-the-line PC that could be upgraded by simply plugging it into a new central processing unit, which meant that the system owner could get the equivalent of a new computer for about $300.

Such consumer-oriented features helped to earn Packard Bell the highest marks in the industry in consumer satisfaction, according to a 1990–91 survey by Verity Group, a market research company. Augmenting Packard Bell's reputation was its comprehensive customer support system. The company offered round-the-clock, toll-free telephone support for buyers of all of its computers. The system, called Infinitech, offered the option of recorded answers to users' technical questions. Furthermore, all Packard Bell systems were backed by a one-year warranty complete with on-site service. Customers could also obtain help through Packard Bell bulletin board services on Prodigy and Compuserve.

Reflecting the wisdom of Packard Bell's overall strategy during the early 1990s, sales rose to more than $900 million in 1992, and then to an estimated $1.25 billion in 1993. Likewise, the company's work force leapt to more than 700. Packard Bell's ace in the hole continued to be its dominance of mass market retail channels. Success in that arena had pushed its overall U.S. market share to 5.3 percent by 1992, followed by an impressive 6.7 percent in 1993, making Packard Bell the fourth-leading personal computer supplier in the United States behind IBM, Apple, and Compaq. Market share gains were becoming increasingly difficult for Packard Bell, though, in light of the fact that its competitors were borrowing heavily from its play book. Indeed, during the early 1990s several of the industry leaders followed Packard Bell's lead by expanding into mass retail channels, offering easy-to-use bundled products, and slashing prices. In turn, Packard Bell began pressuring industry leaders by diversify from its narrow low-cost PC market and using its proven merchandising tactics to penetrate the market's high end.

In addition to broadening the scope of its product line in the early 1990s, Packard Bell began pursuing sales overseas. The company started selling in Europe late in 1991; by 1992 it had found that the strategy that had worked in the United States was also applicable in much of Europe. In fact, in 1992 Packard Bell garnered roughly $100 million—ten percent of sales—from its European operations and expected to double that figure the following year. To that end, in 1993 the company completed a 75,000-square-foot facility in the Netherlands that employed 250 people, including a customer support group providing technical assistance in 12 languages. As it had in the United States, Packard Bell took an early lead in the European mass market computer retail industry. In 1993 it had established 1,500 retail outlets throughout 13 countries.

Although Packard Bell shipped almost two million units per year going into 1994, some analysts doubted the long-term potential of the company's marketing strategy. Because Packard Bell focused on retail sales, its price advantage was increasingly challenged by low-overhead PC makers that sold exclusively through direct mail and catalogs. A corollary of this retail strategy was that Packard Bell suffered relatively higher product-return rates by industry standards due to the liberal product return and exchange policies adhered to by most retail establishments. In 1991, for instance, Packard Bell recorded gross revenue of $819 million, but that was before accounting for $143 million in returns by customers. Despite critics' concerns, Packard Bell continued to outpace analyst projections through 1994 and was constantly adjusting to new market trends.

Evidencing Packard Bell's sensitivity to shifting consumer demands going into the mid-1990s were a number of new products. Most notable was the company's introduction of the first mass-produced, fully configured multimedia system offered through mass marketing channels. The system was offered under different names and with slightly different configurations as part of an effort to appeal to a variety of customer groups. The company also began selling software under the brand name Active Imagination. Offerings included six titles for children that were designed to help build computer skills. In 1994, Packard Bell began selling its Spectria computer line, which Alagem referred to as the "centerpiece of every home." The Spectria included a full-function multimedia PC, CD player, stereo, FM radio, TV and video player, telephone answering system, and fax/modem.

In 1994 Packard Bell more than doubled its 1993 production, shipping 2.1 million units. Gross revenues increased nearly three-fold, to a record $3 billion. Those figures pushed Packard Bell to number three in domestic PC sales, behind Compaq and

IBM. Then, after an incredible 37 percent rate of growth in late 1994 and early 1995, Packard Bell scooped up nearly 13 percent of the U.S. personal computer market and surged to the lead of the industry. In addition, Packard Bell was far and away the leading distributor of PCs through mass retail channels with roughly 50 percent of that market by one estimate. And it was among the leading PC distributors in Europe, where sales were skyrocketing. In 1995 Packard Bell continued to serve as the "industry bellwether," as the *Wall Street Journal* described the company. Early that year, for example, it introduced the first PC with dual CD-ROM drives, one among several new features. Alagem and his partners expected to sustain such impressive growth into the decade, barring an industry downturn.

Further Reading:

Apodaca, Patrice, "Packard Bell Strategy Withstanding Slump," *Los Angeles Times,* January 7, 1992, p. D1.

"Blue-Sky Forecast," *PC Week,* December 6, 1993, p. A7.

Britt, Russ, "1993 Has Been a 'Doubly' Good Year at Packard Bell," *Daily Record-Wooster,* December 20, 1993, section BUS.

Carlton, Jim, "Packard Bell Prospers Despite PC Industry Shake-Up; Computer Maker's Secret of Success: Focusing on the Consumer Market," *Wall Street Journal,* June 14, 1994, p. B4.

Kamionek, Ted, "Packard Bell Launches the New Spectra Line of All-in-One Multimedia Systems," *Business Wire, June 14, 1994.*

Little, Philip, "Packard Bell Establishes European Headquarters in the Netherlands," *Business Wire,* May 20, 1993.

Marks, Don, "Packard Bell Electronics Inc.," *Datamation,* June 15, 1993, p. 103.

Ryan, Ken, "Nobody's Fool: Packard Bell, Pioneer of Computer Retail Distribution, Comes Home to Roost," *HFN: Weekly Newspaper for the Home Furnishing Network,* February 13, 1995, p. 70.

Ryan, Kimberly, "Packard Bell Electronics Inc.," *Datamation,* June 15, 1993, p. 78.

Weiner, Steve, "New Wine in Vintage Bottles," *Forbes,* May 14, 1990, p. 122.

White, Todd, "Postponed Packard Bell IPO Still Can't Find a Date," *Los Angeles Business Journal,* June 8, 1992, p. 22.

——, "Will Packard Bell's Share Sell as Well as Its Inexpensive PCs?" *Los Angeles Business Journal,* April 6, 1992, p. 1.

—Dave Mote

PEARLE VISION™

Pearle Vision, Inc.

2543 Royal Lane
Dallas, Texas
U.S.A.
(214) 277-5000
Fax: (214) 277-5962

Wholly Owned Subsidiary of Grand Metropolitan plc
Incorporated: 1961
Employees: 4,000
Sales: $601 million
SICs: 5955 Optical Goods Stores; 6794 Patent Owners & Lessors

Pearle Vision Inc., a subsidiary of British food conglomerate Grand Metropolitan plc, is one of the largest optical retailers in the world. In 1994 there were more than 900 Pearle Vision stores operating worldwide, including 720 U.S. outlets and about 180 stores in Canada, the Netherlands, and Belgium. About half of those stores were franchised. After reaching a downswing in profits in the late 1980s, Pearle returned to profitability once it restructured its operations during the early 1990s.

Pearle's rapid rise to leadership in the optical retail industry began in 1961, when Dr. Stanley Pearle opened the first Pearle Vision Center in Savannah, Georgia. Although the store was among many optical retail stores competing at the time, Pearle's shop was different and represented a major breakthrough in the eyecare industry. The shop's distinguishing characteristic was that it offered comprehensive, one-stop eyecare: It combined complete eye exams with an extensive selection of eyewear and convenient store hours. Thus, for the first time, a person could go into a store, get an eye exam and prescription, select a pair of glasses and pick up the finished glasses a few days later. The consumer benefited from not having to visit both an optometrist (eye doctor) and an optician (one that makes and sells eyeglasses and contact lenses). Dr. Pearle profited by providing both diagnostic and treatment services.

Pearle's innovative store was a hit, and he enjoyed immense growth and profits during the 1960s and 1970s. But his was not an overnight success story. Pearle was born in Pittsburgh in 1918 and graduated from high school in 1936. Because of the severe recession at the time, he was unable to attend college. Pearle was able to find a job, though, and later started optometry school in Chicago. He graduated in 1940 and headed back to Pennsylvania to take the optometry exam, but he ended up in Texas. ''I went back to Philadelphia to take the Pennsylvania State Board of Optometry exam. In those days, you had to wait two months before you knew whether you passed—an eternity for a young man waiting to start a career,'' Pearle recalled in company annals. ''A fellow optometrist suggested we both go to Texas where they announce the test results the next day. So, I scrounged up $100 for expenses and a train ticket to Texas, took the state board exam, and passed. Although I found out that I had passed the Pennsylvania State Board, I just never left Texas.''

Pearle started out in the optometry business, but his erratic career took several turns. He served a tour a duty with the U.S. Navy during World War II before returning to private practice in Corpus Christi, Texas. In 1948, he joined Lee Optical as a junior partner. He worked at Lee for ten years before striking out on his own in 1958. Pearle was still living in Texas at the time he decided to open his own shop. He was drawn to Savannah, Georgia, however, because he believed that the area offered greater opportunity. The move was profitable for Pearle, whose unique concept flourished. ''My idea was to create modern-looking optical shops that combined top-quality service and products, convenient locations, expanded hours, competitive prices, and a better selection of eyewear styles,'' related Pearle. ''Before that, eyeglass wearers had only a few styles to choose from, and all the dispensing was done out of a small area in the optometrist's office.''

Throughout the 1960s and 1970s, Dr. Pearle added to his chain of Pearle Vision Centers at a rapid clip. In addition to building new outlets, he developed the company by purchasing other optical stores. Importantly, Pearle was joined by two other industry innovators in 1971—Robert Hillman and his partner Larry Kohan. Hillman, the son of an optician, had opened his first eyewear store, in 1966, at the age of 23. Like Pearle Vision, the Hillman-Kohan chain expanded during the late 1960s by innovating. The partners are generally credited with inventing one-hour eyeglasses services and with helping to pioneer the trend toward eyecare superstores. By 1971, the Hillman-Kohan chain had swelled to 17 stores. Pearle became interested in both the stores and their founders. He approached Hillman and Kohan, who agreed to sell their chain to Pearle Vision for $7 million. Hillman and Kohan both stayed on at Pearle Vision and, throughout the 1970s, helped to take the Pearle Vision chain national. Hillman and Kohan left the organization in 1980 and started Eyelab, the first true eyeglasses superstore.

Pearle Vision expanded its one-stop shop outlets across the United States during the 1970s and early 1980s. Throughout the period, Pearle benefited from demographic, legal, and market trends that bolstered overall industry sales and profits. The Federal Government, for example, eased restrictions on advertising by optometrists. In addition, Pearle continued to innovate and create new opportunities. In 1981, for example, Pearle began franchising its stores as opposed to owning all of them: Franchisees paid Pearle a fee to use the respected Pearle Vision name and proven business format, and Pearle trained them and helped with purchasing, marketing, lab processing, distribution, and other aspects of the business. Similarly, in 1984, Pearle introduced its successful Managed Vision Care unit, which offered a comprehensive vision benefit service to managed health care providers. The Managed Vision Care plan allowed managed care companies to provide benefits such as prepaid exams and optical materials for as little as $5 per member per year.

After more than 20 years of steady growth, the Dallas-based Pearle Vision was among the largest optical retailers in the world with stores throughout the United States. But it was destined to increase in size even further. Indeed, in September of 1985, Pearle Vision was purchased by Grand Metropolitan plc. Grand Metropolitan was one of the largest international companies in the United Kingdom and was a global leader in the food and beverage industry. Grand Metropolitan considered Pearle Vision a worthy diversification, and it believed that it could use its own financial might to help Pearle dominate the increasingly consolidated retail optical industry. The 68-year-old Dr. Pearle remained active in the company as a consultant and as a representative in Pearle Vision's government relations.

Backed by Grand's massive capital base, Pearle Vision executives launched an aggressive expansion initiative during the late 1980s. They engineered the acquisition of a number of smaller chains in an effort to boost Pearle's market share and increase the company's economies of scale. By 1990, the Pearle chain had ballooned to more than 1,000 stores, including outlets in Japan and Europe. Unfortunately, an economic downturn, beginning in the late 1980s and dragging through the early 1990s, hurt Pearle's sales. Augmenting Pearle's woes was increasing competition from both small and large rivals. Major chains like Precision LensCrafters and Cole Vision Corp. were aggressively competing with Pearle on a national scale, as were a growing number of giant warehouse and club chains. Likewise, a number of smaller regional operations were pressuring Pearle in local markets. For example, former Pearle Executive Hillman was back in the eyecare game with his latest venture, Hillman Eyes, a growing chain of eyecare discount superstores.

Partly as a result of intense competition and the sluggish economy, but also because Pearle had tried to grow too quickly in the eyes of some observers, Pearle's financial performance deteriorated. Sales rocketed to a record $670 million in 1991 as Pearle's chain of stores vaulted to 1,054. But profits were elusive. The company's financial details were buried in statistics reported by its parent, Grand Metropolitan, but the *Dallas Business Journal* reported that former Pearle executives estimated that Pearle lost money in 1991. Recognizing the urgency of the situation, Grand Metropolitan took bold steps to turn the company around. Grand effectively jettisoned Pearle's existing management team and brought in a new group. Bob Stetson was named president and chief executive and put in charge of the reorganization. Stetson had formerly served as an executive at Burger King, another Grand Metropolitan subsidiary.

Under Stetson's direction, Pearle slashed six of its nine layers of management as part of an effort to bring executives closer to customers. Furthermore, each division of the company was set up as a separate business unit, allowing each a greater degree of autonomy. Pearle laid off about 150 employees, including about 15 percent of the workers at its Dallas headquarters and four percent of its field force. Importantly, Stetson devised an ambitious franchising effort. He announced plans shortly after his arrival to begin selling franchises to people other than optometrists, opticians, and ophthalmologists. In theory, any entrepreneur would be considered a franchisee candidate. The strategy represented Pearle's response to the sweeping industry trend toward discounting. Stetson estimated that the plan could potentially double the number of Pearle outlets within five years and boost system-wide revenues into the $1.5 billion range. An important corollary of the tactic was that in the short term it would bring much needed cash into Pearle's coffers.

Grand Metropolitan didn't like Stetson's strategy. After less than a year, Stetson was replaced by David +Nardle. "It was more of a philosophical difference," explained Ron Nykiel, senior vice-president at Pearle, in the October 2, 1992 *Dallas Business Journal*. "Where Bob wanted quantity, David wanted quality." Nardle sustained Stetson's cost-cutting drive. He also pursued the franchising effort, although he tweaked it slightly. Rather than focusing on selling franchises to new store owners, Pearle would concentrate on making franchisees out of some of its existing store operators. By doing that, Pearle would enjoy an influx of up-front cash from the new store owners, albeit at the expense of long-term corporate revenue and earnings. The effort was also expected to improve the performance of formerly Pearle-owned stores because the new owner would have a greater incentive to run the business more efficiently.

Augmenting the franchise strategy was an ongoing program initiated by Pearle's human resource department in 1991. Vice-president for Human Resources, Roy J. Wilson had spearheaded an effort to change the compensation system for the managers of Pearle-owned stores. He was given the go ahead to implement his program after Pearle executives recognized that franchised stores consistently outperformed company-owned stores in profitability. To improve the performance of Pearle's store managers, Wilson and his subordinates devised a system that would empower the managers to make their own decisions and derive greater benefits from their successes. Part of the program entailed an unlimited bonus influenced by profit figures under the store manager's control. The initial results of the "Optipreneur" program were impressive. In the first few months, the 14 stores tested increased their profits an average of 185 percent. Some store managers earned bonuses of more than $100,000 in just seven months, and the overall test resulted in hundreds of thousands of dollars in extra profits. Wilson began implementing the program system-wide in 1993.

Grand Metropolitan shook up Pearle's management again early in 1994 when it hired Glenn E. Hammerle to take the helm. Hammerle left the CEO slot at Crown books to try his hand at hiking Pearle's performance. Under Hammerle's hand, Pearle continued to restructure its management and incentive systems during the early 1990s. It also streamlined its organization by selling off stores. By late 1994, in fact, the Pearle Vision chain had been reduced to just more than 900—down from a peak of about 1,100. The number of U.S. stores had fallen from 900 to 720. The remainder of Pearle's stores were located primarily in Canada, but also in the Netherlands and Belgium. Although Pearle lost its status as the world's largest optical retailer, in 1994, to LensCrafters, its restructuring paid off. The company reported about $10 million in profit in 1994 from $601 million in sales, which was Pearle's first surplus since 1990.

Industry trends suggested future growth for Pearle going into the mid-1990s. The business was becoming more competitive, but annual U.S. optical sales had surged from $8 billion in 1987 to $13 billion by 1994. Furthermore, large chains like Pearle had increased their share of the market from less than 30 percent in the late 1980s to more than 35 percent going into 1995. Industry sales were expected to continue rising throughout the 1990s and into the 2000s as the eyesight of aging baby boomers, who are generally willing to spend more for designer eyewear, fades. Pearle's prospects were enhanced both by its dominant market presence—Pearle controlled more than five percent of the U.S. optical market in 1995 and was one of only three chains with more than 500 stores—and the fact that its reorganization was largely complete.

Principal Subsidiaries: Pearle Vision Center; Pearle Vision Express.

Further Reading:

Glater, Jonathan D., "Crown Books Chief Quits to Join Pearle Vision," *Washington Post,* January 25, 1994, p. 1B.

Keever, Sue, "A Patriotic Offering from Pearle Vision," *Business Wire,* June 19, 1992.

Laabe, Jennifer J., "Pearle Vision's Managers Think Like Entrepreneurs," *Personnel Journal,* January 1993, p. 38.

Ohr, Erica, "Independents Feel Squeezed as Chains Take Over Their Turf," *Baltimore Business Journal,* October 21, 1994, p. 28.

Pisick, Betsy, "Crown Books CEO Leaves for Pearle Vision Presidency," *Washington Times,* June 25, 1994, p. 5D.

Rigg, Cynthia, "Bob Hillman's Back to Change Eyewear Retailing Yet Again," *Crain's New York Business,* April 24, 1989, p. 3.

Scott, Dave, "Pearle Cuts 15 Percent of Local Work Force," *Dallas Business Journal,* October 2, 1992, p. 1.

Yes Virginia, There Really is a Dr. Pearle, Dallas: Pearle Vision, Inc., 1994.

—Dave Mote

Penn Traffic Company

1200 State Fair Blvd.
P. O. Box 4737
Syracuse, New York 13221-4737
U.S.A.
(315) 453-7284
Fax: (315) 461-2474

Public Company
Incorporated: 1854
Employees: 24,200
Sales: $3.33 billion
Stock Exchanges: New York
SICs: 5141 Groceries, General Line; 5411 Grocery Stores; 5461 Retail Bakeries

Penn Traffic Company is one of the leading food retailers in the eastern United States. In early 1994 it had 232 supermarkets in operation throughout Pennsylvania, Ohio, upstate New York, and northern West Virginia under the names ''Big Bear'' and ''Big Bear Plus,'' ''Quality Markets,'' ''Riverside Markets,'' ''Bi-Lo Foods,'' ''P & C Foods,'' and ''Insalaco's.'' Penn Traffic also operates a wholesale food-distribution business, a discount general-merchandise retail chain, a full-service dairy business in Johnstown, Pennsylvania, and bakery businesses in Syracuse, New York, and Columbus, Ohio.

Until the 1960s Penn Traffic was a general-merchandise department store located in the gritty industrial town of Johnstown, Pennsylvania. Founded in 1854, the store was reincorporated on March 9, 1903, as the successor to Penn Traffic Co., Ltd. The store's headquarters were in Philadelphia, and it was a public company listed on the Philadelphia Stock Exchange. For the fiscal year ending January 31, 1919, sales came to more than $4 million, with posted net earnings of $340,575; ten years later sales had dropped to $3.4 million and net earnings reached only $65,452.

The Great Depression of the 1930s posed the same problems for Penn Traffic as other businesses. In fiscal 1933 the company recorded a loss of $74,670 on earnings of $2 million and did not pay a dividend for the only year since 1910. The next year it rebounded, earning a small profit on even lower earnings, presumably because of stringent economies, and recorded a profit for most of the rest of the decade. In fiscal 1937, however, it listed $184,253 in losses due to the 1936 Johnstown flood.

By fiscal 1949 net sales had reached $9 million and net income $544,283. Thereafter Penn Traffic reported little growth, despite a post-World War II expansion in the national economy; in 1962, net sales crested only slightly above $10.5 million and net income was only $280,963. In 1962, however, Penn Traffic acquired Supervalue Corp.—operators of the ten-store Riverside Markets supermarket chain based in Du Bois, Pennsylvania—for about $2.4 million worth of stock. Penn Traffic, which moved its headquarters to Johnstown the same year, saw its sales immediately triple, although the gain in profit was slight.

In 1968 Penn Traffic acquired the Johnstown Sanitary Dairy and, the following year, the Cresson, Pennsylvania-based Penn Cress Ice Cream. In 1967 it opened a cafeteria in Altoona, Pennsylvania, and in 1968 a second department store in nearby State College. By the end of the decade Penn Traffic was operating 18 food supermarkets, a chain of 11 Dairy Dell combination restaurant/dairy stores, three combination department store/supermarket units in western Pennsylvania, and the two department stores. The central warehouse at Du Bois was enlarged to 182,000 square feet in 1969. In fiscal 1968 the company earned $1,316,234 on net sales of nearly $63.4 million, a profit margin that would prompt it to enter the wholesaling field in 1970.

By late 1971 Penn Traffic was well on its way toward its ninth year in a row of higher sales and earnings. The Riverside Markets chain was growing rapidly, with each location targeted for at least $2 million in sales annually, and the company's initial venture outside Pennsylvania was scheduled for Brookfield, Ohio. Supermarkets accounted for 64 percent of sales in 1970, department stores for 23 percent, and the dairy for about 11 percent. A $3.5-million project was expected to double capacity by mid-1972 at the dairy, which was producing orange juice and a number of other fruit drinks in addition to milk and milk products. Penn Traffic was listed on the American Stock Exchange, with about 19 percent of the common shares held by directors.

In 1979 Penn Traffic acquired Quality Markets, Inc., a chain of 21 supermarkets based in Jamestown, New York, for about $4.5 million. This chain was added to Penn Traffic's 46 supermarkets operating under the Riverside or Bi-Lo names, all of which were self-service and many of which had on-premises bakeries and delicatessen departments. By this time Penn Traffic also operated a third department store as well as the three store units in combination with Riverside supermarkets. Net sales in fiscal 1980 reached $375.6 million, and net income nearly $6.5 million.

Penn Traffic left the department-store business in 1982, when it sold its six department stores and two women's specialty-store leases to Crown America Corp., owners of Hess Department Stores, for about $7.3 million in cash and properties. In that year the 50 Riverside and six Bi-Lo stores added Topco bulk produce to complement approximately 50 private, Riverside-label dry-grocery and snack items; the 20 Quality stores were already marketing Topco products. Penn Traffic's president anticipated a 15 percent annual return on average shareholders' equity and an earnings-per-share growth of 12.5 percent each year.

In fiscal 1983 Penn Traffic opened 17 stores, including 13 acquired from A & P's old Altoona division. However, three unprofitable Youngstown, Ohio, supermarkets were shut down in June 1984; shortly afterwards the company's management acknowledged that profitability had declined during the last six months, a development blamed on high labor costs. In its annual report Penn Traffic declared the intention to concentrate more on wholesaling, which had grown to account for 15 percent of its business. Before the year was out Penn Traffic had closed 19 stores, 17 of which became independent retailers serviced by the company.

By May 1985, Penn Traffic was operating four superstores and had three more in the planning stages in competition with lower-cost operators and depot stores. It also started supplying cigarettes and health and beauty aids to its 23-unit Quality Market chain. The following year it purchased the 15-store food division of Johnstown's Glosser Brothers, which was to be operated as a subsidiary supplied by Penn Traffic's Du Bois warehouse.

Miller, Tabak, Hirsch & Co., a New York City investment group, began a takeover bid for Penn Traffic in 1986, raising its ownership in the company to 7.2 percent of the common stock by midyear. At first management attempted to foil the bid, even soliciting support from the United Food and Commercial Workers Union. Early in 1987, however, Penn Traffic agreed to an offer by an affiliate of Miller, Tabak of $31.60 a share for the 4.2 million shares outstanding. After this leveraged buyout, Penn Traffic went public in a stock and bond offering that raised a significant amount of capital, with Miller, Tabak affiliate retaining 53-percent ownership. Gary Hirsch, chairman of Penn Traffic, controlled 22 percent of the stock in late 1994.

In August 1988 Penn Traffic had purchased a majority interest in P & C Foods Inc., the largest food distributor in central and upstate New York, for $210.6 million. The rest of P & C's stock and equity was bought in 1991 for another $43.8 million, and in 1992 Penn Traffic moved its headquarters from Johnstown to Syracuse, New York. With the P & C acquisition, the number of Penn Traffic retail stores rose to 156. It also supplied 66 franchises and 263 independent stores. Investment analysts questioned, however, the company's longstanding policy of allowing its acquisitions to operate essentially as separate companies, thereby missing opportunities for economies of scale.

In early 1989 Penn Traffic acquired Big Bear Inc., a supermarket chain based in Columbus, Ohio, for about $390 million. And in April of that year Grand Union Co., was sold for $1.2 billion to a group consisting of Penn Traffic, Miller, Tabak, and certain other investors, including Grand Union management. This deal was described by *Supermarket News* as making Penn Traffic the seventh-largest food retailer in the United States, with Grand Union's 306 stores in New York, New Jersey, Vermont, New Hampshire, Massachusetts, Connecticut, and Georgia bringing Penn Traffic's total to 561. Subsequently, however, Penn Traffic's stake in Grand Union was revealed to be only 24.3 percent of the common stock, and by mid-1993 that share had declined to 17.8 percent. In 1993 P & C was supplying bakery products to Grand Union, which supplied commissary products to P & C, one of a few joint buying activities.

These transactions, and especially the leveraged buyout, left Penn Traffic more than $800 million in debt. Moreover, in mid-1992 it had reported losses in 13 of the last 15 quarters and at year end in each of the past four years. By July 1994 long-term debt had climbed to more than $1.1 billion. No dividends had been paid since the company went public in 1987, and none were expected in the near future. Yet investors remained bullish on the stock, bidding it to $30 a share in 1991 and as high as $36 in 1992, compared to a share price of little more than $15 in 1988. One analyst calculated the true value of the stock in 1991 as $74 a share. In 1993 Penn Traffic stock went as high as $45.75 a share, and it traded in about the same range in 1994.

The company climbed into the black in fiscal 1993, earning $3.2 million. Net income rose to $8 million in fiscal 1994, excluding an extraordinary charge of more than $25.8 million due to early retirement of debt. At the end of 1994, Penn Traffic stock began trading on the New York Stock Exchange, and in fiscal 1995 net income of $13.2 million was recorded.

Penn Traffic gained 27 more supermarkets in early 1993 by acquiring Peter J. Schmitt Co., a Buffalo, New York, chain operating under Chapter 11 bankruptcy law protection, for $38 million. Later that year Penn Traffic paid $41 million for Insalaco Markets Inc., a 12-store supermarket chain based in Pittston, Pennsylvania.

Penn Traffic's plans, as stated by Hirsch in 1993, were to spend $600 million over five years to open new stores and remodel both existing stores and the company's distribution centers. During the five years through 1993–94, Penn Traffic opened or remodeled 65 percent of its retail supermarket space, believing that these larger, more modern facilities would enable it to offer a broader variety of specialty departments.

Hirsch also said the company was expanding its private-label program, standardizing its distribution systems, and consolidating and standardizing data processing. A $23-million, 220,000-square-foot perishables distribution center opened in Syracuse in 1993, and work began that year on tripling the 50,000-square-foot perishables facility in Du Bois. Fifteen pharmacies were added to new or existing stores in 1992, with an additional 19 planned for 1993.

Penn Traffic began consolidating its procurement and distribution of nonfood items for all its divisions and Grand Union in August 1993. A Big Bear facility in Columbus, Ohio, was used for general merchandise and a Grand Union in Montgomery, New York, for health- and beauty-care items. This action was expected to substantially increase direct purchases from manufacturers and consequently reduce procurement costs. Both Penn Traffic and Grand Union were expected to increase nonfood space in their stores. In late 1994 Penn Traffic was building a satellite-driven communications network in Syracuse to link its store base. And about 15 new, replacement, or expanded stores in the range of 60,000 to 100,000 square feet in space were to open by January 1996.

Penn Traffic's scope widened again with the announcement on September 30, 1994, that it was buying 45 Acme Markets stores in Pennsylvania and New York from the American Stores Co. for $95.7 million. This brought Penn Traffic's total to 285 retail and wholesale food stores in early 1995.

As of January 1994—prior to the acquisition of the Acme stores—Penn Traffic was operating 77 Big Bear and Big Bear Plus stores, 61 P & C Foods stores, 45 Quality Markets, 23 Bi-Lo Foods stores, and 13 Insalaco's. Its wholesale food-distribution business, the sixth largest in the United States in 1990, served 133 licensed franchises and 119 independent operators. Penn Traffic also operated a discount general-merchandise business with 15 stores, the Johnstown "Sani-Dairy" and bakeries in Syracuse and Columbus under the names "Penny Curtiss" and "Big Bear Bakeries," respectively.

Located primarily in towns and small cities, Penn Traffic's stores often faced little competition. There was no supermarket competition against the stores that garnered more than 20 percent of Penn Traffic's revenues, with the exception of Kroger Co., which competed against the Big Bear stores that represented about 30 percent of company revenues. The smaller stores were generally in areas of low population density. Larger or more affluent areas were better served by full-service supermarkets of up to 64,000 square feet, containing specialty departments such as bakeries, delicatessens, and departments containing fresh seafood and flowers. Penn Traffic's "Plus" format had store sizes ranging from 70,000 to 140,000 square feet and included an expanded variety of nonfood merchandise. Some supermarkets had video-rental departments and banking services provided by automated teller machines.

About 35 percent of Penn Traffic's stores were open 24 hours a day for at least five days per week. Most of the supermarkets were in shopping centers. About 91 percent of the stores used product-scanning systems and proprietary software for inventory and shrinkage controls at both delivery and checkout points. The average store had 37,945 square feet of space and annual sales of $11.8 million.

Almost all of Penn Traffic's licensed independent operators used the company as their primary wholesaler and receiving advertising, accounting, merchandising, consulting, and retail counseling services from Penn Traffic. 73 were leasing or subleasing supermarket buildings and much of the equipment used in the supermarkets from Penn Traffic. The company's wholesale operations accounted for $462 million, or 14.5 percent of total revenues, in fiscal 1994.

Johnstown's Sani-Dairy was one of the largest dairies in Pennsylvania, producing more than 900 dairy and dairy-related products. Penny Curtiss Bakery was primarily supplying P & C stores and affiliated accounts with private-label fresh and frozen bakery products, but was also supplying certain bakery products to Riverside, Quality Markets, and Grand Union stores. Big Bear Bakeries was primarily supplying Big Bear stores with private-label fresh and frozen bakery products. Penn Traffic also operated 15 Harts discount general-merchandise stores averaging 66,000 square feet. 14 were in central and southern Ohio, and the remainder in northern West Virginia.

The principal Pennsylvania distribution facilities were company-owned, 390,000-square-foot and 254,000-square-foot centers in Du Bois. Three other Pennsylvania warehouses were being leased. The main New York distribution facilities were company-owned, 498,000-square-foot and 217,000-square-foot centers in Syracuse, with another 349,000-square-foot distribution center located in Jamestown. The main Ohio distribution facility was a leased 484,000-square-foot center in Columbus. Penn Traffic also owned a 208,000-square-foot center in Columbus and leased two Columbus warehouses with a total of 399,000 square feet of space. The company had a fleet of 326 tractors, 378 refrigerated trailers, and 566 dry trailers.

Principal Subsidiaries: Big M Supermarkets, Inc.; Dairy Dell, Inc.; Sunrise Properties, Inc.; PennWay Express, Inc.; Penny Curtiss Baking Co., Inc.

Further Reading:

Abelson, Alan, "Up & Down Wall Street," *Barron's,* June 29, 1992, pp. 31–32.

Campanella, Frank W., "Penn Traffic to Extend String of Rising Sales and Net," *Barron's,* September 20, 1971, pp. 25, 27.

Dowdell, Stephen, "Penn Traffic's Regional Recipe," *Supermarket News,* October 3, 1988, pp. 1, 9, 62.

Tosh, Mark, "Hirsch's Capital Idea," *Supermarket News,* May 24, 1993, pp. 1, 10–11.

Turcsik, Richard, "Penn Traffic-Led Group to Acquire Grand Union," *Supermarket News,* April 17, 1989, pp. 1, 33.

Welling, Kathryn M., "Dream Themes," *Barron's,* March 8, 1992, p. 14.

—Robert Halasz

Philips Electronics North America Corp.

100 E. 42nd Street
New York, New York 10017
U.S.A.
(212) 850-5000
Fax: (212) 850-5362

Public Subsidiary of Philips Electronics N.V.
Incorporated: 1959 as Consolidated Electronics Industries Corp.
Employees: 35,000
Sales: $5.95 billion
Stock Exchanges: New York
SICs: 3651 Household Audio & Video Equipment; 3634 Electric Housewares & Fans

Philips Electronics North America Corp. (PENAC), a subsidiary of the Netherlands-based electronics giant Philips Electronics N.V., is one of the 100 largest manufacturers in the United States. Its products in consumer electronics, components, semiconductors, communications systems, medical systems, diagnostic imaging systems, and other professional equipment are marketed under such familiar brand names as Philips, Magnavox, and Norelco.

For much of its history—from the late 1950s to the late 1980s—PENAC was essentially operated as a separate entity from its Dutch parent, despite an unusual brand of symbiosis: Dutch shareholders gained from the independent company's growth, and the company benefited from its Dutch relative's expertise in electronic innovation and research. In 1987, however, this unusual arrangement was simplified, as PENAC was once again acquired by N.V. Philips as a wholly owned subsidiary. Even as such, however, the company remained covetous of its hard-earned reputation and success as an independently managed firm.

PENAC's early history is closely linked to that of its parent, Philips Electronics N.V., which was founded as a lamp factory, Philips & Company, in 1891 in Eindhoven. Gerard Philips, a young engineer who saw commercial potential in newly developing electrical technology, formed the partnership with his father, Frederik Philips, to manufacture incandescent lamps and other electrical products.

With constant innovations and new product development—from tungsten filament to argon-filled lamps—the young company survived a difficult childhood. It also began a long process of vertical integration in order to become more self-sufficient, establishing its own argon-production facility and its own glass works by the 1920s. After incorporating as N.V. Philips Gloeilampfabrieken in 1912, the company continued to diversify and grow through World War I and the Depression.

By the 1920s, the company was under the management of Anton Philips, the youngest son of the founding patriarch. In addition to the components on which it had based its early growth—light bulbs, X-ray tubes, and radio valves—Philips manufactured complete products—like radio sets—whenever possible, marking a significant change in management strategy.

Anton Philips was also instrumental in setting up a financial organization that protected the Dutch firm from outside forces, especially German financiers. In 1920 N.V. Gemeenschappelijk Bezit van Aandeelen Philips' Gloeilampenfabrieken (known simply as ''Bezit'') was established as a holding company. Before World War II, Bezit held 89 percent of Philips' shares, with another six percent under the control of General Electric Co. By the late 1950s, Bezit controlled 98 percent of the operating company's shares, and top management held ''priority shares'' that granted them the power to nominate members of the ''board of management.'' The financial grip of Philips was thus secured in the hands of the Dutch.

During the 1920s, the company's headquarters at Eindhoven underwent extensive renovation and expansion, with the construction of additional buildings for new and existing industrial products. Toward the end of the decade, Philips' Lamp Works set up more overseas subsidiaries in Asia and Africa, as well as in Europe and South America in the 1930s.

Despite Depression-driven cutbacks in the 1930s, the company forged ahead with new products such as gas-discharge lamps, X-ray equipment, car radios, telecommunications equipment, welding rods, and electric shavers, all of which ultimately helped alleviate the company's financial difficulties.

An important administrative reorganization occurred just before World War II. Anton Philips retired in 1939 as president, although he remained active in a supervisory role. He was succeeded as president by his son-in-law, Frans Otten, while his son, Frits Philips, was made a director of the company. Under this leadership, the company took precautionary measures against the war that resulted in the formation of North American Philips (NAP), the precursor to Philips Electronics North America Corp. (PENAC).

Indeed, the ominous political developments in Europe at the end of the 1930s prompted management to prepare for the worst. Philips's legal home was shifted to the Dutch island of Curacao off the coast of Venezuela. Philips created a U.S. trust handled by Hartford National Bank and Trust Co. to hold majority interests in North American Philips (NAP). A separate British trust was established to control the company's British operations. When the Nazis invaded in May 1940, Dutch defenses crumbled and the country capitulated within a week. The management of Philips followed the Dutch government into exile in England. Eventually, the top management made its way to the

United States, where NAPC managed operations in non-occupied countries for the duration of the war. Frits Philips, while attempting to maintain as much independence as possible from Nazi authorities, remained behind to manage operations in the Netherlands. After the war, Philips was able to draw from its complex financial network to fully revive operations, even though Eindhoven had been completely demolished. In 1955 Philips repurchased its British businesses, leaving NAP to operate as an independent company until its re-merger with the parent in the late 1980s.

Thus, for more than four formative decades, NAP remained a sort of corporate orphan, invested with many of the character traits of its original parent, but largely independent in its development. Actually, NAP was one in a group of orphans: by 1994, Philips had eight offshoots in the United States, most of which were engaged in war work.

These Philips offshoot companies trod lightly on the turf of other American manufacturers of electrical consumer products. Philips's rather complex presence in the U.S. market enabled the company to skirt the line between being an innocuous, small company and a frightful megalith among electronics concerns. Indeed, Philips received an early slap on the wrist in 1941, when the U.S. Department of Justice filed a light-bulb cartel suit against GE, other electrical producers, and Philips, containing charges of price-fixing and monopolies on patents. Although Philips emerged with few scars, its interests were best served by maintaining a low profile thereafter.

Even with intentions of laying low, Philips's U.S. offshoots—and North American Philips Co. Inc. in particular—emerged as strong market forces after World War II. The company employed a strategy of buying up small, specialized companies and grouping them together to fill specific market niches, from high-fi, X-ray, and lighting equipment to the import and export of specialized components.

This strategy came to a head in 1959, with the incorporation of Consolidated Electronics Industries Corp. (Conelco), a consolidation of a company of that name, Philips Industries, Inc., and Central Public Utility Corp. The first two of these merging companies were already part of the Philips fold: 100 percent of the stock of Philips Industries was owned by Philips's North American trust, and, in turn, Philips Industries owned 64.2 percent of the stock in Philips Electronics, Inc.; Consolidated Electronics, founded in 1919 as Jackson Cushion Spring Co., was 4.4 percent owned by Philips Industries, Inc. and 35.4 percent owned by North American Philips (another ''little Philips'' that wasn't directly involved in this particular merger). Finally, Central Public Utility Corp. was altogether unrelated, but its big cash position amounting to $13 million would provide the Philips cousins with welcome capital for greater productivity capacity and further R&D.

In the 1960s, Consolidated Electronics began a pattern of continued growth and diversification with the 1961 acquisition of Thompson-Hayward Chemical Co. (which it transferred to Philips Electronics & Pharmaceutical Industries Corp., a subsidiary, a year later). Thereafter, the company's electro-mechanical and electronic products soared through numerous new subsidiaries and their wares, including Advance Transformer Co. (fluorescent lamp ballasts, dimming and control systems for fluorescent lamps); Ferroxcube Corp. of America (ferrite memory cores, recording heads for computers); Alliance Manufacturing Co. (specialized fractional and subfractional horse-power motors for use in sound reproduction equipment, time controls); Ohmite Manufacturing Co. (rheostats, resistors, switches, transformers); Chicago Magnet Wire Corp. (insulated copper, other wire); Dialight Corp. (illuminated push-button switches, indicator lights). The company also ventured into popular, jazz, and classical records (Mercury Record Corp.) and passenger bus services (Carolina Coach Co.). Growth was impressive: From 1955 to 1966, Conelco's sales rose from $11 million to more than $300 million.

A whole new level of growth was reached in 1969, when Conelco merged with North American Philips Co. Inc., another ''little Philips'' company, to form North American Philips Corp. (NAP). The new entity combined Conelco's strength in electric-electronic products with NAP's leadership in consumer products and services and professional equipment. Pieter C. Vink, one of the original managers trained by Philips to ply overseas trade after the war, took the helm (after having steered North American Philips for decades). NAP found strength in unity and in its widening variety of products—from the first cassette player marketed in the United States, the Norelco ''Carry-Corder'', to professional equipment such as electronic calculators and computers, training and education systems, broadcast equipment, and electro-optical products such as the popular Plumbicon color-TV camera tubes and cameras.

The merger between publicly owned Conelco and NAP, the privately held subsidiary of Philips, resurrected interest on the part of the press—and investors—concerning NAP's relationship to its original Dutch parent. The merger effectively gave the Dutch concern 66 percent control over the new corporate entity through control of the U.S. Philips Trust. As in other ''little Philips'' operations, many top managers boasted past and ongoing ties to the Dutch parent; and all of Philips's U.S. operations benefited immeasurably from their access to the parent's products and advanced technology. Still, Vink insisted that his company was totally independent, leading *Forbes* magazine to conclude that ''North American Philips is, among other things, a monument to man's ability to maintain a legal fiction despite its obvious unreality,'' in a 1969 article called ''Orphan Grown Up.'' Such skepticism in the press persisted well into the 1980s. In 1980, for example, *Forbes* attributed U.S. investors' coolness toward NAP to the possibility that the Philips Trust, not U.S. investors, stood to gain most from the company's growth. The company's own annual report stated that the purpose of the trust was to pursue the Dutch company's interest in the U.S. market. Analysts throughout Wall Street continued to suggest that the Dutch pulled the strings in the background and that Philips operated as a worldwide conglomerate, whether or not its ownership was fragmented into subsidiaries with varying degrees of autonomy.

Whether or not NAP was part of a conglomerate, expansion over the following two decades was quickly transforming the company into a megalith in its own right. Special emphasis was placed on the lighting industry. In 1970 NAP's Radiant Lamp Corp. subsidiary—which had been acquired by Conelectron in 1968—changed its name to North American Philips Lighting

Corp. A series of acquisitions followed: Verd-A-Fay, the lighting products division of Lear-Siegler Inc. (1971); the Large lamp division and the Lustra Lighting Division of International Telephone and Telegraph Corp. (1973); and Solar Electric Corp. (1980). In 1983 North American Philips Lighting Corp. shone particularly bright, with the acquisition of Westinghouse Electric Corp.'s Lamp Division and the acquisition of a Corning Glass Works glass plant, as well as a merger with the Philips Emet Division of NAP.

Meanwhile, NAP forged ahead in electronics, as well. The company's solid R&D base was supplemented by the market weight of strategic acquisitions: Electra/Midland Corp. (1971); Unelec, Inc. (1972); Magnavox Co. and National Components Industries, Inc. (1974); Airpax Electronics, Inc. and Rohe Scientific Corp. (1976); General Electric Co.'s electronic capacitor manufacturing operation (1978); and a majority stake in the Centralab division of Johnson Controls, Inc. (1980).

Capitalizing on the insatiable American appetite for television, NAP also took bold strides into the TV market. Though Magnavox had been acquired just in time for the collapse of U.S. TV manufacturing, falling into the red for a good part of the 1970s, NAP forged ahead. In 1981 the company acquired General Telephone & Electronics Corp.'s television set business, helping boost its market share of the color TV market to 13.1 percent that year. The company also consolidated TV production in a modern plant in eastern Tennessee and integrated cost-cutting automation. NAP found itself wedged between American competitors and increasingly aggressive Japanese manufacturers. By 1987, its market share had slipped to 9.8 percent, though Philips brands of color TVs still ranked third in the United States, behind RCA and Zenith. By 1988, Philips had developed the first demonstration of high definition TV (HDTV) hardware for U.S. satellite transmission. In a joint venture with Hughes Communications, Inc., a subsidiary of Hughes Aircraft Co., NAP began field testing a HDTV satellite feeder signal system in 1989. Through Broadcast Technology Systems, Inc. (BTS)—a joint venture between Philips and Bosch—the company developed a special high definition video camera to create optimal images for the system.

Though NAP showed tremendous promise for the future, the company was not living up to its potential in the 1980s: its consumer electronics division reported a loss of $12.7 million in 1985 and another loss the following year. In response, the company began a process of consolidation and realignment along core business lines. In 1985 it sold its inter-city bus transportation business (Carolina Coach Co. and Seashore Transportation Co.) as well as its hospital attendant TV business, N.A.P. Commercial Electronics Corp. The following year, several subsidiaries merged: Mepco/Electra Inc. and Centralab Inc., as well as Dialight Corp. and Kulka Smith Inc.

Speculation over NAP's curious relationship to its parent finally came to an end in November 1987, when the company became a wholly owned subsidiary of the Dutch giant. Cees Bruynes, chairman and president of NAP, emphasized that the changes were structural in nature and would not affect ongoing operations and operational responsibilities. Still, a sweeping reorganization was initiated in order to streamline the structure of the company's activities in the Unites States and improve coordination with the Philips Group worldwide.

As part of the new organization, the company appointed a new president. On January 1, 1989, Einar Kloster, a former executive vice-president of the North American Philips Corporation, returned as president of the company, replacing Cees Bruynes. Mr. Bruynes, in turn, was named chairman and CEO of a new subsidiary, Consolidated Electronics Industries Corp., which grouped together those subsidiaries that lay outside the company's core electronics business in an effort to improve NAP's focus and performance. The new subsidiary included the Magnavox defense contracting business, which could not be foreign-owned according to Pentagon rules, and various other businesses, including Anchor Brush toothbrushes, Genie garage door openers, Selmer musical instruments, and Magnavox cable television equipment.

As part of its new American organization, Philips also launched a renewed marketing campaign designed to strengthen the Philips presence and visibility in the United States, the largest consumer electronics market. Indeed, in the past, the American offshoots had suffered from poor marketing and timing of new product introductions. Philips had invented the CD player, for example, and had become a leader in the European market, while players sold under the Magnavox name in the United States had barely managed to capture two percent of the market. The company's VCRs, designed in the early 1980s, endured similar hardship; NAP even refused to market them in the United States, selling machines purchased form Matsushita instead.

The new marketing initiative intended to reverse this pattern by aggressively supporting consumer products under such names as Norelco, Magnavox, Philco, and Sylvania, while greatly enhancing market awareness of other products under the Philips name itself. According to *Television Digest,* immediate results were felt in Philips's color TVs, which saw a rise to 10.7 percent in 1989, from 9.5 percent the previous year, largely due to an ad campaign featuring the Smothers Brothers. Other advertising efforts promoted such products as Norelco's men's and women's electric razors, CleanAir filtering machines, and EZ Irons.

NAP's new image was part and parcel of a general facelift that the parent company underwent well into the 1990s. After reporting heavy losses in 1990, Philips' Board of Directors drafted Jan Trimmer as president to return Philips to profitability. By implementing a so-called Operation Centurion, the company hoped to make itself more responsive to the competitive marketplace by raising productivity, stimulating cost consciousness, and minimizing office bureaucracy. In 1991 the company's name was changed from N.V. Philips Gloeilampenfabrieken to Philips Electronics N.V. Following suit, NAP's name was changed to Philips Electronics North America Corp. to more accurately define its products (especially its renewed emphasis on core consumer electronics) and more closely identify it with the parent company.

Both companies moved to recapture slipping market share in an increasingly competitive electronics arena, especially threatened by Japanese manufacturers. Big Philips's closer ties to its

American subsidiary were a calculated attempt to recapture that pivotal market: "To win the battle in consumer electronics, we have to win in America," a Philips executive told *Business Week* in 1987.

Certainly, Philips's long tradition of innovation and quality gave the company an edge over its competitors. Backed by the tremendous resources and joint projects of its parent—and by the famed Philips Laboratories where it conducted cutting-edge research—Philips Electronics North America Corp. focused on several strategically developed and timed products in the mid-1990s. As early as 1993, the company joined CellularVision and Bell Atlantic in a partnership toward multi-channel, interactive, multimedia services. Meanwhile, expanding on the CD technology it had pioneered, the company moved into CD-I (interactive, multimedia compact disk systems) and a digital videodisc, for which Philips, in alliance with Sony Corp., competed against a Toshiba Corp. / Time Warner Inc. alliance to set industry standards. The company also positioned itself for growing demand in full color, high-resolution, flat panel display systems by entering into a joint venture with Kopin Corp. to develop a new generation of liquid crystal display imaging devices. And in 1995, a joint venture with Cree Research, Inc., made great advances in blue laser diode technology, useful in high density commercial memory systems and for military applications such as lightweight countermeasure systems and covert communications.

These were just some of the innovative products that Philips Electronics North America Corp. is depending on to hold its ground in an increasingly competitive electronics market. With the backing of its impressive parent, renewed marketing program, and focus on its core electronic business, the company stands an excellent chance of setting new standards in the emerging multimedia electronics markets of the 21st century.

Further Reading:

Briggs, Jean A., "Uncle Philips' American Nephew," *Forbes,* April 14, 1980, p. 68.

"Cree Research and Philips Sign Joint Agreement; New Laser Diodes Will Increase Optical Storage Capacity," *Business Wire,* April 4, 1995.

"Diversification Sparks Consolidated Electronics," *Barron's,* January 16, 1967, p. 26.

"Dutch Philips' Defiant U.S. Connection," *Business Week,* March 30, 1981, p. 92.

"How Far Can Philips Elbow Its Way Into the U.S.?" *Business Week,* March 2, 1987, p. 46.

"How Philips Merger Was Born," *Business Week,* April 18, 1959, pp. 172–74.

Levine, Jonathan B., and Robert D. Hof, "Has Philips Found Its Wizard?" *Business Week,* September 6, 1993, p. 82.

"North American Philips Finds Strength in Unity," *Barron's,* October 13, 1969, p. 27.

"North American Philips Listed Among Top 50 U.S. Exporters," *Business Wire,* July 12, 1989.

"Orphan Grown Up," *Forbes,* July 15, 1969, p. 22.

"Philips Demonstrates Full Resolution High Definition Television (HDTV)," *Business Wire,* December 7, 1988.

"Philips of Holland Raises Its U.S. Sights," *Business Week,* January 18, 1958, pp. 104–10.

Robertson, Jack, "Seek Aid to Sell Magnavox; Losses Mount at Philips Defense Unit," *Electronic News,* March 6, 1989, Vol. 35, No. 1748, p. 1.

"What Could Slow Philips' Drive in the U.S." *Business Week,* July 18, 1983, p. 158.

—Kerstan Cohen

Philips Electronics N.V.

Groenewoudseweg 1
5621 BA
Eindhoven
The Netherlands
+31-04-786022
Fax: +31-04-785486

Public Company
Incorporated: 1912 as N.V. Philips Gloeilampenfabrieken
Employees: 249,759
Sales: Dfl 60.98 billion ($33.69 billion)
Stock Exchanges: Amsterdam New York London
SICs: 3645 Residential Lighting Fixtures; 3634 Electric Housewares & Fans; 3651 Household Audio & Video Equipment; 3679 Electronic Components, Not Elsewhere Classified

Inspired by the visions and leadership of several generations of the Philips family, Philips Electronics N.V. (known as Philips Gloeilampenfabrieken, or Philips Incandescent Lamp Works, until 1991) has grown from a small light bulb maker into one of the largest and most successful electronics firms in the world. Throughout the company's history, the family has sustained a strong commitment to technological innovation, market expansion, and stringent management policies.

An efficient organizational structure has helped maintain management's hold on the increasingly gargantuan company. Philips Electronics N.V. acts as the holding company of the Philips group, with nine chief product divisions responsible for global product policy and approximately 60 national organizations responsible for conducting general policy in their respective geographical markets. Into the 1990s, the nine product divisions remained: Communications Systems; Components; Consumer Electronics; Domestic Appliances and Personal Care; Industrial electronics; Lighting; Medical systems; Semiconductors; and Polygram (recorded music and music publishing). Consumer Electronics—with 47 percent of turnover in 1992—remained the most important division, especially as Philips poured new resources into R&D and marketing in order to directly compete with Japanese manufacturers and capture a greater share of that market into the 21st century.

The early years of the company were very much a family affair. On May 15, 1891, Gerard Philips, a young engineer who saw commercial potential in newly developing electrical technology, formed Philips & Company, a partnership with his father, Frederik Philips, to manufacture incandescent lamps and other electrical products. The elder Philips, a wealthy tobacco merchant and banker from Zaltbommel, provided the financing while Gerard contributed the technical expertise.

Philips & Company began operations in a small factory in Eindhoven. Production started in 1892, but the fledgling company encountered problems from the very beginning. The firm could not produce as many lamps as Gerard had forecast, nor did the lamps fetch the price he had expected. Father and son had underestimated the strength of international competition in the young industry, especially from the large German manufacturers who had entered the market in the early 1880s and were already well established.

The company suffered heavy financial losses in 1893, and by 1894 the two men decided to sell the business. That might have been the end of the family's venture into the electrical industry had it not been for the fact that the only offer they received was considered unacceptable by Frederik. After negotiations broke down with the prospective buyer, the Philipses decided to risk everything rather than sell at too low a price.

The company was clearly in need of someone with commercial skills and ambition to make it profitable. Frederik was preoccupied with his banking and commercial interests in Zaltbommel, and, while Gerard possessed the technical ability necessary to manufacture electric light bulbs and other innovative products, he was not by nature a businessman. Frederik thus turned to his youngest son, Anton.

Anton Philips, who was 16 years younger than Gerard, joined the firm in early 1895. Anton had left school early to work in London for a brokerage firm. This brief training in business helped; once he assumed control, Anton began winning the company new customers both at home and abroad. In a few years, the company was growing at a healthy rate.

At the turn of the century the company kept pace with constant innovations in the electrical industry by developing a skilled staff of technical and commercial specialists. When the carbon-filament lamp became obsolete after 1907, Philips and other companies pioneered the development of lamps that used tungsten wire, which produced three times as much light for the same amount of electricity. Philips was also at the forefront of revolutionary improvements in the manufacture of filament wire, which gave rise to the production of incandescent lamps of all types and sizes. In 1912 Philips & Company was incorporated as N.V. Philips Gloeilampenfabrieken and began offering its shares on the Amsterdam Stock Exchange.

As the company grew, it became increasingly evident to both Gerard and Anton that a strong research-and-development capability would be critical to its survival. Consequently, in 1914 Gerard appointed a young physicist, Gilles Holst, to lead the company's research effort. Dr. Holst and his staff worked as a separate organization, reporting directly to the Philips brothers; this laboratory eventually developed into the Philips Research Laboratories.

The Netherlands remained neutral in World War I, to the company's benefit. Shortages of coal for the production of gas resulted in gas rationing, which in turn stimulated the use of electricity. By 1915, Philips had succeeded in producing a small, economical argon-filled lamp that was immediately in great demand.

When Germany prohibited the export of argon gas, Philips avoided a production breakdown by completing its own argon-production facility. Similarly, the glass bulbs used in manufacturing its lamps, which had been obtained from factories in Germany and Austria before the war, suddenly fell into short supply. The brothers decided in 1915 that the supply problem could be solved only by constructing a glass works of their own. That factory opened in 1916, followed shortly by additional facilities for the production of hydrogen gas and corrugated cardboard. These moves were the first steps toward the vertical integration of the company's production processes.

After the war, Philips began to expand its overseas marketing efforts significantly. Before 1914, Philips had autonomous marketing companies in the United States and France. In 1919, La Lumière Economique was established in Belgium, followed by similar organizations set up in 13 other European countries as well as China, Brazil, and Australia.

Research conducted under the direction of Dr. Holst played a critical role in the development of new products during this time. Fields such as X-ray radiation and radio reception were given high priority, resulting a few years later in product-line additions such as X-ray tubes and radio valves.

In 1920 a holding company, N.V. Gemeenschappelijk Benzit van Aandeelen Philips Gloeilampenfabrieken, known as N.V. Benzit, was formed and assumed ownership of Philips. Gerard Philips retired in 1922 and was succeeded as company chairman by Anton, who was 48 years old.

Under Anton's management, the company began to manufacture complete radio sets; it displayed its first model at the Utrecht Trade Fair in September 1927. From then on, rather than manufacturing just electrical components, the company started to manufacture complete products whenever possible—a significant change in management strategy.

During the 1920s, the company's headquarters at Eindhoven underwent extensive renovation and expansion, with the construction of additional buildings for new and existing industrial products. Toward the end of the decade, Philips's Lamp Works set up more overseas subsidiaries in Asia and Africa, as well as in Europe.

The worldwide depression of the 1930s, however, stalled the company's robust expansion, forcing employee layoffs and an administrative reorganization. As a result, new budgeting methods and an improved cost-price calculation were introduced to facilitate a faster response to changing market conditions. Research continued with considerable vigor, producing new products such as gas-discharge lamps, X-ray equipment, car radios, telecommunications equipment, welding rods, and electric shavers, all of which ultimately helped alleviate the company's financial difficulties. And, despite its problems, the company opened a number of new offices in South America.

The international trade barriers erected by many national governments during the 1930s in an attempt to protect domestic industries from foreign competition forced a major change in the structure of the company. As a result of the barriers, it became extremely difficult for Philips to supply its overseas marketing companies from its headquarters in Eindhoven. Management responded by establishing local production facilities in foreign countries.

Anton Philips retired in 1939 as president, though he remained active in a supervisory role. He was succeeded as president by his son-in-law, Frans Otten, while his son, Frits Philips, was made a director of the company.

The ominous political developments in Europe at the end of the 1930s prompted management to prepare for the worst. The North American Philips Corporation (NAPC) was founded in the United States in anticipation of the possible Nazi occupation of the Netherlands. When the Nazis invaded in May 1940, Dutch defenses crumbled and the country capitulated within a week. The management of Philips followed the Dutch government into exile in England. Eventually, the top management made its way to the United States, where NAPC managed operations in nonoccupied countries for the duration of the war. Frits Philips, while attempting to maintain as much independence as possible from Nazi authorities, remained behind to manage operations in the Netherlands.

Philips' activities in the Netherlands suffered seriously as the war progressed. In 1942 and 1943 company factories were bombed by the Allies, and in 1944 the Nazis bombed them a final time as they withdrew. Thus the first order of business after the war ended was reconstruction. By the end of 1946, most of the buildings had been restored and production had returned to its prewar level.

The postwar years were a time of worldwide expansion for the company. The existing Eindhoven-centered management structure was revised to allow overseas operations more autonomy. National organizations, responsible for all financial, legal, and administrative matters, were created for each country in which Philips operated. Manufacturing policy, however, remained centralized, with various product divisions in Eindhoven responsible for overall development, production, and global distribution.

The research arm of the company remained a separate entity, expanding in the postwar years into an international organization with eight separate laboratories in Western Europe and the United States. Philips laboratories also made major technological contributions in electronics, including the development of new magnetic materials, and work on transistors and integrated circuits.

The growth of the Common Market, established in 1958, presented the company with new opportunities. While factories had previously manufactured products solely for local markets, larger-scale production units encompassing the entire European Economic Community were now possible. With export to Common Market countries made easier, a new approach to product development was also necessary. Philips's factories were gradually integrated and centralized into International Production Centers—the backbone of its product divisions—as it made the transition from a market-orientated to a product-oriented business.

Frits Philips was named president in 1961 and managed the firm during a very prosperous decade, so that when, in 1971, Henk van Riemsdijk was appointed president, he took over a company riding the crest of 20 years of uninterrupted postwar success. The 1970s, however, were a difficult time, as competition from Asia cut into Philips' markets. Many of its smaller, less-profitable factories were closed as the company created larger, more efficient units. The company also continued its innovative efforts in recording, transmitting, and reproducing television pictures. In 1972, for example, the company introduced the first video cassette recorder to the market.

In 1977, Nico Rodenburg became president. Under Rodenburg sales grew steadily for most of the late 1970s and early 1980s, but increased profits did not follow. As Japanese companies, with their large, automated plants, flooded the market with inexpensive consumer electronics, Philips, with factories scattered throughout Europe and rising labor costs, saw its market share continue to decline.

The company's fortunes began to change with the appointment of Wisse Dekker as president and chairman of the board in January, 1982. Dekker initiated an ambitious restructuring program intended to control Philips' unwieldy bureaucracy and increasingly haphazard productivity. After only a few months, Dekker had closed more than a quarter of the company's European plants and had significantly pared down its global work force.

Dekker also began to seek acquisitions and joint ventures designed to help concentrate the company's resources on its most profitable and fastest-growing product lines. Philips bought the lighting business of the American company Westinghouse outright, and acquired a 24.5 percent stake in Grundig, the largest West German consumer-electronics firm. In the United States, North American Philips consolidated the operations of its Magnavox consumer-electronics division with the Sylvania and Philco businesses it had already purchased from GTE Corporation, in 1981. Two years later, the company announced a 50-50 joint venture with AT&T to manufacture and market public-telephone equipment outside the United States, a deal it hoped would save millions in research-and-development costs.

When Cornelis van der Klugt assumed the presidency of Philips in 1986, he continued to seek acquisitions and joint ventures to improve the company's market position. Philips's research in solid-state lasers and microelectronics, resulting in advancements in the processing, storage, and transmission of images, sound, and data, also helped regain part of the market lost to the Japanese. This research produced innovative items such as the LaserVision optical disc, the compact disc, and optical telecommunications systems.

Van der Klugt reorganized the company, eliminating an entire layer of management and setting policy by committee. Van der Klugt also made an effort to globalize the company's structure, improving profitability; in 1988 Philips's profits rose 29 percent. Rationalization of operations also played a role in this restructuring. In 1987, Philips geared up for a major international push into consumer electronics, and targeted U.S. markets hoping to broaden its market share in TVs, VCRs, and CD players. Indeed, by 1995, consumer electronics accounted for more than 35 percent of the company's sales revenue.

In response to Japanese competition, van der Klugt also began to drop non-core activities in favor of development in electronics. In late 1989, for example, the company began a graceful withdrawal from the defense market, where it had maintained a leading stride since developing nuclear control instruments (chiefly for nuclear power generation) and fire control and radar instruments for missile systems in the 1950s. Philips sold its Dutch defense electronics subsidiary, Hollandse Signaalapparaten (HSA) to Thomson S.A. of France at the end of 1989 and put other European defense subsidiaries (and interests) up for sale shortly thereafter. Philips also began to share rising research-and-development costs with other large corporations such as AT&T, Siemens A.G., and Whirlpool through joint ventures.

Despite these moves, Philips got slammed in 1990, reporting a loss of $2.2 billion for the year. The board of directors drafted Jan Trimmer as president to return Philips to profitability. Trimmer's expertise, and his long-standing experience at Philips, made him qualified for the task. From 1983 to 1987, he was president and CEO of PolyGram International, the company's music-industry subsidiary; and in 1987 he was promoted to head the high-profile consumer electronics division. Among his many credits, Trimmer was instrumental in spearheading the industry's switch to the digital audio compacts disc (CD), which spun out tremendous profits for Philips throughout the 1980s. With that under his belt, the new president intended to emphasize new developments in CD technology, as well as aggressive R&D in other high-tech areas, to ensure Philips's market leadership going forward.

Trimmer's initiatives were broad, bold, and swift. By implementing a so-called operation Centurion, the company hoped to make itself more responsive to the competitive marketplace by raising productivity, stimulating cost consciousness, and minimizing office bureaucracy. In 1991, the company's name was changed to Philips N.V. In July of that year, the company announced a plan to reduce working capital and the size of its property portfolio by several billions of guilders within several months.

In late 1991, Trimmer beefed up his ambitious reorganization plans for Philips by hiring former Hewlett-Packard executive Frank Carrubba as executive vice-president to take command of virtually every link in the product chain, from research to purchasing and manufacturing, and "fix the whole thing," according to Jonathan B. Levine in a September 6, 1993 *Business Week* article. Carrubba's experience as a star computer engineer at IBM and his reputation as an "agent for change" at Hewlett-Packard prepared him for the challenges at Philips. One of Carruba's first obstacles was to overcome barriers between R&D and product groups and factories, which had repeatedly stalled Philips's introductions of the right products at the right time. In response, Carrubba spearheaded a program of five-year product plans with labs and factories. Other projects initiated by the new VEP included cross-divisional task forces to develop products and businesses in order to bolster high-value, software-rich products and services, as well as R&D

contracts with universities and institutions, with R&D objectives tied to broad corporate strategies in order to compensate for cutbacks in R&D budgets since the 1980s.

Philips supplemented its internal rehabilitation program with new alliances and profit-oriented sales. In 1991 it announced a partnership with Nintendo to develop CD-based video games. Philips also sold most of its computer business and its stake in Whirlpool (appliances) back to that company. In 1992, the company consolidated its VCR and camcorder operations at Grundig, the German electronics manufacturer, while consolidating its 36 percent stake in Grundig with the company's own accounts. Philips also collaborated with Motorola to establish a state-of-the-art facility to manufacture video circuits for the new multimedia CD player. In 1992, Philips sold its Magnavox Electronic Systems units and its interest in Matsushita Electronics. And the following year Philips's music division turned up the volume by adding the revitalized Motown label to its fold of record companies.

Philips continued to ply its strategy of gaining market share by developing new products and then buying into companies that sold them directly to the consumer. In 1992, for example, Philips bought a 25 percent stake in Whittle Communications, a company that produced a news program for American teens and numerous software packages that could be upgraded using Philips' CD-Interactive system. Though such a strategy proved successful in numerous other ventures, Philips wrote off most of its $175 million investment in the failed Whittle venture in 1994.

In the 1990s, Philips placed increasing emphasis on R&D, allotting more than two-thirds of that budget toward research directly linked to the company's products divisions. With consumer electronics still occupying the lion's share of the company's profits, it was not surprising that many key products in the development pipeline were in that division. Such products included: digital compact cassette (DCC), a digital extension of the compact cassette system, providing both recording and playback capabilities; High Definition Television (HDTV), with better clarity of vision and wider screens than conventional televisions; D2MAC, the intermediary stage between traditional television and HDTV; and CD Interactive (CD-i), optical compact disc that merges audio, video, text and graphics into one digital system. Intense research was also conducted toward development of screen telephones, flat panel displays, and multifunctional digital signal processors for multimedia markets—an area of expertise largely assigned to the company's new TriMedia division based in the United States.

Philips's aggressive R&D efforts boosted product development in other divisions as well. The lighting division moved closer to development compact fluorescent and halogen lighting, featuring compact designs and very high efficiency. Other lighting systems combined lighting with security, telephone, environmental, and computer systems. Responding to new burgeoning applications for semiconductors, the company also beefed up its semiconductor research, signing a cooperative agreement with IBM in January 1995 to develop new semiconductors in a jointly owned facility in Germany, while forging ahead in DRAM process know-how.

Despite the company's precedent of excellence and innovation, several of its research endeavors ran into obstacles in the early 1990s, shedding uncertain light on their chances of translating into sure market success. In the area of CD-i and DCC technology, for example, many analysts projected that Philips had missed the opportune time to claim market leadership. CD-i met stringent competition from a flood of other multimedia products, and DCC ran head-on against Sony's MiniDisc system (MD), with which that company was trying to set the industry standard as well. Still, Trimmer insisted that MD and DCC systems each met different consumer needs and that there was room enough for both to succeed in the marketplace. In the closely-related introduction of Multimedia CD (MMCD) products, Philips and Sony eventually joined forces in an attempt to win market share away from a similar product co-developed by Toshiba and Time Warner, Inc. In 1995, Sony and Philips were pushing a single-sided product that could store the equivalent of 135 minutes of a movie (or any combination of images, computing and audio recording power); while the Toshiba/Time Warner product—called a Super Compact Disk—could store much more information with its double-sided format, but required new hardware that was incompatible with older CD-ROMs. Ultimately, the only sure test of market share remained time . . . and marketing prowess, which both Philips and its competitors possessed in equal share.

Still, Philips' future looked bright, not only because of its expertise in lighting systems, but because of its long history of impeccable research and innovation. With its renewed focus on R&D, as well as its aggressive cost-cutting strategies, the company's diverse products in lighting, consumer electronics, domestic appliances, professional systems, and components remained poised for larger market shares. Philips, after all, had developed the cassette tape, the VCR, and the CD, which all became standards in consumer electronics industries. With the advent of a new age in interactive technology, there was no reason to doubt its supremacy in those technologies as well.

Principal Subsidiaries: Nederlandse Philips Bedrijven B.V.; Philips International B.V.; Philips Lighting Holding B.V.; Philips Communication systems International B.V.; Philips Components international B.V.; Philips Consumer Electronics International B.V.; Philips Domestic Appliances and Personal are International B.V.; Philips Industrial Electronics international B.V.; Philips Semiconductors International B.V.; Philips Electronic North American Corp. (U.S.)

Further Reading:

Bouman, P.J., *Anton Philips of Eindhoven,* London: Weidenfeld and Nicolson, 1956.

Fisher, Lawrence M., ''Gateway 2000 Backs Sony/Philips Disk Format,'' *The New York Times,* June 16, 1995, p. D8.

Heerding, A., trans. by Derek S. Jordan, *The History of N.V. Philips' Gloeilampenfabrieken,* Cambridge: Cambridge University Press, 1980.

Levine, Jonathan B., ''Has Philips Found Its Wizard?,'' *Business Week,* September 6, 1993, p. 82.

—updated by Kerstan Cohen

Piggly Wiggly Southern, Inc.

100 Brinson Road
Vidalia, Georgia 30474
U.S.A.
(912) 537-5500
Fax: (912) 537-1211

Wholly Owned Subsidiary of Bruno's Inc.
Incorporated: 1919
Employees: 6,000
Sales: $660 million
SICs: 5411 Grocery Stores

Food retailer Piggly Wiggly Southern, Inc. is an immediate subsidiary of Bruno's Inc., a food and drug chain company which operates and leases food, drug, and liquor stores in five southeastern states, with the heaviest concentration in Alabama, Georgia, and Florida. Bruno's acquired Piggly Wiggly Southern in 1988, adding it to its FoodMax, Food World, Food Fair, and Bruno's Food and Pharmacy franchises. By 1993, 57 Piggly Wiggly supermarkets were in operation, located largely in central and southern Georgia, representing 22 percent of its total number of stores. That year, to cut costs, Bruno's moved the Piggly Wiggly Southern corporate offices to Birmingham, Alabama, integrating them as a unit in its home office. However, it left the Piggly Wiggly distribution center in Vidalia, Georgia, its original base. Bruno's, under competitive pressure from other chains, notably Wal-Mart and Publix, was at that time restructuring its operations, closing unprofitable stores, remodeling others, and altering some of its marketing strategies. It was also recovering from a tragic air crash that in late 1991 had claimed the lives of Angelo and Lee Bruno, son and grandson of the company's founder, and four other company executives. Because of its restructuring, innovations, and the improving economy, the picture for Bruno's and its subsidiaries, including Piggly Wiggly Southern, brightened after 1993.

Although the food store chain concept was invented by A & P in 1859, the self-service food market came into being as a direct result of the first Piggly Wiggly store, established in Memphis, Tennessee by Clarence Saunders in September 1916. Prior to Saunders' introduction of Piggly Wiggly, grocery chains were essentially ''economy stores,'' which had replaced home-delivery and credit sales with a cash-and-carry system but were not planned for self-service. Saunders' first store, the forerunner of contemporary supermarkets, was designed to allow customers access to shelved merchandise which they would select and carry through turnstiles to checkout counters.

The plan was extremely successful, and the original Piggly Wiggly company extended franchises to hundreds of independent grocers who wanted to use the system and operate under the Piggly Wiggly name, giving the company a very complex history. Even some of the leading food chains, like Kroger and Safeway, operated stores under the Piggly Wiggly name before converting their parent stores to self-service. By 1920, stores under the Piggly Wiggly name were doing an aggregate $60 million per year business, with 35 stores in Memphis and hundreds in other cities and towns. The following year, Saunders and his organization had direct control of over 350 Piggly Wiggly stores, and there were many others operating on a royalty basis, paying a half percent of their gross sales to retain the franchise rights.

Among the companies that would eventually operate under the Piggly Wiggly name was the Tanner-Brice Company of Vidalia, Georgia. It was founded in September 1919, by Mitchell F. Brice with the financial backing of E. L. Tanner, his father-in-law. Tanner-Brice was incorporated to wholesale and retail ''groceries, dry goods and merchandise generally.'' Operating in rural Georgia, the company often did business on a bartering rather than a cash basis, particularly with farmers who could exchange eggs and butter for flour or other processed merchandise.

In the 1930s, during the Great Depression, which hit farm areas very hard, the Tanner-Brice Company grew through consolidations and foreclosures. The company had extended credit and had no choice but to seek legal redress when debtors defaulted on loans. The first such business legally conveyed to Tanner-Brice had been managed by a Mr. Sims, a former A & P employee. Thereafter, Tanner-Brice operated its small retail grocery stores under the name Sims Service Stores, Inc., reserving the Tanner-Brice name for its wholesale operation. The typical Sims store, like the one in Dublin, Georgia, was a long and narrow ''shotgun store'' with less than 4,000 square feet of floor space, and although the company started building larger stores nearer the end of the Depression, most of them into the World War II era were still small, ''mom and pop'' operations.

In 1941, under tight money constraints and pressure from such competition as A & P (which had more efficient supply and marketing arrangements) and unable to keep up with the product demands of his customers, Mitch Brice decided to sell his controlling interest in the company in order to concentrate on his other business interests. A salesman named Phil Friese, aware of the company's difficulties, convinced the Schroder Trust Company of New York to take over the firm. At the time, with Friese as the new general manager, Tanner-Brice had 76 retail stores in operation. Brice retained a one-sixth share of the business but stepped down from the company's presidency to devote time to his banking and movie theater interests.

In what proved to be an astute policy, the new owners of Tanner-Brice decided to include existing company supervisors in the firm's restructuring and to institute an optional profit-sharing plan. Credit for these decisions can be given to Hugo

Meyer, who represented the majority stockholders. Meyer also convinced a friend, Gerald H. Achenbach, a Wall Street investment counselor, to take over the Tanner-Brice presidency, surmising that Achenbach's skills and experience would be invaluable in the company's restructuring. Achenbach went to Georgia with the idea of propping up the operation and then moving on, but he ended up staying on with the company until his retirement.

Among other restructuring measures, the new management liquidated the wholesale end of the business because the gross retail sales were 800 percent greater than the wholesale sales. Then, in 1943, Achenbach and his chief associates, who believed that the self-service food market was the best model for future expansion, entered into an agreement with the Piggly Wiggly Corporation. In a policy summary written during that year, Achenbach argued that the Piggly Wiggly arrangement would allow for ''bigness'' without sacrificing ''personal influence'' to impersonal protocols.

On an experimental basis, the company began converting selected Sims stores to Piggly Wigglys, starting with a store in Americus, Georgia, in July 1943. Convinced that the conversions to the Piggly Wiggly format would prove of great benefit to Tanner-Brice, in 1945 the company changed its name to Piggly Wiggly Sims, Inc., joining the two trade names under which it then operated.

Some further adjustments were necessary to keep the company on firm footing. In one problem year, 1946, the company, operating a chain of 36 stores, netted a profit of only $5,000. Financially, the situation improved after 1947, when an outsider from Tennessee, J. A. Crockett, joined the firm and set up a much more effective system of accounting and identifying profit-margin problems. In 1948, the company was able to buy six Piggly Wiggly stores in Macon, Georgia, franchises that also traced their beginning back to 1919, when Clarence Saunders, the Piggly Wiggly originator, advised some Macon merchants to get into the self-service grocery business.

It was also in 1948 that the company warehouse in Vidalia was reorganized by its new superintendent, E. G. Weathers. With the marketing skills of other personnel, including Fred Stewart, D. Larkin Temples, and Weathers' successor, E. K. Stafford, Sr., Piggly Wiggly Sims quickly became one of the most modern and efficient food distribution centers in Georgia.

Throughout the 1940s, Piggly Wiggly Sims had pursued a policy of closing stores that either by size or age presented modernization or expansion problems. The plan had been to remodel select stores in order to make them the most up-to-date supermarkets in their communities. By 1950, firmly convinced that it had made the right decision to make the changeover complete, the company converted its last viable Sims stores to Piggly Wigglys and changed the company name to Piggly Wiggly Southern, Inc. While the conversion and closing policy for a time resulted in a reduction in the total number of stores that Piggly Wiggly Southern operated, falling to a low of 27 stores in 1960, the decline in the total number of stores was misleading, for in 1961 26 stores generated $25 million in sales, while in 1941 76 stores, most of them small, mom and pop stores, had generated a total sales of only $2 million.

In 1952, in a move to centralize it operations, Piggly Wiggly Southern had moved its corporate headquarters into a new building in downtown Vidalia. Two years later it bought a large warehouse, which allowed the company to distribute a greater variety and larger number of foodstuffs. At about the same time, following a policy of employee participation in company policy making, the company extended the previously limited profit-sharing plan to all employees and instituted a pension plan. The company was also flexible and aggressive in its marketing techniques, and throughout the 1950s used such attractions as S & H Green Stamps and price war strategies to keep its customers from defecting to its competitors.

Later in the 1950s, while continuing to expand its self-service food market business, Piggly Wiggly Southern also incorporated two subsidiaries. The first was a printing company operating under the name of Southern Graphic Arts; the second was a chain of auto parts stores operating as Whiteway, Inc. The first of these proved very profitable, and by 1977 it was printing 23 weekly newspapers. However, the Whiteway stores struggled, and after four years of operation had just reached a break-even point. The Whiteway enterprise was then liquidated, after accumulating a before-tax loss of about $600,000.

In the early 1960s, the company realized the need for yet a more efficient, centralized operation. By then it was distributing foods from nine different warehouses scattered around downtown Vidalia. It solved the problem by moving into new buildings outside of Vidalia, built in the green hills that lay in the suburbs to the east. The new office complex and expandable warehouse went into operation in 1967. The offices were comfortable and spacious, while the gigantic, 500,000 square foot warehouse was outfitted with the latest climate control equipment and boasted 65,000 square feet of frozen storage space.

The number of Piggly Wiggly Southern stores continued to increase through both the 1960s and 1970s. Newly started stores were larger and better equipped than the old Sims stores and offered a much greater variety of foods and services. In 1977, the company opened a 40,000 square foot Piggly Wiggly in Augusta, Georgia, about 100 miles north of Vidalia, with such new features as an in-store bakery, a flower shop, and a delicatessen with booths where hungry shoppers could sit and eat lunch or just drink a soda. The store, the 61st operated by Piggly Wiggly Southern, was widely regarded as one of the most beautiful commercial buildings in the South. It was also an instant financial success, recording gross sales of $155,000 in its first week of business, a company record.

Throughout its post World War II expansion, Piggly Wiggly Southern pursued a deliberate policy of promoting from within, and for that reason took special care to groom its employees for potential advancement through the managerial ranks. Among other things, it instituted orientation and self-improvement programs for its employees, designed to make sure that they would have adequate training to take on new responsibilities within the organization. The result was that most all the senior executives in the company had at one time first worked at such lower-end jobs as part-time clerking in one of the old Sims or newer Piggly Wiggly Stores. For example, Ronald A. Frost, who succeeded Achenbach as president, had started in the business by sweeping the floor of his father's store in Wrightsville, Georgia, with a stubby broom.

In the 1980s, Piggly Wiggly Southern became the leading supermarket chain in the central and southern Georgia region. By 1987, it was serving about 765,000 customers weekly. It continued to locate most of its stores in suburban areas, and prided itself on its customer loyalty, derived from its ''long standing commitment to providing a high level of customer service and convenience,'' according to company literature. In that year it was operating 82 retail supermarkets under the Piggly Wiggly name, all located within 175 miles of its distribution center in Vidalia. Stores ranged in size from about 13,000 to 47,000 square feet and averaged around 24,000 square feet. Forty-four of its stores were new or were extensively remodeled or enlarged in the 1980s.

However, the company underwent a restructuring that resulted from a 1986 ownership transfer to the PWS Holding Corporation. PWS acquired control in a managerial buy out scheme organized by Riordan Freeman & Spogli, a Los Angeles banking firm that had invested in other supermarket chains. Shortly after the transfer, new upper echelon managers took over the operation of the business, including, for example, James A. Bolanda, who replaced Frost as CEO and president.

Bruno's, Inc. then acquired Piggly Wiggly Southern in April 1988. At the time, the company's annual sales exceeded $571 million. The transaction brought 58 of the Piggly Wiggly Southern stores under Bruno's corporate umbrella. The price was 2.49 million shares of Bruno's common stock. Bruno's retained some key Piggly Wiggly personnel in middle management, but it replaced the top executives with personnel from its own corporate structure. It named Paul F. Garrison president, then replaced him with William J. White when Garrison was named president of Bruno's newly formed Birmingham division.

Bruno's acquisition of Piggly Wiggly Southern involved a contingent liability suit against PWS Holding, which had broken a lease agreement. In 1991, a judgment of $4.2 million in damages was awarded the plaintiff, reducing Bruno's second quarter profits by about $2.66 million. Through 1992, when Bruno's was still showing ''no momentum'' and the company was reeling from a risky joint venture with Kmart, the wisdom of its Piggly Wiggly investment was in doubt. However, since 1993, it has proved a lucrative transaction and was likely to remain a profitable part of Bruno's business for several years.

Principal Subsidiaries: Georgia Sales Co.

Further Reading:

''A Piggly Wiggly Idea Develops Into a $60,000,000 Business,'' *Current Opinion,* November 1921, pp. 669–70.

''Bruno's After the Crash,'' *Forbes,* July 6, 1992, p. 128.

''Food Distributors: Getting Hyper,'' *Forbes,* January 11, 1988, p. 132.

''It Was Merger, Buyout Time For Firms in 1988,'' *Atlanta Business Chronicle,* June 12, 1989.

Kindel, Stephen, ''Bruno's: On the Mend Slowly,'' *Financial World,* March 30, 1993, p. 20–21.

Lebhar, Godfrey M., *Chain Stores in America: 1859–1962,* 3rd edition, New York: Chain Store Publishing Corporation, 1963.

''Piggly Wiggly Comeback,'' *Business Week,* November 24, 1934, pp. 14–15.

—John W. Fiero

Pillsbury Company

200 South Sixth Street
Minneapolis, Minnesota 55402-1454
U.S.A.
(612) 3304966
Fax: (612) 3307283

Wholly Owned Subsidiary of Grand Metropolitan PLC
Incorporated: 1869 as the Pillsbury Flour Mills Company
Employees: 18,000
Sales: $5.6 billion
SICs: 2041 Flour & Other Grain Mill Products; 2038 Frozen Specialties, Not Elsewhere Classified; 2033 Canned Fruits & Vegetables

Pillsbury is one of America's oldest and best-recognized names in food retailing. From its beginnings in flour milling, but over the course of more than a century, the company evolved over the course of a century into a broader based food producer. In 1989, Pillsbury was acquired by Grand Metropolitan PLC, a diversified British beverage company.

In 1869, after working in his uncle's hardware supply company in Minneapolis, 27-year-old Charles A. Pillsbury bought one-third of a local flour mill for $10,000 and began the Pillsbury Company. Pillsbury and a competitor, the Washburn Crosby Company, formed the Minneapolis Millers Association that same year.

Pillsbury's improvements in milling machinery included the early incorporation of modern equipment for milling the very hard local wheat. These improvements and the purchase of two additional mills allowed him to produce 2,000 barrels of flour a day by 1872. That year he reorganized the company as C.A. Pillsbury and Company, making his father and uncle partners. In addition, he registered the trademark Pillsbury's Best XXXX in 1872.

During the 1880s Pillsbury added six more mills, including one that was then the largest flour mill in the world. This mill was equipped with state-of-the-art machinery, which more than tripled the company's output. Weakened by three mill fires in 1881, Pillsbury Company had just begun to recover, and was buying grain elevators to cut storage costs, when, in 1889, it sold the Pillsbury mills to an English financial syndicate. The syndicate also purchased competing Minnesota mills, elevators, and bordering water-power rights. Pillsbury remained as managing director of the new company, which was called the Pillsbury-Washburn Flour Mills Company Ltd. The company put its new water-power rights to use, and in 1896 the company passed the 10,000 barrel-per-day mark. Pillsbury-Washburn eventually grew, under Pillsbury's leadership, into the world's largest milling company.

During the 1890s the company focused on vertical integration. It began selling flour directly to retailers and stepped up advertising. Pillsbury-Washburn struggled with freight rates and the depressed agricultural economy during the first few years of the 20th century. In 1907, following a poor harvest, it became impossible for the company to mill profitably. Unmet financial obligations forced it into receivership. Charles S. Pillsbury, Charles A. Pillsbury's son, was one of the three men appointed to reorganize the company, which became the Pillsbury Flour Mills Company.

The new company overhauled the mills and the organization that ran them. In addition Pillsbury became a pioneer in product research by building its own laboratory. The firm rebounded and, on June 27, 1923, the Pillsbury Flour Mills Company purchased all remaining assets from the shareholders of Pillsbury-Washburn.

During the 1920s the Pillsburys opened several new plants and began to diversify. By 1932 Pillsbury had expanded into specialized grain products like cake flour and cereals. Expansion continued through 1940 with deals like the $3 million purchase of the Globe Grain and Milling Company and its various plants. The purchase helped Pillsbury set a new flour-milling record of 40,000 barrels a day. Pillsbury also continued manufacturing Globe's line of pancake mixes, biscuit mixes, and pasta.

In 1944 the company changed its name to Pillsbury Mills, Inc. Throughout this period Pillsbury family members had run the company, and in 1940 Philip W. Pillsbury, Charles S. Pillsbury's son, became president. The company limited itself to kitchen staples through the 1940s, but expanded its offerings in that line. Pillsbury began to export its flour, introduced food products for hotels and restaurants, and manufactured food products for U.S. troops during World War II, developing dry soup mixes in addition to its grains.

In the late 1940s Pillsbury ventured into higher-margin convenience products to meet growing consumer demand. Cake mixes were introduced in 1948, and over the next ten years Pillsbury increased the varieties it offered. The company expanded its product line with yet another acquisition, in 1951, of Ballard & Ballard Company and its line of refrigerated foods.

Pillsbury invested heavily in market research and development during the 1950s, and by the end of the decade had broadened beyond baking-related products. The company also continued its vertical integration efforts during the decade, opening milling plants in Canada and increasing its grain storage capacity. The company grew so quickly in the 1950s that by 1963 the Pillsbury name appeared on 127 different products. As the company's marketing and development continued to accelerate through the decade, so did its interest in a bigger market.

In 1959 Pillsbury began purchasing flour mills abroad, including units in Venezuela, El Salvador, Guatemala, Ghana, the Philippines, and Trinidad. In successive years international operations increased to include food companies in France, Australia, and Germany. Fast growth continued, and in 1960 Pillsbury made its first nonfood purchase, Tidy House Products Company, a manufacturer of household cleaners.

Robert J. Keith, who became president in 1966, brought Pillsbury into a new phase of food production. The post-war convenience era culminated in 1967 with the purchase of Burger King, the fast-food restaurant chain. By 1968 Pillsbury also owned interests in a variety of companies, including a computer time-sharing business, a publications division, and a life insurance company.

At the end of its first 100 years the Pillsbury Company had become highly diversified and decentralized in order to handle the variety of management decisions involved with producing flours and instant foods, as well as running restaurant, computer, and publishing operations. Terrance Hanold, who became president in 1967, planned to continue diversifying and increasing independence for managers in the 1970s.

In 1973 William H. Spoor became CEO and Pillsbury entered an era of increasing sales and earnings. Spoor valued diversification and growth through acquisition, but he limited Pillsbury to the food industry. He quickly stripped the company of housing, computer time-sharing, and flower businesses, as well as other businesses unrelated to food processing.

Over the next few years Spoor purchased Totino's Finer Foods and followed this venture into frozen foods with the 1979 purchase of Green Giant, a packager of frozen vegetables. Steak & Ale, Pillsbury's first full-service restaurant chain, was acquired in 1976; the well-timed purchase of HäagenDazs ice cream came in 1983; and Van de Kamp, the seafood company that produced Chicken of the Sea canned tuna followed in 1984. A few weeks after Spoor retired in 1984, Pillsbury announced the purchase of two more restaurant companies: Diversifoods Inc. and QuikWok Inc.

Pillsbury's business boomed during the 1970s, as Spoor solidified Pillsbury's strategy and made several smart purchases. Green Giant and other frozen-food companies gave Pillsbury a much larger share of the food industry and more consistent earnings. Profits in 1976 were divided almost evenly between three groups: consumer foods, agricultural products, and restaurants. By 1984, the agriproducts group had shrunk to only four percent and restaurants provided 53 percent.

The agriproducts group had long been run by Fred C. Pillsbury, Charles S. Pillsbury's brother, who developed cattle feeds from mill by-products before the turn of the century. The division grew to become responsible for the collection, milling, storage, trading, and distribution of grain and feed ingredients. Pillsbury continued to provide about ten percent of U.S. flour into the 1980s, and the division became one of the largest U.S. purchasers of grains and dry beans.

Consumer foods, the company's largest division, marketed Pillsbury's supermarket products. In addition to its domestic subsidiaries, Pillsbury sold grocery items through H.J. Green and Hammond's in the United Kingdom, Erasco and Jokisch in West Germany, Gringoir/Brossard and Singapour in France and Belgium, and Milani in Venezuela. Pillsbury also owned similar operations in Mexico, Guatemala, Jamaica, and the Philippines. In the United States, Pillsbury's line of refrigerated dough, for products like pastries and cookies, was distributed by Kraft Foods for many years. These products accounted for about ten percent of the company's sales.

Pillsbury owed much of the credit for this extraordinary boom to its restaurants. By expanding Burger King's operations and hiring Donald Smith from McDonald's, it became the second largest fastfood chain operator. The purchase of Diversifoods, at $390 million Pillsbury's biggest acquisition, included nearly 400 additional Burger King outlets as well as Godfather's Pizza, Chart House, and Luther's BarBQ. Pillsbury decided to compete with McDonald's not in size but in per unit sales. As Burger King continued to grow, franchising became more common and only 20 percent of the restaurants remained company owned.

John M. Stafford inherited a healthy company when he was appointed president in 1984. Each year between 1972 and 1986 the company set records for both sales and earnings. Pillsbury had a reputation for quiet, conservative growth, despite nearly doubling its earnings between 1980 and 1985, from $100 million to $190 million. Pillsbury finally surpassed its chief competitor, General Mills, during Stafford's first full year. Because Stafford, who came to Pillsbury through Green Giant, expected growth through increased demand for products from the agriproducts and restaurant groups, company structure remained unchanged.

Pillsbury, however, had dramatically changed its position internationally. The company no longer exported flour, since local mills could produce it more efficiently. Instead, the international division began marketing prepared foods and restaurants overseas. By 1984 Pillsbury sold over 200 products in 55 countries and Burger King had restaurants in 22 countries.

Unchecked growth continued in 1985. Cash dividends increased for the 27th consecutive year. Earnings were up 13 percent, another record, and over 400 percent higher than the 1976 level. Pillsbury focused on consumer foods abroad through acquisitions and subsidiary product development. In 1986 the company's international subsidiaries reported a six percent increase in sales, and Pillsbury prepared to market its domestic labels, like HäagenDazs, in Japan and Europe. International sales increased 18 percent the next year.

The mid-1980s brought a gradual reversal of the company's progress, however. Sectors of agriproducts began to report losses, and the company spent heavily on concept development for its restaurants. The success of its Bennigan's restaurant chain covered its start-up costs, but sales for chains like Steak & Ale failed to increase.

Stafford began to shift priorities, albeit conservatively. Bennigan's and Burger King were squeezed to make up for decreasing returns on the smaller restaurant chains. Consumer foods showed a profit gain of 22 percent between 1985 and 1987, and Stafford planned to continue development of Pillsbury's frozen foods and its microwave line, first introduced in 1979.

The corporation continued to have problems secondguessing the fast-paced restaurant industry. Total sales increased five percent, but earnings declined for the first time in 16 years, down 13 percent. Consumer foods and agriproducts remained strong, but the decline in profits prompted further evaluation.

Although acquisitions overseas and in Canada continued, the company announced early in 1988, after a nine-month review, that it would reduce its restaurant division. While it kept Burger King, Bennigan's, Godfather's, and Steak & Ale, the corporation sought to rid itself of company-run units by selling them to franchisers. It also planned to refurbish 145 Burger King units. These modest reductions disappointed some analysts and takeover rumors began to circulate.

Such rumors gained momentum when the board asked William Spoor to return as CEO. Then, the chairman of Steak & Ale and the president of the U.S. foods division left the company, creating the perception of a lack of leadership. In 1988 earnings plummeted to $6.9 million, less than half the level of the year before. Management attributed much of this decline to restaurant-related restructuring changes.

Philip L. Smith, formerly of the General Foods Corporation, became CEO in August 1988. He held the post for five months as he tried to fight off a takeover attempt that had begun in October, when the British distiller Grand Metropolitan PLC first made a $60 per share bid for Pillsbury. For nearly three months after GrandMet's initial offer, Pillsbury fought the takeover. The company tried to arrange a poison pill defense and to spin off Burger King, but it was prevented from doing so by court order.

In 1989, Pillsbury became a part of Grand Metropolitan after shareholders accepted a $66 per share offer. GrandMet was one of the world's leading consumer goods companies, specializing in branded food and drink businesses. The deal, worth $5.75 billion, made GrandMet the eighth largest food manufacturing company in the world. GrandMet's branded consumer foods businesses were organized into two main groups: Pillsbury and GrandMet Foods-Europe. Pillsbury's consumer foods business was organized along major brand groups, including Pillsbury, Green Giant, and HäagenDazs. Burger King became a separate entity within the food sector.

Pillsbury's operations and sales improved following the acquisition. GrandMet's restructuring reduced expenses by about $150 million and eliminated about 3,550 jobs by the middle of 1990. In May 1990 GrandMet released an impressive financial report for the first six months of the fiscal year. Pre-tax profits were up 36 percent and earnings per share increased 25 percent. Furthermore, the company predicted it would turn a profit on the Pillsbury acquisition in its first full fiscal year and would have no problem meeting the corporate goal of 15 percent annual earnings growth.

Pillsbury, under the management of CEO Paul Walsh, planned to move away from commodity products such as flour, and focus on products with established brand names, while expanding into the international market. Toward that end, the company made several significant acquisitions during the 1990s. The company's February 1992 acquisition of McGlynn Bakeries's frozen products division enhanced Pillsbury's bakery division through its marketing of frozen dough products to food service and convenience outlets, as well as bakery mixes to in-store bakeries. The McGlynn products were given the more recognizable Pillsbury brand name.

In November 1993 Pillsbury purchased Roush Products Company, a manufacturer of variety and specialty bread mixes for food service and wholesale bakers. The acquisition also included Country Hearth, a market-leading brand of bread. In 1994 Pillsbury purchased Rudi Foods Inc., a leading producer of partially baked breads for food service and supermarket bakeries. The operations were combined with Pillsbury Bakeries and Foodservice Inc., an entity with annual sales of about $500 million. That same year, Pillsbury acquired Martha White brand baking mixes and flours.

Perhaps one of the most notable acquisitions was Pillsbury's February 1995 acquisition of food conglomerate Pet Inc. for $2.6 billion. The purchase gave Pillsbury such popular brand names as Old El Paso, Progresso, Pet-Ritz, and Downyflake. Moreover, the Pet line enabled Pillsbury to create a more diverse product line, so that the Pillsbury name spanned across supermarket shelves.

In 1994, Pillsbury introduced over 80 new products, including Totino's Select Pizza, Pillsbury Cream Cheese Toaster Strudel, HäagenDazs Sorbet, and Hungry Jack Microwave Syrups. Internationally, Pillsbury products were sold in more than 55 countries. In Japan, Green Giant achieved a market-leading position in the frozen vegetable market and HäagenDazs became the leading brand of premium ice cream. The company planned on expanding its Pillsbury, Green Giant, and HäagenDazs brands into Russia, India, Asia and Latin America.

For over 125 years, Pillsbury has created and marketed some of the best-known brands and products, making the Pillsbury Doughboy and Jolly Green Giant familiar figures in kitchens across America. Under GrandMet, Pillsbury remained a prominent leader in the food industry and was positioned as a powerful competitor in world markets.

Further Reading:

Fusaro, Dave, "The Doughboy Is Smiling Again," *Prepared Foods,* April 1994, p. 30.

Kuhn, Mary Ellen, "Pillsbury Plus Pet Looks Like a Winner," *Food Processing,* February 1995, p. 27.

Papa, Mary Bader, "Run, Doughboy, Run," *Corporate Report-Minnesota,* July 1990, p. 39.

"Pillsbury Acquires Rudi Baked Breads Producer," *Nation's Restaurant News,* July 11, 1994, p. 81.

"Pillsbury Buys Windmill Holdings Unit," *Nation's Restaurant News,* November 29, 1993, p. 30.

Riddle, Judith S., "McGlynn Brings Pillsbury Extra Dough," *Supermarket News,* July 20, 1992, p. 35.

Wiesendanger, Betsy, "Linda Keene: Making a Stale Business Poppin' Fresh," *Sales & Marketing Management,* April 1992, p. 38.

—updated by Beth Watson Highman

PNC Bank Corp.

One PNC Plaza
Fifth Avenue and Wood Street
Pittsburgh, Pennsylvania 15222
U.S.A.
(412) 762-2666
Fax: (412) 762-4507

Public Company
Incorporated: 1983 as PNC Financial Corporation
Employees: 26,400
Total Assets: $75.8 billion
Stock Exchanges: New York
SICs: 6712 Bank Holding Companies; 6021 National Commercial Banks; 6022 State Commercial Banks; 6091 Nondeposit Trust Facilities

PNC Bank Corp. is the 11th largest bank in the United States and one of the premier superregional bank holding companies. PNC has grown rapidly in the 1980s and 1990s mainly through a series of acquisitions, the largest being the 1995 purchase of Midlantic Corp. In an era of heavy bank consolidation brought on by increasing competitive pressures and deregulation, PNC's aggressive acquisition program has enabled it to stay competitive. Increasingly diversified through 1990s nonbank acquisitions, PNC operates in four core businesses: corporate banking, retail banking, investment and trust management, and investment banking.

PNC Bank Corp.'s immediate forerunner was PNC Financial Corporation, formed in 1983 from the merger of two Pennsylvania banking concerns, the Pittsburgh National Corporation and the Provident National Corporation. The Pittsburgh National Bank was incorporated in 1959, but its roots can be traced back to 1852, when steel magnates James Laughlin and B. F. Jones opened the Pittsburgh Trust and Savings in downtown Pittsburgh. PNC Financial's other predecessor, the Provident National Bank, headquartered in Philadelphia, can also be traced to the mid-1800s. In 1847, the Tradesmens National Bank of Philadelphia opened its doors. After more than a century of banking and a series of name changes and acquisitions, it became the Provident National Bank in 1964. The Pittsburgh National Bank and the Provident National Bank combined their extensive banking experience in 1983. At that time, the newly formed bank holding company was no more than a medium-sized regional concern, but it rapidly developed into one of the nation's most powerful superregional banks.

PNC's first chief executive, Merle E. Gilliand, had already served as CEO at Pittsburgh National Bank for 11 years by the time PNC Financial was formed. Gilliand set the tone of PNC's management style, which has been described as "bottom-up management." He surrounded himself with competent senior executives and allowed them to make decisions on their own. This grass roots approach was rare in banking. Gilliand, however, contended that this method provided better service and, over the long run, a better bank. Under Gilliand's leadership, PNC emphasized quality, not size. Nonetheless, this strategy also proved very conducive to growth in the changing markets of the 1980s.

PNC's chief rival in the 1980s was the Mellon Bank. For years, Mellon controlled the large corporate accounts of Pittsburgh's many companies (the city ranked third in the nation in number of corporate headquarters). As a result, PNC was forced to cater to mid-sized companies and to businesses outside of Pittsburgh. But, when Pittsburgh's big companies experienced difficulties in the late 1970s and 1980s, PNC was not as exposed to the "rust belt" problems as the Mellon Bank. PNC, under Gilliand, was content to operate on a smaller scale than its rival, striving to provide all the same services with greater quality.

Banking deregulation allowed, and to some extent encouraged, mergers between banks. As the 1980s wore on, a number of well-run banks found it in their interest to join forces with the PNC group. PNC's acquisition strategy focused on purchasing healthy banks which would add to the corporation's overall strength. In 1984, PNC acquired the Marine Bank of Erie, Pennsylvania. A year later, it acquired the Northeastern Bancorp of Scranton, Pennsylvania. PNC's criteria for acquisitions were strict by industry standards. Acceptable banks were mid-sized, with assets of between $2 and $6 billion, had a solid market share in their operating regions, earned excellent return on equity and on assets, and ideally had expertise in a specific area of financial services which would benefit the entire group. Close attention was also paid to whether or not the bank's management philosophy was compatible with PNC's.

In 1985, Thomas H. O'Brien replaced the retiring Merle Gilliand as CEO at PNC. At 48, O'Brien was the youngest CEO of any major U.S. bank. Ironically, he had started his banking career at PNC's archrival, the Mellon Bank, before earning his MBA at Harvard. O'Brien had risen quickly through the ranks of the Pittsburgh National Bank, eventually heading PNC's merchant banking activities, and finally becoming chairman and chief executive. As the top executive at PNC he continued Gilliand's bottom-up management style. O'Brien would let executives at affiliates implement their own ideas at their own bank without a great deal of interference from the top. As a result of the autonomy PNC gave its affiliated banks, the banking group was an attractive merger partner for exactly the healthy regional banks it wished to acquire. PNC could grow, and the new affiliates could take advantage of the extended services offered by the group. PNC became known for its friendly takeovers of already successful banks.

Under O'Brien's conservative yet aggressive leadership, PNC grew at a tremendous rate. In 1986, the Hershey Bank joined the group. The following year, with the acquisition of Citizen's Fidelity Corporation of Louisville, PNC grew larger than its rival, the Mellon Bank. In 1988, PNC acquired the Central Bancorp of Cincinnati and the First Bank and Trust of Mechanicsburg. While acquisitions normally diluted the value of a corporation's stock for some time, PNC's careful planning allowed it to quickly make up for the dilution. By the late 1980s, Wall Street analysts were so confident in PNC's management that acquisition announcements did not seriously reduce the stock's price.

The relaxation of interstate banking regulations in the United States during this time created a new kind of bank: the superregional. Superregionals operated in a number of states, and began in the late 1980s to compete with the money center banks for a greater share of large corporate business. As mid-sized companies needed more services in the international trade arena, the superregionals became more and more involved there as well. With its network spread throughout Pennsylvania, Kentucky, Ohio, and Delaware, PNC was the premier superregional in the United States by 1987 and had become the nation's 12th-largest banking group. Its assets had more than doubled since 1983, and its earnings were among the highest in the industry.

Like many banks throughout the world, PNC was forced to set aside huge sums as a provision against bad debt in Third World countries in 1987. Unlike many banks, however, the PNC group still earned a substantial profit that year, despite its $200 million increase in loan loss reserves. While two-thirds of U.S. banks actually showed losses, PNC netted more than $255 million for its shareholders that year.

The banking group was very conservative in its lending throughout the 1980s. It set limits for the number of loans allowed to any particular industry and enforced stringent credit criteria. At the same time, PNC was energetic in its marketing. The corporation went after trust and money management business as well as corporate lending. PNC affiliates also showed higher than average earnings from fee income.

PNC suffered a slight setback in 1989 and 1990 when it was caught with millions in nonperforming commercial real estate loans—part of them inherited through its late 1980s acquisitions—resulting in reduced earnings. The company responded by tightening its loan policies and beginning an effort to reduce its dependence on riskier commercial loans in favor of the more dependable consumer sector. A restructuring in 1991 further reflected PNC's desire to diversify its holdings by focusing company's operations on four core businesses: corporate banking, retail banking, investment and trust management, and investment banking. The following year, with assets reaching $45.5 billion, PNC began a program of consolidation in which all its banks and most of its affiliated companies would take on the name PNC Bank. PNC Financial Corporation itself changed its name to PNC Bank Corp. in early 1993.

PNC's desire to diversify was evident in its nonbank acquisitions of the early 1990s. In 1993 PNC acquired the Massachusetts Company to boost its financial services offerings. That year it also acquired the Sears Mortgage Banking Group, a major home mortgage lender, from Sears Roebuck & Co. for $328 million in cash. The move immediately quadrupled PNC's mortgage business, pushing it into the top ten nationwide. In 1994 a third major nonbank acquisition bolstered the bank's asset management area. The purchase of BlackRock Financial Management for $240 million in cash and notes increased PNC's amount of assets under management to $75 billion, the sixth-largest amount among bank asset managers.

These acquisitions, however, would pale in comparison to those overseen by chairman and CEO O'Brien in the mid-1990s. As a prelude, in 1993 PNC purchased First Eastern Corp. of Wilkes-Barre, Pennsylvania, for $330 million, solidifying its holdings in northeastern Pennsylvania. In keeping with his strategy of expanding only within or adjacent to PNC's existing retail banking territory, O'Brien then shifted his attention to the Philadelphia area and New Jersey, long a target for PNC growth. Early in 1995, PNC purchased 84 branches in southern and central New Jersey from Chemical Banking Corp. for $504 million. Then in July of that year, the bank announced it would acquire Midlantic Corp. of Edison, New Jersey, through a $2.84 billion stock swap. Midlantic's $13.7 billion in assets would give PNC a total of $75.8 billion in assets, making it the 11th largest bank in the country. More importantly, PNC had purchased the third largest bank in New Jersey and had achieved a significant presence there.

Through its acquisitions in the early and mid-1990s, PNC Bank Corp. had in many ways created a unique type of bank that could provide a model for others to emulate. It was considered one of the top superregionals in the country with more than 800 branches in the contiguous area of Indiana, Kentucky, New Jersey, Pennsylvania, and Ohio. At the same time, it was building a national and in some cases international presence in the areas of asset management services and investment banking. Its strong regional retail banking operations coupled with its diversified financial services businesses were designed to help it weather banking downturns that have inevitably beset PNC's and other banks' earnings in the past. As barriers to interstate banking continued to fall, however, industry analysts were predicting further bank consolidation, even suggesting that only about five large banks would be left by the end of the 1990s. Whether PNC would be among them remained to be seen.

Principal Subsidiaries: Bank of Delaware Corporation; BHC Holding, Inc.; BHC Securities, Inc.; The Central Bancorporation, Inc.; PINACO; The Central Bank & Trust Company; The Central Trust Co. Central Ohio; PNB Securities Corp.; PNC Bancorp Inc.; PNC Bank (Indiana); PNC Bank (Kentucky); PNC Bank (Pennsylvania); PNC Bank, N.A.; PNC Bank, Northern Kentucky; PNC Bank, South Central; PNC Capital Corp.; PNC Commercial Corporation; PNC Community Development Corp.; PNC Corp.; PNC ESOP Funding Corporation; PNC Financial Services, Inc.; PNC Florida, Inc.; PNC Funding Corp.; PNC International Bank; PNC International Finance, N.V.; PNC Leasing Corp.; PNC Life Insurance Company; PNC National Bank; PNC National Investment Corporation; PNC-NJ N.A.; PNC Realty Corporation; PNC Realty Holding Corporation; PNC Securities Corp.; PNC Trust Company of Florida, N.A.; PNC Venture Corporation; RBS/PNCF Inc.; Sears Mortgage Company.

Further Reading:

Crockett, Barton, ''Has PNC Picked the Wrong Time to Grow in Investment Management?,'' *American Banker,* October 5, 1994, p. 8.

''Forging a New Bank at PNC,'' *United States Banker,* July 1993, pp. 22–24.

Murray, Matt, and Timothy L. O'Brien, ''PNC Bank Corp. Agrees to Purchase Midlantic in a $2.84 Billion Stock Swap,'' *Wall Street Journal,* July 11, 1995, p. A3.

——, ''PNC Is Acquiring Chemical Branches for $504 Million,'' *Wall Street Journal,* March 9, 1995, p. A6.

O'Brien, Timothy L., and Steven Lipin, ''In Latest Round of Banking Mergers, Even Big Institutions Become Targets,'' *Wall Street Journal,* pp. A3, A4.

Olson, Thomas, ''PNC Ensures New Market by Selling Insurance Products,'' *Pittsburgh Business Journal,* July 25–31, 1994, p. 15.

——, ''PNC's Purchase of Sears Mortgage Offers Market Clout,'' *Pittsburgh Business Times,* May 17–23, 1993, p. 5.

''PNC Bank to Buy First Eastern Corp. in $330 Million Deal,'' *Wall Street Journal,* p. B4.

Schroeder, Michael, ''Maybe This Bank Should Have Cried Wolf,'' *Business Week,* September 17, 1990, p. 140.

——, ''A Pittsburgh Bank That's Dazzling the Street,'' *Business Week,* February 29, 1988, p. 84.

Stern, Gabriella, and Robert McGough, ''PNC Agrees to Acquisition of BlackRock,'' *Wall Street Journal,* p. A4.

—updated by David E. Salamie

Porsche AG

Stuttgart
D-7000
Germany
011 711 8270
Fax: 011 711 827 5777
Porsche Cars North America Inc.
P.O. Box 30911
Reno, Nevada 89520
U.S.A.
(702) 348-3000
Fax: (702) 348-3880

Public Company
Incorporated: 1931 as Dr. Ing hc F. Porsche KG
Employees: 8,431
Sales: DM 2.6 billion
Stock Exchanges: Frankfurt
SICs: 5012 Automobiles & Other Motor Vehicles

Porsche AG is legendary for its innovative and beautiful automobile designs. The Porsche 911, first manufactured in 1963, quickly became one of the world's most famous and most recognizable automobiles. The company has also been on the cutting edge of automotive engineering and technology, using the sports car racing circuit to develop and improve products renowned for their high performance and outstanding handling. It is not surprising that Porsche has recorded more victories than any other automobile manufacturer in such classics as the 24 Hour LeMans and the 24 Hour Daytona races.

The founder of the company, Dr. Ferdinand Porsche, was born in Bohemia and studied mechanical engineering in Vienna. In 1923 he traveled to Stuttgart, Germany, and by 1930 the ambitious young man had established his own engineering and design firm there under the name Dr. Ing hc F. Porsche KG. The new firm garnered a reputation for innovative car designs, and when Adolf Hitler came to power in Germany, he summoned Ferdinand Porsche to meet with him, requesting that he find a solution to some of the technical difficulties that were delaying production of the "Volkswagen," or people's car. The famous Volkswagen design had been created in Porsche's office, and as early as 1935 Porsche had designed a special sports version of the car. The Nazi regime initially rejected his application to produce the sporting version, but during the late 1930s Hitler himself approved a contract with Porsche to design a car for the 1939 Auto-Union Grand Prix, a famous motor race from Berlin to Rome.

Porsche's idea for a racing car was based on expanding the capacity of the utilitarian Volkswagen engine by using different valves and cylinder heads and by including a new system known as fuel injection. The car also included a significantly enlarged wheelbase and a unique aerodynamic body design. Although three prototypes of the car were built in early 1939, the beginning of World War II in September of that year led to cancellation of the race and halted further development of the Porsche car. During the war years, the well-known engineer remained in Germany while continuing to work on Hitler's Volkswagen project. On various occasions, he also gave Hitler advice on how to increase the production of military equipment used by the German armed services. At the end of the war, Dr. Porsche was imprisoned in France for a short time because of his association with Adolf Hitler and the Nazi regime.

After World War II, the Porsche design firm relocated to Gmund in Kärnten, Austria, and survived primarily by repairing and servicing different kinds of automobiles. By 1946, however, the Porsche design team was working on various sports and racing car designs. Ferdinand Porsche's son, Ferry Porsche, Jr., insisted on conducting market research in order to determine whether people were willing to buy an expensive, hand-made, high performance sports car. Ferry approached a circle of well-to-do Swiss financiers who agreed to fund production. Working from the basic design model of a Volkswagen Beetle, the company created a lightweight sports car, and the Porsche design office became an automobile factory. The prototype of the Porsche sports car was on the road by March 1948, and small-scale production was initiated by the end of the year. The Gmund plant manufactured five hand-made Porsche cars a month, each with a single aluminum body hand-beaten for hours over a wooden rig by a master craftsman of the art.

Also near the end of 1948, Porsche signed an important agreement with Volkswagenwerk which allowed Porsche to use the larger company's service organization throughout Germany and Austria. In addition, a short time later Porsche moved its growing car production facilities from Gmund to Stuttgart, and occupied the Zuffenhausen factory recently vacated by American occupation forces. This move provided the company with more space and the ability to manufacture more cars. In early 1950 the first Porsche 356 rolled off the Stuttgart production line. By March 1951 the company had manufactured its 500th car, and, a short six months later, the 1,000 Porsche sports car was delivered. Ferdinand Porsche died that year, having seen his vision come to fruition. More than 200 workmen were hammering out hand-made Porsche sports cars, and the company's reputation was growing rapidly. Porsche customers included film and radio stars, as well as financiers and shipping magnates. In a tragic accident, the American film idol James Dean was killed while driving a Porsche Spyder.

By 1952 customers and distributors were frequently requesting a trademark or symbol to adorn the hoods of their automobiles. Dr. Ferry Porsche designed an emblem including both the coat of arms of Stuttgart and the coat of arms of Württemberg, along with the Porsche name. The emblem first appeared in 1953 on the steering wheel hub of a Porsche 356 and has remained unchanged to the present time.

The Dr. Ing he F. Porsche GmbH company celebrated its Silver Anniversary in March 1956 by unveiling the 10,000th Porsche car to leave the production line. In the mid- and late 1950s, nearly 70 percent of all Porsche cars manufactured were exported to eager customers abroad, and between 1954 and 1956 Porsche cars won over 400 international motor races. As the car's popularity continued to increase, different Porsche 356 models were developed, including the 356A and 356B.

In 1960 the company expanded both its physical plant and the number of its employees: a new sales department, service shop, spare parts center, and car delivery department were added, and more than 1,250 factory and office workers helped increase production. Porsche was determined to guard its reputation for reliability and high performance, assigning nearly one of every five workers to quality control. In December 1960 the company produced 39,774 cars, and each of them had earned four quality control certificates, including a certificate for the engine, transmission, general vehicle examination, and measurements. For the fiscal year 1960, Porsche reported revenues totaling DM 108 million.

During the early 1960s, the 356 Porsche remained similar in design to the Volkswagen Beetle and continued to incorporate many of its predecessor's parts. Dr. Ferry Porsche and his management team decided that it was time for an entirely new Porsche design, one that didn't rely heavily on the Volkswagen Beetle. They considered designing a four-seat sedan, but ultimately decided to remain with a two-seat sports car. A low waistline and expanded glass areas gave the new design a more elegant look, and the air-cooled flat engine remained situated in the rear of the car. With many other additions, the unique Type 911 Porsche was introduced in 1964 at a list price of DM 21,000. One year later, the last Porsche 356 model left the factory after almost 20 years of increasing sales. With a total production of 76,302, the Porsche 356 series had made the company famous throughout the world. New Porsche models such as the 912, 924, and 928 soon followed.

Until the 1970s, Porsche KG was under the joint ownership of the Porsche and Piech families, headed by Dr. Ferry Porsche and his sister, Louise Piech, who also owned Porsche Konstruktionen AG in Salzburg, Austria. Dr. Ferry Porsche was still head of the design office, while his two nephews, Ferdinand and Michael Piech, worked in administration. In 1971 revenues reached DM 900 million, and the family decided that the company was growing so rapidly that it needed a thorough reorganization. As a result, the family incorporated its holdings into a single organization with administration centralized in Stuttgart. Dr. Ferry Porsche and his sister presided over an expanded board of directors, and Dr. Ernst Fuhrmann was hired as president of the company. In 1973 the firm went public and became a joint stock company under the name Porsche AG.

During the mid- and late 1970s, Porsche AG committed itself to large-scale research and development in fields related to automotive design and production. Prompted by requests from the German government and numerous private companies, Porsche technicians began expanding their research in engine development to include metrology and vibrations, metal processing, plastics, and welding and bonding techniques. The company opened a Development Center in Weissach, outside of Stuttgart, at a cost of DM 80 million, to test cars and different types of cross-country vehicles. Nearly 4,000 employees worked directly on research and development projects, and data compiled by Porsche was used to fight air pollution and improve auto safety. Porsche's Development Center has garnered such a stellar reputation for its auto engineering design that even Rolls Royce and competitor Mercedes-Benz contract the company for design work.

During the 1970s, Japan developed into one of Porsche's most important foreign markets. Although Porsche sold only 97 cars in Japan in 1970, the repeal of Japanese import restrictions led to a significant sales increase, with sales of Porsche cars jumping from 122 in 1973 to nearly 500 in 1976. By 1978 Porsche was selling more than 900 cars in Japan, which was nearly the same number sold in the United Kingdom and Switzerland. These sales figures are even more impressive when the costs of transport and modifications required by Japanese import law are figured into the price of the cars. A Porsche 930 Turbo, for example, which sold for DM 78,800 in Germany in 1980, was priced at DM 148,000 in Japan.

The 1980s were boom years for Porsche AG. Despite a change in management upon Ernst Fuhrmann's retirement, the company increased production and revenues continued to soar: in fiscal 1981, revenues reached DM 1.5 billion. Of all the cars manufactured in Stuttgart, a total of 70 percent were exported, with the United States accounting for nearly 40 percent of the company's total sales. This successful trend continued throughout the decade: in 1986, for example, Porsche sold a total of 49,976 sports cars, including more than 60 percent to U.S. customers. Models such as the 924, 944, and 928 were introduced during the late 1980s and—along with the 911, perhaps the most popular sports car ever built—contributed to Porsche's seemingly endless string of production successes. By the end of the decade, the United States had developed into Porsche's most important market.

During the 1990s, however, the market collapsed. From its peak of 30,471 sports cars sold in the United States in 1986, Porsche sales amounted to only 4,400 by 1991. Unfortunately, the slide continued. One year later, worldwide sales for the company dropped to 23,060 units, with only 4,133 cars sold in the United States. Some automotive industry analysts blamed a slowdown in the U.S. economy and its negative impact on car imports, while other pointed to the ever-increasing prices for Porsche cars, from $40,000 to $100,000, and growing competition from other sports car manufacturers such as Mazda and Jaguar. A steady loss of top management in the early 1990s exacerbated a deteriorating situation.

In order to reduce costs and increase efficiency, the Porsche and Piech families hired Wendelin Wiedeking, an engineering and manufacturing expert, as chief executive. Wiedeking immediately eliminated overtime for company employees and convinced a majority of them to reduce their daily working hours. He initiated an updated version of the Porsche 911 and planned to introduce a new two-seater sports car with a completely original design and shape. In order to make the car more attractive to U.S. customers, Wendelin promised that Porsche would sell the car at a list price of less than $40,000.

As one of the few remaining small, independent automobile manufacturers, Porsche AG hopes to remain competitive in a volatile industry. The Porsche and the Piech families have the financial resources to weather periods of economic difficulty, as well as an unwavering commitment to the survival of Porsche AG as an independent sports car manufacturer.

Further Reading:

Boshen, Lothar, *The Porsche Book,* New York: Arco, 1984.
Fong, Diana, "A Family Affair," *Forbes,* April 27, 1992, p. 43.
Flint, Jerry, "Porsche Turns," *Forbes,* February 1, 1993, p. 104.
"Life In The Fast Lane," *Economist,* November 6, 1993, p. 84.

—Thomas Derdak

PRIMARK

Primark Corp.

1000 Winter Street, Suite 4300N
Waltham, Massachusetts 02154
U.S.A.
(617) 466-6611
Fax: (617) 890-6190

Public Company
Incorporated: 1981
Employees: 4,200
Sales: $477 million
Stock Exchanges: New York Pacific
SICs: 4581 Airports, Flying Fields, & Services; 7373 Computer Integrated Systems Design; 6719 Holding Companies, Not Elsewhere Classified

Primark Corp. was emerging as a leader in the global information services industry in the mid-1990s. Through its four major divisions, the company focused its information services on financial, weather, and information technology markets. Primark also provided miscellaneous transportation and financial services. Primark was basically a utility company until 1987, when it exited that business and forged into information services.

Primark originated from the early 1980s spin-off of Michigan Consolidated Gas by American Natural Resources. At the time, American Natural Resources was operating two primary subsidiaries: Michigan Consolidated Gas, which was a distributor of natural gas serving the Detroit area, and a sister company that operated an interstate gas pipeline. Although the two companies seemed to complement each other, regulatory constraints were stifling potential synergies. The gas pipeline company, which was regulated at the federal level, was highly profitable. In contrast, Michigan Consolidated had long suffered from tepid earnings and thin rate increases. The main problem was that Michigan regulators had been unsympathetic to rate hike requests because American Natural Resources generated so much profit from its gas distribution company.

Frustrated with the situation, American Natural Resources decided to jettison its lagging Michigan Consolidated Gas subsidiary in 1981. The new enterprise formed the basis for the creation of Primark Corp., which became the parent of Michigan Consolidated Gas in 1982. The new company was initially headed by Robert Stewart, who stayed with the spun-off subsidiary as chairman. Under his direction, Michigan Consolidated thrived. Its early success was primarily the result of rate hikes; Michigan regulators were forced to give Michigan Consolidated rate increases that would allow the company to survive on its own. Although the company continued to churn out sales of about $1.1 billion annually, its profits began to rise. By 1984, in fact, Michigan Consolidated was approaching the maximum return on equity allowed by state regulators.

Stewart recognized early that Michigan Consolidated's prospects for growth were limited. So he formed the holding company Primark as part of his long-term diversification strategy. He planned to use excess cash from Michigan Consolidated to fund acquisitions of non-gas companies that would boost Primark's overall profits. To that end, Stewart and his fellow executives engineered the buyout of several companies in different industries during the early 1980s. They purchased a small California thrift, for example, and a couple of small insurance companies. Among their most notable buyouts was Hospital Satellite Network, a satellite broadcasting service for hospitals that arranged teleconferences and provided medical training programs. Primark bought that start-up company in 1983 with the intention of using its deep pockets to fund its rapid growth.

Although management of those diversified holdings by a gas company seemed like a stretch to some observers, Stewart cited the very strong numbers orientation of his management team. Furthermore, Primark was selective about its acquisitions. In 1984, for instance, the company considered but rejected a proposal to buy Continental Health Care Systems, a producer of mini-computers for hospitals. The end result of Stewart's overall strategy was that sales and profits rose, and Primark's stock price increased sharply between 1981 and 1985. Encouraged by gains, Stewart pursued more acquisitions, beginning with the 1985 buyout of The Aviation Group, a company that provided pilots and maintenance personnel to package air carriers like United Parcel Service, Emery Air Freight, and Purolator Courier. Other major buys included Telerent, which leased televisions, receivers, and satellite equipment to the hotel industry.

By 1987 Primark's portfolio of holdings consisted of Michigan Consolidated, an aviation group that provided cargo aircraft operations and maintenance services, Hospital Satellite Network, and a financial division with leasing, mortgage, and insurance operations. Unfortunately, Stewart's diversification plan began to sour. During the first nine months of 1987, in fact, only Michigan Consolidated and the financial division were profitable. Among other setbacks, The Aviation Group lost its major customer, UPS, which accounted for about 50 percent of that subsidiary's sales. That blow resulted in a $64.4 million restructuring charge related to the division late in 1987. And, while Hospital Satellite Network had a lot of potential, the venture was still in the early stages of growth and was consuming relatively large amounts of capital for expansion.

Primark managed to capture about $1.6 billion in revenues and $51.7 million in net income during 1986. But profits began to slip in 1987 and the company's stock price plunged—the stock dip was also the result of the 1987 stock market crash. Critics charged that Primark's diversification strategy lacked direction, and that the company was failing to realize any benefits from investing excess cash from Michigan Consolidated in its acquisitions. Even Stewart conceded that his plan was not working as he had hoped it would. Stewart had planned for non-gas acquisitions to eventually represent about one-third of the company's profit. By mid-1987, however, they were making up less than ten percent.

To give Primark some direction, the company's board brought in Joseph Kasputys to take control of the operation as president. The 51-year-old Kasputys came to Primark from McGraw-Hill, where he had engineered a huge, two-and-one-half year merger and acquisition campaign that put the company near the top of its industry. Even before his work at McGraw-Hill, Kasputys had demonstrated his abilities in a number of situations. Kasputys was born and raised in New York. He attended Brooklyn College, served in the Navy during the Korean War, and got his master's degree from Harvard in 1967. From Harvard, Kasputys went to work for the Pentagon during the Vietnam War before returning to Harvard to obtain his doctorate in business. He returned to Washington in 1972 and, among other distinctions, served as assistant secretary of the Commerce Department. Throughout the period, he managed to complete 20 years of service in the Armed Forces and retire in 1976 with the rank of Commander. Kasputys would prove to be just as successful in the private sector.

Kasputys took the lead at Primark in August of 1987; Stewart remained as chairman. Less than six months later, Kasputys and the Primark board surprised analysts with the announcement that Primark was going to spin off its core unit, Michigan Consolidated. The idea was to sell Michigan Consolidated, streamline Primark's existing group of companies, and use cash from the sale to acquire new companies. Existing Michigan Consolidated head Alfred Glancy III remained at the helm of his company and was free to focus all of that organization's energy on the gas distribution business. The 63-year-old Stewart retired, and Kasputys became chairman (and, later, chief executive and president) of the slimmed down Primark. The spin-off was completed in may of 1988.

Michigan Consolidated stayed in its home state after the breakup, while Primark's headquarters stayed in McLean, Virginia; they were later moved to Waltham, Massachusetts. Primark's work force shrank from more than 5,000 to about 1,500 following the sale of Michigan Consolidated, and the resultant holding company was reduced to annual revenues of about $100 million. However, the sale left Primark with about $110 million in cash that Kasputys believed he could use, with the help of some lenders, to purchase at least $1 billion worth of new companies. To add to the cash hoard, moreover, Kasputys jettisoned several Primark subsidiaries that did not fit in with his information services focus. He decided to dump Telerent, for instance, and later sold some of the mortgage and insurance businesses. Investors reacted to the split and reorganization positively, as evidenced by a stock price gain of 75 percent during Primark's first year after the sale of Michigan Consolidated.

During 1989 and 1990 Primark dabbled in a number of different industries in an effort to develop some sort of focus. It continued to operate its hospital satellite network but was also engaged in businesses ranging from trucking and aircraft maintenance to gas storage and insurance. Beginning in 1990, though, the company began a concerted effort to focus on one key industry; information services. Kasputys believed that the information services industry offered strong growth potential. To succeed, moreover, Primark would have to target all or most of its investments in that direction. To that end, Primark discontinued its Westmark Mortgage Corp., Triad International Maintenance Corp. (TIMCO) (TIMCO), and General Transport Services subsidiaries in 1992; Primark eventually retained TIMCO as one of its few non-information subsidiaries. Then, in 1993 and 1994, Primark liquidated its remaining life insurance interests.

As Primark jettisoned its holdings, it drew on its hefty cash reserves to begin building itself into a leading information services company. Importantly, Primark purchased Analytical Sciences Corp. (TASC) in 1991 for $167 million. TASC was a Massachusetts-based research and technical services company serving both government and commercial markets. The company was among the leading global providers of advanced, high-end information gathering systems that were purchased by entities like intelligence agencies and military forces. Sales to defense and intelligence communities, in fact, accounted for the bulk of the company's sales. In addition to its core market, TASC also provided systems for various commercial markets, including the airline industry, weather forecasters, and environmental data and surveillance organizations. Furthermore, the company was using its advanced research operation to develop new document imaging systems and software products related to its information markets.

Primark followed the TASC acquisition with the 1992 buyout of Datastream International Ltd. for $191 million. The London-based Datastream was founded in 1964 and was a subsidiary of Dun & Bradstreet Corp. before Primark purchased it. Datastream provided financial information services to investment bankers, brokers, pension fund managers, and insurance companies in 36 countries. Kasputys hoped to use the company to capitalize on the growing trend toward global investing by portfolio managers and other investment professionals. Because most of Datastream's revenues came from outside the United States, Kasputys believed that strong domestic growth opportunities existed. He was also interested in getting the company's giant database of global financial data on, for example, emerging economies. During 1992 and 1993 Datastream posted steady gains under Primark's umbrella. By 1994, in fact, Datastream was providing global financial information and software services to institutional investment and money management professionals in 1,500 organizations in 41 countries on five continents.

In 1994, Primark added another, smaller business to its burgeoning information services portfolio when Datastream purchased Vestek Systems, Inc., for $6.9 million. Founded in 1983, Vestek provided investment information services and software to about 200 organizations in the United States and Canada. Investment professionals used Vestek products and services to construct investment strategies and to help with reporting tasks. Customers included mutual fund managers, bank trust departments, insurance companies, and financial consultants. Before Primark bought it, the San Francisco-based Vestek posted sales of $7 million and employed about 45 people. Kasputys hoped to integrate Datastream's and Vestek's competencies to create a whole that was greater than the sum of its parts. Evidencing that intent was the introduction of Primark's Global Asset Allocation Model in 1995, which was the first product sold as a result of cooperation between Datastream and Vestek; the model was designed to help money managers allocate funds across different asset categories and geographic markets.

Primark was enjoying steady improvements in its information services businesses going into the mid-1990s. Although its chief subsidiary, TASC, was suffering from a downturn in its core defense and intelligence markets, the subsidiary continued to post relatively healthy sales and operating profit growth. Datastream and Vestek posted much stronger gains. Even Primark's major non-information subsidiary, TIMCO (9.7 percent of Primark's 1994 revenues), was enjoying profit increases. Overall, Primark revenues exploded from about $10 million going into the 1990s to $444 million in 1993 and then to $477 million in 1994. More importantly, net income climbed to nearly $14 million in 1994. Meanwhile, Kasputys and his fellow executives hunted for new additions to the Primark information services group.

Further Reading:

Curran, John J., "A Gas Company Whose Profits Glow Brightly," *Fortune,* February 4, 1985, p. 106.

Hinden, Stan, "Primark's Chief Shopping for Strong Growth Companies," *Washington Post,* July 10, 1989, p. E39.

Jaffe, Thomas, "Primark Toes the Mark," *Forbes,* December 12, 1988, p. 301.

Menninger, Bonar, "Diversification Veteran to Try Hand at Primark," *Washington Business Journal,* September 7, 1987, p. 3.

——, "Primark Spins Off Cash Cow, Keeps Its Riskier Units," *Washington Business Journal,* January 18, 1988, p. 1.

Munroe, Tony, "Primark to Buy London Company," *Washington Times,* August 15, 1992, p. B5.

Pham, Ales, "Primark Purchases Data Firm for $191 Million Cash, Debt," *Washington Post,* August 15, 1992, p. F1.

Schneider, Steven L., "Primark Completes Acquisition of Vestek Systems, Inc.," *PR Newswire,* July 1, 1994.

——, "Primark Reports Increased Earnings in 1992," *PR Newswire,* February 19, 1993.

"Top 100: #58 Primark Corp.," *Washington Post,* April 9, 1990, p. E46.

Wernle, Bradford, "Primark Woes Cut the Value of MichCon," *Crain's Detroit Business,* January 18, 1988, p. 1.

—Dave Mote

Puritan-Bennett Corporation

9401 Indian Creek Parkway
P.O. Box 25905
Overland Park, Kansas 66225-5905
U.S.A.
(913) 661-0444
Fax: (913) 661-0234

Public Company
Incorporated: 1913 as Oxygen Gas Company
Employees: 2,600
Sales: $309 million
Stock Exchanges: NASDAQ
SICs: 3841 Surgical & Medical Instruments; 3842 Surgical Appliances & Supplies; 3728 Aircraft Parts & Equipment Not Elsewhere Classified; 2813 Industrial Gases

The Puritan-Bennett Corporation, headquartered in Overland Park, Kansas, with research and manufacturing facilities in the United States, Canada, France, Ireland, and Mexico, is one of the world's leading manufacturers of respiratory products for the health care and aviation markets. The first company to produce oxygen west of the Mississippi, Puritan-Bennett has been known throughout its history as a leader in creating innovative medical technology and is widely recognized for developing such products as the MA-1 Volume Ventilator, which virtually replaced the cumbersome iron lung, and the 7200 Microprocessor Ventilator, which has become one of the most widely used ventilator systems in the world. In addition to being the largest producer of several types of liquid oxygen systems, the company is the world's second largest supplier of diagnostic and therapeutic sleep products. The company's organizational structure consists of the Puritan group, which manufactures mostly home care and gas products; the Bennett group, which oversees most of the company's hospital products; and Aero Systems, which supplies emergency oxygen systems for commercial and private aircraft. Although the company has been traditionally best known for producing life-support equipment for hospitals, the movement of the health care industry as a whole toward home care has brought about a shift in focus. While roughly 60 percent of the company's 1994 total revenue still came from the sale of hospital/physician office products, home care equipment, most of which is used to meet the supplementary oxygen needs of patients suffering from chronic bronchitis, emphysema, and other respiratory diseases, represents the fastest growing segment of the company.

Puritan-Bennett was founded in 1913 by Parker B. Francis as a manufacturer and distributor of oxygen and hydrogen. Although the company, known at the time as the Oxygen Gas Company, originally directed sales toward the welding industry, its founder had the foresight to perceive that the experimental use of nitrous oxide coupled with oxygen would one day replace ether as the anesthetic of choice and place his company at the forefront of the surgical gas industry.

Despite the company's inauspicious first month of operation—$186 in revenue compared to $1,150 in expenses—Francis persevered, and with the onset of World War I, his company received the opportunity to make a vital contribution to the war effort and solidify its financial base at the same time. Not only would large quantities of oxygen and nitrous oxide be needed to provide countless medical services, but hydrogen, a by-product of the oxygen manufacturing process, was in high demand by the military to support the rapidly expanding dirigible business.

Following the war, Francis, an ardent supporter of the newly formed National Anesthesia Research Society, devoted much of his energy to improving the purity and bottling of nitrous oxide. In an effort to distinguish itself from the growing number of "oxygen companies," the company entered the 1920s with a new name, the Kansas City Oxygen Company, as it continued to expand the distribution of its products geographically. In 1923, while the demand for oxygen exceeded the company's production, the demand for hydrogen fell considerably. In an attempt to combat this problem, the company purchased its first oxygen liquefaction plant and entered the liquid oxygen industry. Five years later, Puritan, in conjunction with several other industry leaders, adopted a uniform color scheme for medical gases.

While the Great Depression forced many companies to shut down operations or at least reduce its work force, the Puritan Compressed Gas Corporation, as it became known in 1931, continued to expand and never had to lay off an employee. Moreover, while President Franklin D. Roosevelt had ordered the closing of all the country's banks, the company paid its employees in cash. The company's success was due in part to its ability to take advantage of a number of new market opportunities. For instance, after witnessing several unexplained airplane crashes between 1930 and 1936—accidents that investigators believed were caused by pilots who blacked out at high altitudes because they lacked sufficient oxygen—Francis developed an oxygen mask that helped to solve the problem and paved the way for a new aerospace division for his company at the same time.

In 1937, the destruction of the German hydrogen dirigible, the Hindenburg, brought another opportunity for Puritan to introduce a safer gas product. The tragedy exposed the highly flammable properties of hydrogen and led the U.S. government and private companies to search for better alternatives. The ensuing repeal of the ban on helium enabled Puritan to conduct extensive research in the use of helium/oxygen mixtures in ventilating patients with severe respiratory problems. And in 1938, following widespread customer approval, Puritan added helium to its line of gas products. That same year the company made another entrance into the medical field by manufacturing one of its first pieces of medical equipment, the "Puritan Portable Oxyaerator," an oxygen humidifier. The publicity the company received during the 1930s for its highly successful aviation oxygen masks placed the company at the forefront of oxygen therapy technology.

In 1941, Puritan set up one of the first cascade oxygen filling systems in Baltimore, and by 1944 had begun producing a full line of cylinder valves for both military and civilian uses. The mid-1940s, of course, saw the company devote most of its attention to manufacturing war-related products, supplying the military, medical, and industrial fields with oxygen, medical gases, oxygen equipment, and industrial tools. As the war drew to a close, Puritan took advantage of bargain prices on previously unavailable machine tools of all kinds to build one of the finest machine shops in the industry. The end of the war also enabled the company to return to its emphasis on civilian research. In 1946, Baylor University asked the company to improve upon the non-sterile conditions caused by bringing oxygen cylinders off the street into the hospital nursery. By adapting a special type of coupler used by welders to a piped outlet in the hospital, the company solved the problem and created the first "quick connect" in the medical piping industry. By the end of the decade, the company featured a full line of regulators, flowmeters, and adaptors; in 1951 the company published its first piping systems catalog.

The 1950s proved to be a decade of transition and expansion for the company. In 1956, the company acquired V. Ray Bennett and Associates, Inc.; a year later its name was changed to Bennett Respiration Products, Inc. That same year, Parker B. Francis handed over control of the company to his sons, Parker B. Francis III and John B. Francis, and the company expanded its medical catalog offerings to include almost all of the items that served the medical gas piping industry into the 1990s. Two years later, specially trained and licensed Puritan-Bennett dealers were given the authority to fill gas cylinders within their own locations, significantly reducing the company's overall packaging costs. Another major improvement in efficiency occurred that same year when Pure Maid Products Inc., a wholly owned subsidiary, opened the company's first automated nitrous oxide production facility. Once in full operation, the state-of-the-art plant manufactured nearly 600 percent more gas per day than the one it replaced.

Technological innovation and market expansion also characterized the 1960s. While adding such products as the bubble jet and a heated humidifier to its oxygen therapy line, Puritan introduced a series of new manual resuscitators and suction equipment. Perhaps the most important development of the decade, however, was the 1967 introduction of the MA-1 Volume Ventilator, which assisted a patient's breathing and controlled respiration should the patient stop breathing. By virtually replacing the cumbersome iron lung, the MA-1 not only brought the company to the forefront of this market but made the Bennett name recognizable in the larger medical equipment field. Having exported products to Latin America as early as the 1930s, the company also began placing more of an emphasis on its international business, opening its first Canadian facility in Toronto and its first sales office in the Far East. In 1968, a year that saw revenue surpass the $20 million mark for the first time, the parent company reorganized itself as the Puritan-Bennett Corporation and consolidated its medical marketing department into a single unit.

Profits continued to rise steadily during the next decade as Puritan-Bennett entered the home health care market and made several important acquisitions. After purchasing a number of home care distributorships, the company formed a new marketing department under the name Medical; however, after three years of modest success, all but a single Miami unit were sold. Despite this inauspicious beginning, the company's commitment to alternative health care markets remained strong throughout the decade. Meanwhile, Puritan-Bennett's aviation division was given a boost through the purchase of the Zep Company, the leading manufacturer of oxygen systems for general aircraft, and the Wemac Company, the largest producer of air venting equipments used in the overhead passenger units of commercial and general aircraft. By the end of the 1970s, net sales had climbed to more than $80 million, an increase of nearly 400 percent during the decade.

During the early 1980s, Puritan-Bennett fell behind some of the industry leaders in technology and the company's sales and profits fell accordingly: revenue increased only four percent between 1981 and 1984, and the company lost money in 1982 and 1984. But in 1986, under the direction of president and CEO Burton A. Dole, Jr., the company rebounded strongly, recording a jump of more than 21 percent from the previous year. The turnaround was largely the result of the success of one of the company's best-known products: the 7200 Microprocessor Ventilator. First made available in 1983, the highly sophisticated system of respiratory therapy and monitoring quickly became the most widely used ventilator across the world, capturing a 60 percent share of the international market by the end of the decade. And with the introduction of the CliniVision Respiratory Care Management Information System, a central station patient monitoring system used in hospital intensive care units, as well as several improvements to the PB 7200 series, Puritan-Bennett ended the decade with $226 million in total revenue and a net income of nearly $16 million.

While Puritan-Bennett, as a competitor in a recession-resistant industry, managed to perform well through the end of the 1980s largely on the strength of hospital equipment sales, a number of changes in the health care industry forced the company to begin focusing on its fledgling home care market. With the number of individuals suffering from chronic respiratory impairment on the rise, the appearance of new research confirming the viability of home respiratory care, and pressure from the federal government to curb hospital spending, the company had already laid the groundwork for a home care division in the early 1980s. Its line of home care products was expanded, and a network of referral sources from hospitals and pulmonary physicians was built, fostering a yearly growth of around 20 percent in the home care division in the late 1980s.

As Puritan-Bennett entered the 1990s, the changing face of the health care industry, as well as the uncertainty surrounding U.S. health care reform following the election of the Clinton administration, brought new challenges to the company. Moreover, recessionary economic conditions in Europe during the early 1990s reduced demand for the company's hospital intensive equipment. A tragic fire at Brooklyn, New York's Maimonides Medical Center in September 1993 called into question the safety of some Puritan-Bennett products. Although an independent investigation absolved the company four months later, the initial reports may have prompted the Food and Drug Administration (FDA) to conduct additional investigations at some of the company's other facilities. These investigations occurred before the company had been able to complete its planned improvement programs and resulted in the issue of a consent decree in January 1994. The company was forced to cease shipments from its portable ventilator plant in Boulder, Colorado, and from its FoxS intra-arterial blood gas monitoring operation in Carlsbad, California, until Good Manufacturing Practice (GMP) and Medical Device Reporting (MDR) guidelines were met.

These factors have led Puritan-Bennett to take a number of major actions to better position the company for the future. First, the company has intensified and expanded its efforts to comply with government safety standards. Second, the company closed its Boulder facility and transferred the manufacture of portable ventilators to an International Standards Organization (ISO) certified facility in Ireland. Finally, the company has substantially cut its FoxS operation, while addressing its GMP compliance issues and offering it up for sale, after realizing that it lacked the financial resources to fully develop the high-tech blood gas monitoring system.

Having successfully rejected a hostile takeover attempt by Waltham's Thermo Electron Corporation in December 1994, one that 72 percent of Puritan-Bennett stockholders had favored, the company has taken measures to prepare itself for the changing face of the future health care market in the United States and throughout the world. To that end, the company has focused much of its attention and resources to developing and improving products for the home care segment of the industry so that it will be less vulnerable to changes affecting its life-support equipment. The future performance of the company will depend largely on home oxygen therapy, which has represented three-quarters of its home care business. One of the company's most dramatic areas of potential future growth can be found in its sleep disorder diagnosis and treatment products business. Having grown more than 75 percent in 1994, this segment stands to expand rapidly as a result of the purchase of SEFAM S.A., the leading European supplier of sleep disorder products, that same year. Perhaps the most immediate challenge to the company, though, will be to assure compliance with the ever-changing federal safety requirements.

Principal Subsidiaries: Puritan-Bennett International, Inc.; Puritan-Bennett Canada, Ltd.; Puritan Bennett International Corp.; Puritan-Bennett Aero Systems Co.; Puritan-Bennett UK Ltd.; Puritan-Bennett (HK) Ltd.; Puritan-Bennett France Sarl; Medicomp, Inc. (50%); Puritan-Bennett Italia Srl; Puritan-Bennett Australia Pty. Ltd.; Puritan-Bennett Nederland BV; Puritan-Bennett Holdings Ireland Ltd.; Puritan-Bennett (Ireland) Ltd.; Puritan-Bennett de Mexico Sa de Cv; Puritan-Bennett Helsinki DV; Puritan-Bennett Hoyer GmbH (50%); SEFAM SA (France); Puritan-Bennett France Holdings SA; Puritan-Bennett Ireland Distribution Ltd.

Further Reading:

Burton, Thomas M., "Technology & Health: FDA Alert Cites 2 Puritan-Bennett Devices," *Wall Street Journal,* September 15, 1993, p. 6.

Byrne, Harlan S., "Puritan-Bennett Corp.: It's Out Front Again in a Recession-Resistant Business," *Barron's,* November 6, 1988, pp. 53–54.

Hauser, John R., "How Puritan-Bennett Used the House of Quality," *Sloan Management Review,* Spring 1993, pp. 61–70.

Holmes, Tom, "Puritan-Bennett Corporation: The 75th Anniversary," *Life Line,* April 12, 1988, pp. 1–10.

Steinmetz, Greg, and Barbara Carton, "Thermo Electron Drops Hostile Offer For Puritan-Bennett," *Wall Street Journal,* December 12, 1994, p. A3.

Wood, Carol, "FDA Oversight Spurs Puritan to Pick Ireland," *Denver Business Journal,* December 18, 1994, p. A16.

—Jason Gallman

Quanex Corporation

1900 West Loop South
Suite 1500
Houston, Texas 77027
U.S.A.
(713) 961-4600
Fax: (713) 877-5333

Public Company
Incorporated: 1927 as Michigan Seamless Tube Company
Employees: 2,600
Sales: $699 million
Stock Exchanges: New York
SICs: 3316 Cold-Finishing of Steel Shapes; 3317 Steel Pipe & Tubes; 3353 Aluminum Sheet, Plate & Foil; 3354 Aluminum Extruded Products

Quanex Corporation is a leading U.S. manufacturer of specialized metal products made from carbon and alloy steel and aluminum. Quanex operated through four primary divisions going into the mid-1990s: hot-rolled steel bars; cold-finished steel bars; aluminum products; and steel tubing. Its products were purchased by markets ranging from transportation and defense to energy and construction. After faltering through the early 1980s, Quanex regrouped and established itself as a leader in steelmaking technology and efficiency.

Quanex was incorporated in 1927 in South Lyon, Michigan, as the Michigan Seamless Tube Company. Under the leadership of William N. McMunn, the fledgling start-up profited by reworking used boiler and condenser tubes for resale. Success in that business prompted the company to build a processing mill in 1929 that could produce seamless tubing from solid steel billets. Michigan Seamless managed to survive the 1929 stock market crash and even managed to increase its business during the Great Depression. Indeed, the enterprise began producing tubing made from steel alloys in 1933 and by 1935 was generating more than $1 million in annual sales.

After the Depression, Michigan Seamless enjoyed a sales boom as a result of U.S. government purchases during World War II. Founder McMunn died in 1941 and was replaced by board member W. A. McHattie, who oversaw the company's war effort and would lead the enterprise into the 1970s. Michigan Seamless was a major supplier to the armed forces during the war, and was distinguished as the only company in the nation to be awarded five Army-Navy "E" awards for production and quality of aircraft tubing. Demand for the company's steel products temporarily declined immediately after the war. But the postwar economic boom soon supplanted that market and Michigan Seamless resumed its hearty growth. In 1946, in fact, the company installed a new furnace and processing mill in anticipation of demand growth.

Throughout the 1950s and 1960s Michigan Seamless enjoyed steady gains. Besides expanding its original South Lyon facilities, it also branched out into other regions and markets. In 1956, for example, Gulf States Tube Corporation, an affiliate of Michigan Seamless, was started in Rosenberg, Texas. That division would give Michigan Seamless an important foothold in the oil and gas tubing market. Importantly, Michigan Seamless acquired Standard Tube in 1965, an acquisition that gave Michigan Seamless new operations in Detroit and Shelby, Ohio. Shortly after the purchase, the company was listed on the New York stock exchange. Other acquisitions followed, including the purchase of U.S. Broach and Machine Company in 1968. By that time, Michigan Seamless was making and processing steel in several states and had diversified into a number of different industries.

During the early 1970s Michigan Seamless began developing plans to build a state-of-the-art steel mill in Jackson, Michigan. The MacSteel mill, as it was called, would eventually become a model for other U.S. producers of high-grade engineered steel—such steel was purchased by manufacturers for use in demanding applications like producing ball bearings and camshafts. MacSteel would also form the basis of what would become the company's primary operating division. Shortly after announcing construction of the MacSteel plant, McHattie died in 1972. He was replaced by Carl E. Pfeiffer, a Detroit native and a graduate of Michigan State University. An engineer by training, Pfeiffer joined Michigan Tubeless in 1953 and quickly worked his way to president of the company in 1971 before assuming the chief executive role in 1972.

Pfeiffer oversaw the opening of the MacSteel plant in 1974 and also helped to engineer the acquisition of Viking Metallurgical in 1976. Reflecting the company's growing market and product diversity, Pfeiffer changed the name of the company in 1977 from Michigan Seamless Tube Company to Quanex Corporation. Also in 1977, Quanex moved its headquarters from Michigan to Houston, Texas. Both the name change and the move mirrored the company's growing emphasis on the bustling oil and gas industry, which was demanding large amounts of tubing and other steel goods to build wells and other infrastructure. Indeed, during the energy crises of the late 1970s and early 1980s, consumption of steel by the energy industry boomed and producers like Quanex scrambled to keep pace with spiraling demand.

Encouraged by booming sales to the energy sector, Quanex set its sites on that market in the late 1970s. It purchased the operations of Acquired Pipe Specialties, Inc., of Houston in 1978, for example, before acquiring Leland Tube Company of New Jersey in 1979. At the same time, Quanex jettisoned its comparatively sluggish Standard Tube Division and the U.S. Broach and Machine Company, both of which did not complement the company's energy industry focus. As sales surged,

Quanex expanded. It invested heavily to upgrade its MacSteel plant in Michigan, and even constructed a new welded-oil-tubing manufacturing facility in 1980 in Bellmont, Texas—closer to its primary customer base. In 1981, Quanex completed construction of a heat treating facility in Indiana, and announced an ambitious plan to build a second MacSteel plant in Arkansas. The MacSteel plant would be the centerpiece of Quanex's thriving energy-related steel business, which was accounting for about 50 percent of the company's total revenues by 1981.

Quanex rode into the 1980s on a wave of success that had buoyed the company for more than a decade. Indeed, during the 1970s Quanex achieved average annual sales gains of nearly 22 percent while earnings grew at a compounded rate of nearly 30 percent. Satisfied investors enjoyed fat stock price gains and hefty dividends, and it looked as though the expanding Quanex would continue to excel into the mid-1980s. In 1981, in fact, Quanex posted a record $31.4 million profit. Some of that excess cash was used in 1982 to purchase LaSalle Steel Company, an addition to the company's Indiana-based holdings. Meanwhile, plant expansions and construction of the new MacSteel plant continued.

To the surprise of executives at Quanex and many other companies, the energy industry collapsed in 1982. And it brought down with it several other steel-consuming industries including capital equipment and automotive businesses. Quanex managers were stunned. The company's total order backlog plunged from a whopping $139 million going into 1982 to about $60 million by the year's end. Surplus steel lay rusting on Quanex's lots, forcing Quanex to eventually take a $65 million write-off related to its oil-tubing inventories. The company finished the year with a depressing $34.5 million loss. Flustered Quanex executives quickly exited the depressed market for what is known as end-finished oil tubular goods, and postponed construction on the new MacSteel plant for one year.

Quanex was faced with increasingly intimidating debt obligations as its profits plummeted. Under pressure from investors, the company reorganized and initiated an aggressive campaign to cut costs and reduce its dependency on gasping energy markets. Toward that end, Quanex halted operation at its Oil Country Tubular division late in 1984 and sold a fabricating unit, among other moves. Quanex did, however, resume construction of the Arkansas MacSteel plant in 1984 using funds gleaned from a February 1984 bond offering—Quanex floated $125 million worth of junk bonds in an effort to scale back its massive $176-million debt load. The MacSteel plant opened in 1985, but would operate in the red for a few years and drag down the company's bottom line.

As Quanex sold off divisions, revenues dropped—to about $400 million in 1984 and then to a low of $297 million in 1985. Despite major hurdles, however, the company continued to post profits during the mid-1980s, with the exception of 1986. It used the surplus to pay off its long-term debt, which shrank to about $40 million in 1988. Meanwhile, Pfeiffer and company slashed costs, reorganized to concentrate on specialty and high-margin steel products, and worked to diversify away from the oil business. The number of employees at the company's headquarters was cut from about 100 in the early 1980s to about 30 by the end of the decade, and the percentage of Quanex's sales attributable to the energy industry shrank from half to about seven percent. Quanex made up for that lost market share by entering markets including construction, defense, agriculture, transportation, and others.

Besides expanding into new end markets, Quanex also diversified geographically with sales in Europe and Japan. Furthermore, to divert another inventory disaster such as that suffered in 1982, the company adopted a policy of holding almost no inventory; instead, almost every batch of steel was made to order and was even barcoded with the owner's name and address prior to delivery. Importantly, Quanex began to concentrate on efficiency and customer service as a means of capturing market share and increasing its competitiveness in the increasingly global steel industry. It installed state-of-the-art equipment in its processing mills and shaped its compensation system to promote quality and productivity; workers were paid a bonus according to how much steel they shipped out, less any defective steel that was returned.

Quanex's impressive productivity gains during the 1980s and early 1990s were made possible by its integration of mini-mill technology. During the 1980s, mini-mill steelmaking factories, which use scrap and such techniques as continuous casting, emerged as stellar performers in the steel industry. Indeed, the mini-mill process was used by industry powerhouses such as Nucor to undercut traditional steel manufacturers in commodity steel markets. Quanex added a twist to the mini-mill revolution when it utilized mini-mill techniques to create high-grade, engineered steel. The result was that Quanex was able to produce high-profit steel at a very low cost. By the early 1990s, in fact, Quanex was churning out nearly defect-free steel that required only 1.9 man-hours of labor per ton to produce, as compared to about four man-hours required to create a ton of steel in a traditional, or integrated, steel mill.

As Quanex implemented its unique new strategy, its financial performance rebounded. Sales shot up from $345 million in 1987 to $463 million in 1988, and then to $502 million in 1989. In 1990, moreover, Quanex generated $650 million in sales and nearly $30 million in net income. By that time, Quanex's debt burden had eased and several banks had even approached CEO Pfeiffer about the possibility of a leveraged buyout. Instead, Pfeiffer elected to pour the money back into the company to increase its diversity and to improve productivity. To that end, in 1989 Quanex purchased Nichols-Homeshield for $105 million. Nichols manufactured aluminum sheet for gutters, downspouts, and windows. Quanex invested $60 million to build a new plant for the company and expected to use the new division to penetrate the market for aluminum.

After elevating Quanex to a member of the Fortune 500 in 1991, Pfeiffer relinquished his chief executive duties in 1992 to Robert C. Snyder, an engineer. The 53-year-old Snyder had been serving as president of Leland Tube Co. when it was acquired by Quanex in 1979. After filling key executive slots at several Quanex subsidiaries, he was tapped as Pfeiffer's successor. Snyder came into the job with goals similar to those established by his predecessor. Unfortunately, he also assumed the helm during an economic downturn that was suppressing the overall steel market. Quanex's sales slipped to $572 million in 1992, although the company continued to post relatively strong operating profits. Sales began to pick up the following year, however, and in 1994 reached the record level of $699 million. 1994 earnings reflected big gains in the new Nicols-Homeshield division, as well as recovering steel prices.

Going into the mid-1990s, Quanex was serving four major markets: industrial machinery and capital equipment (32 percent of sales); transportation (29 percent); aluminum products (29 percent); and energy (nine percent). And it was operating its subsidiaries through four major divisions: hot-rolled steel bars; cold-finished steel bars; aluminum products; and steel tubing. Rising steel prices and increased market share in 1995 boded well for Quanex in the short term. Likewise, low debt, ongoing investments in productivity and quality initiatives, and geographic and product diversity suggested long-term growth and stability for the enterprise.

Principal Subsidiaries: MACSTEEL; LaSalle Steel Company; Nichols-Homeshield; Quanex Tube Group.

Further Reading:

Byrne, Harlan S., ''A Specialty Rebound: Quanex Emerges from Steel Slump,'' *Barron's,* June 6, 1988, pp. 38–40.

Cleary, W. F., ''Quanex Announces Management Changes,'' *Business Wire,* September 2, 1992.

Cleary, W. F., and C. A. Meador, ''Quanex Corp. Announces Financial Results,'' *Business Wire,* May 30, 1990.

Galow, Jeff, ''Quanex Sells Bellville Tube Plant,'' *PR Newswire,* April 15, 1993.

Jacobs, Bill, ''Quanex Profits Get Boost from Q-C,'' *Quad-City Times,* December 10, 1994, p. M5.

Nulty, Peter, ''The Less-Is-More Strategy,'' *Fortune,* December 2, 1991, p. 102.

—Dave Mote

Ralston Purina Company

Checkerboard Square
St. Louis, Missouri 63164
U.S.A.
(314) 982-1000
Fax: (314) 982-2134

Public Company
Incorporated: 1894 as Robinson-Danforth Commission Company
Employees: 54,099
Sales: $5.76 billion
Stock Exchanges: New York Midwest Pacific
SICs: 2047 Dog and Cat Food; 3691 Storage Batteries; 2048 Prepared Feeds, Not Elsewhere Classified

The Ralston Purina Company leads the world in two ostensibly disparate categories, dry dog food and dry cell batteries. Over the course of the 20th century, the company evolved from a midwestern U.S. producer of animal feeds into a global consumer products company. Under the direction of Chairman, President and CEO William P. Stiritz from 1981 through the mid-1990s, Ralston shed its U.S. livestock feed business to concentrate on consumer goods, then spun off its grocery products to shareholders as Ralcorp Holdings. As of mid-1995, the company's interests were focused on pet foods sold under the venerable Purina Chow brand as well as Eveready and Energizer batteries and flashlights, which boasted 35 percent of the global battery market.

The multibillion-dollar company of the 1990s was largely the result of the vision of one man: William Henry Danforth. Danforth was so extremely hardworking, religious, and philanthropic, he might almost have been a caricature of the Protestant work ethic if he hadn't done so well by it. Raised and educated in Charleston, Missouri, Danforth earned a degree in mechanical engineering from Washington University in St. Louis, Missouri, in 1892. Within a year of graduating, he joined two church acquaintances in St. Louis in mixing and selling feed for mules and horses. Their blend of oats and corn, billed as ''cheaper than oats and safer than corn,'' sold well among the farmers along the Mississippi River.

The company was incorporated as the Robinson-Danforth Commission Company in 1894. Danforth bought control of the company just two years later. On the very day after the purchase was completed, the company's new mill was destroyed by a tornado. With the help of a sympathetic banker, Danforth rebuilt and the company resumed its pattern of growth. The site of the new mill would years later become company headquarters, known as Checkerboard Square.

In 1898 Danforth discovered a Kansas miller who had found a way to prevent wheat from turning rancid, giving credence to Danforth's corporate slogan, ''Where Purity is Paramount.'' He introduced the miller's hot breakfast cereal made from cracked wheat. A clever marketing strategist, Danforth persuaded Dr. Everett Ralston, the head of a chain of faddish health clubs, to give the cereal his official sponsorship. The doctor agreed on the condition that it be named after him. To take advantage of the growing success of both the cereal and the feeds, Danforth changed the name of his company in 1902 to Ralston Purina, ''purina'' representing a combination of ''pure'' and ''farina'' (grain). He introduced the red-and-white checkerboard logo in 1900 and used it to identify virtually everything related to the company, from delivery trucks, to packaging, to grain elevators. He even wore the ubiquitous checkerboard design on his jacket and socks.

Danforth's expectation that his employees would ascribe to his own strict personal standards earned him the admiration of some and the derision of others. For example, he prohibited smoking anywhere on company premises and rewarded employees who subscribed to his philosophies and went to church regularly. Danforth made his expectations clear to his employees in a weekly inspirational address, and published a compendium of his ideals under the title *I Dare You: Stand Tall, Think Tall, Smile Tall, Live Tall.*

Danforth's European travels during the first two decades of the 20th century served as sources of new technological and marketing ideas, as well as the subject of several published travelogues. During World War I, Danforth went to France as a representative of the Young Men's Christian Association to give the troops moral support. While there, he observed that soldiers referred to rations as ''chow.'' Returning home, he christened his animal feeds ''chows'' and, to clinch the custom, fined employees who continued to use the word ''feed.'' Danforth visited England during the interwar period, where he was introduced to the concept of compressing feed into cubes. In 1921 he began using this technique in the United States. His pellet-shaped feed revolutionized the domestic industry and remained the standard throughout the remainder of the 20th century.

Purina Chow's main competitor, then and for decades to come, was the individual farmer who had always fed his animals ordinary grain. In 1926 Danforth reluctantly purchased a research farm outside St. Louis at the behest of his son Donald Danforth, who had joined the company in 1920. At this facility new products were tested, including feeds with non-grain ingredients like animal by-products and vitamins. Innovative farm management and sanitation techniques were also tested there. While other feed companies diversified, Danforth poured his profits into Purina chows, buying up mills nationwide so that he could adapt his mixtures to the climate-related needs of farmers in each region. This local tailoring was a vital factor in his strategy to boost sales volume—and thus profits—in the low margin livestock feed industry.

By 1930 Ralston Purina's sales had reached $60 million. With the advent of the Great Depression, however, farmers who could no longer afford commercial feed put their livestock back on a homemade diet. Within just two years, Ralston Purina's sales plummeted by two-thirds. Danforth turned to marketing to save his company, persuading the country's most popular cowboy balladeer, Tom Mix, to lend his name to the advertising for Ralston Cereal. Though the inexpensive, nutritious cereal had long been losing money, it soon began to generate a profit.

In spite of the dramatic decline in the animal feed business, Danforth continued to expand the operations of Purina Mills. His confidence paid off in 1933, when sales began to rebound. Donald Danforth succeeded his father as president in 1932, and the older Danforth divided the ensuing 20 years between Ralston Purina and the administration of the Danforth Foundation. Founded in 1927, this charitable organization built chapels on college campuses and in hospitals and gave generously to churches, colleges, and universities.

During World War II, government subsidies fostered tremendous growth in the meat and poultry industries, and farmers increasingly relied on commercially prepared feeds. Ralston Purina's sales more than tripled and, despite price controls, net profits rose nearly 150 percent. Realizing that a farmer with disappointing returns was more likely to blame his feed than other contributing factors, the company began training its local salespeople in the basics of farm management, including breeding and sanitation. Thousands of Ralston Purina dealers became sources of valuable free advice.

Will Danforth soon came to be widely recognized as a public relations genius. Through its experimental farm, the company demonstrated to customers that the nutritional balance offered by Purina chows could produce bigger, healthier animals for less money. Groups toured the farm—at their own expense—led by guides who were well versed in the company's overall philosophy and product line. After the tour, visitors attended a show, complete with chorus line, performed by amateurs from the general office in St. Louis. As more sophisticated feed supplements became available, Ralston Purina added them to its chows, while taking care to maintain the homespun image its customers had come to trust.

With the end of the war, the price of grains began to rise sharply. To raise the operating capital necessary to purchase these raw materials, the Danforths reluctantly took their company public. By 1947 sales of Purina chows, milled in 27 plants nationwide, had topped $200 million.

Between 1947 and 1957 the nation's canine population soared. Purina, which had been feeding hunting and farm dogs for 24 years, saw the opportunity to use its expertise to capture a high-growth, high-profit margin industry. The company undertook the development of an appealing food for domesticated dogs in 1950 and introduced its Purina Dog Chow in 1957. Within 16 months it had become the market leader, a position Ralston Purina never relinquished.

William Danforth's death in 1955 heralded a new era of international expansion. Donald Danforth advanced to chairman of the board, and Raymond E. Rowland was elected president. Under Rowland, Ralston Purina acquired significant interests in feed companies in France, West Germany, and Italy, and bought plants in Mexico, Guatemala, Colombia, Venezuela, and Argentina.

In spite of a disastrous explosion and fire that destroyed much of the company's St. Louis plant in January 1962, Ralston Purina continued to grow. Most of this expansion came from the consumer goods sector. The company increased its share of the American grocery shopper's dollar through burgeoning sales of Chex breakfast cereals and Purina Dog Chow. An acquisition program initiated under R. Hal Dean, who became president upon Donald Danforth's 1963 retirement, also augmented Ralston's consumer goods interests. In 1963, the company exchanged 1.9 million of its own shares for ownership of the Van Camp Seafood Company, canners of Chicken-of-the-Sea tuna and salmon. By the mid-1960s, livestock feeds represented only half of total sales, down from 90 percent.

Dean's acquisitive activities continued with the 1968 purchase of Foodmaker, Inc., a restaurant franchising company that included the Jack-in-the-Box hamburger chain. A hockey fan, Dean bought St. Louis's ailing professional hockey team, the Blues, and renamed their stadium the Checkerdome. Next Ralston Purina purchased Green Thumb, which sold houseplants, for $45 million; a well-known life-sciences testing lab (to be merged with Ralston Purina's own lab) named the WARF Institute; and the Bremner Biscuit Company. New products included Cookie Crisp, which broke records in the children's cereal market. Between 1964 and 1974, the company's sales more than tripled, and in 1976, Dun's Review named Ralston Purina "one of the five best-managed companies this year."

By 1979, however, there were signs of trouble. In one 18-month period, the company's dog foods lost a quarter of their market share to competitors. Dean had opened dozens of new fast-food restaurants in the eastern United States only to find the market there already saturated. Houseplants weren't selling, and too much capital had been invested in shrimp farms, tuna boats, a fledgling soy-isolate business, and packaged fresh mushrooms—all enterprises that later proved minimally or erratically profitable.

Moreover, Ralston Purina had earned a reputation for being closely held, and this policy backfired in November 1978 at a meeting of stock market analysts. When top executives imprudently decided to withhold certain figures, disgruntled analysts went home with Ralston Purina at the top of their sell lists. The company's stock dropped eight percent in just two days.

Although Dean reorganized again and succeeded in selling off some of the company's less-profitable acquisitions, Ralston Purina's earnings were still dropping off in 1981. As Dean prepared to retire, the company took the unusual step of paying each of three outside directors a substantial sum to assist in finding a new president.

Their candidate was William P. Stiritz, a 47-year-old "maverick" who planned a drastic reorganization of his new employer. But first, he had to deal with a major industrial accident. Just one month after he was hired, in January 1981, a Ralston Purina soybean-processing plant in Louisville, Kentucky, leaked an explosive solvent into local sewers. The resulting explosion caused few injuries but cost the company over $40 million in reparations, plus an indictment and fine for failing to notify the proper officials of the leak.

Stiritz's reorganization strategy included a series of major divestitures and acquisitions. Less-profitable subsidiaries, including the St. Louis Blues, the fleet of tuna boats, the fresh mushroom farms, and the soybean-processing business, were shed. In 1985 Ralston Purina sold its Foodmaker restaurant chain for $450 million. In 1988 the company sold its Van Camp Seafood division to a group of investors led by a privately held Indonesian concern for $260 million. Stiritz, whom a 1987 *Fortune* article characterized as a member of "the unsentimental school of executives who believe in running their companies like investment portfolios," even sold the domestic livestock feed business upon which Ralston Purina was founded. Ralston Purina did, however, retain ownership of the famous checkerboard logo, the Purina name, its foreign animal-feeds business, and its pet food interests. In all, the divestitures had accounted for nearly half of the company's sales, but a considerably smaller share of its profits.

In the meantime, Stiritz used the proceeds of these sales (along with a generous dose of long-term debt) to acquire businesses with products complementary to Ralston's lines of food and consumer items. In 1984 the company bought Continental Baking, makers of Wonder Bread and Hostess snack cakes, for $475 million. With the bread industry too intensely competitive to offer much hope of an increase in market share, the new parent focused on expanding Continental's line of baked snack products. Within two years, this strategy had succeeded in raising the division's profit margins.

In June 1986, Ralston Purina purchased Union Carbide Corporation's industry-leading Eveready Battery division for $1.4 billion. The $115 million acquisition of Drake Bakeries, an important competitor in baked snacks, however, drew an antitrust action. While Ralston was compelled to sell Drake in 1987, it was able to realize an after-tax gain of $43 million on the deal.

From 1982 to 1987, Ralston Purina's sales climbed to $5.87 billion and its net income quadrupled to $526.7 million. Stiritz also boosted Ralston Purina's shareholder value through a massive stock repurchase plan. From 1982 to 1991, the leader invested nearly $3 billion in the repurchase of almost half of the company's outstanding shares. His organizational, operational, and strategic moves effected fabulous stock performance: the company's adjusted share price multiplied from $5 to $60.

But a recession in the late 1980s and early 1990s, combined with trends in the pet food business, began to deflate Ralston Purina's high-flying performance. Just as Stiritz's acquisitive scheme to build up Ralston's brand equity came to fruition, recession-battered consumers began to trade down to cheaper private-label products. Ironically, while some shoppers also sought out cheaper foods for their pets, others put their dogs and cats on "superpremium" diets. Influenced by these two trends, Ralston Purina's earnings fell in five of the six years between 1987 and 1994.

The company responded to the challenges of the grocery industry by deftly exiting many of the affected businesses. It distributed 55 percent of its stake in Continental Baking to shareholders in 1993, and accepted a $560 million bid for the remaining shares early in 1995. Stiritz also created a separate subsidiary, Ralcorp Holdings, and spun it off to shareholders early in 1994. The new company combined Ralston Purina's Chex and private-label cereal operations, its cookies and crackers business, the Beech-Nut baby food business it had acquired in 1989, and Colorado's Breckenridge Ski Area. This series of divestitures left Ralston Purina with 15 percent less in annual sales and profits from 1993 to 1994, but was predicted to enable the company to concentrate on its two most profitable businesses, pet food and batteries.

While its reaction to competitive pressures in the pet food industry were judged tardy by some analysts, Ralston Purina attacked on both the premium and budget fronts in the early 1990s. Priced just slightly lower than superpremium leaders Science Diet and Iams, the company's Purina O.N.E. (Optimal Nutritional Effectiveness) brand dog and cat foods vaulted to the top of the supermarket pet food trade, and made significant inroads in the pet shop venue. Moreover, the company sought to appeal to the price-conscious pet owner with the introduction of Alley Cat brand cat food.

The Eveready Battery business proved a boon in the midst of Ralston's other dilemmas. Promoted by the "Energizer Bunny" advertising campaign launched in 1989, Eveready's Energizer brand gained about nine percentage points in domestic market share and 35 percent in worldwide sales from 1989 to 1991. The Energizer brand denoted Eveready's transition from outdated zinc oxide batteries to the faster-growing, higher-margin alkaline category. Energizer's 36.4 percent share of the American battery market mounted a serious challenge to Duracell's 40.4 percent share. From its acquisition in 1986 to 1993, the division's return on assets grew from nine to 14 percent, as CEO Stiritz rationalized operations. The leader also orchestrated geographic expansion through the acquisition of three European firms (including Great Britain's Ever Ready) at a total cost of $480 million.

Further Reading:

Danforth, William H., *I Dare You! Stand Tall, Think Tall, Smile Tall, Live Tall,* St. Louis: William Danforth, 1948.

Desloge, Rick, "Eveready Energizer Charges Closer to Duracell," *St. Louis Business Journal,* June 3, 1991, p. 1A

——, "Ralcorp Strategy: Pearce Will Copy Baby Food Formula," *St. Louis Business Journal,* February 14, 1994, p. 1.

Liesse, Julie, "Purina Bites Back into Pet Food," *Advertising Age,* April 20, 1992, p. 45.

Moore, Thomas, "Old-Line Industry Shapes Up," *Fortune,* April 27, 1987, p. 22.

Oliver, Suzanne, "Out of the Doghouse?," *Forbes,* March 28, 1994, p. 46.

Philpott, Gordon M., *Daring Venture; The Life Story of William H. Danforth,* New York: Random House, 1960.

The Ralston Chronicle, 1894–1994: A Century of Managing Change, St. Louis: Ralston Purina Company, 1994.

Ralston Purina Yesterday, St. Louis: Ralston Purina Company, 1980.

Spirit of Purina Mills, 1894–1994: America's Leader in Animal Nutrition, St. Louis: Max Fisher, 1994.

—updated by April Dougal Gasbarre

RANDOM HOUSE, INC.

Random House, Inc.

201 East 50th Street
New York, New York 10022
U.S.A.
(212) 751-2600
Fax: (212) 572-2593

Private Company
Founded: 1925
Employees: 3,500
Sales: $290 million
SICs: 2731 Book Publishing

The largest general trade book publisher in the English-speaking world, Random House, Inc. posted sales of $290 million in 1992. Working in concert or at times in competition, Random House's 10 independent book groups have represented dozens of the world's most renowned authors and won virtually every distinguished literary award. In the mid-1990s, Random House prepared for the future by establishing a New Media Division to track the latest advances in electronic media and their varied applications for publishing.

When Bennett A. Cerf and Donald S. Klopfer decided to rename their joint publishing venture Random House, Inc. (RH) in 1927, its pedigree was already well established. The 27-year-old Cerf and his 23-year-old partner had purchased the 109-volume Modern Library line in 1925 for $215,000 from the Boni & Liveright publishing firm in New York. Since 1923, Cerf had worked at Boni & Liveright as a vice president (replacing Richard L. Simon, who left to form a joint venture with M. Lincoln Schuster), and he had become increasingly aware of the series' value and potential. When Horace Liveright's financial problems grew untenable and forced him to sell the seven-year-old Modern Library, Cerf and Klopfer jumped at the opportunity.

Inspired by Everyman's Library, founded in 1905 by Londoners Joseph Malaby Dent and Ernest Rhys, Modern Library was already considered a classic in its time. Cerf and Klopfer replaced the company's logo with a leaping torchbearer designed by Lucian Bernhard, bound the books in cloth instead of the original navy lambskin, and recouped their initial investment within two years. The partners soon changed the company's name to ''Random House'' to reflect their intention of publishing a wide array of fiction and nonfiction without limitations. In 1931, Cerf and Klopfer created the Modern Library Giants, ''a collection of the most significant and thought-provoking books in modern literature,'' as a sibling series of longer classics, like Leo Tolstoy's *War and Peace* and Victor Hugo's *Les Miserables.* The partners also produced a few ''deluxe'' editions, like the Rockwell Kent-illustrated version of Voltaire's *Candide* and a lavish version of Mark Twain's *Adventures of Tom Sawyer,* yet these indulgences were discontinued when the Depression took a firm hold of the economy.

Moving into less-expensive trade books, Cerf immediately set out to sign up the day's literati, including playwright Eugene O'Neill and poet Robinson Jeffers. Cerf also flew overseas to secure U.S. publishing rights to James Joyce's *Ulysses.* When his unexpurgated copy of the book was seized by customs as ''obscene'' material upon his return, Cerf and attorney Morris Ernst gained international acclaim by taking the case to court. On December 6, 1933, Judge John Woolsey issued a decision with historic implications by upholding Cerf's right not only to possess the book, but to publish an uncensored version of *Ulysses* in America. Cerf's precedent-setting crusade made RH a household word, and the Modern Library's *Ulysses* was published in 1934.

In 1936, RH purchased Robinson Smith & Robert Haas, Inc. and netted several prominent authors in the process, including Isak Dinesen, William Faulkner, Edgar Snow, and Jean de Brunhoff. The acquisition of de Brunhoff, creator of the popular *Babar* series, proved both timely and prescient, as RH expanded into children's books. After World War II ended, RH sought both domestic and international expansion, beginning with the establishment of Random House Canada and the development of a college books division in 1944. In 1947, after years of research and at a cost of over $500,000, RH published the *American College Dictionary,* the first of its many reference books. Continuing in this vein but directing its efforts toward children, RH's think tank initiated a series of Landmark Books about legendary Americans in 1950. Written by famous authors like Pearl S. Buck, C. S. Forester, and John Gunther, the line was expanded in 1953 to cover historic world events and leaders.

RH's children's division published a picture book in 1957 called *The Cat in the Hat* by Dr. Seuss. Simple and silly, the book was so successful it was reprinted in 1958 as the first of a new line christened ''Beginner Books.'' The series enjoyed huge success, becoming an enduring favorite for new readers and remaining a staple of libraries and bookstores to this day. The same year, RH hired Saxe Commins as its editor-in-chief. ''With Mr. Commins' counsel and Mr. Cerf's instincts,'' Alden Whitman of the *New York Times* observed, ''Random House began to grow into one of the giants of the books business.''

In 1959, RH went public with an offering of over 220,000 shares at $11.25 each, with Cerf selling about a third of his stock (he kept 200,000 shares). Much of the proceeds went into rapid expansion, beginning with the 1960 acquisition of Alfred A. Knopf for about $3 million. In Knopf, RH gained one of the nation's most distinguished and respected publishers. Cerf assured the new subsidiary of complete editorial independence, and he and Knopf forged a close alliance, both professionally and personally, that endured for decades. RH's second major acquisition was textbook producer L. W. Singer, which was followed by Helen and Kurt Wolff's brainchild, the 19-year-old Pantheon Books, in 1961. Andre Schiffrin was named editor-in-chief of Pantheon in 1963 at the age of 28.

In 1965, the first of several significant events affecting RH's future occurred. In a curious role reversal, the acquisitive RH was purchased by Radio Corporation of America (RCA). Cerf became chairman of the board following the sale, and he relinquished the presidency to protege Robert L. Bernstein the next year. Though the buyout was one "of mingled sadness and joy" for Cerf, he was pleased with RH's record earnings and happy to end the company's independence "in a blaze of glory." In 1966, one of the company's crowning achievements came to fruition—the unabridged, 2,059-page *Random House Dictionary of the English Language,* which took more than 10 years to research and compile at an estimated cost of $3 million, was published. It sold well over 500,000 copies within the next five years.

The changing of the guard was nearly complete in 1969, when RH moved from the old Villard House on Madison Avenue—a historic landmark located behind St. Patrick's Cathedral—to the company's current location at 201 East 50th Street. Cerf stepped down as chairman the following year, with his longtime friend and colleague Klopfer taking over. Cerf remained at RH as a senior editor until his death in 1971, at age 73. Called "a glorious amalgam of pragmatist and leprechaun" by John Daly, former host of *What's My Line?*—a television game show on which Cerf had been a panelist for 16 years—the RH founder was a popular man whose funeral was a veritable who's who of the publishing and show business worlds. "I wonder," Eudora Welty mused, "if anyone else of such manifold achievements in the publishing world could ever have so many friends."

With Bernstein and Klopfer running the ship, RH continued to flourish. In 1971, the Modern Library exceeded 400 titles and sold 50 million books. The 1973 acquisition of mass marketer Ballantine Books added considerably to RH's paperback audience. Seven years later, RH was again on the receiving end of a takeover, this time by Advance Publications, Inc., part of the Newhouse family's vast holdings, which purchased the publisher from RCA for $70 million. The next decade was one of extraordinary growth, marked by the 1982 purchase of Fawcett Books, the 1983 founding of Villard Books, and the 1984 acquisition of Times Books from the New York Times Company. In 1985, RH launched its AudioBooks division, drawing on the company's extensive backlist to create abridged and unabridged cassette recordings.

RH continued to expand its reach with the 1986 purchase of Fodor's Travel Guides and the 1987 acquisition of Chatto, Virago, Bodley Head & Jonathan Cape, Ltd., a prestigious British publishing group. "With companies like Bantam and Simon & Schuster becoming more involved overseas, we had a feeling we should do something ourselves," Bernstein told *Publishers Weekly.* As with previous mergers, the companies remained autonomous but also stood to benefit immensely from the alliance for subsidiary rights and other negotiations. Also in 1987, RH's renowned Pantheon Books and the newly acquired Schocken Books were merged editorially.

The following year, RH once again expanded its holdings by acquiring the large, respected Crown Publishing Group, comprised of Crown Books, Clarkson N. Potter, Inc., Harmony Books, and the Outlet Book Company. In 1989, the company experienced its second changing of the guard when Bernstein departed RH after 23 years. His replacement as president, chairman, and CEO was Alberto Vitale, former head of rival Bantam Doubleday Dell (BDD). Among Vitale's immediate concerns were trimming the fat and overhauling RH's operations. Additionally, Vitale focused RH on the 21st century by diversifying into the burgeoning electronic field and developing multimedia products. This year also saw further U.K. expansion with the acquisition of Century Hutchinson, Ltd., which along with the Chatto, Virago, Bodley Head and Cape group became Random House UK, with subsidiaries in Australia, New Zealand, and South Africa.

In his continuing efforts to streamline the company, Vitale set his sights on the ailing Pantheon Books. Since Bernstein—one of Pantheon's most ardent supporters—was gone, the industry was rife with rumors of the imprint's imminent dissolution. Andre Schiffrin, Pantheon's directional force for 28 years, resigned in 1990 after refusing to go along with Vitale's cost-cutting measures. His departure stirred up a storm of controversy, as Studs Terkel (Pantheon's bestselling author), E. L. Doctorow, Barbara Ehrenreich, Kurt Vonnegut, and 350 others staged a demonstration in front of RH's offices, while another 300 writers signed a letter of protest on Pantheon's behalf. In response, Vitale told *Publishers Weekly,* "I want to most emphatically reaffirm Random House's commitment to maintaining Pantheon's position as one of our most prestigious imprints and to insuring its continuity and success in the future." Vitale soon hired Erroll McDonald—who had criticized the demonstrators in an op-ed piece for the *New York Times*—as the new executive editor of Pantheon, and the imprint continued with a smaller staff and fewer projected titles.

In 1992, Vitale raided his former employer's legions to hire William Wright, who became his right-hand man as RH's executive vice president and chief operating officer. Also during this year, RH founded two new imprints under the Ballantine group's umbrella: One World, to produce culturally diverse originals and reprints in hardcover and trade paperback; and Moorings, to publish hardcover and trade paperbacks with a Christian, devotional, or inspirational leaning. Yet 1992's biggest news was the renaissance of the Modern Library, with the reintroduction of 27 volumes, complete with new bindings and reset pages, to celebrate the series' 75th anniversary. Simultaneously, those at Knopf put the finishing touches on the revival of Everyman's Library, the long-dormant hardcover classics once published by Dutton that were the original model for RH's own Modern Library series. Though there was some concern about competition, Jane Friedman, president of RH Audio, posited, "Would [we] have been any happier if some other publisher had brought out Everyman's?"

Once again solidifying assets and looking for more, Vitale engineered the purchase of BDD's Bantam Electronic Publishing in 1993. The move was intended to beef up RH's own electronic division, or as Vitale told *Publishers Weekly,* "to create more critical mass in a field that, while evolving, is here to stay." As proof of his commitment, Vitale formed RH's New

Media Division to ''identify and pursue multimedia opportunities'' and installed Randi Benton as its president. Additionally, RH formed several joint ventures in 1993, including one to distribute the National Geographic Society's books; a second with Broderbund to create and market story-based multimedia software for children; and another between RH's Electronic Publishing division and Prentice Hall to produce and market a line of computer-oriented books under the newly established imprint of Hewlett-Packard Press. RH continued its trend of acquisition and reorganization in 1994 and 1995.

Through the decades, RH has embraced virtually every facet of publishing—from hardcover to electronic media, and from adult to juvenile—and has brought many renowned writers to the attention of a worldwide audience. The small company that was built on the foundation of the Modern Library to publish selected books ''at random'' grew through acquisitions to become a vast empire.

Principal Subsidiaries: Alfred A. Knopf Inc.; Ballantine Books, Inc.; Clarkson N. Potter Inc.; Crown Publishing Group; Fodor's Travel Publications, Inc.; Pantheon Books; Random House AudioBooks; Random House Reference and Electronic Publishing; Random House Inc. Home Video Division; Random House Canada; Alfred A. Knopf Canada; Random House UK.

Further Reading:

Alter, Jonathan, ''The Rumble at Random House,'' *Newsweek,* October 26, 1987, p. 62.

''Bennett Cerf,'' *Current Biography,* New York: H. W. Wilson, 1958, pp. 82–83.

Cerf, Bennett, *At Random: The Reminisces of Bennett Cerf,* New York: Random House, 1977.

Dahlin, Robert, ''Joint Venture Sparks Audubon Book and Tour,'' *Publishers Weekly,* December 7, 1992, pp. 21–22.

Feldman, Gaye, ''A Conversation with Crown's Ann Patty,'' *Publishers Weekly,* August 22, 1994, pp. 22–23.

Giddins, Gary, ''Why I Carry a Torch for the Modern Library,'' *New York Times Book Review,* December 6, 1992, pp. 42–43.

Milliot, Jim, ''Ballantine Publishing Group Posts Record Year in 1993,'' *Publishers Weekly,* January 17, 1994, pp. 20–21.

——, ''Outlet Book Co. Becomes RH Value Publishing,'' *Publishers Weekly,* April 4, 1994, p. 12.

Model, F. Peter, ''A Volvo, Not a Caddy: The Modern Library's Second Coming,'' *Wilson Library Bulletin,* December 1992, pp. 66–68.

Mutter, John, ''Del Rey Creates 'Cybercommunity,' '' *Publishers Weekly,* December 19, 1994, pp. 18–19.

Oder, Norman, ''Looking behind Ann Godoff's Bestselling Spring Leap,'' *Publishers Weekly,* July 4, 1994, pp. 23–24.

''Random and Prentice Hall Sign Joint Deal with Hewlett-Packard,'' *Publishers Weekly,* March 15, 1993, p. 9.

''Random House Acquires Bantam Computer Books,'' *Publishers Weekly,* May 24, 1993, p. 25.

''Random to Distribute National Geographic Titles to Stores,'' *Publishers Weekly,* May 24, 1993, p. 26.

Raymont, Henry, ''Cerf Rites Draw Friends of 'Two Worlds',' *New York Times,* September 1, 1971, p. 40.

Reilly, Patrick M., ''Godoff Named Editorial Chief at Random House,'' *Wall Street Journal,* January 13, 1995, p. B2.

Reuter, Madalynne, ''After the Un-Random Showdown,'' *Publishers Weekly,* October 30, 1987, p. 11.

——, ''Schiffrin to Leave Pantheon Books,'' *Publishers Weekly,* March 9, 1990, p. 10.

——, and Marianne Yen, ''Random House to Acquire Chatto, Virago, Bodley and Cape Group,'' *Publishers Weekly,* May 15, 1987, p. 114.

Shapiro, Laura, ''Publisher at the Barricades,'' *Newsweek,* March 19, 1990, p. 71.

''Short Shrift,'' *Economist,* March 10, 1990, p. 102.

Whitman, Alden, ''Bennett Cerf Dies; Publisher, Writer,'' *New York Times,* August 29, 1971, pp. 1, 56.

—Taryn Benbow-Pfalzgraf

Rayovac Corporation

601 Rayovac Drive
Madison, Wisconsin 53711-2497
U.S.A.
(608) 275-3340
Fax: (608) 275-4577

Private Company
Founded: 1906 as the French Battery Company
Employees: 2,800
Sales: $450 million
SICs: 3648 Lighting Equipment, Not Elsewhere Classified; 3691 Storage Batteries

Rayovac Corporation was the third leading U.S. manufacturer of storage batteries and the leading supplier of hearing aid and computer backup batteries in 1994. It also manufactured flashlights and other miscellaneous items. The company has played a leadership role in the U.S. battery industry throughout the 20th century. After faltering in the late 1970s and early 1980s, Rayovac rebounded and was the fastest growing contender in the industry in the early 1990s. Going into the mid-1990s, the company operated ten plants in the United States and two plants in the United Kingdom, and had international sales and distribution operations in Europe and Asia.

Rayovac's roots reach back to 1906, when entrepreneurs James B. Ramsay, P.W. Strong, and Alfred Landau joined forces to create the French Battery Company. Ramsay, the leader of the operation, was 35 years old at the time and had already established himself as a successful businessman. His gumption, in fact, was evident early; he convinced the University of Wisconsin to admit him when he was a junior in high school, and subsequently became the only person to graduate from the institution who didn't have a high school diploma. After college, Ramsay moved to Medford, Wisconsin, where he started a lumber company and was later elected mayor of the town. He sold the thriving business when he was 35 years old and returned to Madison in search of a new challenge.

After Ramsay returned to Madison, Strong, an old friend, approached him about a business opportunity. The dry cell battery had been invented in the 1800s in France and demand for the technology was beginning to grow in the United States by the early 1900s. Strong was aware of a man in Chicago named Alfred Landau who was manufacturing batteries in his attic and selling them locally. Cursory research convinced Ramsay that it was a good investment. So, in 1906, the three men initiated the French Battery Company. They started with $30,000 working out of Landau's Chicago attic. "The company just happened," Ramsay noted in company annals, "as did the history of the fellow who grabbed such a hold of the bull's tail that he couldn't let go."

Landau's crude manufacturing operation soon outgrew his attic so the men moved the company to a small building in Madison in March of 1906. But orders continued to pour in, many of them unsolicited, and the entrepreneurs were overwhelmed with new accounts. Just three months after they had started the company, sales had far surpassed even their most ambitious projections. In the summer, they moved the operation into a two-story brick building with the help of 12 more investors who supplied about $60,000 in new capital. By that time the company was employing 24 workers. During its first year, the French Battery Company churned out 37,000 battery cells, most of which sold for about 13 cents apiece. To boost revenues, Ramsay hired L.H. Dodge as the company's first salesman in January of 1907. He added three more salesman in the summer of that year.

Ramsay and his cohorts were operating a bare bones operation: They owned one roll-top desk, a typewriter, and about $314 worth of lab equipment going into 1907. But they had invested heavily in inventory in anticipation of growing demand. Unfortunately, some of the materials were found to be unreliable after many batteries had been shipped. Disappointed buyers demanded refunds and the struggling upstart began losing money. Infuriated investors demanded that Landau, who was serving as the official head of the company, resign. Landau returned to France, and Ramsay kept the operation going, although another investor was appointed president. By the end of 1907, the company's books showed a total deficit of $50,000 for the two years of operation. Nevertheless, Ramsay remained committed to the company's success.

To replace Landau's technical expertise, Ramsay called on Dr. Charles F. Burgess, the founder of the chemical engineering department at Ramsay's alma mater. Burgess was intelligent and a perfectionist. He was immediately intrigued by Ramsay's enthusiasm about the operation, despite his belief that the French Battery Company was producing the worst battery on the market. Burgess invested in the company and helped it to upgrade its products. Within a year he believed that the company was offering the best dry cell available in the United States. The company struggled for a few more years, narrowly escaping bankruptcy, before posting its first profit in 1910. Enthusiasm about the surplus was negated, however, by a fire that wiped out French's factory. Importantly, though, French began selling a pivotal new flashlight battery that would eventually bring big profits.

French recovered from the fire and achieved steady profits between 1913 and 1920, despite another fire that virtually leveled the company's new factory in 1915. Burgess became increasingly involved in, and vital to, the company during those years and was elected vice president in 1915. After the 1915 fire, however, relations between Burgess and the company deteriorated. Burgess departed in 1916 to start his own enterprise, although he allowed French to continue manufacturing products under his patents. Burgess was succeeded by his top assistant, Otto E. Ruhoff. Despite management turbulence, French recorded record profits in 1916 of $62,410 from sales of $889,880. That year, moreover, marked the last one in which the company would generate less than one million in sales. Ramsay was elected president of the company in 1918.

Battery sales boomed during World War II because of huge orders from the United States and allied governments. By 1919, the company had established sales branches throughout much of the nation and as far west as Kansas City. An economic downturn in 1920 stalled growth, and wary executives shuttered the company's recently constructed New Jersey manufacturing plant. But the downturn was short-lived. Spurred by new applications for batteries, particularly the radio, demand spiraled during the 1920s and French prospered. French's line of successful batteries was expanded to include Ray-O-Vac (radio batteries), Ray-O-Lite (flashlight cells), and Ray-O-Spark (ignition batteries). Sales topped $3 million in 1923 and production facilities were expanded to meet demand for French's patented batteries. At the peak of activity in the 1920s, when unsolicited orders poured in from around the globe, the company was employing 1,300.

Explosive demand growth during the mid-1920s was driven primarily by the radio, the use of which necessitated batteries. Battery manufacturers were stunned, therefore, when Dr. Samuel Rubin invented technology that made the plug-in electric radio possible. The discovery capped French's growth spurt and even pummeled sales and profits during the late 1920s and early 1930s. Revenues plunged from $4.1 million in 1928 to just $2.1 million in 1933. The industry shakeout left only a dozen beleaguered battery manufacturers intact, one of which was French. Ramsay resigned in 1929, deciding "to make way for a younger man." He remained on the company's board until his death in 1952 at 83 years of age. Ramsay was succeeded by Bill Cargill, an aggressive, flamboyant general manager described by others as larger than life.

Partly as a result of Cargill's sheer energy and charisma, The French Battery Company survived the Great Depression relatively unscathed. Because of the name recognition of its Ray-O-Vac battery, the company officially adopted that name in the early 1930s. Ray-O-Vac's fortunes began to turn in the mid-and late 1930s, partly as a result of new innovations that boosted sales. Interestingly, in 1933, Ray-O-Vac's research team, led by the talented Art Wengel, developed the first portable radio with high fidelity reception. The radio was so small that it could be carried around in a suitcase-style box. In 1937, moreover, Ray-O-Vac patented the first wearable vacuum tube hearing aid. Despite global economic malaise, Ray-O-Vac's sales steadily surged to an impressive $5 million annually by 1936 and continued to grow to more than $8 million by 1941.

In 1939, Ray-O-Vac's Herman R.C. Anthony invented the leak-proof "sealed in steel" dry cell battery, which closely resembled the metal-encased batteries sold throughout much of the mid-1900s. That product played an important role during World War II, as Allied troops used the batteries to power flashlights, radios, walkie-talkies, mine detectors, signal lights, bazookas, and other gear. The company's work force soared from about 1,500 to more than 14,000, including many women and elderly men. Ray-O-Vac's manufacturing facilities, considered war plants, were patrolled by armed military guards. In some of its plants, battery making was discontinued in favor of production of parts for military gear and weaponry. The government purchased an astounding 23 million units of just one type of leak-proof battery during the War, and Ray-O-Vac operated the largest battery plant in the world—the 10-building Signal Battery complex in Milwaukee.

Batteries were rationed to the public during the War, so the loss of government orders following the War was partially replaced by increased consumer demand. After a brief period of reorganization, the company began growing in the wake of the post-war population and economic boom. In an effort to bring some order to the sprawling organization, Cargill realigned Ray-O-Vac in 1946 into six divisions: Lighting Division; Manufacturers Battery Company, which produced radio batteries and related items; Canadian Division; Specialty Battery Division; Export Division; and Research and Development Division. Although sales and profits swelled throughout the late 1940s and into the 1950s, the reorganization eventually proved inefficient. Nevertheless, Ray-O-Vac continued to innovate and set new records. It sold more than 100 million leak proof batteries in 1946, for example, and in 1949 Ray-O-Vac's Dr. W. Stanley Herbert introduced the breakthrough "crown cell" alkaline battery for hearing aids. Also in 1949, the company introduced its hugely popular Sportsman flashlight.

Ray-O-Vac shipped its billionth leak proof battery in 1950. Two years later, Cargill, in ill health, retired and was replaced by Don Tyrrell. Just a few days after the transfer of power, the company's founder, Ramsay, died. Ray-O-Vac was already operating on several continents going into the 1950s. But Tyrrell stepped up international efforts. Notably, he helped to engineer an agreement with a Japanese company to import and distribute Ray-O-Vac products. Ray-O-Vac was soon producing and distributing batteries throughout the Orient. Sales in that region augmented increased efforts in Europe and South America, among other regions. At the same time, Tyrrell spearheaded a diversification effort. Ray-O-Vac's first purchase was Wilson, a safety products company that it bought in 1955. Other acquisitions followed.

The battery industry was transformed during the late 1950s and 1960s by the introduction of the transistor in 1956. The transistor replaced energy-consuming vacuum tubes, thereby making devices smaller and more energy efficient. The invention created a plethora of new market opportunities for companies that were willing to take risks. Elmer Ott succeeded Tyrrell as president in 1957. He continued to diversify the company and to prepare for growth in the popularity of the transistor. Also in 1957, Ray-O-Vac merged with the Electric Storage Battery Co. (ESB), a leading manufacturer of industrial and automotive "wet" batteries. At the time, ESB's sales were $102 million annually—roughly two and a half times as great as Ray-O-Vac's. Ray-O-Vac effectively became a division of ESB. ESB was particularly interested in tapping into Ray-O-Vac's international network, which by the late 1950s spanned 100 different nations and accounted for nearly 25 percent of profits. The Ray-O-Vac name became so well known overseas, in fact, that it was often exploited (illegally) by foreign companies—a humorous example was "Ray-O-Vac Leak Proof Fish Sauce" in China.

In an attempt to adapt to a world increasingly dominated by transistors, Ray-O-Vac introduced a number of low-voltage, miniature battery products during the 1960s, including penlight batteries and super small button batteries. In addition, Ray-O-Vac became a leader in battery-powered lighting systems and devices, including fluorescent camping lanterns, miniature disposable flashlights, and long-lasting boat lamps. Meanwhile, international expansion continued with the development of manufacturing facilities in Iran, for example, and expanded operations in Latin America. Ray-O-Vac was generating annual revenues of about $55 million by 1965, for the first time surpassing World War II sales figures. The company also made national headlines in 1965 because of one of its employees, Doc Swenson. Doc turned 100 in 1965. He had worked for Ray-O-Vac since 1916 and continued to work 40-hour weeks until the age of 90, after which he cut back to 20 hours weekly. Doc, who missed only one-and-one-half days of work during his career, died shortly after his hundredth birthday.

After 44 years of service to Ray-O-Vac, Ott passed the torch in 1967 to Owen Slauson. Under Slauson's direction, Ray-O-Vac aggressively automated its manufacturing operations and continued to pursue global diversity with new factories in the Dominican Republic, Mexico, Africa, Peru, Korea, and other places. In the United States, Ray-O-Vac built a $2 million Engineering and Development Center in Madison, Wisconsin. Innovations stemming from research in the facility included the first heavy-duty all zinc-chloride battery, which was introduced in 1972 and doubled the life of existing general-purpose batteries. The company also continued to diversify by acquiring, among other ventures, fishing tackle companies, plastic and rubber manufacturers, and mining operations. Unfortunately, most of the acquisitions languished and became a drag on Ray-O-Vac's bottom line. In 1979, ESB, which was purchased by INCO Ltd. in 1974, reunited Ray-O-Vac's domestic and international operations and selected Benno A. Bernt as president of the group.

By the early 1980s, Ray-O-Vac was generating about $175 million in annual sales. However, Ray-O-Vac's attempts at geographic diversity and product innovation belied serious structural problems that plagued the company during the 1970s and early 1980s. Indeed, Ray-O-Vac was the undisputed leader of the U.S. battery industry during the 1950s. During the 1960s and 1970s, though, it lost its edge and gradually succumbed to the challenge of competitors like Everready Battery Co and Duracell Inc. Ray-O-Vac's share of the battery market plunged during the period from 35 percent to a measly six percent. Some critics blamed Ray-O-Vac's parent companies for the slide. Others pointed to internal problems that resulted in outdated packaging and stale product offerings in comparison to other battery producers. Most importantly, Ray-O-Vac executives failed to aggressively pursue the emerging market for alkaline batteries, which quickly became the industry standard. Going into the 1980s, sales were falling, Ray-O-Vac was laying off workers, and major long-term customers were dropping the Ray-O-Vac line.

Enter Thomas and Judith Pyle, a husband and wife team with experience selling toiletries, sewing patterns, makeup, and wigs to personal care and consumer products companies. The Pyles, with two other investors, purchased Ray-O-Vac (they changed the name to Rayovac Corporation) from INCO in 1982. The 44-year-old Pyle and his wife became chairman and co-chairwoman and Pyle named himself president and chief executive. They eventually bought out the other two investors and virtually owned the company. The Pyles combined their consumer marketing savvy with Rayovac's untapped manufacturing potential and were able to bring the company back from the edge of disaster. Under their direction, Rayovac introduced a steady stream of innovative products and marketing initiatives. In 1984, for example, the company unveiled its successful WORKHORSE premium flashlight with its ultrabright bulb and lifetime warranty. Likewise, they started selling "Smart Packs" of six to eight batteries instead of the usual two.

The Pyle's strategy was based on experience gleaned from their previous work with consumer products. Judith Pyle called their tactics "nichemanship," meaning that every product, particularly new ones, had to incorporate features, designs, and prices focused tightly on a specifically targeted group of customers. Secondly, new products had to be truly innovative, as opposed to "me-too" entries into the crowded marketplace. To that end, Rayovac, introduced products like the successful Luma 2, the first flashlight with its own emergency backup system; if the batteries failed, a separate lithium-powered system could be activated. Similarly, the Loud 'n Clear hearing aid, unveiled in 1987, represented a breakthrough in hearing-aid zinc battery technology. In the late 1980s, moreover, Rayovac began using the Checkout Pack Merchandising System. That system featured shrink-wrapped battery packages that could be stacked rather than hung on conventional pegboard displays and a new gravity-fed display rack designed for use at check-out counters.

In addition to introducing new products, the Pyles also updated Rayovac's packaging and aggressively sought to recover customers who had dropped their lines. They barraged lost customers in Wisconsin, for example, with letters asking them to start selling Rayovac products again. The effort boosted market penetration in the state from 20 percent to 70 percent within a few years. Meanwhile, Rayovac shuttered some nonperforming operations and expanded through acquisition. During the 1980s, the company's acquisitions included, in 1983, certain Timex battery operations in the United Kingdom; in 1988, Raystone Corp., a manufacturer of battery cells; in 1989, Crompton Vidor, a United Kingdom producer of consumer batteries and flashlights; and the Tekna line of high-tech flashlights. The Pyles also initiated an aggressive quality improvement program designed to improve operations at every organizational level.

The net result of the Pyle's efforts was that Rayovac's sales shot up to $270 million in 1987, reflecting growth of nearly 15 percent in 1985 and 1986. Furthermore, the company's share of the U.S. retail battery market vaulted to 12 percent. Between 1987 and the early 1990s, moreover, Rayovac's market share continued to surge as reported revenues bolted past $450 million. Innovations in the early 1990s included: a new alkaline computer clock battery; a line of ultra-tough flashlights; a WORKHORSE fluorescent lantern; and the Renewal battery, the first reusable, long-life alkaline battery which could be used

25 times or more and was environmentally safe. Importantly, Rayovac signed sports megastar Michael Jordan in a long-term endorsement contract in April of 1995. That major coup had the potential to send Rayovac's market share soaring.

Principal Subsidiaries: Raystone Corp.; Crompton Vidor (U.K.).

Further Reading:

Daggett, John, ''Rayovac Introduces Reusable Alkaline Battery System,'' *PR Newswire,* June 15, 1993.

Gribble, Roger A., ''Workers Essential to Rayovac Quality,'' *Wisconsin State Journal,* February 14, 1993, Section Bus.

''Jordan Joins the Rayovac Team,'' *PR Newswire,* April 11, 1995.

Kueny, Barbara, ''Flashlights of Innovation Illuminate Rayovac's Bottom Line,'' *The Business Journal-Milwaukee,* May 27, 1991, p. 13S.

Millard, Pete, ''Look at the Source: Wisconsin Companies are Developing Technologies to Solve Environmental Problems,'' *Corporate Report Wisconsin,* March 1994, p. 23.

''Reviving Primary Cells,'' *Machine Design,* March 9, 1995, p. 131.

Ruble, Kenneth D., *The Rayovac Story,* Madison, Wisc.: North Central Publishing Company, 1981.

Tracewell, Nancy, ''Enterprising Companies Build for Future During Recessions,'' *Business Journal-Milwaukee,* December 28, 1987, p. B4.

Weiner, Steve, ''Electrifying,'' *Forbes,* November 30, 1987, p. 196.

—Dave Mote

Restaurants Unlimited, Inc.

1818 North Northlake Way
Seattle, Washington 98103
U.S.A.
(206) 634-0550
Fax: (206) 632-3533

Private Company
Incorporated: 1969
Employees: 2,000
Sales: $180 million
SICs: 5812 Eating Places

One of the fastest-growing restaurant companies in the United States, Restaurants Unlimited, Inc. operated more than 20 full-service dining establishments and nearly 300 Cinnabon stores that sold specialty cinnamon rolls. In the course of its growth, Restaurants Unlimited became recognized as a trend-setting industry leader, assembling a diverse collection of restaurants that positioned it as a food-service force to be reckoned with in the 1990s and beyond.

Like most entrepreneurial creations, Restaurants Unlimited had humble beginnings. The company's founder was Richard Komen, whose first foray into business began in the back of a pick-up truck loaded with peanuts. Komen—who led Restaurants Unlimited during its first two formative decades of existence and became arguably the most successful restaurateur in Seattle's history—earned a graduate degree in accounting at the University of Washington, then went on to work as a representative for Associated Grocers, a regional wholesale grocery supplier based in Seattle. In 1961, he stopped by his former university's Husky Stadium, where he talked with members of the school's athletic department about taking over the concession business for Washington Husky football games. Then 28 years old, Komen had $1,000 in savings and no experience in food service, yet his inquiry was a fortuitous one. The concession contract for the 55,000-seat stadium was soon coming up for public bid, and the contract winner would receive a three-year deal to supply the concessions with hot dogs, soft drinks, and peanuts for Washington Husky fans.

Komen bid for the contract despite his lack of experience, his youth, and his limited cash to underwrite the venture. Komen improved his odds by enlisting his uncle, who owned a successful diner in Seattle, as a partner. Six weeks later he was awarded the concession contract for Husky Stadium, beginning with the 1961 season. Concurrent with this first big break, Komen formed Volume Service Company as the corporate entity to operate his concession business. He then spent each Friday night before a Husky game with friends bagging peanuts by hand, gradually emptying the back of his loaded pick-up.

Komen enjoyed considerable success as a concessions operator, and soon gained the food-service contract for the Seattle Center, a vast complex created for the 1962 World's Fair. Several years later, he was awarded the concession business for two ski resorts located near Seattle. Komen and his Volume Service Company rapidly became a recognizable food-service force, moving beyond Washington's borders to gain concession contracts later in the 1960s for Oakland Coliseum in California, the H. Truman Sports Complex in Kansas City, the Fair and Exhibition Center in Louisville, Kentucky, and the Los Angeles Convention Center.

By the beginning of the 1970s, though Volume Service Company had become a highly successful business, Komen's entrepreneurial passions were beginning to pull him in a different direction. One year after he was awarded the concession contract for Husky Stadium, Komen had opened his first restaurant—Hippopotamus—but three years later, in 1965, the restaurant closed its doors, temporarily ending Komen's diversification into the full-service dining business. In 1969, he renewed his efforts at creating a successful restaurant, opening a dining facility called The Red Baron which operated as a division of Volume Service Company. Later that year he formed a new company, Restaurants Unlimited, and focused his efforts on creating a new niche in the food-service industry.

Volume Service Company was sold to Chicago-based Interstate United Corporation in 1972, by which time Komen had intensified his efforts toward becoming a successful restaurateur. In the course of his business travel for Volume Service Company, Komen had noticed two burgeoning dining trends, particularly in California and Hawaii. One was the increasing popularity of restaurants serving steak, prime rib, lobster, and salad in a casual dining atmosphere. The other was the dining public's acceptance of theme restaurants decorated in a distinctive style with a menu that reflected the period and country implied by the decor. Komen combined the two trends and created two restaurants—Horatio's and Clinkerdagger, Bickerstaff & Pett's Public House. These ventures would become the engines that propelled Restaurants Unlimited through the 1970s.

Horatio's and Clinkerdagger, decorated in dark, wood-paneled decor reminiscent of Edwardian English pubs, were both opened in 1971. That same year Raymond Lindstrom, who had spent the previous two years working for restaurants, joined Komen in his drive to build a successful restaurant business. Komen and Lindstrom enjoyed immediate success with their ventures. Seattle residents flocked to the two new restaurants, embracing the concept of steak, lobster, prime rib, and salad served in a decidedly Dickensian atmosphere. Horatio's, which featured seafood, collected $1.2 million in sales after its first year of business, convincing Komen and Lindstrom they had created a successful model that could be replicated.

The two restaurateurs did replicate their success, opening another Clinkerdagger in 1972 in Tacoma and a third in Spokane in 1974. By this time, Komen's dining concept was flourishing, enjoying what Restaurants Unlimited managers would later describe as its heyday. Encouraged by the success of his three Clinkerdaggers and one Horatio's, Komen moved beyond Washington's borders in 1976 by opening a Horatio's in Honolulu, and then he opened a Clinkerdagger in Anchorage the following year. Four more Clinkerdagger restaurants and two more Horatio's would be opened before the end of the decade, extending Restaurants Unlimited's geographic coverage into Oregon and California. By the late 1970s, however, the concept underpinning the success of the restaurants had lost its attractive power—particularly in the case of Clinkerdagger, which stopped growing in 1976 and then limped along for the rest of decade recording limited success.

Public tastes had changed, in terms of both the type of food dining patrons craved and the type of dining atmosphere they desired. Wholesale changes were needed and Komen and Lindstrom knew it, but they were uncertain which direction to go. By 1980, the company's restaurants were merely vestiges of a once-popular chain. Restaurants Unlimited had tapped into the dining trends of the early and mid-1970s, but its establishments were outdated in the 1980s. The fact that Komen and Lindstrom had astutely ascertained what would make a successful restaurant concept during the 1970s gave rise to optimism that they would find a popular entry for the 1980s, but the two restaurateurs struggled, unable to divine a profitable future course for their company.

For a year every outward manifestation of activity came to a halt. Komen and Lindstrom spent the time canvassing the country's restaurants, searching for new a new dining trend to carry their company through the 1980s. Restaurant consultants were hired and design teams were contracted. Finally, after a year of introspective analysis, Komen and Lindstrom built their new restaurant, Morgan's Lakeplace, in December 1981. Ten years had passed since they had opened the first Horatio's and the first Clinkerdagger, Bickerstaff & Pett's Public House. At a cost of $350,000, Morgan's was in many respects the antithesis of Clinkerdagger: dark wood paneling was replaced with lightly colored, weathered wood and large glass windows; beef and rich, butter-based sauces gave way to an eclectic, multinational menu featuring pasta, chicken, seafood, and vegetables. It was a contrast the public applauded.

With Morgan's, Komen and Lindstrom placed an emphasis on food quality rather than restaurant motif, which had been one of the primary attractions of both Clinkerdaggers and Horatio's, and this strategic shift made Morgan's a tremendously popular restaurant. The opening of Morgan's also provided the first indication of what type of restaurant company Restaurants Unlimited was destined to become. Before Morgan's, Restaurants Unlimited had expanded in a manner typical for restaurant chains: the two successful prototypes were duplicated again and again in different areas. This time, however, the company would not repeat the pattern.

Although the original Morgan's proved to be highly successful, it was the only Morgan's restaurant the company ever constructed. Instead, Komen and Lindstrom went on to build a variety of restaurants that, with a few exceptions, operated under different names and were designed specifically for the particular markets they occupied. Moreover, when one brand of restaurant began to decline in popularity, as Clinkerdagger did in the late-1970s, the partners closed the struggling restaurant and reopened it as a different type of restaurant. As a result of these changes, Restaurants Unlimited became less of a restaurant chain and evolved into a family or collection of restaurants.

Soon other Clinkerdagger locations were converted into restaurants more reflective of the 1980s. Restaurants Unlimited's sixth Clinkerdagger, in Beaverton, Oregon, was recast as Hall Street in 1982, for example, while its first Clinkerdagger, in Edmonds, Washington, was changed into a restaurant called Scott's that same year. The success of these new ventures sparked the construction of a wave of new restaurants throughout Restaurants Unlimited's territory, each one slightly different from the rest. Cutter's Bayhouse, a more refined version of Morgan's, was opened in Seattle in 1983, the same year Ryan's opened in Honolulu. Other openings included Skates on the Bay in Berkeley in 1984, Stepps on the Court in Los Angeles in 1985, Stats in Chicago the same year, and Kincaid's in Bloomington, Minnesota, in 1986. Others followed at a rapid pace, enlarging Restaurants Unlimited's geographic scope and financial magnitude.

All told, Restaurants Unlimited created 18 new restaurants during the 1980s, but Komen and Lindstrom were not satisfied with this prodigious program of expansion. Instead, they led Restaurants Unlimited in a new direction by opening a specialty cinnamon roll business in 1985. Cinnabon shops featured oversized cinnamon rolls, which were becoming increasingly popular during the mid-1980s. The first Cinnabon opened in a mall near the airport serving the greater Seattle area. All of the 22 additional Cinnabons opened the following year were located in malls, where customers could watch the rolls being made by hand. This network of "bakeries" provided a new franchise arm for Restaurants Unlimited that complimented the company's growing collection of restaurants. The Cinnabon chain stretched from Hawaii to Illinois after its first year of operation, then 16 more outlets were opened in 1987—blanketing the country with high-profit cinnamon roll businesses.

By the end of 1990, there were 72 Cinnabons scattered throughout the nation, generating roughly 25 percent of Restaurants Unlimited's $100 million in annual sales. The company's restaurant business also recorded a vigorous rate of expansion during the late 1980s, adding six restaurants between 1987 and 1989. Perhaps the most significant of these new dining establishments was a restaurant opened in Seattle in late 1989 called Palomino Euro Bistro—a Mediterranean-style restaurant featuring wood-fired rotisseries and a menu borrowing from Greek, Italian, and other southern European cooking. With the opening of Palomino, Komen and Lindstrom ushered in a new era for their company, one that focused on only a few restaurant "brands." Restaurants Unlimited's management expected Palomino to be the vehicle for the company's new, narrower approach. As one senior company official explained to *Nation's Restaurant News,* the concept was a "horse that we're going to be riding for some time."

A second Palomino was opened in Minneapolis in 1991, then two more were added to the company's collection of restaurants in 1993—one in Palm Desert, California, and another in San Francisco. This new strategy for growth was expected to facilitate the company's expansion and, in the process, turn Restaurants Unlimited into a more typical restaurant chain once again. At the same time, the company made another strategic decision to spend more time and money developing its only self-service restaurant, an all-you-can-eat establishment called Zoopa. Opened in 1990 in Tukwila, Washington, Zoopa enjoyed only modest success during its first year of operation. But the company made several adjustments, particularly in the restaurant's pricing structure, to improve its performance and thus created a solid restaurant brand to expand with in the future.

Also during this time, Restaurants Unlimited opened its most extravagant restaurant to date in Seattle. Called Palisade, the 13,000-square foot, $4.5 million restaurant was opened in 1992 and featured a 1,000-square-foot saltwater pool, a wood-fired rotisserie, and an up-scale menu offering prime rib, chicken, pasta, and seafood. Expected to contribute between $7 and $8 million in sales annually, Palisade represented an exception to Restaurants Unlimited's strategy of relying on its Palomino and Zoopa brands and its Cinnabon chain to fuel the company's growth.

A year after Palisade opened, Lindstrom, president of the company since 1979, was named Restaurants Unlimited's chief executive officer, with Komen retaining his corporate title of chairman. In reference to his promotion, Lindstrom explained to *Nation's Restaurant News,* "We had to send the community and this organization a signal about the succession that is already going on."

As Lindstrom gradually assumed control of the company, Restaurants Unlimited entered the mid-1990s continuing to expand both its restaurant business and its Cinnabon chain. By 1995, there were 276 Cinnabon shops—half of which were franchised—located in 37 states, Canada, and Mexico. Restaurants Unlimited planned to increase the total to 500 by the end of the decade. The company also hoped to exceed the meteoric 25 percent annual sales growth rate Cinnabon recorded during its first decade of existence and build on its $100 million annual sales volume. In order to reach its optimistic goals and become one of the country's leading food-service concerns, Restaurants Unlimited planned to become a publicly owned company by 1998.

Further Reading:

Buck, Richard, "Seattle a 'Must' for Restaurant Professionals," *Seattle Times,* June 14, 1978, p. C13.

Farrell, Kevin, "Ray Lindstrom," *Restaurant Business,* May 20, 1991, p. 113.

Ingle, Schuyler, "King of the New Gourmets," *Weekly,* September 19, 1984, p. 32.

Liddle, Alan, "Restaurants Unlimited Knows: To Err Is Human—to Fix Things Is Divine," *Nation's Restaurant News,* May 18, 1992, p. 18.

——, "Richard Komen: 'Visionary' on the Move," *Nation's Restaurant News,* September 21, 1992, p. 96.

——, "RUI 'brands' Palomino Bistro a Winner, Ready for Breeding," *Nation's Restaurant News,* March 1, 1993, p. 3.

——, "RUI Opens Palisade on Waterfront," *Nation's Restaurant News,* July 20, 1992, p. 3.

——, "RUI Seeks New Growth by Revamping Zoopa," *Nation's Restaurant News,* April 22, 1991, p. 18.

"Lindstrom Named RUI Chief Exec as Part of Company Reorganization," *Nation's Restaurant News,* January 11, 1993, p. 11.

Prinzing, Debra, "Komen Keeps One Menu ahead of a Fickle Clientele," *Puget Sound Business Journal,* July 3, 1989, p. 17A.

"RU Opens Palomino in Minneapolis," *Nation's Restaurant News,* December 9, 1991, p. 32.

"Volume Service Co.," *Seattle Times,* July 11, 1969, p. 16.

Williams, Linda, "Restaurants Unlimited Serves Up Posh Eatery in Tough Times," *Puget Sound Business Journal,* July 3, 1992, p. 16.

Yang, Dori Jones, "Seattle Is on a (Cinnamon) Roll," *Business Week,* February 27, 1995, p. 8.

—Jeffrey L. Covell

Riggs National Corporation

1503 Pennsylvania Avenue N.W.
Washington, District of Columbia 20005
U.S.A.
(202) 835-6000
Fax: (202) 835-6830

Public Company
Incorporated: 1836
Employees: 1,700
Sales: $5 billion
Stock Exchanges: New York
SICs: 6712 Bank Holding Companies; 6021 National Commercial Banks

The Riggs National Corporation operates a leading bank in Washington, D.C. The Riggs National Bank, founded in the first half of the nineteenth century, was a key player in the development of the city of Washington, and also played a role in the history of the United States. Riggs served as the bank of presidents for generations, and provided funds for numerous endeavors of the U.S. government. It remained a pillar of the Washington banking establishment up until the late 1980s and early 1990s, when bad real estate loans threatened its financial viability.

Riggs dates its founding to 1836, when William Wilson Corcoran, a Washington, D.C., financier, opened a note brokerage house. Four years later, Corcoran joined with a partner, George Washington Riggs, Jr., to offer depository and checking services. In 1844 Corcoran & Riggs was selected as the only depository for the U.S. government in Washington. The following year, the company took over the former home and the assets of the failed Second Bank of the United States, located at 15th Street and Pennsylvania Avenue. This structure, which had been created by the same architect who designed the U.S. Capitol, became the headquarters of Corcoran & Riggs for the next 50 years.

In the 1840s Corcoran & Riggs took part in the westward expansion of the United States by supplying funds for the construction of railroads and the purchase of land. In 1845 the bank invested in Samuel P. Morse's telegraph device, which helped to provide communications throughout the newly opened territories. Corcoran & Riggs also sold bonds in London in the latter part of the 1840s to finance the war between the United States and Mexico. These activities established the bank as a presence in international finance.

William Corcoran retired in 1854, and the company he had founded continued on as Riggs & Company under the leadership of his partner. The bank opened a New York branch the following year, which it maintained for 33 years. Throughout the 1850s, Riggs continued its involvement with the historic and political affairs of the United States. The Army Corps of Engineers opened a Riggs account to handle construction of the U.S. Capitol building in 1853. Five years later, Riggs was also instrumental in the restoration of Mount Vernon, George Washington's Virginia home.

In addition, almost all of the country's presidents maintained accounts at Riggs. In 1861 Abraham Lincoln opened his checking account with the bank, shortly before the Civil War broke out. Four years later, in the wake of the war, Riggs opted to remain a private bank, despite the fact that most other American banks chose to become chartered under a new Banking Act.

In 1867 Riggs survived the first of several financial panics that swept the country in the late nineteenth century. A year later the bank supplied $7.2 million in gold to the U.S. government, which it used to purchase Alaska from Russia.

Riggs grew rapidly in the mid-1870s. Between 1873, when Charles Carroll Glover became the bank's chief administrative officer, and 1876, the company's deposits more than doubled. Throughout this decade and the next, Riggs and its officers remained central to the civic development of Washington, D.C. Glover took part in efforts to preserve Rock Creek Park and to create land from the swampy Potomac Flats, while the Riggs family donated funds for a library at Georgetown University.

In 1896—a year in which deposits at Riggs totaled $3.6 million—Riggs & Company changed its name to the Riggs National Bank. The company sold 5,000 shares at $100 each. Two years later, the company began paying dividends.

By the turn of the century, Riggs had become Washington's largest bank. In 1902 Riggs installed a 35-ton vault door to further safeguard the valuables held on its premises. The company moved to strengthen its ties with other banks in New York, and took a leading roll in passage of the Aldrich-Vreeland Act in 1908, a piece of legislation that helped the federal government to resolve a shortage of specie (coin money) and paved the way for the Federal Reserve. As a result of these activities, Riggs National Bank's deposits reached $9 million by 1909.

In 1914 Riggs joined the newly-instituted Federal Reserve System. The company's deposits continued to grow in the next four years as war raged in Europe, and they more than doubled to $21.5 million by the time the conflict was over. Two years later, Riggs offered savings deposit services to its clients for the first time, and in 1921 the company formed a trust department.

In 1923 Riggs returned its first stock dividend, in addition to the cash dividends that it paid. The company's shares were held by 460 stock owners. In the mid-1920s Riggs purchased two other Washington banks. The Hamilton Bank, located on Dupont Circle, and the Northwest National Bank, on the corner of M

Street and Wisconsin Avenue in Georgetown, subsequently became the first Riggs branches.

In 1928 Riggs added another location when it merged with the Farmers and Mechanics Bank of Georgetown. Despite the booming financial markets of the late 1920s, Riggs resisted the temptation to speculate, and thus the company was able to avoid serious damage in the stock market crash of 1929. In fact, Riggs reported net earnings of more than $800,000 in 1929, almost twice the level of 1923.

The country sank into the Depression in the early 1930s. Riggs worked with the Reconstruction Finance Corporation, inaugurated by Herbert Hoover, to try to counteract the country's general economic woes. By 1931 Riggs had grown to include 189 employees. The company provided $500,000 in cash that year to be displayed in another Washington financial establishment—the Perpetual Savings & Loan—when depositors lost confidence in that bank's safety and threatened a run on its funds.

Two years later, Riggs bought the failed Chevy Chase Savings Bank, which it then reopened after the bank holiday declared by President Franklin D. Roosevelt. In 1933 the company became one of the early participants in the new Federal Deposit Insurance Corporation. Riggs retained its state of financial health throughout the mid-1930s, although more than half of Washington's banks had closed in the previous decade.

Riggs National Banks' viability was strengthened in 1934 when it became the second bank to be approved as a Federal Housing Administration mortgager. Two years later, Riggs celebrated its 100th anniversary. Despite the economic woes besetting its industry as a whole in the 1930s, when more than 40 percent of all American banks failed, Riggs ended the decade with assets of $119 million, up from $57 million when the Great Depression began.

As World War II developed, Riggs participated in the sale of war bonds, moving $233 million worth of notes in the course of the conflict. The company also undertook operations to get funds to Allied fighters in Nazi-occupied Europe. In 1943 Riggs began to supply accounting services to the Office of Price Administration, while the company was also approved as a depository for taxes withheld under the new Revenue Act.

In 1944 Riggs opened a branch at the Walter Reed Army Medical Center to ease efforts to supply financial services to the vast number of military personnel stationed in Washington. Among the soldiers who utilized Riggs' services were generals Douglas MacArthur and Chester Nimitz, both of whom appointed Riggs executors of their affairs should they die in battle.

After the war, Riggs continued to alter its activities to meet the changing needs of its customers. Riggs reacted to the booming American economy of the late 1940s by offering a wide variety of consumer loans, including home loans, auto loans, and GI loans. In 1947 Riggs processed a war loan repayment check for $50 million, the largest amount ever drawn on a Washington bank. Riggs took its first tentative step into the computer age in 1948, the first year that the company's general ledger books were done by machine instead of by hand.

Riggs continued to grow and solidify its position in Washington and the world in the 1950s. The company's international division developed a strong relationship with the International Monetary Fund and the World Bank, and the bank also provided services to a large number of embassies located in Washington. The company also expanded its local activities during this time. In 1954 Riggs purchased Washington Loan and Trust; the bank merged with the Lincoln National Bank four years later.

In 1961 Riggs became a television sponsor for the first time, underwriting the "World Concert Series." Two years later, the company took another step toward modernization when customer accounts began to be serviced by computer. By this time, the trust department of Riggs had $1 billion in assets. Five years later, the company could also boast that its loans exceeded half a billion dollars. In that same year, the company opened its 17th branch location, in L'Enfant Plaza. In 1969 Riggs paid out $3.5 million in cash dividends.

The population of the Washington area grew rapidly in the late 1960s, driven by government expansion during Lyndon Johnson's Great Society push. Riggs grew quickly as well. In 1970 the company's total assets passed the $1 billion mark. Because the confines of Washington itself were quite small, however, the bulk of the growth in the Washington area in the 1970s took place in the suburbs of Virginia and Maryland, where Riggs was not able to conduct business. Nevertheless, the bank continued to grow throughout the 1970s, and it reported net income of $21.7 million at the end of 1979.

Riggs increased its international presence in 1980 when the bank opened a branch in London. Later that year Riggs announced that it would reorganize itself into a bank holding company. Riggs hoped to gain flexibility in responding to changes in banking laws, and to make growth and the purchase of other banks easier. By the end of 1980 Riggs had solidified its position as Washington's biggest bank, with assets of $3.1 billion and earnings of $24 million.

In December 1980 Washington media millionaire Joseph L. Allbritton, who had previously owned the *Washington Star*, announced that he planned to take over Riggs. At that time he offered $26.8 million for a majority share in the company. Early in February 1981, Allbritton extended his offer to $67.50 a share, despite the fact that Riggs stock was then trading at about $50 a share. Although the bank's directors initially tried to block Allbritton's takeover by filing suit against it, they withdrew this attempt in the face of shareholder willingness to accept Allbritton's generous offer. In March 1981 Allbritton successfully purchased more than 40 percent of Riggs for over $77 million. On May 31, 1981, the Riggs National Corporation, the bank holding corporation which had been formed to purchase Riggs, took over all of the stock of the Riggs National Bank, and Allbritton assumed the post of chairman of this company.

Over the course of the following year, Riggs sold off its consumer credit business to Citibank, although it began to offer money market accounts to its customers. In November 1983 Riggs enhanced its presence in London with the purchase of the AP Bank, Ltd. The company paid $35.9 million to buy the bank from the Norwich Union Life Insurance Society. Riggs also began to issue notes directly to the Euromarkets in the following year, selling $60 million of floating rate financial instruments.

In the mid-1980s Riggs began to offer customers the option of using automatic teller machines, and the company joined the CIRRUS network. By this time, the company's number of bank branches had reached 28. All of these branches were located in the District of Columbia, despite the fact that many of Riggs' more affluent customers had moved to the suburbs of Washington or Virginia. Many Washington banks followed these customers to outlying areas, opening branches closer to their homes, but Riggs, under Allbritton's leadership, remained reluctant to do so.

Finally, Riggs made a long overdue move into the Maryland and Virginia markets in 1986. The company purchased the Guaranty Bank & Trust Company of Fairfax, Virginia, for $37.8 million. This company was subsequently renamed the Riggs National Bank of Virginia. One year later, Riggs bought the First Fidelity Bank of Rockville and named it the Riggs National Bank of Maryland.

Despite these advances, Riggs suffered other difficulties in the late 1980s. Convinced that the continued growth of the federal government would insulate Washington from the threat of overbuilding, Riggs made a large number of commercial real estate loans. In addition, the company made other bad loans, such as a $90 million portfolio of debts issued to a Texas developer who had only two cars as assets. When Washington's real estate market went into a slump in the early 1990s, the fortunes of Riggs and other Washington banks took a nosedive. By January 1990 Riggs had the third highest level of construction and real estate loans in the country.

Despite this worrisome sign, Riggs continued its efforts to expand its operations, concentrating on markets overseas. In March 1990 the company opened Riggs Asia, Ltd., a deposit-taking company in Hong Kong specializing in international private and commercial banking services, foreign exchange, and the finance of trade. In April of that year, Riggs bought Elders Keep, a trade finance company based in Birmingham, England. Riggs opened a Paris subsidiary, Riggs National Bank Europe (S.A.), seven months later.

In December 1990 Riggs bought the deposits and assets of the failed National Bank of Washington, the oldest bank in Washington, for $33 million. Riggs finished 1990 reporting $57 million in losses. Red ink continued to spill in 1991, and losses mounted to $66 million over the first nine months of the year. Riggs announced in late 1991 that it would try to sell $200 million worth of foreclosed real estate to raise funds, but with the market saturated, prospects for success in this endeavor appeared bleak.

Riggs continued to struggle in 1992. The following year, the company hired a management consultant to help it return to profitability. In the first quarter of 1993, Riggs took a $14 million charge against earnings in order to restructure its operations and cut costs. In addition, the company unveiled a new advertising program that used humor to push its products. Nevertheless, Riggs lost $94 million over the course of the year.

Riggs continued its efforts to return to profitability in 1994. The company got rid of non-performing loans, cut costs, issued new stocks, and strengthened its management. By the end of the year, it was able to report earnings of $34 million. Although the period of the early 1990s had proved perilous for the bank, Riggs had retained its independence and its status as a Washington-owned bank.

Principal Subsidiaries: Riggs National Bank of Washington, D.C.; Riggs National Bank of Virginia; Riggs National Bank of Maryland.

Further Reading:

"Capital Achievement," *Fortune,* May 4, 1981.
Clash, James M., "Tandonitis?," *Forbes,* 1993.
Killian, Linda, "Abe Lincoln Banked Here," *Forbes,* December 9, 1991.

—Elizabeth Rourke

Rock-Tenn Company

504 Thrasher Street
Norcross, Georgia 30071
U.S.A.
(404) 448-2193
Fax: (404) 263-3582

Public Company
Founded: 1898 as Rock City Box Co.
Employees: 5,928
Sales: $705.85 million
Stock Exchanges: NASDAQ
SICs: 2631 Paperboard Mills; 2653 Corrugated & Solid Fiber Boxes; 2657 Folding Paperboard Boxes; 2671 Paper Coated & Laminated Packaging

Rock-Tenn Company is one of the largest U.S. manufacturers of 100 percent recycled paperboard, a product that comprised almost all of Rock-Tenn's paperboard output in 1994. The company also ranked fourth in the United States in the manufacture of the more printable clay-coated recycled paperboard, also made from recovered wastepaper. In the mid-1990s Rock-Tenn was using 69 percent of its paperboard production to make paperboard products. Ranking fourth in the United States in the production of folding cartons, it was the largest U.S. producer of laminated paperboard for the book-cover and furniture markets. Rock-Tenn also was the largest producer of solid-fiber partitions in North America, and also engaged in the manufacture of corrugated sheets and boxes and thermoformed plastic products. Long a privately held company, Rock-Tenn made its first public offering of stock in 1994.

The Rock-Tenn Co. was formed in 1973, the product of a merger between Tennessee Paper Mills Inc. and Rock City Packaging, Inc. Its origins date back to 1898, when the Rock City Box Co. of Nashville, Tennessee, was founded. Among its customers in the mid-1940s were a local boot factory, a local candy manufacturer, a hosiery company, and several shirt manufacturers. The owners, Joe McHenry and A. E. Saxon, who also operated several other business ventures, wanted to sell out and retire. Rock City was attractive to Arthur Newth Morris, owner of the Southern Box Corp., not least for its bank account of $60,000. Morris purchased the company in 1945 for $200,000, making a cash down payment of $50,000.

The 25-year-old Morris had been a printer and part-time Presbyterian minister when he went to work in 1926 for Edwin J. Schoettle, a Philadelphia industrialist who owned a group of box and printing companies that bore his name. For a monthly salary of $350 Morris was expected to manage several hundred employees, some of them more than twice his age. He also traveled along the eastern seaboard, explaining to meatpackers his discovery that they could avoid shrinkage of their hot dogs by putting them in Schoettle's boxes instead of stringing them up like bananas.

By 1935 Morris was making a salary on which he could comfortably support his wife and four children, but he wanted to go into business for himself. Armed with life savings of $5,000 and a $7,500 investment by his boss, he moved to Baltimore. There he managed the J. E. Smith Box & Printing Co. during the day, while running the Southern Box Corp., a company he founded in 1936, at night. Using Smith's presses, die-cutters, and other boxmaking equipment during the evening, Morris began servicing two anchor customers who knew him from his Philadelphia days.

Only six months after Morris had left Philadelphia, Schoettle came to Baltimore to offer him a promotion and a $25,000 salary. When Morris refused, Schoettle offered to sell Morris his own majority share of Southern Box for $25,000. A bank loan helped Morris come up with the money and truly become his own boss. He moved to new quarters for $200 a month, left day-to-day management to one of his employees, and devoted himself to finding new accounts. In its first year the company made a few thousand dollars on sales of $60,000.

By 1942 Morris was doing well enough to open a corrugated box plant and to buy another Baltimore enterprise, the King Folding Box Co., where he installed a corrugated sheet cutter. Morris sold corrugated partitions to major glass companies, which needed them to separate the bottles and glasses they shipped. The following year the name of his enterprise was changed to The Newth-Morris Box Co. In 1944 another branch was opened in Jacksonville, Florida, where the company produced cardboard anti-radar devices for World War II's Army Air Force and popcorn boxes for movie-theater owners.

Morris's purchase of the Rock City Box Co. in 1945 put him in contact with one of its suppliers and his future merger partner: Tennessee Paper Mills. A. L. Tomlinson and John Stagmaier, two of Tennessee Paper's three founders, were Athens, Tennessee, businessmen who already owned box factories. The company's third founder was A. M. Sheperd of Vincennes, Indiana, a boxboard manufacturer. Tennessee Paper Mills was incorporated in 1917 with Stagmaier as president, Tomlinson as vice-president, and Sheperd as general manager. With $300,000 raised from stock offerings, the three men established a paperboard factory in Chattanooga, where operation began in July 1918. By the end of the year the new company had made a handsome net profit of $23,367 on sales of $165,799.

Although the founders originally planned to make board from wheat straw, they turned instead to wastepaper as the primary raw material; thus Tennessee Paper became the first recycled paperboard mill in the South. To reduce its electric bill, the company installed its own steam generating plant in 1926.

Paperboard production averaged 20 tons a day in the early years, reaching an average of 56.77 tons in 1930, the same year that the company produced a record 15,557 tons of product. This figure would not be matched for some time due to the advent of the Great Depression; production dropped to 11,995 tons in 1934. The company remained profitable, however, although only modestly so. As the nation's economy slowly recovered, Tennessee Paper's volume of business increased to meet renewed demand. During 1939 the factory operated at 85 percent capacity, compared to the industry average of 71 percent. In 1941 it operated a record 305 days. Sales volume exceeded $1.7 million in 1945. A second papermaking machine doubled the mill's capacity in 1949.

Beginning in 1954, however, Tennessee Paper began losing customers to lower-cost folding cartons and corrugated and plastic containers. The trend in the business was toward vertical integration. Many paperboard companies acquired—or merged with—their customers. Typically profits were made at the mill level, by selling boxes virtually at cost. The effect on boxmakers was so severe that by 1957 Tennessee Paper was extending credit and loans to its customers in order to keep their accounts.

One of these customers was Rock City. Its consumption of Tennessee Paper's board grew from about 1,000 tons in 1944 to about 37,000 tons in 1972, when it took 44 percent of Tennessee Paper's total boxboard production. Between 1965 and 1968 Tennessee Paper bought 29.5 percent of Rock City's common stock, preparing the way for the eventual merger of the two companies. By then Rock City owed Tennessee Paper more than $4 million in loans.

Morris's burgeoning industrial empire grew both by acquisitions and by establishing new companies. Among the former was the Parks Box & Printing Co., located on a leased 11-acre tract in Norcross, Georgia. This land was purchased in 1957 and gradually became the focal point for management of all the Morris companies. A new 30,000-square-foot warehouse was added to the Norcross facility in 1960.

Each of the Morris companies operated as a separate and virtually autonomous profit center. Rock City opened not only small set-up and folding-carton plants but also facilities in Livingston and Milan, Tennessee, to meet the packaging needs of shirtmakers. A set-up-box division was established in 1955. Rock City Waste Paper Co. collected, sorted, and baled wastepaper for sale to paper mills. Other Morris companies and plants sprouted throughout the South. Sales grew from $8 million in 1959 to $12.9 million in 1967, when all the companies were consolidated into Rock City Packaging, Inc. Morris became chairman of the board and a son-in-law, Worley Brown, became president. Sales volume reached $23 million in 1972.

Meanwhile, in order to meet the competition, Tennessee Paper began buying customers to assure continued markets for its paperboard products. In 1964 it acquired Knoxville Paper Box Co., Inc., a manufacturer of folding and set-up boxes, for about $1 million. In 1969 Tennessee Paper acquired wastepaper factories in Knoxville and Atlanta, and in 1972 it built another wastepaper plant in Chattanooga.

The merger of Rock City Packaging and Tennessee Paper Mills in 1973 gave Morris, Brown, and others who held stock in the former companies a controlling interest in the new corporation, Rock-Tenn Co. Most Tennessee Paper common stockholders received preferred stock in the new company that earned them triple the dividends they had been receiving. Some shareholders, however, opted for cash instead. The president of Tennessee Paper, W. Max Finley, and his immediately family, received common stock in the new company. Finley was elected chairman of the board and Brown became president and chief executive officer.

Reorganization did nothing to slow down expansion. The Crescent Box & Printing Co. of Tullahoma, Tennessee, was acquired in 1973 and Clevepak Corp.'s Conway, Arkansas, folding-carton plant in 1974. By 1976 the company had 29 divisions. Sales in 1974, the first fiscal year after the merger, reached $47.7 million. In 1978 Bradley Currey, Jr., a veteran officer of the Trust Co. of Georgia who had helped effect the merger, became president and chief operating officer of Rock-Tenn. Brown became chairman of the board while remaining chief executive officer. Finley moved to senior chairman of the board. Morris remained chairman of the executive committee until his death in January 1985. Currey later became Rock-Tenn's chairman and chief executive officer as well as its president, posts he still held in 1995.

In 1982 Rock-Tenn's sales volume reached $133 million and its production of recycled paperboard peaked at 180,000 tons, most of which it used itself in the manufacture of folding cartons and containers and corrugated boxes. Its many customers included Coca-Cola, DuPont, and Kentucky Fried Chicken, which it serviced from facilities in Alabama, Arkansas, Georgia, Maryland, Massachusetts, North Carolina, Ohio, Tennessee, and Texas with a work force of 1,700 people. In a 1983 *Atlanta Constitution* interview, Currey attributed the decade-old company's growth to "luck, chance, and circumstance . . . but the success of any company depends on its people." He added that the company had gone to great lengths "to make sure the workers know that we care"—a group of senior executives took a month each year to travel to each of the company's facilities in order to talk to employees and present service awards.

Rock-Tenn made its biggest acquisition ever in 1983, when it paid $40 million to buy 11 Clevepak Corp. plants, seven of which were making partitions to protect glass and plastic containers. Currey said the acquisition would allow Rock-Tenn to capture about one-fourth of the partition market, raise annual revenue to more than $200 million, and increase production of recycled paperboard to 235,000 tons. In 1989 net sales had reached $515.9 million, and net income was $31.1 million. The following year the company dedicated to chairman of the board Finley a 33,000-square-foot office building behind its headquarters in Norcross.

In 1990 Rock-Tenn acquired Allforms Packaging Corp. of Long Island and Box Innards Inc. of Orange, California. The following year it purchased the former Specialty Paperboard Inc. mill in Sheldon Springs, Vermont, and Ellis Paperboard Products Inc. of Scarborough, Maine, a manufacturer of folding cartons and solid-fiber partitions. The Ellis purchase included its Canadian subsidiary, Dominion Paperboard Products Ltd. With these additions Rock-Tenn controlled 60 manufacturing and distribution operations, including eight mills with a total annual production capacity of 607,000 tons of recycled paperboard products. Rock-Tenn now ranked sixth among U.S. producers of recycled paperboard, with market share of 5.7 percent.

Net sales rose from $564.1 million in fiscal 1991, ending September 30, 1991, to $655.5 million in 1992, but dipped to $650.7 million in 1993. Net income rose from $25 million in 1991 to $33.2 million in 1992 before dipping to $25.5 million in 1993. The 1993 figure included unusual after-tax expenses of $5.8 million. Production in fiscal 1994 was 700,000 tons of recycled paperboard, of which 182,000 tons was clay-coated recycled paperboard.

The first public offering of Rock-Tenn stock, amounting to about 14 percent of the shares outstanding, was made in March 1994. A handful of shareholders offered about 3.6 million shares of Class A common stock, while the company itself offered about 900,000 shares. An analysis in *Barron's* described Rock-Tenn's balance sheet as ''attractive'' and said the company was ''more soundly financed than many in its field,'' noting that long-term debt of $51.6 million was only one year's cash flow. Although calling the offering somewhat pricey at $16.50 a share, it noted that ''Rock-Tenn's emphasis on recycling makes it well-suited to customers wishing to appear environmentally responsible, and could also prove profitable if use of woodlands is restricted.'' Officers and directors of Rock-Tenn still controlled about 71 percent of the combined voting power of Class A and B common stock after the offering. Class A stock was selling at $16.75 a share at the end of March 1995.

In December 1993 Rock-Tenn paid $35 million for Les Industries Ling, a Canadian company that used recycled paperboard to make folding cartons. The newly acquired plant, which was to serve as the principal supplier of recycled clay-coated paperboard for Rock-Tenn's Vermont mill, became the company's second-largest folding-carton facility. A year later, Rock-Tenn agreed to acquire Olympic Packaging, an Illinois-based manufacturer of folding cartons, and Alliance Packaging of Winston-Salem, North Carolina. The purchases, which boosted Rock-Tenn's acquisitions of manufacturing operations to 17 in a decade, cost about $75 million.

Questioned by an *Atlanta Constitution* reporter about Rock-Tenn's stock offering, a J. P. Morgan Securities analyst replied, ''They've got a bulletproof balance sheet . . . and are better positioned both financially and strategically than their major peers.'' The same analyst also favored the two 1994 acquisitions, declaring that they would take Rock-Tenn ''to $800 million practically overnight, and the businesses fit extremely well.''

By the middle of the 1990s, Rock-Tenn had 59 facilities in 19 states and Canada. Eight were mills making recycled paperboard, eight were paper-recovery facilities, 39 were converting facilities, and two were distribution facilities. There were seven manufacturing divisions.

Net sales reached $705.8 million during fiscal 1994, constituting an 11.8 percent compounded annual growth rate for the past decade. Net income came to a record $37.5 million. During the fiscal year Rock-Tenn generated over $74 million in cash and invested over $106 million in capital expenditures and acquisitions. Some 86 percent of net sales, but only 39 percent of operating income, came from products converted from paperboard. Of converted-products sales, folding cartons accounted for 52 percent; laminated paperboard, 19 percent; solid-fiber partitions, 17 percent; and corrugated sheets and boxes and plastics, 12 percent.

Principal Subsidiaries: Concord Industries, Inc.; Dominion Paperboard Products, Ltd. (Quebec); Rock-Tenn Co. of Arkansas; Rock-Tenn Co. of Texas; Rock-Tenn Co. Converting Co.; Rock-Tenn Co., Mill Division, Inc.

Further Reading:

Cochran, Thomas N., ''Offerings in the Offing,'' *Barron's,* February 21, 1994, p. 50.

Harte, Susan, ''Rock-Tenn's Public Stock Offering Finances Expansion, Acquisitions,'' *Atlanta Constitution,* December 1, 1994, p. F7.

——, ''Rock-Tenn Plans Another Acquisition,'' *Atlanta Constitution,* December 16, 1994, p. G2.

Herndon, Keith, ''Rock-Tenn Seeks Knockout Punch,'' *Atlanta Constitution,* July 11, 1983, p. C12.

The Rock-Tenn Story, Norcross, Ga.: The Rock-Tenn Company.

—Robert Halasz

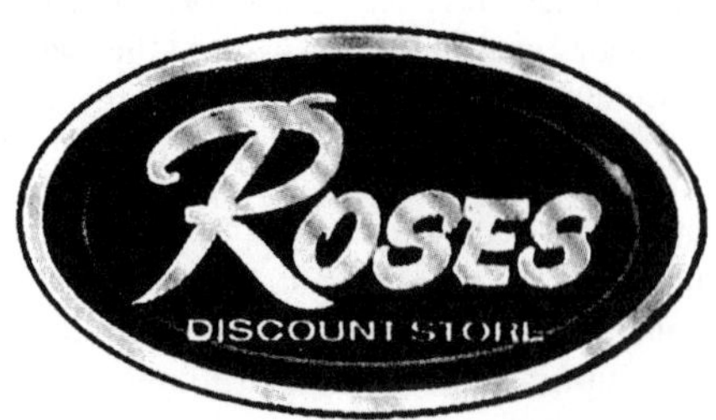

Rose's Stores, Inc.

P.O. Drawer 947
Henderson, North Carolina 27536
U.S.A.
(919) 430-2100
Fax: (919) 492-4226

Public Company
Incorporated: 1927 as Rose's 5-10-25 Cent Stores
Employees: 8,800
Sales: $756 million
Stock Exchanges: NASDAQ
SICs: 5632 Women's Accessory & Specialty Stores; 5611 Men's & Boys' Clothing Stores; 5719 Miscellaneous Home Furnishings Stores; 5945 Hobby, Toy & Game Shops

Rose's Stores, Inc., operates a chain of more than a hundred discount stores in a region extending from Delaware to Georgia and westward to the Mississippi Valley. The 24,000- to 76,000-square-foot stores, which primarily serve populations of less than 50,000 people, carry a wide variety of general merchandise items, including clothing, shoes, household furnishings, small appliances, toiletries, cosmetics, sporting goods, automobile accessories, food, yard and garden products, electronics, and occasional furniture. Since its inception in 1915 as a "5, 10, and 15 Cent Store," the company has restructured itself several times in adapting to an increasingly competitive market. During the 1960s and early 1970s, Rose's expanded into one of the nation's fastest growing variety store chains, ranking in the top ten in sales during the 1960s. But a flood of new competition in the mid-1970s and the ensuing entrance of its two principal competitors—Kmart and Wal-Mart, who now control roughly one-sixth of the $600 billion market—knocked the company out of the top 100 in the mid-1980s and ultimately brought on Chapter 11 bankruptcy in September 1993. However, by redefining itself as a discount merchandiser, downsizing its operations, and tailoring its marketing strategy specifically to the needs of its lower income shoppers, the company successfully emerged from bankruptcy in April 1995, following one of its strongest years in decades.

More than twenty years before Paul H. Rose founded the company that would one day bear his name in more than 250 stores throughout the Southeast, the 12-year-old entrepreneur set up a wooden box in front of a Seaboard, North Carolina drugstore, selling lemonade and cookies supplied by his mother. His first "store" later evolved into a mail order business, in which he advertised a hair straightener in the *Home Folks Magazine.* While the product lived up to its billing, it also served as a hair remover, prompting a visit from the Federal Food and Drug Administration and the end of his fledgling establishment. After attending business school in Virginia, Rose opened a small dry goods store in Littleton, where he put empty shoe boxes on the shelf and wrapped remnants of cloth around pieces of cardboard in order to give the appearance of a fully stocked store. Known for his creative sales promotion, he also held regular "popular girl contests," in which votes were cast by purchasing a specific type of candy, with the results posted each evening to generate interest in the store. Attracting the attention of a New York candy manufacturer, Rose was hired as a candy salesman and wholesale buyer, but he grew tired of the travelling the job demanded and returned to North Carolina to open a chain of his own stores. With the partnership of two other men, he started two United 5 and 10 Cent Stores in Charlotte and Henderson. In 1915, after one of his partners failed to meet his financial commitment, the 34-year-old Rose borrowed $500 to purchase the Henderson unit and opened up the first Rose's 5-10-15 Cent Store.

With his wife Emma assisting him, Rose worked up to 18 hours a day maintaining and improving his store, setting aside nearly all of his profits for future expansion. Living by one of his favorite aphorisms, "Where there's a hill, there's a valley; where there's disappointment, there's a compensating blessing," Rose allowed himself only a $1500 salary during his first year. And in 1916 he added a store in Oxford, 11 miles away, enlisting the managerial services of his 19-year-old brother, Thomas B. Rose, who would later take over the company. By 1921 the Rose operation included a chain of eleven stores, as well as a wholesale warehouse and distribution facility in Henderson known as the Rose Merchandising Company, which kept the stores stocked with about 300 items. With the addition of a traffic department in the mid-1920s, which significantly lowered operation costs by finding the most cost-effective method of transporting goods, Rose added another 19 stores before the first shares of Rose's stock became available for purchase in 1927. With the capital furnished by the new stockholders, Rose's was able to expand at a rate unprecedented by a merchandiser of its kind in the South: during the 18-month period ending in October 1929, Rose's opened approximately one store a month throughout North Carolina, South Carolina, and Tennessee, including a state-of-the art, 7,200 square-foot store in Henderson.

Despite the challenges that accompanied the Great Depression and the entrance of the United States into the Second World War, Rose's continued to prosper, growing into one of the leading variety store chains in the South. While countless businesses collapsed during the 1930s, Rose's not only survived but experienced a steady increase in sales and expansion. In addition to boosting sales from $1.8 million to $5.6 million by the end of the decade, the company surpassed the 100-store mark, extending its operations into the five states of North Carolina, Virginia, South Carolina, Tennessee, and Georgia. A large part of the company's success during this period can be attributed to its commitment to efficiency. The decade saw

Rose's add a company print ship and a 20,000-square-foot consolidated warehouse, enabling the company to reduce office and transportation costs by as much as 40 percent.

As the company entered the 1940s, world events again brought new challenges to the company. As hostilities in Europe grew, Congress passed a draft law that promised to create vacancies in numerous labor and management position within the company. Seeing that the U.S. involvement in World War II was imminent, the company began training women to fill these posts in its 118 stores. And when the war started, Rose's was prepared to make the necessary personnel changes: by 1944, 32 women were serving as managers. The nation's commitment to the war effort, though, brought about a shortage in labor and raw materials for manufacturing suppliers, forcing many suppliers to ration goods to the stores on a quota basis. Despite the fact that stores were rarely fully stocked, sales increased every year during the war and four stores were added.

The end of the war and the economic boon in the U.S. economy that followed enabled the company to implement several innovative management and marketing strategies. In addition to establishing a group health insurance plan and a Profit Sharing Trust Plan, Rose's added a trucking division that shortened the time required to deliver merchandise from the Henderson warehouse to surrounding stores. The appearance of the Rose's stores also underwent a significant change. Until 1947, all of the stores prominently displayed goods in the large windows at the front of the store, an advertising technique that required not only a great deal of merchandise to make them look full but a significant amount of employee time to maintain. When it came time to remodel a store in Durham, Paul Rose went with a new design featuring untrimmed windows that allowed anyone to see directly into the store. The grand opening of the new store was such a success that all future stores were designed according to the ''see-through'' concept. The founder's entrepreneurial drive also brought significant returns on the company balance sheets: in 1948 Rose's generated $17.6 million in sales and recorded its highest net profit in relation to sales, a mark that would stand for nearly two decades.

Rose's moved into the 1950s as a thriving 130-store outfit on its way to becoming a giant in the variety/general merchandise industry. While the company would continue to prosper, it would do so without the leadership that had guided the company through the Great Depression and two wars. With the death of Paul Rose and three other top executives came the need for a new management team. Thomas B. Rose, succeeding his brother as company president, led a new team of managers dedicated to further expansion. In keeping with its strategy of growth through innovation, the company implemented its first computer system in 1953. But the IBM data processing equipment proved unsatisfactory after about a year. Undaunted, company management replaced the machinery with Remington Rand Univac equipment that, after a brief period of transition, proved successful. While making the transition to ''self-service'' stores, the company also added a new 115,000-square-foot warehouse division, Rose Merchandising Company, and introduced luncheonettes, snack bars, and garden shops to its stores. By 1959 sales reached a record high $38.8 million—leading all the country's variety stores in increase of sales for that year. And at that year's Christmas party, President ''T. B'' Rose boldly predicted that the company would surpass the $50 million mark before man reached the moon.

It would take only two years for the prediction to come true, and by the time Neil Armstrong took his historic step, Rose's had nearly quadrupled its volume of sales and had expanded to 183 stores. Having first entered shopping centers in 1947, the company continued its move from the small variety store to the large self-service department store. While improving upon older, small-town units periodically through modernization, new units took the form of large, self-service, junior department stores, located primarily in suburban shopping centers. In the early 1960s, under the direction of president L. H. Harvin, Jr., the company also enlarged its operations through diversification, entering the discount market with the construction of a large store in Spartanburg, South Carolina, in 1961, and adding upscale merchandise to its product line by acquiring the Paul H. Rose Corporation—an offshoot of Rose's founded in the early 1940s—as a subsidiary and opening up three full-line department stores. In an effort to better reflect this broader focus, the company changed its name to Rose's Stores Inc. in 1962.

The early 1970s saw the company continue its transition into a general merchandise superpower. While Rose's had become one of the country's top ten variety store chains in the early 1960s, it exploded into one of the fastest growing general merchandise/variety chains in the South, opening an average of 20 stores a year, each in the 40,000- to 60,000-square-foot range. The company's growth during this period, to be sure, was the result of its strategic move to larger stores. For instance, in 1971 the average sales per store surpassed the $1 millon mark for the first time, and units opened between 1969 and 1972 accounted for half of the company's total sales. Much to the approval of its stockholders and the U.S. financial community, this growth was achieved without making acquisitions or using long-term debt financing. By the time Harvin stepped down as president and CEO in 1979, the company had achieved sales of nearly $500 million, a figure almost ten times larger than when he first took office 16 years earlier. Although sales had continued to climb during the mid- and late 1970s, profits were undercut by a flood of competitors that had moved into the Southeast. Companies such as Edwards, Big-K, Zayres, and Hills, as well as a recessionary economy, slowed Rose's net earnings. For the first time in its history, the company lost money in 1974, as the ratio of net profit to sales dropped to less than two cents on the dollar. And by the end of the decade all of the Paul Rose upscale department stores were closed.

The first major wave of competition called for a new marketing focus, and Lucius H. Harvin III, succeeding his father as president and CEO in 1980, was given the responsibility of redefining the company. He assumed leadership of a company whose growth, according to some analysts, exceeded its ability to keep its existing stores up to date with a changing retail environment. As a result, many of its stores, while large and favorably located, relied on antiquated merchandise assortments and presentations. These problems were compounded by the vast dissimilarity among Rose's stores, which ranged from 4,000 to greater than 60,000 square feet, making it difficult for the company to implement a coherent marketing strategy. With Lucius Harvin at the helm, though, the company restructured itself as a discount store and made changes accordingly. In late

1982, the company initiated a strategic planning process that led to the reshaping of Rose's basic design and conceptual framework: existing stores were remodeled to enhance merchandise display and improve traffic flow; apparel sales were underscored; inventories were augmented. In line with the new focus on discount store business, nearly all of the P. H. Rose variety stores were sold by the end of 1983. The new strategy resulted in a record boon for the company: Rose's stock split twice in 1983, leading to the first public offering of stock since 1927; two years later, the company broke the $1 billion sales barrier.

In 1987, just as Rose's completed a 12-month period in which its stock price increased faster than that of any other southeastern company, the company's customer base was diminished by the opening of 53 new Wal-Mart stores. Although sales continued to climb steadily, net profits declined nearly 25 percent, the direct result of competition and large capital expenditures needed to upgrade the company's distribution and information systems. As the decade drew to a close, sales records continued to be broken, but net profits plummeted as at least two-thirds of the company's 259 stores were engaged in head-to-head competition with their two major competitors, Wal-Mart and Kmart.

In mid-1991 a new management team, led by President and CEO George L. Jones, a former top executive with Target Stores, was selected to help the company reverse the decline brought on by competition. Their plan called for a thorough remerchandising of their stores, which involved eliminating categories of slow-moving merchandise and replacing them with products better suited to Rose's target "value-oriented" customer. For instance, instead of offering a complete line of hardware products, Rose's reduced its line to include a limited number of tools and materials designed for light "do-it-yourself" tasks. On the other hand, the company's traditionally strong departments—toys, health and beauty aids, and lawn and garden, for instance—were expanded. Likewise, the company mounted a "Greatest Deal on Earth" campaign, featuring an assortment of first-quality merchandise at "closeout," or significantly reduced prices, in an attempt to provide attractive opportunities for unplanned purchases. While restructuring its product line, Rose's also took advantage of new technology to improve customer service and store space management, implementing a state-of-the-art computerized price removal and inventory replenishment system.

Despite these efforts, the company continued to lose money and had difficulty maintaining its inventory due to credit problems, leading to poor sales performance. And on September 5, 1993, the company filed a voluntary petition for relief under Chapter 11, Title 11 of the U.S. Bankruptcy Code. After closing more than a hundred stores in the first half of 1994, Rose's secured an exit financing commitment from the First National Bank of Boston and the CIT Group/Business Credit, Inc., calling for a three-year revolving credit agreement that enabled the company to borrow up to $125 million. Under the direction of a new president and CEO, R. Edward Anderson, who took over in August 1994, the company finished the year with sales of $756 million, a decrease of more than 40 percent. However, the company recorded operating profits of $6.6 million, compared to a loss of $27 million the previous year, and entered 1995 with the operating cash flows necessary to emerge from Chapter 11. After turning in its best overall performance in several years, the company looked forward to leaving behind the complicated distractions of financial reorganization and returning to its focus on the operational aspects of the business.

With 75 percent of its stores in direct competition with Wal-Mart or Kmart and 60 percent forced to contend with both, Rose's has attempted to prosper in the mid-1990s by further narrowing its marketing focus within the discount industry, targeting value-conscious lower income consumers by offering special senior citizens' discounts and double-coupon deals, emphasizing closeout merchandise, and prominently displaying discounted goods. "We feel our niche is narrower and more toward the lower end," Anderson told *Discount Merchandiser*'s Pat Corwin in March 1995, "so we want our customers to see value very quickly when they walk into our stores. We don't want it to be subliminal, we want it right in their faces." And with a strong belief that there are people who still believe in the 80-year-old Rose's name, Anderson has predicted that, under stable economic conditions, the company will grow once again.

Further Reading:

"*Chain Store Age Executive* $100 Million Club," *Chain Store Age Executive,* August 1985, pp. 22–30.

Corwin Pat, "Rose's Recovery—Built to Last," *Discount Merchandiser,* March 1995, pp. 26–28, 70.

Folger, J. C., "Unfolding Our History," *Communiques,* Henderson, North Carolina: Rose's Stores, Inc., 1991.

Jones, George, "A Need for Differentiation," *Discount Merchandiser,* December 1993, pp. 68–70.

"Kresge Tops Big Builders," *Chain Store Age Executive,* November 1974, pp. 17, 64.

Marcial, Gene G., "Don't Discount This Discounter," *Business Week,* October 23, 1989, p. 130.

"Rose's: Plans to Emerge from Chapter 11," *Discount Merchandiser,* September 1994, p. 12.

"State of the Industry," *Chain Store Executive Age,* August 1994, pp. 3–25A.

—Jason Gallman

Salomon Brothers

Salomon Inc.

Seven World Trade Center
New York, New York 10048
U.S.A.
(212) 783-7000
Fax: (212) 783-2110

Public Company
Incorporated: 1981
Employees: 9,077
Total Assets: $172.73 billion
Stock Exchanges: New York
SICs: 6211 Security Brokers & Dealers; 5171 Petroleum Bulk Stations & Terminals; 2911 Petroleum Refining; 6719 Holding Companies, Nec

Salomon Inc. is a diversified trading and financial services holding company led by its flagship subsidiary, Salomon Brothers Inc., one of Wall Street's leading securities houses and a worldwide operator through its offices in London, Tokyo, and Hong Kong. The parent company also engages in commodities trading and petroleum refining through its subsidiaries Phibro Energy USA, Inc., Phibro Division of Salomon Inc., and Phibro Energy Production, Inc., a joint venture with Russia. This slightly unusual combination of businesses is the result of the 1981 purchase of Salomon Brothers, then a private partnership, by the commodities company Phibro Corporation. The resulting company was named Phibro-Salomon until 1986, when the firm assumed the name Salomon Inc.

Salomon Brothers may not be Wall Street's most famous name, but this reflects more than anything else the firm's long and continued absence from the retail end of the securities business. Institutional investors and companies in search of an underwriter don't need pithy advertising slogans to catch their attention. Throughout its history, Salomon has worked primarily in the two businesses it knows best—wholesale securities trading and underwriting—and used them to rise from modest beginnings to a position of prominence in the financial community by the 1970s. The firm continued to prosper until a 1991 scandal involving U.S. treasury bonds tarnished the company's reputation and its aftermath threatened to relegate Salomon to second-tier status on Wall Street.

Salomon Brothers was founded in New York City in 1910 when Arthur, Herbert, and Percy Salomon broke away from their father Ferdinand's money-brokerage operation and went into business for themselves. They took with them a $5,000 stake and their father's clerk, Ben Levy, and opened a small office on Broadway near Wall Street. Later that year, they became Salomon Brothers & Hutzler when they brought broker Morton Hutzler into the firm for the sake of his seat on the New York Stock Exchange.

During its infancy, Salomon concentrated on money brokerage, an obscure Wall Street specialty that consisted of arranging loans for securities brokers and trading bonds for institutional clients. The partners branched out into underwriting in 1915 by participating in a $15 million offering of short-term Argentine notes. But expansion of its underwriting activities was limited: underwriting was dominated at the time by a select group of old-line firms. Reputation and connections were essential to building a clientele, and the Salomons had neither.

Salomon Brothers' big break came when the United States entered World War I. The Liberty Loan Act of 1917 unleashed a flood of government securities that needed someone to take them to market; since social connections were not necessary to getting business, Salomon entered the lucrative government-bond market. The firm's expansion continued through the boom years of the 1920s. By 1930, Salomon had opened branches in Boston, Chicago, Philadelphia, Minneapolis, and Cleveland and employed a staff of more than 30 traders and salespeople.

The 1920s are remembered most for the big bull market in stocks, but Salomon entered the equities business tentatively, even then dealing only wholesale. As a result, the firm made little money in the bull market, but also escaped serious damage in the market crash in 1929. Arthur Salomon, in fact, had decreed in 1927 that all of his company's margin accounts be terminated.

The eldest and most forceful personality among the three Salomons, Arthur was without question the firm's dominant partner. A shrewd player of the financial game and a hard worker who held few interests beyond Wall Street, he became known, according to Salomon historian Robert Sobel, "as one of the very few individuals who could see J. P. Morgan without an appointment." His death in 1928 left a power vacuum that was not filled until his nephew William became managing partner 35 years later.

In addition to coping with the Great Depression, Salomon had to deal with an internal struggle in the 1930s centering around Herbert, who considered himself Arthur's natural heir. Herbert was the youngest brother, but Percy was too retiring by nature to assume leadership. Herbert, however, lacked Arthur's *savoir-faire* and failed to earn the confidence of many partners, who found a reluctant leader for their opposition in Ben Levy. The general slump in the bond market increased tensions within the firm, squeezing its profits and forcing it to lay off traders.

The one bright spot in the decade for Salomon came at the end of the capital strike of 1933–35, when the establishment investment banks protested the Roosevelt administration's formation of the Securities and Exchange Commission by refusing to bring new issues to market. In 1935 both the government and the banks were looking for a face-saving end to the moratorium, but Salomon, still an outsider, decided to end it on its own by underwriting a bond issue for Swift & Company, the meat packer. This was the first new debt issue to come to market under the new SEC rules and, though it brought the Salomon name into the spotlight, it caused resentment among the old-line underwriters that would last into the 1950s.

The firm concentrated on government bonds during World War II but did not find them as great a boon as in 1917. After the war, Salomon's power vacuum persisted and the firm lacked strategic direction as a result. Nonetheless, individual departments prospered when left to their own devices. In 1951 Herbert died and Rudolf Smutny became the dominant figure in the firm, becoming senior partner in 1955. Smutny's abrasive manner and questionable business decisions led to his ouster the next year. Percy Salomon's son William, aided by Ben Levy, spearheaded the coup.

William's coming of age in the family business solved the leadership problem that had existed since Arthur's death. William gradually accumulated influence at the firm in the years after Smutny's departure and was named managing partner in 1963. He guided Salomon through a massive expansion marked not by rapid diversification but by an aggressive, no-guts-no-glory approach to fields in which it was already established. According to journalist Paul Hoffman, William once boasted, "We'll bid for almost anything, and we take many baths."

In 1960 the firm moved to shore up a major weakness by starting its own research department, hiring economist Sidney Homer away from Scudder, Stevens & Clark to head it. Two years later, Homer was joined by Henry Kaufman, whose extraordinary ability to forecast interest rates would earn him the nickname "Dr. Gloom" on Wall Street.

In 1962 Salomon pulled a major coup by underwriting an AT&T offering worth $218 million, even though the financial markets were paralyzed at the time by the Cuban Missile Crisis. Also in the autumn of that year, the firm formed, with Blyth, Merrill Lynch, and Lehman Brothers, a group that became known as "the fearsome foursome." This association tried to break the establishment firms' stranglehold on the underwriting business by putting together syndicates that sought to outbid them on major utility-bond issues throughout the decade. Between 1962 and 1964, Salomon more than tripled its underwriting business, from $276 million to $873 million.

Salomon finally began to diversify its activities in the mid-1960s when, aided by the new computer technology on Wall Street, it expanded its block-trading activity on the New York Stock Exchange. In 1965 the firm bought seats on exchanges in Boston, Philadelphia, Washington, and Baltimore and on the Pacific Stock Exchange in Los Angeles. Salomon took advantage of an opportunity created by depressed stock prices in 1969 to expand its merger-and-acquisition activity, forging, among others, the Pepsi-ICI merger and Esmark's acquisition of Playtex. In 1971 the firm opened its first overseas office, in London, and the next year another in Hong Kong; in 1980 it opened a third in Tokyo.

In 1970 the firm finally dropped Morton Hutzler's name (Hutzler had retired in 1929) to mark a new era in Salomon's history. In 1971 the SEC began the process of deregulating brokerage commissions. Fees earned on the largest block trades were the first to be cut loose. Salomon responded by slashing its commission rate 50 percent. When rate structures ended in April 1972, Salomon and archrival Goldman, Sachs led the way in conducting the first major block trades. Soon, however, sluggish stock market conditions made block trading less lucrative, and in 1973 Salomon posted its first money-losing year since 1956.

In 1975 the firm participated in one of the year's major stories when New York City found itself unable to meet its financial obligations and appealed to the state and federal governments for aid. William Simon, a former Salomon partner who was treasury secretary in the Ford administration at the time, said that Washington might organize a "punitive" bailout package to discourage other cities from doing the same in the future. New York state, for its part, formed the Municipal Assistance Corporation (MAC) to generate funds for the city. Salomon, along with Morgan Guaranty Trust, led the syndicate that marketed MAC debt offerings. Salomon also helped underwrite two more major bailouts before the decade was through, for the Government Employee Insurance Company in 1976 and Chrysler Corporation in 1979.

Having transformed Salomon into the second-largest underwriter and the largest private brokerage house in the United States, William Salomon retired in 1978 and was succeeded as CEO by John Gutfreund. Described by *Business Week* as "shrewd, supremely intelligent, cosmopolitan yet street-fighter tough" and as a member of Manhattan high society who would "host extravagant parties straight out of *The Great Gatsby*," Gutfreund had studied literature at Oberlin College and considered teaching English before joining Salomon in 1953. He became a partner in 1963 at the age of 34 and became William Salomon's heir apparent when Simon left to join the federal government in 1972.

Under Gutfreund, Salomon participated in the leveraged-buyout boom of the 1980s, including Xerox's acquisition of Crum & Foster, Texaco's controversial acquisition of Getty Oil, and the mergers between Santa Fe Industries and Southern Pacific and Gulf Oil and Standard Oil of California. The firm was also retained as an adviser by AT&T when the telecommunications giant underwent the largest corporate breakup in United States history. However, the core of Salomon's business remained underwriting and bond trading, as it had been for seven decades. By 1985 Salomon's underwriting business generated 22 percent of all the money raised by American corporations through new issues, while Salomon's high-volume, low-margin approach to the bond business had made it the largest dealer of U.S. government securities.

A seminal event in Salomon's history occurred in 1981, when the company was acquired by Phibro Corporation, a commodities firm. The new entity was known as Phibro-Salomon Inc. until 1986, when Salomon gained control and changed the name of the parent company to Salomon Inc. The merger gave Phibro the diversification it desired and gave Salomon the operating capital it needed for further expansion. But many partners were not pleased by the prospect of becoming salaried employees whose profits would belong to Phibro management and not themselves. William Salomon also expressed displeasure that retired partners received nothing out of the merger deal while general partners like Gutfreund and merger-and-acquisition specialist J. Ira Harris received bonuses of over $10 million. "I would have thought that those of us who had been here 40 years deserved to share in the gain," he told *Business Week*. He and his successor rarely spoke after the merger.

The flight of individual investors that followed the stock market crash of 1987 did not hit Salomon as hard as it did retail-oriented houses like PaineWebber and Merrill Lynch. In fact, it closed out the year as the largest underwriter in the country, and the second-largest in the world after sponsoring $40.3 billion worth of new issues. But Salomon had also announced significant retrenchment plans prior to the crash and laid off 800 employees. Changes in the tax laws and rising interest rates in the first half of 1987 caused a slump in the bond market, seriously affecting Salomon's main business, and competition from Japanese firms further cut into profits. Although the firm could boast of co-managing Conrail's $1.7 billion stock offering (the largest initial public stock offering in history), it also lost $79 million in a post-crash underwriting for British Petroleum and was nearly left with a $100 million loss when Southland Corporation decided to postpone a junk-bond offering in November of that year.

To cope with the slow securities markets, many Wall Street firms turned to merchant banking and junk bonds for revenue. Thanks in part to lower stock prices, mergers and acquisitions increased in 1988. But Salomon, which had always specialized in trading and was plagued by weakness in its merchant-banking division (Salomon's reputation was tarnished by its involvement with two leveraged buyout failures—TVX in 1987 and Revco in 1988) was slow to diversify, and its financial performance suffered. Its underwriting business also suffered, and in 1988 Merrill Lynch overtook Salomon as the nation's top underwriter. Gutfreund came under substantial external and internal criticism for a lack of strategic direction, causing financial journalists to refer to him as "embattled" throughout 1988 and into 1989. Key personnel began to leave, and rumors circulated that Salomon would take itself private or be taken over. One bright spot, however, was its office in Japan, which was headed by Derek C. Maughan. Salomon's Tokyo office was, according to *Business Week*, "Tokyo's largest and most successful foreign brokerage." Given Japan's notoriously clubby business atmosphere, Salomon's success was particularly impressive.

Although it had missed out on the junk bond heyday of the 1980s, Salomon began to succeed in this arena in the early 1990s after the collapse of junk bond pioneer Drexel Burnham Lambert Inc. in February 1990. Drexel's demise left a hole in the secondary market for junk bonds which Salomon was quick to fill. The firm hired several prominent former employees of Drexel, and then purchased for $1 million a critical Drexel junk bond database which contained important information on more than 3,000 issues. These moves enabled Salomon to quickly become a leader in the junk bond market; by March 1991 it had built a $1 billion trading inventory in junk bonds, an impressive increase from its December 1990 level of $400 million. It managed or co-managed such major underwritings as the refinancing of $1.5 billion in RJR Nabisco debt. This expansion of its junk bond business helped Salomon post record pretax earnings of $500 million in the first quarter of 1991, on revenues of $1.2 billion.

The very next quarter, however, saw the beginning of a major scandal that nearly brought Salomon to the same end as Drexel. Treasury rules for auctions of U.S. issues of notes and bonds stipulated that no one purchaser could bid for more than 35 percent of the entire auction offering. Salomon, however, could—and often did—bid for itself, up to 35 percent, and as a broker for one or more clients, up to 35 percent for each client. Salomon circumvented these rules in the May 1991 auction of two-year Treasury notes by submitting false bids in the names of two of its clients, in addition to a 35-percent bid in its own name. When these submissions won the auction, Salomon then entered into its computer fake "sales" from its clients to Salomon. As a result, Salomon controlled $10.6 billion of the total $11.3 billion auction, putting it in a very strong position to squeeze dealers who had taken positions in the when-issued market for the May auction. Salomon could consequently charge higher-than-expected prices to these dealers and make huge profits. Martin Mayer claimed in *Nightmare on Wall Street* that this is precisely what happened.

In part because one of the two Salomon clients whose name the firm used in the May auction submitted a legitimate bid of its own which raised its total bid over 35 percent, the Treasury initiated an investigation. After the probe uncovered in detail what happened in May, found previous instances of similar false bids, and discovered that top officials at Salomon—including Gutfreund—had been told of one of the earlier infractions but had done nothing about it, major changes rippled through the company. In August the famed investor Warren E. Buffett, who was Salomon's largest shareholder with a $700 million stake, took over as Salomon CEO and chairman from Gutfreund, who resigned, as did Thomas Strauss, president of Salomon Inc.; John Meriwether, vice-chairman and supervisor of all of Salomon's proprietary bond trading; and Donald Feuerstein, the firm's general counsel. Paul Mozer, the head government bonds trader and the person who made the false bids, and Thomas Murphy, Mozer's assistant, were fired. Had Buffett not stepped in to take over, observers have speculated that Salomon would have gone under.

Eventually, the following year, the Securities and Exchange Commission imposed $290 million in fines and damages on Salomon for violations of securities laws, the second-largest such fine ever, behind only a $600 million judgment against Drexel. The company was also suspended from its position as primary dealer at treasury auctions for a two-month period. Buffett staved off more severe penalties by fully revealing the company's actions and taking steps to prevent recurrences. Buffett also propped up the financial structure of the company—damaged by the difficulty in gaining credit following the revelation of the scandal—by selling some of Salomon's assets. Also in 1992, Buffett installed Maughan, the former head of Salomon's Tokyo office, as chairman of Salomon Brothers and Robert E. Denham, his long-time attorney, as chairman of Salomon Inc. Buffett remained on the Salomon board of directors and continued to be substantially involved in the company's operation.

The new management had seemed to weather the scandal's aftermath on the basis of two impressive years during which the company returned to its roots in securities trading to great success. In 1992 Salomon posted $550 million in net income on

$1.06 billion in pretax earnings, and in 1993 $827 million on $1.47 billion in pretax earnings. The 1994 results—a $399 million net loss on a pretax loss of $831 million—however, pointed to several weaknesses at Salomon and pressure from an increasingly competitive market. *Business Week* contended that Salomon suffered from weak management at the hands of Maughan, who had never been a trader. Key personnel left Salomon because of a new compensation plan implemented in 1993 that cut traders' bonuses for the benefit of shareholders. Perhaps most importantly, Salomon management had failed to define a clear vision for the company's future. As a result, industry observers, who predicted a mid-1990s shakeout on Wall Street based on an overabundance of traders and underwriters, speculated that Salomon would need to remake itself again in order to survive another crisis—the possibilities included an emphasis on investment banking, a return to a primarily fixed-income trading orientation, or a merger with or acquisition by a commercial bank. It seemed unlikely that Salomon would ever return to its position near the top of Wall Street that it held during the 1980s.

Principal Subsidiaries: Phibro Division of Salomon Inc.; Phibro Energy Production, Inc.; Phibro Energy USA, Inc.; Salomon Brothers Inc.

Further Reading:

Hoffman, Paul, *The Dealmakers: Inside the World of Investment Banking,* Garden City, New York: Doubleday, 1984, 230 p.

Lenzner, Robert, ''The Secrets of Salomon,'' *Forbes,* November 23, 1992, pp. 123–27.

Lewis, Michael, *Liar's Poker: Rising through the Wreckage on Wall Street,* New York: W. W. Norton, 1989, 249 p.

Mayer, Martin, *Nightmare on Wall Street: Salomon Brothers and the Corruption of the Marketplace,* New York: Simon & Schuster, 1993, 272 p.

''Salomon Brothers: Battling Back,'' *Economist,* November 21, 1992, p. 90.

Schifrin, Matthew, ''Solly's Revenge,'' *Forbes,* June 10, 1991, pp. 38–39.

Sobel, Robert, *Salomon Brothers 1910–1985: Advancing to Leadership,* New York: Salomon Brothers Inc., 1986, 240 p.

Spiro, Leah Nathans, ''The Man Who's Filling Meriwether's Loafers at Solly,'' *Business Week,* August 29, 1994, p. 61.

——, ''Turmoil at Salomon: Huge Losses and a Talent Drain Have It Reeling,'' *Business Week,* May 1, 1995, pp. 144–51.

——, and Richard A. Melcher, ''Rescuing Salomon Was One Thing, but Running It . . . ,'' *Business Week,* February 17, 1992, pp. 120–21.

''Taking Arms against a Sea of Troubles,'' *Euromoney,* March 1992, pp. 42–48.

—updated by David E. Salamie

Samsonite Corp.

11200 E. 45th Avenue
Denver, Colorado 80239
U.S.A.
(303) 373-2000
Fax: (303) 373-6300

Public Company
Incorporated: 1912 as Shwayder Trunk Manufacturing Company
Employees: 5,000
Sales: $635 million
Stock Exchanges: NASDAQ
SICs: 3161 Luggage; 5099 Durable Goods, Not Elsewhere Classified

Samsonite is the leading manufacturer of luggage in the world and the top seller of luggage in the United States, Europe, and Japan. In addition to its world-renowned Samsonite label, the company also markets the popular American Tourister brand. Under those names, Samsonite offers a full line of luggage, including softside and hardside suitcases, garment bags, casual bags, business cases, and other travel bags and accessories. Samsonite changed ownership several times during the 1980s and early 1990s before regaining its independence in 1995.

Samsonite owes its start to Colorado native Jesse Shwayder. After growing up in the American West during the late 1800s, Shwayder was working in New York as a salesman for the Seward Trunk and Bag Company by his mid-20s. He was making a lot of money, but he missed Colorado and longed to pursue his dream of starting his own business. Thus, Shwayder quit his job when he was 28 and moved back to Denver. Shortly thereafter, on March 10, 1910, he founded the Shwayder Trunk Manufacturing Company with his life's savings of $3,500. With a work force of ten men, Shwayder began manufacturing what were known as ''suitcases'' in a 50 × 125 foot room that he had rented in downtown Denver. The management philosophy he adopted to guide the firm from day one, according to company annals, was the Golden Rule (do unto others . . .), to which Shwayder adhered tenaciously.

Shwayder burned through most of his $3,500 in savings during his first year of business. He was able to borrow money to stay afloat, however, and had soon turned the corner toward profitability. His brother Maurice joined him in 1912, and together they traveled throughout the region in an effort to drum up sales and keep the business going. A few years later, Sol Shwayder, a third brother, joined the sales team. Shwayder brothers Ben and Mark also jumped on board in 1923; eventually, Mark worked on sales, Maurice and Ben focused on manufacturing, and Sol became the company's attorney. The brothers incorporated in 1912 and, having outgrown their downtown room, moved to larger offices. By 1917 they were selling $76,000 worth of luggage annually throughout the western United States. To keep up with spiraling demand they built a new three-story manufacturing facility. That new plant would also prove inadequate soon, as mail-order advertising expanded the Shwayder's reach eastward across the United States.

The Shwayders' success was no accident. Indeed, Jesse drew from his work experience in New York to develop a strategy that he would pursue from the start. He realized that he was facing stiff competition from deep-pocketed luggage manufacturers. So, rather than trying to compete with other luggage companies on price, he would differentiate his products by quality and charge as high a price as the market would bear. To reflect the quality and durability of their luggage, the Shwayders named their first products ''Samson'' after the powerful Biblical character. Indeed, the chief advantage of the cases was that they could take a lot of punishment and were extremely durable. In 1916, in fact, the Shwayders took a picture that would become an advertising coup. The four brothers and their father, Isaac, stood on a plank positioned atop one of their suitcases above the caption; ''Strong enough to stand on.'' Because the five portly Shwayder men weighed more than 1,000 pounds together, the picture was striking and became an excellent promotional and direct-mail advertising gimmick for several years.

The Shwayders rolled out their first nationally advertised suitcase in 1918. The premium quality case retailed for $4.95 and was advertised in a window at the famous Macy's department store; the suitcase was displayed with a half-ton of sugar resting on top. Boosted by the success of that and other products, Shwayder Trunk revenues rocketed to $300,000 by 1924. In that year, the brothers moved their operation into a gleaming new 80,000 square foot factory in south Denver; that plant was gradually expanded to include a total of 500,000 square feet. The plant was organized to operate on an assembly-line basis, and even incorporated a state-of-the art conveyor system to transport products and materials in the plant. The company boasted in its literature that it built suitcases the same way that Ford built automobiles.

Shwayder Trunk's revenues bolted to more than $1 million during the late 1920s and sales, particularly to the eastern United States, exploded. To keep pace with demand, the Shwayders leased an 85,000 square foot factory near Detroit. With that plant up and running, the company seemed almost unstoppable. Unfortunately, the 1929 stock market crash and succeeding Great Depression quashed that perception. Indeed, Shwayder Trunk's shipments plummeted by 50 percent within a few years. The brothers, scrambling to meet payroll and pay their bills, began trying to supplant lost luggage sales by manufacturing products ranging from license plates and card tables to stilts, doggie dinettes, and sandboxes. To reflect the diversification, the brothers changed the name of their company in 1931 to

Shwayder Brothers, Inc. Interestingly, the Shwayder's card table sales briefly surpassed luggage shipments during the 1930s.

Despite their setbacks in the luggage industry, the Shwayders continued to improve their luggage and invent new travel products. By the 1930s, in fact, the Denver luggage plant was the most modern of its type in the world. From that plant came innovative Samson luggage with exclusive features such as wood-frame construction, super-strong handles, rayon linings, fiber finishes, and secure locks. Specialty fibre finishes were developed by Shwayder Trunk specifically as a covering for Samson suitcases. In 1939 the company introduced a unique suitcase that Jesse dubbed "Samsonite." The suitcase, which was the predecessor to the popular Samsonite Streamlite line, was covered with sturdy vulcanized fiber that was used with a leather binding. The case's tapered shape was destined to become a classic within the industry.

During the early 1940s Shwayder Trunk's factories were converted to produce war materials. Immediately after the war, however, the Shwayders resumed their luggage and folding furniture business and even managed to sell $7 million worth of goods during their first year of postwar production in 1946. During that and the succeeding few years, the brothers integrated into the facilities all of the manufacturing knowledge that they gleaned during war-time production. That allowed them to introduce precision manufacturing methods and to incorporate advanced new synthetic materials into their products. By 1948, sales had shot up to $13 million. The Shwayders then split the company into two divisions: luggage and steel/folding furniture, with the latter division being headquartered at the Detroit factory. The company even opened a second furniture plant in Pennsylvania in 1949.

Shwayder Trunk again converted its manufacturing facilities for war-time production during the Korean War of the 1950s. Although part of that decade was spent building things like bombs and rocket carriers, the brothers managed to increase their luggage and furniture businesses. For example, they began building specialized carrying cases for everything from musical instruments to advanced electronic equipment. And they started producing vinyl clad material for use in automobile interiors. Importantly, the company introduced the Ultralite luggage line in 1956. That luggage was the first to abandon wood-frame construction in favor of magnesium and injection-molded plastics. Also in 1956, Shwayder Brothers expanded out of the United States with a separate Canadian subsidiary and an export sales department focused on Europe. Meanwhile, the flourishing furniture division was consolidated and relocated to a giant production facility in Tennessee.

During the 1960s the company introduced a number of new products under the increasingly popular Samsonite brand name. They brought out several new travel and attaché cases, for example, as well as a line of upscale folding furniture and a successful line of metal patio furniture. The brothers changed the name of the company in 1965 to Samsonite Corporation to capitalize on the now-renowned Samsonite label. Interestingly, the company introduced LEGO by Samsonite in 1960. The snap-together plastic building blocks for children enjoyed immediate acceptance in the North American marketplace and eventually became one of the most popular toys of all time. The stellar success of LEGO prompted Shwayder Brothers to launch more than 50 new toy items before the early 1970s. Lagging performance of the toy division, however, caused the company to jettison the operation in 1972 and focus on furniture and luggage.

Samsonite's gains during the 1960s were achieved under the guiding hand of founder Jesse Shwayder's son, King D. Under King's leadership, Samsonite managed to firmly establish itself as the world's leading manufacturer of molded luggage and attaché cases by the early 1970s. Indeed, the company added manufacturing operations and sales offices throughout Europe and even Japan during the 1960s and enjoyed hefty sales increases in those regions. Having grown to dominate the business luggage markets, Samsonite set its sites on the mushrooming consumer luggage market. To that end, Samsonite introduced a highly successful line of soft-sided luggage during the late 1960s and early 1970s and even built new factories in Arizona and New Mexico dedicated to manufacturing soft-sided luggage. Samsonite simultaneously acquired companies that gave it leading positions in the markets for personal travel luggage-related products (such as leather toiletries kits), as well as redwood patio and casual furniture.

During the 1970s Samsonite intensified its global expansion efforts related to luggage. By the early 1970s, the company was already operating facilities in Osaka and Tokyo, Japan, as well as in Holland, Spain, Britain, Belgium, Germany, and other countries. During the mid-1970s, though, the company acquired competitors or initiated operations in new manufacturing facilities in France, Germany, the Netherlands, Belgium, Mexico, and other places. By the mid-1970s, then, the company had achieved a truly global presence and was the leading manufacturer of luggage in the world. The enterprise, which was still headquartered in Denver, was employing a work force of 5,000 and boasted the largest and most advanced production facilities in the luggage and casual furniture industries.

After operating as an independent under the direction of the Shwayder family for more than 60 years, Samsonite was engulfed in the corporate consolidation and buyout binge of the 1970s. In 1973 Samsonite was purchased by corporate giant Beatrice Foods Co. At the time, Beatrice was still garnering about 75 percent of its sales from various food and chemical divisions; but it had 1,000 locations around the world, 8,000 different products, more than 65,000 employees, and was growing rapidly through acquisition. Beatrice planned to allow Samsonite to continue operating as a relatively autonomous company, and to support its expansion efforts financially. Beatrice became the first of several companies that would own and sell Samsonite in the 1970s and through the early 1990s. During that time, Samsonite would effectively jettison its furniture operations and focus its energy on the global luggage industry.

Samsonite continued to grow under the Beatrice umbrella during the late 1970s by expanding globally and introducing new products. Unfortunately, its momentum began to wane. Although the company remained a world leader in its key markets, by the early 1980s Samsonite was losing ground. Lackluster management had left the company with a dearth of new products, despite access to Beatrice's bank account, and Samsonite was rapidly losing its edge and reputation as an industry innovator. In addition, competition from low-cost foreign producers was chipping away at Samsonite's market share. To rectify the situation, Beatrice brought in 47-year-old Malcom Candlish to lead the company. The British-born Candlish was a seasoned consumer products industry executive. Beatrice wanted him to revive the company and put it unquestionably back on top of the luggage industry.

Candlish took the helm in 1983 and immediately began whipping the company into shape. He laid off about 250 workers, initiated aggressive cost cutting programs, and replaced some of the old guard with new, more aggressive employees. By his own estimate, about half of the company's work force had been replaced by 1989. Candlish also launched a comprehensive study to determine exactly what consumer wanted. That survey lead to the introduction of the 'World's Greatest Garment Bag,' as described in company promotionals, which became a very successful new product. That bag was followed by a string of new soft- and hard-sided luggage products that served to renew Samsonite's innovation edge. By 1986, Samsonite was generating annual sales of about $300 million (50 percent from overseas operations), controlling about 12 percent of the U.S. luggage market, and rapidly improving.

Like its subsidiary, Beatrice was scurrying during the early and mid-1980s to cut costs and refocus its organization. To that end, it sold Samsonite in 1986 to leveraged buyout king Kholberg, Kravis & Roberts. Then, 15 months later, Kholberg spun off Samsonite and eight other companies into a new company called E-II. Six months later E-II was bought out by American Brands, which subsequently was purchased by billionair Meshulam Riklis of Riklis Family Corp. Throughout the buyout melee, Candlish managed to keep his chief executive job and even to improve Samsonite's performance. By 1989, in fact, Samsonite was generating an estimated $430 million in sales worldwide, and Candlish was still working to cut costs and bring out more new products.

As Samsonite continued to post gains in the recession of the late 1980s and early 1990s, its parent company, E-II, floundered and eventually filed for Chapter 11 bankruptcy. "We like to say we have a sick head and a healthy body," said Nick Nell, Samsonite's chief financial officer, in the September 27, 1992, *Denver Post.* Samsonite's revenues leapt up into the $500 million range in 1992 from the sale of approximately ten million pieces of luggage worldwide. Those sales included nearly 70 percent of all the hard-sided luggage sold throughout the world, including such nations as Russia, Argentina, and China. By the early 1990s Samsonite was recognized as a U.S. leader in global marketing.

Following a messy reorganization of E-II, Samsonite emerged as a subsidiary of a new company called Astrum International Corp. Steve Green, former E-II executive, became the new chairman and chief executive of Samsonite. Under his direction, Samsonite continued to grow and to retain its global bent. In 1993 Astrum purchased the American Tourister luggage company to complement Samsonite. That purchase significantly bolstered Samsonite's lead in the domestic luggage market and broadened its scope to include some lower tier segments of the market. The combined operations were generating sales of approximately $600 million annually going into 1994. Samsonite posted record sales in 1994 of $634 million, about $72 million of which was profit.

Samsonite regained its independence for the first time since 1973 when Astrum announced early in 1995 that it was going to split into two companies, one of which would be the new publicly held, independent, Denver-based Samsonite Corporation. The new company retained the Samsonite and American Tourister divisions and related operations. Green expected to stay on as head of Samsonite. Besides expanding into new global markets, Green announced his intention to broaden Samsonite's product line to include luggage racks, golf and ski bags, camping gear, and even computer and camera cases.

Further Reading:

Elder, Drew, "Samsonite Bagging Profits With Innovative Products," *Denver Post,* September 24, 1992, p. C1.

——, "Samsonite Ignores Storm," *Denver Post,* September 27, 1992, p. 1.

Kempner, Michael W., "Astrum International Corp. Announces Spin-Off," *PR Newswire,* April 24, 1995.

Lieb, Jeffrey, "Samsonite To Go Independent," *Denver Post,* April 25, 1995, p. C1.

——, "Samsonite Upbeat on Tourister Deal," *Denver Post,* August 5, 1993, p. C2.

O'Neal, Nan, "Durable Samsonite Chief Vows to 'Set Industry on Fire'," *Denver Business Journal,* January 16, 1989, p. 10.

The Samsonite Story, Denver: Samsonite Corp., 1973.

Skolnik, Rayna, "The Strength Behind Samsonite," *Sales & Marketing Management,* September 1986, p. 40.

—Dave Mote

Sapporo Breweries, Ltd.

10-1, Ginza 7-chome
Chuo-ku, Tokyo 104
Japan
(03) 5423 2111
Fax: (03) 5423 2057

Public Company
Incorporated: September 1949 as Nippon Breweries, Ltd.
Employees: 4,071
Sales: ¥663.9 billion (US $6.65 billion)
Stock Exchanges: Tokyo Osaka Nagoya Sapporo
SICs: 2082 Malt Beverages; 2086 Bottled and Canned Soft Drinks; 2084 Wines, Brandy and Brandy Spirits; 5812 Eating Places; 6531 Real Estate Agents and Managers

Over the course of its more than 100 year history, Sapporo Breweries Ltd. has evolved from a government-owned beer maker into a multi-faceted consumer products concern. In the mid-1990s, its interests included the namesake Sapporo beers and a full line of soft drinks, wine, teas, and coffees, as well as real estate, restaurants, and hotels. Along with Kirin Brewery Co., Asahi Breweries Ltd. and Suntory Ltd., Sapporo ranks among Japan's ''Big Four'' breweries; its flagship Black Label brand beer held 18.2 percent of the country's beer market in 1994.

Beer was introduced to Japan in the mid-1800s. The American largely responsible for renewing trade relations with Japan, Commodore Matthew Perry, brought several cases of beer to Japan as a gift for the Tokugawa Shogunate. The beverage was so well liked that the Japanese government soon decided to establish a brewing industry. After an extensive search for a suitable area, wild hops were found growing on the island of Hokkaido, the northernmost island in the Japanese archipelago. As a result, in 1876 the Commissioner-General for the development of Hokkaido founded Japan's first brewery in the town of Sapporo. (Coincidentally, the global beer capitols of Munich, Milwaukee, and Sapporo are all located along the 45° north latitude.)

The original government facility was designed by the brewmaster Seibei Nakagawa, who had returned to Japan after studying beer-making techniques in Germany. The first product brewed in the factory was called Sapporo cold beer or German beer, and even some of the early labels were printed in German as well as in Japanese.

In 1886 the brewery was sold by the government to Okura-Gumi, a private limited partnership. Two years later, Okura-Gumi itself was purchased by a group of Japanese businessmen, who then reorganized the brewing operations under the name Sapporo Brewery Ltd. A number of other breweries, which would soon figure prominently in Sapporo's development, were also started during this time, including Nippon Brewing Company Ltd., Osaka Brewery, Kirin Brewery Company Ltd., and the Nippon Beer Kosen Brewery.

In the first decade of the 20th century, the Sapporo Brewery, the Nippon Brewing Company, and the Osaka Brewery were amalgamated as the Dai Nippon Brewery Company Ltd. This process of amalgamation and consolidation continued for 20 years until, in 1933, the Nippon Beer Kosen Brewery was also absorbed by Dai Nippon.

During the 1920s and 1930s Japanese militarists, implementing their plan to make Japan the dominant economic power in Asia, began to centralize the brewing industry. By 1943, the merger of all Japanese breweries was virtually complete: Dai Nippon and Kirin were the only two brewing companies left in Japan. In fact, the militarists were powerful enough to force the Sapporo division of Dai Nippon to establish joint ventures in the occupied territories of Korea and Manchuria.

At this stage, local markets were dominated by particular brands. Dai Nippon sold Sapporo beer in the region north of the Kanto district, primarily in Hokkaido. The company also manufactured Yebisu and Asahi brand beers; the former was popular in the Tokyo area and the latter in the Kansai area. Not surprisingly, because of the increased demand for beer (it was rapidly superseding the traditional drink sake), its production continued throughout the war.

The current structure of Japan's brewing industry originated after World War II during the U.S. occupation. In 1949 the Dai Nippon Brewery, which had cornered nearly 70 percent of the beer market in Japan, was divided into Nippon Breweries Ltd. and Asahi Breweries Ltd. Initially, Nippon Breweries marketed beer exclusively under its own brand name; it was not until 1957 that beer displaying the Sapporo label was reintroduced.

Nippon's growth during the postwar period, primarily because of an expanding product line, was impressive; from 1951 to 1981 production at the company's facilities increased by a factor of 15. During that same period, the brewery's sales increased from ¥20 billion to ¥330 billion, and its capitalization from ¥100 million to over ¥14.1 billion.

It was not until 1964 that the Nippon Breweries changed its name to Sapporo Breweries, Ltd. Shortly thereafter, arrangements were made to merge the Sapporo and Asahi breweries. By this time they had become the second and third largest breweries, respectively, in Japan. (Kirin had captured the largest share of the domestic beer market.) However, the merger never materialized.

The formation of a joint venture with Guinness plc, called Sapporo-Guinness, also took place in 1964. This agreement led to the sale of Irish stout in Japan. By 1976 the consumption of stout beer had risen dramatically and a sales war ensued with the Kirin brewery, which had its own version of the beverage. Even though the cost of Guinness's product was twice that of Kirin's, Sapporo managed to maintain about 45 percent of the domestic stout market by relying heavily on Guinness's quality image.

Sapporo entered the wine market in 1971 when it formed a joint venture with Mitsui and Company Ltd. to import both wine and liquor. Sapporo Liquor Company Ltd. first began to import Nicolas, Hoch, and Melini wines. The company then started to produce its own wines at the Katsunuma Winery west of Tokyo in 1976; its Polaire brand of wine would eventually include the top five best sellers in Japan. After the Okayama Winery was established in 1984, a wine cooler, a sparkling wine, and Hyosai, a white brandy, were also added to the growing domestically produced beverage line. In addition, the Sapporo Liquor Company imported Baileys Irish Cream, Bombay Gin, Green Island Rum, and several scotches, including J and B Rare, Dunhill, Knockando, and Spay Royal.

First established in 1908, Sapporo's research and development division was created to breed varieties of barley and hops especially suited to Japan's climate. In the mid-1970s the Sapporo laboratory developed a technique for the ceramic filtration of beer. Since the introduction of pasteurization in the early part of the 20th century, beer had been sterilized by means of a heating process. This was necessary because the yeast residue in beer rendered it unsuitable for extended storage or long-distance transportation. Yet the problem with heating beer was that the high temperature affected its flavor. Sapporo's unique ceramic filtration method removed the yeast residue from beer without having to heat it. The beer was filtered at a constant temperature of zero to one degree centigrade through a long ceramic cylinder; a thin coating of diatomaceous earth in the tube trapped the yeast residue. The first draft beer made with this new process went on the market in 1977, and in 1985 the filtration technology was exported to South Korea and to the Miller Brewing Company in the United States. Even so, Sapporo continued to pasteurize many of its products.

In 1988, Sapporo's research and development department expanded into the propagation of rare orchids for sale in the United States, Europe, and domestically. The Sapporo laboratory also conducted research in such fields as soft drinks, and the application of beer yeast to the development of food seasonings and health food products. Sapporo scientists also investigated the utilization of recent discoveries in biotechnology to develop agricultural chemicals and pharmaceuticals.

Throughout its history, rising prices for raw materials cut into company profits. Sapporo's supply of yeast came from a strain originally developed at the Sapporo laboratory. Although Sapporo brand name beer was brewed exclusively in Japan, much of the barley and hops used in its manufacture were historically imported from Canada, Australia, West Germany, and Czechoslovakia. During the 1970s the Japanese government raised the brewery's already high costs by requiring them to purchase domestically grown barley; this accounted for 20 to 25 percent of the barley used in the entire industry. Originally intended to protect farmers who had switched from the cultivation of rice (which was in surplus) to barley, the domestic strain cost brewers 3.7 times as much as imported ones.

In spite of such roadblocks, Sapporo grew consistently. In fact, from 1985 to 1987 the company enjoyed record sales and earnings. Sapporo attributed its success to reduced materials costs, a decreasing interest payment burden, and effective management of surplus funds. Furthermore, the appreciation of the yen and the consequent lower price of foreign malt also helped boost results.

But as the Japanese beer market fast approached saturation in the late 1980s, Sapporo sought new markets through geographic and product diversification. Having established distributorships in over 30 countries around the world, the company founded its first full-fledged foreign subsidiary in the United States in 1984.

While striving to maintain a premium image for its flagship beers, Sapporo catered to both ends of the Japanese beer market in the late 1980s and early 1990s. The company introduced the gold-labeled Yebisu Beer and the ultra-dry Kissui ale for the upscale market. Around the same time, it inked a contract with the U.S.-based Stroh Brewing Company to import a bargain-priced beer into the country. And after five years of research and development, the company also launched "Drafty," a sparkling alcoholic drink which the company was able to offer at a low price, due to the product's low malt content, which incurred less tax.

The seeds of Sapporo's burgeoning restaurant empire were planted with the establishment of the brewery's first beer hall back in 1899. By 1994, a beer hall division had grown to become Sapporo Lion Limited, a 180-location chain that contributed about five percent of the company's annual revenues and an incalculable amount to Sapporo's brand cachet. Echoing an American trend, the company began to develop several "brew-pubs" featuring boutique beers brewed on site.

Having put its first soft drink, Ribbon Citron, on the market as early as 1909, Sapporo placed ever-increasing emphasis on its nonalcoholic beverage line. By the late 1980s, this product segment included traditional and medicinal teas, Beans brand canned coffees, and a variety of carbonated sodas and mineral waters. The company concentrated on introducing all-natural, wholesome drinks with fruit flavors and light carbonation in the early 1990s.

While real estate still only contributed 6.5 percent of Sapporo's total annual revenues in the mid-1990s, this segment was considered the cornerstone of the company's diversification strategy. Development activities took center stage with the 1994 opening of the Yebisu Garden Place, a downtown Tokyo office complex that featured retail outlets and upscale condominiums that cost the company ¥295 billion and took ten years to complete. The brewer proudly moved its headquarters to the new facility that same year. But far from abandoning its historical birthplace, the company redeveloped its first brewery into what it referred to as a "cultural mall," incorporating public services, retail, and leisure centers.

An especially hot summer spurred demand and boosted domestic beer consumption to record levels in 1994. Sapporo's own four percent year-to-year increase in beer sales contributed to a 10.3 percent overall revenue increase, to ¥663.9 billion that year. However, the company's new president and representative director, Kenzo Edamoto, warned that the long-term beer industry trend was toward marginal growth, hence Sapporo's energetic development of its real estate and other businesses.

Principal Subsidiaries: Sapporo Lion Ltd.; Sapporo Wines Ltd.; Meguro Planning Co., Ltd.; Sapporo Beer's Beverage Co., Ltd.; Sapporo Development Co., Ltd.; Sapporo U.S.A., Inc.

Further Reading:

''Sapporo Beer Wants to Set New Challenges,'' *Yomiuri Report From Japan,* May 19, 1995, p. 3.

Tanaka, Kazuo, *The History of Sapporo Breweries Ltd.* Sapporo-shi: Hokkaido Shinbunsha, 1993.

—updated by April Dougal Gasbarre

Scottish Hydro-Electric PLC

10 Dunkeld Road
Perth PH1 5WA
United Kingdom
(01738) 455040
Fax: (01738) 455045

Public Company
Incorporated: 1989
Employees: 3,525
Sales: £792 million
Stock Exchanges: London
SICs: 4911 Electric Companies and Systems; 5712 Furniture Shops

The smaller of the two Scottish electric companies, Scottish Hydro-Electric PLC generates, transmits, and supplies electricity to the Scottish Highlands and Islands. Hydro-Electric's position in the U.K. electricity industry is unique, serving as it does a region comprising some 25 percent of Britain's total land area—and encompassing some of the United Kingdom's loveliest yet least hospitable terrain—but containing only 3 percent of its population. Though it got a late start relative to electricity suppliers in England and Wales, Scottish Hydro-Electric has, over the past 50 years, brought electricity to the north of Scotland virtually single-handedly, first as a public sector utility and later as a privatized company. The generation and provision of electricity in the Highlands remained the company's core business, but in the 1990s it significantly broadened its market to include areas south of the border.

The harnessing of electricity for public use developed more slowly in Scotland than in England and Wales, where nearly 500 separate electricity suppliers had arisen within just 40 years following the introduction of street lighting in 1881. In Scotland the first electricity was supplied in 1890 via a water turbine at Fort Augustus. The first commercial use of water power in Britain came in 1896, when the British Aluminum Company set up a factory at Foyers on Loch Ness, utilizing the water coursing down the slopes of the Great Glen to power its aluminum smelting. But subsequent development, particularly in the remote and sparsely populated Highlands, was slow. There were few schemes until 1930, when the Grampian Electricity Supply Company began operating projects at Rannoch and Tummel Bridge, Perthshire, and at Luichart, Ross-shire.

These projects were by no means far-reaching, however; as late as 1943, five out of six farms and 99 out of 100 crofts in the Highlands had no link to publicly supplied electricity. In that year the North of Scotland Hydro-Electric Board was established by an act of Parliament. When, five years later, the electricity industry was nationalized, the projects of Grampian Electricity and other independent suppliers came under the jurisdiction of the new board.

The formidable work of harnessing water power in the Highlands now began in earnest. Within Britain, only in the Scottish Highlands could hydro power be utilized so extensively for electricity generation. The Highlands boast some of Britain's highest mountains, large expanses of uninterrupted high ground, vast tracts of moorland, and numerous large and deep lochs. All these features provide ideal conditions for the use of hydro power. At the same time, those very features of the landscape often proved a barrier to development. Coupled with the scattered and isolated nature of Highland settlements, they made transmission of power a difficult task indeed. Nonetheless, work progressed with a labor force averaging between 4,000 and 5,000, and at one time reaching as high as 12,000. By 1965 about half of the area's estimated potential had been realized. This equated to 54 main power stations with a generating capacity of more than 1,000 megawatts, 56 primary dams, 300 kilometers of excavated rock tunnels, 300 kilometers of aqueducts and pipelines, 32,000 kilometers of overhead cables, and 110 kilometers of submarine cables.

Despite its history and even its name, only a proportion of Hydro-Electric's power was generated by water. In 1994, the breakdown of the company's power generation sources was as follows: 16 percent hydro; 51 percent oil and gas; 11 percent coal; 19 percent nuclear; and 3 percent other. However, the use of hydro power fluctuated year by year, sometimes considerably, depending on rainfall; in 1993 the hydro figure had been 26 percent. The high percentage of oil and gas use was accounted for primarily by one station: Peterhead.

In the early 1970s the North Sea oil boom brought rapid development to the northeast of Scotland, and with it a heavily increased demand for electricity. Hydro-powered electricity had served the region previously, but this was inadequate for the surge in requirements for geographical reasons. Scotland's northeast, which mainly consists of a low plateau, is unusual in the Highlands in that it has no proximity to a major river system. Thus plans were laid for Hydro-Electric's major thermal power station.

Begun in 1973 and based at Boddam, near Peterhead, the plant was fully operational by 1982. Originally oil had been the favored fossil fuel, but by the time the project was completed natural gas had become a more popular option for the electricity industry (although the Peterhead plant retained its oil capability). In 1988 Hydro-Electric arranged to buy the entire natural gas yield of the Miller Field in the North Sea, thus securing itself a continuing supply from 1992, when the gas came on stream, until well into the next century.

In the late 1980s Britain's Conservative government laid plans to privatize the electricity industry, and Scottish Hydro-Electric was accordingly incorporated as a private company in 1989.

The company's shares were sold on the stock market in 1991. The privatized electricity industry in Scotland was structured differently than in England and Wales. In Scotland, Hydro-Electric and its southern counterpart ScottishPower were fully integrated: that is, they generated, distributed, and supplied electricity. In England and Wales, however, the system was more fragmented. The electricity generators, principally National Power and PowerGen, produced electricity, which was then distributed via the National Grid to the Regional Electricity Companies (RECs), who in turn supplied electricity to consumers.

The Scottish electricity boards were originally slated to be privatized first, but eventually the government decided to proceed with the English RECs first, at the end of 1990. Hydro-Electric and ScottishPower were offered for sale in the summer of the following year. Some investors argued that in the interim the government changed the rules so that the munificent premiums enjoyed by investors in the RECs were not available to those who invested in Hydro-Electric and ScottishPower. For reasons that have never been entirely clear, shareholders in the English and Welsh companies made five times more in capital gains than their Scottish counterparts. This history of inequity played a part in the controversy that arose in 1994 between Hydro-Electric and the Office of Electricity Regulation (Offer).

Although privatized, Hydro-Electric remained a monopoly supplier of a public utility, and as such was subject to government regulatory control. It was Offer's task to balance the interests of Britain's electricity consumers against those of the industry's shareholders. The job proved to be a particularly sensitive one in 1994, when Offer assessed the position of the electricity industry for the first time since privatization with a view to setting a new round of pricing controls. The English and Welsh RECs were reviewed first, and the consensus among financial analysts was that the RECs had been treated very leniently. Happy shareholders agreed, and the companies' share prices rocketed to record levels. Some politicians and consumer groups were less pleased, however, and Offer was widely criticized.

Suspiciously minded observers speculated that Offer was mindful of that criticism the following month, when the Scottish companies were assessed with quite a different result. (Bowing to pressure, Offer subsequently announced its intention to re-review the English and Welsh companies, but a decision date was not revealed.) The main point of contention was Offer's proposed price formula for electricity distribution, which allowed the RECs a rate of return of 6.5 to 7 percent, ScottishPower 6 percent—and Hydro-Electric 2 percent. Hydro-Electric's share price dropped dramatically after the regulator's announcement.

ScottishPower accepted Offer's decision, but Hydro-Electric protested vigorously. The company claimed that the stringent pricing controls would render it unable to undertake necessary improvements to its distribution network, on which it spent some £50 million a year. Hydro-Electric warned that power cuts would inevitably be suffered in its rural areas. When outraged critics labeled this nothing short of blackmail, Hydro-Electric chief executive Roger Young replied bleakly: "It isn't blackmail, it's a statement of fact." After a month of deliberations, Hydro-Electric refused to accept Offer's price caps, forcing the regulator to refer the matter to the Monopolies and Mergers Commission (MMC) for arbitration.

Since privatization, Hydro-Electric has been increasingly looking to expand its market, in terms of both geography and product. Toward that end, the company began aggressively seeking opportunities south of the border. In 1994/95, Hydro-Electric opened three new power stations in England, each as a 50-50 joint venture with another firm. The biggest project was at Keadby, South Humberside, where Hydro-Electric, in conjunction with Norweb, finished a 680 megawatt combined cycle gas turbine plant, operated through the subsidiary Hydro-Electric Production Services. The other two projects were combined heat and power (CHP) schemes: a 157 megawatt plant built at Sellafield in cooperation with British Nuclear Fuels, and a Dover-based 9 megawatt plant built to deliver steam and electricity to the project's partner, the papermakers Arjo Wiggins Appleton. These three projects together accounted for 15 percent of Hydro-Electric's total generating capacity; add to this electricity generated in Scotland but supplied to England, and Hydro-Electricity's production south of the border rises to 30 percent, or about 2 percent of the entire English market.

In 1993 Hydro-Electric launched an important project as a joint venture with the U.S. oil and gas company Marathon: Vector Gas Ltd. With the gas industry well on the road to deregulation, Hydro-Electric was eager to penetrate a wider energy market. Vector sold gas to commercial and industrial customers throughout the United Kingdom under its "HE Energy" brand. One of the company's highest-profile clients (among the more than 1,000 it served) was beer and leisure industry giant Scottish & Newcastle.

Gaining experience in the retail gas market was an important move for Hydro-Electric, because its core electricity business was in a region where 40 percent—an unusually high percentage—of water and space heating was provided via electricity. Competition from gas was sure to arise in the future, and Hydro-Electric hoped to be able to persuade its electricity customers to become its gas customers too, rather than switching to other suppliers.

Clearly Hydro-Electric viewed its future as stretching beyond the boundaries of its traditional role as electricity supplier to the Highlands. While the company stressed that its commitment to its home base of the north of Scotland remained its first priority, it also became apparent from the firm's initiatives and pronouncements that Hydro-Electric intended to continue to expand beyond its borders and beyond its core business to play a significant role in the production and supply of energy in the United Kingdom.

Principal Subsidiaries: Fellside Heat and Power Ltd. (50 percent); HE Gas Ltd.; Hydro-Electric Energy Ltd.; Hydro-Electric Production Services Ltd.; Hydro-Electric Supply Ltd.; Keadby Power Ltd. (50 percent); Vector Gas Ltd. (50 percent).

Further Reading:

Baur, Chris, "The Words and Pictures of the Noble Adventure," *Hydro-Electric Business*, Spring/Summer, 1993, pp. 20–21.

" 'Blackmail' Claim over Electricity Pricing," *Herald,* December 10, 1994.
Calder, Colin, "Vector Puts New Gas into Brewing," *Hydro-Electric Business,* Spring/Summer, 1994, pp. 30–32.
"Electricity Price Controls Thrown into Confusion," *Scotsman,* November 16, 1994.
"Fifty Years of Hydro-Electric," *Hydro-Electric Business,* Spring/Summer, 1993, pp. 18–19.
"Hydro Drive South Starts to Pay Off," *Scotsman,* December 9, 1994.
"Hydro in Highland Power Cuts Warning," *Times,* December 9, 1994.
"Hydro Is Looking South to Offset Highland Limitations," *Herald,* December 9, 1994.
"Plugging into the Power Profits," *Scotsman,* September 30, 1994.
Power from the Glens, Perth: Scottish Hydro-Electric PLC, n.d.
"Power Struggle," *Herald,* December 10, 1994.
"Scots Electric Shares Slide as Price Curbs Put in Place," *Guardian,* September 30, 1994.
"Scots Power Runs into Littlechild," *Daily Telegraph,* September 30, 1990.
"Scots Power Shares Plunge on Price Review," *Herald,* September 30, 1994.
"Scottish Power Groups Hit by Tougher Price Controls," *Daily Telegraph,* September 30, 1994.
"UK Company News: Scottish Hydro-Electric Declines 23 Percent to Pounds 35 Million," *Financial Times,* December 9, 1994.
"VAT Adds Cold Comfort to Order to Cut Power Bills," *Herald,* September 30, 1994.
Wilkinson, Paul, "Building on Experience at Keadby," *Hydro-Electric Business,* Spring/Summer, 1994, pp. 14–17.

—Robin DuBlanc

Sequa Corp.

200 Park Avenue
New York, New York 10166
U.S.A.
(212) 986-5500
Fax: (212) 370-1969 or 983-2774

Public Company
Incorporated: 1929 as General Printing Ink Corp.
Employees: 10,250
Sales: $1.4 billion
Stock Exchanges: New York
SICs: 2821 Plastic Materials, Synthetic Resins & Nonvulcanizable Elastomers; 3471 Electroplating, Plating, Polishing, Anodizing & Coloring; 3511 Turbines and Turbine Generator Set Units; 3555 Printing Trades Machinery & Equipment; 3714 Motor Vehicle Parts & Accessories; 3724 Aircraft Engines & Engine Parts; 3764 Guided Missile & Space Vehicle Propulsion Units & Propulsion Unit Parts; 3812 Search, Detection, Navigation, Guidance, Aeronautical & Nautical Systems and Instruments; 3841 Surgical & Medical Instruments & Apparatus

Sequa Corporation is a diversified industrial company that produces a broad range of aerospace products, printing machinery, metal coatings, and specialty chemicals. Under its previous names General Printing Ink Corp. and Sun Chemical Corp., Sequa was the world's leading producer of printing inks and organic pigments before its graphic-arts unit was sold in 1986 and aerospace became the company's chief field of operations.

The General Printing Ink Corp. was organized in 1929 from the merger of five companies. These were George H. Morrill Co., established in 1840; Sigmund Ullman Co., established in 1861; Fuchs & Lang Manufacturing Co., established in 1871; Eagle Printing Ink Co., established in 1893; and American Printing Ink Co., established in 1897. The consolidated companies manufactured and distributed news, letterpress, lithographic-process and other printing inks, lithographic machinery and supplies, and related products. The eight principal factories owned by General Printing Ink included two in Chicago and one each in San Francisco and New York City, where the executive offices were also located. The five companies had combined net sales of $9.4 million and net income of $1.3 million in 1928.

According to an article in *Chemical Week,* General Printing Ink's constituent companies largely continued to compete with one another for sales rather than to cooperate and take steps to keep abreast of changing technology. Nevertheless, the amalgamated company made profits and paid dividends throughout the Great Depression of the 1930s. By 1940 it owned two more principal manufacturing plants, including one in Toronto that belonged to General Printing Ink Corp. of Canada, Ltd., a subsidiary organized in 1931. General Printing Ink had net income of $1 million in 1940 on sales of $10.6 million.

In 1945 the company was renamed the Sun Chemical Corp., reflecting its broadened range of interests. A number of companies were acquired—usually through an exchange of stock—and made subsidiaries during this period. These included: in 1945, E. J. Kelly Co., Michigan Research Laboratories, A. C. Horn Co., and Warwick Chemical Co.; in 1946, Hudson Paint & Varnish Co. and C. A. Willey Co.; and in 1947, Electro-Technical Products Co. and Number 113 East Centre Corp.

By 1950 Sun Chemical was divided into groups for graphic arts, paint, industrial finishes, and chemicals, and into divisions for pigments, electro-technical products, and overseas. In addition, the company had nine subsidiaries. Sun Chemical and its subsidiaries owned or leased 42 plants and facilities, including three in Canada. With these acquisitions, net sales climbed from $17.5 million in 1945 to $35.5 million in 1949. Net profit also increased during this period, from $770,000 to $1.5 million.

With 32 divisions and subsidiaries in 1954 and, in addition to its manufacturing plants, 30 warehouses and 60 sales offices, Sun Chemical was a sprawling giant difficult to keep under control. However, with the exception of a subsidiary that manufactured printing-machinery equipment, all used raw materials based on oil, resins, and pigments. During 1954 Sun consolidated its products and selling organizations into three groups: chemicals (principally waxes); graphic arts; and structural waterproofing, paints, and products finishing. A management committee was established in 1953 to administer corporate policy.

Norman Alexander was president of Ansbacher-Siegle Corp., a producer of organic pigments for inks, paints, plastics, and cosmetics, when he acquired control of Sun Chemical, becoming its president in 1957. The son of a spats manufacturer, Alexander directed the family garment business before amassing a fortune in other manufacturing interests, real estate, and movie distribution. After he took control of Sun, the company bought Ansbacher-Siegle. A lawsuit by Sun stockholders charged Alexander with profiteering by buying Ansbacher-Siegle for what they claimed was an unreasonably high price. The suit eventually was settled by a court-approved compromise.

When Alexander took over Sun Chemical it ranked second among U.S. printing-ink producers and increasingly was falling behind the leader, Interchemical Corp. Sales were stagnant, and management was paying out big dividends rather than setting aside money to modernize the company's aging factories. Net income sank from $2.1 million in 1955 to $1.1 million in 1958. One problem was that the business was overly decentralized; for example, there were 28 ink centers, each purchasing raw materials from its own sources, and the smaller operations especially were unable to keep up with technological changes. The Warwick Chemicals operation, however, became in the mid-1950s the first supplier of thermosetting resins for wash-and-wear white shirts.

During Alexander's first decade directing Sun Chemical, he sold off or dissolved more than a third of the company. He concentrated on expanding its ink-and-pigment operations, buying private companies in this field throughout the world. By the end of 1960 Sun Chemical held 15 wholly owned active subsidiaries, including two in Canada and one in Venezuela. It also had a majority or half interest in eight companies in Australia, England, France, Mexico, and the United States. The Graphic Arts Group made inks for all printing processes and machinery for graphic arts. The Packaging Materials Group made a variety of films, fabrics, tapes, coatings, and other materials. The Chemical Group produced pigments and paints, textile and paper chemicals, textile-printing colors, and color dispersions. In all, Sun Chemical and its subsidiaries owned or leased 60 plants.

In 1960 Sun Chemical established a corporate research program. Two years later, the staff moved into a building in Carlstadt, New Jersey. By 1966, when Sun was spending between 2.5 and 3 percent of its annual sales on research, the research center housed 90 scientists and technicians. Much of its effort was directed toward the ink operations, which had been consolidated with centralized purchasing. A major emphasis was on developing polyamide resins for flexographic inks and on developing inks for a prospective electrostatic textile-printing machine. Sun had become the first supplier of ink for new machines performing electrostatic printing on fruit and plywood.

Although graphic arts remained Sun's largest group, chemicals was the fastest growing in the mid-1960s, with sales doubling every three years. Sun was the world's leading supplier of resins for permanent-press systems. In 1963 it introduced its Permafresh 183 glyoxal-based resin for the Koratron permanent-press process and carbonate-type resins for white goods. These resins were made by the chemicals group, then sold to the graphic-arts group. The chemicals group's researchers also were developing water repellents and high-performance pigments for the automobile and plastics industries.

Sun's overseas operations grew in the late 1950s and early 1960s. By 1966 it had added joint ventures in Italy, Spain, and Japan to its international interests. A second Mexican factory, opened in 1965, was the largest ink plant in Latin America. A new Venezuelan ink factory replaced the existing one, and another ink plant opened in Colombia as a joint venture. In all, Sun Chemical recorded an increase in sales from $73.4 million in 1965 to $108.1 million in 1969, and an even more impressive gain in per-share earnings from $1.01 to $2.17.

Sun Chemical had sales of $121.9 million in 1971. About half that sum came from inks. The company also was diversifying into related businesses, especially peripheral printing equipment. In addition, it was the chief supplier of machines for imprinting labels on two-piece, seamless beverage and aerosol cans. At the end of 1972 Sun acquired Standard Kollsman Industries Inc., a manufacturer of automotive parts, optical and aviation instruments, and electronic components, in a transaction valued at about $10.3 million in common stock. This purchase, which concluded a protracted struggle for control of the company, formed the basis for the establishment of instrumentation and automotive groups within Sun Chemical and included Kollsman System-Tecknik GmbH, the company's German subsidiary.

The Standard Kollsman purchase helped boost Sun Chemical's net sales from $136.9 million in 1972 to $246.5 million in 1973, and its net income from $4.9 million to $7 million. Graphic-arts materials and equipment accounted for two-thirds of all sales in 1974, by which time a Graphic Systems Group had been added to the company's operations. This group manufactured cylindrical decorators, photocomposition machines, automatic newspaper-handling systems, and computerized text-editing systems, and it also distributed electronic color scanning and separation equipment.

By the mid-1970s the company's investment in Suncure, a newly developed instant drying, solventless, ultraviolet cured ink, was paying off. There were a number of economic advantages to this process and a major environmental one: no smoke or toxic hydrocarbon emissions. Enthusiastic investors bid Sun Chemical's stock from about $11 to $27 a share in 1976, one of the best performances on the New York Stock Exchange that year. The outlook was also good for Sun's pigments, used in printing inks, paintings and coatings, plastics, cosmetics, and textiles. Alexander sought to make the company the largest domestic pigment producer by 1983. A $30-million Sun manufacturing complex in Muskegon County, Michigan, was expected to be the world's largest facility solely devoted to the production of organic pigments.

The company's expansion continued throughout the late 1970s. Net sales grew from $337.5 million in 1977 to $468.7 million in 1979, and net income from $15.3 million to $24.5 million. New subsidiaries were established in Bermuda, Chile, and Panama. By 1980 Sun had become the world's leading producer of printer's inks. Alexander, who now owned 34 percent of the company (compared to about 20 percent in 1966), had acquired more than 20 companies since taking charge of Sun and was engaged in his biggest takeover scheme, a contest for control of Chromalloy American Corp., three times the size of Sun Chemical.

Chromalloy held more than 140 businesses at the time, including drilling muds for the oil industry, textiles and apparel, coatings for turbines and other metal products, and financial services. It also owned a barge line plying the Mississippi River and its tributaries. Sun Chemical purchased a 5.2-percent interest in Chromalloy in February 1979, increasing its share to 18 percent before the end of the year. Further purchases of stock in late 1981 and early 1982 increased its share to 36 percent, despite litigation by Chromalloy directors, and Alexander became its chief executive officer in mid-1982.

Sun Chemical found itself on the receiving end of a takeover bid in 1986. A Japanese company, Dainippon Ink and Chemicals, Inc. offered to buy Sun in April for $77 a share, or $600.6 million, then sweetened its offer in May to $85 a share, or $663 million. Alexander, although a long-time friend of Dainippon's president, rejected the bid and raised his own stake in Sun to nearly 47 percent. In August, however, he agreed to sell Sun's graphic-arts materials group to Dainippon for $550 million. At the time this group was accounting for 61 percent of Sun's total sales and 57 percent of its operating profit.

Dainippon's cash offer enabled Sun Chemical to purchase the outstanding 56 percent of Chromalloy's shares for about $267 million in a 1986 stock swap and merge it into the parent company. It also made possible a cash offer for all the outstanding shares of Atlantic Research Corp., a producer of solid-propellant rocket motors and gas generators for short-to-intermediate tactical missiles like the shoulder-fired Stinger and the Tomahawk cruise missile. Sun already held an 18.6 percent stake in the company. After initial resistance, Atlantic Research in December 1987 accepted a sweetened offer of $31 a share—about 2.7 times book value and totaling about $307 million.

With the acquisition of Chromalloy and Atlantic Research, Sun was not so much a producer of chemicals as of military hardware; the company's name was changed to the Sequa Corp. to reflect this change in focus. Its acquisitions enabled net sales to rise from $371.4 million in 1986 to $1 billion in 1987. In 1990 Sequa's net sales reached a peak of almost $2 billion, but thereafter military cutbacks resulting from the end of the Cold War devastated the company's balance sheet. Sales dropped from $1.9 billion in 1991 to $1.4 billion in 1994, and the company was in the red all four years, with the deficit increasing from $6.6 million in 1991 to nearly $64 million in 1993 before falling to $25.8 million in 1994.

Not all the drop-off in sales was due to military cutbacks. In August 1991 Sequa announced it was discontinuing six business units that had combined sales of $145 million during the first six months of the year. These included Valley Line Co., an inland barge transportation business; Sabine Towing & Transportation Co., a tanker and tank-barge firm; Sequa Engineered Services, producer of oil-well equipment and pump parts; and Sequa Capital Corp., a leasing and financial-services company. CSX Corp. bought Valley Line, which owned and operated 912 barges and 29 tow boats. The sale of Sabine was completed in 1992 for $36 million. In January 1994 Sequa sold ARC Professional Services Group to Computer Sciences Corp. for more than $64 million.

Sequa's woeful 1993 performance was partly due to an eight-week-long suspension of operations mandated by the Federal Aviation Administration at its Chromalloy Gas Turbine Corp. unit in Orangeburg, New York. A federal investigation of the work done in this plant for the repair of jet-engine parts led to the suspension and a $5 million fine. Sequa reported a loss of $18.5 million for the second quarter of 1993 and suspended dividend payments for the foreseeable future. Its common stock, which traded as high as $85 in 1990, dipped as low as $18 that year. In August 1994 the company announced that Chromalloy Gas Turbine again was profitable. Sequa sold three Gas Turbine units in 1994 for net cash proceeds of $57.2 million.

Aerospace was Sequa's leading business segment in 1994. Gas Turbine, the company's largest operating unit, accounted for 42 percent of all sales and revenues that year. This unit was a leader in the development and use of advanced metallurgical and other processes to manufacture, repair, and coat blades, vanes, and other components of gas-turbine engines used for military and commercial jet aircraft and for other industrial purposes.

ARC Propulsion, a supplier of solid-rocket-fuel propulsion systems since 1949, accounted for ten percent of 1994 sales and revenues. This unit was a leading developer and manufacturer of advanced rocket-propulsion systems, gas generators, and auxiliary rockets. Besides propulsion systems for tactical weapons, the unit was producing small liquid-fueled rocket engines for a number of space satellite systems worldwide. The Kollsman division was supplying electro-optical and electronic systems for military weapons and was designing and manufacturing aircraft instruments and related test equipment.

Machinery and metal coatings accounted for 15 percent of the company's business in 1993. Precoat Metals, the largest Sequa unit in this business segment, was a leader in the application of protective coatings to continuous steel and aluminum coil. The Can Machinery unit included Rutherford, the world's leading manufacturer of equipment to coat and decorate two-piece beverage cans. Europe-based Materiels Equipements Graphiques was supplying equipment for web-offset printing presses.

The chief operation in the specialty-chemicals segment was Warwick International, which accounted for 12 percent of Sequa's sales and revenues in 1994. Warwick was a leading producer and supplier of TAED, a bleach activator for European powdered laundry-detergent products. Sequa Chemicals was manufacturing high-quality performance-enhancing chemicals used in the textile and graphic-arts industries. Other Sequa units were Casco Products, manufacturer of automotive cigarette lighters, power outlets, and electronic sensing devices; Northern Can Systems, manufacturer of easy-open steel lids for cans; Kollsman Manufacturing Co., Inc., a subsidiary that produced medical diagnostic instrumentation; and Centor, a real-estate holding company owning and operating, among other properties, the 18-story Chromalloy Plaza Building in Clayton, Missouri.

In 1994 Chromalloy Gas Turbine Corp. was operating more than 50 plants in 13 states and six foreign countries, of which about half were owned and the remainder leased. ARC's chief installations were two leased manufacturing plants in Gainesville, Virginia, and Camden, Arkansas. Kollsman's properties included two plants in New Hampshire and one in Wichita, Kansas. Precoat Metals owned five manufacturing facilities in Missouri, Illinois, and Mississippi. Sequa's specialty chemicals segment owned a plant in Chester, South Carolina, and two in Great Britain.

In the mid-1990s Norman E. Alexander was approaching his 40th year at the helm of the company. He was also its principal stockholder. At the end of 1992 Alexander owned 35.8 percent of Sequa's stock and controlled 49.1 percent of its voting power. Sequa's long-term debt was $590.6 million in mid-1994.

Principal Subsidiaries: Atlantic Research Corp.; Casco Products Corp.; The Centor Co.; Chromalloy Gas Turbine Corp.;

Kollsman Manufacturing Co.; Northern Can Systems, Inc.; Sequa Chemicals, Inc.; Warwick International Ltd.

Further Reading:

Bernstein, Peter W., ''Norman Alexander Just Won't Go Away,'' *Fortune,* January 28, 1980, pp. 82–85, 87.

''Clinic Tightens Family Ties,'' *Business Week,* May 15, 1954, pp. 136, 138–140.

''Holders Clear Merger of Sun Chemical Corp. and Standard Kollsman,'' *Wall Street Journal,* January 2, 1973, p. 36.

Irving, John, ''Sun Projects 6–8 Percent Growth for Pigments,'' *Journal of Commerce,* September 27, 1978, pp. 3, 5.

Kiesche, Elizabeth S., ''Sequa's Cabrey: The Art of the Sale,'' *Chemical Week,* July 4–11, 1990, pp. 50, 52.

Meier, Barry, ''Sun Chemical Will Sell Group for $550 Million,'' *Wall Street Journal,* August 19, 1986, p. 13.

Scott, Robert D., Jr., ''Sun Chemical Corporation,'' *Wall Street Transcript,* May 29, 1972, pp. 28620–21.

''Sun Begins to Shine,'' *Chemical Week,* July 9, 1966, pp. 33–34, 36, 38, 40, 42, 44.

Tanzer, Andrew, ''With Friends Like These,'' *Forbes,* June 30, 1986, pp. 31–32.

Wyatt, Edward A., ''Speaking of Dividends,'' *Barron's,* August 16, 1993, p. 46.

—Robert Halasz

Shawmut National Corporation

777 Main Street
Hartford, Connecticut 06115
U.S.A.
(203) 728-2000
Fax: (203) 240-7707

Public Company
Incorporated: 1988
Employees: 9,565
Sales: $1.07 billion
Stock Exchanges: New York
SICs: 6712 Bank Holding Companies; 6021 National Commercial Banks; 6022 State Commercial Banks

Shawmut National Corporation is one of New England's largest banking companies, offering financial products and services in consumer banking, commercial markets, investment and trust services, and financial institutions. The company focuses on the consumer market, small- to medium-sized companies, and the insurance industry. Shawmut also offers financial services to correspondent banks, state and local governments, and select niches in national markets. The 1988 merger between the Connecticut-based, $14.1 billion Hartford National Corporation and the $10.4 billion, Massachusetts-based Shawmut Corporation positioned the present company as one of the 20 largest bank holding companies in the United States. Into the 1990s, Shawmut continued to pursue strategic growth in order to remain competitive in the dog-eat-dog dynamics of the banking industry.

Shawmut's diversified portfolio of businesses fall under four main business lines. Its Consumer Banking division claimed the leading market share position in southern New England, engaging in business with more than one million households—roughly one in five households in Connecticut and Massachusetts—according to a company source in November 1994. That division's four business segments—Community Banking, Small Business Banking, the Shawmut Mortgage company, and the Installment Finance Division—satisfied the transaction, credit, savings, and investment needs of both target and mass-market consumer groups as well as small businesses.

Shawmut's Commercial Markets business line provided commercial and asset-based lending, investment, and cash management services to companies in southern New England as well as to large, national companies in selected industries.

The company's Investment Services and Trust line distributed a range of asset management and administrative services to a variety of institutional and retail customers. By 1994, Shawmut ranked number one in New England private banking. Its Personal Investment Services division was designed to establish investment relationships earlier in individuals' life cycles, then nurture relationships over time, ultimately funneling clients to Personal Trust. The Institutional Investment Services, on the other hand, competed for institutional asset management business by capitalizing on the strength of Shawmut's diverse financial services franchise.

Finally, Shawmut's Financial Institutions business line was broken down into specialized segments designed to service clients in the insurance industry, corporate trust, government finance, and correspondent banking. The Insurance Industry division provided credit and cash management services to insurance companies. Corporate Trust provided trustee and agency services to issuers of debt, while acting as claims, disbursement, exchange and ballot agent for companies in bankruptcy proceedings. Government Finance provided credit, fiscal advisory, and investment management services to state and local governments. Correspondent Banking provided check processing, selected cash management services, and other services to banks, savings and loans, cooperatives and credit unions.

These services owed much of their breadth to the February 29, 1988, merger between Shawmut Corporation and the Hartford National Corporation, which consolidated both institutions' vast assets under the single roof of the new Shawmut National Corporation. More than a doubling of means, however, the merger invested the story of Shawmut's past with dual historical roots. Thereafter, the history of Shawmut would encompass the legacy of both its Massachusetts lineage—dating back to Boston in 1836—along with its Connecticut ancestry—bringing the narrative back to Hartford in 1792. A quick survey of these dual roots sheds greater light on the recent development—and future possibilities—of the Shawmut banking tree.

The Massachusetts branch of Shawmut's history—from which the current company inherited its name—began with the founding of the Warren Bank in Boston in 1836, when operations began in a rented room on the second floor of an office building on State Street in Boston. It was a time of general economic prosperity throughout the nation; the pace of financial growth and business prosperity was matched only by the bustle of Boston's port. New schools and universities, industries, modes of transportation from shipping to railroads, and infrastructure projects all helped spur a bustling banking industry. When the federal charter of the Second Bank of the United States expired in 1836, Warren Bank was one in the flurry of new state bank charters. Within two months after the petition was submitted to the state legislature in February 1836, Warren Bank was granted a charter. Upon opening its doors for business, Warren bank competed with twenty-eight other active banks in the Boston business community.

Less than a year later, the new bank adopted the name Shawmut, beginning a long history of growth and change under that name. The Shawmut tribe of Native Americans had inhabited the pre-colonial area around Boston, describing it with the southern Algonquin word, ''Mushauwomuk,'' meaning ''broad low valley.'' Records dating back to 1630 identified the peninsula later named Boston as Shawmut. The sachem, or leader, of the Shawmut tribe was Chief Obbatinewat, whose strength and historical significance were portrayed by the Native American bust adorning all Shawmut locations, as well as by the distinctive Shawmut logo designed in the Chief's image.

The newly chartered bank's board of directors—many of whom were influential figures in the insurance industry—elected as president their respected colleague, Benjamin T. Reed, a director of the Warren insurance company, Central Wharf merchant, treasurer of the newly established Eastern Railroad, former Whig legislator, and colleague of the bank's founder, John L. Dimmock. With the aid of Thomas Drown as his hand-picked cashier, and other associates, the fledgling bank seemed well positioned for a promising future.

Any early success for Shawmut was quickly hampered by the Panic of 1837, which precipitated the failure of numerous banks and other businesses in quick succession. As lending risks skyrocketed, specie assumed premium value, and notes plummeted, driving the banking industry into a hole. Of the 126 Massachusetts banks operating at the outset of the Panic, 23 had gone out of business within seven years. Shawmut suffered with the rest, but managed to survive, thanks in part to Reed's insistence on joining the Associated Banks of Boston, an ad hoc group of banks that agreed to accept each other's notes in order to uphold bank credit and avoid bank rushes. After braving the general recession that lingered into the mid-1840s, Reed began pushing for expansion, moving Shawmut into larger offices in 1846 and fostering steady—if not astronomical—growth until his resignation in 1847.

Reed's immediate successors steered Shawmut on a path of steady growth into the mid-1850s. John Gardner, elected president in May 1848, developed Shawmut's interests in the burgeoning wool and cotton trade. When the discovery of gold in California sent shock waves through a financial community closely geared to the value of specie, Gardner maintained conservative banking practices at Shawmut. By the time he resigned his post in 1853, his successor, Albert Fearing, was on steady ground. Though Fearing's 20-month term was the shortest in the bank's history, he engineered Shawmut's first capital increase, raising $250,000 in less than eight months. When Fearing resigned to join a competing firm in November 1854, Shawmut had taken its first big steps toward the terrain of big banks.

By the mid 1850, bankers had started seeking new solutions to bank problems; the rising use of checks drawn against demand deposits, for example, called for new procedures to replace the entrenched system of note redemption. Meanwhile, the prevalent Suffolk System of note redemption—by which Suffolk Bank enjoyed disproportionate benefits from its role as middleman in the note-redemption services of all Massachusetts banks—was under strain. In March 1856, Shawmut joined 29 city banks in the Boston Clearing House, an operation designed to provide a more efficient and safer method of clearing checks.

The Civil War was the straw that finally broke the back of the old banking system. Abraham Lincoln's secretary of the Treasury, Salmon P. Chase, enacted legislation to change the banking system so that the federal government could more efficiently raise funds for the war effort. Chase proposed a system of national banks that would operate under federal law and that could issue national bank notes to serve as United States currency. From 1863 to 1865, Congress enacted three National Bank Acts to that effect, each consecutively giving federally chartered banks more autonomy. On November 22, 1864, the Comptroller of the Currency in Washington, D.C., issued Shawmut's federal charter, initiating a period of reorganization and, ultimately, of growth for Shawmut under the management of William Branhall.

From the late 1860s until the turn of the century, Shawmut continued to grow under the presidency of John C. Cummings, Jr., as the banking industry in general moved from the post-Civil-War period and into the era of modern banking. The effects of the civil war dominated banking priorities for well over a decade. Major concerns remained reducing inflation and controlling the stock of money in circulation. Meanwhile, the seeds of modern banking began to sprout, as deposits and investments grew steadily in tandem with rapid industrial development. Shawmut's loans grew in diversity and size, railroad securities became keystones in its portfolio, and the bank's services expanded beyond local markets. In 1893 the Shawmut board of directors appointed James P. Stearns to the newly created post of vice-president. Cummings needed all the help he could get, as the nation fell into a panic-driven depression that year, driving key railroads out of business and sending tremors through the entire financial market. Though these and other rigors—such as the Spanish-American War—strained Shawmut, the bank held up relatively well: by 1897, Shawmut's capital had swelled to $1 million, with more than $9 million in deposits.

The turn of the century marked an unprecedented period of mergers in the banking industry as industrial growth reached new and, at times unmanageable, levels. Under the direction of Stearns, who became president in 1898, Shawmut joined the bandwagon and enjoyed rapid growth through acquisitions. In 1897 a surfeit of national banks in the Boston area had resulted in a flat market, prompting savings institutions and investors to seek a demand-driven remedy. The private investment firm of Kidder, Peabody and Company helped organize a merger of several of Boston's key banks—including Boston National, Hamilton National, Market National, and many others, including Shawmut. In October 1898, it was announced that Shawmut would be the successor bank; and a month later, Shawmut effected a reorganization whereby the Shawmut National Bank liquidated its assets and was rechartered as the National Shawmut Bank, with capital of $3 million. Such an enormous leap in size afforded Shawmut a wholly new level of power to continue its expansion. Until 1907, the bank did just that, benefiting from alliances with other financial institutions such as Kidder, Peabody, and delving into new markets such as foreign investments, utilities, and mines.

Though Shawmut had grown into a market leader, it was far from immune to the Panic of 1907, which fell on the heels of the famous run on the Knickerbocker Trust Company of New York. While institutions hoarded their assets in reaction to money shortages and a panicky demand for gold, many banks demanded payments of loans from even their most reliable clients.

Shawmut's president, William A. Gaston, resisted panic, working instead in cooperation with federal regulators in the formulation of national policies that would regulate the banking industry and, in the long term, benefit Shawmut. These initiatives included the Federal Reserve Act, which established the Federal Reserve System and enlarged the scope of national banks. In addition, with the involvement of the United States in World War I, Shawmut supported Liberty Loan Act bond drives and pushed for developments in international finance that ultimately led to Shawmut's Foreign Department.

Postwar peace afforded time for consolidation, adjustment, and rapid economic growth (the so-called era of "good times"), conditions that Alfred L. Aiken's administration embraced with zeal. In *Shawmut: 150 Years of Banking 1836–1986,* Asa S. Knowles described Aiken as "a president of promotional and salesmanship skills." Indeed, under his tenure during the 1920s, Shawmut augmented its Savings Department and its Foreign Department; organized the Shawmut Bank Investment Trust; shared profits with management; merged with the Citizens National Bank; and in May 1929, entered into an agreement with Kidder, Peabody and Co. to underwrite the issue of 200,000 shares at the new $25 par value, crowning the bank's remarkable trajectory of growth.

The bank's path toward success over the next three decades encountered some rocky spots, as well. In order to survive the Depression, Shawmut not only absorbed substantial loan losses, but also cut back on expenses, such as discontinuation of the 1926 Plan for Additional Compensation for Executive Management. Even with the reassurance of the Federal Reserve system and the Reconstruction Finance Corporation (implemented under President Hoover), Shawmut was not immune to worsening conditions that led to panic and an industrywide run on banks in 1933. A series of responses and regulatory moves ensued, including The Bank Holiday, which forced Shawmut to temporarily close on March 3, 1933; The Banking Act of 1933, which restricted bank activity and forced Shawmut National Bank to divest itself of the Shawmut Corporation; the establishment of the Federal Deposit Insurance Corporation, which required Shawmut and all other banks in the Federal Reserve System to become members by January 1, 1934; and other regulatory measures.

Just as Shawmut began adjusting to the changes and regulations spawned by the Depression, World War II brought a whole new set of challenges and opportunities. Starting in the latter half of 1939, industrial production skyrocketed. Shawmut engaged in several new lines of business, from government securities and obligations and deposits, to V (later VT) loans used by contractors to fill war orders. From 1939 to 1945, Shawmut's assets had grown from more than $229 million to well over $462 million.

The early 1950s saw the advent of a new era, as Walter Borden assumed presidency of Shawmut. During the postwar era, Shawmut's activities reflected rapid growth in the national economy, a new character in New England commerce, and the need to expand the both the scope of banking services and their geographical range.

The late 1950s and early 1960s marked years of transition for Shawmut. Horace Schermerhorn's administration was responsible for expanding the loan and trust operations of Shawmut, promoting the growth of the Association, and developing the status of Shawmut as a Boston, state, and regional force.

Many of Shermerhorn's initiatives set the ground for the establishment of Shawmut Association, Inc., the most momentous development of the 1960s and early 1970s at Shawmut. Lawrence H. Martin, president from 1962 to 1972, was instrumental in reshaping the Shawmut public image and drafting the blueprint that would define the bank as a diversified holding company. In 1965 the loosely grouped Association became the Shawmut Association, Inc., a bank holding company that controlled all the Association banks and National Shawmut itself. That same year, the Board of Directors of National Shawmut approved the establishment of a separate international division that would be known as the Shawmut International Corporation. By the end of 1971, assets of the National Shawmut Bank alone had reached $1.37 billion.

The 1970s posed a new set of challenges, as the United States fell into a recession that endured a good part of the decade. The Arab Oil embargo of 1973 underlined the fragility of global markets, while rampant inflation added to the tremors that were felt throughout the banking industry. At Shawmut, D. Thomas Trigg's administration faced these difficulties by diversifying beyond New England and emphasizing efficient deployment of personnel. Many of the changes that were implemented during his presidency, from 1972 to 1980, helped position Shawmut for its 1988 merger with Hartford National Corp. to catapult its leadership beyond regional markets and into the ranks of a national leader among bank holding companies.

Strategic moves included expansion of marketing, with the establishment of the Market Research Division in 1972; more aggressive loan practices; and technological advances in electronic data processing and the implementation of Customer Account Processing Services (CAPS) in the late 1970s. In 1975 Shawmut Association, Inc. was renamed Shawmut Corporation, and its expansion of banking operations continued in the form of mergers with bank holding companies rather than the simpler acquisition of independent banks.

These and other initiatives paid off: total corporation assets reached $3.4 billion by the end of 1980, giving Shawmut the momentum it would use to continue expanding through the 1980s.

That expansion culminated in Shawmut Corporation's 1988 merger with Hartford National Corporation, with its own historical narrative dating back to the founding of the Hartford National Bank in 1792—the fifth bank to be chartered in the United States. The young bank grew at a steady pace and made several key acquisitions before the Depression. In 1915 Hartford National Bank merged with Aetna National Bank (established in 1792) into Hartford-Aetna National Bank. Under the National Bank Act of 1923, Hartford National Bank & Trust Co. was formed through a consolidation of Hartford-Aetna National Bank and the United States Security Trust Co.

The bank managed to survive the Depression and continued to expand through acquisitions from the early 1930s to the 1950s. Bankers Trust Co. was merged in 1933. The July 1949 merger with First National Bank of Hartford set the stage for an impressive series of mergers and acquisitions in the 1950s and early 1960s: East Hartford Trust Co. (1950); National Bank of Commerce and New London City National Bank (1953); Connecticut River Banking Company and Travelers Bank & Trust Company (1954); Uncas-Merchants National Bank of Norwich, Central National Bank & Trust Co., and Middletown National Bank (1955); Windsor Trust Co. (1956); Torrington National Bank & Trust Co. (1958); First National Bank (1960); and Cargill Trust Co. (1964).

In 1968 the bank effected a plan of reorganization which established the holding company, Hartford National Corp., as the umbrella that would cover the growing number of affiliates in the Hartford financial family. During most of the 1970s, Hartford was battered by economic recession, and, in 1975, by a drop in real estate shares (REITs) that lost one-third of total assets.

In 1982 Connecticut National Bank of Bridgeport merged into Hartford National Bank, which then changed its name to Connecticut Bank to become Hartford National Corp.'s biggest subsidiary for the remainder of the decade. Other key mergers and acquisitions of the 1980s included Mattatuck Bank & Trust Co. (1983); FirstBancorp., whose three subsidiaries became part of Connecticut National Bank (1984); Seymour Trust Co. (1985); Provident Institution for Savings, First BanCorporation, First New England Bankshares Corp., and Peoples Bank (1986).

By the mid-1980s, Hartford National Corp. could look back on the losses of the 1970s and the recuperation of the early 1980s and consider itself a "bunch of survivors," according to Robert L. Newell, chairman and CEO, in a December 1984 *United States Banker* article. Newell and President Joel B. Alvord—who would become president of Shawmut after the 1988 merger—teamed up for aggressive but conservative growth, aspiring to keep balance sheets "elegantly balanced."

With the passage of regional interstate banking legislation in 1985, Hartford National's "elegance" made the bank holding company a perfect match for a merger with Shawmut, springing both parties into the ring with the heavyweights of banking on a national scale. And once Alvord had taken the helm as chairman at the newly formed Shawmut National Corp. (with Gunner S. Overstrom named president and chief operating officer in August 1988) his fighting skills were promptly put to the test. By 1988, problem assets peaked at $1.7 billion, placing Shawmut on the list of banks regulators deemed doomed to fail. Overstrom set about aggressively realigning the company to better compete in its key strategic markets.

For all his good intentions and experience at Hartford National, Alvord was faced with a tough beginning at Shawmut. In March 1990, he and other top officials of the company were charged in a shareholder lawsuit with artificially inflating the bank's earnings during 1989 and concealing evidence that its loan portfolio had substantially suffered. By the end of that month, Shawmut said that the examination by Federal banking regulators had prompted it to revise its 1989 earning to show a loss of $129.9 million, in stark contrast to the profit of $201.7 million reported in January of that year. Still, the bank began a plan to cushion additional losses by trimming expenses, and to temporarily reduce its quarterly dividend and its overall size. By most accounts, in a banking environment where the ability to keep growing through acquisitions meant life or death, Shawmut's slip could have spelled disaster. "The longer Shawmut stays in the doghouse, the more opportunities will be missed. A New England bank that cannot make acquisitions is likely to be sold," said Kidder, Peabody & Co. banking analyst George Bicher.

Shawmut took several steps to regain its lost balance. In 1990 assets were reduced from $28 billion to $24 billion, and the following year its credit card business was sold at a gain of $68 million. The company consolidated banking subsidiaries from 12 down to 3 in 1990. It also conformed to more rigorous regulations, such as those governing lending practices, credit review, liquidity planning, and management of information systems.

In the middle of 1991, Shawmut and Bank of Boston Corp. began intense negotiations for a merger that would have created new England's largest financial institution. After Bank of Boston issued an ultimatum to accept or reject the plan in January 1992, Shawmut called it quits. While some analysts regarded Shawmut's decision as a sign of renewed confidence and the ability to compete on its own, others considered the rejection a lost opportunity to begin a whole new era of growth. "By rejecting Bank of Boston's offer, Alvord and Shawmut's board are gambling that the bank's fortunes, and the region's economy, will improve enough that they might get a better offer from another bank sometime in the future," wrote Doug Bailey in the *Boston Globe*.

Alvord's gamble in turning down the Bank of Boston deal proved prescient, as Shawmut's continued recovery over the following two years led to numerous advantageous acquisitions. One of the first steps in that recovery process was a realignment of the organization's management team, with Alvord placing new executives in key positions, including David L. Eyles as vice-chairman and chief credit policy officer in February 1992.

In 1993 Shawmut continued to bolster its strength. Several product introductions attracted new business, including the introduction of seven mutual funds through branches (February); a certificate of deposit with a return linked to the performance of the S&P 500 (March); the Shawmut Target Investment Plan, a goal-oriented savings program matching customers' long-term goals to specific savings schedules. That year, Shawmut also made definite agreements to acquire the following banks: New Dartmouth Bank of Manchester; Peoples Bancorp of Worcester, Massachusetts; and Gateway Financial of Norwalk, Connecticut. Finally, that same year, Connecticut National Bank—Shawmut's largest bank subsidiary—changed its name and more than 1,000 branch signs to Shawmut Bank in order to more closely associate the bank with the parent company. These and other strategic changes paid off: in October 1993, Shawmut reported a third-quarter profit of $71.1 million, more than five times the earnings for the same period of the previous year.

The number of banks acquired in 1993 paled in comparison to the flood of acquisitions—and potential income boosts—of 1994. Those acquisitions and purchases included 10 branches of Northeast Savings located in eastern Massachusetts and Rhode

Island; Cohasset Savings Bank of Cohasset, Massachusetts; West Newton Savings Bank of West Newton, Massachusetts; Northeast Savings Bank of Hartford, Connecticut; Guardian Bank, FSB, of Boca Raton, Florida; the Processing Services Division of Poorman-Douglas Corporation, Portland, Oregon; Barclays Business Credit of Glastonbury, Connecticut; and Old Stone Trust Company based of Providence, Rhode Island. In all, concluded or announced agreements for the year increased Shawmut's asset base by $10 billion, according to a company report.

Not all Shawmut's deals proceeded as smoothly as planned, though. In the summer of 1994, the corporation agreed to buy out Northeast Federal Corp. in a $172 million stock-swap arrangement. As Shawmut's stock prices skidded to from late 1994 into the beginning of 1995, however, their low prices triggered a provision in the agreement permitting Northeast to call off the deal. Well into 1995, Shawmut's stock showed continued volatility and the company refused to sweeten its deal, casting uncertain light on the future of the deal.

Meanwhile, the Shawmut's Northeast dealings were overshadowed by one of the most momentous merger arrangements in the organization's history: on February 12, 1995, Shawmut announced an agreement to merge with the Fleet Financial Group, an agreement that would create one of the ten largest banking companies in the nation, with more than $80 billion in assets. The merger, expected to be completed in the fourth quarter of 1995, would impose widespread change throughout Shawmut, with projections that almost ten percent of the total workforce of the two banks would be cut in a restructuring that would cost up to $400 million. The group's new name would be Fleet Financial Group, centered in Boston.

Many analysts hailed the news as the beginning of a strong new era for Shawmut. John Carusone, president of the Hartford-based Bank Analysis Center told *Journal Inquirer,* that Northeast shareholders should be ecstatic, as the Shawmut stock they receive as part of the takeover deal should see a jump start from the Fleet deal. Beyond the effect on Northeast shareholders, the effect on the Shawmut National Corp. at large would remain shady—though promising—until the new entity had time to sort out its reorganization and adapt to a rapidly changing financial marketplace. One thing remained certain: Shawmut's trademark logo of Chief Obbatinewat would ride into the 21st century on a much bigger monetary horse than the Chief, or any of Shawmut's legacy of leaders, could have imagined.

Principal Subsidiaries: Hartford National Corp.; Shawmut Trust Co.; Shawmut National Trust Co.; Shawmut Corp.; Shawmut Investment Advisers, Inc.; Shawmut New Hampshire Corp.; Shawmut Bank NH; Shawmut Bank Connecticut, National Association; Shawmut Mortgage Co.; Shawmut Brokerage, Inc.; Shawmut Trust Company of Rhode Island; Shawmut Capital Corp.; Shawmut Bank, National Association; Shawmut Bank, FSB.

Further Reading:

A Background and Information Guide to Shawmut National Corporation and *The Shawmut Fact Book, November, 1994,* Boston: Shawmut National Corporation, 1994.

Bailey, Doug, "Investors Sue Shawmut for Misstatement," *Boston Globe,* March 15, 1990, p. 49.

——, "Shawmut Rejects Merger with Bank of Boston; The Merger That Wasn't," *Boston Globe,* January 16, 1992, p. 1.

Blanton, Kimberly, "Price Dispute Stalls Shawmut's Buyout of Northeast Federal," *Boston Globe,* January 12, 1995, p. 34.

Carey, Mary Agnes, "The Signs, They Are A-Changin'," *Hartford Courant,* July 28, 1992, p. D1.

"Connecticut National Bank to Launch Intensive Advertising Campaign Announcing Name Change to Shawmut," *PR Newswire,* December 28, 1992.

Cranmore, J. J., "The Fleet-Shawmut Merger: Breaking New Banking Ground," *Connecticut Law Tribune,* May 15, 1995, p. 26.

Faust, William H., and Arthur Eilerston, "You've Got a Logo, You Need a Brand," *ABA Banking Journal,* October, 1994, p. 86.

"Fleet to Buy Shawmut—Creates One of Ten Biggest U.S. Banks," *Deutsche Press-Agentur,* February 21, 1995.

French, Howard, "The 'Other' Deal Is Still On: Merger Won't Affect Shawmut's Plan to Buy Out Northeast Federal," *Journal Inquirer,* February 22, 1995, p. A1.

Gold, Jacqueline S., "CEO Has Resilient Shawmut Poised to Either Swallow or Be Swallowed," *American Banker,* February 4, 1994, p. 4.

Johnson, Joanne, "Shawmut Profit up Fivefold," *Hartford Courant,* October 14, 1993, p. C1.

Knowles, Asa S., *Shawmut: 150 Years of Banking 1836–1986,* Boston: Houghton Mifflin Company, 1986, 517 p.

Quint, Michael, "New Report Shows Loss at Shawmut," *New York Times,* March 22, 1990, p. D1.

Roberts, Paul Craig, "The Fed's Sham Settlement with Shawmut," *Business Week,* January 24, 1994, p. 22.

"Shawmut National Corporation Announces Introduction of Shawmut Mutual Funds," *PR Newswire,* February 23, 1993.

"Shawmut Strives for Fed Approval," *Regulatory Compliance Watch,* May 9, 1994, Vol. 4, No. 18, p. 4.

Wade, Alan, "Hartford's Elegant Balance," *United States Banker,* December 1984, p. 43.

Zuckoff, Mitchell, "Shawmut Bolsters Top Team," *Boston Globe,* February 11, 1992, p. 41.

—Kerstan Cohen

The Sherwin-Williams Company

101 Prospect Avenue, Northwest
Cleveland, Ohio 44115-1075
U.S.A.
(216) 5662000
Fax: (216) 5663310

Public Company
Incorporated: 1884
Employees: 17,886
Sales: $3.1 billion
Stock Exchanges: New York
SICs: 2851 Paints & Allied Products; 5231 Paint, Glass & Wallpaper Stores

The Sherwin-Williams Company, ''America's Paint Company,'' is the largest producer of paints, varnishes, and specialty coatings in the United States. It also produces related home improvement items, motor vehicle finishes, and refinish products, as well as industrial finishes for original equipment manufacturers of metal, plastic, and wood products. Its products are sold through 2,046 company-operated stores, as well as mass merchants, independent paint and hardware stores, and a direct sales staff.

The story of The Sherwin-Williams Company began in 1866, when Henry Sherwin used his life savings of $2,000 to buy a partnership in the Truman Dunham Company of Ohio. The firm was a distributor of pigments, painting supplies, oils, and glass. In four years, this original partnership was dissolved, and Sherwin organized a paint business with new partners, Edward P. Williams and A. T. Osborn. The new business was called Sherwin-Williams & Company. In 1873 the company purchased its first factory, on the Cuyahoga River in Cleveland, Ohio. The factory manufactured paste paints, oil colors, and putty. The company's first manufactured product, Guaranteed Strictly Pure Raw Umber in Oil, came off the line in that year.

In the paint industry in the 1870s, painters had to buy the ingredients and mix their own paint each day. At this time prepared paints—paints that were ready-mixed—were concocted and sold by individual dealers who mixed a few popular colors. These premixed paints were available only during the busy spring painting season. Moreover, in those days, oil and pigment had to be ground together into a paste. The paste was then thinned with more oil, thinners, and dryers. Customers brought their own containers to stores and filled them as needed. Paints had to be stirred continuously to prevent the pigment from sinking to the bottom of the container. In addition, the paint had to be used quickly or it dried out. For these reasons, paints were seldom shipped far from where they were made. The first patent for ready-mixed paint was taken out in 1867 by D.R. Averill of Newburg, Ohio, improving upon the existing mixing processes.

In 1877, Sherwin-Williams & Company developed the first patented reclosable paint can. This revolutionized the way paint could be used, and more importantly, reused over a period of time. During the 1880s the company continued to develop new products for the paint industry. At the beginning of the decade it improved its liquid paint formula. After two years of test marketing under the Osborn label, it introduced SWP—Sherwin-Williams Paint—the first mixed paint to receive considerable public acceptance.

In 1884 the partnership was dissolved and Sherwin and Williams incorporated as The Sherwin-Williams Company. In the same year, Inside Floor Paint was introduced. This new product encouraged the notion that specific paints should be used for specific purposes. During 1884, Percy Neyman was hired by Sherwin-Williams as the first paint chemist in the industry. Neyman contributed greatly to Sherwin-Williams research and development of new products for the paint industry.

Sherwin-Williams had always been committed to finding and developing new markets for paint products. In 1888, the company saw the possibility of marketing paints and coatings to the railroad industry. It opened a manufacturing facility in Chicago to serve the Pullman Company, and to better serve the farm-implement and carriage industries. In those days, Pullman required as many as 20 coats of highquality finishes for the elaborate interiors of the Pullman cars. Sherwin hired George A. Martin, an ambitious young man, to run the new facility. Martin later served as the third president of the company.

Marketing and advertising quickly became critical to the growing company. Seeing the need to make people aware of its products, in 1890 the company formed a department devoted exclusively to advertising and to publicizing Sherwin-Williams and its products. George Ford was hired to head the department. A year later, a sales agency was opened in Worcester, Massachusetts, which was the model for the company's successful concept of the ''company store.'' In 1905, the ''Cover the Earth'' trademark was first introduced.

Walter H. Cottingham became the second president of the company in 1909. Sherwin then became chairman of the board of directors. Cottingham strove throughout his career to inspire his workers to attain their maximum potential. Cottingham was adept at launching successful sales campaigns. He was also known as a writer and orator and wrote a collection of ''inspirational'' editorials and papers on a variety of subjects.

In the early part of the 20th century Sherwin-Williams began acquiring other companies to meet the increasing demand for a variety of different paints and related products. In 1917, under Cottingham's guidance, the company bought the Martin-Senour Company, of Chicago. Three years later, in 1920, the company went public, selling $15 million in preferred stock. Proceeds from the sale were used to purchase the Acme Quality Paint Company, of Detroit; a new plant in Oakland, California; and to expand various existing facilities.

When Cottingham retired in 1922, Martin—who had become vice-president and general manager in 1920—took over the leadership of the company. During Martin's tenure as president, Sherwin-Williams developed nitro-cellulose lacquer and synthetic enamel. These products made possible the brilliant finishes that covered cars during the 1920s. Such products also reduced from 21 days to a few hours the drying time of newly painted cars.

George A. Martin, like Cottingham, believed in strong advertising for his company and its products. He sponsored the "Metropolitan Opera Auditions of the Air," a successful radio program that ran for years. Also during Martin's presidency, Sherwin-Williams bought several other high-quality, nationally known companies. Among them were The Lowe Brothers Company, of Dayton, Ohio, and The John Lucas Company, of Philadelphia. Both were innovative companies.

Martin's vision focused on finding ways to expand the company and increase its profits. He believed that Latin Americans would respond favorably to high-quality paint products. In 1929 Sherwin-Williams bought the Bredell Paint Company of Havana and enlarged it. Martin expanded the company's manufacturing facilities and established plants in Buenos Aires and Sao Paulo.

For Sherwin-Williams, the early 1940s brought an opportunity to participate heavily in America's World War II effort. Sherwin-Williams, along with other paint companies, supplied camouflage paints for the armed forces, and it was said that the U.S. invasion of North Africa was delayed while waiting for the delivery of camouflage paints with which to provide proper field cover. The company also received a commission to load shells, anti-tank mines, and aerial bombs. To meet this demand, the company constructed and managed a plant in Carbondale, Illinois.

In 1940, Arthur W. Steudel, a Cleveland native, succeeded Martin as president. Steudel worked his way up in the company through the dye, chemical, and color division. He had many visionary ideas about paint retailing and merchandising, and the company's profits increased under Steudel. He served as president until 1961, at which time he became chairman and chief executive officer.

Sherwin-Williams continued to introduce new products to the consumer during this time. Kem-Tone, the first emulsion-based, fast-drying paint for the do-it-yourself market was introduced in 1941 and met with remarkable success. Kem-Tone helped deal with the raw material shortage that the nation faced after the war. That same year, the company introduced the Roller-Koater, the first applicator that was not a brush and was later developed and refined into the paint roller commonly used today. Soon thereafter, the company introduced Kem-Glo, a porcelain-like enamel and Super Kem-Tone, a high-quality interior paint that had a synthetic rubber content. The prefix "Kem" indicated that the paints were "chemically involved materials." Product development, crucial to the expansion and success of the company, continued into the 1960s, as the company gained a new president, E. Colin Baldwin, and was listed for the first time on the New York Stock Exchange in 1964. In 1971 Sherwin-Williams introduced POLANE, a coating designed to efficiently cover metal surfaces but found to work exceedingly well on plastics as well.

In the 1970s, however, the company began to experience substantial losses. In 1977, on revenues of $1 billion, Sherwin-Williams reported a loss of $8.2 million. Dividends were suspended, and the company's borrowings increased dramatically during this time. In the period from 1967 through 1978, in fact, Sherwin-Williams's long-term debt increased from zero to $242 million. In addition, by 1978 Gulf & Western Industries held 13.47 percent of Sherwin-Williams' outstanding stock, and rumors of a takeover loomed.

Shifts in management also occurred. Walter O. Spencer, CEO since 1971, resigned in 1978 and was replaced, on an interim basis, by William C. Fine. The company found a new permanent leader in January 1979, when John G. Breen, formerly an executive vice-president for Gould Inc., a Minneapolis battery manufacturer, became president and CEO. In a short time, Breen managed to bring the company back to financial stability and avert the threatened Gulf & Western takeover. Breen first persuaded Gulf & Western Chairman Charles Bludhorn to sell his company's Sherwin-Williams shares, convincing Bludhorn that Gulf & Western's holdings were a liability and that Sherwin-Williams would be unable to recover financially while the threat of takeover loomed. Bludhorn was likely swayed to a greater extent by the fact that his Sherwin-Williams shares were no longer a sound investment. Next, Breen reshuffled Sherwin-Williams management, replacing several vice-presidents, decentralizing responsibility, and discontinuing about 1,000 slow-selling products. Breen also cut the company's long-term debt. In the first half of 1980, Breen's policies yielded a 57 percent improvement in earnings over the same period the year before. In 1979, Sherwin-Williams sales were $1.19 billion, and by 1985 they had reached $2.17 billion. Moreover, net income rose from six cents to $1.60 per share between 1978 and 1985. Breen served as president until 1986, when he became chairman, retaining the office of CEO. Thomas A. Commes became president.

Acquisitions in the 1980s included the popular Dutch Boy line of paints and its manufacturing facilities, as well as Dupli-Color Products Company, which specialized in automotive paints. In 1984, to reach markets outside the continental United States, the company entered into a partnership known as BAPCO with C-I-L, Inc. of Canada, a subsidiary of England's Imperial Chemical Industries PLC. The new concern was eventually acquired in its entirety by C-I-L, as Sherwin-Williams gradually divested its chemical operations.

During this time, sales of house paints decreased, due largely to the use of alternative surface finishes, such as pre-finished aluminum and plastic surfaces, in the construction of homes. Sherwin-Williams responded to this trend by going after market share and substantially increasing its advertising budget from $4 million in 1989 to $125 million in 1990. This strategy was well-timed, as increasingly popular discount and home decorating chains that catered to the do-it-yourself market preferred to rely on one or two major suppliers that sold national brands and provided national distribution, rather than hundreds of smaller, local paint companies.

Moreover, in 1990 Sherwin-Williams added the well-known Krylon and Illinois Bronze lines of aerosol paints to its holdings. And with the 1990 purchase of the architectural coatings business of DeSoto, Inc., Sherwin-Williams gained its biggest chunk of market share. It paid $67 million for the business, which traced its roots back to 1910 and eventually became as one of the largest paint manufacturers in the country, supplying private label paints for such chains as Sears and Home Depot. The addition of DeSoto made Sherwin-Williams the world's largest supplier of custom paints for the private-label market. The following year, the company purchased the Cuprinol brand name of premium stains, liquid sealers, and other coatings products from the Darworth Company of Connecticut, as well as two coatings business units from Cook Paint and Varnish Company.

The acquisitions paid off well for Sherwin-Williams. According to a 1992 article in *Business Week,* industry sales fell 0.2 percent in 1991, due to national economic recession, but revenues at Sherwin-Williams were up 2.9 percent, excluding acquisitions. For the first two quarters of 1991, in fact, the company's profits climbed 23 percent to $68 million on sales of $1.37 billion. As Sherwin-Williams celebrated its 125th anniversary that year, it had become one of only a few companies to lead its chosen industry for more than a century.

By 1993, Sherwin-Williams was reporting earnings of $165 million on sales of $2.9 billion, and its balance sheet was almost debt-free. Indeed, in the 15 years since Breen took over, revenues more than doubled, while profits increased almost tenfold. In new product development, the company introduced Ever-Clean, a premium latex interior wall paint with superior stain resistance and washability characteristics. The new paint was launched in 1994 as part of a national advertising campaign which was the largest in the company's history. Also that year, Sherwin-Williams acquired the assets of The Old Quaker Paint Company for an undisclosed amount. This purchase brought Sherwin-Williams into the residential construction market of southern California.

To support the company's growth and keep its operations running at top performance, Sherwin-Williams had a software designer help develop an automated control system for its distribution centers. Known as the Automated Warehouse Control System (AWCS), the system became fully operational in all its distribution centers in 1994. Using bar-code technology and portable radio frequency, it significantly improved the efficiency and accuracy of processing orders. For example, workers received electronic orders via a hand-held machine incorporating a radio, a computer terminal, and a scanner. The computer sent orders ranking each tasks priority and recalculated the list each time a task was completed. When trucks were unloading at the warehouse, the computer determined where to put the goods based on what space was free at that moment, eliminating the need to hold a particular slot empty until a truck was unloaded.

The early and mid-1990s saw a decline in new housing starts and thus proved challenging to the construction and building materials industries. Sherwin-Williams, along with most companies competing in that business sector, felt the effects in the form of reduced stock prices. Nevertheless, Sherwin-Williams remained in a strong financial position; having avoided long-term debt and gained market share, the company was able to respond effectively to the shifting economic environment and was still intent on serving as ''America's Paint Company.''

Principal Subsidiaries: Contract Transportation Systems Co.; Dupli-Color Products Company; Sherwin-Williams International Company; DIMC, Inc.; Interiors Guild, Inc.; MTM Development Corporation; Sherwin-Williams Acceptance Corporation; SWIMC, Inc.; Sherwin-Williams Canada, Inc.; 147926 Canada Inc.; The Sherwin-Williams Co. Resources Limited (Jamaica); Sherwin-Williams (Caribbean) N.V. (Curaçao); Sherwin-Williams (West Indies) Ltd. (Jamaica); Sherwin-Williams Foreign Sales Corporation Limited (Virgin Islands); Sherwin-Williams do Brasil Industria e Comercio Ltda. (Brazil); Compañia Sherwin-Williams, S.A. de C.V. (Mexico); Sherwin-Williams Cayman Islands Ltd. (Grand Cayman).

Further Reading:

Dyer, Davis and Kathleen McDermott, *America's Paint Company: A History of Sherwin-Williams,* Cambridge, Mass.: Winthrop Group, Inc., 1991, 109 p.

Feldman, Amy, ''The House that Jack Rebuilt,'' *Forbes,* April 25, 1994, pp. 91–93.

Harrison, Kimberly P., ''Sherwin-Williams to Stash $250MM for Acquisitions,'' *Crain's Cleveland Business,* September 27, 1993, p. 1.

Madigan, Kathleen, ''Masters of the Game: CEOs Who Succeed in Business When Times are Really Trying,'' *Business Week,* October 12, 1992, pp. 110–16.

Schlenberg, Fred, ''Cleveland, Part I: 'Not Just Great, But the Greatest','' *American Paint & Coatings Journal,* January 5, 1987.

——, ''Cleveland, Part II: Sherwin, Williams . . . and Fenn,'' *American Paint & Coatings Journal,* January 19, 1987.

——, ''Cleveland, Part III: Era of the Empire Builders,'' *American Paint & Coatings Journal,* February 2, 1987.

''Sherwin-Williams Acquires Old Quaker Paint Co.,'' *American Paint & Coatings Journal,* September 12, 1994, p. 17.

Shingler, Dan, ''Cash-Rich Sherwin Ripe for Deal-Making,'' *Crain's Cleveland Business,* May 29, 1995, p. 2.

—Virginia L. Smiley
updated by Beth Watson Highman

ShowBiz Pizza Time, Inc.

4441 West Airport Freeway
P.O. Box 152077
Irving, Texas 75015
U.S.A.
(214) 258-8507
Fax: (214) 258-8545

Public Company
Incorporated: 1980
Employees: 14,000
Sales: $267.8 million
Stock Exchanges: NASDAQ
SICs: 5812 Eating Places; 6794 Patent Owners & Lessors

ShowBiz Pizza Time, Inc. is the only child-oriented restaurant entertainment chain in the United States; it's slogan is "Where a kid can be a kid." Aimed at families with children between the ages of two and 12, the restaurants augment a pizza and sandwich menu with games, rides, and animated musical and comic entertainment. Stage shows feature life-size, computer-controlled robotic characters, the most famous of which is Chuck E. Cheese, the chain's rodent mascot. As of March 1995, ShowBiz operated a system of 328 Chuck E. Cheese's restaurants in 45 states, with 1994 sales of $267.8 million. Of the restaurants, 227 were company operated; the other 101 were run by franchisees. In 1994, ShowBiz sold its 27 Monterey's Tex-Mex Cafe restaurants as part of a repositioning effort in the face of increased competition and decreased revenues.

The history of ShowBiz Pizza Time, Inc. follows two companies, each operating a chain of pizza/entertainment centers. The first company, Pizza Time Theatre Inc., operated Chuck E. Cheese's Pizza Time Theatre outlets between 1977 and 1984. The second company, ShowBiz Pizza Time Inc., operated ShowBiz Pizza Place outlets. ShowBiz Pizza Time's parent company, Brock Hotel Corp., purchased Pizza Time Theatre in 1984 and operated ShowBiz and Chuck E. Cheese's outlets under its ShowBiz Pizza Time division until 1988 when it spun off that division. ShowBiz Pizza Time became a publicly traded company in 1989.

The concept for the novel mixture of games, pizza and electronic animals originated with Nolan Bushnell, the founder of Atari video games. In the mid-1970s, teenagers were flocking to game arcades to test their reflexes on the latest craze: video games. The revenues generated by the quarters slotted into those games were huge, and, according to a 1982 *Fortune* article, Bushnell "wanted to operate and take in those quarters." But he wanted something different than the typical game arcade. He came up with the idea of using the games to fill the 20-minute wait for a pizza order to be prepared. By banning unaccompanied teenagers and adding automated entertainers for younger children, he hoped to attract families and avoid having the pizza entertainment centers turn into teenage hangouts.

The Warner Corporation agreed to build one restaurant after buying Atari from Bushnell for $28 million in 1976. The first Chuck E. Cheese's Pizza Time Theatre opened in May 1977, in San Jose, California, as a division of Atari. After a year of operation, Bushnell left Atari and bought the Pizza Time restaurant and the rights to the idea from Warner for $500,000. He then began looking for franchisees.

One person interested in such a franchise was Robert Brock, whose Dallas-based company, Brock Hotel Corp., had 1978 profits of $4.6 million. In 1979, Brock signed a co-development agreement with Bushnell to build Pizza Time restaurants and sign up franchisees in areas he knew from his Holiday Inns and their restaurants. Before the 1980 date for opening his first restaurant, however, Brock was introduced to a Florida inventor, Aaron Fechter. Fechter's company, Creative Engineering Inc., produced animated characters and singing robots for amusement parks. Brock thought the robots were better than those used by Pizza Time and tried to get out of the contract with Bushnell. When Bushnell refused, Brock and Fechter went ahead and negotiated a preliminary agreement. Early in 1980, Brock told Bushnell their agreement was cancelled. Bushnell sued for breach of contract and Brock countersued for misrepresentation. Brock and Bushnell eventually reached a legal settlement under which Brock could use the Pizza Time Theatre concept by paying fees based on a percentage of the annual gross revenues of the first 160 ShowBiz restaurants.

Brock opened his first ShowBiz Pizza Place in March 1980, incorporating under the name ShowBiz Pizza Time, Inc. in Kansas. The restaurant's electronic host was Billy Bob Brokali, a large bear with an ironic smile. That same year, Bushnell's Pizza Time Theatre showed a profit for the first time and, in 1981, Bushnell took Pizza Time Theatre public. Both companies expanded quickly, building restaurants primarily in the Midwest, Southwest, and on the West Coast.

The two companies were battling for a very lucrative market. In 1981, according to the 1982 *Fortune* article, ShowBiz restaurants averaged $1.45 million in revenues and Chuck E. Cheese's outlets averaged $1.19 million each. This compared to average sales that year of $320,000 at PepsiCo Pizza Hut restaurants and $1.1 million at McDonald's outlets. Part of the reason was size: the typical ShowBiz and Chuck E. Cheese's unit was between 10,500 and 11,000 square feet and could serve 400 to 500 customers per restaurant, compared to about 100 customers for most pizza chain units. The second reason for their success was all those quarters being played on the video games, which brought in over 25 percent of sales revenues. Of course, the restaurant/entertainment centers were also more expensive to build and outfit. The *Fortune* article reported that "a ShowBiz unit cost $1.25 million, including $90,000 for eight animals and their stage effects plus $200,000 for 50 video games and 30 amusement-park devices for children. Pizza Time Theatres, slightly larger, cost $1.6 million each."

The two chains offered customers a similar experience, with very few distinctions other than their entertainment. Most notably, the restaurants were big and loud; an article in *Inc.* described Pizza Time Theatres as "Las Vegas casinos for kids." In the dining area, customers sat at tables, ate pizza, and watched large, wildly costumed robot animals sing and perform skits. On one of the three stages at ShowBiz, the Rock-A-Fire Explosion Band—consisting of a gorilla, a bear, a mouse, and a dog—performed songs from the 1960s to attract parents. In another room, adults had the alternative of watching soap operas on wide-screen television. At Chuck E. Cheese's, the big rodent led sing-alongs and cracked jokes while customers in other lounges were entertained by robotic animals resembling human entertainers such as Dolly Parton and Elvis. Above the sounds of the songs and jokes rang the bells, whistles, and shouts from the game area, at which youngsters played video and other arcade games and romped about on kiddie rides. A merchandise booth at most restaurants sold hats, T-shirts, stuffed animals, and other toys.

Despite the restaurants' popularity, there was skepticism among some financial analysts regarding their staying power, given emerging competition that offered better games and better food. But the trouble, when it came, was not from the video-game manufacturers and other companies who had opened a few competing outlets. By the mid-1980s, the video game craze was over. ShowBiz and Pizza Time Theatre began losing the teen market, and the food and other entertainment was not enough to draw new or return customers. Each company also carried large debts as a result of their rapid expansion.

When Pizza Time Theatre went into bankruptcy in 1984, Brock Hotel Corp. promptly bought up its competitor's assets. But Brock soon found the two pizza chain subsidiaries were draining his company's resources. To avoid bankruptcy itself, Brock Hotel Corp. underwent a refinancing. Between 1986 and 1988, according to *Restaurant Business,* The Hallwood Group made an equity investment in the company, receiving 14 percent ownership and control of the board of directors. Robert Brock resigned and, in 1985, Richard Frank, an experienced restaurant executive, was hired to head up the ShowBiz Pizza Time division as president and chief operating officer. In 1986 he was named chairman and chief executive officer of the restaurant division. When Frank assumed control, ShowBiz Pizza Time operated 262 restaurants: 107 Chuck E. Cheese's (30 company-owned and 77 franchised) and 155 ShowBiz units (95 company-owned and 60 franchised).

Frank began by initiating customer research, which found that although younger children liked the restaurants, their parents did not. There was too much noise, the food was mediocre, and, because there were no service personnel, parents had to order and serve themselves. Frank decided to reposition the restaurants as places to take the family and to concentrate on kids ages 2 to 12 and their parents.

His strategy was to improve the food quality and make the outlets attractive to parents as well as their kids. Beginning with company-owned units, ShowBiz increased the lighting, added windows, and hired service personnel to deliver the food. Restaurants reduced the number of video games, offered more rides and games for the under-12 set, and installed games of skill to attract more fathers. Moreover, the company improved the pizza and expanded the menu, installed self-serve drink stations, moved the salad bars into the middle of the room to make them more accessible, built a two foot high wall around the toddler area and put windows in the wall between the dining area and game rooms so parents could keep an eye on their children but not hear all the noise.

Frank also implemented a new marketing approach, advertising special price deals in newspaper inserts several times a year. Television spots focused less on the animal characters and more on parents and children having fun together at the restaurant. His plan required putting money into existing outlets in addition to opening new ones. He also designed a new, smaller prototype (8,500 square feet) which could be built for roughly half the cost of the old format.

In 1988, Brock Hotel Corp. changed its name to Integra-A Hotel and Restaurant Company, and spun off ShowBiz Pizza Time through a stock swap with shareholders. As reported in *Nation's Restaurant News,* for every ten shares of Integra they held, shareholders received about four shares of ShowBiz. A lawsuit arose from the Hallwood Group refinancing and ShowBiz divestiture in which plaintiffs alleged violation of Texas security laws and fraudulent transfer. Among its allegations, a group of Integra stockholders claimed that the stock options, warrants, and preferred stock they received in the refinancing became worthless when ShowBiz, which by 1988 was the biggest revenue producer in Integra, was spun off to common stock holders, primarily the restaurant management and The Hallwood Group. ShowBiz maintained that the suit had no basis, and the case remained in litigation in the mid-1990s.

The independent ShowBiz also purchased Integra's Mexican dinner chain, Monterey House, with 58 restaurants. ShowBiz attempted to broaden Monterey's base of blue-collar, low-income adults by attracting more families with an expanded Tex-Mex menu, modernized furniture and brighter, lighter dining areas. However, by the end of 1989, there was no improvement in sales and the company decided to convert 26 of the units to a trendier concept, Monterey's Tex-Mex Cafes, and close the rest. In addition to Richard Frank, the new company's management team consisted of Terry Spaight, president and chief operating officer; Matthew Drennan, executive vice-president and director of operations for Monterey; and Michael Magusiak, chief financial officer. In 1989, ShowBiz became a publicly traded company on the NASDAQ stock market.

Frank's efforts to understand and please his customers appeared to be working. By the middle of 1990, the company's stock was selling at $25.25 (up from $5.25 at the beginning of 1989 when the company went public), after 17 quarters of increased same-store sales. Deciding it was necessary to create a single, stronger identity for marketing, Frank moved to unite his two pizza chains under the Chuck E. Cheese's name. Within two years the company had converted the animated characters in all its own ShowBiz restaurants to Chuck E. Cheese and his friends. It also had moved into New England and the midatlantic regions of the country and was opening between 20 and 30 new outlets a year.

With an increasing employee base, ShowBiz established Chuck E. Cheese's University to train its operations and technical managers. New managers went through three weeks of hands-on training in guest relations, personnel management, food quality, and entertainment. Technical managers spent two weeks learning the basics of operating the rides, games, and animated stage shows.

Frank's strategy of reinvesting in the existing restaurant base, developing new locations, and accelerating debt repayment continued to be successful. ShowBiz reported 28 consecutive quarters of same-store sales increases with a net income of $15.5 million on revenues of $253.1 million in 1992. However, when the company announced lower-than-expected second quarter earnings in June 1993, its stock dropped 35 percent to $18.75 a share. In a *Wall Street Journal* article appearing the Monday after the drop, the company attributed lower sales to ineffective advertising and a slowdown in unit remodeling. Analysts also pointed to the introduction and growth of new commercial indoor playgrounds at restaurants such as McDonalds, which attracted families with young children and provided the first real competition to ShowBiz's entertainment center concept.

Believing in the soundness of the Chuck E. Cheese's concept, Frank continued his customer-oriented policies, remodeling and refining existing restaurants. In 1993, smoking was banned in most of the restaurants. The company spent a year planning the change after an earlier attempt resulted in a significant drop of sales at smoke-free outlets. This time, Frank emphasized preparing customers for the change and stressing the move was being made for the kids' sakes. The desire of parents for safe environments for their children also led to the new ''Kid Check'' child identification policy. Upon entering a restaurant, adults and children had their wrists stamped with matching invisible ink codes to show they were together. Codes were checked when an adult left the premises with a child to make sure the codes were the same.

When research revealed that customers thought they were spending too much for what they got at Chuck E. Cheese's, Michael Magusiak, who was named president in 1994, began testing a value-pricing strategy. The resulting policy of having customers buy discounted game tokens when purchasing a meal rather than at a change dispenser allowed parents to pay for everything at one time—and actually brought in more revenues. The remodeling of units proceeded with updated decor, more game packages for older children, and new proprietary Chuck E. games for youngsters. A new play attraction, Skycrawl, was introduced as free entertainment. New menu items aimed at both children and their parents were also tested. These included pizzas topped with traditional kids' foods, such as french fry and hamburger pizza or macaroni and cheese pizza, as well as a Southwestern chicken pizza for adults. During 1994, 22 units were upgraded and 12 more were opened, a much slower rate than in previous years. The company also restructured its management, reducing to two the levels between top management and restaurant managers, and sold its Monterey's Tex-Mex Cafes. However, it retained a 12.5 percent equity interest in River Associates, Inc., the company purchasing the Monterey's chain.

Despite its problems in the early 1990s, ShowBiz's new policy of renovation, cautious growth, and aggressive marketing was seen by many of the company's institutional investors as the right approach for keeping the kids' market. ''They got caught in a really competitive environment and maybe started doing things a bit late, but when they realized something needed to be done, they did it,'' one analyst noted in the *Dallas Morning News*. By the mid-1990s, the remodeled restaurants were generating sales at a double-digit pace and the company had a cash flow of over $30 million. In shopping centers and suburbs around the country, Chuck E. Cheese continued to be a big draw. As Jonathan Clements wrote in *The Wall Street Journal* after an afternoon at one of the chain's outlets with his five-year-old daughter, ''Kids love Chuck E. Cheese's. And as any parent knows, kids may not make money, but they sure help decide how it gets spent.''

Further Reading:

''Business Brief: ShowBiz Pizza Time Inc.: Firm To Sell Most Assets Of Monterey's Tex-Mex Line,'' *Wall Street Journal,* November 17, 1993.

Cheney, Karen, ''Kids' Chains Hit Growth Spurt,'' *Restaurants & Institutions,* April 15, 1993, pp. 12–14.

''Chuck E. Cheese: Repositioning Helped the Chain Please Parents and Young Children,'' *Restaurants & Institutions,* August 1, 1993, p. 38.

Clements, Jonathan, ''Heard on the Street: Kids Love Chuck E. Cheese's, Prompting Some To Look Beyond ShowBiz Parent's Profit Slide,'' *Wall Street Journal,* March 31, 1994, p. C4.

Coll, Steve, ''When The Magic Goes,'' *Inc.,* October 1984, p. 83–95.

Farrell, Kevin, ''ShowBiz Pizza Time Grows Up,'' *Restaurant Business,* June 10, 1988, pp. 133–136.

Jeffrey, Don, ''ShowBiz Back in Limelight After Years of Bad Reviews,'' *Nation's Restaurant News,* May 18, 1987, p. 246.

Kinkead, Gwen, ''High Profits from a Weird Pizza Combination,'' *Fortune,* July 26, 1982, pp. 62–66.

Labate, John, ''Companies to Watch: ShowBiz Pizza Time,'' *Fortune,* May 17, 1993, p. 102.

Marcial, Gene G., ''Food-Plus-Fun Finds New Fans,'' *Business Week,* July 2, 1990, p. 78.

Power, William, ''ShowBiz Pizza's Meltdown Has Connoisseurs Reviewing Their Lists of Trendy Restaurants,'' *Wall Street Journal,* June 14, 1993, p. C2.

Prewitt, Milford, ''ShowBiz Parent Merges Concepts Into One Big Pie,'' *Nation's Restaurant News,* September 10, 1990, p. 12.

——, ''Wall Street Cheers ShowBiz Turnaround,'' *Nation's Restaurant News,* June 4, 1990.

Romeo, Peter, ''ShowBiz Flexes Independence in Bid to Rejuvenate Monterey,'' *Nation's Restaurant News,* April 3, 1989, p. 18.

——, ''ShowBiz Pizza Time Tries Expansion Drive,'' *Nation's Restaurant News,* October 12, 1987, p. 3.

Ruggless, Ron, ''New ShowBiz Prexy Shifts Focus to Refining, Remodeling,'' *Nation's Restaurant News,* June 20, 1994, p. 1.

Taub, Stephen, ''A Noisy Decline,'' *Financial World,* November 30, 1983, pp. 40–43.

''This Little Family Got Its Wrists Stamped,'' *Restaurant Business,* October 10, 1994, p. 26.

Troy, Timothy, ''Integra Board Named in Suit,'' *Hotel & Motel Management,* February 24, 1992, p. 1, 42.

Woodard, Tracey Taylor, ''Monterey House Goes Tex-Mex,'' *Nation's Restaurant News,* October 2, 1989, p. 1.

—Ellen D. Wernick

Skidmore, Owings & Merrill

224 S. Michigan Ave.
Suite 1000
Chicago, Illinois 60604
U.S.A.
(312) 554-9090

Private Company
Incorporated: 1936
Operating Revenues: $80 million
Employees: 660
SICs: 8712 Architectural Services; 8711 Engineering Services

Skidmore, Owings & Merrill is one of the most prestigious and successful architectural and engineering firms in the United States. Many of the distinguished buildings in the Chicago Loop and those that grace the city's skyline, including the AT&T Corporate Center, the Brunswick Building, the Inland Steel Building, the John Hancock Center, and the tallest building in the world, the Sears Roebuck Tower, were built by Skidmore, Owings & Merrill. Well known for its clean, geometric designs, during the 1970s and 1980s the firm was the pre-eminent champion of a style of architecture that dominated the landscape of great cities worldwide. Unfortunately, when the style of architecture promulgated by Skidmore, Owings & Merrill was eclipsed by other styles during the late 1980s and early 1990s, the company was hit hard by a decrease in new contracts.

While studying architecture and design in Paris during the late 1920s, Louis Skidmore met some of the architects who were planning the Century of Progress Exposition scheduled for 1933 in Chicago. Through his connections, Skidmore was appointed the chief architect for the exposition and hired Nathaniel Owings, his brother-in-law, to help him design the layout and buildings for the entire site.

After the exposition was over, the two men went their separate ways, but they joined together again in 1936 to establish a design firm in Chicago. Named Skidmore and Owings, the company began to draft designs for corporate clients they had met during the Century of Progress Exposition. By the end of the year, the firm had grown large enough for the partners to hire three employees to help with drafting new designs. In 1937 the firm opened an office in New York City, primarily to assist the American Radiator Company in designing a new office building. Using their corporate contacts and emphasizing the experience they had gained from the Century of Progress Exposition in Chicago, the two men won the contract to design the 1939–40 New York World's Fair. In 1939 engineer John Merrill joined the firm as partner, and the name was changed to Skidmore, Owings & Merrill.

By the early 1940s, the firm had developed its own architectural style, emphasizing clean lines and functional designs. It secured its most important contract during this time—the design of part of the facilities used in the Manhattan Project in Oak Ridge, Tennessee—which catapulted the firm into national prominence. Skidmore and Owings also articulated the guiding principles upon which the firm's architectural designs would be based; these included group projects, innovative designs, social change, and "showmanship." By promoting these principles the firm grew rapidly, and after the war ended Skidmore, Owings & Merrill was selected to build such prestigious buildings as Lever House in New York City, the H. J. Heinz plant in Pittsburgh, and Mount Zion Hospital in San Francisco.

The decade of the 1950s was the beginning of the firm's golden era. By 1950 the firm had grown to include seven partners, one of whom was Gordon Bunshaft. Bunshaft had joined the firm in 1937, and by 1950 he had assumed leadership of the New York office with its staff of approximately 40 architects and designers. Under his direction, the firm began to win numerous large institutional and corporate contracts. The Lever House contract in New York propelled Skidmore, Owings & Merrill into corporate architecture and interior design, and the firm soon garnered a reputation as the leading exponent of an architectural style promulgated by Mies van der Rohe and Le Corbusier.

With accolades heaped upon its distinctively modern designs, the firm became the first to receive an invitation to exhibit at the Museum of Modern Art in New York City. By 1952 the company numbered 14 partners and over 1,000 employees, with offices in Chicago, New York, San Francisco, and Portland, Oregon.

During the late 1940s, the firm's wealthier corporate clients began to provide funds for such items as plants, sculptures, paintings, and various other decorative objects to provide an attractive atmosphere in their workplaces; they also began to request that Skidmore, Owings & Merrill purchase or design furniture that was particularly comfortable, so that employee morale would remain high and performance during long hours remain effective. Adequate lighting and suitable coloring also became concerns. With more and more clients requesting such services, Skidmore, Owings & Merrill became one of the first architectural firms to include interior design in its contracts, attending to space, lighting, color, furniture, and the overall effect of the enclosed environment.

The combination of architectural design and interior design was reflected in the company's projects during the 1950s. In association with a Turkish firm, Sedat Eldem, Skidmore, Owing & Merrill was contracted to design and decorate the Istanbul Hilton Hotel. Situated on a site overlooking the Bosporus Strait that separates the continents of Asia and Europe, the Istanbul Hilton was a combination of modern architectural and traditional design. The building was constructed of reinforced concrete, with a rigid rectilinear form and a rising facade of recessed balconies. In contrast, the interior of the hotel was embellished with rich and lushly textured materials and colors incorporating traditional Turkish motifs. Completed in 1955, the Istanbul Hilton was hailed as one of the great architectural and interior design achievements of Skidmore, Owings & Merrill.

Another landmark building designed by Skidmore, Owings & Merrill was the Chase Manhattan Bank. The firm was commissioned to design both a sixty-story downtown headquarters and a smaller office located at 410 Park Avenue. The larger building would include the bank's executive offices, and the smaller midtown office was to be used primarily for customer transactions.

Skidmore, Owings & Merrill encouraged Chase to adopt a contemporary design for its offices and to incorporate art into the interior as an element integral to the design of the building. The curator of the Museum of Modern Art was brought in to provide advice in purchasing an art collection; the collection was not only well received by art critics, but also established a precedent for other corporate art collections. When the building was completed in 1959, the exterior was sparse and minimalist while the interior was rich in color and texture—and one of the best art collections in the country.

During the 1960s, the company continued its innovative designs both for corporate and institutional commissions. In 1962 Skidmore, Owings & Merrill designed the buildings for the U.S. Air Force Academy in Colorado Springs, Colorado. In 1965 the firm designed the Brunswick Building in Chicago, the entire community at the University of Illinois at Chicago, and the library and museum at the Lincoln Center for the Performing Arts in New York. Perhaps the firm's most distinctive architectural and interior design of this period was the Businessmen's Assurance Company of America. Located in Kansas City, Missouri, and completed in 1963, the design was a strikingly successful mix of contrasting styles and periods, with cool, clear lines on the exterior of the building and a tapestry of Native American artifacts such as Apache baskets, Navaho jewelry, and old arrowheads decorating the interior. One of the notable awards received by Skidmore, Owings & Merrill during this decade was from the American Institute of Architects. Presented by the membership to the firm, it was the first award for architectural excellence presented by the Institute.

In the 1970s Skidmore, Owings and Merrill reached the peak of its influence. In 1970 and 1971 the firm designed the John Hancock Center in Chicago, Regenstein Library at the University of Chicago, One Shell Plaza in Houston, the Bank of America Building in San Francisco, the Library at Northwestern University in Evanston, Illinois, and the Lyndon Baines Johnson Memorial Library at the University of Texas in Austin. In 1974 the firm designed the Hirshhorn Museum and Sculpture Garden in Washington, D.C., and the Sears Roebuck Tower in Chicago, the tallest building in the world. One of the most interesting commissions received during this period was the rehabilitation of one floor of a corporate complex in New York City, for the insurance company Alexander & Alexander. Skidmore, Owings & Merrill combined Queen Anne chairs with glass-topped dining tables to create a remarkable balance between old and new designs.

In 1977 the firm won an important commission to design the National Commercial Bank in Jidda, Saudi Arabia. The clients requested that the firm design one of its greatest buildings, and the result was not disappointing. The triangular twenty-seven story building, situated on a site directly overlooking the Red Sea, was a stunning merger of traditional Islamic elements with modern design and the capacity for modern electronic banking. The facade was interrupted by interlocking incisions and different elevations, giving the impression both of mystery and severity. The interior design was considered one of the best ever conceived by the firm. Furniture was designed in France, Italy, and the United States; carpets were purchased from Hong Kong; woodwork was commissioned from Germany; and fifteen different types of marble were used in decorating the interior, along with one hundred different kinds of fabrics and more than twenty-five types of wood. Individual executive offices were designed to have their own unique furniture, carpet, and wall coverings. Completed in 1982, this project was the last of the firm's historic designs and signaled the end of an era. The founders had all retired, and Gordon Bunshaft also retired with the completion of the National Commercial Bank.

By the mid-1980s, architectural design and engineering were fully integrated with interior design, and the firm offered a wide range of services, including architectural design, civil engineering, electrical engineering, equipment planning, fire protection engineering, landscape architecture, mechanical engineering, plumbing engineering, site planning, space planning, and structural engineering. With such an inclusive list of services for clients, Skidmore, Owings & Merrill continued to grow, relying heavily on increasing commissions from outside the United States. In 1986 the firm opened its first overseas office, in London, and counted more than 1,400 employees in nine locations.

During the late 1980s, the firm designed the AT&T Corporate Center in Chicago and Rowes Wharf in Boston, two of the most impressive buildings of that era. With the advent of Postmodernism, however, Skidmore, Owings & Merrill's dedication to Modernism began to seem outdated, and the company found itself struggling for lucrative commissions. New management was brought in to solve the problem, but a crisis in the commercial real estate market further exacerbated the firm's declining fortunes.

Sales dropped precipitously from a total of $134 million in 1990 to $63 million by 1992, necessitating massive layoffs: between 1990 and 1992 employment dropped from 1,623 to 687.

In 1991 the position of chairman was assumed by David Childs, a long-time employee at Skidmore, Owings & Merrill. Within a short time, Childs had successfully steered the firm toward designing and building institutional projects, such as transportation facilities, airports, and religious buildings. Examples of his influence include the Chicago Transit Authority building, the Commonwealth Edison building, also located in Chicago, and the Islamic Center in New York.

Further Reading:

Slavin, Maeve, *Davis Allen: 40 Years of Interior Design at Skidmore, Owings & Merrill,* New York: Rizzoli, 1990.

—Thomas Derdak

Smith Corona Corp.

65 Locust Avenue
New Canaan, Connecticut 06840-4725
U.S.A.
(203) 972-1471

Public Company
Incorporated: 1985
Employees: 3,000
Sales: $278 million
Stock Exchanges: New York
SICs: 3579 Office Machines, Not Elsewhere Classified; 3955 Carbon Paper and Inked Ribbons; 2675 Die-Cut Paper and Board: 2678 Stationery Products

Smith Corona is a world-famous designer, manufacturer, and marketer of portable and compact electronic typewriters, personal word processors, electronic reference products, and accessories. Having achieved considerable success in the typewriter business beginning in the late 19th century, the company saw its fortunes decline in the late 1980s, when personal computers, capable of performing more sophisticated word processing functions, began to replace the typewriter in the office as well as the home. To offset the effects of this trend, Smith-Corona branched out into word processing and computer products in the early 1990s but eventually filed for bankruptcy in 1995, hoping to restructure and reemerge a more stable corporation.

Smith Corona was established in 1886 as the Smith-Premier Typewriter Company. Its founders were four brothers formerly in the gun manufacturing business: Lyman, Wilbert, Monroe, and Hurlburt Smith. The typewriter concept had first been introduced ten years earlier at the Centennial Exhibition in Philadelphia, and a designer and inventor named Alexander Brown became intrigued by the newfangled writing machine. Brown had studied the device and decided that he could build a better one himself. Not overly concerned with portability, he aimed to build an office writing machine that would be solid, durable, and attractive.

When Lyman and Wilbert Smith hired Brown to help redesign a gun for them, Brown presented them with his typewriter idea and they agreed to finance its production. Brown's typewriter, like the others of its day, was a "blind" writing machine: the typist could not see what he typed without lifting the carriage. It had a double keyboard, with "a key for every character." Reflecting the classical style of the era's office architecture, it featured fluted pillars resembling Ionic columns and a frame decorated with flowers and cattails. The Smiths named the typewriter and their new company Smith-Premier, achieving immediate success with the public for what became the most popular double-keyboard machine in America.

During this time, the typewriter was becoming standard office equipment, but the typewriter industry had no standard keyboard. Each of the 30 emerging typewriter manufacturers in the United States arranged the letters on the keyboard in its own way, leaving the public bewildered. There was great variation in the way the machines operated as well. Some manufacturers produced double keyboard machines without shifting ability, while others had single-keyboard machines with the shift function. Some machines were capable of producing only capital letters; others printed both capital and lowercase letters.

Some of these problems were alleviated in 1893 when Smith-Premier merged with six other leading manufacturers to form the Union Typewriter Company of America, based in Syracuse, New York. Headed by the Smith brothers, Union Typewriter proceeded to make the Smith-Premier the most popular of the "blind" writing machines. The company's slogan claimed, "The pen is mightier than the sword, but the Smith-Premier type writer bends them both!" By 1894, more than 60,000 No. 1 Smith-Premiers were sold. In fact, throughout the 1890s, Smith-Premier sales were second only to Remington's typewriters.

An industry standard among typewriter keyboards finally materialized in 1895. The following year, the first "visible" typewriter was introduced, allowing the typist to see what he typed without lifting the carriage. Its introduction to the market caused a rift at Union Typewriter, since, while the Smith brothers quickly recognized the new machine's advantages, their associates did not. The disagreement prompted the Smith brothers to resign and start a new venture; the L.C. Smith & Brothers Typewriter Company of Syracuse was founded on January 27, 1903 to manufacture "visible" typewriters.

To produce such high-quality machines in great quantities, L.C. Smith & Brothers soon found that they needed a new factory. Eager to commence construction, company president L.C. (Lyman) Smith had a crew begin digging the foundation for the factory in March 1903, before the architect had even finished his drawings. Throughout the construction, in fact, the architects rushed to stay ahead of the builders who not only erected the plant but laid a branch railroad and stretched a bridge across a nearby creek to bring materials to the site. The factory was finished in December 1903, and Carl Gabrielson, who had accompanied the Smith brothers from Union Typewriter, took over the designing of the company's new product. Late in 1904, he developed a visible single keyboard typewriter; eventually, visible typewriters would come to dominate the market and blind writing machines would fall into disuse.

During this time, another typewriter company was also achieving considerable success. In 1906, the Corona Typewriter Company introduced its Corona model, a light-weight, 3-bank portable typewriter. By 1914, Corona was the leading manufacturer of portable typewriters. Though typewriter production practically ground to a halt in Europe during the First World War, American typewriter production did not suffer as much since the United States entered the war relatively late. Moreover, American exports continued for a significant time during the war years and the Corona, in particular, achieved immense popularity. It was a favorite of the military and the journalists at the front. British forces used the portable Corona in the trenches and in patrol aircraft. Many important documents were typed or duplicated on Coronas, including the surrender papers for German South West Africa.

Corona typewriters won fame and success in peacetime also, and without substantially changing their design. Despite the dramatic technological change between the two World Wars, the Corona portable's design survived as the industry standard. Part of Corona's peacetime renown came during the Dempsey-Firpo fight in 1924 when Firpo knocked Dempsey through the ropes onto a Corona portable typewriter. Dempsey climbed back into the ring and was able to continue the fight. Surprisingly, the Corona on which the heavyweight had landed continued to work as well as it had before. This incident gave Corona a new slogan, "Dempsey knocked out Firpo, but he could not knockout Corona!"

In the 1920s, the typewriter industry underwent dramatic changes. In 1923, there were over 300 kinds of typewriters on the market, most of them American; by 1929, the market had consolidated considerably and only five kinds of typewriters were being manufactured in the United States. One of the successful mergers of this decade resulted in the January 1926 formation of the L.C. Smith & Corona Typewriter Company, occasioned when Corona merged with L.C. Smith and Brothers, giving the new business the second half of the most recognized name in typewriters.

After the stock market crashed in 1929, sales of typewriters to businesses declined sharply, and, suffering some setbacks in the wake of the Great Depression, Smith & Corona responded with a major change in strategy: the company began to market portable typewriters to the home in addition to the office. Departing from its practice of focusing on a basic black model of typewriter geared toward business use, Smith & Corona began marketing entire lines of brightly colored portable typewriters, as well as new models, branded Silent L.C. Smith and Sterling, which were quieter than their predecessors. Other new brand names included the Clipper and the Zephyr. The company also made an acquisition during this time, taking over the Portable Adding Machine Company in 1934.

During World War II, as the country's industrial sector shifted its focus to assist with the war effort, the U.S. government ordered major manufacturers to cease production of typewriters. Smith & Corona's facilities were converted for the production of percussion primers for bombs as well as rifles. The company's sales force was kept busy helping the government purchase used typewriters. By 1943, however, the armed forces' demand for rifles was filled, and they again needed writing machines. Smith & Corona was asked to return to making typewriters; fortunately, it had saved the necessary manufacturing equipment.

Smith & Corona became known as Smith-Corona in 1946 and in 1953 was renamed Smith-Corona Inc. During the postwar years, the company worked to meet the challenge of the newest technology, the electric typewriter, which began to dominate the market in 1948. In 1955, Smith-Corona introduced an electric typewriter for the office. The result of a decade of research, the new machine featured a scientifically sloped keyboard fitted to natural finger movements, more controls in the keyboard area than any other electric typewriter, and automatic repeat actions on all keys. Continuing to branch out into other areas, Smith-Corona merged with Marchant Calculators in September 1958; the resulting company, Smith-Corona Marchant Inc. (SCM), became world renowned as an aggressive and diversified corporation.

Throughout the 1960s, Smith-Corona Marchant competed in the electric typewriter, home, and office equipment markets and increased sales both at home and abroad. Their electric typewriters of the 1960s and early 1970s featured a smaller compact design and keys that were more easily depressed than their predecessors. By 1974, Smith-Corona had become a division of Kleinschmidt and had ceased to manufacture manual and electric standard office typewriters, concentrating instead on portable machines and compact electric typewriters.

That year, Smith-Corona also filed a complaint against Brother Industries Ltd., beginning a 20-year imbroglio between itself and the Japanese competitor. Specifically, Smith-Corona's complaint charged Brother with "dumping" portable typewriters, exporting the machines for sale in the United States at prices below cost. Arguing that Brother was in violation of the Antidumping Act of 1921, Smith Corona saw its sales decline in the face of what it deemed an unfair trade practice. In 1979, the U.S. government imposed an import fee on Brother's typewriters, and throughout the 1980s the courts modified these antidumping orders and import fees to include new products such as Brother electronic typewriters and word processors.

Then an ironic role reversal occurred that complicated matters further. In 1985 Smith Corona was incorporated as a wholly owned subsidiary of SCM Corp., and the following year, the London-based conglomerate, Hanson PLC, acquired SMC Corp. Adapting to an increasingly global economy, Smith Corona began manufacturing typewriters in Singapore for export to the United States, gradually eliminating jobs at its factory in Cortland, New York, and bolstering its work force at its Singapore plant. At the same time, Brother Industries opened a plant in Bartlett, Tennessee, where it manufactured 600,000 typewriters annually for the U.S. market. It was Brother's turn to file dumping complaints against Smith Corona, and the fight continued.

Also during this time, Smith Corona was struggling to adapt to the changes wrought by the personal computer (PC) revolution. Under increasing pressure from recent innovations and changing economic conditions, the company undertook a variety of efforts to meet the challenges of the new era. It introduced several word processing machines, hoping to entice consumers with their facility of use and low price. However, few anticipated the speed with which the quality of PCs would go up and prices would come down.

Nevertheless, in 1989, Smith Corona led the personal word processor (PWP) market. That year, the company introduced the portable, economical PWP 270, marketing it to those waiting for laptop PC prices to drop, as well as to those already convinced of the benefits of a PWP. Smith Corona hoped to win over the former group with the PWP 270's spelling, merging, and automatic saving capabilities, in addition to the letter quality printer that came in the same package. The company also marketed the first laptop PWP, dubbed the 270LT, that year. Despite these innovations and high hopes, the spring of 1989 saw the beginning of a strong and steady decline in Smith Corona stock prices that lasted through July 1990. The growth of the PC industry and the competition from overseas were taking their toll on Smith Corona's finances. In June 1989, Hanson PLC spun off 53 percent of Smith Corona stock in a public offering, and Smith Corona laid off ten percent of its work force.

In 1990, Fred Feuerhake, vice-president of marketing for Smith Corona, stated in *Dealerscope Merchandising* magazine that the industry was ''in a period of transition between typewriters and word processors.'' Though he had not lost faith in the typewriter, he predicted that the greatest growth in sales would be in word processors. Still, Feuerhake believed that there was a niche for Smith Corona among consumers who wanted word processing capability without the complexities and expense of a PC. The only obstacle to the success of this strategy was an unexpected drop in PC prices.

A drop in PC prices was observed in a July 1990 report in *Business Week,* which also noted that manufacturers were making the more powerful PCs easier to operate and less intimidating. The PWP market, once forecast at 1.2 million units per year, had peaked at 250 thousand units per year. Although revenues of the PWP market increased from 1990 to 1991, sales of PWPs and typewriters were poor overall throughout the early 1990s.

Smith Corona responded by entering into the competitive PC market. In April 1991, the company introduced a seven-model line of PCs called Simply Smart. The Simply Smart line was intended for first-time users and buyers looking for a PC that was easy to use and inexpensive. At that time, Smith-Corona CEO Lee Thompson told *Dealerscope Merchandising* that, despite this development, his company was not abandoning the typewriter or word processor markets. Computers are ''a logical extension of our line,'' Thompson said, ''not a replacement for other products within our line. We strongly believe in the continuing need for the typewriter and will maintain our lead position in the market place.''

In 1992, Smith Corona introduced the PC340 as its top-of-the-line word processor. The PC340 was faster and therefore more competitive than previous models, featured easy, one-touch access to Smith Corona's proprietary PWP Word Processing 6.0 program, and came with a generous software package that included Microsoft Windows and some graphics programs. That year, the company also announced that it was moving its manufacturing operations to Mexico. The company maintained that this would result in a ten to 12 percent reduction in costs.

In February 1994, Smith Corona and Brother Industries finally ended years of litigation over the dumping issue. In a joint statement, the companies admitted that it was better to direct their energies toward the marketplace rather than the courtroom. They asked the commerce department to cease their investigations of typewriter dumping and revoke the added import taxes.

Despite the end of its litigation woes, however, Smith Corona still faced financial challenges. In October 1994, the company reported that its fiscal first quarter profit had decreased 70 percent. Poor sales and low competitor prices were blamed for the net income drop from $4 million in the fiscal quarter ended September 30, 1993 to $1.2 million in the same quarter in 1994. Typewriter and PWP sales were down 15 percent from the previous year. After a 100-year history of manufacturing in the United States, Smith Corona moved the last of its U.S. production from New York to Mexico.

On July 5, 1995, the Smith Corona Corporation filed for bankruptcy protection in Delaware. Typewriters, the product so successfully manufactured and marketed by Smith Corona in its various incarnations for more than a century, were becoming obsolete. Despite the company's forays into word processors, facsimile machines, and other office products, customers still associated Smith Corona with typewriters and typewriters had remained the core of the company's business. Smith Corona planned to stabilize its operations, obtain additional financing, and restructure. At the end of June 1995, new management took over and Smith Corona hired R.H. Stengel & Company to turn its finances around. The company that had once declared, ''The pen is mightier than the sword, but the Smith-Premier Typewriter bends them both!'' had seen the computer replace both pen and typewriter.

Principal Subsidiaries: SCM Office Supplies, Inc.; SCM (United Kingdom) Ltd.; Histacount Corp.; Smith Corona Overseas Holdings, Inc.; Smith Corona Private Ltd.; Smith Corona (Canada) Ltd.; Smith Corona Australia PTY Ltd.; Smith Corona France S.A.R.L.; Smith Corona GmbH.

Further Reading:

Beeching, Wilfred A., editor, *Century of the Typewriter,* London: William Heinemann, Ltd, 1974, 276 p.

''CES Wrap Up: Smith Corona Adapts to Changing Market,'' *Dealerscope Merchandising,* July 1990, p. 50.

''Computer Reviews: On the Right Track,'' *Dealerscope Merchandising,* June 1992, pp. 56–60.

Hays, Laurie, ''Smith Corona Net Decreased 70% in Fiscal 1st Period,'' *The Wall Street Journal,* October 26, 1994, p. B 12.

''Home Office Retailing: 7 New PCs Debut from Smith Corona,'' *Dealerscope Merchandising,* May 1991, p. 22.

''Home Office Retailing: Smith Corona Assails 'Predatory Conduct,' '' *Dealerscope Merchandising,* September 1991, p. 70.

Mares, G.C., *The History of the Typewriter: Successor to the Pen,* Arcadia, Calif.: Post-Era Books, 1985, 314 p.

Masi, Frank, T., ed., *The Typewriter Legend,* Secaucus, N.J.: Matsushita Electric Corporation of America, 1985, 132 p.

Naj, Amal Kumar, ''Smith Corona, Brother Industries End 14 Years of Litigation Over Dumping,'' *The Wall Street Journal,* February 8, 1994, p. A5.

Novack, Janet, ''It's Like a Big Balloon,'' *Forbes,* July 20, 1992, p. 48.

''Oh, Brother!: Dumping Lawsuit Defies All Sense,'' *Far Eastern Economic Review,* March 10, 1994, p. 7.

''Product Applications: Smith Corona Offers First Laptop Personal Word Processor—The PWP 270LT,'' *Dealerscope Merchandising,* December 1989, p. 59.

Reich, Robert B., ''Dumpsters: The End of an Unfair Trading Practice,'' *New Republic,* June 10, 1991, pp. 9–10.

''Selling Points: A Laptop for Less,'' *Dealerscope Merchandising,* October 1989, p. 72.

''Typewriter Market: The Fight Over What's Left!'' *Purchasing,* October 22, 1992, p. 65, 67.

Vogel, Todd, and Mark Maremont, ''Smith Corona's Market is Tapping Out,'' *Business Week,* July 16, 1990, p. 31.

Zuckerman, Laurence ''Smith Corona, Another Victim Of Computer Age, Seeks Help,'' *New York Times,* July 6, 1995.

—John Myers-Kearns

Softbank Corp.

3-42-3
Nihonbashi-Hanacho
Chuoku Tokyo 103
Japan
(81) 3-5642-8020

Public Company
Incorporated: 1981
Employees: 1,700
Sales: $900 million
SICs: 5045 Computers Peripheral Equipment & Software

Softbank Corp. ranked as Japan's largest software wholesaler and top publisher of computer magazines and books. The company also gained a reputation as a notable software venture capitalist. In 1995, Softbank marked its thirteenth anniversary and its first year as a publicly traded business by posting over $900 million in annual sales. The Tokyo-based firm was founded and led by Masayoshi Son (rhymes with "lone"), a self-promoting 34-year-old whose rapid rise earned him the nickname "the Bill Gates of Japan." Son possessed a rare combination of character traits as an inventor, businessman, and "consummate salesman." Although he hailed from a country that was not often distinguished for encouraging entrepreneurship, the editors of *Business Week* ranked him one of the best entrepreneurs of 1994. Son was often cited as a driving force behind the development of Japan's $2.75 billion PC software market, of which his company controlled a sizable share. Although the firm diversified widely during its relatively brief history, software wholesaling still accounted for over half of annual revenues in 1994.

Son was born in 1957 to Japanese citizens of Korean descent. By his own account, his early years were characterized by second-class citizenship and poverty. In a 1992 interview with Alan M. Webber of the *Harvard Business Review,* he acknowledged that, like many other Koreans in Japan, his entire family had assumed a Japanese surname, Yasumoto, in order to better assimilate into society. Son's family was able to move out of a squatter town and into the middle class by the time he reached the age of 13. At 16, Son traveled to the United States to attend high school.

The youngster flourished in his new environment, resuming his Korean surname and breezing through three grades to graduate from his California high school within a couple of weeks. Son attended Holy Names College for two years, then transferred to the University of California at Berkeley. It was there that, with the help of some professors of microcomputing, he made his first $1 million at the age of 19 by developing a pocket translator. Son sold the patent for his device to Sharp Corp., which marketed it as the Sharp Wizard. By the time he was 20, Son had earned another million importing used video game machines from Japan.

Although Son realized that it would be relatively easy to launch a business in the United States, the budding entrepreneur also knew that the Japanese culture tended to produce employees who were likely to be more loyal and work harder than their American counterparts. Consequently, he decided to return to his homeland upon his graduation from college. He spent the next 18 months researching 40 different business options ranging from software development to hospital management. Using a matrix, Son ranked each one against 25 of his own "success measures." He described a few of these to Webber in the *Harvard Business Review* interview: "I should fall in love with [the] business for the next 50 years at least;" "the business should be unique;" and "within 10 years I wanted to be number one in that particular business." The field he chose—wholesaling personal computer (PC) software—met the majority of his criteria. At the time, most software developers did not have the capital to promote their products to hardware manufacturers, and most hardware manufacturers and retailers did not have software to run on their machines. Son hoped to carve out a profitable niche as a liaison between the two groups.

At first, his Softbank Corp. was more spectacle than substance. Using a combination of previously earned and borrowed funds, Son purchased one of the biggest display areas available at a 1981 consumer electronics show in Tokyo. Having absolutely no product to offer, Son called all 12 of the software vendors he knew at the time and offered to display their wares at his booth *gratis.* Not surprisingly, many jumped at the opportunity. Although his exhibit, which featured a large banner proclaiming a "revolution in software distribution," caught many attendees' attention, most already had their own contacts with software vendors. The show earned the fledgling entrepreneur only one contact; luckily, it was with Japan's foremost PC retailer, Joshin Denki. Son negotiated exclusive rights to purchase software for the chain, then parlayed that top-notch industry connection into exclusive contracts with other firms, including Hudson Software, the country's largest vendor. Over the course of its first year in business, Softbank's monthly sales mushroomed from $10,000 to $2.3 million. By 1983, the company served over 200 dealer outlets.

By that time, Son was already pursuing additional business interests in the broader field he called "computing infrastructure." He first diversified into publishing. His first two magazine titles, *Oh!PC* and *Oh!MZ,* lost hundreds of thousands of dollars in their inaugural months due to lack of interest. But Son feared that if he dropped these sidelines clients would smell trouble, so instead he revamped the layout and threw the weight of an expensive television advertising campaign behind the project. By the early 1990s, the flagship *Oh!PC* enjoyed a circulation of about 140,000 and had become the forerunner of a stable of 20 Softbank-published periodicals, including the Japanese edition of *PC Week.* Writing for *Forbes* in 1992, Andrew Tanzer noted that "the magazines rather shamelessly promote products Son distributes," an accepted practice in Japan. By the early 1990s, the division had also put out over 300 computing books and become Japan's leading publisher of high-tech magazines.

A lengthy bout with hepatitis sidelined Son from 1983 through 1986. Although he gave up Softbank's presidency during this period, Son kept tabs on the company via computer and telecommunications equipment installed in his hospital room. His prolonged recuperation apparently gave him time to conjure up new ideas. Upon his return to Softbank's helm, Son invented a "least-cost routing device" that came to form the basis of the company's DATANET telephone data division. The idea evolved when Japan's telephone monopoly, Nippon Telegraph & Telephone Corp. (NTT), was joined by three new common carriers—DDI Corporation, Teleway Japan, and Japan Telecom—in 1986. Although they offered lower long-distance rates, the inconvenience of dialing the three newcomers' additional four-digit prefixes deterred many customers from signing on. Son's computerized invention, which he described as about "the size of two cigarette packs," would automatically choose the cheapest carrier and route, then dial the appropriate number. Periodic on-line updates kept the routers' rate information current. Softbank offered the devices free to telephone customers and made money by collecting royalties on common carriers' increased billings. In the early 1990s, Son expanded the business by offering routers installed in new telephones and fax machines.

Seeking ways to invest his profits—and perhaps to erect a bulwark against getting bypassed in the distribution chain—Son soon earned renown as a venture capitalist and corporate "matchmaker." Early deals paired U.S. software vendors with Japanese partners who modified American computer applications for sale in Japan. Softbank made commissions on the matchmaking, then distributed the newly modified products.

The "marriages" got bigger in the early 1990s. In 1991, Son arranged two major computer networking alliances that combined the resources of a coterie of well-known rivals. The lead company in the first venture was BusinessLand Inc., a top systems integrator in the United States. It owned 54 percent of the $20 million venture, appropriately named BusinessLand Japan Co. Softbank held another 26 percent of the equity, while Toshiba Corp., Sony Corp., Canon Inc., and Fujitsu Ltd. each controlled five percent. Unlike its California-based majority partner, BusinessLand Japan eschewed the retail market in favor of corporate customers. While some analysts observed that the new venture's Japanese participants would give it a leg up on pre-existing competitors like America's Electronic Data Systems (EDS), IBM Corp., and Digital Equipment Corp., others noted a conflict of interest in having computer manufacturers among BusinessLand Japan's investors. In fact, the venture failed and was liquidated within a year.

Nonetheless, Son had no trouble convincing many of those same corporations to invest in a second endeavor that same year. America's Novell Inc. owned 54 percent of and lent its name to the venture, Novell Japan Ltd. Softbank held 26 percent of the new company, while hardware manufacturers NEC, Toshiba Corp., Fujitsu Ltd., Canon Inc., and Sony Corp. each chipped in four percent of the equity. Although each of the latter five partners produced its own version of the networking system, all were compatible. The coalition sold network operating systems, peripherals, cables, transceivers, boards, and other network-related products. Since, according to Son's estimate, less than five percent of Japan's PCs were networked in 1990, the allies expected to make Novell's NetWare the industry standard there. Son predicted that the Japanese computer networking industry would "grow like hell" in a 1992 interview for the *Harvard Business Review.* This prediction came true: by 1994, Novell Japan Ltd. boasted $130 million in annual sales.

That same year, Son engineered what *Business Week* called a "sweeping alliance" involving Cisco Systems Inc., Fujitsu Ltd., Toshiba Corp., and a dozen other Japanese firms. The partners anted up a total of $40 million to fund the launch of Nihon Cisco System, which planned to distribute internetworking systems in Japan.

Although he was widely hailed as a "whiz kid," Son was not infallible. Within just six months in 1991, he allegedly lost $10 million in a bungled on-line shopping venture. Systembank, a joint venture with H. Ross Perot's Perot Systems, was intended to provide systems integration for large Japanese corporations. According to a February 1995 article in the *New York Times,* Systembank was "quietly disbanded." In 1994, Son convinced NTT to invest $200,000 in a "video on demand" alliance. The proposed interactive system would allow subscribers to request movies and other media at their leisure. Son boldly predicted that the joint venture would have 10 million customers by the turn of the century. But NTT, which had a similar agreement with Microsoft Corporation, did not plan to have the necessary infrastructure (i.e., fiber optic cable to households) ready for another five to ten years, which pushed back Son's anticipated timetable substantially.

Son's first post-graduate American venture, Softbank Inc., was formed in 1993 with the cooperation of Merisel Inc., Phoenix Technologies Ltd., and telemarketer Alexander and Lord. The new subsidiary planned to distribute software through the interactive Softbank On-Hand Library service. Softbank Inc.'s vice-president, Meg Tuttle, described the demo disks as "adware." Reviewer Steve Bass of *PC World* "fell in love" with the $10 CD-ROMs, which allowed users to "test-drive" over 100 programs, then order and pay for the selected software on-line. Several big-league computer companies, including Apple Computer, Inc., IBM Corp., and Ingram Micro Inc., had already launched similar promotions. But other analysts and competitors ballyhooed the idea. For example, David Goldstein, president of Channel Marketing, told *PC Week*'s Lawrence Aradon that offering software on compact disks would become "the Edsel of the computer industry." The venture's direct competition with one of Softbank's most important consumer groups, software retailers, broke what Steve Hamm of *PC Week* called one of Son's golden rules: "don't compete with clients or suppliers." By early 1995, in fact, a number of industry analysts pronounced the venture defunct for that very reason.

Son took Softbank Corp. public in 1994 in an offering that valued the company at $3 billion. The founder retained a 70 percent interest in his company. Coming off the late 1994 loss of a bidding war for the U.S. magazine publishing operations of Ziff Communications Co., Son acquired that firm's trade show division for $202 million. The subsidiary's name was changed from ZD Expos to Softbank Expos. Early in 1995, Softbank made a major addition to that interest with the $800 million purchase of a package of 17 computer trade shows from Sheldon Adelson's Interface Group. The acquisition, which was financed with at least $500 million in debt and a new offering of Softbank Corp. shares, nearly doubled Softbank's U.S. operations.

The acquisition included the Las Vegas Comdex show, which was characterized in a 1995 *Wall Street Journal* article as ''a huge draw in the computer industry.'' Launched in 1979, Comdex attracted 195,000 attendees and 2,200 exhibitors to its November 1994 show. Although it remained popular, the event's high prices had come under criticism in recent years. Some major exhibitors, including Compaq, Packard Bell, Oracle, and Seagate Technologies, had already opted out of the show by the time Softbank took over. Son expressed confidence that he could revitalize the event without a total revamp, citing the fact that exhibit space for the 1995 show was already 90 percent booked by the previous spring. Expansion plans for the new businesses included the first French Softbank Expo in 1995 and the premier Japanese and British Comdexes in 1996.

In 1995, 37-year-old Son predicted to Steve Hamm of *PC Week* that he would ''do something big'' while in his 40s. While it seemed likely that he would stay within the bounds of the computer industry, potential rivals within that very broad category were expected to keep a close eye on the movements of this innovative competitor.

Further Reading:

Aragon, Lawrence, ''Off and Running,'' *PC Week,* March 14, 1994, p. A1.

Bass, Steve, ''Hot Picks for the Home Office,'' *PC World,* March 1995, p. 241.

''The Best Entrepreneurs,'' *Business Week,* January 9, 1995, p. 112.

Burke, Steven, ''$20 Million Joint Venture Gives BusinessLand Foothold in Japan,'' *PC Week,* June 11, 1990, p. 119.

Hamilton, David P., ''Comdex Owner Doesn't Plan to Alter Show,'' *Wall Street Journal,* February 21, 1995, p. A13B.

Hamm, Steve, ''The Rising Son,'' *PC Week,* April 10, 1995, p. A1.

Holyoke, Larry, ''Japan's Hottest Entrepreneur Hits the U.S.,'' *Business Week,* February 27, 1995, p. 118G.

Patch, Kimberly, '' 'Virtual Shopping' Via CD-ROM,'' *PC Week,* July 12, 1993, p. 6.

Pollack, Andrew, ''Computer Exhibition Purchased,'' *New York Times,* February 14, 1995, pp. C1(N), D1(L).

——, ''A Japanese Gambler Hits the Jackpot with Softbank,'' *New York Times,* February 19, 1995, sec. 3, p. 10.

Smith, Dawn, ''Demo Disk Double-Take,'' *Marketing Computers,* October 1993, pp. 18–19.

Tanzer, Andrew, ''Hot Hands,'' *Forbes,* May 11, 1992, p. 182.

Umezawa, Masakuni, ''The New Golden Age of Wireless,'' *Tokyo Business Today,* November 1994, pp. 10–12.

Webber, Alan M., ''Japanese-Style Entrepreneurship: An Interview with Softbank's CEO, Masayoshi Son,'' *Harvard Business Review,* January–February 1992, pp. 93–103.

—April D. Gasbarre

Southern Electric PLC

Southern Electric House
Westacott Way
Littlewick Green
Maidenhead
Berkshire SL6 3QB
United Kingdom
(01628) 822166
Fax: (01628) 584400

Public Company
Incorporated: 1989
Employees: 7,642
Sales: £1.78 billion
Stock Exchanges: London
SICs: 4911 Electric Companies and Systems; 1731 Electrical Contracting; 5722 Household Appliance Shops

Southern Electric PLC was the second-largest regional electricity company in England and Wales, serving 2.5 million domestic, commercial, and industrial customers. Its 16,900-square-kilometer region extended from London in the east to Somerset in the west, and from Oxfordshire in the north to the Isle of Wight in the south. Originating in the public sector as the Southern Electricity Board, Southern Electric was privatized, along with the whole of Britain's electricity industry, in 1989. Since then the company has increasingly become involved in separate but related business opportunities. By 1995, Southern Electric's subsidiary interests included utility contracting, investments in power generation projects, environmental engineering, electrical retailing, and supplies of natural gas. In addition, as the electricity industry became increasingly deregulated, Southern Electric began competing directly with other distributors to capture a wider customer base. Southern Electric's principal activity remained, however, its core business of marketing and distributing electricity to central southern England.

Electricity was first harnessed for practical use in the United Kingdom in the late nineteenth century, with the introduction of street lighting in 1881. By 1921 over 480 authorized but independent electricity suppliers had arisen throughout England and Wales, resulting in a rather haphazard system operating at different voltages and frequencies. In recognition of the need for a more coherent, interlocking system, the Electricity (Supply) Act of 1926 created a central authority to encourage and facilitate a national transmission system. This objective of a national grid was achieved by the mid-1930s.

The state consolidated its control of the utility with the Electricity Act of 1947, which collapsed the distribution and supply activities of 505 separate bodies into 12 regional area boards, at the same time assigning generating assets and liabilities to one government-controlled authority. A further Electricity Act, in 1957, created a statutory body, the Central Electricity Generating Board (CEGB), which dominated the whole of the electricity system in England and Wales. As generator of virtually all the electricity in the two countries as well as owner and operator of the transmission grid, CEGB supplied electricity to the area boards, which they in turn distributed and sold within their regions.

Such was the situation for 30 years, until the government raised the idea of privatizing the electricity industry in 1987. The proposal was enshrined in the Electricity Act of 1989, and a new organizational scheme was unveiled. The CEGB was splintered into four divisions, destined to become successor companies: National Power, PowerGen, Nuclear Electric, and the National Grid Company (NGC). The generators National Power and PowerGen were to share between them England and Wales's fossil-fueled power stations; Nuclear Electric was to take over nuclear power stations; and the NGC was to be awarded control of the national electricity distribution system. The 12 area boards, Southern Electric among them, were converted virtually unchanged into 12 regional electricity companies (RECs), and these were given joint ownership of the NGC. Southern Electric was incorporated as a private company in 1989, and its shares, along with those of the other RECs, were the first to be sold to the public, at the end of 1990.

The provision of electricity consists of four components: generation, transmission, distribution, and supply. In England and Wales, generation is the province of National Power, PowerGen, and Nuclear Electric. Transmission is the transfer of electricity via the national grid, through overhead lines, underground cables, and NGC substations. Distribution is the delivery of electricity from the national grid to local distribution systems operated by the RECs. Supply, a term distinct from distribution in the industry, refers to the transaction whereby electricity is purchased from the generators and transmitted to customers. Under the terms of their licenses, the generators may supply electricity directly to consumers, but that right is comparatively little exercised; their usual customers are the RECs, who in turn sell the electricity to the end users.

A new trading market was devised with the privatization scheme for bulk sales of electricity from generators to distributors—the pool. A rather complicated pricing procedure exists in the pool, according to which each generating station offers a quote for each half-hour of the day, based on an elaborate set of criteria including the operating costs of that particular plant, the time of day, the expected demand for electricity, and the available capacity of the station. The NGC arranges these quotes in a merit order and makes the decisions regarding which plant to call into operation when. The pool system is not relied upon exclusively, however, as the generators and distributors frequently make contractual arrangements for a specified period of time as a means of mutual protection against fluctuations in the pool price. Southern Electric's contracts with the generators were arranged for periods of anywhere from one to 15 years.

The privatized Southern Electric took as its core business that of the former Southern Electricity Board, in which fully 60 percent of its staff was employed—supplying electricity from the National Grid to its 2.5 million customers via 71,000 kilometers of cables, both above and below ground, and about 51,000 substations. All in all, the company dealt with over 5,000 megawatts of electricity per year. This immense and complex network cost the company about £100 million each year in development and maintenance costs. About 40 percent of Southern Electric's customers were private homes, 35 percent offices and shops, and 25 percent factories and farms.

The deregulation of the electricity industry changed the face of the business. Under the state-controlled system, customers and suppliers were matched on a purely geographical basis. Beginning in 1991, however, consumers with larger electricity requirements of over one megawatt, including hospitals, industrial sites, and ports, were free to choose their own suppliers. From 1994, customers demanding more than 100 kilowatts, such as superstores and office buildings, had a similar freedom of choice, and come 1998 a completely free market would be in operation. In this new environment Southern Electric had to compete not only with the other RECs but also with suppliers of other forms of energy, such as British Gas.

In the light of the new competitive era, Southern Electric targeted three key areas in its marketing strategies—industrial, commercial, and domestic—offering free specialist advice to each sector to attract customers. Industrial applications of electricity were myriad and could be refined to suit individual needs with an eye to energy efficiency and cost savings. Southern Electric's clients in this sector included such varied corporations as Parrs Quality Confectionery Ltd., Westinghouse Brakes Ltd., and BICC-Vero Electronics Ltd.

In its bid for commercial clients, Southern Electric offered a range of specialist advisory services, including its Building Energy Appraisal Service (BEAS) and Energy Efficient Design (EED). The company also advised on such applications of electricity as space heating, water heating, ventilation and air conditioning, catering, and lighting. Southern Electric won clients in commercial fields as diverse as education, retailing, leisure, and health care. In the domestic sphere, Southern Electric concentrated on providing information and advice to woo customers to electricity in preference to other energy sources where choice was possible, as in cooking, heating, and water heating.

Privatization and increased competition also allowed Southern Electric to move beyond its core business and expand into other, related ventures. Southern Electric Contracting Ltd., which began as a branch of Southern Electric PLC, moved to subsidiary status in 1992. Its business ran the gamut of electrical design and installation work, encompassing everything from domestic needs—such as insulation, fitted kitchens, replacement doors and windows, and rewiring—to complex and often dangerous work for the petrochemical industry. The subsidiary also boasted a public lighting division that was the largest contractor of its kind for local authorities' street lighting, a security systems area, and a datacom division. Operating not only in Southern Electric's traditional region but in Edinburgh, Leeds, Birmingham, and Middlesbrough as well, the subsidiary's clients included public utilities, government departments, universities, and health authorities.

M. P. Burke PLC was a post-privatization acquisition. The company was established in 1983 in Yorkshire as a general civil engineering firm, but over the years it became a specialist in utility contracting for the water, gas, electricity, telecommunications, and cable TV industries. Southern Electric Power Generation Ltd., formed in 1992, was Southern Electric's entry into the field of energy generation. During its short existence the subsidiary has invested, as full or part owner, in four combined cycle gas turbine (CCGT) or combined heat and power (CHP) projects. Thermal Transfer Ltd., which was established in 1972 and was later added to Southern Electric's stable, was an environmental engineering company serving the heating, ventilation, and air conditioning markets. The company also served the pharmaceutical, biotechnology, microelectronics, and food industries with design and installation of sterile facilities and mechanical and electrical services. It counted among its clients Bass Brewers, British Aerospace, and Motorola.

In a 1992 joint venture with Phillips Petroleum Company United Kingdom Ltd., Southern Electric formed Southern and Phillips Gas Ltd. Phillips, with its history of oil and gas exploration and production in North Sea fields, provided the gas, while Southern Electric controlled the service, sales, and marketing end of the business. The alliance enabled Southern Electric to offer its customers a choice of energy supply. Clients included Oxford University, Toys 'R' Us, bookseller W. H. Smith, and local government authorities.

Southern Electric also owned, in conjunction with fellow RECs Eastern Electricity and Midlands Electricity, the appliance retailing operation Powerhouse. Formed as a partnership between Southern and Eastern in 1992 and originally known as E & S Retail Ltd., the company had more than 300 outlets in the South, the Midlands, and East Anglia. Powerhouse was the third-largest electrical retail group in the U.K., but nonetheless was the most disappointing performer in Southern Electric's portfolio, consistently making losses.

On the whole, however, Southern Electric had fared well since privatization: in 1994 its profits were the highest of all the RECs. This success was due in part to the company's own efforts. Like virtually all privatized companies in Britain, Southern Electric instituted a rigorous program of cost-cutting and efficiency improvement after leaving the public sector. Procedures were streamlined, management structures pared, and fully one quarter of its staff was cut—with more jobs likely to be eliminated in the future.

Another cause of Southern Electric's consistently rising profits was the straightforward expedient of higher prices charged to customers—a sensitive issue for all connected with the industry. Because electricity is an essential utility in the modern world, the privatized industry remains subject to governmental control through the Office of Electricity Regulation (Offer). Offer's task is to ensure that the electricity companies provide a fair deal to customers while at the same time not unduly depressing profits to the detriment of shareholders. Offer's role in maintaining this balance is a highly controversial subject. For example, many observers maintain that the RECs have enjoyed a very easy ride since privatization. Some 80-95 percent of the RECs' profits derive from the distribution side of their core business. Since privatization, the companies have been permitted to raise their distribution prices by an average of 1.1 percent over inflation every year. This situation, commented the *Independent,* "has proved a virtual license to print money."

Offer's first post-privatization review of the industry came in August 1994. The stock market was wary, and the RECs' share prices fluctuated, but in the end Offer was extremely lenient with the RECs, allowing them a significantly higher price cap than had been anticipated. Indeed, many consumer groups and some politicians were outraged by the decision, believing that Offer had weighted the balance too far in favor of the profit motive. Offer was apparently not impervious to this criticism, because some months later, in the spring of 1995, the regulator unexpectedly announced that it would re-review the electricity companies with the intention of tightening price controls. A decision date was not announced. The prolonged suspense returned the stock market to a state of uncertainty.

In one possible scenario, much favored by consumer groups, Offer would limit pricing to four percent below inflation as well as insist that the RECs provide cash rebates to customers, although at least one REC publicly questioned the legality of this proposal. If Offer and the RECs should find themselves unable to reach an agreement, the Monopolies and Mergers Commission would have to step in to arbitrate—resulting in a long, drawn-out process to no one's advantage. Already the uncertainty has delayed indefinitely the proposed privatization of the National Grid, jointly owned by the 12 RECs.

The extent to which Southern Electric would suffer if Offer chose to take a hard line was unknown, though it was clear that the company had prospered since privatization and possessed healthy cash reserves. Curbed profits in the company's core business were more than likely; serious damage to Southern Electric's financial well-being was not. In any event, financial analysts agree that the way forward for the privatized utilities will be largely through the growth of their non-regulated activities, and here Southern Electric appeared well positioned, with its newer ventures increasingly contributing to the company's profits. M. P. Burke and the company's contracting business were performing particularly well. Southern Electric was virtually certain to achieve its stated aim of generating 15 percent of its profits from its non-core businesses by the year 2000. Thus, although Southern Electric's traditional role of providing electricity to central southern England would remain the company's mainstay for the foreseeable future, its penetration into new markets and its diversification in the ever more competitive energy industry should afford Southern Electric new opportunities for corporate growth.

Principal Subsidiaries: M. P. Burke PLC (70 percent); National Grid Holding PLC (11 percent); Powerhouse Retail Ltd. (36 percent); Southern and Phillips Gas Ltd. (50 percent); Southern Electric Contracting Ltd.; Southern Electric Power Generation Ltd.; Thermal Transfer (Holdings) Ltd.

Further Reading:

"Power Firms Spurn Concern over Bills by Pegging Prices," *Guardian,* March 4, 1994.

Reguly, Eric, "Southern Electric Plans to Eliminate 1,200 More Jobs," *Times,* December 14, 1994.

"Southern Chief Warns Regulator over Service Standards," *Guardian,* June 24, 1994.

"Southern Electric Powers On to Lift Payout and Profit," *Times,* June 24, 1994.

"Southern Electric Surges to £222 Million," *Independent,* June 24, 1994.

"Southern Electric's Buyback Triggers a Buzz," *Independent,* May 4, 1994.

"Southern Seeks Efficiency Reward," *Daily Telegraph,* June 24, 1994.

This Is Southern Electric, Maidenhead: Southern Electric PLC, 1993.

"UK Company News: Southern Electric up at £222 Million," *Financial Times,* June 24, 1994.

Waller, Martin, "Eastern Doubts Legality of Electricity Bill Rebates," *Times,* April 10, 1995.

Waller, "Work Resumes on Flotation of Grid," *Times,* April 3, 1995.

—Robin DuBlanc

Southern Indiana Gas and Electric Company

20 Northwest Fourth Street
Evansville, Indiana 47741
U.S.A.
(812) 424-6411
Fax: (812) 464-4554

Public Company
Incorporated: 1912 as Public Utilities Company
Employees: 5,500
Sales: $234 million
Stock Exchanges: New York
SICs: 4931 Electric & Other Services Combined

Southern Indiana Gas and Electric Company (SIGECO) is an electric and gas utility company serving the southwest portion of the state of Indiana. In 1995 the utility was providing electricity to about 120,000 electricity customers and about 100,000 gas customers. It was also operating nonregulated businesses related to real estate, facility design, and alternative energy products. SIGECO is distinguished as a low-cost supplier of power in comparison to other U.S. utility companies.

SIGECO was founded in 1912 by the merger of three southwestern Indiana energy companies: Evansville Gas Light Company; Brush Light and Power Company; and Evansville Public Service Company. Those companies had been serving southwest Indiana since before the Civil War. Evansville Gas Light Company, in fact, was formed in 1852 by several businessmen, in the southwestern Indiana city of Evansville, who organized the company to light stores and streets in the downtown area. The company started out extracting and refining a gaseous byproduct of coal combustion, and then delivering the fumes to gas-burning street and store lamps. The venture's innovative system soon gained widespread acceptance and new gas manufacturing facilities were constructed to serve a broader area. The *Evansville Journal* during the 1950s described the gas manufacturing facilities as "on a slightly larger scale than those of Cleveland, Ohio."

Evansville Gas Light Company illuminated the streets of Evansville for 30 years before electricity emerged as a commercially viable lighting and energy source in the area. In 1882, the Brush Light and Power Company began lighting streets electrically in Evansville. One year later, Brush Light and Evansville Gas joined forced to create the Evansville Gas and Electric Light Company. Evansville Gas brought 30 years of experience in Evansville to the table, while Brush Light boasted expertise related to the energy supply of the future. The new company expanded rapidly during the late 1880s and 1890s, supplying gas and electricity to light streets and buildings, power factories, and even energize homes. Indeed, an increasing number of homes near the turn of the century were enjoying the benefits of electricity. The typical household still used coal for heating and cooking, and ice for refrigeration. But many homes also had a few electric incandescent bulbs for reading and, in some cases, an electric iron to help with the laundry.

Evansville prospered around the turn of the century. Because of its convenient location on the Ohio River, the town had long served as an important regional hub of commerce. During the late 1800s and early 1900, moreover, the city evolved into a hearty manufacturing town. Evansville's population more than doubled in just more than ten years during the height of its growth. At the same time, new uses for gas and electricity proliferated. By the early 1900s, gas and electricity was being used for thousands of industrial, commercial, institutional, and consumer applications.

Spiraling power consumption led to the emergence of the third energy start-up in Evansville in 1909—Evansville Public Service Company. Although that company initially promised to bring much-needed competition to the local gas and electricity market, it soon became apparent that the two companies would be providing overlapping infrastructure and services. To achieve economies of scale, Evansville Public Service merged with Evansville Gas and Electric Light in 1912 to form Public Utilities, a holding company developed to buy the outstanding stock of both companies. C.B Cobb was named as the company's first president. Simultaneously, the new holding company purchased Southern Indiana Traction Company, a local transportation utility; it wasn't until 1920 that the organization's name was changed to the more appropriate Southern Indiana Gas and Electric Company. Also in 1912, a fire destroyed the utility's downtown Evansville offices, which were quickly rebuilt.

SIGECO expanded at a rampant clip during the 1910s and 1920s by purchasing other utility companies in the southwest Indiana area. As demand for electricity and gas escalated, the company's facilities, sales, and profits surged. At the same time, economies of scale and new generation and distribution technology allowed the company to reduce its rates. Between 1916 and 1926, for example, SIGECO's electricity sales more than doubled while both gas and electricity prices dropped more than ten percent. As noted in company annals, Edison's prophecy that one day only the rich would burn candles was becoming true. Not only had it become more expensive to burn candles for light than to use electricity, but consumers were discovering that they could heat their homes, cook, and run new appliances with electricity and gas.

The 1930s became known as the "golden age" of the gas and electricity industry in southwest Indiana. During that period, demand for power from the industrial sector rocketed. Industrial growth, in fact, was a welcome reprieve to a woodworking region that had nearly depleted its rich forests. Factories sprang up in the region that were producing automobiles and vehicle parts, industrial equipment, and heavy appliances. Besides increased demand for electricity from the companies building those products, the consumers of many of those goods demanded more power to run them. The result was that demand for electricity in southwestern Indiana was doubling every ten to 12 years during the late 1920s and 1930s, despite the Great Depression.

SIGECO scrambled during the 1930s to build new infrastructure to keep pace with racing demand. As the Depression wore on, the utility invested millions of dollars in new facilities and equipment. The heart of its system became the giant Ohio River Station generation plant, which was built during the mid-1920s and expanded throughout the 1930s. Hundreds of miles of new above-ground power lines, supported by tall pine poles, were strung throughout the cities and countryside. Likewise, miles of underground natural gas pipelines were laid with the help of new gas-powered heavy equipment. SIGECO's expansion was made possible by its conversion from horse-drawn wagons to gas-powered trucks. Those trucks were instrumental in building and repairing the infrastructure that allowed SIGECO to generate and deliver gas and electricity throughout Evansville and surrounding areas during the 1930s and 1940s.

SIGECO and the Evansville area suffered a major setback in 1937 that temporarily squelched the company's ambitious growth plans. A record-breaking flood inundated the region, wreaking about $17 million in property damage and flooding out about one-third of the homes in Evansville. Despite the flooding, SIGECO managed to continue supplying electricity to many of its customers from the Ohio River Station. As recorded in company annals, the January 28 *Evansville Courier* wrote of SIGECO's efforts: "in this period of stress and strain let us remember that our light and power service is not being maintained without heroic action. Some 60 workers are virtually entombed at the utility plant where they fight 24 hours in the day to maintain service. Food and water get to them by boat through window tops. Workers dig coal from underwater pits to keep up this power."

SIGECO recovered from the 1937 flood and enjoyed steady demand growth during the 1940s, particularly given a population surge in Evansville during this time, upon the establishment of an important shipbuilding enterprise for the war effort. Growth was also strong following World War II, when the postwar economic and population boom resulted in a rapid escalation of power consumption. In fact, it became clear during the early 1950s that SIGECO might have trouble meeting the demand for natural gas. The problem was that its main gas works, which had been the key gas production and supply facility for years, had become obsolete. To solve the problem, SIGECO invested heavily to add underground gas storage facilities to feed its main pipeline system, and closed the original gas works. That effort had the added benefit of allowing SIGECO to purchase surplus gas when prices were low. At the same time, SIGECO recognized that it needed to augment its electricity generating facilities. The company again added to the Ohio River Station, among other moves, and built a new plant called the Culley Station.

By the 1960s SIGECO had established itself as a key supplier of gas and electricity to Evansville and surrounding southwest Indiana areas. The company benefited from generally positive industry trends throughout the 1950s and 1960s, in fact, that created a boon for the electricity industry. SIGECO's growth during that period and into the 1970s was typical of many other power companies that vastly expanded their infrastructure and increased sales to meet surging demand. Unfortunately, the power industry experienced turbulence beginning in the 1970s. Efforts by the Organization of Petroleum Exporting Countries (OPEC) shocked the United States into the reality that natural energy sources were not unlimited. SIGECO, like other power companies at the time, was forced to change its mindset. Conservation became key, as reflected in the company's consumer education initiatives and efforts to increase the energy efficiency of its end users.

SIGECO was also influenced during the 1970s by new environmental laws. Legislation that proliferated during that period effectively forced the company to revamp its facilities to generate less pollution. Those costs, combined with increased fuel prices, caused energy prices to rise. SIGECO, however, was sheltered from most negative effects by its status as a government-regulated utility. Still, its rates increased, spelling an end to the rapid demand growth that the company experienced during the 1950s, 1960s, and early 1970s. Despite comparatively sluggish demand growth, SIGECO managed to post revenue and profit gains during the late 1970s and early 1980s. Revenues surged from $94 million in 1977 to $118 million in 1979, and then to $154 million in 1980 as OPEC influences eased. Meanwhile, net income bounced from about $15 million to $21 million and the company's customer base rose to about 163,000.

During the 1980s SIGECO benefited from reduced energy prices and moderate demand growth. The company also expanded by acquiring other companies, thus broadening its customer base throughout southwest Indiana. By 1987, SIGECO's potential customer base encompassed a 2,250-square mile area with a population of about 350,000 people in 74 cities and communities. SIGECO was supplying electricity to more than 110,000 customers, including nonresidential users, and was selling gas to about 68,000 customers in 40 communities. In 1988, SIGECO purchased the service territory of Hoosier Gas Corporation, which boosted its gas customer base to more than 90,000. As a result of that and other acquisitions, SIGECO's revenues surpassed $230 million in the late 1980s, up from about $190 million in the mid-1980s. The late 1980s were also marked by the retirement of Alva Bertrand Brown, who had served as chairman of the board and/or chief executive officer for 35 years, presiding over much of the company's growth.

SIGECO, like other government-regulated utilities, maintained a relatively stable course during the late 1980s and early 1990s. Sales hovered around $230 million, while profits grew from around $30 million in the late 1980s to more than $35 million annually during the early 1990s. The profit gain was partially attributable to SIGECO's cost-cutting and efficiency initiatives, which earned the company recognition as a low-cost leader in the utility industry. Indeed, going into the mid-1990s SIGECO was ranked in the bottom 12 percent of all U.S. utility companies for operating costs as a percentage of sales, and it charged among the lowest rates for electricity and natural gas in the nation. It was also among the top in the industry in terms of customer satisfaction. Among other miscellaneous credits, SIGECO maintained a cutting-edge fleet of vehicles that used compressed natural gas as fuel and was also helping to convert many area school buses to compressed natural gas.

By 1994 SIGECO was serving more than 120,000 electricity customers and more than 100,000 natural gas consumers. 1994 sales reached a recorded $261 million as net income surpassed $41 million. By that time, SIGECO was employing a work force of 5,500 people throughout southwest Indiana. Under the leadership of Ronald G. Reherman, the company continued to boast a healthy balance sheet and to cement its status as a low-cost provider of gas and electricity in comparison to other U.S. utilities.

In addition to its core utility operations, which were facing increasing competition from alternative providers, SIGECO began a push during the early 1990s to diversify into nonregulated businesses. To that end, the company established three subsidiaries: Southern Indiana Properties, Inc., a real estate division created in 1985; Southern Indiana Minerals, Inc., a division created in 1994 to market coal combustion by-products; and Energy Systems Group, Inc., which was incorporated in 1994 to design and recommend building upgrades that would pay for themselves through lower energy consumption. Gains from those subsidiaries, combined with healthy regional growth and positive returns from SIGECO's long-standing gas and electricity operations, suggested ongoing success for the 83-year-old utility in 1995.

Principal Subsidiaries: Southern Indiana Properties, Inc.; Southern Indiana Minerals, Inc.; Energy Systems Group, Inc.

Further Reading:

Goebel, A.E., ''Southern Indiana Gas and Electric Company Reports Fourth Quarter Results,'' *PR Newswire,* January 29, 1993.

''Southern Indiana Gas and Electric Co.,'' *Indianapolis Business Journal,* March 12, 1990, p. 21A.

SIGECO: Celebrating 75 Years; Southern Indiana Gas and Electric Company 1987 Annual Report, Evansville, Ind.: Southern Indiana Gas and Electric Company, 1988.

—Dave Mote

Standard Commercial Corporation

2201 Miller Road
Wilson, North Carolina 27893
U.S.A.
(919) 291-5507
Fax: (919) 237-1109

Public Company
Incorporated: 1916 as Standard Commercial Tobacco Co.
Employees: 2,280
Sales: $1.04 million
Stock Exchanges: New York
SICs: 5159 Farm-Product Raw Materials, Not Elsewhere Classified; 2281 Yarn Spinning Mills

Until early 1995, Standard Commercial Corporation oversaw two international service-related businesses in two very different fields: leaf tobacco and wool. It is the world's second largest leaf tobacco importer and exporter, and was one of the world's ten largest wool merchants until it sold those interests in order to focus on tobacco. Buying leaf from tobacco growers around the world, Standard sells the product to cigarette companies for blending. Leaf dealing is sufficiently complex that only a handful of companies do it, and such industry giants as R.J. Reynolds contract for the leaf product with companies like Standard Commercial.

Standard Commercial was founded in the early 1900s by Turkish immigrant Ery Kehaya, Sr., the son of a revered teacher of religion and ethics and his wife, also from a family of religious educators and prelates. Kehaya grew up in a tobacco-growing region of Turkey along the Black Sea. Although Kehaya was groomed for a role in the church, and educated by his uncle, an archbishop in a Macedonian diocese, the young man's interests soon lead him in other directions. After traveling extensively and studying at the Sorbonne in Paris, Kehaya arrived in the United States and became a U.S. citizen. He initially found work as a waiter in a Greek-Turkish restaurant in New York City. However, the industrious young man had greater aspirations.

In New York at the time, several small factories had been established at which cigarettes were rolled by hand, using tobaccos imported from the Orient. Several tobacco importers frequented the restaurant at which Kehaya worked, and, having become acquainted with some of them, Kehaya was once prevailed upon to help sell one importer's tobacco stock to the factories. Kehaya accepted the offer, and received a commission for his sales. With the money he earned, he decided to leave the restaurant and get into the tobacco business himself.

The few thousand dollars Kehaya had earned by 1912 became the start-up capital for his new enterprise: Standard Commercial Tobacco Company. Garnering a solid reputation for the good quality of its imported Oriental tobacco, the company saw steadily increasing sales and was incorporated in Delaware in 1916. That year, as a testament to Kehaya's business acumen, Standard Commercial entered into a contract to provide Oriental leaf tobacco to R.J. Reynolds Tobacco Company. When offered a commission on the purchases, Kehaya said that he would prefer to be paid with interest in Reynolds, a company he believed offered tremendous opportunity for growth. He was right; his original shares in Reynolds would over the next ten years be worth about $5 million.

In 1917, Kehaya married Grace Whitaker, the daughter of a prominent North Carolina tobacco manufacturer. During this time, on the brink of U.S. involvement in World War I, Standard Commercial met with some misfortune. Kehaya had decided to diversify his interests, and his company had purchased two steamships, one of which was dubbed the *Grace.* However, that sideline business came to an abrupt end, as Kehaya and Grace, on their honeymoon, learned that their two ships had been sunk by the Germans. Also during this time, as Bolshevik forces overthrew Kerensky's regime in Russia, Standard Commercial's large store of tobacco in Russia was threatened with confiscation. While U.S. businesses, investors, and banks with holdings in Russia were losing fortunes daily, Kehaya came up with a unique plan. While other companies tried and failed to move merchandise out of Russia via railroads and established trade channels, he arranged for barges to move his tobacco up the Volga River to the White Sea and then on to the Arctic Ocean, on their way to the North Pole. Through this less travelled, and therefore unguarded, route, the tobacco reached its destination safely.

During the 1920s, Standard Commercial expanded the scope of its operations worldwide, purchasing a cigarette manufacturer in Hamburg, Germany, and establishing offices and processing plants in Korea. In fact, much of Kehaya's early work involved some real pioneering. For example, after securing a contract with a Japanese company for the export of tobacco grown in Korea, Kehaya and his wife lived in a railroad car in rural Korea for more than a year in 1922, overseeing the project, which involved teaching Korean farmers to grow tobacco.

By 1928, Standard's net worth had risen to $12 million and the company gained a listing on the New York Stock Exchange. However, the price of leaf tobacco had been depressed, and the United States was on the brink of a stock market crash that would result in the Great Depression. Having borrowed more than $15 million to purchase some Turkish tobacco, Standard was rocked soon thereafter, when the bank was forced to request repayment of the loan at maturity. Kehaya was forced to choose between selling the tobacco at the current prices and losing millions of dollars, or asking for an extension, risking the possibility of being denied further credit and potentially damaging Kehaya's reputation.

Kehaya opted to repay the loan, and toward that end he sold tobacco at record-low prices, divested many capital investments, and reduced his own salary significantly, asking his colleagues to do likewise. The Depression thus hit Kehaya and Standard very hard. But while the company founder lost much in the way of personal assets, Standard Commercial, unlike many larger corporations, survived.

As political and economic conditions overseas grew increasingly complex, Standard shopped stateside for opportunities in the 1930s. The company purchased a controlling interest in the Axton-Fisher Tobacco Company of Louisville, Kentucky, which produced the increasingly popular "Twenty Grand" cigarette brand for ten cents a pack, undercutting the more expensive brands of Camel, Lucky Strike, and Chesterfields. Standard also entered into an agreement with the Jas I. Miller Tobacco Company, purchasing and processing some of that company's products.

Since Axton-Fisher continued to prosper in the mid-1930s, Standard borrowed money to buy up its remaining stock. However, the acquisition soon soured, when, in 1937, a devastating flood hit the Ohio Valley, submerging the warehouse in which Axton-Fisher stored its redried tobacco. Costly efforts were made to salvage the tobacco, but Standard's losses and debt load were mounting.

Standard Commercial and the once-promising Axton-Fisher eventually went into bankruptcy. At that point, the Bank of America came to the rescue, becoming Axton-Fisher's majority shareholder and taking over its management, while Standard Commercial tended to its own problems. In 1944, the Bank of America decided to sell Axton-Fisher's physical assets to Phillip Morris and to liquidate all assets. As the minority shareholder of Axton-Fisher, Kehaya found an interested buyer in the Jas. I. Miller Co., which paid a good price for the tobacco inventory and helped Standard Commercial to withstand the disaster, albeit so heavily scaled-down in size and scope that in the mid-1940s the company was not much more than a handful of employees and the founder's will to reemerge.

The onset of World War II also complicated matters for Standard Commercial. Greece, Bulgaria, and Turkey had been the company's major sources for tobacco leaf prior to the war, and when Greece and Bulgaria came under German occupation, they ceased shipments. Moreover, the company's Mediterranean ports serving Turkey were also disrupted by the war. With great effort, Standard managed to get some of its stores of tobacco out of Russia during this time and also received shipments of Oriental tobacco from Rhodesia.

By 1947, with continued assistance from the Bank of America, all of Standard's outstanding debts from the Axton-Fisher disaster were paid, and, with the end of the war, the company was ready to regain its momentum. By the end of the decade, the company had reestablished relations in the East and in Europe and had reinitiated trade with Greek and Turkish markets, and formed a joint venture in Greece that was the largest of its kind at the time.

Establishment of Standard's foreign presence continued in the 1950s. In 1953, Standard formed a subsidiary in Valuz, called Eryka International, AG, to oversee purchases and sales of tobacco in the Eastern block countries, but many of Standard's dealing during this time took the form of partnerships, as had their 1955 venture to import tobacco from Thailand. With deals of such magnitude, Standard and its partners found that they needed to form a substantial subsidiary to oversee Far Eastern operations. In 1957, the Trans-Continental Leaf Tobacco Company (TCLTC) company was formed as a joint venture with the Elia Salzman Tobacco Co. Ltd. Elia Salzman, whose name the partner company bore, had founded his company in London, selling Indian tobacco in the United Kingdom and elsewhere. A formidable presence and an industry legend, Salzman could, according to Kehaya, "tear a thick phone book in half with his bare hands," and was proficient in the Russian, German, French, Turkish, Greek, and English languages. Salzman's company oversaw TCLTC's Indian business, while Standard Commercial was responsible for its business in the Orient.

In the midst of these complex foreign affairs, Standard's founder suffered a stroke, and his son, Ery W. Kehaya, was named president. The younger Kehaya had been hard at work with the company since 1945, starting out on the docks and then helping with an ultimately unsuccessful tobacco farming project in California, before becoming established in company's sales force in the 1950s.

The late 1950s and early 1960s saw the rise to prominence of TCLTC. That company took over Salzman's tobacco interests in Rhodesia and then signed a ten-year contract with the Thailand Tobacco Monopoly for exclusive rights to the export of all surplus flue-cured tobaccos. The company was also contracting with the Japan Monopoly Corporation during this time for export of their burley to Europe. Moreover, having purchased tobaccos from Thai Company, Thapawong, Ltd. for some years, TCLTC signed with them in 1962 to form a joint company, Siam Tobacco Export Corporation, which built a factory and over time bought out curing stations in order to produce and acquire its own tobaccos as security against years of small crops. TCLTC entered the Philippines in the late 1950s, exporting that country's first shipments of flue-cured tobaccos, and entered Taiwan in 1960, striking a deal with the Taiwanese Monopoly to export surplus tobaccos in Europe, Indonesia, and the United States. Business with India was ceased for some years after the death of Salzman in 1963, but would later be reestablished with the acquisition of Siemssen Threshie & Co. in the 1970s. By the mid-1960s, TCLTC had accounts in Mexico, Brazil, Argentina, and Europe, as well as smaller operations in Pakistan, Ceylon, Ghana, and Indonesia.

Meanwhile, Standard Commercial explored untapped sources such as Uganda and Tanzania in 1964. While Uganda's potential exports were ceased under the Amin regime, Tanzania proved a particularly prosperous exporter for Standard Commercial. In the late 1960s, Standard became interested for the first time in cigar tobacco and began buying it in Paraguay, Mexico, Brazil, and the Philippines, delegating responsibility for the cigar business to the German subsidiary Werkhof GmbH. However, Standard Commercial soon became dissatisfied with the operation, which proved too small to handle all of the business demands, and a more suitable arrangement was found in partnering Werkhof with the East Asiatic Co. of Copenhagen. Standard would later reacquire these cigar interests, which became known as LEAFCO, in 1982 and relocate all such operations as a division in Copenhagen.

After years of global expansion and a slowdown in the early 1970s, Standard Commercial decided to enhance its presence in the United States. In 1974, they engaged with Imperial Tobacco in establishing facilities in Wilson, North Carolina. The company also established a branch office in Richmond, Virginia. Moreover, Standard Commercial acquired the outstanding shares of its former joint venture, TCLTC, in 1975, making it a wholly owned subsidiary.

Acquisitions in the 1970s included Andrew Chalmers International, Ltd., which was eventually merged with Siemssen to form Standard Commercial (U.K.). Standard also acquired a 51 percent interest in Swiss company Spierer Freres, which moved Oriental leaf out of markets in Turkey and Greece. Jas. I. Miller Tobacco Company, Standard's frequent partner in deals, was purchased in 1978. This North Carolina-based company gave Standard a firmer presence in the United States, adding a processing factory and some great employees to the company. In 1981, Marvin Coghill was named president of Standard Commercial, as Kehaya ascended to the position of chairman.

When sanctions against Rhodesia, which had since become known as Zimbabwe, were lifted in 1979, Standard reviewed its options and decided to acquire a 49 percent interest in a plant called Tobacco Packers. Toward that end, Standard partnered with Zimbabwe's largest locally owned public company, T.A. Holdings. In 1984, Standard acquired British Leaf Tobacco Co. of Canada Ltd., which would later be merged with Standard Commercial Co. of Canada Ltd. Moreover, the company also solidified its stateside presence during this time, buying up the remaining land and buildings of Jas. I. Miller's Springfield, Kentucky facilities, after a destructive fire destroyed most of the processing machinery there. Standard eventually installed all new equipment at the Springfield facility, just in time for the 1983 burley processing season. The facility secured Standard's place in Kentucky's burley markets. That year, the company's net profit was $11.4 million.

Standard Commercial's focus changed drastically in the late 1980s. Though there had always been a need for leaf dealing, the U.S. cigarette market was shrinking, as increasingly health-conscious Americans began kicking the smoking habit. In fact, cigarette consumption domestically had been dwindling since 1981. Standard had to either downsize accordingly or widen its interests.

One of Standard's closest competitors in leaf dealing during this time, Dibrell Brothers, had diversified into the manufacturing of ice cream freezers. Standard took another direction, however. Beginning in 1986, the company spent $35 million for acquisitions in the wool industry, adding four wool trading and processing companies in 1987 alone, and the company began buying and processing wool for a long list of customers, primarily overseas. By 1988, wool accounted for 44 percent of the company's sales. Standard's global contacts in banks and business helped guide this growth.

Wool trading in the late 1980s was similar to tobacco trading in the 1950s: very fragmented. No single company owned more than ten percent of the wool business in the Free World. Nevertheless, Standard had plants in Australia, France, and Argentina by 1988, and by 1990 had acquired seven wool dealers and processors to become one of the largest entities in that market. Wool accounted for half of its $936 million in revenues in fiscal 1989.

But, just as its production was soaring, the demand for wool plunged. Prices collapsed globally and Standard was in a position eerily similar to the one its founder had faced in the Depression. Stuck with a lot of wool, few buyers and bad prices, the company had to devise a plan. Although the company tended to avoid retaining large inventories, it waited out the depressed prices, and by 1991 was able to move from a $4.3 million loss in 1991 to $6.2 million in operating profits in 1992.

Luckily, the company's tobacco business was reviving at the same time. Tobacco was then accounting for two-thirds of Standard's revenues. Foreign sales, particularly of American blends and low-tar products, increased so much that Standard's tobacco revenues increased 140 percent between 1990 and 1992. In fact, American blends represented about 30 percent of tobacco consumed worldwide in 1991, and Standard was one of that product's major exporters.

Early 1993 saw competitor Dibrell Brothers seek a merger with Standard Commercial; any tentative agreements reached, however, were scrapped the next year by Standard. Dibrell maintained a 9.9 percent stake in Standard, but opted to explore mergers with other companies instead. Also during this time, the domestic cigarette market was suffering as U.S. legislators debated enacting laws to regulate tobacco content and impose federal excise taxes on cigarettes and other tobacco products. Moreover, an oversupply of tobacco hurt everyone in the industry in 1993 and 1994, and Standard joined its competitors when it sold its inventory at a loss to manufacturers. Referring to 1994 as a "year of unprecedented difficulty," president and CEO J. Alec G. Murray pledged to divest those interests not crucial to Standard's role as wool and tobacco. However, in March 1995, Standard decided to sell its wool trading and processing business. Given the severe state of flux in the tobacco trade in the United States, the future seemed uncertain for the company, but Standard vowed to focus on improving risk management, reducing inventory, improving profitability, and strengthening its management structure in hopes of a turnaround.

Principal Subsidiaries: W.A. Adams Company; Jas. I. Miller Tobacco Company Inc.; Standard Commercial Tobacco Co. Inc.; Standard Commercial Services Inc.; Spierer Freres & Cie S.A. (Switzerland); Standard Commercial Tobacco Company of Canada Ltd.; Transconti Srl (Italy); Werkhof GmbH (Germany); Standard Commercial Tobacco Company (UK) Ltd.; Trans-Continental Leaf Tobacco Corporation; Transcatab SpA (Italy); Trans-Continental Participacoes e Empreendimentos Ltda. (Brazil); Transhellenhic Tobacco S.A. (Greece); World Wide Tobacco España S.A. (Spain).

Further Reading:

Cone, Edward, "Turning Over a New Leaf," *Forbes,* April 4, 1988, p. 87.

Cochran, Thomas, "Hardly a Wool Gatherer," *Barron's,* January 22, 1990, p. 42.

Dubashi, Jagannath, "Standard Commercial: Investing Without Getting Fleeced," *FW,* August 4, 1992, p. 14.

"Standard Commercial Corporation Reports Third Quarter and Nine Months Results," *PR Newswire,* February 8, 1995.

"Standard Commercial Settles Tax Dispute, Pays IRS $1.3 Million," *Wall Street Journal,* January 3, 1985, p. 2.

—Carol I. Keeley

Starbucks Corporation

2203 Airport Way South
Seattle, Washington 98134
U.S.A.
(206) 447-1575
Fax: (206) 442-7756

Public Company
Incorporated: 1985
Employees: 11,000
Sales: $284.9 million
Stock Exchanges: NASDAQ
SICs: 5499 Miscellaneous Food Stores; 5149 Groceries & Related Products Nec

Starbucks Corporation is the leading roaster, retailer, and brand of specialty coffee in North America. From a single small store that opened in 1971 to more than 535 locations in 1995, Starbucks has led a coffee revolution in the United States.

Starbucks was founded in Seattle, Washington, a haven for coffee aficionados. The city was noted for its coffee before World War II, but the quality of its coffee had declined so much by the late 1960s that resident Gordon Bowker made pilgrimages to Vancouver, British Columbia, to buy his beans there. His point of reference for the beverage was dark, delicious coffee he had discovered in Italy. Soon Bowker, then a writer for *Seattle* magazine, was making runs for friends as well. When *Seattle* folded, two of Bowker's friends, Jerry Baldwin, an English teacher, and Zev Siegl, a history teacher, also happened to be seeking new ventures; the three banded together and literally built their first store by hand. They raised $1,350 apiece, borrowed another $5,000, picked the name Starbucks—for the punchy "st" sound and its reference to the coffee-loving first mate in *Moby Dick*—then designed a two-tailed siren for a logo and set out to learn about coffee.

Siegl went to Berkeley, California, to learn from a Dutchman, Alfred Peet, who ran Peet's Coffee, which had been a legend among local coffee drinkers since 1966. Peet's approach to coffee beans became the cornerstone for Starbucks's reputation: high-grade arabica beans, roasted to a dark extreme by a trained perfectionist roaster. Starbucks bought its coffee from Peet's for its first nine months, giving away cups of coffee to hook customers. The plan worked. By 1972 the three founders had opened a second store in University Village and invested in a Probat roaster. Baldwin became the young company's first roaster.

Within its first decade, Starbucks had opened stores in Bellevue, Capitol Hill, and University Way. By 1982 the original entrepreneurs had a solid retail business of five stores, a small toasting facility, and a wholesale business that sold coffee primarily to local restaurants. The first of the company's growth versus ethos challenges came here: how does one maintain a near fanatical dedication to freshness in wholesale? Starbucks insisted that the shelf life of coffee is less than 14 days after roasting. As a result, they donated all eight-day-old coffee to charity.

In 1982 Starbucks hired Howard Schultz to manage the company's retail sales and marketing. While V.P. of U.S. operations for Hammarplast, a Swedish housewares company, and working out of New York, Schultz met the Starbucks trio and considered their coffee a revelation. (He had grown up on instant.) He and his wife packed up and drove 3,000 miles west to Seattle to join Starbucks.

There were other changes taking place at Starbucks at the same time. Siegl had decided to leave in 1980. The name of the wholesale division was changed to Caravali, out of fear of sullying the Starbucks name with less than absolute freshness. Blue Anchor, a line of whole-bean coffees being prepackaged for supermarkets, was relinquished. Starbucks learned two lessons from their brief time in business with supermarkets: first, supermarkets and their narrow profit margins were not the best outlet for a coffee roaster who refused to compromise on quality in order to lower prices, and second, Starbucks needed to sell directly to consumers who were educated enough to know why the coffee they were buying was superior. In 1985 Starbucks bought Peet's Coffee, which had by then become a five-store operation itself.

Meanwhile, in 1983 Schultz had taken a buying trip to Italy, where another coffee revelation took place. Wandering the piazzas of Milan, Schultz was captivated by the culture of coffee and the romance of Italian coffee bars. Milan had about 1,700 espresso bars, which were a third center for Italians, after work and home. Schultz returned home determined to bring Italian coffee bars to the United States, but found his bosses reluctant, being still more dedicated to retailing coffee. As a result, Schultz left the company to write a business plan of his own. His parting with Starbucks was so amicable that the founders invested in Schultz's vision. Schultz returned to Italy to do research, visiting hundreds of espresso and coffee bars. In the spring of 1986, he opened his first coffee bar in the Columbia Seafirst Center, the tallest building west of Chicago. Faithful to its inspiration, the bar had a stately espresso machine as its centerpiece. Called Il Giornale, the bar served Starbucks coffee and was an instant hit. A second was soon opened in Seattle, and a third in Vancouver. Schultz hired Dave Olsen, the proprietor of one of the first bohemian espresso bars in Seattle, as a coffee consultant and employee trainer.

A year later, Schultz was thriving while Starbucks was encountering frustration. The wholesale market had been reconfigured by the popularity of flavored coffees, which Starbucks resolutely refused to produce. The company's managers were also increasingly aggravated by the lack of wholesale quality control, so they sold their wholesale line, Caravali, to Seattle businessman Bart Wilson and a group of investors. In addition, Bowker was interested in leaving the company to concentrate on a new project, Red Hook Ale. Schultz approached his old colleagues with an attractive offer: how about $4 million for Starbucks? They sold, with Baldwin staying on as president of the Peet's Coffee subsidiary and Olsen remaining as Starbucks's coffee buyer and roaster. In 1987 the Il Giornale shops changed their names to Starbucks, and the company became Starbucks Corporation and prepared to go national.

In August 1987 Starbucks Corporation had 11 stores and fewer than 100 employees. In October of that year it opened its first store in Chicago, and by 1989 there were nine Chicago Starbucks, where employees trained by Seattle managers served coffee roasted in the Seattle plant.

Their methods were costly, using high-grade arabica beans and expensive dark roasting, while suffering the financial consequences of snubbing the supermarket and wholesale markets. Nevertheless, Starbucks's market was growing rapidly: sales of specialty coffee in the United States grew from $50 million in 1983 to $500 million five years later.

In 1988 Starbucks introduced a mail order catalogue, and by the end of that year, the company was serving mail-order customers in every state and operating a total of 26 stores. Because the company's reputation grew steadily by word of mouth, it spent little on ads. Schultz's management philosophy, "hire people smarter than you are and get out of their way," fed his aggressive expansion plans. Industry experts were brought in to manage Starbucks's finances, human resources, marketing, and mail-order divisions. The company's middle ranks were filled with experienced managers from such giants as Taco Bell, Wendy's, and Blockbuster. Schultz was willing to lose money while preparing Starbucks for explosive growth. By 1990 he had hired two star executives: Howard Behar, previously president of a leading developer of outdoor resorts, Thousand Trails, Inc.; and Orin Smith, chief financial and administrative officer for Danzas, USA, a freight forwarder.

Starbucks installed a costly computer network and hired a specialist in information technology from McDonald's Corporation to design a point-of-sale system via PCs for store managers to use. Every night, stores passed their sales information to Seattle headquarters, which allowed planners to spot regional buying trends almost instantly. Starbucks lost money while preparing for its planned expansion, including more than $1 million in 1989 alone. In 1990 the headquarters expanded and a new roasting plant was built. Nevertheless, Schultz resisted both the temptation to franchise and to flavor the beans. Slowly, the chain developed near-cult status.

Starbucks also developed a reputation for treating its employees well. In 1991 it became the first privately owned company in history to establish an employee stock option program that included part-timers. Starbucks also offered health and dental benefits to both full- and part-time employees. As a result, the company has a turnover rate that is very low for the food service industry. Employees were rigorously trained, completing at least 25 hours of coursework on topics including the history of coffee, drink preparation, and how to brew a perfect cup at home. The company went public in 1992, the same year it opened its first stores in San Francisco, San Diego, Orange County, and Denver. Its stores totaled 165 by year's end. The company began special relationships with Nordstrom's and Barnes & Noble, Inc., offering coffee to shoppers at both chains.

Growth mandated the opening of a second roasting plant, located in Kent, Washington, by 1993. After 22 years in business, Starbucks had only 19 individuals it deemed qualified to roast coffee. One of the 19 was Schultz, who considered it a tremendous privilege. Roasters were trained for more than a year before being allowed to roast a batch, which consists of up to 600 pounds of coffee roasted for 12 to 15 minutes in a gas oven. The beans make a popping sound, like popcorn, when ready, but roasters also use sight and smell to tell when the beans are done to perfection. Starbucks standards required roasters to test the roasted beans in an Agron blood-cell analyzer to assure that each batch is up to standards. If not, it's discarded.

Starbucks's first East Coast store opened in 1993, in a premier location in Washington D.C. The chain had 275 stores by the end of 1993 and 400 by August 1994. Sales had grown an average of 65 percent annually over the previous three years, with net income growing 70 to 100 percent a year during that time. Starbucks broke into important new markets in 1994, including Minneapolis, Boston, New York, Atlanta, Dallas, and Houston, and purchased the Coffee Connection, a 23-store rival based in Boston, for $23 million, making it a wholly owned subsidiary. Smith was promoted to president and COO and Behar became president, international. Starbucks also announced a partnership with Pepsi-Cola to develop new ready-to-drink coffee beverages. In the summer of 1995, Starbucks and Pepsi test-marketed a cold coffee-based beverage called Mazagran in the Santa Monica area.

In early 1995 Starbucks made an $11 million minority investment in Noah's New York Bagels, a small retailer with high growth potential. Starbucks broke into new markets including Pittsburgh, San Antonio, Las Vegas, and Philadelphia. By April 1995, the company had 539 Starbucks stores, a national mail-order operation, and a specialty sales group.

Principal Subsidiaries: The Coffee Connection; Starbucks New Venture Company.

Further Reading:

Abramovitch, Ingrid, "Miracles of Marketing: How to Reinvent Your Product," *Success,* April 1993, p. 22–26.

Brammer, Rhonda, "Grounds for Caution," *Barron's,* August 15, 1994, p. 20.

Cuneo, Alice, "Starbucks' Word-of-Mouth Wonder," *Advertising Age,* March 7, 1994, p. 12.

Frank, Stephen, "Starbucks Brews Strong Results Analysts Like," *Wall Street Journal,* July 14, 1994, p. C1.

Harris, John, "Cuppa Sumatra," *Forbes,* November 26, 1990, p. 213–14.

Jones Yang, Dori, "The Starbucks Enterprise Shifts into Warp Speed," *Business Week,* October 24, 1994, p. 76–78.

Robinson, Kathyrn, "Coffee Achievers," *Seattle Weekly,* August 2, 1989.

Schultz, Howard, "By Way of Canarsie, One Large Hot Cup of Business Strategy," *New York Times,* December 14, 1994, p. C1, 8.

Whalen, Jeanne, "Starbucks, Pepsi Tackle Coffee Venture," *Advertising Age,* August 1, 1994, p. 44.

—Carol I. Keeley

Stone & Webster, Inc.

One Penn Plaza
250 West 34th Street
New York, New York 10119
U.S.A.
(212) 290-7500
Fax: (212) 290-7507

Public Company
Incorporated: 1889 as The Massachusetts Electrical Engineering Company
Employees: 5,000
Sales: $818 million
Stock Exchanges: New York Boston
SICs: 8711 Engineering Services, Construction and Civil Engineering, Building Construction Consultants; 8742 Management Consulting Services; 4222 Refrigerated Warehousing and Storage; 1311 Crude Petroleum and Natural Gas; 1381 Drilling Oil and Gas Wells

Stone & Webster, Inc., one of the nation's engineering giants, has since 1889 offered its customers in the United States and the world engineering, design, construction, consulting, and environmental services to build electric power plants, petrochemical plants and refineries, factories, infrastructure, and civil works projects. It has also engaged in activities in cold storage warehousing, real estate, and oil and natural gas. In 1994, the company derived about 91 percent of its $818 million in annual revenues from engineering, with the remainder from cold storage and other activities.

Stone & Webster helped build substantial portions of the nation's power production infrastructure, including coal, oil, natural gas, nuclear, and hydroelectric plants constituting around 20 percent of U.S. generating capacity. The company played a significant role in the nation's defense efforts during World War I and II and afterwards, helping develop the A-Bomb, constructing large shipyards, and creating alternate means of production of strategic materials such as synthetic rubber. Much of the world's capacity in petrochemical and plastics development was also developed as a result of Stone & Webster efforts.

The company's founders were two electrical engineering graduates from the Massachusetts Institute of Technology (MIT), Charles A. Stone and Edwin S. Webster, who had been graduated for just one year when they started their own firm, the Massachusetts Electrical Engineering Company. Electrical engineering was a new field in the 1880s—Thomas Edison had patented the incandescent lamp only a decade earlier—and Stone and Webster opened their doors in spite of discouraging advice from respected mentors such as Professor Charles Cross, who told them that "there might be enough electrical consulting work to support one of you, but not both."

From the company's start in Boston in 1889, however, there was work for both, work which initially involved small jobs such as testing equipment and performing feasibility studies. Stone and Webster soon developed original testing systems, and expanded their test activities to encompass the complete range of electrical equipment.

A year after the company, which became known as Stone & Webster, opened for business, the company obtained its first significant contract, with the S.D. Warren Company in Maine, to design and install a direct current generating plant associated with a dam, along with a transmission line to the Warren paper mill a mile distant. In this task and those that followed, the new engineering company hired part-time university students, beginning a relationship with the Boston academic community which would continue into the 1990s.

By the early 1900s, Stone & Webster had diversified rapidly, involving itself in engineering, building, constructing, and managing power plants, and developing a name for its ability to build and operate integrated systems fueled either by coal or hydroelectric generation. Initial start-up operations were handled by the company's plant betterment division, which created and used an early form of quality control. In addition to its plant operations, the company also installed and managed lighting systems and electric-powered street railway systems.

By 1906, a number of major engineering projects were in process in six states, with several others being planned. To handle the load, Stone & Webster formed its first subsidiary, Stone & Webster Engineering Corporation, which managed all engineering, construction, and purchasing activities. Corporation activities underwent rapid growth, and by 1910 some 14 percent of the nation's total electrical generating capacity had been designed, engineered, and built by Stone & Webster.

After the onset of World War I, Stone & Webster took on a variety of military assignments, including designing and building new arsenals, military bases, airfields, and camp facilities, as well as the massive Hog Island Shipyard at Philadelphia, which employed 35,000 workers and had more launching ways than the three largest British shipyards combined. Once open, Hog Island completed 82 ships in two and one-half years.

In the post-armistice years and into the next decade, the company continued to grow and expand in the United States as well as abroad, constructing increasingly larger power plants and stations and transmission lines, as well as laboratories, factories, sugar refineries, warehouses, and a variety of other facilities. By 1920, the company also began building what at that time was the world's longest continuous tunnel, an 18.2 mile water tunnel which doubled the supply of Catskill water to Manhattan.

That year, Stone & Webster also managed 59 utility companies in 18 states and held a financial interest in many of them. As the decade moved on, growing national energy needs resulted in a need for increased availability of financing, and Stone & Webster responded in 1927 by merging with a 41 year-old investment banking organization to create a new investment subsidiary. During the next three years, the subsidiary participated as a principal in originating and underwriting more than a billion dollars in security issues, and participating in the sale of nearly one-quarter of all new offerings syndicated in the United States.

In 1929, Stone & Webster decided for the first time to offer its stock to the public at $100 a share. However, in the words of former company President William F. Allen, Jr., in an address to the Newcomen Society, "that was not, perhaps, the greatest piece of timing." Only a few months later, the stock market crashed, eventually bringing the value of Stone & Webster stock to the low teens during the worst years of the Depression.

The 1930s were particularly challenging years for Stone & Webster. While the momentum in construction built by long-term contracts signed in the boom years of the late 1920s carried the company through 1931, new business became increasingly difficult to secure. During the early part of the decade the company built, among other projects, the Rock Island Dam (the first to cross Washington's Columbia River), the 50-story RCA building in New York City, and a natural gas pipeline in Texas and New Mexico; however, by 1934 the company had far fewer contracts and had reduced its staff to 263.

Moreover, with the 1930 acquisition of Engineers Public Service, a utility holding company, Stone & Webster had itself become a utility holding company. When the Public Utilities Holding Company Act was passed just five years later, Stone & Webster was forced to choose between remaining a holding company or focusing on the engineering and construction business. The company opted to divest itself of its utility holdings.

Through the mid-1930s the company continued to be active in appraisals and studies for major clients and in designing and constructing plants. As the decade drew to a close, the chemical industry began to undergo a rapid expansion, and Stone & Webster established a petroleum division.

America's entry into World War II brought a dramatic increase in demand for all types of engineering and construction, and Stone & Webster became intensely involved in the war effort. According to former Stone & Webster President Allen, "few elements of war production were not impacted in a significant way by Stone & Webster."

Typical Stone & Webster wartime assignments included the design and construction of cartridge case plants, a complete steel foundry, a plant to produce bombsights and other equipment, a plant furnishing fire-control instruments, a facility producing aircraft superchargers, and three TNT-production plants, in addition to meeting demands for infrastructure and power facilities.

The company was also called upon to engage in more creative projects. For example, since the Japanese invasion of Southeast Asia had eliminated virtually all of the world's access to natural rubber, Stone & Webster was asked to develop a production process for synthetic rubber technology, and the company subsequently designed or built all U.S. plants for the production of butyl rubber.

Perhaps the most creative Stone & Webster wartime effort was its involvement in the Manhattan Project, which created the atomic bomb. Beginning in early 1942, company efforts resulted in the establishment of a completely separate engineering organization employing 800 engineers and draftsmen, which examined ways to obtain large quantities of fissionable uranium-235, built an electromagnetic separation plant, and constructed a city in Oak Ridge, Tennessee, which ultimately housed 75,000 workers.

These extensive efforts were undertaken despite the complexities that often follow a change in organizational leadership, for in 1941, after 52 years, founder Charles Stone passed away; five years later, partner Edwin Webster retired from his position as chairman of the board.

Immediately after the end of the war, demand for Stone & Webster services rose rapidly among U.S. public utilities. Under the leadership of Texan George Clifford, the company began to build interstate gas pipelines and compressor stations, and also became the largest single stockholder in the Tennessee Gas Transmission Company (Tenneco). Unique solutions were devised to problems related to the need to store natural gas under extreme pressure in stainless steel containers underground. The company built the world's largest turbine manufacturing plant, and also continued to concentrate heavily on power generation. In 1949, Stone & Webster accounted for some 16 percent of the steam electric generating capacity being generated in the United States.

The company was also retained on tasks that helped shift the nation's economy from a defense to a civilian basis, such as estimating the costs of deactivation and stand-by maintenance of defense plants and shipyards, providing technical advice and services on Japanese reparations, evaluating the mobile equipment that remained in overseas theaters, and continuing work at Oak Ridge.

During the 1950s and 1960s, Stone & Webster was perhaps the most significant engineering company to be involved in the nation's developing nuclear power industry. Chosen after a competition with 90 other companies to build the nation's first nuclear power plant in Shippingport, Pennsylvania, Stone & Webster was subsequently selected to design and supervise the construction of a large accelerator at the Brookhaven National Laboratory, design the neutron shield tank for the nuclear-powered merchant ship N.S. Savannah, and engineer and construct a prototype Army atomic energy power plant.

The steady demand for electric power generation also meant an increase in construction contracts for more conventional power plants. By the early 1950s, Stone & Webster had built 27 separate hydroelectric plants constituting five percent of U.S. capacity; steam power plants aggregating six million kilowatts in capacity; and some 6,000 miles of power transmission lines.

During this time, the company also obtained a variety of chemical process contracts in the United States, Canada, Japan, and in other countries, to meet the worldwide demand for plastics. Under the "process" category, the company designed ethylene plants, oil refineries, artificial gas producing plants, paper mills, specialized processing and purification facilities, extraction plants, and breweries. From 1950 through 1970, for example, the company designed 22 petrochemical plants in Japan alone.

As the 1960s drew on, however, the company's petrochemical and plastics activity began to slow, as U.S. refinery capacity caught up with customer demand and declined accordingly. To smooth the impact of these fluctuations, the company diversified its process interests, developing, for example, a more extensive relationship with the paper industry. During the decade, for example, the company designed the first commercial mill which made pulp from hardwood trees.

Slowing business activity also resulted in some conceptual restructuring within the company, including an effort to standardize designs in areas of proven success and placing a greater emphasis on the use of project work teams which combined staff with differing specialized skills. The increased emphasis on teaming fit well with Stone & Webster's need to address problems that developed in the energy supply sector in the mid- to late 1960s, and was used in the design of synthetic natural gas plants, a liquified natural gas distribution center, and demonstration projects in coal and oil gasification.

During the 1970s, major world events including the two OPEC oil embargoes, corresponding uncertainty in the chemical process industry with respect to feedstock supplies, increasing public opposition to the use of nuclear power, and an increasing environmental awareness brought difficulties as well as new business opportunities for Stone & Webster.

The high prices that followed the embargoes, for example, constrained energy demand and thus reduced the need for new electric generating capacity. Utilities looked into every possible alternative to meet demand, short of constructing major new baseload stations, resulting in "one of the severest drop-offs in building in the history of the engineering-construction industry," according to former Stone & Webster President William Allen in *Public Utilities Fortnightly.* An equally severe, simultaneous downturn in international construction compounded the problem.

Stone & Webster's difficulties with constructing conventional power plants were matched by its problems in nuclear construction. By the late 1970s, the company had attained a central role in the nuclear power industry—a significant portion of all nuclear energy in the United States was being generated at plants designed and generated by Stone & Webster. In 1975 the company had even been selected to construct the Clinch River Breeder Reactor. However, increasing public opposition to the construction of nuclear plants, lengthy delays brought by challenges before Public Utility Commissions, and corresponding increases in plant construction costs, capped by the incident at Three Mile Island in 1979, brought about a moratorium on the construction of large nuclear plants and the cancellation of many existing orders.

The company began to respond to these challenges during the remainder of the 1970s and the early 1980s. Stone & Webster met its clients' reluctance to build by improving engineering and construction efficiencies through the use of computer-assisted design and innovative working agreements with contractors and the building trades unions, as well as by providing services that kept plants operating safely, efficiently, and for a longer time than originally intended.

To further survive in this complex business environment, Stone & Webster began to more intensely solicit government and international business, increase its activity in the area of environmental protection and alternative energy production, continue its activity in extending the lives of existing power plants, and develop other areas of diversification as long as they did not distract from the company's core business, engineering. The company also began to phase out those parts of the company unrelated to core activities that were no longer considered financially viable, such as its securities subsidiary.

In the 1990s, Stone & Webster faced a business environment in which its core activities of power plant and petrochemical plant construction were lagging, and new areas targeted for growth had not yet fulfilled their potential. As a result, company stock performance was sluggish, and in response, in 1992, a stockholder group headed by corporate gadfly Bob Monks attacked Stone & Webster management, asserting that the company had not exploited its assets to keep its stock prices high and inquiring as to growth plans the company intended to institute in order to raise stock value. Over the two years that followed, Monks brought suit in federal court and also took action before the Securities and Exchange Commission on issues related to Stone & Webster's performance, but both the court and the SEC rejected his assertions.

In 1994, the company registered a net loss of $7.8 million despite revenues of over $818 million. Recognizing that a need existed to improve its financial picture, Stone & Webster opted for a further change in its traditional marketing strategy. The company centered its hopes for future growth on a broader expansion of its core businesses into global markets, a cutback in its dependence on power generation, and the expansion of its environmental and transportation efforts.

By the year 2000, remarked President and CEO Bruce Coles, Stone & Webster's engineering and construction efforts were projected to move from 80 percent dependence on the power market to between 30 and 50 percent. Government contracts in transportation and the environment were expected to constitute another 17 to 25 percent of revenues, with 16 to 25 percent from process activities, and eight to 15 percent from the industrial sector. Coles estimated that some 40 percent of Stone & Webster's business would take place overseas by 2000.

In the mid-1990s, new Stone & Webster environmental services contracts included an exclusive licensing arrangement with Texaco entered into in 1994 to help develop and market the High Rate Bioreactor (HRB), which used bacteria to detoxify industrial and municipal wastes. Stone & Webster was also involved in the U.S. Department of Energy's nuclear cleanup efforts at Hanford, Washington, and Rocky Flats, Colorado; water and sewer cleanup programs including the cleanup of New York and Boston harbors, the development of a land-based sludge disposal system for New York City; and the expansion of the wastewater treatment system at Disney World in Florida.

Stone & Webster's infrastructure and transportation activities during this time included the engineering and design of railway and other large transit systems, including part of the Washington, D.C. metro; major airport improvements in Denver and Miami; bridge construction, such as the eight mile-long bridge linking Prince Edward Island to the Canadian mainland; roadway upgrading, including work on the New Jersey Turnpike; and other services.

Moreover, the company's advanced computer applications efforts included the use of three-dimensional models; expert systems which monitored, diagnosed, and recommended solutions in areas from equipment vibration to chemical plant processing; and advanced controls that continuously monitored all plant operations.

Despite its challenges, Stone & Webster still had considerable strengths on which to draw, and once the impact of strategies responsive to the business environment of the 1990s had been put in place, company officials and outside observers appeared reasonably optimistic about the company's prospects as it moved on into its second century. "This is a company with a bright future, facing a world filled with opportunities," Coles commented, adding, "but first there are some fundamental changes, changes that we have begun, that must work their way through our company."

Principal Subsidiaries: Stone & Webster Engineering Corp.; Stone & Webster Management Consultants, Inc.; Stone & Webster Advanced Systems Development Services, Inc.; Stone & Webster Advanced Technology Applications, Inc.; Stone & Webster Development Corp.; Stone & Webster Overseas Group, Inc.; Stone & Webster, Canada, Ltd.; Stone & Webster Oil Company, Inc.; Commercial Cold Storage, Inc.; Sabal Corp.

Further Reading:

Allen, William F., Jr., "Evolution in an Industry—As Seen By an Engineer," *Public Utilities Fortnightly,* July 20, 1989, p. 15.

——, *Stone & Webster: A Century of Service,* Exton, Penn.: The Newcomen Society of the United States, 1989.

Keller, David Neal, *Stone & Webster: 1889–1989,* New York: Stone & Webster, 1989.

Marcial, Gene G., "Monks the Gadfly Lands On Stone & Webster," *Business Week,* January 10, 1994, p. 57.

Savitz, Eric J., "Rebuilding America: It's the Kicker in Stone and Webster's Future," *Barron's,* May 11, 1992, p. 15.

—Bob Swierczek

Tennant Company

701 North Lilac Drive
P.O. Box 1452
Minneapolis, Minnesota 55440
U.S.A.
(612) 540-1200
Fax: (612) 540-1437

Public Company
Incorporated: 1969
Employees: 1,750
Sales: $281 million
Stock Exchanges: NASDAQ
SICs: 3589 Service Industry Machinery Nec

Tennant Company is the world's foremost manufacturer of floor maintenance equipment, including sweepers, scrubbers, and burnishers, in a variety of ride-on and walk-behind models. Tennant dominates the U.S. market with an estimated 65 percent of market share and holds 25 percent of the market worldwide. Tennant produces heavy duty floor cleaning machines that are used to maintain indoor and outdoor surfaces in factories, shopping malls, stadiums, and airports. Over half of the company's total sales are placed by U.S. heavy industry, although products are distributed in 60 countries. The biggest single users of Tennant's products are auto and aerospace companies, along with federal and local governments.

Tennant Company was founded in Minneapolis in 1870 by an Irish immigrant named George Henry Tennant. Tennant had opened a sawmill and woodshop to supply the growing number of houses with hardwood floors, wooden downspouts, and rain gutters. Over the next 30 years the woodworking shop expanded, surviving several fires, and by the turn of the century had become one of the leading manufacturers of hardwood flooring in the Upper Midwest. Many of the original G. H. Tennant hardwood floors can still be found in the stately homes along the main streets of Minneapolis and St. Paul.

The innovation that would shape Tennant's business and revolutionize floor care was a classic example of ingenuity born of frustration. In 1932 a local high school janitor weary of laboring over floors on his hands and knees discovered a way to "dry clean" his floors. He fashioned a scouring contraption from a coffee can wrapped in steel wool that he hooked up to an old washing machine motor. The janitor demonstrated his idea to a neighbor, who just happened to be a shop foreman at Tennant. Tennant acquired the rights to manufacture the machine, and within a few years, a variation of the janitor's model formed the backbone of the company's business.

Tennant had developed a floor finishing and treating system based on oils and sealers to be applied with a buffer. Along with the floor-care machine, the "Tennant Floor Maintenance System" flourished, and by 1940, over 100,00 square feet of wooden floors in bakeries, schools, and factories were maintained with its products. Tennant continues to manufacture floor coatings, which make up approximately seven percent of its sales, although the waxes and varnishes of the 1930s have long since given way to a sophisticated array of urethane and epoxy finishes.

The outbreak of World War II ushered in a new era for Tennant. As defense plants sprang up, heavy duty machines were required to keep those installations immaculate. Tennant responded with the production of the Model K, a much larger machine with a wider cleaning path. The product line was expanded to include scarifiers, a series of outdoor machines that could be used to route and loosen up the surfaces of airport ramps, bridges, and highways. Tennant also participated in the war effort by subcontracting parts for the Norden bombsight manufactured by Honeywell. During this period, sales went from $330,000 in 1938 to $1 million in 1945.

The postwar period witnessed a continuation of Tennant's explosive growth. Ongoing innovations in equipment created increased demand, and the market for scrubbers and sweepers rapidly expanded. A landmark event was the invention of the first vacuumized power sweeper in 1947 by Ralph Peabody, a Tennant Company engineer. The sweeper revolutionized industrial floor maintenance by controlling dust dispersion during sweeping. The Model 36, as it was called, formed the prototype of a long line of sweepers, scarifiers, and scrubbers. 1950 marked the introduction of sweepers with front wheel steering, and in 1953 Tennant launched the first mechanically raised hopper, followed by the first hydraulically driven sweeper in 1961.

As a result of Tennant's rapid expansion in the 1950s, the company outgrew its plant in Minneapolis and relocated to a larger headquarters in suburban Minneapolis in 1957. Since that time, Tennant has added five other facilities in the greater suburban area of the Twin Cities. In 1969 Tennant went public with its first stock offering and made its first major acquisition with the purchase of Taylor Material Handling in Michigan.

The 1960s and 1970s were decades of prosperous growth for Tennant. In the early 1960s, Tennant took the first steps to carve out a stronger niche for the company's products in Europe by granting a license to its importer, R. S. Stokvis Company, to manufacture the company's products in Holland. By 1970, Tennant had bought out the license agreement from Stokvis in a takeover of Stokvis/De Nederlandsche Kroon Rijwiefabrieken and formed a wholly owned subsidiary, Tennant NV, based in Uden, the Netherlands.

Looking toward expansion in the Pacific, Tennant embarked upon a joint venture with Fuji Heavy Industries in Japan in 1964. In the long term, this relationship did not live up to its initial promise as Fuji was less than aggressive in promoting and distributing Tennant's products. In Australia, too, during this same period, sales failed to advance as expected under Tennant's national distributor, Clark Equipment. In the mid-1970s, Tennant phased out Clark and began selling directly. Sales increased from $750,000 in 1976 to $11 million by 1994.

In the United States, Tennant further solidified its position as an industry leader by introducing service and parts through authorized service dealers around the country. Unlike its major competitors, Tennant also maintains its own direct sales force, which actively seeks out new markets and customer feedback. In this way, the sales force not only sells Tennant's products and services, but also serves as a sounding board for customer concerns. Tennant's sales force promotes the company's complete product line out of three regions (western, central, and eastern), and works in tandem with service representatives in these areas.

A major turning point for Tennant Company took place in 1979, when the company launched an all-out quality improvement campaign after a thorough evaluation of the company's operations by quality expert Philip Crosby. While Tennant's sales were booming at the time, CEO Roger Hale and other senior managers were keenly aware that American companies were quickly losing their competitive edge in the global marketplace. At the same time, Hale was detecting warning signs about Tennant's quality as complaints came in from Japanese customers about sweepers leaking hydraulic oil. Strangely enough, U.S. customers hadn't bothered to protest the same leaks, which Hale took as an indication of American complacency to issues of quality. Then came the news that Toyota's lift-truck division was planning to enter the floor sweeper business. With a formidable Japanese competitor looming on Tennant's horizon, Hale and other Tennant executives moved quickly to explore dramatic quality improvements.

Tennant's extensive rework stations were the first target. These areas, where 20 of the company's top mechanics worked overtime to get faulty machines ready for shipping, took up 15 percent of assembly space, and an average of 33,000 hours was spent annually on manufacturing rework, a practice that was considered standard across U.S. industry. Resolving to do it right the first time, Hale transferred rework mechanics to assembly to catch mistakes on the line from the beginning.

Tennant's vast number of suppliers posed another problem. Supplied parts represented 65 percent of the average cost of a sweeper or scrubber, and with so many suppliers, there were inevitable inconsistencies in parts and inadequate training for assemblers. Tennant carefully weeded out its suppliers and reduced their numbers from 1,100 in 1980 to 250 in 1992. The number of defects dropped dramatically. Employees were also trained in statistical process control (SPC), a method of monitoring defects and setting goals to reduce them. According to *Training* in 1990, SPC allowed the company to cut by half the number of inspectors of parts manufacturing.

In a further effort to reduce errors, small teams of managers and workers were formed to focus on how procedures could be improved. These small groups became a way of life at Tennant and encouraged regular employee feedback in all areas of the business. Management also relied on the team process to stay in touch with day-to-day operations. The 1993 edition of *The 100 Best Places to Work in America* gave Tennant high marks for management responsiveness and general working conditions. The report also highlighted the incentive programs and recognition program that have helped prompt greater employee participation in the quality improvement campaign.

Roger Hale, a great-grandson of Tennant's founder, who had led the company since 1976, embraced the quality philosophy with the fervor of a missionary. His account of how the company transformed itself, *Quest for Quality (How One Company Put Theory to Work),* published in 1989, became required reading for other companies interested in quality management. Tennant also sponsored an annual conference on quality. In addition to the extensive training introduced for company employees, a department was created to run external training programs for companies eager to emulate Tennant's approach.

Tennant's quality campaign not only produced savings for the company, but also translated into tangible benefits for its customers. Tennant's products were more reliable, and during the 1980s prices on some machines actually went down. Warranty coverage was extended. Tennant's sweepers and scrubbers were featured in *Fortune's* 1988 roundup of topnotch U.S. products in an article entitled "What America Makes Best." According to *Management Accounting* in 1992, Tennant significantly improved product quality and reduced total quality costs from 17 percent of sales in 1980 to 2.5 percent of sales in 1988.

As part of its ongoing quality improvement campaign, Tennant was investing what *Barron's* called "an incredibly high level" of revenues, close to five percent, in new product research and development. By the mid-1990s, the company had cut its product development cycle in half, from four to two years. Some of the more innovative products to emerge in this period were environmentally safe resurfacing coatings and a heavy duty machine for use in airports to pick up and recycle the de-icing fluids sprayed on planes before take-off.

Tennant weathered the recession of the early 1990s with minor layoffs and a slump in sales of its floor coatings products. Overall sales in 1991 dropped six percent to $144 million and earnings were off by approximately 25 percent. As a way to invigorate its quality efforts, Tennant launched a "Preeminence 2000" campaign in 1992 to define a strategy to "propel the company into the next century." The company's mission was to be the preeminent company in the industry with the goal of doubling sales by the millennium. Continued diversification and expansion of overseas sales seemed to be the key to prosperity despite a stagnant market at home.

Under Hale's leadership, Tennant had moved to expand international sales, initially concentrating on Europe. Using its base in the Netherlands as a springboard, Tennant had gradually assumed ownership of the Stokvis organizations in Germany (1978), the United Kingdom (1982), and France (1994), establishing direct sales and service operations in all four countries. A fifth direct sales office in Spain got its start in 1991 and had more than doubled in size four years later.

Tennant Australia, a wholly owned subsidiary, became a full sales, marketing, and service organization and the first to offer service 24 hours a day, seven days a week. In 1989, after ending its 25-year joint venture with Fuji Heavy Industries, Tennant formed Tennant Japan K.K. and with its master distributor, Nippon Yusoki Company, Ltd., initiated direct imports from the United States to Japan. In 1992 Tennant formed Tennant Company Japan Branch to sell commercial floor care equipment. In 1994 overseas sales accounted for $72 million, or 25 percent of revenues.

Tennant's significant inroads into the commercial market were enhanced by the acquisition in 1994 of Castex, the world leader in carpet maintenance equipment. Castex itself had widened its scope in 1989 by taking over Nobles Industries, which offered much broader established distribution channels for its line of hard floor maintenance equipment. Castex/Nobles was integrated with Tennant Trend, which was acquired in 1989, and these operations were consolidated in a new manufacturing facility in Michigan. Castex complemented Tennant's product line with a wide range of walk-behind scrubbers, sweepers, and wet/dry vacuums, as well as carpet extractors and floor polishers, appropriate for use in commercial settings such as office buildings, hospitals, and supermarkets.

Tennant's ambitious program to dominate the commercial floor equipment market was further bolstered with the purchase of Eagle Floor Care, Inc., a manufacturer of propane burnishers that same year. By the end of 1994, commercial floor maintenance equipment sales had more than tripled since the year before due to marketplace acceptance of the new acquisitions.

1994 was a banner year for Tennant in more ways than one. Sales of $281 million were up 27 percent over 1993, with sales in North America registering a 33 percent increase. That same year, Tennant was the first non-Fortune 500 company to receive *Purchasing* magazine's Medal of Professional Excellence. Other recipients of the award include Motorola, Hewlett Packard, Chrysler, and General Electric. *Purchasing* made special note of the company's outstanding performance in the areas of supplier relations, product teams, and quality. This type of recognition signaled that Tennant Company was well on its way to its goal of being the preeminent company in non-residential floor maintenance products by the year 2000.

Principal Subsidiaries: Tennant Co. Australia; Tennant Maintenance Systems Ltd. (U.K.); Tennant N.V. (Netherlands).

Further Reading:

Carr, Lawrence, and Thomas Tyson, ''Planning Quality Cost Expenditures,'' *Management Accounting,* October 1992, pp. 52–56.

Hale, Roger L., ''Tennant Company: Instilling Quality from Top to Bottom,'' *Management Review,* February 1989, p. 65.

Hale, Roger L., and Douglas Hoelscher, *Quest for Quality: How One Company Put Theory to Work,* Minneapolis: Tennant Company, 1989.

Hale, Roger L., Kowal, Ronald; et al., *Made in the U.S.A.: How One American Company Helps Satisfy Customer Needs through Strategic Supplier Quality Management,* Minneapolis: Tennant Company, 1991.

Hequet, Marc, ''Selling In-House Training Outside,'' *Training,* September 1991, pp. 51–56.

Knowlton, Christopher, ''What America Makes Best,'' *Fortune,* March 28, 1988, pp. 40–53.

Levering, Robert, and Milton Moskowitz, *The 100 Best Companies to Work for in America,* New York: Doubleday, 1993, pp. 447–50.

Oberle, Joseph, ''Employee Involvement at Tennant,'' *Training,* May 1990, pp. 73–79.

Palmer, Jay, ''Come the Recovery . . . and Tennant Seems Poised to Clean Up,'' *Barrons,* February 3, 1992, pp. 17, 36.

Porter, Anne Millen, ''Does Quality Really Affect the Bottom Line?'' *Purchasing,* January 16, 1992, pp. 61–64.

Raia, Ernie, ''Medal of Excellence: Swept Away by Tennant,'' *Purchasing,* September 22, 1994, pp. 37–45.

''Sweeper Manufacturer Writes the Book on Quality,'' *Diesel Progress, Engines and Drives,* April 1993, p. 18.

Tennant Anniversary Book: 1870–1995, Minneapolis: Tennant Company, 1995.

—Leslie D. Hyde

Terra Industries, Inc.

600 Fourth Street
Sioux City, Iowa 51101
U.S.A.
(712) 277-1340
Fax: (712) 233-3648

Public Company
Incorporated: 1964 as Terra Chemicals International, Inc.
Employees: 2,400
Sales: $1.67 billion
Stock Exchanges: New York Toronto Pacific
SICs: 2873 Nitrogenous Fertilizers; 2874 Phosphatic Fertilizers; 2879 Agricultural Chemicals, Nec; 5191 Farm Supplies

Terra Industries, Inc., is one of the nation's largest producers and marketers of nitrogen fertilizer, crop protection products, seed, and services for farmers, dealers, and professional growers. Terra supplies dealers and growers with more than 5,000 different products, as well as feed ingredients and application services. The company also produces and markets nitrogen products and methanol for the industrial sector.

"Anything we're not the largest in, we probably have a goal to get there in the near future," Terra President Burton Joyce told David Hendee of the *Omaha World Herald* on May 3, 1995. Indeed, that year the company ranked as North America's third-largest producer of anhydrous ammonia and the largest manufacturer of nitrogen solutions—both fertilizer products especially useful in corn farming. Terra also boasted the market's largest company-owned farm service center network, with more than 350 locations; second place as a supplier of crop production inputs to North American growers and dealers; a leading position in methanol production; and a well-respected profile in the development of environmentally friendly dry flowable technology for crop protection products.

Terra's activity falls into three main lines of business. The distribution segment sells crop inputs—fertilizers, crop protection products, and seed services—to agricultural, turf, ornamental, and other growers, and to dealers. Terra's nitrogen production facilities, marketed under the Terra Nitrogen name, convert natural gas, air, and water into nitrogen fertilizer, animal feed, and industrial products in the form of anhydrous ammonia, nitrogen solutions, urea, and other ammonia derivatives. Finally, Terra's methanol production line is growing rapidly to supply fuel companies with products to meet increasing demand for cleaner-burning fuels.

The company's roots go back to 1964, when Terra Chemicals International, Inc., broke ground for a large nitrogen fertilizer manufacturing complex at Port Neal, Iowa. Shortly thereafter, Terra began selling fertilizers and crop protection products through Grand Forks Seed Company and other established outlets in Iowa and Wisconsin.

The young company moved quickly to expand its product line and sales territory. By 1967, the Port Neal site was producing sizable amounts of nitrogen-based fertilizer, and within a decade, the company entered into a joint venture with W. R. Grace and Gulf Oil Chemical Co. to obtain an interest in another fertilizer plant in Woodward, Oklahoma. (Terra eventually became the sole owner of that facility in 1988.)

With the 1977 acquisition of Memphis-based Riverside Chemical Company, Terra greatly expanded both its capacity and its geographical reach. The addition of Riverside's 45 farm service centers to Terra's fold made it one of the nation's largest independent producers and distributors of fertilizer, agricultural chemicals, and seed.

In 1981 Terra became a wholly owned subsidiary of Plateau Holdings, an umbrella company for mining and natural resources, to begin a decade of vastly accelerated growth and diversification. Plateau, which was jointly owned by Minerals and Resources Corporation Limited (Minorco Inc., U.S.A.) and Hudson Bay Mining and Smelting Co., Ltd. (HBMS), created a new company, Inspiration Resources Corp., as a holding company for Terra and several other natural resources ventures.

Within two years, a reorganization realigned the corporate chips, making HBMS and Trend International Ltd. (TIL) wholly owned subsidiaries of Inspiration. In 1984 Inspiration traded shares of TIL and Trend Exploration Ltd. (TEL)—formerly one of its wholly owned subsidiaries—with Danville Resources, Inc., which, in turn, exchanged its shares of TIL and TEL for shares in Madison Resources, Inc. Thus, Terra's parent, Inspiration, ended up holding a 73 percent interest in Madison, including its wholly owned subsidiaries, TIL And TEL. Despite this session of "musical shares" and the diversification of Inspiration into everything from copper mining to ammonia production, the Terra subsidiary continued to focus primarily on agricultural markets.

A series of strategic acquisitions, paired with renewed emphasis on aggressive distribution channels, propelled new growth for Terra in the mid 1980s. The company began operating a dry and liquid flowable crop protection formulation facility in Blytheville, Arkansas in 1984. In 1985 Terra acquired the agricultural products division of Sohio Chemical Company, augmenting its direct sales contact with farm customers through the division's 118 retail farm service centers across Michigan, Ohio, Indiana, Illinois, Missouri, and Kansas. That year, the company also changed its name to Terra International, Inc., in anticipation of broader markets.

As markets for base metals took a beating in the early 1980s, Terra's parent felt the heat. Inspiration suffered consecutive losses of $83 million in 1983 and $101 million in 1984, for example, largely due to sagging copper prices (which adversely affected the company's Consolidated Copper Corp. and Hudson Bay Mining & Smelting Co. Ltd. subsidiaries). A 1985 company report noted that Inspiration was attempting to lessen its dependence on copper by increasing its interests in oil, gas, agricultural, and chemical businesses. This trend spelled good news for Terra, which would benefit from the parent's search for "inspiration" in agribusiness. In a 1986 speech to shareholders, Reuben F. Richards, Inspiration's chairman, said that the corporation's prospects for profitability hinged greatly on the ability of Inspiration Copper to secure substantial labor cost reductions and a strong performance by Terra International's agricultural business.

By the early 1990s, with the base metals market still weighing down on Inspiration's recovery, the company focused its efforts on agribusiness, beginning to divest or discontinue other operations in areas such as mining and base metal refining. In 1990 the company wrote off its equity investment in western Gold Exploration and Mining Co. Limited Partnership (Westgold). That year, Inspiration also discontinued its coal operations. Such divestment continued in August 1991, when Inspiration sold its base metals business, principally its wholly owned subsidiary Hudson Bay Mining and Smelting Co. Ltd., and related metals marketing and trading operations to Minorco (U.S.A.). Within a year, the parent company also sold certain leased rail assets and, by 1992, had discontinued the leasing and construction materials businesses as well as equity interests in a copper alloy producer, an undeveloped beryllium mine property, and its gold mining affiliate.

These changes were accompanied by organizational shifts as well. In August 1991, Inspiration named W. Mark Rosenbury as vice-president and chief financial officer of the newly reconstituted company, with its new emphasis on fertilizer and other agribusiness units operated by Terra International, Inc. Terra's ascent was not complete until Inspiration moved its corporate offices from New York to Sioux City, Terra's headquarters, and, finally, until IRC's shareholders approved a name change for the parent company to Terra Industries Inc. in May 1992. The new name recognized Terra's focus on agribusiness with the sale/discontinuance of its natural resources and other businesses. "We have transformed ourselves from a metal and mining company to one of the nation's leading producers and marketers of fertilizers, crop chemicals and seed. Terra, the Latin world for 'land,' has been known and respected for over 25 years in the agricultural community," president and CEO Burton M. Joyce said at the annual meeting in May 1992. Essentially, the parent company had developed along the lines of its most successful subsidiary.

In 1992 Terra decided to diversify into methanol production, announcing plans on December 1 to begin production of the chemical at its Woodward, Oklahoma, nitrogen fertilizer manufacturing facility. Scheduled for completion in the first quarter of 1994, the $15.5 million project was designed for a capacity of 400 tons of methanol per day, a relatively small production quantity by industry standards. Still, the company focused not on volume but on efficiency, devising a production process by which methanol and ammonia could be processed simultaneously, using synergy to save energy. "Terra will be one of the smallest methanol producers, but likely one of the most efficient," Joyce said, according to *PR Newswire*. By diversifying into methanol, while increasing its storage capacity, Terra hoped to reduce the impact of fertilizer market seasonality on its profits, Joyce said.

Terra also moved toward market stability through sheer volume, effecting a virtual explosion of growth in its nitrogen fertilizer business in 1993. With that year's acquisition of ICI Canada's Lambton Works facility near Sarnia, Ontario, Terra increased its nitrogen fertilizer capacity by 50 percent, making it the fourth-largest nitrogen solutions producer and the fifth-largest anhydrous ammonia producer in North America. The ICI acquisition also included interests in 32 farm service centers, or "Agromarts," in Ontario, New Brunswick, and Nova Scotia.

Terra continued to expand its geographical reach with the 1993 acquisition of the business and most of the assets of Asgrow Florida Company (AFC), a subsidiary of the Upjohn Company and a distributor of fertilizer, crop protection products, and seed to the vegetable and ornamental markets in Florida. Initially operating under the Terra Asgrow Florida name, the combined organization resulted in a broader range of products and services for Florida vegetable, citrus, ornamental, and other growers. For Terra, it marked yet another new frontier; in 1993 the company announced plans to broaden its agrichemical operations into the Southwest and Far West as well.

Such explosive growth in fertilizers was, unfortunately, interrupted by a tragic fertilizer explosion at Terra's Port Neal plant in Iowa in December 1994. The accident took the lives of four employees, injured 19 people, unleashed a cloud of potentially dangerous ammonia gas that caused the evacuation of a nearby town, and rendered the 325,000-ton-a-year plant inoperable for nearly one year.

Terra's Port Neal explosion created shock waves on various fronts, including trading floors. While personnel tried to assess the damage and the cause of the explosion—and whether the plant would reopen—Terra stock plunged, while Terra's main competitors, Cominco Fertilizers Ltd. of Calgary and Chicago-based Vogoro Corp. saw their shares jump in brisk trading.

Tremors from the explosion also shook up investigators and regulatory boards. In January 1995, the Iowa Occupational Safety and Health Administration (IOSHA) filed an affidavit alleging that Terra had hindered inspections of the blast, whereupon Terra filed a court motion disputing the state's charges. By May, the dispute had escalated, with Terra denying IOSHA's allegations that the company hindered inspections and contesting the $460,000 fine that the state agency proposed. Into 1995, the dispute fueled other, related disputes in the media, including the extent of federal regulation and oversight in an era when Congress displayed an anti-regulatory mood. In 1990 Congress had created a five-member, independent Chemical Safety and Hazard Investigation Board as part of the Clean Air Act amendments. By 1995, the new panel—which would have investigated cases similar to Terra's—hadn't yet been sworn in; the Office of Management and Budget made moves to block the panel and transfer its intended responsibilities to the existing U.S. Environmental Protection Agency and OSHA. Thus, the

Terra explosion highlighted not only ambiguities regarding that company's safety policies, but those of the federal government as well.

Despite the legal and financial setbacks of the Port Neal explosion, Terra enjoyed a year of solid growth in 1994, reporting a net income of $56.6 million, or 78 cents a share, for the year, compared with net income of $22.8 million for 1993. Despite a $7 million charge in the fourth quarter to cover uninsured costs from the explosion, the company said business interruption insurance and property damage insurance would enable it to rebuild the facility.

Moreover, Terra continued to grow through strategic acquisitions, shooting to the top echelon of North American nitrogen product and methanol production with its 1994 acquisition of Agricultural Minerals and Chemicals Inc. (AMCI). The combination of both companies' production facilities resulted in an annual production capacity of 2.7 million tons of ammonia, of which 1.6 million tons were upgraded into 3.0 million tons of nitrogen solutions, and over 700,000 tons of urea. The combined methanol production capacity of the company reached 320 million gallons a year. To help finance the AMCI acquisition, Terra successfully issued 9.7 million common shares, raising $113 million and immediately adding to earnings per share. ''Geographically, these businesses fit well, and operationally we'll realize synergies that will benefit both sides of the business combination,'' Joyce announced in an October 1994 company news release.

Positioning itself for still wider markets, in June 1994 Terra announced that it had signed a letter of intent to acquire a one-third interest in Royster-Clark, Inc., a farm service distribution network located on the East Coast. The terms of the agreement provided Terra with the option of increasing its ownership position to majority holder within five years. In a June 1994 news release, Joyce said that the new alliance afforded Terra Products growth potential in new markets, such as the East Coast—particularly the Carolinas—where Royster-Clark had a strong presence.

These new markets laid a fertile groundwork for Terra's continued growth into the 21st century. Moreover, the methanol market, which the company had entered in 1992, showed particular promise as requirements of the Clean Air Act caused gasoline producers to build inventories of methanol for use in formulating methyl-tertiary-butyl-ether (MTBE), a clean burning fuel additive, in anticipation of increased demand.

Through clearly stated growth strategies, Terra stood ready to meet the challenges of the dynamic fertilizer industry. The company would increase revenues by exploiting the resources of the newly acquired AMCI; by serving new markets in turf, nursery and vegetation management; and by acquiring additional farm service centers across broader geographical regions. The company also planned to save costs by increasing production of higher margin products, including expanded urea production, Riverside brand chemicals, and Terra brand seed. With a longer-term goal of establishing a Terra farm center, or an affiliated dealer, in each of the major agricultural counties in North America, Terra had broad fields to sow, and just the right materials to do the sowing.

Principal Subsidiaries: Hudson Holding Corporation; Hudson Bay Gold Inc.; Inspiration Coal Inc.; Inspiration Coal Development Company; Inspiration Gold Incorporated; Terra International, Inc.; El Rancho Rock & Sand, Inc.; Inspiration Consolidated Copper Company.

Further Reading:

Beeman, Perry, ''Bumpy Ride for Terra Probe,'' *Des Moines Register,* January 22, 1995, p. G1.

Hendee, David, ''Terra to Expand through Global Sales,'' *Omaha World Herald,* May 3, 1995.

——, ''Iowa Says Terra Isn't Cooperating; Firm Denies Slowing Probe of Plant,'' *Omaha World Herald,* January 7, 1995, p. 1.

Jordan, Carol L., ''Profit Prospects Hinge in Agri, Copper Businesses: Inspiration,'' *American Metal Market,* May 16, 1986, Vol. 94, p. 5.

Munford, Christopher, ''Inspiration to Cut Costs, Staff; Consolidation Under Way after Sizable 2d-Quarter Loss,'' *American Metal Market,* August 16, 1991, Vol. 99, No. 157, p. 2.

—Kerstan Cohen

Thermo King Corporation

314 West 90th Street
Minneapolis, Minnesota 55420
U.S.A.
(612) 887-2200
Fax: (612) 887-2615

Wholly Owned Subsidiary of Westinghouse Electric Corporation
Incorporated: 1938 as U. S. Thermo Control Company
Employees: 4,200
Sales: $877 million
SICs: 3585 Refrigeration & Heating Equipment; 3433 Heating Equipment Except Electric & Warm Air Furnaces

Thermo King Corporation, a technological leader in mobile temperature control, revolutionized the eating habits of the world. Truck and trailers fitted with Thermo-King self-powered refrigeration units cooled meats, poultry, fruits, and vegetables and permitted consumers to begin enjoying fresh food grown beyond their immediate vicinities. From 13 plants, Thermo King manufactures mobile temperature control equipment for trucks, trailers, and seagoing containers, as well as air conditioning equipment for buses and rail cars. The company also maintains an extensive distribution and service network, developed during the first years of production. A profitable company for parent Westinghouse, Thermo King had a record setting year in 1994: revenue grew 22 percent to $877 million and operating profit rose 19 percent to $130 million.

The Minnesota-based company began with a collaboration between entrepreneur Joseph Numero and self-taught engineer Frederick McKinley Jones. Having found early success in real estate, manufacturing, and finance, Numero had the means to retire by the time he was 25 years old. Instead, he studied law at the University of Minnesota. Although he passed the bar exam and was eligible to practice law, he was not able to graduate, since he was still a few credit hours short of the undergraduate degree requirements. This problem, however, paled in comparison to another event; in 1929 the stock market crashed, wiping Numero out financially.

During the Great Depression, one of the few industries that thrived was the motion picture business, and an old school friend of Numero's got him interested in the business possibilities of "talkie" motion pictures. The motion picture sound industry's two major manufacturers at the time were Western Electric and RCA, which leased, rather than sold, their equipment to theater owners. Determining that he could produce less expensive equipment of a higher quality, Numero founded Ultraphone Sound Systems Inc. to develop, manufacture, and sell motion picture sound equipment. Specifically, Numero sought to replace earlier sound systems, consisting of phonograph turntables and loud speakers, with a better, sound-on-film system. And he needed a technical expert to facilitate the shift from sound-on-record to the electronic-sound-track equipment.

Frederick McKinley Jones provided that expertise and much more. Jones, the son of an Irish father and African American mother, was on his own at an early age. By the time he was 16 years old he was foreman in an automobile repair shop in Cincinnati, across the Ohio River from Covington, Kentucky, where he was born. He was passionate about race cars and designed and built them for his boss, until a dispute arose over whether or not Jones, a black man, should be allowed to attend the races in which his cars were running.

Quitting his job, Jones left Cincinnati and traveled, working at a series of repair jobs. One of those jobs led Jones to a farm in Hallock, Minnesota, where he was put in charge of maintaining all equipment at the 300,000-acre farm. He next went to work at a garage and farm implement shop, where he again began building and this time racing dirt track cars. Since he was living in the snow belt, he also experimented with early snowmobile design. During World War I, Jones served as a mechanic and electrician in France, returning to Hallock in 1919. Although he had only a few years of formal education, he had a broad range of interests and gained expertise by watching others, asking questions, reading books and magazines, and by practice.

It was motion pictures that led Jones to the next phase of his life, a 30-year business relationship and friendship with Joseph Numero. The Hallock movie house, like many other small theaters, had difficulty making the expensive switch over from silent films to "talkies." While working as a projectionist there, Jones volunteered to build a version of a sound-movie machine. Using such materials as disks from a plow and a leather machine belt to drive them, he pieced together a sound-on-record projection system for the Grand Theater. When the industry upgraded to sound-on-film, Jones again went to work and ground a glass towel rod into the lens needed to produce the sound. The system he created rivaled the quality of those that commercial manufacturers were leasing to movie houses. Word of the homemade sound system Jones fabricated reached Minneapolis, and when Joseph Numero heard how well it worked he sent a letter to the Hallock theater asking the maker to come to Minneapolis.

When Jones arrived at Ultraphone Sound Systems Inc. in 1930, he again encountered the racism so prevalent in the United States at the time, as he was immediately informed that there were no janitorial jobs available at the company. Nevertheless, Jones produced the letter Numero had sent to the Hallock theater, and was eventually introduced to the other engineers. Soon after going to work for Ultraphone, Jones was appointed chief engineer.

The sound-on-film systems Jones developed were sold throughout the Midwest, including Chicago. However, the company experienced intense competition from Westinghouse and RCA, and was also plagued with a six-year patent infringement lawsuit filed by Western Electric and American Telephone & Telegraph that was eventually settled out of court. In the meantime, in order to offset such challenges, Ultraphone sought to introduce other industry-related products such as ticket dispensing machines. Also during this time Jones became interested in designing air conditioning systems. According to one anecdote, he was inspired one summer evening while sitting in his car by a lake; he had to roll up the windows to keep mosquitos out and, of course, the car became unbearably warm with the windows shut. Jones did develop such a system but had difficulty persuading Numero that his automobile air conditioner would sell.

Then, in 1938, Numero found himself in a friendly golf course wager that changed the direction of the company. Upon hearing that one of his golf foursome had lost a truck load of poultry to the heat, Numero prodded another of the four, an air conditioning man, to create a reliable cooling system for the transport company. Experiments with transport air conditioning previously had met with limited success due to the damage caused by the vibration of the trucks and the lack of an independent power source. Numero said, in jest, that if the air conditioning expert could not come up with something, then he would. Numero's trucking friend took him seriously. What had begun as a joke resulted in a transport refrigeration business.

In a 1949 *Saturday Evening Post* article, Steven M. Spencer noted that Jones was ''largely responsible for the gasoline-powered automatic refrigerators that now keep thousands of tons of food fresh on long hauls from farm to packing house to consumer.'' Options for keeping perishable goods cool over a long distance haul in the 1930s were limited to old-fashioned ice and salt methods or to electric refrigeration units which required layovers at power sources. However, Jones applied his knowledge of race car shock proofing and automobile air conditioning to the transport refrigeration project. The result was a 2,200-pound apparatus mounted under a trailer. A four-cylinder, gasoline-powered engine drove the compressor and a starter-generator-flywheel combination controlled the engine and the expansion thermostat. That first model cost $30,000 to build and was sold for $1,500. Following test runs Jones pared the weight down by 400 pounds, and the transport company bought several more of the refrigeration units. Numero sold Ultraphone to RCA along with the patents on the electronic-sound-track equipment and the ticket dispensing machine, borrowed $10,000 on his life insurance, and formed the U. S. Thermo Control Company.

Since the early product—first called the Thermotrol and soon renamed Thermo-King—tended to collect dirt and mud from the road and was also susceptible to excessive heat and damage from road debris, Jones soon returned to the drawing board. He redesigned the unit, mounting it on the upper front of the trailer where it was cooled by the truck's motion through the air. The gas engine, compressor, and condenser were mounted on the outside of a truck, while the evaporation coils were placed inside the truck's trailer. The new model weighed 950 pounds thanks to the light weight aluminum compressor; the use of the porous alloy was considered unwise by some who believed the refrigerant would leak from the compressor.

The world was skeptical about this new form of transport refrigeration. In 1988 Numero told Irene Clepper of *Air Conditioning, Heating and Refrigeration News,* ''The saying about the world beating a path to your door if you invent a better mousetrap—don't believe it. You have to sell the idea. I can't think of any invention that didn't have its trial and tribulations in reaching the market. We certainly had ours.'' In order to get the product on the road, Numero made a deal with Armour, a meat packing company. He agreed to install, without charge, refrigeration units in two of their trucks and guaranteed to reimburse them for any loses due to equipment failure. The experiment succeeded and Armour ordered eight more units; however, Thermo Control's first real breakthrough came during World War II.

The entry of the United States into World War II precipitated the shutdown of plants not necessary for the war effort. Numero considered re-enlisting in the military and even went to Washington D.C. to offer his services. While he was there he followed up a lead on a military refrigeration contract; as a result, Numero did not join the service but began to manufacture refrigeration units for the Army. Jones's light weight, portable refrigeration units performed so well in the field they became designated equipment for all the armed forces. Variations of the Thermo-King units were used all over Europe and Africa, as well as in the South Pacific, cooling everything from drinking water to blood plasma. Military personnel in field hospitals, repair shops, and transport trucks were made more comfortable, and cockpits and engine nacelles of B-29s were also cooled by Thermo's Control systems. Thermo Control sales to the military during the war topped $10 million.

After World War II, Jones and U.S. Thermo Control Co. developed refrigerated containers that could be moved from one kind of transportation to another, from train to ship to truck. Myron Green, who founded the company along with Numero, pioneered a nationwide service and distributorship system. (Green would later serve as company president from 1963 to 1975.) In 1948 the company established a training school for refrigeration mechanics. By 1949 sales climbed toward $4 million, the company employed 200 people, and more than 5,000 trucks and trailers on roadways in North and South America, Europe, and in the Middle East carried Thermo-King refrigeration units.

The ability to keep food fresh or frozen in transport propelled the growth of the frozen food and supermarket industries beginning in the 1950s. Thermo King grew along with these industries: plants in Minneapolis and St. Paul employed about 450 persons during peak production times. In 1956 the company needed more space and purchased a 90,000-square-foot plant in Bloomington, Minnesota. In the mid-1950s the company took the name of its successful product and was renamed Thermo King Corporation. By 1960, Thermo King had net earnings of $1.5 million.

The 1960s ushered in a new era for the privately held company. In February of that year, engineering genius Fred Jones died. And soon thereafter Numero sold Thermo King to Westinghouse Electric Corporation for approximately $35 million. Numero continued as company president until 1963 and then served as honorary chairman, when Myron Green, who had been serving as executive vice-president, was named to the presidency.

But with the progress of 1950s and the 1960s also came some troubling times. Labor strikes were called against the company in 1958, 1960, 1963, and 1966; each strike lasted longer than the one before it. Another dark period for the company occurred in 1966 when an airplane crash in Japan killed three top company officials and 35 key dealers on a Far Eastern tour.

Despite its problems Thermo King continued to grow and thrive. By the late 1970s Thermo King had plants in Georgia, Puerto Rico, Belgium, and Brazil. Cooling and heating products powered by diesel, gasoline, propane, and electricity were used in more than 60 countries in trucks, shipboard containers, fishing vessels, railway cars, warehouses, and cargo planes.

Thermo King annual sales had climbed to the $300-$400 million range by the late 1980s. About 2,700 persons were employed worldwide and plants had been added in the Dominican Republic, Ireland, and Spain. The main office in Bloomington included a manufacturing plant, an engineering test facility, a parts distribution center, and a training school for transport refrigeration engineers. Jim Jones noted in a 1987 *Star Tribune* article: ''The company has outlasted such one-time giants in mechanical refrigeration as Frigidaire and International Harvester.'' The company that Numero had founded was a multimillion-dollar business when he died in 1991.

James F. Watson Jr., appointed president of Thermo King in 1993, continued the international focus of the company. That year Thermo King had nearly half the Japanese market in transport refrigeration. In the next year dealer networks in Eastern Europe and Asia increased by 36 percent. The international emphasis appeared to be working: sales of products and services and operating profit increased each year during the period from 1992 to 1994.

Indeed, Thermo King was a bright spot for parent Westinghouse. The conglomerate had lost billions due to its troubled financial services unit and slow down in the environmental clean-up sector. As part of Chairman Michael H. Jordan's efforts to turn Westinghouse around, layoffs and divestitures ensued; however, Westinghouse retained a few main businesses including Thermo King. While Westinghouse reduced its debt from $9.9 billion in 1991 to $3 billion in 1995, Thermo King began cost cutting measures of its own and expected to save $16.5 million in 1995 and $27 million in 1996 with its new purchasing program.

The refrigeration industry itself faced dramatic changes in the 1990s, particularly in the face of environmental concerns. Specifically, chlorofluorocarbons (CFCs) and halons, commonly used in the refrigeration industry, were found to be depleting the earth's ozone layer. The Montreal Protocol, a global agreement to ban CFCs, was signed in 1987, and the U.S. deadline for the production phase-out of CFCs was set for December 31, 1995. Options left for users of refrigerants included: recycling CFCs, rebuilding equipment for use with ozone-friendly refrigerants, and developing new types of products. In 1994, Thermo King completed development of components and refrigeration units using ozone-friendly chemicals.

As Thermo King headed toward the 21st century, it faced yet another potentially dramatic change. In August 1995, Westinghouse announced its agreement to buy CBS Inc., the well-known broadcasting company, for $81 a share, or $5.4 billion. According to a *Wall Street Journal* article during this time, Westinghouse was ''expected to put its Thermo-King refrigeration-equipment business up for sale, which could bring as much as $1 billion to help fund the [CBS] purchase.'' Regardless, it appeared that Thermo King would continue to look to the global marketplace, along with competitors Carrier Transicold Corporation and Mitsubishi Heavy Industries, as the source of the majority of its new revenues in the future.

Further Reading:

Chanen, David, ''Refrigeration Pioneer Myron Green Dies,'' *Star Tribune* (Minneapolis), December 5, 1994, p. 4B.

Clepper, Irene, ''Founder of Transport Refrigeration Tells Story of War, Fame,'' *Air Conditioning, Heating & Refrigeration News,* August 15, 1988, pp. 28–32.

Edson, Lee, ''The Biggest Chill,'' *Across The Board,* March 1994, pp. 36–40.

Foster, Jim, ''Watson Works to Motivate People,'' *Star Tribune* (Minneapolis), May 10, 1993, p. 4D.

''Frederick McKinley Jones: Black Genius,'' *Gopher Historian,* Fall 1969, pp. 1–4.

Hays, Jean, ''Industry Leaders Starting to Sweat As Chlorofluorocarbon Ban Nears,'' *Journal of Commerce & Commercial,* July 23, 1993, p. 7A.

Huffman, Jim, ''Plane Crash in Japan Kills Bloomington Firm Officers,'' *Minneapolis Tribune,* March 6, 1966.

Jones, Jim, ''Thermo King Owes a Lot to Founder's Hot Idea,'' *Star Tribune* (Minneapolis), June 15, 1987, p. M1.

Kelley, John, ''Orient Overseas Buying Reefer Boxes,'' *Journal of Commerce & Commercial,* August 31, 1987, p. 3B.

Mackay, Harvey, ''No More Room for the 'Us Vs. Them' Mentality,'' *Star Tribune* (Minneapolis), January 5, 1995, p. 2D.

Paul, Herb, ''Thermo Control Company Buys Baker Plant in Bloomington,'' *Minneapolis Star,* May 2, 1956.

Robinson, Duncan, ''Thermo King Targets Ex-USSR Market,'' *Journal of Commerce & Commercial,* June 18, 1992, p. 2B.

Shelsby, Ted, ''Westinghouse Says Earnings to be Much Lower Than Expected,'' *Baltimore Sun,* September 18, 1993.

Sinker, Howard, ''Sixty Years After Finishing Program, He'll Get Law Degree,'' *Star Tribune* (Minneapolis), May 9, 1988, p. 1A.

Spencer, Steven M., ''Born Handy,'' *Saturday Evening Post,* May 7, 1949.

Swanson, Gloria M., and Margaret V. Ott, *I've Got an Idea: The Story of Frederick McKinley Jones,* Minneapolis: Runestone Press, 1994, 94 p.

''Thermo King Founder Joseph Numero Dies,'' *Star Tribune* (Minneapolis), May 9, 1991, p. 6B.

Wickland, John, ''Million Dollar Cooler Firm Started as Joke,'' *Minneapolis Tribune,* May 28, 1950.

Wiegner, Kathleen K., ''Some Irish Luck,'' *Forbes,* March 7, 1988, p. 8.

Zeidler, Susan, ''Westinghouse to Cut 1,200 More Jobs, Take Charge,'' *Reuter Business Report,* January 26, 1995.

—Kathleen Peippo

Ticketmaster Corp.

3701 Wilshire, 7th Floor
Los Angeles, California 90010
U.S.A.
(213) 381-2000
Fax: (213) 386-1244

Private Company
Incorporated: 1982
Sales: $200 million
SICs: 7822 Theatrical Producers & Services; 7999 Amusement & Recreation, Not Elsewhere Classified

Ticketmaster Corp. is the largest ticket distribution company in the United States, completely dominating its market niche. It was selling more than $1 billion worth of ticket annually in the early 1990s for events ranging from professional wrestling matches to rock concerts and operas. Ticketmaster fielded 30 million telephone calls in 1994 and generated revenues of about $200 million. Going into the mid-1990s, the company was expanding into other entertainment and media-related ventures. A privately held company, Ticketmaster's employment statistics are unavailable.

Ticketmaster was started by two Arizona State University students who were looking for a solution to a problem they encountered when buying concert tickets. At the time, the buyer of a ticket was forced to select from the seats that had been allotted to the particular vendor from whom he or she was purchasing the ticket. If the vendor was nearly sold out, the buyer might be forced to buy bad seats even though better seats were available through other ticket sellers. Melees occasionally erupted when ticket buyers, after standing in line for hours at one place, found that the vendor was sold out or that better seats were available elsewhere. The system was also inefficient for promoters and owners of venues, who often had difficulty selling all of their tickets, despite unmet demand.

In 1978, the two budding entrepreneurs developed a solution to the problem. They created an innovative computer program that networked several computers in such a way that a person buying an event ticket at a box office could quickly select from the total reserve of seats available. Thus, efficient computerized ticket vending was born, and Ticketmaster—the company that sprouted from student innovation—became one of several small vendors in the late 1970s and early 1980s that pioneered the industry. When it was starting out, in fact, Ticketmaster was just one of many small ticket-vending companies competing for a small share of the industry; the business had come to be dominated by ticket distribution giant Ticketron. Nevertheless, Ticketmaster, with its unique computer-based vending system, managed to increase its ticket sales to about $1 million annually by 1981. That amount was still less than one percent of the business controlled by Ticketron, however.

Ticketmaster's fate was changed in 1982, when Chicago investor Jay Pritzker purchased it. Pritzker, the wealthy owner of the Hyatt Hotel chain, paid $4 million for the entire company. He immediately brought in Fred Rosen as chief executive to manage the operation. Rosen, an attorney and former stand-up comic, brought energy and vision to the enterprise. He believed that the future of the ticket industry was in concert sales, rather than sporting events. That was partly because sporting event-goers often were able to circumvent service fees charged by ticket sellers by purchasing season tickets. But his feeling also arose from his observations about the dynamics of the concert industry. Indeed, if concert fans wanted to see a show badly enough, they would buy on impulse and would be willing to pay higher prices for tickets. Furthermore, the giant lines that formed at box offices for rock concerts indicated a great need for Ticketmaster's computerized service.

Besides new computer and information technologies, other forces were at work in the ticket industry in the early 1980s that boded well for an innovator like Ticketmaster. In fact, the rock concert industry, among other entertainment businesses, was becoming much more complicated. Prior to the 1970s, bands were paid a lump sum—usually in cash just a few minutes before they went on stage—by the promoter of the concert. The promoter would agree beforehand to pay the band, say, $20,000, and any money left over would be used to pay the promoter's expenses and profit.

In the 1970s, however, bands started demanding more. They started charging minimum appearance fees, for example, and wanted a cut of the money generated from concessions and parking. The demands were partly the result of a feeling by top bands that promoters were often taking advantage of them. But it was also caused by the increased cost of traveling and putting on a show; fans came to expect much more in the way of expensive sound systems and special effects, for example.

One result of the new demands was that, after a concert, the band's manager and the promoter typically negotiated, or argued, about exactly how much the promoter and other involved parties would be paid. The new system increased the bargaining power of the bands, eventually boosting their take to 75 percent or more of the gross receipts. Meanwhile, the promotion industry was pinched. Many promoters saw their profit margins deteriorate to as little as one percent, despite the fact that they were still bearing much of the risk of a failed concert. To get the big name bands, however, promoters had to be willing to accept that risk and honor many of the group's requirements.

That was the environment still evolving when Rosen took the helm at the fledgling Ticketmaster. Realizing the folly of trying to compete with the mammoth Ticketron using conventional industry tactics, he devised a strategy that exploited the frustrations of the promoters. He effectively offered to limit inside charges—the money taken from promoters and facility owners—thus reducing the promoter's risk. He would accomplish this by raising service charges on individual ticket sales and giving promoters a percentage of the proceeds. In return, the promoters agreed to give Ticketmaster the exclusive rights to ticketing for their shows. To boost service fees, Rosen implemented new sales techniques, particularly telephone sales service that gave customers an alternative to standing in line. For the convenience, Ticketmaster was able to charge as much as a 30 percent premium, or higher in some instances.

Many promoters gave exclusive rights to Ticketmaster. Indeed, besides guaranteed fees, the promoters benefited from Ticketmaster's state-of-the-art ticketing system. The company's computers could sell 25,000 tickets in just a few minutes, if necessary, which substantially reduced the promoter's advertising and related costs and improved customer satisfaction with the overall event. The arrangement worked so well that Ticketmaster was eventually able to secure long-term contracts with several major promoters for handling ticketing for all of their events. Promoters also viewed Ticketmaster as preferable alternative to the giant Ticketron, which many promoters believed had become arrogant and sloppy.

Despite steady gains, Ticketmaster lost money in the late 1970s and early 1980s as it scrambled to implement its expensive strategy. By the mid-1980s, though, the company was posting profits. To boost sales and market share, Ticketmaster began buying out smaller competitors in an effort to broaden its reach into major cities. It acquired Datatix/Select-A-Seat in Denver, for example, and SEATS in Atlanta. As it bought up more companies and drove others out of business, the number of competitors in the industry declined. At the same time, Ticketron's supremacy was rapidly waning. Besides complacency, part of Ticketron's problem was that it lacked the investment capital afforded by Ticketmaster's deep-pocketed owner. Its ticketing systems soon became obsolete in comparison to those in use at Ticketmaster.

By the late 1980s, Ticketmaster had become a top player in the ticketing business and Ticketron was scurrying to duplicate Rosen's successful revenue-sharing strategy. But it was too late; Ticketmaster had mastered the recipe and was rapidly increasing the number and size of its contracts. In fact, Ticketmaster's relationship with, and control over, its promoters had evolved to the point where Ticketmaster was deeply entwined in the promotion business. That involvement was evidenced by a relationship in Seattle that finally ended in a lawsuit. In 1989, Ticketmaster made a loan and credit line guarantee valued at $500,000 to two of the area's top promoters. The promoters used the money to start a new operation promoting concerts in The George, a facility in central Washington. In that same year, one of the promoters launched another venture, PowerStation, to sell tickets in competition with Ticketmaster. Enraged Ticketmaster executives responded by withholding cash from the promoter's ticket sales through Ticketmaster. The promoter sued and finally settled with Ticketmaster out of court, but the PowerStation was shuttered and both promoters left the concert business.

By the end of the 1980s, Ticketmaster was selling more than $500,000 worth of tickets annually. Ticketron was still considered an industry power, but its status was diminished and its long-term prospects were dismal. The only other competition consisted of a smattering of local and regional companies struggling to combat Ticketmaster. Ticketmaster finally delivered the crowning blow to Ticketron in 1991, when it purchased some of the company's assets and effectively rendered the company no more than a lesson in corporate history. Questions were raised about whether or not the buyout would give Ticketmaster a monopoly on the industry, but the U.S. Department of Justice approved the deal. With Ticketron out of its way, Ticketmaster was virtually dominant and its sales began rising rapidly toward the $1 billion mark.

Because it had so much control in the ticket industry, Ticketmaster came under fire from numerous critics following the demise of Ticketron. Some fans complained that Ticketmaster was raising its fees, reflecting a monopoly on the industry. Similarly, some promoters argued that Ticketmaster wielded too much power and that it was willing to abuse that power to get its way. Finally, some rock bands complained that Ticketmaster was gouging their profits with excessive fees, knowing that the bands had nowhere else to turn. Ticketmaster countered, citing rising operating costs and relatively modest overall company profits. Still, criticism continued.

Band discontent with Ticketmaster's tactics culminated in one of the most visible disputes with Ticketmaster on record: a complaint filed with the Justice Department by the popular rock band Pearl Jam, alleging that Ticketmaster engaged in monopolistic practices. Pearl Jam wanted Ticketmaster to drop its service fees to $1.80 per ticket, but the company refused to drop below $2.50. Pearl Jam rejected the offer and threatened to work without Ticketmaster. The band planned to find venues, such as fairgrounds and racetracks, that were not subject to Ticketmaster's exclusive contracts. Their efforts eventually failed and their concert tour fell apart. That's when the band filed the complaint, and the Justice Department launched an investigation.

Ticketmaster argued that from about $1 billion worth of tickets sold in 1993, it generated revenues of $191 million in 1993, only $7 million of which was earned as net profit. That amounted to less than ten cents in profit per ticket. Critics complained that Ticketmaster was simply concealing the profitability of the business, but Rosen and his fellow executives were adamant that the industry was still competitive. "Fifteen years ago, there was another company everybody said had a monopoly—Ticketron," said Larry Solters, Ticketmaster spokesperson, in the July 31, 1994 *News & Observer.* He added, "Ticketmaster did ticketing better. And I wouldn't be surprised if somebody else comes up with a better system someday. There are a million ideas out there. . . . It's not that tough."

After posting record sales and profits in 1993, Ticketmaster's fate was changed again when Paul Allen beat out several big-name media companies in a bid to purchase a controlling stake in the company for about $300 million. The 40-year-old Allen had gained fame as the cofounder of software superstar Microsoft. Since cashing out of that venture, he had assembled an interesting portfolio of investments, many of which were generally related in some way to the emerging information highway. He also owned the Portland Trailblazers basketball team and a charitable foundation, among many other interests. Allen retained Rosen as CEO, but he had new plans for the company. In fact, he wanted to increase the company's sales three- to five-fold within three to five years and expand into different distribution avenues. Potential sales routes included interactive television and on-line computer services, among others.

Ticketmaster sold a whopping 52 million tickets to entertainment and sporting events in 1994 and captured about $200 million in revenues. Having nearly cornered the ticket market, it was setting its sites on several media-related ventures. Ticketmaster already was distributing a regional monthly events guide to about 600,000 customers, and it planned to piggyback off of that venture to create a new entertainment magazine. The company was also working on a new online service, in essence hoping to position itself as a sort of one-stop shopping center for entertainment/event needs, although Rosen had yet to reveal his specific strategy by the mid-1990s.

Further Reading:

Andrew, Paul, "Paul Allen's Ticket to Future," *Seattle Times,* November 23, 1993, p. E1.

Corr, O. Casey, "Big-Ticket Troubles: Concert Industry Rolls in Money, but Where Is it All Going," *Seattle Times,* August 21, 1994, p. A1.

Francis, Mike, "Paul Allen Slowly, Surely Steps Into Public Light," *Oregonian,* August 14, 1994, p. F1.

Gaulin, Jacqueline, "Consumer Groups Go After Ticketmaster," *Washington Times,* March 22, 1995, p. B7.

Menconi, David, "TicketMaster's Money Tree—A Giant With it Made in the Shade," *News & Observer* (Raleigh, N.C.), July 31, 1994, p. G1.

Spring, Greg, "Ticketmaster Sets Sights On New Ventures," *Los Angeles Business Journal,* February 13, 1995, p. 6.

—Dave Mote

The Timberland Company

200 Domain Drive
Stratham, New Hampshire 03885
U.S.A.
(603) 772-9500
Fax: (603) 773-1640

Public Company
Incorporated: 1978
Employees: 7,000
Sales: $637.5 million
Stock Exchanges: New York Pacific Chicago
SICs: 3143 Men's Footwear, Except Athletic; 3144 Men's Boots, Casual or Dress; 2386 Women's Footwear, Except Athletic; 2329 Women's Leather or Canvas Boots

The Timberland Company's ascension in the rugged footwear industry was sometimes rocky, but savvy marketing, excellent products, and extraordinary luck eventually turned an obscure bootmaker into a worldwide symbol of rustic chic. The first hint of widespread interest came in the early 1980s, when Italian trendsetters made Timberland hiking boots the ultimate in style and sophistication. The resultant European buying frenzy sent American retailers scrambling for Timberland footwear, sparking the first of many fashion booms. Although Timberland became a household name through a fluke of fashion, the company's outdoor footwear and accessories also became synonymous with quality, dependability, and a return to nature. In 1993, Timberland became the leading producer of rugged footwear in Italy and the United States with net sales of $418.9 million. Continuing its spectacular climb in 1994, Timberland reached $637.5 million in net sales by year's end, an astonishing 52 percent leap from 1993.

In 1952 Nathan Swartz, a shoe stitcher by trade, bought half-interest in the Abington Shoe Company of Abington, Massachusetts. Within three years, Nathan acquired the remaining interest in the company for $20,000 and brought his youngest son, 19-year-old Sidney, aboard. Within the year, Nathan's elder son, Herman, returned from a stint in the navy and joined the business too. For the next decade, father and sons produced and sold handmade footwear to discount outlets and stores that put house labels on them. In 1965, after researching alternatives to the expensive art of hand-stitching soles and uppers together, the Swartzes purchased an injection-molding machine—a new binding process that chemically molded and attached soles to uppers. Injection molding not only produced footwear for 50 cents less per pair, but it also allowed Abington to charge about 20 cents more because the new footwear had some water resistance. Now selling boots for $5.75 a pair wholesale, Abington was able to generate a small profit rather than just breaking even.

In 1968 Nathan retired, leaving Abington in his sons' capable hands. Two years later, the brothers moved the company to New Hampshire and set their sights on producing tough, thoroughly waterproof boots capable of standing up to the worst weather and the ravages of time. Surprisingly, they found a prototype right under their noses—Abington's maintenance man wore rugged workboots year-round that were comfortable, durable, water-resistant. The boots, made in Canada and distributed in the United States by the Vermont-based Dunham company, inspired fierce loyalty in their owner. The Swartzes bought a pair, dissected them, and were determined to make their own, even better version.

After persuading Goodyear to design a synthetic rubber sole capable of withstanding the harshest elements, the Swartzes used injection molding to bond the polyurethane soles to genuine blond leather uppers. To test for water resistance, the brothers tried everything from weighting boots with metal and submerging them in a bucket to filling the boot itself with dyed water and waiting for leaks. The result was Abington's first truly waterproof boots, which the company began marketing under the brand name "Timberland" in 1973 and guaranteed as water-resistant. Targeted at blue-collar workers and sold in Army-Navy stores, Timberland boots were a serendipitous hit on college campuses.

Never big on advertising, Abington hired the Boston firm of Marvin & Leonard to help market Timberland boots. Len Kanzer, the agency's president, convinced the Swartzes to appeal to upscale buyers via ads in the *New Yorker.* As a result, Timberland boots sold remarkably well at high-brow retailers like Bergdorf Goodman, Lord & Taylor, and Saks Fifth Avenue, and the company produced 5,000 pairs in 1974. By 1975, production jumped to 25,000 and sales neared the million-dollar mark. By the late 1970s, the company was producing 400,000 pairs of Timberlands annually, which prompted the Swartz brothers to consider expanding their product line. Abington Shoe Company's principal output was now Timberland boots, with no-name boots amounting to only about 20 percent of 1978's production. Now on the map with its own brand, Abington discontinued manufacturing for others and concentrated on Timberland boots.

While diversifying was indeed a gamble, Herman and Sidney decided to risk it. First, taking full advantage of their rugged footwear's brand recognition, they renamed the Abington Shoe Company as The Timberland Company and incorporated in 1978. The newly christened company then introduced its first casual shoes for men with handsewn uppers, solid brass eyelets, and water-resistant full-grain leather. Next came 1979's boating or "deck" shoe, which went toe-to-toe with the industry leader—Sperry's perennially popular Top-Sider brand. Timberland aggressively marketed its product, polling dozens of sailors and eventually winning endorsements from hardcore yachters William F. Buckley Jr. and Ted Kennedy.

Also in 1979, an Italian goods distributor named Giuseppe Veronesi visited Timberland's New Hampshire factory and ordered 3,000 pairs of boots. Veronesi, the president of Ritz Firma, a subsidiary of FinRitz SpA (which was responsible for the Louis Vuitton brand and Ralph Lauren's Polo line for women), figured Timberland boots would be a perfect fashion accessory for well-heeled Italians. After testing the market in *haute couture* shops in Milan and Rome, Veronesi soon began selling Timberland boots in boutiques throughout Italy. Though Timberland products were still selling well in America's pricey department stores, the Italian craze caused even more U.S. retailers to jump on the Timberland bandwagon. Now grossing in the neighborhood of $14 million, Timberland was becoming known worldwide. Boot production rose to 1.8 million pairs in 1983, with a price tag between $70 and $80 per pair in the United States, and nearly double that in Europe.

In 1984, Timberland was flushed with success and poised for more. As a company on the move, moreover, it had caught the interest of several acquisitive conglomerates. The VF Corp., which had holdings including Lee Jeans, was the first to approach the Swartzes with a buyout offer of $60 million. Herman, nearing 60 years of age, wanted to accept the package and retire. Sidney, however, was not interested in selling and wanted Timberland to raise its own funds for a major expansion. Before the brothers could reach a compromise, the offer was withdrawn. Despite what may have been a lost opportunity, it was business as usual at Timberland. The company planned a further expansion into international markets, hoping to capitalize on its continued boom in Italy, where 490,000 Timberland boots were exported in 1984. Soon Timberland began shipping products to France, Germany, Hong Kong, Switzerland, and Turkey. Not only did Italian sales continue to climb, reaching 540,000 in 1985, but worldwide sales soon hit $68 million.

In the early months of 1986, Timberland was again faced with the possibility of acquisition. This time a former partner of Morgan Stanley & Company proffered a bid of about $60 million. Again, the brothers were at odds: Herman for the buyout, and Sidney steadfastly against it. In order to reach an agreement, Sidney sought financing and came up with $34.5 million from Merrill Lynch to purchase Herman's share of Timberland for roughly $30 million. Herman left Timberland and retired, while Sidney became president and CEO of the company.

After 30 years, Herman was no longer at his brother's side as Sidney moved forward with both domestic and international expansion. In 1986, Timberland hoped to claim $20 million worth of the lucrative Japanese consumer goods market. Sidney's 29-year-old son Jeffrey joined the company as head of the international sales division to help steer the company's growing Asian and European presence. Less than a year after Herman sold his stake in Timberland and retired, Merrill Lynch sold 3.35 million Timberland shares, roughly 30 percent of their holdings, at $14 each in an initial public offering. When Sidney and Jeffrey made a public offering on the American Stock Exchange in mid-1987, they kept the "B" shares, with 10 votes each, in the family, and dispersed only "A" shares, which held one vote apiece.

Meanwhile, Timberland's expansion continued unabated, and the Swartzes started to lose control of their vast empire. By rapidly introducing 160 new models, bringing Timberland's total product line to about 500, the company caught its factories unprepared. Inventory control and customer service suffered, frustrating retailers and consumers. Despite the fact that revenues climbed by 24 percent and total sales reached $85 million by the end of 1986, profits fell 14 percent to $4.8 million. In an effort to stem manufacturing and customer service problems, Timberland created a worldwide customer relations department in 1987 to make good on its commitment to quality products and service.

Also in 1987, Marvin & Leonard Advertising made Timberland the first boot producer to advertise its products on television. One memorable commercial featured rural bootleggers extolling the virtues of Timberland boots for hiding from Treasury agents in swamps. The wry ads gained plenty of attention, propelled sales, and solidified Timberland's reputation as a producer of fashionable footwear.

In 1988, the company entered the men's and women's clothing and accessories market. "Versus Ralph Lauren, we have a degree of authenticity," Jens Bang, Timberland's executive vice-president, explained to *Advertising Age.* The clothing, like Timberland footwear, "would perform under extreme conditions and are good-looking, too." Though sales sputtered initially, apparel and accessories eventually claimed about 20 percent of Timberland's net sales. Later that year, the company began opening specialty stores: the first on Newbury Street in Boston; a second on Madison Avenue in New York City; and a third on New Bond Street in London.

Finishing the year with profits of $8 million on revenues of $133 million, Timberland also posted record exports of $39 million. The majority of exports were still shipped to Italy—528,000 pairs of footwear worth $21 million wholesale. Despite runaway sales, however, Timberland's profit margin continued to erode; from 1987 to 1989, profits fell from $9.4 to $6.4 million. The company had too many products, too little focus, and even less corporate restraint. "I nearly drove this company under the ground," Sidney Swartz admitted to *Forbes* in 1989. Though his ideas and intentions were good, the reality of Timberland's rapid expansion had proved burdensome for a company still adjusting to its previous growth. "My optimism sometimes gets the better of me," Sidney said as he envisioned Timberland backpacks, canoes, and sleeping bags. "And we're not ruling out mountain bikes."

Luckily for Sidney, his son was a capable business manager. The two set out to regain control of their product line and eliminate costly manufacturing snafus. The company also stopped trying to capture two disparate markets—the fashion elite who wore Timberland boots simply for effect and the outdoor crowd who wore them to get fit and explore the natural world. Eschewing trends, the company stepped up advertising to the outdoorsy men and women its rugged footwear was originally designed for. Integrating its marketing efforts, Timberland also began to stress corporate responsibility and a growing community awareness. The company reemphasized its commitment to consumers interested in hiking, climbing, camping, adventure travel, and environmental protection by backing local and national service organizations like the Wilderness Society, the Boston-based City Year, and Alaska's legendary Iditarod dogsled race.

Timberland's growing relationship with City Year was not just public relations posturing; what began as a request for 50 pairs of boots had turned into a $1 million investment by 1992, enabling the company to expand into four states. "As a company," Jeffrey noted, "we have a responsibility and an interest in engaging the world around us. By doing so, we deliver value to our four constituencies: consumers, shareholders, employees, and the community." The company furthered this commitment by granting all employees between 16 and 32 hours of paid time off each year for community service. The Swartzes also broadened their sensitivity to environmental issues by joining the EPA's Green Lights Program, Businesses for Social Responsibility (BSR), and the Coalition for Environmentally Responsible Economies (CERES) in 1992 and 1993.

In 1989 sales topped $156 million, of which exports represented 30 percent—despite Timberland's withdrawal from China after the Tiananmen Square massacre. In 1991, 31-year-old Jeffrey Swartz was named Timberland's chief operating officer. Overseeing daily operations, Jeffrey implemented several corrective measures to restructure the company, cut waste, boost profits, and maintain shipping schedules. The biggest of these adjustments was the switch from assembly-line manufacturing to teamwork, which cut production time by as much as two-thirds. This year also featured two other milestones: the company's commencement of trading on the New York Stock Exchange, and the fall debut of *Elements: The Journal of Outdoor Experience,* Timberland's slick, 32-page biannual magazine. Translated into four languages and distributed in nine countries, the magazine's content was written by celebrated outdoor enthusiasts and edited by mountaineer John Harlin III.

By 1992, Timberland's print and media gambits carried the company logo and a social message, like the "Give Racism the Boot" campaign it ran in the United States and Europe. Complete with billboards in New York City, as well as t-shirts, posters, and pins (proceeds from the sale of which went to City Year), the campaign fueled company growth of 22 percent in the first half of the year. To keep its lead in the footwear and apparel industry, Timberland started retooling factories with the latest technology and applied a few tricks of the trade learned from Japanese manufacturers. "Companies that don't adapt won't be around," Sidney told *U.S. News and World Report.* "It's Darwinism at its best. We will adapt and we will survive." By the end of 1992, Timberland's sales topped $291 million, and its products were sold in 50 countries, 12 retail stores, and over 225 department store "concept" shops worldwide.

As the 1990s progressed, the popularity of Timberland's footwear spawned many imitators. Adidas, Nike, and Reebok all came out with rugged footwear in an attempt to compensate for sluggish athletic shoe sales. According to market analyst Scott Davis in *USA Today,* however, "Timberland is No. 1 in this market. Everyone else is playing catch-up." As proof, Timberland stock rose 280 percent in 1993 and was named one of the NYSE's "best stocks" by *Business Week.* Near the end of the year, Timberland's creative advertising campaigns once again struck a chord with television viewers when Mullen Advertising introduced its inspired Muddy Waters campaign. Rife with shots of Mother Nature's mood swings, the quirky, pun-filled commercials drew cheers from fellow agencies and consumers alike.

Timberland's 1994 revenues were even more incredible, partly due to a sizeable increase in its advertising budget, which reached between $18 and $25 million worldwide. Timberland's increasingly aggressive media blitzes paid off handsomely. The Swartzes strengthened Timberland's market share even more by slashing prices, by as much as 25 percent, on Weatherbuck casuals, with plans for more "value pricing." Domestic production climbed from 3 to 5 million pairs annually; combined with improved inventory control and faster delivery, this production helped Timberland secure more business in the American Midwest and South, the company's fasted-growing regions for the third quarter of 1993.

While several prominent athletic shoe manufacturers continued to expand their rugged footwear lines, even Harley Davidson and Caterpillar announced their intentions to join the fray. Yet Jeffrey Swartz was not overly concerned: "We transcend language and geography," he told *USA Today* at the end of 1993. "We represent something that's more than a product; it's also a point of view. Whether it's the '60s or '70s, whether it's grunge or hip-hop or be-bop, it still snows and it still rains and you're going to get dressed for the snow and the rain." Timberland's revenues bore this out, and the company maintained its quest to make even better products. One advance was Timberland's introduction, in January 1995, of its exclusive Active Comfort Technology (ACT), which was soon to become part of its high-performance hunting and hiking boots.

Community service, too, became a bigger part of Timberland's corporate life. The company made a $5 million pledge to City Year in 1994 and participated in several area events, including the Seacoast Hospice clean-up, a City Year-sponsored "Serv-A-Thon" at the Thurgood Marshall School in Atlanta, and work at the YMCA's Camp Gundalow in both 1993 and 1994. In the latter effort, Jeffrey Swartz and his three young sons (ages six, four, and one) were among over 175 Timberland employees who pitched in to help prepare Camp Gundalow for the upcoming summer season. "As an employee, you don't draw strength from some corporate guy making a speech," Jeffrey told a local newspaper covering the event.

Entering the mid-1990s, the Swartz family had evolved from producers of sturdy, unglamorous work boots to become the titans of the rugged outdoor footwear market. The company experienced rough times during the late 1980s, as Sidney explained to *USA Today:* "Frankly, we didn't have a disciplined approach or business sense about us," he admitted. "We were very driven, but didn't know where we were going." Timberland overcame this difficult period, however, and appeared firmly focused on the future.

Principal Subsidiaries: Timberland Aviation Inc.; Timberland Direct Sales Inc.; Timberland Europe Inc.; Timberland International Inc.; Timberland Manufacturing Co.; Timberland Overseas Co.; Timberland Scandinavia Inc.; Timberland World Trading Co.

Further Reading:

Angrist, Stanley W., ''Betting the Company,'' *Forbes,* April 25, 1983, pp. 109–110.

Benoit, Ellen, ''When the Shoe Fits,'' *Forbes,* September 16, 1985, p. 194.

Conklin, Michele, ''How Three Shoe Manufacturers Found their Pots of Gold,'' *Madison Avenue,* October 1985, p. 49–50.

Cook, William J., ''Four Better Mousetraps,'' *U.S. News & World Report,* Aust 24, 1992, pp. 52–55.

Greenwald, John, ''Timberland Hits Its Stride,'' *Time,* November 29, 1993, p. 63.

Hill, Julie Skur, ''Japan is Next for Timberland,'' *Advertising Age,* October 27, 1986, p. 62.

Lippert, Barbara, ''Blues Power,'' *ADWEEK,* November 15, 1993, p. 42.

Maremont, Mark, ''Timberland Comes Out of the Woods,'' *Business Week,* September 13, 1993, p. 78.

Meeks, Fleming, ''Sidney Swartz' Dolce Vita,'' *Forbes,* July 10, 1989, pp. 56–57.

Rosato, Donna, and Judith Schroer, ''Timberland Steps Into Fashion, *USA Today,* December 14, 1993, p. B1.

Sloan, Pat, ''Timberland Tries on Clothes,'' *Advertising Age,* Augst 22, 1988, p. 51.

''Timberland Launches Anti-Racism Ads,'' *Sporting Goods Business,* February 1993.

''Timberland: Walking Tall,'' *The Economist,* Augst 4, 1990, pp. 56–57.

—Taryn Benbow-Pfalzgraf

Tombstone Pizza Corporation

101 Harlem Avenue
Glenview, Illinois 60025
U.S.A.
(708) 646-2000
Fax: (708) 646-3901

Wholly Owned Subsidiary of Kraft General Foods Inc.
Founded: 1962
Employees: 1,600
Sales: $190 million (estimated)
SICs: 2038 Frozen Specialties; 2013 Sausages and Other Prepared Meats

''What do you want on your Tombstone?,'' an executioner asks a condemned man. ''Cheese and pepperoni,'' the man replies in a memorable television commercial for the fastest-growing frozen pizza manufacturer in the United States. Tombstone Pizza Corporation, a subsidiary of Kraft General Foods Inc., grew out of the hit product of a northern Wisconsin tavern to become a national phenomenon. In 1995, Tombstone announced that its product had earned the number one ranking in a year-long Nielsen poll of frozen pizza consumers nationwide.

Tombstone's history was as unique and humorous as its name. In the 1960s, brothers Joseph ''Pep'' and Ronald Simek ran a neighborhood tavern called the Tombstone Tap on the outskirts of Medford, Wisconsin. The local watering hole, which sold beer at a dime a glass, was so named not because of any occult interests on the part of its owners, but rather because it was located across from a cemetery. One night, while letting loose to the ''Peppermint Twist,'' Pep got a bit carried away and fell, breaking his leg. For the next six weeks, he hobbled about on crutches and was confined to the tavern's minuscule back kitchen. With nothing better to do, Pep relieved his boredom by experimenting with various pizza recipes as a snack for Tombstone Tap's patrons. Remembering some delicious pizza he had tried during a recent visit to the Windy City, Pep decided to produce a Chicago-style pizza and experimented with crust thickness, spices, sauces, and toppings until it was just right.

By 1962, 35-year-old Pep had perfected his pizza with a secret slew of spices, tangy sauce, real Wisconsin cheese, and lean meats. Once the pizzas were served at Tombstone Tap, customers could not get enough. Word quickly spread about the terrific pizza at Tombstone, and by 1963 other local taverns commissioned the Simeks to make pizzas for them to freeze and serve later. Pep and Ron, along with their wives, Joan and Frances, began making pies in earnest from the living quarters attached to the Tap. Folks referred to their products as ''Tombstone's'' or ''Tombstone'' pizza, and the unlikely name stuck.

From the beginning, the Simeks went about their enterprise with a singularity of purpose: to create the tastiest, best pizza possible, whether it was served to the tavern's customers or frozen for delivery. Even their method of delivery was unique and stylish—packed in dry ice, the handmade pizza pies were delivered in a snazzy 1959 Cadillac. Yet demand quickly exceeded the car's capabilities, and the Simeks took out a $5,600 loan to buy their first refrigerated truck in 1966. The truck had the capacity to carry up to 1,800 frozen pizzas to neighboring taverns, campgrounds, gas stations, bowling alleys, and other clients.

The following year, the Simeks faced a daunting decision—whether to continue with their burgeoning wholesale pizza business or concentrate on running the tavern. They decided on the former and converted the rooms attached to the back of the Tap into a small factory, where they produced pizzas until clients from distant counties began calling with orders. Once again, demand overtook supply and the Simeks' back rooms-turned-factory would no longer suffice. They built their first large-scale manufacturing facility in 1968 and set their sights on conquering the entire state of Wisconsin by way of Milwaukee, the nation's highest seller of sausage-topped frozen pizzas, some 250 miles away.

By 1970, frozen pizzas had become a $100-million industry. Within three years, Tombstone Pizza's reputation had once again exceeded its manufacturing capability and Pep and Ron needed to enlarge their factory in northern Wisconsin. The pizza-making business continued to grow unabated, and the Simeks found themselves putting additions on the Medford facility practically every year. In addition, the brothers found it increasingly difficult to control some of their independent distributors and to closely monitor sales and receipts. In 1975, Pep and Ron hired a 32-year-old named Grant White, who had previously tended bar at the Tap, as Tombstone's salaried sales manager. Another former bartender, D. David ''Dewey'' Sebold, also 32 years old, was hired to realign the company's field sales team. Sebold, who had organized and run a sales force for pharmaceutical giant Ciba-Geigy, convinced the Simeks that they would regulate their deliveries more easily by replacing the varied distributorships with their own specially trained sales force.

Taking Dewey's advice, Tombstone commenced its direct-store-delivery (DSD) service in 1976, taking pizzas directly from the manufacturing plant to designated distribution points, where the Tombstone sales force took over by driving the refrigerated trucks to supermarkets, convenience stores, and other retail customers. By delivering its products in this manner, Tombstone ensured that its pizzas were fresher, plus it carried lower inventory and saved money by reducing out-of-stock situations and labor costs. Tombstone was in control of the entire process from start to finish, which insured quality pizzas and prompt distribution. The practice was reminiscent of the early days, when Tombstone Pizzas arrived at the customer's door from the back of the Simeks' 1959 Cadillac. Although refrigerated trucks replaced the Cadillac and drivers with a regular route replaced Ron and Pep, the personal touch survived.

However, DSD service was difficult and costly to implement. For example, within the year Tombstone went from 20 independent route salesmen with complete discretion and autonomy to over 140 routers with 20 supervisors, 19 district managers, and 4 regional managers. And to make the Tombstone brand of customer service clear, salespeople underwent a five-week training program headed up by White, who traveled the state for months looking for recruits. Moreover, not all customers were impressed with DSD service, and some refused to carry Tombstone products because of the company's insistence on direct delivery. One case in point was the Dominick's supermarket chain, which operated through independent brokers and maintained its own storage facilities. Dominick's management believed DSD created undue congestion, ample opportunities for theft, and unfair brand positioning. Yet after dodging Tombstone's sales proposals for two years, Dominick's relented because of consumer demand. ''Customers wanted Tombstone real bad,'' Larry Nauman, vice president of advertising and public relations for Dominick's Finer Foods, told *Inc.* in 1982. ''We were losing action without handling it.''

In the remainder of the 1970s, Tombstone entered several new markets, including Denver, Minneapolis, St. Louis, and Chicago. In 1979, the company diversified a bit by bringing out a smoked beef product called Tombstone Beef Sticks. The onset of the 1980s found Tombstone evolving from state to regional to national pizza supplier. By 1981, sales had mushroomed to $62 million in the billion-dollar frozen pizza market, a 27 percent increase from the previous year's $49 million. Tombstone's success, the result of its superior products and homespun philosophy, allowed it to take business away from its large and well-established competition one slice at a time. Big names like Pillsbury and General Mills offered dozens of frozen products, including pizza, in a dizzying array of brands. ''We're basically a single-product company,'' Sebold, now Tombstone's executive vice president and general manager, told *Inc.* in 1982. ''We don't have the luxury of bringing out a new specialty product each week, and we can't compete with larger companies by cutting prices.'' White, director of the sales force, concurred: ''Being a one-product company can sometimes be a negative, but it's also a plus,'' he explained, ''because it's hard to lose perspective on what we're selling.''

Tombstone pizzas sold like hotcakes in 17 states, and not as an inexpensive commodity, but as a high-quality specialty product worthy of its purchase price. Tombstone's premium products included only 100 percent real cheese (other brands often used artificial or cheese substitutes), and the company made its own Canadian bacon, pepperoni, and sausage. In a 1982 *Quick Frozen Foods* editorial, Sebold blamed the industry's decline in shipments of 15 million tons from the previous year on the widespread use of bargain-basement selling tactics: ''The pizza industry must upgrade itself considerably to be in position for the upcoming economic recovery. It must offer quality, not price; convenience, not confusion; service, not lip service; merchandising expertise, not forced distribution; innovative products, not me-too products; and profit, not margin-devastating deals.'' At the time of Sebold's comments, Tombstone's primary competitors, Jeno's and the Pillsbury-owned Totino's, were engaged in a messy court battle many felt undermined the industry itself.

Since food stores now accounted for a majority of its business, Tombstone hired Charles Stoeringer, a former marketing manager for the Green Giant Company. Stoeringer convinced the Simeks that it was more important than ever for Tombstone's sales force to maintain its edge over competitors. Though many companies adopted ''quality'' as a buzzword, Stoeringer helped Tombstone earn the distinction. For example, Tombstone goods were packaged in clear plastic instead of boxes, Tombstone drivers personally arranged products on customers' shelves rather than simply dropping off sealed cartons, and salespeople were encouraged to offer demonstrations to clients. Under Stoeringer's tutelage, Tombstone hired the Minneapolis-based Campbell-Mithun Inc. advertising agency to help coordinate its marketing efforts in the traditional venues of newspapers, television, and coupon promotions.

From 1976 to 1983, Tombstone grew by more than 25 percent each year. This growth led the company to acquire and customize a new manufacturing facility in Sussex, Wisconsin, and to install an on-line computer system for marketing forecasts, reports, and sales figures. Both the Sussex plant and the new data processing system added dramatically to Tombstone's capabilities, just in time for the company's penetration of the Columbus, Ohio, and Kansas City frozen pizza markets. In 1984, the year a Gallup poll ranked pizza as the favorite take-out food in America, Tombstone's revenue surpassed $100 million.

Yet consumers' tastes were not restricted to frozen pizza products, but also included pizza from restaurant chains and local pizzerias as well as the newest craze, do-it-yourself pizza kits with crust, sauce, and cheese included. Discussing the competition between frozen suppliers and pizza chains, Sebold told *Quick Frozen Foods,* ''I think they're great for business. . . . You have to recognize what business they're in; they're in the franchise business, not the pizza business. At Pizza Hut, pizza is one of their mainstays, but they have everything from lasagna to sandwiches. . . . So you're measuring a certain dollar volume that isn't solely pizzas. You're measuring restaurant sales.'' As the pizza craze continued, even supermarket delis joined the fray by offering their own freshly prepared pizzas for customers to simply pop in the oven.

''Frozen pizza is a mature category,'' Sebold admitted to *Quick Frozen Foods* in 1985, ''but with good marketing—not giveaways and short-term strategies—there's plenty of growth left in the industry.'' To take advantage of this growth, Tombstone introduced another beef stick product under the ''Snappy'' brand, followed by Tombstone Beef Jerky, the ''DoubleTop'' 12-inch pie, and revamped packaging that included a toll-free consumer hotline. Also in 1985, the Medford fleet service facility was opened to maintain Tombstone's trucks, and the company entered two far-flung new markets, Dallas (the nation's top-selling area for frozen pizza) and Phoenix. By this time, Tombstone serviced 45,000 retailers in 22 midwestern and western states and was closely chasing the nation's top frozen pizza suppliers, Totino's and Jeno's, which were both now owned by Pillsbury.

In 1986, the $7 billion Kraft General Foods corporation made the Simeks an attractive buyout offer which gave the company the potential for almost unlimited growth. All of Tombstone's 1,000 employees, including management, were assured of their positions—only Pep and Ron would no longer be a part of the company under the acquisition's terms. The brothers ultimately decided they were ready to leave the pizza-making business and entrust their company to Kraft's considerable power and expertise. Tombstone Pizza became "a freestanding operating unit" of Kraft and its parent company, Dart & Kraft Inc. Tombstone marketing specialist Cathryn Pernu told the *Wausau Daily Herald* that this time the Simeks, who had turned down several buyout offers in the past, "felt they had paid their dues. Selling just seemed to be more attractive than before." When Pep stepped down as chairman and Ron as president, Dewey Sebold, formerly executive vice-president and general manager, took the helm of Tombstone as it became Kraft's newest subsidiary. For its part, Kraft had recently bought about 30 companies and was in the market for a premium pizza manufacturer after its own boxed brand failed. Kraft's media relations coordinator, Paul Johnson, said Tombstone's "amazing growth record" had impressed Kraft. Kraft also welcomed the opportunity to use its own cheeses on Tombstone's pizza varieties.

By 1987, the Medford factory was renovated to add 10,000 square feet of productive capacity and its equipment was brought up to speed with the latest technology. A similar renovation took place in Sussex, as the four-year-old facility tripled its size. Both factories braced for the flood of orders from the company's latest product launch, the first Tombstone microwave pizza. The next year Tombstone ventured west all the way to Seattle, the biggest market for frozen pizza with Canadian bacon in the United States, and conquered Texas with the addition of the Austin and San Antonio markets. At this point Tombstone occupied markets in 23 states. Also in 1988 came the news of Kraft General Foods's merger with Philip Morris, the huge tobacco corporation.

Still coming up with new ways to serve its consumers, Tombstone added a crispy 12-inch thin-crust pizza to its line in 1989, the same year the company's headquarters was moved from Wisconsin to Glenview, Illinois. Tombstone added Portland and North and South Carolina to its ever-expanding market in 1990. As Americans became more concerned about the calories, cholesterol, and fat in the foods they ate, Tombstone introduced the health-conscious 12-inch Tombstone Light pizza. Later that year, the Chicago advertising agency Foote, Cone & Belding introduced the witty "What do you want on your Tombstone?" commercials, startling and amusing viewers nationwide. The campaign was so successful that it spawned several variations as well as imitations over the next several years.

Due in part to its creative television advertising and local and regional marketing efforts, Tombstone maintained its spectacular growth into the 1990s. In 1991, the company launched another new variety, the 12-inch Tombstone Special Order Pizza, to compete with carryout and delivery pizzas from local restaurants. The company also expanded its markets throughout the United States, including Detroit, Roanoke, Richmond, Baltimore, Washington, D.C., Birmingham, Memphis, New Orleans, and Little Rock.

By 1992, with its expansion into major metropolitan areas in Florida, Pennsylvania, New Mexico, and California, Tombstone's sales areas encompassed about 70 percent of the country's households. By 1994, Tombstone's distribution pushed into the remaining East Coast states, completing its national network. That same year its latest innovation, the Tombstone For One pizza, made its debut. As the company entered the mid-1990s, sales maintained their upward swing and Tombstone Pizza's brand recognition continued to grow. The tasty pizzas from the Tombstone Tap had come a long way to reach homes across America.

Further Reading:

Benner, Jacqueline, "Pizza Standard Changes Outrage Processes," *Quick Frozen Foods,* November 1983, pp. 35–36.

Caron, Tom, "A Franchise Forgotten," *Quick Frozen Foods,* July 1983, pp. 15, 53.

Dagnoil, Judann, and Julie Liesse, " 'Healthy' Frozen Foods Launch Offensive," *Advertising Age,* September 2, 1991, pp. 1, 45.

Delano, Sara, "Rolling in Dough," *Inc.,* November 1982, pp. 67–70.

Demarest, Dusti, "Tombstone Sold to Kraft," *Wausau Daily Herald,* July 1986, pp. 1A–2A.

"Frozen Pizza," *Consumer Reports,* May 1986, pp. 327–331.

"Frozen Pizza Sales Still Soft as Billion Dollar Market Holds," *Quick Frozen Foods,* August 1985, pp. 72–76.

"Frozen Pizza War Is Heating Up," *Quick Frozen Foods,* July 1982, pp. 51–52, 196.

Heitzman, Beth, "Best Clients: Tombstone Pizza," *Adweek,* November 16, 1992, p. 20.

Liesse Erickson, Julie, "Frozen Pizza Makers Smell Success," *Advertising Age,* September 12, 1988, p. 86W.

Mogelonsky, Marcia, "Let Them Eat Pizza," *American Demographics,* March 1995, p. 10.

Neiman, Janet, "Jeno's Unit Joins Pizza Battles," *Advertising Age,* July 11, 1983, p. 24.

Parsons, Heidi, "Imaginative Marketers Paint New Picture of Frozen Pizza," *Quick Frozen Foods,* August 1985, pp. 38–42.

Prime, Jamison S., "Americans Hunger for a More Homey Pizza," *Wall Street Journal,* June 29, 1993, p. B6.

"Promotions Breathe Life into Retail Sales," *Quick Frozen Foods,* July 1983, pp. 17–19.

Strazewski, Len, "Four Davids Reject Goliath-like Paths," *Advertising Age,* October 12, 1987, pp. S4–S9.

Sebold, D. David, "Partners in Pizza: Has the Trade Been Ignored?," *Quick Frozen Foods,* July 1982, p. 14.

"Tombstone Buys Ad in Yellow Pages," *Supermarket News,* June 7, 1993, p. 31.

"Tombstone Pizza Marketing Basics Spice up Growth," *Quick Frozen Foods,* July 1983, pp. 40–44.

"When 'Fresh' Is Really Frozen: Pizza's Ingredients of Success," *Quick Frozen Foods,* July 1984, pp. 44F–44I.

—Taryn Benbow-Pfalzgraf

Topps Company, Inc.

One Whitehall Street
New York, New York 10004
U.S.A.
(212) 376-0300
Fax: (212) 376-0573

Public Company
Incorporated: 1947 as Topps Chewing Gum Inc.
Employees: 1,075
Sales: $268.04 million
Stock Exchanges: NASDAQ
SICS: 2759 Commercial Printing, Not Elsewhere Classified; 2067 Chewing Gum; 2064 Candy and Other Confectionery Products

Topps Company, Inc. is one of the most recognized makers and marketers of trading cards and bubble gum in the world. With products sold in 40 countries, a variety of entertainment licenses including exclusive license arrangements with virtually all the players in Major League Baseball, the National Football League, the National Basketball Association, and the National Hockey League, and trading card sales in the millions, the company that introduced baseball cards as premiums to sell gum has become part of Americana. Topps' popular BAZOOKA Bubble Gum is almost as familiar to consumers as its trading cards; in fact, BAZOOKA's aroma was one of those most frequently cited in a study of smells that elicit memories. Besides trading cards and bubble gum, Topps has marketed high-quality color comic books, collectibles, and candies. Since 1966, Topps has manufactured its gum at its plant in Duryea, Pennsylvania. Since that time, the company has established candy manufacturing plants in Scranton, Pennsylvania, and the Republic of Ireland. Though it faces greater competition than it did in the early years, Topps has retained the economic and imaginative leadership of its field.

The company was founded in 1938 by four brothers experienced in marketing tobacco, fuel, and other products. Abram, Ira, Philip, and Joseph Shorin named their organization the ''Topps Chewing Gum Inc.'' after their ambition to produce the best chewing gum available, adding an extra ''p'' for distinction. The company's first product, single pieces of chewing gum selling for a penny apiece, promptly became popular throughout the country.

When sugar was rationed during World War II, the fledgling Topps Chewing Gum company bought smaller candy companies, closed them, and used their sugar quotas. With such ingenuity and with the popular slogan, ''Don't Talk, Chum. Chew Topps Gum'' (reflecting the wartime campaign for reminding civilians to keep closemouthed regarding war information), the company was able to thrive while larger gum manufacturers had to cease operations.

To improve business after the war, the Shorin brothers introduced BAZOOKA Bubble Gum. (The BAZOOKA Joe comics found inside the wrapper were introduced later, in 1953, and the main character, BAZOOKA Joe, was modelled after co-founder Joseph E. Shorin.) Topps also soon introduced ''Magic Photos,'' its first picture products. These cards featured 252 different subjects, including 19 baseball greats. The cards appeared blank when taken from the packages, but when moistened they revealed black-and-white photos ''magically.''

In the same year the Topps Chewing Gum's major competitor, the Bowman Gum Company, began to market baseball and football cards as premiums. Baseball cards had first been offered as premiums in cigarette packs during the late 1880s, but the practice had been given up during World War I's raw material shortages. Topps was intrigued by the premium idea but needed to obtain the legal rights to depict the players and teams. Sy Berger, hired in 1947 to assist with a promotional campaign for Topps salesmen, personally took up the challenge, overseeing the signing of many sport figures of the time to individual contracts. Topps was able, therefore, to enter the baseball card business in 1951.

In that year the Topps Chewing Gum Company, began marketing two 52-card sets, known to collectors in the 1990s as ''Blue Backs'' and ''Red Backs,'' which were designed so that a game of card-baseball could be played by those who had collected all 52 in the set. Each card featured a hand-colored picture of a player and instructions on how to play the card-baseball game.

In 1952, Topps introduced the familiar format for its baseball cards, though their size was somewhat larger than the eventual standard. Sy Berger designed these cards to have color pictures of the players with their team emblems on the front and the players' personal history and playing statistics on the back.

During this time, Topps was working on obtaining rights to feature players and logos, while also working to standardize its cards. From 1952 through 1955, Topps competed intensely with Bowman for contracts, and by the end of that period, Topps had managed to secure most of them, purchasing remaining contracts from Bowman. In fact, in January 1956, Topps bought the Bowman company itself, and from that year until 1980 Topps had virtually no competition in the sports trading card market. Standardization efforts were also complete, and in 1957, Topps introduced the standard 2.5 by 3.5 inch cards and began replacing the hand-tinted pictures with color photographs taken by Topps photographers at spring training camps as well as during the official season.

The 1950s also saw Topps enhance its trading card lines with new product lines featuring notable football, hockey, and basketball players. After two years of experimentation, Topps entered the football card market in earnest in 1951 with a 75-card set of college players. Although its football card line would not reappear until the college All-Americans series of 1955, Topps issued football cards every year thereafter. In 1956, Topps sold its first NFL set. Topps also began to compete with the Parkhurst Company for market share in hockey card business; Topps introduced a set limited to players from the Boston Bruins, Chicago Blackhawks, Detroit Red Wings, and New York Rangers in 1954. The next Topps hockey set came out in 1957, and thereafter sets were issued each season through 1981. Finally, in 1957 Topps began to market NBA basketball cards. Since these were only mildly successful, another full set of basketball cards was not produced until 1969.

By the early 1960s Topps baseball cards were a well established part of American culture, and production was increasing annually.

Football and hockey cards were also selling, particularly after Parkhurst discontinued its hockey line following the 1963–64 season. In 1968, Topps formed a joint venture with the Canadian company O-Pee-Chee to better reach markets for hockey cards in Canada; this relationship continued until 1993.

Topps also began including premiums inside packages of trading cards to entice their young customers. From 1961 until 1971 various lines of Topps cards included collectible items such as stamps or specially embossed cards. Other premium experiments in the 1970s included Topps Story Booklets, Topps Baseball Tattoos, Topps Coins, Topps Posters, Topps Puzzles, and Wacky Packages. Moreover, the company bolstered its lines at the end of the 1974 season to include "Traded" cards for players who had changed teams. This would become standard practice for the sports card industry.

In 1975, the Fleer trading card company filed a $17.8 million federal antitrust suit against Topps and the Major League Baseball Players Association. Specifically, Fleer alleged that Topps' exclusive contracts with the players kept competitors from the baseball card market. Four years of litigation later, Judge Clarence C. Newcomer ruled against Topps and the Players Association in a district court in Philadelphia. Newcomer ordered Topps not to enforce the exclusivity clauses in its contracts and required the Players Association to review applications for licenses to market cards and to enter into at least one agreement by 1981. While the industry would change considerably as a result of the ruling, the damages awarded to Fleer amounted to only $3 plus attorney's fees.

In 1980, with company sales at $60 million, Arthur Shorin, son of founder Joseph Shorin, became chairman and CEO of the company. The younger Shorin had begun working for Topps in 1958, and had gained experience in every department, noting in a 1995 interview in *Topps Magazine,* "I came up principally through the marketing and sales route, but also did my time in manufacturing."

Arthur Shorin's first years as CEO were filled with challenges. As such competitors as Fleer and Donruss (and eventually Upper Deck) were entering the baseball card market, Topps was experiencing some problems. First, the company was focusing on a new product, chocolate bubble gum, to help grow its sales, and that product was failing to provide results; Shorin would later recall, "I don't know a lot about racing, but that was the wrong horse to bet on." Moreover, the company had become unwieldy, with a huge work force and little focus. Shorin promptly jettisoned the chocolate gum scheme and began scaling down the work force and implementing cost cutting measures.

His company was also involved in an appeal of the antitrust suit brought by Fleer. In August 1981, Newcomer's ruling that Topps and the Players Association had violated antitrust violations was overturned. However, the Third U.S. Circuit Court of Appeals in Philadelphia did not prevent the Players Association from licensing more than one company in the future, encouraging increased competition with Topps. Sy Berger noted at the time that "The Supreme Court confirmed the Court of Appeals decision by not hearing the case. . . . The one thing that the law said is that Topps does not have a monopoly, that others could enter the field and if they worked as hard as Topps, took as long as Topps, maybe they could do as well as Topps."

Basketball and hockey cards were underperforming during this time. After experimenting with its line of basketball cards, introducing an unusual 176-card set of larger cards displaying pictures of three players, the company returned the cards to their normal size and tried distributing them in a different way, tailoring various sets for different geographic regions. After these experiments failed to bring NBA card sales to an acceptable level, Topps left the basketball card market in 1982 and did not return for ten years. Topps likewise bowed out of the hockey card market during this time, while the company's Canadian partner, O-Pee-Chee, continued these efforts.

Despite such difficulties, Topps was on the rebound by 1984; indeed, baseball card collecting in the 1980s was rapidly becoming an investment market in addition to a hobby. Periodicals emerged featuring price information and describing industry trends. Computer hotlines and investment advising groups helped investors pick out the best cards for their money. In fact, throughout the decade, rookie baseball cards outperformed all other comparable investments—including corporate bonds, common stocks, treasury bills, U.S. coins, and diamonds. During this time, however, Topps underwent a dramatic change. In conjunction with the company's law firm, Forstmann, Little & Company, Topps management took the company private, paying just $98 million in a leveraged buyout. Three years later, Topps became publicly held again, selling a limited amount of stock that raised $22 million. In 1988, to reward loyal shareholders who weren't seeing increased stock prices during this transition, Topps borrowed $140 million in order to pay out a special dividend.

By the late 1980s, Topps was reporting a negative net worth, resulting from a heavy debt load and the instability of the trading card market. Indeed, analysts had began warning investors of a potential decline in the value of their baseball memorabilia. Others, however, remained more optimistic about the future of Topps and its competitors. Topps did, in fact, have a good cash flow, and baby-boomer fathers, it seemed, were getting their children interested in card collecting as an investment.

Because Topps' major competitors were concentrating their efforts on higher priced cards and their high-bidding collectors,

Topps came to virtually own the market for less expensive cards. Topps even improved the paper stock of the inexpensive cards and boosted prices from 50 cents for 16 cards to 55 cents for 15. At the peak of the baseball memorabilia market, Topps sales rose 28 percent for the fiscal year ending February 1990.

Moreover, to compete with Upper Deck, which was offering trading cards of a higher quality, Topps introduced premium Stadium Club baseball packs in 1991. The innovative cards featured "full-bleed" photographs rather than the traditional ones with cropped borders, glossier laminates, and gold foil stamping. They proved especially popular with collectors, many of whom bid as much as $12 for a pack of 15. Topps introduced Stadium Club lines of its hockey cards the following year.

The company's Bowman subsidiary was experiencing improved sales as well. Topps had brought Bowman back into the baseball card market in 1989, with disappointing results, but in 1992 Topps reduced the Bowman set and added new sets featuring retired ball players. The subsidiary's sales went up, establishing a new card brand for Topps.

By 1992, Topps was free from debt and it resumed its marketing of Topps basketball cards. In addition, the company issued an Archives set which showed NBA stars from the 1980s as they would have appeared had the company kept up the NBA line. Football card lines were also resumed and enhanced. But the company's most profitable line remained its baseball cards, consisting of four brands: Topps, Bowman, Stadium Club, and Stadium Club Dome; these brands were augmented in 1993, when the company premiered its Baseball's Finest line.

Baseball cards remained the biggest seller as the company approached the mid-1990s. However, after being deluged by all of the new cards marketed by Topps and other companies in these years, collectors staged a rebellion of sorts in 1992, and overall sales for the sports card business dropped 20 percent. Topps' profits decreased by 65 percent in the fiscal year ending February 1993, and the following year its stock value fell significantly also.

The baseball strike that began August 11, 1994 didn't help matters. Nevertheless, Topps' response to the strike was unique. The company simulated full season statistics for the backs of its cards by means of a software program that calculated what players might have done if not for the strike. Other new developments at Topps during this time included a move from its old Brooklyn headquarters to new corporate offices in lower Manhattan.

Topps also made efforts at diversifying in the face of a stagnant baseball card market. Indeed, by the mid-1990s, Topps had become quick to introduce trading cards that capitalized on fads unrelated to sports. For example, after learning that children were increasingly interested and apprehensive about the war in the Persian Gulf, Topps took only six weeks to introduce its Desert Storm line of trading cards. Other lines featured pop music stars and characters from such films as *Jurassic Park.*

The company's success was something in which its executives and visionaries took pride. In his introduction to *Topps Baseball Cards: The Complete Picture Collection, A 40 Year History,* Sy Berger, vice-president of sports and licensing at Topps, wrote: "I must confess that I am proud of what we have achieved. I feel we have given Young America a wholesome interest; we have satisfied the desires of those who are prone to collect; and for the nostalgia buff, we have made something that he can reflect on." Moreover, CEO Shorin remained optimistic about the company's future, asserting in a 1995 *Topps Magazine* article: "Anyone who doesn't think the [recent] unrest has caused real damage to the industry can sell his or her brain for shoe leather. But I think the hobby is resilient, as are the fans, and creativity still works."

Principal Subsidiaries: Topps International, Inc.; Topps Ireland Ltd.; Bowman Gum, Inc.; Goudey Gum, Inc.; Topps Comics, Inc.

Further Reading:

Ambrosius, Greg, "Leading Topps Profitably into the 21st Century," *Topps Magazine,* July 1995, pp. 14–15.

——, "One on One with Sy Berger," *Topps Magazine,* July 1995, pp. 16–18.

——, "The History of Topps," *Topps Magazine,* July 1995, pp. 8–13.

Baldo, Anthony, "Topps' Stock: The Game Is Over," *Financial World,* April 5, 1988, p. 18.

Bleiberg, Robert M., "Topp of the Market? Baseball Cards Can't Keep Going Up Forever," *Barron's,* June 27, 1988, p. 9.

Jaffe, Thomas, "Topps Pick," *Forbes,* April 30, 1990, p. 456.

Krause, David S., "Baseball Cards Bat .425," *Money,* June 1988, pp. 140–146.

Lazo, Shirley A., "Payment By Topps A Strikeout Victim," *Barron's,* December 19, 1994, p.32.

Lesly, Elizabeth, "A Burst Bubble At Topps," *Business Week,* August 23, 1993, p. 74.

McLoone, Margo, and Alice Siegel, *Sports Cards, Collecting, Trading, and Playing,* New York: Random House, 1979, 78 p.

Rubel, Chad, "Players' Strike Hurting Baseball Card Sales," *Marketing News,* January 30, 1995, p. 2.

Slocum, Frank, *Topps Baseball Cards: The Complete Picture Collection, A 40 Year History, 1951–1990,* New York: Warner Books, 1990.

Teitelbaum, Richard S., "Timeliness Is Everything," *Fortune,* April 20, 1992, pp. 120–121.

"Tempting Takeover Morsels That Could Gain 38% Plus," *Money,* September 1994, p. 62.

Topps Football Cards: The Complete Picture Collection: A History, 1956–1986. New York: Warner Books, 1986, 350 p.

—John Myers-Kearns

TORRINGTON

The Torrington Company

59 Field Street
Torrington, Connecticut 06790
U.S.A.
(203) 482-9511
Fax: (203) 496-3642

Wholly Owned Subsidiary of Ingersoll-Rand Company
Incorporated: 1898 as The Torrington Company of Maine
Employees: 11,000
Sales: $1.26 billion
SICs: 3562 Ball & Roller Bearings

A leading manufacturer of anti-friction bearings and a Fortune 500 company, The Torrington Company sold its products, which also included an array of metal parts and assemblies, to a variety of major global industries. Originally a sewing needle manufacturer, Torrington diversified and grew over the years, becoming a discernibly different company with each passing decade. During the 1930s, the company diversified into anti-friction bearings and from that point forward evolved into the formidable force it represented during the 1990s.

Yankee inventiveness, a familiar theme in American lore, manifested itself in classic fashion on two notable occasions during the 19th century, both which occurred in the state of Connecticut, where the drive for technological advancement and the spirit of innovation were firmly rooted in the hearts of its citizens. Connecticut was home to several inventive ''Nutmeggers,'' including Samuel Colt, who developed the first revolver, Eli Whitney, whose invention of the cotton gin revolutionized the cotton industry, and Elias Howe, a transplanted ''Nutmegger'' from neighboring Massachusetts who made his life's discovery in New Hartford, Connecticut, where he recorded the first of two landmark achievements that would launch the predecessor to The Torrington Company into business.

In 1846, Elias Howe designed an early version of the sewing machine. Howe's invention represented a historic advancement in technology to be sure, but there were critical problems with his new machine that made its usefulness not quite the labor-saving device it purported to be. The chief problem with Howe's machine was the ineffectiveness of the needles it employed; Howe, in essence, had created a razor without the blades. In the years following his discovery, the sewing needles that existed were imprecise pins of steel hammered out essentially the same way a blacksmith formed a horseshoe. It was a crude method that produced imperfect results, frequently leaving the purchasers of Howe's machine with broken needles they had pounded out by hand. Twenty years would pass before a suitable solution was found.

The solution arrived—at first unbeknownst to its creators—in 1864, when another transplanted ''Nutmegger,'' a former Vermont toolmaker, Orrin L. Hopson, and his associate, Herman P. Brooks, made their own pivotal discovery in Waterbury, Connecticut. Hopson and Brooks developed and patented a machine that year described as ''An Improvement in Pointing Wire for Pins,'' which perhaps was as specific a use for the machine as the two inventors had in mind. Their machine could compress a section of steel but for what purpose and to whose interest, they were unclear. The two designers of the wire-compressing machine decided to leave Waterbury to find a market for their invention. Hopson and Brooks, who reacted to their discovery with a decided entrepreneurial bent, had settled by 1866 in Wolcottville, Connecticut, by which time they had determined that the marketability of their invention was not the machine itself but the products it could manufacture: sewing machine needle blanks.

In Wolcottville, the central part of the city of Torrington, which had been for years a hub of numerous light-manufacturing activities, Hopson and Brooks convinced seven local businessmen that their machine could produce sewing machine needle blanks superior to those already in existence. A company called Excelsior Needle Company was organized in February 1866 to create a manufacturing concern inspired by Hopson's and Brooks' machine and what it could produce. Hopson and Brooks received 100 of the 800 shares composing Excelsior Needle stock, relinquished their patent rights for $5,000, and left the realization of their invention's potential in the hands of Achille F. Migeon, Excelsior Needle's president, and Charles Alvord, the company's secretary and treasurer.

Migeon and Alvord wasted no time in getting the business started, obtaining a two-story, 16-room building for $3,000 six days after they were elected to their posts. The wood framed structure became Excelsior Needle's first factory. By 1868, two years after beginning business, Excelsior Needle had produced enough sewing needles to begin selling them to sewing machine manufacturers, the largest of which was the Singer Company. Two years later, when roughly 700,000 sewing machines were being manufactured each year, fueling demand for Excelsior Needle's products, the fledgling manufacturing concern had sold enough needle blanks to warrant the relocation of its operations to larger quarters closer to rail transportation.

By the mid-1870s, Excelsior Needle was churning out 30,000 sewing needles a day, six days a week, and generating approximately $75,000 a year in sales. Soon thereafter, the company's sales volume rose even further above that level. The solid foundation Excelsior Needle had established during its first decade—by helping to create a new American industry—provided a stable springboard for growth that carried the company through the 1880s and toward its first defining decade.

During the 1890s, Excelsior Needle diversified its business line, expanded its business overseas, and established the first of many acquisitions. Perhaps the most notable change that occurred during the decade was a symbolic one—the first link to The Torrington Company. In 1890, before Torrington entered the scene, Excelsior Needle absorbed Springfield, Massachusetts-based National Needle Company, a competing needle manufacturer that had first opened its doors 18 years earlier, in 1873. The addition of National Needle's assets and its 175 employees occurred during the same year that Excelsior Needle located to a larger factory for the second time to provide for the company's burgeoning growth.

Growth was the dominant theme during the decade, engendering a more well-rounded and financially sound company. As the 1890s progressed, Excelsior Needle diversified into a number of new areas, including the manufacture of knitting machine latch needles and the manufacture of heavy hook needles used in the mass production of shoes and other leather goods. Excelsior Needle continued to diversify, forming a subsidiary named Torrington Swaging Company, to manufacture spokes for bicycle wheels. (This was in response to a new feature of the sewing machine industry that took shape during the 1890s: Sewing machine manufacturers, led by the Singer Company, had begun to manufacture bicycles in increasing numbers.) Excelsior Needle also acquired controlling interest in two sales organizations—Boston-based S.M. Supplies Company and New York City-based C.B. Barker & Company—and moved beyond U.S. borders for the first time with the establishment of American Supplies Company in England.

Near the turn of the century, the steady growth during the 1880s and the multifarious outbursts of diversification and expansion during the 1890s had combined to create a prodigious manufacturing force with annual sales amounting to $768,000 by 1898. Much had transpired during the company's first 30 years of business: It had evolved from a small entrepreneurial company that manufactured sewing machine needle blanks to a diversified manufacturing concern which, by the century's conclusion, derived only 25 percent of its sales from the production of sewing needles.

Much, however, remained to be accomplished. Migeon and Alvord, still heading the company after three decades, looked to expand further, but the two executors of Excelsior Needle determined that the scope of their operations exceeded the financial clout of their local community. In pursuit of capital then, all the assets of Excelsior Needle were transferred in 1898 to The Torrington Company of Maine, organized two days prior to the transfer for just that purpose. Excelsior Needle acted as the operating company of its parent company, The Torrington Company of Maine, until 1917, when the directors of both companies decided to form a single corporate entity, The Torrington Company of Connecticut. Federal tax laws, however, stipulated that the exchange would result in the payment of capital gains tax, something the directors of the company wished to avoid, so for the next 19 years there were two Torringtons—The Torrington Company of Maine, which acted as a holding company for the second company, and The Torrington Company of Connecticut. Excelsior Needle, meanwhile, disappeared as a distinct corporate entity, continuing on merely as the "Excelsior Plant."

During the two decades bridging the formation of The Torrington Company of Connecticut in 1917 and its dissolution in 1936 when The Torrington Company of Maine absorbed its assets, the diversified manufacturing concern grew in stature, recording notable successes and a share of failures during an era pocked by global conflict. World War I brought Torrington into a new business line when the government requested that the well-known needle manufacturing concern begin producing surgical needles, a complex product to manufacture that Torrington had little interest and no experience in making. Before the war, Europe, particularly England, had been the primary source for surgical needles for the United States, but when World War II broke out, the supply of surgical needles into the United States slowed to a trickle. Torrington compensated for the precipitous drop in surgical needle imports, but only at the government's request. Spark plugs and marine engines, shipped to Torrington's subsidiary in England, and the production of 75 millimeter shells were also included in the company's war-time contributions, but unlike many other manufacturing concerns, Torrington was able to conduct business on a fairly normal level throughout the war, emerging from the war years as strong, if not stronger, than it had entered them.

After the war, Torrington recorded its first debilitative blunder during the 1920s when it began selling electrically-powered vacuum cleaners. This debacle of the decade was offset by rousing success in producing wheel spokes for automobile wire wheels. By the 1930s, the Great Depression had created a need for Torrington to search for new business, the pursuit of which led to the most defining moment in the company's history. The epiphany that forever changed Torrington's future and the answer to the company's need for new business had roots stretching back 20 years earlier, back to 1912, when Torrington had acquired a small ball bearing business through an affiliation with an automobile ignition coil and spark plug manufacturer. Initially Torrington's ball bearing business represented a relatively small and insignificant facet of the company's business, but by the mid-1920s it had evolved into a respectably-sized manufacturing operation that produced a wide range of bearings and provided the foundation for a new, larger segment of Torrington's business in the 1930s.

The person charged with drumming up new business during the Depression was a research engineer named Edmund K. Brown. He developed a new type of bearing for the company—a needle bearing—that eventually predicated the bulk of Torrington's business. On the heels of Brown's discovery came an important acquisition in 1935, when Torrington acquired the Bantam Ball Bearing Company. Brown's needle bearing and the addition of Bantam Ball Bearing signalled the beginning of a new era for Torrington, a future in which the production of bearings would fuel the company's growth and lift Torrington into the upper echelon of U.S. manufacturers.

This new chapter in the history of Torrington began with a decided flourish during World War II when the company once again manufactured surgical needles to supply the nation's wartime needs. In contrast to World War I, however, Torrington invested considerable effort toward manufacturing its new line of products—bearings. Needle bearings were supplied to the government for a variety of purposes, especially for uses in military aircraft and in B-29 bombers in particular, giving the company's bearing business sufficient momentum to emerge during the postwar era as the driving force propelling the company's growth.

During the two decades following the conclusion of World War II, Torrington's bearing business evolved into the company's mainstay product line, eclipsing the fabrication of needles as the company's primary source of revenue. By 1965, the sale of bearings accounted for more than 60 percent of Torrington's total sales, with needles, sold primarily to the textile and shoe industries, accounting for 30 percent of the company's sales volume.

The U.S. bearing industry by this point was a $1 billion business, having tripled in size since World War II. As a leading producer of a broad line of anti-friction bearings, including needle, ball, roller, and specialty bearings, Torrington had benefited immeasurably from the prolific growth of the bearing industry, while the company's host of other products buttressed its financial performance. In addition to bearings, Torrington's eight domestic plants were devoted to the manufacture of nuts, screws, bolts, metal specialties, spokes and nipples, drill bits, surgeon needles, hooking and felting needles, swaging machines, and a special purpose sewing machine, lending a diversity to the company's business lines that insulated it from cyclical economic conditions to a large extent. Beyond U.S. borders, the Torrington empire comprised manufacturing facilities in England, Canada, Germany, Brazil, Italy, Portugal, and in Japan, giving the company a sizeable presence in key international markets. The domestic and international operations created a solid manufacturing entity that flourished during the 1960s. Sales, which stood at $33.6 million in 1950, totaled $67.5 million in 1960, then shot upward to $93.4 million in 1965. The following year, Torrington celebrated two century marks by reaching its 100th anniversary in business as well as reaching over $100 million in sales. By all accounts, Torrington was a thriving manufacturer—a company that had earned the respect of competitors—and now, as it mapped its course for its second century of business, it began to attract the attention of a handful of suitors intent on acquiring the venerable manufacturing concern.

Against the backdrop of a nationwide trend of mergers and acquisitions, the directors of Torrington realized that refusing every bid offered for the company was implausible and, perhaps, imprudent. In 1968 then, Torrington's management settled on Ingersoll-Rand, a diversified manufacturer of machinery, tools, and construction equipment. Through an exchange of stock valued at over $200 million, Torrington became an autonomous subsidiary of Ingersoll-Rand that year, embarking on its second century of business under the corporate umbrella of its parent.

As an autonomous subsidiary of Ingersoll-Rand, Torrington's second century began much as the first one had ended, with long-time Torrington officials presiding over the company's activities. New corporate headquarters were completed in 1970, marking the beginning of a decade that would see Torrington's financial performance sputter in the face of recessive economic conditions. Favorable developments came in the form of Torrington's involvement in the manufacture of steering column universal joints for the automotive industry and the continuing success of its needle bearing manufacturing business. Despite these developments, though, profits lagged throughout the decade, leading Ingersoll-Rand to exert its authority over Torrington for the first time by the decade's conclusion. Torrington's needle making business, an intrinsic and formative facet of the company's existence since its inception, was abandoned in 1980 after 114 years of contributing to the company's growth. Since the Ingersoll-Rand merger, Torrington's needle business had produced lackluster results and it was decided that both Torrington's and Ingersoll-Rand's future goals could best be accomplished without the business first launched by Migeon and Alvord.

Stripped of its needle business, Torrington entered the 1980s as primarily a bearing manufacturer, with needle bearings accounting for 49 percent of the company's sales and heavy bearings contributing another 30 percent. After several years of corporate restructuring, Torrington became a considerably larger bearing manufacturer when the company acquired Fafnir Bearing Company in 1985. Formed, like Torrington, in Connecticut, Fafnir had evolved into a leading bearing producer from its origination in 1911, becoming by the mid-1980s a precision ball bearing manufacturer serving the aerospace, machine tool, industrial, and agricultural industries with distinction. When the two bearing producers were combined in 1985, adding Fafnir's seven manufacturing facilities to Torrington's already numerous manufacturing facilities, the result was the largest bearing manufacturing company in North America and one of the largest in the world, with total sales amounting to roughly $750 million.

The addition of Fafnir provided a powerful boost to Torrington's stature as a bearing manufacturer, coming in a decade during which the company also hailed the accomplishment of significant developmental work in ceramic and sensor bearings. These achievements helped reduce the sting of the lamented divestment of its needle business. By the end of the 1980s, however, Torrington's situation had once again soured, as U.S. competitors in the $3 billion bearing business railed against unfair foreign competition. Torrington was among the pack charging that Asian and European bearing producers were selling bearings below their manufacturing cost, an illegal practice that carried into the early 1990s.

As Torrington sought to bring a favorable conclusion to the contentious legal debate addressing unfair trade practices, the company entered the mid-1990s as a stalwart industry leader. Part of Ingersoll-Rand's Bearings, Locks, and Tools business group, Torrington charted its future course beyond the mid-1990s, buoyed by its more than 125 years of successfully navigating through unseen waters. This legacy of success promised to serve the company well in the years to come, adding a rich history of experience to surmount whatever obstacles loomed in the future.

Principal Subsidiaries: Kilian Manufacturing Corporation; Torrington Holdings, Inc.; Torrington France, S.A.R.L.; Torrington, Inc. (Canada); Torrington Industria e Comercio Ltda (Brazil); Torrington Beteiligungs GmbH (Germany); Torrington GmbH (Germany); Torrington Nadellager GmbH (Germany); The Torrington Company Limited (England).

Further Reading:

''Century-Old Torrington Rolls Toward New Growth,'' *Barron's,* September 25, 1967, p. 43.

''Ingersoll-Rand Company,'' *Wall Street Transcript,* July 13, 1970, pp. 21,145.

''Ingersoll-Rand, Torrington Agree on Merger Plan,'' *Wall Street Journal,* October 11, 1968, p. 4.

Lieberthal, Edwin M., *Progress Through Precision.* Torrington, Conn.: The Torrington Company, 1992.

Loehwing, David A., ''On the Ball,'' *Barron's,* October 25, 1965, pp. 3, 14, 16, 18.

Perham, John C., ''Less Friction,'' *Barron's,* March 5, 1962, p. 3.

Sherman, Joseph V., ''Shape of Things to Come,'' *Barron's,* June 29, 1970, p. 11, 13.

''Torrington Co.'' *Automotive News,* March 7, 1994, p. 16.

''Torrington Co.'' *Magazine of Wall Street,* June 17, 1961, p. 389.

—Jeffrey L. Covell

Trader Joe's Co.

P.O. Box 3270
Pasadena, California 91031
U.S.A.
(514) 861-9481
Fax: (514) 861-7053

Public Company
Incorporated: 1967
Employees: 2,200
Sales: $600 million
SICs: 5499 Miscellaneous Food Stores

Trader Joe's operates a chain of unique grocery stores that have been described as a cross between a discount warehouse club and a gourmet deli. The company has grown steadily since its inception through innovation and sharp management techniques. In 1994 there were about 75 Trader Joe's stores operating in the western United States from San Francisco to Phoenix. The company, distinguished by its practice of carrying zero debt, was purchased in 1979 by the Albrechts, a wealthy and secretive German family, making financial information difficult to obtain.

Although Trader Joe's was not officially founded until 1967, its origins can be traced back to the Pronto Markets chain of food stores that were started in the late 1950s. Pronto Markets was initiated by the Rexall Drug Co. in 1957. The venture reflected the intent of Rexall, an operator of a chain of drug stores, to get in on the burgeoning convenience and corner foodstand market. Rexall appointed Joe Coulombe to head up the new division. Coulombe was only 26 years old at the time and had been with Rexall for only three years. Nevertheless, his managers were impressed with his performance and believed that he could handle the job. During the late 1950s and early 1960s Coulombe managed to build Pronto into a chain with a considerable presence in Orange County, California.

Despite its expansion, Pronto was experiencing growing profit pressures by the mid-1960s as a result of increased competition. Southland Corp.'s successful 7-Eleven chain, in particular, was bearing down on smaller competitors like Pronto and was even planning an aggressive expansion in Pronto's region. Rexall elected in 1966 to jettison its Pronto Markets division and escape the convenience store industry. Coulombe, still at the helm, was faced with a choice—attempt a buyout of the chain that he had built and remain as chief executive, or bail out and look for a new niche in the retail industry. Coulombe took an extended Caribbean vacation before deciding to stick with Pronto. With the financial backing of Bank of America, he purchased Pronto from Rexall and went to work.

Coulombe knew when he bought Pronto that the strategy he had used to grow the business in the past would be ineffective in the face of growing competition. 7-Eleven was targeting his customers, and his organization lacked the resources to compete with the national chain. The ever-innovative Coulombe considered two prevalent social trends as he devised a new marketing scheme. First of all, consumers were becoming increasingly educated and sophisticated, and were expecting more from their shopping experiences. Secondly, the surge in global travel, made possible by plummeting jumbo jet airfares, was exposing Americans to new foods. Coulombe decided to develop a food store at which well-educated, well-traveled, but not necessarily wealthy people could buy foods that would impress themselves and their friends. "I wanted to appeal to the well-educated and people who were traveling more," he explained in the October 2, 1989 *Forbes,* "like teachers, engineers and public administrators. Nobody was taking care of them."

Coulombe's initial concept was to reposition Pronto as an upscale food market/convenience store located near educational centers. That decision was influenced by the health of the liquor business at the time, which, for Pronto, was still very profitable. That scheme was scrapped in 1971, however, when the aerospace industry collapsed and the local Orange County economy plunged. The recession squarely hit Coulombe's targeted customers, who weren't throwing many parties. To overcome the slowdown, Coulombe drew on his own travel experiences and fashioned a sort of combination health food shop and liquor store during the early 1970s. He ordered unique food items from different parts of the world to attract customers, and he labeled the foods with sprightly, entertaining labels like "Kiwi From Paradise juice," and "Look Ma! No Refined Sugar!" Coulombe's new Trader Joe's stores experimented with all types of health foods and beverages, and generally avoided marketing mammoths like Coca-Cola and Budweiser.

Among Coulombe's most successful tactics in the early 1970s was his biting journal *Fearless Flyer* (originally called *Trader Joe's Insider Report*), which aroused environmental awareness through stinging commentary on conservation issues. Distributed to the general public, the *Flyer* brought hordes of environmentally conscious customers into Trader Joe's, which began stocking increasing amounts of vitamins, biodegradable products, and health foods. Focused on that key market, Trader Joe's boosted sales and profits steadily until 1976. In that year, California legislators deregulated the supermarket industry. The change boded poorly for Trader Joe's liquor segment. Indeed, since the Great Depression the state had effectively subsidized the sale of milk and liquor by markets. Many smaller convenience stores, in fact, had come to rely on milk and liquor sales, even to the point of advertising other items below cost just to get customers in their shops. Deregulation quashed that practice, and many mom-and-pop stores failed.

As the giant supermarkets flexed their muscles in the newly deregulated grocery industry, Trader Joe's quickly adapted to the new environment. Coulombe rejected traditional convenience store inventory and began to market Trader Joe's as an upscale, but value-oriented, seller of trendy, hard-to-find beers and wines. The strategy was a success and Trader Joe's maintained its profitability. Trader Joe's continued to selling its inexpensive, unique wines and imported cheeses and coffees as it had since the early 1970s. But Coulombe gradually began expanding the chain's inventory to include a wide array of singular nuts, pastas, fish, vegetables, and prepared snacks and meals. In 1979 Trader Joe's was purchased by the Karl and Theo Albrecht, members of the secretive, billionaire Albrecht family in Germany. The Albrechts retained Coulombe as CEO.

During the early and mid-1980s Coulombe continued to perfect Trader Joe's inventory and market position and to slowly grow the California chain. He gradually moved away from the intense environmental rhetoric in the *Fearless Flyer,* for example, and evolved with his core market. That meant positioning the Trader Joe's stores to appeal the emerging upwardly mobile, or "Yuppie," crowd which was exhibiting increasingly sophisticated shopping patterns. Unique beers and wines remained a major attraction, but Coulombe also began bringing in more perishables and unique dry food items. The *Fearless Flyer* continued to be a primary marketing tool, but it was toned down and used to provide entertaining and useful information such as health tips and new store items; "I wanted it to be a marriage of *Consumer Reports* and *Mad Magazine,*" Coulombe said in a June 5, 1995 *Business Week* article.

Importantly, Coulombe bolstered the attraction of his inventory by keeping a sharp focus on value and targeting the well-educated but less-than-affluent consumer. Wines and other alcoholic beverages were often displayed in cases and most stores had only a few rows of shelving. And while the average store size increased during the 1970s and 1980s, the average Trader Joe's store was still only about 6,000 square feet by the late 1980s—about half the size of the typical Los Angeles supermarket. Although his strategy of maintaining a continually changing inventory may have seemed like an expensive and daunting proposition to larger markets and superstores, Coulombe managed to keep prices low. Trader Joe's efficiency was partly the result of its cash policy; the company paid cash for all purchases and funded growth internally as well as through the deep-pocketed Albrecht family. Innovative, low-cost advertising was a major money saver as well.

Also minimizing expenses was the company's unusual purchasing program. The store's own branded items—fresh salsa and unique pastas, for example—were supplied by a constantly changing set of small, independent contractors. The foods they supplied were often discontinued items that Trader Joe's bought at a discount. Those contractors and other suppliers were found by Trader Joe's own buying team, which traveled throughout America and Europe in search of interesting items and bargains. The result of Coulombe's innovative inventory and pricing strategy was huge profit margins. In 1989, Trader Joe's chalked up an estimated $150 million in sales. That figure reflected gross sales of more than $800 per square foot—extremely high compared to grocery industry norms. Furthermore, because its stores were usually located on non-prime real estate, the company's fixed overhead was relatively low.

By the late 1980s the nearly 60-year-old Coulombe had built Trader Joe's into a chain of 30 outlets, most of which were in the Los Angeles and San Diego regions. Besides his efforts at Trader Joe's, moreover, Coulombe became involved with Denny's Restaurants Inc. as a board member in the early 1980s and had been instrumental in taking the company private in a $700 million buyout. "I was approaching coronary age and I wanted to retire," Coulombe recalled in the February 26, 1990, *Los Angeles Business Journal.* "But I wanted to leave the company in good hands," he added In 1988 Coulombe selected 55-year-old John V. Shields to succeed him at the helm. Following a short transition period, Coulombe stepped aside and the Albrecht family welcomed Shields as the new chief.

Shields had known Coulombe for about 40 years when he joined Trader Joe's. The two had met in 1950 as fraternity brothers at Stanford University and had kept in touch over the years; Coulombe had always been impressed by Shield's retail sense. Shield's first exposure to retailing occurred at Stanford, where he worked as a salesman at a men's clothing store. After college he accepted a job with R.H. Macy in New York and set a goal of becoming senior vice-president by the age of 40. He began by turning around the women's department, converting it from a money loser into one of the store's most profitable departments. Following similar feats, he was promoted to senior vice-president before he was 40. In 1978 he took a job at Mervyn's and helped that retail chain grow from 38 stores to 180 within nine years. He next move was to Trader Joe's.

Shield's maintained much of Trader Joe's unique product mix and marketing strategy, as evidenced by a transaction conducted shortly after he took control of the chain. In a rapid-fire deal, Trader Joe's wrote a check for $1 million worth of wine from the Napa Valley Mihaly winery. The winery had just been purchased by a group of Japanese investors who planned to make sake, or rice wine, at the winery. They didn't need the inventory of wines that were popular in the United States, so Trader Joe's moved quickly in a deal that brought it 240,000 bottles of wine at a bargain price. "We never buy anything unless we've tasted it, and we turn down more than 90 percent of the wine that is offered to us," Shields said in the *Los Angeles Business Journal* article, "but we knew we wanted the Mihaly inventory . . . if we didn't move fast, someone else might have." A similar deal about the same time brought 3,000 cases of a mid-level chardonnay to Trader Joe's; Trader Joe's was selling the bottles for $2.99 while nearby liquor stores were charging $8.50.

Deals like these kept Trader Joe's cash registers ringing into the early 1990s. Indeed, despite an economic downturn and another depression in the California defense industry, the Trader Joe's units continued to perform. Inventory was broadened to include a variety of wines, nuts, cheeses, dairy products, frozen foods, candies, bakery items, juices, and even dog food. Moreover, Trader Joe's became the largest retailer of pistachio nuts, whole bean coffee, and brie in California, and was among the largest retailers of maple syrup and wild rice, among other distinctions. Meanwhile, Shields was working to expand the enterprise. By late 1991 there were 43 Trader Joe's operating in California, including several new units in the San Francisco Bay area. Total sales for the company were topping $250 million annually, and the average size of the outlets had grown to about 7,500 square feet.

Shield's stepped up Trader Joe's expansion activity in 1992 and 1993, moving outside of California into Phoenix and growing the chain to 59 stores by late 1993. By that time, the chain was generating revenues of about $500 million annually (about 40 percent of which came from imported goods) and was eyeing expansion possibilities in Seattle and Portland. Trader Joe's inventory had swelled to include about 1,500 items in each store, including many goods from former Soviet-bloc countries like Hungary and Czechoslovakia. The company was also boosting purchases from Caribbean nations as a result of new trade agreements signed by the United States in that region. Its major advertising tool continued to be its *Fearless Flyer* and word-of-mouth, but it was also promoting through radio spots and ads in local media by the mid-1990s.

Trader Joe's grew to about 65 outlets in 1994 and grossed about $600 million, representing average annual per-store sales growth of about ten percent over the past five years. The company began establishing stores in Seattle late in 1994 and planned to open 15 to 20 outlets in Oregon and Washington within a few years. By mid-1995, in fact, Trader Joe's was operating 72 outlets and was generating an estimated $1,000 per square foot. Evidencing the rising popularity of Trader Joe's was the circulation of the *Fearless Flyer,* which had grown to 800,000 before rising delivery costs forced the company to begin distributing it in the stores rather than through the mails. By 1996, moreover, Shields was expecting to expand in the Northeast, with plans to build at least 50 new Trader Joe's stores in that region within five years.

Further Reading:

Armstrong, Larry, ''Trader Joe's Atlantic Overtures,'' *Business Week,* June 5, 1995, pp. 86–87.

Frook, John Evan, ''A Well-Developed Sense of Retailing Trade Winds,'' *Los Angeles Business Journal,* February 26, 1990, p. 22.

Goodman, Stephanie, ''Trader Joe's Thrives on Inconsistency,'' *Adweek's Marketing Week,* April 24, 1989, p. 32.

Hicks, Larry, ''Yuppie Foods at Bargain Prices,'' *Sacramento Bee,* November 20, 1991, p. D1.

Hill, Jim, ''Trader Joe's On Way to Portland Area,'' *Oregonian,* January 25, 1995, p. B16.

Law, Steve, ''Trader Joe's Sprouts in Portland'' California Grocer Takes Aim at Nature's Niche,'' *Business Journal-Portland,* July 26, 1993, p. 1.

Lazzareschi, Carla, ''BeGATTing An End To Food Fight Era,'' *Los Angeles Times,* December 10, 1993, p. D1.

Paris, Ellen, ''Brie, But Not Budweiser,'' *Forbes,* October 2, 1989, p. 235.

Retchin, Mark, ''Back at the Helm,'' *Orange County Business Journal,* August 6, 1990, p. 9.

Sanchez, Jesus, ''Trader Joe's Looks East: 68-Store Grocery Firm Plans to Conquer New Markets,'' *Los Angeles Times,* February 27, 1995, p. D1.

Sather, Jean, ''Trader Joe's Will Open String of Gourmet-Food Emporiums,'' *Puget Sound Business Journal,* March 10, 1995, p. 1.

Shiver, Jube, Jr., ''Pacific Enterprises Appoints Trader Joe's Founder to Oversee its Ailing Retail Chains,'' *Los Angeles Times,* March 12, 1992, p. D1.

—Dave Mote

Transamerica Corporation

600 Montgomery Street
San Francisco, California 94111
U.S.A.
(415) 983-4000
Fax: (415) 983-4234

Public Company
Incorporated: 1928
Employees: 10,800
Total Assets: $40.39 billion
Stock Exchanges: New York Pacific London Amsterdam Basel Frankfurt Geneva Paris Tokyo Zurich
SICs: 6311 Life Insurance; 7359 Equipment Rental & Leasing, Nec; 6141 Personal Credit Institutions

Transamerica Corporation is involved, largely through semi-independent subsidiaries, in life insurance, financial services, and real estate services. Through its Transamerica Life Insurance Companies subsidiary, it is the eighth-largest life insurer in North America, and its life insurance operations generated 48 percent of Transamerica's 1994 earnings. Financial services operations generated 40 percent of 1994 earnings, and centered around consumer and commercial lending, as well as the leasing and managing of transportation equipment. Transamerica Financial Services ranks fourth in the United States in consumer lending; Transamerica Commercial Finance is a leading commercial lender in the United States and the largest in Canada; Transamerica Leasing has the second-largest fleet of container equipment for rail, steamship, and motor carriers in the world. Real estate services comprise Transamerica's smallest general area of operation, with 12 percent of 1994 earnings. Transamerica Real Estate Tax Service is one of the leading real estate tax operations in the United States, while Transamerica Realty Services oversees a real estate and mortgage portfolio that includes the holdings of both Transamerica's parent company and its subsidiaries.

When Peter Amadeo Giannini, the son of Italian immigrants, began dreaming of his career in turn-of-the-century San Francisco, he had not set his heart on building a banking empire. Instead, at the age of 12 he was sneaking out of his home at night to work in his stepfather's produce business and, by the age of 19, was a full partner. His early success at this business allowed him to retire at the age of 31 with a modest, but comfortable, fortune. His foray into the banking world did not begin until several years later when he received a legacy from his father-in-law, Joseph Cuneo, who had made Giannini a director of his Columbus Savings and Loan Society, a building and loan association in San Francisco. Giannini's career in banking lasted for over forty years, and during this time he established the Transamerica Corporation.

After Giannini was appointed a director of Columbus Savings and Loan he became immersed in a number of disagreements with other directors of the bank over policy issues. He consequently left the Savings and Loan Society and established his own banking business which was located directly across the street from Columbus Savings and Loan. Giannini organized the Bank of Italy with $150,000 in capital contributed by his stepfather and ten friends. He envisioned the bank as an institution for the "little fellow," and the bank subsequently made loans to merchants, farmers, and laborers who were mostly of Italian descent.

Ironically, the San Francisco fire and earthquake of 1906 established Giannini's reputation in the banking world. As he stood amid the rubble of his bank on the morning of the earthquake, he was able to salvage over $2 million in gold and securities. In order to avoid the looters who were running through the city, he hid his bank's resources under piles of vegetables in a horse-drawn cart borrowed from his former produce business. Giannini immediately alerted his depositors that their savings were safe and began making loans to businessmen who had lost their savings and their companies.

Giannini's success as a banker is also clearly evidenced by his anticipation of the 1907 stock market crash, and his accumulation of gold before the crash. When the crash came Giannini was able to pay his depositors in cash while other banks were using certificates for cash. From this experience, Giannini realized that only larger banks would ensure security, and therefore he began purchasing small banks and converting them into branches of the Bank of Italy. With these acquisitions Giannini established the first branch banking policy in California.

The Bank of Italy grew so rapidly that by 1919 Giannini was able to form Bancitaly Corporation to organize the expansion. In 1928 Bancitaly Corporation was followed by Transamerica Corporation, which was formed as a holding company for all Giannini's banking, insurance, and industrial concerns.

Giannini's expansion into other areas of the financial services had established him as a leader in the financial services field. By 1929 he had moved into the New York banking scene and purchased the solidly established Bank of America. The following year after this important acquisition, all of Giannini's banks were consolidated into Bank of America National Trust and Savings Association. Transamerica played the role of parent company throughout this period.

In 1931, just a year after the consolidation of his banks under Bank America, Giannini retired and left the top post to Elisha Walker, a Wall Street investment banker. Walker did his best to break up this "empire" created by Giannini. Not surprisingly, Giannini forced Walker out in what was called a "furious proxy battle" at the 1932 annual meeting.

During the previous few decades Giannini's operations had been closely observed by both Wall Street and regulatory branches of the U.S. government; Giannini's success had found critics within both these institutions. Throughout the 1930s Transamerica experienced problems with regulatory procedures and changes enacted by the government. In 1937 Transamerica sold 58 percent of its stock in Bank America, although it still controlled the board of directors. At the time of his death in 1949, Giannini was embroiled in a fight with the Federal Reserve Board as to whether or not Transamerica had violated the Clayton Anti-Trust Act in creating a ''credit monopoly'' by placing directors on the boards of banks in the huge chain owned by Bank of America. It was the Reserve Board's belief that Transamerica still controlled the bank even after the 1937 split.

The split between Bank of America and Transamerica was present throughout World War II until 1956 when Congress passed the Bank Holding Company Act, which did not allow bank holding companies the right to involve themselves in industrial activities. By this time, Transamerica was a holding company for several industrial concerns as well as the successful Occidental Life Insurance Company. As a result of the passage of this Act, Transamerica sold its banks, forming Western Bancorporation, and was left with Occidental Life and other smaller concerns under its direction.

While the litigation continued over Bank of America, Transamerica was resourcefully building up its life insurance business through Occidental Life. By the early 1960s Occidental Life had assets of $751 million. The success of Occidental Life was due largely to its ability to make the most of a sale. In the post war 1930s Occidental was selling term life insurance to California families. Since term life insurance carried lower premiums than full life insurance, other insurance companies dismissed this type of sale as a trivial pursuit, but Occidental banked on high-volume sales that would eventually be converted into full life insurance as the policyholder's income increased, thus making up for the initially low profit. This method worked. Occidental's insurance sales increased from $1 billion in 1945 to $6 billion in 1955 to $16 billion in 1965.

Due to the success of Occidental Life it is not surprising that in 1959 President Horace W. Brower was interested in expanding the company's financial services and moving toward ''modern merchandising techniques.'' When Brower rose to the chairman's seat, he looked outside the company to find a ''hard-nose financial man'' who could successfully run the company as president. The man Transamerica found was John R. Beckett, a 42-year old investment banker and vice-president of Blyth and Company's San Francisco office. Beckett was considered to be extremely conversant with the world of finance and negotiations, an important quality since Brower was ready to begin a major acquisition program for Transamerica Corporation.

The plan at Transamerica during this time was to create a financial institution where people could do all their business, something of a ''department store of finances.'' It was Beckett's belief that people wanted ''convenience and service,'' and he was willing to provide such banking. Beckett's concern centered on the fact the financial service industry changed quickly, and he was determined to stay ahead of his competitors.

Occidental Life was used as a base for changing Transamerica into a holding company not only for insurance but also for other companies within the service field. Beckett was interested in companies that would ''work in harmony with one another in the market place.'' The first major acquisition after Beckett became president was Pacific Finance Corporation in 1961, and additional acquisitions focused on land, title insurance, and mortgage banking companies. New credit card, leasing, and life insurance operations were also started during the 1960s. By 1969 Transamerica was considered a large service conglomerate. To his credit, Beckett changed the dependency on Occidental from 75 percent of the company's profits to just over 50 percent by 1966.

Beckett saw the transformation of Transamerica not only as a chance for consumers to do business with a ''friendly'' full-service bank, but also as a way to impress upon customers the importance of using these services over and over again. Beckett compared Transamerica to General Electric: ''We hope it will be like the family that buys a refrigerator from G.E. If they like the product and the price, and they get good service, they'll go back to G.E. when they need a new stove. . . . That's exactly what we're trying to do in financial services.''

Beckett's attempts to enlarge Transamerica resulted in the company being labeled a conglomerate, but Beckett strongly disagreed with this image. Beckett saw managers of conglomerates as ''opportunists, people who make acquisitions strictly on an ad hoc basis. They move too quickly, pay too much, use funny accounting, and don't look for long-range values. Eventually their bubbles will burst.'' In contrast, Beckett believed that he was acquiring companies slowly and in concert with a plan to provide a full-line financial services company.

According to Beckett's plan, financial services also included leisure time services for consumers such as movies and travel. In 1967 Transamerica acquired United Artists and in 1968 Trans International Airlines and Budget Rent-a-Car. United Artists would prove to be the acquisition of the 1960s that resulted in financial difficulties for Transamerica.

United Artists, created in 1919 by such movie stars and directors as Douglas Fairbanks, Sr., Mary Pickford, Charlie Chaplin, and D. W. Griffith, looked like a profitable acquisition in 1968, but in 1970, two years after Beckett became chairman, Transamerica's earnings dropped by half because of an $18 million loss due to several unsuccessful films. Beckett, although caught by surprise by the large loss at United Artists, eventually saw the film company turn into a very profitable business by the late 1970s with such successful films as *Rocky, Coming Home,* and *One Flew over the Cuckoo's Nest.*

Along with these successes, however, there was also unrest within United Artists; the management who had initially sold the film company to Transamerica was now interested in buying it back. Beckett fought back, telling *Fortune* magazine that if ''the people at United Artists don't like it, they can quit and go off on their own.'' That is exactly what they did.

Beckett claimed that he would never sell United Artists, but in 1981 it was sold for $380 million under the direction of president James R. Harvey, who took over in January 1981 when Beckett became chairman. Harvey was an executive vice-president under Beckett and had been with the company since 1965. Harvey's goal for Transamerica was to concentrate primarily on financial services and insurance. Over the next several years, Harvey would pursue this goal by making an enormous number of acquisitions ($1.7 billion worth) while at the same time divesting Transamerica of a host of operations that fell outside the newly defined operational area ($1.5 billion worth).

Trans International Airlines and Budget Rent-a-Car were both sold in 1986, and Transamerica Title was sold in 1990. By 1991 Harvey was chairman of Transamerica, and Frank C. Herringer had taken over as president and CEO. Herringer continued Harvey's program to remake Transamerica with the 1993 divestiture of the firm's property and casualty insurance operations. Initially the company attempted to find a private buyer for the unit, which was in a segment of the insurance industry that had been performing poorly, but there were no takers. So the firm spun off the operation early in 1993 through an initial public offering. Transamerica retained a 26 percent stake in the new company, known as TIG Holdings Inc., which it then sold through a second public offering later in the year, marking its complete exit from the business. Transamerica used the money generated by the offering—about $1 billion—to pay down its debt and invest in its remaining operations.

The company suffered a setback in the financial services area in 1994 when it decided to sell its mutual funds business, Transamerica Fund Management Company. The operation was not as effective as some other mutual funds companies in that it was unable to develop methods to sell the funds other than through Transamerica's own insurance agents. The buyer of Transamerica's mutual funds business, John Hancock Mutual Life Insurance Co., in fact sold two-thirds of its funds through channels other than its own agents. The unit sold for $100 million.

More than offsetting this development, however, was Transamerica's 1995 purchase of a $1 billion portfolio of home equity loans from the ITT Corporation. Transamerica's leasing operations also received a major boost in 1994 with the acquisition of a British counterpart, Tiphook PLC, for more than $1 billion in cash. The acquisition strengthened Transamerica's position in the international transportation equipment leasing market, as well as making it number two in the industry worldwide. Overall, the company's success in its latest transformation was evident in the record gross revenues of $5.35 billion and record net income of $427.2 million in 1994.

Principal Subsidiaries: Transamerica Finance Group, Inc.; Transamerica Financial Services; Transamerica Commercial Finance Corporation; Transamerica Leasing Inc.; Transamerica Real Estate Tax Service; Transamerica Realty Services; Transamerica HomeFirst, Inc.; Transamerica Life Companies; First Transamerica Life Insurance Company; Transamerica Investment Services, Inc.

Further Reading:

Carlsen, Clifford, "Transamerica Set to Shed Unprofitable Unit," *Insurance,* January 22, 1993, p. 4A.

Dolan, Carrie, "Transamerica Unit Fetches about $1 Billion," *Wall Street Journal,* April 20, 1993, p. A3.

Gilpin, Kenneth N., "ITT Reported in $1 Billion Loan Sale to Transamerica," *New York Times,* April 1, 1995, pp. 35, 37.

Koster, George H., *The Transamerica Story: 50 Years of Service and Looking Forward,* San Francisco: Transamerica Corporation, 1978, 96 p.

McGough, Robert, "John Hancock Is Planning to Acquire Transamerica Corp.'s Mutual Funds," *Wall Street Journal,* October 18, 1994, p. C18.

—updated by David E. Salamie

Tultex Corporation

P.O. Box 5191
Martinsville, Virginia 24115
U.S.A.
(703) 632-2961
Fax: (703) 632-8000

Public Company
Incorporated: 1937 as Sale Knitting Company
Employees: 7,500
Sales: $503.9 million
Stock Exchanges: New York
SICs: 2253 Knit Outerwear Mills; 2329 Men's/Boys' Clothing, Not Elsewhere Classified; 2339 Women's/ Misses' Outerwear, Not Elsewhere Classified

The Tultex Corporation is a leading marketer of fleeced sportswear and licensed sports apparel. The company is a vertically-integrated manufacturer of sweatshirts, sweatpants, and other athletic wear. Throughout most of its history, Tultex concentrated on producing fleeced goods in factories in Virginia and North Carolina. In the 1990s, however, the company branched out to other, fast-growing sportswear lines, and began to make and sell products in locations outside the United States.

Tultex was originally founded as an outgrowth of another textile manufacturing company, the Pannill Knitting Company, which was founded in 1926. This firm was owned and run by William L. Pannill, who had gotten his start in a Mayodan, North Carolina, cotton-spinning mill. At that time, textile mills in the northeast dominated the market for knit underwear. Pannill decided that mills in the south should move in on this lucrative niche, and he got himself a low-level job as a janitor in a plant in Utica, New York, in order to observe how knit underwear was manufactured. After watching and learning all that he could, Pannill returned to the south to inaugurate his new business.

Pannill chose to locate his business in rural Martinsville, Virginia, a town situated in the foothills of the Blue Ridge mountains, near the North Carolina border. The inhabitants of this area were diligent, tradition-minded workers, willing to toil for low wages without demanding union benefits. Pannill hoped to hire the wives of men who worked in the area's other industry, furniture-making, to work in his mill. In this way, he hoped to make his products competitive by keeping his costs low.

In the early 1930s textile manufacturers in New England introduced fleece-lined sweatshirts, knit products in which one side of the nap had been roughed up to produce a thick insulation. Soon after these products came to the attention of Pannill, he began to make them at one of his company's buildings in Martinsville.

In August 1937 Pannill put his son-in-law, E.A. Sale, who had married his daughter Lucy, in charge of this new operation. A new company was organized and given the name Sale Knitting Company. Sale was given a share in the company, and stock was sold to other citizens of the town.

By the end of 1937 the Sale company had outgrown its cramped quarters, and the fleece machines were moved into a new 30,000-square-foot space specially built for this purpose. This move marked the separation of Sale's operations from those of its parent company. The new enterprise, which had 50 employees, manufactured fleece-lined union suits as well as sweatshirts. The company's products came in four colors: white, ecru, silver grey, and gunmetal.

Three years later, Sale added on to its physical plant once again. In addition, Sale purchased an old silk factory that it used for knitting machines. Also in 1941, Sale commissioned the Henry J. Tully Corporation, based in New York, as the exclusive sales agent for its fleece products.

While the United States was engaged in World War II, Sale fulfilled orders for the government, producing sweatshirts in olive drab. In the wake of the war, the company continued to expand the number of colors in which its products were available. Sale transferred its dying activities from their small facility in Martinsville to a larger facility in town. This allowed Sale to introduce fleece products in red, gold, and royal blue by 1949. Within three years, this advance had transformed the sweatshirt from a purely functional product to a fashionable item as well.

In 1953 Sale's founding president retired. He turned the reins of the company over to another Pannill son-in-law, William F. Franck. In addition, Sale's selling agent, the Henry J. Tully Corporation, bought a majority interest in the firm. Four years after this transfer of ownership, Sale Knitting moved to a new building, once a tobacco warehouse, in Martinsville. This move enabled Sale to consolidate many of the processes that had previously taken place in different locations, such as knitting and dyeing.

Demand for Sale's products continued to be strong throughout the 1960s, and the company expanded its production facilities several times. In 1963 Sale constructed a $3.5 million cutting and sewing plant. Three years later, the company bought a building in South Boston, a nearby Virginia town, that had once been owned by a tobacco company. Sale installed a sewing operation at this site, which employed 250 people. In 1969 Sale built a modern dyeing facility.

Sale underwent a corporate transformation and expansion of its activities in the 1970s. In 1971 the company added a packing and distribution center, based around a conveyor belt system, to its site in Martinsville. Also in that year, Sale merged with the Henry J. Tully Corporation, its sales agent and part-owner, and changed its name to the Tully Corporation of Virginia.

As part of this transaction, Tully came into possession of two additional companies, the Roanoke Fashions Group and Tulstar Factors, Inc. The Roanoke Fashions Group ran four mills, located in Roanoke, Lakeside, Chilhowie, and Bastian. With the acquisition of these properties, Tully greatly increased its knitting, cutting, sewing, and dyeing abilities.

In 1973 Tully entered a new field when it purchased yarn-producing mills to augment its fleece production facilities. In this way, the company hoped to become a fully integrated manufacturer, better able to control the cost of its primary raw material. The move into yarn gave Tully the ability to control every step of production, from spinning yarn to packaging the final product. Tully first entered the yarn business in May 1973, when it bought two factories owned by Roxboro Cotton Mills, which made up the Natural Yarn Division of Indian Head, Inc. This purchase enabled Tully to meet its need for 100 percent cotton yarn.

In addition, Tully bought Kings Mills, Inc., which ran 13,500 spindles in Kings Mountain, North Carolina. In 1974 Tully purchased Sawyer Industries, Inc., a modern open-ended spinning plant located in Rockingham, North Carolina. Its operations, which enabled Tully to enter the synthetic and blended yarn markets, were consolidated into the rest of Tully's activities over the course of the next three years.

In the summer of 1976 Tully moved its yarn headquarters to Gastonia, North Carolina. A short time later, Tully changed its name to the Tultex Corporation, and the Tultex Yarn Group was created. Tultex made another yarn acquisition in that year when it bought four-fifths of Sunburst Yarns, Inc., a maker of solution-dyed synthetic yarns.

In the late 1970s Tultex found demand for its sweatshirts and sweatpants increasing on the strength of the growing popularity of jogging and other fitness exercises. The company worked to expand the fitness-wear concept into the fashion field as well, and took a number of steps to increase its production facilities.

In 1978 Tultex expanded its manufacturing capacity by buying a sewing operation located in Reidsville, North Carolina, from Camor Industries. Also at that time, Tultex began to plan a new corporate headquarters building to be located in Martinsville, on the former site of a hospital. This move prompted a range of improvements to be made to the town's center.

In September 1980 Tultex bought the Peerless Spinning Corporation, which ran a fine-combed yarn plant in Lowell, North Carolina, for nearly $2 million. One month later, Tultex announced that it would start trading its stocks on the American Stock Exchange, under the symbol "TTX."

Tultex initiated several other business moves in 1980 as well, including a sewing operation located in the Vesta-Meadows of Dan area. In March 1980 Tultex made another major acquisition when it bought the Athletic Textile Company, Inc. This property was subsequently merged into Reidsville Fashions, Inc., and the combined operations were given Athletic's name. At the end of that year, Tultex's sales had reached $181.7 million, and the company reported earnings of $7.5 million for 1980.

A year later, Tultex consolidated its Athletic Textiles unit into the rest of its operations. Tultex also sold its Sunburst Yarns subsidiary to the Amoco Fabrics company in 1981. The company reported sales of $210 million at the end of 1981, with earnings of $10 million.

In 1982 Tultex expanded its production capacity for fleece apparel further when it purchased the Washington Mills Company for $19 million. With this acquisition, Tultex took over apparel and yarn plants in Mayodan, North Carolina. Tultex installed Swiss spinning machines equipped with rotors that turned 80,000 times a minute, and robot arms to fill spindles. The company was thus able to increase the mill's output by 60 percent while cutting the work force from 250 to 100.

In addition, the Washington Mills purchase gave Tultex plants in Asbury, Dobson, Marion, and Spindale, North Carolina. Earlier in 1982, the Spindale plant had started a centralized cutting operation after its conversion to a dyeing and finishing operation in the mid-1970s. At the end of 1982, Tultex reported sales of $231 million, and profits of $12.7 million.

In 1983 Tultex took steps to enhance the fashion end of its line. The company signed a licensing agreement with Nautilus to manufacture a line of Nautilus sportswear as part of an effort to differentiate its sweatshirts from those produced by factories overseas, where labor costs were lower. Although many other American apparel makers found their market share severely eroded by foreign imports, Tultex continued to maintain a strong presence in the fleece-wear field, in part because sweatshirts and sweatpants required little labor to make. Another factor hindering overseas production was the weight of the products. The sweatshirts were so heavy that shipping them across the ocean became prohibitively expensive.

In 1984 Tultex reorganized its corporate structure once again. Up until that time, the company had continued to operate Sale Knitting, Washington Mills, and Roanoke Fashions under their original names, as separate and independent entities. In 1984, however, all company operations took on the Tultex name, unifying operations that stretched across Virginia and North Carolina and employed more than 8,000 people.

Tultex also moved to consolidate its operations, focusing exclusively on fleeced products. The company eliminated other product lines that were not returning profits. It also sold several money-losing operations, including two North Carolina sewing plants. In addition, Tultex tried to cut costs by decreasing the number of managers it employed. In May 1985 Tultex moved over to the New York Stock Exchange as the company reported $9.7 million in income for the previous year.

In 1986 the company began to automate its administrative, financial, operations, sales, and marketing functions, using computers to coordinate its different areas. Tultex also discontinued a $26-million line of non-fleece knit goods so it could concentrate on its more popular fleece-lined sweat items. The following year, Tultex launched a campaign to fully modernize its manufacturing plants, installing jet dyeing technology that allowed for greater color control.

These upgrades enabled Tultex to survive a shake-out in the fleecewear industry later in the decade. Still, two other major

American underwear producers entered the fleecewear market, and Tultex anticipated further competition from abroad. To meet these challenges, the company strengthened its balance sheet and planned further modernization.

A key facet of this program was unveiled in 1989, when Tultex completed a new distribution center with three mechanized storage and retrieval systems, cranes, racks, and conveyors, all controlled by computers. Despite the availability of this high-tech facility, Tultex was forced to postpone use of it until April 1991 because of glitches in the facility's operating software.

As Tultex moved into the 1990s, the company underwent a series of management renewals. A new "vision" for the future was adopted that sought to integrate the needs of all of the company's constituent parts, including shareholders, employees, customers, and communities. In addition, the company inaugurated "Team Tultex," in which employees got together in task forces to work on problems faced by Tultex.

At the end of 1991, Tultex made further headway in its effort to increase marketing tie-ins when it signed an agreement with Levi-Strauss to make fleece goods under its Brittania label. Later, Tultex began to market clothes under the Levi label as well. Tultex moved even further in this direction in 1992. At that time, the company decided to broaden its product line, adding licensed sports apparel to its fleece items. To do this, Tultex purchased Logo 7, Inc., based in Indianapolis, for $58 million. Logo 7 made products emblazoned with professional and college sports logos. Tultex also enhanced its own ability to screen print clothing by opening a new plant in Martinsville. In June 1992 Tultex purchased Universal Industries, Inc., located in Mattapoisett, Massachusetts. This company, for which Tultex paid $11.1 million, made hats and caps decorated with the names of professional sports teams.

Tultex hopes to use these acquisitions to diversify its product line, which was vulnerable to competition from lower-cost products, and step up its emphasis on marketing. While fleece products had helped Tultex to thrive in the past, the company felt that it needed to lessen its dependence on fleecewear. Accordingly, the portion of its sales contributed by fleecewear fell from 95 percent in 1991 to 65 percent in 1992, as sales of hats and t-shirts expanded rapidly.

Tultex launched a new advertising campaign in 1992, dubbed "Tulavision," to promote its new line of products. This program used television commercials, aired on various cable channels, to push the company's products. The quarterback of the Dallas Cowboys was signed to be a company spokesman and promote the Logo Athletic line.

To enhance sales overseas, Tultex signed an agreement with the Nissan Trading Company, Ltd., in which Nissan earned the right to distribute Tultex Maximum Sweats and Discus Athletic products in Japan. Tultex hoped that such agreements would enable it to sell more goods in Europe, Canada, and Japan in the coming years. In addition, the company announced a willingness to manufacture products in areas outside its Virginia and North Carolina home base, prioritizing profits over geographical loyalties.

As Tultex moved into the mid-1990s, the company continued its efforts to become a major marketer of licensed sportswear. In preparation for a shake-out in its industry, Tultex attempted to cut costs and streamline operations. After sales dropped and unsold inventory accumulated in the second half of 1993, Tultex announced that it would implement a reduced work schedule in an effort to avoid further accumulation of unsold goods.

Such steps allowed Tultex to reduce inventories by $27 million the following year. Nevertheless, the company's results suffered in 1994 as a baseball strike and a hockey lockout cut into demand for its sports-related items. Despite these difficulties, however, logo goods still accounted for the fastest-growing segment of Tultex's sales. As Tultex moves into the late 1990s, it looks to these new product lines, as well as its traditional strength in fleecewear, to allow it to thrive in the coming years.

Principal Subsidiaries: AKOM, Ltd. (Cayman Islands); Tulstar Factors, Inc.; Dominion Stores, Inc.; Tultex International, Inc.; Logo 7, Inc.; Universal Industries, Inc.; Tultex Canada, Inc.

Further Reading:

Baldwin, William, "Golden Fleece," *Forbes,* August 1, 1983.
"Tultex Corp.," *Barron's,* February 8, 1988.

—Elizabeth Rourke

UNITED MERCHANTS

United Merchants & Manufacturers, Inc.

1650 Palisade Ave.
Teaneck, New Jersey 07666
U.S.A.
(201) 837-1700
Fax: (201) 837-9015

Public Company
Incorporated: 1922 as Cohn-Hall-Marx Co.
Employees: 1,500
Sales: $98.3 million
Stock Exchanges: New York Pacific
SICs: 3961 Costume Jewelry and Costume Novelties, Except Precious Metal; 5621 Women's Clothing Stores; 5632 Women's Accessory and Specialty Stores

At one time United Merchants & Manufacturers, Inc. (UM&M) was one of the biggest companies in the garment industry, with annual sales of textiles and apparel exceeding $1 billion. By 1995, however, the firm that a 1989 *Forbes* article called "The Incredible Shrinking Company" had been in bankruptcy proceedings twice since 1977, having lost money in every year since 1985. Although it sold off unprofitable divisions to stay afloat, UM&M continued to remain in the red through the mid-1990s; independent auditors then considered the company's survival doubtful.

United Merchants & Manufacturers began as Cohn-Hall-Marx in 1912, a New York City textile converter. As a converter, it bought unfinished fabrics (known as "gray goods") from textile mills and sent them to finishing plants to dye or print the fabrics according to specifications. Then it sold these finished goods to apparel manufacturers or retail stores. Because a converter requires no manufacturing facilities, it can make a big return on small capital if it comes up with a popular design or color combination. Between 1916 and 1923 Cohn-Hall-Marx reported annual profits ranging from $290,967 to $844,275.

Investment bankers at the Boston office of Kidder, Peabody & Co. approached the owner of Cohn-Hall-Marx and proposed a merger of their converting business with manufacturing plants. Advantages of such a consolidation included greater efficiency and flexibility, better cost control, and the ability to deliver new styles more quickly. Accordingly, with a $20-million investment from Kidder, Peabody, United Merchants & Manufacturers was incorporated in 1928 to acquire interests in New York City textile-selling houses or converters and to purchase plants bleaching dye and prints and mills specializing in products being sold by the selling houses.

Cohn-Hall-Marx's president, Lawrence Marx, ran day-to-day operations at UM&M until 1938, with the rank of vice-president. Jacob W. Schwab, a cousin of Marx and the company's original treasurer, was president of UM&M from 1939 to 1959. His son, Martin J. Schwab, became treasurer in 1955 and attained the presidency in 1968.

While the core business remained Cohn-Hall-Marx, UM&M quickly purchased three textile mills in South Carolina and plants in Jewett City, Connecticut, and New Bedford and Fall River, Massachusetts. Its first headquarters were in Boston but were moved to New York in 1931. Company assets were given as $24.3 million in 1930. During the first seven months of 1931, UM&M made a profit of $1.2 million, but in the fiscal year ending July 31, 1932—a severe Depression year—the company suffered a loss of over $2.2 million. It rebounded the following year, earning more than $1.4 million.

By 1935 UM&M had net sales of nearly $35 million and had acquired a silk- and rayon-weaving plant in Louiseville, Quebec. The company expanded into the factoring field that year, through the creation of United Factors Corp., a subsidiary of Cohn-Hall-Marx. As factors, United handled the accounts receivable of a roster of clients, guaranteeing they would be paid when due. Since many of UM&M's customers were poorly financed apparel manufacturers, factoring enabled the company to exploit the experience of its salesmen in rating the creditworthiness of their customers. The first dividend on UM&M's common stock was paid in 1936, when the company had about 2,400 stockholders.

By 1940 UM&M and its associated companies owned and operated, through subsidiaries, 12 plants, including a cotton mill and finishing plant constructed in Buenos Aires, Argentina, in 1936. This made the company one of the first U.S. textile firms to expand outside North America. In addition to units manufacturing and converting textiles and related fabric products, a subsidiary was producing chemicals for use in the textile industry. The company was listed on the New York Stock Exchange by 1940. Sales were flat in the late 1930s, however. UM&M lost money in fiscal 1938 and paid no dividend on common stock in 1938 and 1939.

Like the country as a whole, UM&M was not able to put the Depression behind it until World War II. Net sales, stagnant until fiscal 1941, reached $66.9 million in 1942, $98.2 million in 1943, and $125.6 million in 1944. Net sales reached $211.5 million in 1948, while net income rose from $3.8 million in 1942 to $22 million in 1948. In 1945 UM&M acquired Union-Buffalo Mills Co., a manufacturer of cotton cloth with three plants near Union, South Carolina. By mid-1949 UM&M held 34 subsidiaries in the United States, Canada, Argentina, Uruguay, and Venezuela, not including subsidiaries of these subsidiaries. Together, they operated 13 weaving plants, seven finishing plants, and five miscellaneous plants and warehouses.

Jacob Schwab was one of the highest-paid executives in the United States, earning $440,542 in 1946.

UM&M became a major retailer with the acquisition and growth of Robert Hall Clothes, Inc. and Case Clothes, Inc. These discount clothing chains stemmed from a single store opened in Waterbury, Connecticut, in 1940. Merged in 1948 as Robert Hall, the chain had 75 stores and was operating coast-to-coast by mid-1949. Its annual sales were estimated at between $50 million and $75 million. Locating at first in lofts and hanging clothes on pipe racks, Robert Hall hewed to a cash-and-carry, no-frills strategy that enabled it to hold its average mark-up to about 21 percent, compared to 40 percent or more for the average full-service clothing store. In 1946 Robert Hall started its own men's topcoat and suit factories, but the women's lines were purchased on the open market. The 200th store opened in 1955.

The company's growth continued to be robust in the 1950s. Net sales of $215 million in fiscal 1950 increased to $500.1 million in 1960. By then UM&M had 21 weaving plants—including two in Rio de Janeiro, Brazil—and ten finishing plants. It was now merchandising and marketing woolen and worsted fabrics as well as manufacturing and selling cotton, silk, and rayon textile fabrics under trademarks that included "Cohama," "Ameritext," "Juilliard," and "Comark." Between 1959 and 1960 UM&M acquired an English textile converter and—jointly with Swiss interests—a Scottish silk-dyeing company. Robert Hall had grown into a 327-store chain. Net profits, however, rose only from $10.8 million to $14.4 million between 1950 and 1960 and dipped below $10 million during 1952–54.

In 1964 UM&M was among the five largest domestic producers of fiberglass industrial fabrics to be charged by the U.S. Justice Department with conspiring with distributors and each another to fix prices and rig bids. After the companies pleaded no contest to criminal charges in 1965, the federal government sought double damages in civil suits. In July 1966 UM&M agreed to pay $250,000 to settle the case.

In 1966 *Financial World* reported that UM&M had "finally broken out of its earnings rut," increasing profits in fiscal 1965 to $3.13 a share, compared to the previous high of $2.44 a share in 1956. This increase was attributed to modernized production facilities and tightened internal controls as well as heavy demand, both military—due to the Vietnam War—and civilian. As a result the company's stock price had climbed to $36.50 after spending most of the previous decade in the teens.

Textile production and related activities accounted for about half of 1965's record sales volume of $559.7 million. The Robert Hall chain, consisting of 384 stores, accounted for 30 percent, and foreign textile operations the remaining 20 percent. The company's merchandising and distributing units were taking 45 percent of its weaving-plant output and 90 percent of its finishing-plant output. Sales included a variety of cotton, silk, wool, synthetic and fiberglass textiles, plastic products, and chemical specialties, including acrylic polymers and resins for making durable-press apparel. UM&M was also providing financing and factoring services for textile firms.

By 1975 UM&M was the nation's third-largest publicly owned textile company and its largest factoring company. Among its 70 manufacturing facilities, it held 19 weaving mills, 13 finishing factories, and 7 synthetic-yarn plants. Textiles were also being produced in Japan, England, and Colombia under joint ventures. There were also 16 merchandising and distributing units, including two in France, which acted as the company's converters. UM&M also had five research and five chemical units, plus five commercial factoring and financing offices. Its United Factors subsidiary had an annual volume of $1.4 billion and was so successful in analyzing creditworthiness that its losses were averaging less than one-quarter of one percent. Another subsidiary was performing other financial services, such as managing credit-card charges for several hundred department stores. The number of Robert Hall stores had reached 436.

Net sales of $787 million in fiscal 1972 was a record, but net income of $15.3 million was well below the high of $24.1 million recorded in 1966. In fiscal 1974 net income was $30.9 million, double the 1972 figure. Nevertheless, for the first five years of the 1970s, UM&M's annual return on investment averaged less than five percent compared to an average return of more than 11 percent in 1974 for all manufacturing companies. Another troubling figure was the $226 million in long-term debt, about 43 percent of the company's total capital and a sharp rise from $99 million in 1966.

UM&M lost $26.3 million in fiscal 1975 and $19.8 million in fiscal 1976, despite record sales volume in the latter year of more than $1 billion. To improve the situation, the company brought in new managers, closed some unprofitable operations, and consolidated profit centers. To reduce short-term debt, it sold its equipment-leasing business to Crocker National Bank for about $50 million, and a financing operation to Citicorp for $51 million. But turning around Robert Hall was a tougher problem. This subsidiary had earned $14 million as late as 1969, but it lost about $21 million in 1975 and a whopping pretax $41.8 million in 1976, despite having closed 135 unprofitable stores. The low-budget retailer specializing in men's suits and coats had been slow to move into shopping centers and suffered from a dowdy, Depression-era image.

A former Sears merchandise executive brought in to manage Robert Hall stocked the stores with a wider array of wearing apparel, including more infant's and children's wear, men's leisure clothes, and jeans and tops for young people. By mid-1977, however, UM&M, still hemorrhaging, had omitted its quarterly dividend and two of its debt securities had been downgraded by Moody's Investor Service. Accordingly, Martin Schwab decided to close the remaining Robert Hall stores—which had lost $100 million since 1974—and also decided to sell the lucrative factoring division to Crocker. George L. Staff, the president and chief operating officer Schwab had hired in November 1975, was dismissed.

Only a month later, on July 12, 1977, UM&M filed for protection under Chapter 11 provisions of the federal bankruptcy act. Although UM&M listed assets of $566.5 million and liabilities of only $381.3 million on March 31, 1977, it told a federal judge it was unable to pay its debts as they matured. In the biggest auction of retail-store merchandise ever, the contents of 367 Robert Hall stores were sold in the summer of 1977 for $35 million.

UM&M lost $191.8 million in fiscal 1978. The liquidation of Robert Hall, costing more than $100 million, was its biggest expense. The factoring division brought more than $160 million in its sale to Crocker. Some foreign textile operations also were shed. In June 1978, the end of its fiscal year, UM&M emerged from Chapter 11 bankruptcy on schedule—the biggest company ever to do so—having deposited $195.9 million to cover initial payments to creditors and other expenses. Under the plan, creditors were to be paid 35 percent in cash and the rest in annual installments. UM&M had paid about half of its debt of $410 million by May 1982, when it adopted a plan to eliminate the rest by issuing about 1.25 million shares of common stock and a cash payment of about $66 million. Manufacturers Hanover Trust Co. extended a loan for this payment, secured by UM&M's receivables.

A reorganized UM&M soon attracted the interest of an Israeli investment group composed of Libora, N.V., a Netherlands Antilles holding company, and Piryon Investment Trust Co., an Israeli public company. Eventually the group's holdings were sold to Uzi Ruskin, a citizen of both the United States and Israel who became a company director in 1980. Backed by Israeli investors, Ruskin bought $3 million more of UM&M stock in 1981, raising his stake in the company to 17 percent. He became its president in 1982.

Ruskin and his backers apparently were attracted to UM&M because of its $187 million in tax-loss credits against future earnings. However, he was unable to turn the company around. It lost $24.8 million on continuing operations in fiscal 1980, $7.3 million in 1981, and $44 million in 1982. The tax credits were spent on acquiring losers, according to a critical *Forbes* article. The worst of these was Jonathan Logan Inc., purchased in a 1984 hostile takeover for $195 million. A big apparel manufacturer with brand names like Misty Harbor, Act III, Rose Marie Reid, and Villager, Jonathan Logan proved unprofitable at the purchase price, which included $99 million in new bank loans and the issuance of high-yield bonds. In 1986, for example, Logan lost $36 million when including interest costs of more than $51 million.

To keep the company afloat Ruskin first sold one-sixth of UM&M's costume-jewelry unit to the public and closed the company's South American operations, some of its textile-printing plants, and a dyeing-and-finishing unit. In 1988–89 he sold the fiberglass-fabrics division, a shoe-and-handbag division, and part of the home-furnishings group. He raised more than $100 million, but in fiscal 1989 the company still carried an operating loss of $29 million. This sum did not include $35 million in interest payments on the company debt of $264 million. By the end of 1989 a share of UM&M was trading for about $2, compared to $21.50 in 1986. At this price Ruskin and his supporters felt confident enough to raise their stake in the company to about 30 percent. However, a proposal by Ruskin in September 1989 to acquire majority control of the company and pay for it with a new preferred-stock issue was rejected by company directors as too complex. Three of the four outside directors resigned in November.

Early in 1990 UM&M sold its Decora and Misty Harbor divisions for $33.6 million in order to reduce its debt. However, in November the company again filed for Chapter 11 protection because it was unable to repay $11.6 million on a maturing debenture. The petition included two subsidiaries—Jonathan Logan and United Merchants Trucking Inc.—but not Victoria Creations Inc., its costume-jewelry subsidiary.

UM&M emerged from bankruptcy in August 1992 but defaulted in January 1993, when it could not make a bond-interest payment due at the beginning of the year to CIT Group/Commercial Services, a unit of CIT Group Holdings, Inc. The restructuring agreement ending bankruptcy had required the company to reduce its debt to CIT to $88 million by the end of 1992, but UM&M still owed about $95 million at year's end. However, CIT agreed to continue to advance money to UM&M.

For fiscal 1993 UM&M registered a loss of $25.2 million, compared to a loss of $33 million the previous year. In November 1993 CIT agreed that if UM&M reduced its debt of $124 million to $60 million by mid-1994, it would forgive $30 million of the remaining debt and accept a long-term subordinated income note for the other $30 million. To pay for the latter, UM&M borrowed money from Foothill Capital and sold its Uniblend yarn division and Clarkesville Mill division for about $8.3 million. UM&M reported a loss of only $752,000 in fiscal 1994, but accounting changes masked a loss from continuing operations of $23.2 million. For the second straight year independent auditors expressed "substantial doubt" that the company could continue as a going concern.

In August 1994 UM&M settled a $22 million dispute with the International Ladies Garment Workers Union (ILGWU). The company had argued that its liability to pay this pension-plan sum had been wiped out by Chapter 11 reorganization. After a bankruptcy judge rejected the argument, UM&M issued ILGWU a contingent-income note due June 30, 2019.

UM&M closed its last remaining operation in the apparel textile division, South Carolina's Buffalo Mill, in early 1995, the last Jonathan Logan unit, Rose Marie Reid, having been sold in 1992. This left as its chief asset Victoria Creations, Inc., a 79-percent-owned subsidiary based in Providence, Rhode Island. Manufacturers of women's accessories, Victoria Creations lost $9.1 million in fiscal 1991, $7.4 million in fiscal 1992, and $1.6 million in fiscal 1993.

With the sale of Buffalo Mills, UM&M's only businesses consisted of Victoria Creations and a chain of 51 discount retail stores. Victoria Creations was one of the leading designers, manufacturers, and distributors of costume jewelry in the United States and also an exporter of such products. Its range of costume jewelry included relatively expensive items sold under the Bijoux Givenchy, Richelieu, and Karl Lagerfeld trade names. The retail chain consisted, in 1994, of 40 stores selling women's apparel and 11 selling women's accessories. About 60 percent of the apparel items were being sold under the Jonathan Logan name and most of the accessories were being manufactured by Victoria Creations.

UM&M registered a net loss of $18.8 million in fiscal 1994 on net sales of $98.3 million. Its long-term debt was about $150 million and its common stock was quoted at 12.5 cents a share at the end of the first quarter of 1994. Ruskin owned or controlled 6.5 percent of the common stock in September 1994, while Menachem Atzmon controlled 32.2 percent. By mid-1994

UM&M had a tax-loss carryforward of about $300 million that could be used to shelter future profits. The company said it was shifting the focus of its businesses to financial services and took steps in 1994 to establish a reinsurance business. Company headquarters, previously located in Manhattan's garment district, moved to Teaneck, New Jersey, in the early 1990s.

Principal Subsidiaries: Victoria Creations, Inc.

Further Reading:

Barmash, Isadore, "United Merchants, Citing Losses, Files Voluntary Bankruptcy Action," *New York Times,* July 13, 1977, p. D1.

Bingaman, R. P., Jr., "United Merchants & Manufacturers," *Wall Street Transcript,* June 17, 1968, p. 13580.

"Bloodbath at UMM," *Forbes,* August 15, 1976. p. 44.

Lappen, Alyssa A., "The Incredible Shrinking Company," *Forbes,* December 11, 1989, pp. 207, 210.

"The Lure Is Price, Not Glamor," *Business Week,* April 23, 1955, pp. 46, 51–52.

"United Merchants' Record Recovery," *Business Week,* July 31, 1978, pp. 77–78.

"United Merchants—Trade Complex," *Financial World,* May 11, 1966, pp. 12, 22.

"Up in the Loft," *Time,* April 25, 1949, pp. 86, 88.

Vanderwicken, Peter, ". . . And So UMM Decided to Trim Its Capital Budget," *Fortune,* September 1975, pp. 124–29, 167–68.

Wallach, Jack B., "Bargains—But No Basements," *Nation's Business,* February 1949, pp. 72–75.

Yaeger, Deborah Sue, "United Merchants Emerges, with Cheers and Tears, from Chapter 11 Proceedings," *Wall Street Journal,* July 3, 1978, p. 4.

—Robert Halasz

UNUM Corp.

2211 Congress Street
Portland, Maine 04122
U.S.A.
(207) 770-2211
Fax: (207) 770-4387

Public Company
Founded: 1985
Employees: 5,760
Total Assets: $13.13 billion
Stock Exchanges: New York
SICs: 6311 Life Insurance; 6321 Accident & Health Insurance; 6719 Holding Companies Not Elsewhere Classified

UNUM Corp. is, through its various subsidiaries, the leading provider of disability insurance in the United States and the United Kingdom. UNUM also provides services in the realms of employee benefits, long-term care, retirement products, and specialty risk offerings. The company grew explosively between the mid-1980s and mid-1990s as an innovator in the disability insurance industry.

UNUM Corp. was formed late in 1985 as the successor to the Union Mutual Life Insurance Company. At the time, Union Mutual was a relatively modest regional insurance company based in Portland, Maine. The company had operated in the area since before the Civil War. Over the years it had expanded its offerings to include various medical and life insurance plans as well as pension and investment products. By the early 1980s Union Mutual was managing assets of approximately $2.3 billion and employing a work force of about 1,900. Although it was a leader in the long-term disability insurance segment of the industry, the company was not viewed as a competitor with major national or international prospects. Moreover, it was gradually being overshadowed by much larger insurance companies with national marketing programs and increasingly automated operations.

In recognition of the encroaching threat to the company, executives in 1982 took measures to shift Union Mutual's focus away from market segments that were becoming dominated by the major national insurers. They also decided to take the company public (Union Mutual Life Insurance Company was a mutual company, meaning that it was owned by its policyholders). In 1986 Union Mutual changed its name to UNUM, the Latin word for the numeral one. UNUM's directors also hired James F. Orr III to help Chief Executive Colin Hampton oversee its transition from a mutual to a public company. Hampton, who had served as UNUM's leader for 15 years, believed that going public would bring much-needed expansion capital into the company. He also felt that Union Mutual would benefit from the accountability imposed by a corporate structure.

The 43-year-old Orr was an executive at Connecticut Bank & Trust before joining UNUM. He had recently helped to complete the merger of that bank and The Bank of New England, and UNUM directors felt that his background complimented their situation. Orr, who had been a track star at Villanova University in the 1960s, was recognized as an intelligent, frank, even-tempered achiever. He welcomed the move to Maine for both personal and professional reasons. "The company was in a very, very exciting period of transition—demutualization. It was the first, if not only, major demutualization in insurance that's ever taken place," Orr recalled of the move in the October 1990 *Business Digest of Southern Maine.* "The lifestyle in Maine was also appealing. My family and I had been coming to the Maine coast for 25 or 30 years, so putting it all together was just a tremendous opportunity."

In November 1986 UNUM distributed its entire net worth of $700 million to its policyholders. The company simultaneously sold new shares to new shareholders, a move that brought $700 million into the corporation's coffers. Although demutualization eventually proved to be a wise move, the transition was sometimes turbulent. Policyholders and employees were not accustomed to having the company's business scrutinized by the general public. As a result, Orr was deluged with complaints at times. "Looking back on it, I think we all underestimated how difficult it would be to get the people in the company oriented to having a new stakeholder group out there, namely, our shareholders," Orr noted in the *Business Digest of Southern Maine.* Orr helped smoothed the transition by increasing the size of performance-based incentives for employees, a program that Hampton started.

In addition to his efforts to engineer the transition to a public company, Orr began to aggressively reorganize and reposition UNUM to compete and grow. Within a year of his arrival—Orr officially assumed the chief executive slot in 1987—he slashed $25 million out of UNUM's annual expenses by trimming back the work force and dumping some of the organization's slumping divisions.

Union Mutual had been trying exit various nonperforming businesses since the early 1980s. Orr intensified that effort in 1986, and UNUM eventually bailed out of several of its core businesses, including life insurance, general investment contracts, and individual annuities and pensions. Most importantly, Orr and fellow executives decided to eliminate the company's involvement in the medical insurance business. Orr poured the resources saved from that business segment into sales and marketing programs for its remaining products.

With its diversified lines of insurance and financial products largely eliminated, UNUM had become primarily a provider of long-term disability insurance. UNUM sold most of its policies to groups—a company's employees, for example—but also registered sales to individuals and small businesses like medical practices. These agreements stipulated that, when a policyholder was out of work for an extended period due to a disability, UNUM would pay a percentage of the person's salary for a predetermined time period until the individual could return to work. In 1988 non-disability businesses still accounted for roughly two-thirds of UNUM's $1.5 billion in annual premiums. But nearly all of its $129 million in aftertax income came from disability premiums. Cognizant of this state of affairs, Orr continued to reduce UNUM's large pension and individual life businesses.

Orr's decision to concentrate on the long-term disability market was influenced in part by UNUM's established leadership position in the relatively small industry. In addition, the long-term disability market was growing quickly in comparison to most other types of insurance. Between 1962 and 1986, in fact, the number of Americans prevented from working because of a disability more than doubled to 9.3 million, a rate of growth that outstripped population growth more than four-fold. Some industry observers noted that, although sales of disability policies were increasing at a rapid rate of about 15 percent annually, the potential U.S. market of 117 million (by one estimate) was only 36-percent-saturated by the late 1980s.

Between 1985 and 1988 UNUM significantly bolstered its lead in the U.S. disability insurance market. By early 1989, UNUM's portfolio held a heady 30 percent of all U.S. disability policies and had captured about 17 percent of industry revenues. UNUM's market share was a whopping four times larger than that of its four largest competitors combined. It achieved those gains by underpricing the competition. One reason for the company's impressive performance was its $13 million annual investment in what it called "benefits management," which cut UNUM's claim payouts through investigation and reduction of false claims. The program also helped clients to secure Social Security payments owed to them. UNUM's competition scrambled to match the company's efficiency. Allstate Insurance Co., for example, cut its policy prices by 15 percent in the mid-1980s in an effort to lure away UNUM policyholders. It was unable to post profits, though, and Allstate dropped out of the business in 1988.

As UNUM's disability business surged, so did its revenues and profits. Between 1987 and 1990 sales rose from about $1.6 billion to roughly $2.2 billion. Profits, moreover, jumped from just under $100 million in 1987 to $160 million in 1989 and then to nearly $220 million in 1990. Orr was confident about UNUM's future prospects for the early and mid-1990s: "When we go into a marketplace, we want to stake out a leadership position," he asserted in *Forbes.* That confidence was reflected in Orr's vision of the company's standing in the latter part of the 1990s. Aside from dominance of the U.S. disability market, that vision included charitable efforts in the local community, a healthy corporate culture and work force, and international expansion. One key action meant to help the company meet the latter goal was the 1990 purchase of National Employers Life Assurance Co. Ltd., the largest disability provider in the United Kingdom.

UNUM's most powerful competitive advantage during the late 1980s and early 1990s was its coveted database. First established in the early 1970s, by the beginning of the 1990s the UNUM database consisted of information on 26,000 clients and 2.8 million insured individuals. Using the detailed information base, UNUM was able to precisely measure risks of disability stemming from numerous occupational, social, economic, and geographic factors. Such data gave UNUM an edge over its competitors in valuing risks, pricing policies, and creating specialized products for small niche markets. During the early 1990s, UNUM's database advantage was reflected by a 15 percent return on equity from its long-term disability business, a rate of return significantly higher than the industry average.

As a result of increased operational efficiency and intense market focus, UNUM's sales and profits continued to surge during the early 1990s. Annual revenues bolted to more than $3 billion in 1992 and then to $3.4 billion in 1993 as net income jumped to $300 million. By 1993, moreover, UNUM's asset base had grown to nearly $12.5 billion. Part of the growth was attributable to various acquisitions and joint ventures. In December 1992, for example, UNUM finalized an agreement with Equitable, a leading U.S. insurance company, to have Equitable's 8,300-member sales force sell only disability products designed by UNUM. The same year, UNUM purchased Duncanson & Holt, Inc., a leading accident and health reinsurance underwriting manager. That acquisition increased UNUM's reach in the United States, Great Britain, Canada, and Singapore. Similarly, in 1994 UNUM established UNUM Japan Accident Insurance Company Limited, a Japanese subsidiary.

After posting successive and impressive gains throughout the late 1980s and early 1990s, UNUM stumbled in 1994. Assets and sales increased, but net income dropped to $154 million and the company experienced its first stock price drop (of 14 percent) since it had gone public in 1986. The slide was primarily the result of setbacks related to UNUM's individual disability business. The company suffered serious losses from that segment during 1994, prompting executives to announce late in 1994 that UNUM would no longer market individual, noncancelable disability products in the United States. The losses occurred, in part, because of significantly increased claims by UNUM-insured doctors, which accounted for about 15 percent of the company's business. UNUM believed that changes in the profession gave doctors more reasons to claim disability payments—which were often $20,000 to $30,000 per month—rather than recover and return to work. UNUM lost $61.7 million from the segment in the third quarter of 1994 alone, a figure that prompted it to lay off 350 workers.

Going into the mid-1990s UNUM barely resembled the mutual company that had preceded it in the mid-1980s. Still focused primarily on long-term disability insurance, UNUM conducted business through seven major subsidiaries with offices in North America, Europe, and the Pacific Rim. Despite setbacks in 1994, UNUM's long-term prospects were favorable. UNUM continued to dominate the growing disability insurance niche on the strength of a healthy balance sheet, increasing globally diversification, and aggressive pursuit of fast-growing market niches that complimented its core operations.

Principal Subsidiaries: UNUM Life Insurance Company of America; First UNUM Life Insurance Company; Commercial Life Insurance Company; UNUM Limited (United Kingdom); Duncanson & Holt, Inc.; Colonial Life & Accident Insurance Company Limited; and UNUM Japan Accident Insurance Company Limited.

Further Reading:

Cox, Brian, ''UNUM to Leave Individual Non-cancelable DI Market,'' *National Underwriter Life & Health-Financial Services Edition,* November 14, 1994, p. 3.

Eleazer, Carol A., ''UNUM and The Equitable Form Strategic Alliance,'' *Business Wire,* December 10, 1992.

Ellman, Mark, Guy Davis, Fran Brennan, and Ward Graffam, ''UNUM to Focus on Permanent Health Insurance in U.K.; Plans to Sell U.K. Life, Pensions and Mortgage Businesses,'' *Business Wire,* September 26, 1990.

French, Dorry, ''Unum's Long Term Orr-Ganizer,'' *Business Digest of Southern Maine,* October 1990, p. 2.

Gribbel, Susie L., and Gretchen McLain, ''UNUM Creates Related Businesses Division to Pursue External Growth; Brennan Selected to Direct New Operation,'' *Business Wire,* September 13, 1988.

Jereski, Laura, ''We Understand Risk,'' *Forbes,* March 20, 1989, pp. 127–128.

Kerr, Peter, ''Less is Key to an Insurer's Success,'' *The New York Times,* February 10, 1993, p. D1.

Libbey, Robert E., ''UNUM Announces 1994 Earnings,'' *Business Wire,* February 8, 1995.

McGough, Robert, ''Yankee Clipper: UNUM Sails the Fast Tack From Its Home Port in Maine,'' *Financial World,* June 11, 1991, p. 38.

—Dave Mote

Value Merchants Inc.

710 N. Plankinton Avenue
Milwaukee, Wisconsin 53203
U.S.A.
(414) 274-2575
Fax: (414) 274-2930

Private Company
Incorporated: 1944
Employees: 2,200
Sales: $363 million
Stock Exchanges: New York
SICs: 5331 Variety Stores

Value Merchants Inc.'s Everything's A Dollar subsidiary operated more than 250 discount stores throughout the nation going into the mid-1990s. Founded in 1944, the company grew modestly during the first couple decades of its existence. During the late 1980s and early 1990s, however, Value Merchants grew explosively. Its rapid expansion ultimately exposed weaknesses in the company, though. In 1993 Value Merchants filed for Chapter 11 bankruptcy protection. The company was still struggling to reorganize and recover in 1995.

Value Merchants Inc. was formerly known as the Wisconsin Toy Company. The name was changed in 1990 when Steven Appel became chief executive of the concern. He replaced Philip Cohen, who had served as CEO of the company since 1960 (his father had founded the organization). During the mid-1900s the Cohens built their enterprise into a successful U.S. toy wholesaler. Philip Cohen took the operation public in 1969—it was incorporated at that time as Wisconsin Toy Company—in a transaction that shifted ownership to a holding company, but he continued to successfully run the organization.

By the 1980s, in fact, Wisconsin Toy was one of the largest competitors in its specialized niche. Wisconsin Toy's annual sales were about $25 million by the early 1980s, about $800,000 of which was netted as income. In addition to its Milwaukee headquarters, the company had a sales office and showroom in New York City and maintained distribution centers in New Jersey and San Francisco. The company profited by purchasing large quantities of close-out inventory from a wide variety of toy makers, including major manufacturers in the United States and Asia. It sold the merchandise to U.S. retailers—including several major retail chains—who used the inexpensive items to promote foot traffic in their stores and boost sales of goods that had higher profit margins.

Until 1984 Wisconsin Toy sold its merchandise only at the wholesale level. Executives chartered a new course for the company in 1985. Rather than sell their goods to other retailers, who usually increased the price, they reasoned that they could sell directly to the public at wholesale prices. In 1985 Wisconsin Toy opened its first retail outlet—a Toy Liquidators discount store in Virginia. The success of that store prompted the company to open four more outlets in Indiana within a year and to plan launches of several more shops in 1986 and 1987. Cohen, who turned 68 in 1987, remained on the management team, but his role was reduced. In 1987 Leslie Mendelsohn was named president of the company. Mendelsohn, age 40, had served as an executive at Federal Wholesale Company, a West Coast toy wholesale company.

By June of 1987 Wisconsin Toy operated 50 Toy Liquidators retail outlets. In an effort to raise $15 million to $18 million of capital for expansion, Wisconsin Toy's parent company, Zilber Ltd., took the company public. Additional stores were acquired or built. Although sales and profits in 1986 remained at 1984 and 1985 levels, revenues bolted about 70 percent in 1987 and net income surged to a record $2.3 million. Although Wisconsin's wholesale operations continued to account for the majority of sales and earnings, the company was clearly headed in a new direction; away from wholesaling and toward the growing U.S. discount retail market. Because of its access to low-cost toys and other merchandise, Wisconsin Toy seemed well positioned to compete.

During the late 1980s Wisconsin Toy added 40 more Toy Liquidator establishments to its portfolio, bringing the size of its Toy Liquidators chain to 90 by 1990. In 1989 Wisconsin Toy generated $53 million in sales (fiscal year ending January 31) and earned nearly $3.6 million in net income. But while the company's growth during the late 1980s was impressive, it was a mere prelude to the expansion that would occur during the early 1990s. In 1989 Wisconsin Toy departed from its historic emphasis on toys. It purchased Everything's A Dollar Inc. (EAD), a chain of about 60 discount retail stores that had previously been a Wisconsin Toy customer. The shops were similar to Toy Liquidators, except that they sold all kinds of different merchandise ranging from shampoo and sunglasses to toys and mustard.

The EAD concept was relatively simple. The company purchased huge lots of items at cut-rate prices. The goods were typically excess inventory or items that had run their course in the mainstream marketplace. The products were shipped to stores and sold, on average, for a small profit. The draw for customers was that virtually every item in the store cost one dollar. The concept was especially attractive to teenagers, who could walk into an EAD shop with five dollars and leave with a bag full of goods. But the dollar strategy had also proved increasingly popular with other segments of the value-oriented shopping population that were looking for low-cost gifts and household goods.

EAD stores were typically about 3,000 to 4,000 square feet in size. Most of them were located in large metropolitan shopping malls rather than the low-rent discount factory outlets in which Toy Liquidators were stationed. Neon lights or back-lit glass blocks near the entrance enticed buyers, and progressive decor and lively music inside facilitated an atmosphere of impulse buying. Indeed, the stores relied on high volumes of impulse purchases to squeeze a profit out of the low-priced goods. While the typical customer transaction was only a little more than $5, an average new store was projected to register more $1 million in sales during the first year of operation.

The EAD acquisition effectively doubled the size of Wisconsin Toy's swelling retail division. Moreover, the EAD stores seemed like a perfect compliment to Wisconsin Toy's existing operations. EAD provided a huge new distribution channel for the company's wholesale purchasing division and added a new dimension to its discount retail business. At the time, the dollar discount concept was just beginning to get popular and the potential of the industry seemed huge. Wisconsin Toy hoped to parlay its experience in the wholesale business into a leadership position in the rapidly growing industry. To do that, it would need to expand rapidly to sustain its lead over its discount retail peers.

To guide Wisconsin Toy's evolution into a large discount retailer, Wisconsin Toy's directors hired Wisconsin native Steven Appel, a self-described hard worker with average technical skills. Appel grew up in a working class household, married at the age of 18, and was a working father by the time he entered the University of Wisconsin at Milwaukee in 1960. Appel took on a full course load despite his responsibilities. To accomplish the feat, he learned to negotiate with his professors. At the beginning of each semester he approached them with a proposition: He would attend all classes and take all the exams if they would not require him to turn in homework assignments. If the professor refused, he simply dropped the class and added a different one.

Appel graduated in four years with a degree in accounting, a profession that his father had urged him to pursue because he had a friend that was a successful accountant. After graduation, Appel accepted a job as a staff accountant with Arthur Anderson & Co. His penchant for hard work served him well and he steadily progressed through the ranks. "For the first time in my life, I was exposed to the vastness of the world," Appel recalled in *Business Journal-Milwaukee.* "I also realized how much I could grow if I committed myself to a career with Arthur Andersen and, despite average technical skills, I believe my sheer desire helped form a strong work ethic and channel my interpersonal skills to achieve my goals." Appel's energy and drive was also evident in his personal life; he managed to qualify for the Boston Marathon at the age of 41 with a 26-mile time of three hours and three minutes.

By 1987 Appel served as managing director of Arthur Anderson's financial consulting services division. Among the companies he advised was Wisconsin Toy Company. Executives there were impressed by his work and eventually approached him about joining the company. Appel accepted and joined Wisconsin Toy in 1989 as chief operating officer. When Cohen officially retired as CEO in June 1990, Appel took the reins. By that time the Wisconsin Toy Company operated nearly 150 stores, including more than 60 EAD and 80 Toy Liquidators (some of the toy retail outlets were called Toys Unlimited). To reflect Wisconsin Toy Company's growing emphasis on retail and general merchandise, Appel changed the organization's name to Value Merchants Inc. in July 1990.

Under Appel's direction, Value Merchants intensified its expansion efforts during the early 1990s in an attempt to assume a dominant position in the discount bulk merchandise industry. It purchased the remaining 20 percent of the EAD chain that it didn't own and added 100 new stores during 1991. By the end of that year, Value Merchants held more than 200 EAD stores stretching from New York to Florida and as far west as Texas. By April 1992 Value Merchants owned 230 EAD stores and 110 Toy Liquidator establishments. It made further plans for growth, pursuing experiments with such new types of EAD outlets as a 9,000-square-foot superstore on the East Coast and downtown shops in Miami.

Value Merchants' financial figures mirrored the blistering growth rate. Although the company's debt load increased, sales doubled in 1990 (fiscal 1991 ending January 31) to a whopping $140 million. During 1991, moreover, revenues bolted to $235 million and revenues vaulted to a peak of $9.2 million. Investor enthusiasm sent the company's stock price rocketing to more than $34 per share.

Value Merchants continued to add outlets at a fast pace throughout 1992. By the end of the year, in fact, the company boasted a network of 540 locations in more than 40 states. That explosive growth, however, belied serious structural problems in the Value Merchants organization. In 1992 the company's financial performance began to slide as the profitability of its stores waned. It became apparent to investors that executives had tried to grow too quickly and had neglected to ensure that existing operations remained profitable. "Nobody held a gun to their head and said grow by 300 stores," noted one analyst in 1993 in the *Business Journal-Milwaukee.* "They obviously bit off more than they could chew." Value Merchants' stock price plunged to $7.75 per share in January 1993. Appel quickly squelched 1993 expansion plans and laid off workers at the company's Milwaukee headquarters.

Appel took responsibility for Value Merchants' problems, but he also pointed to some untimely setbacks that had rocked the company. The company, for example, had expected to have access in April 1991 to an $85 million financing package that would be used to fund store openings and infrastructure plans. When the money was delayed until August of that year, a severe cash crunch ensued. One result was that several stores opened late in the year and missed out on most of the important Christmas season. At the same time, Value Merchants invested heavily in advanced computer systems and new satellite distribution facilities designed to support its swelling national retail chain. Analysts noted that while such steps were perhaps necessary to manage the company's growth, the short time period involved required that the execution be flawless.

Although Value Merchant's revenues ballooned to $364 million in fiscal 1993, it posted a discouraging $8 million deficit. Worried investors pressured company executives to bandage bleeding balance sheets. But the company's problems only worsened. Appel responded by shuttering some unprofitable stores and working to increase the performance of the existing chain. The effort was insufficient. Faced with looming deadlines for payments to creditors, Value Merchants and its EAD subsidiary filed for bankruptcy in December 1993. The move allowed the company to keep cash flow from its Christmas sales while it worked to reach an agreement with creditors in 1994.

During 1994 Value Merchants jettisoned its original toy wholesale purchasing division and the remaining 84 Toy Liquidators outlets. Consolidated Stores Corp. bought the chain and Value Merchants used the cash from the sale to reduce its debt. The company also eliminated more than 150 EAD outlets. Entering 1995, Value Merchants consisted of a chain of about 265 EAD outlets, roughly half the number it operated during the peak of its expansion in 1992. Value Merchants eventually proposed an agreement with creditors during 1994 that would give them ownership of most of the company. ''This plan is the culmination of an aggressive effort to improve the financial condition and future prospects of Value Merchants and to deal equitably with stake holders,'' Appel said in December 1994 in the *Business Journal-Milwaukee*. The long-term future of the discounter was still in doubt going into 1995.

Principal Subsidiaries: Everything's A Dollar Inc.

Further Reading:

''The CEOs of Wisconsin: Steven Appel,'' *Business Journal-Milwaukee,* March 27, 1993, section 3, p. 10.

Chua, Linus, ''Single-Price Shops Try to Buck the Chain Stores,'' *Business Journal-Milwaukee,* August 22, 1992, p. 1.

Dires, Michael, ''Shades of CEO: Heart and Soul—How Who They are Plays a Role in How They Lead,'' *Business Journal-Milwaukee,* March 27, 1993, section 3, p. 9.

''Hot Shots Number 37: Value Merchants Inc.,'' *Business Journal-Milwaukee,* July 30, 1990, section 3, p. 27.

Kane, Tim, ''Dollar Store Company Targets Shoppers Out for a Bargain,'' *Capital District Business Review,* October 5, 1992, p. 2.

Kass, Mark, ''Limited Value? Fiscal Loss, Layoffs Dog Value Merchants as Firm Disappoints Wall Street,'' *Business Journal-Milwaukee,* January 30, 1993, p. 1.

——, ''New Chapter in Value Merchants Saga,'' *Business Journal-Milwaukee,* December 18, 1993, p. 1.

——, ''Too Few Bargains? Value Merchants Creditors Wary,'' *Business Journal-Milwaukee,* December 3, 1994, p. 1.

Kastel, Gary I., ''Value Merchants, Inc. Completes Sale of Its Toy Operations to Unit of Consolidated Stores Corp.,'' *Business Wire,* May 17, 1994.

——, ''Value Merchants, Inc. Reports 58 Percent Increase in March Sales,'' *Business Wire,* April 9, 1992.

Olson, Jon, ''Hot Shots—Wisconsin's Best-Performing Public Companies: #13 Value Merchants Inc.,'' *Business Journal-Milwaukee,* July 29, 1991, section 3, p. 16.

Pereira, Miriam, ''Everything's A Dollar Capitalizes on Excess Retail Inventory,'' *South Florida Business Journal,* December 16, 1992, p. 6.

Spivak, Cary, ''Zilber's Wisconsin Toy Files for Initial Public Offering,'' *Business Journal-Milwaukee,* May 18, 1987, p. 8.

Storm, Sheila, ''Mankato's $1 Store is 1st in Minnesota,'' *Successful Business,* January 13, 1992, p. 1.

—Dave Mote

Vendex International N.V.

P.O. Box 7997
1008 AD Amsterdam
The Netherlands
31 20 549 0500
Fax: 31 20 646 1954
or
Vendamerica Inc.
104 Field Point Rd.
Greenwich, Connecticut 06830
U.S.A.
(203) 629-4676
Fax: (203) 629-2273

Public Company
Founded: 1887
Operating Revenues: NLG 10.4 billion
Employees: 78,500
Stock Exchanges: Amsterdam

Vendex International N.V. is one of the largest retail operations in The Netherlands. The Vendex empire is vast, with 1,660 retail outlets including food stores, large department stores, and specialty stores in jewelry, sporting goods, photography and electronics, pet products, hard goods, fashion, and home furnishings. The company also has substantial business interests in maintenance services, temporary-help services, insurance, and real estate. In addition to its extensive holdings throughout the Netherlands, Vendex operates businesses in France, Belgium, Germany, Spain, Sweden, and the United States.

The founders of the company that eventually became Vendex, Willem Vroom and Anton Dreesmann, had extensive retail experience, having clerked in various food stores and dry goods stores for years. After the two young men met they formed a close friendship; ambitious and energetic, they decided to open a department store of their own. When the first Vroom & Dreesmann retail store opened in downtown Amsterdam in 1887, bundles of soap and candles, swatches of clothing material, and brooms were just some of the items sold by the new company to the general public.

From that date to the beginning of World War I, Vroom & Dreesmann department stores expanded throughout The Netherlands. Both of the founders came from close-knit families, and the two men were able to convince their relatives to operate each new store that was opened. The stores were typically co-owned by Vroom & Dreesmann and the chosen relative, but individually managed by the relative, who was given a great deal of autonomy. Vroom & Dreesmann relied heavily on the idea of familial responsibility to assure the success of each new store.

The First World War and the Second World War hurt the company not only in loss of revenue but also in loss of personnel to the tragedies of both conflicts. Yet Vroom & Dreesmann continued to grow. People still needed soap, shoes, and toilet paper, and Vroom & Dreesmann stores were there to provide these necessities, although without the direction of the founders, who had passed away some time before.

Throughout the 1950s and into the 1960s, Vroom & Dreesmann department stores operated within a highly decentralized corporate structure. During the early 1960s, the Vroom & Dreesmann group decided to impose some order on the company by organizing the stores by region, in a first step toward a more centralized and more efficient operational structure. In 1973 the regional groups merged to form a united Vroom & Dreesmann Group. Anton Dreesmann's grandson, who was also named Anton Dreesmann, became chairman of the newly restructured company.

With a Ph.D. in Economics and Law, and having taught as a professor at the University of Amsterdam, Anton Dreesmann was well prepared to assume the leadership of Vroom & Dreesmann. He immediately began to overhaul the organization and administration of the firm, implemented standardized operating procedures, and initiated a bold expansion strategy. Seeking to diversify from the traditional department store business, Dreesmann moved into the fields of food retail, fashion, banking, hardware retail, jewelry retail, maintenance services, mail order services, employment services, catering services, and electronic retail. The acquisition of such well-known firms as Kreymborg, Claudia Strater, Edah, Staal Bankiers, Vedior, Vedelectric, Siebel, and Nederlands Talen Institut was financed most through debt.

During the late 1970s, the government in The Netherlands revised the corporate tax structure as a means of financing social programs, and companies such as Vroom & Dreesmann were faced with a significant increase in their taxes. In response, Dreesmann began seeking overseas partners and acquisitions. He established a U.S. subsidiary, Vendamerica, to analyze trends in American retailing, and in 1978 he negotiated a major agreement with Dillard's Department Stores. According to the agreement, Vroom & Dreesmann paid approximately $24 million for more than one million non-voting shares of stock; in return, Dreesmann was made a member of Dillard's Board of Directors. In 1979 Dreesmann purchased Ultralar, a major Brazilian department store chain.

During the 1980s, Dreesmann continued to pursue an aggressive expansion strategy, although at a somewhat slower pace. In 1980 he attempted to acquire 50 percent of W. R. Grace's retailing operations. Grace, one of the largest conglomerates in the United States, was initially receptive to Dreesmann's overtures, but after months of intense negotiations, the two companies could not reach a mutually satisfactory agreement. During the same year, Dreesmann expanded into the Far East by purchasing a three percent interest in UNY, one of Japan's largest retailers, which operated numerous superstore and specialty store outlets. Other notable purchases during this time included a 50 percent stake in the Brazilian branch of the Sears department store chain and the acquisition of Perry Sports, one of the largest and most successful sports retail store chains in The Netherlands.

From 1982 through the remainder of the decade, the company focused on implementing a comprehensive reorganization plan. This involved organizing the company's businesses into separate operating divisions, with the retail trading division comprising food stores, department stores, specialty fashion, specialty hard goods, and specialty home furnishings, and the business services division comprising maintenance services, employment services, and miscellaneous services. The divisions were under the direction of the holding company, which changed its name to Vendex International B.V. in 1985. Throughout these changes, Anton Dreesmann remained firmly in control of the company, especially since the Dreesmann family retained a majority of the firm's stock.

Revenues and profitability continued to grow as a result of Dreesmann's expansion strategy. In 1987 Vendex acquired a 50 percent interest in B. Dalton, a huge bookstore chain in the United States, and a 32 percent stake in the College Book Stores of Barnes & Noble, another large American retail bookseller. Vendex also acquired numerous European companies in unrelated industries, including a Belgian furniture store chain and a Dutch travel agency.

By the late 1980s, however, Vendex was experiencing serious financial problems. Having concentrated for years on its highly successful expansion strategy, the company failed to adapt to changes in the domestic market, especially in the retailing industry. This, combined with a slowdown in the Dutch economy, led to declining sales. The company's heavy debt load and high interests rates also contributed to significant losses in certain sectors of its business. Compounding these problems was the poor health of Dreesmann, who suffered a series of debilitating strokes.

In 1988 Dreesmann appointed Arie Van der Zwan to take his place as chairman of Vendex. Van der Zwan, also an economics professor, began to improve the company's operational efficiency by taking drastic measures, which included layoffs of almost 18 percent of the company's retail employees. Dreesmann was furious. Highly regarded for his employee relations policies—and called "Uncle Anton" by his workers—Dreesmann returned to Vendex despite his failing health. He immediately fired Van der Zwan, and implemented his own reorganization and revitalization strategy.

In 1990 Dreesmann selected Jan Michiel Hessels to succeed him as chairman of Vendex. Hessels had obtained a law degree from the University of Leiden and had extensive administrative experience in companies such as Akzo, Delimaatschappij, and Deli Universal. Hessels's assignment was to revitalize the company through a three-pronged strategy: divest unprofitable, noncore businesses; restructure the retail department store division by concentrating on improved profitability and domestic acquisitions; and reduce corporate debt.

In 1990 Vendex discontinued almost all of its operations in Brazil, including its retail department store operations, banking operations, and hard goods retail operation, primarily due to declining profits and the instability of the Brazilian economy. The company also disposed of some holdings in banking, mail order services, and real estate operations within The Netherlands and reduced its interest in Barnes & Noble, the U.S. bookstore chain. In 1991, after its American home center retail store chain, Mr. Goodbuys, filed for Chapter 11 bankruptcy, Vendex ceased all operations of the company. Vendex sold its shares in Dillard's department stores, reaping a healthy profit from its investment, and reduced its share in Software, Etc., another American investment.

Hessels's strategic moves paid off handsomely. Vendex International's total income increased from NLG 164 million in 1990 to more than NLG 340 million in 1995. Part of this improvement resulted from an increase in profits reported by Vroom & Dreesmann department stores, which shot up from NLG 7 million in 1990 to NLG 86 million in 1995, and by an improvement in the company's debt-to-equity ratio, which decreased from 234 percent at the end of 1991 to just 48.4 percent in 1995.

In 1995 Vendex reported that approximately 72 percent of net sales and nearly 75 percent of its operating income came from its retail division, while the remainder was derived from the business services division. The company operated a total of 655 food stores and 121 franchise pet food retail stores, and had more than 11 percent of the total food retail market in The Netherlands. Edah, the company's largest retail food store chain, which operated medium-sized supermarkets, was listed as the third-largest food retail store in the country in 1995.

Vendex International's department store operation was led by Vroom & Dreesmann, which had a 40 percent share of the total department store market in The Netherlands. With 62 stores across the country, Vroom & Dreesmann department stores sold a wide variety of merchandise, including clothing, toys, and telecommunications equipment. The company's specialty store operations were equally diverse, with product lines including lingerie, camping accessories, jewelry, and home furnishings. Companies within the Vendex specialty retail family included such well-known names as Kreymborg, Kien, America Today, Perry Sport, the Siebel Group, and Kijkshop/Best-Sellers.

Vendex's business services operation was led by Cemsto, the largest cleaning service firm in the country, which had more than 11,000 employees. Most of Cemsto's cleaning services were contracted by large buildings, housing corporations, and other business enterprises. Vendex's Employment services sector operated 474 offices throughout The Netherlands, Belgium, Luxembourg, France, and Germany. Vedior International, which provided employment services such as helping people find temporary jobs or training the long-term unemployed to find work, was considered one of the most innovative firms in the field.

With Hessels firmly in control, Vendex International's future looks bright. The company continues to grow within a small geographical area by adapting to the changing conditions of the European marketplace. As long as management remains flexible, and Vroom & Dreesmann retains its pre-eminent position among department stores, Vendex International will continue to be a Dutch success story.

Principal Subsidiaries: Edah; Konmar; Basismarkt; Dagmarkt; Battard; Eda Belgium; Eda France; Pet's Place; Vroom & Dreesmann; Kreymborg; Hunkemoller; Kien; Claudia Strater; America Today; Perry Sport; The Siebel Group; Kijkshop/Best-Sellers; The Dixon's Group; The Stoutenbeck Group; Cemsto; Holland Partners; Eijssink; Van Heusden; Zidkenhuis Diensten Groep; Tecso Antoine Petit; Restoplan (50%); Nedsafe; Receptionelle; Dick van Troost; Eventure; Groene Team (50%); Domesta; AVO; ASB/Vedior; Dactylo; Project Partners; Compuhelp; Gregg; ASB Interim; Intertra France; Regit France; ADHOC Germany; Markgraaf; F.A.A.; Bakker Continental.

—Thomas Derdak

Waban Inc.

One Mercer Road
P.O. Box 9600
Natick, Massachusetts 01760
U.S.A.
(508) 651-6500
Fax: (508) 651-7437

Public Company
Incorporated: 1983 as HomeClub Inc.
Sales: $3.65 billion
Employees: 16,000
Stock Exchanges: New York
SICs: 5031 Lumber, Plywood and Millwork; 5039 Construction Materials; 5122 Drugs, Proprietaries and Sundries; 5141 Groceries, General Line

Waban Inc. consists of two warehouse merchandising businesses: HomeBase and BJ's Wholesale Club. In 1994 HomeBase, one of the nation's four largest home-improvement merchandisers with a warehouse format, ranked as the second-largest operator of home-improvement stores in the western United States. BJ's Wholesale Club, which sells food and general merchandise, was the nation's third-largest membership warehouse chain the same year. As of 1992 Waban was the sixth-largest business based in Massachusetts.

Waban's rise to prominence was a rapid one. The HomeBase part of the business was founded by Robert McNulty and George Handgis as HomeClub Inc. Based in Fullerton, California, HomeClub opened its first two warehouse outlets in the California communities of Fountain Valley and Norwalk in October 1983. Warehouse-format home centers typically offer lower prices than traditional home-improvement and building supply stores and lumber yards. They also typically offer greater product selection and in-stock merchandise. The home-center warehouse format generally serves do-it-yourself customers as well as professional contractors and facility managers.

A high-school dropout and Vietnam veteran with experience in home-improvement retail stores, McNulty was the active partner in the fledgling business. Armed with $4.5 million in start-up funds from venture-capital investors, he regularly put in 90- to 100-hour workweeks. By the end of 1985 the HomeClub chain had grown to 18 stores, with 18 more stores planned to open in 1986. These stores were open to all, but nonmembers paid five percent more for purchases than fee-paying members. The company reported sales of $90.5 million in the six months ending July 28, 1985, with net income (excluding an extraordinary item) of $1.7 million.

McNulty's plans for national expansion were scotched by a disappointing response to HomeClub's initial public offering of stock in October 1985. Lacking what he called the ''deep pockets'' needed to go nationwide, he agreed the following month to sell the company to discount merchandiser Zayre Corp. for Zayre common stock valued at between $147 million and $151 million. McNulty calculated his projected profit from Zayre stock and options at $6.5 million. Sixty-five of his employees also owned HomeClub shares that they swapped for Zayre stock after the deal was ratified in January 1986.

Zayre, with headquarters in Framingham, Massachusetts, was then operating self-service discount department stores and off-price specialty stores. In announcing the acquisition, Zayre's president said it was ''part of the company's long-term strategy to become a diversified, value-based chain-store retailer.'' HomeClub maintained its headquarters in Fullerton and McNulty continued to lead the company after the purchase. He resigned in 1986 to pursue other business ventures and was replaced by Herbert J. Zarkin, who remained president until 1988. By late 1988 HomeClub had expanded greatly, with annual sales of more than $750 million.

Zayre introduced the warehouse-club concept to New England by founding BJ's Wholesale Club in 1984. In that year it opened three 100,000-square-foot facilities. Patterned after such competitors as The Price Co.'s Price Club and Wal-Mart's Sam's Club, BJ's typically offered a wide array of merchandise in self-service no-frills facilities. Establishments confined product choice to brand-name leaders and refused to accept credit cards. Its goal was to achieve high sales volumes and rapid inventory turnover, attracting customers from supermarkets, discount stores, office-supply stores, consumer electronics stores, automotive stores, and wholesale distributors and jobbers. The reference to ''wholesale'' in the company name was primarily a marketing device, for the operation was directed principally, if not wholly, toward retail sales. As a membership club, BJ's charged its customers an annual fee. This fee was originally $30. It dropped to $25 for a time, but the $30 membership fee was eventually reinstated.

A computer-management executive named Mervyn Weich was appointed to run the operation. Headquarters were established in Natick, Massachusetts. By mid-1987, 15 BJ stores were in operation in the East and Midwest, and annual sales rose from $350 million in 1986 to $580 million in 1987. The company, however, posted a loss. Weich (who later opened a rival operation called Wholesale Depot) resigned at the end of June 1987 and was replaced by John F. Levy. An analyst for a brokerage house told a *Boston Globe* reporter at the time, ''if I were senior management, I would have hoped BJ's had accomplished more by this time, given the money thrown into it.''

By the end of 1988 the number of BJ stores had grown to 22 in 11 states. Sales volume reached $827 million that year, placing BJ's fifth in the nation among warehouse clubs. In late 1989 its stock consisted of about half food and half general merchandise, with small businesses representing about ten percent of the customers but about half of total sales. A representative store, like the 107,000-square-foot facility in Weymouth, Massachusetts, stocked 3,500 items in bulk, including television sets, exercise equipment, power tools, clothing, books, tires, and housewares. Goods were typically stacked almost to the ceiling in plain steel racks.

Profitability remained elusive, however, even though sales reached $1.1 billion in 1990. In the face of stiff competition from other warehouse clubs entering New England and the Middle Atlantic states, BJ's had been forced to restrict its markup to only eight to ten percent above cost. An industry analyst told the *Boston Globe* that although the club had cut costs to the bone and raised efficiency, it was failing to attract repeat business because it was not introducing new products. By contrast, the HomeClub organization, with about the same sales volume in 55 stores, had established itself as a moneymaker.

Following Zayre's acquisition of HomeClub, it was consolidated with BJ's into a single warehouse-club division. This division became Waban Inc. in 1989, the year Zayre, which was renamed TJX Cos., spun it off as a separate company. Based at BJ's Natick headquarters, Waban was named for a nearby Massachusetts village. Zayre stockholders received one Waban share for every two Zayre shares they owned. Most stockholders sold their shares, which fell from an initial price of $18 a share to about $14.50 in the next few months. Some brokers and analysts were bullish on the new company's potential, though, noting that it had a debt-to-capital ratio of only 11 percent and a price-earnings ratio lower than its competitors.

Waban's first months of operation proved difficult. Net income fell from $28.8 million in 1989 to $18.4 million in 1990. Management attributed the profit drop to a decision to set aside money for needed substantial long-term investments, but analysts noted stiff competition from HomeClub's archrival, Home Depot. The price of Waban stock fell as low as $4.63 a share in 1991. In March of that year HomeClub terminated its membership fee in an effort to increase its customer base. The more than one million current members were issued refund vouchers of $10 to $15, redeemable at all warehouses. The name of the chain was changed to HomeBase in 1992 in order to remove any remaining perception that it had a membership policy.

HomeClub had 70 stores in operation in the West when, in mid-1991, it opened its first midwestern location. The new store was located in Toledo, Ohio, at the site of a former BJ's establishment. The company's president foresaw the possibility of opening 150 HomeClubs over a 10-year period in the Midwest, where the warehouse-club format had not been widely tested. HomeClub also began a campaign to attract women by offering more home-decor items, including Oriental rugs.

Midwestern expansion proved a mistake. HomeClub entered the Chicago area in 1991 by revamping failed BJ's stores. It abandoned Chicago two years later, turning over leases on five of its six stores in the metropolitan area to Home Depot. The warehouse chain—now HomeBase—also closed its two Toledo stores at this time. While their operations were profitable, the stores did not return profits high enough to satisfy Waban. BJ's, which had grown to 28 stores by mid-1991 and had added fresh-meat departments and in-store bakeries to its stores, sold one of its four Chicago-area outlets that year while turning over the other three to HomeClub. Waban's retreat from the Midwest was based on its conclusion that this region was not as interested in the warehouse concept as the East and West.

In 1992 BJ's reached sales volume of $1.79 billion, but average sales of $48 million for its 39 stores trailed the results posted by competing warehouse-club chains. In May 1993 Levy was replaced as chief executive officer of Waban by Zarkin, who had been serving as president of BJ's since 1990. Levy acknowledged that "results have fallen short of the board's goals," an outcome industry analysts described as a sure sign of a shakeout in the warehouse-format industry. One analyst told the *Boston Globe* that "BJ's clubs and HomeBase stores just aren't quite up to par with the execution of Sam's Club or a Home Depot."

The subsequent restructuring of Waban included a decision to spend $100 million to close or relocate 24 HomeBase stores (including the Chicago-area stores). HomeBase's operating income for the third quarter of the fiscal year had declined to $8.4 million from $14.8 million in the previous year's third quarter, despite an increase of four percent in total sales. Zarkin said Waban sought to build "HomeBase into a major regional home-improvement retailer in the western United States, a position similar to that held by BJ's Wholesale Club as the dominant membership warehouse club in the Northeast."

At the end of 1993 there were 82 HomeBase stores in 11 western states; 51 were in California. Sales volume (excluding the 24 stores closed or to be closed) came to $1.6 billion, and operating income was $42.7 million. A net loss was recorded, however, because of a $60.2-million post-tax reserve set aside for restructuring. The average HomeBase store occupied 101,000 square feet.

Waban's evaluation was that the division was falling short in providing service to the casual do-it-yourself customer. Company strategy, as approved in the November 1993 restructuring plan, called for an increase in customer service by hiring more salespeople, an aggressive marketing campaign, cost-cutting via centralization of merchandise replenishment and reduction of freight costs, and selective price increases. A satellite-television network was used to broadcast product-knowledge training sessions to all the stores. The restructuring plan also called for the closing of 16 HomeBase stores, mostly older units with undesirable buildings or unacceptable retail locations.

BJ's Wholesale Club, meanwhile, had 52 stores in 12 eastern seaboard states ranging from Maine to Florida at the end of 1993. It also had 2.6 million club members. The average store occupied 110,000 square feet. BJ's made plans to open about 15 new warehouse clubs each year during the mid-1990s, virtually all of them in the Northeast. Since BJ's appeal was based on low prices and high volume, it constantly sought to reduce its operating costs and pass savings along to its members. Sales volume in 1993 came to $2 billion, while operating income reached $45.2 million.

Supermarket-style conveyers and sophisticated scanning technology at BJ's checkouts resulted in significant cost reductions in 1992 and 1993. New products and services added in the early

1990s included fresh meat and bakery departments, optical centers, cellular-phone sales booths, lottery-ticket counters, an auto-buying service, a travel service, and novel departments like ''Pop'n Fudge,'' which offered fresh gourmet popcorn and homemade fudge. A BJ's credit card was introduced in late 1993.

BJ's recorded annual double-digit growth in total sales and operating profit during 1991–93. It was able to drive down costs during this period by flowing a greater percentage of its goods through its cross-docking facilities and centralizing many labor-intensive activities in those facilities. It paid manufacturers a lower price for freight because they were not shipping to each club individually. This process also allowed BJ's to maintain lower inventory levels, thereby enabling the clubs to operate more efficiently and reduce interest costs.

For the fiscal year ended January 29, 1994, Waban grew in sales volume by 6.9 percent, reaching nearly $3.6 billion. While the company recorded its first loss ($17.8 million), the drop was attributed to a restructuring charge of $60.2 million to reposition HomeBase; otherwise the company recorded a profit comparable to the previous year's $44.2 million. For the fiscal year ended January 28, 1995, sales volume rose slightly, to $3.65 billion, while net income increased significantly, to nearly $65 million. Waban's long-term debt was $259 million in October 1994.

Listed on the New York Stock Exchange, Waban common stock reached a high of $26.50 a share in 1992. At the end of 1994 it was trading at about $16 a share, but by the end of March 1995 it had risen to about $19 a share. As of that date no dividend had ever been paid out by Waban.

Principal Subsidiaries: HomeBase; BJ's Wholesale Club.

Further Reading:

Berkman, Leslie, ''HomeClub Chief a Man on the Go,'' *Los Angeles Times,* November 21, 1985, section IV, pp. 1, 17.

Biddle, Frederic, ''BJ's Chief Is Ousted by Parent Company,'' *Boston Globe,* May 26, 1993, pp. 1, 51.

——, ''Waban Inc. to Take $100M Charge in Unit's Restructuring,'' *Boston Globe,* November 17, 1993, p. 61.

Brumback, Nancy, ''Zayre Seeks Wholesale Club Sales,'' *Boston Globe,* March 18, 1984, p. A7.

Gilbert, Les, ''Halpin Targets National Status, Enters Midwest,'' *HFD,* July 8, 1991.

Laderman, Jeffrey, ''This Zayre Spinoff Could Spin Gold,'' *Business Week,* November 13, 1989, p. 128.

Mehegan, David, ''BJs Girds for Wholesale Attack,'' *Boston Globe,* October 24, 1989, p. 25.

Schmeltzer, John, ''Home Base Leaves; Home Depot Lands,'' *Chicago Tribune,* November 17, 1993, section III, p. 3.

Snyder, Sarah, ''Who's In, Who's Out,'' *Boston Globe,* July 1, 1987, p. 65.

—Robert Halasz

Wabash National Corp.

1000 Sagamore Parkway South
Lafayette, Indiana 47905
U.S.A.
(317) 448-1591
Fax: (317) 447-9405

Public Company
Incorporated: 1991
Employees: 3,400
Sales: $562 million
Stock Exchanges: New York
SICs: 3715 Truck Trailers; 3714 Motor Vehicle Parts & Accessories; 6159 Miscellaneous Business Credit Institutions; 5012 Distribution of Trailers for Trucks

Wabash National Corporation—one of the largest manufacturers of semi-trailers in the world—designs, manufactures, and markets standard and customized truck trailers, including dry freight vans, refrigerated trailers, and bimodal (road and rail) trailers, as well as parts and related equipment. The company also manufactures fiberglass-reinforced plastic and aluminum plate trailers, as well as RoadRailer, a patented type of trailer which can be quickly and inexpensively attached to a train car. Constant innovation to meet customer needs, worker training and motivation programs, flexible manufacturing schedules, and partnerships with leading transportation companies fueled Wabash's rise. In the early 1990s, the company's primary customers were truckload carriers, less-than-truckload carriers, leasing companies, private fleets, railroads, and package carriers. A subsidiary, Wabash National Finance Corp., provided leasing and financing to customers. In 1995, Wabash recorded more than $500 million in annual revenue and employed about 3,400 people. *Inc.* magazine named Wabash co-founder and Chief Executive Officer Donald J. (Jerry) Ehrlich its 1992 Entrepreneur of the Year. In 1993, *Forbes* included Wabash on its list of America's top 200 small companies. The next year, Wabash shipped more truck trailers than any other American manufacturer, according to *Southern Motor Cargo Magazine.*

Wabash was co-founded in April 1985 by Jerry Ehrlich, formerly the president of Monon Corp., an Indiana-based trailer manufacturer. Two years earlier, corporate raider Victor Posner had acquired Monon's parent company, Evans Products Co., and had proceeded to sell off its assets to pay debt. As Monon declined, Ehrlich repeatedly offered to buy the company but to no avail. Thus, Ehrlich and two fellow ex-Monon Corp. executives, Ronald J. Klimara and William M. Hoover, started their own company. They were soon joined by 14 other former Monon employees.

Ehrlich and his associates established their company in Lafayette, Indiana, about 30 miles south of Monon Corp. and approximately 65 miles northwest of Indianapolis. In need of manufacturing facilities, Wabash initially leased a 450,000 square-foot abandoned factory then used by local farmers to store corn. The executives' experience and contacts helped Wabash acquire its start-up capital: $2 million in equity from Washington D.C. investors Steven and Mitchell Rales, a $3 million industrial revenue bond, and a $5 million line of credit from a local bank. Wabash's first trailer was reportedly built on two sawhorses and was finished in August 1985. Its first customer was Sears, Roebuck & Co., a former customer of Monon, which ordered ten trailers from Wabash.

With Ehrlich as Wabash's president, and Hoover and Klimara as vice-presidents of sales and finance, respectively, Wabash began to grow rapidly. Its client list soon expanded to include Heartland Express Inc., Schneider National Inc., and Dart Transit Co. In 1986, the company generated sales of $70 million from more than 15,000 trailers. That year the company also purchased a more suitable factory in the same area for about $2.5 million. Ehrlich later noted that lower interest rates, down considerably from their levels in the late 1970s and early 1980s, helped the company buy more equipment.

Ehrlich attributed a great part of the company's early success to its focus on expanding product lines. In an interview for the Lafayette *Courier and Journal,* he cited Wabash's "ability to design specialized semitrailers for several industries," noting that this ability minimized risk by allowing the company to rely less on one industry and one segment of the economy.

Product innovation in response to industry needs, in fact, became a distinguishing factor at Wabash. Until the mid-1980s, trailer sides were commonly built of long, overlapping sheets of aluminum-covered plywood about 1.5 inches in thickness. Standard pallets, upon which shipping loads were placed, were 44 inches wide, and two pallets could thus travel side by side, lengthwise, on the 99 inch-wide trailer floor. However, under this system, a rip in the trailer side more than two feet long would threaten the trailer's structural soundness, and 11 inches of interior width space alongside the pallets was wasted. When trucking firm Dart Transit Co. called for a more efficient use of space and materials, Wabash responded with the aluminum plate trailer.

Wabash's design consisted of a series of side-by-side, four-foot-wide aluminum panels, joined to aluminum posts on the outside of the trailer. The walls were half an inch wide, making the interior of the trailer 101 inches wide, which allowed a company to load one pallet the long way and one the wide way, resulting in only one inch of wasted space. The walls were flexible, deflecting instead of bending if the truck were to hit a wall. And even if one panel did rip, it could be easily replaced. The new design thus reduced maintenance costs and also reduced water damage to freight. In fact, Rod Ehrlich, Jerry's brother and the company's head of engineering, later reported that water damage claims with the new design were one-fifteenth the number encountered by Wabash competitors. Wabash patented the design, and, as competitors were either unable or unwilling to invest in the design, Wabash captured 90 percent of the aluminum plate trailer market by 1992.

Another of Wabash's best-known products was RoadRailer, a trailer design for which Wabash acquired the rights to build and market in 1991. The RoadRailer trailer could be attached to the back of semis or locomotives and could thus ride across highways on trailer tires, as a typical semi-trailer would, or across railroad track via the trailer's air suspension system, which would lift its back and raise it onto a set of railroad wheels for attachment to other train cars. Moreover, RoadRailer could be transferred between railroads and highways wherever the two met, unlike other intermodal trailers, which required special equipment or loading facilities to make the transfer.

As customers began buying RoadRailer, Wabash introduced modified versions for new purposes, including a smaller RoadRailer, a refrigerated Roadrailer, and also the AutoRailer, a trailer that could fully enclose up to six autos for transport. With AutoRailer, an automaker or shipper could drive three vehicles onto a rack in the trailer, placing them end to end. When an electric system then raised the rack to the top level and locked it, three more cars could be driven in under the top level. With AutoRailer's air-ride suspension, autos did not have to be tied to racks, but could be locked into place with a nylon belt wrapped over one tire. The AutoRailer was then shut, and the cars were ready for shipment to dealers via railroad or highway. Since cars were not tied to racks and were totally enclosed from the factory until their final destination, damage to the vehicles was minimized. When the vehicles arrived at their final destination, moreover, dealers could simply drive the cars out of AutoRailer.

To meet customer needs, Wabash also developed many other unique trailers. One such trailer contained a deep well which could hold large sheets of glass. A retractable floor could cover the well, allowing conventional cargo to be transported on another leg of the trip. Another new model used a new "axleless" suspension system, based on technology used by Walt Disney Co. to haul laundry at Disney World. Each wheel was individually suspended, allowing the trailer floor to drop just above pavement level. A third trailer used smaller tires, lowering the trailer floor about ten inches for loading cargo. The trailer included a pneumatic lift to raise it ten inches so it could be loaded at conventional loading docks as well.

In addition to product innovation, Wabash's rapid growth was attributed to marketing strategy. Wabash decided early on that it would identify and target fast-growing firms within key sectors of the worldwide transportation economy; by seeking to understand what drove each company's productivity and then engineering products to improve this productivity, the company would bring in key customers.

To produce customized products, Wabash engaged a flexible, but cost-efficient manufacturing system, which included extensive use of computer systems. In fact, through the mid-1990s, almost all of the company's products were designed on computer systems, which could directly transfer design information to computers on the factory floor. The company's computer-controlled machine tools could then change the shape of parts with just 15 seconds of startup time, instead of the 30 minutes required to make the change manually. This allowed the company to create custom parts, while keeping costs low. It also let Wabash quickly make parts only when needed, avoiding storage and material costs created by extra inventory.

In order to generate still higher profit margins, Wabash also sought to work more closely with its customers. Commenting on the gains to be had from meeting customer needs, Ehrlich told *Inc.* in 1992 that he hoped to "get to the point where we're producing 100% proprietary products and we're the single source of supply in 100% of the cases." In order to achieve such high percentages, Wabash focused on being willing and able to design products to meet specific needs as well as on forging good customer relations, since customers had to be willing to share sensitive information about their business and allow Wabash to check its products on the road. Praising Wabash's efforts, Heartland Express President Russ Gerdin told *Inc.* in December 1992 that when he took his specific needs to other manufacturers, they often told him, " 'It can't be done.' Wabash says, 'Let's see what we can do'."

Some of Wabash's key "partners" during this time included Heartland, Federal Express, Swift Transportation, Triple Crown Services (a railroad/highway shipper owned by Conrail and Norfolk Southern) and Schneider National, one of the largest truckload carriers in the United States. In fact, Schneider National became Wabash's biggest customer, accounting for more than one-sixth of its sales from 1992 through 1994. Schneider allowed Wabash to monitor the performance of its trailers, and a top Schneider executive occasionally visited Wabash employees to stress how important they were to Schneider's success.

Schneider, along with other trucking companies and railroads, began moving toward intermodal shipping in the early 1990s. Intermodal shipping involved shipping products over railroads for part of the trip and over highways for the remainder of the trip. Railroads could haul goods long distances more cheaply than could trucking companies, who hauled them more quickly and more flexibly over short distances. With the RoadRailer trailer, Wabash had positioned itself well to benefit from the shift toward intermodal shipping.

Finally, Wabash considered its worker training programs as imperative to its success. Under the programs, a coordinator assigned to one of several workgroups taught new employees the handful of jobs in that area, such as installing trailer roofs. Workers were allowed to shift between workgroups every year, thus widening the scope of their experience. They also went through quality training, based on the principles of W. Edwards Deming.

Wabash offered its employees interest-free loans so that they could purchase computers with the same hardware and software the company used. Moreover, the company offered voluntary classes, on employees' time, about such subjects as finance, quality, problem solving, team building, and manufacturing. In the early 1990s, around nine of every ten employees attended such classes, and top students qualified for a thorough, two-year program taught by professors at Purdue University. By 1992, more than 100 employees had graduated from the program.

Employees who attended finance courses could better understand the financial figures that Ehrlich posted each month on the side of a trailer. Such numbers were important to workers, who shared ten percent of the company's pre-tax profits. Wabash also tied its matching of employees' 401(k) retirement plans to its pre-tax profits. As long as Wabash made money, it matched 30 percent of employee contributions. Wabash would then increase that number by one percent for every .25 percent increase in pre-tax profit above five percent on sales. Thus, if the company made a seven percent pre-tax return on sales, it would match 38 percent of employees' contributions. Employees met several times with a 401(k) consultant and could have their families join meetings. They could also sign up for a personal finance class taught by a local accountant. With its work force thus encouraged to learn about Wabash's 401(k) plan, its participation rate was much higher than the national average in the mid-1990s. The number of employees at Wabash grew steadily, rising to approximately 3,400 by 1995.

As Wabash's product line expanded, so did its manufacturing facilities, which were enlarged to include 12 buildings and 917,000 square feet. Wabash bought a second manufacturing facility in Lafayette in 1994, moving into a vacant General Foods building. In 1995, Wabash opened its new plant in Lafayette with 500,000 square feet of manufacturing space, tripling its capacity from just two years earlier. And Wabash would need the capacity, since its backlog of orders more than doubled in 1994, reaching $1 billion by the year's end.

Wabash also grew by licensing overseas companies to produce its products. In 1992, the company signed its first agreement to allow RoadRailer production outside the United States, covering Australia. By the end of 1994, Wabash had entered into licensing agreements with six firms in 19 countries, including China, India, and Taiwan. In return for the right to use RoadRailer technology, those companies agreed to pay Wabash royalties based on sales.

Wabash's sales and net profits grew quickly during its first decade. In 1990, the company had more than $170 million in sales and a pretax income of nearly $5 million. The company raised more than $39 million by offering stock to the public in November 1991. Wabash issued additional shares of stock to the public in 1993 and 1994 to raise money for its manufacturing operations and to create its subsidiary, Chicago-based Wabash National Finance Corp., formed to allow customers to finance the purchases of Wabash trailers. By 1994, its third year of operations, WNFC contributed eight percent of Wabash's earnings.

Principal Subsidiaries: Wabash National Finance Corp.

Further Reading:

Bonney, Joseph. "Santa Fe Tests AutoRailer Trailers," *American Shipper,* October 1994, p. 60.

Burke, Jack, "Wabash National's 'Mega-Wedge' the Main Attraction in Expo Equipment," *Traffic World,* April 18, 1994.

Harper, Doug, "RoadRailer Again Rises From Ashes," *Journal of Commerce,* December 9, 1993, p. 8A.

McKinney, Jeff, "Wabash National Banks on Experience," *Journal and Courier (Lafayette, Ind.),* May 10, 1987.

"Not Just Your Ordinary 401(k)," *Inc.,* November 1993, p. 128.

Shaffer, David J., "German Trailer Order a Giant Step Forward for Wabash National," *Indianapolis Star,* December 24, 1994, p. C6.

Smith, Bruce C., "Governor Lauds Industrial 'Triple Crown'," *Indianapolis Star,* July 29, 1994, p. D1.

Vantuono, William C., "RoadRailer Hits The Big Time," *Railway Age,* October 1994.

Welles, Edward O., "Least Likely to Succeed," *Inc.,* December 1992, pp. 74–86.

—Kurt Moeller

Walbro Corporation

6242 Garfield Street
Cass City, Michigan 48726-1397
U.S.A.
(517) 872-2131
Fax: (517) 872-2301

Public Company
Incorporated: 1950
Employees: 2,300
Sales: $325.20 million
Stock Exchanges: NASDAQ
SICs: 3592 Carburetors, Pistons, Rings & Valves; 3714 Motor Vehicle Parts & Accessories

Walbro Corporation, a manufacturer and designer of fuel systems for automotive and outdoor power equipment, is headquartered in Cass City, Michigan, with subsidiaries throughout the world. Initially a small engine carburetor manufacturer, Walbro now has a separate subsidiary which focuses on small engine fuel systems—Walbro Engine Management—and another subsidiary for automotive systems—Walbro Automotive. Walbro Engine Management is a world leader in small engine carburetors, especially diaphragm carburetors. Walbro Automotive is a leader in fuel efficient technology with an international profile and huge growth potential. Automotive products account for more than 60 percent of Walbro Corp.'s overall sales.

Walbro was founded by Walter E. Walpole in 1950 in Fenton, Michigan. Walpole left college in his freshman year and entered the business world as a messenger at a Chicago bank. He eventually worked his way up to become secretary treasurer of the carburetor division of the Borg-Warner Corp. Walpole's real goal, however, was to have his own company, and he created Walbro to fulfill this dream. Walpole hoped that his company would become the major supplier of carburetors for small power tools, lawnmowers, and outboard motors.

Walpole was betting that the postwar economic boom would mean more homes and leisure time, which would translate into a high demand for products requiring small engines. If these products were to become indispensable to the American way of life, Walbro would have a growing market for its specifically designed carburetors. Walpole was willing to cash out his pension and mortgage his own home, putting his family of five children in financial jeopardy, to finance his dream. The dream seemed a long way off during the early years of the company, when Walpole experienced frustration and mounting debts during the three years it took to make his first sale.

The first significant event that helped to reverse Walbro's poor fortunes came in 1954, when Walbro moved from Fenton to Cass City, Michigan. Cass City and Walpole had something to offer each other. The city needed new industry and Walbro needed space at a reasonable rate. The Cass City Industrial Development Corporation offered Walpole a 6,000-square-foot building and five acres of land for nominal rent. Not everyone in Cass City thought that Walbro represented a sensible gamble for the town. Walpole had to convince the city that his company could provide them with a future, even though Cass City's main banker assured them that Walpole and his company were all but bankrupt. Despite the gloomy appraisal of the local bank and the fact that the company was indeed in poor financial shape, Walpole managed to find local investors to the tune of $25,000. A $1,000 investment made in the company in 1954 was estimated to have a value of $150,000 by the late 1980s. Since many of the initial investors were still shareholders 30 years later, it would appear that some Cass City merchants hit the jackpot when they invited Walbro to move to their town.

In 1957 Walbro began designing fuel systems for automobiles. Eventually the automotive industry was to become a major growth area for Walbro, but small engines for power tools, lawnmowers, and outboard motors continued to be the most significant sector throughout the 1960s and 1970s. Most of Walbro's automotive products were designed as aftermarket products. It would be over 20 years before the company made significant inroads to the original products market in the automotive sector.

In 1972 Walbro became a public company. Walbro sold stock in order to raise money to finance joint ventures and expand outside of the U.S., as well as to develop new products especially for the automotive sector. Walbro developed a fuel injection system in the 1980s for what became the company's first major foray into the automotive original equipment market.

Walbro's sales in 1972 were approximately $10 million, with modest growth expected. After twenty years of building the company into one of the leading fuel system manufacturers for small engines, Walpole was taking his biggest gamble since mortgaging his home back in the early 1950s. He placed his bets on two things: that demand would grow for more ecologically sound emissions; and that Japan would emerge as the automotive giant of the next few decades. Walpole's gamble paid off in both respects. The company's Asian connections have expanded to include joint ventures in Korea, Singapore, and China. Research and development investments made during the 1970s also paid off as Walbro was poised to fill orders for fuel supply systems that would meet higher emissions standards. Nevertheless, Walpole's decision to finance these developments by taking the company public proved to have complications after his death.

Walpole, the company's founder and first president, had seen Walbro through the lean years into a period of global expansion and successful joint ventures during the 1970s. Walpole died in 1987, but his family continued to influence Walbro. Walpole's son-in-law Bert Althaver became president and CEO, while his sons Robert and Forrest became vice-presidents. In addition to the continuity of the family connection, Walbro continued to enjoy a close relationship with its home base of Cass City, Michigan. Perhaps because the company came so close to failing before Cass City made its offer, Walbro continued to think in terms of the good of the community, or its "stakeholders" rather than simply its shareholders. Forrest Walpole expressed his father's feelings about the company in an interview for *Inc.* in 1989: "We give people jobs that create some meaning in life, and we think serving the wider community is what business is all about." This relationship was tested in the early 1990s, when the company faced a hostile takeover attempt soon after the death of Walter Walpole.

Eight months after the founder's death, Althaver received a copy of a 13D schedule filed with the Securities and Exchange Commission which notified him that New York-based UIS had acquired over 6.8 percent of Walbro common stock. Accompanying the schedule 13D was a letter from UIS president Andrew Pietrini suggesting that he and Althaver meet to discuss mutual areas of interest. Althaver interpreted this letter as an attempt to buy the company out from under him.

Rather than taking time to consider the possible advantages of a buyout, Althaver phoned Pietrini the next day to tell him that Walbro was not interested. One week later, after persistent attempts by Pietrini to convince Althaver to cooperate, UIS made a formal tender offer to buy the company. By this time UIS owned 288,000 shares, or 8.6 percent, of Walbro stock. UIS advertized in the *Wall Street Journal* offering shareholders $27.25 each for their outstanding shares. UIS's strategy was to purchase 61 percent of the shares in order to control Walbro; however, Walbro management viewed this limited share purchase as a tactical error on the part of UIS. Had UIS offered all shareholders a chance to cash out, the offer may have met with more success. Instead, the UIS offer seemed to insure that one-third of existing shareholders would be left out of the deal, so it garnered little sympathy from shareholders. Walbro management took advantage of the situation to gain additional leverage with major shareholders, undermining UIS's claim that its offer was in the best interest of both companies.

Althaver knew that it was not going to be easy to fight off the UIS siege. He hired investment banking firm Goldman and Sachs and a New York law firm to help organize a strategic defense against the takeover. In the end, however, Althaver credited the local and family continuity for saving the company. Management and the board of directors owned 17 percent of the stock at the time of the takeover bid, so they had more breathing room than other boards who were faced with similar situations. In addition, another 10 to 15 percent of the shares were held by other members of the Cass City community, thanks to Walter Walpole's early agreement to sell a stake in Walbro to Cass City residents. In order to ward off UIS, Walbro drew up shareholder agreements which insured that approximately 30 percent of the shares would not be sold before the end of the year. John Haire, owner of the *Cass City Chronicle,* stated that there was "a unanimity of support" for Walbro, and the town's stockholders signed pledges not to sell.

Confident that there was a healthy base of stockholders who would not sell out, the board created more shares and looked for a large capital base that could keep these new shares in friendly hands. Goldman and Sachs helped to map out this most costly phase of the strategy. As Althaver told the story to *Ward's Auto World:* "We ended up with General Electric Credit Corp. We put together a deal in one week where they bought $35 million in preferred stock, convertible into what amounted to a million shares of common. . . . There was no agreement they had to vote in any given way. [But] that meant the company had shares in friendly hands that was very close to 50 percent. The importance of the GE [loans] was of course the million shares and the million votes it represented."

Although Walbro was able to ward off the hostile takeover from UIS, the cost was enormous. The fees to Goldman and Sachs alone were about $1 million. According to Goldman and Sachs, only five percent of companies survived takeover bids in anything like their pre-takeover shape. If General Electric Credit Corp. represented a white knight for Walbro, it was a white knight with a price tag. General Electric Credit Corp.'s role in the affair was very profitable both in terms of the dividends it received—essentially interest on what was in fact a loan—and in fees for structuring the deal, which totalled approximately $1.5 million. Although UIS was unsuccessful in its takeover bid, the enterprise was also profitable for them. With various lawsuits pending and threatened, the two companies came to an agreement that enabled Walbro to buy back the UIS shares at a considerable profit to UIS. UIS agreed to sell its 8.6 percent of Walbro stock, most of which it had purchased at around $22.15 per share, back to Walbro for $25.50.

When Althaver finally met the man who had cost him so much money there was little open hostility between the two parties. Pietrini for his part was unapologetic, contending that UIS's bid would have been advantageous to Walbro. As Pietrini described the takeover bid in *Forbes:* "They represented a fit for us. . . . [Walbro] management would have continued, and they would have had liquidity as well." However, Walbro's escape from UIS was greeted with glee by the Cass City faithful and by corporate watchers everywhere who held a soft spot for the perceived underdog.

Althaver himself was less gleeful than most after having saved the company. Before the fight with UIS Walbro had a long-term debt-to-equity ratio of two percent, but this ratio ballooned to 71 percent as a result of paying out $5 million in expenses and borrowing much more than that to buy back stock. Then Walbro laid off 75 workers in 1989, undermining the euphoria in the community. The debt load and the layoffs at Walbro, when contrasted with the profits gained by almost all other players in the takeover drama, made it difficult for Althaver to view the defeat of the UIS bid as a victory for Walbro.

Althaver feared that the huge debt would affect Walbro's research and development expenditures, which he considered the linchpin of the company's success and growth potential. He also was wary of the possibility of facing another hostile takeover in the future, asserting that no public company was safe as long as the board owned less than 51 percent of the shares. Putting all of these fears behind them, the board went ahead and sold yet more stock in the early 1990s to finance continued research and global expansion.

Walbro bounced back from the anxiety-filled years following the 1987 takeover bid with record sales and profits in the 1990s. The company was able to capitalize on tougher fuel emission standards by developing highly efficient fuel systems that decreased waste and small engine systems that used alternative fuels such as methanol. An electronics division was added to Walbro in 1993 and expanded in 1994, committing the company to electronic fuel injection technology.

The high-water mark for Walbro's success in the automotive sector was its fuel modules for the Chrysler Cirrus, *Motor Trend*'s "car of the year" for 1994. Success with Walbro systems on the Cirrus led Chrysler to make Walbro the supplier of fuel modules for its immensely popular minivan series—another coup for Walbro. The company developed other new products for the automotive sector in the 1990s as well, including plastic fuel tanks, which were lighter and produced lower hydrocarbon emissions than traditional models. Walbro built an entire plant for construction of plastic fuel tanks without any customers to by the new product. The new tanks were used by Ford in its 1994 minivans, thereby vindicating Walbro's faith in its new product by assuring several hundred thousand units of sales for at least three years.

While the automotive sector heated up domestically, Walbro also concentrated on the international prospects for its small engine products. For example, it entered into a joint venture in the 1970s with a Japanese carburetor manufacturer. The new company later became a wholly owned subsidiary with facilities in Singapore, Europe, and Mexico. Walbro was particularly aggressive in China, where production of two-wheeled vehicles escalated dramatically during the 1990s to surpass Japan as the world leader in 1993.

Walbro purchased 60 percent of Fujian Hualong Carburetor in China in 1994. Later Walbro purchased 40 percent of Korea Automotive Fuel Systems Ltd. No matter where the Asian market expanded, Walbro had a legitimate stake and could reasonably expect to reap the rewards of diligently forged international ties. Walbro did not neglect the European market, either. In 1995 Walbro purchased the Fuel Systems Division of Dyno Industrier AS of Oslo, Norway. Earlier Walbro had forged joint ventures with Italian and French firms.

When Walbro faced the hostile takeover threat from UIS in 1987, it was a much smaller company than it would become just eight years later. Althaver's efforts to keep Walbro independent would seem to have been justified given the exceptional growth and profitability of the company. Company founder Walter Walpole's foresight in developing the automotive sector, investing heavily in research and development, and forging international connections assured Walbro a lucrative future.

Principal Subsidiaries: Walbro Automotive; Walbro Engine Management; Walbro Korea Ltd.; Walbro Canada.

Further Reading:

Fitzgerald, Edmund, "Walbro Boss Beat Raid, Saved Company Town," *Automotive News,* September 12, 1988, p. 3J.

Jaffe, Thomas, "Cleaner Air Company (II)," *Forbes,* September 14, 1992, p. 562.

Lowell, John, and Michael Arnholt, "The Hostile Takeover," *Ward's Auto World,* July 1988, pp. 91–2.

Meeks, Fleming, "Invasion of the Company Snatchers," *Forbes,* December 12, 1988, pp. 106–8.

"Walbro Buys Dyno Fuel Tank Business," *Chemical Marketing Reporter,* January 9, 1995, p. 13.

Walbro History for Publication, Cass City, Mich.: Cass City Historical Society, February 20, 1995.

Welles, Edward O., "Under Siege," *Inc.,* July 1989, pp. 46–59.

—Donald C. McManus and
Hilary Gopnik

Wascana Energy Inc.

1777 Victoria Avenue
P.O. Box 1550
Regina, Saskatchewan S4P 3C4
Canada
(306) 781-8200
Fax: (306) 781-8364

Public Company
Incorporated: 1973 as Saskatchewan Oil and Gas Corporation
Employees: 650
Sales: C$437.6 million
Stock Exchanges: Montreal Toronto
SICs: 1311 Crude Petroleum & Natural Gas; 1381 Drilling Oil & Gas Wells

Wascana Energy Inc. is involved in the exploration, development, and marketing of crude oil and natural gas in northwestern Canada. Originally called the Saskatchewan Oil and Gas Corporation, it was created as part of an initiative to establish state-owned enterprises, which would take advantage of Saskatchewan's natural resources to diversify the province's predominantly agricultural economic base. A major petroleum concern in Saskatchewan, Wascana has also broadened its mission by expanding operations geographically to other provinces and abroad to South America, Africa, Asia, and Europe.

Saskatchewan became a Canadian province in 1905. As a remote plain region, its almost complete dependence on agriculture exposed the province to severe economic fluctuations. In the 1970s, the province made efforts to stabilize its economy by diversifying its agricultural base and developing an industrial and manufacturing sector. A new opportunity emerged in the growing world market for mineral resources such as potash, oil, and uranium. The region proved rich in minerals and the provincial government established a number of Crown Corporations to develop this natural resource base; among them was the Saskatchewan Oil and Gas Corporation.

Volatility in the world petroleum industry, subsequent price increases, and questions about the dependability of foreign oil supplies made the new company's formation timely. Foreign dominance of Canadian oil production became a government policy issue of major concern that would continue into the 1990s. Because of the agriculture's increasing reliance on mechanized, gasoline fueled equipment, an additional boon was seen for the Province of Saskatchewan in developing its own source of petroleum.

March 1975 marked the end of the first full year of operation for Saskatchewan Oil and Gas. All of the activities necessary to establish a major capital-intensive business were begun. The company grew from one to 22 employees, as senior management positions were filled, support staff hired, and permanent office space found. The company began land acquisition, geological appraisal, exploratory drilling, field production, and property acquisition, as well as the development of administrative and accounting systems. By fiscal year end, the corporation had spent C$2.8 million on 949,599 acres of land in Saskatchewan and C$0.8 million on 63,680 acres in neighboring Alberta. Management began a program to acquire reserves and spent C$8.6 million to purchase proven producing properties from outside operators.

The first crude sales began in May 1974. Sales reached as much as 1,590 barrels per day, and the average price per barrel was C$6.07 gross and C$3.21 net. By fiscal year end, a capacity of 2,240 barrels a day was achieved. Revenue for the first full fiscal year was C$356,631, with a net loss of C$236,577.

The corporation grew significantly over the next year. By 1976 fiscal year end, the company had doubled its exploratory acreage, drilled over three times the number of wells from the year before, tripled the funds spent on the acquisition of reserves, and increased oil production almost nine-fold. The number of employees grew from 22 to 44. Net income for the year was positive for the first time, with a total of C$360,201. Gross revenue was almost ten times that of the year before at C$3.4 million.

One major and five smaller acquisitions increased the company's reserves by nearly 22 million barrels during this time. The purchase of Atlantic Richfield Canada Limited's Saskatchewan interests for C$23.3 million provided the bulk of the expansion. Another C$1.3 million in smaller purchases accounted for a little more than a million barrels of the new reserves. Production averaged more than 2,500 barrels per day over the year and capacity more than quadrupled to 11,000 barrels per day by fiscal year end. To handle the increasing responsibilities, a formal production department with ten employees was established in July 1975. Also in 1975, Kywan Petroleum Ltd., a wholly owned subsidiary, was incorporated to perform oil and gas exploration and development outside of Saskatchewan.

In 1976 and 1977, the corporation continued to expand steadily. The number of wells drilled almost doubled and production more than tripled to 3.3 million barrels. Revenue more than tripled to C$14.3 million. Price per barrel increased to C$8.05, almost two dollars more than the previous year's price. Export restrictions, however, were reducing demand for the company's medium gravity crude and the corporation made a strategic decision to begin investing in heavy oil extraction. The province was rich in heavy oil, but these reserves were not as developed as lighter crude reserves because heavy oil was more difficult to produce and refine than medium and light crudes. Heavy oil was normally found in thin, unconsolidated sand formations and was extremely viscous, making development and refining more difficult than for lighter crudes. The corporation decided to explore new technologies that would make development of this resource viable.

The fourth full year of operation for Saskoil, as the corporation now referred to itself, was a significant one in terms of profitability and new investments. Net revenue income increased to C$5.7 million, almost 26 percent of gross revenues, compared to eight percent the year before. Saskoil attributed this success to unprecedented production volumes, which accounted for 60 percent of the revenue increase, and a C$1.57 increase in wellhead price per barrel. C$8 million in capital investments was financed through re-investment of cash flow from operations.

Saskoil was not alone in its success during this period. The late 1970s were boom years for the upstream industry. Increased revenues from OPEC crude oil price hikes engendered high profits that allowed greatly expanded exploration programs. The expansion was further fueled by fear of middle eastern dominance in the petroleum industry and a desire to garner as much control of the outstanding resources as possible. Heavy investment in capital-intensive projects set the scene for the problems that many in the industry faced as a result of declining oil prices and the global economic recession of the early 1980s.

In keeping with its strategy to invest in heavy oil extraction, Saskoil undertook a major experimental project with two other investors in June 1977. Saskoil, Texasgulf Inc., and Total Petroleum Ltd. each took a one-third working interest at a cost of C$1.4 million in the leasehold, wells, and steam-generating equipment of the pilot North Battlefield Heavy Oil Project. The project was formed to explore techniques to reduce the viscosity of heavy crude so that it could be extracted by conventional pumping techniques. Already in operation seasonally since 1974, the facility was slated for expansion by the new investors, making it operational year-round.

By 1979, Saskoil was the third largest owner of oil produced in Saskatchewan, drilled the second largest number of wells and largest number of exploratory wildcat wells. Saskoil, along with Gulf Canada Resources Inc. and Petro Canada Exploration Inc. as one-third investors, began an eight-year project to identify and develop heavy oil reserves in a largely unexplored area of west central Saskatchewan. The Province of Saskatchewan was also an investor in the C$100 million project. The investment was made as a hedge against the declining reserves of light and medium crude oil. The high costs associated with the production of heavy oil and technological research to reduce costs were justified as a necessary part of a forward-looking strategy to ensure crude supply in a volatile and foreign-dominated oil market.

In 1980, business was still booming. The company reported capital expenditures equal to 2.5 times cash flow. Investments had been doubling every one or two years as the company pursued its goal of becoming a major presence in the oil and gas industry in Saskatchewan. While production of light and medium crude declined due to reserve depletion, heavy oil production had increased 75 percent over the previous year. The Saskatchewan Heavy Oil Project was successfully on balance and continued to grow. Net revenues were up 20 percent over 1979. A formal research and development division was formed in anticipation of increasing importance of enhanced oil recovery technology.

In the early 1980s, recession, severe price restrictions, and higher taxes from Canada's National Energy Program (NEP) cut into the profitability of the North American petroleum industry. While foreign crude sold for $C41.30 per barrel in 1981, Saskatchewan crude was limited to C$21.30 per barrel by the NEP. Moreover, the federal Import Compensation Program made foreign crude cheaper than Canadian crude for Canadian refineries. Fifty percent of Saskatchewan production suitable for Canadian refineries was stopped in response to the NEP restrictions. In 1981, Saskoil had a loss in net income of C$6.2 million, down from C$5.7 million profit the year before. The bulk of the loss was due to the 12 percent Petroleum and Gas Revenue Tax. The tax cost Saskoil C$3.7 million in 1981, wiping out its C$2.9 million net earnings before the tax. The tax was estimated to have cost oil companies operating in Canada a collective C$2.5 billion a year from 1980 to 1985.

At C$2.9 million before the Petroleum and Gas Revenue Tax, Saskoil's earnings were still down by almost half from the previous year. Saskoil production fell 40 percent below expected levels and 20 percent below the production level of the year before. An additional problem for producers in Saskatchewan was the cut back in production by the Province of Alberta in reaction to the NEP measures. The high sulfur content of crude from Saskatchewan required blending with the sweeter crude from Alberta to be suitable for Canadian refineries. Lack of availability of Alberta crude reduced the volume of marketable Saskatchewan crude. There was much negotiation between producers, the provincial government, and federal government concerning the NEP. Hoping for a favorable outcome from negotiations, Saskoil decided to maintain its exploration pace. The North Battlefield Heavy Oil Project doubled. Saskoil also joined a group of companies planning to construct a heavy oil upgrading facility to make it suitable for refining.

In 1982, a change in provincial government created a "significant change in purpose and direction, characterized by a shift in focus away from its previous 'invest to grow' mandate to one emphasizing profit and return on investment," according to Saskoil's 1982 annual report. Prices declined as a result of a world oil glut, an economic recession, and declining demand. The company shifted emphasis from exploration to production and continued to focus on heavy oil. Production was up by 18 percent over 1981 and the company realized a modest profit of C$1.6 million. Relief from taxes through the May 1982 NEP Update and a government price supplement added C$4.9 million to cash flow, a million dollars less than the previous year's loss. Soft demand and declining prices put the Enhanced Oil Recovery and heavy oil upgrading projects under scrutiny as demand for secondary products in the future was unstable.

The following year, Saskoil had a record after-tax income of C$30.9 million. Demand for Saskoil's heavier crude was boosted by a major road repaving project in the United States requiring large amounts of asphalt. An amendment to the NEP, giving the world price to oil discovered after March 1974, applied to about 60 percent of Saskoil's production and further boosted revenues.

In late 1985, world oil prices decreased precipitously to under US$20 a barrel due to increased OPEC production. Most of the provisions of the Canadian NEP were dismantled in 1985 by the Progressive-Conservative government. OPEC countries had indicated that they would continue producing at that level until non-OPEC countries dropped their production levels to what OPEC considered a fair proportion of the world supply. An expected change in the royalty rates in Saskatchewan added to the uncertainty of the future outlook for the company.

In the same year, Saskoil made its first public offering and was privatized under the Oil and Gas Corporation Act of 1985. The initial public offering was considered a success and the C$110 million in shares were subscribed within several days. The Province of Saskatchewan retained a 7.35 percent stake in Saskoil.

In 1986, crude prices dropped significantly and continued to be volatile into the 1990s. Natural gas prices dropped as well. The deregulation of the United States petroleum industry and the Free Trade Agreement between the United States and Canada further increased competition. The downward pressure on prices and profitability was evident in the bankruptcies, cost-cutting, and mergers that characterized the industry. Saskoil began an expansion through acquisition that continued into the 1990s. In 1987, Saskoil bought all issued and outstanding shares of Thomson-Jenson Petroleum Limited and Thomson-Jenson Energy Limited from the Thomson Organization PLC for C$65.8 million. In 1988, the company began an international exploration program as larger reserve investment opportunities declined in western Canada. In 1989, Saskoil increased its medium gravity crude reserves by C$7.3 million and bought ICG Resources Ltd. for C$105 million to expand the percentage of its production operated by Saskoil. The company continued its commitment to heavy oil investment by acquiring heavy crude production properties in Northwest Saskatchewan from Gulf Canada Resources Limited for C$34 million in 1990 and Moose Jaw Asphalt Limited for C$10.9 million in 1991. Also in 1991, Saskoil acquired light crude oil assets in Southeast Saskatchewan from Esso Resources Canada Limited for C$75.8 million. In 1992, Saskoil acquired Broad Street Oil & Gas of Columbus, Ohio, to expand marketing opportunities in the Mid-west and California.

In 1993, Saskoil changed its name to Wascana Energy Inc. The change was intended to reflect the company's diversified business and growing role outside Saskatchewan. Wascana's activities by then had grown to include crude oil and natural gas exploration and development in Canada and abroad, a full range of crude and natural gas marketing activities, transportation and an interest in cogeneration. Since 1990, however, the company had been reporting a net loss in earnings.

A net gain of C$49 million was welcome news in 1994, especially after a net loss the previous year of C$34 million. C$37 million of the gain was due to the sale of non-core properties. Wascana's 1994 annual report was entitled "Back to the Basics" and detailed a renewed focus on "economically replacing reserves and efficiently producing and marketing crude oil and natural gas." Wascana sold Broad Street Oil & Gas, exited from the cogeneration project, reduced exploration in foreign countries to two principal areas, and consolidated the London office into Canadian operations. Dramatic improvement in profitability in 1994 and the introduction of significant measures to stabilize Wascana's performance put the company in a good position for the immediate future. Still, sustained competition, rationalization in the industry and the threat of takeover, even for a company of Wascana's size, continued to present significant challenges.

Principal Subsidiaries: Wascana Energy Marketing Inc.; Moose Jaw Asphalt Inc.

Further Reading:

Boras, Alan, "Huge Oil Find: Grad & Walker Field Contains 135 Million Barrels," *Calgary Herald,* February 14, 1995, p. 1.

"Free at Last," *The Economist,* April 6, 1985, p. 67.

Jeffrey, Tim, "Wascana Energy Announces Year End 1994 Results," *Business Wire,* February 20, 1995.

Yergin, Daniel, *The Prize,* New York: Simon & Schuster, 1992.

—Katherine Smethurst

Western Publishing Group, Inc.

444 Madison Avenue
New York, New York 10022
U.S.A.
(212) 688-4500
Fax: (212) 688-5025

Public Company
Incorporated: 1910 as Western Printing & Lithographing Co.
Employees: 5,000 (4,200 full-time)
Sales: $613.5 million
Stock Exchanges: NASDAQ
SICs: 2678 Stationery, Tablets and Related Products; 2731 Books: Publishing or Printing and Publishing; 2759 Commercial Printing

Western Publishing Group, Inc. is the holding company for Western Publishing Co., Inc., the largest creator, publisher, manufacturer, printer, and marketer of children's books in the United States. It is also engaged in printing and in producing and marketing stationery and paper goods. In 1994 it sold other extensive interests, including its games and puzzles businesses, direct-marketing activities, and some of the businesses in the advertising specialty division of its Penn Corp. subsidiary.

The company traces its beginnings to Edward Henry (E.H) Wadewitz and his brother Al. The two men bought a financially troubled Racine, Wisconsin business called West Side Printing Co. for $2,504 in 1907. Neither of them knew anything about the printing business prior to the acquisition, but they obviously had some canny business sense, for in 1908 they made a respectable profit on only $5,000 in sales. One of E.H.'s first actions was to obtain accurate figures for all operations and overhead in order to establish the true cost of filling an order. During its first full year the company moved to bigger quarters, hired several new employees, and installed a cylinder press, two smaller presses, and an automatic power cutter.

The business was incorporated in 1910 as the Western Printing & Lithographic Co. The name was a reflection of another acquisition—its first lithographic offset press. Roy A. Spencer, a journeyman printer recruited from a local newspaper, became president, with E.H. as secretary-treasurer. Sales topped $127,000 by 1914, when the company installed a larger offset press and added electrotyping and engraving departments. Two years later it acquired the assets of Hamming-Whitman Publishing Co., a Chicago publisher of children's books that had defaulted on its bills, and transformed it into a subsidiary named Whitman Publishing Co. Western introduced boxed games and jigsaw puzzles in 1923. With sales topping $1 million for the first time in 1925, it added another subsidiary, the Western Playing Card Co.

Sales passed $2.4 million in 1928, the year Western opened a small printing plant in Chicago and produced its ten-millionth children's book. The following year it purchased a Chicago-based producer and seller of engraved stationery and greeting cards. In 1932 the Whitman Big Little Book line made its debut with *Adventures of Dick Tracy.* The following year Western won exclusive book rights to all Walt Disney licensed characters. In 1934 Western established an eastern printing plant in Poughkeepsie, New York. The facility became a major preparation and production source for Dell's comic books and paperbacks over the course of its first year of operation.

Western began a fruitful collaboration with Simon and Schuster's juvenile book division in 1938 and soon evolved into the division's sole creative and production source. Executives of the two companies decided to issue 25-cent books for children called Little Golden Books, each with 42 pages, 16 of them in full color. Within five months of publication of the first run in 1942, three editions totaling 1.5 million books had sold out.

Big and Giant Golden Books were introduced in 1944, and Deluxe Golden Books in 1946. Golden Books became the first children's books to appear at supermarket checkout counters. By the mid-1950s Simon and Schuster had published more children's books than all other publishers combined.

Western added another major printing plant with the 1945 acquisition of the Wolff Printing Co. of St. Louis. Guild Press, Inc., a publisher of Catholic books, religious greeting cards, and gift wrap, was purchased in the early 1950s. A new specialty printing plant was built in Hannibal, Missouri, in 1955. Western reached sales of $63 million in 1957, the year it celebrated its 50th anniversary. In the same year the company acquired Kable Printing Co., a large rotogravure magazine printer.

Western and Pocket Books, Inc. formed a new company—Golden Press, Inc.—at the end of 1958 following their joint purchase of all Golden Book properties from Simon and Schuster. The arrangement called for Western to continue creating and manufacturing Golden Books and for Pocket Books to promote, sell, and distribute them. The companies quickly reaped the benefits of their arrangement. By 1959 over 150 Little Golden Book titles had sold at least a million copies, and over 400 of the more than 1,000 Golden Book titles were in print in 13 different languages. The 16-volume Golden Book Encyclopedia, introduced in 1960, enjoyed sales of 60 million in two years, while sales of Golden Press books reached almost $39 million in 1960.

Western offered common stock to the public for the first time in 1960, when the name Western Publishing Co. was adopted. Almost 80 percent of the common stock remained in management and employee hands, however. By this time Western had established itself as a giant in the publishing industry. It was the largest creator, producer, and publisher of juvenile books in the United States, the largest producer and distributor of children's games made from paper and paper products, and the largest creator and producer of comic books. It had operated profitably in every year since 1907 and had paid dividends every year since 1934. Net sales rose from $40.5 million in 1950 to $123.8 million in 1960, while net income rose from $3.1 million to $7.4 million in the same period.

The following year Western opened another printing plant, in Cambridge, Maryland. It also acquired several companies, including Odyssey Press, a publisher of high school and college textbooks, in 1970.

Western earned 65 percent of its total revenues in 1963 from juvenile literature (including games), 25 percent from commercial printing, and 10 percent from books for other publishers and miscellaneous activities. Whitman alone accounted for 35 percent of the company's revenues. By contrast, the company's half-share in Golden Press, Inc. had become a burden. Golden Press lost money in 1961 and 1962, and in 1963 its sales plummeted to $22.5 million from $32.9 million the previous year. In 1964 Western bought the other half-share from Pocket Books for 276,750 shares of its common stock, a purchase valued at nearly $7.4 million. Odyssey was given the job of selling and distributing adult Golden Books, while Western took over the task of handling the children's titles.

Western Printing & Lithographing was the largest company unit in 1965, accounting for about 40 percent of sales. Another of the 14 active subsidiaries—Artists & Writers Press, Inc.—created books for publishers and commercial customers. These included not only the Golden Books, but also Betty Crocker cookbooks and the Arts of Mankind series for Golden Press and a four-volume Harper Encyclopedia of Science for Harper & Row. Other subsidiaries carved out strong positions as well. Capitol Publishing, purchased in 1961, was an originator and producer of educational materials and games for children, including toys and novelty products. The Kable Printing division produced more than 125,000 monthly magazines and other periodicals and a substantial volume of catalogues. The Watkins-Strathmore Co., acquired in 1957, also produced children's books and games, including "Magic Slate." Whitman, meanwhile, published almost every type of juvenile and adolescent books, numismatic books and coin cards, and a wide variety of games, playing cards, crayons, and gift wrapping. Other Western businesses included a Canadian subsidiary (established in 1959) and a French company (established in 1960).

Golden Press was one of 18 book publishers charged by the Justice Department in 1967 with illegally fixing prices of library editions of children's books. Each agreed to the terms of a consent judgment that forbade them from submitting rigged bids or conspiring with book wholesalers to fix prices for sales to schools, libraries, and government agencies.

Western departed from ink-on-paper acquisitions for the first time in 1968 when it purchased Skil-Craft Playthings, Inc., for 100,000 shares of common stock. The Chicago-based company was a leader in craft kits and a manufacturer of laboratory science sets for children.

In 1970 Western's sales were up for the seventh straight year, to $171.5 million, but its net income of $3.9 million was below levels posted during the previous decade. This was attributed to one-time factors such as acquisition of a computerized typesetting facility and an 11-week strike. Still, the company took several measures to boost its income. A strict cost-control program was adopted, and the Hannibal plant was closed. By mid-1974 employment had been reduced by 1,500. Net income that year was $10.1 million on sales of $215.6 million. Consumer products accounted for 62 percent of Western's sales and 91 percent of pretax profits.

In 1971 Western reached an agreement with the Children's Television Workshop to collaborate on a number of products, including Golden Books featuring Jim Henson's Sesame Street Muppets. Big Little Books were a hit after their 1973 reintroduction. Dell Publishing Co. agreed in 1974 to a 10-year printing contract with Western estimated in excess of $50 million, and in the same year construction was begun in Fayetteville, North Carolina, on a new Western consumer products distribution and game-and-puzzle assembly center.

In 1976 Gerald J. Slade, chairman and president of Western, attributed some of the company's financial gains to its strategy, initiated in 1971, of emphasizing direct-mail selling in place of traditional distribution channels like department and discount stores and supermarkets. By 1976 direct marketing accounted for about one-fourth of Western's consumer product sales, which accounted for 70 percent of the company's total sales. A hot direct-mail item was the Betty Crocker Recipe Card Program, through which millions of customers were sent monthly packets of recipes. Net income of $10.8 million in 1976 on $237.3 million of sales was a company record.

Western's history as an independent company came to an end in 1979 when it was acquired by the toy and entertainment company Mattel, Inc. for $120.8 million in cash and stock. The new administration stressed market research and new product development in consumer products and involved Western's creative staff in commercial printing. In 1980 Western launched the Sesame Street Book Club and relocated Skil-Craft's manufacturing plant from Chicago to Fayetteville. Sales reached a record $277.9 million in 1981.

Mattel's investment soon turned sour in the eyes of company management. In fiscal 1983 (ending January 31, 1983) Western registered sales of $246 million. But the company posted an operating loss of $2.4 million after a $7.5 million charge relating to the closing of its Poughkeepsie printing plant. Suffering from its own financial problems and strapped for cash, Mattel sold Western in December 1983 to Richard A. Bernstein, a New York City real estate investor, for $75 million as well as the assumption of certain liabilities later reckoned at $40 million. Bernstein reincorporated the firm as the Western Publishing Group, with headquarters in his Newsweek Building on Manhattan's Madison Avenue. Western Publishing Co., now a subsidiary, continued to be based in Racine.

A self-made multimillionaire, Bernstein made his first fortune by purchasing commercial real estate during New York City's fiscal crisis of the mid-1970s, an experience that convinced him "the herd is always wrong." After purchasing Western, he made a number of changes. To cut printing costs, he invested in more efficient machines that reduced waste. The savings were used to moderate price increases in the Golden Books series and thus raise its market share. Videocassettes featuring Golden Book characters were introduced, and by the end of 1985 2.5 million copies of the original series of eight had been shipped. Western began developing games and producing them under license for companies like Hasbro and Tonka. The company also moved into what Bernstein called ''sponsored publishing''—developing storybooks inscribed with company logos as promotional items. In 1986 it bought Penn Corp., a producer of paper party goods and advertising specialties, for $108 million.

When Bernstein took Western public in April 1986, he made more than $70 million on his original investment of $5 million while still retaining 21 percent of the stock. The company continued to do well; for the fiscal year ending January 31, 1989, earnings were nearly $30 million on sales of $551 million. The following year, however, sales dropped to $508 million and earnings were down to $23 million. Analysts noted that sales of Pictionary, a popular Western board game introduced in 1987, fell from $118 million to $42 million. In fiscal 1991 (ending January 31, 1991) earnings were down to $8 million on sales of $491 million. By late 1991 a share of Western stock, which had once traded as high as $28, was down to $9.

Western celebrated the 50th anniversary of the introduction of Little Golden Books in 1992. A boxed set of the 12 original titles was offered for $19.95. Special volumes of all-time favorites and new books by the nation's most popular artists and illustrators of children's books were produced to mark the occasion. A new Golden Little Nugget Book line sold more than 1.9 million units in six months. The following year Golden management decided to sell a line of trade books for children for the first time. These titles were published under the imprint Artists and Writers Guild Books.

Western enjoyed a recovery in fiscal 1992 and 1993, with net income of $13.7 million and $17.5 million, respectively, on net sales of $552.4 million and $649.1 million, respectively. In 1993, however, company fortunes took a disastrous turn. A $21.8-million writedown was taken on the advertising specialty division, which Western had decided to dismantle. The company also spent $10 million to test a concept whereby Western would run bookstores inside Toys ''R'' Us stores, but the merchandiser ultimately decided it could sell books without Western's help. Another $20 million was added to costs because of Bernstein's efforts to expand Western products into discount stores, supermarkets, and drugstore chains as well as toy and book stores. The direct-marketing division also lost money in its effort, begun in 1990, to market a school book club. For fiscal 1994 (ending January 29, 1994) the company lost $55.8 million on net income of $613.5 million.

Western's big loss raised its debt to $250 million. Because of negative cash flow, its bonds were downgraded to junk grade. Bernstein, unable to sell the company, embarked on a major restructuring effort. In April 1994 he sold its games-and-puzzles business to Hasbro Inc. for $105 million. The Fayetteville distribution and manufacturing facility, whose operations were geared to games and puzzles, was also put on the block. The school book club division was sold to Troll for $4.3 million. Western also sold the Ritepoint and Adtrend businesses of Penn Corp.'s advertising specialty division and agreed to sell its direct-marketing continuity-club business. The company staff was reduced by roughly 28 percent. Bernstein said, however, that the company would continue to develop book sections within stores. It announced the introduction of 100 Just For Kids sections in Wal-Mart stores. These sections would feature video and music as well as books.

During the first three quarters of 1994, Western lost $11.6 million on revenues of $303.9 million. Its common stock, traded as high as $21 a share in 1993, was below $10 in April 1995. No dividend had been paid since Bernstein acquired the company from Mattel in 1984. In April 1994 Bernstein owned or controlled nearly 20 percent of the common stock. The Gabelli Group held about 17 percent, while Prudential Insurance Co. of America owned 8.6 percent. Long-term debt was $249.8 million.

At the end of 1994 Western Publishing Co. continued to create, publish, manufacture, print, and market children's books under such imprints as Golden Books and Little Golden Books. It also produced a variety of activity books and products including coloring books, paper-doll books, pop-up books, crayons, and boxed activity products. Prerecorded video and audio cassettes for children were being produced for children under the Golden Book Videos and Golden Music trademarks. Coin-collecting products and other special-interest products were produced and marketed under the company's Whitman trademark, and adult nonfiction books were sold under the Golden Guides trademark. Western also was involved in selling arts-and-crafts products under three trademarks and prerecorded audio cassette tapes packaged with books under its Book 'n' Tape trademark. The Penn Corp. subsidiary continued to design and produce quality decorated paper tableware, party accessories, invitations, giftwrap products, stationery, and giftware under the Beach and Contempo trademarks and the Renner Davis name. Three Golden Book Showcase stores—Schaumberg, Illinois; Burbank, California; and Rockefeller Center in New York City—were opened as well in the early 1990s.

Principal Subsidiaries: Penn Corp.; Western Publishing Co., Inc.; Western Publishing (Canada) Inc.

Further Reading:

''Betty Crocker to Little Lulu—They Help Western Publishing Grow,'' *Barron's,* July 8, 1974, pp. 22, 31.

Brown, Anthony D., ''Western Publishing Co.,'' *Investment Dealers' Digest,* September 13, 1965, pp. 40–42.

Chakravarty, Subrata N., ''The Herd Is Always Wrong,'' *Forbes,* October 3, 1988, pp. 143, 146–147.

Goddard, Connie, ''Fifty Years of Books 'For the Masses,' '' *Publishers Weekly,* June 22, 1992, pp. 28–30.

''Mattel Inc. Sets Plan to Acquire Publishing Firm,'' *Wall Street Journal,* January 10, 1979, p. 2.

Samuels, Gary, ''Sorry About That, Folks,'' *Forbes,* August 29, 1994, pp. 53, 56.

''The Westerner: Commemorative Issue,'' Racine, Wisconsin: Western Publishing Co., 1982.

—Robert Halasz

White Consolidated Industries Inc.

11760 Berea Road
Cleveland, Ohio 44111
U.S.A.
(216) 252-3300
Fax: (216) 252-3311

Division of Electrolux Group
Incorporated: 1876 as White Sewing Machine Company
Employees: 26,704
Sales: $4.75 billion
SICs: 5064 Electrical Appliances Television & Radio

White Consolidated Industries Inc. (WCI), part of the Electrolux Group since 1986, manufactures and markets a wide variety of appliances for Electrolux's North American operations. Perhaps most recognized in the United States among WCI's holdings are the brand names of Viking and White sewing machines, Eureka vacuum cleaners, appliances under the Philco, White-Westinghouse, and Tappan names, and Poulan/Weed Eater chainsaws and trimmers.

The man whose name the company bears, Thomas H. White, was 22 years old when he invented a single-thread sewing machine small enough to fit in the palm of a hand. In 1858, with a patent and a partner, White began making "The New England Sewing Machine," which sold for $10. By 1866, sales were hot enough to prompt White to move from his native Massachusetts to Cleveland, Ohio, to be closer to his suppliers and markets. The White Mfg. Co. changed its name to the White Sewing Machine Company when it became incorporated in 1876.

While the founder's love was truly sewing machines, and he pursued many related innovations, his sons became interested in other types of machinery, such as steam-powered automobiles. The early days of the 20th century were explosive with growth for the company. Indeed, White diversified as early as 1903—making roller skates, automatic lathes, kerosene lamps, and even cars. When White's sons couldn't convince their father that the steam automobile was worth keeping in production, Windsor and Walter White spun that product division off from White, forming the White Motor Corporation in 1906. The White Sewing Machine Co. then turned its attention back to its original product.

Meanwhile, White's sewing machine innovations piled up, including the progenitor to the portable sewing machine, the first furniture-style sewing machine cabinets, the first full rotary mechanism, and, in the 1920s, an electric motor. Naturally, all of these advances made the company's sewing machines even more popular, so in 1923, White Sewing stopped manufacturing its other product lines and focused on sewing machines and accessories. The next year, it signed a contract with Sears, Roebuck & Co to supply them with private-label machines: over the next 12 years, White supplied Sears with about 20 percent of their sewing machine output. By 1926, White had acquired Theodore Kundtz Furniture Factory, which made White's sewing furniture; King Sewing Machine Co.; and, from Sears, the Domestic Sewing Machine Co. Eventually a subsidiary, which became known as Standard Sewing Equipment Corporation, was formed.

With the Great Depression came renewed interest in home sewing. White continued to innovate, introducing the first sewing machine outside of its traditional black models, which was made of a magnesium alloy and was also much lighter than its forebears. This product did well enough to warrant the formation of a second subsidiary in 1939, White Sewing Machine Products Limited, in Canada.

During World War II, like many U.S. companies, White turned over its manufacturing for the purpose of producing goods to aid the war effort. Production was high enough to necessitate a move to a bigger plant in 1949. A new administration building was completed in 1951.

The world was a changed place by then, as a strong demand for consumer goods ensued. While White had improved its production methods significantly, and 2,000 machines were rolling forth a day, imported machines from Germany, Italy, and Japan, had begun to swamp the U.S. market, and it was becoming impossible to compete with their prices. In fact, White spent on materials alone what a finished, imported sewing machine cost in the United States. Even though the company had a hearty $20 million in sales in 1954, it reported a $440,667 net loss and had been on an earning slide for the past six years. In such a changing industry, and world, White could no longer afford to remain a one-product company. When Sears, which represented 40 percent of White's business in the early 1950s, gave its manufacturing contract to the Japanese, the company fully realized the need to diversify.

Enter Edward Reddig, an accountant who, upon becoming White's president in 1955, led the charge with a single-mindedness that bordered on ruthless, according to many. Reddig quickly arranged to have White's machines manufactured overseas, to company specifications, and began slashing costs back home, a program that included firing one-third of White's work force.

Reddig also launched an intensive acquisition campaign. The plan was diversity and the targets were largely appliance concerns. White merged with or acquired roughly 14 companies in 1960 alone. By 1964, the parent company had changed its name to White Consolidated Industries, or WCI, a reflection of its rainbow of acquisitions, which included: the Kelvinator Appliance Division, from American Motors; Gibson, which was then

Westinghouse's appliance division; and Franklin Appliance Division of Studebaker.

Reddig's recipe was to target companies that were sickly, but not terminal; pay bargain-basement prices for them; and then slash overhead, excess product lines, and employees until they were lean and profitable. One of his targets, Franklin, for example, had lost money in 1964 and 1965, and then had turned a pale profit in 1966; this record was typical of the kind of purchase Reddig sought. As an example of his tenacity in reducing costs, 70 percent of Kelvinator's administrative staff was terminated in the first month after takeover. Among newly acquired companies, research and development was often halted and computer operations were often junked. Reddig attributed his style to his tenure at Arthur Anderson & Co. in Chicago, during the 1930s, where he was assigned to enter big companies and crack the books. In 1967, WCI acquired Hupp Corporation, a maker of electric appliances, air conditioners and rangers.

By the decade's end, WCI had a comprehensive line of tools, valves, household appliances, and machinery. And its sewing machine operations, being handled overseas, were still regarded as the most innovative in the business. White sewing machines introduced the first overlock system designed for a home sewing machine, the first numbered tension dials, and a recessed cutting system. By 1968, WCI's sales were $830 million; stunning when compared with the $29 million reported in 1963, or even the $172 million from the year before.

By 1968, WCI was operating from four basic divisions: machinery and equipment; valves, controls and instrumentation; sewing and knitting machinery; and industrial supplies. The machinery and equipment group accounted for about 55 percent of WCI's sales in 1967, valves contributed roughly 20 percent of sales, and about 14 percent of sales came from the sewing division.

In early 1970, WCI was approached by its offspring, White Motor Corporation, which proposed a merger. However, the Justice Department soon forced the two to separate, ruling that the resulting company would have had a monopoly, particularly in light of the fact that WCI then owned 30 percent of Allis-Chalmers Mfg. Co. Allis was a competitor with White Motor in several arenas, and had a few years earlier moved for an antitrust injunction to stop WCI from acquiring further stock. The ultimate scraping of that venture cost WCI dearly; it lost $63 million when it divested White Motor Corp.

Another milestone came in 1975, with the purchase of Westinghouse's major appliance business. This division was in the red at the time and pulling on Westinghouse's capital. Despite the fact that the appliance industry was in a slump at this time, Reddig accepting the $700 million acquisition price, since the division would double WCI's appliance business overnight, and add 60 percent to WCI's overall volume. The purchase meant taking more of a punch than was WCI's habit, as the company usually planned one year per company for turnaround. While Kelvinator was coaxed from a $47 million loss in 1947 to breaking even at the end of the next year, Westinghouse would require more work. As more than 60 percent of its business at the time was in manufacturing private label appliances for Sears, Montgomery Ward, and J.C. Penney, among others, WCI welcomed the opportunity to purchase a brand that would help it compete with appliance giants General Electric and Whirlpool.

During this time, White Motor was doing so poorly the Justice Department reversed its opposition to the WCI merger in 1976, arguing that White Motor would fail without it. Then, in a stunning blow, the directors of WCI voted the merger down. After the White Motor merger was voted down in his absence—the board claimed it was unhappy with the proposed financing—Reddig retired from WCI. By 1976, WCI had doubled its sales and earnings within four years, passing the billion dollar mark. Reddig had transformed WCI from a $20 million sewing machine company into a $1.2 billion presence.

Succeeding Reddig was a three-man team, which initially carried on some of Reddig's plans, such as the 1977 acquisition of Sundstrand Corporation's machine-tool business, which had been losing money. Nevertheless, a parting of philosophies was evident in that, besides being no longer a one-man operation, the new team believed in the value of marketing. Part of its plan for turning the new Westinghouse appliance business around was to spend heavily on advertising.

At that point, WCI ranked third in appliances, behind General Electric and Whirlpool, who priced aggressively. Unlike Reddig, the new management at WCI was willing to sell more actively and loosen the reigns on cost in order to compete. Although an engineering staff was established, and WCI stepped up its advertising budget, the company managed to avoid spending as much on ads as its competitors did, since it sold about half its appliances as private-label brands through the mass merchandisers. By the late 1970s, WCI was a big-league manufacturer of major home appliances, but still not a household word. Then, in 1979, WCI purchased General Motor's Frigidaire division for about $120 million; the company's appliance business then boomed, and meant it was closing in on the competition.

WCI bought the American Tool Company in 1980. Between 1975 and 1985, its sales jumped from $1.2 billion to more than $2 billion. In fact, by 1983, WCI was the nation's third largest manufacturer of refrigerators, stoves, and air conditioners. The company's 84 plants were scattered across the continent, each run with basic autonomy. However, while appliances were profitable, sales weren't exploding and machine tools weren't doing well, so WCI's management trio began hunting for a new business to add to the family. In 1983, the company sold its Sarco subsidiary, a textile machinery division, and closed its steel industry equipment unit.

The company focused on three divisions in 1985: home products, which contributed about 76 percent of sales; machine and metal-basting divisions, providing 12.1 percent of sales; and the general industrial and construction equipment division pitching in the rest. The home products division was an umbrella for the widely known Kelvinator, Gibson, Hamilton, Frigidaire, Bendiz, Philco and White-Westinghouse brands. That year, WCI decided to combine the divisions' four major brands into a single operating unit, to be run out of Columbus, Ohio. Prompting this radical move was the fact that the market had suffered decreasing profits and increasing competition for the previous six months, and WCI was pressed to cut costs. Thus, one effective cost-cutter would be to improve the efficiency of its manufacturing.

While tackling this massive change, another dramatic change occurred. AB Electrolux of Sweden, the largest manufacturer of appliances in Europe, needed to widen its place in the U.S. market. WCI seemed the perfect ambassador. Electrolux approached WCI in 1986, with what was then a very fair offer. After some minor disagreement, the merger took place. Electrolux at that time had sales of $4.6 billion, and its only other holding in the United States was Tappan, a maker of ranges and microwaves, acquired in 1979.

After the takeover, WCI was subjected to a bit of its own medicine, as the company was trimmed and unified, and made more efficient. Underutilized plants were boarded up and product lines were enhanced, in a shift from the no-frills philosophy instilled by Reddig. Electrolux had become the world's largest maker of major appliances, with $9 billion in sales by 1987. Having been cash-strapped just before the transaction, WCI benefited from the financial resources of its new parent.

WCI was soon able to acquire Design & Manufacturing's (D&M) dishwasher business, begin building a new highly modern refrigerator plant, and hire a new head for its marketing sector. It also worked on reducing its distribution costs, a real killer in the industry. The sizable D&M deal alone gave WCI a quarter of the country's dishwasher business, making it second only to General Electric. WCI was fortunate to have such a wealthy parent at a time when so many costly changes were needed; working on brand-name recognition alone cost a fortune. WCI had long staked its fortunes on look-alike models for private labels, which kept costs down; to suddenly invert this strategy and develop distinct products readily recognized and popular with the public was a big change. In the early and mid-1990s, home appliances and products continued to WCI's largest sector. Although little information on WCI was made available after the Electrolux acquisition, judging by Eletrolux's continued growth and health, White was surely thriving as well.

Principal Subsidiaries: Frigidaire Company; The Eureka Company; Schrock Cabinet Company; American Yard Products; Poulan/Weed Eater; Americold; Baring Industries; Beam Industries; Challenge Industries, Inc.; Dimas; Dito Dean Food Prep; Dometic Corporation; Euroclean; Husqvarna Forest & Garden Company; The Kent Company; Partner Industrial Products; Richards-Wilcox; VWS; Wascator Manufacturing; Washex Machinery Company.

Further Reading:

Donnelley, Richard, "White Consolidated Buys Firms to Make Them Pay," *Barron's,* December 20, 1963, pp. 22, 25.

DuPont, Ted, "Fueled by its Swedish Parent, America's #3 Appliance Maker is Coming on Strong," *HFD,* December 14, 1987, pp. 1, 96, 97, 103.

Fountain, Ronald, "From Dance to Deal: The White Consolidated Takeover," *Planning Review,* May/June, 1988, pp. 8–15.

Groseclose, Everett, "The Road to the Top: Ed Reddig is Abrasive, Profane and Ruthless, But He Gets Results," *The Wall Street Journal,* October 12, 1971, pp. 1, 27.

"Growing Big by Playing It Tough," *Business Week,* August 3, 1968, pp. 106–108.

Malester, Jeff, "WCI Melds 4 Brands' Offices," *HFD,* July 1, 1985, pp. 1, 95, 96.

Nossiter, Daniel, "Wizard White," *Barron's,* March 21, 1983, pp. 20, 24.

"One Man's Poison," *Forbes,* January 15, 1975, pp. 30, 31.

"Rebuilding with Imported Wares," *Business Week,* May 23, 1959, pp. 50–55.

"The Difference at White Consolidated," *Business Week,* September 26, 1977, pp. 135, 138.

"White Consolidated Meets White Motor," *Business Week,* April 26, 1976, pp. 96, 97.

"White Consolidated's New Appliance Punch," *Business Week,* May 7, 1979, pp. 94–98.

"White Motor Merger is Put off by Court: Antitrust Suit Filed," *The Wall Street Journal,* January 28, 1971, p. 12.

Winter, Ralph, "White Motor's Purchase Killed by Consolidated," *The Wall Street Journal,* May 4, 1976, p. 4.

—Carol I. Keeley

WOODWARD®

Woodward Governor Co.

5001 North Second Street
P.O. Box 7001
Rockford, Illinois 61125-7001
U.S.A.
(815) 877-7441
Fax: (815) 877-0001

Public Company
Incorporated: 1902
Employees: 3439
Sales: $374 million
Stock Exchanges: NASDAQ
SICs: 3511 Turbines & Turbine Generator Sets; 3519 Internal Combustion Engines, Not Elsewhere Classified; 3625 Relays & Industrial Controls; 3714 Motor Vehicle Parts & Accessories

Woodward Governor Co. is the world's oldest and largest manufacturer of controls for prime movers, which are machines that convert either heat or hydraulic energy into mechanical or electrical energy. The company designs and manufactures controls for all types and sizes of steam and diesel engines, hydraulic turbines, aircraft propellers, and industrial and aircraft gas turbines. Woodward Governor is also distinguished by a unique and proven management philosophy.

The company that would become Woodward Governor was founded in 1870 by Amos W. Woodward. Woodward was descended from the Woodward family that helped to settle Watertown, Massachusetts, in the 1630s. Born in 1829 in Winthrop, Maine, Woodward attended Kents Hill Academy for only one term. In that short time, however, he mastered higher mathematics and physics and was considered by many to be a genius. Woodward eventually went to work in a factory in Massachusetts before migrating to the Midwest in 1856. An inveterate tinkerer and inventor, Woodward managed to earn a modest salary by selling his innovations. He also held various mechanic jobs. It was through one of those positions, in fact, that he became intrigued with a major dilemma of the day: how to control the speed at which waterwheels turned.

Woodward solved the problem by designing a mechanism—the mechanical noncompensating waterwheel governor—in 1869. He received a patent for the device in 1870 and started a company to manufacture the governors. Despite the usefulness of Woodward's invention, the new company struggled. Besides lacking capital, Woodward also lacked the desire to build a profitable business. Like many other inventors, he was more interested in developing new ideas. Fortunately, his son Elmer Woodward had a greater knack for business. Elmer had started working in his father's shop as a boy and had, like his father, shown himself to be gifted in math and physics. On one occasion, for example, Elmer devised a contraption that automatically controlled the cutting speed and feeder of a machine that he was operating. Elmer was caught reading a book while the machine worked away.

Elmer Woodward's desire for learning stemmed from what he considered a poor formal education. To make up for the deficiency, he spent years studying technical books after dinner until midnight. As he got older, he became increasingly involved in the company's business affairs. It was then that the enterprise began to prosper. In 1891, the business had three employees and was selling about $8,000 worth of governors annually. During the 1890s, though, the company grew and even expanded into a larger manufacturing facility. At the same time that he was helping to run the business, Elmer Woodward, like his father, continued to invent. Importantly, in 1898, when he was 36 years old, Elmer received a patent for a governor that was an improvement over the one his father had designed. The breakthrough device gave the company an important advantage in the burgeoning market for governors needed to control new hydro power electric generators.

In 1902 Amos and Elmer Woodward incorporated as Woodward Governor Company. By that time they were employing 25 men at their Rockford, Illinois, manufacturing facility. As the hydro electric power market surged during the 1910s and 1920s, so did Woodward Governor's sales. The company also expanded overseas into Europe, Japan, New Zealand, and elsewhere throughout the world. Indeed, by the 1920s the company was making more than 35 percent of its sales to foreign buyers. In 1910 Woodward Governor moved its operations to a new five-story plant. Elmer Woodward continued to tweak and improve the company's governors in an effort to meet new needs in the marketplace, helping the company's revenues to climb. Amos Woodward died in 1919, a few years short of his 90th birthday, and his son continued to lead Woodward throughout the 1920s. Early in 1929, when he was 67 years old, Elmer Woodward hired son-in-law Irl Martin to take over day-to-day operations, while he continued to design new products and make pivotal contributions to the company well into his 70s.

By 1929, Woodward Governor was employing 50 workers and had established itself as a leader in the design and manufacture of prime mover controls. Unfortunately, the company's fortunes were about to change for reasons outside of its control. The stock market crash of 1929 quashed demand for Woodward's waterwheel and hydro power governors. Martin was faced with a crisis, his handling of which would demonstrate his legendary management abilities and philosophies. Rather than lay off staff, Martin called all of the workers together and offered them a choice: either fill existing orders and hope for more, or keep everyone on the payroll at 20 hours per week and at a cut in pay until business improved. The workers elected to scale back hours and pay. Until the crisis was over, Elmer Woodward paid much of their wages out of his own pocket—a practice that was, and still is, almost unheard of in any kind of corporation. It was later discovered that Woodward had borrowed against his own life insurance to meet the payroll.

The company's shipments began to pick up in 1932 and 1933, although the company was still lagging. Woodward and Martin realized that the company would be forced to find new sources of revenue to supplant lost demand. To that end, Woodward began developing a governor to control diesel engines that were being used at the time as auxiliary systems in hydro-electric plants. Under his supervision, the company perfected a governor for diesel engines in 1933 that would become the core of the company's product line for several years. The pivotal breakthrough provided an important boost to the company's sagging bottom line. In fact, Woodward Governor's elated workers were soon making up for lost time with 60-hour weeks. Unfortunately, the Federal government, concerned with underemployment, forced the company to cut them back to 40 hours. Martin feared that the company would be unable to meet demand, but their workers, realizing the urgency of the situation, continued to work 60 hours per week at only 40 hours of pay.

Woodward Governor introduced another major product breakthrough in 1934: a governor that could control the pitch of an airplane propeller. An aviation company had approached the company about creating such a control, and several of the company's younger members had gone to work to design the contraption. Unable to solve the problem, they eventually called on 73-year-old Elmer Woodward to finish the job. Within several months his team delivered a perfected governor that would give Woodward Governor a much-needed entry into the aviation industry.

Although sales surged during the mid-1930s as a result of the new innovations, the company's equipment and facilities had depreciated by the end of the decade. Rather than borrow the cash to renew the plant, Martin again called the employees together. They all agreed that everyone in the company should forego a pay raise in order to pay cash for new equipment. Thus, Woodward Governor emerged from the Depression with a broader product line, new equipment, little debt, and a family-like bond between labor and management that would distinguish the company in American industry.

Much of Woodward Governor's success in the 1930s, and even throughout the mid-1900s, was attributable to Martin's unique management techniques. In the 1930s, for example, Martin realized that some of his skilled machinists and mechanics were not producing as much as he believed they could. He believed the problem was psychological and was attributable to the workers' poor self image. To solve the problem, he instituted a dress code that included a tie and smock, and began requiring that all employees remain neatly shaven. The workers also agreed to begin keeping their work areas extremely clean and neat. Worker productivity improved greatly and, according to Martin, the workers began to realize the true value of their contribution to the company and society. Among other of Martin's management innovations was aptitude testing, which was used to help determine where a worker would perform most effectively and happily. He also introduced a cutting edge health insurance program that focused on personal preventive medicine.

On December 31, 1940, 78-year-old Elmer Woodward, or ''Pops'' as he had come to be called, worked a full day, returned home, and then died of a heart attack. His exemplary service to the company spanned 64 years. Among other attributes, the soft-spoken Elmer was known for treating all men as his equal, regardless of position or stature, as well as for earning the respect of all those who knew him. Irl Martin assumed complete leadership of the company after Elmer's death, just as Woodward Governor was entering the greatest growth phase in its history. Indeed, WWII placed huge demands on the company's production facilities as orders for its advanced propeller controls boomed; the advantage that the controls offered was that they reduced vibration in airplanes and ships by synchronizing and phasing the propellers of two or more engines.

Woodward Governor continued to innovate during the war, introducing, for example, the first aircraft turbine control in 1943, and sales skyrocketed. Amazingly, the company's ranks swelled from just 50 in 1935 to more than 1,600 during the war's peak. The explosive growth virtually changed the face of the company, which had moved its operations into a large new factory at the very start of the war. Again, Martin consulted his workers about the new facility and they all agreed to forgo some compensation to build it. The facility was completely state-of-the-art, and was designed with worker productivity and satisfaction in mind. The plant became much less crowded after the war, when the work force shrank to a more manageable 500. Although demand faded during that period, sales growth resumed in the wake of the postwar economic boom of the 1950s and 1960s.

During the late 1940s, Martin instituted what would become one of his most noted management schemes; The Corporate Partnership. This plan lead to a number of innovative management solutions. For example, Martin was concerned about the problem of determining equitable pay rates for everyone in the company, including himself. After much thought, he decided to present a solution to the employees. Under the new system, every employee, or ''member,'' would receive no more and no less than ten times that of the least valuable category of worker. In addition, a bonus system was put in place. At the end of each year, workers and management would rank everyone in their department according to a given set of criteria. The rankings were combined and every employee then received a ranking within the entire company. That rank was used, and continued to be used in the 1990s, to determine an employee's percentage of the aggregate annual bonus.

During the mid-1950s Woodward Governor expanded its product line to include main fuel controls for aircraft gas turbines and electronic analog controls. Among the recognized innovations during the 1950s and 1960s were: the electrical cabinet actuator in 1957; the first truly electric governor in 1960; fuel valves for aerodrive turbines in 1962; control for turboprop engines in 1964; and a unique new electronic control system in 1965. As demand for the company's products increased, Martin expanded the company. In 1955 Woodward Governor built a new factory in Fort Collins, Colorado. Subsequently, Martin oversaw the installation of production facilities throughout the world in The Netherlands, England, Japan, and Australia. By the late 1960s, Woodward was generating annual revenues of about $70 million.

Although the 65-year-old Martin officially retired from the presidency in 1960, he remained as chairman of the board and led Woodward Governor into the 1970s. The company continued to introduce new products during the early 1970s and to strengthen its Corporate Partnership program. In fact, Martin became a sought-after speaker in the Midwest by groups wanting to hear about his unique management philosophy. Unfortunately, Martin's health began deteriorating in 1975. He resigned in March 1976 and died on April 22 after 55 years of service to Woodward Governor.

Martin was succeeded by Calvin C. Covert. Covert had joined the company in 1942, going to work in the lowly 'snagging' room, where he shaved rough spots off of castings. "One day Mr. Martin came out and said, 'Sonny boy, you made'," Covert recalled in the January 1988 *Rockford Magazine.* Covert continued, "I said, 'made what.' And he said, 'I gave you one of the dirtiest jobs. Now what the hell do you want to do?' " That began Covert's rise up the corporate ladder. By the time he took the helm in 1976, he had been working in top management for most of his career. Under his direction, Woodward Governor continued to create new products and to refine its management techniques. Major new products in the 1970s included an eight-bit microprocessor synchronizer and a digital synchronizer for aircraft. Covert also stepped up Woodward Governor's international expansion in 1977 with a new plant in Brazil.

The company thrived under Covert's leadership. It experienced a downturn in its important turbine division in the early 1980s, but by the mid-1980s its sales were approaching the $200 million mark. That improvement was accomplished with the help of Robert Pope, who was brought in from outside the company in 1983 to act as president, while Covert remained at Woodward Governor as chairman of the board. Under Pope's leadership, the company whipped its internal operations into shape and stepped up its growth pace in the mid-1980s. Indeed, $100 invested in Woodward Governor in 1976 would have grown to nearly $1,500 by 1988. That growth was largely the result of an economic upswing and increased demand from defense and aerospace industries during the mid- and late 1980s. Woodward Governor's sales leapt 13 percent in 1987 to $275 million as net earnings rose 37 percent to $24 million. By the end of the decade, moreover, the company was generating more than $300 million in revenues annually.

Although Woodward Governor was helped by strong markets during much of the 1980s, its success was also attributed to its proven management style, which was getting increased attention within American industry as a result of the company's ability to compete with Japan and other countries. As it turned out, Woodward Governor had long been practicing management techniques (such as employee empowerment and performance-based incentives) that were emerging as major trends in the 1980s. For example, the company's president received only $247,000 in total salary and bonuses in 1986, in keeping with the company rule of not making more than ten percent of the lowest job category. Likewise, new Woodward Governor employees were brought into the company by way of a solemn ceremony; other employees attended, and even joined in prayer, as the new employees were inducted into the Woodward "family." And, while Woodward Governor's workers received only about 80 to 90 percent of the salary of their U.S. industrial counterparts, their bonuses consistently placed them well above the national average in compensation.

Woodward Governor entered the 1990s with record sales and profits; revenues hit $362 million in 1991. Unfortunately, waning defense and aerospace markets were beginning to take their toll on the company's bottom line. Woodward Governor had been trying to reduce its dependence on the aircraft market since the mid-1980s, when over 60 percent of sales were attributable to that sector. But by the early 1990s the company was still getting more than 50 percent of its revenues from the aircraft market and was scurrying to beef up its activity in other sectors. Similarly, the company had seen the percentage of its sales attributable to defense markets fall from 20 percent in 1990 to less than 15 percent by 1993. To make up for the shortfall, Woodward Governor began concentrating on its industrial controls division, its only major segment other than aircraft controls.

Sagging key markets hurt Woodward Governor in 1993 and 1994. Sales slipped to $333 million in 1994, and the company posted its first loss since 1940. By that time, John Halbrook had been brought on board as president and chief executive. Under his leadership, the company instituted aggressive cost-cutting measures in 1994 that resulted in a $24 million restructuring charge, which pinched its net earnings. The charge also forced the company to cut its aircraft division work force by 20 percent, resulting in one of the biggest layoffs ever conducted by the organization. Covert passed away in December of 1994 at the age of 70, and Halbrook assumed his position as chairman, announcing his commitment to continue cutting costs and improving the company's market stance.

Despite setbacks going into the mid-1990s, Woodward Governor continued to research and introduce new products. It brought out innovative new digital controls in 1992 and 1993, for example, and had several advanced devices for both aircraft and industrial markets under development. With facilities throughout Illinois, Woodward Governor's aircraft controls division remained a leader in the production of high quality fuel controls and control systems for aerospace customers in both commercial and military markets. Similarly, its industrial controls division was supporting offices and plants throughout the United States and Europe, as well as in Japan and Singapore. Moreover, Woodward Governor was a top global supplier of hydromechanical governors and analog controls for products including off-road machinery, locomotives, gas and steam industrial turbines, hydroelectric machinery, and more.

Further Reading:

Anason, Dean, "This Isn't the Place to Rest," *Atlanta Business Chronicle,* May 26, 1995, p. 1B.

Bremner, Brian, "Caught in Crunch: Growth Crimps Woodward Governor," *Crain's Chicago Business,* January 25, 1988, p. 20.

A Gentleman Named Woodward, Rockford, Ill.: Woodward Governor Company, 1974.

McGough, Robert, "How to Win the Class Struggle," *Forbes,* November 3, 1986, p. 153.

Osbourne, Randy, "An Officer and a Gentleman," *Rockford Magazine,* January 1988.

Palmer, Ann Therese, "Cost Controls Key for Woodward Governor," *Crain's Chicago Business,* February 6, 1995, p. 24.

Pride, Jackie, "Woodward Eliminates 200 Jobs," *Wausau Daily Herald,* April 2, 1993, Business Sec.

Spivak, Cary, "Woodward Shifts Facilities to Handle Product Demand," *Crain's Chicago Business,* January 27, 1986, p. 18.

Weingarten, Paul, "Woodward's Way," *Chicago Tribune Magazine,* July 29, 1984.

Woodward Governor Company: 125 Years, Rockford, Ill.: Woodward Governor Company, 1994.

—Dave Mote

York International Corp.

631 S. Richland Avenue
P.O. Box 1592-364M
York, Pennsylvania 17405-1592
U.S.A.
(717) 771-7890
Fax: (717) 771-7440

Public Company
Incorporated: 1895 as York Manufacturing Co.
Sales: $2.42 billion
Employees: 13,800
Stock Exchanges: New York
SICs: 3433 Heating Equipment, Except Heating and Warm Air Furnaces; 3564 Industrial and Commercial Fans and Blowers and Air Purification Equipment; 3585 Refrigeration and Heating Equipment

York International Corp. is a global manufacturer of heating, ventilating, air-conditioning, and refrigeration products. It manufactures heating, air-conditioning, and thermal-storage equipment for factories, stores, hospitals, universities, office buildings, shopping malls, airports, marine vessels, and residences. It also manufactures refrigeration and gas-compression equipment for industries processing food, beverages, chemicals, and petrochemicals. In 1993, the company's products were in use in such diverse locations as the British Houses of Parliament, the World Trade Centers of both New York and Tokyo, NASA's Vehicle Assembly Building at Cape Canaveral, Florida, the Los Angeles International Airport, the Sydney Opera House, the Hong Kong Exposition Centre, and the English Channel Tunnel.

The York Manufacturing Co. was founded in York, Pennsylvania, in the fall of 1874 by six men. It became a partnership in 1885, the year that the company built its first ice machine for a customer in Mississippi. During the winter, people in the North were generally content with ice harvested and stored from frozen rivers and lakes, but York persevered in developing various ways to make and store ice. In 1897 ice making and refrigeration comprised York's product lines; all other product lines were sold or discontinued.

York's first link between refrigeration and industrial air conditioning came in 1903, when the company installed a large system for dehumidifying blast-furnace air in a factory operated by Carnegie Steel Co. Its first public venture in air-conditioning was in 1914, when it air conditioned the Empire Theatre in Montgomery, Alabama. York's first air-conditioning for an office building was in 1923, for the San Joaquin Light and Power Co. in Fresno, California. By that time, the company's facilities consisted of 154 buildings on about 17 acres in York. Although York had sold products overseas in Japan as far back as 1898, it did not open its first foreign office in Europe until 1923, in London. Soon after, York created a refrigeration system for an English dairy which then grew to be the largest in the world and helped make milk pasteurization a reality.

In 1927 the company was reincorporated in Delaware, with nine affiliated companies, and was renamed the York Ice Machinery Corp. During the mid-1920s, York built its first single-room air conditioner, which weighed 600 pounds. Since there was little residential market for such a behemoth, the company concentrated on installing air conditioners in commercial establishments through its Yorkaire line. These units included high-speed lightweight compressors using freon or ammonia. During the late 1920s, York made the St. Anthony Hotel in San Antonio the first completely air-conditioned hotel in the United States.

York's sales grew from nearly $2.2 million in fiscal 1915 to $8 million in fiscal 1920 and to a peak of $17.5 million in fiscal 1929. In the depths of the Great Depression, business slumped to $7.4 million in fiscal 1933, and deficits were recorded in 1933, 1934, and 1935. Yet the company had grown significantly during the early 1930s. By the mid-1930s there was a second plant, adjacent to York, and offices in 64 U.S. cities and 21 foreign cities. In 1937, sales rebounded to the 1929 peak of $17.5 million. Significant successes included more than 1,000 York air-conditioning installations functioning in France by 1940, as well as complete cooling systems for the first fully air-conditioned train and for the Capitol in Washington.

During World War II, York installed air-conditioning and refrigeration equipment aboard the ships of six countries and at military sites ranging from headquarters operations to strategic outposts and the front lines. The company's naval-training school graduated 1,200 petty officers trained to operate and maintain refrigeration and air-conditioning machinery aboard ships. The water used to cool the nuclear reactor at Hanford, Washington (which produced the plutonium for one of the two atomic bombs dropped on Japan) passed through a York refrigeration plant. Net sales of the company, which was renamed the York Corp. in 1942, grew to a wartime peak of $38.4 million in 1945.

York's business continued to boom with new innovations in the late 1940s and early 1950s. Its first automatic ice makers for hotels, restaurants, and hospitals, were introduced in 1948. Hermetically-sealed cooling circuits for room air conditioners were brought to market in 1950 as were improved heat pumps for year-round comfort in the early 1950s. York also introduced a residential air-conditioning unit to sell for under $1,000, installed, in 1950. This unit was designed to cool the average five-room house. The first single-stage, high-speed centrifugal refrigeration compressor made its debut in 1954, the year in which net sales reached a record $93.3 million and net income reached a record $2.9 million. Manufacturing facilities were located in several other U.S. cities, and in Nottingham, England.

Borg-Warner Corp., a diversified Chicago-based manufacturing company known best for its automotive parts, acquired York in 1956. York shareholders received a half-share of Borg-Warner common stock and $2 in cash for each share of York common stock. York became a Borg-Warner division.

Business boomed in the late 1950s and throughout the 1960s as both individuals and companies increasingly relied on "man-made weather." Installed gas-powered cooling equipment, for example, doubled between 1958 and 1960, and York was one of three firms producing the major share of such larger equipment. Although the division concentrated more on industrial and commercial business than it did on residential sales, one of its fastest-selling new products in 1961 was the Sunline rooftop air conditioner, which took up no interior space and was almost invisible from the ground because of its low-silhouette design. York installed the world's largest water-cooled air-conditioning system at the World Trade Center in New York City in 1968, weighing 49,600 tons.

In 1966 York's air-conditioning sales were running 15 percent above a year earlier, with new orders jumping 48 percent.

An independent 1970 market-projection report had more good news: air-conditioning sales were said to be rising even faster than the industry annual growth rate of 10 to 15 percent, and there was a record order backlog. In October 1972, work began on a $12-million air-conditioning plant in Madisonville, Kentucky. A new York heat pump was in production in 1977. Expected to improve the division's sales in residential housing, this pump, besides removing the heat from within a house in summer, acted to warm the house in the winter months.

By 1981, York was the second-largest maker of air-conditioning and related equipment in the United States, having in that year acquired Westinghouse Electric Corp.'s air-conditioning division. However, by 1985, Borg-Warner was considering selling its air-conditioning unit (now called Borg-Warner Environment). Its operating profit of $6.5 million in 1984 was only two percent of Borg-Warner's total, while its debt of $60 million was 17 percent of the parent company's total. It lost $1.2 million in 1985.

After failing to make a profitable deal, Borg-Warner spun off the unit in 1986 to shareholders by distributing one share for every ten shares of Borg-Warner held by investors. (A "spin-off" is a form of company divestiture that results in a subsidiary or division becoming an independent company.) A former helicopter designer, Stanley Hiller, Jr., took over management at the head of a group investing $2 million in the new York International Corp., which became the largest independent publicly traded firm in the heating and air-conditioning field. "The company's been on a self-destruct course for several years," Hiller told a *Business Week* reporter.

Despite York's existing debt, Hiller paid $37 million to buy Bristol Compressors Inc., a manufacturer of hermetic compressors, and also purchased Frick Industrial, Inc. and Frigid Coil/Frick, designers of industrial refrigeration machinery and heat-transfer equipment. Hiller envisioned great opportunities overseas, a higher degree of vertical integration, and more emphasis on new products and research and development. In a 1988 *Wall Street Transcript* interview, he disclosed that York's debt had been refinanced in Europe and proclaimed the company to be "in an excellent financial position."

York went private in 1988, when an investor group headed by Citicorp Capital Investors Ltd. paid shareholders $761.6 million in cash and $90.2 million in debentures. Citicorp and affiliates of Prudential Insurance Co. of America were the main investors, together holding nearly 70 percent of equity. In this reorganization, the company assumed a heavy burden of debt. It reported a 1991 loss of $4.3 million, despite a tripling of operating income over 1990's total to $13 million, because of a charge of $17.3 million for debt restructuring.

In October 1991, York became a public company once more, offering more than 12 million shares at $23 a share. By March 1992, when 19.8 million of the 20.8 million remaining shares were offered at $31.75 a share, York stock was selling at $34 a share. The funds from this offering allowed the company to raise its credit standing to investment grade BBB and refinance $400 million of $650 million in bank debt at lower interest rates. York was described as the most profitable, fastest-growing company in its industry in 1993. Its stock hit a 32-month high of nearly $41 a share in August 1994. York's long-term debt was $280.6 million at the end of 1994.

York signed a $750-million, five-year agreement in June 1992 to build a manufacturing plant for milk refrigeration units in Russia that would eliminate 80 percent of the annual milk spoilage in Russia, which was said to be about half of the total amount of milk produced. Other projects abroad included a cooling system for Saudi Arabia's Jiddah Airport, a water-chilling system for the English Channel Tunnel, and Norway's largest ammonia refrigeration plant, for the 1994 Winter Olympics. In 1994, York introduced the first-ever natural-gas heating and cooling system in the form of its Triathlon heat pump, powered by a revolutionary small Marathon engine. About 25,000 units were expected to be sold over the next three years, with at least three-quarters expected to be residential sales.

York also foresaw a big market in retrofitting existing industrial and commercial cooling systems to eliminate chlorofluorocarbons. Production of these chemicals was banned by 1996 in many countries because of their role in thinning the earth's atmospheric ozone layer. York claimed to have the industry's broadest line of equipment using alternative refrigerants.

York's net income (excluding extraordinary items and accounting changes) soared to $69.3 million in 1992 from $13 million in 1991, while its sales rose from $1.65 billion to $1.94 billion. In 1993, sales passed $2 billion for the first time, and net income reached nearly $75.5 million. Sales passed $2.4 billion in 1994, and net income rose to nearly $89.8 million. Of the 1994 revenue total, commercial products accounted for nearly $1.16 billion, residential products for $795 million, and refrigeration products for $469 million. Repair and replacement business accounted for an estimated 50 percent of total sales in 1993. U.S. revenue accounted for 56 percent of the total and international operations for 44 percent in 1994. International operations were expected to comprise more than half of total revenue by 2000. The company entered 1995 with a backlog of $779 million in orders.

York had operations in more than 120 countries in 1994, including sales and service organizations. Residential products, which consisted of central air-conditioning and heat pumps, furnace units, and hermetic compressors, were being marketed under the York, Luxaire, Fraser-Johnston, Moncrief, Homeair, and Bristol trademarks. Commercial products, which included equipment for heating, air conditioning, process cooling, and thermal storage, were being marketed under the York, Luxaire, Fraser-Johnston, Miller-Picking, and Tempmaster trademarks. Refrigeration and gas-compression equipment designed for industry were being marketed under the York, York Food Systems, Frick, Frigid Coil, Imeco, Reco, and Recold trademarks.

A 71-acre site owned by the company in York, Pennsylvania, continued to be the site of its headquarters in 1994 and also the site of its largest manufacturing facility, occupying about 1.5 million square feet. York also owned 13 other manufacturing facilities: seven in the United States, two in Mexico, and one each in England, France, Australia, and Uruguay. In addition, the company leased for its own use six manufacturing facilities and about 90 facilities for sales and service offices and regional warehouses. York also was taking part in four joint ventures with companies in Egypt, Malaysia, and Taiwan.

Principal Subsidiaries: Airchal Industries, S.A.; Codorus Acceptance Corp.; Frigid Coil/Frick Inc.; IMECO, Inc.; Miller-Picking, Inc.; Viron, Inc.; YIHC, Inc.; York Food Systems International Ltd.

Further Reading:

''Borg-Warner Corp. Would Acquire York Corp. in Proposed Merger,'' *Wall Street Journal,* April 6, 1956, p. 5.

Brennan, Robert J., ''York International Sets New Offering That Undoes LBO,'' *Wall Street Journal,* March 2, 1992, p. 5A.

Byrne, Harlan S., ''York International,'' *Barron's,* August 16, 1993, pp. 33–34.

Eklund, Christopher S., ''Stan Hiller Is Old-Fashioned: He Fixes Broken Companies,'' *Business Week,* March 31, 1986, pp. 74–75.

Goodwin, William, ''CIBC Leads Refinancing for York International,'' *American Banker,* July 2, 1992, p. 14.

Weinberg, Neil, ''York's Hot Prospects,'' *Forbes,* August 16, 1993, p. 138.

''York International Corporation,'' *Wall Street Transcript,* February 8, 1988, p. 88358.

—Robert Halasz

Zenith Electronics Corporation

1000 Milwaukee Avenue
Glenview, Illinois 60025-2493
U.S.A.
(708) 391-7000
Fax: (708) 391-7253

Wholly Owned Subsidiary of LG Electronics Inc.
Incorporated: 1923 as Zenith Radio Corporation
Sales: $1.47 billion
Employees: 25,000
Stock Exchanges: New York
SICs: 3651 Household Audio and Video Equipment; 3671 Electron Tubes; 3663 Radio and T.V. Communications Equipment

Zenith Electronics Corporation is recognized primarily as a manufacturer of high-quality consumer electronics products. From its start Zenith advertised that its reputation would be built and sustained by the superior workmanship, reliability, and innovation of all products bearing the Zenith name. The company became a huge American success as a top producer first in the radio industry and later in television. Low-priced imports from Asia, however, began to rock Zenith in the mid- to late 1970s. Although continuing to produce innovative products including the high-definition television (HDTV) technology chosen as the standard by the industry alliance in the United States, Zenith posted losses nine out of the ten years from 1985 to 1994. With no end in sight to the mounting losses, and needing capital to upgrade its plants, Zenith sold a controlling interest to South Korea-based LG Electronics Inc. in 1995.

Zenith's beginnings were very modest. Two ham radio operators, Karl E. Hassel and R. H. G. Mathews, began manufacturing radio equipment at a kitchen table in 1918 under the name Chicago Radio Laboratory. Hassel ran an amateur radio station with the call letters 9ZN, from which they named their first product Z-Nith—the origin of the later name "Zenith." These two men were joined by Commander Eugene F. McDonald Jr. in 1921. McDonald, already a self-made millionaire when he joined the company, was pivotal to Zenith's growth. He was much more than a financial backer. McDonald's flamboyant style was echoed in the company's dramatic advertising methods and this style, coupled with innovative genius and an ability to sense changes in public tastes, meant that for more than three decades, in the public perception McDonald was Zenith.

McDonald was counterbalanced by Hugh Robertson, who joined the company as treasurer in 1923. Robertson's financial expertise and careful planning led Zenith through many difficulties, including the Great Depression. 1923 was significant in many other ways. The company was incorporated as Zenith Radio Corporation that year, and 30,000 shares of stock were issued at $10 per share, with the largest single block going to McDonald. At that time, Zenith Radio Corporation took over sales and marketing for the Chicago Radio Laboratory, a maker of radio equipment. Zenith later acquired all of Chicago Radio Laboratory's assets and officially began to manufacture under its own name.

Soon McDonald, who preferred to be addressed as "The Commander" (as a lieutenant commander in the Navy during World War I he was entitled to the name), began to show his flair for drama. He persuaded Admiral Donald B. MacMillan to take a shortwave radio with him on his Arctic expedition. MacMillan's transmissions proved exciting demonstrations of the efficiency of shortwave communication. In addition to his advertising schemes, McDonald organized and became president of the National Association of Broadcasters in 1923.

Meanwhile, Zenith's inventors and technicians were developing landmark products. In 1924 Zenith introduced the world's first portable radio. Then in 1925, McDonald helped MacMillan organize another expedition, this time to the North Pole. McDonald was part of the expedition as a ship commander, but went only as far as Greenland. His shortwave radio broadcasts of Eskimos singing into the microphone was a great success, and Zenith's advertising always reminded the public that Zenith shortwave radios were the choice of the Arctic explorers.

More innovations followed. In 1926 Zenith introduced the first home radio receiver that operated directly from regular AC electric current, and automatic push-button tuning came in 1927. By the late 1920s Zenith was in 12th place in a $400 million industry.

But when the Great Depression hit after the stock market crash of 1929, the radio industry was thrown into chaos. Zenith's sales went from $10 million in 1929 to less than $2 million in 1932. Although the company suffered five successive years of losses, Treasurer Hugh Robertson managed to get the company through without borrowing until profitability returned.

McDonald, even during those times, did not give up his attempts to get Zenith technology into new areas. In 1934, he sent a wire to all U.S. oil and tire companies: "Watch absence of people on streets between eleven and eleven thirty during presidential talk." After the talk, he sent letters urging them to become Zenith auto-radio dealers and get rich.

One of McDonald's most popular ideas during the 1930s was the "big black dial" for radios. Its large clock-style numbers were designed to be read from a distance or without glasses. McDonald also promoted portable shortwave radios for $75—predecessors of Zenith's famous Trans-Oceanic radios—an idea that was ridiculed at the time but was extremely successful in the end.

Zenith management valued and encouraged worker loyalty. Therefore, when the company began to be profitable again in 1936 for the first time in five years, Zenith paid its workers, rather than its stockholders, a dividend, in appreciation for sticking out the tough times of little money. Net sales of $8.5 million in 1936 resulted in net income of $1.2 million. By 1937 sales were up to almost $17 million, and net income was nearly $2 million.

By the late 1930s, Zenith was exporting to 96 countries and was a pioneer in television and FM broadcasting. In 1939 Zenith's station W9XZV, the first all-electronic television station, went on the air. This was followed the next year by W9XEN, one of the first FM stations in the United States. By 1941 Zenith had risen to second place in a $600 million industry, behind only RCA.

Although World War II meant a decline in normal consumer business, this decline was more than offset by war production. Zenith manufactured radar, communications equipment, and high-sensitivity frequency meters. Net sales were $23.8 million in 1941, and $34.2 million in 1942, with $1.4 million in net income that year.

Zenith's major product outside of war-related materials during World War II was a highly successful line of hearing aids that retailed for $40. A miniature adaptation of a radio receiving set, it made hearing assistance affordable for thousands of people. Zenith became the largest marketer of hearing aids in the world, outselling all other companies combined.

Once it was able to resume civilian research and production, Zenith concentrated on improving television, even though McDonald had resisted television for almost a decade. The company introduced its first line of black-and-white television receivers in 1948. Also in 1948, in order to meet an immediate increased demand, Zenith purchased the Rauland Corporation, a noted Chicago manufacturer of television picture tubes. One year after this purchase, the combined talents of the Zenith and Rauland researchers produced the nonreflective "black-tube."

While Zenith continued research and development on color television throughout the early 1950s, and even participated in the development of industry standards for a compatible color television system, it still did not get into the color-TV market. McDonald was even more adamant about color television than he had been about black-and-white, saying "someday, the technical and service problems of color TV will be solved. When that day comes, we will offer you a line of outstanding color sets. In the meantime, we will not try to make an experimental laboratory of dealers and the public. We will keep color in our laboratories until it is ready." Zenith continued to work on its black-and-white televisions, inventing the first wireless remote control in 1956, and held the leading position in black-and-white television from 1959 on.

The color television breakthrough came in 1961, when Zenith introduced a ten-receiver line of color sets. Demand for these sets grew so quickly that it had to expand its facilities. Also that year Zenith's experimental stereophonic FM broadcasting system was approved by the FCC as the national standard.

Color television improvements continued steadily. In 1969 Zenith introduced the patented Chromacolor picture tube, which set the standard for brightness in the color-TV industry for many years. In 1970, the company received awards from the American Association for the Advancement of Science in recognition of its years of technological achievements. By 1972, the year it introduced a line of 25-inch television, Zenith was number one in production of color television sets.

Enormous profitability led to expansion. In 1971 Zenith acquired a 93 percent interest in Movado-Zenith-Mondia Holding, a watch manufacturer. It also acquired a one-third interest in a Venezuelan television company in 1974, and significantly increased its U.S. product distributors. Zenith was able to maintain the leading position in the fiercely competitive U.S. color-television market between 1972 and 1978, but was overtaken by RCA in 1979.

Domestic competition, however, did not prove to be Zenith's greatest problem. Manufacturers in Japan, Taiwan, and Korea began selling great numbers of electronic consumer goods in the United States at prices below what American companies could afford to offer. Zenith's then-chairman, John Nevin, filed suits against the Japanese and testified in Congress, accusing the Japanese of dumping goods on the American market at below-cost prices. Nevin's demand that the federal government enforce its antidumping laws was finally met, but not before significant damage had been done.

In 1977, Zenith sold most of its domestic hearing aid instrumentation operation. Also that year, Zenith contracted with Japan's Sony Corporation to market Sony's Betamax home video television recorder in the United States under the Zenith label. By 1978, Zenith had sold most of its Movado watch assets and laid off 25 percent of its American workers, having established plants in Mexico and Taiwan. The latter move was intended to take advantage of the cheaper labor available in those countries and to address the increasing price competition.

Zenith President and CEO Revone Kluckman realized that action outside Washington was needed to combat the pricing crisis. Kluckman was credited with refocusing Zenith's competitive energies from legal battles back to the factory floor by implementing cost-cutting measures and improved manufacturing procedures.

A sweeping reorganization also began in 1978. The corporate structure was rebuilt along product lines, with each group receiving a charter to move aggressively into new businesses. Jerry Pearlman, then a senior Zenith finance executive, later chairman and president, was instrumental in pushing for one business in particular: computers. In 1979, Zenith acquired the Heath Company, a long-time maker of do-it-yourself electronic kits. The shrewd and inexpensive ($64.5 million) purchase occurred right after Heath announced its first personal computer kit and only months after Apple introduced its first personal computer.

Zenith Data Systems, a wholly owned subsidiary, was born after the Heath acquisition. The parent company required that any new business tap at least two of three Zenith capabilities: technology, manufacturing, and distribution. Zenith Data Systems was a perfect match on all three counts. The first Zenith computer, the Z-100, was introduced in 1981; 35,000 Z-100s were shipped that first year.

In addition to complete computer systems, Zenith began to sell video terminals compatible with virtually all personal computers on the market. These became very successful, as were the components Zenith sold to other computer companies. Zenith also entered the market for decoders for the growing cable TV and wireless markets.

Nevertheless, the early success of Zenith Data Systems was not enough to offset the impact of price competition in the consumer electronics business. The company suffered a net loss of $24 million on revenues of $1.2 billion in 1982 and did not pay a dividend that year for the first time in almost half a century.

Zenith continued to push for cost reductions. These were achieved through the use of robotics and other improvements in design and manufacturing, which led to a higher sales volume to offset lower prices. By 1983, although it lacked the advertising dollars to mount the campaigns of other industry manufacturers, Zenith Data Systems boasted an installed base of 95,000 microcomputers. Computer sales mounted to $135 million that year, and Zenith was profitable. It also celebrated a short-lived victory in an antitrust suit against Japanese television manufacturers that year, a suit later overturned on appeal.

Zenith worked to win large contracts with educational institutions and the federal government, greatly broadening its impact on the personal computer market. It also held a virtual monopoly on the do-it-yourself computer market through more than 70 Heathkit Electronic Centers. Whereas overall computer sales accounted for 1.4 percent of Zenith sales in 1979 (exclusively Heath), they were up to 15 percent in 1984. Also in 1984, the electronics industry adopted the Zenith-developed system for MTS stereo TV broadcast and reception. It was another profitable year, marked by a name change from the long outdated Zenith Radio Corporation to Zenith Electronics Corporation.

The roller coaster went down again for Zenith in 1985. Although computer-products sales rose from $249 in 1984 to $352 million in 1985, computer sales did not offset the $125 million loss in consumer electronics. The company was nearly $8 million in the red at year's end.

In 1986 Zenith introduced more new products than at any time in its history, especially in the home entertainment and computer improvement areas. Record numbers of video cassette recorders were shipped, up 34 percent, and cable operations were up 16 percent. Foreign operations brought in 13 percent of overall revenues. Computer systems and components were up 56 percent to $548 million, accounting for 29 percent of total sales (consumer electronics figured at 64 percent and components, at seven percent, made up the rest). Nevertheless, 1986 was another year of losses—of $10 million—due to pricing pressures and lower profit margins. Japanese, Taiwanese, and Korean prices in the United States were ten percent lower in 1986 than in 1985.

Zenith chairman Jerry Pearlman eventually asked the federal government to once again monitor foreign manufacturers' illegal dumping of inexpensive TV sets on the American market. His request did little good, however, because the government took years to investigate and act on the charges. As Zenith continued to lose money, pressure from investors to sell its consumer electronics unit mounted. Pearlman, however, could not attract an acceptable bid.

In 1988 Zenith reported a modest $12 million profit, ending a four-year streak of losses. But the company was saddled with heavy debt (incurred primarily in financing the growth of its computer business), and competition in both the consumer electronics and computer industries was heating up.

It was becoming increasingly evident to Pearlman that Zenith's continued participation in two tough business areas was hurting the company's competitiveness; while both were over $1 billion in sales by 1988, neither was profitable. In 1989 Pearlman and the Zenith board suddenly decided to sell Zenith's computer business to Paris-based Groupe Bull. Zenith used the $500 million it received from Bull to pay off its short-term debt and some of its long-term obligations as well. Zenith management hoped this trimming would improve its ability to compete in consumer electronics in the 1990s.

But starting with 1989, Zenith posted five straight years of heavy losses—the smallest, the 1991 loss of $52 million; the largest, the 1992 loss of $106 million. In the midst of these losses—primarily caused by continued depressed prices for televisions—the company moved forward with the development of new, innovative products.

The company's most publicized foray involved high-definition television (HDTV), the super-sharp digital television technology that was supposed to replace the standard analog television. With the prodding of the U.S. government, which feared that Japanese manufacturers would completely dominate the television industry unless American companies moved quickly to develop HDTV, three company partnerships were formed in the late 1980s, each working on their own HDTV standard. Zenith and its partner AT&T Microelectronics developed a digital transmission technology that was among the finalists for adoption. In 1993, however, the government wanted to speed up the adoption process by having all seven company finalists cooperate on developing a digital HDTV system, forming the "Grand Alliance." The following year, Zenith's transmission system was chosen by the alliance to be the U.S. standard to be submitted to the Federal Communications Commission for final approval. With the alliance arrangement, Zenith would receive a royalty for its role—a slice of perhaps $10 to $20 per television set—but could not expect a sizable return on its $15 million HDTV investment until after 2000 when the market for HDTV sets approached that of regular TVs.

With its HDTV payoff years away, Zenith faced a proxy fight in 1991 from a dissident stockholder dissatisfied with the management of the company. Pearlman was able to ward off this attempt for his ouster by wooing a foreign investor. South Korea-based Lucky-Goldstar Group, a huge conglomerate and maker of low-end consumer electronics products, purchased a five percent stake in the company for $15 million. The purchase initiated some small cooperative ventures between the two firms.

Starting in 1992, Zenith attempted to improve operating results through a series of reengineering efforts initiated by the firm's president and chief operating officer, Albin F. Moschner. In addition to reducing its work force by 25 percent over the next two years, the program aimed to improve new product development and get products to market faster, increase quality, and establish greater integration between factories. These efforts, however, did not produce immediate results, and continuing pressure from shareholders over the lack of improvement led the Zenith board of directors to begin a program of closely monitoring Pearlman's performance through frequent and lengthy meetings and the tracking of numerous performance measures. A further blow came in early 1993 when one of Zenith's creditors, the Bank of New York, found the company in violation of the net worth covenant in its credit agreement.

Zenith's performance did improve in 1994, but not enough to put it back in the black. The company continued to suffer from price erosion—$48 million worth—brought on by its foreign competitors, leading to another loss, this time of $14.2 million. This represented a $83 million improvement over 1993 results, partly attributed to savings of $40 million in costs from the reengineering efforts.

Early in 1995, Pearlman retired as CEO, naming Moschner to the position, and also announced he would retire as chairman at the end of the year. Shortly thereafter, Moschner and Pearlman revealed that the firm planned to concentrate on the production of large-screen TV sets, those with screens larger than 30 inches. This segment of the market was predicted to enjoy much greater revenue growth than the industry overall. In order to begin production of the large-screen TVs, Zenith needed $150 million to upgrade its production facilities, money it did not have and needed to secure from the outside. Once again, Zenith turned to the Lucky-Goldstar Group, now known as LG Group, for an infusion of cash. LG Electronics Inc., a subsidiary of LG Group, acquired a nearly 58 percent controlling interest in Zenith through the purchase of $351 million in Zenith stock. The last of the American-controlled television manufacturers was thus in the hands of foreign ownership. Through the sale, Zenith acquired the immediate capital it needed for its plans to produce large-screen picture tubes and large-screen TV sets. The deal was synergistic in that Zenith would also be able to make large-screen picture tubes for Goldstar TVs sold via LG's distribution system to such emerging markets as Latin America and Asia. The cash infusion and the potential for further LG investment in Zenith if the need arose placed Zenith in a stronger position to survive until it could benefit from its commitment to large-screen TVs and from its investment in HDTV.

Principal Subsidiaries: Zenith Distributing Corporation; Zenith Electronics Corporation of Arizona; Zenith Electronics Corporation of Texas; Zenith International Sales Corporation; Zenith Microcircuits Corporation; Zenith Video Tech Corporation; Zentrans, Inc.; Zenith Radio Canada Ltd.; Cable Productos de Chihuahua, S.A. de C.V. (Mexico); Electro Partes de Matamoros, S.A. de C.V. (Mexico); Partes de Television de Reynosa, S.A. de C.V. (Mexico); Productos Magneticos de Chihuahua, S.A. de C.V. (Mexico); Teleson de Mexico, S.A. de C.V.; Zenco de Chihuahua, S.A. de C.V. (Mexico); Zenith Taiwan Corporation.

Further Reading:

Carey, Susan, "South Korean Company Seeks Control of Zenith, Last of the U.S. TV Makers," *Wall Street Journal,* July 18, 1995, pp. A3, A4.

Dobrzynski, Judith H., "How to Handle a CEO," *Business Week,* February 24, 1994, pp. 64–65.

Miller, James P., "HDTV Panel Picks Zenith Signal System," *Wall Street Journal,* February 17, 1994, p. B6.

Miller, James P., "Zenith's Pearlman Plans to Step Down as CEO, Chairman," *Wall Street Journal,* February 24, 1995, pp. B2, B8.

Therrien, Lois, "HDTV Isn't Clearing Up Zenith's Picture," *Business Week,* February 25, 1991, pp. 56–57.

——, "Zenith Wishes on a Lucky-Goldstar," *Business Week,* March 11, 1991, p. 50.

Zenith: Highlights of the First 60 Years, Glenview, Ill.: Zenith Radio Corporation, 1978.

—updated by David E. Salamie

INDEX TO COMPANIES AND PERSONS

Listings are arranged in alphabetical order under the company name; thus Eli Lilly & Company will be found under the letter E. Definite articles (The) and forms of incorporation that precede the name (A.B. and N.V.) are ignored for alphabetical purposes. Company names appearing in bold type have historical essays on the page numbers appearing in bold. Updates to entries that appeared in earlier volumes are signified by (upd.). The index is cumulative with volume numbers printed in bold type.

INDEX TO INDUSTRIES

Index to Industries

BEVERAGES

CHEMICALS

CONGLOMERATES

CONSTRUCTION

CONTAINERS

DRUGS

ELECTRICAL & ELECTRONICS

ENGINEERING & MANAGEMENT SERVICES

ENTERTAINMENT & LEISURE

FINANCIAL SERVICES: BANKS

FINANCIAL SERVICES: NON-BANKS

FOOD PRODUCTS

FOOD SERVICES & RETAILERS

HEALTH & PERSONAL CARE PRODUCTS

HEALTH CARE SERVICES

HOTELS

INFORMATION TECHNOLOGY

INSURANCE

LEGAL SERVICES

MANUFACTURING

MATERIALS

MINING & METALS

PAPER & FORESTRY

PERSONAL SERVICES

PETROLEUM

PUBLISHING & PRINTING

REAL ESTATE

RETAIL & WHOLESALE

RUBBER & TIRE

TELECOMMUNICATIONS

TEXTILES & APPAREL

TOBACCO

TRANSPORT SERVICES

UTILITIES

WASTE SERVICES

NOTES ON CONTRIBUTORS

Notes on Contributors

BELSITO, Elaine. Free-lance writer.

BERRY, Pam. Free-lance writer and editor.

CANIPE, Jennifer Voskuhl. Free-lance writer and researcher.

COHEN, Kerstan. Free-lance writer and French translator; editor for *Letter-Ex* poetry review.

COVELL, Jeffrey L. Free-lance writer and corporate history contractor.

CRAIG, William O. Part-time researcher at a major Washington news bureau and free-lance writer for various clients, including the Smithsonian Institution, the Library of Congress, and the National Science Foundation; former journalist and federal government information director.

DERDAK, Thomas. Free-lance writer and adjunct professor of philosophy at Loyola University of Chicago; former executive director of the Albert Einstein Foundation.

DUBLANC, Robin. Free-lance writer and copyeditor in Yorkshire, England.

FIERO, John. Free-lance writer, researcher, and consultant; Professor of English at the University of Southwestern Louisiana in Lafayette.

GALLMAN, Jason. Free-lance writer and graduate student in English at Purdue University.

GASBARRE, April Dougal. Archivist and free-lance writer specializing in business and social history in Cleveland, Ohio.

GOPNIK, Hilary. Free-lance writer.

GUARDIANO, John. Director of Economic Research for the Washington, D.C.-based Center for American Eurasian Studies and Relations (CAESAR); Arlington, Virginia-based free-lance writer who writes often about business and economic issues.

HALASZ, Robert. Former editor in chief of *World Progress* and *Funk & Wagnalls New Encyclopedia Yearbook;* author, *The U.S. Marines* (Millbrook Press, 1993).

HECHT, Henry. Editorial consultant and retired vice-president, editorial services, Merrill Lynch.

HIGHMAN, Beth Watson. Free-lance writer.

HOLLEY, Val O. Biographer and free-lance writer living in Washington D.C.

HUGHES, Terry W. Educator and free-lance writer with special interests in education, home video, home audio, motion pictures, woodworking, and historic preservation.

HYDE, Leslie. Free-lance writer in Washington, D.C. who has worked extensively as an editor and translator in Rome and Paris.

JACOBSON, Robert R. Free-lance writer and musician.

KEELEY, Carol I. Free-lance writer and researcher; columnist for *Neon;* researcher for *Ford Times* and *Discovery.* Contributor to *Oxford Poetry,* 1987, and *Voices International,* 1989.

McMANUS, Donald. Free-lance writer.

MOELLER, Kurt. Former newspaper reporter and a graduate business student at Indiana University.

MONTGOMERY, Bruce P. Curator and director of historical collection, University of Colorado at Boulder.

MOTE, Dave. President of information retrieval company Performance Database.

MYERS-KEARNS, John. Free-lance writer.

PEIPPO, Katherine. Minneapolis-based free-lance writer.

PFALZGRAF, Taryn Benbow. Free-lance editor, writer, and consultant in the Chicago area.

ROULAND, Roger. Free-lance writer whose essays and journalism have appeared in the *International Fiction Review, Chicago Tribune, and Chicago Sun-Times.*

ROURKE, Elizabeth. Free-lance writer.

SALAMIE, David E. Part-owner of InfoWorks Development Group, a reference publication development and editorial services company.

SMETHURST, Katherine. Free-lance writer.

SWIERCZEK, Bob. Journalist and policy analyst; currently writing for several publications in Washington, D.C.

TROESTER, Maura. Free-lance writer based in Chicago.

WERNICK, Ellen D. Free-lance writer and editor.